C000142957

ISBN 978-0-331-77862-5
PIBN 11053158

THE

COLONIAL LAWS

OF

NEW YORK

FROM THE

YEAR 1664 TO THE REVOLUTION,

INCLUDING THE

CHARTERS TO THE DUKE OF YORK, THE COMMISSIONS AND INSTRUCTIONS TO COLONIAL GOVERNORS, THE DUKE'S LAWS, THE LAWS OF THE DONGAN AND LEISLER ASSEMBLIES, THE CHARTERS OF ALBANY AND NEW YORK AND THE ACTS OF THE COLONIAL LEGISLATURES FROM 1691 TO 1775 INCLUSIVE.

VOLUME V.

TRANSMITTED TO THE LEGISLATURE BY THE COMMISSIONERS OF STATUTORY REVISION, PURSUANT TO CHAPTER 125 OF THE LAWS OF 1891

ALBANY:
JAMES B. LYON, STATE PRINTER.
1894.

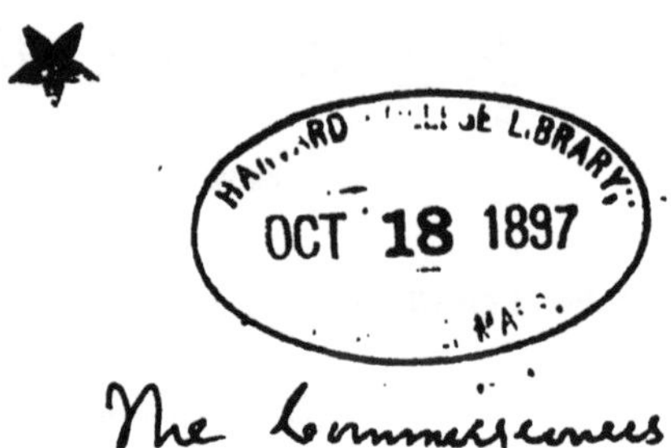

THIRTY-FIRST ASSEMBLY.

Second Session.

(Begun Nov. 21, 1769, 10 George III, Cadwallader Colden, Lieut. Governor.)

[CHAPTER 1406.]

[Chapter 1406 of Van Schaack, where the title only is printed.]

An Act for collecting the Duty of Excise on Strong Liquors retailed in this Colony from the first Day of January one thousand seven hundred and seventy to the first Day of January one thousand seven hundred and seventy one, inclusive.

[Passed, December 30, 1769.]

BE IT ENACTED by his Honor the Lieutenant Governor the Council and the General Assembly, and it is hereby enacted by the Authority of the same that Cornelius Clopper shall be and hereby is appointed Commissioner for collecting the Duty of Excise of and from the several Retailers of Strong Liquors within the City and County of New York from the first Day of January in the Year of our Lord one thousand seven hundred and seventy, to the first Day of January which will be in the Year of our Lord one thousand seven hundred and seventy one.

AND BE IT FURTHER ENACTED by the Authority aforesaid that the said Commissioner shall as soon after the Publication of this Act as he shall judge convenient, appoint the several Retailers within the said City and County, and direct and ascertain what each Retailer shall pay for the said Duty from the first Day of January one thousand seven hundred and seventy, to the first Day of January one thousand seven hundred and seventy one.

AND BE IT ENACTED by the Authority aforesaid that the several and respective Persons herein after named shall be and hereby are appointed Commissioners for collecting the Duty of Excise of and from the several and respective Retailers of Strong Liquors within the several and respective Counties of this

Colony herein after mentioned, and the Harbours, Bays an Rivers respectively thereunto adjoining or belonging Viz't

For the City and County of Albany, Peter Lansing and Guy-bert G Marselis Esquires.

For the Borough of West Chester, Nathaniel Underhi Esquire

For the Manor of Philipsburgh and Yonkers in the County o West Chester, William Davids and Isaac Deane Esquires.

For the Manor of Cortlandt in the County of West Chester, Charles Moore and Hackaliah Browne Esquires.

And for the remaining Part of West Chester County Edward Stephenson and John Thomas Junior Esquires.

For Kings County Theodorus Polhemus Esquire.

For Queens County Benjamin Townshend and Samuel Clowe Esquires.

For Dutchess County Cornelius Lister, Peter Harris and Ben jamin Akins Esquires.

For Ulster County Joseph Gasherie, and James Mc Clagr Esquires.

For Orange County, David Puy for Haverstraw Precinct; fo Orange Town John Perry, for Goshen Precinct Benjamin Tusteen and for Cornwell Precinct Daniel Coleman Esquires.

For Richmond County, Hezakiah Wright, Jacob Rezeau, an Richard Conner Esquires.

And for Suffolk County, Richard Floyd, Samuel Landon and Malby Gelston Esquires.

AND BE IT ENACTED by the Authority aforesaid, that th aforesaid several and respective Commissioners or the majo Part of them respectively shall as soon as they conveniently ca after the Publication of this Act meet at the County Hall of thei several and respective Counties or at such other Place or Place as they the said Commissioners shall respectively appoint fo putting in execution the Powers and Authorities given by thi Act, at which Time, or at such other Times as they shall judg necessary, the said Commissioners, or the major Part of then respectively shall for their own Counties and Districts severall and respectively fix the Number and appoint the several Retailer within their several and respective Counties and Districts, an direct and ascertain what each Retailer shall pay for the sai Duty of Excise from the first Day of January one thousand seve hundred and seventy to the first Day of January one thousan seven hundred and seventy one. PROVIDED ALWAYS AND BE IT FURTHER ENACTED by the Authority aforesaid, that no Retailer in any of the Cities or Counties of this Colony shall pay under the sum of twenty shillings for the said Duty of Excise, except those who shall retail Strong Liquors not to be drank in their Houses, and such as may retail strong Liquors at or near the County Hall in Suffolk County during the sittings of their Courts, or other Public Meetings there, who shall be rated at the discretion of the respective Commissioners and that all those who have heretofore been Retailers of Strong Liquors in this Colony shall not pay less for the said Duty than they did in the Year of our Lord one thousand seven hundred and sixty nine, but as much more as the Commissioner or Commissioners for the City County or District, where such Retailers may reside, shall think reasonable.

AND BE IT FURTHER ENACTED by the Authority aforesaid, that the said several Commissioners shall on or before the first Day of of January in the Year of our Lord one thousand seven hundred and seventy one, render just true and particular Accounts on Oath to the Treasurer of this Colony of all the Sums of Money to be raised by virtue of this Act on the several Retailers within the Cities, Counties and Districts for which they are respectively appointed Commissioners as aforesaid, specifying the Names of every Retailer, and the Sums they have respectively been rated at, and pay the same to the said Treasurer of this Colony for the Time being deducting therefrom only such Sum or Sums as is by this Act allowed such Commissioner or Commissioners for the management of the said Duty. and in order the better to secure the payment of the Sums to be raised by virtue of this Act.

BE IT FURTHER ENACTED by the Authority aforesaid that the said Commissioners before they take upon themselves the execution of the Powers and Authorities given by this Act shall respectively enter into Bonds to the Treasurer of this Colony for the Time being in the Sums following, that is to say.

The said Cornelius Clopper in the Penal Sum of one thousand six hundred Pounds.

The said Peter Lansing, and Guysbert G Marselis in the Penal Sum of three hundred Pounds.

The said Nathaniel Underhill in the Penal Sum of twenty Pounds.

The said William Davids and Isaac Deane in the Penal Sum of forty Pounds.

The said Charles Moore, and Hackaliah Browne in the Penal Sum of forty Pounds.

The said Edward Stephenson and John Thomas Junior in the Penal Sum of one hundred Pounds.

The said Theodorus Polhemus, in the Penal Sum of sixty Pounds.

The said Benjamin Townshend and Samuel Clowes in the Penal Sum of one hundred and sixty Pounds.

The said Cornelius Lister, Peter Harris and Benjamin Akins in the Penal Sum of two hundred Pounds.

The said Joseph Gasherie and James M. Clagry, in the Penal Sum of one hundred and fifty Pounds.

The said David Puy, John Perry, Benjamin Tusteen and Daniel Coleman in the Penal Sum of twenty Pounds each of them.

The said Hezakiah Wright, Jacob Rezeau and Richard Conner in the Penal Sum of forty Pounds.

The said Richard Floyd, Samuel Landon, and Malby Gelston in the Penal Sum of one hundred Pounds.

CONDITIONED that the said respective Commissioner or Commissioners his or their Executors or Administrators shall render a just and true Account upon Oath to the Treasurer of this Colony of all the sums that may by him or them be raised in virtue of this Act upon the several Retailers of Strong Liquors within the City, County or District for which he or they are or is appointed Commissioner or Commissioners, and well and truly pay the same except the Sum allowed him or them by this Act to the Treasurer of this Colony for the Time being on or before the first Day of January in the Year of our Lord one thousand seven hundred and seventy one: which Bond shall be delivered to and remain with the Treasurer of this Colony for the Time being, and upon performance of the Conditions of the same respectively shall be delivered up to be cancelled, but if Default shall be made in the performance of the Condition of any or either of the said Bonds, it shall and may be Lawful to and for the Treasurer of this Colony for the Time being, and he is hereby directed and required after the expiration of three Callender Months from the said first Day of January in the Year of our Lord one thousand seven hundred and seventy one to cause Suits to be brought in the Name of the Treasurer of the Colony of New York upon each and every of the said Bonds so forfeited and prosecute the same to effect, and no Suit to be brought upon any or either of the said Bonds shall be abated or discontinued by the Death or removal of the Treasurer of this Colony, but shall be continued and prosecuted to effect by the new Treasurer, in the Name of the Treasurer of the Colony of New York.

AND BE IT FURTHER ENACTED by the Authority aforesaid that the said Commissioners shall be allowed and may deduct out of the Sum to be by them respectively laid on the several Retailers within the City County or District for which they are respectively appointed Commissioners the following Sums for their Trouble and Charges in the execution of the Powers vested in them by this Act, that is to say.

The said Cornelius Clopper the Sum of fifty Pounds for incidental Charges and his Commissions.

The said Peter Lansing and Guysbert G Marselis the Sum of twenty eight Pounds.

The said Nathaniel Underhill the Sum of one Pound four Shillings.

The said William Davids and Isaac Deane the Sum of three Pounds ten Shillings.

The said Charles Moore and Hackaliah Browne the Sum of three Pounds ten Shillings.

The said Edward Stephenson, and John Thomas Junior the Sum of ten Pounds.

The said Theodorus Polhemus the Sum of five Pounds.

The said Benjamin Townshend and Samuel Clowes the Sum of ten Pounds.

The said Cornelius Lister, Peter Harris and Benjamin Akins the Sum of fifteen Pounds.

The said Joseph Gasherie and James Mc Clagry the Sum of eight Pounds.

The said David Puy, John Perry, Benjamin Tusteen, and Daniel Coleman the Sum of six Pounds.

The said Hezakiah Wright, Jacob Rezeau, and Richard Conner the Sum of three Pounds.

The said Richard Floyd, Samuel Landon, and Malby Gelston the Sum of nine Pounds.

AND BE IT FURTHER ENACTED by the Authority aforesaid that the several and respective Retailers of Strong Liquors shall pay the several and respective Sums of Money to be laid on them by virtue of this Act, unto the aforesaid several and respective Commissioners on or before the first Day of December one thousand seven hundred and seventy, for securing which payment the said Commissioners shall respectively oblige the said several and respective Retailers to give such Security as they the said Commissioners shall judge necessary. PROVIDED that such Retailer in the City of New York as shall be rated three Pounds and under, and such in the several Counties as shall be rated at thirty Shillings and under, shall not be permitted to retail unless they immediately pay the several and respective Sums they shall be rated at to the aforesaid Commissioners any Thing herein before contained to the contrary notwithstanding.

AND BE IT FURTHER ENACTED by the Authority aforesaid that in Case any Person or Persons whomsoever other that such as the said Commissioners shall permit shall presume to sell any Strong Liquors by retail directly or indirectly, the Offender or Offenders shall for each such Offence forfeit the Sum of six Pounds to be recovered by the said Commissioner or Commissioners respectively on the Oath of any one credible Witness in a Summary Way in the Cities of New York and Albany and Borough of West Chester before the Mayor or Recorder and one or more Aldermen of the said Cities and Borough respectively, and in the several Counties before any Justice of the Peace within the said several Counties respectively, and if upon Conviction the said Forfeitures be not paid, the same shall be levied on the Goods and Chattels of the Offender or Offenders by Warrant or Warrants under the Hands and Seals of the Person or Persons before whom such Conviction shall happen, and if no Goods and Chattels are found on which to distrain, it shall and may be lawful for the Person or Persons who heard and determined the same, to commit the Offender or Offenders to Goal without Bail or Mainprize for the Space of three Months unless the Penalties are sooner discharged, and the said respective Magistrates shall be and are hereby fully impowered directed and required to hear and determine those Matters in the Manner aforesaid, and to give Judgment if need be, to award Execution thereon and to issue a Warrant or Warrants for the commitment of Offenders as the Case may require, one third of which Forfeiture shall be to the Informer or Informers, one third to the said Commissioners, and one third to the Poor of the Town Manor or Precinct where the Offence shall be committed, to be paid into the Hands of the Church Wardens or Overseers of the Poor of the said respective Place or Places by the Officer or Officers by whom the same shall be levied; any Thing in any of the Acts of this Colony to the contrary notwithstanding.

AND BE IT FURTHER ENACTED by the Authority aforesaid that the several Retailers who shall be permitted and allowed to retail by the said Commissioner or Commissioners shall before they do so retail any Strong Liquors enter into Recognizance, that is to say in the Cities of New York and Albany and Borough of West Chester before the respective Mayors thereof and in the several Counties in this Colony before two Justices of the Peace in the Penal Sum of twenty Pounds with sufficient Sureties in the like Sum, conditioned to keep an orderly House, according to Law during the Time they shall be permitted to retail as aforesaid, and thereupon the said respective Mayors or the said Justices shall grant to such Person or Persons who have entered into such Recognizance a Licence under his or their Hands and Seals to retail Strong Liquors in such House and Place as shall be mentioned therein during the continuance of this Act, which Recognizances are to be lodged by the Person or Persons before whom the same shall be taken Vizt. in the Cities of New York and Albany and Borough of West Chester with the Town Clerks, and in the several Counties with the respective Clerks thereof, and upon Complaint of the Breach of the said Condition it shall be lawful for the said Mayor and Aldermen of New York and Albany, and Borough of West Chester respectively or the greater Number of them, and in the Counties for the Justices of the General and Special Sessions of the Peace to suppress the Licence or Licences of such Offender or Offenders.

AND BE IT ENACTED by the Authority aforesaid that in case any of the persons who shall be permitted to retail Strong Liquors as aforesaid by the said Commissioner or Commissioners shall presume to retail before he she or they have obtained a Licence and entered into Recognizance to keep an orderly House as aforesaid, he she or they so offending shall respectively forfeit the Sum of six Pounds for each Offence, to be recovered in a summary Way in the Manner before directed, one half thereof to the Informer, and the other half to the Poor of the Town Manor or Precinct where the Forfeiture shall arise: and that the Expence of being qualified to retail may be within the Bounds of moderation.

BE IT ENACTED by the Authority aforesaid that no more shall be taken for a Licence and Recognizance in the Cities of

New York and Albany and Borough of West Chester than the usual and accustomed Fees, and in the respective Counties than the Sum of three Shillings

AND BE IT ENACTED by the Authority aforesaid that such Persons permitted to retail as aforesaid by the said Commissioner or Commissioners who retail Strong Liquors not to be drank in their own Houses but carried elsewhere shall not be obliged to enter into the Recognizance and take Licence as aforesaid, any Thing contained in this Act to the contrary notwithstanding.

AND BE IT ENACTED by the Authority aforesaid that in Case of the Death of any of the aforesaid Commissioners, the surviving Commissioner or Commissioners where such Death may happen shall be and hereby is and are entitled to the whole Reward, and vested with the same Powers and Authorities to execute this Act as if no such Death had happened, and in Case of the Death or refusal of all the Commissioners of any of the respective Cities Counties and Districts, then the Sheriff or Sheriffs for the Time being of the Cities Counties or Districts where such Death or refusal shall happen, shall be and hereby is and are vested with all the Powers and Authorities given to the Commissioners by this Act, be under the same Regulations, and entitled to the same Rewards to all Intents, Constructions and purposes whatsoever as if they had been particularly named and appointed in this Act, any Thing in this Act to the contrary notwithstanding.

AND BE IT FURTHER ENACTED by the Authority aforesaid that all the Monies to be paid to the Treasurer of this Colony by virtue of this Act or recovered upon any of the aforesaid Bonds, shall remain in the Hands of the Treasurer of this Colony for the Time being to be disposed of as is or shall be directed by any Act or Acts passed or to be passed for that purpose.

AND BE IT ENACTED that the Retailers in the City of New York shall pay the Excise in three several Payments or sooner as the Commissioner and they shall agree.

PROVIDED ALWAYS that Nothing in this Act shall be construed to make void abridge, or any wise lessen the several Rights and Privileges granted unto the Cities of New York and Albany and Borough of West Chester by their respective Charters, any Thing contained in this Act to the contrary thereof notwithstanding.

[CHAPTER 1407.]

[Chapter 1407 of Van Schaack, where the title only is printed. See chapter 1357. Continued by chapter 1465.]

An Act further to continue an Act intitled "An Act for granting to his Majesty the "several Duties and Impositions on Goods, "Wares and Merchandizes, imported into this "Colony therein mentioned."

[Passed, December 30, 1769.]

WHEREAS the several Duties and Impositions on Goods, Wares and Merchandizes imported into this Colony, and granted for the support of the Government of his late Majesty King George the second by the abovementioned Act, have by several subsequent Acts been continued to the first Day of January next ensuing; and the General Assembly being willing to make Provision for the further Support of his Majesty's Government of this Colony.

BE IT THEREFORE ENACTED by his Honor the Lieutenant Governor, the Council and the General Assembly, and it is hereby enacted by the Authority of the same, that the abovementioned Act intitled "An Act for granting to his Majesty the "several Duties and Impositions on Goods, Wares and Merchan-"dizes imported into this Colony therein mentioned." passed in the twenty seventh Year of his late Majesty's Reign shall be and hereby is continued, and every Clause, Matter and Thing therein contained enacted to be and remain in full Force to all Intents, Constructions and purposes whatsoever until the first Day of January which will be in the year of our Lord one thousand seven hundred and seventy one inclusive.

PROVIDED ALWAYS that so much of the first Clause or Section of said Act, as relates to European or East Indian Goods imported from the British Islands into this Colony shall be construed taken and deemed to be from the British Islands in America only, any Thing in the said Act to the contrary thereof notwithstanding.

[CHAPTER 1408.]

[Chapter 1408 of Van Schaack, where the act is printed in full. See chapter 1196.]

An Act to continue an Act intitled "An "Act for the punishment of Persons in the "City of New York, who shall by false pre- "tences, obtain any Goods, Wares or Mer- "chandizes from any Person, with Intent to "cheat or defraud such Person," with an Addition thereto.

[Passed, December 30, 1769.]

BE IT ENACTED by his Honor the Lieutenant Governor, the Council and the General Assembly, and it is hereby enacted by the Authority of the same, that the Act intitled An Act for the punishment of Persons in the City of New York who shall by false pretences obtain any Goods Wares or Merchandizes from any Person, with Intent to cheat or defraud such person, passed in the third Year of his present Majesty's Reign shall be and hereby is continued in full Force and Virtue to all Intents and Purposes from the first Day of January next, until the first Day of January which will be in the Year of our Lord one thousand seven hundred and eighty inclusive.

AND WHEREAS Doubts and Scruples have arisen whether Monies are or shall be deemed or counted Goods and Merchandizes BE IT ENACTED by the Authority aforesaid that all persons obtaining Money by false Pretences or Tokens shall be liable to the like Punishment as Persons are in the City of New York who shall by false Pretences obtain any Goods, Wares or Merchandizes from any Person with Intent to cheat or defraud such Person or Persons.

[CHAPTER 1409.]

[Chapter 1409 of Van Schaack, where the title only is printed. See chapter 1268. Continued by chapter 1512.]

An Act to continue an Act intitled "An "Act for the better regulating the Publio "Roads in the City and County of New York "and to levy Money to defray the Expence "thereof."

[Passed, December 30, 1769.]

BE IT ENACTED by his Honor the Lieutenant Governor, the Council and the General Assembly, and it is hereby enacted by the Authority of the same that the Act intitled "An Act for the "better regulating the Public Roads in the City and County of "New York, and to levy Money to defray the Expence thereof." passed in the fourth Year of his present Majesty's Reign shall be and hereby is continued, and every Clause, Article, Matter and Thing in the said Act contained enacted to be and remain in full Force and Virtue to all Intents, Constructions and Purposes whatsoever until the first Day of January which will be in the Year of our Lord one thousand seven hundred and seventy two, except so much of the second Clause of the said Act as is therein expressed and contained in the Words following to wit "And "if any Person or Persons shall lay out any Road or Roads "through his her or their Lands, and leave the same open for "common use by the space of three Months, the said Commis- "sioners are hereby impowered immediately thereafter to record "all and every such Road and Roads in the Manner hereinafter "directed; which being so recorded shall be deemed Publick "Roads and Highways to all Intents Constructions and Purposes "whatsoever."

[CHAPTER 1410.]

[Chapter 1410 of Van Schaack, where the act is printed in full. Expired January, 1772. Revived and continued by chapter 1522.]

An Act for the more effectual prevention of Fires in the City of New York.

[Passed, December 30, 1769.]

WHEREAS the many instances of the great Destruction made by Fire in many Populous Cities, makes it highly necessary to use all possible precaution against the like Calamities in this City. AND WHEREAS the storing of Pitch Tar, Turpentine, Rosin, Spirits of Turpentine or Shingles in any Houses, Store Houses, Cellars or other Places within this City, may be of very bad Consequences in Case of Fire breaking out at or near the Place where any such commodities are stored. AND WHEREAS the firing and discharging of Guns, Pistols, Rockets, Crackers, Squibs, and other Fireworks in the City of New York, may not only be likely to do personal Injuries to the Inhabitants and others, but the City may be in danger of being set on Fire by such Practices for Remedy whereof.

BE IT ENACTED by his Honor the Lieutenant Governor, the Council and General Assembly and it is hereby enacted by the

Authority of the same that from and after the first Day of January next no Pitch, Tar, Turpentine, Rosin or Spirits of Turpentine or Shingles shall or may be put in any Place in the City of New York to the Southward of Fresh Water, other than in such proper place or places to be appointed and approved of by the Mayor Aldermen and Commonalty of the City of New York in Common Council convened under the Penalty of ten Pounds for every Offence or Refusal to remove the same to be levied by Warrant under the Hand and Seal of one or more of his Majesty's Justices of the Peace for the City and County of New York by distress and Sale of the Goods and Chattels of the Offender upon due Conviction upon Oath or upon the View of one or more of such Justices of the Peace, rendering the Overplus if any be to the Owner, and for want of such Distress the Offender shall be imprisoned by Warrant from the said Justice or Justices, who are hereby impowered and required to issue such Warrant until payment as aforesaid, which said Forfeitures shall be paid to the Church Wardens of the City of New York for the Time being for the use of the Poor of the said City. PROVIDED ALWAYS that it shall and may be lawful to and for such of the Inhabitants of the said City who are Ship Chandlers to have near their Doors in the open Street, and not in any Building or Inclosure a small Quantity of Pitch Tar Rosin and Turpentine not exceeding in the whole at any one Time twenty Barrels in order the more readily and handily to supply the Merchant Ships, and others who may have Occasion for small Quantities of such Commodities any Thing herein before contained to the contrary thereof in any wise notwithstanding.

AND BE IT FURTHER ENACTED by the Authority aforesaid that if any Person or Persons of what Age Sex or Quality soever from and after the said first Day of January shall Fire and discharge any Gun, Pistol, Rocket, Cracker, Squib, or other Fire Work in any Street, Lane or Alley, Garden or other Inclosure or from any House or in any other Place where Persons frequently walk to the Southward of Fresh Water, that then every such person or persons so offending and being thereof convicted before one or more Justice or Justices of the Peace for the said City and County of New York either by the Confession of the Party or Parties so offending or the Oath of one or more Witness or Witnesses (which Oath the said Justice or Justices of Peace is and are hereby impowered and required to Administer) shall for every such Offence forfeit the Sum of twenty Shillings, the said Forfeitures to be levied by distress and sale of the Goods and Chattels of every such Offender by Warrant under the Hand and Seal of the said Justice or Justices of the Peace before whom such Conviction or Convictions shall be as aforesaid made, the which Forfeitures to be to the use of the Poor of the said City of New York; and if the said Offender or Offenders shall not pay the said Forfeiture or Forfeitures upon Conviction as aforesaid, and want of sufficient distress whereon the same can be made, that then every such Justice or Justices of the Peace is and are hereby impowered and required by Warrant under his or their Hands and Seals to commit every such person or persons so as aforesaid offending to the Common Goal of the City and County of New York, there to remain without Bail or Mainprize for the Space of ten Days unless such Forfeiture or Forfeitures be sooner paid: But in Case such Offender or Offenders in the Premises last abovementioned shall happen to be a Slave or Slaves and the Forfeiture or Forfeitures aforesaid on Conviction as aforesaid shall not be forthwith paid, that then it shall and may be lawful to and for such Justice or Justices before whom the Conviction shall be to cause such Slave or Slaves to be publickly Whiped on the naked Back such Number of Stripes as he or they shall think proper not exceeding thirty nine, which Punishment shall be in lieu and stead of the said Forfeiture; This Act to be of force from the first Day of January one thousand seven hundred and seventy, to the first Day of January which will be in the year of our Lord one thousand seven hundred and seventy two.

[CHAPTER 1411.]

[Chapter 1411 of Van Schaack, where the act is printed in full. See chapter 890.]

An Act to encourage the destroying of Wolves in the County of Albany.

[Passed, December 30, 1769.]

WHEREAS an Act intitled An Act to encourage the destroying of Wolves in the County of Albany passed in the twenty fourth Year of his late Majesty's Reign will expire the first Day of January next, and the said Act having been found useful, and would be more so provided a greater Reward was allowed for destroying of Wolves and Whelps than is therein mentioned.

BE IT THEREFORE ENACTED by his Honor the Lieutenant Governor, the Council and the General Assembly, and it is hereby enacted by the Authority of the same, that from and after the first Day of January next and during the continuance of this Act every Person whether a Christian or Slave who shall kill or destroy a Wolf or it's Whelp in the County of Albany shall have & receive the Reward following,— that is to say; for every grown Wolf, the Sum of twenty Shillings and for every Wolf under the Age of one Year the Sum of fifteen Shillings, and that every Native free Indian, shall have and receive one half of the said Reward for Wolves killed and destroyed by them, and to the End the Reward above mentioned may be truly paid and discharged.

BE IT ENACTED by the Authority aforesaid that the Person or Persons killing or destroying a Wolf or Wolves, and carrying the Head or Heads thereof, with the intire Skin thereon within three Days after killing the same to a Justice of the Peace residing in the said County, the said Justice shall and hereby is obliged thereupon to give a Certificate thereof gratis, and to mention therein the Name or Names of the Person or Persons that killed such Wolf or Wolves, the Time when, and to distinguish whether the same were full grown, or under the age of one Year: after which the Ears of the Wolf or Wolves so certified are to be cut off in the presence of the said Justice, and such certificate being produced to the Supervisors of the said County the said Supervisors shall and hereby are obliged at their annual Meetings to order the Treasurer of the said County to pay unto the Person or Persons who so killed or destroyed the same, or to his or their Assigns the Reward allowed and extablished by this Act, and the said Reward shall be a County Charge, and raised together with the other necessary and contingent Charges of the said County; this Act to be in force from the first Day of January next, until the first Day of January one thousand seven hundred and seventy five.

[CHAPTER 1412.]

[Chapter 1412 of Van Schaack, where the act is printed in full. See chapter 483.]

An Act to continue an Act intitled An Act to revive an Act intitled An Act to impower the Justices of the Peace of the County of Albany living or dwelling in the Township of Schenectady in the said County to regulate the Streets and Highways and to prevent Accidents by Fire in the said Town.

[Passed, December 30, 1769.]

WHEREAS an Act intitled An Act to revive an Act intitled An Act to impower the Justices of the Peace of the County of Albany living or dwelling in the Township of Schenectady in the said County to regulate the Streets and Highways and to prevent Accidents by Fire in the said Town passed in the thirty third Year of his late Majesty's Reign will expire on the first Day of January next unless the same be continued.

BE IT THEREFORE ENACTED by his Honor the Lieutenant Governor the Council and the General Assembly and it is hereby enacted by the Authority of the same that the abovementioned Act shall be, and hereby is continued from the first Day of January next until the first Day of January which will be in the year of our Lord one thousand seven hundred and seventy five.

[CHAPTER 1413.]

[Chapter 1413 of Van Schaack, where the title only is printed. Amended by chapter 1496. Expired January 1, 1773.]

An Act impowering the Justices of the Peace living or dwelling in the Township of Schenectady in the County of Albany to establish and regulate a Night Watch, appoint Firemen and other Purposes therein mentioned.

[Passed, December 30, 1769.]

WHEREAS the establishing a Watch and appointing Firemen to manage the Fire Engine in the Township of Schenectady will tend to the safety and preservation of the Inhabitants thereof in their Persons and Effects.

BE IT THEREFORE ENACTED by his Honor the Lieutenant Governor, the Council and the General Assembly, and it is hereby enacted by the Authority of the same that it shall and may be Lawful to and for the Justices of the Peace living or dwelling in the Township of Schenectady or the Major Part of them to meet together in the said Township with all convenient Speed, after the publication of this Act, and they are hereby required and directed then and there at such Meeting to order establish and regulate a Night Watch not exceeding six Men and an Officer for each Night out of the Inhabitants of the said Township, who shall and are hereby required and directed in their Turns in the Night Time to keep Watch and Guard the said Township in such Manner and at such Times and Places as the said Justices or the major Part of them shall order and direct.

AND BE IT FURTHER ENACTED by the Authority aforesaid that it shall and may be Lawful to and for the said Justices of the Peace or the major Part of them living or dwelling in the said Township of Schenectady to make establish and ordain such Rules Orders Ordinances and Regulations in respect of the Government, Conduct, Duty and Behaviour of the said Watch and Watchmen, and to impose and establish such reasonable Fines, Penalties and Forfeitures upon them or any of them for Default or Neglect of the Duties, Businesses and services thereby to be enjoined or required from them as to the said Justices or the major Part of them shall from Time to Time seem meet and convenient. PROVIDED ALWAYS that no greater Fine, Penalty or Forfeiture than six Shillings on an Officer and three Shillings on every other Person or Watchmen shall be imposed for neglecting or non-attending on Watch when warned.

AND BE IT FURTHER ENACTED by the Authority aforesaid that from and after the publication of this Act it shall and may be Lawful to and for the Justices of the Peace dwelling or residing in the said Township of Schenectady or the major Part of them and they are hereby required with all convenient Speed thereafter to elect nominate and appoint a sufficient Number of strong, able, discreet, honest and sober Men willing to accept, not exceeding twenty in Number, out of the Inhabitants of the said Township to have the Care, Management, working and using the said Fire Engine, and the other Tools and Instruments for extinguishing of Fires that may happen within the said Township who are hereby required and enjoined always to be ready both by Day and Night to manage, work, and use the said Fire Engine and the other Tools and Instruments for the Extinguishing of Fires that may happen or break out in the said Township; and in order to compel and oblige the Firemen so to be elected nominated and appointed as aforesaid to be diligent, industrious and vigilent in the execution and discharge of their Office and Duty.

AND BE IT FURTHER ENACTED by the Authority aforesaid, that the Justices of the Peace living or dwelling in the said Township of Schenectady, or the major Part of them are hereby authorised and impowered to remove and displace all or any of the Firemen so as aforesaid to be elected nominated or appointed, when and as often as they shall think fit, and others in the Room or Places of such as they shall remove or displace to elect nominate appoint and put in from Time to Time as they the said Justices of the Peace for the Time being or the major Part of them shall see convenient.

AND BE IT FURTHER ENACTED by the Authority aforesaid that the Persons so to be elected, nominated or appointed Firemen as aforesaid, and each and every of them from Time to Time during their continuance in the Office of Firemen and no longer, shall and hereby are declared to be freed, exempted and Privileged from the several Offices of Constable and Surveyor of the Highways, and of and from serving as Jurors, and of and from serving in the Militia, or any of the Independant Companies of or in the said Township, or any or either of them, except in cases of Invasion, or other imminent Danger.

AND BE IT FURTHER ENACTED by the Authority aforesaid, that it shall and may be lawful to and for the Justices of the Peace aforesaid or the Major Part of them, to make establish and ordain such Rules, Orders, Ordinances and Regulations in respect of the Government Conduct, Duty and Behaviour of the Persons from Time to Time to be by them elected nominated or appointed Firemen by virtue of this Act for the purposes aforesaid.

AND BE IT FURTHER ENACTED by the Authority aforesaid, that this Act shall be in force from the Publication thereof until the first Day of January which will be in the Year of our Lord one thousand seven hundred and seventy three.

[CHAPTER 1414.]

[Chapter 1414 of Van Schaack, where the act is printed in full. See chapter 1286.]

An Act to prevent Damages by Swine in that Part of the Manor of Rensselaerwyck called Claverack.

[Passed, December 30, 1769.]

WHEREAS an Act intitled An Act to prevent Damages by Swine in that Part of the Manor of Rensselaerwyck therein mentioned is by experience found to be a useful and beneficial Law, and the extention thereof to that Part of the Manor of Rensselaerwyck called Claverack will therefore be serviceable to the Inhabitants there

BE IT THEREFORE ENACTED by his Honor the Lieutenant Governor, the Council and the General Assembly, and it is hereby enacted by the Authority of the same that the said Act intitled. "An Act to prevent Damages by Swine in that Part of the Manor of Rensselaerwyck therein mentioned passed in the sixth Year of his present Majesty's Reign shall be and is hereby extended to that Part of the Manor of Rensselaerwyck called Claverack.

[CHAPTER 1415.]

[Chapter 1415 of Van Schaack, where the title only is printed. See chapter 1123. Expired January 1, 1772.]

An Act to continue an Act intitled, an Act to revive an Act intitled an Act for the better relief of the Poor in Dutchess County.

[Passed, December 30, 1769.]

BE IT ENACTED by his Honor the Lieutenant Governor the Council and the General Assembly and it is hereby enacted by the Authority of the same that the Act intitled An Act to revive an Act entitled an Act for the better relief of the Poor in Dutchess County shall be and hereby is continued, and every Clause Article and Thing therein contained enacted to be and remain in full force from the first Day of January next until the first Day of January which will be in the Year of our Lord one thousand seven hundred and seventy two.

[CHAPTER 1416.]

[Chapter 1416 of Van Schaack, where the act is printed in full. See chapter 1203.]

An Act to revive an Act intitled An Act to prevent the Diging of Pits for the taking of Deer in Queens and Suffolk Counties.

[Passed, December 30, 1769.]

WHEREAS an Act intitled An Act to prevent the diging of Pits for the taking of Deer in Queens and Suffolk Counties passed the eleventh of December one thousand seven hundred and sixty two expired by it's own Limitation on January the first in the Year one thousand seven hundred and sixty five, and the same having been found very useful and necessary.

BE IT THEREFORE ENACTED by his Honor the Lieutenant Governor, the Council and the General Assembly and it is hereby enacted by the Authority of the same that the abovementioned Act intitled An Act to prevent the Diging of Pits for the taking of Deer in Queens and Suffolk Counties, shall be and hereby is revived, and every article Matter and Clause therein contained, enacted to be and remain in full Force from the Publication hereof, until the first Day of January which will be in the Year of our Lord one thousand seven hundred and seventy five.

[CHAPTER 1417.]

[Chapter 1417 of Van Schaack. where the act is printed in full. See chapters 482 and 898.]

An Act to continue an Act intitled "An "Act to prevent the setting on Fire or burn-"ing the old Grass on Hampstead Plains with "an Addition thereto."

[Passed, December 30, 1769.]

BE IT ENACTED by his Honor the Lieutenant Governor the Council, and the General Assembly, and it is hereby enacted by the Authority of the same, that the Act intitled "An Act to pre-"vent the setting on Fire or burning the old Grass on Hamp-"stead Plains," passed in the twelfth Year of the Reign of his late Majesty King George the first, and by several subsequent Acts continued to the first Day of January in the Year of our Lord one thousand seven hundred and seventy, shall be and hereby is further continued and every clause Article Matter and Thing therein contained, enacted to be of full Force and Virtue to all Intents, Constructions and purposes whatsoever, until the first Day of January which will be in the Year of our Lord one thousand seven hundred and eighty.

AND WHEREAS several of the Persons appointed in the said Acts to put the same in execution with respect to the extinguishing of Fire, are either dead or removed from the respective Plantations where they formerly resided, by which means the good Ends and purposes thereby intended, may be frustrated, for preventing whereof.

BE IT ENACTED by the Authority aforesaid that the Persons hereafter named Viz't William Cornell Junior, Benjamin Cheesman, John Williams, Richard Townsend Junior, Thomas Willits, Solomon Powell, Richard Willits, John Robbins, Silas Smith, Richard Powell, James Seaman, John Birdsal, John Jackson Esquire, David Batty, John Hall, and David Beadle, shall be and hereby are appointed to put in execution the several Powers and Authorities given by the said first mentioned Act, to the Persons therein appointed for that Purpose, and the said Persons above named are hereby vested with as full Power and Authority in that respect, as if they had been appointed in and by the said first mentioned Act, any Thing therein contained to the contrary notwithstanding.

[CHAPTER 1418.]

[Chapter 1418 of Van Schaack, where the act is printed in full. See chapters 599 and 692.]

An Act to continue an Act intitled An Act to prevent the Penning and folding of Sheep and Neat Cattle feeding on Hampstead Plains.

[Passed, December 30, 1769.]

WHEREAS an Act intitled An Act to prevent the Penning and folding of Sheep and Neat Cattle feeding on Hampstead Plains passed in the seventh Year of his late Majesty's Reign, and by several subsequent Acts continued to the first Day of January in the Year of our Lord one thousand seven hundred and seventy, and the said Act having been found beneficial.

BE IT THEREFORE ENACTED by his Honor the Lieutenant Governor, the Council and the General Assembly, and it is hereby enacted by the authority of the same that the abovementioned Act, intitled, An Act to prevent the Penning and folding of Sheep and Neat Cattle feeding on Hampstead Plains shall be, and hereby is continued and every Clause, Article, Matter and Thing therein contained enacted to be of full Force and Virtue to all Intents Constructions and purposes whatsoever until the first Day of January which will be in the Year of our Lord one thousand seven hundred and eighty.

[CHAPTER 1419.]

[Chapter 1419 of Van Schaack, where the act is printed in full.]

An Act to enable the Freeholders and Inhabitants of the several Towns, therein mentioned in the County of Suffolk to elect a greater Number of Constables in their respective Townships.

[Passed, December 30, 1769.]

WHEREAS several of the Towns in the County of Suffolk have considerably increased in Number of Inhabitants, and their out Settlements are become more extensive, whereby the Constables Fees are greatly augmented, and the Service of all process from the Justices of the Peace is attended with greater difficulty and uncertainty, it is therefore conceived beneficial that their Liberty in this respect should be enlarged.

BE IT THEREFORE ENACTED by his Honor the Lieutenant Governor, the Council and General Assembly and it is hereby enacted by the Authority of the same, that from and after the Publication of this Act, it shall and may be Lawful to and for the Freeholders and Inhabitants of the said Towns, and they are hereby impowered, yearly at the Times already fixed and settled for the Public Town Meetings in their respective Townships, either by Patents or any Act or Acts of the Legislature of this Colony, to elect and choose by a Majority of Voices the following Number of Constables in their respective Townships (if it shall seem expedient to them) in the manner and proportion herein directed and no otherwise (to wit) for the Township of Southold not exceeding six, for the Township of Southampton not exceeding four, for the Township of Huntington not exceeding three, and for the Township of Brookhaven not exceeding four, and every person so elected as aforesaid shall serve as Constable for the then ensuing Year, or until there be another chosen and qualified according to Law, in his Room and Stead, and every person so chosen, who shall refuse or neglect to qualify and serve as above directed, when thereunto required, by any one Justice of the Peace, shall forfeit the Sum of five Pounds with Costs, to be recovered by Warrant issued by said Justice, directed to the Constable thereafter to be appointed, by distraining the Goods and Chattels of the Offender, and the said Constable after six Days Public Notice is given by him, that the Goods distrained are to be sold shall make Sale thereof, and return the Overplus (if any there be) to the Owner or Owners: and the Forfeiture to be applied by the said Justice, for the use of the Poor of that Town or Precinct where such Forfeiture shall arise, and in Case of such Refusal or Denial as aforesaid, it shall and may be Lawful for any two Justices of the Peace of the Town where it happened, to appoint some fit person or persons to execute the Office of Constable for the Place or Places where such Refusal or Neglect shall be made, by virtue of this Act as aforesaid, and every such Constable or Constables, so elected chosen or appointed as aforesaid, shall have the same Powers, and be subject to the same Fines and Forfeitures, as the other Constables for the several Towns and Precincts in the said County are vested with, or liable to, any Law Usage or Custom to the contrary notwithstanding.

[CHAPTER 1420.]

[Chapter 1420 of Van Schaack, where the act is printed in full. See chapter 1106.]

An Act to continue an Act intitled An Act to prevent Damages by Swine in the County of Orange, and some Parts of Ulster County so far as the same relates to Ulster County.

[Passed, December 30, 1769.]

WHEREAS the above mentioned Act is found by experience to be a useful and Beneficial Law for the Inhabitants of those Parts of the County of Ulster to which the same doth extend; and as the same will expire on the first Day of January next unless continued.

BE IT THEREFORE ENACTED by his Honor the Lieutenant Governor, the Council and the General Assembly and it is hereby enacted by the Authority of the same, that the said Act intitled An Act to prevent Damages by Swine in the County of Orange and some Parts of Ulster County, and every Article, clause, matter and Thing therein contained so far as the same relates to those Parts of Ulster County as are therein mentioned, shall and hereby is continued to be in full Force until the first Day of January which will be in the Year of our Lord one thousand seven hundred and seventy five.

[CHAPTER 1421.]

[Chapter 1421 of Van Schaack, where the act is printed in full.]

An Act to enable the Supervisors of the County of Orange to hold their annual Meetings at or as near the Center of said County as conveniently can be for the good of the Public Service.

[Passed, December 30, 1769.]

WHEREAS the Court House at Orange Town being the place appointed for annual Meeting of the Supervisors for the County of Orange in October is found by experience to be very inconvenient on account of it's situation for Remedy whereof.

BE IT ENACTED by his Honor the Lieutenant Governor the Council and the General Assembly, and it is hereby enacted by the Authority of the same, that it shall and may be Lawful for the Supervisors of said County of Orange and they are hereby directed to meet at the House of Daniel Coe at Cakiate in said County on the first Tuesday of October next, and from thence to adjourn to any other Place as near the Center of said County as shall seem most convenient to them for the good of the Public Service, any Law, Usage or Custom to the contrary thereof in any wise notwithstanding.

[CHAPTER 1422.]

[Chapter 1422 of Van Schaack, where the title only is printed.]

An Act for making a further provision of two thousand pounds for furnishing his Majesty's Troops quartered in this Colony with Necessaries for one year.

[Passed, January 5, 1770.]

BE IT ENACTED by his Honor the Lieutenant Governor the Council and the General Assembly, and it is hereby enacted by the Authority of the same, That the Treasurer of this Colony shall pay and he is hereby directed and required out of any Monies now in the Treasury, and not already appropriated for

Support of Government, to pay such Sum or Sums of Money as shall from Time to Time be necessary for quartering his Majesty's Troops in this Colony, on Warrant or Warrants to be drawn for that purpose by his Honor the Lieutenant Governor or Commander in chief for the Time being by and with the Advise & Consent of his Majesty's Council: provided the whole Sum so to be drawn for does not exceed the Sum of one thousand pounds.

AND BE IT ENACTED by the Authority aforesaid, That the Treasurer of this Colony, shall pay, and he is hereby directed & required, out of the Loan Office Bill now before this House for emitting Bills of Credit to the Amount of one hundred and twenty thousand pounds, as soon as it shall be passed into a Law and the Money issued; to pay such further Sum or Sums of Money, as shall from Time to Time be necessary for the quartering his Majesty's Troops in this Colony for one Year from the first Day of January one thousand Seven hundred and Seventy on Warrant or Warrants, to be drawn for that purpose, in the Manner herein before directed: provided the whole Sum so to be drawn for does not exceed the Sum of one thousand pounds

AND BE IT ENACTED by the Authority aforesaid that both the aforesaid Sums of Money shall be replaced, in the Treasury, out of the first Money arising from the Interest of the Loan Office Bill aforesaid and that the Treasurer shall keep exact Books of his payments by Virtue of this Act, and a true and just Account thereof shall render upon Oath to the Governor or Commander in chief for the Time being, the Council, or General Assembly, when by them or any of them thereunto required.

[CHAPTER 1423.]

[Chapter 1423 of Van Schaack, where the title only is printed. Repealed by the king February 14, 1770, but provided for by chapter 1472.]

An Act for emitting the Sum of one hundred and twenty thousand Pounds in Bills of Credit to be put out on Loan, and to appropriate the Interest arising thereon to the payment of the Debts of this Colony and to such Public Exigencies as the Circumstances of this Colony may from Time to Time render necessary.

[Passed, January 5, 1770.]

WHEREAS from the great decay of Trade, and the insolvency of the late Treasurer, and other Difficulties a deficiency has arisen in the Public Funds. AND WHEREAS the Funds granted for the support of his Majesty's Government in and over this Colony have of late been reduced one half, which Deficiency this Colony in it's present Circumstances is unable to discharge unless it be done by the means of a Loan of Money. AND WHEREAS also there is a great want of Specie or other Medium of Trade in this Colony, whereby the Inhabitants labour under insuperable Difficulties, and many of them are utterly ruined by being obliged to sell considerable Estates greatly under the real value thereof, and the Merchants rendered unable to make Remittances to Great Britain as without such Medium, Bills of Exchange cannot be purchased, wherefore as well to revive the Commerce, Trade, and Navigation of this Colony as to promote the improvement and Settlement thereof the General Assembly pray that it may be enacted.

I BE IT THEREFORE ENACTED by his Honor the Lieutenant Governor the Council and the General Assembly, and it is hereby Enacted by the Authority of the same, that Bills of Credit to the value of one hundred and twenty thousand Pounds Current Money of New York shall after the first Day of April next be printed as follows Vizt five thousand Bills each of the value of ten Pounds. six thousand Bills each of the value of five Pounds, six thousand Bills each of the value of three Pounds, five thousand Bills each of the value of two Pounds, six thousand Bills each of the value of one Pound, eight thousand Bills each of the value of ten shillings, and eight thousand Bills each of the value of five shillings, upon which Bills shall be impressed the Arms of the City of New York on the Right side of every of the said Bills and the said Bills shall be in the form following.

"By a Law of the Colony of New York this Bill shall be "received in all Payments in the Treasury for ——. ——. ——. "——. New York the tenth Day of June, one thousand seven hun-"dred and seventy." Which Bills shall be numbered by Henry Holland, or Walter Franklin, or Isaac Low or Theophilact Bache and signed by any two of them, and by the Treasurer or Loan Officer to whom by this Act the said first Signers are directed to deliver them.

II AND BE IT ENACTED that the said first signers are hereby directed and impowered upon the delivery to them of the said Bills by the Printer thereof to administer to him and he is hereby directed to take an Oath or Affirmation in the Words

4

following. "I A. B. do declare that from the Time that the Letters were set, and fit to be put in the press for printing the Bills "of Credit now by me delivered to you until the Bills were "printed, and the Letters afterwards distributed into the Boxes, "I went at no Time out of the Room in which the said Letters "were without locking them up so as they could not be come at "without Violence, a false Key or other Art then unknown to "me, and therefore to the best of my knowledge no Copies were "printed off but in my presence, and that all the Blotters and "other Papers whatsoever impressed by the said Letters whilst "set for printing the said Bills, to the best of my knowledge, are "here delivered to you, together with the Stamps; and in all "Things relating to this Affair, I have well and truly demeaned "myself according to the true Intent and meaning of the Law in "that Case made, to the best of my knowledge and understanding, so help me God." Which Printer at the Time he has Orders to print the said Bills shall have a Copy of this Oath that he may govern himself accordingly. PROVIDED ALWAYS that if any unforseen Accident has happened he may have the Liberty of making an Exception thereof in his Oath, he declaring fully how it was, and if any more of the said Bills are printed than by this Act is directed, when the said Henry Holland, Walter Franklin, Isaac Low, Theophilact Bache or any two of them have signed the Number hereby directed to be issued, they shall immediately burn and destroy all the remainder.

III AND BE IT ENACTED by the Authority aforesaid that Elisha Gallaudet or such other Person as the Major Part of the said first Signers of the said Bills of Credit shall agree with shall engrave according to the Directions he shall receive from the Majority of the said first Signers twenty eight Stamps for the Sides of the said Bills, and fourteen Stamps for the Arms of the City of New York and shall deliver them to the Treasurer who shall in the Presence of the Majority of the said Signers deliver them unto Hugh Gaine the Printer of this Colony upon his Receipt for the same, and when the said Hugh Gaine has finished and compleated the printing the Quantity and Sorts of Bills hereby directed to be struck and issued, he shall re-deliver the said Stamps to the said Signers and Treasurer, who are hereby directed and required to seal them up with their several Seals, and they are so to remain in the Treasury until they shall be ordered to be made use of by any future Act of Assembly, and the Receipt of the said Treasurer to the said Hugh Gaine shall be a sufficient discharge for such re-delivery. But in Case of the Death Sickness or inability of the said Hugh Gaine to print the said Bills, then the Majority of the said Signers shall appoint another Printer for the Service aforesaid in his Place, which Printer so appointed shall take the Oath as above directed.

IV BE IT ALSO ENACTED that before the said Signers do receive any of the said Bills they shall (before any of the Magistrates of the City of New York) each of them take an Oath or Affirmation well and truly to perform what by this Act they are enjoined as their Duty, and will knowingly sign no more Bills of Credit than what by this Act is directed.

AND BE IT ENACTED that the said first Signers shall out of the Bills of Credit by them numbered and signed as aforesaid, deliver to the Loan Officers herein after mentioned on producing the Certificates of Qualification herein after directed, in the Sums and Quotas following, to wit:

TO the Loan Officers of the City and County of New York to and for the Purposes herein after mentioned, the Sum of forty thousand Pounds.

TO the Loan Officers of the City and County of Albany to and for the Purposes herein aftermentioned the Sum of twenty thousand Pounds.

TO the Loan Officers of Kings County to and for the Purposes herein aftermentioned the Sum of five thousand one hundred and sixty eight Pounds.

TO the Loan Officers of Queens County to and for the purposes herein aftermentioned the Sum of ten thousand seven hundred and twelve Pounds.

TO the Loan Officers of Suffolk County to and for the Purposes herein aftermentioned the Sum of nine thousand two hundred Pounds.

TO the Loan Officers of Richmond County to and for the Purposes hereinafter mentioned the Sum of three thousand two hundred and forty eight Pounds.

TO the Loan Officers of West Chester County to and for the Purposes herein after mentioned the Sum of ten thousand seven hundred and twelve Pounds.

To the Loan Officers of Dutchess County to and for the purposes herein after mentioned the Sum of eight thousand five hundred and sixty Pounds.

TO the Loan Officers of Orange County to and for the purposes herein aftermentioned the Sum of three thousand two hundred Pounds.

TO the Loan Officers of Ulster County to and for the purposes herein aftermentioned the Sum of nine thousand two hundred Pounds. For which respective Sums the said Treasurer shall give his receipt, and the Loan Officers respectively shall give receipts to the said first Signers indorsed on the Clerks certificate, and other Qualification herein after directed, which Receipts shall be to the same first Signers their Executors and Administrators a sufficient Discharge if otherwise they have well and truly performed the Duty enjoined them by this Act.

VI AND BE IT ALSO ENACTED that before the said Loan Officers do respectively enter upon their said Office every of them shall give Bond to his Majesty his Heirs and Successors, with such sufficient Security as shall be approved of by any one or more of the Judges of the inferior Court of the County together with the Majority of the Supervisors of the same County, and in the City of New York by any one or more of the Judges of the Supreme Court, signified by signing such his or their approbation on the Back of the said Bond, which Bond shall be in the full sum by this Act committed to his charge with Condition for the true and faithful performance of his Office and Duty, and that without favour Malice or Partiality.

VII. AND BE IT ENACTED that each Loan Officer respectively shall take take the following Oath or Affirmation. "I A B "will according to the best of my Skill and knowledge faithfully "impartially and truly demean myself in discharge of the Trust "committed to me as one of the Loan Officers for the ——. ——. "——. of ——. ——. —— by the Laws of this Colony in that "behalf made according to the purport true Intent and meaning "of the said Laws, so as the Public may not be prejudiced by "my Consent privity or procurement, so help me God." Which Oath or Affirmation shall be administred by any Justice of the Peace and indorsed on the Back of the said Bond, and signed by such Justice and the Loan Officer.

VIII AND BE IT ENACTED that the aforesaid Bond indorsed with the Approbation and Affidavit or Affirmation aforesaid shall be lodged with the Clerk of the County, who upon Receipt thereof shall give the Loan Officer a Certificate that such Bond indorsed as aforesaid is lodged with him, which

Certificate is to be delivered to the first Signers as aforesaid, on their delivering to him the Bills of Credit aforesaid, which Bond and Indorsements shall be recorded by the Clerk, and in Case of the Forfeiture of the same Bond, the Majority of the Supervisors with any one or more of the Judges of the Inferior Courts of the Counties respectively are hereby impowered to order the same to be put in suit, and the Monies recovered by virtue thereof shall be applied to the use of the County, on Consideration of the County's making good the Deficiencies of the Borrowers in the same, as in this Act is hereafter directed PROVIDED ALWAYS that in the City and County of New York the Justices and Vestrymen of the same City and County shall have all the Powers by this Act given to the Judges of the Inferior Courts and Supervisors in the other Counties of this Colony, which Justices and Vestrymen of the City and County of New York shall also perform all the Duties and Services and be liable to all the Pains, Penalties and Forfeitures which the Judges aforesaid and supervisors of the other Counties are to perform and be subject to by virtue of this Act, and in Case of any Deficiency of the Borrowers, they shall Cause such Deficiency, to be assessed levied and raised in such Manner as they assess, levy and raise the Tax for Minister and Poor.

IX AND BE IT ENACTED by the Authority aforesaid that on the last Tuesday of April next the Judges of the Inferior Courts or any one or more of them, together with the Supervisors (or the Majority of them) of the several Counties respectively of this Colony, shall meet at the Court House of the Counties respectively where the Majority of them shall elect and choose two sufficient Freeholders of the respective Counties to be Loan Officers for the same Counties. PROVIDED ALWAYS that nothing in this Clause shall be construed to extend to the Cities and Counties of New York and Albany.

X AND BE IT ENACTED by the Authority aforesaid that the Vestrymen of the City and County of New York, and Supervisors of the several Counties of this Colony shall at every of their Meetings with the Judge or Judges aforesaid directed by this Act, in the first Place take the Oath or Affirmation before any Justice of the Peace in the Words following. "I. A. B. will "according to the best of my Judgment and knowledge well and "truly execute the Trust reposed in me by an Act of the General "Assembly of this Colony intitled. AN ACT for emitting the

"Sum of one hundred and twenty thousand Pounds in Bills of "Credit to be put out on Loan, and to appropriate the Interest "arising thereon to the payment of the Debts of this Colony, and "to such Public Exigencies as the Circumstances of this Colony "may from Time to Time render necessary, and that without any "Favour, Malice or Partiality, so help me God."

XI AND BE IT ENACTED by the Authority aforesaid that the Loan Officers of each of the Cities and Counties aforesaid respectively when elected appointed and qualified according to the Directions of this Act shall be Bodies Politick and Corporate in fact and in Law, that is to say.

The Loan Officers for the City and County of New York shall be one Body Politick and Corporate by the Name of the Loan Officers of the City and County of New York.

The Loan Officers for the City and County of Albany shall be one Body Politick and Corporate by the Name of the Loan Officers of the City and County of Albany.

The Loan Officers for Kings County shall be one Body Politick and Corporate by the Name of the Loan Officers of Kings County.

The Loan Officers for Queens County shall be one Body Politick and Corporate by the Name of the Loan Officers of Queens County.

The Loan Officers for Suffolk County shall be one Body Politick and Corporate by the Name of the Loan Officers of Suffolk County.

The Loan Officers for Richmond County shall be one Body Politick and Corporate by the Name of the Loan Officers of Richmond County.

The Loan Officers for West Chester County shall be one Body Politick and Corporate by the Name of the Loan Officers of West Chester County.

The Loan Officers for Dutchess County shall be one Body Politick and Corporate by the Name of the Loan Officers of Dutchess County.

The Loan Officers for Orange County shall be one Body Politick and Corporate by the Name of the Loan Officers of Orange County.

The Loan Officers for Ulster County shall be one Body Politick and Corporate by the Name of the Loan Officers of Ulster County.

With full power to every of the said Bodies Politick to use a Common Seal, and by the same Seal, and in the Name of such

Body Politick to grant Receipts receive Mortgages, and again to grant the same away, to sue and to be sued, and generally with all such Powers as are necessary to be used for the due Execution of the Trust reposed in the said Loan Officers by this Act, any Law usage or Custom to the contrary in any wise notwithstanding.

XII AND BE IT ENACTED by the Authority aforesaid that when the said Loan Officers respectively have qualified themselves as above in this Act is directed they shall receive the said Bills of Credit signed by two of the four Signers first named as aforesaid which Bills the Loan Officers respectively shall divide betwixt them, and each of them sign his dividend thereof which Bills of Credit so signed by two of the four first Signers herein before named, and by one Loan Officer shall be let out to such as shall apply for the same, and can and will give Security to the said Loan Officers by Mortgage on Lands, Lots, Houses or other valuable Improvements lying in the same City or County, they the said Loan Officers first giving Public Notice (as in other Cases by this Act directed for Notices) by Advertisements set up, that on a certain Day (at least ten Days after setting them up) they will be ready to receive Borrowers qualified according to the Directions of this Act, and as on that Day Borrowers do offer their Names, and Sums they demand shall be orderly entered down in the Minute Book of proceedings, and every one shall be served according to the Priority of their Demand if reasonable Objection be not against the Title and Value of the Lands offered to be mortgaged, or some other sufficient Reason, which shall be entered also in the Minute Book of proceedings. PROVIDED ALWAYS, that if upon the first Day so many Borrowers do offer as to demand a greater Sum than the whole Sum in that County to be lent out, then and in that Case every such Borrower shall be abated of the Sum he demanded proportionately.

XIII AND BE IT ENACTED that the said Loan Officers respectively before they accept of any Lands, Lots, Houses or other Improvements in Mortgage for any of the said Bills they shall first view what is so offered in Mortgage or make due enquiry into the value thereof and then shall examine the Titles thereto by perusing the Deeds, Patents, Surveys and other Writings and Conveyances by which the same is held, and by which the value and Quantity may be the better known, and the said

Loan Officers respectively are hereby also impowered and required to administer to all persons applying for any of the said Bills as aforesaid the following Oath (or Affirmation if Quakers) to wit, "I A. B. am bona fide seized in fee Simple of the Lands. "Tenements and Hereditaments by me now offered to be Mort-"gaged in my own Right and to my own use, and the same were "not conveyed to me in Trust for the use of any Person nor with "Intent to borrow any Sum or Sums of Money upon the same, "for the use of any other Person or Persons whatsoever, and the "premises are free and clear from any other or former Gift, "Grant, Sale, Mortgage, Judgment, Extent, Recognizance or "other Incumbrance whatsoever to my knowledge except the "Rent issuing thereout to our Lord the King, so help me God."

XIV AND BE IT ENACTED by the Authority aforesaid that the Loan Officers of the said Cities and Counties respectively upon finding Borrowers qualified, and the Loan Officers being satisfied as aforesaid, are hereby required, and by virtue of this Act have full Power to lend out the Bills delivered to them as aforesaid at the Interest of five per Cent per Annum for the Term of fourteen Years from the last Tuesday of June next to come to be paid in again by payments to be made as herein after directed in Sums not exceeding three Hundred Pounds and not under fifty Pounds (unless the Proportion as aforesaid be less) to any one Person, the said Loan Officers taking security for the same by way of Mortgage as aforesaid of at least double the Value in Lands Tenements and Hereditaments, and of at least three Times the Value in Houses within the said respective Cities and Counties, and administring an Oath or Affirmation to the Borrower as aforesaid, and the said Mortgage shall be executed before two or more lawful Witnesses signing thereto, and the Substance thereof shall be Minuted in a Book to be by the said Loan Officers kept for that purpose in each respective City and County, for the making of which Mortgage and Minute the Borrower shall pay to the said Loan Officers the Sum of four Shillings and no more, which Mortgage and Minute shall be and each of them are hereby declared to be Matter of Record and an attested Copy of the said Mortgage if in being or of the said Minute in Case the Mortgage is lost under the Hands of the Loan Officers, and Seal of the Loan Office shall be good Evidence of the said Mortgage in any Court within this Colony.

XV. AND BE IT ENACTED by the Authority aforesaid that the Interest of the Money lent out as aforesaid shall be payable Yearly on the last Tuesday of June to the Loan Officers, and the Principals of all the Monies lent out as aforesaid shall be paid in again in the Manner following that is to say, one tenth Part of the principal Money on the last Tuesday of June which will be in the Year of our Lord one thousand seven hundred and seventy five. one other tenth Part thereof on the last Tuesday of June which will be in the Year of our Lord one thousand seven hundred and seventy six, one other tenth Part thereof on the last Tuesday of June which will be in the Year of our Lord one thousand seven hundred and seventy seven one other tenth Part thereof on the last Tuesday of June which will be in the Year of our Lord one thousand seven hundred and seventy eight one other tenth Part thereof on the last Tuesday of June which will be in the Year of our Lord one thousand seven hundred and seventy nine one other tenth Part thereof on the last Tuesday of June which will be in the year of our Lord one thousand seven hundred and eighty one other tenth Part thereof on the last Tuesday of June which will be in the Year of our Lord one thousand seven hundred and eighty one, one other tenth Part thereof on the last Tuesday of June which will be in the Year of our Lord one thousand seven hundred and eighty two, one other tenth Part thereof on the last Tuesday of June which will be in the Year of our Lord one thousand seven hundred and eighty three, and the remaining tenth Part thereof on the last Tuesday of June which will be in the Year of our Lord one thousand seven hundred and eighty four, and the respective Loan Officers at the lending of the Money are hereby required to take the Security for the same accordingly, and the said Loan Officers for every Sum paid to them shall give to the payer a Receipt and shall also enter one Minute of the same payment on the Back of the Mortgage, and another Minute thereof in the Book of Accounts by them to be kept, and that without any Fee or Reward. But if the Borrower his Heirs Executors or Administrators shall see Cause to pay in a fourth or a half or three Quarters or the whole of the Principal due to the said Loan Officer on any last Tuesday of June before the said last Tuesday of June one thousand seven hundred and eighty four, the said Loan Officers are hereby impowered and required to receive the same on the last Tuesday of June annually, and no other Day of the Year unless so many do offer payment on that Day, that the Loan Officers cannot within the Day receive the whole, and in that Case they are to continue to receive until all that on that Day offered have paid in the Monies so offered, and unless he brings along with him another sufficient Borrower to give new Security to the Satisfaction of the Loan Officers for the whole of the Money by him paid in, and in that Case the Loan Officers shall accept thereof on any of their stated Days of meeting, and when the whole Principal and Interest is paid the said Loan Officers shall if required give the Party paying a Release of the Mortgage given by the Borrower and shall tear off the Name and seal and make an Entry in the Margin of the Mortgage and in the Margin of the Minute made thereof, that such a Day and Year such Release was made, for which Release the Releasee shall pay the Sum of two shillings and no more, and when any Parts of the Principals are paid in as aforesaid before the said last Tuesday of June one thousand seven hundred and eighty four the Loan Officers shall at the end of that Meeting compute the Sum of the whole Principals so paid in, and give Public Notice of the Sum by Advertisements set up, and that on that Day Week they will be ready to receive Borrowers of the said Monies, to whom the said Loan Officers shall lend the same out, and in the lending and taking security shall conform themselves (as near as the Circumstances of the Case can admit) to the Directions herein before prescribed and if any Monies still remain in their Hands for want of Borrowers, they shall set up Advertisements of the Sum thereof and continue to do the like at the End of every of their stated Meetings.

XVI AND BE IT ENACTED that in case any Loan Officer shall die or remove or neglect delay or refuse or omit performing the Duty required or enjoined him by this Act or shall behave himself in his Office with Favour, Affection, Partiality or Malice whereby the Public or any private Person may be injured, upon Report or Complaint made thereof to any two or more of the Judges aforesaid of the respective Counties, or to the Justices and Vestrymen of the City of New York to which he belongs, the said Judges are hereby required and commanded to issue out their Precepts to call together the Judges and Supervisors of the same County to meet at such Time and Place as in the said Precept shall be appointed to hear and determine summarily, upon the said Report or Complaint, and upon sufficient Proof made to any or more of the said Judges with the major Part of the said Supervisors of any Death, Removal, Failure, or Neglect in the said Office as aforesaid, then and in that Case the said Majority of the Supervisors with Concurrence of one or more of the Judges aforesaid shall proceed in Manner as herein before directed to elect and choose and are hereby required and commanded to elect and choose a Loan Officer in the Room and stead of such deceased or absent Person or omitter or Defaulter which Loan Officer, so chosen as aforesaid having entered into Bond and been qualified in like manner as other Loan Officers are by this Act directed shall then have all the Powers, Privileges and Advantages and be subject to all the Pains, Penalties and Forfeitures which any of the Loan Officers of the County elected as aforesaid are vested with entitled to, charged with or Subject to by virtue of this Act.

XVII AND BE IT ENACTED that if any of the Loan Officers hereafter to be elected and appointed by virtue of this Act shall at any Time hereafter desire to be discharged of and from the said Office, he applying to any one or more of the Judges aforesaid for that purpose, he or they shall upon that Application issue their Precept to summon the Judges aforesaid and Supervisors to meet at a Place and Day by the said Precept prefixed, to whom when met the said Loan Officer shall produce or render an Account of his proceedings in his said Office, and if it appear upon Examination that the said Loan Officer hath faithfully demeaned himself in the Discharge of his said Office according to the true Intent and Meaning of this Act, then and in such Case such Loan Officer shall by the Majority of the Supervisors with the concurrence of the said Judges be discharged of and from his said Office, and another fit Person shall be by them elected and appointed to supply his place, who shall take the same Oath or Affirmation, give the like Security, be under and subject to the like Penalties, Restrictions and Regulations, and receive the same salaries and Advantages whatsoever as the other Loan Officers for that County by virtue of this Act are liable subject or intitled unto.

XVIII AND BE IT ENACTED by the authority aforesaid that when a Loan Officer shall be chosen and qualified as herein is directed in the Place of a former Loan Officer, such former Loan Officer his Executors or Administrators shall upon Demand deliver to the new Loan Officer chosen in his Place and qualified as aforesaid, all the Monies, Books, and Papers that were in such former Loan Officers Custody belonging to his Office upon Oath before any Justice of the Peace and in Case any such former Loan Officer, or his Executors or Administrators shall deny delay or refuse to make such Delivery on Oath when demanded as aforesaid, the Bond of such former Loan Officer shall be forfeited.

XIX BE IT ALSO ENACTED that if any Borrower shall neglect to bring in and pay, or cause to be brought in and paid yearly and every Year on the last Tuesday of June or within twenty two Days thereafter on one of the Days which the Loan Officers aforesaid are by this Act directed to attend the respective Loan Offices, the yearly Interest due by his Mortgage and also the Part of the Principal as it becomes payable, then and in either of these Cases the Loan Officers to whom such mortgage was granted shall be seized of an absolute indefeazable Estate in the Lands, Houses, Tenements, and Hereditaments thereby Mortgaged to them their Successors and Assigns to the uses in this Act mentioned, and the Mortgagor his or her Heirs and Assigns shall be utterly foreclosed and barred of all equity of Redemption of the Mortgaged Premises any Law usage or Custom or Practice in Courts of Equity to the contrary notwithstanding.

XX BE IT FURTHER ENACTED that the said Loan Officers respectively shall attend the Loan Office every Year to receive the Monies by this Act directed to be paid into them upon the last Tuesday of June, and thereafter on the Tuesday in each Week for the Term of three Weeks.

XXI AND BE IT ENACTED that the said Loan Officers shall in the Evening of the last of the Tuesdays aforesaid, yearly and every Year give sufficient Directions which they are to take care shall be observed for fixing up Advertisements at three of the most Public Places in at least three or more distinct Towns or Precincts of the County where the Premises are situate of all the Lands contained in the Mortgages whereof the Equity of Redemption is foreclosed, describing the Quantity and situation of the same, and that on the last Tuesday of December next following they are to be sold at the Court House of the respective County where the Lands lye by way of Public Vendue to the highest Bidder.

XXII BE IT LIKEWISE ENACTED that the Loan Officers of the respective Cities and Counties aforesaid shall on the said last Tuesday of December yearly expose the Lands in the Mortgages foreclosed as aforesaid to sale by way of Public Vendue, and upon Sale shall convey them to the highest Bidder or Bidders, who shall pay for their Deeds five shillings, and the Buyer or Buyers shall and may hold and enjoy the same for such Estate as they were sold clearly discharged and freed from all Benefit and Equity of Redemption, and all other Incumbrances made and Suffered by the Mortgagor his or her Heirs or Assigns, and such Sales shall be available in Law and Equity.

XXIII AND BE IT ENACTED that the Money or Price for which the Premises are sold shall upon the Sale thereof be paid to the said Loan Officers out of which they shall retain in their Hands what has not been paid in of the whole Principal lent together with the Interest that has become due thereon and might become due until the last Tuesday of June next, as also the Expence of the Advertisements, and of the Sale the same not exceeding fifteen Shillings and the Remainder (if any be) the Loan Officers shall pay to the Mortgagor his or her Heirs or Assigns. PROVIDED ALWAYS that if a Person Offers at the Time of the Sale to borrow (on sufficient Security within this Act) the whole Principal that is to be retained out of the price and lent out again, then and in that Case the Loan Officers shall not retain Interest beyond the Day of Sale. PROVIDED ALSO that if the Buyer incline to be the Borrower of the Principal or Principals that is or are to be paid in by him and lent out again, and if the Loan Officers be satisfied of the Security to be given by him in Manner aforesaid he shall be preferred to any other Borrower. PROVIDED LIKEWISE that the Loan Officers shall not be obliged to take Notice of any Assigns of the Mortgagor, unless they enter a Notice of their Right with the said Loan Officers at or before the Time of Sale which Notice the Loan Officers shall enter on the Mortgage and Minute thereof on Demand, the Assignee paying one Shilling for the same and Assigns shall be preferred according to the Priority of their Entries of such Notices.

XXIV AND BE IT ENACTED that after any Lands Houses, Tenements or Hereditaments are mortgaged according to the Directions of this Act, if it shall appear to the Loan Officers upon Good and sufficient Grounds (which they shall insert in the

Minute Book of their proceedings) that the Mortgagor had no good Right or Title to the Premises Mortgaged or has otherwise broke the Covenants of his Mortgage, so that the Public may be in danger of losing the Monies or any part thereof, advanced to Loan upon the Credit of the Premises, it shall and may be lawful to and for the said Loan Officers, and they are hereby impowered and required to commence an Action or Actions of Debt or Covenant upon the said Mortgage against the Mortgagor his or her Heirs Executors or Administrators, and the same to prosecute to Judgment in any Court of Record for the Recovery of the whole Monies lent upon the Mortgage and Interest become due, and that shall become due until the last Tuesday of June next following the Judgment with Costs and Charges by all lawful Ways and means whatsoever, in which Action or Actions the Mortgagor shall be held to special Bail, and the Court in which such Action is brought is, and the Judges thereof in vacation are hereby authorized and directed to give such short Days for the Rules of Pleading thereon, that Judgment or a Tryal and final Determination may be had the first Court after the Court at which the Defendant first appeared to the same Action, and such Action shall be brought (if the Defendant be found within this Colony) in the County where the Cause of Action arises.

XXV AND BE IT ENACTED that the aforesaid Bills of Credit to be made and issued by virtue of this Act, when signed by any two of the first Signers aforesaid, and the Treasurer or one Loan Officer shall be received by the said Loan Officers for and during the Term of fourteen Years, and by the Treasurer of this Colony for and during the said Term and for one Year thereafter.

XXVI AND BE IT ENACTED that if any Person or Persons whatsoever shall presume to counterfeit any of the Bills of Credit issued by virtue of this Act, or shall alter any of the said Bills issued as aforesaid so that they shall appear to be of greater value than by this Act the same Bill or Bills so altered were enacted signed or Numbered to pass for, or shall knowingly pass or give in payment any of the Bills aforesaid so counterfeited or altered every Person guilty of Counterfeiting or altering of any of the said Bills as aforesaid or of knowingly passing or giving in payment any such counterfeit or altered Bills, shall be guilty of Felony and being thereof convicted shall suffer the Pains of Death without the Benefit of Clergy, and though such counterfeiting, altering or knowingly passing Counterfeit or altered Bills shall be done out of this Colony, yet any Grand Jury within this Colony is hereby impowered to present the same and to set forth in the Indictment the Place where by their Evidence it appeared that the Fact was committed which Indictment is hereby declared good notwithstanding that the Place alledged be out of this Colony, and the Petty Juries on the Tryals of all such foreign Issues shall be returned from the Body of the City and County of New York, any Law usage or Custom to the contrary notwithstanding.

XXVII AND BE IT ALSO ENACTED that the respective Loan Offices in this Colony shall be kept at the Court House of each respective County or at some other convenient Place near the same, and the said Loan Officers shall so soon as the said Bills are signed and delivered to them set up Advertisements of the first Day of their attending the Loan Office for the purposes herein before mentioned, and shall duly attend the same on that first Day and on every Tuesday and Wednesday in each Week for the Space of four Weeks thereafter, if there be Occasion of their sitting so long; and the said first Signers aforesaid as soon as they can fix the Day upon which they can deliver the said Bills to the Loan Officers, shall send Notice by Letters to them to come and receive the Bills at that Day.

XXVIII. AND BE IT ENACTED that the Loan Officers respectively shall retain in their Hands so much of the Interest Monies paid in to them as will pay them their respective Salaries appointed by this Act, and the remainder of the said Interest Monies shall be annually paid to the Treasurer of this Colony on or before the last Tuesday of the Month of August and the said Treasurer's Receipt shall be to the said Loan Officers, and every of them their Heirs, Executors and Administrators a sufficient Discharge.

XXIX. AND BE IT FURTHER ENACTED that the Yearly Salaries of the Loan Officers aforesaid for the Services required of them by this Act shall be as follows, to wit

For every of the Loan Officers of the City and County of New York forty Pounds.

For every of the Loan Officers of the City and County of Albany thirty Pounds.

For every of the Loan Officers of Kings County ten Pounds.

For every of the Loan Officers of Queens County sixteen Pounds.

For every of the Loan Officers of Suffolk County sixteen Pounds.

For every of the Loan Officers of Richmond County nine Pounds.

For every of the Loan Officers of West Chester County sixteen Pounds.

For every of the Loan Officers of Dutchess County sixteen Pounds.

For every of the Loan Officers of Orange County ten Pounds.

For every of the Loan Officers of Ulster County sixteen Pounds.

XXX AND BE IT ENACTED by the Authority aforesaid that the Supervisors and Judges aforesaid of the several Counties of this Colony shall on the last Tuesday of June which will be in the year of our Lord one thousand seven hundred and seventy one, and yearly thereafter on the last Tuesday of June, meet together with the said Loan Officers at the Court House of the County, and the majority of the Supervisors with one or more of the Judges aforesaid shall carefully inspect and examine the Mortgages, Minutes and Accounts of the Loan Officers, to find whether they have been in any way faulty or negligent in their Offices, and if they find so, then to choose others in their Places as aforesaid, when also if any Deficiency has happened by a Borrowers not having Right to the Lands Mortgaged, or by the selling thereof for a less Price than what before is mentioned or any other way whatsoever, then they the said Supervisors or the majority of them with the Concurrence of one or more of the said Judges shall cause all such Deficiencies to be assessed and levied of the County, as the other County Charges, so that the whole of such Deficiencies be paid in to the said Loan Officers by the last Tuesday of June then next following.

XXXI AND BE IT ENACTED by the Authority aforesaid that in Case one or more of the said Judges, and a majority of the Supervisors aforesaid shall not meet on the last Tuesday of June next to come, or in Case they shall not meet Yearly on the last Tuesday of June, or in Case they shall not meet when summoned by a Precept of one or more of the said Judges for the several Purposes in this Act mentioned, every of them in either of these Cases that are absent unless detained by Sickness shall forfeit the Sum of three Pounds, and the Judge or Judges then attending shall issue his or their Precept to one or more Constables to summon the Judges and Supervisors to attend that

Day Week for the Purposes aforesaid under double the Penalty aforesaid, which each neglecting then to attend if duly summoned shall also forfeit, though a sufficient Number do appear; And in Case a sufficient Number do not then appear the Judge or Judges appearing shall proceed in like manner from Week to Week till a full Number of Supervisors do appear to perform the Duty for which they before ought to have met. And in Case the said Supervisors or Vestrymen or either of them when a majority of them are met shall neglect or refuse to take the Oath or Affirmation herein prescribed, or neglect or refuse to do the Duty enjoined them by this Act when met, or shall on any Pretence whatsoever on the Day of their annual Meeting, neglect or omit the causing to be assessed levied and raised the whole Deficiencies that have happened by any of the Means aforesaid, every of them neglecting their Duty herein, shall forfeit to his Majesty the Sum of five Pounds; all which Penalties before in this Clause mentioned are to be recovered before any one of his Majesty's Justices of the Peace within the City or County where such Forfeiture shall arise, one half to the use of such Judge or Judges and Supervisors of the same County endeavouring to perform their Duty herein, who will Sue and inform against the rest, and prosecute their Suit to effect, and the other half to be paid to the Treasurer, and applied towards cancelling the Bills of Credit in such Manner as shall be directed by Act or Acts of the General Assembly.

XXXII AND BE IT ENACTED that all and every the Sums of Money which may at any Time afterwards be recovered by the Loan Officers aforesaid of such Persons as have been the occasion of such Deficiencies as aforesaid shall be applied to the use of such County and the Judge or Judges and Supervisors are hereby impowered to take all lawful Ways and Means in the Name of the said Loan Officers to recover the same.

XXXIII AND BE IT ENACTED by the Authority aforesaid that it shall and may be lawful for the said Loan Officers to let out upon Loan any of the said Bills of Credit in such Manner as they shall think best upon security of good Plate to be delivered to them at six Shillings per Ounce, to be paid in again to the said Loan Officers on the last Tuesday of June then next with a Years Interest at five per Cent for the same, and in Case of Non-payment at any of the two first stated Days of Meeting of the

Loan Officers, then the said Loan Officers are to sell the same Plate in such Manner, and upon the same Day as they are directed to sell the Lands of the Mortgages forfeited as aforesaid and they are to return the overplus to the Owner (if any be) after payment of the Principal and Charges with Interest past and to come until the last Tuesday of June then next to come unless a Borrower offers at Time of Sale as in Case of Lands herein before mentioned, any Thing in this Act to the contrary notwithstanding.

XXXIV. AND BE IT ENACTED that if any of the said Monies shall remain in the Hands of the Loan Officers four Weeks after the first Day of letting it out for want of Borrowers, it shall be lawful for them to let out the same on good security by Mortgage of Lands in the County or on Plate as aforesaid to any Person who will borrow the same in any Sums though they be upwards of three Hundred Pounds.

XXXV. BE IT ENACTED by the Authority aforesaid that if any of the Bills of Credit shall remain four Weeks over and above the four Weeks aforesaid that is to say in all eight Weeks in the Hands of the Loan Officers for want of Borrowers after the first Day of letting out as aforesaid, then and in that Case the said Loan Officers or one of them, by the Consent of the other to be entered and signed in the Minute Book of proceedings shall carry it to the Loan Officers of the next County or Counties where there were more Monies demanded in Loan than there were Monies to lend, and deliver it to the Loan Officers of such next County, upon their Receipt for the same, and their entering a Memorandum of it in the Minutes of their Proceedings, which Loan Officers to whom such Sum is brought, shall accept thereof and shall set up Advertisements thereof, and therein assign a Day in the next Week for Borrowers to offer and shall proceed in the lending this further Sum in their County as nearly as Circumstances of Things can admit in the like Manner as they proceeded in lending the first Sum, of which Transposition of those Monies the Loan Officers of the several Counties shall give Notice in writing signed by them to the Treasurer at the Time of their paying to him the first Interest Monies thereafter, of which Notices to him he shall enter Memorandums in his Books of Accounts the better to ascertain the Interest he is to receive yearly from the respective Counties, and the principal Sums that the Counties are finally to cancel.

XXXVI. AND to prevent Frauds that may happen by Executors or Administrators in their nonpayment of any Part of the Money borrowed as aforesaid by their respective Testators or Intestates. BE IT ENACTED that if any Person or Persons that shall become Borrowers of the Bills issued by virtue of this Act, and shall afterwards make his her or their last Will and Testament in due form of Law, thereby devising the Premises so mortgaged to any other Person or Persons, leaving personal Estate sufficient to pay his or her debts, with an Overplus not otherwise in the said Will disposed of, and not expressly providing in other Manner by the said Will, in such Case it shall be understood that the Devisor intended that the Mortgage Money in arrear at the Time of his Death should be PAID out of his Personal Estate and his Executor or Executors shall be accordingly compelled to pay the same thereout in aid of such Devisee or Devisees. But in Case the said last Will was made before the premises were mortgaged then it shall be understood that the Testators intent was (unless otherwise expressed in such Will) that the Devisee or Devisees should pay the residue of the Mortgage Money in arrear at the Time of such Testator's Death, and in Case any Executor or Executors contrary to the Intent of this Act, having Effects sufficient, shall permit a sale to be made of the Premises mortgaged, such Devisee or Devisees may immediately have his her or their Action either in proper person or by Guardian or next Friend if under age, against such Executor or Executors, and recover double the Damages sustained with Costs of Suit; and in Case any Executor or Executors shall in such Case be a purchaser of the Premises so mortgaged, or any other in Trust for him or for his use, he or they shall be deemed seized of the premises for the use of the Devisee or Devisees, and such Executor or Executors, and their Trustees, are hereby disabled from making any Conveyance thereof from such Devisee or Devisees, and if any such Conveyance is made the same is hereby declared fraudulent and void against such Devisee or Devisees.

XXXVII. AND BE IT ENACTED that in Case any Mortgagor die intestate, the Mortgage Money aforesaid or any Part thereof being in arrear and unpaid, and leaving personal Estate sufficient to pay his Debts with an Overplus, his Heir at Law being under age when any Part of the said Mortgage Money shall become due, in such Cases the Mortgage Monies shall be paid out of the Personal Estate if sufficient and the profits of the Premises Mortgaged shall be applied towards Repayment of the said Monies to such Person or Persons as may be entitled to the same where it so happens that the Part of the Personal Estate coming to the said Heir at Law is not sufficient to discharge such Mortgage, and in Case the Profits of the Mortgaged Premises shall not be sufficient to make such Re-payment, the Heir at Law shall be compelled to make it up with Interest, when he she or they come of Age, and where any Sale shall happen to be made pursuant to the Tenor of this Act, after the Death of the Testator or Intestate because of the Deficiency of the Personal Estate of the Testator or Intestate, his or her Heirs or Devisees being then under Age, in such Case the Monies arising by such Sale after the Deduction of the principal, Interests and Costs due to the said Loan Office, shall be placed out to Interest by the Executors or Administrators for the Benefit of such Heir or Devisee or Person entitled to such Lands.

XXXVIII. AND BE IT ENACTED by the Authority aforesaid that the Borrowers may pay their Interest and Principals in any of the Bills of Credit of this Colony, or in Silver or Gold, or Lyon Dollars, and the Treasurer and Loan Officers shall accept thereof in lieu of the Bills issued by virtue of this Act.

XXXIX AND BE IT ENACTED by the Authority aforesaid that if any Person shall falsely swear or Affirm in any of the Cases where an Oath or Affirmation is required to be taken by this Act, or shall Willfully and knowingly act contrary to the Oath or Affirmation he has before taken, such Offence is hereby declared to be Perjury and the Offender being convicted thereof shall suffer all the Pains and Penalties of Perjury which by the Laws of Great Britain can be inflicted.

XL AND BE IT FURTHER ENACTED that all Judges and Justices in this Colony shall and they are hereby directed to construe this Act most favourably for the prosecutor, and most strongly against the Offender, and shall allow him or her no Essoin Protection or Wager of Law nor more than one Imparlance, and shall endeavor the Execution of this Act according to the true Intent and Meaning thereof, notwithstanding the want of apt Words to express the same, and if Mischiefs should happen which may affect the Public or any Private Person or the Credit of the Bills issued by virtue of this Act against which no Remedies are expressly provided by this Act, but if there happen to be Remedies against like Mischiefs they the said Judges and Justices shall construe and extend the like Remedies to and for the like Mischiefs according to the true Intent and meaning of this Act, any Law usage or Custom to the contrary notwithstanding.

XLI AND BE IT ENACTED that the first Signers of the Bills shall preserve one Copy of each Impression of the Bills hereby issued, upon which they shall remark how the Bills are numbered, and shall deliver those Copies to the Treasurer to be carefully preserved for the better discovery of Counterfeits, if any should happen to be made of the said Bills any Thing herein contained to the contrary notwithstanding.

XLII. AND BE IT ALSO ENACTED by the Authority aforesaid that the Bills of Credit issued by virtue of this Act shall be cancelled in like Manner as the Bills of Credit were cancelled that were emitted by virtue of an Act intitled, An Act for the more effectual cancelling the Bills of Credit of this Colony passed the eighth Day of April one thousand seven hundred and forty eight and that the Representatives in General Assembly for the Time being for the City and County of New York shall and are hereby impowered to cancel the same as by the said Act is directed.

XLIII AND BE IT ENACTED by the Authority aforesaid that on the last Tuesday of April next one or more of the Judges of the Inferior Court for the County of Orange together with the supervisors (or the major Part of them) shall meet at the dwelling House of Daniel Coe in Haverstraw Precinct in the said Colony, when the Majority of them shall elect and choose two sufficient Freeholders of the said County to be Loan Officers for the said County, and that the Supervisors and Judges aforesaid of the said County shall on the last Tuesday of June which will be in the year of our Lord one thousand seven hundred and seventy one, meet at the Court House at Orange Town with the Loan Officers of the said County, and the Year following at the Court House at Goshen, and so alternately each year during the Continuance of this Act.

XLIV. AND BE IT ENACTED by the Authority aforesaid that Theodorus Van Wyck, Andrew Barclay and Nicholas Governeur shall be the Loan Officers for the City and County of New York, any Thing in this Act to the contrary thereof in any wise notwithstanding.

XLV. AND BE IT ENACTED by the Authority aforesaid that John H. Ten Eyck and Harmanus Wendell shall be the Loan Officers for the City and County of Albany, and that in Case of the Death or refusal of either or both of them, the Judges and Supervisors of the said City and County shall appoint others, as is directed by this Act in the other Counties, any Thing in this Act to the contrary notwithstanding.

XLVI. BE IT ALSO ENACTED that the Interest of the Money arising by virtue of this Act shall be and remain in the Treasury until it shall be disposed of by Act or Acts hereafter to be passed for that purpose.

[CHAPTER 1424.]

[Chapter 1424 of Van Schaack, where the title only is printed. Repealed by the king March 14, 1770, provided for by chapter 1473.]

An Act to facilitate and explain the Duty of the Loan Officers in this Colony.

[Passed, January 5, 1770.]

I BE IT ENACTED by his Honor the Lieutenant Governor, the Council and the General Assembly, and it is hereby enacted by the Authority of the same that for the greater uniformity in the Securities to be taken in the Loan Offices for the Money to be lent by virtue of an Act of the General Assembly of this Colony intitled, "An Act for emitting the Sum of one hundred and "twenty thousand Pounds in Bills of Credit to be put out on "Loan and to appropriate the Interest arising thereon to the "payment of the Debts of this Colony, and to such Public Exigen- "cies as the Circumstances of this Colony may from Time to "Time render necessary." The Mortgages for the Money by virtue of the said Act lent, shall be in the Form following, Vizt:

THIS INDENTURE made the Day of in the year of the Reign of our Sovereign Lord George the third by the Grace of God of Great Britain France and Ireland, King, Defender of the Faith, &c Annoq. Domini one thousand seven hundred and BETWEEN of the County of of the one Part, and the Loan Officers of the said of of the other Part. WITNESSETH that the said for and in Consideration of the Sum of by the Loan Officers of the of to him well and truly in Hand paid, whereof he grants the Receipt and acknowledges himself to be therewith contented, and for himself his Heirs Executors and Administrators releases and discharges the Loan Officers of the of and their Successors thereof forever HATH Granted Bargained Sold, Released Enfeoffed and Confirmed, and by these Presents doth Grant Bargain, Sell, Release, Enfeof, and Confirm to the Loan Officers of the of and their Successors and Assigns forever All that TOGETHER with all and all Manner of Woods, Underwoods, Trees, Mines, Minerals, Quarries, Hawkings, Huntings, Fowlings, Fishings, Buildings, Fences, Improvements, Hereditaments and Appurtenances whatsoever to the same belonging or in any ways appertaining, and all the Estate Right, Title, Interest, possession, property, Claim and Demand of the said and his Heirs to the above Bargained Premises and every Part thereof. TO HAVE AND TO HOLD the above Bargained Premises to the Loan Officers of the of their Successors and Assigns forever to the uses and purposes mentioned in an Act of the General Assembly of this Colony passed in the tenth Year of the Reign of King George the third Intitled. "An Act for emitting the Sum of one hundred and "twenty thousand Pounds in Bills of Credit to be put out on "Loan, and to appropriate the Interest arising thereon to the "payment of the Debts of this Colony, and to such Public exigen- "cies as the Circumstances of this Colony may from Time to "Time render necessary" and the said for himself his Heirs Executors and Administrators does Covenant, Grant, Bargain, and Agree to and with the Loan Officers of the of and their Successors that at and before the Time of the Ensealing and Delivery hereof he the said stood lawfully seized of the abovebargained Premises of a good sure perfect absolute and indefeazible Estate of Inheritance in the Law in Fee Simple, and that the same then were free and clear of all former and other Gifts, Grants, Bargains, Sales, Leases, Releases, Judgments, Extents, Recognizances, Dowers, Entails and other Incumbrances in the Law whatsoever PROVIDED ALWAYS, and these Presents are upon this Condition, that if the said his Heirs Executors, Administrators or Assigns do pay or cause to be paid to the Loan Officers of the of the Interest at the Rate of five per Cent of the said Principal Sum of on the last Tuesday of June yearly until the last Tuesday of June which will be in the Year of our Lord one thousand seven hundred and seventy four inclusive; and if the said or his aforesaids shall pay to the Loan Officers of the of the one tenth Part of the said Principal Sum of on the last Tuesday of June which will be in the Year of our Lord one thousand seven hundred and seventy five, together with the Interest due on the said Principal Sum of and one other tenth Part of the said Principal Sum on the last Tuesday of June which will be in the Year of our Lord one thousand seven hundred and seventy six together with the Interest then due, and one other tenth Part of the said Principal Sum on the last Tuesday of June which will be in the Year of our Lord one thousand seven hundred and seventy seven together with the Interest then due, and one other tenth Part of the said Principal Sum on the last Tuesday of June which will be in the Year of our Lord one thousand seven hundred and seventy eight, together with the Interest then due, and one other Tenth Part of the said Principal Sum on the last Tuesday of June which will be in the Year of our Lord one thousand seven hundred and seventy nine, together with the Interest then due, and one other tenth Part of the said Principal Sum on the last Tuesday of June which will be in the Year of our Lord one thousand seven hundred and eighty, together with the Interest then due, and one other tenth Part of the said Principal Sum on the last Tuesday of June which will be in the Year of our Lord one thousand seven hundred and eighty one, together with the Interest then due, and one other tenth Part of the said Principal sum on the last Tuesday of June which will be in the Year of our Lord one thousand seven hundred and eighty two together with the Interest then due, and one other tenth Part of the said Principal Sum on the last Tuesday of June which will be in the Year of our Lord one thousand seven hundred and eighty three, together with the Interest then due, and the Remainder of the said Principal Sum on the last Tuesday of June which will be in the Year of our Lord one thousand seven hundred and eighty four together with the Interest then due thereon according to the true Intent and meaning of the said Act of General Assembly, then the above Grant, Bargain and Sale and every Article and Clause thereof shall be void, but if Failure be made in any of the Payments abovementioned then the above Bargain and Sale is to remain in full Force and Virtue and the said for himself his Heirs and Assigns doth agree to be absolutely barred of all equity of Redemption of the Premises within twenty two Days after such Failure; and the said for himself his Heirs, Executors and Administrators does Covenant Grant, Bargain, promise and agree to and with the Loan Officers of the of . and their Successors well and truly to pay to them all and every of the Sums of Money above-mentioned at the Times on which the same ought to be paid as aforesaid, and that the above Bargained premises upon the Sale thereof pursuant to the Directions of the said Act will yield the Principal and Interest aforesaid remaining unpaid at the Time of such Sale and until the last Tuesday of June next after the Day of Sale together with fifteen Shillings for the charge of such Sale IN WITNESS whereof the Parties to these Present Indentures have interchangeably set their Hands and Seals the Day and Year first above written.

SEALED and DELIVERED in the presence of

II. AND BE IT ENACTED by the Authority aforesaid that Hugh Gaine shall print forty eight hundred Copies of the said Mortgages, and bind so many of them into a Book together with six Leaves of clean Paper for an Alphabet for the use of the Loan Office of each County, that there may be a Mortgage for every fifty Pounds of Bills of Credit given to the Loan Office of that County, and the Number remaining he shall give in loose Sheets in the like proportion to each of the Loan Offices in order therewith (if there should be Occasion) to give attested Copies of the original Mortgages to the Buyers of any of the Mortgaged Lands, which Books together with the said loose Sheets are to be delivered by the Printer to the first Signers of the Bills, by them with the Bills to be delivered to the Loan Officers of each County.

III. AND BE IT ENACTED that no Mortgage shall be taken in the Loan Offices but by filling up one of the Blanks of the said Book of Mortgages none of them shall be defaced nor torn out, except the Seal when the Mortgagor pays off the whole Principal and Interest of the Mortgage, and the Loan Officers shall proceed in the taking of the Mortgages from the Beginning of the Book forward numbering the Mortgages as they are taken and inserting the Mortgagors Name and Number in the Alphabet under the Letter answering the Mortgagor's Sirname.

IV. BE IT ENACTED that the Printer shall also bind up ten Books of clean paper one for the use of each Loan Office, and to contain about two third Parts of the bigness of the Book of Mortgages for the same County to be delivered as aforesaid with the Book of Mortgages.

V. BE IT ENACTED that the Loan Officers shall in one End of the last Book minute the Substance of each Mortgage to wit, the Number thereof, the Date, the Mortgagor's Name, the Sum lent, and the Boundaries of the Lands Mortgaged: and when the one Loan Officer has the Custody of the Book of Mortgages, the other shall have the Custody of this Book, that Fire or other Accidents which may happen may be guarded against, and the Printer shall make an Alphabet, to it like to that of the Book of Mortgages, and to prevent any Deception of the Mortgagor, he shall examine, or see the Minute examined with the Original Mortgage, and he with the Witnesses shall sign to the same.

VI AND BE IT ENACTED that the Loan Officers, beginning at the other End of the said Book shall insert the Minutes of their proceedings therein, to wit.

1st: The Days they meet, Place, House, and Loan Officers present.

2d: If any is absent, shall the next Time minute the Cause of his Absence.

3d. Shall enter the Hour that every one demands the Loan of Money, and the Quantity he demands.

4th; Shall enter down the Reason why a Prior Demander had not the Money according to his Demand, and the Substance of Examinations for clearing Titles and Value.

5th: Shall enter down the Monies received from the first Signers of the Bills and the Monies delivered to, or received from the Loan Officers of another County, and the Day when, with Copy of the Notice thereof to be delivered to the Treasurer, and when that Notice was delivered to the Treasurer and by whom.

6th; The last Day of their four Days of Meeting for receiving of Monies yearly, they shall enter whose Mortgages are foreclosed and the Numbers and Sums of them.

7th; Shall enter the Orders for, and Copies of the Advertisements of Sale and Places at which they were to be set up, and Persons Names that are to set them up.

8th; Shall enter the Buyer's Name of Lands and price sold for and payment of the Overplus to whom it belongs, with the Time and Witnesses of such payment.

9th; In Case any Principals or Part thereof are paid in before the Times of Payment in the Mortgages, the Totals of such Principals so paid in shall be entered in this Book, with Copy of the Advertisement of lending out again, and on the Day of Demand advertised, the Names of the Demanders thereof, and they shall in that Case proceed as before.

10th: Shall enter the Cause of all Suits, and the Informations they have received and of whom, and how, at length, or if too long refer to them in Papers apart minuting the Substance.

11th: Shall enter their Meetings with the Justices and Supervisors, and Persons present, together with the Minutes of all acted with them, particularly, what were the Deficiencies laid before them, what was resolved on for the Assessing and levying them, who for assessing them, who for neglecting or delaying it.

12th: Every other Thing remarkable that has any relation to their Office, and not otherways directed about shall be entered in the Minute Book of their Proceedings except their Accounts.

VII. AND BE IT ENACTED that the Printer shall also bind up other ten Books of clean Paper, one of them for the use of each Loan Office about two thirds of the bigness of the Book of Mortgages for the same County to be delivered as aforesaid with the Book of Mortgages.

VIII. BE IT ENACTED that therein shall be entered all the Accounts of the Loan Office; That at the Beginning there shall be an Alphabet wherein shall be inserted every Man's Name, and the Leaf wherein his Account stands, and that this Book be kept in the fairest and best Method that the Loan Officers can, and it is to remain in the Custody of him who has the Minutes of the Mortgages and proceedings.

IX. AND BE IT ENACTED that the Deeds to be granted by the Loan Officers for any Lands to be sold by them, whereof the Equity of Redemption is foreclosed shall be in Form following to wit.

THIS INDENTURE made the Tuesday of in the Year of the Reign of our Sovereign Lord George the third by the Grace of God of Great Britain France and Ireland King Defender of the Faith &c Annoq. Domini one thousand seven hundred and BETWEEN the Loan Officers of the of of the one Part, and of the other Part WITNESSETH that the Loan Officers of of for and in Consideration of the Sum of to them in Hand paid whereof they grant the Receipt and discharge the said his Heirs Executors and Administrators thereof forever HAVE pursuant to an Act of the General Assembly of this Colony intitled, "An Act for emitting the sum of one "hundred and twenty thousand Pounds in Bills of Credit to be "put out on Loan and to appropriate the Interest arising thereon "to the payment of the Debts of this Colony, and to such Public "Exigencies as the Circumstances of this Colony may from Time "to Time render necessary." Granted, Bargained, Sold, Released, Enfeoffed and Confirmed, and by these presents do Grant, Bargain, sell Release Enfeoff and Confirm unto the said his Heirs and Assigns, all that TOGETHER with all and all Manner of Woods Underwoods, Trees, Mines, Minerals, Quarries Hawkings, Huntings, Fowlings, Fishings, Fences, Improvements, Hereditaments and Appurtenances whatsoever to the same belonging or in any wise appertaining and all the Estate Right Title Interest, Claim possession property and Demand whatsoever of the Loan Offices of of and their Successors to the above bargained Premises and every Part thereof.

TO HAVE AND TO HOLD the above bargained premises and every Part thereof with the Appurtenances to the said his Heirs and Assigns to the sole and only proper use Benefit and Behoof of the said his Heirs and Assigns forever

IN WITNESS Whereof the Loan Officers of the of have hereunto set the Seal of their Corporation together with their Hands the Day and Year above written.

SEALED and DELIVERED in the presence of.

To which Deed the Loan Officers are to put only one Seal as the Seal of the Loan Office, and jointly take off the Seal from the Wax, and all sign their Names.

X. AND BE IT ENACTED that upon every Sale of Lands the Loan Officers shall fill up one of the loose Sheets of Blank Mortgages like to the Original Mortgage and attest the same as a true Copy under their Hands and the Seal of the Loan Office, and give it instead of the Original Mortgage for Evidence of the Title of the Buyer, and the Bond to be entered into by the Loan Officers shall be in the Form following Vizt

KNOW ALL MEN by these Presents that we are held and firmly Bound unto our most gracious Sovereign Lord George the third by the Grace of God of Great Britain France and Ireland King Defender of the Faith &c in the Sum of to be paid unto our most gracious sovereign Lord the King and his Successors, to the which payment well and truly to be made and done we bind ourselves our Heirs, Executors, and Administrators, and every of us and them jointly and severally firmly by these Presents sealed with our Seals and dated the Day of in the Year of his Majesty's Reign Annoq. Domini one thousand seven hundred and

THE CONDITION of the above Obligation is such that if the above Bounden shall well and truly perform the Office and Duty of One of the Loan Officers of the of and shall demean himself therein without favour Malice or Partiality then the above Obligation to be void, otherwise to remain in full Force and Virtue.

SEALED and DELIVERED in the presence of

XI AND BE IT ENACTED and declared that in Case of the Forfeiture of such Bond as aforesaid the Suit thereon shall be staid on the Defendant's paying or tendring in Court to pay the Damages arisen by the Breach of the Condition of the Bond sued, with the Costs to that Time, and if Judgment be had thereon, a Jury shall enquire of the Damages according to the Form of the Statute in that Case made and provided.

XII BE IT ENACTED for the better satisfaction of the Loan Officers as to the Title and value of what is offered in Mortgage by Borrowers, the Loan Officers or either of them are hereby authorized and impowered to examine the Borrower and Witnesses upon Oath, or Affirmation if Quakers, concerning the same, a brief Minute of which Examinations, and of the Names of the Persons so examined, they shall enter into their Minute Book of proceedings.

[CHAPTER 1425.]

[Chapter 1425 of Van Schaack, where the title only is printed.]

An Act to impower the Mayor Recorder and Aldermen of the City of New York, or the major Part of them to order the raising a Sum not exceeding sixteen Hundred Pounds for the uses therein mentioned.

[Passed, January 5, 1770.]

WHEREAS the providing a sufficient Number of Watchmen, and lighting of Lamps within the City of New York, has not only been found convenient but also necessary for the safety of it's Inhabitants and others.

I BE IT THEREFORE ENACTED by his Honor the Lieutenant Governor, the Council, and the General Assembly, and it is hereby enacted by the Authority of the same, that the Mayor

Recorder and Aldermen of the City of New York for the Time being or the Major Part of them, whereof the Mayor or Recorder to be one, shall have full power and Authority, and are hereby fully impowered and authorized on the second Tuesday in this present Month of January, or within ten Days thereafter to order the raising a sum not exceeding sixteen hundred Pounds, by a Tax upon the Estates Real and Personal of all and every the Freeholders, Freemen, Inhabitants, Residents, and Sojourners within the City of New York on the South side of Fresh Water for the payment of so many Watchmen as the Mayor, Aldermen and Commonalty of the City of New York shall think necessary for guarding the City and for purchasing Oil, providing Lamps, and for repairing and attending the Lamps which now are or hereafter may be erected and add the same sum of sixteen hundred Pounds to the Sum which shall be raised for the Minister and Poor of the said City, which Tax so to be laid shall be rated and assessed at the same Time, and by the Vestrymen who shall rate and assess the Tax for the Minister and Poor of the said City, and shall be rated together in one Assessment made of the whole the Vestrymen first taking the Oath prescribed to be taken in and by an Act intitled, "An Act to enable the Inhabi-"tants of the City of New York to choose two Vestrymen for "each respective Ward within the said City," made and passed in the nineteeneth Year of the Reign of his late Majesty King George the second and the Tax so to be laid shall be collected levied and paid at the same Time as the Tax for the Maintenance of the Minister and Poor of the said City hath been accustomed into the Hands of the Church Wardens of the said City for the Time being who are hereby required and directed to pay the same into the Hands of the Chamberlain of the said City, to be by him paid as he shall be directed by Warrant or Warrants of the said Mayor Aldermen and Commonalty in Common Council convened for the uses aforesaid.

II AND BE IT FURTHER ENACTED by the Authority aforesaid that over and above the Sum of Sixteen hundred Pounds to be levied and paid by virtue of this Act the Sum of three Pence in the Pound as a Reward to the Constables for their Trouble shall be assessed levied and paid to the respective Constables for collecting and paying the same and no more, according to the true Intent and meaning of this Act, any Thing herein or in any other Act or Acts contained to the contrary hereof in any wise notwithstanding.

III. AND BE IT FURTHER ENACTED by the Authority aforesaid that if the said Mayor, Recorder or Aldermen, Church Wardens, Vestrymen or Constables of the said City of New York who are hereby authorized impowered and required to take effectual Care that this Act be executed according to the true Intent and meaning thereof, or any of them shall deny refuse or delay to perform execute or comply with all or any of the Powers Authorities and Duties in this Act given and required to be done and performed by them or either of them, and thereof shall be lawfully convicted in any Court of Record in this Colony, he or they so denying refusing or delaying to perform the Duties as aforesaid shall suffer such Pains and Penalties by Fine and Imprisonment as by the discretion of the said Court shall be adjudged.

IV. AND BE IT FURTHER ENACTED by the Authority aforesaid that if any Person or Persons shall Willfully break or damage any of the Lamps now erected or hereafter to be erected within the said City, he she or they so offending shall forfeit the Sum of twenty Pounds for every Lamp he she or they shall damage or break as aforesaid to be levied by Warrant or Warrants under the Hands and Seals of two or more of his Majesty's Justices of the Peace for the City and County of New York by distress and Sale of the Offender's Goods and Chattels on due conviction made upon the Oath of one or more credible Witness or Witnesses rendering the Overplus if any there be, to the Owner or Owners, and for want of such distress the Offender or Offenders shall be imprisoned by Warrant under the Hands and Seals of the said Justices who are hereby required to issue the same for the space of three Months unless the said Forfeiture or Forfeitures be sooner Paid, which Forfeitures shall be applied towards providing and repairing of Lamps and paying the Watchmen.

V. AND BE IT FURTHER ENACTED by the Authority aforesaid that all such Persons as shall be employed to guard the said City and attend the Lamps shall be under the Direction of and obey such Orders as they shall from Time to Time receive from the Mayor, Aldermen and Commonalty of the said City, any Custom Law or usage to the contrary thereof in any wise notwithstanding.

[CHAPTER 1426.]

[Chapter 1426 of Van Schaack, where the title only is printed.]

An Act to enable the Mayor Recorder Aldermen and Commonalty of the City of Albany for the Time being or the Major part of them to order the raising a Sum not exceeding two hundred and fifty pounds for the Uses therein mentioned

[Passed, January 5, 1770.]

WHEREAS the establishing of a regular well constituted Night Watch in the City of Albany will tend to the Safety and preservation of the Inhabitants in their persons and Effects

BE IT THEREFORE ENACTED by his Honor the Lieutenant Governor the Council and the General Assembly, and it is hereby enacted by the Authority of the same that the Mayor, Recorder Aldermen and Commonalty of the City of Albany for the Time being or the Major part of them whereof the Mayor or Recorder to be one shall have full power and Authority and are hereby fully impowered and authorized at any Time before the last Day of February one thousand seven hundred and seventy to order the raising a Sum not exceeding two hundred and fifty pounds by a Tax upon the Estates real and personal of all and every the Freeholders Freemen and Inhabitants Residents and Sojourners within the City of Albany living within Half a Mile from the River for the payment of so many Watchmen as the Mayor, Aldermen and Commonalty of the said City in common Council convened shall think necessary for guarding the said City which Tax so to be laid shall be rated and assessed at the same Time and by the Assessors who shall rate and assess the Tax which shall be raised by Virtue of an Act of the Governor the Council and the General Assembly of the Colony of New York entitled, "An Act for the better explaining and more effectual puting in "Execution an Act of the General Assembly made in the third "Year of the Reign of their late Majesties, King William & "Queen Mary, entitled "An Act for defraying the public and "necessary Charges throughout this province and for maintain-"ing the poor and preventing Vagabonds" made and passed the Nineteenth of June one thousand seven hundred and three the Assessors first taking the Oath prescribed to be taken by the last mentioned Act and the Tax so to be laid shall be collected levied and paid by the same Collector and at the same Time as the Tax raised by Virtue of the Act aforesaid hath been accustomed and shall be paid into the Hands of the Chamberlain of the said City to be by him paid as he shall be directed by Warrant or Warrants of the said Mayor Recorder Aldermen and Commonalty in common Council convened for the Uses aforesaid

AND BE IT FURTHER ENACTED by the Authority aforesaid that the Collector shall retain in his Hands three pence in the pound of every pound so raised by Virtue of this Act as a Reward for his Trouble in collecting and paying the same and no more

AND BE IT FURTHER ENACTED by the Authority aforesaid that if the said Mayor, Recorder Aldermen & Commonalty, Assessors or Collectors of the said City of Albany who are hereby authorized impowered and required to take effectual Care that this Act be executed according to the true intent and Meaning thereof, or any of them shall deny refuse or delay to perform execute or comply with all or any of the powers Authorities and Duties in this Act given and required to be done and performed by them or either of them and thereof shall be lawfully convicted in any Court of Record in this Colony he or they so denying refusing or delaying to perform the Duties as aforesaid, shall suffer such pains and penalties by Fine and Imprisonment as by the Discretion of the said Court shall be adjudged.

AND BE IT FURTHER ENACTED by the Authority aforesaid that if any person or persons shall neglect or refuse to pay the several Rates and Assessments wherewith he or they shall be charged by this Act for or in respect of his and their Goods and Chattels Lands or Tenements upon Demand of the Collector appointed to receive the same that then it shall and may be lawful to and for such Collector and he is hereby required for non payment thereof by Warrant under the Hand of the Mayor Recorder Aldermen and Common Council of the said City for the Time being, or the Major part of them to distrain the person or persons so refusing or neglecting to pay by his or their Goods or Chattels or distrain in and upon the Messuages, Lands and Tenements so charged and the Goods and Chattels then and there found and the Distress so taken to carry away and the same to expose to Sale within the said City for the payment of the said Rate or Assessment; and the Overplus coming by the said Sale, if any be over and above the Charges of taking and carrying away the said Distress to be immediately returned to the Owner thereof

AND BE IT FURTHER ENACTED by the Authority aforesaid that all such persons as shall be employed to guard the said City shall be under the Direction of, and Obey such Orders as they shall from Time to Time receive from the Mayor Aldermen and Commonalty in Common Council convened any Custom Law or Usage to the Contrary in anywise Notwithstanding

[CHAPTER 1427.]

[Chapter 1427 of Van Schaack, where the title only is printed.]

An Act for the Payment of the Salaries of the Several Officers of this Colony, and other Purposes therein mentioned

[Passed, January 27, 1770.]

BE IT ENACTED by his Honor the Lieutenant Governor the Council and the General Assembly, and it is hereby enacted by the Authority of the same that the Treasurer of this Colony, shall and hereby is directed and required out of the Monies arisen or which may arise by Virtue of the following Acts Vizt. An Act Intitled. "An Act further to continue an Act intitled an Act "for granting to his Majesty the several Duties and Impositions "on Goods Wares or Merchandizes imported into this Colony "therein mentioned." An Act intitled "An Act for collecting "the Duty of Excise on Strong Liquors retailed in this Colony "from the first Day of January one thousand seven hundred and "seventy, to the first Day of January one thousand seven and "seventy one inclusive." and an Act intitled. "An Act for regu- "lating the Sale of Goods to be sold at Public Vendue Auction or "Outcry within this Colony," and out of the Monies which may arise by virtue of a Bill passed this House intitled. "An Act to "restrain Hawkers and Pedlars from selling without Licence" when the same shall pass into a Law, to pay.

UNTO the Executors or Administrators of his late Excellency Sir Henry Moore Baronet for administring the Government of this Colony from the first Day of September one thousand seven hundred and sixty nine, to the eleventh Day of said Month after the Rate of two thousand Pounds per Annum, the sum of sixty Pounds five Shillings and three Pence three Farthings.

UNTO the Executors or Administrators of his said late Excellency for Firewood and Candles for his Majesty's Fort George in the City of New York from and to the Time aforesaid after the Rate of four hundred Pounds per Annum the sum of twelve Pounds three Shillings and one penny.

UNTO his Honor the Lieutenant Governor for his Administring the Government of this Colony from the twelfth Day of September one thousand seven hundred and sixty nine to the first Day of September which will be in the year one thousand seven hundred and seventy after the Rate of two thousand Pounds per Annum.

UNTO his said Honor for providing FireWood and Candles for his Majesty's Fort George in the City of New York from the twelfth Day of September one thousand seven hundred and sixty nine, to the first Day of September one thousand seven hundred and seventy after the Rate of four hundred Pounds per annum.

UNTO the Honorable Daniel Horsemanden Esquire as Chief Justice of the Supreme Court of this Colony and for going the Circuits from the first Day of September one thousand seven hundred and sixty nine to the first Day of September one thousand seven hundred and seventy, after the Rate of three hundred Pounds per annum.

UNTO the Honorable David Jones Esquire one of the Puisne Justices of the Supreme Court of this Colony, and for going the Circuits from and to the Time aforesaid after the Rate of two hundred Pounds per Annum.

UNTO the Honorable Robert R Livingston Esquire, one other of the Puisne Justices of the Supreme Court of this Colony and for going the Circuits from and to the Time aforesaid after the Rate of two hundred Pounds per Annum.

UNTO the Honorable George D Ludlow Esquire the other Puisne Justice of the Supreme Court of this Colony, and for going the Circuits from the sixteenth Day of December one thousand seven hundred and sixty nine to the first Day of September one thousand seven hundred and seventy after the Rate of two hundred Pounds per annum.

UNTO the Executors of the late Honorable William Smith Esquire third Justice of the Supreme Court of this Colony, and for his going the Circuits from the first Day of September one thousand seven hundred and sixty nine to the twenty second Day of November following after the Rate of two hundred Pounds per Annum.

UNTO the Secretary of this Colony for the Time being for engrossing and enrolling the Acts of the General Assembly from the first Day of September one thousand seven hundred and sixty nine to the first Day of September one thousand seven hundred and seventy, after the Rate of thirty Pounds per Annum.

UNTO the Clerk of the Council for the Time being for his Services in that Station from and to the Time aforesaid the Sum of thirty Pounds.

UNTO the Door keeper of the Council for the Time being for his Services in that Station from and to the Time aforesaid the Sum of twenty Pounds.

UNTO Hugh Gaine as Public Printer of this Colony for his Services in that Station from and to the Time aforesaid after the Rate of fifty Pounds per Annum

UNTO the said Hugh Gaine for extraordinary Services performed by him the Sum of Seventy five Pounds.

UNTO John Kipp as Gauger of Liquors subject to a Duty within this Colony or to the Gauger thereof for the Time being from and to the Time aforesaid after the Rate of thirty Pounds per Annum.

UNTO Thomas Hill and Josias Smith Land and Tide Waiters, or to the Land and Tide Waiters for the Time being for their Services in that Station from and to the Time aforesaid after the Rate of fifty Pounds per Annum to each of them.

ALL which aforesaid Several Sums of Money shall be paid by the Treasurer on Warrant or Warrants to be issued by his Honor the Lieutenant Governor or the Commander in Chief for the Time being by and with the Advice and Consent of his Majesty's Council of this Colony and the Receipts of the several Persons indorsed on the said Warrants shall be to the Treasurer good Vouchers and Discharges for so much as shall be thereby acknowledged to be received.

AND BE IT ENACTED by the Authority aforesaid that the Treasurer shall be and hereby is directed and required out of the Funds aforesaid to pay the several Allowances following, to wit.

UNTO Abraham Lott Esquire Treasurer of this Colony for his Services in that station from the first Day of September one thousand seven hundred and sixty nine, to the first Day of September one thousand seven hundred and seventy, after the Rate of two hundred Pounds per Annum.

UNTO the said Treasurer for the Extraordinary Services which he is now obliged to perform beyond the usual Duty of his Office after the Rate of the further Sum of one hundred Pounds.

UNTO Robert Charles Esquire Agent of this Colony, or to the Agent for the Time being in Great Britain from the first Day of September, one thousand seven hundred and sixty nine, to the first Day of September one thousand seven hundred and seventy after the Rate of five hundred Pounds per Annum.

UNTO John Tabor Kemp Esquire for Extraordinary Services performed by him as Attorney General of this Colony from and to the Time aforesaid after the Rate of one hundred and fifty Pounds per Annum.

UNTO Edmond Seaman Esquire as Clerk to the General Assembly for his Services in that Station from the first Day of September one thousand seven hundred and sixty nine to the first Day of September one thousand seven hundred and seventy, twenty Shillings per Diem payable upon a Certificate from the General Assembly signed by the Speaker for the Number of Days he has or may serve the General Assembly.

UNTO the said Edmond Seaman for sundry Disbursements by him made for the use of the General Assembly the Sum of twenty five Pounds ten shillings.

UNTO Gerard Bancker as Assistant Clerk to the General Assembly for his Services in that Station from the eighteenth Day of April one thousand seven hundred and sixty nine to the first Day of September one thousand seven hundred and seventy, twenty Shillings per Diem, payable upon a Certificate from the General Assembly signed by the Speaker for the Number of Days he has or may serve the General Assembly.

UNTO Alexander Lamb Door keeper of the General Assembly for his Services in that Station from the first Day of September one thousand seven hundred and sixty nine to the first Day of September one thousand seven hundred and seventy, six Shillings per Diem payable upon a Certificate from the General Assembly signed by the Speaker for the Number of Days he has or may serve the General Assembly.

UNTO the said Alexander Lamb for providing Fire-Wood and sundry Necessaries for the use of the General Assembly the Sum of fifty Pounds.

UNTO John Martin as Gunner and keeper of the Colony Stores from the twenty eighth Day of July one thousand seven hundred and sixty nine to the twenty eighth Day of July one thousand seven hundred and seventy, after the Rate of twenty Pounds per Annum.

UNTO William Scott Serjeant at Arms for his Services in that Station from the fourth Day of April one thousand seven hundred and sixty nine to the first Day of September one thousand seven hundred and seventy, four shillings per Diem, payable upon a Certificate from the General Assembly signed by the Speaker for the Number of Days he has or may serve the General Assembly.

UNTO James Wilmot for attending and keeping open the Library for the use of the General Assembly, from the fourth Day of April one thousand seven hundred and sixty nine to the first Day of September one thousand seven hundred and seventy, five shillings per Diem payable upon a Certificate from the General Assembly signed by the Speaker for the Number of Days he has or may serve the General Assembly.

AND BE IT ENACTED by the Authority aforesaid that for answering the Expences of Contingencies and extraordinary Emergencies that have or may happen for the Service of this Colony from the first Day of September one thousand seven hundred and sixty nine to the first Day of September one thousand seven hundred and seventy. Warrants may issue for the same on the Treasurer from Time to Time, if drawn by his Honor the Lieutenant Governor, or the Commander in Chief for the Time being, with the Advice and Consent of his Majesty's Council which the Treasurer is hereby Ordered and directed to pay out of the Monies arising by virtue of the Acts herein before mentioned. Provided the Amount of the said Warrants, does not exceed the Sum of one hundred Pounds.

AND BE IT ENACTED by the Authority aforesaid that the Treasurer of this Colony shall out of the Funds aforesaid pay the several Sums following.

UNTO Andrew Gautier and Jonathan Hampton for repairs done by themselves and sundry other Persons to Fort George and the Barracks and Materials found by them as per their Accounts the Sum of three hundred and forty eight Pounds, nine Shillings.

UNTO Richard Nicholls Register and John McKesson Deputy Register in the Court of Admiralty for Charges incurred in prosecuting of Pirates at a Court of Admiralty held in the City of New York, the Sum of thirty four Pounds nineteen Shillings.

UNTO Thomas Ludlow Junior Marshall for Charges attending the Execution and hanging in Chains Joseph Anderson lately executed for Piracy, the Sum of forty six Pounds one Shilling and eleven Pence.

UNTO Sarah Brock for the use of a Room for the Committee of Privileges and Elections the Sum of five Pounds.

UNTO his Honor the Lieutenant Governor to defray the Expence of keeping one Interpreter and two Smiths at Niagara and Detroit in the Year one thousand seven hundred and sixty nine agreeable to a Resolution of the General Assembly in May last the Sum of one hundred and fifty Pounds.

[CHAPTER 1428.]

[Chapter 1428 of Van Schaack, where the title only is printed. Repealed by the king June 7, 1771.]

An Act more effectually to enable Persons to recover Debts in this Colony on Promisory Notes.

[Passed, January 27, 1770.]

WHEREAS in and by a certain Act of the Governor the Council and the General Assembly of this Colony passed the twenty fourth Day of December in the eighth Year of his present Majesty's Reign intitled. "An Act to declare the extension of "several Acts of Parliament made since the establishment of a "Legislation in this Colony and not declared in the said Acts to "extend to the Plantations." it is among other Things Enacted that the first second and third Clauses of a certain Act of Parliament passed in the third and fourth Years of the Reign of Queen Anne, intitled. "An Act for giving like Remedy upon "Promissory Notes as is now used upon Bills of Exchange and "for the better payment of Inland Bills of Exchange." shall be deemed to be in full force and effect within this Colony: By the third of which clauses of the said Act of Parliament so extended as aforesaid it is enacted that all and every Action upon such Promissory Notes and Assignments thereof, shall be commenced sued and brought within such Time as is appointed for commencing and suing Actions upon the Case by the Statute made in the one and twentieth Year of the Reign of King James the first intitled, "An Act for the Limitation of Actions and for "avoiding of Suits in Law," AND WHEREAS many such Promissory Notes had been nearly of six Years standing at the Time that the said third Clause of the said Statute was so extended as aforesaid, and consequently before the Inhabitants of this Colony could generally be apprized thereof, many such Notes of Hand, and the Assignments thereof have by the said Extension become irrecoverable to the great Loss of many, and the utter Ruin of some, AND WHEREAS also the very great Scarcity of Cash, and the Poverty of the numerous new settlers in this Colony have not only rendered the giving and taking of Promissory Notes, and Assignments of Promissory Notes to the Amount of many thousand Pounds absolutely necessary, but have also unavoidably occasioned longer Credits on such Promissory Notes after the same became payable than is permitted by the above recited third Clause of the said Act of Parliament extended as aforesaid. In Order therefore not only to prevent many heavy and great Losses that may be occasioned to Honest, Humane and Ignorant Creditors who have not sued on such Promissory Notes according to the Terms prescribed by the said above recited third Clause of the said Act of Parliament but also to encourage the growth and Settlement of the Colony, to increase the Number of his Majesty's good Subjects within the same, and augment the Revenue of the Crown.

BE IT ENACTED by his Honor the Lieutenant Governor the Council and the General Assembly, and it is hereby enacted by the Authority of the same that every Person and Persons to whom any Sum or Sums of Money on or by virtue of any such Promissory Note or Notes, Assignment or Assignments thereof as aforesaid is or are claimed to be due to him her or them, either in his her or their own Right, or as Executor or Executors,—Administrator or Administrators to any other Person or Persons shall and may sue for recover and receive the Monies made payable thereby respectively as fully and effectually as he she or they could or might have done had not the said above recited third clause of the said Acts been extended in Manner aforesaid any Thing in the said Clause to the contrary thereof in any wise notwithstanding. PROVIDED that Suit or Suits for that Purpose be commenced before the first Day of January which will be in the Year of our Lord one thousand seven hundred and seventy two, and not afterwards, but that from and after the said first Day of January in the Year of our Lord one thousand seven hundred and seventy two, the said recited third Clause of the said Act shall have it's full operation and extent, any Thing herein contained to the contrary thereof in any wise notwithstanding.

[CHAPTER 1429.]

[Chapter 1429 of Van Schaack, where the act is printed in full. See chapter 1308.]

An Act to revive and continue an Act intitled "An Act to prevent Frauds by the "adulteration of Pot Ash and Pearl Ash."

[Passed, January 27, 1770.]

BE IT ENACTED by his Honor the Lieutenant Governor the Council and the General Assembly and it is hereby enacted by the Authority of the same, that the Act intitled. "An Act to pre- "vent Frauds by the Adulteration of Pot Ash and Pearl Ash." passed in the seventh Year of the Reign of his present Majesty shall be and hereby is revived from the Publication hereof, until the first Day of January which will be in the Year of our Lord one thousand seven hundred and seventy five.

[CHAPTER 1430.]

[Chapter 1430 of Van Schaack, where the act is printed in full. Revived and continued by chapter 1519.]

An Act to prevent Frauds in Bar Iron exposed to Sale in this Colony.

[Passed, January 27, 1770.]

WHEREAS the Bar Iron exposed to Sale in this Colony is oftentimes of a very bad Quality and not well manufactured by means whereof the purchasers are deceived and the Exporters of the same suffer Great Losses and the Credit thereof is much lessened at foreign Markets for Remedy whereof

BE IT ENACTED by his Honor the Lieutenant Governor the Council and the General Assembly and it is hereby enacted by the Authority of the same that all Bar Iron whatsoever made in America and exposed to Sale within this Colony or exported from it after the first day of May next shall be hammered and drawn of an equal width and thickness throughout the whole Bar as nearly as may be and that every Bar of Iron so exposed to Sale shall be Stamped or marked with the Name of the Furnace or Forge or Owner or Owners of the Works where the same shall be made at Large and the Letter F,—as near together as may be if it shall be of that Quality and the Bar Iron called Bloomery Iron shall be stamped or marked in like manner as above directed and the Letter B,— and that all persons whatsoever exposing to Sale or purchasing or exporting any Bar Iron of American make not duly marked as aforesaid shall forfeit the Sum of three Shillings for every Bar of Iron exposed to Sale or purchased or exported the one half thereof to the Informer or Informers and the other half thereof to the Use of the poor of the City, Manor Borough Town or precinct where such Forfeiture shall arise to be recovered before any one Justice of the peace of the place or places aforesaid together with the Costs of Suit

AND BE IT ENACTED by the Authority aforesaid that this act shall be and remain in Force until the first day of January one thousand seven hundred and seventy two.

[CHAPTER 1431.]

[Chapter 1431 of Van Schaack, where the act is printed in full.]

An Act appointing Commissioners to meet with Commissioners who are or may be appointed by the Neighbouring Colonies to fix on a General Plan for the Regulation of the Indian Trade.

[Passed, January 27, 1770.]

WHEREAS his Majesty has been graciously pleased to direct that the Regulation of the Indian Trade for the future shall be left to the Colonies. AND WHEREAS it is conceived that the good Purposes of the design cannot be fully answered without the Harmonious co-operation of the Neighbouring Colonies concerned therein, for the obtaining of which

BE IT ENACTED by his Honor the Lieutenant Governor the Council and the General Assembly and it is hereby enacted by the Authority of the same that Philip Livingston Henry Holland, Isaac Low, John Alsop, William McAdam and John Thurman or any three of them, the Survivor or Survivors of them be and they are hereby appointed Commissioners on the Part of this Colony and are fully authorized and impowered to meet and confer with Commissioners who are or may be appointed by the Neighbouring Colonies to fix on a general Plan for the Regulation of the Indian Trade.

AND BE IT FURTHER ENACTED by the Authority aforesaid that the said Commissioners or such of them as shall meet any Commissioners who may be appointed by the Neighbouring Colonies do with all convenient Speed after such Meeting or

Meetings make full and perfect Report or Reports of such Regulations or Plan as they shall or do fix, or agree upon in conjunction with such other Commissioners as are or may be appointed by the Neighbouring Colonies to the Governor or the Council when thereunto required or to the General Assembly of this Colony which may be then sitting or to the first General Assembly of this Colony which may sit thereafter in order that a proper Law or Laws may be passed conformable thereto.

AND BE IT FURTHER ENACTED by the Authority aforesaid that Provision shall be made for paying the reasonable Expences that shall accrue on the Part of this Colony in performance of the service aforesaid when the Amount thereof shall be known by some future Act or Acts to be passed for that purpose.

[CHAPTER 1432.]

[Chapter 1432 of Van Schaack, where the act is printed in full. See chapter 1351.]

An Act to revive an Act intitled. "An "Act to prevent the Defaults of Grand and "Petit Jurors, Constables and other Per"sons." with an Addition thereto.

[Passed, January 27, 1770.]

WHEREAS an Act intitled, "An Act to prevent the Defaults "of Grand and Petit Jurors, Constables and other persons." passed in the eighth year of his present Majesty's Reign, expired by it's own Limitation on the first Day of January in this present Year one thousand seven hundred and seventy, and the same being found useful and necessary.

BE IT THEREFORE ENACTED by his Honor the Lieutenant Governor, the Council and the General Assembly and it is hereby enacted by the Authority of the same, that the abovementioned Act intitled. "An Act to prevent the Defaults of Grand and Petit "Jurors, Constables and other Persons," shall be, and hereby is revived, and every Article Matter and Clause therein contained, enacted to be and remain in full force from the Publication hereof, until the first Day of January which will be in the Year of our Lord one thousand seven hundred and seventy five.

PROVIDED that Nothing in the aforementioned Act contained, shall be construed to extend to any Fine above the Sum of ten Pounds, or to any Court for the tryal of Causes to the value of ten Pounds and under.

[CHAPTER 1433.]

[Chapter 1433 of Van Schaack, where the act is printed in full. Continued by chapter 1466. Revived and amended by chapter 1604.]

An Act to restrain Hawkers and Pedlars within this Colony from selling without Licence.

[Passed, January 27, 1770.]

BE IT ENACTED by his Honor the Lieutenant Governor the Council and the General Assembly and it is hereby enacted by the Authority of the same that from and after the twenty fifth Day of March next there shall be answered and paid to his Majesty his Heirs and Successors by every Hawker, Pedlar, Petty Chapman or any other Trading Person or Persons going from Town to Town, or to other Mens Houses and travelling either on Foot or with Horse, Horses or otherwise within this Colony of New York (except as hereafter is excepted) carrying to sell or exposing to sale any Goods Wares and Merchandizes a Duty of eight Pounds, for every Person travelling on Foot, per Annum, and that every Person so travelling with Horse or other Beast bearing or drawing Burden, shall pay the sum of eight Pounds per Annum for each Horse or other Beast bearing or drawing Burden with which he or she shall travel over and above the said first mentioned Duty of eight Pounds; And for every Waggon, Cart, Sled or other Carriage by Land or Water the further sum of five Pounds per annum, over and above the aforesaid Duty.

AND BE IT ENACTED by the Authority aforesaid that every Pedlar, Hawker, or Petty Chapman, and other Trading Person or Persons so travelling as aforesaid within this Colony shall take a Licence from the Treasurer of this Colony for the Time being, and in order thereto shall deliver unto the said Treasurer a Note in Writing, under his or her Hand, or under the Hand of some Person by him her or them Authorized in that behalf, how and in what manner he or she will travel and trade, whether on Foot, or with one or more Horses or other Beast bearing or drawing Burden or with any Sort of Carriage as aforesaid, and according to such Notification, he or she shall pay unto the said Treasurer for the Time being the Sum or Sums abovementioned, and upon Payment thereof to the said Treasurer he is to give a Licence under his Hand and Seal to the Person or Persons making such payment to travel with his or her Wares for sale for the Term of one year, or during the continuance of this Act, either single or with one or more Horses or with any Carriage as aforesaid according to the sum of Money paid by such Person or Persons for which Licence there shall be paid by the Person to whom the same shall be granted the Sum of three Shillings and no more, over and above the Duties aforesaid, and which Licence and method of obtaining and granting thereof shall be good and effectual and that the Treasurer for the Time being shall keep a distinct Account of the Duties to be received by virtue of this Act.

AND BE IT ENACTED by the Authority aforesaid that if any Hawker, Pedlar or Petty-Chapman from and after the said twenty fifth Day of March and during the continuance of this Act be found trading as aforesaid without or contrary to such Licence, such Person shall for each and every such offence forfeit and pay the Sum of ten Pounds current Money of this Colony, to be recovered before any Justice of the Peace within this Colony in a summary Way with Costs of Suit, the one Moiety thereof to the Informer, and the other Moiety to the Poor of the Town or place wherein such Offender shall be discovered, and that every Person so trading who upon Demand made by any Justice of the Peace, Sheriff, Constable or any other Person within this Colony where he or she shall so trade, shall refuse to produce or shew his her or their Licence for so trading, to be granted as aforesaid, that then the Person so refusing shall forfeit Ten Pounds to be paid to the Overseers of the Poor where such Demand shall be made, to the use of the Poor of the place, and for nonpayment thereof shall suffer one Months Imprisonment.

AND BE IT FURTHER ENACTED by the Authority aforesaid that if any Person or Persons shall forge or Counterfeit a Licence or Licenses to travel with such forged or Counterfeited Licence for the purposes aforesaid, such person shall forfeit the sum of fifty Pounds, one Moiety thereof to his Majesty his Heirs and Successors to be applied as the Governor or Commander in Chief for the Time being, the Council and the General Assembly of this Colony shall hereafter think fit, and the other half to him or them that prosecute or sue for the same to be recovered by Action of Debt, Bill, plaint or Information in the Supreme Court or any of the Inferior Courts within this Colony in which no Essoin Protection, Wager of Law, or more than one Imparlance shall be allowed.

AND BE IT FURTHER ENACTED by the Authority aforesaid that if any Person or Persons shall be sued, molested or troubled for putting in Execution any of the Powers contained in this Act, or for doing any Matter or Thing pursuant thereto, such person or persons shall and may plead the General Issue, Not Guilty, and give the special Matter in Evidence, and if the Plaintiff or Plaintiffs shall become Non-Suit, or discontinue his or their Action, or if a Verdict pass against him or them, the Defendant shall recover treble Costs, for which Execution shall issue in such Manner as in other Cases where Costs are allowed to Defendants.

AND BE IT FURTHER ENACTED by the Authority aforesaid that it shall and may be Lawful for any Person or Persons whatsoever to seize and detain any such Hawker, Pedlar or Petty-Chapman, or other trading Person or Persons as aforesaid who shall be found trading without a Licence contrary to the true Intent and meaning of this Act, and him her or them so seized to carry before one or more of his Majesty's Justices of the Peace of the County or Place where such Offence or Offences shall be committed, which said Justice or Justices of the Peace is and are hereby authorized and strictly required (either upon the Confession of the party offending or due proof by any one or more credible Witnesses upon Oath, which Oath he or they is and are hereby impowered to Administer, " that the Person so " brought before him or them, had so traded as aforesaid." and if no such Licence shall be produced by such Offender before the said Justice or Justices) by Warrant under his or their Hands and Seals, or under the Hand and seal of one of them, to cause the said Sum of ten Pounds to be forthwith levied by distress and Sale of the Offenders Goods, Wares and Merchandizes rendering the Overplus if any be to the Owner or Owners thereof after true Deduction for the reasonable Charge of taking the said Distress, and out of the sale to pay the said respective Penalties and forfeitures aforesaid.

AND in Order to prevent the giving of any unnecessary Trouble to any Person or Persons who shall suspect any such Hawker, Pedlar, Petty-Chapman or other Trading Person, trading without a Licence.

BE IT ENACTED by the Authority aforesaid that upon refusal of producing such Licence to any Person or Persons demanding the same, and it be afterwards produced to the Justice or Justices, such Offenders for such Refusals shall forfeit and pay to the person or persons demanding the same the sum of three Pounds current Money aforesaid.

PROVIDED ALWAYS and be it enacted by the Authority aforesaid that neither this Act nor any Thing therein contained shall extend to prohibit any Person from selling any Fish, Fruit or Victuals, or to hinder any Person or Persons who are the real Workers, or makers of any Goods or Wares of his her or their own manufacturing in any Public Market, Fair or elsewhere, nor any Tinker, Glazier, Cooper, Plummer, Taylor, or other Person usually trading in mending or making of Cloaths, Kettles, Tubs, or Household Goods whatsoever, from going about and carrying with him or them proper Materials for making and mending the same.

PROVIDED ALSO and be it Enacted by the Authority aforesaid that neither this Act nor any Thing therein contained shall extend or be construed to give any Power for the Licencing any Hawker, Pedlar or Petty-Chapman to sell or expose to sale any Wares or Merchandizes in the Cities of New York and Albany, any Thing herein contained to the contrary notwithstanding.

AND BE IT ENACTED by the Authority aforesaid that the Treasurer of this Colony is hereby impowered and directed to give unto Andrew Baron of South-Hampton on Nassau Island a Licence to travel as a Pedlar in this Province without Fee or Reward, and free from the Duties mentioned in this Act, which said Licence shall fully exempt the said Andrew Baron from all the Fines, Forfeitures and Penalties by this Act imposed, any Thing herein contained to the contrary in any wise notwithstanding.

This Act to continue in Force from the twenty fifth Day of March next to the twenty fifth Day of March which will be in the Year of our Lord one thousand seven hundred and seventy one.

[CHAPTER 1434.]

[Chapter 1434 of Van Schaack, where the title only is printed. Amended by chapter 1477. This act expired January 1st, 1772. Re-enacted by chapter 1510.]

An Act for the Inspection of Sole Leather in the City of New York.

[Passed, January 27, 1770.]

WHEREAS for want of a Law to inspect Sole Leather vended in the City of New York, great Frauds and abuses have been committed by selling the same before it is sufficiently tanned or properly dryed; for remedy whereof.

BE IT ENACTED by his Honor the Lieutenant Governor the Council and the General Assembly, and it is hereby enacted by the Authority of the same that Thomas Warner, and Benjamin Stout shall and hereby are authorized and appointed to inspect and seal all Sole Leather that shall be manufactured within the City of New York or imported from any other Part or Parts of this Colony, or of the Neighbouring Colonies at any Time or Times from and after the first Day of May next, which said Officers before they do any Thing in execution of the said Office shall respectively take an Oath before any Magistrate of the City of New York in the Words following Vizt. "I, A. B. do swear that I will faithfully truly and impartially according to the best of my Judgment skill and understanding execute do and perform the Office and Duty of an Inspector and examiner of Sole Leather, and I will not directly or indirectly buy or sell any Sole Leather during the Time that I continue Inspector of the same except for the private use of my Family according to the true Intent and meaning of an Act intitled. "An Act for the Inspection of Sole Leather in the City of New York." so help me God."

AND BE IT FURTHER ENACTED by the Authority aforesaid that from and after the said first Day of May next no sole Leather manufactured in this Colony, or any of the Neighbouring Colonies shall be sold disposed of or applied to use by any Person or Persons whatsoever within the City of New York until the same shall have been first inspected and sealed by one of the said Persons hereby appointed for that Purpose, upon Pain of forfeiting forty shillings for every offence to be sued for and recovered by Action of Debt with Costs of suit in a summary way by any Person who will sue and prosecute for the same before any Justice of the Peace within the City of New York to be levied by process to be directed to the sheriff or any of the Constables of the City commanding them or either of them to levy the same by distress and sale of the Offenders Goods and Chattels, one half of the said Penalty or Forfeitures when so recovered as aforesaid to be applied by the Person recovering the same to his or her own use and the other half thereof when so recovered to be paid by him or her to the Church Wardens of the said City for the use of the Poor thereof.

AND BE IT FURTHER ENACTED by the Authority aforesaid that there shall be paid to the Inspector and Sealer for every side of Leather that shall be so inspected and sealed two Pence, one half thereof by the Seller, and the other half by the Purchaser.

AND BE IT FURTHER ENACTED by the Authority aforesaid that the said Inspectors shall and are hereby required to provide themselves respectively with proper Seals for the Purpose aforesaid, and to impress on every Side of Sole Leather which shall be deemed good and Merchantable the Letters of their Christian and Sirnames with New York at full length: And if any Person or Persons shall presume to Counterfeit the same by making any Impression or Mark on any Sole Leather, he or they so offending shall forfeit and pay for every Offence the Sum of ten Pounds to be sued for recovered and applied in manner aforesaid. PROVIDED NEVERTHELESS that all Sole Leather which shall not bear the Inspection aforesaid may be used for any other Purposes except being worked up into Shoes, Boots and Buckets, provided the same be marked by either of the Inspectors aforesaid with his Name and the Letter B, who are hereby required to keep a proper Instrument for that Purpose, any Thing in this Act contained to the contrary in any wise notwithstanding.

AND BE IT FURTHER ENACTED by the Authority aforesaid that this Act and every Clause Matter and Thing therein contained shall be and remain in full Force and Effect from and after the first Day of May next until the first Day of January which will be in the Year of our Lord one thousand seven hundred and seventy two.

[CHAPTER 1435.]

[Chapter 1435 of Van Schaack, where the title only is printed. Repealed by the king the 6th of June, 1770.]

An Act declaring certain Persons therein mentioned incapable of being Members of the General Assembly of this Colony.

[Passed, January 27, 1770.]

WHEREAS by the Ancient Usage of Parliament, the Judges of the Courts of King's Bench, Common Pleas, and Exchequer in England, and by Statute Law the Judges of the Court of Sessions or Justiciary or Baron of the Exchequer in Scotland, are declared incapable of being elected, or of sitting or voting as Members of the House of Commons.

AND WHEREAS notwithstanding so wise laudable and Constitutional an Example from the Mother Country, some of the Judges of the Supreme Court have been suffered to sit and vote as Members of former General Assemblies for this Colony, for remedy whereof.

BE IT ENACTED by his Honor the Lieutenant Governor, the Council and the General Assembly and it is hereby enacted by the Authority of the same that for the future no Judge of the Supreme Court of this Colony shall be capable of being elected or of sitting or voting as a Member of this or any other General Assembly, Any Law Usage or Custom to the Contrary hereof in any wise Notwithstanding.

[CHAPTER 1436.]

[Chapter 1436 of Van Schaack, where the title only is printed. See chapter 1392.]

An Act to amend an Act intitled. "An "Act for regulating the Sale of Goods to be "sold at Public Vendue, Auction or Outcry "within this Colony."

[Passed, January 27, 1770..]

WHEREAS it is found by experience that the Duties imposed on all Goods sold or exposed to sale at Public Vendue, Auction or Outcry within this Colony by the abovementioned Act intitled, "An Act for regulating the Sale of Goods to be sold at Public "Vendue Auction or Outcry within this Colony." doth not answer the good intention of the Legislature, for Remedy whereof.

BE IT ENACTED by his Honor the Lieutenant Governor, the Council and the General Assembly and it is hereby enacted by the Authority of the same that all Goods, Chattels, Wares, Merchandizes and Effects whatsoever, which are now subject and liable to a Duty of five per Cent, shall or may at any Time or Times, from and after the Publication hereof, and during the continuance of the abovementioned Act be sold or exposed to sale, at Public Vendue, Auction or Outcry within this Colony by any Vendue Master or Vendue Masters, Auctioneer or Auctioneers or by any other Person or Persons whomsoever be and hereby are declared and made subject to no more Duty than three Pounds for every one hundred Pounds of the Value or price at which the same shall be sold or exposed to sale as aforesaid and after the same Rate for every greater or lesser Sum to be paid by such person or persons who shall so sell or expose the same to Sale as aforesaid, any Thing in the said Act mentioned to the Contrary in any wise notwithstanding.

[CHAPTER 1437.]

[Chapter 1437 of Van Schaack, where the act is printed in full. See chapter 1490.]

An Act impowering and directing the Treasurer of this Colony to sue for Duties still due to the late Treasurer of this Colony, and other Purposes therein mentioned.

[Passed, January 27, 1770.]

WHEREAS it appears by the Accounts of Abraham Lott Esquire the present Treasurer of this Colony that many Persons still remain indebted for Duties which arose and became due to Abraham DePeyster Esquire deceased late Treasurer of this Colony, and still remain unpaid.

BE IT THEREFORE ENACTED by his Honor the Lieutenant Governor the Council and the General Assembly and it is hereby enacted by the Authority of the same that the present Treasurer of this Colony or the Treasurer for the Time being shall and he is hereby directed and required in the Name of the Treasurer of this Colony with all convenient speed after the Publication of this Act to order Suits to be brought against all and every Person indebted for any of the Duties aforesaid, and that no Suit shall be discontinued or cease on the Death or Removal of such Treasurer but shall continue until the same be prosecuted to effect.

AND BE IT FURTHER ENACTED by the same Authority that the Treasurer of this Colony for the Time being shall also and he is hereby impowered and required in Manner as above directed to sue for any Debts due and in Arrear upon any Act or Acts of this Colony passed for the purpose of laying Duties on Strong Liquors retailed in this Colony.

AND WHEREAS it appears by the said Accounts that David Johnston Esquire stands indebted to this Colony for Duties in the sum of one hundred Pounds and that he detains the same in Hand to satisfy him for the like Sum due from the Colony to the Estate of his late Brother John Johnston as Colonel in Chief of the Forces in the pay of this Colony in the Year one thousand seven hundred and fifty nine, to whom he is Heir at Law.

AND WHEREAS there also appears to be due from the Estate of James Stevenson Esquire late of the City of Albany deceased the sum of fifty six Pounds thirteen shillings and eight Pence for the Duty of Excise by him received in the Year one thousand seven hundred and forty seven, which his Executors also retain in their Hands for the like Sum allowed the said James Stevenson by an Act passed the ninth Day of April in the Year of our Lord one thousand seven hundred and forty eight which remains unpaid to this Day: And as these accounts cannot now be settled without the Aid of the Legislature.

BE IT THEREFORE FURTHER ENACTED by the Authority aforesaid that it shall and may be lawful for the Treasurer of this Colony to liquidate and settle the said two Accounts with the said David Johnston & the said Executors of James Stevenson Esquire deceased, by giving the respective Parties Credit in his or their Accounts for the Sums due from them to the Colony, and charging them with the Sum due from the Colony as if the same had been really paid.

[CHAPTER 1438.]

[Chapter 1438 of Van Schaack. where the act is printed in full.]

An Act to prevent the Abuse of Writs and Plaints in Replevin.

[Passed, January 27, 1770.]

WHEREAS frequent abuses have been committed in the Execution of Writs of Replevin by Sheriffs making deliverance notwithstanding due Notice and claim of Property have been interposed by the Defendant or Possessor; for the more effectual prevention whereof for the future.

BE IT ENACTED by his Honor the Lieutenant Governor, the Council and the General Assembly, and it is hereby enacted by the Authority of the same, that if at any Time hereafter, on a Writ or Plaint of Replevin the Defendant in Replevin, or possessor, shall claim property in the Thing whereof Deliverance is sought; and the Sheriff either by himself his under Sheriff, or Bailif, having due notice, shall nevertheless proceed to make deliverance, and dispossess such Defendant thereof, before the Claim of property shall be enquired into, or tried, as the Law directs; such Sheriff, for every such Offence, shall incur and forfeit the Penalty of one hundred Pounds to be recovered by any Person who shall sue for the same, in any Court of Record within this Colony, by Bill, Plaint, or information, wherein no Essoin, Protection or Wager of Law, nor more than one Imparlance shall be allowed, one half of which Penalty shall be for the use of the Person who shall sue for the same, and the other half shall be applied towards the Support of government.

[CHAPTER 1439.]

[Chapter 1439 of Van Schaack, where the act is printed in full. Confirmed by the king the 7th of June, 1771. See chapter 293.]

An Act to enable all Persons who are his Majestys' liege Subjects either by Birth or Naturalization to inherit and hold Real Estates notwithstanding any Defect of purchases made before Naturalization within this Colony.

[Passed, January 27, 1770.]

WHEREAS it was enacted by a Law of this Colony passed on the fifth Day of July in the Year of our Lord one thousand seven hundred and fifteen, that all foreign Protestants then inhabiting this Colony, should upon the Terms therein mentioned enjoy the Rights, Privileges and Advantages of natural Born Subjects. AND WHEREAS divers persons have since come into this Colony and purchased or acquired by Patent Real Estates here, some of whom were before naturalized only in other Colonies, and others became afterwards naturalized in this Colony, and such Estates are now held and claimed under such Grants or purchases by his Majesty's natural Born Subjects or such as are naturalized and as the greater Number of these are poor Persons and will be utterly ruined if advantage is taken of the Alienism of any such purchaser or Patentee, Wherefore in tender commisseration of all Persons holding or claiming by such defective Title, and confiding in his Majesty's great Bounty the General Assembly humbly pray that it may be enacted.

AND BE IT ENACTED by his Honor the Lieutenant Governor, the Council and the General Assembly and it is hereby enacted by the Authority of the same that the Title and Claim of every Inhabitant of this Colony who is now his Majesty's natural born Subject under any Patent or Purchase of Lands Tenements, and Real Estate granted to or made by an Alien at any Time inhabiting this Colony since the fifth Day of July in the Year of our Lord one thousand seven hundred and fifteen, shall not be defeated merely upon the Pretence of Alienism in the Grantee or Purchaser or any person holding as by Descent or otherwise since such Grant or purchase, but that such Title shall be adjudged to be good, the Plea or Pretence of Alienism in such Case notwithstanding.

PROVIDED ALWAYS that nothing herein contained shall be construed to extend to any Lands or Tenements heretofore Vested in the Crown by Office found, or which after such finding have been regranted to any of his Majesty's natural born Subjects; nor shall this Act be in force until the same shall be approved of by his Majesty.

[CHAPTER 1440.]

[Chapter 1440 of Van Schaack, where the act is printed in full. See chapters 1075 and 1396.]

An Act to amend an Act intitled. "An "Act more effectually to prevent the killing "of Deer and firing the Woods within this "Colony," so far as the same relates to the Counties of Suffolk and Queens.

[Passed, January 27, 1770.]

WHEREAS in and by the aforesaid Act intitled "An Act more "effectually to prevent the killing of Deer and firing the Woods "within this Colony." passed in the thirty second Year of the Reign of his late Majesty King George the second, it is provided and enacted that if any Person or Persons after the Publication thereof should kill or destroy any wild Buck, Doe or Fawn, or any other sort of Deer whatsoever at any Time in the Months of January, February, March, April, May or June, every such Person should for every such Offence forfeit the Sum of three Pounds for every such Buck, Doe or Fawn or other Deer so killed or destroyed as aforesaid contrary to the true Intent and Meaning of the said Act, which penalty is found not to answer the good Purposes intended by the said Act in the Counties of Suffolk and Queens.

BE IT THEREFORE ENACTED by his Honor the Lieutenant Governor, the Council and the General Assembly, and it is hereby enacted by the Authority of the same, that if any Person or Persons after the Publication of this Act shall kill or destroy any Wild, Buck, Doe, Fawn, or any other sort of Deer whatsoever at any Time in the Months of January, February, March, April,

May or June, every such Person shall for every such Offence, forfeit the sum of forty shillings with Costs of Suit, and shall be committed by any Justice of the Peace of the County where such Offence shall happen to the common Goal of such County there to remain for the Space of thirty Days without Bail or Mainprize for every such Buck, Doe, Fawn or other Deer so killed or destroyed as aforesaid contrary to the true Intent and meaning of this Act, and the said forty Shillings to be recovered and applied as in and by the said in part recited Act is directed, and for want of Effects to answer the aforesaid Fine of forty shillings and Costs to be continued in the Common Goal of the County where such Offence shall be committed for the space of one Month longer than aforesaid, if not sooner discharged by paying the said Fine of forty shillings and Costs, and for the better convicting of Offenders against this Act.

BE IT ENACTED by the Authority aforesaid that every Person in whose Custody shall be found or who shall expose to sale any Green Deer Skins, fresh Venison, or Deers Flesh at any Time in any of the Months before mentioned and shall be convicted thereof by the Oath of one Credible Witness, or by the Confession of the Party shall be deemed and adjudged Guilty of the Offence.

AND BE IT FURTHER ENACTED by the Authority aforesaid that every Constable being thereto Authorized by the Warrant of one or more Justices of the Peace under his or their Hands and Seals shall and may have full power and Authority at any Time in any of the Months before mentioned and hereby is required to enter into and search in such Manner and with such Power as where such Goods are Stolen, or suspected to be stolen, the House, or Houses, Out Houses or other places belonging to such suspected Persons, and in Case any Green Deers Skin, fresh Venison, or Deers Flesh shall there be found, such Officer shall apprehend such Offender and carry him before some Justice of the Peace of the same County, and shall be convicted by the said Justice of such Offence who on such Conviction shall be subject, and liable to the Forfeiture and penalty hereby inflicted for the killing of any one Deer in the same Manner as if thereof convicted as aforesaid, any Law Usage, or Custom to the contrary in any wise notwithstanding

[CHAPTER 1441.]

[Chapter 1441 of Van Schaack, where the act is printed in full. Amended by chapter 1493.]

An Act to establish the Rates to be taken for Wharfage of ships and other Vessels, and the Rates to be taken for Cranage within the City of New York.

[Passed, January 27, 1770.]

WHEREAS it hath been found by Experience that the Wharfs fronting the East and Hudson's Rivers in the City of New York have been greatly serviceable, and very much conduced to the Ease, Benefit, Increase, and Advantage of Trade and Navigation, to and from the said City, in the lading and unlading of Ships and other Vessels, and for as much as the Owners and Proprietors thereof have been at a very great Expence not only in the making erecting and building, but also in maintaining and keeping the same from Time to Time in good and sufficient Repair, to answer the Purposes aforesaid; and that the same tending to the advancement of Trade, ought to meet with due and proper Encouragement for their Maintenance and support.

AND WHEREAS the Laws heretofore made for establishing the Rates to be taken for the wharfage of Ships and other Vessels using the said Wharfs have not fully answered all the good purposes thereby intended.

I BE IT THEREFORE ENACTED by his Honor the Lieutenant Governor the Council and the General Assembly, and it is hereby enacted by the Authority of the same that it shall and may be Lawful to and for the present Owners and Proprietors of the said mentioned Wharfs, or the Owners or Proprietors thereof, for the Time being to ask, demand, take and receive to and for their several and respective uses for all Ships and Vessels using or that shall use the same, from and after the Publication hereof, the Wharfage and Rates following, that is to say, for each Ship or other Vessel of sixty Tons or upwards whilst careening, loading, unloading or lying fast to either of the said Wharfs after the Rate of three Shillings Current Money of this Colony for each Day.

II. BE IT FURTHER ENACTED that every Ship or other Vessel, which at any Time after the Publication hereof, shall only lie fast to any or either of the said Wharfs, shall be obliged to move off from thence in order to make Room for and suffer any other ship or Vessel to load unload or careen thereat, and on refusal or Failure so to do, after Notice and Request thereof to the Master or Commander, or to any one of the Owners of such Ship or other Vessel or either of them he or they shall Forfeit and pay to the Owner or Owners of said Wharf the Sum of three Pounds.

III BE IT FURTHER ENACTED that all and every Ship or other Vessel that shall make fast to any other Ship or Vessel that shall be fastened to any or either of the Wharfs aforesaid and shall continue so to lie fastened, or shall so load, unload or careen, shall be subject and liable to pay, and shall pay the one half Part of the Rates that such Ship or other Vessel so fastened should and would have been liable to pay, in case she were fastened to any or either of the said Wharfs, and there loaded unloaded and careened.

IV. BE IT FURTHER ENACTED by the Authority aforesaid, that all Ships and other Vessels under the Burthen of sixty Tons, and of twenty five Tons and upwards, shall pay for lying fast, loading, unloading, and careening one half Part of the Rates, for the purposes herein before mentioned, and all Vessels under twenty five Tons, for lying fast, loading unloading or careening, one fourth Part of the Rates for the Purposes herein before first mentioned.

V. AND BE IT FURTHER PROVIDED AND ENACTED that all Coasting Vessels lying fast at any or either of the said Wharfs, and not being actually loading, unloading or careening, shall on request make loose and move off, to make Room for and suffer any Sea Vessel or Vessels paying a higher Rate to come in her and their Place and Places, and that on Neglect or Refusal so to do, the Master, Commander or Owner of every such coasting Vessel or Vessels shall pay such Rate and Rates as the Sea Vessel or Vessels would have been liable to pay which really and bona fide was or were intended to be loaded, unloaded or careened there.

VI. AND BE IT FURTHER ENACTED by the Authority aforesaid that it shall and may be lawful to and for the Owner and Owners respectively of every Crane that now is or hereafter shall be made, erected and built on any or either of the Wharfs aforesaid, or on any Part thereof, to ask, demand, take, and receive, to and for his, her, and their several and respective use and uses, from the Master, Commander or Owners of all Ships and other Vessels that shall use or employ such Crane or Cranes the Rates following that is to say, for taking out and puting in the Mast of any Ship or other Vessel the Sum of thirty shillings; For taking out, or puting in the Mast of any Ship or other Vessel the Sum of twenty five shillings current money aforesaid

VII AND WHEREAS it may be difficult as well as inconvenient for the Owners and Proprietors of the several Wharfs aforesaid personally to attend collect and receive the Rates due, and to grow due for wharfage of Ships and other Vessels. BE IT THEREFORE ENACTED by the Authority aforesaid, that it shall and may be lawful to and for the Owner or Owners of the said Wharfs for the Time being to appoint a proper and fit Person to be the Wharfinger or Overseer thereof, for and during his or their Will and Pleasure, and shall and may at his or their like will and pleasure, displace and remove such Person so appointed, other and others in his and their Room and stead, when and as often as to him or them shall seem meet to appoint, and such Person so appointed Wharfinger shall while he continues in that Office have the Power of ordering and regulating of the Wharf he shall be so appointed for as aforesaid, and of the Births of all such Ships and other Vessels as shall load, unload, careen or fasten to the same, and moreover shall have full Power and Authority either in his own Name or in the Names of the Owners and Proprietors of the said Wharfs to ask sue for, demand and receive the Wharfage thereof, as it shall become due.

VIII. AND WHEREAS the Wharfs aforementioned are often so incumbered by Lumber Millstones or other Merchandize that by means thereof the loading and unloading of Vessels is very much incommoded, and the passing and repassing of Carts and Carriages is very much impeded, retarded and hindered. BE IT THEREFORE ENACTED by the Authority aforesaid that if any or either of the said Wharfs shall at any Time or Times hereafter be so incumbered as to Subject the same to any or either of those Inconveniencies, the Owner or Wharfinger of such Wharf and Wharfs respectively for the Time being, shall either personally warn or by Notice in Writing to be left at the Place of Residence of the Owner or Owners of such Lumber or other Goods, their Factor or Factors, require him or them to remove the same from thence within a reasonable Time, and if the same shall not be removed accordingly the Owner of said Wharf, or Wharfinger is hereby impowered to remove the same, and keep them in his Custody till the whole Charges attending the removal be paid by the Owner or Claimer of such Goods, and in Case the Owner or Factor is not to be found, the Owner of said Wharf or Wharfinger shall and may at his discretion, remove the said Goods as before directed.

IX PROVIDED ALWAYS, AND BE IT ENACTED by the same Authority that Nothing herein contained, shall impair the Right which the Mayor Aldermen and Commonalty of the City of New York have to the Docks and Slips herein before mentioned, but the same shall be saved to them and their Successors as fully as if this Act had not passed.

This Act to be and continue of force from the Publication thereof to the first Day of January which will be in the Year of our Lord one thousand seven hundred and eighty.

[CHAPTER 1442.]

[Chapter 1442 of Van Schaack, where the title only is printed.]

An Act to enable the Mayor Recorder and Aldermen of the City and County of New York to raise and pay into the Treasury the Arrears of Taxes due from the said City and County.

[Passed, January 27, 1770.]

WHEREAS it appears by the Accounts of Abraham Lott Esquire Treasurer of this Colony, that the said City and County of New York is in arrear the Sum of eight thousand six hundred and eighty Pounds three shillings and six Pence half penny for Taxes laid by several Acts of Assembly for cancelling Bills of Credit emitted by this Colony.

BE IT ENACTED by his Honor the Lieutenant Governor the Council and the General Assembly, and it is hereby enacted by the Authority of the same that the Mayor Recorder and Aldermen of the City of New York, or any five of them (whereof the Mayor or Recorder to be one) shall and they are hereby enabled authorised directed and required at any Time after the Publication of this Act, and before they cause any Part of the aforesaid Sum to be raised diligently and strictly to examine how such Deficiencies or Arrears have happened; and if it shall appear that any particular Person or Persons, Collector or Collectors of any or either of the Wards within the City of New York have been deficient in collecting and paying any of their Quotas or Shares of the said several and respective Taxes laid by the several beforementioned Acts on which the aforesaid Arrearages have arisen, such Deficiency or Deficiencies so discovered shall be laid on, levied and collected from such particular Person or Persons, Collector or Collectors of any or either of the Wards where such Deficiency or Deficiencies, hath or have happened, and in Case of Failure of Payment the said Mayor Recorder and Aldermen or any five of them, (whereof the Mayor or Recorder to be one) are hereby fully authorized and impowered to convene before them such particular Person or Persons, Collector or Collectors, and to cause them to give Information upon Oath relative to such Arrears of Taxes as aforesaid that they may thereby be enabled to liquidate the Sum or Sums such Delinquent or Delinquents is or are to pay, and if any such Person or Persons, Collector or Collectors shall refuse or Neglect to appear before the said Mayor Recorder and Aldermen being duly required by them so to do, or shall refuse when he or they shall or do appear to give such Information as aforesaid, each Person so refusing shall for every such Offence forfeit the sum of one hundred Pounds current Money of this Colony to be recovered by Action of Debt to be brought by and in the Name of the Treasurer of this Colony and applied towards discharging the Arrears of Taxes now due from said City.

AND BE IT FURTHER ENACTED by the Authority aforesaid that in Case any of the said particular Person or Persons Collector or Collectors who shall appear to have any Part of the said Arrears in their Hands shall neglect or delay to make their respective payments to the Treasurer of this Colony (for such Arrears as shall be liquidated by the said Mayor Recorder and Aldermen, and appear to be in the Hands of such Person or Persons Collector or Collectors) for the Space of three Months next after the Publication of this Act, that the said Treasurer of the Colony shall be and hereby is enabled directed and required in his own Name to commence Actions for the same in the Supreme Court of this Colony within one Month after such Default made by any such particular Person or Persons, Collector or Collectors and prosecute the same to effect, and in Case the Treasurer of this Colony shall neglect his Duty herein all such Sum or Sums of Money so liquidated as aforesaid and unpaid shall be deemed, taken and esteemed to be in his Hands and he shall be chargeable therewith as if he had actually received the same.

AND BE IT FURTHER ENACTED by the Authority aforesaid that the said Arrear of Taxes which shall appear to be justly due owing unpaid and in arrear from the several and respective

Wards within the said City, shall be raised assessed and levied by a Public Tax upon the Estates real and personal of all and every the Freeholders Inhabitants and Residents within the several and respective Wards aforesaid according to the several Proportions which are still due unpaid and in Arrear from the said several and respective Wards and shall be collected gathered in and paid unto the Treasurer of this Colony, one half thereof by the first Tuesday in November which will be in the Year of our Lord one thousand seven hundred and seventy, and the other half thereof by the first Tuesday in November which will be in the Year of our Lord one thousand seven hundred and seventy one, any Thing herein before contained to the contrary thereof in any wise notwithstanding.

[CHAPTER 1443.]

[Chapter 1443 of Van Schaack, where the act is printed in full. See chapter 33 and chapter 812.]

An Act to amend an Act intitled "An "Act for settling a Ministry and raising a "Maintenance for them in the City of New "York, County of Richmond, West Chester "and Queen's County, and an Act intitled. "An Act to enable the Inhabitants of the "City of New York to choose annually two "Vestrymen for each respective Ward within "the said City." so far as the same relates to the election of the Church Wardens and Vestrymen of the City of New York.

[Passed, January 27, 1770.]

WHEREAS by the third Clause in the Act intitled "An Act "for settling a Ministry and raising a Maintenance for them in "the City of New York. County of Richmond, West Chester and "Queens County," it is therein enacted that the respective Justices of every City and County aforesaid, or any two of them shall every Year issue out their Warrants to the Constable to summon the Freeholders of every City County and Precinct aforesaid together on the second Tuesday in January for choosing ten Vestrymen and two Church Wardens. AND WHEREAS by the first Clause in an Act intitled. "An Act to enable the Inhabitants of "the City of New York to choose annually two Vestrymen for "each respective Ward within the said City." it is therein enacted that on the second Tuesday in January next, and on the second Tuesday in January in every Year forever thereafter, there shall be chosen fourteen Vestrymen, that is to say, two Vestrymen for each and every Ward within the said City. To render the said Time commodious and convenient for the Inhabitants of the said City.

BE IT ENACTED by his Honor the Lieutenant Governor the Council and the General Assembly, and it is hereby enacted by the Authority of the same, that from and after the Publication of this Act the Justices of the Peace for the City and County of New York or any two of them shall every Year issue their Warrants to the Constables of each respective Ward at least two Days before the Day of Election for choosing Aldermen and other Officers, to summon the Freeholders of the said City and County to meet at the City Hall in the said City on the same Day on which the Aldermen, Assistants and other Officers of the said City are elected and then and there to choose by plurality of Voices two Church Wardens, and Overseers of the Poor, and fourteen Vestrymen, two for each Ward of said City, any Thing in the said Acts contained to the contrary in any wise notwithstanding.

[CHAPTER 1444.]

[Chapter 1444 of Van Schaack, where the act is printed in full. See chapter 1355.]

An Act to revive and continue an Act intitled. "An Act to ascertain the size of "Casks in which white Bread shall be packed "within the City of New York and to regulate the Manner in which the same shall be "sold."

[Passed, January 27, 1770.]

BE IT ENACTED by his Honor the Lieutenant Governor, the Council and the General Assembly and it is hereby enacted by the Authority of the same that the Act intitled. "An Act to ascertain the size of Casks in which white Bread shall be packed "within the City of New York and to regulate the manner in "which the same shall be sold." passed in the eighth Year of his present Majesty's Reign shall be and hereby is Revived, and every clause Matter and Thing therein contained, enacted to be and remain of Force from the Publication hereof until the first Day of January which will be in the Year of our Lord one thousand seven hundred and seventy five.

[CHAPTER 1445.]

[Chapter 1445 of Van Schaack, where the act is printed in full. See chapters 941, 1104, 1259.]

An Act to revive an Act intitled an Act to enable the Mayor, Deputy-Mayor, Recorder, and Aldermen of the City of New York for the Time being or the Major Part of them to raise a Tax for mending and keeping in repair the Public Wells and Pumps in the said City to the South of Fresh Water and other Purposes therein mentioned, with an Addition thereto.

[Passed, January 27, 1770.]

WHEREAS an Act intitled "An Act to enable the Mayor, "Deputy Mayor, Recorder and Aldermen of the City of New York "for the Time being or the Major Part of them to raise a Tax for "mending and keeping in repair the Public Wells and Pumps in "the said City to the South of Fresh Water and other Purposes "therein mentioned," passed in the twenty seventh Year of the Reign of his late Majesty King George the second, and since continued by an Act intitled. "An Act further to continue an Act intitled. "An Act further to continue an Act intitled An Act to "enable the Mayor, Deputy Mayor, Recorder and Aldermen of "the City of New York for the Time being, or the Major Part of "them to raise a Tax for mending and keeping in Repair the "Public Wells and Pumps in the said City to the South of Fresh "Water with an Addition thereto," expired on the first Day of this instant Month of January; and the same having been found useful and necessary.

BE IT THEREFORE ENACTED by his Honor the Lieutenant Governor, the Council and the General Assembly and it is hereby enacted by the Authority of the same that the said two Acts shall be and hereby are revived and every Clause Matter and Thing in the said two Acts contained enacted to be and remain in full Force from the Publication hereof until the first Day of January which will be in the Year of our Lord one thousand seven hundred and eighty.

AND WHEREAS the Money in the first mentioned Act is ordered to be laid on the second Tuesday in January which Time in this present year was elapsed before the passing this Act.

BE IT THEREFORE ENACTED by his Honor the Lieutenant Governor the Council and the General Assembly and it is hereby enacted by the Authority of the same, that it shall and may be lawful to and for the Mayor, Deputy Mayor or Recorder together with three or more Aldermen of the said City at any Time within ten Days after the Publication of this Act to order the raising for this present Year a Sum not exceeding two hundred Pounds, for the uses in the said first Act mentioned, to be raised in the same Manner as the Monies in the said Act are yearly directed to be raised.

[CHAPTER 1446.]

[Chapter 1446 of Van Schaack, where the act is printed in full.]

An Act to enable the Supervisors of the several Counties of this Colony therein mentioned to take Security of their respective County Treasurer before he enters upon the execution of his Office.

[Passed, January 27, 1770.]

WHEREAS several of the Counties within this Colony have sustained considerable Losses by the Insolvency and Misconduct of the Treasurers of the said Counties for remedy whereof for the future.

BE IT ENACTED by his Honor the Lieutenant Governor the Council and the General Assembly and it is hereby enacted by the Authority of the same, that every Treasurer hereafter to be chosen in each respective County within this Colony immediately after he shall be elected Treasurer for such County, and before he shall enter upon the Business of the said Office of Treasurer shall enter into Bond or Obligation with sufficient Security to the Supervisors of each respective County for the Time being in such Sum as the Supervisors for the Time being shall think proper well and faithfully to execute the Office of Treasurer of such respective County according to the Directions of the several Laws of this Colony in such Case made and provided.

AND BE IT FURTHER ENACTED by the Authority aforesaid that if the Treasurer of each respective County shall not comply with the Condition of the Bond or Obligation above directed to be given, whereby the Penalty of such Bond or Obligation shall be forfeited in such Case it shall and may be lawful for the Supervisors of each respective County for the Time being by the Name or Names of the Supervisors of such County to commence an Action of Debt on such Bond or Obligation against such Treasurer and his Security or Securities or either of them, or their respective Heirs, Executors or Administrators in any Court of Record within this Colony, and that the Monies that shall be recovered in any such Suit or Action shall be applied towards defraying the necessary Charges of such respective County.

PROVIDED ALWAYS that Nothing in this Act shall be construed to extend to the Treasurer or Chamberlain of the City and County of New York.

[CHAPTER 1447.]

[Chapter 1447 of Van Schaack, where the title only is printed. The acts revived are chapters 1121, 1143, 1166, 1315, 1369. This act expired the 1st of January, 1771, and was re-enacted by chapter 1475.]

An Act to revive the several Acts therein mentioned relative to Publick Highways in the County of Albany.

[Passed, January 27, 1770.]

WHEREAS the Act intitled. "An Act for regulating, clear-"ing and further laying out Public Highways throughout the "City and County of Albany," passed in the thirty third year of "his late Majesty's Reign, and the Act intitled. "An Act for "altering and explaining Part of an Act intitled An Act for "regulating clearing and further laying out Public Highways "throughout the City and County of Albany." passed in the first Year of his present Majesty's Reign, and the Act intitled. "An "Act to amend an Act intitled An Act for regulating, clearing "and further laying out Public Highways throughout the City "and County of Albany." passed in the second Year of his present Majesty's Reign. also the Act intitled. "An Act to impower the "Justices of the Peace in the County of Albany in General Ses-"sions, to appoint Commissioners to lay out new Roads or High-"ways in the said County." passed in the Seventh Year of his present Majesty's Reign, and also an Act intitled "An Act to "amend an Act intitled An Act for regulating clearing and "further laying out Public Highways throughout the City and "County of Albany." passed in the ninth Year of his present Majesty's Reign, have all expired on the first Day of January one thousand seven hundred and seventy.

BE IT THEREFORE ENACTED by his Honor the Lieutenant Governor, the Council and the General Assembly, and it is hereby

Enacted by the Authority of the same that the said several abovementioned Acts shall be and hereby are revived, and every Clause, Article, Matter and Thing in the said several Acts contained, enacted to be and remain in full force and virtue to all intents Constructions and Purposes whatsoever from the Publication hereof until the first Day of January which will be in the Year of our Lord one thousand seven hundred and seventy one.

[CHAPTER 1448.]

[Chapter 1448 of Van Schaack, where the act is printed in full. See chapter 1403.]

An Act to amend an Act intitled, "An "Act to enable the Freeholders and Inhabit- "ants of the Manor of Rensselaerwyck to "elect six Assessors three Collectors, eight "Constables, two Clerks, Pound Masters, "Fence Viewers and Surveyors of the "Highways."

[Passed, January 27, 1770.]

WHEREAS in and by an Act intitled "An Act to enable the "Freeholders and Inhabitants of the Manor of Rensselaerwyck "to elect six Assessors, three Collectors eight Constables, two "Clerks, Pound Masters, Fence Viewers, and Surveyors of the "Highways," it is enacted that the Supervisor and Treasurer for the said Manor shall annually be elected and chosen at the present dwelling House of Rebecca Dox in the said Manor. AND WHEREAS it is conceived that it will be more convenient for the Freeholders and Inhabitants of the said Manor to meet as well for the Election of a Supervisor and Treasurer as for electing all other the Officers mentioned in the said Act at the dwelling House of Rebecca Lombus at Cralo in the said Manor.

BE IT THEREFORE ENACTED by his Honor the Lieutenant Governor the Council and the General Assembly and it is hereby enacted by the Authority of the same, that the next annual Meeting of the Freeholders and Inhabitants of the said Manor of Rensselaerwyck for electing the several Officers in the said Act mentioned shall be held at the dwelling House in the possession of Rebecca Lombus at Cralo in the said Manor, which shall continue to be the place of annual Meeting for electing the Officers aforesaid for the said Manor, until such Time as a majority of the Freeholders and Inhabitants thereof at any such Meeting shall agree upon some other Place of Meeting for the following Year;

And then such Place so to be agreed upon, shall be the place of annual Meeting for the purposes aforesaid until altered as aforesaid, any Thing in the said Act contained to the contrary thereof in any wise notwithstanding.

AND BE IT FURTHER ENACTED by the Authority aforesaid that the Supervisor of the said Manor shall Publickly read this Act, at the next annual Meeting of the Freeholders and Inhabitants of the said Manor for electing of the Officers aforesaid. This Act to be in force from the Publication hereof, till the first Day of January which will be in the Year of our Lord one thousand seven hundred and seventy seven.

[CHAPTER 1449.]

[Chapter 1449 of Van Schaack, where the act is printed in full.]

An Act to prevent Accidents by Fire in that Part of the Manor of Rensselaerwyck therein mentioned.

[Passed, January 27, 1770.]

WHEREAS there are many dwelling Houses and other Buildings in that Part of the Manor of Rensselaerwyck contiguous to the City of Albany and on both Sides of the Street or Road leading from the said City to Water Vliet, and as many Persons there do not use that Precaution necessary against Accidents by Fire which may prove fatal as well to themselves as to the Inhabitants of said City, it is therefore become highly necessary to provide against the same.

BE IT THEREFORE ENACTED by his Honor the Lieutenant Governor, the Council and the General Assembly, and it is hereby enacted by the Authority of the same, that the Freeholders and Inhabitants within that Part of the Manor of Rensselaerwyck on both Sides of the Street or Road leading from the City of Albany to Water Vliet, be and are hereby impowered and directed as soon as conveniently may be after the Publication of this Act to assemble and meet together at the House at present occupied by Rebecca Dox within the Bounds aforesaid, and then and there by Majority of Voices elect and choose two sufficient able and discreet Persons being Freeholders to be Overseers of the Chimneys and Ovens in the said District, which Persons so chosen shall be Overseers as aforesaid from the Time of such their appointment until the first Tuesday in October next, and the said Freeholders and Inhabitants are hereby impowered and directed

aforesaid or to the Major Part of them after retaining six Pence out of every Pound so collected for his or their Trouble in collecting the same, to be by the said Justices or the Major Part of them laid out and they are hereby directed and required with all convenient Speed after the Money so raised as aforesaid shall come to their Hands to lay out the same in purchasing a Fire Engine, and in building a House for the same and for purchasing Leather Buckets to be lodged in such convenient Place in said Township as the said Justices shall direct, and to be used by the Inhabitants thereof in extinguishing of Fires that may happen within the same.

[CHAPTER 1431.]

[Chapter 1451 of Van Schaack, where the title only is printed. Repealed by chapter 1617.]

An Act for the better laying out, regulating, and keeping in Repair the Common and Public Highways in such Precincts in the County of Ulster as are therein mentioned.

[Passed, January 27, 1770.]

WHEREAS an Act was passed in the sixth Year of his present Majesty's Reign intitled, "An Act for the better clearing, mend-"ing, and further laying out Public High Roads and others in the "County of Ulster." which will continue by it's own Limitation to the first Day of January in the Year of our Lord one thousand seven hundred and seventy six, AND WHEREAS it has been found by Experience that although the said Act is well calculated to execute the intended Design in divers Parts of the said County; yet that sundry Amendments and Alterations are requesite for the more effectual Improvement of the Roads in the Precincts of New Windsor, Wallkill and New Burgh which from their peculiar State require a different Provision in sundry Instances.

BE IT THEREFORE ENACTED by his Honor the Lieutenant Governor the Council and the General Assembly, and it is hereby Enacted by the Authority of the same, that every Person compellable to Work on any Road within either of the said Precincts shall actually work for each Day he is obliged to work eight Hours, and for Default shall be liable to pay a Fine of six Pence for every Hour: To be recovered in the Manner directed for not Working on the Highways by the Act abovementioned, with the Charges of the Prosecution therefor.

AND WHEREAS according to the said Act no Difference is made between the Rich and the Poor; but they are (contrary to common Justice) obliged to work every Year an equal Number of Days; and as it is conceived that if the People were not to work as great a Number of Days on the Roads as by the abovementioned Act they are obliged to, and instead thereof Labourers were employed to work for Wages, the necessary Design of improving the Public Roads, would be much more effectually answered.

BE IT THEREFORE ENACTED by the same Authority that every Inhabitant within the said Precincts being a Freeholder, or Housekeeper shall be obliged to work four Days only in each Year instead of six: and every Person being a Labourer or Tradesman and no Freeholder or Housekeeper only two Days in each Year: and that Persons that live with and Labour for their Parents or Masters, and not being Freeholders shall be exempted from the Burthen of working upon, or contributing to the Charge of maintaining, the Public Roads within the Precincts aforesaid. And in Order that a Sum of Money may be annually raised in each of the said Precincts for paying such Labourers as may be employed in working and improving the Public Roads as aforesaid.

BE IT ENACTED by the Authority aforesaid, that when and as often as the Collector of each of the said Precincts shall receive the Rate List for collecting the necessary and contingent Charges of the said County, he shall annually within five Days thereafter lay the same before the Assessors of the same Precincts respectively who shall within ten Days after meet together and therefrom, form a distinct Roll or Rate List, and make particular Assessments therein upon every Inhabitant being a Freeholder or Housekeeper of the same Precincts respectively for paying the Expence of the Highways within the same Precinct, which Assessment shall be made with due respect (according to the best of their Skill and Understanding) to the comparative Abilities of the Inhabitants therein assessed, and as near as possible agreeable to the Assessments made upon them in the Tax Lists for raising the other necessary and contingent Charges of the County; and the sum so to be annually assessed upon and raised in each Precinct, shall be a sum equal to the Amount of six Shillings for every Inhabitant living within the same, who is either a Freeholder or Housekeeper with the addition of two

Pence in every Pound for the Collector's Trouble in collecting the same.

AND BE IT ALSO ENACTED by the same Authority, that when the said Assessors have formed the Roll of Assessment hereby directed, they shall sign and deliver the same to the respective Collectors, and such Roll so signed shall be as sufficient a Warrant for collecting the respective Rates therein mentioned as the Rate List and Warrant from the Supervisors is for collecting the necessary and contingent County Charge, and that the several Rates therein mentioned shall be recoverable in the same Manner as the said County Rates now are.

AND BE IT FURTHER ENACTED by the same Authority that the Inhabitants being Freeholders or Housekeepers of each of the said Precincts shall at their next and every subsequent annual Meetings respectively choose by plurality of Voices three commissioners of Highways in the Room and stead of the present Commissioners who shall, have all the Powers given to, and, perform the Duties enjoined upon Commissioners of Highways by virtue of the Act abovementioned, and every future Vacancy of the Place of any Commissioner or Commissioners shall be supplied by an Election of some other fit Person or Persons in his or their stead in the Manner thereby directed; And the Commissioners of every Precinct by major Voice are hereby authorized to divide the same into Districts and describe the same in Writing to be by them subscribed and filed with and entered by the Clerk of each respective Precinct in the Town Books, and for every such District the Freeholders and Housekeepers thereof may at their next and every subsequent annual Meeting choose one Overseer who shall have all the Powers given and perform all the Duties enjoined by the said Act on Overseers or Surveyors of the Highways; which Overseers Together with the Commissioners by major Voice shall make a just and equitable Partition of the Money so to be raised as aforesaid upon the same Precinct among the several Districts thereof, and if either of the said Overseers shall die within the Year or be disabled from executing his Office, another shall be appointed in his Room by the Commissioners of the Precinct where such Death or Disability shall happen, or by the Major Part of them.

AND BE IT FURTHER ENACTED by the Authority aforesaid, that the Money so to be assessed, when collected shall be put into the Hands of the Clerks of the Precincts respectively, who shall keep true Books and Accounts of the Receipt and Disbursement of the same, and shall pay the Shares of each District to the Overseer thereof from Time to Time according to the Warrant of the Commissioners, or of the Majority of them, under their Hands and Seals to be applied according to the Discretion of the Overseers in hiring Labourers, Teams, Carriages, and Instruments for the uses aforesaid; and every Overseer may retain for his own attendance and Labour in overseeing the Persons hired to work upon the Road five shillings for every Day of actual Service; and in every such Day there shall be actually employed under him not less than eight hired Persons without Teams, nor less than six with two Teams and Carriages, which Labourers, and Teams and Carriages shall be hired by the said Overseers respectively in the cheapest and most reasonable Manner: Of all which Services and of their Disbursements the same Overseers respectively shall keep true and exact Accounts and return the same upon Oath to the Commissioners of the Precinct when by them or the Major Part of them they shall be severally thereunto required.

AND BE IT FURTHER ENACTED by the same Authority, that it shall be lawful for any Person compellable to work on the Roads as aforesaid to commute for and pay Money at the Rate of three shillings a Day instead of labouring on the Road, which Money shall be paid to the Clerk of the Precinct, and be applied for the Improvement of the Roads of the Precinct in which the Person or Persons paying the same may dwell: PROVIDED ALWAYS that no Person shall be excused from working upon the same Roads according to the Direction of the Overseer or Overseers thereof unless at the Time of his being summoned he shall produce a Certificate under the Hand of the Clerk of the Precinct to prove the actual payment of the Money according to the Directions of this Act, or shall then pay the same to the Overseer so warning him to work, who shall account with the said Clerk for the same.

AND BE IT FURTHER ENACTED by the same Authority that if the Inhabitants of either of the said Precincts at any subsequent annual Town Meeting shall by Major Voice resolve to raise for the Purposes aforesaid in Manner above directed any sum not less than what the Quota of the Precinct would amount to according to the Rates herein before prescribed, and the same shall be entered upon the Town Books, then the said Assessors and Collectors shall and may proceed to an Assessment and Collection of the same in the Manner herein before directed for the uses abovementioned and in every such Case none of the Inhabitants of the same shall be compellable to work upon the same Roads; any Thing herein contained to the contrary thereof in any wise notwithstanding.

AND BE IT ALSO ENACTED by the same Authority, that every Commissioner and Precinct Clerk shall before he proceeds to the Execution of the Power given to him by this Act, take an Oath before any one of his Majesty's Justices of the Peace of the said County well and faithfully to perform the same according to the best of his Skill and Understanding; And the Overseers respectively of the said Precincts before they enter upon the Execution of their Office shall take the following Oath, to wit, That in the Distribution of the Money to be raised by virtue of this Act among the different Districts in his Precinct he will act fairly and impartially, according to the best of his Skill and understanding, and will render to the Clerk of the Precinct a true Account of all such Sum and Sums of Money as shall be by him received or disbursed by virtue of this Act within one Month after the Determination of his Office of Overseer. And every Commissioner for refusing or neglecting to serve shall forfeit five Pounds, and every Assessor for refusing or neglecting the Duty enjoined on him by this Act five Pounds, and every Overseer five Pounds to be recovered in a summary Way before any one of his Majesty's Justices of the Peace by any person who will sue for the same, one third Part whereof shall be to the Person suing for the same and the other two third Parts to be paid to the Clerk of the Precinct where such Forfeiture shall be made, and applied to the Uses prescribed by this Act in manner aforesaid.

BE IT FURTHER ENACTED by the same Authority that the Commissioners for laying out Roads for the Towns of Hurley and Marble Town are hereby authorized and impowered to lay out a Road leading from the King's Road near the old House of Andries De Witt Esquire in Marble Town to the King's Road or Highway leading from the New Paltz to Kingston, so as to be most convenient for the Inhabitants requiring the same to pass to the Green Kill Mills. PROVIDED ALWAYS that the same Road so to be laid out shall not exceed two Rods in Breadth, and that the Commissioners in laying out the same shall govern themselves in the same Manner as is directed in and by the Act abovementioned, and that the said Road shall not be considered as a common Public Highway to be supported at the Expence of the County, but as a Road for the use of a Neighbourhood only.

AND BE IT ALSO ENACTED by the same Authority that this Act shall continue and be in Force till the first Day of January which will be in the Year of our Lord one thousand seven hundred and seventy six, and no longer.

[CHAPTER 1452.]

[Chapter 1452 of Van Schaack, where the act is printed in full. See chapter 1375.]

An Act for charging the Care of providing for the Relief of the Poor in the Town of Kingston in Ulster County upon the Trustees of the Freeholders and Commonalty of the said Town, and for compelling Constables to execute their Offices.

[Passed, January 27, 1770.]

WHEREAS an Act was passed in the ninth Year of his present Majesty's Reign intitled an Act for the Relief of the Poor in the Counties of Ulster and Orange and to enable the Freeholders and Inhabitants of the several Towns and Precincts thereof to elect Overseers of the Poor at their Annual Meetings.

AND WHEREAS particular Elections meerly for that purpose in the Town of Kingston where there are already annual Elections of Trustees who can and usually have performed the Office of Overseers of the Poor will create an unnecessary Waste of Time to the Inhabitants.

BE IT THEREFORE ENACTED by his Honor the Lieutenant Governor, the Council and the General Assembly, and it is hereby declared and enacted by the Authority of the same that from and after the Publication of this Act the Trustees of the Freeholders and Commonalty of the Town of Kingston aforesaid shall perform the Duty enjoined by the said Act upon the Overseers of the Poor, and that the Powers thereby given for making prudential Rules and Orders with respect to the Poor and their Children and for compelling Persons to work who have no visible way of gaining an honest Livelihood, shall be vested in the said Trustees or the major Part of them who shall and may regulate the annual Elections for Constables and other Officers of the said Town and finally determine upon all Disputes concerning the same: and if any Person chosen to the Office of a Constable shall not in two

Days next after Notice thereof from the Clerk of the sa'd Town take the Oath of Office required by Law, he shall incur alty of three Pounds to be recovered with Costs of S Name of the Person acting as President of the Trustees for the Time being, who shall sue for the same before a his Majesty's Justices of the Peace for the said county which said Penalty shall be applied for the use of the P said Town as other Monies raised for that purpose pu the said Act are. Provided that the Constable so chosen within the said Town on Lands held or which have l under the same before the passing of this Act or up within the Bounds of the said Town held by Grants pr Charter incorporating the said Town.

[CHAPTER 1453.]

[Chapter 1453 of Van Schaack, where the title only is printed. to the manor of Cortlandt, by chapter 1500, and to the city and county of Albany, with an addition, by chapter 1526. This act expired the 1st of January, 1773, and re-enacted by chapter 1624.]

An Act for the better regulation of the Public Inns and Taverns in the Counties of Ulster and Orange.

[Passed, January 27, 1770.]

WHEREAS though the original Design of instituting Inns and Taverns was that Travellers might be accommodated with Necessaries and Conveniencies, yet so laudable a Design has been perverted to the most michievous Purposes in society, by furnishing Means, for the entertainment of Idle and dissolute Youth to the Ruin of Families and the great Injury of the Public.

BE IT THEREFORE ENACTED by his Honor the Lieutenant Governor, the Council and the General Assembly and it is hereby enacted by the Authority of the same that from and after the first Day of January next, if any Person or Persons, keeping a Public Inn or Tavern in either of the Counties of Ulster or Orange shall sell give or otherwise furnish any Quantity of Strong Liquors to any Person under the Age of sixteen Years whereby such Person shall be Intoxicated or shall suffer such Person under the age of Sixteen Years to play at any Game within the House, Out House or the appurtenances thereunto belonging of such Innholder or Tavernkeeper, he she or they so offending shall forfeit and pay for every such Offence the sum of five Pounds to be sued for and recov--ed by the Parent or Guardian of such person under the sixteen Years, by Action of Debt in a Summary way with f Suit, before any Justice of the Peace of the County uch Offence shall be committed, one half of such For- to be applied to the use of the Person so suing for and ng the same, and the other half thereof to be paid into nds of the Overseers of the Poor in such Town or Pre- here the Offence shall have been committed to be applied Maintenance of the Poor thereof.

BE IT FURTHER ENACTED by the Authority afore- t every Person who shall after the said first Day of Jan- xt, keep any Inn or Tavern in either of the said Counties ue of any Licence pursuant to the Laws of this Colony, ave all his Measures for Liquor and for Provender for or other Cattle of such Sizes and Dimensions respectively contain the full Quantities respectively which shall be ---- for or required by any Person or Persons asking for or requiring the same to be ascertained according to the respective Quantities of Measures established in the City of New York on Pain of forfeiting the sum of forty shillings to be recovered by any Person or Persons who will sue and prosecute for the same in Manner aforesaid for his or their own use.

AND BE IT FURTHER ENACTED by the Authority afore- said that every Person and Persons after the said first Day of January next keeping any Public Inn or Tavern in either of the said Counties shall keep two good spare Beds, one whereof to be a Feather Bed, with good and sufficient sheeting and covering for such Beds respectively and good sufficient Provision for four persons and also good and sufficient stabling and Provender of Hay in the Winter, and Hay or Pasturage in the Summer, and Grain for four Horses or other Cattle for the accommodation of Travellers their Horses and Cattle upon Pain of forfeiting for every Offence the sum of twenty shillings, to be sued for recovered and applied as in the last mentioned section of this Act is directed. PROVIDED ALWAYS, AND IT IS HEREBY ENACTED that whereas in some Parts of the said Counties of Ulster and Orange, so little resort is had to Some Inns or Taverns as would make the last mentioned Regulation Burthensome; and yet it being necessary that in those places some Sort of Enter- tainment should be provided for persons carrying their Produce to Market; it shall therefore be in the discretion of the Major

Part of the Justices of the Peace of each respective Town and Precinct, if there are three or more Justices in such Town or Precinct, and if not, then in the Discretion of the Major Part of the Justices of the said Town or Precinct, and the Justice or Justices of the next adjacent Town or Precinct, to exempt by writing under their Hands and Seals one or more Inholders or Tavern-keepers in every such Town or Precinct from being subject to the Regulation prescribed in and by the last abovementioned section of this Act, any Thing therein contained to the contrary thereof in any wise notwithstanding.

AND BE IT ALSO ENACTED by the Authority aforesaid that the Clerk of each respective Town and Precincts within the Counties aforesaid shall publickly read this Act at the next annual Town or Precinct Meeting for which he is Clerk, and so every Year during the continuance of this Act.

AND BE IT ENACTED by the Authority aforesaid that this Act shall continue in force from the first Day of January next 'till the first Day of January which will be in the Year of our Lord one thousand seven hundred and seventy three.

[CHAPTER 1454.]

[Chapter 1454 of Van Schaack, where the act is printed in full. See chapter 1375.]

An Act to amend an Act intitled, An Act for the relief of the Poor in the Counties of Ulster and Orange, and to enable the Freeholders and Inhabitants of the several Towns and Precincts thereof to elect Overseers of the Poor at their annual Meetings so far as the same relates to the County of Ulster.

[Passed, January 27, 1770.]

WHEREAS in and by the abovementioned Act among other Things, it is enacted that the Freeholders and Inhabitants of the respective Towns and Precincts within the Counties of Ulster and Orange may and are thereby impowered at their annual Meetings for choosing Supervisors and other Officers, to agree on such Sum or Sums of Money as they may think proper for the Sustenance of the Poor, binding Out as Apprentices the Children of such Parents as are unable to maintain them, and for compelling such Persons to work as have no visible Way of gaining an honest livelyhood in the Course of the ensuing Year, and for an Allowance to their Clerk, and that a Copy of the Entry, respecting the Sum or Sums so agreed to be raised for the Purposes aforesaid shall be forthwith delivered, signed by the said Clerks respectively and the Overseeres of the said Towns or Precincts, to the Supervisors or one of them who shall lay the same before the Supervisors of the respective Counties aforesaid at their first annual Meeting, and that the same Sum or Sums shall be levied upon the Freeholders and Inhabitants of the said Towns and Precincts respectively, as Part of the necessary and Contingent Charge of the said Counties, and paid and applied as in and by the said Act is directed. AND WHEREAS the Town of Hurley long since duely Incorporated under the Great Seal of this Colony, and several other of the Towns in the said County of Ulster hold their annual Meetings by virtue of their respective Charters and some of them after the Day of the first annual Meeting of the Supervisors of the County of Ulster aforesaid, by reason of which the Freeholders and Inhabitants of the said Towns are deprived of the Benefit of the said. Act, for Remedy whereof.

BE IT ENACTED by his Honor the Lieutenant Governor, the Council and the General Assembly, and it is hereby enacted by the Authority of the same, That the Time for laying the Copies of the Entries of such Sum or Sums of Money as shall be agreed upon to be raised by virtue of the said Act, and for the purposes therein mentioned before the Supervisors of the said County of Ulster, shall be at the second annual Meeting of the said Supervisors instead of the first as directed in and by the said Act, any Thing therein contained to the contrary thereof in any wise notwithstanding.

AND BE IT FURTHER ENACTED by the Authority aforesaid that the Supervisors of the said County of Ulster shall not hold their second Meeting for settling the contingent Charges of said County till after the second Tuesday in June in every Year to the Intent that the said incorporated Town of Hurley and the several other Towns in the County of Ulster aforesaid, holding their annual Elections by virtue of Charters as aforesaid may be enabled to take the Benefit of the abovementioned Act.

[CHAPTER 1455.]

[Chapter 1455 of Van Schaack, where the title only is printed. See chapter 1290. Amended by chapter 1502. Repealed by chapter 1616.]

An Act to amend an Act intitled. "An Act for the better laying out, regulating and keeping in repair Common, Public and Private Highways on the North Side of the Highlands in the County of Orange.

[Passed, January 27, 1770.]

WHEREAS by the thirteenth Section of an Act intitled. "An " Act for the better laying out, regulating and keeping in Repair " Common Public and Private Highways on the North side of the " Highlands in the County of Orange," passed the twenty third Day of December one thousand seven hundred and sixty five, it is among other Things enacted that the Bridges and Causeways in the said Act particularly mentioned, should be made and kept in repair by a Public Tax upon the Precincts of Goshen and Cornwall, and that all other Bridges and Causeways in the precinct of Goshen which the Commissioners of Goshen or the Major Part of them for the Time being should think proper should be made and kept in repair by a Public Tax. And all other Bridges and Causeways in the Precinct of Cornwall which the Commissioners of Cornwall or the Major Part of them should think proper should also be made and kept in repair by a Public Tax. AND WHEREAS it is thought proper for the present that no Bridges or Causeways should be made or kept in repair by a Public Tax other than those particularly mentioned in the Said Act, and a Bridge over the Outlet of the Drowned Lands.

BE IT THEREFORE ENACTED by his Honor the Lieutenant Governor the Council and the General Assembly, and it is hereby enacted by the Authority of the same, that no other Bridge or Causeway in the said Precincts except those particularly mentioned in the said Act, and the Bridge and Causeway across the Walkill at the Outlet of the Drowned Lands shall be made or kept in repair by a Public Tax.

AND BE IT FURTHER ENACTED by the authority aforesaid that every Person who by this Act is obliged to work on Highways and does dwell in that Part of the Precinct of Cornwall within the following Bounds (to wit) Beginning on the West Side of the Murderers Creek where the reputed Line of Jurisdiction between the Counties of Ulster and Orange crosses the same from thence Southwesterly along the West Side of the said Creek till it comes opposite to the North End of Schunamuck Hill or Mountain then along the West Side of said Hill or Mountain to the Southerly End of it so as to include all the Inhabitants that live on the West Side of said Hill, and from thence to and including the House in which John Smith now lives, and from thence to the Division Line of Cornwall and Goshen Precincts, and from thence along the last mentioned Line till it intersects the said reputed Line of Jurisdiction between the said Counties of Ulster and Orange, and from thence along the said last mentioned Line to the place of beginning and also every Person who by this Act is obliged to work on Highways and doth dwell in the said Precinct of Goshen to the Eastward of the Walkill, and to the North Eastward of the following Line (to wit) beginning at the Black Walnut Island, and from thence to and including the House of Captain John Wisner, from thence to and including the House of Francis Armstrong from thence to and including the House of John Sayrs, from thence to and including the House of Timothy Clarke Junior, from thence to and including the House in which John Perham now lives, from thence to the House in which James Jackson now lives, and from thence to the said Division Line of the Precincts of Goshen and Cornwall except the Inhabitants of those Districts which work on the Road from Captain Nathaniel Roe Junior to Sterling Iron Works shall during the Continuance of this Act work one Day in a Year between the first Day of April, and the first Day of July on the Water Side Roads in the Precinct of Cornwall from the said Division Line of the said Precincts near Barnabas Horton Junior down to New Windsor and the Road from the said Division Line of the said Precincts near Barnabas Manneys, and along by Stephen Gilbert's down to New Windsor, and that Captain John Wisner, Captain Elihu Mervin, Mr Zachariah Dubois, and Mr John Wells are hereby directed and required by the first Day of April next, and that as often as they shall think necessary to view the said Roads, and that they or any three of them shall give directions to every Overseer in the Said Precincts of Goshen or Cornwall, who are obliged to work on the said Roads, what place they shall work upon, and in Case any Overseer shall refuse or neglect to Work according to such Directions, he shall forfeit the sum of five Pounds.

AND BE IT FURTHER ENACTED by the Authority aforesaid that every Overseer within the said Precinct that shall not give Notice to the Persons within his District who are obliged to work on Highways to work five Days in a year, or if any Overseer shall not fine every Person who shall neglect or refuse to work on the Highways at the Time and Place he shall be directed to work, or if any Overseer shall neglect to lay out the Money arising by every Fine on the Highway within his District, or where the Person ought to have Worked and within twenty five Days after the Time in which the Person fined should have worked said Overseer in each of the above Cases shall forfeit the Sum of five Pounds.

AND BE IT FURTHER ENACTED by the Authority aforesaid that no greater or other Fees or Charges shall be allowed or taken for altering or laying out any Highway than the following to wit, to each Commissioner and Justice six Shillings per Day; to the Justices for issuing their Warrant to Summon a Jury three Shillings; to the Sheriff, his Deputy or a Constable for Summoning a Jury six Shillings; for his Attendance on the Jury each Day four Shillings; to each Jury Man four Shillings per Day; to Captain John Wisner, Captain Elihu Mervin, Mr Zachariah Dubois, and Mr John Wells each four Shillings per Day as a reward for their Care and Trouble in doing the Business required by this Act, which Fees or charges shall be raised upon the respective Precincts of Goshen and Cornwall as the other Charges of the said Precincts are raised.

BE IT FURTHER ENACTED by the Authority aforesaid that every Male Freeholder and Inhabitant and no other person within the said Precincts between the Age of twenty one Years and sixty Years shall either in Person or by an able and sufficient Man in his Room be obliged to work five Days in a year upon the Highways, any Law, usage or Custom to the contrary thereof in any wise notwithstanding.

WHEREAS it has been found by experience to be extremely Difficult for the Overseers to deliver in upon Oath an Account in the Manner and at the Time directed by the tenth Section of the aforesaid Act, to prevent such Difficulties for the future.

BE IT FURTHER ENACTED by the Authority aforesaid that instead of the Account to be delivered under Oath in the said tenth Section mentioned every Overseer shall deliver an Account on or before the last Tuesday in March in every Year to one or more of the Commissioners of the Precinct to which he doth belong, and shall take an Oath before the said Commissioner, who is hereby impowered to administer the same, in the Words following, to wit, I, A. B. declare upon the holy Evangelists that this Account now delivered by me contains the Names of all the Persons within my District which by this Act are obliged to work on Highways that each Person therein named has worked himself or by a Man in his stead five Days since the first Day of April last and at least to the amount of eight Hours in each Day three of which Days work were done between the first Day of April and the first Day of July, or I have laid out the Fines of such Persons that have not worked agreeable to this Act on the Highway within my District and within twenty five Days after the Time in which such Persons as I have fined ought to have worked according to the best of my knowledge and understanding, so help me God. And if any Overseer shall neglect or refuse to deliver an Account or take the Oath hereby required, he shall forfeit the Sum of five Pounds, which forfeiture with all others herein before mentioned shall be recovered and applied as by the aforesaid Act is directed.

AND BE IT FURTHER ENACTED by the Authority aforesaid that when the Commissioners or the Major Part of them in the respective Precincts for which they shall be chosen, shall stop up or alter any Road already laid out, and lay out another in the stead of it, the said old Road so stopped up shall belong to the Person or Persons through or on whose Land the same did run if such Person or Persons do not insist on pay for the Land over which the new Road may run; but if pay shall be insisted upon for the Land over which the new Road shall be laid then the Jury to be summoned by virtue of the aforesaid Act for ascertaining the Value of the same shall take a View of both Roads and fix such Value to each of the said Roads as they shall think reasonable and the Person or Persons through or on whose Land the Old Road run shall pay such Sum or Sums of Money to the Commissioners of the said Precinct where such old Road lay to be applied towards paying for the Lands on which the new Road or alteration shall be made Provided the Person or Persons through or on whose Land ye old Road run agreed that the said old Road, should be stopped up, previous to such Alteration, and if the said Person or Persons through or on whose Land the said old Road shall run, shall refuse or neglect within six Months thereafter to pay such Sum or Sums of Money to the Commissioners aforesaid or one of them as the Jury shall fix as the Value of the Old Road, then it shall and may be lawful for the Justices who attended the Jury on valuing the said Road or either of them to issue Execution for the said Sum or Sums, with the Costs thereon accrued, as is usual in other Cases.

This Act to continue in force three Years from the Publication thereof, and no longer.

[CHAPTER 1456.]

[Chapter 1456 of Van Schaack, where the act is printed in full. See chapter 1381.]

An Act more effectually to prevent Damages by Swine in the County of Orange.

[Passed, January 27, 1770.]

WHEREAS by an Act passed in the ninth Year of his Present Majesty's Reign, the Freeholders of the Township of Marbletown, and the Freeholders of the Precincts of Goshen and Cornwall respectively or the Major Part of them at their annual Meetings for election of Town Officers are impowered to make such prudential Rules, Orders and Regulations for restraining of Swine from running at large, or for compelling the Owner or Owners of such Swine who shall thereafter commit Damages to make satisfaction to such Person or Persons who shall sustain the same or otherwise as by them shall be thought most convenient; which said Act being found by Experience to be ineffectual for the good Purposes thereby designed in the said Precincts of Goshen and Cornwall in Orange County.

BE IT THEREFORE ENACTED by his Honor the Lieutenant Governor, the Council and the General Assembly, and it is hereby enacted by the Authority of the same, that from and after the Publication of this Act it shall and may be lawful for all and every of the Inhabitants living in the said County of Orange to take, keep or impound in any Pound or Place within the County aforesaid, and in the Precinct in which he she or they shall reside, all such Swine great or small which shall or do get into any of his her or their Cornfields, Orchards, Gardens, Meadows or other improved Lands until the Owner or Owners of such Swine shall pay and satisfy the Person or Persons who shall take and impound them the Damages done by the said Swine together with the Costs of advertising and keeping them and one Shilling a Head for the Trouble of impounding them if in the Precincts of

Goshen or Cornwall, and three Shillings a Head if in the Precincts of Haverstraw or Orange Town, which Damages, Costs of Advertising and keeping the said Swine shall be ascertained by any three Freeholders living in the Precinct where such impounding shall happen.

AND BE IT FURTHER ENACTED by the Authority aforesaid that in Case the Owner or Owners of any Swine, taken, kept or impounded by virtue of this Act, shall or do not within twenty four Hours after Notice personally given to the Owner or Owners thereof, or by a Notice left at his, her or their Place of abode with some of the Family of suitable Age of such taking keeping or impounding such Swine, redeem his her or their Swine by paying the Penalties imposed by this Act; or in Case the Owner or owners of such Swine be not known the Person or Persons so taking and impounding such Swine shall advertise them for four Days in two of the most Public Places near to where the said Swine may be impounded and then shall sell them at Public Vendue, unless they shall be sooner redeemed by paying the Penalties as aforesaid.

AND BE IT FURTHER ENACTED by the Authority aforesaid that if any Swine shall be sold by virtue of this Act, the overplus Money (if any) after deducting all Damages and Costs shall be returned to the Owner or Owners of such Swine provided the same shall be demanded within six Months after such impounding, and if no demand shall be made the Overplus shall be given to the Overseers of the Poor of the Precinct where such impounding may happen, to be applied towards the Maintenance of the Poor within the same.

AND BE IT FURTHER ENACTED by the Authority aforesaid that if any Swine (except sucking Pigs) not having their Noses ringed so as to prevent them from Rooting shall hereafter run at large in the Precincts of Haverstraw and Orange Town, in the Town of Goshen or in Florida, between the House of William Thompson Esquire, and the House of Mr Garret Bloom it shall and may be lawful for any person or Persons to take up and impound any such Swine, and In Case the Owner or Owners of such Swine shall not within twenty four Hours after Notice given to him her or them thereof, or a Notice left at his her or their Place of abode with some of the Family of suitable Age redeem the said Swine by paying one Shilling a Head for the trouble of impounding them, or in Case the Owner or Owners of such Swine shall not be known, the Person or Persons so taking and impounding such Swine, shall advertise them for four Days in two of the most Public Places near to where the said Swine may be impounded and shall then sell them, and after deducting one shilling a Head for impounding such Swine and three Shillings a Head for keeping and advertising them, the Overplus Money (if any) shall be disposed of as is above directed, any Thing in the said in part above recited Act contained to the contrary hereof in any wise notwithstanding.

AND BE IT FURTHER ENACTED by the Authority aforesaid that this Act shall continue and be in force from the Publication thereof until the first Day of January one thousand seven hundred and eighty and no longer.

CHAPTER 1457.

[Chapter 1457 of Van Schaack, where the act is printed in full. This act expired the 1st of January, 1773, and was continued by chapter 1587.]

An Act for the more equal Taxation of Estates in Orange County.

[Passed, January 27, 1770.]

WHEREAS the ascertaining the Quotas of proportions of each respective Precinct in the County of Orange towards the Taxes, Rates and Contingent County Charges to be assessed and raised upon the said County, hath hitherto been attended with great Difficulty and Uncertainty; and given Occasion for Disputes and Discontent, for preventing whereof for the future.

BE IT ENACTED by his Honor the Lieutenant Governor, the Council and the General Assembly, and it is hereby enacted by the Authority of the same that from henceforth the Taxes, Rates and Contingent County Charges to be assessed levied and raised upon the said County of Orange shall be sustained by, assessed raised and levied upon the several Precincts of the said County in the Quotas and Proportions following, that is to say, If at any Time the sum of three thousand six hundred and fifty Pounds should be raised upon the said County twelve hundred and fifty Pounds shall be levied and assessed upon the Precinct of Goshen, six hundred and ninety Pounds upon the Precinct of Cornwall, six hundred and twenty Pounds upon the precinct of Haverstraw, eight hundred Pounds upon the Precinct of Orange Town, and two hundred and ninety Pounds upon the Precinct of Minisink, and so in all Cases where a greater or less Sum shall be levied upon the said County, the same shall be assessed and raised by and upon the said several Precincts in the Proportion which each of the said several sums hereby affixed and declared to be the Quota of the said respective Precinct do bear to the said sum of three thousand six hundred and fifty Pounds which Proportion shall remain and continue as a nominal Rule and Standard for ascertaining and apportioning the Shares and Quotas of the said respective Precincts towards all Taxes Rates and Contingent County Charges hereafter to be assessed levied and raised upon the said County.

And for the more just and equal Assessment and Collection of the Taxes or Rates to be imposed upon the said several Precincts in the said County of Orange. BE IT FURTHER ENACTED that every Person subject to such Tax or Charge, shall at all Times when required by the Assessors of the Precinct wherein he resides, or either of them give him or them a view of all the improved Land in his Occupation and a just Account of all the Horses Cattle and Chattels which are his Property, and ought to be subject to such Tax or Charge, and if any Person shall secret or conceal from the Assessors any Part of his improved Land Horses, Cattle or Chattels, which ought to have been subject to such Tax or Charge he shall forfeit for every such Concealment four Times the Amount or Value of the Tax which ought to have been assessed on the Land Horses Cattle or Chattels so concealed, which Forfeiture upon the Conviction of the Offender before any Justice of the Peace of the said County by the Oath of one or more Witnesses shall be levied and raised by the Collector of the Precinct together with the Costs of the Conviction in the same manner the Tax ought to have been levied and raised had no such Fraud been committed and one half of the Penalty arising from every such Conviction shall be for the use of the Person who shall sue for the same, and the other half shall be applied to the use of the Poor of the Precinct wherein such Penalty shall have been incurred. Provided always that nothing herein contained shall be construed to oblige any Person to give in any Account of any Sums of Money due to him, or of his Household Furniture, Jewels, Plate or wearing Apparel.

AND BE IT FURTHER ENACTED by the Authority aforesaid that when any Tax or charge is to be raised and levied upon the said County, the Supervisors of the several Precincts shall at their Meetings fix and ascertain the several Quotas or shares of each Precinct towards such Tax or charge agreeable to the Rule and Proportion in this Act directed and prescribed, and the Assessors of each Precinct (after having taken the following Oath before one of his Majesty's Justices of the Peace for the said County to wit, I A. B. do solemnly and sincerely Swear that I will well and truly, equally and impartially according to the best of my skill knowledge, and Judgment assess every Part of the Real Estate Wood Land only excepted, and also every Part of the Personal Estate of every Person within the Town or Precinct for which I am chosen assessor, and of all such as have Estates therein and do not reside there, so help me God.) shall proceed to rate and assess every Inhabitant of each Precinct a just Proportion according to the value of the rateable Part of his Estate of the sum to be levied and raised in each respective Precinct, and when the same is compleated the Assessors for each respective Precinct shall form a Tax Roll for their several Precincts specifying the Name of each Inhabitant, the sum at which his rateable Estate is computed, and the Amount of the Tax at which he is assessed.

AND BE IT FURTHER ENACTED by the Authority aforesaid that the Assessors of the several Precincts hereafter mentioned shall be allowed and paid by their respective Precincts for their services in that Office for every Day they shall respectively be actually employed therein in the Manner following, that is to say, each of the Assessors of the Precinct of Cornwall six shillings per Day, and each of the Assessors of the Precincts of Haverstraw and Orange Town four shillings per Day, which several allowances shall from Time to Time as they shall become due be levied and raised upon the said respective Precincts in the same Manner as the other contingent County Charges are or shall be raised and levied in the said Precincts respectively.

AND BE IT FURTHER ENACTED by the Authority aforesaid that this Act shall continue in force from the Publication hereof until the first Day of January which will be in the Year of our Lord one thousand seven hundred and seventy three and no longer.

[CHAPTER 1458.]

[Chapter 1458 of Van Schaack, where the act is printed in full. See chapter 801. By chapter 1619 all acts relating to the highways so far as they concern the Borough of Westchester, are repealed.]

An Act to revive an Act intitled "An Act "for the better clearing regulating and fur-"ther laying out Public Highways in the "County of West Chester." with some Alterations.

[Passed, January 27, 1770.]

WHEREAS an Act intitled. "An Act for the better clearing, regulating and further laying out Public Highways in "the "County of West Chester." passed in the nineteenth Year of his late Majesty's Reign expired by it's own Limitation on the first Day of December one thousand seven hundred and fifty-five, and the same having been continued by several subsequent Acts until the first Day of January one thousand seven hundred and seventy, which said Act having been found very useful.

BE IT THEREFORE ENACTED by his Honor the Lieutenant Governor the Council and the General Assembly and it is hereby enacted by the Authority of the same that the above mentioned Act intitled. "An Act for the better clearing regulating and fur-"ther laying out Public Highways in the County of West Chester." shall be and hereby is revived and every Article, Matter and Clause therein contained enacted to be and remain in full force from the Publication hereof until the first Day of January which will be in the Year of our Lord one thousand seven hundred and eighty.

AND BE IT FURTHER ENACTED by the Authority aforesaid that the several Persons herein after named to wit For West Chester and Fordham, Walter Brigs, Anthony Bartow and James Ferris. For East Chester John Townshend, Charles Vincent, Thomas Butler and Edward Burling. For New Rochelle and Pelham, Jacobus Bleeker, Peter Flandereau, Philip Pell and Richard Willis. For Rye and White Plains Gabriel Lynch, Job Hadden, and John Thomas Junior. For Mamaroneck Benjamin Griffin, Daniel Barker, and Reuben Bloomer. For Bedford Zebediah Mills, Abraham Miller Nehemiah Lownsberry and Stephen Holmes. For North Castle Benjamin Smith, Moses Quinby and David Daton, For Salem Josiah Gilbert, James Brown and

Solomon Close. For the Manor of Cortlandt, Philip Verplank, Pierre Van Cortlandt Joseph Sherwood and Hackeliah Brown. For the lower Part of the Manor of Philipsburg James Van Cortlandt, Frederick Philips and Benjamin Fowler. For the upper Part of said Manor William Davids, Isaac Deane, and Gilbert Drake; and for the East Patent and old Pound Ridge, John Crawford Hezekiah Wood and Joseph Lockwood shall be and hereby are appointed Commissioners to regulate and lay out Highways in the said County for the places for which they are respectively appointed, and shall be and hereby are vested with as full power and Authority for that End to all Intents Constructions and purposes whatsoever as if they had been actually named and appointed in and by the aforesaid Act, any Thing in the aforesaid Act to the contrary notwithstanding.

AND BE IT FURTHER ENACTED by the Authority aforesaid, that the Commissioners or the Major Part of them for the Manor of Cortlandt in said County shall from Time to Time during the Continuance of this Act enter in Writing all the Highways or Roads by them laid out altered or Stopt up and sign the same by putting their Names thereto, and cause the same to be entered in the Record of the said Manor, or in the County Record, and the several Clerks are hereby directed and required to record the same, and whatsoever the said Commissioners shall do according to the powers given them in this Act being so entered in the Record of said Manor, or in the County Record shall be deemed valid and good to all Intents and purposes whatsoever, any Law, Usage or Custom to the contrary notwithstanding.

[CHAPTER 1459.]

[Chapter 1459 of Van Schaack, where the act is printed in full.]

An Act to impower the Freeholders and Inhabitants of Rykes Patent, in the Manor of Cortlandt, in West Chester County to Elect annually, one Supervisor and such other Officers as are therein mentioned.

[Passed, January 27, 1770.]

BE IT ENACTED by his Honor the Lieutenant Governor the Council and the General Assembly and it is hereby Enacted and declared by the Authority of the same, that for the better defraying the common and necessary Charges of Rykes Patent in the Manor of Cortlandt in West Chester County it shall and may be lawful for the Freeholders and Inhabitants thereof by Majority of Voices to elect and choose Yearly and every Year within the said Patent on the first Tuesday in April, one Clerk, one Supervisor, one Constable, one Assessor, one Collector, one Poor Master, two Fence Viewers, one Pound Master, and one or more Surveyors of the Highways who shall have the same Powers Authority, Office, and Function, and do and perform the same Services and be liable to the same Pains and Penalties as the like Officers by the Laws of this Colony have, do, perform, or are liable to.

[CHAPTER 1460.]

[Chapter 1460 of Van Schaack, where the act is printed in full. Revived by chapter 1700.]

An Act to impower the Freeholders of the Town of Huntington in the County of Suffolk to make prudential Orders for the better regulating, collecting, and parting their Sheep, feeding on the Plains and other Common Lands in the said Town, and to sell such stray Sheep as shall be left at the Time of parting.

[Passed, January 27, 1770.]

WHEREAS there is a large Tract of Pine Plain and other Common Lands within the Township of Huntington which said plain and Common Lands are claimed by a great Number of People of the said Town, and are made use of as a Common pasture for their Sheep, and as it is necessary the Freeholders of the said Town should be impowered to make such Rules and Regulations in respect to their collecting and parting their Sheep and disposing of the stray Sheep, that shall be left at such parting.

BE IT THEREFORE ENACTED by his Honor the Lieutenant Governor the Council and the General Assembly and it is hereby enacted by the Authority of the same, that the Freeholders of the said Town of Huntington are hereby impowered at their Annual Town Meeting to make and establish such prudential, Orders, Rules and Regulations as the Major Part of the Freeholders assembled shall think fit with respect to the Parting and separating their Sheep feeding on the Plain and Common Lands aforesaid, and also to impose such Penalties on the Offenders against the said Orders, Rules and Regulations as the Majority of the Freeholders in the said Town so assembled, shall from Time to Time judge necessary. PROVIDED the Penalty does not exceed the sum of twenty shillings for each Offence, which said Orders, Rules and Regulations being entered on the Public Register of said Town, shall be good and valid to all Intents and Purposes, until they shall be altered or made void by the Majority of the said Freeholders.

AND BE IT FURTHER ENACTED by the Authority aforesaid, that the Freeholders of the said Town when assembled as aforesaid, shall be and hereby are enabled to elect and make choice of one or more Person or Persons to demand, sue for, and receive all the Penalties and Forfeitures which shall be incurred by the Breach of the said Orders, Rules and Regulations of the said Town, which said Penalties and Forfeitures so recovered shall be applied to such Uses, as the Majority of the Freeholders of said Town shall order and direct.

AND BE IT FURTHER ENACTED by the Authority aforesaid that the Freeholders of the said Town when Assembled as aforesaid shall be and hereby are further enabled and impowered to elect and make choice of one or more persons to sell and dispose of all such stray Sheep as shall be left at such Time of Parting, and within ten Days after the sale thereof shall pay the Money arising by such Sale as aforesaid into the Hands of the Town Clerk of the said Town, with each and every Sheep's Artificial Ear Mark and Brand as near as may be, and the Sum that each Sheep sold for, retaining in his or their Hands, for the service aforesaid, the sum of four Pence for each Sheep so sold as aforesaid; and the said Town Clerk shall make a full Entry thereof at large in a Book provided by him for that purpose, and the Money to be paid by said Clerk unto the Person or Persons who are the proper Owners of the aforesaid Sheep. PROVIDED he or they make application within twelve Months after the aforesaid Entry, and in Case all or any of the Money shall be left in the Clerks Hands after the expiration of twelve Months as aforesaid he is hereby directed to pay the same into the Hands of the Trustees or Overseers of the Poor of the said Town, and shall be applied for the use of the Poor in such Manner as the Majority of the said Trustees or Overseers of the Poor shall think fit, and the said Clerk shall retain in his Hands for his Service the Sum of four Pence for each Sheep entered as aforesaid.

BE IT FURTHER ENACTED by the Authority aforesaid, that this Act shall be and continue in Force from the Publication hereof, until the first Day of January which will be in the Year of our Lord one thousand seven hundred and seventy five.

[CHAPTER 1461.]

[Chapter 1461 of Van Schaack, where the act is printed in full. See chapter 1344.]

An Act to amend an Act intitled "An Act "authorizing certain Persons therein named "to settle the Line of Division between the "Counties of Kings and Queens County, as "far as the Townships of Bushwick and "Newtown extend."

[Passed, January 27, 1770.]

WHEREAS Disputes and Controversies have arisen between the Freeholders and Inhabitants of the Townships of Newtown and Bushwick relating to such Expences, Costs and Charges, as have arisen in consequence of an Act intitled. "an Act Authoris-"ing certain Person therein named to settle the Line of Division "between the Counties of King's and Queen's County, as far as "the Townships of Bushwick and Newtown extend." for Remedy whereof.

BE IT ENACTED by his Honor the Lieutenant Governor the Council and the General Assembly, and it is hereby enacted by the Authority of the same, that Samuel Smith and Tallman Waters Esquires of Queens County, and John Lefferts Esqr., and Leffert Lefferts (of Bedford) Esquire both of King's County or the Majority of them are hereby appointed Commissioners to examine settle and finally determine all such Expences Costs and Charges as have arisen in consequence of the abovementioned Act, in the Manner as specified and directed in the said Act and the said Commissioners or the Majority of them are hereby impowered to order the Supervisors of the said Counties respectively to raise all such Sum and Sums of Money as they shall agree upon in proportions and Manner as the said Act directs; which Supervisors respectively are hereby required to levy the same in the usual Manner the other Taxes are raised by Warrant or Warrants to the Assessors and Collectors of such Town or Towns as they shall direct and appoint, who are hereby required to execute the same, and pay all such Money to the Trustees of the respective Towns that were appointed for that purpose or any of them, to be by them applied for defraying the Expences that have accrued in the settlement of the said Line; and the said Commissioners or the Majority of them are hereby authorized and impowered to meet for that purpose, at such Place or places within either of the said Counties, and as often as they shall think proper and to summon and order the said Trustees of the said Towns or any of them, or any other persons, to attend at such Meetings, with their Accounts Papers and other Evidences as they shall think proper to direct: and that the Commissioners, or a Majority of them shall make such their Agreement or determination within eight Months from the passing of this Act, and in case the said Commissioners or the Major Part of them cannot agree in the Settlement as aforesaid, that in such Case the said Commissioners or the Major Part of them are hereby impowered to nominate and appoint another Person to assist them in the aforesaid settlement, who is hereby vested with the same Power and authority as the other Commissioners are, which are appointed by this Act any Thing herein contained to the contrary notwithstanding.

AND BE IT ENACTED by the Authority aforesaid that if the supervisors Assessors, Collectors or Trustees of the respective Counties or Townships shall neglect or refuse to do and perform what is herein required of him or them, they shall respectively forfeit the sum of twenty Pounds, to be recovered by any person that will sue for the same with Costs of suit .

[CHAPTER 1462.]

[Chapter 1462 of Van Schaack, where only part of this act is printed. Naturalization acts being all alike it was deemed unnecessary to print them at large.]

An Act for naturalizing Frederick Koose John Stone, Godfried Shoe, John Karne, Hannis Albrant, Hannis Alt, Han Ury Creitz, Jacob Seber, Augustus Eikler, Conradt Smith, John Everhart Coghnot, George Ecker, Hannis Hartel, John Brader, Philip Pilet, George Rupert, George Sharpe, Hendrick Hann, John Seabalt, Nicholas Bradhour, George Bronce, George Skink, Jacob Becker, John Farlinger, George Binder, Frederick Waggoner, Matthias Kough, Adam Garlogh, Peter Young, Peter Gronce, Peter Forster, George Flunean, Simon Shreider, John Frederick Tolle, John Marchel, Konrat Louwer, William Petrie, James Colon, George Colon, Jonas Colon, Elizabeth Allen, Samuel Isaacs and Peter Surget.

[Passed, January 27, 1770.]

WHEREAS the above named Persons have by their several Petitions presented to the General Assembly desired they may be naturalized and become his Majesty's liege Subjects and settlers in this Colony.

BE IT THEREFORE ENACTED by his Honor the Lieutenant Governor the Council and the General Assembly, and it is hereby enacted by the authority of the same, that the before mentioned several Persons, and each and every of them shall be and hereby are declared to be naturalized to all Intents Constructions and purposes whatsoever, and from henceforth, and at all Times hereafter shall be entitled to, have and enjoy all the Rights, Liberties, Privileges and Advantages, which his Majesty's Natural born Subjects in this Colony have and enjoy, or ought to have and enjoy, as fully to all Intents and purposes whatsoever, as if all and every of them had been born within this Colony.

PROVIDED ALWAYS and it is hereby further enacted by the Authority aforesaid, that each of the above mentioned Persons shall take the Oaths appointed by Law instead of the Oaths of Allegiance and supremacy, subscribe the Test, and make, repeat Swear to, and subscribe the abjuration Oath, in any of his Majesty's Courts of Record within this Colony; which Oaths the said Courts are hereby required upon application to them made, to administer, take subscriptions, and cause the Names of the Persons so swearing and Subscribing to be entered upon Record in the said Courts, and the said before mentioned Persons are hereby each of them required to pay the several Sums here after mentioned, that is to say, To the Speaker of the General Assembly the Sum of ten Shillings to the Judge of such Court the sum of six Shillings, and to the Clerk of such Court the sum of three Shillings.

AND BE IT FURTHER ENACTED by the Authority aforesaid that if the said Persons or any of them having so sworn and subscribed as aforesaid, shall demand a Certificate of his or her or their being entered upon Record in the manner before directed, the Court or Courts, in which such Oaths and subscriptions shall be made are hereby directed and required to grant such under the Hand of the Judge, and seal of the said Court or Courts in which such Oaths and Subscriptions as aforesaid shall be made, countersigned by the Clerk of the said Courts, for which Certificate each of them shall pay over and above the Sums abovementioned the sum of six Shillings, one half to the Judge of such Court or Courts, and the other half to the Clerk thereof, which Certificate or Certificates shall be at all Times to the Person or Persons therein named a sufficient Proof of his her or their being naturalized by virtue of this Act, in as full and effectual a Manner as if the Record aforesaid was actually produced by the Person or Persons so named in such Certificates.

PROVIDED ALSO, AND BE IT ENACTED by the Authority aforesaid that such of the persons hereby naturalized, as shall not take the Oath, Test and Abjuration in manner herein before directed within twelve Months next after the Publication hereof shall have no manner of Benefit by this Act, any Thing herein contained to the contrary notwithstanding.

AND BE IT ENACTED by the same Authority that the Public Printer of this Colony shall and hereby is directed and required to print this Act as if the same was a Public Law of this Colony.

[CHAPTER 1463.]

[Chapter 1463 of Van Schaack, where the title only is printed. This act was continued by chapter 1480, to expire the 1st of May, 1772. Repealed by the king the 7th of June, 1771.]

An Act for the Relief of Insolvent Debtors within the Colony of New York with respect to the Imprisonment of their Persons.

[Passed, January 27, 1770.]

WHEREAS many Persons by Losses and other Misfortunes are rendered incapable of paying their whole Debts, and though they are willing to make the utmost Satisfaction they can, are nevertheless detained in Prison by their Creditors. AND WHEREAS such unhappy Debtors have always been deemed the proper Objects of Public Compassion, therefore for the Relief of such Prisoners who shall be willing to satisfy their Creditors as far as they are able.

BE IT ENACTED by his Honor the Lieutenant Governor the Council and the General Assembly, and it is hereby enacted by the Authority of the same, that if any Person or Persons now charged in Execution or having been committed for the space of six Months or longer upon any Writ or Writs of Capias for any sum or sums of Money not exceeding in the whole the Sum of fifty Pounds; or having been committed in like Manner for the space of twelve Months or longer for any sum or sums of Money not exceeding in the whole the Sum of one hundred Pounds, and in like Manner for the space of two Years or longer for any sum or sums of Money not exceeding in the whole, the sum of two hundred Pounds Current Money of this Colony from and after the Publication hereof, shall be minded to deliver up to his her or their Creditors, all his her or their Effects towards the Satisfaction of the Debts wherewith he she or they stand charged, it shall and may be lawful for such Prisoner to exhibit a Petition to any of the Courts of Law within this Colony from whence the Process issued, upon which he she or they was or were taken or charged in Execution or other Process as aforesaid certifying the Cause or Causes of his or her or their Imprisonment, and an Account of his her or their whole Real and Personal Estate with the Dates of the Securities wherein any Part of it consists and the Deeds or Notes relating thereunto, and the Names of all the Witnesses to the same so far as his her or their knowledge extends thereto, and upon such Petition the Court may and is hereby required by Order or Rule of Court to cause the Prisoner to be brought up, and the several Creditors at whose suit he she or they stand charged as aforesaid, and all other his or her Creditors that are or can be known to the Court to be summoned to appear personally or by their Attorney in Court at a Day to be appointed for that purpose, and upon the Day of such appearance if any of the Creditors summoned, refuse or neglect to appear upon Affidavit made of the due Service of such Rule or Order, or upon Affidavit made that the Creditor or Creditors are not to be found, the Court shall in a Summary way examine into the Matter of the said Petition and hear what can or shall be alleged on either Side, for or against the Discharge of such Prisoner, and upon such his Examination the Court may and are hereby required to administer or tender to the Prisoner an Oath or Affirmation to the Effect following, which Oath or Affirmation the said Court is hereby impowered to administer. "I A B. do solemnly swear in the presence of almighty God (or being of the People called Quakers do sincerely and truly declare and Affirm) that the Account by me now delivered is a just and true Account of all my Creditors, and the Monies owing to the best of my knowledge or Remembrance by me, and that the Inventory and Account now delivered by me is a just and true Account of all my Estate Real and Personal both in Law and Equity, either in possession, Reversion or Remainder, the necessary wearing Apparel of myself, my wife and Children excepted; and that I have not directly or indirectly, sold, leased Assigned, or otherwise disposed of, or made over, either in trust for myself or otherwise except as set forth in the same Account any Part of my Estate real or Personal for my future Benefit, or in order to defraud my Creditors. so help me

God." And in Case the Prisoner shall in open Court take the said Oath or Affirmation, and upon such Examination, and his or her taking the said Oath or Affirmation, the Creditors shall be satisfied with the Truth thereof, the Court may immediately order the Lands, Goods, and effects contained in such Accounts, or so much of them as may be sufficient to satisfy the Debts wherewith he or she is or shall be charged together with Costs of Suit, and the Fees due to the keeper of the Goal or Prison from which the Prisoner was brought, to be by a short Indorsement on the Back of such Petition signed by the Prisoner assigned to the said Creditors or one or more of them in Trust for the rest of them, or to some proper Person to be by the said Court appointed in Trust for all the Creditors, And by such Assignment, the Estate Interest and Property of the Lands, Goods, Debts and Effects so assigned shall be vested in the Person or Persons to whom such Assignment is or shall be made, who may take possession of, or sue for the same in his or their own Name or Names in like Manner as Assignees or Commissioners of Bankrupts, to which Suit no Release of the Prisoner his or her Executors or Administrators, or any Trustee for him or her subsequent to such Assignment shall be any Bar, and immediately upon such Assignment executed, the said Prisoner shall be discharged out of Custody by order of Court and such Order shall be a sufficient Warrant to the Sheriff, Gealer or Keeper of such Prison to discharge the said Prisoner if detained for the Causes mentioned in such Petition and no other, and he is hereby required to discharge and set him at Liberty forthwith without Fee, nor shall such Sheriff or Goaler be liable to any Action of Escape or other Suit or Information upon that Account and the Person or Persons to whom the Effects shall be Assigned paying the Fees to the Goaler or Keeper of the Prison in whose Custody the Party discharged was, shall and are hereby required to divide the Effects so assigned among the Creditors, and all the Persons for whom they shall be intrusted in proportion to their respective Debts: But in Case the Person or Persons at whose Suit such Prisoner was charged in Execution or in Custody upon other Process as aforesaid, or any other Creditors shall not be satisfied with the Truth of such an Oath or Affirmation, but shall desire further Time to inform himself of the Matters contained therein the said Court may and shall remand the said Prisoner, and direct the said Prisoner and the Person or Persons dissatisfied with such Oath or Affirmation to appear at another Day to be appointed by the said Court sometime within the Term next following the Time of such Examination, and if at such second Day so to be appointed the Creditor or Creditors dissatisfied with such Oath or Affirmation shall make Default in appearing, or in Case he or they shall appear, but shall be unable to discover any Estate or Effects of the Prisoner omitted in such his or her Petition, or to shew any Probability of his or her having been foresworn or to have declared falsely in the said Oath or Affirmation, then the said Court shall immediately cause the said Prisoner to be discharged, upon such Assignment of his or her Effects in Manner as aforesaid unless such Creditor or Creditors do insist upon his or her being detained in Prison, and do agree by writing under his or her Hand to pay and allow any Sum of money that shall be assessed by the said Court not exceeding the Sum of three shillings and six pence per Week unto the said Prisoner to be paid the Monday of every Week so long as he or she shali continue in Prison at his her or their Suits. On Failure of the payment of which Weekly sum at any Time, the said Prisoner shall forthwith upon application to the Court be discharged by such Order as aforesaid; but in Case the said Prisoner shall refuse to take the Oath or Affirmation, or having taken the same shall be detected of Falsity therein, he or she shall be presently remanded.

AND BE IT FURTHER ENACTED by the Authority aforesaid that no Person to be discharged by this Act shall at any Time hereafter be imprisoned by reason of any Judgment or Decree obtained for payment of Money, only, or for any Debt Damage Costs, Sum or Sums of Money contracted, incurred, occasioned, owing or growing due before the Time of his or her Discharge, but that upon every Arrest, every such Judgment or Decree for such Debts, Damages, Contempts, Cost, Sum or Sums of Money, it shall and may be lawful for any Judge of the Court where the process issued, upon shewing the Duplicate of such Prisoner's Discharge or Discharges, to release and Discharge out of Custody such Prisoner or Prisoners as aforesaid, and the Judge is hereby impowered so to do, so as every such Prisoner or Prisoners arrested or detained upon Execution or other Process as aforesaid do give a Warrant of Attorney to appear to every such Action and plead thereunto.

AND BE IT FURTHER ENACTED by the Authority aforesaid that if any Action of Escape, or any Suit or Action be brought against the Judge of any Court or any Justice of the Peace, or any Sheriff, Goaler or Keeper of any Prison for performing their Office in pursuance of this Act they may plead the General Issue, and give this Act in Evidence, and if the Plaintiff be non-Suited or discontinue his Action, or Verdict pass against him, or Judgment upon Demurrer, the Defendant shall have treble Costs, PROVIDED that this Act shall not extend to discharge any Person out of Prison who shall stand chargeable at the Suit of the Crown only.

PROVIDED ALWAYS and be it further Enacted by the Authority aforesaid that notwithstanding the Discharge of the Person of such Prisoner or Prisoners as aforesaid all and every Debt or Debts due and owing from the said Prisoner or Prisoners, and all and every Judgment or Judgments had and taken, and Decree obtained against him or her shall stand and be good and effectual in the Law to all Intents and Purposes against the Lands, Tenements, Hereditaments, Goods and Chattels of the said Prisoner so discharged as aforesaid which he she or they, or any Person or Persons in Trust for him her or them at the Time of such Discharge, hath or have, or at any Time hereafter shall or may be in any wise seized, or possessed of interested in or intitled to either in Law or Equity except the necessary wearing apparel of the said Debtor his Wife and Children and it shall and may be lawful to and for such Creditor or Creditors of such Prisoner or Prisoners so discharged as aforesaid his her or their Executors or Administrators to take out a new Execution against the Lands, Tenements Hereditaments Goods and Chattels of such Prisoner or Prisoners (except as before excepted) for the Satisfaction of his her or their Debts in such Sort, Manner and fform, as he she or they might have done if the Person or Persons of such Prisoner or Prisoners had never been taken in Execution, or other process as aforesaid, any Law, Usage or Custom to the contrary in any wise notwithstanding.

PROVIDED ALWAYS and be it further Enacted by the Authority aforesaid that if any such Person who shall take such Oath or Affirmation as aforesaid shall upon any Indictment for perjury in any Matter or particular contained in the said Oath or Affirmation be convicted by his or their own Confession or by Verdict of twelve Men, as he or she may be, by force of this Act, the Person so convicted shall suffer all the Pains and Forfeitures which may by Law be inflicted on any Person convicted of Wilful perjury, and shall likewise be liable to be taken on any Process de Novo, and charged in Execution for the said Debt in the same

Manner as if he or she had never been discharged or taken in Execution before, and shall never after have the Benefit of this Act.

PROVIDED ALSO and be it further Enacted by the Authority aforesaid that if the Effects so assigned shall not extend to satisfy the whole Debts due to the Creditors of the Person or Persons so discharged, and the Fees due to the Attornies, Sheriffs and other Officers of the Court with the Goaler, there shall be an Abatement in proportion, and such Officers shall come in as a Creditor for what shall be then due to him for his Fees in proportion with the other Creditors.

AND BE IT FURTHER ENACTED by the Authority aforesaid that when there are mutual Debts between the Debtor or Debtors, and his, her or their Creditors, or if either Party sue or be sued as Executor or Administrator, where there are mutual Debts between the Testator or Intestate and either Party, one Debt shall be set against the other, and such Matter may be given in Evidence upon the General Issue or pleaded in Bar, as the Nature of the Case shall require so as at the Time of the pleading the General Issue, where any such Debts of the Plaintiff his Testator or Intestate is intended to be insisted on in Evidence Notice shall be given of the Particular sum or Debts so intended to be insisted on, and upon what Account it became due, otherwise such Matter shall not be allowed in Evidence upon the General Issue. PROVIDED that where any Rent shall be due from any Prisoner or Prisoners at the Time of his or their respective Discharges, no Goods or Chattels then lying or being in or upon their respective Tenements or Lands so in Lease, or liable to be distrained shall be removed or disposed of without the Consent of the Landlord or Person to whom the Rent is due until the same (not exceeding one Years Rent) be paid or satisfied, and that the Landlord may use all Lawful Ways for the having and recovering his Rent so as that the same exceed not one years Rent by Distress or otherwise as he might have had, or could have done before the making of this Act, any Thing herein contained to the contrary in any wise notwithstanding.

AND BE IT FURTHER ENACTED by the Authority aforesaid that John Cox, Samuel Stitt, Sarah Mc. Culluem, John Belfield, Thomas Dods, and Hugh Cosgriff now confined in Goal in the City of New York shall be and hereby are intitled to all the Relief, Advantage and Benefit that other Insolvent Debtors are intitled to by this Act, to all Intents, Constructions and Purposes whatsoever although their Debts do exceed the Sum of two hundred Pounds, any Thing in this Act contained to the contrary in any wise notwithstanding

AND BE IT FURTHER ENACTED by the Authority aforesaid that this Act shall continue in force from the Publication thereof until the first Day of May one thousand seven hundred and seventy one.

[CHAPTER 1464.]

[Chapter 1464 of Van Schaack, where the title only is printed. Repealed by the king the 7th of June, 1771.]

An Act for the relief of James DePeyster of the City of New York Merchant and Insolvent Debtor and others therein named.

[Passed, January 27, 1770.]

WHEREAS James DePeyster of the City of New York Merchant among other Debts is considerably indebted to the Estate of Abraham DePeyster Esquire deceased late Treasurer of this Colony, as well on Account of private Dealings between them as for Public Duties, and by an Act of the Legislature of this Colony intitled "An Act for the more effectual vesting the real "and Personal Estate whereof Abraham De Peyster Esquire late "Treasurer of this Colony died seized and possessed in Trustees "for the payment of his Debts." made and passed in the eighth year of his Majesty's Reign, the Estate of the said Abraham De Peyster is vested in John Cruger, Philip Livingston, Leonard Lispenard, Henry Holland and William Bayard Esquires in Trust for the Purposes there in mentioned, and the said James De Peyster by his humble Petition to the General Assembly having represented that Becoming Insolvent by a Series of Losses and Misfortunes he with the concurrence of many of his Creditors hath endeavoured to take the Benefit of the Acts of the Legislature heretofore provided for the relief of Insolvent Debtors; but that on application to the Trustees of the Estate of the said late Treasurer they declined subscribing his Petition for that Purpose, conceiving they were unauthorized without a further act of the Legislature, and that while his former Petition praying that the said Trustees might be enabled to compound with him, was under consideration in General Assembly the Acts for the relief of Insolvent Debtors, expired whereby he must be reduced to the necessity of continuing in his present unhappy situation unless relieved by the Interposition of the Legislature, the General Assembly therefore pray that it may be enacted.

AND BE IT ENACTED by his Honor the Lieutenant Governor the Council and the General Assembly, and it is hereby enacted by the Authority of the same, that it shall and may be lawful to and for the said Trustees of the Estate of the said Abraham De Peyster, or the Major part of them, or the Major Part of the Survivors of them, and they are hereby authorized and directed to compound with the said James De Peyster, in the Manner by this Act prescribed, for and concerning all Monies which were due and owing from him to the said late Treasurer at his decease, as well on Account of the Private Dealings and Transactions which subsisted between them, as for Duties due and owing from the said James De Peyster to this Colony.

AND BE IT FURTHER ENACTED by the Authority aforesaid that it shall and may be lawful to and for the said James De Peyster in conjunction with the said Trustees of the Estate of the said late Treasurer or the Major Part of them, and such other of the Creditors of the said James De Peyster as shall be desirous to have the Benefit of this Act to present a Petition to the Supreme Court or in the Vacation to two or more of the Judges thereof; praying that the Estate of the said James De Peyster may be assigned and delivered to such Person or Persons as the said Petitioners or the Majority of them in respect to their Demands shall nominate to receive and dispose of the same for the use of all the Creditors of the said James De Peyster.

AND BE IT FURTHER ENACTED by the Authority aforesaid that the said James De Peyster within two Days after the presenting such Petition, shall deliver in writing to the said Court or Judges a full and true Account of all his Creditors, and the Monies owing to them by him, and also a full and true Inventory and Account of all his Estate, both real and personal in Law and Equity, and all Books Vouchers and Securities relating to the same, except the necessary Apparel and Bedding of himself his Wife and Children, on which the said Court or Judges are hereby required to administer and tender to him an Oath to the following Effect. ".I. James De Peyster do Solemnly Swear that "the Account by me delivered is a just and true Account of all "My Creditors, and the Monies owing to the best of my knowl-"edge and remembrance by me, and that the Inventory and "Account delivered by me is a just and true Inventory and "Account of all my Estate real and personal both in Law and "Equity either in possession, Reversion, or Remainer, the Wear-"ing Apparel and Bedding of myself my Wife and Children "excepted and that I have not directly or indirectly sold, leased "assigned or otherwise disposed of, or made over either in Trust "for myself or otherwise, except as set forth in the same Account "any Part of my Estate real and personal, for my future Benefit, "or in order to defraud my Creditors, So help me God." which Oath being taken by the said James DePeyster, notice shall be given by the Petitioners to all the Creditors of the said James DePeyster, by advertising the same in one or more of the Public News Papers to shew Cause if any they have, by such a Day as shall be appointed by the Court, or two or more of the Judges, why an Assignment of the Estate of the said James DePeyster should not be made, and he thereupon discharged from his Debts, at which Day it shall and may be lawful to and for one fourth Part of the Creditors of the said James DePeyster in respect to the amount or value of all the Debts due and owing by him to signify in Writing under their Hands their dissent to his being so discharged and in that Case the said Court or Judges are hereby prohibited and disabled from giving the said James DePeyster or his Petitioning Creditors any Benefit or Relief by this Act: but if at the Day so to be appointed such dissent shall not be shewn by one fourth Part of the Creditors of the said James DePeyster as aforesaid: and no other sufficient Cause to the contrary appear, the said Court or any two of the Judges shall direct a legal Grant or Assignment of all the Estate of the said James DePeyster both in Law and Equity to be made by him to the Persons nominated for that purpose by the Petitioners or a Majority of them, in respect to the Amount of their just Demands.

AND BE IT FURTHER ENACTED by the Authority aforesaid that such Assignees shall have full power and Authority in their own Names to sue for and recover all and every Part of the real and Personal Estate, Rights and Outstanding Debts, so to them to be assigned by the said James DePeyster, and to grant sell and dispose of such real Estate, and to make and execute good and Sufficient Deeds and Conveyances for the same, and to refer to Arbitration, settle Compound or agree with any Person indebted to the said James DePeyster or claiming or possessed of any part of his real Estate in such Manner, and on such Terms and Conditions as they shall conceive to be just and reasonable; and shall proceed to convert the Estate of the said James DePeyster into Money, as soon as conveniently may be, and shall within the Space of one Year and an half proceed to make a Dividend of all the Monies which shall arise or come to their Hands out of the said Estate so to be assigned first giving three Months notice of the Time and Place of making such Dividend by advertising the same in one or more of the Public Newspapers, and if the whole be not then collected and settled shall within the Space of one Year thereafter make a Second Dividend of what Monies may come to their Hands after the first, and so from Year to Year until a final Settlement and a just and equal Dividend of the whole Estate be made.

AND BE IT FURTHER ENACTED that if any Controversy shall arise between the said Assignees, and any Creditor of the said James De Peyster concerning any Debt due from him; for the more easy and speedy determination thereof the Assignees shall nominate two referrees not being Creditors, and the Creditor whose Debt is in controversy shall nominate two others, and their Names separately written on four pieces of paper as nearly of the same size as possible shall be rolled up in the same manner, and put into a Covered Box and from thence one of the Assignees shall draw out three of the said Pieces of paper, and the Persons whose Names are so drawn shall finally settle such controversy, and if any Referree so appointed shall refuse or be incapable of acting in a reasonable Time, a new choice shall be made in the same manner, and in Case any Creditor shall refuse to nominate Referrees on his part, the Assignees are hereby impowered to nominate them for him.

AND BE IT FURTHER ENACTED that in Case any Part of the Real Estate of the said James DePeyster to be so assigned, shall be held by him in Fee Tail, in possession, Reversion or Remainder (except the said Estate be so entailed by his Majesty or his Royal Predecessors, and the Reversion remaining in his Majesty his Heirs or Successors) that the Assignees shall have power in Order to save the Trouble and Expence of a common recovery, to grant, sell, and dispose of all such Estate and make a good Title for the same to any purchaser thereof in fee Simple, and all Persons who do or shall claim any Right Title or Interest in and to such Estate, by virtue of such Entail, shall be and are hereby effectually barred from claiming or recovering the same.

AND BE IT FURTHER ENACTED that the Assignees to be so appointed by virtue of this Act shall have full power and authority by and with the free and voluntary consent of the said

Insolvent's Wife, to dispose of the Real Estate so to be assigned by him, discharged and free of any Claim of Dower by her.

AND BE IT FURTHER ENACTED that the Assignees shall immediately after the Assignment to them made, take an Oath to be administered by the Court, or any one of the Judges, well and faithfully to manage the said Insolvents Estate, and keep and render a true Account of all that shall come to their Hands of the same; and for that purpose shall keep regular Books of Accounts to which every Creditor may at all Times have recourse, and for their Care and trouble shall be allowed out of the said Insolvent's Estate, such a Consideration as the Petitioners, or the Major Part of them shall agree and fix upon.

AND BE IT FURTHER ENACTED that for the more full discovery of the said Insolvent's Estate, the Court or any one of the Judges, at the request of the Assignees shall have full power and are hereby required to summons and examine on Oath any Person whomsoever known or suspected to detain any Part of the said Insolvent's Estate, or to be indebted thereto; and in Case any person on such Summons, shall refuse to attend, having no reasonable excuse, or shall refuse to be Sworn, or if a Quaker to affirm; then it shall be lawful for the said Court, or any one of the Judges, to commit the Person in contempt to Goal, till he shall submit to be examined concerning what he may know of the said Insolvent's Estate or Effects; and if any such Person shall Wilfully and knowingly swear or Affirm falsely, the Person so offending shall incur the same Pains and Penalties as those who are convicted of wilful and corrupt Perjury.

AND BE IT FURTHER ENACTED that the said Insolvent having given up his Estate and conformed in all Things to the Directions of this Act shall be discharged and acquitted from all Debts due from him at the Time of the Assignment or contracted for before that Time, though Payable afterwards and if sued or prosecuted for any such Debt or Contract, it shall and may be lawful for him to plead the General Issue, and give the special Matter in Evidence.

PROVIDED ALWAYS and be it further Enacted that before such Release and acquittal shall be good and available in the Law, every Petitioning Creditor of the said Insolvent shall be obliged to swear that the sum annexed to his Name in the Account so to be exhibited of all the Creditors is justly due to him or will become due to him at some future Time ascertaining when; but if the Creditor be out of this Colony, and Petitions by his Attorney, instead of the Affidavit of the Principal, it shall suffice if the Attorney swears, that he verily believes that the Sum claimed by him is justly due to his principal. PROVIDED ALSO that the Trustees of the Estate of the said late Treasurer, shall not be held to swear or attest to the Debt due from the said Insolvent to them as Trustees; but having ascertained the same in the best manner they are able, their Subscription of the said Petition shall be effectual, without any further attestation.

AND BE IT FURTHER ENACTED that if the said Insolvent shall be Guilty of Perjury, by concealing any Part of his Estate or Effects; or shall after the Assignment of his Estate by Virtue of this Act receive any Debt or Debts due to him, before such Assignment or shall secrete any Books, Vouchers, Writings or other Things appertaining to his Estate with an Intent to defraud his Creditors; he shall in any such Case be deemed and adjudged Guilty of Felony, without Benefit of Clergy; but his Estate shall nevertheless be distributed among his Creditors.

PROVIDED ALWAYS and be it further Enacted that after deducting all such Costs Charges and Expences as shall be necessarily laid out and expended by the said Assignees together with their Commissions for their Care and Trouble therein, the residue of the Estate of the said Insolvent shall be equally divided among the Creditors in proportion to their respective Debts, in which Dividend no preference shall be given to Debts due by Specialty or on Judgment, or otherwise howsoever, but if there should be an Overplus after all the Creditors are fully satisfied their just Demands, it shall be paid by the Assignees to the said Insolvent his Executors or Administrators.

AND BE IT FURTHER ENACTED by the Authority aforesaid, that if any Person shall be sued for any Matter or Thing to be done in pursuance of this Act, it shall be lawful for him to plead the General Issue, and give the Special Matter in evidence.

AND BE IT FURTHER ENACTED by the same Authority that it shall and may be lawful to and for Daniel Hauxhurst and Jacob Kemper Insolvent Debtors of the City of New York to take the Benefit of the several Acts continued by an Act intitled. "An Act to continue the several Acts therein mentioned respect-"ing the Relief of Insolvent Debtors," passed the Nineteenth Day of December one thousand seven hundred and sixty six, and which are expired by their own Limitation as fully and effectually as if the said Acts respecting the relief of Insolvent Debtors were now in actual and full force

AND BE IT ALSO ENACTED by the same Authority that Whereas it appears by the Oath of William Hauxhurst an Insolvent Debtor, that there was due to him at the Time of his becoming Insolvent the Sum of eight hundred and forty two Pounds, eighteen Shillings, and ten Pence half penny from the said Daniel Hawxhurst; that it shall and may be lawful to and for the Assignees of the said William or the Major Part of them to join in a Petition with the said Daniel, and with the Creditors of said Daniel in order to his obtaining the Benefit of said Acts, provided that it appears to them or the major Part of them by the Books of said William or otherwise that the said sum of eight Hundred and forty two Pounds eighteen Shillings and ten pence half penny, was actually due from the said Daniel to the said William, at the Time that the said William became Insolvent, or for so much thereof as to the said Assignees shall appear to be actually due from the said Daniel to the said William; and that the Assignees of the said William Hauxhurst shall certify under their Hands to the Judge or Judges to whom such Petition shall be preferred the Sum that to them appears due from the said Daniel to the said Assignees, which certificate shall be as full and effectual as if the said Assignees had taken the Oath prescribed by the said Acts or one of them for Petitioning Creditors to take, any Thing in the said Acts to the contrary hereof notwithstanding.

AND BE IT FURTHER ENACTED by the Authority aforesaid that this Act shall continue and be in full force until the first Day of January one thousand seven hundred and seventy one as to the Liberties of the Creditors Petitioning, and no longer; but shall continue, and be in full force as to the Power of every Court, Person, assignee or Assignees appointed by this Act until a full and final settlement and Division shall be by them made according to the true Intent and meaning of this Act.

THIRTY-FIRST ASSEMBLY.

Third Session.

(Begun Dec. 11, 1770, 11 George III, John Earl of Dunmore, Governor.)

[CHAPTER 1465.]

[Chapter 1465 of Van Schaack, where the title only is printed. Continued by chapter 1509.]

An Act further to continue an Act intitled. "An Act for granting to his Majesty the "several Duties and Impositions on Goods, "Wares and Merchandizes imported into this "Colony therein mentioned."

[Passed, December 22, 1770.]

WHEREAS the several Duties and Impositions on Goods, Wares and Merchandizes imported into this Colony, & granted for the support of the Government of his late Majesty King George the second by the abovementioned Act, have by several subsequent Acts, been continued to the first Day of January next ensuing, and the General Assembly being willing to make Provision for the further support of his Majesty's Government of this Colony.

BE IT THEREFORE ENACTED by his Excellency the Governor, the Council, and the General Assembly, and it is hereby enacted by the Authority of the same, That the abovementioned Act intitled "An Act for granting to his Majesty the several "Duties and Impositions on Goods Wares and Merchandizes "imported into this Colony therein mentioned." passed in the twenty seventh Year of his late Majesty's Reign, shall be and hereby is continued, and every Clause Matter and Thing therein contained, Enacted to be and remain in full force, to all Intents, Constructions and purposes whatsoever, until the first Day of February which will be in the Year of our Lord one thousand seven hundred and seventy two inclusive. PROVIDED ALWAYS that so much of the first Clause or Section of said Act, as relates to European or East India Goods imported from the British Islands into this Colony shall be construed taken and deemed to be from the British Islands in America only; any Thing in the said Act to the contrary hereof notwithstanding.

[CHAPTER 1466.]

[Chapter 1466 of Van Schaack, where the title only is printed. See chapter 1433. This act was continued by chapter 1520.]

An Act to continue an Act intitled "An "Act to restrain Hawkers and Pedlars "within this Colony, from selling without "Licence."

[Passed, December 22, 1770.]

WHEREAS the Act intitled "An Act to restrain Hawkers and " Pedlars within this Colony from selling without Licence," will expire by it's own Limitation on the twenty fifth day of March next unless continued.

BE IT THEREFORE ENACTED by his Excellency the Governor the Council and the General Assembly, and it is hereby enacted by the Authority of the same, That the said Act intitled "An Act to prevent Hawkers and Pedlars within this Colony "from selling without Licence." shall be and hereby is continued from the expiration thereof, until the first Day of February which will be in the Year of our Lord one thousand seven hundred and seventy two, any Thing in the said Act contained to the contrary hereof in any wise notwithstanding.

[CHAPTER 1467.]

[Chapter 1467 of Van Schaack, where the title only is printed.]

An Act for collecting the Duty of Excise on Strong Liquors retailed in this Colony from the first Day of January in the Year of Lord one thousand seven hundred and seventy one, to the first Day of February one thousand seven hundred and seventy two inclusive.

[Passed, December 22, 1770.]

BE IT ENACTED by his Excellency the Governor, the Council, and the General Assembly, and it is hereby Enacted by the Authority of the same. That Cornelius Clopper shall be and hereby is appointed Commissioner for collecting the Duty of Excise of and from the several Retailers of Strong Liquors within the City and County of New York from the first Day of January in the Year of Our Lord one thousand seven hundred and seventy one, to the first Day of February which will be in the year of our Lord one thousand seven hundred and seventy two inclusive.

AND BE IT FURTHER ENACTED by the Authority afore-said the said Commissioner shall as soon after the Publi-his Act as he shall judge convenient appoint the seve-rs within the said City and County, and direct and what each Retailer shall pay for the said Duty from ay of January one thousand seven hundred and sev-o the first Day of February one thousand seven hun-wenty-two inclusive.

E IT FURTHER ENACTED by the Authority afore-e several and respective Persons herein after named d hereby are appointed Commissioners for collecting Excise of and from the several and respective Retail-g Liquors within the several and respective Counties ny herein after mentioned, and the Harbours, Bays respectively thereunto adjoining or belonging Vizt. ity and County of Albany Peter Lansing and Guysbert Esquires.

Borough of West Chester Nathaniel Underhill Esquire.

For the Manor of Philipsburg and Yonkers in the County of West Chester William Davids and Isaac Dean Esquires.

For the Manor of Cortlandt in the County of West Chester Charles Moore and Hackaliah Brown Esquires, and

For the remaining Part of West Chester County Edward Stephenson and John Thomas Junior Esquires.

For King's County, Theodorus Polhemus Esquire.

For Queens County Benjamin Townshend and Samuel Clowes Esquires.

For Dutchess County, Cornelius Lister, Peter Harris, Benjamin Akins, John Ryder and Lewis Barton Esquires.

For Ulster County, Joseph Gasherie and James Mc Claghry Esquires.

For Orange County. for Haverstraw Precinct David Puy, For Orange Town John Perry, for Goshen Precinct Benjamin Thurston, for Cornwall Precinct Daniel Coleman Esquires.

For Richmond County, Hezekiah Wright, Jacob Rezeau and Richard Conner Esquires.

And for Suffolk County, Richard Floyd, Samuel Landon and Malby Gelston Esquires.

AND BE IT ENACTED by the Authority aforesaid that the aforesaid several and respective Commissioners, or the major Part of them respectively shall as soon as they conveniently can after the Publication of this Act meet at the County Hall of their several and respective Counties or at such other Place or Places as they the said Commissioners shall respectively appoint for putting in Execution the Powers and Authorities given by this Act, at which Time or at such other Times as they shall judge necessary, the said Commissioners or the major Part of them respectively shall for their own Counties and Districts severally and respectively fix the Number and appoint the several Retailers within their several and respective Counties and Districts, and direct and ascertain what each Retailer shall pay for the said Duty of Excise from the first Day of January one thousand seven hundred and seventy one, to the first Day of February one thousand seven hundred and seventy two. PROVIDED ALWAYS and be it further Enacted by the Authority aforesaid. That no Retailer in any of the Cities or Counties of this Colony shall pay under the Sum of twenty Shillings for the said Duty of Excise except those who shall retail Strong Liquors not to be drank in their Houses, and such as may retail Strong Liquors at or near the County Hall in Suffolk County during the sitting of their Courts or other Public Meetings there, who shall be rated at the discretion of the respective Commissioners, and that all those who have heretofore been Retailers of Strong Liquors in this Colony shall not pay less for the said Duty than they did in the Year of our Lord one thousand seven hundred and seventy, but as much more as the Commissioner or Commissioners for the City County or District where such Retailers may reside shall think reasonable.

AND BE IT FURTHER ENACTED by the Authority aforesaid, That the said several Commissioners shall on or before the first Day of February one thousand seven hundred and seventy two, render just true and particular Accounts on Oath to the Treasurer of this Colony of all the Sums of Money to be raised by virtue of this Act on the several Retailers within the Cities Counties and Districts for which they are respectively appointed Commissioners as aforesaid specifying the Names of every Retailer, and the Sums they have respectively been rated at, and pay the same to the said Treasurer of this Colony for the Time being, deducting therefrom only such Sum or Sums as is by this Act allowed Such Commissioner or Commissioners for the management of the said Duty.

AND in order the better to secure the payment of the Sums to be raised by virtue of this Act. BE IT FURTHER ENACTED by the Authority aforesaid. That the said Commissioners before they take upon themselves the execution of the Powers and Authorities given by this Act, shall respectively enter into Bonds to the Treasurer of this Colony for the Time being in the Sums following. That is to say.

The said Cornelius Clopper in the Penal Sum of one thousand six hundred Pounds.

The said Peter Lansing and Guysbert G Marcelis in the Penal Sum of three hundred Pounds.

The said Nathaniel Underhill in the Penal Sum of twenty Pounds.

The said William Davids and Isaac Dean in the Penal Sum of forty Pounds.

The said Charles Moore and Hackaliah Brown in the Penal Sum of forty Pounds.

The said Edward Stephenson and John Thomas Junior in the Penal Sum of one hundred Pounds.

The said Theodorus Polhemus in the Penal Sum of sixty Pounds.

The said Benjamin Townshend and Samuel Clowes in the Penal Sum of one hundred and sixty Pounds.

The said Cornelius Lister, Peter Harris, Benjamin Akins, John Ryder and Lewis Barton in the Penal Sum of two hundred Pounds.

The said Joseph Gasherie and James Mc. Claghry in the Penal Sum of one hundred and fifty Pounds.

The said David Puy, John Perry, Benjamin Thurston, and Daniel Coleman in the Penal Sum of twenty Pounds each of them.

The said Hezekiah Wright, Jacob Rezeau, and Richard Conner in the Penal Sum of forty Pounds

And the said Richard Floyd, Samuel Landon and Malby Gelston in the Penal Sum of one hundred Pounds.

Conditioned that the said respective Commissioner or Commissioners his or their Executors or Administrators shall render a just and true Account upon Oath to the Treasurer of this Colony of all the Sums that may by him or them be raised in virtue of this Act upon the several Retailers of Strong Liquors within the City County or District for which he or they is or are appointed Commissioner or Commissioners, and well and truly pay the same, except the Sum allowed him or them by this Act, to the Treasurer of this Colony for the Time being on or before the first Day of February in the Year of our Lord one thousand seven hundred and seventy two, which Bond shall be delivered to and remain with the Treasurer of this Colony for the Time being, and upon performance of the Condition of the same respectively shall be delivered up to be cancelled; but if Default shall be made in the performance of the Condition of any or either of the said Bonds it shall and may be lawful to and for the Treasurer of this Colony for the Time being, and he is hereby directed and required after the expiration of three Callender Months from the said first Day of February in the Year of our Lord one thousand seven hundred and seventy two to cause Suits to be brought in the Name of the Treasurer of the Colony of New York, upon each and every of the said Bonds so forfeited, and prosecute the same to effect, and no Suit to be brought upon any or either of the said Bonds shall be abated or discontinued by the Death or removal of the Treasurer of this Colony, but shall be continued and prosecuted to effect by the new Treasurer in the Name of the Treasurer of the Colony of New York.

AND BE IT FURTHER ENACTED by the Authority aforesaid, that the said Commissioners shall be allowed and may deduct out of the Sum to be by them respectively laid on the several Retailers within the City County or District for which they are respectively appointed Commissioners the following Sums for their Trouble and Charges in the Execution of the Powers vested in them by this Act. That is to say.

The said Cornelius Clopper the Sum of fifty Pounds for incidental Charges and his Commissions.

The said Peter Lansing and Guysbert G Marcelis the Sum of twenty eight Pounds.

The said Nathaniel Underhill the Sum of one Pound four Shillings.

The said William Davids and Isaac Dean the Sum of three Pounds ten Shillings.

The said Charles Moore and Hackaliah Brown the Sum of three Pounds ten Shillings.

The said Edward Stephenson and John Thomas Junior the Sum of ten Pounds.

The said Theodorus Polhemus, the Sum of five Pounds.

The said Benjamin Townshend and Samuel Clowes the Sum of ten Pounds.

The said Cornelius Lister, Peter Harris, Benjamin Akins, John Ryder and Lewis Barton the Sum of fifteen Pounds.

The said Joseph Gasherie and James Mc. Claghry the Sum of eight Pounds.

The said David Puy, John Perry, Benjamin Thurston, and Daniel Coleman the Sum of six Pounds.

The said Hezekiah Wright, Jacob Lezeau, and Richard Conner the Sum of three Pounds.

And the said Richard Floyd, Samuel Landon and Malby Gelston the sum of nine Pounds.

AND BE IT FURTHER ENACTED by the Authority aforesaid that the several and respective Retailers of Strong Liquors shall pay the several and respective Sums of Money to be laid on them by virtue of this Act unto the aforesaid several and respective Commissioners on or before the first Day of December one thousand seven hundred and seventy one; for securing which payment the said Commissioners shall respectively oblige the said several and respective Retailers to give such Security as they the said Commissioners shall judge necessary. PROVIDED that such Retailer in the City of New York as shall be rated six Pounds and under, and such in the several Counties as shall be rated at three Pounds and under shall not be permitted to retail unless they immediately pay the several and respective Sums they shall be rated at, to the aforesaid Commissioners, any Thing herein before contained to the contrary notwithstanding.

AND BE IT FURTHER ENACTED by the Authority aforesaid that in Case any Person or Persons whomsoever other than such as the said Commissioners shall permit shall presume to sell any Strong Liquors by retail directly or indirectly, the Offender or Offenders shall for each such Offence forfeit the Sum of six Pounds to be recovered by the said Commissioner or Commissioners respectively, on the Oath of any one Credible Witness in a Summary way in the Cities of New York and Albany, and Borough of West Chester before the Mayor or Recorder and one or more Aldermen of the said Cities and Borough respectively, and in the several Counties before any Justice of the Peace within the said several Counties respectively, and if upon Conviction the said Forfeitures be not paid the same shall be levied on the

Goods and Chattels of the Offender or Offenders by Warrant or Warrants under the Hands and Seals of the Person or Persons before whom such Conviction shall happen, and if no Goods and Chattels are found on which to distrain it shall and may be lawful for the Person or Persons who heard and determined the same to commit the Offender or Offenders to Goal without Bail or Main Prize for the space of three Months unless the Penalties are sooner discharged, and the said respective Magistrates shall be and are hereby fully impowered directed and required to hear and determine those Matters in the Manner aforesaid, and to give Judgment if need be to award Execution thereon and to issue a Warrant or Warrants for the commitment of Offenders as the Case may require one third of which Forfeiture shall be to the Informer or Informers, one third to the said Commissioners, and one third to the Poor of the Town Manor or Precinct where the Offence shall be committed to be paid into the Hands of the Church Wardens or Overseers of the Poor of the said respective Place or Places, by the Officer or Officers by whom the same shall be levied, any Thing in any of the Acts of this Colony to the contrary notwithstanding.

AND BE IT FURTHER ENACTED by the Authority aforesaid, that the several Retailers who shall be permitted and allowed to retail by the said Commissioner or Commissioners shall before they do so retail any Strong Liquors enter into Recognizance, that is to say, in the Cities of New York and Albany and Borough of West Chester before the respective Mayors thereof, and in the several Counties in this Colony, before two Justices of the Peace in the Penal Sum of twenty Pounds with sufficient Sureties in the like Sum, conditioned to keep an orderly House according to Law during the Time they shall be permitted to retail as aforesaid, and thereupon the said respective Mayors or the said Justices shall grant to such Person or Persons who have entered into such Recognizance a License under his or their Hands and Seals to retail Strong Liquors in such House and Place as shall be mentioned therein during the continuance of this Act, which Recognizances are to be lodged by the Person or Persons before whom the same shall be taken vizt. in the Cities of New York and Albany and Borough of West Chester with the Town Clerks, and in the several Counties with the respective Clerks thereof, and upon Complaint of the Breach of the said Condition it shall be lawful for the said Mayor and

Aldermen of New York and Albany and Borough of West Chester respectively or the greater Number of them, and in the Counties for the Justices of the General and special Sessions of the Peace to suppress the Licence or Licences of such Offender or Offenders.

AND BE IT ENACTED by the Authority aforesaid that in Case any of the Persons who shall be permitted to retail Strong Liquors as aforesaid by the said Commissioner or Commissioners shall presume to retail before he she or they have obtained a Licence and entered into Recognizance to keep an orderly House as aforesaid he she or they so offending shall respectively forfeit the Sum of six Pounds for each Offence, to be recovered in a Summary way in the Manner before directed, one half thereof to the Informer, and the other half to the Poor of the Town Manor or Precinct where the Forfeiture shall arise. And that the Expence of being qualified to retail may be within the Bounds of Moderation.

BE IT ENACTED by the Authority aforesaid, that no more shall be taken for a Licence and Recognizance in the Cities of New York and Albany, and Borough of West Chester than the usual and accustomed Fees, and in the respective Counties than the Sum of three Shillings.

AND BE IT ENACTED by the Authority aforesaid that such Persons permitted to retail as aforesaid by the said Commissioner or Commissioners who retail Strong Liquors not to be drank in their own Houses, but carried elsewhere shall not be obliged to enter into the Recognizance and take Licence as aforesaid, any Thing contained in this Act to the contrary notwithstanding.

AND BE IT ENACTED by the Authority aforesaid that in Case of the Death of any of the aforesaid Commissioners, the surviving Commissioner or Commissioners where such Death may happen, shall be, and hereby is and are entitled to the whole Reward and vested with the same Powers and Authorities to execute this Act as if no such Death had happened, and in Case of the Death or Refusal of all the Commissioners of any of the respective Cities Counties and Districts, then the Sheriff or Sheriffs for the Time being for the Cities Counties or Districts where such Death or Refusal shall happen, shall be, and hereby is and are vested with all the Powers and Authorities given to the Commissioners by this Act, be under the same Regulations and entitled to the same Rewards to all Intents, Constructions and purposes whatsoever, as if they had been particularly named and appointed in this Act, any Thing in this Act to the contrary notwithstanding.

AND BE IT FURTHER ENACTED by the Authority aforesaid that all the Monies to be paid to the Treasurer of this Colony by virtue of this Act, or recovered upon any of the aforesaid Bonds shall remain in the Hands of the Treasurer of this Colony for the Time being to be disposed of, as is, or shall be directed by any Act or Acts, passed or to be passed for that purpose.

AND BE IT ENACTED that the Retailers in the City of New York shall pay the Excise in three several payments, or sooner as the Commissioner and they shall agree. PROVIDED ALWAYS that Nothing in this Act shall be construed to make void, abridge or any wise lessen the several Rights and Privileges granted unto the Cities of New York and Albany and Borough of West Chester by their respective Charters, any Thing contained in this Act to the contrary thereof notwithstanding.

[CHAPTER 1468.]

[Chapter 1468 of Van Schaack, where the act is printed in full. See chapter 1373.]

An Act to continue an Act intitled "An "Act to prevent Frauds by Bills of Sale "which shall be made and executed after the "first Day of March in the Year of our Lord "one thousand seven hundred and sixty nine, "in the Counties therein mentioned."

[Passed, December 22, 1770.]

WHEREAS an Act intitled "An Act to prevent Frauds by "Bills of Sale which shall be made and executed after the first "Day of March in the Year of our Lord one thousand seven hun- "dred and sixty nine in the Counties therein mentioned." passed in the ninth year of his present Majesty's Reign, will expire by it's own Limitation on the first Day of January next, and the same having been found very useful and necessary.

BE IT THEREFORE ENACTED by his Excellency the Governor, the Council and the General Assembly, and it is hereby Enacted by the Authority of the same. That the abovementioned Act shall be and hereby is continued, and every Article Matter and Clause therein contained Enacted to be and remain in full force until the first Day of February which will be in the Year of our Lord one thousand seven hundred and seventy five.

THIRTY-FIRST ASSEMBLY.

Fourth Session.

(Begun Jan. 1, 1771, 12 George III, William Tryon, Governor.)

[CHAPTER 1469.]

[Chapter 1469 of Van Schaack, where the title only is printed.]

An Act to impower the Mayor, Recorder and Aldermen of the City of New York, or the Major Part of them to order the raising a Sum not exceeding sixteen hundred Pounds, for the uses therein mentioned.

[Passed, January 12, 1771.]

WHEREAS the providing a sufficient Number of Watchmen and lighting of Lamps within the City of New York, has not only been found convenient, but also necessary for the safety of it's Inhabitants and others.

BE IT THEREFORE ENACTED by his Excellency the Governor, the Council, and the General Assembly, and it is hereby Enacted by the Authority of the same, that the Mayor, Recorder and Aldermen of the City of New York, for the Time being, or the major Part of them, whereof the Mayor or Recorder to be one, shall have full Power and Authority, and are hereby fully impowered and authorized, on the second Tuesday in this present Month of January, or within ten Days thereafter to order the raising a Sum not exceeding sixteen hundred Pounds, by a Tax upon the Estates real and personal of all and every the Freeholders, Freemen, Inhabitants, Residents, and Sojourners within the City of New York on the South Side of Fresh Water, for the payment of so many Watchmen as the Mayor Aldermen and Commonalty of the City of New York shall think necessary for guarding the City, and for purchasing Oil, providing Lamps, and for repairing and attending the Lamps which now are or hereafter may be erected, and add the same Sum of Sixteen hundred Pounds to the Sum which shall be raised for the Minister and Poor of the said City; which Tax so to be laid, shall be rated and assessed at the same Time, and by the Vestry-Men who shall rate and assess the Tax for the Minister and Poor of the said City, and shall be rated together in one Assessment made of the whole, the Vestrymen first taking the Oath prescribed to be taken in and by an Act intitled, "An Act to enable the Inhabitants of the City of New "York to choose annually two Vestrymen for each respective "Ward within the said City." made and passed in the nineteenth Year of the Reign of his late Majesty King George the second, and the Tax so to be laid shall be collected, levied and paid at the same Time as the Tax for the Maintenance of the Minister and Poor of the said City hath been accustomed into the Hands of the Church Wardens of the said City for the Time being, who are hereby required and directed to pay the same into the Hands of the Chamberlain of the Said City, to be by him paid as he shall be directed by Warrant or Warrants of the said Mayor Aldermen and Commonalty in Common Council convened for the uses aforesaid.

AND BE IT FURTHER ENACTED by the Authority aforesaid that over and above the Sum of sixteen hundred Pounds, to be levied and paid by virtue of this Act, the Sum of three Pence in the Pound as a Reward to the Constables for their Trouble shall be assessed levied and paid to the respective Constables for collecting and paying the same and no more, according to the true Intent and meaning of this Act, any Thing herein, or in any other Act or Acts contained to the contrary hereof in any wise notwithstanding.

AND BE IT FURTHER ENACTED by the Authority aforesaid that if the said Mayor, Recorder or Aldermen, Church Wardens, Vestrymen or Constables of the said City of New York, who are hereby authorized, impowered and required to take effectual Care that this Act be executed according to the true Intent and Meaning thereof, or any of them shall deny, refuse or delay to perform, execute or comply with all or any of the Powers, Authorities and Duties in this Act given and required to be done and performed by them or either of them, and thereof shall be lawfully convicted in any Court of Record in this Colony, he or they so denying refusing or delaying to perform the duties as aforesaid shall suffer such Pains and Penalties by Fine and Imprisonment as by the Discretion of the said Court shall be adjudged.

AND BE IT FURTHER ENACTED by the Authority aforesaid, that if any Person or Persons shall Wilfully break or damage any of the Lamps now erected or hereafter to be erected within the said City, he, she or they so offending shall forfeit the

Sum of twenty Pounds for every Lamp he she or they shall damage or break as aforesaid, to be levied by Warrant or Warrants under the Hands and Seals of two or more of his Majesty's Justices of the Peace for the City and County of New York by Distress and Sale of the Offender's Goods and Chattels, on due Conviction made upon the Oath of one or more credible Witness or Witnesses, rendering the Overplus if any there be, to the Owner or Owners; and for want of such Distress, the Offender or Offenders shall be imprisoned by Warrant under the Hands and Seals of the said Justices who are hereby required to issue the same, for the Space of three Months, unless the said Forfeiture or Forfeitures be sooner paid: which Forfeitures shall be applied towards providing and repairing of Lamps, and paying the Watchmen.

AND BE IT FURTHER ENACTED by the Authority aforesaid that all such Persons as shall be employed to guard the said City, and attend the Lamps shall be under the Direction of, and obey such Orders as they shall from Time to Time receive from the Mayor, Aldermen and Commonalty of the said City, any Custom Law or Usage to the contrary thereof in any wise notwithstanding.

[CHAPTER 1470.]

[Chapter 1470 of Van Schaack, where the title only is printed.]

An Act to enable the Mayor, Recorder Aldermen and Commonalty of the City of Albany for the Time being or the major Part of them to order the raising a Sum not exceeding two hundred and fifty Pounds for the Purposes therein mentioned.

[Passed, January 12, 1771.]

WHEREAS the establishing of a regular well constituted Night Watch in the City of Albany will tend to the safety and preservation of the Inhabitants in their Persons and Effects.

BE IT THEREFORE ENACTED by his Excellency the Governor the Council and the General Assembly, and it is hereby Enacted by the Authority of the same, That the Mayor, Recorder Aldermen and Commonalty of the City of Albany for the Time being, or the major Part of them whereof the Mayor or Recorder to be one shall have full power and Authority and are hereby fully impowered and Authorized at any Time before the last Day of February one thousand seven hundred and seventy one to order the raising a Sum not exceeding two hundred and fifty Pounds by Tax upon the Estates Real and Personal lying and being within the said City of all and every the Freeholders, Freemen, Inhabitants, Residents and Sojourners living within half a Mile from the River, for the payment of so many Watchmen as the Mayor Aldermen and Commonalty of the said City in Common Council convened shall think necessary for guarding the said City, which Tax so to be laid shall be rated and assessed at the same Time and by the Assessors who shall rate and Assess the Tax which shall be raised by virtue of an Act of the Governor, the Council and the General Assembly of the Colony of New York intitled. "An Act for the better explaining and more "effectual putting in execution an Act of the General Assembly "made in the third Year of the Reign of their late Majesties "King William and Queen Mary intitled an Act for defraying "the Public and necessary charge throughout this Province, and "for maintaining the Poor and preventing Vagabonds," made and passed the nineteenth of June one thousaid seven hundred and three; the Assessors first taking the Oath prescribed to be taken by the last mentioned Act, and the Tax so to be laid shall be collected levied and paid by the same Collector and at the same Time as the Tax raised by virtue of the Act aforesaid, hath been accustomed, and shall be paid into the Hands of such Person as the Mayor Aldermen and Commonalty of the said City or the Major Part of them in Common Council convened shall appoint to be by him paid as he shall be directed by Warrant or Warrants of the said Mayor Recorder Aldermen and Commonalty in Common Council convened for the uses aforesaid.

AND BE IT FURTHER ENACTED by the Authority aforesaid That the Collector shall retain in his Hands three Pence in the Pound of every Pound so raised by virtue of this Act as a Reward for his Trouble in collecting and paying the same and no more

AND BE IT FURTHER ENACTED by the Authority aforesaid. That if the said Mayor Recorder Aldermen and Commonalty Assessors or Collectors of the said City of Albany who are hereby authorized impowered and required to take effectual Care that this Act be executed According to the true Intent and meaning thereof or any of them shall deny refuse or delay to perform execute or comply with all or any of the Powers Authorities and Duties in this Act given and required to be done and performed by them or either of them and thereof shall be lawfully convicted in any Court of Record in this Colony, he or they so denying refusing or delaying to perform the Duties as aforesaid shall suffer such Pains and Penalties by Fine and Imprisonment, as by the discretion of the said Court shall be adjudged.

AND BE IT FURTHER ENACTED by the Authority aforesaid That if any Person or Persons shall neglect or refuse to pay the several Rates and Assessments wherewith he or they shall be charged by this Act for or in respect of his and their Goods and Chattels Lands or Tenements upon Demand of the Collector appointed to receive the same. That then it shall and may be lawful to and for such Collector, and he is hereby required, for nonpayment thereof by Warrant under the Hand of the Mayor Recorder Aldermen and Common Council of the said City for the Time being or the Major Part of them to distrain upon the Goods and Chattels of the Person or Persons so refusing or Neglecting to pay, and for want of Goods or Chattels, to distrain in and upon the Messuages Lands and Tenements so charged, and the Goods and Chattels then and there found, and the Distress so taken to carry away and the same to expose to sale within the said City for the payment of the said Rate or Assessment, and the Overplus if any be, over and above the Charges of taking and carrying away the said Distress to be immediately returned to the Owner thereof.

AND BE IT FURTHER ENACTED by the Authority aforesaid, That all such Persons as shall be employed to guard the said City shall be under the direction of, and obey such Orders as they shall from Time to Time receive from the Mayor Aldermen and Commonalty in Common Council convened, any Custom Law or Usage to the contrary in any wise notwithstanding.

[CHAPTER 1471.]

[Chapter 1471 of Van Schaack, where the act is printed in full. See chapter 942.]

An Act to amend an Act intitled "An "Act to enable the Freeholders and Inhabit-"ants of the Townships of Rochester and "Marble Town to choose and elect at their "annual Town Meetings two Constables for "each Town."

[Passed, January 12, 1771.]

WHEREAS in and by an Act intitled "An Act to enable the "Freeholders and Inhabitants of the Township of Rochester and

"Marble Town to choose and elect at their annual Town Meet-"ings two Constables for each Town." it is enacted that the Freeholders and Inhabitants of the said Townships of Rochester and Marble Town respectively shall at their annual Meetings for electing Town Officers, choose and elect two Constables for each of the said Townships respectively: and the said Townships becoming more extensively inhabited, it is found necessary that one more Constable should be chosen for each of them.

BE IT THEREFORE ENACTED by his Excellency the Governor, the Council and the General Assembly, and it is hereby Enacted by the Authority of the same. That the Freeholders and Inhabitants of the said Townships of Rochester and Marble Town respectively for the future shall at their annual Meetings for electing Town Officers, elect and choose by plurality of Voices, three Constables for each of the said Townships respectively instead of two, as in and by the said Act is directed, and such Person or Persons so elected and chosen as aforesaid shall serve as Constables for the then ensuing Year, until there be others chosen in their room and Stead, and every such Person or Persons so chosen and elected as aforesaid who shall refuse or neglect to qualify and serve as is above directed shall forfeit for every such Offence the sum of forty Shillings, to be recovered before any one of his Majesty's Justices of the Peace for said County by the Overseers of the Poor of the Township where such Refusal or Neglect may happen, to be applied to the use of the Poor of the Township where such forfeiture may arise; and in which Case it shall and may be lawful for any two Justices of the Peace for the said County of Ulster to appoint some fit Person or Persons to execute the Office of Constable for the said Place or Places where such Refusal or Neglect shall happen, until a new Election shall be made by virtue of this Act as aforesaid, and every Constable or Constables so elected chosen or appointed as aforesaid shall have the same Powers and be subject to the same Fines and Forfeitures as the other Constables for the several Towns Manors and Precincts in the said County are invested with and liable to.

[CHAPTER 1472.]

[Chapter 1472 of Van Schaack, where the act is printed in full. Amended by chapter 1760. See chapter 1509.]

An Act for emitting the Sum of one hundred and twenty thousand Pounds in Bills of Credit to be put out on Loan and to appropriate the Interest arising thereon to the payment of the Debts of this Colony, and to such Public Exigencies as the Circumstances of this Colony may from Time to Time render necessary.

[Passed, February 16, 1771.]

WHEREAS from the great Decay of Trade, and the insolvency of the late Treasurer, and other Difficulties a Deficiency has arisen in the Public Funds. AND WHEREAS the Funds granted for the support of his Majesty's Government in and over this Colony have of late been reduced one half which Deficiency this Colony in it's present Circumstances is unable to discharge unless it be done by the Means of a Loan of Money. AND WHEREAS also there is a great Want of Specie or other Medium of Trade in this Colony whereby the Inhabitants labour under insuperable Difficulties, and many of them are utterly ruined by being obliged to sell considerable Estates greatly under the real value thereof, and the Merchants rendered unable to make Remittances to Great Britain as without such Medium Bills of Exchange cannot be purchased: Wherefore as well to revive the Commerce Trade and Navigation of this Colony as to promote the Improvement and settlement thereof, the General Assembly pray that it may be Enacted.

I BE IT THEREFORE ENACTED by his Excellency the Governor the Council and the General Assembly, and it is hereby Enacted by the Authority of the same. That Bills of Credit to the value of one hundred and twenty thousand Pounds Current Money of New York forthwith after the Publication hereof be printed as follows Vizt. five thousand Bills each of the value of ten Pounds, six thousand Bills each of the value of five Pounds, six thousand Bills each of the value of three Pounds, five thousand Bills each of the value of two Pounds, six thousand Bills each of the value of one Pound, eight thousand Bills each of the value of ten Shillings, and eight thousand Bills each of the value of five Shillings, upon which Bills shall be impressed the Arms of the City of New York on the Right Side of every of the said Bills; and the said Bills shall be in the form following.

"By a Law of the Colony of New York this Bill shall be "received in all payments in the Treasury for ···,···,···,··· "New York the ···,···. Day of ···,···. one thousand seven hun-"dred and seventy one, which Bills shall be numbered by Henry "Holland or Walter Franklin or Theophylact Bache or Samuel Verplank, and signed by any two of them, and by the Treasurer, to whom by this Act the said first Signers are directed to deliver them.

II AND BE IT ENACTED that the said first Signers are hereby directed and impowered upon the Delivery to them of the said Bills by the Printer thereof to Administer to him and he is hereby directed to take an Oath or Affirmation in the Words following.

"I A. B. do declare that from the Time that the Letters were "set, and fit to be put in the press for printing the Bills of "Credit now by me delivered to you until the Bills were printed, "and the Letters afterwards distributed into the Boxes, I went "at no Time out of the Room in which the said Letters were with-"out locking them up, so as they could not be come at without "Violence a false Key, or other Art then unknown to me, and "therefore to the best of my knowledge no Copies were Printed "off but in my presence, and that all the Blotters and other "Papers whatsoever impressed by the said Letters, whilst set for "printing the said Bills to the best of my knowledge are here "delivered to you together with the Stamps; and in all Things "relating to this Affair I have well and truly demeaned myself "according to the true Intent and Meaning of the Law in that "Case made and provided to the best of my knowledge and "understanding so help me God."

Which Printer at the Time he has Orders to print the said Bills shall have a Copy of this Oath that he may govern himself accordingly. PROVIDED ALWAYS that if any unforeseen Accident has happened he may have the Liberty of making an exception thereof in his Oath, he declaring fully how it was, and if any more of the said Bills are printed than by this Act is directed when the said Henry Holland, Walter Franklin, Theophylact Bache, Samuel Verplank, or any two of them have signed the Number hereby directed to be issued they shall immediately burn and destroy all the Remainder.

III AND BE IT ENACTED by the Authority aforesaid that Elisha Galludet or such other Person as the Major Part of the said first Signers of the said Bills of Credit shall agree with, shall engrave according to the Directions he shall receive from the Majority of the said first Signers twenty eight Stamps for the Sides of the said Bills, and fourteen Stamps for the Arms of the City of New York and shall deliver them to the Treasurer, who shall in the presence of the Majority of the said Signers deliver them unto Hugh Gaine the Printer of this Colony upon his Receipt for the same, and when the said Hugh Gaine has finished and compleated the printing the Quantity and Sorts of Bills hereby directed to be struck and issued, he shall re-deliver the said Stamps to the said Signers and Treasurer, who are hereby directed and required to seal them up with their several Seals and they are so to remain in the Treasury until they shall be ordered to be made use of by any future Act of Assembly, and the Receipt of the said Treasurer to the said Hugh Gaine shall be a sufficient Discharge for such re-delivery. But in Case of the Death, Sickness or inability of the said Hugh Gaine to print the said Bills, then the Majority of the said Signers shall appoint another Printer for the Service aforesaid in his place which Printer so appointed shall take the Oath as above directed.

IV. BE IT ALSO ENACTED that before the said Signers do receive any of the said Bills they shall (before any of the Magistrates of the City of New York) each of them take an Oath or Affirmation well and truly to perform what by this Act they are enjoined as their Duty, and will knowingly sign no more Bills of Credit than what by this Act is directed.

V. AND BE IT ENACTED that the said Treasurer shall out of the Bills of Credit so signed and numbered as aforesaid deliver to the Loan Officers herein after mentioned on producing the Certificates of Qualification herein after directed in the Sums and Quotas following to wit.

To the Loan Officers of the City and County of New York to and for the Purposes hereinafter mentioned the Sum of thirty eight thousand Pounds.

To the Loan Officers of the City and County of Albany to and for the purposes therein after mentioned the Sum of twenty thousand Pounds

To the Loan Officers of King's County to and for the purposes herein after mentioned the Sum of five thousand one hundred and sixty eight Pounds.

To the Loan Officers of Queen's County to and for the purposes herein after mentioned the Sum of ten thousand seven hundred and twelve Pounds.

To the Loan Officers of Suffolk County to and for the purposes herein after mentioned the Sum of nine thousand two hundred Pounds.

To the Loan Officers of Richmond County to and for the purposes herein after mentioned the Sum of three thousand two hundred and forty eight Pounds.

To the Loan Officers of West Chester County to and for the purposes herein after mentioned the Sum of ten thousand seven hundred and twelve Pounds.

To the Loan Officers of Dutchess County to and for the purposes herein after mentioned the Sum of ten thousand five hundred and sixty Pounds.

To the Loan Officers of Orange County to and for the purposes herein after mentioned the Sum of three thousand two hundred Pounds.

To the Loan Officers of Ulster County to and for the purposes herein after mentioned the Sum of nine thousand two hundred Pounds.

For which respective Sums the said Loan Officers respectively shall give Receipts to the said Treasurer indorsed on the Clerks Certificate and other Qualification herein after directed which Receipts shall be to the said Treasurer his Executors and Administrators a sufficient Discharge if otherwise he has well and truly performed the Duty enjoined by this Act.

VI. AND BE IT ALSO ENACTED that before the said Loan Officers do respectively enter upon their said Office every of them shall give Bond to his Majesty his Heirs and Successors with such sufficient Security as shall be approved of by one or more of the Judges of the Inferior Court of the County, together with the Majority of the Supervisors of the same County, and in the City of New York by any one or more of the Judges of the Supreme Court signified by signing such his or their Approbation on the Back of the said Bond, which Bond shall be in the full Sum by this Act committed to his charge with Condition for the true and faithful performance of his Office and Duty, and that without favour Malice or Partiality.

VII. AND BE IT ENACTED that each Loan Officer respectively shall take the following Oath or Affirmation.

"I A B. will according to the best of my Skill and knowledge "faithfully impartially and truly demean myself in discharge of "the Trust committed to me as one of the Loan Officers for "the of by the Laws of this Colony in that "behalf made, according to the purport true Intent and meaning "of the said Laws, so as the Public may not be prejudiced by my "Consent privity or procurement, so help me God."

Which Oath or Affirmation shall be administered by any Justice of the Peace, and indorsed on the Back of the said Bond, and signed by such Justice and the Loan Officer.

VIII AND BE IT ENACTED that the aforesaid Bond indorsed with the approbation and Affidavit or Affirmation aforesaid shall be lodged with the Clerk of the County who upon Receipt thereof shall give the Loan Officer a Certificate that such Bond indorsed as aforesaid is lodged with him, which Certificate is to be delivered to the said Treasurer on his delivering to the Loan Officer the Bills of Credit aforesaid which Bond and Indorsements shall be recorded by the Clerk, and in Case of the forfeiture of the same Bond, the Majority of the supervisors with any one or more of the Judges of the Inferior Courts of the Counties respectively, are hereby impowered to order the same to be put in Suit, and the Monies recovered by virtue thereof shall be applied to the use of the County on Consideration of the County's making good the Deficiencies of the Borrowers in the same as in this Act is hereafter directed. PROVIDED ALWAYS that in the City and County of New York the Justices and Vestrymen of the same City and County shall have all the Powers by this Act given to the Judges of the Inferior Courts and Supervisors in the other Counties of this Colony, which Justices and Vestrymen of the City and County of New York shall also perform all the Duties and Services and be liable to all the Pains Penalties and Forfeitures which the Judges aforesaid, and Supervisors of the other Counties are to perform and be subject to by virtue of this Act, and in Case of any Deficiency of the Borrowers they shall cause such Deficiency to be assessed levied and raised in such Manner as they assess levy and raise the Tax for Minister and Poor.

IX. AND BE IT ENACTED by the Authority aforesaid that on the first Tuesday of March next the Judges of the Inferior

20

Courts or any one or more of them together with the Supervisors (or the Majority of them) of the several Counties respectively of this Colony shall meet at the Court House of the Counties respectively where the Majority of them shall elect and choose two sufficient Freeholders of the respective Counties to be Loan Officers for the same Counties. PROVIDED ALWAYS that Nothing in this Clause shall be construed to extend to the City and County of New York, the City and County of Albany, the County of Dutchess, the County of Ulster, and the County of Orange.

X AND BE IT ENACTED by the Authority aforesaid that the Vestrymen of the City and County of New York and Supervisors of the several Counties of this Colony shall at every of their Meetings after the said first Tuesday in March with the Judge or Judges aforesaid directed by this Act, in the first Place take the Oath or Affirmation before any Justice of the Peace in the Words following.

"I A B. will according to the best of my Judgment and knowl-"edge well and truly execute the Trust reposed in me by an Act "of the General Assembly of this Colony intitled An Act for "emitting the Sum of one hundred and twenty thousand Pounds "in Bills of Credit to be put out on Loan and to appropriate the "Interest arising thereon to the payment of the Debts of this "Colony, and to such Public Exigencies as the Circumstances of "this Colony may from Time to Time render necessary. And "that without any favour Malice or Partiality, so help me God"

XI AND BE IT ENACTED by the Authority aforesaid. That the Loan Officers of each of the Cities and Counties aforesaid respectively when elected, appointed and qualified according to the Directions of this Act shall be Bodies Politick and Corporate in fact and in Law, that is to say.

The Loan Officers for the City and County of New York shall be one Body Politick and Corporate by the Name of The Loan Officers of the City and County of New York.

The Loan Officers for the City and County of Albany shall be one Body Politick and Corporate by the Name of. The Loan Officers of the City and County of Albany.

The Loan Officers for King's County shall be one Body Politick and Corporate by the Name of The Loan Officers of King's County.

The Loan Officers for Queen's County shall be one Body Politick and Corporate by the Name of The Loan Officers of Queen's County.

The Loan Officers for Suffolk County shall be one Body Politick and Corporate by the Name of The Loan Officers of Suffolk County.

The Loan Officers for Richmond County shall be one Body Politick and Corporate by the Name of The Loan Officers of Richmond County.

The Loan Officers for West Chester County shall be one Body Politick and Corporate by the Name of The Loan Officers of West Chester County.

The Loan Officers for Dutchess County shall be one Body Politick and Corporate by the Name of The Loan Officers of Dutchess County.

The Loan Officers for Orange County shall be one Body Politick and Corporate by the Name of The Loan Officers of Orange County, and,

The Loan Officers for Ulster County shall be one Body Politick and Corporate by the Name of The Loan Officers of Ulster County.

With full Power to every of the said Bodies Politick to use a common Seal, and by the same Seal and in the Name of such Body Politick to grant Receipts, receive Mortgages, and again to grant the same away, to sue and be sued, and generally with all such Powers as are necessary to be used for the due Execution of the Trust reposed in the said Loan Officers by this Act, any Law usage or Custom to the contrary in any wise notwithstanding.

XII AND BE IT ENACTED by the Authority aforesaid That when the said Loan Officers respectively have qualified themselves as above in this Act is directed they shall receive the said Bills of Credit signed by two of the four Signers first named as aforesaid and Treasurer, which Bills of Credit so signed shall be let out to such as shall apply for the same, and can and will give security to the said Loan Officers by Mortgage on Lands, Lots, Houses or other valuable Improvements lying in the same City or County, they the said Loan Officers first giving Public Notice as in other Cases by this Act directed for Notices, by Advertisements set up, that on a Certain Day, at least ten Days after setting them up, they will be ready to receive Borrowers qualified according to the Directions of this Act, and as on that Day Borrowers do offer, their Names and Sums they Demand shall be orderly entered down in the Minute Book of proceedings, and every one shall be served according to the Priority of their Demands if reasonable Objections be not against the Title and Value of the Lands offered to be Mortgaged or some other sufficient Reason which shall be entered also in the Minute Book of proceedings PROVIDED ALWAYS that if upon the first Day so many Borrowers do offer as to demand a greater Sum than the whole Sum in that County to be lent out, then and in that Case every such Borrower shall be abated of the Sum he demanded proportionably.

XIII. AND BE IT ENACTED that the said Loan Officers respectively before they accept of any Lands, Lots, Houses, or other Improvements in Mortgage for any of the said Bills, they shall first view what is so offered in Mortgage or make due enquiry into the value thereof, and then shall examine the Titles thereto by perusing the Deeds, Patents Surveys and other writings and Conveyances by which the same is held and by which the value and Quantity may be the better known, and the said Loan Officers respectively are hereby also impowered and required to administer to all Persons applying for any of the said Bills as aforesaid the following Oath or Affirmation if Quakers to wit.

"I A B. am Bona fide seized in Fee Simple of the Lands Tene-"ments and Hereditaments by me now offered to be mortgaged "in my own Right, and to my own use, and the same were not "conveyed to me in Trust for the use of any Person nor with "Intent to borrow any Sum or Sums of Money upon the Same for "the use of any other Person or Persons whatsoever, and the "premises are free and clear from any other or former Gift, "Grant, Sale Mortgage, Judgment, Extent, Recognizance, or "other Incumbrance whatsoever to my knowledge, except the "Rent issuing thereout to our Lord the King, so help me God."

XIV. AND BE IT ENACTED by the Authority aforesaid that the Loan Officers of the said Cities and Counties respectively upon finding Borrowers qualified, and the Loan Officers being satisfied as aforesaid are hereby required, and by virtue of this Act have full Power to lend out the Bills delivered to them as aforesaid at the Interest of five per Cent per Annum for the Term of fourteen Years from the third Tuesday of April next to come, to be paid in again by payments to be made as herein after directed in sums not exceeding three hundred Pounds, and not under twenty five Pounds (unless the Proportion as aforesaid be less) to any one

Person, the said Loan Officers taking Security for the same by way of Mortgage as aforesaid, of at least double the value in Lands Tenements and Hereditaments, and of at least three Times the Value in Houses within the said respective Cities and Counties, and administring an Oath or Affirmation to the Borrower as aforesaid, and the said Mortgage shall be executed before two or more lawful Witnesses signing thereto, and the Substance thereof shall be Minuted in a Book to be by the said Loan Officers kept for that purpose in each respective City and County, for the making of which Mortgage and Minute the Borrower shall pay to the said Loan Officers the Sum of four Shillings and no more, which Mortgage and Minute shall be and each of them are hereby declared to be matter of Record and an attested Copy of the said Mortgage if in being, or of the said Minute in Case the Mortgage is lost under the Hands of the Loan Officers and Seal of the Loan Office, shall be good Evidence of the said Mortgage in any Court within this Colony.

XV AND BE IT ENACTED by the Authority aforesaid, That the Interest of the Money lent out as aforesaid shall be payable yearly on the third Tuesday of April to the Loan Officers; and the principals of all the Monies lent out as aforesaid shall be paid in again in the manner following, that is to say, one tenth Part of the Principal Money on the third Tuesday of April which will be in the Year of our Lord one thousand seven hundred and seventy six, one other tenth Part thereof on the third Tuesday of April which will be in the Year of our Lord one thousand seven hundred and seventy seven, one other tenth Part thereof on the third Tuesday of April which will be in the Year of our Lord one thousand seven hundred and seventy eight, one other tenth Part thereof on the third Tuesday of April which will be in the Year of our Lord one thousand seven hundred and seventy nine, one other tenth Part thereof on the third Tuesday of April which will be in the Year of our Lord one thousand seven hundred and eighty, one other tenth Part thereof on the third Tuesday of April which will be in the Year of our Lord one thousand seven hundred and eighty one, one other tenth Part thereof on the third Tuesday of April which will be in the Year of our Lord one thousand seven hundred and eighty two. one other tenth Part thereof on the third Tuesday of April which will be in the Year of our Lord one thousand seven hundred and eighty three, one other tenth Part thereof on the third Tuesday of April which will be in the Year of our Lord one thousand seven hundred and eighty four. and the remaining tenth Part thereof on the third Tuesday of April which will be in the Year of our Lord one thousand seven hundred and eighty five. And the respective Loan Officers at the lending of the Money are hereby required to take the Security for the same accordingly, and the said Loan Officers for every Sum paid to them shall give to the payer a Receipt and shall also enter one Minute of the same payment on the Back of the Mortgage, and another Minute thereof in the Book of Accounts by them to be kept, and that without any Fee or Reward. But if the Borrower his Heirs, Executors or Administrators shall see Cause to pay in a fourth, or a half, or three Quarters or the whole of the principal due to the said Loan Officer on any third Tuesday of April before the said third Tuesday of April one thousand seven hundred and eighty five. the said Loan Officers are hereby impowered and required to receive the same, on the third Tuesday of April annually, and no other Day of the Year unless so many do offer payment on that Day, that the Loan Officers cannot within the Day receive the whole; and in that Case they are to continue to receive until all that on that Day offered, have paid in the Monies so offered, and unless he brings along with him another sufficient Borrower to give new Security to the satisfaction of the Loan Officers for the whole of the Money by him paid in, and in that Case the Loan Officer shall accept thereof, on any of their stated Days of Meeting, and when the whole Principal and interest is paid, the said Loan Officers shall if required give the party paying a Release of the Mortgage given by the Borrower, and shall tear off the Name and Seal, and make an Entry in the Margin of the Mortgage, and in the Margin of the Minute made thereof, that such a Day and Year such Release was made, for which Release the Releasee shall pay the Sum of two Shillings and no more, and when any Parts of the Principals are paid in as aforesaid before the said third Tuesday of April one thousand seven hundred and eighty five, the Loan Officers shall at the End of that meeting compute the Sum of the whole principals so paid in and give Public Notice of the Sum by Advertisements set up, and that on that Day Week they will be ready to receive Borrowers of the said Monies, to whom the said Loan Officers shall lend the same out, and in the lending and taking Security shall Conform themselves, as near as the Circumstances of the Case can admit, to the Directions herein before prescribed, and if any Monies still remain in their Hands for want of Borrowers, they shall set up Advertisements of the Sum thereof, and continue to do the like at the End of every of their stated Meetings.

XVI. AND BE IT ENACTED That in Case any Loan Officer shall die or remove or neglect delay or refuse, or omit performing the Duty required or enjoined him by this Act, or shall behave himself in his Office with favour affection Partiality or Malice whereby the Public or any Private Person may be injured, upon Report or Complaint made thereof to any two or more of the Judges aforesaid of the respective Counties, or to the Justices and Vestrymen of the City of New York, to which he belongs, the said Judges are hereby required and commanded to issue out their precepts to call together the Judges and Supervisors of the same County, to meet at such Time and Place as in the said Precept shall be appointed to hear and determine Summarily, upon the said Report or Complaint and upon sufficient Proof made to any one or more of the said Judges with the Major Part of the said Supervisors of any Death, Removal, Failure or Neglect in the said Office as aforesaid, then and in that Case the said Majority of the Supervisors with Concurrence of one or more of the Judges aforesaid shall proceed in manner as herein before directed to elect and choose, and are hereby required and commanded to elect and choose a Loan Officer in the Room and stead of such deceased or absent person or Omitter or Defaulter, which Loan Officer so chosen as aforesaid having entered into Bond and been qualified in like Manner as other Loan Officers are by this Act directed, shall then have all the Powers, Privileges and Advantages, and be subject to all the Pains, Penalties and Forfeitures which any of the Loan Officers of the County elected as aforesaid are vested with, entitled to, charged with, or subject to by virtue of this Act.

XVII AND BE IT ENACTED That if any of the Loan Officers hereafter to be elected and appointed by Virtue of this Act shall at any Time hereafter desire to be discharged of and from the said Office he applying himself to any one or more of the Judges aforesaid for that purpose, he or they shall upon that application issue their precept to summon the Judges aforesaid and Supervisors to meet at a place and Day by the said precept prefixed, to whom when met, the said Loan Officer shall produce or render an Account of his proceedings in his said Office, and if it appear upon examination that the said Loan Officer hath faithfully demeaned himself in the Discharge of his said Office according to the true Intent and meaning of this Act, then and in such Case such Loan Officer shall by the Majority of the Supervisors with the Concurrence of the said Judges be discharged of and from his said Office, and another fit Person shall be by them elected and appointed to supply his place who shall take the same Oath or Affirmation, give the like security, be under and subject to the like Penalties, Restrictions and Regulations, and receive the same Salaries and Advantages whatsoever as the other Loan Officers for that County by virtue of this Act are liable, subject or entitled unto.

XVIII. AND BE IT ENACTED by the Authority aforesaid that when a Loan Officer shall be chosen and Qualified, as herein is directed in the place of a former Loan Officer such former Loan Officer, his Executors or Administrators shall upon Demand deliver to the new Loan Officer chosen in his Place and qualified as aforesaid, all the Monies Books and Papers that were in such former Loan Officer's Custody, belonging to his Office upon Oath before any Justice of the Peace, and in Case any such former Loan Officer, or his Executors or Administrators, shall deny delay or refuse to make such Delivery on Oath when demanded as aforesaid, the Bond of such former Loan Officer shall be forfeited.

XIX. BE IT ALSO ENACTED That if any Borrower shall neglect to bring in and pay or cause to be brought in and paid Yearly and every Year on the third Tuesday of April or within twenty two Days thereafter, on one of the Days which the Loan Officers aforesaid are by this Act directed to attend the respective Loan Offices, the Yearly Interests due by his Mortgage and also the Part of the Principal as it becomes payable, then and in either of these Cases, the Loan Officers to whom such Mortgage was granted shall be seized of an absolute indefeazible Estate in the Lands, Houses, Tenements and Hereditaments thereby Mortgaged to them, their Successors and Assigns to the uses in this Act mentioned, and the Mortgagor his or her Heirs and Assigns shall be utterly foreclosed and barred of all equity of Redemption of the mortgaged premises, any Law usage or Custom, or Practice in Courts of Equity to the contrary notwithstanding.

XX. BE IT FURTHER ENACTED That the said Loan Officers respectively shall attend the Loan Office every year to receive the Monies by this Act directed to be paid into them upon the third Tuesday of April, and thereafter on the Tuesday in each Week for the Term of three Weeks.

XXI. AND BE IT ENACTED That the Loan Officers shall in the Evening of the last of the Tuesdays aforesaid Yearly and every Year give sufficient Directions, which they are to take care shall be observed for fixing up Advertisements at three of the most Public Places in at least three or more distinct Towns or Precincts of the County where the premises are situate of all the Lands contained in the Mortgages whereof the equity of Redemption is foreclosed as aforesaid describing the Quantity and situation of the same and that on the last Tuesday of June in the same Year they are to be sold at the Court House of the respective County where the Lands lye by way of Public Vendue to the highest Bidder.

XXII. BE IT LIKEWISE ENACTED That the Loan Officers of the respective Cities and Counties aforesaid shall on the said last Tuesday of June Yearly expose the Lands in the Mortgages foreclosed as aforesaid to sale by way of Public Vendue and upon Sale shall convey them to the highest Bidder or Bidders who shall pay for their Deeds five Shillings and the Buyer or Buyers shall and may hold and enjoy the same for such Estate as they were sold clearly discharged and freed from all Benefit and Equity of Redemption, and all other Incumbrances made and suffered by the Mortgagor, his or her Heirs or Assigns and such Sales shall be available in Law and Equity.

XXIII. AND BE IT ENACTED That the Money or Price for which the Premises are sold shall upon the Sale thereof be paid to the said Loan Officers, out of which they shall retain in their Hands, what has not been paid in of the whole principal lent, together with the Interest that has become due thereon and might become due until the third Tuesday of April next thereafter, as also the Expence of the Advertisements, and of the Sale, the same not exceeding fifteen Shillings, and the remainder (if any be) the Loan Officers shall pay to the Mortgagor his or her Heirs or Assigns. PROVIDED ALWAYS That if any Person or Persons Offer at the Time of the sale to borrow (on sufficient security within this Act) the whole Principal that is to be retained out of the Price and lent out again, then and in that Case the Loan Officers shall not retain Interest beyond the Day of Sale. PROVIDED ALSO that if the Buyer incline to be the Borrower of the Principal or Principals that is or are to be paid in by him and lent out again, and if the Loan Officers be satisfied of the Security to be given by him in manner aforesaid, he shall be preferred to any other Borrower. PROVIDED LIKEWISE That the Loan Officers shall not be obliged to take Notice of any Assigns of the Mortgagor, unless they enter a Notice of their Right with the said Loan-Officers at or before the Time of Sale, which Notice the Loan-Officers shall enter on the Mortgage and Minute thereof on demand the Assignee paying one shilling for the same and Assigns shall be preferred according to the Priority of their Entries of such Notices.

XXIV AND BE IT ENACTED That after any Lands, Houses, Tenements or Hereditaments are mortgaged according to the Directions of this Act, if it shall appear to the Loan Officers upon good and sufficient Grounds (which they shall insert in the Minute Book of their Proceedings) that the Mortgagor had no good Right or Title to the Premises Mortgaged, or has otherwise broke the Covenants of his Mortgage so that the Public may be in danger of losing the Monies or any Part thereof advanced in Loan upon the Credit of the Premises it shall and may be lawful to and for the said Loan Officers, and they are hereby impowered and required to commence an Action or Actions of Debt or Covenant upon the said Mortgage against the Mortgagor his or her Heirs Executors or Administrators, and the same to prosecute to Judgment in any Court of Record for the recovery of the whole Monies lent upon the Mortgage and Interest become due, and that shall become due until the third Tuesday of April next following the Judgment with Costs and Charges by all lawful ways and Means whatsoever, in which Action or Actions the Mortgagor shall be held to special Bail, and the Court in which such Action is brought is and the Judges thereof in vacation are hereby Authorized and directed to give such short Days for the Rules of pleading thereon, that Judgment or a Tryal and final Determination may be had the first Court after the Court at which the Defendant first appeared to the same Action.

XXV AND BE IT ENACTED that the aforesaid Bills of Credit to be made and issued by virtue of this Act when signed by any two of the first Signers aforesaid and the Treasurer, shall be received by the said Loan Officers for and during the Term of fourteen Years, and by the Treasurer of this Colony for and during the said Term, and for one Year thereafter.

XXVI AND BE IT ENACTED that if any Person or Persons whatsoever shall presume to counterfeit any of the Bills of Credit issued by virtue of this Act, or shall alter any of the said Bills issued as aforesaid so that they shall appear to be of greater value than by this Act the same Bill or Bills so altered were enacted signed or Numbered to pass for, or shall knowingly pass or give in payment any of the Bills aforesaid so counterfeited or altered every Person Guilty of Counterfeiting or altering any of the said Bills as aforesaid, or of knowingly passing or giving in payment any such counterfeit or altered Bills, shall be guilty of Felony, and being thereof convicted shall suffer the Pains of Death without the Benefit of Clergy, and though such counterfeiting altering or knowingly passing Counterfeit or altered Bills shall be done out of this Colony, yet any Grand Jury within this Colony is hereby impowered to present the same, and to set forth in the Indictment the Place whereby their Evidence it appeared that the Fact was committed, which Indictment is hereby declared good notwithstanding that the Place alledged be out of this Colony, and the Petty Juries on the Tryals of all such foreign Issues shall be returned from the Body of the City and County of New York, any Law, Usage or Custom to the contrary notwithstanding.

XXVII. AND BE IT ALSO ENACTED that the respective Loan Offices in this Colony shall be kept at the Court House of each respective County, or at some other convenient place near the same, and the said Loan Officers shall so soon as the said Bills are signed and delivered to them set up Advertisements of the first Day of their attending the Loan Office, for the purposes herein before mentioned, and shall duly attend the same on that first Day, and on every Tuesday and Wednesday in each Week for the space of four Weeks thereafter, if there be occasion of their sitting so long, and the said Treasurer as soon as he can fix the Day upon which he can deliver the said Bills to the Loan Officers, shall send Notice by Letter to them to come and receive the Bills at that Day.

XXVIII AND BE IT ENACTED that the Loan Officers respectively shall retain in their Hands so much of the Interest Monies paid in to them as will pay them their respective Salaries appointed by this Act, and the remainder of the said Interest Monies shall be annually paid to the Treasurer of this Colony on or before the last Tuesday of the Month of July, and the said Treasurer's Receipt shall be to the said Loan Officers and every of them their Heirs, Executors and Administrators a sufficient Discharge.

XXIX AND BE IT FURTHER ENACTED That the Yearly Salaries of the Loan Officers aforesaid for the Services required of them by this Act shall be as follow. to wit.

For every of the Loan Officers of the City and County of New York forty Pounds.

For every of the Loan Officers of the City and County of Albany thirty Pounds.

For every of the Loan Officers of King's County ten Pounds.

For every of the Loan Officers of Queen's County sixteen Pounds.

For every of the Loan Officers of Suffolk County sixteen Pounds.

For every of the Loan Officers of Richmond County nine Pounds.

For every of the Loan Officers of West Chester County sixteen Pounds.

For every of the Loan Officers of Dutchess County sixteen Pounds.

For every of the Loan Officers of Orange County ten Pounds.

For every of the Loan Officers of Ulster County sixteen Pounds.

XXX. AND BE IT ENACTED by the Authority aforesaid That the Supervisors and Judges aforesaid of the several Counties of this Colony shall on the first Tuesday in October which will be in the Year of our Lord one thousand seven hundred and seventy two, and Yearly thereafter on the first Tuesday in October meet together with the said Loan Officers at the Court House of the County, (except the Judges and Supervisors of Suffolk County, who shall meet on the last Tuesday in October; the Judges and Supervisors of Ulster County on the third Tuesday in June; and the Judges and Supervisors of Dutchess County on the first Tuesday in June). and the Majority of the Supervisors with one or more of the Judges aforesaid shall carefully inspect and examine the Mortgages, Minutes and Accounts of the Loan officers to find whether they have been in any way faulty or negligent in their Offices, and if they find so, then to choose others in their Places as aforesaid: when also if any Deficiency has happened by a Borrower's not having Right to the Lands mortgaged or by the selling thereof for a less Price than what before is mentioned, or any other way whatsoever, then they the said Supervisors or the Majority of them with the concurrence of one or more of the said Judges shall cause all such deficiencies to be assessed and levied of the County, as other County Charges, so that the whole of such Deficiencies be paid into the said Loan Officers by the third Tuesday of April then next following.

XXXI. AND BE IT ENACTED by the Authority aforesaid That In Case one or more of the said Judges and a Majority of the Supervisors aforesaid shall not meet on the first Tuesday of March next to come, or in Case they shall not meet yearly on the first Tuesday in October, or on the several and respective Tuesdays herein before appointed for the Counties of Suffolk, Ulster and Dutchess, or in Case they shall not meet when summoned by a Precept of one or more of the said Judges for the several Purposes in this Act mentioned, every of them in either of these Cases that are absent unless detained by sickness shall forfeit the Sum of three Pounds, and the Judge or Judges then attending shall issue his or their Precept to one or more Constables to summon the Judges and Supervisors to attend that Day Week for the purposes aforesaid, under double the Penalty aforesaid, which each neglecting then to attend if duly summoned shall also forfeit, tho' a sufficient Number do appear. And in Case a sufficient Number do not then appear the Judge or Judges appearing shall proceed in like Manner from Week to Week till a full Number of Supervisors do appear to perform the Duty for which they before ought to have met. And in Case the said supervisors or Vestrymen or either of them, when a Majority of them are met, shall neglect or refuse to take the Oath or Affirmation herein prescribed or neglect or refuse to do the Duty enjoined them by this Act when met, or shall on any pretence whatsoever on the Day of their annual Meeting, neglect or omit the Causing to be assessed levied and raised the whole Deficiencies that have happened by any of the means aforesaid, every of them neglecting their Duty herein shall forfeit to his Majesty the Sum of five Pounds, all which Penalties before in this Clause mentioned are to be recovered before any one of his Majesty's Justices of the Peace within the City or County where such Forfeiture shall arise, one half to the use of such Judge or Judges and Supervisors of the same County endeavouring to perform their Duty herein, who will Sue and inform against the rest, and prosecute their Suit to effect, and the other half to be paid to the Treasurer and applied towards cancelling the Bills of Credit in such manner as shall be directed by Act or Acts of the General Assembly.

XXXII AND BE IT ENACTED That all and every the Sums of Money which may at any Time afterwards be recovered by the Loan Officers aforesaid of such Persons as have been the Occasion of such Deficiencies as aforesaid shall be applied to the use of such County, and the Judge or Judges and supervisors are hereby impowered to take all lawful ways and means in the Name of the said Loan Officers to recover the Same.

XXXIII AND BE IT ENACTED by the Authority aforesaid That it shall and may be Lawful for the said Loan Officers to let out upon Loan any of the said Bills of Credit in such Manner as they shall think best upon Security of good Plate to be delivered to them at six Shillings per Ounce to be paid in again to the said Loan Officers on the third Tuesday of April then next with a Years Interest at five per Cent for the same, and in Case of non-payment at any of the two first stated Days of Meeting of the Loan Officers, then the said Loan Officers are to sell the same Plate in such Manner, and upon the same Day as they are directed to sell the Lands of the Mortgages forfeited as aforesaid, and they are to return the Overplus to the Owner (if any be) after payment of the principal and charges with Interest past and to come until the third Tuesday of April then next to come, unless a Borrower Offers at Time of Sale as in Case of Lands herein before mentioned, any Thing in this Act to the contrary notwithstanding.

XXXIV AND BE IT ENACTED That if any of the said Monies shall remain in the Hands of the Loan Officers four Weeks after the first Day of letting it out, for want of Borrowers, it shall be lawful for them to let out the same on good security by Mortgage of Lands in the County, or on Plate as aforesaid to any Person who will borrow the same in any Sums though they be upwards of three hundred Pounds.

XXXV. BE IT ENACTED by the authority aforesaid That if any of the Bills of Credit shall remain four Weeks over and above the four Weeks aforesaid, that is to say in all eight Weeks in the Hands of the Loan Officers for want of Borrowers after the first Day of letting out as aforesaid, then and in that Case the said Loan Officers or one of them by consent of the other to be entered and signed in the Minute Book of proceedings, shall carry it to the Loan Officers of the next County or Counties where there were more Monies demanded in Loan than there were Monies to lend and deliver it to the Loan Officers of such next County, upon their Receipt for the same, and their entering a Memorandum of it in the Minutes of their proceedings, which Loan Officers to whom such Sum is brought shall accept thereof, and shall set up Advertisements thereof, and therein assign a Day in the next Week for Borrowers to offer, and shall proceed in the lending this further Sum in their County as nearly as Circumstances of Things can admit, in the like Manner as they proceeded in lending the first Sum, of which transposition of those Monies, the Loan Officers of the several Counties shall give Notice in writing signed by them to the Treasurer at the Time of their paying to him the first Interest Monies thereafter, of which Notices to him, he shall enter Memorandums in his Books of Accounts the better to ascertain the Interest he is to receive yearly from the respective Counties, and the Principal Sums that the Counties are finally to cancel.

XXXVI. AND to prevent Frauds that may happen by Executors or Administrators in their non payment of any Part of the Money borrowed as aforesaid by their respective Testators or Intestates BE IT ENACTED That if any Person or Persons that shall become Borrowers of the Bills issued by virtne of this Act, and shall afterwards make his her or their last Will and Testament in due form of Law, thereby devising the Premises so mortgaged to any other Person or Persons, leaving Personal Estate sufficient to pay his or her Debts with an overplus not otherwise in the said Will disposed of, and not expressly providing in other manner by the said Will, in such Case it shall be understood that the Devisor intended that the Mortgage Money in arrear at the Time of his Death should be paid out of his Personal Estate, and his Executor or Executors shall be accordingly compelled to pay the same thereout in aid of such Devisee or Devisees. But in Case the said last Will was made before the premises were mortgaged, then it shall be understood that the Testators Intent was (Unless otherwise expressed in such Will) that the Devisee or Devisees should pay the Residue of the Mortgage Money in Arrear at the Time of such Testator's Death, and in Case any Executor or Executors contrary to the Intent of this Act having Effects sufficient, shall permit a Sale to be made of the premises mortgaged such Devisee or Devisees may immediately have his her or their Action either in proper Person or by Guardian or next Friend if under Age, against such Executor or Executors, and recover double the Damages sustained with Costs of suit, and in Case any Executor, or Executors shall in such Case be a purchaser of the Pemises so mortgaged or any other in Trust for him, or for his use, he or they shall be deemed seized of the Premises for the use of the Devisee or Devisees, and such Executor or Executors and their Trustees are hereby disabled from making any Conveyance thereof, from such Devisee or Devisees, and if any such Conveyance is made, the same is hereby declared fraudulent and Void against such Devisee or Devisees.

XXXVII AND BE IT ENACTED That in Case any Mortgagor die Intestate, the Mortgage Money aforesaid, or any Part thereof being in arrear and unpaid and leaving personal Estate sufficient to pay his Debts with an Overplus, his Heir at Law being under age when any Part of the said Mortgage Money shall become due, in such Cases the Mortgage Monies shall be paid out of the Personal Estate if sufficient, and the profits of the Premises mortgaged shall be applied towards repayment of the said Monies to such Person or Persons as may be entitled to the same, where it so happens that the Part of the Personal Estate coming to the said Heir at Law is not sufficient to discharge such Mortgage, and in Case the Profits of the Mortgaged Premises shall not be sufficient to make such Repayment, the Heir at Law shall be compelled to make it up with Interest, when he she or they come of age, and where any Sales shall happen to be made pursuant to the Tenor of this Act after the Death of the Testator or Intestate, because of the Deficiency of the personal Estate of the Testator or Intestate, his or her Heirs or Devisees being then under Age, in such Case the Monies arising by such Sale after the Deduction of the Principal Interests and Costs due to the said Loan Office, shall be placed out to Interest by the Executors or Administrators for the Benefit of such Heir or Devisee, or Person intitled to such Lands.

XXXVIII AND BE IT ENACTED by the Authority aforesaid that the Borrowers may pay their Interest and Principals in any of the Bills of Credit of this Colony, or in Silver or Gold, or Lyon Dollars, and the Treasurer and Loan Officers shall accept thereof in lieu of the Bills issued by virtue of this Act.

XXXIX. AND BE IT ENACTED by the Authority aforesaid That if any Person shall falsely swear or Affirm in any of the

Cases where an Oath or Affirmation is required to be taken by this Act or shall Wilfully or knowingly Act contrary to the Oath or Affirmation he has before taken, such Offence is hereby declared to be perjury, and the Offender being convicted thereof shall suffer all the Pains and Penalties of Perjury, which by the Laws of Great Britain can be inflicted.

XL. AND BE IT FURTHER ENACTED That all Judges and Justices in this Colony shall and they are hereby directed to construe this Act most favourable for the prosecutor, and most strongly against the Offender, and shall allow him or her no Essoin, Protection or Wager of Law, nor more than one Imparlance, and shall endeavour the execution of this Act according to the true Intent and meaning thereof notwithstanding the want of apt Words to express the same, and if Mischiefs should happen, which may affect the Public or any private Person or the Credit of the Bills issued by virtue of this Act, against which no Remedies are expressly provided by this Act; but if there happen to be Remedies against like Mischiefs, they the said Judges and Justices shall construe and extend the like Remedies to and for the like Mischiefs, according to the true Intent and meaning of this Act, any Law, usage or Custom to the contrary notwithstanding.

XLI AND BE IT ALSO ENACTED by the Authority aforesaid That the Bills of Credit issued by virtue of this Act shall be cancelled in like Manner as the Bills of Credit were cancelled, that were emitted by virtue of an Act intitled "An Act for the "more effectual cancelling the Bills of Credit of this Colony". passed the eighth Day of April one thousand seven hundred and forty eight; and the Act intitled "An Act to amend an Act inti-"tled An Act for the more effectual cancelling the Bills of Credit "of this Colony." passed the fourth Day of July one thousand seven hundred and fifty three.

XLII. AND BE IT FURTHER ENACTED by the Authority aforesaid That the Loan Officers for the County of Orange shall be elected and chosen in the following Manner that is to say one of the said Loan Officers being a sufficient Freeholder shall be chosen at the Court House in Goshen Town on the first Tuesday in March next by the two Supervisors of Goshen and Cornwall Precincts, and the Judges and such as are Justices of the Quorum for said County dwelling and residing in said two Precincts by the Plurality of Votes of those that shall meet at said Election, and the other Loan Officer being a sufficient Freeholder, shall in like manner be chosen at the Court House in Orange Town on the first Tuesday in March next by the two Supervisors of Haverstraw and Orange Town Precincts, and the Judges, and such as are Justices of the Quorum for said County dwelling and residing in said last mentioned Precincts, and that the Supervisors and Judges of the said County shall on the first Tuesday of October which will be in the Year of our Lord one thousand seven hundred and seventy two, meet at the Court House at Orange Town with the Loan Officers of the said County, and the Year following at the Court House at Goshen, and so alternately each Year during the continuance of this Act.

XLIII. AND BE IT ENACTED by the Authority aforesaid That Theodorus Van Wyck, Andrew Barclay, and Nicholas Governeur Esquires shall be the Loan Officers for the City and County of New York any Thing in this Act to the contrary thereof in any wise notwithstanding.

XLIV. AND BE IT ENACTED by the Authority aforesaid That John H. Ten Eyck and Hermanus Wendell Esquires shall be the Loan Officers for the City and County of Albany, and Richard Snediker and Jacobus Swartwout Esquires shall be the Loan Officers for the County of Dutchess, and Christopher Tappen and Joseph Gasherie Esquires shall be the Loan Officers for the County of Ulster, and that in Case of the Death or refusal of any of them the Judges and Supervisors of the said City and County of Albany and the Judges and Supervisors of the said Counties of Dutchess and Ulster respectively shall appoint others as is directed by this Act in the other Counties, any Thing in this Act to the contrary notwithstanding.

XLV. AND BE IT FURTHER ENACTED by the Authority aforesaid That the respective Loan Officers within this Colony for the Time being shall permit and suffer any Person or Persons at seasonable Times to search and view the Books of Mortgages in their Hands and Custody, upon their paying one Shilling for the search, and the Mortgages entered as aforesaid shall be of equal force and validity, and have the same effect as those entered in the Register of the respective Counties.

XLVI. BE IT ALSO ENACTED That the Interest of the Money arising by virtue of this Act shall be and remain in the Treasury until it shall be disposed of by Act or Acts hereafter to be passed for that purpose.

[CHAPTER 1473.]

[Chapter 1473 of Van Schaack, where the act is printed in full.]

An Act to facilitate and explain the Duty of the Loan Officers in this Colony.

[Passed, February 16, 1771.]

I. BE IT ENACTED by his Excellency the Governor the Council and the General Assembly, and it is hereby Enacted by the Authority of the same That for the greater uniformity in the Securities to be taken in the Loan Offices for the Money to be lent by virtue of an Act of the General Assembly of this Colony intitled. "An Act for emitting the Sum of one hundred and "twenty thousand Pounds in Bills of Credit to be put out on "Loan, and to appropriate the Interest arising thereon to the "Payment of the Debts of this Colony, and to such Public Exigen- "cies as the Circumstances of this Colony may from Time to Time "render necessary." The Mortgages for the Money by virtue of the said Act lent, shall be in the form following vizt.

THIS INDENTURE made the .... Day of .... in the .... Year of the Reign of our Sovereign Lord George the third, by the Grace of God of Great Britain France and Ireland King Defender of the Faith &c. Annoq. Domini one thousand seven hundred and .... BETWEEN.......... of the County of .... of one Part, and the Loan Officers of the said .... of .... of the other Part WIT- NESSETH That the said .... for and in Consideration of the Sum of .... by the Loan Officers of the .... of .... to him well and truly in Hand paid, whereof he grants the Receipt and acknowledges himself to be therewith contented, and for himself his Heirs, Executors and Adminis- trators releases and discharges the Loan Officers of the .... of .... and their Successors thereof forever. HATH Granted, Bargained. Sold, Released Enfeoffed and Confirmed, and by these presents DOTH Grant Bargain, Sell, Release Enfeoff and Confirm to the Loan Officers of the .... of .... and their Successors and Assigns for ever all That .... TOGETHER with all and all Manner of Woods, Underwoods, Trees, Mines, Minerals, Quarries Hawkings, Huntings, Fowlings, Fishings, Buildings, Fences, Improvements, Hereditaments and Appurtenances whatsoever to the same belonging or in any ways appertaining, and all the Estate, Right, Title, Interests, possession, property Claim and Demand of the said .... and his Heirs to the above Bargained Premises and every Part thereof TO HAVE AND TO HOLD the above bargained Premises to the Loan Officers of the .... of .... their Successors and Assigns forever to the uses and purposes mentioned in an Act of the General Assembly of this Colony, passed in the eleventh Year of the Reign of King George the third intitled, "An Act for emitting the Sum of one hundred and twenty thou- "sand Pounds in Bills of Credit to be put out on Loan, and to "appropriate the Interest arising thereon to the payment of the "Debts of this Colony, and to such Public Exigencies as the "Circumstances of this Colony may from Time to Time render "necessary." and the said .... for himself his Heirs, Executors and Administrators, does Covenant, Grant, Bargain and agree, to and with the Loan Officers of the .... of .... and their Successors that at and before the Time of the ensealing and delivery hereof he the said .... stood lawfully seized of the above bargained Premises of a good sure perfect absolute and indefeazible Estate of Inheritance in the Law in Fee Simple, and that the same then were free and clear of all former and other Gifts, Grants, Bargains, Sales, Leases, Releases, Judgments, Extents, Recognizances, Dowers, Entails and other Incumbrances in the Law whatsoever. PROVIDED ALWAYS and these presents are upon this Condition, That if the said .... his Heirs Executors, Administrators or Assigns do pay or cause to be paid to the Loan Officers of the .... of .... the Interest at the Rate of five per cent of the said Principal Sum of .... on the third Tuesday of April yearly until the third Tuesday of April which will be in the Year of our Lord one thousand seven hundred and seventy five inclusive, and if the said .... or his aforesaids shall pay to the Loan Officers of the .... of .... the one tenth Part of the said Principal Sum of .... on the third Tuesday of April which will be in the Year of our Lord one thousand seven hundred and seventy six together with the Interest due on the said Principal Sum of .... and one other tenth Part of the said Principal Sum on the third Tuesday of April, which will be in the Year of our Lord one thousand seven hundred and seventy seven together with the Interest then due, and one other tenth Part of the said Principal Sum on the third Tuesday of April which will be in the Year of our Lord one thousand seven hundred and seventy eight, together with the Interest then due, one other tenth Part of the said Principal Sum on the third Tuesday of April which will be in the Year of our Lord one thousand seven hundred and seventy nine, together with the Interest then due, and one other tenth Part of the said Principal Sum on the third Tuesday of April which will be in the Year of our Lord one thousand seven hundred and eighty, together with the Interest then due, and one other tenth Part of the said Principal Sum on the third Tuesday of April which will be in the Year of our Lord one thousand seven hundred and eighty one, together with the Interest then due, and one other tenth Part of the said Principal Sum on the third Tuesday of April which will be in the Year of our Lord one thousand seven hundred and eighty two, together with the Interest then due, and one other tenth Part of the said Principal Sum on the third Tuesday of April which will be in the Year of our Lord one thousand seven hundred and eighty three together with Interest then due, and one other tenth Part of the said Principal Sum on the third Tuesday of April which will be in the Year of our Lord one thousand seven hundred and eighty four, together with the Interest then due, and the Remainder of the said Principal Sum on the third Tuesday of April which will be in the Year of our Lord one thousand seven hundred and eighty five. together with the Interest then due thereon, according to the true Intent and meaning of the said Act of General Assembly, then the above Grant Bargain and Sale and every Article and Clause thereof shall be void. But if failure be made in any of the payments abovementioned, then the above bargain and Sale is to remain in full Force and virtue and the said .... for himself his Heirs and Assigns doth agree to be absolutely barred of all equity of Redemption of the premises within twenty two Days after such Failure. and the said .... for himself his Heirs Executors and Administrators does Covenant, Grant, Bargain, Promise and agree to and with the Loan Officers of the .... of .... and their successors well and truly to pay to them all and every of the Sums of Money abovementioned at the Times on which the same ought to be paid as aforesaid, and that the above bargained Premises upon the Sale thereof pursuant to the Directions of the said Act, will yield the Principal and Interest aforesaid remaining unpaid at the Time of such

Sale and until the third Tuesday of April next after the Day of Sale together with fifteen Shillings for the Charge of such Sale. IN WITNESS whereof the Parties to these Present Indentures, have hereunto interchangeably set their Hands and Seals the Day and Year first above Written

SEALED and DELIVERED in the presence of.

II. AND BE IT ENACTED by the Authority aforesaid that Hugh Gaine shall print six thousand Copies of the said Mortgages, and bind so many of them into a Book together with six Leaves of clean Paper for an Alphabet for the use of the Loan Office of each County that there may be a Mortgage for every twenty five Pounds of Bills of Credit given to the Loan Office of that County, and the Number remaining he shall give in loose Sheets in the like Proportion to each of the Loan Offices in Order therewith (if there should be Occasion) to give attested Copies of the Original Mortgages to the Buyers of any of the mortgaged Lands which Books together with the said loose Sheets are to be delivered by the Printer to the Treasurer of this Colony, by him with the Bills to be delivered to the Loan Officers of each County.

III. AND BE IT ENACTED that no Mortgage shall be taken in the Loan Offices, but by filling up one of the Blanks of the said Book of Mortgages, none of them shall be defaced nor torn out, except the Seal when the Mortgagor pays off the whole Principal and Interest of the Mortgage, and the Loan Officers shall proceed in the taking of the Mortgages, from the Beginning of the Book forward, numbering the Mortgages as they are taken, and inserting the Mortgagor's Name, and the Number in the Alphabet under the Letter answering the Mortgagor's Sirname.

IV. AND BE IT ENACTED That the Printer shall also bind up ten Books of Clean Paper, one for the use of each Loan Office, and to contain about two thirds of the bigness of the Book of Mortgages for the same County to be delivered as aforesaid with the Book of Mortgages.

V. BE IT ENACTED That the Loan Officers shall in one End of the last Book, minute the Substance of each Mortgage to wit. The Number thereof, the Date, the Mortgagor's Name, the Sum lent, and the Boundaries of the Lands mortgaged, and when the one Loan Officer has the Custody of the Book of Mortgages, the other shall have the Custody of this Book, that Fire or other Accidents which may happen may be guarded against, and the Printer shall make an Alphabet to it, like to that of the

Book of Mortgages, and to prevent any deception of the Mortgagor, he shall examine or see the Minute examined with the Original Mortgage and he with the Witnesses shall sign to the same.

VI. AND BE IT ENACTED That the Loan Officers beginning at the other End of the said Book, shall insert the Minutes of their proceedings therein, to wit.

1st. The Days they meet, Place, House, and Loan Officers present.

2d. If any is absent shall the next Time minute the Cause of his absence.

3d. Shall enter the Hour that every one demands the Loan of Money, and the Quantity he demands.

4th. Shall enter down the Reason why a Prior demander had not the Money according to his demand, and the Substance of Examinations for clearing Titles and value.

5th. Shall enter down the Monies received from the Treasurer, and the Monies delivered to or received from the Loan Officers of another County, and the Day when, with Copy of the Notice thereof to be delivered to the Treasurer, and when that Notice was delivered to the Treasurer and by whom.

6th. The last Day of their four Days of meeting for receiving of Monies yearly, they shall enter whose Mortgages are foreclosed, and the Numbers and Sums of them.

7th. Shall enter the Orders for, and Copies of the Advertisements of Sale, and places at which they were to be set up, and Persons Names that are to set them up.

8th: Shall enter the Buyer's Name of Lands and Price sold for, and payment of the Overplus to whom it belongs, with the Time and Witnesses of such payment.

9th. In Case any Principals or Part thereof are paid in before the Times of payment in the Mortgages, the Totals of such Principals so paid in shall be entered in this Book with Copy of the Advertisement of lending out again, and on the Day of Demand advertised the Names of the Demanders thereof and they shall in that Case proceed as before.

10th. Shall enter the Cause of all Suits and the Informations they have received, and of whom and how at length, or if too long refer to them in papers apart, minuting the substance.

11th. Shall enter their Meetings with the Judges and Supervisors, and persons present, together with the Minutes of all acted with tnem, particularly what were the Deficiencies laid before them, what was resolved on for the Assessing and levying them, who for assessing them, who for neglecting or delaying it.

12th: Every other Thing remarkable that has any relation to their Office, and not otherwise directed about, shall be entered in the Minute Book of their Proceedings except their Accounts.

VII AND BE IT ENACTED that the Printer shall also bind up other ten Books of clean paper, one of them for the use of each Loan Office, about two thirds of the bigness of the Book of Mortgages for the same County to be delivered as aforesaid with the Book of Mortgages.

VIII BE IT ENACTED that therein shall be entered all the Accounts of the Loan Office, That at the Beginning there shall be an Alphabet wherein shall be inserted every Man's Name, and the Leaf wherein his Account stands, and that this Book be kept in the fairest and best method that the Loan Officers can, and it is to remain in the Custody of him who has the Minutes of the Mortgages and proceedings.

IX AND BE IT ENACTED that the Deeds to be granted by the Loan Officers for any Lands to be sold by them, whereof the Equity of Redemption is foreclosed, shall be in form following, to wit.

THIS INDENTURE made the .... Tuesday of .... in the .... Year of the Reign of our Sovereign Lord George the third by the Grace of God of Great Britain, France and Ireland King Defender of the Faith &c. Annoq. Domini, one thousand seven hundred and .... BETWEEN the Loan Officers of the .... of .... of the one Part, and .... of the other Part WITNESSETH That the Loan Officers of the .... of .... for and in Consideration of the Sum of .... to them in hand paid whereof they grant the Receipt and discharge the said .... his Heirs Executors and Administrators hereof forever. HAVE pursuant to an Act of the General Assembly of this Colony intitled. "An Act for emitting the Sum of one hundred and twenty thousand Pounds in Bills of Credit to be put out on Loan, and to appropriate the Interest arising thereon to the payment of the Debts of this Colony and to such Public Exigencies as the Circumstances of this Colony may from Time to Time render necessary." granted bargained sold, released enfeoffed and confirmed, and by these presents do grant, bargain, sell, Release, enfeoff and confirm unto the said .... his Heirs and Assigns All that .... TOGETHER with all and all Manner of Woods, Underwoods, Trees, Mines, Minerals, Quarries, Hawkings, Huntings, Fowlings, Fishings, Fences, Improvements, Hereditaments and Appurtenances whatsoever to the same belonging or in any wise appertaining, and all the Estate Right Title Interest Claim possession property and demand whatsoever of the Loan Officers of the .... of .... and their Successors to the above bargained Premises and every Part thereof. TO HAVE AND TO HOLD the above bargained premises and every Part thereof with the Appurtenances to the said .... his Heirs and Assigns, to the sole and only proper use Benefit and Behoof of the said .... his Heirs and Assigns forever IN WITNESS whereof the Loan Officers of the .... of .... have hereunto set the Seal of their Corporation together with their Hands the Day and Year above written.

SEALED and DELIVERED in the presence of

To which Deed the Loan Officers are to put only one Seal as the Seal of the Loan Office, and jointly take off the Seal from the Wax, and all sign their Names.

X. AND BE IT ENACTED That upon every Sale of Lands the Loan Officers shall fill up one of the loose Sheets of Blank Mortgages like to the Original Mortgage and attest the same as a true Copy under their Hands and the Seal of the Loan Office, and give it instead of the Original Mortgage for Evidence of the Title of the Buyer, and the Bond to be entered into by the Loan Officers shall be in the form following vizt.

KNOW ALL MEN by these Presents That we .... are held and firmly Bound unto our most gracious Sovereign Lord George the Third by the Grace of God of Great Britain France and Ireland King Defender of the Faith &c. in the Sum of .... to be paid unto our most gracious Sovereign Lord the King and his Successors, to the which payment well and truly to be made and done, we bind ourselves, our Heirs Executors and Administrators and every of us and them jointly and severally firmly by these Presents, sealed with our Seals and dater the .... Day of .... in the .... Year of his Majesty's Reign Annoq Domini one thousand seven hundred and ....

THE CONDITIONS of the above Obligation is such that if the above Bounden .... shall well and truly perform the

Office and duty of one of the Loan Officers of the .... of .... and shall demean himself therein without favour Malice or Partiality, then the above Obligation to be void, otherwise to remain in full force and virtue.

SEALED and DELIVERED in the presence of.

XI. AND BE IT ENACTED and declared that in Case of the Forfeiture of such Bond as aforesaid, the Suit thereon shall be staid on the Defendants paying or tendering in Court to pay the Damages arisen by the Breach of the Condition of the Bond sued, with the Costs to that Time, and if Judgment be had thereon, a Jury shall enquire of the Damages according to the Form of the Statute in that Case made and provided.

XII. BE IT ENACTED for the better satisfaction of the Loan Officers as to the Title and value of what is offered in Mortgage by Borrowers, the Loan Officers or either of them are hereby authorized and impowered to examine the Borrower and Witnesses upon Oath or Affirmation if Quakers, concerning the same, a brief Minute of which Examination, and of the Names of the Persons so examined they shall enter into their Minute Book of proceedings.

[CHAPTER 1474.]

[Chapter 1474 of Van Schaack, where the title only is printed.]

An Act for making a further Provision of two thousand Pounds for furnishing his Majesty's Troops quartered in this Colony with Necessaries for one Year.

[Passed, February 16, 1771.]

BE IT ENACTED by his Excellency the Governor the Council and the General Assembly, and it is hereby Enacted by the Authority of the same. That the Treasurer of this Colony shall pay, and he is hereby directed and required (out of the Interest Money arising from the Bill now depending for emitting Bills of Credit to the amount of one hundred and twenty thousand Pounds.) to pay, such Sum or Sums of Money as shall from Time to Time be necessary for Quartering his Majesty's Troops in this Colony for one Year from the first Day of January one thousand seven hundred and seventy one, on Warrant or Warrants to be drawn for that purpose, by his Excellency the Governor or Commander in Chief for the Time being by and with the Advice and Consent of his Majesty's Council, provided the whole Sum so to be drawn for, does not exceed the Sum of two thousand Pounds.

AND BE IT ENACTED by the Authority aforesaid that the Treasurer shall keep exact Books of his payments by Virtue of this Act, and a true and just Account thereof shall render upon Oath to the Governor or Commander in Chief for the Time being, the Council or the General Assembly, when by them or any of them thereunto required.

[CHAPTER 1475.]

[Chapter 1475 of Van Schaack, where the title only is printed.]

An Act for the payment of the Salaries of the several Officers of this Colony, and other purposes therein mentioned.

[Passed, February 16, 1771.]

BE IT ENACTED by his Excellency the Governor the Council and the General Assembly, and it is hereby Enacted by the Authority of the same That the Treasurer of this Colony shall and hereby is directed and required out of the Monies arisen or which may arise by virtue of the following Acts Vizt: An Act intitled. "An Act further to continue an Act intitled An Act for "granting to his Majesty the several Duties and Impositions on "Goods Wares and Merchandizes imported into this Colony "therein mentioned". an Act intitled. "An Act for collecting the "Duty of Excise on strong Liquors retailed in this Colony from "the first Day of January in the Year of our Lord one thousand "seven hundred and seventy one, to the first Day of February "one thousand seven hundred and seventy two inclusive." an Act intitled "An Act for regulating the Sale of Goods to be sold "at Public Vendue, Auction or Outcry within this Colony." an Act intitled. "An Act to amend an Act intitled An Act for regu-"lating the sale of Goods to be sold at Public Vendue Auction "or Outcry within this Colony." An Act intitled. "An Act to "continue An Act intitled An Act to restrain Hawkers and Ped-"lers within this Colony from selling without License." and an Act intitled "An Act for raising six thousand Pounds by way "of Lottery for the Purposes therein mentioned," to pay.

UNTO his Honor Lieutenant Governor Cadwallader Colden Esquire for his administering the Government of this Colony from the first Day of September one thousand seven hundred and seventy, to the eighteenth Day of October following after the Rate of two thousand Pounds per Annum.

UNTO his said Honor for Fire Wood and Candles for his Majesty's Fort George in the City of New York from and to the Time aforesaid after the Rate of four hundred Pounds per Annum.

UNTO his Excellency the Right Honorable John Earl of Dunmore for Fire-Wood and Candles for his Majesty's Fort George in the City of New York from the eighteenth Day of October one thousand seven hundred and seventy, to the first Day of September one thousand seven hundred and seventy one, after the Rate of four hundred Pounds Per Annum.

UNTO the Honorable Daniel Horsemanden Esquire as Chief Justice of the Supreme Court of this Colony, and for going the Circuits from the first Day of September one thousand seven hundred and seventy, to the first Day of September one thousand seven hundred and seventy one after the Rate of three hundred Pounds per Annum.

UNTO the Honorable David Jones Esquire one of the Puisne Justices of the supreme Court of this Colony, and for going the Circuits from and to the Time aforesaid after the Rate of two hundred Pounds per Annum.

UNTO the Honorable Robert R Livingston Esquire one other of the Puisne Justices of the supreme Court of this Colony and for going the Circuits from and to the Time aforesaid after the Rate of two hundred Pounds Per Annum.

UNTO the Honorable George D Ludlow Esquire the other Puisne Justice of the Supreme Court of this Colony and for going the Circuits from and to the Time aforesaid after the Rate of two hundred Pounds per Annum.

UNTO the Secretary of this Colony for the Time being for engrossing and enrolling the Acts of the General Assembly, from and to the Time aforesaid after the Rate of forty Pounds per Annum.

UNTO the Clerk of the Council for the Time being for his Services in that Station from and to the Time aforesaid the Sum of thirty Pounds.

UNTO the Doorkeeper of the Council for the Time being for his Services in that Station from and to the Time aforesaid the Sum of thirty Pounds.

UNTO Hugh Gaine for services performed as Public Printer of this Colony from and to the Time aforesaid the Sum of one hundred and fifty Pounds.

UNTO John Kip as Gauger of Liquor subject to a Duty within this Colony or to the Gauger thereof for the Time being from and to the Time aforesaid after the Rate of thirty Pounds per Annum.

UNTO Thomas Hill and Josias Smith Land and Tide Waiters, or to the Land and Tide Waiters for the Time being for their Services in that Station from and to the Time aforesaid after the Rate of fifty Pounds per Annum to each of them.

ALL which aforesaid several Sums of Money shall be paid by the Treasurer on Warrants issued by his Excellency the Governor or the Commander in Chief for the Time being by and with the Advice and Consent of his Majesty's Council of this Colony, and the Receipts of the several Persons endorsed on the said Warrants shall be to the Treasurer good Vouchers and Discharges for so much as shall be thereby acknowledged to be received.

AND BE IT ENACTED by the Authority aforesaid, That the Treasurer shall be, and hereby is directed and required out of the Funds aforesaid to pay the several Allowances following to wit.

UNTO Abraham Lott Esquire Treasurer of this Colony for his Services in that Station from the first Day of September, one thousand seven hundred and seventy, to the first Day of September one thousand Seven hundred and Seventy one, after the Rate of two hundred Pounds per Annum.

UNTO the said Treasurer for the extraordinary Services which he is now obliged to perform beyond the usual Duty of his Office after the Rate of the further Sum of one hundred Pounds.

UNTO the Agent of this Colony in Great Britain from the twenty first Day of December one thousand seven hundred and seventy, to the first Day of September one thousand seven hundred and seventy one after the Rate of five hundred Pounds per Annum.

UNTO John Tabor Kemp Esquire for extraordinary Services performed by him as Attorney General of this Colony from the first Day of September one thousand seven hundred and seventy to the first Day of September one thousand seven hundred and seventy one after the Rate of one hundred and fifty Pounds per Annum.

UNTO Edmund Seaman Esquire as Clerk to the General Assembly for his Services in that Station from and to the Time aforesaid twenty Shillings per Diem payable upon a Certificate from the General Assembly signed by the Speaker for the Number of Days he has or may serve the General Assembly.

UNTO the said Edmund Seaman for Sundry Disbursements by him made for the use of the General Assembly the Sum of fifty four Pounds six Shillings and two Pence.

UNTO Gerard Bancker as Assistant Clerk to the General Assembly, for his services in that Station from and to the Time aforesaid twenty Shillings per Diem payable upon a Certificate from the General Assembly signed by the Speaker for the Number of Days he has or may serve the General Assembly.

UNTO the said Gerard Bancker for Services performed by him respecting the Settlement of the Jersey Line the Sum of three Pounds.

UNTO Alexander Lamb Doorkeeper of the General Assembly for his Services in that Station from and to the Time aforesaid six Shillings per Diem payable upon a Certificate from the General Assembly signed by the Speaker for the Number of Days he has or may serve the General Assembly.

UNTO the said Alexander Lamb for providing Fire Wood and sundry Necessaries for the use of the General Assembly the Sum of fifty five Pounds.

UNTO William Scott Serjeant at Arms for his Services in that Station from and to the Time aforesaid four Shillings per Diem payable upon a Certificate from the General Assembly signed by the Speaker for the Number of Days he has or may serve the General Assembly.

UNTO John Martin as Gunner and Keeper of the Colony Stores from the twenty eighth Day of July one thousand seven hundred and seventy to the twenty eighth Day of July one thousand seven hundred and seventy one after the Rate of twenty Pounds per Annum.

AND BE IT ENACTED by the Authority aforesaid That for answering the Expences of Contingencies, and extraordinary Emergencies that have or may happen for the Services of this Colony from the first Day of September one thousand seven hundred and seventy to the first Day of September one thousand seven hundred and seventy one, Warrants may issue for the same on the Treasurer from Time to Time if drawn by his Excellency the Governor or Commander in Chief for the Time being with the Advice and Consent of his Majesty's Council, which the Treasurer is hereby ordered and directed to pay out of the Monies arising by virtue of the Acts herein before mentioned. Provided the amount of the said Warrants do not exceed the Sum of one hundred Pounds during that Time.

AND BE IT ENACTED by the Authority aforesaid, That the Treasurer of this Colony shall out of the Funds aforesaid pay the several Sums following, to wit

UNTO Jacob Walton Esquire for purchasing Timber and Plank, and for making Gun Carriages, and Platforms for the Guns in the Fort and Battery in the City of New York the Sum of one thousand Pounds.

UNTO Robert Mc. Ginnos in Consideration of the many Hardships he suffered in the Service of this Colony during the last War, in the loss of his Arm &c. twenty five Pounds.

UNTO Alexander Whyte late Captain in the Service of this Colony for Money advanced by him for the use of his Company in the Year one thousand seven hundred and sixty four, the Sum of forty seven Pounds fourteen Shillings and three Pence.

UNTO Henry Dawson late Captain in the Service of this Colony for Money advanced by him for the use of his Company in the Year one thousand seven hundred and sixty four, the Sum of fifty Pounds seven Shillings and five Pence.

UNTO Barnaby Byrne late Captain in the Service of this Colony for Money advanced by him for the use of his Company in the Year one thousand seven hundred and sixty four, the Sum of twenty nine Pounds nine Shillings and one penny.

UNTO John Grant late Captain in the Service of this Colony for Money advanced by him for the use of his Company in the Year one thousand seven hundred and sixty four, the Sum of fifty Pounds eighteen Shillings and ten Pence.

UNTO Alexander Charles as Administrator to the late Robert Charles Agent for this Colony in Great Britain or his Order the sum of three hundred and fifty four Pounds three Shillings and four Pence New York Currency as a reward for the said Agent's Care, Trouble and Diligence in attending upon his Majesty and his Ministers of State, in that Station, from the first Day of September one thousand seven hundred and sixty nine, to the fifteenth Day of May one thousand seven hundred and seventy.

UNTO the said Alexander Charles or his Order, as Administrator as aforesaid the further Sum of three hundred and fifty two Pounds seventeen Shillings and two pence Sterling for Sundry Disbursements made by the said Agent from the first Day of January one thousand seven hundred and sixty six to the first Day of May one thousand seven hundred and seventy.

UNTO James DeLancey and Jacob Walton Esquires for Monies advanced by them for the Freight of the Statues of his Majesty and Lord Chatham, and for erecting the same in this City, the Sum of eight hundred and eight Pounds six Shillings and seven Pence, including the Sum of two hundred Pounds which has been paid them by the Treasurer in consequence of a Vote of the General Assembly made during the last Session.

UNTO John Cruger Esquire for Services performed by him as Agent on the Part of this Colony in managing the Controversy about the Boundary or Partition Line between the Colonies of New York and New Jersey the Sum of one hundred Pounds.

UNTO John De Noyellis and William Wickham Esquires for their Expences and Disbursements in running the Line of Partition between the Colonies of New York and New Jersey as decreed by his Majesty's Commissioners in the Year one thousand seven hundred and sixty nine, and pursuant to an agreement entered into by three of the Agents of New York, the Committee of Correspondence and the said John DeNoyellis Esquire; and by four of the Agents of New Jersey the Sum of two hundred and fifty six Pounds eleven Shillings and ten Pence one farthing.

UNTO the said John De Noyellis Esquire for his Attendance and Expences in New York during the Negotiation of the said Agreement from the twenty third Day of January one thousand seven hundred and seventy, to the twenty seventh Day of April following being ninety seven Days the sum of seventy seven Pounds twelve Shillings.

UNTO John Cruger Esquire Speaker of the General Assembly to be laid out in the necessary Repairs about Fort George in this City, the House therein, and for Removing the Barracks out of the said Fort, and erecting them on some other place a Sum not exceeding twelve hundred and seventy five Pounds.

UNTO Simon Metcalfe for his Services and Expences in Surveying running and marking out a Line of Boundary between this Colony and the Indian Country pursuant to an Agreement made with the Indian Nations at a Treaty held at Fort Stanwix in the

Year one thousand seven hundred and sixty eight the Sum of two hundred and fifty Pounds including one hundred Pounds which was paid him by the Treasurer in consequence of a Vote of the General Assembly made in the Year one thousand seven hundred and sixty eight.

UNTO his Excellency the Governor or Commander in Chief for the Time being to defray the Expence of keeping two Interpreters and two Smiths at Niagara and Detroit in the Year one thousand seven hundred and seventy, the Sum of two hundred Pounds agreeable to a Resolution of the General Assembly the twenty fourth Day of January one thousand seven hundred and seventy.

UNTO his Honor the Lieutenant Governor Cadwallader Colden Esquire for Money paid to Michael Cummins for discovering the Publisher of the Paper signed a Son of Liberty pursuant to a Resolution of the General Assembly of the Nineteenth Day of December one thousand seven hundred and sixty nine the Sum of one hundred Pounds.

AND BE IT ENACTED by the Authority aforesaid, That the Treasurer shall, and he is hereby directed to keep exact Books of his several Receipts and payments in virtue of this Act, and shall render true and distinct Accounts thereof upon Oath to his Excellency the Governor or Commander in Chief for the Time being, the Council, or the General Assembly when by them or any of them thereunto required.

[CHAPTER 1476.]

[Chapter 1476 of Van Schaack, where the act is printed in full. See chapters 1188, 1481. This act not of force until an act similar to this is passed by the Legislature of New Jersey, nor until both acts were confirmed by the king.]

An Act for establishing the Boundary or Partition Line between the Colonies of New York and Nova Caesarea or New Jersey, and for confirming Titles and Possessions.

[Passed, February 16, 1771.]

WHEREAS the Boundary or Partition Line between the Colonies of New York and Nova Caesarea or New Jersey from the station on Hudsons River to the station on Delaware River not being duly ascertained, and the Extent of their respective Jurisdictions remaining uncertain and the due and regular Administration of Government in both Colonies being by that means greatly obstructed; the respective Legislatures of both the said Colonies did by Acts for that purpose passed concur in submitting the Title and property of the Lands affected by the said Boundary or Partition Line in both Colonies to such a method of Decision as his most Gracious Majesty should think proper by his Royal Commission or otherwise to institute and appoint of which Acts his Majesty was pleased to declare his approbation, and by his Royal Commission under the Great Seal of Great Britain bearing Date the seventh Day of October in the seventh Year of his Reign did authorize and appoint certain Persons therein named or any five of them to be his Majesty's Commissioners for ascertaining settling and determining the Boundary aforesaid between the said two Colonies. AND WHEREAS a sufficient Number of the Commissioners named in the said Commission on the seventh Day of October in the Year of our Lord one thousand seven hundred and sixty nine did determine that the Boundary or Partition Line between the said Colonies of New York and New Jersey should be a direct and Straight Line from the Fork or Branch formed by the Junction of the Stream or Waters called the Nahackamack with the River called Delaware or FishKill in the Latitude of forty one Degrees twenty one Minutes and thirty seven Seconds as found by the Surveyors appointed by the said Commissioners to a Rock on the West Side of Hudson's River marked by the said Surveyors in the Latitude of forty one Degrees being seventy nine Chains and twenty seven Links to the Southward on a Meridian from Sneyden's House formely Corbets; from which Determination the Agents for both the said Colonies appealed to his Majesty in his privy Council. AND WHEREAS several Tracts of Land to the Northward of the said Partition Line so decreed by the said Commissioners have been heretofore taken up or sold and hitherto and still are held and possessed by virtue of Titles derived from and under the Government of New Jersey or the General Proprietors of the same or some or one of them to wit, One Tract of Land on the sixth Day of November one thousand seven hundred and eighteen, Surveyed and afterwards returned for John Decker for one thousand Acres with the usual Allowance for Highways; Another Tract on the eleventh Day of October one thousand seven hundred and eleven surveyed and afterwards returned for William Tidsworth for three hundred and fifty Acres with the usual Allowance for Highways. Another Tract on the twenty ninth Day of July one thousand seven hundred and thirty one surveyed and afterwards returned for Samuel Green for seven hundred and eighty three Acres with the usual Allowance for Highways and two other Tracts of Land mentioned to contain together five hundred Acres besides the usual allowance for Highways surveyed and returned for Johannes Westphalia, Clause Westphalia, Simon Westphalia, Tunis Quick, Remora Quick, and Cornelius Doutcher, only about one hundred Acres of which last mentioned two Tracts are now held and possessed by virtue of the said Survey the remainder thereof being now held and possessed by Persons claiming under the Colony of New York; Another Tract of Land at the North East End of the Long Pond surveyed and returned for or at the Request of Peter Schuyler, containing four hundred and two Acres and forty nine hundredths of an Acre strict Measure which after Allowance for Highways was to remain for three hundred and eighty three Acres and thirty two hundreths of an Acre. And also another small Tract of Land surveyed the twelfth Day of July one thousand seven hundred and sixty three for John and Gertrude Schuyler situate adjoining the Tract last abovementioned and containing thirteen Acres and fifty nine hundreths of an Acre; Several other Tracts of Land sold and conveyed by the Devisees of James and Mary Alexander to sundry Persons on the thirteenth Day of December one thousand seven hundred and sixty two, to wit, to Elijh Inman one hundred and one Acres and seven hundreth Parts of an Acre, to Hannah Fargeson, one hundred and twenty three Acres and fifty one hundreth Parts of an Acre, to George Kimber one hundred and sixty one Acres and seventy four hundreth parts of an Acre, to Hezekiah Lorin ninety seven Acres and fourteen hundreth Parts of an Acre, to Inman Walling sixty six Acres and ninety three hundredth parts of an Acre, to Benjamin Van Vleet one hundred and four Acres and thirty five hundreth Parts of an Acre, to Bryant Hammell one hundred and thirty five Acres, to James Clerk one hundred and four Acres and fifty six hundreth Parts of an Acre, to Jacobus Rosekrans one hundred and seventy three Acres and thirty five hundreth Parts of an Acre, to Johannes Westbrook one hundred Acres, to John Davis one hundred and fifty two Acres, to Jacob Middagh two hundred and thirteen

Acres and seventy six hundreth Parts of an Acre, and to Josias Cole one hundred Acres, and another Tract of fifty Acres sold and conveyed by Andrew Johnson to George Kember on the eighth Day of August one thousand seven hundred and fifty nine, a Part of which lies to the Southward of the said Partition Line, Another Tract of eighty seven Acres and fifty six hundreth Parts of an Acre sold and conveyed by Benjamin Thompson to Johannes Westbrook on the fourth Day of May one thousand seven hundred and sixty three, two other Tracts of Land sold and Conveyed by James Alexander, William Burnet and James Parker to Richard Gardner on the thirtieth Day of March one thousand seven hundred and fifty three, the one Tract containing one hundred and seventy Acres, and the other eight Acres another Tract of forty Acres and sixty three hundreth Parts of an Acre sold and conveyed by the Devisees of James and Mary Alexander to the said Richard Gardiner on the third Day of January one thousand seven hundred and sixty three, and another Tract of one hundred and seventy three Acres sold and conveyed by the said Devisees of the said James and Mary Alexander to Joseph Barton on the sixteenth Day of December one thousand seven hundred and sixty two, Part whereof lays to the Southward of the said Partition Line; another Piece of Land containing about one Acre, sold and conveyed by David Ackerman to Jacobus Van Boskirk on the twelfth Day of February one thousand seven hundred and sixty two also several other Tracts of Land purchased surveyed and located for the Proprietors of the Sterling Iron Works to wit, one Tract containing fifty Acres surveyed the tenth Day of November one thousand seven hundred and thirty six to Cornelius Board and Timothy Ward, six small Tracts containing in the whole twenty seven Acres and seventy two hundreths of an Acre surveyed the twelfth Day of February one thousand seven hundred and thirty eight, to the said Board and Ward, six other Tracts of Land containing in the whole three hundred and seventy one Acres and fifty three hundreths of an Acre surveyed the twenty third Day of July one thousand seven hundred and forty to Timothy Ward William Smith and Company, and another Tract of ten Acres and eight tenths of an Acre surveyed the twenty ninth Day of November one thousand seven hundred and fifty seven to William Hauxhurst, three other Tracts of Land containing in the whole one hundred and thirty one Acres and twenty five hundreths of an

Acre surveyed to James Burling the seventeenth Day of May one thousand seven hundred and fifty, and another Tract containing ten Acres and twenty nine hundreths of an Acre surveyed to William Hauxhurst the twentieth Day of July one thousand seven hundred and sixty one, one other Tract of Land sold and conveyed to John Barberie and Peter Fauconier to John Sobrisco on the sixth Day of November one thousand seven hundred and twenty four containing six hundred and thirty Acres, one other Tract of Land sold and conveyed by Magdalen Valleau to Coenrad Wannemaker on the twenty third Day of May, one thousand seven hundred and fifty three containing one hundred and five Acres: One other Tract of Land sold and conveyed by Richard Gardner to Elijah Reeve on the eighth Day of June one thousand seven hundred and sixty two containing one hundred and twenty seven Acres and forty eight hundreths of an Acre, also three other Tracts of Land surveyed the thirteenth Day of April one thousand seven hundred and sixty eight to William Hauxhurst containing one hundred Acres and ninety eight hundreths of an Acre strict Measure after the usual Allowance for Highways. AND WHEREAS several other Tracts of Land to the Southward of the said Partition Line so decreed by the said Commissioners, have been heretofore patented and hitherto and still are held and possessed by virtue of Titles derived under the Government of New York to wit, sundry Tracts of Land included in the following Bounds, Beginning at the aforesaid Rock on the West Side of Hudson's River in the Latitude of forty one Degrees and runs from thence southerly along Hudson's River to the South East Corner of the Land now in the possession of Mattys Bogert, and from thence Westerly along the south Side of the said Mattys Bogert's Land and along the Lines of the Lands now in the possession of Isaac Westervelt and Gerrit Westervelt to the Tene Kill and then along the said Kill to the Dwars Kill, and from thence along the said Dwars Kill to Demerest's Kill or Hackinsack River, and from thence along the said River to the Mouth of Pascack River, and then along the said Pascack River till it comes to the Lands of David Demerest whereon the said Demerest's Mill stands, and then Westerly round his Lands and including the same to the said Pascack River and then along the said Pascack River to the said Partition Line decreed as aforesaid and then along the said Partition Line to the Place of beginning; and another Tract of Land sold and conveyed by Benjamin

Ask and Lancaster Syms to Thomas Dekay containing one thousand three hundred and twenty Acres, Part of which lies to the Northward of the said Partition Line: And two other Tracts of Land sold and conveyed by Hendrick Van DeLinde to Frederick Ortendike by Deed bearing Date the thirtieth Day of May one thousand seven hundred and thirty five the one containing two hundred and eighty five Acres, and the other containing one hundred and eighty Acres; and another Tract of Land sold by Abraham Vanhorne and Catharine his Wife, to John Fasheur and Cornelius Haring by Deed bearing Date the twenty second Day of May one thousand seven hundred and fifty two containing one hundred and eighty five Acres be the same more or less; And another Tract of land sold and conveyed by Samuel Verbryck and Susannah his Wife to John Fasheur by Deed bearing Date the nineteenth Day of May one thousand seven hundred and fifty nine containing two hundred and sixty five Acres and three fourths of an Acre good Measure, Part whereof lies to the Northward of said Partition Line: And another Tract of Land sold and conveyed by Benjamin Van DeLinde to William Haldron by Deed bearing Date the eighteenth Day of December one thousand seven hundred and sixty containing two hundred and fifty eight Acres; and another Tract of Land being the remainder of the unsold Lands of so much in Samuel Bayard's Patent as is contained in a Deed from Hendrick Van DeLinde to Roelof Van De Linde, Benjamin Van De Linde and Samuel Verbryck, bearing Date the thirtieth Day of June one thousand seven hundred and sixty; And another Tract of Land sold and conveyed by Robert Campbell to Andries Picterson by Deed bearing Date the twenty first Day of August one thousand seven hundred and sixty two, containing one hundred and fifty Acres: And another Tract of Land sold and conveyed by Henry Van DeLinde and Ariaentje his Wife to Abraham Post by Deed bearing Date the twelfth Day of January one thousand seven hundred and sixty containing one hundred and fifty Acres: And another Tract of Land sold and conveyed by Benjamin Van DeLinde to Gerret Ackerson and Gerret Haring by Deed bearing Date the fourth Day of May one thousand seven hundred and fifty nine containing three hundred and forty eight Acres: And also a Piece of Land now in the Possession of William Bayard Esquire being Part of a Tract of Land formerly granted by Letters Patent under the Great Seal of the Province of New York to Daniel Honan and Michael Hawden lying adjoining to the South Side of the said Partition Line and bounded to the South East by the Land in Possession of John Fasheur, and to the South West by the Land in the Possession of William Haldron. AND WHEREAS it is conceived just and equitable that the present Possessors of the said Lands on each Side of the said Partition Line, who have not only purchased the same for a valuable Consideration, but many of them have laid out all their Substance in the Improvement thereof should be secured in the Enjoyment of the Fruits of their Labour and Industry.

BE IT THEREFORE ENACTED by his Excellency the Governor, the Council and the General Assembly, and it is hereby Enacted by the authority of the same That the said Partition Line so decreed by the said Commissioners is and shall forever hereafter remain and be the Boundary and Line of Partition between this Colony and the Colony of New Jersey.

AND BE IT FURTHER ENACTED by the authority aforesaid That Samuel Gale, William Wickham and John De Noyellis Esquires, or any two of them shall be and hereby are appointed Commissioners to join with such as may be appointed on the Part of the Colony of New Jersey to ascertain and mark the said Partition Line so that it may be sufficiently known and distinguished, and the said Commissioners are hereby directed and required to mark the beforementioned Rock on the West Side of Hudson's River marked by the Surveyors in the Latitude of forty one Degrees with a Straight Line throughout it's Surface, passing through the Place marked by the Surveyors, and with the following Words and Figures to wit LATITUDE 41° NORTH, and on the South Side thereof the Words NEW JERSEY, and on the North Side thereof the Words NEW YORK, and to mark every Tree that may stand in the said Line with five Notches and a Blaze on the North West and South East Sides thereof, and to put up Stone Monuments at one Mile distance from each other along the said Line, and to number such Monuments with the Number of Miles the same shall be from the beforementioned marked Rock on the West Side of Hudson's River, and mark the Words NEW JERSEY on the South Side and the Words NEW YORK on the North Side of every the said Monuments: the one half of the Expence whereof shall be paid by this Colony, out of any Monies which may be in the Treasury upon Warrant to be issued by the Governor or Commander in Chief of this Colony for the Time being with the advice and Consent of his Majesty's Council, Provided the Sum so to be drawn for, does not exceed the Sum of one hundred Pounds.

AND BE IT FURTHER ENACTED by the Authority aforesaid. That the several and respective Patentees, Vendees, Possessors and Claimants of all and every the said Tracts of Land to the Northward of the said Boundary or Partition Line which are now held and possessed in virtue of Titles derived under the Government of New Jersey as above described, and their Heirs and Assigns shall severally hold and forever enjoy the Property of all, and any, and every of the said Tracts of Land so as aforesaid respectively purchased and possessed as fully and in the same Manner to all Intents and purposes whatsoever as if the same had by virtue of this Act been determined to be within the Colony of New Jersey, without any Let, Suit, Disturbance or Molestation of any Person or Persons claiming or to claim by from or under any Patent or Patents or by virtue of any Title derived under the said Government of New York.

PROVIDED ALWAYS and be it further Enacted by the Authority aforesaid. That it shall and may be lawful to and for any Person or Persons claiming Titles under the said Government of New Jersey, or the General Proprietors of the same or some or one of them to any of the aforesaid Lands or Tenements hereby intended to be secured to the Purchasers and Possessors under the said Government of New Jersey to the Northward of the said Boundary or Partition Line, to commence, sue, prosecute and maintain any Writ, Suit, or Action for the Recovery of their Rights, This Act being only designed to confirm the Titles to such Lands to the Northward of the said Partition Line as are in Manner aforesaid actually held and possessed under the Government of New Jersey, against all Claims of any Person or Persons Claiming or to Claim by virtue of any Title or Titles derived under the said Government of New York, but not to determine the particular Rights of the Claimants of such Lands under the Government of New Jersey.

PROVIDED ALWAYS that this Act shall not be in force or take Effect until the Governor or Commander in Chief for the Time being, the Council and the General Assembly of the Colony of New Jersey do pass an Act similar to this Act and thereby confirm the Titles of such Persons as hold Lands under the

Government of New York to the Southward of the said Partition Line in the same Manner as those holding Lands under the Government of New Jersey to the Northward of the said Line are hereby secured, nor until his Majesty shall have given his Royal Assent both to this Act, and such other Act to be passed by the Governor or Commander in Chief for the Time being, the Council and the General Assembly of the Colony of New Jersey as aforesaid

[CHAPTER 1477.]

[Chapter 1477 of Van Schaack, where the title only is printed. Expired the 1st of January, 1772; provided for by chapter 1510.]

An Act to amend an Act intitled. "An "Act for the Inspection of Sole Leather "within the City of New York."

[Passed, February 16, 1771.]

WHEREAS by Part of the fourth Section of the Act intitled. "An Act for the Inspection of Sole Leather in the City of New "York," it is therein provided, "that all Sole Leather which "shall not bear the Inspection aforesaid may be used for any "other purpose except being worked up into Shoes, Boots, and "Buckets, provided the same be marked by any of the Inspectors "aforesaid with his Name and the Letter B. who are thereby "required to keep a proper Instrument for that purpose." AND WHEREAS the same has not been found to answer the good Purposes thereby intended.

BE IT THEREFORE ENACTED by his Excellency the Governor the Council and the General Assembly, and it is hereby Enacted by the Authority of the same. That all Sole Leather which shall not bear the Inspection as in the said Act is directed may be used for any other Purpose except being worked up into Shoes, Boots, and Buckets provided the same be marked by either of the Inspectors aforesaid with his Name and the Letters BAD, who are hereby required to keep a proper Instrument for that Purpose. And if any Person or Persons shall presume to work up into Shoes, Boots or Buckets, such Sole Leather as shall be marked with the Letters BAD as aforesaid he or they so offending shall forfeit and pay for every Offence the Sum of ten Pounds to be sued for, recovered and applied, as in the said Act is directed, anything in the said Act contained to the contrary notwithstanding.

[CHAPTER 1478.]

[Chapter 1478 of Van Schaack, where the act is printed in full. See chapter 1363.]

An Act to revive an Act intitled "An Act "for the better Determination of personal "Actions depending upon Accounts."

[Passed, February 16, 1771.]

WHEREAS an Act intitled "An Act for the better determination of Personal Actions depending upon Accounts." passed the thirty first Day of December one thousand seven hundred and sixty eight expired by it's own Limitation on the first Day of January, one thousand seven hundred and seventy one, and the same having been found very useful and necessary.

BE IT THEREFORE ENACTED by his Excellency the Governor, the Council and the General Assembly, and it is hereby Enacted by the Authority of the same, That the above mentioned Act intitled "An Act for the better determination of Personal "Actions depending upon Accounts." shall be, and hereby is revived, and every Article, Matter and Clause therein contained enacted to be and remain in full force, from the Publication hereof until the first Day of February, which will be in the Year of our Lord one thousand seven hundred and eighty.

[CHAPTER 1479.]

[Chapter 1479 of Van Schaack, where the title only is printed. Expired the 1st of January, 1772. Provided for by chapter 1533.]

An Act to amend an Act intitled, "An "Act the better to ascertain the Quality of "Pot and Pearl Ashes."

[Passed, February 16, 1771.]

WHEREAS it has been found by experience that the Manufactures of Pot and Pearl Ashes are highly advancive of the Interests of this Colony, and the future Increase of those Commodities is likely to be best promoted by rendering the Exportation of them as profitable as possible to the Manufacturers. And Whereas from the Increase of those Articles heretofore, the Office of Inspector is become more lucrative than it was originally intended to be, the Trouble attending the Inspection thereof being also considerably diminished by the Skill which the Manufacturers have acquired in distinguishing between the different Qualities of those Commodities.

BE IT THEREFORE ENACTED by his Excellency the Governor, the Council and the General Assembly, and it is hereby Enacted by the Authority of the same, That from and after the Publication of this Act, the Inspector or Officer for viewing essaying and examining Pot and Pearl Ashes shall not receive more than four Pence per hundred Weight for performing the Services required of him in and by the first Section of an Act intitled. "An Act the better to ascertain the Quality of Pot and "Pearl Ashes." and also for the additional Service of repacking the said Pot and Pearl Ashes, and putting the Casks in such Condition as they may be in when they shall be brought to him for Inspection. PROVIDED that if the said Casks shall then require any further Cooperage to qualify them for Shipping, or if any such Casks shall be incapable of being rendered fit for Shipping, such further Cooperage or such new Casks if necessary shall be at the Expence of the vender, any Thing in the said Act or herein to the contrary notwithstanding.

[CHAPTER 1480.]

[Chapter 1480 of Van Schaack, where the title only is printed. This act was repealed by the king.]

An Act to amend and continue an Act intitled "An Act for the Relief of Insolvent "Debtors within the Colony of New York, "with respect to the Imprisonment of their "Persons".

[Passed, February 16, 1771.]

WHEREAS the Act intitled, "An Act for the Relief of Insolv-"ent Debtors within the Colony of New York with respect to the "Imprisonment of their Persons." passed in the tenth Year of his present Majesty's Reign, is thought necessary for the Relief of such unhappy Debtors, who being willing to satisfy their Creditors as far as they are able, are nevertheless detained in Prison by their Creditors.

BE IT THEREFORE ENACTED by his Excellency the Governor the Council and the General Assembly, and it is hereby Enacted by the Authority of the same, That the said Act shall be and hereby is continued, and every Clause Article Matter and Thing therein contained, Enacted to be and remain in full force and virtue to all Intents, Constructions and Purposes for the Time herein after limited.

PROVIDED NEVERTHELESS, AND BE IT ENACTED by the Authority aforesaid. That Nothing in that Act shall be construed to impower any Creditor or Creditors of such Prisoner or Prisoners so discharged, his her or their Executors or Administrators to take out new Executions against any Lands, Tenements, Hereditaments, Goods or Chattels (Reversions and Remainders excepted) such Prisoner or Prisoners shall or may acquire after his her or their Discharge, any Thing in the said Act to the contrary notwithstanding.

AND BE IT ENACTED by the Authority aforesaid That Thomas Robinson Senior, Abraham Governeur, John Cox & Thomas Robinson Junior, shall and hereby are entitled to all the Benefits and liable to all the Penalties, that Insolvent Debtors were entitled and liable to, by an Act intitled. "An Act for the "Relief of Insolvent Debtors, and for repealing the Acts therein "mentioned" passed the nineteenth Day of May one thousand seven hundred and sixty one, they taking the Oath, and Conforming to the Directions of the said Act.

AND BE IT FURTHER ENACTED by the Authority aforesaid That Nicholas Wortman now confined in New York Goal for a Trespass shall be and hereby is discharged from his Imprisonment, and freed from any further prosecution for said Trespass.

AND BE IT FURTHER ENACTED by the Authority aforesaid, That this Act shall be and remain in full force until the first Day of May, one thousand seven hundred and seventy two.

[CHAPTER 1481.]

[Chapter 1481 of Van Schaack, where the act is printed in full. See chapters 1188, 1476.]

An Act to amend an Act, entitled, "An "Act for submitting the Property of the "Lands which are held or claimed by Grants "under the Great Seal of this Colony, and "are affected by the Controversy about the "Boundary or Partition Line between this "Colony and the Colony of New Jersey to "such a Method of Decision as his most "Gracious Majesty shall think proper by his "Royal Commission or otherwise to appoint, "and for defraying the Expence to accrue on "the part of this Colony on the final Settlement of the said Land."

[Passed, February 16, 1771.]

WHEREAS the Number of Agents appointed in said Act are the equal Number of Six; And Whereas they may on a Division be equally divided by that Means the trust reposed in them by said Act be greatly frustrated for prevention whereof for the future

BE IT ENACTED by his Excellency the Governor the Council and the General Assembly and it is hereby enacted by the Authority of the same that to the number of Agents appointed by the said Act, entitled, "An Act for submitting the Property of "the Lands which are held or claimed by Grants under the "Great Seal of this Colony and are affected by the Controversy "about the Boundary or Partition Line between this Colony and "the Colony of New Jersey to such a Method of Decision as "his Most Gracious Majesty shall think proper by his Royal "Commission or otherwise to appoint and for defraying the "Expense to accrue on the part of this Colony on the final Set-"tlement of the said Line" the following Persons be appointed as an additional Number of Agents, to wit, Benjamin Seaman James Jauncey and Simon Boerum Esquires who shall Act in Conjunction and be vested with all the powers and Authorities to all Intents, Constructions and purposes Whatsoever as the other Agents have that were originally appointed by the aforesaid Act, any thing in the said Act to the Contrary hereof in any wise Notwithstanding

[CHAPTER 1482.]

[Chapter 1482 of Van Schaack, where the act is printed in full.]

An Act further to regulate the Inspection and branding of Flour.

[Passed, February 16, 1771.]

BE IT ENACTED by his Excellency the Governor, the Council and the General Assembly, and it is hereby enacted by the Authority of the same. That all Flour whatever brought into the City of New York for sale and exportation not manufactured within this Colony, shall if good and merchantable have the Name of the Colony where such Flour was manufactured, added to the Mark or Brand wherewith the Flour manufactured within this Colony is by Law directed to be branded: and the Inspectors of Flour which now are or hereafter may be appointed for the City of New York, are hereby required and Commanded to govern themselves according to the true Intent and meaning of this Act.

AND BE IT ENACTED by the Authority aforesaid that if any Dispute shall arise between the Owner or Possessor of any Flour offered to be inspected and the Inspector or Inspectors, concerning the Place where such Flour offered for inspection was manufactured that the Owner or possessor thereof shall prove by himself or one credible Witness upon Oath or Affirmation before any Justice of the Peace to the best of his knowledge or Belief where such Flour was Manufactured or made. And Be it enacted that from and after the first Day of June next no Inspector of Flour appointed for the City of New York, shall brand or mark as inspected any Cask of Flour whereever manufactured, unless the initial Letter of the Christian Name and the Sirname at Length of the Manufacturer are first branded thereon

This Act to remain and be in force until the first Day of January, one thousand seven hundred and seventy five

[CHAPTER 1483.]

[Chapter 1483 of Van Schaack, where the act is printed in full. This act expired January 1st, 1773. Extended to the county of Westchester by chapter 1524. Revived by chapter 899.]

An Act to appoint Inspectors of Flour and Repackers of Beef and Pork in the several Counties therein mentioned.

[Passed, February 16, 1771.]

WHEREAS Flour Beef and Pork are frequently shipped and laden on board of Vessels at sundry Places in several Counties of this Colony in order to be exported out of this Colony; but by reason of there being no Inspectors of Flour or Repackers of Beef and Pork in either of the said Counties, the Owners of the said Flour Beef and Pork are obliged to unload the same at the City of New York to have the Flour inspected, and the Beef and Pork repacked, which is attended with much trouble and Expence.

To remedy which inconvenience, be it enacted by his Excellency the Governor the Council and the General Assembly, and it is hereby Enacted by the Authority of the same, That John Rooseboom, Peter Vosburgh, and John A Van Alen, shall be and hereby are appointed the Officers for viewing and examining all such Flour, and That the said John Roseboom, Peter Vosburgh, and John A Van Alen, shall be and hereby are appointed Repackers of Beef and Pork intended to be shipped or laden on board of any Vessel in the City or County of Albany, to be thence exported out of this Colony; and that John Arthur, Edward Hallack and Lawrence Van Gaasbeek shall be and hereby are appointed the Officers for viewing and examining all Flour, and that William Rose, Samuel Denton and Teunis Hooghteling, shall be and hereby are appointed Repackers of Beef and Pork intended to be shipped or laden on Board of any Vessel in the County of Ulster to be thence exported out of this Colony; and that Henry Wiesner Junior and Roelof Van Houten shall be and hereby are appointed the officers for viewing and examining all Flour, and that Moses Hatfield and Edward W. Kiers shall be and hereby are appointed Repackers of Beef and Pork intended to be shipped or laden on board of any Vessel in the County of Orange to be thence exported out of this Colony, and that Zachariah Van Voohees, Peter P. Van Kleek and William Radlif shall be and hereby are appointed the Officers for viewing and examining all Flour, and that the said Zachariah Van Voorhees, Peter P. Van Kleek and William Radlif shall be and hereby are appointed Repackers of Beef and Pork intended to be shipped or laden on board of any Vessel in the County of Dutchess to be thence exported out of this Colony.

AND BE IT FURTHER ENACTED by the Authority aforesaid That the said several Inspectors of Flour hereby appointed shall respectively have the same Powers and proceed in the viewing and examining of Flour in the same Manner as the like Officers in the City of New York may or ought to do by Law, and shall be and hereby are made subject and liable to the same Regulations, Penalties and Forfeitures, and all Disputes between any of the Inspectors of Flour hereby appointed, and the possessor of such Flour relating to the Finess or goodness thereof shall be determined in the same Manner as is directed in and by an Act intitled "An Act to prevent the exportation of unmerchantable "Flour and the false taring of Bread and Flour Casks," upon application to any Justice of the Peace for the County where such Flour shall be inspected.

AND BE IT FURTHER ENACTED by the Authority aforesaid That if any or either of the Officers hereby appointed shall become incapable or neglect or refuse to execute his or their said

Offices or Misbehave therein or shall happen to die then and so often and from Time to Time in such Case it shall and may be lawful to and for the Justices of the Peace of the County for which such Officer or Officers is or are appointed at their General Sessions to supply his or their place by some other fit and capable Person or Persons to execute the said Office or Offices until another be appointed by Act or Acts hereafter to be passed for that purpose.

AND BE IT FURTHER ENACTED by the Authority aforesaid That before the said Inspectors of Flour hereby appointed shall respectively do any Thing in the execution of their said Office they shall each of them respectively take an Oath or if a Quaker an Affirmation before one of the Judges of the Inferior Court of Common Pleas for the County for which they are respectively appointed Inspectors in the Words following.

"I A B do Swear (or Affirm) that I will faithfully truly and "Impartially according to the best of my Judgment Skill and "understanding execute do and perform the Office and Duty of "an Inspector and Examiner of Flour according to the true "Intent and meaning of two several Acts of this Colony, the one "intitled An Act to prevent the exportation of unmerchantable "Flour and the false taring of Bread and Flour Casks, and the "other intitled, An Act to amend an Act intitled An Act to "prevent the exportation of unmerchantable Flour, and the false "taring of Bread and flour Casks And further that I will not "inspect any Cask of Flour unless the initial Letter of the "Christian Name and the Sirname at Length of the Manufac-"turer are first branded thereon: and that I will brand every "Cask of Flour by me inspected with the Name of the County "where manufactured so help me God."

AND BE IT FURTHER ENACTED by the Authority aforesaid That the said Repackers hereby appointed shall respectively before he or they do any Thing in their said Office take an Oath or if a Quaker an Affirmation before one of the Judges of the Inferior Court of Common Pleas for the County for which they are respectively appointed Repackers of Beef and Pork in the Words following.

"I A B do Swear (or Affirm) that during the Time I am a "Packer or Repacker of Meat in the County for which I am "appointed, I will not directly or indirectly by myself or by my

"Consent privity or procurement brand or cause or suffer to be "branded any Casks containing Beef or Pork which shall be "repacked by me or in my presence in any other than in the "Manner following that is to say on such only as contain that "which is Bona fide and in fact sound and really good the Initial "Letters of my Christian and Sirname the Name of the County "for which I am appointed, with the words New York thereunder, "and no Brand or Brands whatsoever on Casks which contain "unsound or unmerchantable Meat, so help me God."

AND BE IT FURTHER ENACTED by the Authority aforesaid That the said Packers or Repackers of Meat shall not put their respective Brands before mentioned on any Cask or Barrel containing Meat which shall contain less (if of Beef than two hundred and twenty Pounds, if of Pork than two hundred and ten Pounds, and every Barrel or Cask shall be well and sufficiently hooped with at least ten Hoops, and so tight as to hold Pickel, and there shall not be put in any such Barrel or Cask of Pork more than four half heads, and of Beef, not more than two Shins, and there shall be used at least an half Bushel of Salt in repacking of every such Cask or Barrel of Meat as aforesaid, and half Barrels in the same Proportion.

AND BE IT FURTHER ENACTED by the Authority aforesaid that no Beef or Pork to be repacked by virtue of this Act shall be repacked until the same has laid in Salt at least twelve Days before such repacking, and that if any of the said Packers or Repackers appointed or which shall be appointed by virtue of this Act shall not in every respect in the execution of his Office act agreeable to the Directions herein prescribed he or they so offending shall forfeit and pay for every such Offence the Sum of five Pounds to be recovered in a summary way before any one of His Majesty's Justices of the Peace in the County where such Offence shall be committed with Costs of Suit for the use of the Person or Persons who shall Sue for and recover the same.

AND BE IT ALSO ENACTED by the Authority aforesaid That all Flour examined and inspected as aforesaid, and that all Beef and Pork repacked and branded as aforesaid by virtue of this Act in any of the Counties aforesaid shall and may be exported in any Vessel or Vessels from thence to Places out of this Colony as well as if the same had been examined and inspected, repacked and branded in the City of New York, any

issued by the Governor or Commander in Chief of this Colony for the Time being with the advice and Consent of his Majesty's Council, Provided the Sum so to be drawn for, does not exceed the Sum of one hundred Pounds.

AND BE IT FURTHER ENACTED by the Authority aforesaid. That the several and respective Patentees, Vendees, Possessors and Claimants of all and every the said Tracts of Land to the Northward of the said Boundary or Partition Line which are now held and possessed in virtue of Titles derived under the Government of New Jersey as above described, and their Heirs and Assigns shall severally hold and forever enjoy the Property of all, and any, and every of the said Tracts of Land so as aforesaid respectively purchased and possessed as fully and in the same Manner to all Intents and purposes whatsoever as if the same had by virtue of this Act been determined to be within the Colony of New Jersey, without any Let, Suit, Disturbance or Molestation of any Person or Persons claiming or to claim by from or under any Patent or Patents or by virtue of any Title derived under the said Government of New York.

PROVIDED ALWAYS and be it further Enacted by the Authority aforesaid. That it shall and may be lawful to and for any Person or Persons claiming Titles under the said Government of New Jersey, or the General Proprietors of the same or some or one of them to any of the aforesaid Lands or Tenements hereby intended to be secured to the Purchasers and Possessors under the said Government of New Jersey to the Northward of the said Boundary or Partition Line, to commence, sue, prosecute and maintain any Writ, Suit, or Action for the Recovery of their Rights, This Act being only designed to confirm the Titles to such Lands to the Northward of the said Partition Line as are in Manner aforesaid actually held and possessed under the Government of New Jersey, against all Claims of any Person or Persons Claiming or to Claim by virtue of any Title or Titles derived under the said Government of New York, but not to determine the particular Rights of the Claimants of such Lands under the Government of New Jersey.

PROVIDED ALWAYS that this Act shall not be in force or take Effect until the Governor or Commander in Chief for the Time being, the Council and the General Assembly of the Colony of New Jersey do pass an Act similar to this Act and thereby confirm the Titles of such Persons as hold Lands under the

Government of New York to the Southward of the said Partition Line in the same Manner as those holding Lands under the Government of New Jersey to the Northward of the said Line are hereby secured, nor until his Majesty shall have given his Royal Assent both to this Act, and such other Act to be passed by the Governor or Commander in Chief for the Time being, the Council and the General Assembly of the Colony of New Jersey as aforesaid

[CHAPTER 1477.]

[Chapter 1477 of Van Schaack, where the title only is printed. Expired the 1st of January, 1772; provided for by chapter 1510.]

An Act to amend an Act intitled. "An "Act for the Inspection of Sole Leather "within tho City of New York."

[Passed, February 16, 1771.]

WHEREAS by Part of the fourth Section of the Act intitled. "An Act for the Inspection of Sole Leather in the City of New "York," it is therein provided, "that all Sole Leather which "shall not bear the Inspection aforesaid may be used for any "other purpose except being worked up into Shoes, Boots, and "Buckets, provided the same be marked by any of the Inspectors "aforesaid with his Name and the Letter B. who are thereby "required to keep a proper Instrument for that purpose." AND WHEREAS the same has not been found to answer the good Purposes thereby intended.

BE IT THEREFORE ENACTED by his Excellency the Governor the Council and the General Assembly, and it is hereby Enacted by the Authority of the same. That all Sole Leather which shall not bear the Inspection as in the said Act is directed may be used for any other Purpose except being worked up into Shoes, Boots, and Buckets provided the same be marked by either of the Inspectors aforesaid with his Name and the Letters BAD, who are hereby required to keep a proper Instrument for that Purpose. And if any Person or Persons shall presume to work up into Shoes, Boots or Buckets, such Sole Leather as shall be marked with the Letters BAD as aforesaid he or they so offending shall forfeit and pay for every Offence the Sum of ten Pounds to be sued for, recovered and applied, as in the said Act is directed, anything in the said Act contained to the contrary notwithstanding.

the Supreme Court of this Colony, and in that Case such Deed or the Record thereof may be read as Evidence in any of the Courts of Law in this Colony.

[CHAPTER 1485.]

[Chapter 1485 of Van Schaack, where the title only is printed. Repealed by the king the 9th of June, 1772.]

An Act to prevent abuses committed by Tenants, or by other Persons entering and keeping possession of Messuages Lands and Tenements before a legal Title to the same is obtained.

[Passed, February 16, 1771.]

WHEREAS it frequently happens within this Colony that Lessees or Tenants for Years or at Will hold over the Tenements to them demised after the determination of such Leases, and also that Persons enter into possession of Lands or Tenements without legal Titles for remedy whereof for the future.

BE IT ENACTED by his Excellency the Governor the Council and the General Assembly, and it is hereby Enacted by the Authority of the same, That every Lessor or Landlord in this Colony, having leased or demised any Lands or Tenements to any Person or Persons for a Term of one or more Years or at Will shall demand and require his Lessee or Tenant to remove from and leave the same, and upon the Lessee or Tenants refusing to comply therewith in three Months after such Notice given in Writing or fixed up on some Public Place on the Premises, it shall and may be lawful to and for such Lessor or Landlord to complain thereof to any Justice of the Peace of the City, Town or County where the demised Premises are situate, and upon due Proof made before the said Justice, that the said Lessor had been quietly and peaceably possessed of the Lands or Tenements so demanded to be delivered up, that he had demised the same under certain Rents or otherwise to the then Tenant in possession or some Person or Persons under whom such Tenant Claims, or came into possession and that the Term for which the same was demised is fully ended, that then and in such Case it shall and may be lawful for the said Justice to whom Complaint shall be made as aforesaid to notify any two or more Justices who are hereby required to associate themselves with him forthwith to issue their Warrant in nature of a Summons directed to the

Sheriff of the County, thereby commanding him to cause twelve Substantial Freeholders to appear before the said Justices within six Days next after issuing the Summons, and also give Notice in writing to the Lessee Tenant or other Person in possession, or put up such Notice at some Public Place on the Premises, at the same Time to appear before them the said Justices and Freeholders to shew Cause if any he has why restitution of the possession of the demised Premises should not be forthwith made to such Landlord or Lessor, and if upon hearing the Parties, or in Case of the Tenant's or other Person's claiming or coming into possession under the said Lessee or Tenant, neglect to appear after being summoned or notified as aforesaid, it shall appear to the said Justices and Freeholders, the said Freeholders being first duly sworn, that the Lessor or Landlord had been possessed of the Lands or Tenements in Question, that he had demised the same for a Term of Years or at Will to the Person in possession or some other under whom he or she claims or came into possession at a certain Yearly or other Rent, and that the Term is fully ended, that he had demanded of the Lessee or other Person in possession as aforesaid to leave the premises three Months before such Application to the said Justices, that then and in every such Case, it shall and may be lawful for the said three Justices to make a Record of such finding by them the said Justices and Freeholders, and the said Freeholders shall assess such Damages as they think Right, against the Tenant or other Person in possession as aforesaid for the unjust Detention of the demised premises from the Lessor thereof, for which Damages and reasonable Costs Judgment shall be entered by the said Justices, which Judgment shall be final and conclusive to the Parties, and upon which the said Justices shall and they are hereby enjoined and required to issue their Warrant under their Hands and seals directed to the Sheriff of the County commanding him forthwith to deliver to the Lessor full possession of the demised premises aforesaid and to levy the Costs taxed by the Justices and Damages, so by the Freeholders aforesaid assessed of the Goods and Chattels of the Lessee or Tenant or other Person in possession as aforesaid any Law Custom or usage to the contrary notwithstanding.

AND BE IT FURTHER ENACTED by the Authority aforesaid that if any Person or Persons whatsoever shall or do hereafter enter and peaceably take and detain possession without violence of any Lands or Dwelling House, Out House, or any other Building whatsoever without the Consent of the Owner it shall and may be lawful to and for the Owner of such Lands or dwelling House, Out House or other Building to complain thereof to any one Justice of the Peace as herein before is directed, and the said Justices shall proceed as aforesaid, and if it shall appear to the said Justices and Jury that the Owner aforementioned had been possessed of the Lands or Tenements in Question, and had demanded of the Person so entering as aforesaid to leave the Premises before such application, that then and in such Case it shall and may be lawful for the said three Justices to make a Record thereof, and the Jury to assess the Damages, and for granting Restitution of the Premises and the Recovery of such Damages, and reasonable Costs the said Justices shall proceed as herein before is particularly enjoined and required: this Act to be in force from the Publication hereof until the first Day of February one thousand seven hundred and seventy three.

[CHAPTER 1486.]

[Chapter 1486 of Van Schaack, where the act is printed in full. See chapter 908. Continued by chapter 1574.]

An Act to amend an Act intitled "An Act to prevent Frauds in Debtors". by extending the same to Executors and Administrators residing out of this Colony whose Testators or Intestates have Effects within the same.

[Passed, February 16, 1771.]

WHEREAS it frequently happens that Executors and Administrators after being duly qualified remove out of this Colony leaving the Estates of their Testators or Intestates in the Hands and possession of other Persons, by Means whereof the Creditors of such Testators or Intestates are put to great Trouble and Expence in the recovery of their just Debts, and many Times by such Means intirely lose the same, to prevent which for the future.

BE IT ENACTED by his Excellency the Governor the Council and the General Assembly, and it is hereby Enacted by the Authority of the same, That the Lands Effects Goods and Chattels of all and every Testator and Testators Intestate and Intestates, situate lying or being within this Colony, the Executor or Executors, Administrator or Administrators (whether with the

Will annexed or otherwise) of which Testator or Testators, Intestate or Intestates now are or hereafter shall be residing dwelling or living out of this Colony, shall be liable to be taken and seized for the payment of Debts in the same Manner and Form as is directed ordered and appointed in and by the aforesaid Act intitled, "An Act to prevent Frauds in Debtors," with respect to the Effects Goods and Chattels of Persons residing out of this Colony.

AND BE IT ENACTED by the Authority aforesaid That instead of the Oath ordered to be taken in and by the aforesaid Act intitled, "An Act to prevent Frauds in Debtors", as the Foundation for proceeding against the Effects of absconding Debtors as is in & by the said Act directed, the Person or Persons applying for an Attachment or Attachments against the Lands Goods, Chattels and Effects of Testator or Intestates where the Executor or Executors, Administrator or Administrators of such Testator or Testators, Intestate or Intestates, dwell, live or reside out of this Colony, shall make an Affidavit, or Affirmation in Cases where by Law an Affirmation is allowed, That the Testator or Testators, Intestate or Intestates at the Time of his her or their Death, was or were, honestly justly and bonafide indebted to such Person or Persons, in the Sum of ——.——.——. Current Money of New York, over and above all Discounts, and that the same (at the Time of taking such Oath or Affirmation) still remains due owing and unpaid. This Act to continue of force until the first Day of February one thousand Seven hundred and Seventy three.

[CHAPTER 1487.]

[Chapter 1487 of Van Schaack, where the act is printed in full.]

An Act to prevent the Inconveniencies arising from Delays of Causes after Issue joined.

[Passed, February 16, 1771.]

WHEREAS many great inconveniencies have arisen to the Inhabitants of this Colony by means of delaying the Trials of Causes between Party and Party after Issue joined, for Remedy whereof.

BE IT ENACTED by his Excellency the Governor the Council and the General Assembly, and it is hereby Enacted by the Authority of the same. That where any Issue is or shall be joined in any Action or Suit at Law in any Court of Record within this Colony, and the Plaintiff or Plaintiffs in any such Action or Suit hath or have neglected, or shall neglect to bring such Issue on to be tried according to the Course and practice of the said Courts respectively, it shall and may be lawful for the Judge or Judges of the said Courts respectively at any Time after such Neglect upon Motion made in open Court (due Notice having been given thereof) to give the like Judgment for the Defendant or Defendants in every such Action or Suit, as in Cases of Nonsuit unless the said Judge or Judges shall upon just Cause, and reasonable Terms allow any further Time or Times for the Trial of such Issue; and if the Plaintiff or Plaintiffs shall neglect to try such Issue within the Time or Times so allowed then and in every such Case the said Judge or Judges shall proceed to give such Judgment as aforesaid.

PROVIDED ALWAYS and be it Enacted by the Authority aforesaid, That all Judgments given by virtue of this Act shall be of the like force and Effect as Judgments upon nonsuit, and of no other force or effect.

PROVIDED ALSO, That the Defendant or Defendants shall upon such Judgment be awarded his her or their Costs in any Action or Suit where he she or they would upon Nonsuit be entitled to the same, and in no other Action or Suit whatsoever.

AND BE IT FURTHER ENACTED by the Authority aforesaid, That from and after the first Day of May one thousand seven hundred and seventy one, no Indictment, Information or Cause whatsoever shall be tried before any Judge or Judges of any Court of Record within this Colony, where the Defendant or Defendants reside above forty Miles from the Place where the Court is held in which such Cause shall be tried, unless Notice of Trial in Writing has been given at least fourteen Days before such intended Trial.

AND BE IT FURTHER ENACTED by the Authority aforesaid, That in Case any Party or Parties shall have given such Notice of Trial as aforesaid, and shall not afterwards duly countermand the same in writing at least six Days before such intended Trial every such Party shall be obliged to pay unto the Party or Parties to whom such Notice of Trial shall have been given as aforesaid the like Costs and Charges, as if such Notice of Trial had not been countermanded.

[CHAPTER 1488.]

[Chapter 1488 of Van Schaack, where the act is printed in full. Continued by chapter 1575.]

An Act for the apprehending of Persons in any County or Place, upon Warrants granted by Justices of the Peace of any other County or Place.

[Passed, February 16, 1771.]

WHEREAS it frequently happens that Persons against whom Warrants are granted by the Justices of the Peace for the several Counties within this Colony, escape into other Counties or Places out of the Jurisdiction of the Justices of the Peace granting such Warrants, and thereby avoid being punished for the Offences wherewith they are charged

For remedy whereof. BE IT ENACTED by his Excellency the Governor the Council and the General Assembly, and it is hereby Enacted by the Authority of the same, that from and after the first Day of May next, in Case any Person against whom a Warrant shall be issued in any Criminal Matter or Breach of the Peace, by any Justice or Justices of the Peace of any City, County, Borough, Town Manor or Place, out of the Jurisdiction of the Justice or Justices granting such Warrant as aforesaid, it shall and may be lawful for any Justice or Justices of the Peace of the City, County, Borough, Town, Manor or Place where such Person shall escape, go into, reside or be, and such Justice or Justices is and are hereby required upon Proof being made upon Oath, of the Hand Writing of the Justice or Justices granting such Warrant to indorse his or their Name or Names on such Warrant, which shall be a sufficient Authority to the Person or Persons bringing such Warrant, and to all other Persons to whom such Warrant was originally directed, to execute such Warrant in such other City, County, Borough, Town, Manor or Place out of the Jurisdiction of the Justice or Justices granting such Warrant as aforesaid, and to apprehend and carry such Offender or Offenders before the Justice who indorsed such Warrant or some other Justice or Justices of such other City, County, Borough, Town, Manor or Place where such Warrant was indorsed in Case the Offence for which such Offender shall be so apprehended in such other City County, Borough, Town,

Manor or Place as aforesaid shall be bailable in Law and such Offender shall be willing and ready to give Bail for his appearance at the next General or Quarter Sessions of the Peace to be held in and for the City, County, Borough, Town, Manor or Place where the Offence was committed, such Justice or Justices of such other City, County Borough, Town, Manor or Place before whom such Offender or Offenders shall be brought, shall and may take Bail of such Offender or Offenders, for his or their appearance at the next General or Quarter Sessions of the Peace to be held in and for the City, County, Borough, Town, Manor or Place where such Offence was committed in the same Manner as the Justices of the Peace of the City, County, Borough, Town, Manor or Place should or might have done in such proper City, County, Borough, Town, Manor or Place, and the Justice or Justices of such other City, County, Borough Town, Manor, or Place so taking Bail as aforesaid, shall deliver the Recognizances together with the Examination or Confession of such Offender or Offenders, and all other proceedings relating thereto to the Constable or other Person or Persons so apprehending such Offender or Offenders as aforesaid who are hereby required to receive the same, and to deliver over such Recognizance, Examination and other Proceedings to the Clerk of the Peace of the City, County, Borough, Town Manor or Place where such Offender or Offenders is or are required to appear by virtue of such Recognizance, and such Recognizance, Examination or Confession shall be as good and effectual in Law to all Intents and purposes, and of the same Force and validity as if the same had been entered into taken or acknowledged before a Justice or Justices of the Peace in and for the proper City, County, Borough, Town, Manor or Place where the Offence was committed, and the same proceedings shall be had thereon, and in case such Constable or other Person to whom such Recognizance, Examination, Confession or other Proceedings shall be so delivered as aforesaid shall refuse or neglect to deliver over the same to the Clerk of the Peace of the City, County, Borough, Town, Manor or Place where such Offender is required to appear by virtue of such Recognizance, such Constable or other Person shall forfeit the Sum of ten Pounds, to be recovered against him before any one of his Majesty's Justices of the Peace by any Person or Persons who will prosecute or sue for the same and in Case the Offence for which such Offender or Offenders shall be apprehended and taken in any City County Borough, Town Manor or Place shall not be bailable in Law, or such Offender or Offenders shall not give Bail for his appearance at the next General or Quarter Sessions of the Peace to be held in and for the City, County, Borough Town, Manor or Place where the Offence was committed to the Satisfaction of the Justice before whom such Offender or Offenders shall be brought in such other City, County, Borough, Town, Manor or Place, then and in that Case the Constable or other Person or Persons so apprehending such Offender or Offenders, shall carry and convey such Offender or Offenders before one of his Majesty's Justices of the Peace of the proper City, County, Borough Town Manor or Place where such Offence was committed there to be dealt with according to Law.

AND IT IS HEREBY ENACTED by the Authority aforesaid, That no Action of Trespass, false Imprisonment, Information or Indictment, or other Action shall be brought sued commenced or prosecuted by any Person or Persons whatsoever against the Justice or Justices who shall indorse such Warrant, for or by reason of his or their indorsing such Warrant PROVIDED NEVERTHELESS That such Person or Persons shall be at liberty to bring or prosecute his or their Action or suit against the Justice or Justices who originally granted such Warrant in the same Manner as such Person or Persons might have done in Case this Act had not been made.

AND BE IT FURTHER ENACTED by the Authority aforesaid that this Act shall be and remain in force until the first Day of February one thousand seven hundred and seventy three.

[CHAPTER 1489.]

[Chapter 1489 of Van Schaack, where the act is printed in full.]

An Act to prevent the taking and destroying of Salmon in Hudson's River.

[Passed, February 16, 1771.]

WHEREAS it is thought that if the Fish called Salmon which are very plenty in some of the Rivers and Lakes in this and the neighbouring Colonies were brought into Hudson's River, that they would by spawning there, soon become numerous to the great Advantage of the Public.

AND WHEREAS a Number of Persons in the County of Albany propose to make the Experiment, and defray the Expence attending the same; In order that the good Design may be more effectually carried into Execution, it is conceived necessary that a Law should be passed for prohibiting the taking and destroying the said Fish for a Term of Years.

BE IT THEREFORE ENACTED by his Excellency the Governor, the Council and the General Assembly, and it is hereby Enacted by the Authority of the same, That if any Person or Persons after the Publication of this Act, and for and during the Term of five Years next to come shall take any Salmon in Hudson's River, or in any River, Creek or Brook emptying itself into the same, and kill or destroy the same every such Person shall for every Salmon he or she shall so take and kill or destroy, forfeit the Sum of ten Pounds to be recovered with Costs of suit by any Person who shall sue for the same before any one of his Majesty's Justices of the Peace in any of the Counties within this Colony, who is hereby impowered and required to hear and determine the same.

[CHAPTER 1490.]

[Chapter 1490 of Van Schaack, where the act is printed in full. See chapters 1346 and 1437.]

An Act for the more effectual Recovery of Duties arisen in the late Treasurer's Time and remaining still unpaid.

[Passed, February 16, 1771.]

WHEREAS it appears by the Report of Abraham Lott Esquire the present Treasurer of this Colony that the Duties arisen in the late Treasurer's Time and remaining in arrear and unpaid amount to a considerable sum, the Recovery of which or great Part thereof is attended with many Difficulties for the following Reasons.

1st: For that all Sums under ten Pounds arising from the several Acts of the Legislature of this Colony are by the said Acts directed to be immediately paid to the Treasurer, which will be presumed to have been done unless a Bond or Note for the same, or some other full proof of the sum for Duties still being due and unpaid is offered.

2dly: For that the said several Acts of the Legislature of this Colony direct all sums for Duties above the Sum of ten Pounds to be paid in three Months, and a Bond or Bill to be taken for securing the payment thereof at the Discretion of the Treasurer.

3dly. That although the late Treasurer had in most if not all Instances procured the Manifest or Report of the Master, Mate or Purser of every Vessel having dutiable Goods on Board agreeable to the Directions of the several Duty Acts and opened Entries to be signed by the Merchant Factor or Person importing the said Dutiable Goods, yet in many Instances those Entries were opened for one particular Person or Company (as are the Words of the Manifest) which Company is not known, and many of the said Entries are not signed by the Merchant, Factor, or Person importing, and the said late Treasurer conceiving the said particular Entries to be the Bill directed by the said Duty Acts by him to be taken to secure the said Duties has altogether omitted to take any Bonds or other Bills to secure the said Duties, of which many Persons now in arrear for Duties do avail themselves. In Order therefore that Justice may be done to the Public and the Duties now in arrear and unpaid effectually recovered and collected.

BE IT ENACTED by his Excellency the Governor the Council and the General Assembly, and it is hereby Enacted by the Authority of the same, That in any Action or Suit already commenced or hereafter to be commenced by Abraham Lott Esquire the present Treasurer of this Colony or the Treasurer of this Colony for the Time being in virtue of an Act passed the third Day of February in the year of our Lord one thousand seven hundred and sixty eight intitled "An Act directing the Executors "named in the last Will and Testament of Abraham DePeyster "Esquire deceased late Treasurer of this Colony and Frederick "DePeyster Esquire to deliver all Public Monies in their Hands "to the present Treasurer of this Colony, and for other Purposes "therein mentioned," an Act passed the thirty first Day of December in the aforesaid Year of our Lord one thousand seven hundred and sixty eight intitled "An Act for amending an Act "intitled "An Act directing the Executors named in the last Will "and Testament of Abraham DePeyster Esquire deceased late "Treasurer of this Colony, and Frederick DePeyster Esquire to "deliver all Public Monies in their Hands to the present Treas-"urer of this Colony, and for other Purposes therein mentioned"

And an Act passed the twenty seventh Day of January in the Year of our Lord one thousand seven hundred and seventy intitled, "An Act impowering and directing the Treasurer of this "Colony to sue for Duties still due to the late Treasurer of this "Colony, and other purposes therein mentioned," it shall be and is hereby declared to be full and sufficient Proof in Law to entitle the said Treasurer to recover, to produce in support of such Action or Actions the said Entries in the said late Treasurer's Books signed by the Defendant or Defendants their Testator or Intestate, and proving by one or more credible Witnesses the Hand Writing of such Defendant or Defendants their Testator or Intestate, unless such Defendant or Defendants shall shew to the Satisfaction of the Jury trying such Action or Actions that such Defendant or Defendants their Testator or Intestate have well and truly paid and satisfied the said Duties for which such Action or Actions was brought.

AND BE IT FURTHER ENACTED by the Authority aforesaid. That in all Instances where the said Entries are not signed by the Merchant Factor or Person importing the said Dutiable Goods, and where there is no other Proof to charge such Person or Persons with the said Duties, than the Manifest in the late Treasurer's Books Sworn to by the Master Mate or Purser of the Ship or other Vessel in which such dutiable Goods were imported, it shall and may be lawful to and for the said Abraham Lott the present Treasurer, or the Treasurer for the Time being, and he is hereby directed and required, except where Suit is already commenced to signify in Writing to such Person or Persons, that he she or they by the respective Manifests in which he she or they is or are named appears to have imported into this Colony at the Times in the Manifest mentioned, the several dutiable Goods in the respective Manifests mentioned for which the Duties appear to be in Arrear and unpaid, and that unless he she or they do within fifteen Days after the Receipt of such Notice pay the same or make an Affidavit before one of the Judges of the Supreme Court of this Province, or the Mayor of the City of New York proving that the said Duties are well and truly paid and satisfied and in what manner, or that he she or they was or were not the Importer or Importers of the said Goods, and did not receive the same either by himself herself or themselves or any other Person for him her or them, and deliver the said Affidavit to the said Abraham Lott, or to the Treasurer for the Time being, that a suit will be commenced for the Recovery thereof, which Affidavit if made and delivered to the said Treasurer within the Time, and according to the Form aforesaid shall be received and accepted by the said Treasurer as a full and compleat Discharge and acquittance to such Person or Persons. But in Case the said Duties so demanded shall not be paid nor the Affidavit made and delivered within the Time limitted in the said Notice, that then it shall be lawful for the said Abraham Lott the present Treasurer or the Treasurer for the Time being, and he is hereby required and directed immediately to commence Suits for the Recovery of such Duties, in which Action or Actions so to be commenced or already commenced it shall be, and it is hereby declared to be sufficient Proof to support the said Action or Actions and entitle the said Treasurer to recover, to shew the said Manifest or Manifests, and prove the Hand Writing of the late Treasurer Signed to the Certificate at the Foot thereof certifying the same was sworn to before him, unless such Defendant or Defendants prove the same Duties have been paid and satisfied, or at the Trial make such Affidavit as the said Treasurer is herein before directed to request and accept; and produce at least one Credible Witness, who will swear in open Court that he verily believes the Contents of such Affidavit to be true; in which Case the Jury shall find for the Plaintiff six Pence Damages only, and thereupon the Plaintiff shall recover his Costs, to be taxed as in any other Cause; any Law, Custom or usage to the contrary notwithstanding. PROVIDED ALWAYS that Nothing in this Clause shall extend to preclude or debarr any Defendant or Defendants already sued for any Duties, the Proof of which rests in the said Manifests only, from making such Affidavit or Affidavits (as the Treasurer is required to ask of such Defendant or Defendants before suit brought.) in order to discharge themselves of the said Suit and the Costs that may accrue thereon, provided such Affidavit or Affidavits are made and delivered to the said Abraham Lott the present Treasurer or the Treasurer for the Time being at least twenty Days before the next sittings of the Supreme Court of Judicature of this Province.

AND BE IT FURTHER ENACTED by the Authority aforesaid that in all Instances where any Person or Company are named in any Manifest or Manifests in any of the late Treasurer's Books, it shall and may be lawfull for the said Abraham Lott the present Treasurer or the Treasurer for the Time being, and he is hereby directed and required to make demand of the said Person or Persons, so named in the said Manifest or Manifests, of the said Duties in arrear and unpaid, and requesting such Person or Persons within fifteen Days to pay his Part and Proportion thereof if any due, and by his Affidavit to be taken before one of the Judges of the said Supreme Court, or the Mayor of this City if necessary to discharge himself and to designate whose Names should have been inserted in the said Manifest for the said Company, and in what Proportion or proportions they were interested in the said Dutiable Goods mentioned in the said Manifest or Manifests, and if the said Person or Persons shall not pay his Proportion of the Duties so in Arrear, and make the said Affidavit, then and in such Case it shall be lawful to and for the said Abraham Lott the Present Treasurer or the Treasurer for the Time being immediately to commence Suit for the Recovery thereof and prosecute the same to effect in such Manner as by this Act is herein before directed. And in Case such Affidavit as is herein before required shall be made, then the said Abraham Lott the present Treasurer or the Treasurer for the Time being is hereby impowered required and directed to notify such Person or Persons charged with any Duties in and by the said Affidavit in like Manner as by this Act he is directed to notify other Persons who appear to be in Arrear for Duties by the Manifests in the late Treasurer's Books, and if they shall not acquit and discharge themselves from the said Duties within the like Time and in the like Manner as the said other Debtors are by this Act directed to do, then and in such Case it shall and may be lawful for the said Abraham Lott the present Treasurer or the Treasurer for the Time being immediately to commence Suit against such Person or Persons charged by the said Affidavit, in which Action or Suit it shall be sufficient Evidence to support the said Suit and to entitle the said Treasurer to recover to produce the said Affidavit prove the Hand of the Judge or Mayor before whom the same was taken, to produce the Manifest in the late Treasurer's Books, and prove the Hand Writing of the said late Treasurer signed to the Certificate at the Foot of the said Manifest certifying that the same was sworn to before him, unless such Defendant or Defendants prove the same Duties paid, or make Affidavit discharging themselves from the said Duties and produce at least one credible Witness to swear he or they verily believe the Contents of such Affidavit to be true in such Manner as is herein before directed, in which Case as before the said Treasurer shall recover six Pence Damages only, with his full Costs to be taxed any Law usage or Custom to the contrary thereof in any wise notwithstanding.

AND BE IT ALSO ENACTED That no Suit or Suits to be commenced in virtue of this Act shall be discontinued on Account of the Death or Removal of the present or any succeeding Treasurer of this Colony; but such Suit or Suits shall continue and be prosecuted to effect by the Treasurer for the Time being as if no such Death or Removal had happened.

AND BE IT FURTHER ENACTED by the Authority aforesaid. That this present Act shall be accepted taken and reputed to be a general and Public Act of Assembly, and it is hereby declared to be a General and Public Act of Assembly, of which all and every the Judges and Justices of this Colony in all Courts, and all other Persons shall take Notice on all occasions whatsoever relating to the same, any Thing herein contained to the contrary thereof in any wise notwithstanding.

[CHAPTER 1491.]

[Chapter 1491 of Van Schaack, where the title only is printed. Revived and continued till the 1st of November, 1772, with additions by chapter 1535.]

An Act for raising and collecting the Arrears of Taxes due to this Colony from the City and County of New York.

[Passed, February 16, 1771.]

WHEREAS it appears from the Books of the Treasurer of this Colony that there is a very considerable Sum of Money still due owing and unpaid from the City and County of New York for the arrears of Taxes laid by several Acts of Assembly passed for that purpose from the Year one thousand seven hundred and sixty two to the Year one thousand seven hundred and sixty seven inclusive. AND WHEREAS, in and by a certain Act intitled. "An Act to enable the Mayor, Recorder and Aldermen of "the City and County of New York to raise and pay into the "Treasury the Arrears of Taxes due from the s'd City & County" made passed and published on the twenty seventh Day of January in the year of our Lord one thousand seven hundred and seventy. The Mayor Recorder and Aldermen of the City of New

York or any five of them whereof the Mayor or Recorder was to be one, should be and thereby were enabled authorized directed and required at any Time after the Publication of the said Act diligently and strictly to examine how such Deficiency or Arrears had happened, and if it should appear that any particular Person or Persons Collector or Collectors of any of the Wards within the said City had been deficient in collecting or paying any of their Quotas of the said Taxes such Deficiency or Deficiencies so discovered should be laid on levied and collected from such Person or Persons Collector or Collectors of any of the Wards where such Deficiency had happened, and the said Mayor Recorder and Aldermen or any five of them, of which the said Mayor or Recorder was to be one, were also thereby impowered to convene before them such particular Person or Persons, Collector or Collectors and to cause them to give Information upon Oath relative to such Arrears of Taxes that they the said Mayor Recorder and Aldermen, or any five of them, of which the said Mayor or Recorder was to be one might thereby be enabled to liquidate the sum or sums such Delinquent or Delinquents was or were to pay, and it was in and by the said Act further Enacted, that the said Arrears of Taxes which should appear to be justly due owing unpaid and in arrear from the several and respective Wards within the said City should be raised assessed and levied by a Public Tax upon the Estates Real and Personal of all and every the Freeholders Inhabitants and Residents within the several and respective Wards according to the several Proportions which were still due unpaid and in arrear from the said several and respective Wards. AND WHEREAS the Mayor Recorder and Aldermen by virtue of the Act aforesaid caused the several Collectors of the several and respective Wards within this City to appear before them and caused all due Inquiry to be made in order to find how, in what manner, and by what means the several Arrears of Taxes aforesaid happened, and in whose Hands the same remained, upon which Inquiry and Examination it appeared to the said Mayor Recorder and Aldermen that there remained due unpaid and in arrear of the Taxes laid upon the East Ward within the Periods aforesaid the Sum of two hundred Pounds twelve shillings and five Pence, which Deficiency happened by reason of the several Persons upon whom the same was laid having proved Insolvent or having absconded before payment thereof by means whereof the same and every Part of the said Sum became irrecoverable from the several Persons upon whom the same was originally assessed and laid. ALSO that there remained due in arrear and unpaid of the said Taxes from the South Ward the sum of thirty nine Pounds eight shillings and seven pence three Farthings which Deficiency happened in the same Manner and was occasioned by the same Means as the Deficiency happened in the East Ward as aforesaid, and that the same is now also irrecoverable from the several Persons upon whom the same was assessed and laid, Also that there remained due unpaid and in arrear of the said Taxes from the West Ward the Sum of sixty nine Pounds fifteen Shillings and eight Pence And from the North Ward the Sum of two hundred and sixty seven Pounds, eight shillings and two pence, which Deficiencies of the said West and North Wards happened in the same Manner, and was Occasioned by the like Means as the Deficiencies before mentioned happened in the East and South Wards, and are in like manner irrecoverable from the several Persons upon whom the same was heretofore assessed and laid. ALSO that there remained due unpaid and in arrear of the said Taxes from the Dock Ward the Sum of three hundred and fifty one Pounds eight shillings and five Pence half Penny, of which Sum one hundred and nine Pounds thirteen Shillings and eleven pence half penny was occasioned by the like Means, and that the Deficiency of that Sum happened in the same Manner as the Deficiencies happened in the East, West, North and South Wards as before mentioned and is in like Manner irrecoverable from the several and respective Persons upon whom the same was assessed and laid, and that the sum of two hundred and forty one Pounds fourteen shillings and six pence residue of the said Sum of three hundred and fifty one Pounds eight shillings and five Pence half Penny remains outstanding in good Hands and is recoverable from the several and respective Persons upon whom the same was originally laid and assessed or from their several and respective Heirs Executors or Administrators. ALSO that there remained unpaid due and in arrear of the said Taxes from the Harlem Division of the Out Ward the sum of eighty nine Pounds four shillings and four Pence of which Deficiency sixteen Pounds and five Pence was occasioned by the same Means as the Deficiencies herein before mentioned were occasioned, in the East, West, North and South Wards, and the remaining Deficiency being seventy three Pounds three Shillings and eleven

Pence was occasioned by the Death of John Myer Junior insolvent who was collector of that Division for the years one thousand seven hundred and sixty two, one thousand seven hundred and sixty three, and one thousand seven hundred and sixty six, and who as such received the said Sum of seventy three Pounds three Shillings and eleven Pence and never paid the same into the Treasury, by means whereof the whole Deficiency of the Harlem Division of the said OutWard being Eighty nine Pounds four shillings and four Pence is now wholly irrecoverable from the several Persons who ought to pay the same. ALSO that there remained due unpaid and in arrear of the said Taxes from the Bowry Division of the Outward the Sum of one thousand and twenty six Pounds twelve Shillings and one Penny, of which Deficiency it appeared that there was remaining in the Hands of Obadiah Wells two hundred and twenty Pounds and four Pence part thereof which he had received when Collector of the said Division and had not accounted for, also in the Hands of Elias Anderson the further sum of two hundred and forty three Pounds eleven Shillings and eleven Pence other Part of the said Deficiency which he had received when Collector of the said Bowry Division of the Out Ward and had not accounted for. ALSO that the further sum of two hundred and seventy four Pounds thirteen shillings and ten Pence, other Part of the said Deficiency was occasioned by the same Means as the several Deficiencies herein beforementioned were occasioned in the East West North and South Wards, and that the same and every Part thereof is at present irrecoverable from the several and respective Persons upon whom the same was originally laid and assessed, and that the further Sum of two hundred and eighty eight Pounds six Shillings being the remainder of the Deficiency of the Bowry Division of the said OutWard remains still outstanding, but in good Hands, and that the same is at present recoverable from the several and respective Persons upon whom the same was originally laid and assessed or from their several and respective Heirs, Executors or Administrators. AND ALSO that there remained due unpaid and in arrear from Montgomerie's Ward the sum of four thousand one hundred and one Pounds, thirteen shillings and ten Pence, of which said Deficiency it appeared that there was remaining in the Hands of Amos Dodge the Sum of eight hundred and thirty four Pounds fourteen Shillings and six pence, part thereof, which he had received while Collector of the said Ward and had not accounted for. ALSO that the further sum of eight hundred and sixty two Pounds eleven Shillings and ten pence other Part of the said last mentioned Deficiency was occasioned by the same means as the several Deficiencies before mentioned were occasioned in the East West North and South Wards, as is herein beforementioned, and that the same and every part thereof is irrecoverable at present from the several and respective Persons upon whom the same was originally laid and assessed, and that the Sum of two thousand four hundred and four Pounds seven Shillings and six Pence being the remaining Part of the said last mentioned Deficiency remains still outstanding uncollected and in good Hands, and that the same and every Part thereof is now recoverable from the several and respective Persons upon whom the same was originally laid and assessed or from their several and respective Heirs, Executors or Administrators.

BE IT THEREFORE ENACTED by his Excellency the Governor, the Council and the General Assembly, and it is hereby Enacted by the Authority of the same That it shall and may be lawful for the Mayor, Recorder and Aldermen or any five of them of which the Mayor or Recorder to be one, within one Month after the Publication of this Act to order the raising the aforesaid sum of two hundred Pounds twelve Shillings and five Pence herein before mentioned being the Deficiency of the Proportion of Taxes heretofore laid upon the East Ward of the said City, and which is as aforesaid, at present irrecoverable from the Persons upon whom the same was originally laid and assessed, and that by a Tax upon the Estates real and personal of all and every of the Freeholders Inhabitants and Residents within the said East Ward; also the aforesaid Sum of thirty nine Pounds eight Shillings and seven Pence three Farthings herein also beforementioned, being the Deficiency of the Proportion of Taxes heretofore laid upon the South Ward of the said City, and as aforesaid now irrecoverable from the several Persons upon whom the same was originally laid and assessed, and that by a Tax upon the Estates real and Personal of all and every of the Freeholders Inhabitants and Residents within the said South Ward; also the sum of sixty nine Pounds fifteen shillings and eight Pence herein also before mentioned, being the Deficiency of the Proportion of Taxes heretofore laid upon the West Ward of the said City and which is now irrecoverable from the several

Persons upon whom the same was Originally laid and assessed, and that by a Tax upon the Estates real and Personal of all and every of the Freeholders, Inhabitants and Residents within the said West Ward, also the sum of two hundred and sixty eight Pounds eight shillings and two Pence herein also before mentioned being the Deficiency of the Proportion of Taxes heretofore laid upon the North Ward of the said City, which is as aforesaid now irrecoverable from the several Persons upon whom the same was originally laid and assessed, and that by a Tax upon the Estates, real and personal of all and every of the Freeholders Inhabitants and Residents within the said North Ward, also the Sum of one hundred and nine Pounds thirteen Shillings and eleven Pence half Penny, being that Part of the Deficiency of the Proportion of Taxes heretofore laid upon the Dock Ward of the said City which has been occasioned by the Insolvency and absconding of the several Persons upon whom that Sum was laid and assessed, and which is at present irrecoverable from the several Persons upon whom the same was so as aforesaid formerly laid and assessed, and that by a Tax upon the Estates real and Personal of all and every of the Freeholders Inhabitants and Residents within the said Dock Ward, also the Sum of eighty nine Pounds four Shillings and four Pence herein before mentioned being the Deficiency of the proportion of Taxes heretofore laid upon the Harlem Division of the Out Ward of the said City which is now irrecoverable from the several Persons who ought to pay the same; and that by a Tax upon the Estates real and Personal of all and every of the Freeholders Inhabitants and Residents within the Harlem Division of the said OutWard, also the Sum of two hundred and seventy four Pounds thirteen Shillings and ten pence being that Part of the Deficiency of the Proportion of Taxes heretofore laid upon the Bowry Division of the said Out-Ward which is by reason of the Insolvency of the several Persons upon whom the same was originally laid, now become irrecoverable from the several Persons who were heretofore chargeable with the payment thereof and that by a Tax upon the Estates real and personal of all and every of the Freeholders Inhabitants and Residents within the said Bowry Division of the Out Ward. And Also the sum of eight hundred and sixty two Pounds eleven shillings and ten pence being that Part of the Deficiency of the proportion of Taxes heretofore laid upon Montgomerie's Ward in the said City, which was occasioned by the

Insolvency and absconding of the several Persons upon whom the same was originally laid and by that means became and now is irrecoverable from them, and that also by a Tax upon the Estates real and personal of all and every of the Freeholders Inhabitants and Residents within the said Montgomerie's Ward, Pursuant to which Order when made as aforesaid the Mayor of the said City for the Time being shall within two Days thereafter issue his Warrants to the Assessors of each of the several Wards aforesaid for the Time being to make such Assessments, and if any or either of the said Assessors shall neglect refuse or delay to make such Assessment within fifteen Days thereafter and to deliver the same to the several Collectors of the several Wards aforesaid, they and each of them so neglecting refusing or delaying shall respectively forfeit the Sum of fifty Pounds to be recovered by Action of Debt in the Supreme Court of this Colony in the Name of the City Treasurer for the Time being who is hereby authorized and impowered to prosecute for the same in his own Name, which Fine or Fines when recovered shall be applied to the use of the Poor of this City, and the said Mayor for the Time being is also hereby required at the same Time that he issues his Warrants to the Assessors as aforesaid also to issue Warrants to the several Collectors of the several Wards aforesaid thereby commanding, ordering and directing them to collect in the several Sums that shall be assessed and laid upon the several and respective Persons in the said Assessments mentioned and if any Person or Persons in the said Assessments mentioned shall neglect refuse or delay to pay the Sum or Sums annexed to his or their Name or Names that upon such Neglect refusal or delay the said Collectors are and each of them is hereby respectively authorized and impowered to levy the same by Distress and sale of the Goods and Chattels of such Person or Persons who shall as aforesaid neglect refuse or delay to pay the same, returning to the Owner the Overplus if any be (the Charges of such Distress and Sale, and such Tax being first deducted) all which several sums of Money so as aforesaid to be assessed levied collected and Paid in manner and form as aforesaid shall be paid by the several Collectors aforesaid unto the Treasurer of this Colony on or before the first Day of November which will be in the Year of our Lord one thousand seven hundred and seventy one.

AND BE IT ENACTED by the Authority aforesaid that the said Mayor Recorder and Aldermen or any five of them, of which the Mayor or Recorder to be one shall have power and Authority by virtue of this Act, and they are hereby authorized impowered and required immediately after the making of such Order as aforesaid to summon the several Assessors of the several Wards aforesaid to appear before them at such Place as they shall think proper, and then and there to administer to each and every of the said Assessors an Oath well truly equally impartially and in due proportion according to the best of their understanding to assess and rate all and every of the Freeholders Inhabitants and Residents of the respective Wards of which they are respectively Assessors towards raising the several Deficiencies herein before ordered to be raised by a Tax upon Estates real and Personal within the several Wards aforesaid, and for the several Sums in Manner and Form as is herein before mentioned.

AND BE IT FURTHER ENACTED by the Authority aforesaid that over and above the several Sums herein before ordered to be raised levied and paid by virtue of this Act, the Sum of six pence in the Pound for the several Collectors shall be assessed levied and paid to the several Collectors for collecting and paying the same, any Thing herein contained to the contrary in any wise notwithstanding.

AND BE IT FURTHER ENACTED by the Authority aforesaid that the several and respective Collectors of the DockWard, Montgomerie's Ward, and the Bowry Division of the Out Ward of the said City for the Time being are hereby authorized impowered required and directed to collect in and receive from the several Persons upon whom the same was severally laid and assessed, or from their respective Heirs, Executors or Administrators, the several Sums due from them and each of them as their Proportion of the several Deficiencies of the Taxes heretofore laid and assessed upon the Inhabitants Freeholders and Residents of the said Wards by the several Acts heretofore passed for that Purpose, and which said several Deficiencies being to wit, for the Dock Ward two hundred and forty one Pounds fourteen shillings and six Pence; for Montgomerie's Ward two thousand four hundred and four Pounds, seven Shillings and six Pence; and for the Bowry Division of the Out Ward two hundred and eighty eight Pounds six Shillings appeared to the said Mayor Recorder and Aldermen who were impowered by the Act herein before mentioned intitled. "An Act to enable the " Mayor Recorder and Aldermen of the City and County of New " York to raise and pay into the Treasury the Arrears of Taxes "due from the s'd City & County," to examine how such Deficiencies or arrears had happened, that the three several Sums last mentioned were remaining outstanding in good Hands tho' uncollected, and that the same and every Part thereof were recoverable from the several and respective Persons upon whom the same were originally laid and assessed or from their several and respective Heirs Executors or Administrators.

AND BE IT ENACTED by the Authority aforesaid, that the several Tax Books made by the former Assessors of the Dock Ward, Montgomerie's Ward, and the Bowry Division of the Out Ward of the said City of New York in which Books are contained the several Names of the several Persons, and the several Sums annexed to each Name that each Person is to pay of the aforesaid three last mentioned Deficiencies of two hundred and forty one Pounds fourteen shillings and six pence in the Dock Ward, two thousand four hundred and four Pounds seven Shillings and six Pence in Montgomerie's Ward, and two hundred and eighty eight Pounds six Shillings in the Bowry Division of the Out Ward, shall be delivered by the Mayor Recorder and Aldermen with whom the same are now remaining unto the present Collectors of the said Dock Ward, Montgomerie's Ward, and the Bowry Division of the Out Ward of the said City, in order to enable them to collect the said Deficiencies from the Persons upon whom the same were originally laid and from whom or from their Heirs Executors or Administrators the same can still be recovered and collected in, and the said three last mentioned Collectors are, and each of them is hereby authorized enabled and impowered in case any of the Persons who ought to pay their Quota's of the last mentioned deficiencies or the Heirs, Executors or Administrators of such of them as are dead, shall refuse neglect or delay to pay the same after being requested by the said Collectors so to do, to levy the same by Distress and sale of the Goods and Chattels of such Person or Persons who shall as aforesaid neglect refuse or delay to pay the same restoring to the Owner or Owners the overplus if any be, such Tax and the charge of such Distress and sale being first deducted.

AND BE IT ENACTED by the Authority aforesaid that the three sums herein before last mentioned shall be collected in by the several Collectors herein before last mentioned, and by them also paid unto the Treasurer of this Colony on or before the said first Day of November one thousand seven hundred and seventy one, and if any or either of the Collectors of the several Wards within this City shall neglect refuse or delay to pay unto the Treasurer of this Colony the several Sums herein before ordered directed and required to be by them received and collected in within two Months after the said first Day of November one thousand seven hundred and seventy one, it shall and may be lawful for the Treasurer of this Colony for the Time being, and he is hereby authorized impowered and required to commence Actions of Debt against each and every of the said Collectors so refusing neglecting or delaying payment as aforesaid in his own Name in the Supreme Court of this Colony or in Default thereof that the Sum or Sums remaining unpaid shall be deemed Assets in the Hands of the said Treasurer, and he shall be chargeable therewith as if he had actually received the same.

AND BE IT ENACTED by the Authority aforesaid that from and after the Publication of this Act it shall and may be lawful to and for any Collector of Taxes in the City of New York to require and demand the Taxes that shall be assessed and laid on any real Estate in the City of New York by virtue of this Act and mentioned in the Tax list to him delivered or that has been heretofore laid upon any real Estate within the Dock Ward, Montgomerie's Ward, and the Bowry Division of the Out Ward of the said City which shall appear by the Tax Lists to be delivered him by the Mayor Recorder and Aldermen as aforesaid to be unpaid still due and in arrear, and to have been heretofore assessed and laid on any real Estate therein, to demand and require the same of and from the Person and Persons now in possession of such real Estate, and in Case of nonpayment thereof to levy the same by Distress and Sale of the Goods and Chattels found upon the real Estate so taxed rendering the Overplus (if any be) after deducting the said Tax and the Charges of such Distress and sale to the Owner or Owners thereof, and in Case of nonpayment of such Taxes by the Person or Persons in possession of such real Estate or Estates, and for want of Sufficient Goods and Chattels on the Premises whereon the same can be levied by Distress as aforesaid, that then it shall and may be lawful to and for Such Collector to require and demand the said Tax of and from such Person or Persons who shall be named in such Tax Roll as the Owner or Owners, Proprietor or Proprietors of such real Estate or Estates in whatsoever Ward he she or they may dwell and reside, and in Case of nonpayment thereof to levy the same by

Distress and Sale of the Goods and Chattels of such Owner or Owners rendering the Overplus (if any be) after deducting such Tax and the Charges of such Distress and Sale to the Owner or Owners thereof.

AND BE IT FURTHER ENACTED by the authority aforesaid that where any real Estate shall be taxed by virtue of this Act, or where any real Estate has already been taxed in the Dock Ward, Montgomerie's Ward, and in the Bowry Division of the Out Ward of the said City, and the said Tax not paid, and no Goods or Chattels to be found on the Premises whereon the same can be levied by Distress and the Owner thereof shall reside out of the City of New York, that it shall and may be lawful in such Case to and for the Collector of such Tax wherever he can find the Owner of such real Estate so taxed in the City of New York to sue and prosecute him or her for the same in his own Name before the Mayor, Recorder or any one of the Aldermen of the said City in the same Manner as suits to the value of ten Pounds and under are prosecuted before them in which Action it shall be sufficient for the Plaintiff to alledge that the real Estate of the Defendant was taxed, and that the same remains unsatisfied and not paid, and that no Distress can be found whereon to levy the same whereby the Plaintifs Action accrued according to the Form of this Act, without setting forth the special Matter; And the said Mayor, Recorder and Aldermen or either of them are hereby authorized and required to hear and determine such Suit or Suits, and to proceed therein in like Manner as is directed for the Trial and proceedings in Causes to the value of ten Pounds and under. PROVIDED that Nothing in this Act contained shall be construed to affect any Contract or Agreement that has been or shall be made between any Landlord and Tenant about the payment of Taxes, but that they shall be chargeable and answerable to each other, in the same Manner as if this Act had never been made, and in Case any Taxes shall be paid by any Person when by Agreement or by Law the same ought to have been borne and paid by some other Person, that the Person so paying shall and may have such Remedy over against the Person chargeable with the payment of such Tax as he or she could have had if this Act had never been made any Thing herein before contained to the contrary thereof in any wise notwithstanding.

PROVIDED ALWAYS that every Collector before he enters upon the execution of the Powers given to him by this Act shall give such Security for the due performance of the same, to the Mayor, Aldermen and Commonalty of the City of New York as they shall Judge sufficient, and upon his refusal the said Mayor Aldermen and Commonalty shall appoint another Collector to execute the Powers in this Act in his stead who will give such security as aforesaid, any Law Usage or Custom to the contrary Notwithstanding.

[CHAPTER 1492.]

[Chapter 1492 of Van Schaack, where the act is printed in full.]

An Act for the better Regulation of the Election of Officers in the City of New York chosen by virtue of the Charters granted to the said City, and other purposes therein mentioned.

[Passed, February 16, 1771.]

WHEREAS in and by the Charter granted to the City of New York by his late Majesty George the second of Glorious Memory bearing Date the fifteenth Day of January in the fourth Year of his said Majesty's Reign, it is among other Things therein appointed and ordained that the Freemen of the said City being Inhabitants and the Freeholders of each respective Ward in the said City shall and may assemble themselves and meet together on the Feast Day of Saint Michael the Arch Angel at such Time of the Day and such Public Place in each of the said Wards as each respective Alderman for each respective Ward for the Time being shall appoint, and then and there by plurality of Voices or Votes to elect and choose out of the Inhabitants of each respective Ward being Freeholders there or Freemen of the said City (except the Outward) for the ensuing Year, one Alderman and one Assistant two Assessors one Collector, and two Constables, and for the said Outward four Assessors two Collectors and four Constables, but the value of the Freehold upon which such Freeholders shall Vote, nor the Time that such Freemen so choosing shall be Freemen of the said City before the Time of such Election is not ascertained or declared by the said Charter for want of which many Evils may arise to the Inhabitants of the said City, for preventing whereof.

BE IT ENACTED by his Excellency the Governor, the Council and the General Assembly and it is hereby Enacted by the

Authority of the same, That from and after the Publication of this Act no person shall Vote as a Freeholder for any of the said Officers but such as shall have Lands or Tenements to the value of forty Pounds in Freehold lying and being in such Ward in the said City where he shall vote, and shall have possessed the same one Month before the Day of such Election for such Officers; unless he holds his Estate by Descent or Devise: And that no Person shall vote as a Freeman of the said City for any of the said Officers but such who shall have been Freemen of the said City for at least three Months before the Day of such Election, and shall have actually resided in the Ward in the said City in which he shall so vote for one Month next immediately before the Day of such Election; and that every Elector before he is admitted to Poll at the said Election shall if required by the Candidates or any of them or the Officer who shall preside at such Election, first take the Oath or Oaths herein after mentioned or one of them; or being one of the People called Quakers or Unitas Fratrum shall solemnly affirm the Effect thereof, that is to say, if the said Elector Votes as a Freeholder the Oath following.

"You shall swear or affirm that you are a Freeholder in the "Ward in which you now Offer to vote and have Lands or Tene- "ments to the value of forty Pounds lying in the said Ward, that "you do not hold the same in Trust for any Body Politick or "Corporate, or for any Pious or Religious use whatsoever, and "that you have possessed the same for one Month, next before "the Day of this Election, (except he has his Freehold by Descent "or Devise) and that you have not been before Polled at this "Election, nor have you procured this Freehold under any Obli- "gation or Promise to re-convey the same to the Seller after this "Election, so help you God."

AND if the said Elector shall Vote as a Freeman, the Oath herein aftermentioned, or being one of the People called Quakers or Unitas Fratrum shall solemnly affirm the Effect thereof, that is to say.

"You do swear or affirm that you are a Freeman of the City "of New York, and have been so three Months now last Past "and have actually resided in the Ward in which you now offer "to Vote one Month next before the Day of this Election, and "that you have not been before Polled at this Election, so help "you God."

Which Oath or Affirmation every Officer who shall preside at the said Election is hereby authorized and impowered to administer and take, and if any Person or Persons shall refuse or neglect to take the Oaths hereby respectively appointed to be taken or being one of the People called Quakers or Unitas Fratrum shall refuse or neglect to make such solemn Affirmation as aforesaid, being required as aforesaid, then and in every such Case the Vote or Poll of such Person or Persons so neglecting or refusing, shall be and the same is hereby declared to be Null and Void and as such shall be rejected and disallowed, any Charter Law Usage or Custom to the contrary thereof in any wise notwithstanding.

AND BE IT FURTHER ENACTED by the Authority aforesaid, That if any Person or Persons shall Wilfully, falsely and corruptly take the said Oaths or Affirmations set forth and appointed in and by this Act or either of them, and be thereof lawfully convicted by Indictment, or if any Person or Persons shall corruptly procure or suborn any other Person to take the said Oaths or Affirmations or either of them whereby he shall wilfully and falsly take the said Oaths or Affirmations and the Person so procuring or suborning shall be thereof convicted by Indictment, every Person so offending shall for every such Offence incurr and suffer such Penalties Forfeitures and Disabilities as Persons convicted of Wilful, and corrupt Perjury at the Common Law.

AND for the better ascertaining in what right each of the said Electors votes at such Elections that is to say whether as a Freeholder or Freeman BE IT FURTHER ENACTED by the Authority aforesaid that every Person who shall Vote at the said Elections shall before his Vote is taken publickly declare in what Right he votes, whether as a Freeholder or Freeman or both, and in Case any Elector shall refuse or neglect to make such Declaration in what Right he votes being thereunto required by the Candidates or either of them, or the Officer who shall preside at the said Election, then and in such Case the Poll or Vote of such Person or Persons so neglecting or refusing shall be and the same is hereby declared to be Null and Void and as such shall be rejected and disallowed, any Charter Law, Usage or Custom to the contrary thereof in any wise notwithstanding.

AND BE IT FURTHER ENACTED by the Authority aforesaid that no Person or Persons holding Lands Tenements or Hereditaments in Trust for any Body Politick or Corporate or for any Religious or Pious use or purpose, shall in virtue of such Trust be qualified to vote for the aforesaid Officers which shall hereafter be chosen for the said City.

AND WHEREAS it may be doubted whether any Person having Mortgaged his Lands should not by reason of such Mortgage be debarred from voting as a Freeholder. BE IT THEREFORE FURTHER ENACTED by the Authority aforesaid, That if the Mortgagor his Heirs or Assigns be in the actual possession or take the Profits of the Lands so mortgaged such Mortgage shall not debarr him or them from voting, but if the Mortgagee his Heirs or Assigns, be in the actual possession, or take the Profits of the Lands so mortgaged to their own use, then such Mortgagee his Heirs or Assigns being in possession or taking the Profits as aforesaid shall have the Right of voting thereon.

AND WHEREAS by the above recited Charter the Division Line between the West Ward and North Ward in the said City is a Line running from the Middle of New Street at the North End thereof to the Rear of the dwelling House formerly in the Possession of Domini Du Bois, and from thence to run all along the Rear of the Houses that Front the Broad Way up to the North Part of the Rear of Spring Garden House, and from thence to run up a Line as the Broadway runs to the End thereof including the said BroadWay and John Harris his House and to include all other Houses thereafter to be built fronting the said Broadway, and from the North End of the Broad Way to continue and run a Line as the said Street runs until it comes directly opposite to Bestevars Killitie or Rivulet: By which Line of Division most if not all the Lots of Ground fronting the BroadWay lay partly in the WestWard and partly in the NorthWard and the Freeholders of the said Lots have heretofore Voted for Officers chosen by virtue of the said Charters in both the said Wards which is thought unreasonable as they are Taxed only in the West Ward where their Houses are and not in the North Ward into which the Rear of their Lots Extend.

BE IT THEREFORE FURTHER ENACTED by the Authority aforesaid that every Person and Persons seized of a Freehold Estate of and in any Houses or Lots of Ground of Value sufficient by this Act to entitled him or them to a Vote lying and being on the East Side of the BroadWay in the City of New York and fronting thereto shall vote on their said Estate of Freehold for the Officers which shall hereafter be chosen by virtue of the

Charters granted to the said City in the West Ward only, and not in the North Ward of the said City, altho' their Lots of Ground fronting the said Broad Way should extend therein, any Charter Law Usage or Custom to the contrary thereof in any wise notwithstanding.

AND WHEREAS it hath heretofore been customary and usual for the Aldermen of each respective Ward in the said City to preside at the Election of the said Officers for each Ward as the Returning Officer, and to take the Votes and Poll of the Electors, and it has very frequently happened that the Alderman himself is a Candidate in the said Election, and it being thought unreasonable that any Candidate for any Office should be the presiding Officer at the Election for such Office, for Remedy whereof in the Premises and that all future Elections of the said Officers may be had with the utmost fairness and impartiality.

BE IT THEREFORE FURTHER ENACTED by the Authority aforesaid that the Mayor Aldermen and Commonalty of the City of New York or the major Part of them in Common Council convened shall and may on such Day in the Month of September in every Year hereafter as to themselves shall seem meet at least eight Days before the Day of Election fix upon a proper Place in each respective Ward where such Election shall be held and nominate and appoint a fit and discreet Person for each respective Ward in the said City to preside at and be the Returning Officer of the said Elections of the said Officers which shall be chosen for the said City in the said Month of September for the Year next ensuing to see that the same is fairly conducted and had, and to return the Officers that shall be duly chosen, which Person so to be nominated and appointed for each Ward, shall be a resident in the Ward for which he shall be so appointed and a Freeholder there, or a Freeman of the said City, which said Persons so to be nominated and appointed shall respectively appoint a Clerk, or Clerks as they respectively shall think proper to take the Poll at the respective Elections at which they shall respectively preside, which Clerks shall take the Poll in the presence of the said presiding Officer and be sworn by him truly and indifferently to take the same and to set down the Name of each Voter, and in what Right he voted, and for whom he shall Poll, And in Case it should so happen that any of the said Aldermen Assistants, Assessors, Collectors or Constables so chosen should happen to die or remove out of the said City before the Day appointed by the said Charter for the annual Election of such Officers, by which the Election of another in the Room and place of him so dying or removing shall become necessary, that then and in such Case, it shall and may be lawful to and for the Mayor of the said City for the Time being, or his Deputy on such Day as to him shall seem meet previous to the said Election to nominate and appoint some fit and discreet Person being a Resident in the Ward in which such Election shall be made and a Freeholder there or a Freeman of the said City to preside at and be the Returning Officer of the said Election who shall have the like Power and Authority and proceed in the same Manner in such Election as is given and prescribed to the Persons who shall be appointed to preside at the annual Elections of the said Officers for the said City in the Month of September, any Charter Law, Usage or Custom to the contrary in any wise notwithstanding.

AND BE IT FURTHER ENACTED by the Authority aforesaid that in Case any of the said Persons so to be appointed by the said Mayor Aldermen and Commonalty of the City of New York in Common Council convened as aforesaid to preside at the said Annual Elections should happen to die or remove out of the said City, or be otherwise rendered incapable of attending the said Election before the Day on which the same is to be held that then and in such Case it shall and may be lawful to and for the said Mayor, Aldermen, and Commonalty of the City of New York or the major Part of them convened in Common Council to appoint another fit Person being a Resident in the Ward in which such Election shall be made and a Freeholder there or a Freeman of the said City to preside at the said Election in the Room and Stead of the said Person so dying removing or being rendered incapable of attending the said Election and so as often as such Cases shall happen, And should it so happen that the presiding Officer which in the Cases herein abovementioned is to be nominated and appointed by the Mayor of the said City for the Time being or his Deputy should die or remove out of the said City or be otherwise rendered incapable of attending the said Election before the Day on which the same is to be held, that then and in such Case it shall and may be lawful to and for the Mayor of the said City for the Time being or his Deputy to appoint another fit Person being a resident in the Ward in which such Election shall be made and a Freeholder there or a Freeman of the said City to Preside at the said Election in the Room and Stead of the said Person so dying removing or being rendered incapable of attending the said Election and so as often as such Cases shall happen, And in Case the said Mayor Aldermen and Commonalty of the City of New York or the Major Part of them in Common Council convened, or the Mayor of the said City for the Time being or his Deputy or either of them shall neglect to appoint such Persons to preside at the Elections of the said Officers as aforesaid, or should such Presiding Officer chosen as aforesaid or any of them not attend, or do the Duty of their said Office, that then the said Elections of the said Officers shall be made and had according to the directions of the Charters granted to the said City any Thing herein contained to the contrary thereof in any wise notwithstanding.

AND BE IT FURTHER ENACTED by the Authority aforesaid, That each respective Clerk who shall be employed by such presiding Officers as aforesaid to take the Votes or Poll of the Electors and who shall perform that Service shall be paid by the said Mayor, Aldermen, and Commonalty of the City of New York the Sum of twenty Shillings lawful Money of New York.

AND BE IT FURTHER ENACTED by the Authority aforesaid, That if any Person or Persons who shall be appointed as aforesaid to preside at the Elections of the Officers herein before mentioned shall neglect or refuse to execute the said Office every such Person or Persons shall pay as a Fine for every such neglect or refusal the Sum of twenty Pounds Current Money of this Colony for the use of the Corporation of the said City to be levied by Warrant under the Seal of the said City, signed by the Mayor thereof for the Time being.

AND BE IT FURTHER ENACTED by the Authority aforesaid that no Freeholder or Freeholders whatsoever of the City and County of New York shall be entitled to vote for the Election of Church Wardens and Vestry Men of the City of New York who are in and by an Act intitled "An Act to amend an Act intitled "an Act for Settling a Ministry and raising a Maintenance for "them in the City of New York County of Richmond West "Chester and Queen's County. and an Act intitled. An Act to "enable the Inhabitants of the City of New York to choose "annually two Vestrymen for each respective Ward within the "said City so far as the same relates to the Election of the "Church Wardens and Vestrymen of the City of New York." to be chosen on the same Day on which the Aldermen Assistants and other Officers of the said City are elected unless such Freeholder or Freeholders shall be duly qualified in the same manner as in and by this Act the Freeholders of this City and County are directed to be qualified in order to entitle them to a Vote for Aldermen Assistants and other Officers of this City, and that they and each of them who shall offer to vote for the Election of Church Wardens and Vestrymen as aforesaid shall if required by any or either of the Candidates first take the Oath herein before prescribed to be taken by every Freeholder who shall Vote for the Election of Aldermen Assistants and other Officers of the City as aforesaid.

AND BE IT ALSO ENACTED by the Authority aforesaid that the Election and Elections of Church Wardens and Vestrymen hereafter to be made shall begin precisely at eleven of the Clock in the forenoon of each Day of Election at the City Hall of the said City of New York under the inspection of the Mayor, Deputy Mayor and Recorder of the said City, or either of them for the Time being who are hereby authorized and impowered to sit and preside as Judge or Judges of every such Election hereafter to be held and if no Poll shall be demanded within two Hours thereafter it shall and may be lawful for the Mayor Deputy Mayor Recorder or either of them to declare who are duly elected as Church Wardens and Vestrymen for the said City of New York. But if any Poll shall be demanded within the said two Hours that then and in such Case the Mayor Deputy Mayor, Recorder or either of them shall appoint a Clerk and administer to him the Oath herein before prescribed and order to be taken by the Clerks to be appointed by the presiding Officers at Elections hereafter to be held for the Choice of Aldermen Assistants and other Officers of the City, as is herein beforementioned set forth and prescribed, and shall then immediately proceed to take the Votes of such Freeholders as shall offer to vote for Church Wardens and Vestrymen, provided such Freeholders be qualified as is herein before directed; and in Case all the Votes cannot be taken in one Day then the said Mayor, Deputy Mayor, Recorder or either of them may and are hereby required to adjourn the Poll to the next Day, and that the said Mayor Deputy Mayor, Recorder or either of them shall not close the Poll as long as any Voters are ready and offer to give their Votes, nor until the Mayor, Deputy Mayor, Recorder or either of them shall have caused Proclamation to be publickly and openly made for all Persons who have not voted to give their Votes or that the Poll will be Closed, neither shall the Poll be closed until such Proclamation is made as aforesaid and no voters duly qualified according to the directions of this Act shall appear and offer to vote within fifteen Minutes from the Time of the Making of such Proclamation any Law Usage or Custom to the contrary thereof in any wise notwithstanding.

AND BE IT FURTHER ENACTED by the Authority aforesaid That this Act and every Matter and Thing therein contained shall be in force from the Publication thereof to the first Day of February which will be in the Year of our Lord one thousand seven hundred and seventy four.

[CHAPTER 1493.]

[Chapter 1493 of Van Schaack, where the act is printed in full.]

An Act to amend an Act intitled "An "Act to establish the Rates to be taken for "wharfage of Ships and other Vessels, and "the Rates to be taken for Cranage within "the City of New York."

[Passed, February 16, 1771.]

WHEREAS Doubts have arisen as to the Person or Persons liable to pay the Rates of Wharfage established in and by an Act intitled. "An Act to establish the Rates to be taken for Wharf-"age of Ships and other Vessels, and the Rates to be taken for "Cranage within the City of New York." passed the twenty seventh Day of January one thousand seven hundred and seventy.

BE IT THEREFORE ENACTED by his Excellency the Governor the Council and the General Assembly and it is hereby Enacted by the Authority of the same that the Master or Commander, Owner or Owners of every Vessel using any of the Wharfs mentioned in the said Act, and in case of his or their absence out of this Colony, his or their Agent or Agents, Factor or Factors to whom such Vessel shall be consigned or addressed shall be liable to pay the Sum due for the Wharfage of such Vessel after the Rates established in and by the said Act, either to the Owner or Owners of such Wharf, or to the Wharfinger in behalf of such Owner or Owners. PROVIDED that such Factor or Factors Agent or Agents shall be liable to pay the same, only where an Account shall be delivered to, or in case of absence left at his or their House, and the Money demanded of him or them, before the sailing or Departure of such Vessel from Port: any Thing in the said Act, or herein to the contrary notwithstanding.

[CHAPTER 1494.]

[Chapter 1494 of Van Schaack, where the act is printed in full. Revived by chapter 1758.]

An Act for the more effectual Punishment of Persons who shall be guilty of any of the Trespasses therein mentioned in the Cities of New York and Albany, and Township of Schenectady.

[Passed, February 16, 1771.]

WHEREAS some evil minded and Mischievous Person or Persons have of late made a Practice of Breaking glass Windows, Porches, Knockers of Doors and committing other Trespasses and Enormities and damaging Signs in the said Cities and Township, which Practice may not only be dangerous to the Persons of the Inhabitants from Stones and other Things being thrown into their Houses, but injurious to their Properties, and to the Disturbance of the Peace of the said Cities and Township, for the more effectual Punishment of such Offenders for the future.

BE IT ENACTED by his Excellency the Governor the Council and the General Assembly, and it is hereby Enacted by the Authority of the same. That if any Person or Persons of what Age soever from and after the Publication of this Act shall wilfully break any Glass Window or Windows, Porch or Porches, Knocker or Knockers, or break any outside Fixture of any House or damage any Sign belonging to any House or Building in the Cities of New York, and Albany and Township of Schenectady, that then every such Person or Persons so offending and being thereof convicted before one or more Justice or Justices of the Peace in either of the places aforesaid, either by the Confession of the Party or Parties so offending, or the Oath of one or more Credible Witness or Witnesses (which Oath the said Justice or Justices of the Peace is and are hereby impowered and required to administer) shall for every such Offence as aforesaid forfeit the Sum of ten Pounds to be levied by distress and sale of the Goods and Chattels of every such Offender or Offenders by Warrant under the Hand and seal of the said Justice or Justices of the Peace before whom such Conviction or Convictions shall be as aforesaid made, the said Forfeitures to be one half to the Informer or Informers and the other half to the use of the Poor of the said Cities or Township respectively, and if the said Offender or Offenders shall not pay the said Forfeiture or Forfeitures upon Conviction as aforesaid and want of sufficient distress whereon the same can be made, that then every such Justice or Justices of the Peace is and are hereby impowered and required by Warrant under his or their Hands and Seals to commit every such Person or Persons so as aforesaid Offending to the Common Goal of the said Cities respectively, there to remain without Bail or Main Prize for the space of one Month unless such Forfeiture or Forfeitures be sooner paid. But in Case such Offender or Offenders shall happen to be a Slave or Slaves and the Forfeiture or Forfeitures aforesaid on Conviction as aforesaid shall not be forthwith paid, that then it shall and may be lawful to and for such Justice or Justices before whom the Conviction shall be, to cause such Slave or Slaves to be publickly whipped on the naked Back such Number of Stripes as such Justice or Justices shall think proper not exceeding thirty nine, which Punishment shall be in lieu and stead of the said Forfeiture or Forfeitures.

AND WHEREAS the Mischiefs aforesaid are generally committed in the Night Time when the Offenders cannot easily be known in Order therefore that this Act may have the good Effect intended by it. BE IT FURTHER ENACTED by the Authority aforesaid that it shall and may be lawful to and for any Sheriff, Constable, Marshal, or Watchman of the said Cities respectively, or the Watchman or Constable of the Township of Schenectady who shall see any Person or Persons commit either or any of the Mischiefs or Trespasses in either of the places aforesaid, if such Person or Persons so offending shall be unknown to such Sheriff, Constable, Marshal or Watchman to seize, secure, and detain such Offender or Offenders unknown to him Or them as aforesaid until they can discover the Name or Names of such Offender or Offenders or until the next Morning if the Offence shall be committed in the Night, and the Offender or Offenders shall refuse to tell his or their Name or Names, when such Offender or Offenders shall be carried before some Justice of the Peace for the aforesaid Places respectively, who on Conviction of such Offender or Offenders in the Premises as aforesaid shall proceed against him or them in the Manner as herein before is directed for such Offences. And in Case any Person or Persons shall commit either or any of the Mischiefs or Trespasses in either of the Places aforesaid in the presence of any Sheriff Constable, Marshal or Watchman of the said Places, and shall be known to such Sheriff Constable, Marshal or Watchman, that then every such Sheriff Constable, Marshal and Watchman shall and is hereby required speedily to make Information before some Justice of the Peace for the said Places respectively in order that the Offender or Offenders may by such Justice be convicted thereof and punished for the same in manner and form as in and by this Act is directed.

AND BE IT FURTHER ENACTED by the Authority aforesaid, That this Act nor any Thing herein contained shall bar or exclude any Person or Persons from his her or their Damages done by any Person or Persons as aforesaid, but that the same may be had and recovered in the same Manner as if this Act had never been passed and that this Act shall remain of force from the Publication hereof until the first Day of February which will be in the Year of our Lord one thousand seven hundred and seventy three.

[CHAPTER 1495.]

[Chapter 1495 of Van Schaack, where the title only is printed. See chapters 1121, 1143, 1166, 1315, 1369, 1447.]

An Act to revive the several Acts therein mentioned relative to Highways in the County of Albany.

[Passed, February 16, 1771.]

WHEREAS the Act intitled "An Act for regulating, clearing "and further laying out Public Highways throughout the City "and County of Albany" passed in the thirty third Year of his late Majesty's Reign, and the Act intitled. "An Act for altering "and explaining part of an Act intitled An Act for regulating, "clearing, and further laying out Public Highways throughout "the City and County of Albany." passed in the first Year of his present Majesty's reign, and the Act intitled. "An Act to amend "An Act intitled an Act for regulating clearing and further lay- "ing out Public Highways throughout the City and County of "Albany." passed in the second Year of his present Majesty's Reign, also the Act intitled. "An Act to impower the Justices of "the Peace in the County of Albany in General Sessions to "appoint Commissioners to lay out new Roads or Highways in "the said County." passed in the seventh Year of his present Majesty's Reign, and also an Act intitled. "An Act to amend an Act intitled "an Act for regulating, clearing and further laying "out Public Highways throughout the City and County of "Albany." passed in the ninth year of his present Majesty's Reign have all expired on the first Day of January one thousand seven hundred and seventy one.

BE IT THEREFORE ENACTED by his Excellency the Governor the Council and the General Assembly, and it is hereby Enacted by the Authority of the same, that the said several abovementioned Acts shall be, and hereby are revived and every Clause, Article Matter and Thing in the said several Acts contained, enacted to be and remain in full force and virtue to all Intents, Constructions and purposes whatsoever from the publication hereof until the first Day of January which will be in the Year of our Lord one thousand seven hundred and seventy two.

[CHAPTER 1496.]

[Chapter 1496 of Van Schaack, where the act is printed in full. See chapter 1413.]

An Act to amend and explain an Act intitled. "An Act impowering the Justices of "the Peace living or dwelling in the Township of Schenectady in the County of "Albany to establish and regulate a Night "Watch, appoint Firemen, and other Pur- "poses therein mentioned."

[Passed, February 16, 1771.]

WHEREAS in and by an Act intitled, "An Act impowering the "Justices of the Peace living or dwelling in the Township of "Schenectady, in the County of Albany to establish and regulate "a Night-Watch appoint Fireman and other Purposes therein "mentioned." passed the thirtieth Day of December, one thousand seven hundred and sixty nine, it is among other Things enacted, That it should and might be lawful to and for the Justices of the Peace living or dwelling in the Township of Schenectady, or the major Part of them to meet together in the said Township with all convenient Speed after the Publication of that Act, and they were thereby required and directed then and there at such Meeting to order, establish and regulate a Night Watch not exceeding six Men and an Officer for each Night out of the Inhabitants of the said Township, who should and were thereby directed and required in their Turns in the Night Time to keep Watch and guard the said Township in such Manner, and at such Time and places as the said Justices or the Major Part of them should order and direct. AND WHEREAS tho' it was intended by the said Law, that no Person but those living within the Townspot, should be obliged to watch and Guard the said Town; yet it has been otherwise understood by many; which has created great Disputes and controversies as well among the Justices as others the Inhabitants of the said Township and has in a great Measure prevented the putting in Execution that Salutary Law.

BE IT THEREFORE ENACTED by his Excellency the Governor the Council and the General Assembly, and it is hereby enacted and declared by the Authority of the same, That none of the Inhabitants of the said Township, who reside one half of an English Mile or upwards distant from the Dutch Church in said Town shall be subject or obliged to guard or Watch said Town; and that the Night Watch mentioned in the aforesaid Act and thereby ordered and directed to be established shall be composed of such Inhabitants only as dwell and reside on the South Side of the Mohawks River & within one half of an English Mile distant from said Church any Thing in the said Act contained to the contrary in any wise notwithstanding.

[CHAPTER 1497.]

[Chapter 1497 of Van Schaack, where the title only is printed.]

An Act to raise a Sum not exceeding forty Pounds within the Township of Schenectady for repairing the Watch House in the said Township.

[Passed, February 16, 1771.]

WHEREAS the Watch House in the Township of Schenectady is very much out of repair, and the same being found useful, it is become necessary that a Sum of Money be raised for the reparation thereof.

BE IT THEREFORE ENACTED by his Excellency the Governor the Council and the General Assembly, and it is hereby Enacted by the Authority of the same, That it shall and may be lawful to and for the Assessors of the Township of Schenectady, and they are hereby directed and required within four Months next after the Publication of this Act to assess, and cause to be levied and collected of and from the several Freeholders and Inhabitants dwelling and residing within the said Township the Sum of forty Pounds, which Sum shall be assessed raised levied and collected in the same Manner as the other necessary and contingent Charges of the said Township are assessed levied and collected.

AND BE IT FURTHER ENACTED by the Authority aforesaid, That the Money to be raised by this Act shall by the Collector or Collectors of the said Township as soon as collected be paid unto the Justices of the Peace residing within the Township aforesaid or to the major Part of them after retaining six Pence out of every Pound so collected for his or their Trouble in collecting the same, to be by the said Justices or the major Part of them laid out and they are hereby directed and required with all convenient speed after the Money so raised as aforesaid shall come to their Hands, to lay out the same in repairing the said Watch House.

[CHAPTER 1498.]

[Chapter 1498 of Van Schaack, where the act is printed in full. See chapter 1377.]

An Act to revive and continue an Act, intitled. "An Act to appoint an Inspector of "Hemp in the County of West Chester."

[Passed, February 16, 1771.]

WHEREAS the Act intitled. "An Act to appoint an Inspector "of Hemp in the County of West Chester." hath expired by its own Limitation on the first Day of January one thousand seven hundred and seventy one; and the same having been found useful and necessary.

BE IT THEREFORE ENACTED by his Excellency the Governor the Council and the General Assembly, and it is hereby Enacted by the Authority of the same. That the abovementioned Act and every Thing therein contained shall be, and hereby is revived and continued to be and remain in full force, from the Publication hereof, until the first Day of February which will be in the Year of our Lord one thousand seven hundred and seventy five.

[CHAPTER 1499.]

[Chapter 1499 of Van Schaack, where the title only is printed.]

An Act to enable the Freeholders and Inhabitants of Rumbout Precinct in Dutchess County to elect a Collector in the Room of the one discharged by the Court to collect the Arrears of the Poor Tax.

[Passed, February 16, 1771.]

WHEREAS the Inhabitants of Rumbout Precinct in Dutchess County, did on the first Tuesday in April last, pursuant to the Directions of the Act of the Lieutenant Governor, the Councll and the General Assembly in that Case made elect and appoint a Collector to Collect in the Taxes assessed and laid for the support of the Poor, and other contingent Charges in the last Year, which person so chosen as aforesaid was for certain Reasons discharged from his said Office of Collector by a Court of Sessions of the Peace held for the said County of Dutchess, by which means the Taxes that were laid and Assessed in Rumbout Precinct as aforesaid remain uncollected.

For a Remedy in the Premises BE IT ENACTED by his Excellency the Governor, the Council, and the General Assembly, and it is hereby Enacted by the Authority of the same, That it shall and may be lawful to and for the Inhabitants of Rumbout Precinct aforesaid, and they are hereby required and authorized on Tuesday the fifth Day of March next by a majority of Voices to elect and appoint a Collector in the said Precinct in the Room and stead of the Person appointed Collector and discharged as aforesaid, to collect in the Taxes that were assessed and laid in the said Precinct in the last Year for the support of the Poor and other contingent Charges, which Person who shall be elected and appointed as aforesaid a Collector by virtue of this Act, shall have the same Power and authority to perform execute and serve, and be lyable to the same Pains and Penalties for neglect of duty as the Collector Chosen for the said Precinct on the first Tuesday in April in every year is by any Act or Acts of this Colony.

AND BE IT FURTHER ENACTED by the Authority aforesaid, That the Person who shall be elected and appointed a Collector as aforesaid by virtue of this Act shall and he is hereby required to pay such Taxes as shall be by him collected for the purposes aforesaid into the Hands of the Treasurer of the said County on or before the first Day of October next.

[CHAPTER 1500.]

[Chapter 1500 of Van Schaack, where the title only is printed. See chapter 1453.]

An Act to extend an Act intitled "An "Act for the better regulation of the Public "Inns and Taverns in the Counties of Ulster "and Orange," to the Manor of Cortlandt in the County of West Chester.

[Passed, February 16, 1771.]

BE IT ENACTED by his Excellency the Governor the Council and the General Assembly, and it is hereby Enacted by the Authority of the same That the Act intitled "An Act for the "better regulation of the Public Inns and Taverns in the Counties "of Ulster and Orange," passed the twenty seventh Day of January one thousand seven hundred and seventy shall extend to the Manor of Cortlandt in the County of West Chester. PROVIDED ALWAYS that the said Act shall not be in force in the said Manor till the first Day of May next, any Thing herein contained to the contrary thereof in any wise notwithstanding.

[CHAPTER 1501.]

[Chapter 1501 of Van Schaack, where the title only is printed. Expired the 1st of February, 1773. Provided for by chapter 1607.]

An Act to prevent the firing of Guns, Pistols, Squibs and other Fire Works at the Times and Places therein mentioned within this Colony.

[Passed, February 16. 1771.]

WHEREAS great Damages are frequently done on the eve of the last Day of December, and on the first and second Days of January, commonly called New Years Days, by persons going from House to House, with Guns and other Fire Arms and being often intoxicated with Liquor, have not only put the Inhabitants in great Terror, but committed many Mischiefs, for the prevention whereof for the future.

BE IT ENACTED by his Excellency the Governor, the Council and the General Assembly, and it is hereby Enacted by the Authority of the same that if any Person or Persons of any Age or Quality whatsoever shall fire or discharge any Gun, Pistol, Rocket, Cracker, Squib or other fire Work in any House Barn or other Building or before any Door or in any Garden, Street, Lane or other Inclosure on the said Eve or Days within the County of Richmond; and in the Precincts of Haverstraw and Orange Town in the County of Orange, that then every such Person or Persons so offending, and being thereof convicted before one or more Justice or Justices of the Peace in the County or Precincts where such Offence shall be committed either by the Confession of the Party or Parties so offending, or the Oath of one or more Witnesses, which Oath said Justice or Justices of the Peace is and are hereby impowered and required to administer, shall for every such Offence forfeit the Sum of twenty Shillings with Costs of Suit: the said Forfeiture to be levied by distress and sale of the Goods and Chattels of every such Offender, by Warrant under the Hand and Seal of the said Justice or Justices of the Peace before whom such Conviction or Convictions shall be as aforesaid made, the which Forfeitures to be to the use of the Poor of the Town or Place wherein such Offender shall be discovered, and if the said Offender or Offenders shall not pay the said Forfeiture or Forfeitures upon Conviction as aforesaid, and, for want of sufficient Distress whereon to levy the same, than then every such Justice or Justices of the Peace is and are hereby impowered and required by Warrant under his or their Hands and Seals to commit every such Person or Persons so as aforesaid offending, to the common Goal of the County where the said Forfeiture shall arise, there to remain without Bail or Mainprize for the Space of one Month unless such Forfeiture or Forfeitures be sooner paid. but in Case such Offender or Offenders in the Premises last above mentioned shall happen to be a slave or slaves and the Forfeiture or Forfeitures aforesaid on Conviction as aforesaid shall not be forthwith paid, that then it shall and may be lawful to and for such Justice or Justices before whom the conviction shall be, to cause such Slave or Slaves to be publickly whipped on the naked Back, such Number of Stripes as he or they shall think proper not exceeding thirty nine which Punishment shall be in lieu and instead of the said Forfeiture: This Act to be in force from the publication hereof until the first Day of February which will be in the Year of our Lord one thousand seven hundred and seventy three.

[CHAPTER 1502.]

[Chapter 1502 of Van Schaack, where the title only is printed. See chapter 1455. Repealed by chapter 1616.]

An Act to amend the Act therein mentioned relative to High Ways in the County of Orange.

[Passed, February 16, 1771.]

WHEREAS by the second section of an Act intitled "An Act "to amend an Act intitled An Act for the better laying out, "regulating and keeping in repair common, public and private "Highways on the North side of the Highlands in the County of "Orange." passed the twenty seventh Day of January one thousand seven hundred and seventy, it is among other Things Enacted that every Person who is obliged to work on Highways, and does dwell within certain Bounds in the said Section mentioned, shall work one Day in every Year on the Water side Roads in the Precinct of Cornwall; And Whereas many Persons choose rather to pay Money than be obliged to work on the said Roads.

BE IT THEREFORE ENACTED by his Excellency the Governor, the Council and the General Assembly, and it is hereby Enacted by the Authority of the same. That each Person who by the said Act is obliged to work one Day in a year on the said Water side Roads in the Precinct of Cornwall or on the New Road hereafter mentioned, shall be excused from working on the same provided he will (before the Day appointed for him to work,) pay the Sum of three shillings to the Overseer of the District in which he doth belong.

AND BE IT FURTHER ENACTED, That every Overseer shall pay all the Money which he shall or may receive for excusing Persons from working on the said Water side Roads or for Fines for their not working thereon into the Hands of Colonel Benjamin Tusteen, John Brewster, or Zachariah Dubois, who are hereby directed to lay out the same in repairing the said Water side Roads in such Manner as they or any two of them shall think proper, and to render an Account thereof on Oath to the Justices of the Annual Town Meetings of the Precincts of Goshen and Cornwall.

AND BE IT FURTHER ENACTED by the Authority aforesaid, That Captain John Wiesner, Captain Elihu Mervin, Zachariah Dubois and John Wells, or the major Part of them shall order any three of the Overseers of the Districts that are obliged to work on the said Water side Roads to work with the Men of their respective Districts on the New Road which turns out of the Goshen Road opposite to Carpenter's Mills, and runs by Sharrick Van Deursen's to the Landing at New Cornwall; which Days work shall be in lieu of the one Day which they are obliged to work on the said Water side Roads, any Thing in this or the above in part recited Act contained to the contrary notwithstanding.

AND BE IT FURTHER ENACTED by the Authority aforesaid, That instead of the Account which by the said Act was to be delivered by each Overseer in the Precincts of Goshen and Cornwall to one of the Commissioners of the Precinct to which they belonged, every Overseer shall on or before the first Tuesday in November in every Year deliver an Account to one of the Commissioners of the Precinct to which he doth belong, and shall take an Oath before the said Commissioner who is hereby impowered to administer the same in the Words following to wit. "I A B. do declare upon the Holy Evangelists that this Account "now delivered by me contains the Names of all the Persons "within my District which by Law are obliged to work on High-"ways, that each Person therein named has worked himself or "by a Man in his stead, five Days since the first Day of April "last, and at least to the amount of eight Hours in each Day "three of which Day's work were done between the first Day of "April and the first Day of July, and the other two Days between "the said first Day of April and the tenth Day of October, or I "have laid out or disposed of agreeable to Law the Fines of such "Persons as have not worked, and the Monies by me received for "excusing Persons from working as aforesaid, and that within "twenty-five Days after the Time in which such Person as I have "fined ought to have worked, according to the best of my knowl-"edge and belief, so help me God." Provided always, That Nothing herein contained shall exempt the Overseers of Roads in the said Precincts from delivering in their Accounts on the last Tuesday of March next as in and by the said in Part recited Act they are directed.

AND BE IT FURTHER ENACTED, That instead of one of the Water side Roads which in the second Section of the said Act is to begin at the Division Line of the said Precincts near Barnabas Manneys, the Inhabitants which are obliged to work on the Water side Roads shall begin to work on the Road at the Division Line of the said Precincts near John Manneys, and so along by Stephen Gilberts down to New Windsor.

AND BE IT FURTHER ENACTED by the Authority aforesaid. That every Person within the Precinct of Goshen who is obliged to work on Highways to the South of a Line from Black Walnut Island, thence along by Captain John Wiesner's Francis Armstrong's, John Sayre's, Timothy Clark Junior's the House in which John Perham now lives, and the House in which James Jackson now lives, (except such of the Inhabitants as live in the Mountains) shall work one Day in making a new Bridge near the Widow Dekay's Mill, and in making or repairing the Bridge by Richard Dowdle's Mill: and that Richard Edsall Esquire is hereby directed and required at his discretion to give Directions to every Overseer in the said Precinct of Goshen, who are obliged to work on the said Bridges, when he with the People of his District shall work, and on which Bridge he shall work, and in Case any Overseer shall refuse or neglect to work within eight Days thereafter on said Bridge, he shall forfeit the Sum of five Pounds, which Forfeiture shall be recovered and applied as other Forfeitures by the aforesaid Act are directed. Provided nevertheless that each Person who by this Act is obliged to work on the said Bridges shall be excused from working on the same provided he will before the Day appointed for him to work pay the sum of three Shillings to the Overseer of the District to which he doth belong.

AND BE IT FURTHER ENACTED That every Overseer shall pay all the Monies which he shall or may receive for excusing Persons from working on the said Bridges or for Fines for their not working thereon into the Hands of the said Richard Edsall who is hereby directed to lay out the same in making or repairing the said Bridges, as he in his Discretion shall think proper. This Act to continue in Force from the Publication thereof to the twenty seventh Day of January which will be in the Year of our Lord one thousand seven hundred and seventy three

[CHAPTER 1503.]

[Chapter 1503 of Van Schaack, where the act is printed in full. See chapter 1005.]

An Act to amend an Act intitled. "an "Act to encourage the taking and destroying "of Wild Cats in the County of Suffolk."

[Passed, February 16, 1771.]

WHEREAS the aforesaid Act passed in the twenty ninth Year of the Reign of his late Majesty King George the second has been found beneficial to the Inhabitants of the said County: But it appears from experience that the Bounty therein given is not a sufficient Encouragement to the Inhabitants to make it their Business to destroy such Wild Cats, so as wholly to extirpate them.

BE IT THEREFORE ENACTED by his Excellency the Governor the Council and the General Assembly, and it is hereby enacted by the Authority of the same, That from and after the Publication hereof, the Reward for taking killing and destroying any such Wild Cats as are described in the said Act shall be and hereby is encreased to the Sum of twelve Shillings for each grown Wild Cat, and for every such Catling to the Sum of six Shillings Current Money of this Colony over and above the Reward already allowed by the Act aforesaid and the Money raised in the manner therein directed, and that every Certificate to be granted by any Justice of the Peace in pursuance of the said Act, shall be in the Words following.

"I A B. one of his Majesty's Justices of the Peace of the County "of Suffolk do hereby certify that C. D. brought the Skin of a "Wild Cat before me, and that I have strictly examined him and "carefully enquired into the Circumstances thereof, and that it "is a (Grown Cat or Catling), and was killed by him in the said "County, on or about the ——.——.——. Day of ——.——.——. "last (or Instant) and that I have cut off the Ears, and burnt "them, this ——.——.——. Day of ——.——.——. One thousand "seven hundred and ——.——.——.——

A. B.

[CHAPTER 1504.]

[Chapter 1504 of Van Schaack, where the title only is printed. See chapter 1354. Repealed by the King the 19th of June, 1772.]

An Act to amend an Act intitled "An Act "for the more effectual vesting the Real and "Personal Estate whereof Abraham DePeyster Esquire late Treasurer of this Colony "died seized and possessed in Trustees for "the payment of his Debts."

[Passed, February 16, 1771.]

WHEREAS in and by one certain Act of the Governor the Council and the General Assembly of this Colony made and passed the sixth Day of February in the eighth Year of his present Majesty's Reign intitled. "An Act for the more effectual vest-"ing the Real and Personal Estate whereof Abraham De Peyster "Esquire late Treasurer of this Colony died seized and possessed "in Trustees for the payment of his Debts", it is among other Things in Substance recited. That William Axtell of the City of New York Gentleman on the sixth Day of February in the Year of our Lord one thousand seven hundred and sixty seven for the proper Debt of James De Peyster therein named by his certain Bond or Obligation became bound to Lewis Paintard also therein named for the payment of sixteen hundred and fifty four Pounds nineteen shillings with Lawful Interest on the first Day of April then next, when in Fact and Truth the Condition of the said Bond is for the performance of a Collateral Duty to wit for the payment of the like sum with Lawful Interest on the said first Day of April then next unto the Honorable Charles Ward Apthorpe Esquire in the said Act also named, for the payment of which the said Lewis Paintard became bound together with the said James De Peyster and at his request, and for his proper Debt unto the said Charles Ward Apthorpe Esquire by Bond bearing date the thirty first Day of October, in the said Year of our Lord one thousand seven hundred and sixty six; And also with further Condition intended to indemnify the said Lewis Paintard against all Costs and Damages that might accrue to him by reason of his being so bound to the said Charles Ward Apthorpe Esquire. AND WHEREAS it is also among other Things in and by the said Act recited. That the said Abraham

De Peyster on the sixth Day of February in the Year of our Lord one thousand seven hundred and sixty seven by his certain Bond or Obligation became Bound to the said William Axtell in the Penal sum of three thousand three hundred and nine Pounds eighteen shillings with Condition for payment either by the said James DePeyster or Abraham DePeyster of the said Sum of sixteen hundred and fifty four Pounds nineteen shillings with Interest thereon on or before the said first Day of April then next AND WHEREAS also it is in substance among other Things enacted in and by the said Act, That the Trustees therein named and thereby vested with the Estate of the said Abraham DePeyster should among other applications thereby directed, apply the Monies arising by the sale of the Real and Personal Estate of the said Abraham DePeyster thereby so vested in them for discharging so much of the said Debt therein supposed to be due from the said William Axtell for and on Account of the said James DePeyster to the said Lewis Paintard as the Securities delivered to him by the said James DePeyster should fall short of paying. AND WHEREAS it is now shewn by the said Lewis Paintard that at the Time when the said William Axtell made and executed to him the above mentioned Bond with the Condition thereto above in Substance set forth the said Lewis Paintard among other securities then in his Hands had a Mortgage to him from the said James DePeyster on a certain Vessel and her Cargo belonging to the said James De Peyster (and other Parts of his Property) then lying in the Port of New York ready for sailing on a Voyage, and worth upwards of four thousand Pounds, and made and executed with Intent to secure to the said Lewis Paintard the payment of all Monies due to him from and to indemnify him against the said Debt due to the said Charles Ward Apthorpe Esquire as well as against every other Engagement in which the said Lewis Paintard stood bound for the said James DePeyster, and that the said Mortgage and other Securities were amply sufficient for that purpose. That the said Lewis Paintard nevertheless at the special Instance and request of the said James DePeyster and William Axtell in order to permit the said Vessel to sail on her intended Voyage, gave up the said Vessel and her Cargo, and discharged them from the said Mortgage in Exchange for the said Bond from the said William Axtell to him. That the Securities remaining in his Hands after giving up the said Vessel and Cargo were justly and equitably his property according to the Contract subsisting between him and the said James DePeyster so far forth as to entitle him the said Lewis Paintard to apply the Monies to arise therefrom solely to the discharge of the Ballance that should appear to be due to him from the said James DePeyster on the several Engagements which the said Lewis Paintard had entered into for the said James DePeyster to other Persons than the said Charles Ward Apthorpe Esquire and to hold the said William Axtell by virtue of his said Bond to him the said Lewis Paintard to the full Discharge of the Principal Interest and Costs so due to the said Charles Ward Apthorpe Esquire from him the said Lewis Paintard as before and herein after is mentioned, That to compel the Application of the said Securities to the Discharge of the said last mentioned Debt, and to indemnify the said William Axtell in the Manner directed by the said Act would work the most manifest loss and Injury to him the said Lewis Paintard contrary to the clear Right vested in him by virtue of his Contracts with the said James De Peyster and the said William Axtell, which would be the more distressing to him the said Lewis Paintard as the said Charles Ward Apthorpe Esquire has sued and prosecuted him to a Judgment for the said Debt due to him. That although the said Lewis Paintard upon being thus sued brought his Action at Law against the said William Axtell on his said Bond to the said Lewis Paintard, yet that the said Trustees conceiving that they cannot safely discharge the said Debt due to the said Charles Ward Apthorpe Esquire until application of the said Securities be first made to answer that Purpose as far as they will extend, and conceiving also that they are bound by the said Act to indemnify the said William Axtell, have brought their Bill in equity against him and the said Lewis Paintard, and have obtained his Majesty's Writ of Injunction and thereby stayed his said Suit at Law against the said William Axtell. In as much therefore as should the said Act be carried into execution according to the Letter thereof, the said Lewis Paintard would not only remain exposed to have Execution taken out against him by the said Charles Ward Apthorpe Esquire but would also be put to very considerable Costs and Expences contrary to the true Intent and meaning of the said in part recited Act. AND WHEREAS the said Lewis Paintard has offered the said Trustees to perform on his Part what is in and by this Act herein after required of him, on Condition of their performing on their Parts what is herein after required of them, which Offer for want of sufficient Authority they are unable to comply with

BE IT THEREFORE ENACTED by his Excellency the Governor the Council and the General Assembly, and it is hereby enacted by the Authority of the same, That the said Lewis Paintard shall with all convenient speed render upon Oath to the said Trustees a full true and perfect Account of all and Singular the Dealings and Transactions between him and the said James DePeyster as well on Account of the aforesaid Engagements of the said Lewis Paintard for the said James DePeyster as all other Matters and Things between them, whereon any Ballance has arisen or shall arise in favour of the said Lewis Paintard, and also of all the aforesaid Securities now remaining in his Hands, and shall in due form of Law assign over unto the said Trustees the said Ballance and also assign to them all and singular the said Securities and the Monies due and to grow due thereon, and all and singular the Lands Tenements Hereditaments and real Estate thereby or by any of them assigned or conveyed to the said Lewis Paintard, and that they the said Trustees shall on such Assignment as aforesaid pay and satisfy unto the said Lewis Paintard the full amount of the said Ballance that shall appear to be due to him, and also all his Costs Charges and Expences which he has been put to in and about recovering any Monies on the said securities or any or either of them, and all such other Costs Charges and Disbursements as he should be entitled to were he to make up such Account with the said James DePeyster, and also all his Costs of Suit and Disbursements in his said suit against the said James DePeyster, and also in the said Chancery suit and in his said suit at Law against the said William Axtell, and shall also pay and satisfy to the said Charles Ward Apthorpe Esquire all and singular the Principal Interest and Costs due and to grow due on the said Judgment obtained by him against the said Lewis Paintard in full discharge of the said Lewis Paintard, the said several Payments to be made by the said Trustees out of any Monies now in their Hands or that shall hereafter come to their Hands and arisen or that shall arise out of or by or from the Estate of the said Abraham DePeyster so vested in them as aforesaid, or by from or out of the Securities so to be assigned to them by the said Lewis Paintard as aforesaid, the said in Part recited Act or any Clause Matter or Thing in the same contained to the contrary hereof in any wise notwithstanding

AND BE IT FURTHER ENACTED by the Authority aforesaid that the said Ballance, Securities and Sum and Sums of Money, and Lands and Tenements mentioned in the said securities or any or either of them shall immediately on such Assignment as aforesaid vest in and be recoverable by the said Trustees as fully and absolutely, and in the same Manner, and to the same uses intents and purposes as any and every Part of the Real and Personal Estate of the said Abraham DePeyster is or are vested in and recoverable by them by virtue of the said in Part recited Act, any Clause Matter or Thing in the said first mentioned Act contained, or any Law usage or Custom to the Contrary thereof in any wise notwithstanding.

AND BE IT FURTHER ENACTED that the said Trustees immediately upon their having received a sufficient sum of Money in their Hands arising from such securities so to be assigned to them as aforesaid to discharge the several Monies hereby made payable to the said Charles Ward Apthorpe Esquire, and the said Lewis Paintard the securities so to be assigned to them yet remaining in their Hands shall be by them assigned over and delivered to the Assignees appointed by virtue of a Certain other Act intitled. "An Act for the relief of James DePeyster of the "City of New York Merchant an insolvent Debtor and others "therein named," who are hereby impowered to sue for and recover the same as Assignees as aforesaid to be applied by them as by the said last mentioned Act is directed with respect to the Estate of the said James DePeyster, any Thing in this or in any of the abovementioned Act or any Law Usage or Custom to the Contrary thereof notwithstanding.

[CHAPTER 1505.]

[Chapter 1505 of Van Schaack, where the title only is printed.]

An Act for confirming to the Assignees therein named the Estate of Cornelius C Wynkoop, and of Mary Catharine his Wife, heretofore assigned for the Benefit of his Creditors, and for the Relief of the said Cornelius C. Wynkoop and the said Creditors.

[Passed, February 16, 1771.]

WHEREAS Cornelius C Wynkoop of the City of New York Merchant, having become indebted in sundry Sums of Money which he was unable to pay did assign his Estate to Benjamin Booth, Sampson Simpson and John Taylor as Assignees for the Benefit of all his Creditors, and Mary Catharine the Wife of the said Cornelius did with her Husband convey her real Estate to the said Assignees for the same purposes, the Assignees and Creditors of the said Cornelius allowing to her some Articles of Household Furniture in lieu thereof, and the said Creditors by their Petition to two of the Judges of the Mayor's Court of the City of New York intended to procure to the said Cornelius the Benefit of an Act of the Legislature of this Colony intitled. "An " Act to continue the several Acts therein mentioned respecting " the Relief of Insolvent Debtors." and of the several Acts therein mentioned.

AND WHEREAS the said Cornelius C Wynkoop and Mary Catharine his Wife the said Assignees and sundry Other Creditors of the said Cornelius C Wynkoop by their humble Petition to the General Assembly have represented that some Mistakes had arisen and been made in the proceedings by them had on the beforementioned Act of the Legislature of this Colony which may render the same of none Effect, and leave the said Cornelius exposed to all his Creditors and subject the other Petitioners to lose the Benefit of a considerable real and Personal Estate which would pay a large Dividend to all the Creditors of the said Cornelius C Wynkoop unless relieved by the Interposition of the Legislature, the General Assembly therefore pray that it may be Enacted.

AND BE IT ENACTED by his Excellency the Governor the Council and the General Assembly, and it is hereby Enacted by the Authority of the same, (any Misprisons or Mistakes in the proceedings of the said Assignees or Creditors of the said Cornelius C Wynkoop or of any other Person on the beforementioned Act of the Legislature of this Colony notwithstanding.) That all and singular the Real and Personal Estate conveyed by the said Cornelius C Wynkoop and Mary Catharine his Wife to the said Assignees or by their Order and Direction for the Benefit of the said Creditors is hereby fully confirmed to the said Assignees their Heirs and Assigns, and that Benjamin Booth, Sampson Simpson and John Taylor the said Assignees and the Survivors and Survivor of them shall have full power and Authority in their own Names or in the Names or Name of the Survivors or Survivor of them to sue for and recover all and every Part of the Real and Personal Estate of the said Cornelius C Wynkoop and Mary Catharine his Wife assigned to them for the Benefit of the said Creditors, and to grant bargain sell and dispose of the same and to make and execute good and sufficient Deeds and Conveyances for the same in Fee Simple and to proceed to convert the

Estate of the said Cornelius C Wynkoop and Mary Catharine his Wife into Money as soon as conveniently may be for the general Benefit and advantage of all the Creditors of the said Cornelius C Wynkoop.

AND BE IT FURTHER ENACTED by the Authority aforesaid that the said Assignees and the Survivors and Survivor of them, for the full Execution of the Trust reposed in them by the said Cornelius C Wynkoop and his Creditors, shall and may have and exercise all the Powers and Authorities which were heretofore given to any Assignee or Assignees of Insolvent Debtors by the several Acts of the Legislature of this Colony, which were continued by an Act intitled "An Act to continue the several Acts "therein mentioned respecting the relief of Insolvent Debtors," passed the nineteenth Day of December one thousand seven hundred and sixty six, and which are expired by their own Limitation, and as to a Division of the said Estate shall conform to the Directions of the said Acts as fully and effectually as if all the said Acts respecting the Relief of Insolvent Debtors were now in full Force.

AND BE IT ENACTED by the Authority aforesaid that the said Cornelius C Wynkoop having given up and regularly conveyed together with his said Wife Mary Catharine to the said Assignees or to any Person or Persons by their Order for the Benefit of his Creditors all his her and their Estate both Real and Personal (except the said Articles of Household Furniture mentioned in the herein before in Part recited Petition) shall be fully and absolutely discharged from all Debts or Demands due from him at the Time of the Assignment by him made to the said Assignees, or contracted before that Time though payable afterwards, and that if the said Cornelius C Wynkoop is or hereafter shall be sued or prosecuted for any such Debt Demand or Contract it shall and may be lawful for him to plead the general Issue and give the special Matter in Evidence.

AND BE IT FURTHER ENACTED by the Authority aforesaid, That if any Person or Persons shall be sued for any Matter or Thing to be done in pursuance of this Act, it shall and may be lawful for him or them to plead the general Issue and give the special Matter and this Act in Evidence.

AND BE IT FURTHER ENACTED that this Act shall be and continue in full force as to the Power of every Court and also as to the Power of all and every Assignee or Assignees, person or persons interested or concerned in or with the Estate of the said

Cornelius C Wynkoop and Mary Catharine his Wife or either of them until a full and final Settlement and Division of the same shall be made according to the true Intent and Meaning of this Act.

[CHAPTER 1506.]

[Chapter 1506 of Van Schaack, where the title only is printed.]

An Act for the Relief of Elizabeth Seabury an Insolvent Debtor.

[Passed, February 16, 1771.]

WHEREAS the said Elizabeth Seabury and sundry of her Creditors, by their Petition to the General Assembly did set forth. That the Reverend Samuel Seabury her late Husband deceased was at the Time of his Death considerably indebted as well by Bond as otherwise to divers Persons, and having left his Widow the said Elizabeth sole Executrix of his Will, she took upon herself the Administration thereof, and made the most of his Estate by sale except as to some of the Movables which she retained in her own Hands for the purpose of keeping House, and except a small Piece of Land in the Town of Hempstead, which she herself purchased for one hundred Pounds to erect a Dwelling House on, which House she afterwards did erect, and in the doing thereof received considerable Help and Assistance from the People of the Parish. That the said Elizabeth Seabury lately finding that the Debts due from her Testator on Bonds had accumulated so much by their growing Interest as to render her unable fully to discharge them together with some Debts of her own, contracted for her necessary Subsistance, conveyed all her Estate Real and Personal to Samuel Clowes and Richard Hewlett Esquires as Trustees for the Benefit of her own and her said Husbands Creditors, which Estate it is supposed will amount to about four hundred and thirty Pounds, besides which there is a Debt due of about one hundred and forty Pounds to her Testator in the Colony of Connecticut. That the Petitioners from the best Computation they can make, suppose there is due from the said Elizabeth both as Executrix of her said Husband, and in her own Right about seven hundred and twenty Pounds, near if not quite three fourths of which whole Sum is due to the said Petitioning Creditors, who are willing and desirous to have her Estate proportionably distributed among all her Creditors, and that she be thereupon discharged and pray that the Petitioners may be relieved in the Premises.

BE IT THEREFORE ENACTED by his Excellency the Governor the Council and the General Assembly, and it is hereby Enacted by the Authority of the same That the said Elizabeth Seabury in order to the obtaining a full Discharge from all her Creditors as herein after directed, shall deliver in writing to one of the Judges of the Supreme Court of this Province, or to any one of the Judges of the Inferior Court of Common Pleas in and for Queens County, a full just and true Inventory and Account according to the best of her knowledge, as well of all the Debts she owes both in her own Right and as Executrix of her said Husband, and of the Persons to whom the same are due respectively, as of all the Estate Real and Personal which she hath already conveyed as aforesaid to the said Trustees named in the said Petition, and of all such other Estate Chattels and Effects Real and Personal (except the wearing Apparel of the said Elizabeth) which the said Elizabeth hath as well in her own Right, as that which she hath in her Right as Executrix of her said Husband (if any such Estate still remaineth in her Hands) and on the Delivery of such Accounts as aforesaid she the said Elizabeth shall take an Oath to be administred by the Judge to whom such Account or Accounts shall be delivered, to the Effect following, that is to say That such Account or Accounts do contain to the best of her knowledge and Belief a full just and true Account of all the Persons to whom the said Elizabeth either in her own Right or as Executrix of her said Husband stands indebted, and of the Sums respectively due to them, and that she hath not, either of her own or her said Husbands Estate, any Thing more than what is mentioned and specified in such Account except her wearing Apparel, and that she hath not concealed or made over any of her own or her said Testators Estate or Effects directly or indirectly with intent to defraud any of his or her Creditors, or in Trust for herself or otherwise howsoever (except to the said Trustees as aforesaid.)

BE IT FURTHER ENACTED by the Authority aforesaid, That before the said Elizabeth Seabury shall be discharged by virtue of this Act such and so many of the Creditors of the said Samuel Seabury at the Time of his Death, and the Creditors of the said Elizabeth Seabury in her own Right who have become Petitioners to the General Assembly as aforesaid, and such other of the said Creditors as shall or may hereafter prefer a Petition to the Judge aforesaid, to whom such Accounts shall be delivered as aforesaid, praying for the Discharge of the said Elizabeth Seabury under this Act, if any such other Creditors shall so Petition whose Debts remaining due, shall in the whole, amount at least to two equal third Parts of all the Money due and owing from the said Elizabeth, both as Executrix of her said Husband and in her own Right, shall respectively make Oath to the Amount of their respective Demands aforesaid, before such Judge to whom such Accounts as aforesaid shall be delivered by the said Elizabeth Seabury; And the Proportion of two thirds as aforesaid shall be determined from the Sums respectively to be Sworn to by the Creditors, and the whole Amount of the Debts that shall be sworn to by the said Elizabeth Seabury as aforesaid, unless where any Debt so to be sworn to by her, shall appear to such Judge on the Oath of the said Creditors respectively to be more or less than the Debt so to be Sworn to by the Creditors respectively, and in such Case, the Debt sworn to by the Creditors respectively shall be the Rule for ascertaining the said Proportion of two thirds of the whole.

BE IT FURTHER ENACTED by the Authority aforesaid, That when and as soon as the said Elizabeth Seabury shall have complied with the Directions herein before mentioned in this Act, and the said Proportion of two thirds of the whole Debts shall be fixed and ascertained, in the Manner herein before directed; then such Judge to whom such Accounts as aforesaid shall be delivered, is hereby required to give to her the said Elizabeth Seabury a Certificate thereof and a Discharge under his Hand and Seal, and she the said Elizabeth Seabury shall from thenceforth by virtue of this Act be fully and absolutely released and discharged as well of and from all the Debts which she owes as Executrix of the last Will and Testament of her said Husband, as of and from all such Debts which she Owes in her own Right and for and on her own Account to any Person or Persons whatsoever, And in all Suit or Suits brought or to be brought against her the said Elizabeth for any Debt due from her either in her own Right, or as Executrix of her said Husband before such Discharge, she shall and may plead the General Issue and give this Act in Evidence, and the Judges Certificate and Discharge aforesaid shall be in all Courts on the Trial of such Issue sufficient Evidence of such her Discharge under this Act.

BE IT FURTHER ENACTED by the Authority aforesaid that from and immediately after the said Judge giving such Certificate and Discharge as aforesaid, agreeable to the Directions of this Act, they the said Samuel Clowes and Richard Hewlett shall be and are hereby declared to be absolutely vested with all such Estate which hath been already conveyed to them as aforesaid by the said Elizabeth Seabury, and the Monies which have arisen or shall arise from the Sale thereof; as also with a full Right and Title to all such other Estate and Effects which shall be mentioned and specifyed in the Inventory and Account to be rendered as aforesaid by the said Elizabeth Seabury. IN TRUST for the Benefit of all the Creditors of the said Samuel Seabury deceased, whose Debts remain unpaid, and for all the Creditors of her the said Elizabeth in her own Right in proportion to their respective Debts and to no other use Intent or Purpose whatsoever, and the said Trustees are hereby authorized required and directed after such Estate and Effects shall be vested in them by virtue of this Act to sell the same and to pay the Monies that have already arisen or shall arise from the Sale of the said Estate conveyed to them as aforesaid, and such other Estate as shall be mentioned in the said Inventory proportionably among all the said Creditors; and the said Trustees are hereby required respectively to take an Oath before such Judge to whom the Inventory and Account aforesaid shall be rendered, well and faithfully to execute the Trust hereby reposed in them to the best of their Skill and understanding, and shall keep just and true Books of Accounts of the same. PROVIDED ALWAYS that such of the said Creditors, who shall not have Sworn to their respective Debts before the said Judge in the Manner aforesaid, shall be obliged to make Oath of the Amount of their respective Demands before he she or they shall be entitled to receive their respective Dividends aforesaid.

AND BE IT FURTHER ENACTED by the Authority aforesaid, That before any Dividend be made pursuant to this Act, the said Trustees shall advertise the Time and Place for making such Dividend at least for one Month, in one of the Public News Papers of this Colony, and that all Monies which in virtue of the said original Trust have already been received, and which in virtue of this Act shall hereafter be received by the said Trustees or either of them within three Months next after the said Elizabeth Seabury's procuring such Certificate and Discharge as aforesaid, shall be proportionably paid to, and divided in Manner aforesaid, among all the said Creditors within ten Days after the expiration of the said three Months, and such other Monies as the said Trustees shall receive on Account of their Trust aforesaid within six Months next after the Expiration of the said three Months, shall be paid and divided proportionably as aforesaid within ten Days next after the Expiration of the said six Months, the said Trustees giving the like Notice as aforesaid of the Time and Place for making such second Dividend, and all such other Monies as the said Trustees shall receive on account and by virtue of their Trust aforesaid, within one Year next after the Expiration of the said six Months shall be divided among the Creditors as aforesaid within ten Days next after the Expiration of the said Year on the like Notice as aforesaid, and all such other Monies as the said Trustees shall receive on Account and by virtue of their Trust aforesaid within one year next after the Expiration of the said one Year shall be divided among the Creditors as aforesaid within ten Days next after the Expiration of the said Year on the like Notice as aforesaid. PROVIDED ALWAYS that before such Dividend be made respectively it shall and may be lawful for the said Trustees to retain in their Hands all reasonable Expences which they have been or shall be put to in the Execution of the said Trust, and they shall and may also recover by suit in their own Names or in the Name of the Survivor of them all and every of the Debts that shall be due at the Time of the said Elizabeth's Discharge, to the said Elizabeth either in her own Right or as Executrix of the Last Will and Testament of her said Husband and if the said Elizabeth Seabury or any one of the Creditors aforesaid who shall make Oath respecting their Demands as aforesaid shall knowingly swear false in the Premises, the Person and Persons so Offending and being thereof convicted, shall be deemed Guilty of wilful and corrupt Perjury and be subject to Punishment as in Cases of Perjury.

[CHAPTER 1507.]

[Chapter 1507 of Van Schaack, where the title only is printed. Confirmed by the King.]

An Act to impower Philip Van Cortland, the eldest Son and Heir at Law of Mary Walton Hughes, Tenant in Tail of a certain House and Lot of Ground in the City of New York, to hold the same in Fee Simple.

[Passed, February 16, 1771.]

WHEREAS Philip Van Cortland of Queen's County on Nassau Island and Province of New York Esquire hath by Petition represented to the General Assembly that by virtue of the Last Will and Testament of his Grandfather William Ricketts deceased, his Mother Mary Walton the present Wife of the Reverend Philip Hughes became vested with an Estate in Fee Tail of and in all that certain House and Lot or Piece of Land situate in the City of New York, bounded Westerly in Front on John's Street, Northerly on Nassau Street, Easterly by the Lots of Crolius, Turk, Hubbard and others, and Southerly by an Oil-Mill and sundry Lots, which said House and Lot of Ground are now in the possession of Jacob Le Roy of the City aforesaid Merchant, That he the said Philip Van Cortland is the eldest Son and Heir at Law of the said Mary Walton Hughes, and hath procured a Release from his said Mother and her Husband the said Philip Hughes for the abovementioned Premises. That he the said Philip Van Cortland being then ignorant that he held the same in Fee Tail charged the said Premises with the payment of sundry large Sums of Money which he had undertaken to pay in discharge of Debts due from his late Father Stephen Van Cortland Esquire and which by law he was not compellable to satisfy. That his said Mother now dwells and resides at a great Distance from the said City of New York, is infirm, and not capable of being removed here by reason whereof the said Philip Van Cortland is prevented from pursuing the said Intail to be docked agreeable to the Forms prescribed by the Common Law, and being thereby exposed to great difficulties, prays that by an Act for that purpose to be made and passed he may be vested with an Estate in Fee Simple of and in the Premises aforesaid. WHEREFORE as the said Philip Van Cortland cannot procure the said Intail to be docked agreeable to the Forms of the Common Law, and the Prayer of the said Petition being therefore proper to be granted.

BE IT ENACTED by his Excellency the Governor the Council, and the General Assembly, and it is hereby Enacted by the Authority of the same. That the Estate Tail in the Premises aforesaid created by the said last Will and Testament of the aforenamed William Ricketts deceased, shall cease determine and be absolutely void, and that the said Philip Van Cortland shall hold the same and every Part thereof with the Hereditaments and appurtenances thereunto belonging in Fee Simple.

AND BE IT FURTHER ENACTED by the Authority aforesaid, That every Lawful Act and Deed heretofore made done or suffered by the said Philip Van Cortland to charge the said

Premises with the payment of any Sum or Sums of Money shall be deemed, and are hereby declared to be as valid and effectual to all Intents and Purposes as if the said Philip Van Cortland had always held the said House Lot of Ground and Premises aforesaid in Fee Simple.

PROVIDED ALWAYS NEVERTHELESS that Nothing in this Act contained shall be construed to confirm the original Title which the said Philip Van Cortland or those under whom he holds, claim or claimed to the said Premises or to bar the Right which any other Person or Persons may have to the same, it being the Intent of this Act not to give the said Philip Van Cortland Title to the said Premises, but to alter the Estate by which he claims to hold the same from a Fee Tail to a Fee Simple. PROVIDED ALSO that this Act shall not be enforced until the same shall have received the Royal Approbation.

[CHAPTER 1508.]

[Chapter 1508 of Van Schaack, where only a portion of the act is printed.]

An Act for naturalizing the several Persons therein named.

[Passed, February 16, 1771.]

WHEREAS John Cook, George Cook, John Smith, Peter Witmur, Michael Kesmer Junior, Jacob Walter, Jacob Meyars, Christiaen Shutz, Jacob Schith, Jacob Creighoof, Michal Walliser, Johannes Walter, Andreas Fort, John Casper Pere, Jacob Graaf, John Bartholomew, Michael Riche, Conradt Moore, Martin Simson, Philip Kileman, Martin Lasler, George Hough, William Shouman, Jacob Waggoner, Jacob Bickle, George Tundell, John Smith, Adam Plank, Daniel Feick, Michael Heigle, Godfrid Easy, Michael Myar, Andreas Schough, Francis Fry, John Halth, Christian Schick, George Schinck, John Rush, Peter Bos, Ignace Labat, Joseph Simons, Anthony Betellbrunt, Jacob Hoghstrasser, Johan Adam Frank, Michael Shadwell, David Shadwell, Frederick Wolfe, Lewis Fueter, Peter Anckten, John Quithlot and Frederick Myer, have by their Petition presented to the General Assembly desired they may be naturalized and become his Majesty's liege Subjects within this Colony.

BE IT THEREFORE ENACTED by his Excellency the Governor, the Council and the General Assembly, and it is hereby Enacted by the Authority of the same. That the before named John Cook, George Cook, John Smith, Peter Witmur Michael

Kesmer Junior, Jacob Walter, Jacob Meyars, Christiaen Shutz, Jacob Schith Jacob Creighoof, Michael Walliser, Johannes Walter, Andreas Fort, John Casper Pere, Jacob Graaf, John Bartholomew, Michael Riche, Conradt Moore, Martin Simson, Philip Kileman, Martin Lasler, George Hough, William Shouman, Jacob Waggoner, Jacob Bickle, George Tundell, John Smith, Adam Plank, Daniel Feick, Michael Heigle, Godfrid Easy, Michael Myar, Andreas Scough, Francis Fry, John Halth, Christian Schick, George Schinck, John Rush, Peter Bos, Ignace Labat, Joseph Simons, Anthony Betellbrunt, Jacob Hoghstrasser, Johan Adam Frank, Michael Shadwell David Shadwell Frederick Wolfe, Lewis Fueter, Peter Anckten, John Quithlot and Frederick Myer and each and every of them shall be and are hereby declared to be naturalized to all Intents constructions and purposes whatsoever, and from henceforth and at all Times hereafter shall be entitled to have and enjoy all the Rights Liberties Privileges and Advantages which his Majesty's natural born Subjects in this Colony have and enjoy, or ought to have and enjoy as fully to all Intents and Purposes whatsoever as if all and every of them had been born within this Colony.

PROVIDED ALWAYS and it is hereby further Enacted by the Authority aforesaid. That each of the above mentioned Persons shall take the Oaths appointed by Law instead of the Oaths of Allegiance and Supremacy, subscribe the Test and make, repeat, swear to and subscribe the abjuration Oath, in any of his Majesty's Courts of Record within this Colony which Oaths the said Courts are hereby required upon Application to them made to administer, take the subscriptions, and Cause the Names of the Persons so swearing and subscribing to be entered upon Record in the said Courts, and the said before mentioned Persons are hereby each of them required to pay the several Sums hereafter mentioned, that is to say, to the Speaker of the General Assembly the sum of ten shillings, to the Judge of such Court the sum of six Shillings, and to the Clerk of such Court the Sum of three Shillings.

AND BE IT FURTHER ENACTED by the Authority aforesaid, That if the said Persons or any of them having so sworn and subscribed as aforesaid shall demand a Certificate of his or their being entered upon Record in the Manner before directed, the Court or Courts in which such Oaths and subscriptions shall be made are hereby directed and required to grant such under the Hand of the Judge and Seal of the said Court or Courts in which such Oaths and subscriptions as aforesaid shall be made, countersigned by the Clerk of the said Courts; for which Certificate each of them, shall pay over and above the Sums abovementioned the Sum of six Shillings one half to the Judge of such Court or Courts, and the other half to the Clerk thereof, which Certificate or Certificates shall be at all Times to the Person or Persons therein named a sufficient Proof of his or their being naturalized by virtue of this Act in as full and effectual a Manner as if the Record aforesaid was actually produced by the Person or Persons so named in such Certificate.

PROVIDED ALSO and be it Enacted by the Authority aforesaid That such of the Persons hereby naturalized as shall not take the Oath Test and abjuration in Manner herein before directed within twelve Months next after the Publication hereof, shall have no Manner of Benefit by this Act, any Thing herein contained to the contrary notwithstanding.

AND BE IT ENACTED by the same Authority, That the Public Printer of this Colony shall and hereby is directed and required to print this Act as if the same was a Public Law of this Colony.

[CHAPTER 1509.]

[Chapter 1509 of Van Schaack, where the title only is printed. See chapter 1465. Continued by chapter 1573.]

An Act further to continue an Act intitled. "An Act for granting to his Majesty "the several Duties and Impositions on "Goods, Wares and Merchandizes imported "into this Colony therein mentioned."

[Passed, January 22, 1772.]

WHEREAS the several Duties and Impositions on Goods, Wares and Merchandizes imported into this Colony and granted for the Support of the Government of his late Majesty King George the second, by the abovementioned Act have by several subsequent Acts been continued to the first Day of February next ensuing, and the General Assembly willing to make Provision for the further Support of his Majesty's Government of this Colony.

BE IT THEREFORE ENACTED by his Excellency the Governor, the Council and the General Assembly, and it is hereby enacted by the Authority of the same, That the above mentioned Act, intitled "An Act for granting to his Majesty the several

"Duties and Impositions on Goods, Wares and Merchandizes "imported into this Colony therein mentioned," passed in the twenty seventh Year of his late Majesty's Reign, shall be, and is hereby continued, and every Clause Matter and Thing therein contained, Enacted to be and remain in full Force to all Intents Constructions and purposes whatsoever until the first Day of February which will be in the Year of our Lord one thousand seven hundred and seventy three inclusive. PROVIDED ALWAYS, That so much of the first clause or Section of said Act as relates to European or East India Goods, imported from the British Islands into this Colony, shall be construed, taken and deemed to be from the British Islands in America only, any Thing in the said Act to the contrary hereof notwithstanding.

[CHAPTER 1510.]

[Chapter 1510 of Van Schaack, where the act is printed in full. See chapters 1434-1477.]

An Act for the Inspection of Sole Leather in the City of New York.

[Passed, January 22, 1772.]

BE IT ENACTED by his Excellency the Governor the Council, and the General Assembly, and it is hereby enacted by the Authority of the same, That Thomas Warner and Benjamin Stout, shall, and hereby are authorized and appointed to inspect Seal and Weigh all Sole Leather that shall be manufactured within the City of New York, or imported from any other Part or Parts of this Colony, or of the Neighbouring Colonies at any Time or Times after the publication of this Act, which said Officers before they do any Thing in Execution of the said Office, shall respectively take an Oath before any Magistrate of the City of New York in the Words following vizt: "I. A. B. do swear that "I will faithfully, truly, and impartially according to the best of "my Judgment, Skill and understanding, execute, do, and per- "form the Office and Duty of an Inspector and examiner of Sole "Leather, and will not directly or indirectly buy or sell any Sole "Leather, during the Time that I continue Inspector of the same, "except for the private use of my Family according to the true "Intent and meaning of an Act, intitled, "An Act for the Inspection of Sole Leather in the City of New York." "so help me God."

AND BE IT FURTHER ENACTED by the Authority aforesaid, That from and after the Publication of this Act, no sole Leather manufactured in this Colony or any of the Neighbouring Colonies, shall be sold, disposed of, or applied to use by any Person or Persons whatsoever within the City of New York until the same shall have been first inspected, sealed and weighed by one of the said Persons hereby appointed for that Purpose, upon Pain of forfeiting forty shillings for every Offence, to be sued for and recovered by Action of Debt, with Costs of Suit in a summary way by any Person who will Sue and prosecute for the same, before any Justice of the Peace within the City of New York, to be levied by Process to be directed to the Sheriff or any of the Constables of the City, commanding them or either of them to levy the same by distress and sale of the Offenders Goods and Chattles, one half thereof when so recovered to be paid by him or her to the Church Wardens of the said City for the use of the Poor thereof.

AND BE IT FURTHER ENACTED by the Authority aforesaid, That there shall be paid to the Inspector Sealer and weigher of every Side of Leather that shall be so inspected sealed and weighed three Pence, one half thereof by the Seller, and the other half by the Purchaser.

AND BE IT FURTHER ENACTED by the Authority aforesaid, That the said Inspectors shall, and are hereby required to provide themselves respectively with proper Seals for the purpose aforesaid, and to impress on every Side of Sole Leather which shall be deemed dry, good and Merchantable, the Letters of their Christian and Sirnames with New York at full Length, and the weight thereof; And if any Person or Persons shall presume to counterfeit the same, by making any Impression or Mark on any Sole Leather, he or they so offending, shall forfeit and pay for every Offence the Sum of Ten Pounds to be sued for, recovered, and applied in Manner aforesaid. PROVIDED NEVERTHELESS, That all Sole Leather which shall not bear the Inspection aforesaid, may be used for any other purposes, except being worked up into Shoes Boots and Buckets, provided the same be marked by either of the Inspectors aforesaid with his Name, and the Letters BAD who are hereby required to keep a proper Instrument for that purpose; and if any Person or Persons shall presume to work up into Shoes, Boots or Buckets, such Sole Leather as shall be marked with the Letters BAD as aforesaid he or they so Offending shall forfeit and pay for every

Offence the Sum of Ten Pounds, to be sued for, recovered and applied in Manner aforesaid any Thing herein contained to the contrary notwithstanding.

This Act to continue in full Force from the Publication thereof to the first Day of February, one thousand seven hundred and seventy seven.

[CHAPTER 1511.]

[Chapter 1511 of Van Schaack, where the title only is printed.]

An Act to impower the Mayor Recorder and Aldermen of the City of New York, or the Major Part of them to order the raising a Sum not exceeding Sixteen hundred Pounds for the uses therein mentioned.

[Passed, January 22, 1772.]

WHEREAS the providing a sufficient Number of Watchmen, and lighting of Lamps within the City of New York has not only been found convenient, but also necessary for the safety of its Inhabitants and others.

BE IT THEREFORE ENACTED by his Excellency the Governor the Council and the General Assembly, and it is hereby enacted by the Authority of the same, That the Mayor Recorder and Aldermen of the City of New York for the Time being, or the major Part of them, whereof the Mayor or Recorder to be one, shall have full Power and Authority, and are hereby fully impowered and authorized on the second Tuesday in this present Month of January or within ten Days thereafter, to order the raising a Sum not exceeding sixteen hundred Pounds by a Tax upon the Estates real and personal of all and every the Freeholders, Freemen, Inhabitants Residents and Sojourners within the City of New York on the South Side of Fresh Water, for the payment of so many Watchmen as the Mayor Aldermen and Commonalty of the City of New York shall think necessary for guarding the City, and for purchasing Oil, providing Lamps, and for repairing and attending the Lamps which now are, or hereafter may be erected, and add the same sum of sixteen hundred Pounds to the sum which shall be raised for the Minister and Poor of the said City, which Tax so to be laid, shall be rated and assessed at the same Time, and by the Vestrymen who shall rate and Assess the Tax for the Minister and Poor of the said City and shall be rated together in one Assessment made of the whole, the Vestrymen first taking the Oath prescribed to be taken in and by an Act intitled, "An Act to enable the Inhabitants of the City of New York to choose annually two Vestrymen for each respective Ward within the said City," made and passed in the nineteenth Year of the Reign of his late Majesty King George the second; and the Tax so to be laid shall be collected levied and paid at the same Time as the Tax for the Maintenance of the Minister and Poor of the said City hath been accustomed into the Hands of the Church Wardens of the said City for the Time being, who are hereby required and directed to pay the same into the Hands of the Chamberlain of the said City, to be by him paid as he shall be directed by Warrant or Warrants of the said Mayor, Aldermen and Commonalty in Common Council convened for the uses aforesaid.

AND BE IT FURTHER ENACTED by the Authority aforesaid, that over and above the Sum of sixteen hundred Pounds to be levied and paid by virtue of this Act, the Sum of three Pence in the Pound as a Reward to the Constables for their Trouble shall be Assessed levied and paid to the respective Constables for collecting and paying the same and no more, according to the true Intent and meaning of this Act: any Thing herein, or in any other Act or Acts contained to the Contrary hereof in any wise notwithstanding.

AND BE IT FURTHER ENACTED by the Authority aforesaid That if the said Mayor Recorder or Aldermen, Church Wardens, Vestrymen, or Constables of the said City who are hereby Authorized impowered and required to take effectual Care that this Act be executed according to the true Intent and meaning thereof, or any of them shall deny, refuse or delay to perform, execute, or comply with all or any of the Powers, Authorities and Duties in this Act given and required to be done and performed by them or either of them, and thereof shall be lawfully convicted in any Court of Record in this Colony, he or they so denying refusing or delaying to perform the Duties as aforesaid shall suffer such pains and Penalties by Fine and Imprisonment, as by the Discretion of the said Court shall be adjudged.

AND BE IT FURTHER ENACTED by the Authority aforesaid; That if any Person or Persons shall Wilfully break or damage any of the Lamps now erected or hereafter to be erected within the said City, he she or they so offending shall forfeit the Sum of twenty Pounds for every Lamp he she or they shall

Damage Or break as aforesaid, to be levied by Warrant or Warrants under the Hands and Seals of two or more of his Majesty's Justices of the Peace for the City and County of New York, by Distress and Sale of the Offender's Goods and Chattels on due Conviction made upon the Oath of one or more credible Witness or Witnesses, rendering the Overplus if any there be to the Owner or Owners, and for want of such Distress the Offender or Offenders shall be imprisoned by Warrant under the Hands and Seals of the said Justices, who are hereby required to issue the same, for the space of three Months, unless the said Forfeiture or Forfeitures be sooner paid: which Forfeitures shall be applied towards providing and repairing of Lamps, and paying the Watchmen.

AND BE IT FURTHER ENACTED by the Authority aforesaid, That all such Persons as shall be employed to guard the said City, and attend the Lamps shall be under the Direction of, and obey such Orders as they shall from Time to Time receive from the Mayor, Aldermen and Commonalty of the said City, any Custom Law or Usage to the contrary thereof, in any wise notwithstanding.

[CHAPTER 1512.]

[Chapter 1512 of Van Schaack, where the title only is printed. See chapter 1409.]

An Act to revive an Act intitled "An Act "for the better regulating the Public Roads "in the City and County of New York, and to "levy Money to defray the Expence thereof."

[Passed, January 22, 1772.]

WHEREAS an Act intituled, "An Act for the better regulating "the Public Roads in the City and County of New York, and to "levy Money to defray the Expence thereof," passed in the fourth Year of his present Majesty's Reign, and since continued by an Act intitled, "An Act to continue an Act "intitled an Act for the better regulating the Public Roads "in the City and County of New York and to levy Money "to defray the Expence thereof," passed in the tenth Year of his present Majesty's Reign, except so much of the second Clause of the said Act, as is therein expressed and contained in the Words following to wit, "And if any Person or Per"sons shall lay out any Road or Roads through his her or their

"Lands and leave the same open for common use by the space of "three Months, the said Commissioners are hereby impowered "immediately thereafter to record all and every such Road and "Roads in the Manner herein after directed which being so "recorded shall be deemed public Roads and Highways to all "Intents Constructions and purposes whatsoever." expired on the first Day of this Instant Month of January, and the same having been found useful and necessary.

BE IT THEREFORE ENACTED by his Excellency the Governor, the Council, and the General Assembly, and it is hereby enacted by the Authority of the same, That the first above recited Act, except so much of the second Clause thereof abovementioned and expressed, and which was excepted in the second above recited Act, shall be and hereby is and every Clause Matter and Thing in the said first recited Act contained except as above excepted, enacted to be and remain in full force from the Publication hereof, until the first Day of February which will be in the Year of our Lord one thousand seven hundred and seventy three.

[CHAPTER 1513.]

[Chapter 1513 of Van Schaack, where the title only is printed.]

An Act for making a further Provision of two thousand Pounds for furnishing his Majesty's Troops quartered in this Colony with Necessaries for one Year.

[Passed, February 26, 1772.]

BE IT ENACTED by his Excellency the Governor, the Council and the General Assembly, and it is hereby enacted by the Authority of the same, That the Treasurer of this Colony shall pay, and he is hereby directed and required out of the Interest Money arising by virtue of the Act intitled "An Act for emitting "the sum of one hundred and twenty thousand Pounds in Bills "of Credit to be put out on Loan, and to appropriate the Interest "arising thereon to the payment of the Debts of this Colony, and "to such public Exigencies as the Circumstances of this Colony "may from Time to Time render necessary," to pay such Sum or Sums of Money as shall from Time to Time be necessary for quartering his Majesty's Troops in this Colony for one Year from the first Day of January one thousand seven hundred and seventy two, on Warrant or Warrants to be drawn for that purpose, by his Excellency the Governor, or Commander in Chief for the Time being, by and with the Advice and consent of his Majesty's Council, provided the whole Sum to be drawn for does not exceed the Sum of two thousand Pounds.

AND BE IT ENACTED by the Authority aforesaid That the Treasurer shall keep exact Books of his payments by virtue of this Act and a true and just Account thereof shall render upon Oath to the Governor or Commander in Chief for the Time being, the Council or the General Assembly, when by them or any of them thereunto required.

[CHAPTER 1514.]

[Chapter 1514 of Van Schaack, where the title only is printed.]

An Act for collecting the Duty of Excise on Strong Liquors retailed in this Colony from the first Day of February one thousand seven hundred and seventy two to the first Day of February one thousand seven hundred and seventy three inclusive.

[Passed, February 26, 1772.]

BE IT ENACTED by his Excellency the Governor the Council and the General Assembly, and it is hereby enacted by the Authority of the same, That Cornelius Clopper shall be and hereby is appointed Commissioner for collecting the Duty of Excise of and from the several Retailers of Strong Liquors within the City and County of New York, from the first Day of February in the Year of our Lord one thousand seven hundred and seventy two, to the first Day of February which will be in the Year of our Lord one thousand seven hundred and seventy three inclusive.

AND BE IT FURTHER ENACTED by the Authority aforesaid, That the said Commissioner shall as soon after the Publication of this Act as he shall judge convenient, appoint the several Retailers within the said City and County, and direct and ascertain what each Retailer shall pay for the said Duty from the first Day of February one thousand seven hundred and seventy two, to the first Day of February one thousand seven hundred and seventy three inclusive.

AND BE IT FURTHER ENACTED by the Authority aforesaid that the several and respective Persons herein after named, shall be and hereby are appointed Commissioners for collecting the Duty of Excise of and from the several and respective

Retailers of Strong Liquors within the several and respective Counties of this Colony herein after mentioned, and the Harbours Bays and Rivers respectively thereunto adjoining or belonging. Vizt.

For the City and County of Albany Peter Lansingh, and Guysbert G Marselis Esquires.

For the Borough of Westchester Nathaniel Underhill Esquire.

For the Manor of Philipsburgh and Younkers in the County of West Chester William Davids and Isaac Deane Esquires.

For the Manor of Cortland in the County of West Chester Heckaliah Browne Esquire, and for the remaining Part of West Chester County Stephen Ward and John Thomas Junior Esquires.

For Kings County Theodorus Polhemus Esquire.

For Queens County Benjamin Townshend and Samuel Clowes Esquires.

For Dutchess County Cornelius Luyster, Benjamin Akins, John Ryder, Lewis Barton and Myndert Van Kleek Esquires.

For Ulster County, Joseph Gasherie and James McClaghry Esquires.

For Orange County; for Haverstraw Precinct David Puy, for Orange Town John Perry, for Goshen Precinct Benjamin Thurston, for Cornwall Precinct Daniel Coleman Esquires.

For Richmond County, Hezekiah Wright Jacob Rezeau and Richard Conner Esquires.

And for Suffolk County Colonel William Smith, Samuel Landon and Malby Gelston Esquires.

AND BE IT FURTHER ENACTED by the Authority aforesaid That the aforesaid several and respective Commissioners, or the Major Part of them respectively shall as soon as they conveniently can, after the Publication of this Act, meet at the County Hall of their several and respective Counties, or at such other place or places as they the said Commissioners shall respectively appoint for putting in execution the Powers and Authorities given by this Act, at which Time or at such other Times as they shall judge necessary the said Commissioners or the major Part of them respectively shall for their own Counties and Districts, severally and respectively fix the Number and appoint the several Retailers within their several and respective Counties and Districts, and direct and ascertain what each Retailer shall pay for the said Duty of Excise from the first Day of February one thousand seven hundred and seventy two, to the first Day of February, one thousand seven hundred and seventy three,

PROVIDED ALWAYS, And be it further Enacted by the Authority aforesaid that no Retailer in any of the Cities or Counties of this Colony shall pay under the Sum of twenty Shillings for the said Duty of Excise, except those who shall retail Strong Liquors not to be drank in their Houses, and such as may retail Strong Liquors at or near the County Hall, in Suffolk County during the sitting of their Courts, or other Public Meetings there, who shall be rated at the discretion of the respective Commissioners, and that all those who have heretofore been Retailers of Strong Liquors in this Colony shall not pay less for the said Duty than they did in the Year of our Lord one thousand seven hundred and seventy; but as much more as the Commissioner or Commissioners for the City County or District where such Retailer may reside shall think reasonable.

AND BE IT FURTHER ENACTED by the Authority aforesaid, That the said several Commissioners, shall on or before the first Day of February one thousand seven hundred and seventy three, render just true and particular Accounts on Oath to the Treasurer of this Colony of all the Sums of Money to be raised by virtue of this Act, on the several Retailers within the Cities Counties, and Districts for which they are respectively appointed Commissioners as aforesaid specifying the Names of every Retailer, and the Sums they have respectively been rated at, and pay the same to the said Treasurer of this Colony for the Time being, deducting therefrom only such Sum or Sums as is by this Act allowed such Commissioner or Commissioners for the Management of the said Duty.

AND in order the better to secure the payment of the Sums to be raised by virtue of this Act. BE IT FURTHER ENACTED by the Authority aforesaid, That the said Commissioners before they take upon themselves the Execution of the Powers and Authorities given by this Act, shall respectively enter into Bonds to the Treasurer of this Colony for the Time being in the Sums following, that is to say.

The said Cornelius Clopper in the Penal Sum of one thousand six hundred Pounds.

The said Peter Lansingh and Guysbert G Marcelis in the Penal Sum of three hundred Pounds.

The said Nathaniel Underhill in the Penal Sum of twenty Pounds.

The said William Davids and Isaac Deane in the Penal Sum of forty Pounds.

The said Hackaliah Brown in the Penal Sum of Forty Pounds

The said Stephen Ward and John Thomas Junior in the Penal Sum of one hundred Pounds,

The said Theodorus Polhemus in the Penal Sum of Sixty Pounds.

The said Benjamin Townshend and Samuel Clowes in the Penal Sum of one hundred and sixty Pounds.

The said Cornelius Luyster, Benjamin Akins, John Ryder, Lewis Barton and Myndert Van Kleek in the Penal Sum of two hundred Pounds.

The said Joseph Gasherie and James McClaghry in the Penal Sum of one hundred and fifty Pounds.

The said David Puy, John Perry, Benjamin Thurston and Daniel Coleman in the Penal Sum of twenty Pounds each of them.

The said Hezekiah Wright, Jacob Rezeau and Richard Conner in the Penal Sum of forty Pounds.

And the said William Smith, Samuel Landon and Malby Gelston in the Penal Sum of one hundred Pounds.

CONDITIONED that the said respective Commissioner or Commissioners his or their Executors or Administrators shall render a just and true Account upon Oath to the Treasurer of this Colony of all the Sums that may by him or them be raised in virtue of this Act, upon the several Retailers of Strong Liquors within the City County or District for which he or they is or are appointed Commissioner or Commissioners, and well and truly pay the same except the sum allowed him or them by this Act, to the Treasurer of this Colony for the Time being on or before the first Day of February in the Year of our Lord one thousand seven hundred and seventy three, which Bond shall be delivered to and remain with the Treasurer of this Colony for the Time being, and upon performance of the Condition of the same respectively, shall be delivered up to be cancelled; but if Default shall be made in the performance of the Condition of any or either of the said Bonds, it shall and may be lawful to and for the Treasurer of this Colony for the Time being and he is hereby directed and required after the expiration of three Callender Months from the said first Day of February in the Year of our Lord one thousand seven hundred and seventy three, to cause Suits to be brought in the Name of the Treasurer of the Colony of New York, upon each and every of the said Bonds so forfeited, and prosecute the same to effect, and no Suit to be brought upon any or either of said Bonds shall be abated or discontinued by the Death or Removal of the Treasurer of this Colony, but shall be continued and prosecuted to effect by the new Treasurer, in the Name of the Treasurer of the Colony of New York.

AND BE IT FURTHER ENACTED by the Authority aforesaid, That the said Commissioners shall be allowed and may deduct out of the Sum to be by them respectively laid on the several Retailers within the City County or District for which they are respectively appointed Commissioners, the following Sums for their Trouble and Charge in the Execution of the Powers vested in them by this Act, that is to say.

The said Cornelius Clopper the Sum of fifty Pounds for incidental Charges and his Commission

The said Peter Lansing and Guysbert G Marcelis the sum of twenty eight Pounds.

The said Nathaniel Underhill the Sum of one Pound four shillings.

The said William Davids and Isaac Deane, the sum of three Pounds ten Shillings.

The said Hackaliah Brown the sum of three Pounds ten Shillings.

The said Stephen Ward and John Thomas Junior the Sum of ten Pounds.

The said Theodorus Polhemus the Sum of five Pounds.

The said Benjamin Townshend and Samuel Clowes the Sum of ten Pounds.

The said Cornelius Luyster, Benjamin Akins, John Ryder, Lewis Barton and Myndert Van Kleek the Sum of fifteen Pounds.

The said Joseph Gasherie and James McClaghry the Sum of eight Pounds.

The said David Puy, John Perry, Benjamin Thurston and Daniel Coleman the sum of six Pounds.

The said Hezekiah Wright, Jacob Rezeau and Richard Conner the Sum of three Pounds.

And the said William Smith, Samuel Landen and Malby Gelston the Sum of ten Pounds.

AND BE IT FURTHER ENACTED by the Authority aforesaid, That the several and respective Retailers of Strong Liquors, shall pay the several and respective Sums of Money to be laid on them by virtue of this Act unto the aforesaid several and respective Commissioners, on or before the first Day of December one thousand seven hundred and seventy two, for securing which payment the said Commissioners shall respectively oblige the said several and respective Retailers to give such Security as they the said Commissioners shall judge necessary, Provided that such Retailer in the City of New York as shall be rated at six Pounds and under, and such in the several Counties as shall be rated at three Pounds and under shall not be permitted to retail, unless they immediately pay the several and respective Sums they shall be rated at, to the aforesaid Commissioners, any Thing herein before contained to the Contrary notwithstanding.

AND BE IT FURTHER ENACTED by the Authority aforesaid, That in Case any Person or Persons whomsoever, other than such as the said Commissioners shall permit, shall presume to sell any Strong Liquors by retail, directly or indirectly, the Offender or Offenders shall for each such Offence forfeit the Sum of Six Pounds to be recovered by the said Commissioner or Commissioners respectively on the Oath of any one credible Witness in a summary way, in the Cities of New York and Albany and Borough of West Chester before the Mayor or Recorder, and one or more Aldermen of the said Cities and Borough respectively, and in the several Counties before any Justice of the Peace within the several Counties respectively; and if upon Conviction, the said Forfeitures be not paid, the same shall be levied on the Goods and Chattels of the Offender or Offenders by Warrant or Warrants under the Hands and Seals of the Person or Persons before whom such Conviction shall happen; and if no Goods and Chattels are found on which to distrain it shall and may be lawful for the Person or Persons who heard and determined the same, to commit the Offender or Offenders to Goal, without Bail or Mainprize for the Space of three Months unless the Penalties are sooner discharged, and the said respective Magistrates, shall be, and are hereby fully impowered, directed, and required to hear and determine those Matters in the Manner aforesaid, and to give Judgment if need be, to award Execution thereon, and to issue a Warrant or Warrants for the Commitment of Offenders, as the Case may require, one third of which Forfeiture shall be to the Informer or Informers, one third to the said Commissioners and the other third to the Poor of the Town Manor or Precinct where the Offence shall be committed to be paid into the Hands of the Church Wardens or Overseers of the Poor of the said respective place or places, by the Officer or Officers by whom the same shall be levied, any Thing in any of the Acts of this Colony to the contrary notwithstanding.

AND BE IT FURTHER ENACTED by the Authority aforesaid, that the several Retailers who shall be permitted and allowed to retail by the said Commissioner or Commissioners shall before they do so retail any Strong Liquors enter into Recognizance, that is to say, In the Cities of New York and Albany and Borough of West Chester before the respective Mayors thereof, and in the several Counties in this Colony, before two Justices of the Peace in the Penal Sum of twenty Pounds, with sufficient Sureties in the like Sum, Conditioned to keep an orderly House according to Law, during the Time they shall be permitted to retail as aforesaid, and thereupon the respective Mayors or the said Justices shall grant to such Person or Persons who have entered into such Recognizance, a Licence under his or their Hands and Seals to retail Strong Liquors in such House and place as shall be mentioned therein during the continuance of this Act, which Recognizances are to be lodged by the Person or Persons before whom the same shall be taken vizt. In the Cities of New York and Albany and Borough of West-Chester with the Town Clerks, and in the several Counties with the respective Clerks thereof, and upon Complaint of the Breach of the said Condition, it shall be lawful for the said Mayor and Aldermen of New York & Albany, & Borough of West Chester respectively, or the greater Number of them, and in the Counties for the Justices of the General and special Sessions of the Peace to suppress the Licence, or Licences of such Offender or Offenders.

AND BE ENACTED by the Authority aforesaid, That in Case any of the Persons who shall be permitted to retail Strong Liquors as aforesaid by the said Commissioner or Commissioners shall presume to retail before he she or they have obtained a Licence, & entered into Recognizance to keep an orderly House as aforesaid, he she or they so offending shall respectively forfeit the Sum of six Pounds for each Offence to be recovered in a Summary way, in the Manner before directed, one half thereof to the Informer, and the other half to the Poor of the Town, Manor or Precinct where the Forfeiture shall arise.

AND that the Expence of being qualified to retail may be within the Bounds of Moderation.

BE IT ENACTED by the Authority aforesaid that no more shall be taken for a Licence and Recognizance in the Cities of

New York and Albany and Borough of West Chester than the usual and accustomed Fees and in the respective Counties than the Sum of three Shillings.

AND BE IT ENACTED by the Authority aforesaid, That such Persons permitted to retail as aforesaid by the said Commissmissioner or Commissioners who retail Strong Liquors not to be drank in their own Houses but carried elsewhere shall not be obliged to enter into Recognizances, and take Licence as aforesaid, any Thing contained in this Act to the contrary notwithstanding.

AND BE IT ENACTED by the Authority aforesaid That in Case of the Death of any of the aforesaid Commissioners, the surviving Commissioner or Commissioners where such Death may happen shall be, and hereby is and are entitled to the whole Reward, and vested with the same powers and Authorities to execute this Act as if no such Death had happened, and in Case of the Death or Refusal of all the Commissioners of any of the respective Cities, Counties and Districts, then the Sheriff or Sheriffs for the Time being for the Cities Counties or Districts where such Death or Refusal shall happen, shall be and hereby is and are vested with all the Powers and Authorities given to the Commissioners by this Act, be under the same Regulations, and entitled to the same Rewards to all Intents, Constructions and purposes whatsoever, as if they had been particularly named and appointed in this Act, any Thing in this Act to the contrary notwithstanding.

AND BE IT FURTHER ENACTED by the Authority aforesaid, That all the Monies to be paid to the Treasurer of this Colony, by virtue of this Act, or recovered upon any of the aforesaid Bonds, shall remain in the Hands of the Treasurer of this Colony for the Time being, to be disposed of as is or shall be directed by any Act or Acts passed, or to be passed for that purpose.

AND BE IT ENACTED by the Authority aforesaid, That the Retailers in the City of New York shall pay the Excise in three several payments or sooner, as the Commissioner and they shall agree. PROVIDED ALWAYS that Nothing in this Act shall be construed to make void, abridge, or any wise lessen the several Rights and Privileges granted unto the Cities of New York and Albany and Borough of West-Chester by their respective Charters, any Thing contained in this Act to the contrary thereof notwithstanding.

[CHAPTER 1515.]

[Chapter 1515 of Van Schaack, where the act is printed in full.]

An Act to lay a Duty of Tonnage on Vessels for Defraying the Expence of the Light House at Sandy Hook.

[Passed, February 26, 1772.]

WHEREAS it is very reasonable that the Expence of maintaining the Light-House, should be paid by those who receive the immediate Benefit thereof, and for whose use it was erected.

BE IT THEREFORE ENACTED by his Excellency the Governor, the Council and the General Assembly, and it is hereby enacted by the Authority of the same, That all Vessels as often as they shall come into the Port of New York during the continuance of this Act shall pay a Tonnage of one Penny half Penny for every Ton such Vessel and Vessels shall measure according to the Rule hereafter mentioned, except the Vessels herein particularly excepted.

AND BE IT ENACTED by the Authority aforesaid. That the following Vessels shall be exempted from the said Duty of Tonnage, All Whaling Vessels during the Time such Vessels are employed in coasting or Whaling, and all coasting Vessels that shall not exceed eighty Tons Burthen, Carpenter's Tonnage, and shall be wholly owned by Persons dwelling and residing within the Limits of Cape Henry Westward and Southward, and New Hampshire Eastward, both inclusive, and that the same shall be actually loaded at, and come from some Port or Harbour within the Limits aforesaid, and shall return from hence to the place from whence she came, or some other place within the Limits aforesaid, and there unload whatever Goods or Merchandize she took in, in this Colony.

AND BE IT ENACTED by the Authority aforesaid, That every Master of such Vessel shall if required make Oath before Josias Smith, Clerk of the Master and Wardens of the Port of New York, or the Clerk of the said Master and Wardens for the Time being, who is hereby impowered to administer the same, "That "according to the best of his knowledge and belief, such Vessel "is a coasting Vessel, within the true Intent and Meaning of this "Act." and in Case such Master shall refuse to take such Oath as aforesaid, he shall be liable to pay the Duty of Tonnage and Penalties imposed by this Act.

AND BE IT ENACTED by the Authority aforesaid, That every Master or Commander of any Vessel subject to the said Duty of Tonnage, who shall not within forty eight Hours after his Arrival into the Port of New York, make Report to the Clerk of the Master and Wardens of the Port of New York aforesaid of his Arrival and of the Burthen of his Vessel, shall forfeit and pay for every such Neglect and Omission the Sum of ten Pounds.

AND to the End the Dimensions of the Vessels hereby made subject and liable to pay the said Duty of Tonnage, may be known with the greater Ease. BE IT ENACTED by the Authority aforesaid That every Master or Commander of Vessels so liable to the said Duty, shall within three Days after the Arrival of such Vessel in this Colony make Report of the Dimensions thereof to the Person hereinafter appointed to receive the said Duty of Tonnage and at the same Time make Oath before him, or if a Quaker an Affirmation in form following, to wit. "I. A. B. Master or Commander of the............do swear, (or "affirm) that her Length upon the Main Deck from the after Part "of the Stem to the after Part of the Stern Post is.............. "and that her Breadth upon the Midship Beam outside of both "Wales, after taking off four Inches for the thickness of one "Wale is..................and no more," and if a single Deckt Vessel, "the depth of the Hold is................and no more." which Form being entered in a Book to be kept for that purpose the Blanks thereof are properly to be filled up, and being sworn or affirmed to by such Master or Commander, he is likewise to sign the same.

AND BE IT ENACTED by the Authority aforesaid, That if any Master or Commander of Vessels hereby made liable to pay the said Duty of Tonnage, shall neglect or refuse to make Report on Oath or Affirmation in Manner and in the the Time beforementioned, it shall be lawful for the Person qualified to receive the said Duty to cause a sworn Shipwright or other fit Person on Oath to repair on board such Vessel immediately to survey and take the exact Dimensions of such Vessel, and compute the Contents of her Tonnage, according to the Rule herein after prescribed and to make Report thereof to him accordingly: and the Master or Commander, of such Vessel or Vessels shall be subject and obliged to pay not only the full Duty of Tonnage, but likewise the Charges of surveying, which however shall not exceed the Sum of ten Shillings.

AND to prevent Frauds in making such Report as aforesaid. BE IT ENACTED by the Authority aforesaid. That if it should be suspected a short Report hath been made of any Vessel subject to the said Duty of Tonnage, it shall be lawful for the Officer qualified to receive the said Duty, either Personally or by a fit Person on Oath, to survey and measure the Vessel so suspected; and if it be found she hath been reported short, the Master or Commander thereof who made such short Report shall forfeit for every Ton so reported short five Shillings.

BE IT ENACTED by the Authority aforesaid, That the said Duty of Tonnage of all and every Vessel by this Act subject to pay the same, shall be paid by the respective Master Owner or Factor thereof, within six Days after her Arrival in this Colony, and every Master Owner or Factor of such Vessel who shall fail to make such payment as aforesaid within the Time above mentioned shall pay double the Tonnage herein before directed.

AND to prevent Disputes concerning the Contents of Vessels hereby made liable to the said Duty of Tonnage. BE IT ENACTED by the Authority aforesaid, That the same shall be computed in Manner following, that is to say, three fifths of the Beam to be deducted from the Length of the Main Deck, the remainder multiplied by the Breadth of the Beam, that sum to be multiplied by half the Breadth of the Beam for the Depth of the Hold, that divided by ninety five to be the Contents of the Vessel, but if a single Deckt Vessel to multiply her Length and Breadth by her depth in the Hold from Skin to Skin and divide as above.

AND to the End the good Intent of this Act may not be defeated BE IT ENACTED by the Authority aforesaid. That if any Officer belonging to his Majesty's Customs in this Colony shall clear any Vessel by this Act liable to the said Duty of Tonnage, before it shall appear to such Officer by a Certificate or a Receipt under the Hand of the Person hereby appointed to receive the said Duty, that the same is paid and discharged for such Vessel, every such Officer of the Customs so clearing such Vessel without such Certificate or Receipt as aforesaid, shall forfeit and pay double the sum that ought to have been paid for the Tonnage of such Vessel so cleared contrary to the Meaning of this Act, to be received and applied in Manner herein after directed.

AND BE IT FURTHER ENACTED by the Authority aforesaid, That Josias Smith Clerk of the Master and Wardens of the

Port of New York, or in Case of his Death or Removal such other person as they shall appoint, shall be and hereby is appointed authorized impowered and required to receive and collect the Duty of Tonnage to arise by virtue of this Act, and if need be to sue for the same in his own Name, to administer the Oaths and Affirmations, and receive the Report beforementioned: and also to sue in his own Name for the Fines and Forfeitures that shall be incurred by any Person or Persons whatsoever for breach of this Act, or any Part thereof; and further to do and perform all other Acts proper and necessary for securing and collecting the said Duty, and upon recovering it from any Master Owner or Factor, he is to give a Certificate or Receipt unto him or them for the same, gratis; but for the Report and Oath or Affirmation abovementioned, he may demand and receive one Shilling and no more, and he is hereby enjoined to keep exact Books of the said Duty of Tonnage and of what shall from Time to Time arise by the same, and to render Accounts thereof upon Oath to the Governor or Commander in Chief, the Council or the General Assembly when by them or any of them thereunto required.

AND BE IT ENACTED by the Authority aforesaid That the said Duty of Tonnage, and all Fines and forfeitures that shall or may arise for any Breach of this Act shall be sued for and recovered before the Mayor, Recorder and Aldermen of the City of New York, or any two or more of them, whereof the Mayor or Recorder to be one.

AND BE IT ENACTED by the Authority aforesaid, That all the Money to arise by virtue of this Act shall be paid to the Master and Wardens of the said Port of New York (the said Clerk for the Time being first deducting for his Trouble in collecting the said Money the sum of thirty Pounds per Annum, and so in proportion for a greater or lesser Time) to be by them applied for and towards the maintaining supporting and defraying the Expences of the Light-House, as the purchase of Oil, Tallow or Coal, the hire of proper Persons to take care that the Lights are properly kept up, the Lanthorn kept clean, and the Light-House, and Dwelling House built near it for the reception of the Persons to have the care thereof, kept in good Repair: and also for and towards placing and keeping in repair such and so many Buoys as they shall from Time to Time think necessary.

AND BE IT ENACTED by the Authority aforesaid, that if any Person or Persons shall wilfully remove, damage or destroy any Buoys so placed as aforesaid or shall attempt the same, he or they so offending, shall forfeit for every Offence the sum of fifty Pounds, which Forfeiture the Master and Wardens aforesaid are hereby impowered to sue for in any Court of Record in this Colony, and when recovered shall be applied in Manner herein before directed.

AND BE IT FURTHER ENACTED by the Authority aforesaid, that the said Josias Smith or the Clerk of the Master and Wardens of the Port of New York for the Time being, shall previous to the taking on him the Execution of the Trust in him reposed by this Act take an Oath before the Mayor or Recorder of the City of New York that he will faithfully and honestly execute what is of him required by this Act, and shall also enter into Recognizance before the said Mayor or Recorder in the Sum of five hundred Pounds with one surety in the Sum of two hundred and fifty Pounds. Conditioned that he will faithfully and Honestly execute what is of him required by this Act, and that he will pay all the Monies by him to be received by virtue thereof to the said Master and Wardens of the Port of New York except the Allowance made him by this Act: and the said Master and Wardens of the Port of New York are also hereby enjoined to keep regular Accounts of all their Receipts and payments in virtue of this Act and to render Accounts on Oath to the Governor or Commander in Chief, the Council and the General Assembly, when by them or any of them, they shall be thereunto required; This Act to be in force from the publication thereof until the first Day of February one thousand seven hundred and seventy seven.

[CHAPTER 1516.]

[Chapter 1516 of Van Schaack, where the act is printed in full. Continued by chapter 1693.]

An Act to regulate the Sale of Goods at Public Vendue, Auction, or Out-cry within this Colony.

[Passed, February 26, 1772.]

BE IT ENACTED by his Excellency the Governor, the Council and the General Assembly, and it is hereby enacted by the Authority of the same, That all Goods Chattels, Wares, Merchandizes and Effects whatsoever, which shall or may at any Time or Times from and after the Publication hereof and during the Continuance of this Act be sold at Public Vendue Auction or Out-cry within this Colony by any Vendue Master or Vendue Masters Auctioneer or Auctioneers, or by any other Person or Persons whomsoever shall be, and hereby are declared and made subject to a Duty of two Pounds for every one hundred Pounds of the Value or Price at which the same shall be sold as aforesaid, and after the same Rate for every greater or lesser Sum, to be paid by such Person or Persons who shall so sell the same as aforesaid.

PROVIDED ALWAYS and it is hereby enacted by the Authority aforesaid That all Goods belonging to the Crown, or seized by any Public Officer or Officers for or on Account of any Forfeiture or Forfeitures, Penalty or Penalties, Houses, Lands, Ships and Vessels, Goods and Effects of deceased Persons, or Goods distrained for Rent, or taken in Execution Effects of Insolvent Debtors, Household Goods, Utensils of Husbandry, Goods condemned as Prize, Goods damaged at Sea and sold on Account of the Owners or Insurers within twenty Days after the same shall be landed under the inspection of the Master and Wardens of the Port of New York, Horses, Neat Cattle, Hogs, Sheep, and all kinds of Grain, shall in no wise be subject to, but are hereby altogether exempted and declared free from the Duty abovementioned, any Thing herein before contained to the contrary in any wise notwithstanding.

AND in order more effectually to secure the Duty hereby imposed as aforesaid BE IT ENACTED by the Authority aforesaid, That no Vendue Master or Vendue Masters Auctioneer or Auctioneers or any other Person or Persons whatsoever shall presume to sell or dispose of any Goods Chattels, Wares, Merchandizes or Effects (except such as are herein before excepted,) at Public Vendue Auction or Out-cry, unless he she or they first enter into Recognizance to our Sovereign Lord the King his Heirs and Successors before any one of the Judges of the Supreme Court of this Colony or the Mayor or Recorder of the City of Albany or one of the Judges of the Inferior Court of Common Pleas in the other Counties, in the Penal Sum of five hundred Pounds Current Money of this Colony, with two Sufficient Securities each in the Sum of two hundred and fifty Pounds, like Money conditioned for the payment of the Duties herein before mentioned to the Treasurer of this Colony for the Time being, and in all Things well and faithfully to behave according to the true Intent and Meaning of this Act which Recognizance shall be filed with the said Judge, or with the Mayor or Recorder of the City of Albany, or with the Judge of the Inferior Court in the Counties before whom it shall be taken, and every such Vendue Master or Vendue Masters Auctioneer or Auctioneers, and every other Person or Persons, who shall at any Time or Times during the continuance of this Act, either for him her or themselves, or on his her or their own Account, or for or on Account of any other Person or Persons whomsoever sell or dispose of, any Goods Chattels Wares, Merchandizes or Effects (except as is before excepted) at Public Vendue, Auction or Out-cry shall at or within twenty Days after the expiration of every three Months after the commencement of this Act, render a just exact and true Account in writing upon Oath, to the Treasurer of this Colony for the Time being, or to the Mayor or Recorder for the City of Albany, or in the Counties before one of the Judges of the Inferior Court of Common Pleas (who are hereby respectively Authorized and impowered to administer such Oath.) of all and singular the Goods, Wares, Merchandizes and Effects with the Amount thereof, which he she or they shall have so sold and disposed of, at Public Vendue, Auction or Out-cry at each such sale as aforesaid and shall within twenty Days thereafter pay to the said Treasurer for the Time being the Sum of two Pounds out of every hundred Pounds value, for every such respective Sale, and at the same Rate for a greater or lesser Value, which Oath shall be in the following Words, vizt. I. A. B. do swear upon the Holy "Evangelists of Almighty God that the Account now exhibited "by me and to which I have subscribed my Name contains a just "and true Account of all the Goods, Wares Merchandizes and "Effects sold by me or any Person or Persons under me within "the Time in the said Account mentioned, which are liable to the "Duty imposed by an Act intitled, An Act to Regulate the Sale "of Goods at Public Vendue Auction or Out-cry within this "Colony, so help me God". And if the said Vendue Master or Vendue Masters, Auctioneer or Auctioneers neglect or refuse to deliver such Account on Oath, and pay the Duty within the Time limited as aforesaid he she or they so neglecting or refusing shall respectively forfeit the Sum of one hundred Pounds for every Offence, which Forfeiture the Treasurer of this Colony for the Time being is hereby impowered and directed to sue for in any Court of Record in this Colony, and when recovered shall remain in the Treasury till disposed of by Act or Acts hereafter to be made for that purpose.

AND BE IT ENACTED by the Authority aforesaid that any Person or Persons presuming to sell or dispose of any Goods

Wares or Merchandizes (except as before excepted) unless entering into Recognizance as above directed shall forfeit the sum of fifty Pounds for every Offence to be recovered and applied in the manner above directed.

AND BE IT FURTHER ENACTED by the Authority aforesaid, That the Treasurer of this Colony for the Time being shall keep exact and distinct Accounts of the Monies arising and to arise from Time to Time by virtue of this Act which Monies shall remain in the Hands of the Treasurer till disposed of by Act or Acts hereafter to be made for that purpose.

PROVIDED ALWAYS And be it Enacted by the Authority aforesaid that the said Vendue Master or Vendue Masters, Auctioneer or Auctioneers or any other Person or Persons for them or either of them in the City of New York, shall not expose to sale any Goods, Wares or Merchandizes liable to the Duty aforesaid but at their respective Houses or Stores except Rum, Sugar, Molasses, Indigo, Cotton, Coffee, Wine, Brandy, and Cordage under the Penalty of ten Pounds for every Offence to be recovered and applied in the Manner before directed; This Act to be in force until the first Day of February which will be in the Year of our Lord one thousand seven hundred and seventy five.

[CHAPTER 1517.]

[Chapter 1517 of Van Schaack, where the act is printed in full.]

An Act for the better preventing frivolous and vexatious Suits.

[Passed, February 26, 1772.]

BE IT ENACTED by his Excellency the Governor the Council and the General Assembly, and it is hereby enacted by the Authority of the same. that from and after the publication hereof, where several Persons shall be made Defendants to any Action or Plaint of Trespass, Assault, False Imprisonment, or Ejectione firmae, and any one or more of them shall be upon the Trial thereof acquitted by Verdict, every Person or Persons so acquitted shall have and recover his Costs of Suit in like Manner as if a Verdict had been given against the Plaintiff or Plaintiffs, and acquitted all the Defendants, unless the Judge before whom such Cause shall be tried, shall immediately after the Trial thereof in open Court certify upon the Record under his Hand, that there was a reasonable Cause for the making such Person or Persons a Defendant or Defendants to such Action or Plaint.

AND BE IT FURTHER ENACTED by the Authority aforesaid, that if at any Time hereafter any Person or Persons shall commence or prosecute in any Court of Record any Action, Plaint or Suit, wherein upon any Demurrer, either by Plaintiff or Defendant, Demandant or Tenant, Judgement Shall be given by the Court against such Plaintiff or Demandant, or if at any Time after Judgment given for the Defendant in any such Action Plaint or Suit, the Plaintiff or Demandant shall sue any Writ or Writs of Error to annul the said Judgment, and the said Judgment shall be afterwards affirmed to be good, or the said Writ of Error shall be discontinued, or the Plaintiff shall be nonsuit therein, the Defendant or Tenant in every such Action Plaint, Suit or Writ of Error shall have Judgment to recover his Costs against every such Plaintiff or Plaintiffs, Demandant or Demandants, and have Execution for the same by Capias ad Satisfaciendum, Fieri facias,—or Elegit.

AND BE IT FURTHER ENACTED by the Authority aforesaid, that from and after the Publication hereof, in all Actions of Waste wherein the single value or Damage found by the Jury, shall not exceed the Sum of twenty Nobles, and in all Suits upon any Writ or Writs of Scire facias, and Suits upon Prohibitions, the Plaintiff obtaining Judgment or any Award of Execution after Plea pleaded, or Demurrer joined therein, shall likewise recover his Costs of Suit, and if the Plaintiff shall become non-Suit or suffer a Discontinuance, or a Verdict shall pass against him, the Defendant shall recover his Costs, and have execution for the same in like Manner as aforesaid.

AND for preventing Wilful and malicious Trespasses BE IT FURTHER ENACTED that in all Actions of Trespass to be commenced or prosecuted from and after the publication hereof in any Court of Record wherein at the Trial of the Cause it shall appear and be certified by the Judge under his Hand, upon the Back of the Record.— that the Trespass upon which any Defendant shall be found guilty, was wilful and malicious, the Plaintiff shall recover not only his Damages, but his full Costs of Suit, any former Law to the contrary notwithstanding.

PROVIDED ALWAYS that Nothing herein contained shall be construed to alter the Laws in being as to Executors or Administrators, in such Cases where they are not at present liable to the payment of Costs of Suit.

AND BE IT FURTHER ENACTED that in all Actions to be commenced in any Court of Record from and after the publication hereof, if any Plaintiff happen to Die after an interlocutory Judgment, and before a final Judgment obtained therein, the said Action shall not abate by reason thereof, if such Action might be originally prosecuted or maintained by the Executors or Administrators of such Plaintiff; and if the Defendant die after such interlocutory Judgment, and before final Judgment therein obtained, the said Action shall not abate if such Action might be originally prosecuted or maintained against the Executors or Administrators of such Defendant; and the Plaintiff, or if he be dead after such interlocutory Judgment, his Executors or Administrators shall and may have a Scire facias against the Defendant if living after such interlocutory Judgment, or if he died after, then against his Executors or Administrators to shew Cause why Damages in such Action should not be Assessed and recovered by him or them, and if such Defendant his Executors or Administrators shall appear at the Return of such Writ, and not shew or alledge any Matter sufficient to arrest the final Judgment, or being returned warned, or upon two Writs of Scire facias, it be returned, that the Defendant, his Executors or Administrators had Nothing whereby to be summoned, or could not be found in the County, shall make Default, that thereupon a Writ of inquiry of Damages shall be awarded, which being executed and returned Judgment final shall be given for the said Plaintiff, his Executors or Administrators, prosecuting such Writ or Writs of Scire facias, against such Defendant his Executors or Administrators respectively.

AND BE IT FURTHER ENACTED by the Authority aforesaid, that if there be two or more Plaintiffs or Defendants, and one or more of them should die; if the Cause of such Action shall survive to the surviving Plaintiff or Plaintiffs, or against the surviving Defendant or Defendants, the Writ or Action shall not be thereby abated, but such Death being suggested upon the Record, the Action shall proceed at the suit of the surviving Plaintiff or Plaintiffs, against the surviving Defendant or Defendants.

AND BE IT FURTHER ENACTED that in all Actions which from and after the publication hereof, shall be commenced or prosecuted in any Court of Record upon any Bond or Bonds, or on any penal Sum for non-performance of any Covenants or Agreements in any Indenture, Deed or Writing contained, or upon any Bond or Bonds, with any Condition other than for payment of Money, the Plaintiff or Plaintiffs may assign as many

Breaches as he or they may think fit, and the Jury upon Trial of such Action or Actions shall and may assess, not only such Damages and Costs of Suit as have heretofore been usually done in such Cases, but also Damages for such of the said Breaches so to be Assigned, as the Plaintiff upon the Trial of the Issues shall prove to have been broken, and that the like Judgment shall be entered on such Verdict as heretofore hath been usually done in such like Actions, and if the Judgment shall be given for the Plaintiff on a Demurrer, or by Confession, or Nihil dicit, the Plaintiff upon the Roll may suggest as many Breaches of the Covenants, Conditions and Agreements as he shall think fit, upon which shall issue a Writ to the Sheriff of that County where the Action shall be brought to summon a Jury to Appear in the Court where the Action shall be brought, if such Court sits in the same County where the Action shall be brought, or in Case the Court in which the Action is brought does not sit in the County where the Action is laid, then before the Justices or Justice of Assize or Nisi prius of that County where the Action shall be brought, to inquire of the Truth of every one of those Breaches, and to Assess the Damages that the Plaintiff shall have sustained thereby, in which Writ if to be executed before the Justices of Assize or Nisi prius, it shall be commanded to the said Justices or Justice of Assize or Nisi prius that he or they shall make a Return thereof to the Court from whence the same shall issue, at the Time in such Writ mentioned, and in Case the Defendant or Defendants after such Judgment entered, and before any Execution executed, shall pay unto the Court where the Action shall be brought to the use of the Plaintiff or Plaintiffs, or his or their Executors or Administrators, such Damages so to be assessed, by reason of all or any of the Breaches of such Covenants, together with the Costs of Suit, a stay of Execution of the said Judgment shall be entered upon Record, or if by reason of any Execution executed the Plaintiff or Plaintiffs, or his or their Executors or Administrators shall be fully paid or satisfied all such Damages so to be assessed, together with his or their Costs of suit, and all reasonable Charges and Expences for executing the said Execution, the Body, Lands or Goods of the Defendant shall be thereupon forthwith discharged from the said Execution, which shall likewise be entered upon Record, but notwithstanding in each Case such Judgment shall remain, continue and be as a further Security to answer to the Plaintiff or Plaintiffs, and his or their Executors or Administrators, such Damages as shall or may be sustained for further Breach of any Covenant or Covenants, Condition or Conditions, in the same Indenture Deed or Writing contained, upon which the Plaintiff or Plaintiffs may have a Scire facias upon the said Judgment against the Defendant, or against his Heir Terre-Tenants, or his Executors or Administrators suggesting other Breaches of the said Covenants or Agreements and to summon him or them respectively to shew Cause why Execution shall not be had or awarded upon the said Judgment, upon which there shall be the like proceeding as was in the Action of Debt upon the said Bond or Obligation for assessing of Damages upon Trial of Issues joined upon such Breaches or inquiry thereof. upon a Writ to be awarded in Manner as aforesaid, and that upon payment or Satisfaction in manner as aforesaid of such future Damages, Costs and Charges as aforesaid all further proceedings on the said Judgment are again to be stayed, and so toties quoties, and the Defendant his Body, Lands or Goods shall be discharged out of Execution as aforesaid.

[CHAPTER 1518.]

[Chapter 1518 of Van Schaack, where the act is printed in full.]

An Act to confirm certain Acts and Orders made by Justices of the Peace being of the Quorum, notwithstanding any Defect in not expressing therein that such Justices of the Peace are of the Quorum.

[Passed, February 26, 1772.]

WHEREAS Authority is given by divers Laws to two or more Justices of the Peace, whereof one or more are to be of the Quorum. AND WHEREAS divers Acts, Orders, Adjudications, Warrants and other Instruments done, made and executed, by two or more Justices of the Peace without expressing that they are, or that one of them is of the Quorum, have been, and may be for that Reason only, impeached set aside, and vacated.

BE IT ENACTED by his Excellency the Governor the Council and the General Assembly, and it is hereby enacted by the Authority of the same, That from and after the publication hereof, no Act order, Adjudication, Warrant or other Instrument already made done or executed, or hereafter to be made done or executed by two or more Justices of the Peace, which doth not express that one or more of the Justices is or are of the Quorum, shall be impeached, set aside, or vacated for that Defect only any Law Usage or Custom to the contrary notwithstanding.

[CHAPTER 1519.]

[Chapter 1519 of Van Schaack, where the act is printed chapter 1480.]

An Act to revive an Act in[illegible] "Act to prevent Frauds in Barr I[illegible] "to sale in this Colony."

[Passed, Februar

BE IT ENACTED by his Excellency the Governor and the General Assembly and it is hereby enac[illegible] Authority of the same, that the Act intitled "An Ac[illegible] "Frauds in Barr-Iron exposed to sale in this Colony the tenth Year of the Reign of his present Majesty, hereby is revived from the Publication hereof until [illegible] of February, which will be in the Year of our Lord [illegible] seven hundred and eighty.

[CHAPTER 1520.]

[Chapter 1520 of Van Schaack, where the title only is printed. See chapter 1488. Continued by chapter 1604.]

An Act further to continue an Act entitled. "An Act to restrain Hawkers and "Pedlars within this Colony from selling "without Licence."

[Passed, February 26, 1772.]

WHEREAS the Act intitled. "An Act to restrain Hawkers "and Pedlars within this Colony from selling without Licence." will expire by its own Limitation on the first Day of February 1772.

BE IT THEREFORE ENACTED by his Excellency the Governor the Council and the General Assembly, and it is hereby enacted by the Authority of the same, that the said Act intitled "An Act to restrain Hawkers and Pedlars within this Colony "from selling without Licence." shall be and hereby is continued from the expiration thereof until the first Day of February one thousand seven hundred and seventy three, any Thing in the said Act contained to the contrary hereof in any wise notwithstanding.

[CHAPTER 1521.]

[Chapter 1521 of Van Schaack, where the act is printed in full. See chapter 1363.]

An Act to amend an Act intitled "An Act "for the better determination of Personal "Actions depending upon Accounts."

[Passed, February 26, 1772.]

WHEREAS the aforesaid Act intitled "An Act for the better determination of Personal Actions depending upon Accounts is confined to the Supreme Court of this Colony. AND WHEREAS the same Reasons exist for investing the Inferior Courts of Common Pleas in this Colony, and the Mayor's Courts of the Cities of New York and Albany, with the same Powers as are in and by the said Act given unto the Supreme Court of this Colony.

BE IT THEREFORE ENACTED by his Excellency the Governor the Council and the General Assembly, and it is hereby enacted by the Authority of the same, That the aforesaid Act intitled. "An Act for the better determination of Personal Actions depending upon Accounts." and every Article, Clause and Thing therein contained shall be and hereby is extended to the Inferior Courts of Common Pleas in this Colony, and the Mayor's Courts of the Cities of New York and Albany and the Judges of the said Inferior Courts and Mayor's Courts of the Cities of New York and Albany are hereby vested with the like Powers and Authorities as are given unto the Judges of the Supreme Court of this Colony in and by the aforesaid Act intitled "An Act for the better determination of personal Actions depending upon Accounts." any Thing therein contained to the contrary thereof in any wise notwithstanding.

PROVIDED ALWAYS That Nothing in this Act contained shall be construed to extend to any other Suits or Actions than those, the Parties in which both reside in the County where the same is or are brought.

[CHAPTER 1522.]

[Chapter 1522 of Van Schaack, where the act is printed in full. See chapter 1410.]

An Act to revive and continue an Act Intitled "An Act for the more effectual pre- "vention of Fires in the City of New York."

[Passed, February 26, 1772.]

WHEREAS an Act intitled "An Act for the more effectual "prevention of Fires in the City of New York." expired on the

[CHAPTER 1519.]

[Chapter 1519 of Van Schaack, where the act is printed in full. See chapter 1430.]

An Act to revive an Act intitled. "An "Act to prevent Frauds in Barr Iron, exposed "to sale in this Colony."

[Passed, February 26, 1772.]

BE IT ENACTED by his Excellency the Governor the Council and the General Assembly and it is hereby enacted by the Authority of the same, that the Act intitled "An Act to prevent "Frauds in Barr-Iron exposed to sale in this Colony." passed in the tenth Year of the Reign of his present Majesty, shall be and hereby is revived from the Publication hereof until the first Day of February, which will be in the Year of our Lord one thousand seven hundred and eighty.

[CHAPTER 1520.]

[Chapter 1520 of Van Schaack, where the title only is printed. See chapter 1433. Continued by chapter 1604.]

An Act further to continue an Act entitled. "An Act to restrain Hawkers and "Pedlars within this Colony from selling "without Licence."

[Passed, February 26, 1772.]

WHEREAS the Act intitled. "An Act to restrain Hawkers "and Pedlars within this Colony from selling without Licence." will expire by its own Limitation on the first Day of February 1772.

BE IT THEREFORE ENACTED by his Excellency the Governor the Council and the General Assembly, and it is hereby enacted by the Authority of the same, that the said Act intitled "An Act to restrain Hawkers and Pedlars within this Colony "from selling without Licence." shall be and hereby is continued from the expiration thereof until the first Day of February one thousand seven hundred and seventy three, any Thing in the said Act contained to the contrary hereof in any wise notwithstanding.

[CHAPTER 1521.]

[Chapter 1521 of Van Schaack, where the act is printed in full. See chapter 1363.]

An Act to amend an Act intitled "An Act "for the better determination of Personal "Actions depending upon Accounts."

[Passed, February 26, 1772.]

WHEREAS the aforesaid Act intitled "An Act for the better determination of Personal Actions depending upon Accounts is confined to the Supreme Court of this Colony. AND WHEREAS the same Reasons exist for investing the Inferior Courts of Common Pleas in this Colony, and the Mayor's Courts of the Cities of New York and Albany, with the same Powers as are in and by the said Act given unto the Supreme Court of this Colony.

BE IT THEREFORE ENACTED by his Excellency the Governor the Council and the General Assembly, and it is hereby enacted by the Authority of the same, That the aforesaid Act intitled. "An Act for the better determination of Personal Actions depending upon Accounts." and every Article, Clause and Thing therein contained shall be and hereby is extended to the Inferior Courts of Common Pleas in this Colony, and the Mayor's Courts of the Cities of New York and Albany and the Judges of the said Inferior Courts and Mayor's Courts of the Cities of New York and Albany are hereby vested with the like Powers and Authorities as are given unto the Judges of the Supreme Court of this Colony in and by the aforesaid Act intitled "An Act for the better determination of personal Actions depending upon Accounts." any Thing therein contained to the contrary thereof in any wise notwithstanding.

PROVIDED ALWAYS That Nothing in this Act contained shall be construed to extend to any other Suits or Actions than those, the Parties in which both reside in the County where the same is or are brought.

[CHAPTER 1522.]

[Chapter 1522 of Van Schaack, where the act is printed in full. See chapter 1410.]

An Act to revive and continue an Act Intitled "An Act for the more effectual pre- "vention of Fires in the City of New York."

[Passed, February 26, 1772.]

WHEREAS an Act intitled "An Act for the more effectual "prevention of Fires in the City of New York." expired on the

first Day of this Instant Month of January, and the same having been found useful and Necessary.

BE IT THEREFORE ENACTED by his Excellency the Governor the Council and the General Assembly, and it is hereby enacted by the Authority of the same That the said Act shall be, and hereby is revived, and every Clause Matter and Thing in the same contained, enacted to be and remain in full force from the Publication hereof until the first Day of February in the Year of our Lord one thousand seven hundred and Seventy Seven.

[CHAPTER 1523.]

[Chapter 1523 of Van Schaack, where the title only is printed.]

An Act to enable the Mayor Recorder, Aldermen and Commonalty of the City of Albany for the Time being or the Major Part of them to order the raising a Sum not exceeding one hundred and fifty Pounds for the Purposes therein mentioned.

[Passed, February 26, 1772.]

WHEREAS the Establishment of a regular well constituted Night-Watch and Lighting of Lamps within the City of Albany has not only been found convenient, but also necessary for the safety of it's Inhabitants and others.

BE IT THEREFORE ENACTED by his Excellency the Governor the Council and the General Assembly, and it is hereby enacted by the Authority of the same, That the Mayor, Recorder Aldermen and Commonalty of the City of Albany for the Time being, or the Major Part of them whereof the Mayor or Recorder to be one, shall have full power and Authority and are hereby fully impowered and authorized at any Time before the last Day of March one thousand seven hundred and seventy two, to order the raising a Sum not exceeding one hundred and fifty Pounds by a Tax upon the Estates real and personal lying and being within the said City, of all and every the Freeholders, Freemen, Inhabitants Residents and Sojourners living within half a Mile from Hudson's River for the payment of so many Watch-men as the Mayor Aldermen and Commonalty of the said City in Common Council convened shall think necessary for guarding the said City and lighting the said Lamps which Tax so to be laid shall be rated and assessed at the same Time, and by the Assessors who shall Rate and Assess the Tax which shall be raised by virtue of an Act of the Governor the Council and the General Assembly of the Colony of New York intitled "An "Act for the better explaining and more effectual putting in "Execution an Act of the General Assembly made in the third "Year of the Reign of their late Majesties King William and "Queen Mary, intitled an Act for defraying the Public and "Necessary Charge throughout this Province and for maintain-"ing the Poor and preventing Vagabonds." made and passed the nineteenth Day of June one thousand seven hundred and three, the Assessors first taking the Oath prescribed to be taken by the last mentioned Act, and the Tax so to be laid shall be collected levied and paid by the same Collector and at the same Time as the Tax raised by virtue of the Act aforesaid hath been accustomed and shall be paid into the Hands of such Person as the Mayor Recorder Aldermen and Commonalty of the said City or the Major Part of them in Common Council convened shall appoint to be by him paid as he shall be directed by Warrant or Warrants of the said Mayor, Recorder Aldermen and Commonalty in Common Council convened for the uses aforesaid.

AND BE IT FURTHER ENACTED by the Authority aforesaid that the Collectors shall retain in his Hands three Pence in the Pound of every Pound so raised by virtue of this Act as a Reward for his Trouble in collecting and paying the same and no more.

AND BE IT FURTHER ENACTED by the Authority aforesaid, That if the said Mayor Recorder Aldermen and Commonalty, Assessors or Collectors of the said City of Albany, who are hereby authorized impowered and required to take effectual care that this Act be executed according to the true Intent and meaning thereof or any of them shall deny, refuse or delay to perform execute or comply with all or any of the Powers Authorities and Duties in this Act given and required to be done and performed by them or either of them and thereof shall be lawfully convicted in any Court of Record in this Colony, he or they so denying refusing or delaying to perform the Duties as aforesaid shall suffer such Pains and Penalties by Fine and Imprisonment as by the Discretion of the said Court shall be adjudged.

AND BE IT FURTHER ENACTED by the Authority aforesaid That if any Person or Persons shall neglect or refuse to pay the several Rates and Assessments wherewith he or they shall be charged by this Act for or in respect of his and their Goods and Chattles, Lands or Tenements upon Demand of the

Collector appointed to receive the same, that then it shall and may be lawfull to and for such Collector, and he is hereby required for nonpayment thereof, by Warrant under the Hand of the Mayor Recorder Aldermen and Commonalty of the said City for the Time being or the Major Part of them to distrain upon the Goods and Chattels of the Person or Persons so refusing or neglecting to pay, and for want of Goods or Chattels to distrain in and upon the Messuages Lands and Tenements so charged, and the Goods and Chattels then and there found and the Distress so taken to carry away, and the same to expose to sale within the said City for the payment of the said Rate or Assessment, and the Overplus if any be, over and above the Charges of taking and carrying away the said Distress to be immediately returned to the Owner thereof.

AND BE IT FURTHER ENACTED by the Authority aforesaid That all such Persons as shall be employed to guard the said City shall be under the Direction of and obey such Orders as they shall from Time to Time receive from the Mayor, Recorder, Aldermen and Commonalty in Common Council Convened and Custom Law or Usage to the contrary in any wise notwithstanding.

[CHAPTER 1524.]

[Chapter 1524 of Van Schaack, where the act is printed in full. See chapter 1483.]

An Act to extend to the County of Westchester an Act intitled "An Act to appoint "Inspectors of Flour and Repackers of Beef "and Pork in the several Counties therein "mentioned."

[Passed, February 26, 1772.]

BE IT ENACTED by his Excellency the Governor, the Council and the General Assembly and it is hereby enacted by the Authority of the same. That the Act intitled. "An Act to "appoint Inspectors of Flour and Repackers of Beef and Pork, "in the several Counties therein mentioned." passed the sixteenth Day of February, one thousand seven hundred and seventy one, shall immediately after the Publication hereof extend to the County of Westchester.

AND BE IT ENACTED by the same Authority, That John Johnson of the Manor of Cortlandt Gilbert Merritt, Gilbert Horton and Benjamin Ferris shall be and hereby are appointed the Officers for viewing and examining all such Flour, and that

Daniel Strang of the Manor of Cortlandt, and the said Gilbert Merritt, Gilbert Horton and Benjamin Ferris shall be and hereby are appointed Repackers of Beef and Pork intended to be shipped or laden on Board of any Vessel in the County of Westchester to be thence exported out of this Colony, and shall respectively have the same powers, proceed in the viewing and examining of Flour in the same Manner, and be subject to the same Forfeitures as the several Officers named in the abovementioned Act are, any Thing in the abovementioned Act to the contrary notwithstanding.

[CHAPTER 1525.]

[Chapter 1525 of Van Schaack, where the act is printed in full.]

An Act to enable the Justices, Church-Wardens and Vestry of the Parish of West-Chester in the County of West Chester to raise a Sum not exceeding five hundred Pounds for the purposes therein mentioned.

[Passed, February 26, 1772.]

WHEREAS the want of proper Regulations for relieving the Poor in the Parish of West Chester has not only occasioned many Inconveniencies as well as much Expence to the Inhabitants of the said Parish, but has also prevented the Monies expended from fully answering the humane and benevolent purposes for which they were intended; for Remedy whereof, and in order to make a suitable Provision for the impotent poor, to provide Work for such as are able and cannot otherwise get Employment, and to establish a place of Correction for idle and disorderly Persons within the said Parish.

BE IT ENACTED by his Excellency the Governor, the Council and the General Assembly and it is hereby enacted by the Authority of the same, That the Justices of the Peace dwelling within the said Parish, that is to say within Westchester East-chester, Yonkers and the Manor of Pelham, and the Church Wardens and Vestry of the said Parish for the Time being or the major Part of them annually elected by the Inhabitants thereof, shall be authorized and impowered, and they are hereby directed and required within some convenient Time after the Publication of this Act to raise a Sum not exceeding five hundred Pounds by a Taxation on the Inhabitants of the said Parish, which Tax shall be assessed by the said Justices. Church Wardens and Ves-

AND BE IT FURTHER ENACTED by the Authority aforesaid, that if at any Time hereafter any Person or Persons shall commence or prosecute in any Court of Record any Action, Plaint or Suit, wherein upon any Demurrer, either by Plaintiff or Defendant, Demandant or Tenant, Judgement Shall be given by the Court against such Plaintiff or Demandant, or if at any Time after Judgment given for the Defendant in any such Action Plaint or Suit, the Plaintiff or Demandant shall sue any Writ or Writs of Error to aunul the said Judgment, and the said Judgment shall be afterwards affirmed to be good, or the said Writ of Error shall be discontinued, or the Plaintiff shall be nonsuit therein, the Defendant or Tenant in every such Action Plaint, Suit or Writ of Error shall have Judgment to recover his Costs against every such Plaintiff or Plaintiffs, Demandant or Demandants, and have Execution for the same by Capias ad Satisfaciendum, Fieri facias,—or Elegit.

AND BE IT FURTHER ENACTED by the Authority aforesaid, that from and after the Publication hereof, in all Actions of Waste wherein the single value or Damage found by the Jury, shall not exceed the Sum of twenty Nobles, and in all Suits upon any Writ or Writs of Scire facias, and Suits upon Prohibitions, the Plaintiff obtaining Judgment or any Award of Execution after Plea pleaded, or Demurrer joined therein, shall likewise recover his Costs of Suit, and if the Plaintiff shall become non-Suit or suffer a Discontinuance, or a Verdict shall pass against him, the Defendant shall recover his Costs, and have execution for the same in like Manner as aforesaid.

AND for preventing Wilful and malicious Trespasses BE IT FURTHER ENACTED that in all Actions of Trespass to be commenced or prosecuted from and after the publication hereof in any Court of Record wherein at the Trial of the Cause it shall appear and be certified by the Judge under his Hand, upon the Back of the Record.— that the Trespass upon which any Defendant shall be found guilty, was wilful and malicious, the Plaintiff shall recover not only his Damages, but his full Costs of Suit, any former Law to the contrary notwithstanding.

PROVIDED ALWAYS that Nothing herein contained shall be construed to alter the Laws in being as to Executors or Administrators, in such Cases where they are not at present liable to the payment of Costs of Suit.

AND BE IT FURTHER ENACTED that in all Actions to be commenced in any Court of Record from and after the publication hereof, if any Plaintiff happen to Die after an interlocutory Judgment, and before a final Judgment obtained therein, the said Action shall not abate by reason thereof, if such Action might be originally prosecuted or maintained by the Executors or Administrators of such Plaintiff; and if the Defendant die after such interlocutory Judgment, and before final Judgment therein obtained, the said Action shall not abate if such Action might be originally prosecuted or maintained against the Executors or Administrators of such Defendant; and the Plaintiff, or if he be dead after such interlocutory Judgment, his Executors or Administrators shall and may have a Scire facias against the Defendant if living after such interlocutory Judgment, or if he died after, then against his Executors or Administrators to shew Cause why Damages in such Action should not be Assessed and recovered by him or them, and if such Defendant his Executors or Administrators shall appear at the Return of such Writ, and not shew or alledge any Matter sufficient to arrest the final Judgment, or being returned warned, or upon two Writs of Scire facias, it be returned, that the Defendant, his Executors or Administrators had Nothing whereby to be summoned, or could not be found in the County, shall make Default, that thereupon a Writ of inquiry of Damages shall be awarded, which being executed and returned Judgment final shall be given for the said Plaintiff, his Executors or Administrators, prosecuting such Writ or Writs of Scire facias, against such Defendant his Executors or Administrators respectively.

AND BE IT FURTHER ENACTED by the Authority aforesaid, that if there be two or more Plaintiffs or Defendants, and one or more of them should die; if the Cause of such Action shall survive to the surviving Plaintiff or Plaintiffs, or against the surviving Defendant or Defendants, the Writ or Action shall not be thereby abated, but such Death being suggested upon the Record, the Action shall proceed at the suit of the surviving Plaintiff or Plaintiffs, against the surviving Defendant or Defendants.

AND BE IT FURTHER ENACTED that in all Actions which from and after the publication hereof, shall be commenced or prosecuted in any Court of Record upon any Bond or Bonds, or on any penal Sum for non-performance of any Covenants or Agreements in any Indenture, Deed or Writing contained, or upon any Bond or Bonds, with any Condition other than for payment of Money, the Plaintiff or Plaintiffs may assign as many

Breaches as he or they may think fit, and the Jury upon Trial of such Action or Actions shall and may assess, not only such Damages and Costs of Suit as have heretofore been usually done in such Cases, but also Damages for such of the said Breaches so to be Assigned, as the Plaintiff upon the Trial of the Issues shall prove to have been broken, and that the like Judgment shall be entered on such Verdict as heretofore hath been usually done in such like Actions, and if the Judgment shall be given for the Plaintiff on a Demurrer, or by Confession, or Nihil dicit, the Plaintiff upon the Roll may suggest as many Breaches of the Covenants, Conditions and Agreements as he shall think fit, upon which shall issue a Writ to the Sheriff of that County where the Action shall be brought to summon a Jury to Appear in the Court where the Action shall be brought, if such Court sits in the same County where the Action shall be brought, or in Case the Court in which the Action is brought does not sit in the County where the Action is laid, then before the Justices or Justice of Assize or Nisi prius of that County where the Action shall be brought, to inquire of the Truth of every one of those Breaches, and to Assess the Damages that the Plaintiff shall have sustained thereby, in which Writ if to be executed before the Justices of Assize or Nisi prius, it shall be commanded to the said Justices or Justice of Assize or Nisi prius that he or they shall make a Return thereof to the Court from whence the same shall issue, at the Time in such Writ mentioned, and in Case the Defendant or Defendants after such Judgment entered, and before any Execution executed, shall pay unto the Court where the Action shall be brought to the use of the Plaintiff or Plaintiffs, or his or their Executors or Administrators, such Damages so to be assessed, by reason of all or any of the Breaches of such Covenants, together with the Costs of Suit, a stay of Execution of the said Judgment shall be entered upon Record, or if by reason of any Execution executed the Plaintiff or Plaintiffs, or his or their Executors or Administrators shall be fully paid or satisfied all such Damages so to be assessed, together with his or their Costs of suit, and all reasonable Charges and Expences for executing the said Execution, the Body, Lands or Goods of the Defendant shall be thereupon forthwith discharged from the said Execution, which shall likewise be entered upon Record, but notwithstanding in each Case such Judgment shall remain, continue and be as a further Security to answer to the Plaintiff or Plaintiffs, and his or their Executors or Administrators, such Damages as shall or may be sustained for further Breach of any Covenant or Covenants, Condition or Conditions, in the same Indenture Deed or Writing contained, upon which the Plaintiff or Plaintiffs may have a Scire facias upon the said Judgment against the Defendant, or against his Heir Terre-Tenants, or his Executors or Administrators suggesting other Breaches of the said Covenants or Agreements and to summon him or them respectively to shew Cause why Execution shall not be had or awarded upon the said Judgment, upon which there shall be the like proceeding as was in the Action of Debt upon the said Bond or Obligation for assessing of Damages upon Trial of Issues joined upon such Breaches or inquiry thereof. upon a Writ to be awarded in Manner as aforesaid, and that upon payment or Satisfaction in manner as aforesaid of such future Damages, Costs and Charges as aforesaid all further proceedings on the said Judgment are again to be stayed, and so toties quoties, and the Defendant his Body, Lands or Goods shall be discharged out of Execution as aforesaid.

[CHAPTER 1518.]

[Chapter 1518 of Van Schaack, where the act is printed in full.]

An Act to confirm certain Acts and Orders made by Justices of the Peace being of the Quorum, notwithstanding any Defect in not expressing therein that such Justices of the Peace are of the Quorum.

[Passed, February 26, 1772.]

WHEREAS Authority is given by divers Laws to two or more Justices of the Peace, whereof one or more are to be of the Quorum. AND WHEREAS divers Acts, Orders, Adjudications, Warrants and other Instruments done, made and executed, by two or more Justices of the Peace without expressing that they are, or that one of them is of the Quorum, have been, and may be for that Reason only, impeached set aside, and vacated.

BE IT ENACTED by his Excellency the Governor the Council and the General Assembly, and it is hereby enacted by the Authority of the same, That from and after the publication hereof, no Act order, Adjudication, Warrant or other Instrument already made done or executed, or hereafter to be made done or executed by two or more Justices of the Peace, which doth not express that one or more of the Justices is or are of the Quorum, shall be impeached, set aside, or vacated for that Defect only any Law Usage or Custom to the contrary notwithstanding.

[CHAPTER 1519.]

[Chapter 1519 of Van Schaack, where the act is printe chapter 1430.]

An Act to revive an Act i "Act to prevent Frauds in Barr "to sale in this Colony."

[Passed, Febru

BE IT ENACTED by his Excellency the Governo and the General Assembly and it is hereby ena Authority of the same, that the Act intitled "An A "Frauds in Barr-Iron exposed to sale in this Colon the tenth Year of the Reign of his present Majesty hereby is revived from the Publication hereof until of February, which will be in the Year of our Lord seven hundred and eighty.

[CHAPTER 1520.]

[Chapter 1520 of Van Schaack, where the title only is printed. See chapter 1438. Continued by chapter 1604.]

An Act further to continue an Act entitled. "An Act to restrain Hawkers and "Pedlars within this Colony from selling "without Licence."

[Passed, February 26, 1772.]

WHEREAS the Act intitled. "An Act to restrain Hawkers "and Pedlars within this Colony from selling without Licence." will expire by its own Limitation on the first Day of February 1772.

BE IT THEREFORE ENACTED by his Excellency the Governor the Council and the General Assembly, and it is hereby enacted by the Authority of the same, that the said Act intitled "An Act to restrain Hawkers and Pedlars within this Colony "from selling without Licence." shall be and hereby is continued from the expiration thereof until the first Day of February one thousand seven hundred and seventy three, any Thing in the said Act contained to the contrary hereof in any wise notwithstanding.

[CHAPTER 1521.]

[Chapter 1521 of Van Schaack, where the act is printed in full. See chapter 1363.]

An Act to amend an Act intitled "An Act "for the better determination of Personal "Actions depending upon Accounts."

[Passed, February 26, 1772.]

WHEREAS the aforesaid Act intitled "An Act for the better determination of Personal Actions depending upon Accounts is confined to the Supreme Court of this Colony. AND WHEREAS the same Reasons exist for investing the Inferior Courts of Common Pleas in this Colony, and the Mayor's Courts of the Cities of New York and Albany, with the same Powers as are in and by the said Act given unto the Supreme Court of this Colony.

BE IT THEREFORE ENACTED by his Excellency the Governor the Council and the General Assembly, and it is hereby enacted by the Authority of the same, That the aforesaid Act intitled. "An Act for the better determination of Personal Actions depending upon Accounts." and every Article, Clause and Thing therein contained shall be and hereby is extended to the Inferior Courts of Common Pleas in this Colony, and the Mayor's Courts of the Cities of New York and Albany and the Judges of the said Inferior Courts and Mayor's Courts of the Cities of New York and Albany are hereby vested with the like Powers and Authorities as are given unto the Judges of the Supreme Court of this Colony in and by the aforesaid Act intitled "An Act for the better determination of personal Actions depending upon Accounts." any Thing therein contained to the contrary thereof in any wise notwithstanding.

PROVIDED ALWAYS That Nothing in this Act contained shall be construed to extend to any other Suits or Actions than those, the Parties in which both reside in the County where the same is or are brought.

[CHAPTER 1522.]

[Chapter 1522 of Van Schaack, where the act is printed in full. See chapter 1410.]

An Act to revive and continue an Act intitled "An Act for the more effectual pre- "vention of Fires in the City of New York."

[Passed, February 26, 1772.]

WHEREAS an Act intitled "An Act for the more effectual "prevention of Fires in the City of New York." expired on the

first Day of this Instant Month of January, and the same having been found useful and Necessary.

BE IT THEREFORE ENACTED by his Excellency the Governor the Council and the General Assembly, and it is hereby enacted by the Authority of the same That the said Act shall be, and hereby is revived, and every Clause Matter and Thing in the same contained, enacted to be and remain in full force from the Publication hereof until the first Day of February in the Year of our Lord one thousand seven hundred and Seventy Seven.

[CHAPTER 1523.]

[Chapter 1523 of Van Schaack, where the title only is printed.]

An Act to enable the Mayor Recorder, Aldermen and Commonalty of the City of Albany for the Time being or the Major Part of them to order the raising a Sum not exceeding one hundred and fifty Pounds for the Purposes therein mentioned.

[Passed, February 26, 1772.]

WHEREAS the Establishment of a regular well constituted Night-Watch and Lighting of Lamps within the City of Albany has not only been found convenient, but also necessary for the safety of it's Inhabitants and others.

BE IT THEREFORE ENACTED by his Excellency the Governor the Council and the General Assembly, and it is hereby enacted by the Authority of the same, That the Mayor, Recorder Aldermen and Commonalty of the City of Albany for the Time being, or the Major Part of them whereof the Mayor or Recorder to be one, shall have full power and Authority and are hereby fully impowered and authorized at any Time before the last Day of March one thousand seven hundred and seventy two, to order the raising a Sum not exceeding one hundred and fifty Pounds by a Tax upon the Estates real and personal lying and being within the said City, of all and every the Freeholders, Freemen, Inhabitants Residents and Sojourners living within half a Mile from Hudson's River for the payment of so many Watch-men as the Mayor Aldermen and Commonalty of the said City in Common Council convened shall think necessary for guarding the said City and lighting the said Lamps which Tax so to be laid shall be rated and assessed at the same Time, and by the Assessors who shall Rate and Assess the Tax which shall be raised by virtue of an Act of the Governor the Council and the General Assembly of the Colony of New York intitled "An "Act for the better explaining and more effectual putting in "Execution an Act of the General Assembly made in the third "Year of the Reign of their late Majesties King William and "Queen Mary, intitled an Act for defraying the Public and "Necessary Charge throughout this Province and for maintain-"ing the Poor and preventing Vagabonds." made and passed the nineteenth Day of June one thousand seven hundred and three, the Assessors first taking the Oath prescribed to be taken by the last mentioned Act, and the Tax so to be laid shall be collected levied and paid by the same Collector and at the same Time as the Tax raised by virtue of the Act aforesaid hath been accustomed and shall be paid into the Hands of such Person as the Mayor Recorder Aldermen and Commonalty of the said City or the Major Part of them in Common Council convened shall appoint to be by him paid as he shall be directed by Warrant or Warrants of the said Mayor, Recorder Aldermen and Commonalty in Common Council convened for the uses aforesaid.

AND BE IT FURTHER ENACTED by the Authority aforesaid that the Collectors shall retain in his Hands three Pence in the Pound of every Pound so raised by virtue of this Act as a Reward for his Trouble in collecting and paying the same and no more.

AND BE IT FURTHER ENACTED by the Authority aforesaid, That if the said Mayor Recorder Aldermen and Commonalty, Assessors or Collectors of the said City of Albany, who are hereby authorized impowered and required to take effectual care that this Act be executed according to the true Intent and meaning thereof or any of them shall deny, refuse or delay to perform execute or comply with all or any of the Powers Authorities and Duties in this Act given and required to be done and performed by them or either of them and thereof shall be lawfully convicted in any Court of Record in this Colony, he or they so denying refusing or delaying to perform the Duties as aforesaid shall suffer such Pains and Penalties by Fine and Imprisonment as by the Discretion of the said Court shall be adjudged.

AND BE IT FURTHER ENACTED by the Authority aforesaid That if any Person or Persons shall neglect or refuse to pay the several Rates and Assessments wherewith he or they shall be charged by this Act for or in respect of his and their Goods and Chattles, Lands or Tenements upon Demand of the

Collector appointed to receive the same, that then it shall and may be lawfull to and for such Collector, and he is hereby required for nonpayment thereof, by Warrant under the Hand of the Mayor Recorder Aldermen and Commonalty of the said City for the Time being or the Major Part of them to distrain upon the Goods and Chattels of the Person or Persons so refusing or neglecting to pay, and for want of Goods or Chattels to distrain in and upon the Messuages Lands and Tenements so charged, and the Goods and Chattels then and there found and the Distress so taken to carry away, and the same to expose to sale within the said City for the payment of the said Rate or Assessment, and the Overplus if any be, over and above the Charges of taking and carrying away the said Distress to be immediately returned to the Owner thereof.

AND BE IT FURTHER ENACTED by the Authority aforesaid That all such Persons as shall be employed to guard the said City shall be under the Direction of and obey such Orders as they shall from Time to Time receive from the Mayor, Recorder, Aldermen and Commonalty in Common Council Convened and Custom Law or Usage to the contrary in any wise notwithstanding.

[CHAPTER 1524.]

[Chapter 1524 of Van Schaack, where the act is printed in full. See chapter 1483.]

An Act to extend to the County of Westchester an Act intitled "An Act to appoint "Inspectors of Flour and Repackers of Beef "and Pork in the several Counties therein "mentioned."

[Passed, February 26, 1772.]

BE IT ENACTED by his Excellency the Governor, the Council and the General Assembly and it is hereby enacted by the Authority of the same. That the Act intitled. "An Act to "appoint Inspectors of Flour and Repackers of Beef and Pork, "in the several Counties therein mentioned." passed the sixteenth Day of February, one thousand seven hundred and seventy one, shall immediately after the Publication hereof extend to the County of Westchester.

AND BE IT ENACTED by the same Authority, That John Johnson of the Manor of Cortlandt Gilbert Merritt, Gilbert Horton and Benjamin Ferris shall be and hereby are appointed the Officers for viewing and examining all such Flour, and that

Daniel Strang of the Manor of Cortlandt, and the said Gilbert Merritt, Gilbert Horton and Benjamin Ferris shall be and hereby are appointed Repackers of Beef and Pork intended to be shipped or laden on Board of any Vessel in the County of Westchester to be thence exported out of this Colony, and shall respectively have the same powers, proceed in the viewing and examining of Flour in the same Manner, and be subject to the same Forfeitures as the several Officers named in the abovementioned Act are, any Thing in the abovementioned Act to the contrary notwithstanding.

[CHAPTER 1525.]

[Chapter 1525 of Van Schaack, where the act is printed in full.]

An Act to enable the Justices, Church-Wardens and Vestry of the Parish of West-Chester in the County of West Chester to raise a Sum not exceeding five hundred Pounds for the purposes therein mentioned.

[Passed, February 26, 1772.]

WHEREAS the want of proper Regulations for relieving the Poor in the Parish of West Chester has not only occasioned many Inconveniencies as well as much Expence to the Inhabitants of the said Parish, but has also prevented the Monies expended from fully answering the humane and benevolent purposes for which they were intended; for Remedy whereof, and in order to make a suitable Provision for the impotent poor, to provide Work for such as are able and cannot otherwise get Employment, and to establish a place of Correction for idle and disorderly Persons within the said Parish.

BE IT ENACTED by his Excellency the Governor, the Council and the General Assembly and it is hereby enacted by the Authority of the same, That the Justices of the Peace dwelling within the said Parish, that is to say within Westchester East-chester, Yonkers and the Manor of Pelham, and the Church Wardens and Vestry of the said Parish for the Time being or the major Part of them annually elected by the Inhabitants thereof, shall be authorized and impowered, and they are hereby directed and required within some convenient Time after the Publication of this Act to raise a Sum not exceeding five hundred Pounds by a Taxation on the Inhabitants of the said Parish, which Tax shall be assessed by the said Justices. Church Wardens and Vestry or a Major Part of them in a Manner as nearly proportioned as may be to the respective Rates and Quotas assessed and imposed on the Inhabitants of the said Parish at the last Assessment made for the County of Westchester by the Supervisors of said County, and shall be levied and collected by Warrant from the said Justices, Church Wardens and Vestry, or a major Part of them, directed to the Collector or Collectors of the said Parish in like Manner as the necessary and contingent County Charges have heretofore been levied and collected within the said Parish; And the said Sum being so assessed levied and collected the Justices, Church Wardens and Vestry within the said Parish for the Time being or the major Part of them are Authorized and directed with Part of the said Money to purchase a Lot of Ground within the said Parish and thereon to erect and build a House with Appartments suitable for the purposes herein after mentioned, which said Lot so purchased shall be vested in and held by the said Justices, Church Wardens and Vestry their Successors and Assigns for the Time being, who are hereby impowered to take and hold such Estate in Trust for the Uses and purposes in this Act mentioned forever.

AND BE IT FURTHER ENACTED by the Authority Aforesaid, That the Justices of the Peace, Church Wardens, and Vestry of the said Parish for the Time being or a major Part of them shall from Time to Time take Order for the Relief of the lame, old, blind, and such other Poor as are not able to work, and also for setting to work all such other persons, married or unmarried who have no visible Means to Maintain themselves, and shall in like manner be empowered to purchase Materials and stuff whereon to set them at work, and to bind poor Children Apprentices until each Boy shall attain to the age of twenty one, and each Girl to the age of eighteen Years.

AND BE IT FURTHER ENACTED by the Authority aforesaid, That the Buildings to be erected in manner aforesaid, shall be also a House of Correction, for the Direction and Superintendency over which the said Justices, Church Wardens and Vestry for the Time being or a major Part of them shall appoint such Person or Persons as Overseers and with such Allowance as they shall think proper; and to which House of correction it shall be lawful for any one Justice of the Peace dwelling in the said Parish to commit idle, disorderly, and vagrant Persons, that is to say all such who not having wherewith to maintain themselves, live idle without Employment, and also all such as go about within the said Parish to beg or gather Alms (the said Offenders being thereof first convicted before the said Justice by his own View or Confession or Oath of one Witness) and the said Offenders being so committed, it shall be lawful to keep them to hard Labour for the Space of one Month, and if they shall afterwards repeat the same Offense, they may again be committed, and besides being put to hard Labour, they may be punished by Whipping in such manner as the said Justices, Church Wardens and Vestry for the Time being, or a major Part of them shall direct.

[CHAPTER 1526.]

[Chapter 1526 of Van Schaack, where the title only is printed. See chapter 1453. Expired the 1st of January, 1778. Provided for by chapter 1624.]

An Act to extend an Act intitled "An "Act for the better regulation of the Public "Inns and Taverns in the Counties of Ulster "and Orange." to the City and County of Albany with an Addition thereto.

[Passed, February 26, 1772.]

BE IT ENACTED by his Excellency the Governor the Council and the General Assembly, and it is hereby enacted by the Authority of the same, that a certain Act of the Legislature of this Colony passed the twenty seventh Day of January one thousand seven hundred and seventy intitled. "An Act for the better "regulation of the Public Inns and Taverns in the Counties of "Ulster and Orange." shall be and hereby is extended to the City and County of Albany, any Thing in the said Act to the contrary hereof notwithstanding.

PROVIDED ALWAYS, that Nothing in the said Act shall be construed to abridge or diminish the rights of the Corporation of the City of Albany.

[CHAPTER 1527.]

[Chapter 1527 of Van Schaack, where the act is printed in full. See chapter 726.]

An Act to amend an Act intitled "An "Act for returning Neat Cattle and Sheep to "their Owners." so far as it relates to Suffolk, Queens and Westchester Counties.

[Passed, February 26, 1772.]

WHEREAS by the Second Section of the Act intitled, "An Act for returning Neat Cattle and Sheep to their Owners." passed the twenty seventh Day of November, one thousand seven hundred and forty one, it is enacted that if no Owner or Owners shall appear to claim the said Neat Cattle within the space of one Year after the first Notice given to the Clerk, then the possessor or possessors are thereby required to sell them at Vendue to the highest Bidder, which being found inconvenient, to prevent the same for the future.

BE IT ENACTED by his Excellency the Governor, the Council and the General Assembly, and it is hereby enacted by the Authority of the same, That if no Owner or Owners shall appear to claim the said Neat Cattle in either of the Counties of Suffolk, Queens and Westchester, after the first Notice given to the Clerk as by the aforesaid Act is directed, that in such Case the possessor or Possessors of them are hereby directed to sell them at Public Vendue to the highest Bidder, on the first Tuesday of May then next following, first giving notice, at least fourteen Days, as is directed by the abovesaid Act, and the Money arising from such Sale or Sales, shall be kept and disposed of according to the Direction of the above recited Act, any Thing contained in the said Act to the contrary in any wise notwithstanding

[CHAPTER 1528.]

[Chapter 1528 of Van Schaack, where the act is printed in full.]

An Act to prevent the use of Spirituous Liquors at Vendues in the Counties of Ulster and Orange.

[Passed, February 26, 1772.]

WHEREAS the use of Spirituous Liquors at Vendues hath heretofore been productive of Evil consequences by intoxicating the Bidders; who in such Condition frequently bid high and extravagant Prices for Articles of small value and of which they don't Stand in need, to the great distress of many poor Families: And in as much as the Laws for the Prevention thereof in the Counties of Ulster and Orange are expired.

BE IT THEREFORE ENACTED by his Excellency the Governor the Council and the General Assembly and it is hereby enacted by the Authority of the same, That if any Person or Persons whomsoever shall presume after the first Day of March next to give or sell any Spirituous Liquors at any Vendue within either of the said Counties of Ulster or Orange, or shall procure the same to be done by any other Person or Persons either at the House or place where such Vendue may be held, or at any other place within one Mile of such Vendue under any pretence whatsoever contrary to the true Intent and meaning of this Act, such person or persons shall forfeit and pay the sum of five Pounds for each person to whom he or they shall sell or give Spirituous Liquors as aforesaid to be recovered in distinct suits before any one of his Majesty's Justices of the Peace for the County where the Offence shall be committed, together with Costs of Suit; the one half of said Forfeitures to be for the use of him or them who shall sue for the same, and the other Half for the use of the Poor of the Town Manor or Precinct where such Forfeiture shall arise.

AND BE IT FURTHER ENACTED by the Authority aforesaid, That this Act shall be in force until the first Day of March which will be in the Year of our Lord one thousand seven hundred and eighty. Provided always, that no Penalty shall be incurred by this Act, if the Person or Persons to whom such Spirituous Liquor shall be sold, shall not be a Bidder at such Vendue, either by himself, or any other Person for him.

[CHAPTER 1529.]

[Chapter 1529 of Van Schaack, where the act is printed in full. See chapter 1311.]

An Act to revive and continue an Act intitled, "An Act for laying out regulating "and keeping in repair common and Public "Highways in the County of Cumberland."

[Passed, February 26, 1772.]

WHEREAS an Act intitled. "An Act for laying out regulating "and keeping in Repair common and public Highways in the "County of Cumberland." made and passed the nineteenth Day of December in the seventh Year of his present Majesty's Reign expired on the first Day of January one thousand seven hundred and seventy one. AND WHEREAS the said Act has been found Beneficial to the Inhabitants of the said County of Cumberland.

BE IT THEREFORE ENACTED by his Excellency the Governor the Council and the General Assembly, and it is hereby enacted by the Authority of the same. That the aforesaid Act intitled. "An Act for laying out regulating and keeping in repair "common and Public Highways in the County of Cumberland." shall be and hereby is revived and continued, and every Article Matter Clause and Thing therein contained is hereby enacted to be remain and continue in full force and virtue to all Intents and purposes whatsoever until the first Day of February which will be in the Year of our Lord one thousand seven hundred and Seventy seven.

[CHAPTER 1530.]

[Chapter 1530 of Van Schaack, where the act is printed in full.]

An Act for regulating of Inns and Taverns in the County of Cumberland.

[Passed, February 26, 1772.]

WHEREAS there is at present no Law to regulate the keeping of Taverns and Inns in the County of Cumberland, by means whereof many improper persons have set up Inns and Taverns in the said County, which has a manifest Tendency to encourage Gameing Drunkenness and Idlenesess to the great Scandal of Religion and Impoverishment of many of the Inhabitants of the said County.

BE IT THEREFORE ENACTED by his Excellency the Governor, the Council and the General Assembly, and it is hereby enacted by the Authority of the same. That the Court of General Sessions of the peace for the said County of Cumberland, shall be and hereby are Authorized and impowered to grant Licenses at their said Court of General Sessions to such persons as the Justices of the said Court shall think proper to sell and retail Strong Liquors within the said County, which Licences so to be granted, or a Note or Minute thereof shall from Time to Time be entered by the Clerk of the said Court of General Sessions of the Peace, in the Records of the said Court.

AND BE IT FURTHER ENACTED by the Authority aforesaid. That it shall and may be lawful for the Justices of the said Court to demand and receive for every such Licence as shall be granted by them as aforesaid, the Sum of three Shillings and no more, and for the Clerk of the said Court to demand and receive for entering the said Licences or a Minute thereof in the Records of the said Court the sum of two Shillings and no more.

AND BE IT FURTHER ENACTED by the Authority aforesaid That from and after the next Court of General Sessions of the peace to be holden for the said County of Cumberland no person or persons within the said County, shall sell by retail any Rum, Brandy, Wine or Spirits of any kind under the Quantity of one Quart, nor any Cyder, Strong Beer, Metheglin or any such Strong Liquor or any mixt Liquors directly or indirectly, under the Quantity of five Gallons, except thereunto licenced as herein is before directed, on pain of forfeiting the Sum of twenty Shillings Current Money of this Colony for every Offence to be recovered by Action of Debt or otherwise before any one Justice of the Peace of the said County with Costs of Suit by any person or persons that shall or will sue for the same, one half of which Forfeiture shall be paid to the person or persons that shall sue for the same, and the other half shall be paid to the Overseers of the Poor of the said County for the Time being to be applied by them for the use of the Poor of the said County, provided the person or persons Transgressing be duly convicted of such Offence within two Months after the same shall be committed.

AND BE IT FURTHER ENACTED by the Authority aforesaid, That all such Licences shall be made to continue for one Year only from the Date thereof, and that the Justices of the said Court of General Sessions of the Peace for the said County shall cause this Act to be publickly read once in every Year in the said Court of Sessions.

AND BE IT FURTHER ENACTED that this Act shall continue in Force until the first Day of February which will be in the Year of our Lord one thousand seven hundred and seventy seven.

[CHAPTER 1531.]

[Chapter 1531 of Van Schaack, where the title only is printed.]

An Act for confirming to Zebulon Williams, second Son of Temperance the Daughter of John Williams late of Jericho in the Bounds of Oyster Bay in Queen's County in the Province of New York Yoeman deceased, and to Robert Williams, second Son of Hannah another Daughter of the said John Williams, who were heretofore respectively called Zebulon Seaman, and Robert Seaman, the Sirname of Williams which they have lately respectively assumed conformable to the last Will and Testament of the said John Williams devising to them certain Lands in the Township of Oyster Bay, in the Parish of Hempstead.

[Passed, February 26, 1772.]

BE IT ENACTED by his Excellency the Governor the Council and the General Assembly, and it is hereby enacted by the

Authority of the Same, that it shall and may be lawful to and for the said Zebulon and Robert and each of them respectively to bear and use the Sirname of Williams instead of the Sirname of Seaman: and that the said Zebulon and Robert, shall and may respectively, by the respective Names of Zebulon Williams and Robert Williams sue and be sued, implead and be impleaded, answer and be answered unto, defend and be defended in all Courts and elsewhere in all Manner of Actions, Suits, Complaints, Pleas, Causes, Matters and Demands whatsoever.

AND BE IT FURTHER ENACTED by the Authority aforesaid, That in all Actions, Suits and Pleadings hereafter to be had or brought by or against them the said Zebulon and Robert or either of them upon or by virtue of any Bond, Covenant, Specialty, or other Writing whatsoever made or given by or to them or either of them by the Sirname of Seaman, it shall be sufficient to alledge, that such Bond Specialty or other Writing was made or given to or by the said Zebulon Williams or Robert Williams by the Name of Zebulon Seaman or Robert Seaman.

PROVIDED ALWAYS that Nothing herein contained shall prejudice the Right of his Majesty his Heirs and Successors, or any Body Politic or Corporate or any Person whomsoever, nor shall this Act be of force until the same shall have obtained his Majesty's Royal Approbation.

[CHAPTER 1532.]

[Chapter 1532 of Van Schaack, where the title only is printed. The act suspended is chapter 656.]

An Act to impower Justices of the Peace Mayors Recorders and Aldermen to try Causes to the Value of five Pounds and under and for suspending an Act therein mentioned.

[Passed, March 12, 1772.]

WHEREAS it has been found by experience that the impowering Justices of the Peace, Mayors Recorders and Aldermen to try Causes to the Value of five Pourds and under has been greatly advantageous to the Inhabitants of this Colony, and for which they are very solicitous, as being enabled thereby, speedily and at small Expence to come at Justice.

BE IT THEREFORE ENACTED by his Excellency the Governor the Council and the General Assembly, and it is hereby enacted by the Authority of the same That all Actions, Cases and Causes of Debt, Trespass, Trespass upon the Case and Replevin wherein the Sum or Thing demanded for Cause of Action or Ballance due on any Specialty or Obligation shall not exceed the sum of five Pounds (except such Actions as are hereby excepted) shall after the Publication hereof be, and hereby are made cognizable before any one Justice of the Peace of any of the Counties, or the Mayor, Recorder or Aldermen of the Cities of New York and Albany, and Borough of Westchester respectively within this Colony; and the said Justices, Mayors, Recorders and Aldermen are hereby respectively impowered and required to hold Court for the tryal of such Causes, and be vested with all such power and Authority as may be necessary to maintain Order and Decency as is usual in other Courts of Record within this Colony, and to sign all Process which shall issue out of such Court, and upon application to either of them made for the recovery of any such Debt or Demand to issue a Summons or Warrant as the Case may require directed to a Constable or other proper Officer of the City Town, Manor, Borough, Precinct or District where the Defendant dwells or can be found commanding him to bring or cause such Defendant to come and appear before him at the Time and in the manner following, that is to say, in Case where such process shall be in the Nature of a Warrant forthwith after the service thereof; but where the Summons shall be issued, then on some certain Day therein to be expressed, not less than six, nor more than twelve Days from the service of such Summons, and at the Time appointed for hearing such Cause, or on such other Day as such Court shall think reasonable to appoint not exceeding six Days; the said Court shall proceed to hear and examine the Allegations and Evidences of the Plaintiff and Defendant, and within twelve Days thereafter give Judgment thereon in such manner as shall appear to the Court agreeable to Equity and Justice together with such Costs as are herein after allowed. PROVIDED ALWAYS If it shall so happen that at the Time the Warrant is served the Magistrate who issued the same be abroad or so circumstanced as not to be able to hear and try the Cause in such Case it shall and may be lawful for the Officer serving such Warrant to carry the Defendant before any other Magistrate of the said City County or Place who shall and may take Cognizance of the said Cause and proceed to a final Determination thereof in the same Manner as he could or might have done if he had issued such Warrant by which such Defendant shall be arrested.

AND BE IT ENACTED by the Authority aforesaid, That the Process against all Freeholders and Inhabitants having Families shall be by Summons only, except as is hereafter excepted, and served on the Person of the Defendant, or a Copy thereof left at his or her House or place of abode in the presence of some of the Family of suitable Age and discretion (who shall be informed of the Contents thereof) at least six Days before the Time of hearing, and the Officer serving such Summons shall, upon the Oath of his Office, endorse the Manner in which he has executed the same and sign his Name thereto, and in Case the Defendant doth not appear at the Time and Place appointed in such Summons and it shall appear by the Return endorsed thereon that the said Summons was duly served upon the Person of the Defendant in Manner aforesaid and no sufficient Reason appearing to the Court why the Defendant did not appear at the Time appointed, then the said Court shall proceed to hear try and determine the Cause and issue Execution thereon in the same Manner as if such Defendant had actually appeared; But in Case a Copy of the Summons was left at his or her House or place of abode in Manner aforesaid and the Office endorse such Return thereon as he is above directed, if then the Defendant doth not appear at the Time and Place appointed in the Summons and no Sufficient Reason be offered to the Court why he does not appear then in such Case the Court shall issue a Warrant and proceed in the same Manner as is above directed. PROVIDED ALWAYS that where any Parties shall agree to enter the Cause without any Process, the Court shall proceed to tryal in the same Manner as if a Summons or Warrant had issued.

PROVIDED ALSO and be it enacted by the Authority afore. said. That if any such Plaintiff or his Attorney so applying shall upon Oath or Affirmation declare That he or she does really and sincerely believe, that if such Process be only by summons against such Freeholder or Inhabitant having a Family, he or she will be in Danger of losing the Debt or Demand thereby; or doth really and sincerely believe that such Freeholder or Inhabitant will depart the City County or Borough or otherwise abscond before such Time, then the Court shall issue a Warrant in such Manner as if the Defendant had not been a Freeholder or Inhabi. tant having a Family; and if any Defendant shall require a longer Time than is first appointed by the Court, and will if required give sufficient Security to appear and stand tryal on such other

Day as shall be appointed then the Court is hereby impowered and required to adjourn the tryal of such Cause to any Day the Court shall judge most convenient not exceeding twelve Days, nor less than three from that Time, unless the Court and Parties shall otherwise agree.

PROVIDED ALWAYS that where the Plaintiff in any Cause or Action to be brought by virtue of this Act, shall be a non-resident of the City County or Borough and shall give Security to pay all Damages and Costs of Suit, in Case judgment shall be given against him that then he may have a Warrant returnable immediately and the Court in which such Cause is to be tryed shall not adjourn the same for more than three Days, unless the Parties agree to allow a longer Time.

AND BE IT ENACTED by the Authority aforesaid That in every Action that shall hereafter be brought in this Colony by virtue of this Act, it shall and may be lawful for either of the parties to the Suit, to demand of the said Justice Mayor Recorder or Alderman, that such Action be tryed by a Jury, and upon such Demand the said Justice, Mayor, Recorder or Alderman is hereby required to issue a Warrant to the Constable or other Officer of the City, Borough, Town, Manor, Precinct or District, where the same may happen, commanding him to return at such certain Time and place as shall be expressed in the Warrant on the same Day in which such Cause is to be tryed, a List or Panel of the Names of not more than eighteen nor less than twelve good and lawful Men of the City Borough or County respectively, being Freeholders or Freemen unless the Parties in such suit agree to a lesser Number, and unless they further consent that such returning Officer shall summon a Jury at his Discretion, then the Name of each and every Person who shall be returned in such Pannel as aforesaid shall be written in several and distinct Pieces of Paper, being all as near as may be of equal size and Bigness, and shall be delivered unto the Justice, Mayor, Recorder or Alderman, before whom such Cause is to be tried by the Constable or other proper Officer returning such Pannel or some Agent of his or theirs respectively, and shall by them be rolled up all as near as may be in one and the same Manner, and put together in a Box to be by him or them provided for that purpose, and then unless the Tryal be adjourned such Justice, Mayor, Recorder or Alderman, or such indifferent Person as he shall appoint shall draw out the said Papers one after another until the whole shall be drawn, and write the Names of said Persons on a List or Pannel in the same Order in which they shall be drawn out of the said Box, and the first six of the said Persons on the said List or Pannel, shall be the Jury appointed to try the Cause unless any of them shall be challenged, then such further Number of them in the same Order as they shall stand upon the said Pannel. shall be added to them as will make up the Number six after all Causes of challenge allowed as fair and indifferent by such Justice, Mayor, Recorder or Alderman as aforesaid, whereupon such Justice, Mayor, Recorder or Alderman shall issue his Precept commanding such Constable or other returning Officer to cause such persons to come before him, at such Time and Place as shall be expressed in such Precept, and in Case any of them are absent, and cannot be found, then to summon such other Person or Persons whose Name or Names are incerted on such Pannel next after such absent Person or Persons not challenged and set aside as aforesaid, and to proceed to summon them in the same Manner and order until the full Number of six shall appear, to each of whom the said Justice Mayor, Recorder or Alderman shall administer an Oath in the following Form. "You shall well and truly try this Matter in Difference between A. B. Plaintiff and C. D. Defendant, and a true Verdict shall give according to Evidence, so help you God." PROVIDED ALWAYS That upon a Jury being demanded of either of the Magistrates of the City and County of New York the said Magistrate shall issue a Warrant to a Constable or other Officer of the said City and County commanding him to summon twelve Good and lawful Men of the said City being Freeholders or Freemen of the said City to be and appear before such Magistrate issuing such Warrant at such certain Time and place as shall be expressed in such Warrant to make a Jury for the Tryal of the Cause between the Parties mentioned in the said Warrant, which Officer shall at the return of the said Warrant return a pannel of the Names of the Jurors he shall so Summon by virtue thereof when the Name of each and every Person who shall be returned in such Pannel shall be written on several and distinct pieces of Paper as near of one Size and bigness as may be and shall be delivered to the Mayor Recorder or Alderman before whom such Cause is to be tryed by the Constable or other proper Officer returning such Pannel or some Agent of his or theirs respectively and shall by them be rolled up all as near as may be in one and the same Manner and put together in a Box or some other convenient Thing, and when such Cause shall be brought on to be tryed, then such Mayor Recorder or Alderman or such indifferent person as he shall appoint shall draw out six of the said papers one after another, and if any of the Persons whose Names shall be so drawn shall not appear, or be challenged and set aside, then such further Number thereof shall be drawn as shall make up the Number six, who do appear after all Causes of Challenge allowed, as fair and indifferent, and the said six Persons so first drawn and appearing, and approved as indifferent shall be the Jury who shall try the Cause, to each of whom the said Mayor, Recorder or Alderman shall administer the Oath above directed, and after the six Persons have taken the Oath aforesaid, they shall set together and hear the several Proofs and Allegations of the Parties which shall be delivered in public in their presence, after which they shall be kept together in some convenient place until they all agree upon a Verdict which shall be given in to the said Justice Mayor, Recorder or Alderman who is hereby required to give Judgment agreeable to such Verdict and to award Execution in the Manner herein after directed; The Costs of the Jury to be paid with the other Costs by the party against whom their Verdict shall be found. PROVIDED ALWAYS That no Oath or Affirmation of the Parties or Exparte Affidavit of any other Person shall be allowed or given in Evidence in any Suit to be brought by virtue of this Act unless the Parties agree to admit of such Evidence

AND BE IT FURTHER ENACTED, That every Person or Persons whose Name or Names shall be so drawn and summoned as aforesaid, or supoened as a Witness, and who shall not appear, or appearing shall refuse to serve or give Evidence upon Oath made by some credible Person, that such Person so making Default or refusing to give Evidence had been lawfully summoned as aforesaid shall forfeit and pay for Every such Default, unless some reasonable Cause of his Absence shall be proved by Oath Affidavit or Affirmation to the Satisfaction of the Court, such Fine or Fines not exceeding the Sum of forty Shillings not less than ten Shillings, as the said Court shall think reasonable to inflict or assess, and to issue his Warrant to levy the same.

AND BE IT ENACTED by the Authority aforesaid, That if the Plaintiff in any such Suit or Action shall be nonsuited, or discontinue or withdraw his suit, without the Leave of the Defendant, then Judgment shall be given against him for the Costs accrued, or if he shall appear to be indebted to the Defendant, then Judgment shall be given against him for the Debt or Demand and Costs as the Case may require, and whenever judgment shall be given against either Plaintiff or Defendant in any of the beforementioned Cases, the Justice, Mayor, Recorder or Alderman that pronounced the said Judgment, shall grant Execution thereupon, directed to one of the Constables or other proper Officer of the said City Borough Town Manor Precinct or District commanding him to levy the debt or Demand and Costs on the Goods and Chattels of the Person against whom such Execution shall be granted, and for want of sufficient Effects whereon to levy the Execution, to take the Body of the Person against whom such Execution shall be granted, and him or her convey and deliver to the keeper of the Common Goal of the City Borough or County, which said Constable or other proper Officer after his taking such Goods and Chattels into his Custody by virtue of such Execution shall immediately give Public Notice by an Advertisement put up at the most public place of the City, Borough Town, Manor, Precinct or District where such Goods shall be taken of the Sorts of the Goods, and the Time and Place where and when they shall be exposed to Sale, at last five Days before the Time appointed for selling them, and at the Time and place so appointed for selling them, shall expose them to sale by Public Vendue to the highest Bidder and pay the Money according as shall be directed in the Warrant or Writ of Execution, and return the Overplus if any be, to the Owner, and that not exceeding twenty Days after the Receipt of such Execution. AND for want of sufficient Goods and Chattels whereon to levy the Execution, the Constable or other proper Officer to whom any such Execution shall be directed, shall accordingly to the Tenor of the said Execution, take the Body of the Person against whom any such Execution shall be granted, and convey and deliver him or her to the keeper of the common Goal of that City, Borough or County, which said Goal-keeper is hereby Commanded to keep such Prisoner in his safe Custody in the Common Goal until the Debt or Demand with the Costs shall be fully paid or until he or she shall be from thence delivered by due Course of Law. PROVIDED NEVERTHELESS that no Execution of any Judgment given by virtue of this Act shall issue against any Freeholder or Inhabitant having a Family in less than two Months after giving the said Judgment, unless the Party in whose favour judgment shall be given, shall make it appear to the said Court on Oath or Affirmation that he or she is in danger of losing their Debt or Demand if such Delay be allowed in which Case the Justice Mayor Recorder or Alderman shall issue his Warrant of Execution immediately as herein before directed, unless the Party against whom such Judgment shall be given, shall thereupon give security to the Party in whose favour Judgment went to pay the full of the Debt or Demand and Costs at or before the expiration of two Months. PROVIDED ALSO, That where any Judgment shall be given for any Debt or Demand that does not exceed forty shillings Execution may issue after fourteen Days.

AND BE IT ENACTED by the Authority aforesaid That if any Person or Persons whatsoever shall commence, sue or prosecute any Suit or Suits for any Debt or Demand made Cognizable as aforesaid, in any other Manner than is directed by this Act, and shall obtain a Verdict or Judgment thereon for a Debt or Damages which without Costs of Suit shall not amount to more than five Pounds (not having Caused an Oath or Affirmation to be made before the obtaining a Writ, and filed the same in the Clerks Office, that he she or they so making Oath or Affirmation did truly believe the Debt due or Damages sustained exceeded the sum of five Pounds) he she or they so prosecuting shall not recover, nor have any Costs in such Suit, any Law usage or Custom to the contrary in any wise notwithstanding. PROVIDED ALWAYS that neither this Act nor any Thing herein contained shall be deemed construed or understood to extend to such Actions wherein his Majesty his Heirs or Successors may be concerned, or where the Title of Lands shall any wise come in question, or any Action or Actions of Defamation or Slander. PROVIDED ALSO that Nothing in this Act shall extend to Matters of Account where the Sum Total of such Account shall exceed in the Amount of value thereof the sum of twenty Pounds, and that Account proved to the satisfaction of the said Court, and that no Justice of the Peace being a Tavernkeeper shall try any Cause by virtue of this Act, neither shall the Mayor Recorder or Aldermen of the City and County of New York try any Cause in any Tavern whatsoever, any Thing herein to the contrary notwithstanding.

AND BE IT FURTHER ENACTED That when in any Action of Trespass to be brought by virtue of this Act, the Defendant shall justify, upon Plea of Title, that he shall then enter into a Recognizance to make good his Title in Manner as is directed, in and by an Act of this Colony for preventing of Trespasses, passed in the eleventh Year of the Reign of his late Majesty King William the third otherwise the Justice Mayor, Recorder or Alderman shall proceed to hear try and determine the Cause, as if no such Plea had been made.

AND BE IT FURTHER ENACTED by the Authority aforesaid That all and every the Sum and Sums of Money under the Value of five Pounds to be sued for and recovered in any Court of Record, by virtue of any Law of this Colony, shall and hereby are made cognizable before any one Justice, Mayor, Recorder or Alderman in Manner as aforesaid, any Thing in the said Acts mentioned to the contrary in any wise notwithstanding. AND ALSO That where in any Precinct District or other exempt Jurisdiction; no such Constable or other proper Officer shall be chosen and appointed, that then and in such Case, the Justice Mayor Recorder or Alderman (upon Application made to them) or any of them for any Precept to be served therein, are hereby authorized and impowered to depute and order the next Constable to the Defendant of such District Precinct or exempt Jurisdiction who is hereby required to execute the same unless some other Person shall voluntarily consent to be deputed for that purpose.

AND BE IT ENACTED by the Authority aforesaid That no greater or other Fees shall be allowed taxed or taken in Actions brought in the Manner by this Act directed than as in this Act is appointed to be taken Vizt: JUSTICES FEES — a Summons ninepence, a Warrant one shilling, a Judgment one Shilling, Administring every Oath or Affirmation six pence, every Execution one Shilling and six pence, a Summons for Evidence six pence, issuing the Venire Facias to summon a Jury one Shilling, swearing the Jury one Shilling and six Pence. EVIDENCES. Attending on Summons or otherwise two Shillings per Day, and so in proportion for a longer or shorter Time. CONSTABLE, or other proper Officer for serving every Warrant Summons or Execution for one Miles Travel or under one Shilling, for every Mile more six pence, serving every Execution, for every Pound one Shilling, summoning every Jury three Shillings. JURIES, for all Causes tried one Shilling per Man, when summoned and the Cause not tried six pence per Man, provided that the whole Costs to be recovered or allowed in any one Cause or Action, shall not exceed the Sum of forty shillings, and no more than one shilling to be allowed for summoning each Witness and PROVIDED that Nothing herein contained shall extend to oblige any Member of his Majesty's Council, any Judge of the County Courts, the Mayors and Recorders of the Cities of New York and Albany or any Justice of the Peace who shall be a Member of the General Assembly to take Cognizance of any Causes Matters or Things as are by this Act provided for, but that they shall be at liberty at all Times to act therein or not, as to them shall seem fitting, any Thing herein contained to the contrary notwithstanding.

AND BE IT ENACTED by the Authority aforesaid That one certain Act entitled "An Act for establishing and regulating " Courts to determine Causes of forty Shillings and under in this " Colony." passed in the eleventh Year of his late Majesty's Reign, shall be immediately after the commencement of this Act suspended, and every Clause Article, Matter and Thing in the said Act contained hereby made null and void during the continuance of this Act. PROVIDED ALWAYS and be it enacted by the Authority aforesaid, that all suits already commenced before any Mayor Recorder Alderman or Justice of the Peace within this Colony by virtue of or under the said Act last abovementioned, and also all suits which have been commenced in any of the Inferior Courts of Common Pleas, or Mayor's Court within this Colony, tho' the Sum or Thing sued for be under the Value of five Pounds, shall and may be proceeded into Judgment and Execution in the same Manner as fully and effectually as if this Act never had passed, any Thing herein contained to the contrary thereof in any wise notwithstanding.

AND BE IT FURTHER ENACTED That from and after the Publication hereof no Writ of Certiorari, or writ of Error shall be issued out of the Supreme Court of this Colony in any suit wherein a final Judgment shall be given by any Justice, Mayor, Recorder or Alderman in a civil Matter cognizable before them or any of them, unless one of the Parties in such Suit shall within one Month after such final Judgment shall be given, make Affidavit before one of the Judges of the Supreme Court, or one of the Judges of the Inferior Court of Common Pleas of the County, or Commissioner for taking affidavits to be read in the Supreme

Court where such Judgment shall be given, and in Case such Affidavit shall be made before one of the Judges of the County or such Commissioner, such Affidavit shall be transmitted to one of the Judges of the Supreme Court, satisfying such Judge that there is reasonable Cause for granting a Writ of Certiorari or Writ of Error, to remove such Judgment, either for Error therein, or some unfair Practice in the Justice, Mayor, Recorder or Alderman who shall have tried the same, which shall be particularly specified therein, and the Judge or Commissioner before whom such Affidavit shall be made, shall keep a true Copy thereof, to be delivered to the adverse party, when he shall be thereunto required.

AND BE IT FURTHER ENACTED, That in Case any Person being a Party in such Suit, shall procure any Writ of Certiorari, or Writ of Error, otherwise than is herein above directed shall forfeit the Sum of five Pounds to be recovered with Costs of Suit, before any one Justice of the Peace, Mayor, Recorder, or Alderman within this Colony, by the adverse party, Plaintiff or Defendant in such original Suit for his own use, and if such Judgment shall be confirmed, then the Party procuring such Writ of Certiorari or Writ of Error, shall pay all Costs of defending such Suit in the Court above, to be taxed by one of the Judges of the said Court, and if the Judgment shall be reversed, the Person in whose favour such Judgment shall be reversed shall in like Manner have his Costs to be taxed as aforesaid, and recovered by Certificate from such Judge, before any one Justice of the Peace, Mayor, Recorder or Alderman in the County or City in which such Cause shall have been tried.

AND BE IT FURTHER ENACTED by the same Authority That if it shall appear that any Justice, Mayor, Recorder or Alderman having tried a Cause and given Judgment thereon and that he has wilfully been guilty of unjust Practices that in such Case, the Justices of the Supreme Court shall direct the Attorney General to prosecute such Justices Mayor Recorder or Alderman so offending by Information on behalf of the Crown according to the ordinary Course of Law.

AND BE IT FURTHER ENACTED by the Authority aforesaid, That this Act be of force from the Publication hereof, until the first Day of February which will be in the Year of our Lord one thousand seven hundred and eighty.

[CHAPTER 1533.]

1533, of Van Schaack, where the act is printed in full. Revived 1730.]

An Act the better to ascertain the Quality of Pot and Pearl Ashes.

[Passed, March 12, 1772.]

ENACTED by his Excellency the Governor the Council General Assembly, and it is hereby enacted by the .y of the same, that no Person or Persons whatsoever .ip any Pot or Pearl Ashes for Exportation, before he rst submit the same to the view and Examination of the hereinafter named, who shall try the same by starting it the Casks, and then carefully examine, inspect, and sort me, in three different Sorts, if necessary; that he shall put each Sort by itself into tight Casks, well hooped and coopered which he shall distinguish by the Words. "first Sort," "Second Sort," or "third Sort," with the Word "Pot" or "Pearl" as the same may be, branded in plain legible Letters, together with the initial Letter of his Christian Name and his Sirname and the Words "New York." in full length on each of the Casks, for which Trouble, and also for the additional Service of repacking the said Pot and Pearl Ashes, and putting the Casks in such Condition as they may be in when they shall be brought to him for inspection and for weighing the same, and delivering to the proprietor an Invoice or Weigh Note under his Hand of the Weight of each Cask; the said Officer shall have and receive four Pence for every hundred weight; one half to be paid by the purchasor, and the other half by the Vender. Provided that if the said Casks shall be incapable of being rendered fit for shipping, such further Cooperage, or such new Casks if necessary, shall be at the Expence of the Vender.

AND BE IT ENACTED by the Authority aforesaid, that the said Officer at the Time of starting the said Pot or Pearl Ashes out of the Cask or Casks to inspect the same, shall weigh the said Cask or Casks, and mark the just and true Weight with a Marking Iron on each Head thereof. PROVIDED ALWAYS, and be it enacted by the Authority aforesaid, that if any Dispute should happen to arise between the said Officer and possessor of such Pot or Pearl Ashes concerning the Quality thereof, upon application to one of the Magistrates of the City of New York he shall and hereby is required to issue his Warrant to three indifferent judicious Persons of Skill and Integrity to view and search the said Pot or Pearl Ashes, one of them to be named by the possessor of such Pot or Pearl Ashes, the second to be named by the Officer, and the third Person to be named by the said Magistrate, which three Persons shall be duly sworn carefully to examine the said Pot or Pearl Ashes, and make Report forthwith according as they find the same; and the said Magistrate is hereby impowered and required to give Judgment agreeable to the Report of the Persons so named, or to the Report of any two of them, and in Case the said Pot or Pearl Ashes are judged to be of the Quality or Qualities as distinguished by the said Officer, the said Magistrate is hereby authorized to direct the said Pot or Pearl Ashes to be branded by the said Officer, agreeable to such Distinction and shall also award, and order the Owner or possessor of said Pot or Pearl Ashes, to pay the said Officer six Pence for each hundred weight for all such Pot or Pearl Ashes as shall be so judged as aforesaid, with reasonable Costs and Charges; but in Case the said Pot or Pearl Ashes upon Trial shall be found to differ in Quality from the said Inspectors Judgment thereon the Charges of prosecution shall be paid by the Officer.

AND BE IT ENACTED by the Authority aforesaid that such Officer shall have full power and Authority by virtue of this Act, and without any further or other Warrant, to enter on board any Ship Sloop or Vessel whatsoever, lying or being in the Harbour of said City to search her, and make discovery of any Pot or Pearl Ashes shipped or Shipping on board any such Vessel for exportation out of this Colony, and if said Officer shall on such Search, discover any Cask or Casks of Pot or Pearl Ashes, not branded as before directed, the Person or Persons so shipping the same shall forfeit all and every Cask or Casks of Pot or Pearl Ashes so shipped or Shipping, and not branded in the Manner before directed; and the Master or Commander of any such Vessel who shall receive any such Cask or Casks of Pot or Pearl Ashes not branded as aforesaid, shall forfeit and pay for each Cask so received on board his Vessel, the Sum of five Pounds, and if any Master of such Vessel, or any of his Servants or Seamen shall obstruct or hinder the said Officer in making such Search as aforesaid, every Person so offending, shall forfeit the sum of ten Pounds.

AND BE IT ENACTED by the Authority aforesaid, that Abraham De La Montagne shall be and hereby is appointed the Officer for viewing and examining all Pot and Pearl Ashes, that are intended to be shipped for Exportation directly from the Port of New York, and if the said Officer hereby appointed, shall by any Accident be rendered incapable, or neglect to execute the said Office or Misbehave himself therein, or shall happen to die, then, and so often, and from Time to Time in such Cases, it shall and may be lawfull to and for the Mayor, Recorder and Aldermen of the City of New York or the Major Part of them to supply his place by some other fit and capable Person who shall thereupon be the Officer for putting this Act in execution, until another be appointed by Act or Acts hereafter to be passed for that purpose, which Officer so appointed shall have the same Powers, and be liable to the same Penalties, as the Officer particularly appointed by this Act, any Law, Usage or Custom to the contrary notwithstanding: But before the said Officer hereby, or hereafter to be apointed, shall do any Thing in execution of the said Office, he shall take an Oath before the Mayor or Recorder of the City of New York, in the Words following. vizt: "I. A. B. "do swear that I will faithfully truly and impartially according "to the best of my Judgment, Skill and understanding, execute, "do and perform the Office and Duty of an Inspector and Exam-"iner of Pot and Pearl Ashes according to the true Intent and "Meaning of an Act intitled "An Act the better to ascertain the "Quality of Pot and Pearl Ashes." and I will not directly or indirectly by myself or by any Person for me, buy or sell any "Pot or Pearl Ashes during the Time that I continue Inspector of "the same, for my own Account, or upon the Account of any "other Person or Persons whatsoever, so help me God."

AND BE IT FURTHER ENACTED by the Authority aforesaid, that if the aforesaid Officer, not then employed in the Examination of Pot or Pearl Ashes according to the Powers and Authorities given by this Act, shall on Application to him made for the Examination of any Pot or Pearl Ashes as aforesaid, refuse neglect, or delay to proceed to such Examination for the Space of three Hours after such Application so made, the said Officer so refusing, neglecting or delaying to make such Examination shall for each Offence forfeit the Sum of twenty Shillings, to the use of the Person or Persons so delayed.

AND BE IT ENACTED by the Authority aforesaid, that if any Person or Persons shall counterfeit any of the aforesaid

Brand Marks, or impress or brand the same on any Cask of Pot or Pearl Ashes, he, she, or they, being thereof legally convicted shall forfeit and pay the Sum of fifty Pounds.

AND BE IT ENACTED by the Authority aforesaid, that if any Person or Persons shall empty any Cask or Casks of Pot or Pearl Ashes branded as aforesaid in order to put in other Pot or Pearl Ashes for Sale for exportation without first cutting out the said Brand Marks, the said Person or Persons so offending shall respectively forfeit the Sum of fifty Pounds.

AND BE IT ENACTED by the Authority aforesaid, that all the Fines and Forfeitures mentioned in this Act, shall be recoverable in the same Manner as other Debts of the same value are recovered by the Laws of this Colony, by Suit, Bill, Plaint or Information, wherein no Essoin, Protection or Wager of Law, or any more than one Imparlance shall be allowed; the one half of all which Fines and Forfeitures, except such as are herein before otherways applied, when recovered shall be immediately paid into the Hands of the Treasurer of this Colony towards the support of the Government thereof, and the other half to the Officer or other Person who shall sue for the same.

AND BE IT ALSO ENACTED by the same Authority that no Pot or Pearl Ashes shall be exported from the City of Albany to any place beyond this Colony unless the same shall have first been there inspected Branded and marked as by this Act is directed to be done in the City of New York, and have the Name of the Inspector hereby appointed for the City of Albany marked thereon, and the Inspector for the City of Albany shall be Jeremiah Van Rensselaer, who shall take the same Oath that the Inspector for the City of New York is required by this Act to take, which Oath shall be Administered by the Mayor, Recorder or any one of the Aldermen of the City of Albany and the said Inspector shall demean himself in the Duties and Execution of his Office in the same Manner as by this Act is required of the Inspector for the City of New York and be liable to the like Pains and Penalties and have the like Rewards for his Trouble.

BE IT ALSO ENACTED by the same Authority, that all or any of the Pot or Pearl Ashes so inspected in the City of Albany as by this Act is directed and required may be shipped from the said City of Albany in Vessels going immediately from thence to any Place or Port beyond this Colony without undergoing a re-inspection in the City of New York, any Thing in this Act to the contrary hereof notwithstanding.

PROVIDED NEVERTHELESS, that if any Pot or Pearl Ashes shall be inspected in the City of Albany, and be branded and marked as by this Act is required, and be afterwards shipped for Exportation from the City of New York, that the same shall be there re-inspected before it shall be from thence exported to any place or Port beyond this Colony.

AND BE IT ENACTED by the Authority aforesaid that this Act shall commence from the passing thereof, and be of force until the first Day of January which will be in the Year of our Lord one thousand seven hundred and seventy five.

[CHAPTER 1534.]

[Chapter 1534 of Van Schaack, where the act is printed in full. See chapters 17, 333 and 1719.]

An Act to divide the County of Albany into three Counties.

[Passed, March 12, 1772.]

WHEREAS a Law was passed in this Colony on the first Day of October in the Year of our Lord one thousand six hundred and ninety one, intitled. "An Act to divide the Province and Dependencies into shires and Counties." according to which the County of Albany was to contain the Manor of Rensselaerwyck, Schenectady and all the Villages Neighbourhoods and Christian Plantations on the East side of Hudson's River from Roelof Janse's Creek; and on the West side from Sawyer's Creek to the utmost End of Saratoga. AND WHEREAS by one other Law intitled. "An Act for annexing that part of the Manor of Livingston " which now lies in Dutchess County unto the County of Albany." passed the twenty seventh Day of May, one thousand seven hundred and seventeen. AND WHEREAS the Lands within the County of Albany are more extensive than all the other Counties of this Colony taken together, and altho' the Inhabitants thereof are already very numerous and continue to increase; yet it is conceived that the settlement of the Country would proceed with much greater Rapidity, to the vast augmentation of his Majesty's Revenue and the Benefit of the Colony, if a suitable partition was made of the said Lands and new Counties created; The Number of Inhabitants and their great Distance from each other rendering the Administration of Justice extreamly Difficult and Burthensome; many People as County Officers, Jury-Men, Suitors and Witnesses being obliged to travel near two hundred Miles to the City of Albany where the County Goal is, and where the Courts of Common pleas Sessions of the Peace, Oyer and Terminer and general Goal delivery are held, so that the Inhabitants instead of having Justice distributed according to our excellent Constitution as it were at their Doors, are from the enormous Extent of the said County of Albany, exposed to great Hardships, and lesser Crimes pass unnoticed, and Crimes of the most atrocious Nature frequently go unpunished for the Want of the Attendance of Witnesses upon Grand Juries sitting, and coming from places remote from those where the Offences were committed, and Sheriffs and Coroners are discouraged from executing both Civil and Criminal process and the Expence of attending the Courts often exceeds the value of the Thing in demand and great default of Justice is occasioned, and as the Power of the Justices of the Peace in the Determination of small Causes to two Pounds and under is commensurate with the County, the people either as Parties or Witnesses are sometimes compelled to such remote Attendance, and to such a waste of Time as discourages the Settlement of the country; Wherefore that an adequate Remedy may be applied to these and many other Evils too Tedious to be particularly enumerated.

BE IT ENACTED by his Excellency the Governor the Council and the General Assembly, and it is hereby enacted by the Authority of the same, That the County of Albany shall be henceforth restricted to the Bounds and Limits following to wit. On the South, and on the West Side of Hudsons River by the County of Ulster as Ascertained by the first beforementioned Act intitled. "An Act to divide the Province and Dependencies into "shires and Counties." and on the West by Delaware River and the West Branch thereof as far up as a certain small Lake called Utsayntho, and thence by a Line North twenty five Degrees East until it be intersected by a West Line drawn from the North West Corner of the old Schoharie Patent, thence East to the North East Corner of the said Schoharie Patent, thence to the North West Corner of the Township of Duanesburgh, thence along the North Bounds thereof to the North East Corner of the same thence on the same Course with the said North Bounds of Duanesburgh to the Mohawk River, thence North until it intersects a West Line drawn from Fort George near Lake George. thence East until it intersects a North Line drawn from that high Falls on Hudson's River which lays next above Fort

Edward, thence South to the said Falls thence along the East Bank of Hudson's River to a certain Creek called Stoney Creek thence East five hundred and ten chains, thence South to the North Bank of Batten Creek thence up along the North Bank of said Creek until the said Creek intersects the South Bounds of Prince Town, thence along the same to the South East Corner thereof, thence East to the West Bounds of the County of Cumberland, thence Southerly and Easterly along the West and South Bounds thereof to Connecticut River, thence along the said River to the North Bounds of the Colony of Connecticut, thence along the North and West Bounds of the same to the County of Dutchess, thence along the North Bounds of the said County of Dutchess to Hudson's River, and thence by a Straight Line to the North East Corner of the County of Ulster on Hudson's River.

AND BE IT FURTHER ENACTED by the same Authority. That all the Lands lying within this Colony to the Westward of the County of Albany as by this Act restricted, and to the Westward of the North Line from the Mohawk River abovementioned continued to the North Bounds of this Province, shall be one Separate and distinct County, and be called and known by the Name of the County of Tryon.

AND BE IT ENACTED by the same Authority. That all the Lands lying within this Colony to the Northward of the County of Albany as restricted by this Act, and to the Eastward of the County of Tryon, and to the Westward and Northward of the Counties of Cumberland and Gloucester shall be one separate and distinct County, and be called and known by the Name of the County of Charlotte.

AND BE IT FURTHER ENACTED by the same Authority, That until Goals for the said Counties of Charlotte and Tryon shall be erected, the several Sheriffs and Officers, and Ministers of Justice having process, and the Custody of Prisoners may make use of the present Goal of the County of Albany, and the Goaler thereof shall receive the prisoners and be as Answerable for them as if they were delivered to his Care by the Sheriff or other Officer of the said County of Albany.

AND BE IT FURTHER ENACTED by the same Authority. That Nothing in this Act shall be construed to affect any Suit or Action already commenced, or to be commenced before the first Day of January which will be in the Year of our Lord one thousand seven hundred and seventy three, so as to work a Wrong or prejudice to any of the parties therein, nor to Affect any Criminal or other proceeding on the Part of the Crown already began, nor any Recognizance when relative thereto, but all such Civil & Criminal proceedings shall and may be carried on to tryal and final Determination as tho' this Act had never been passed, nor shall any of the Lines so assigned for the Limits of either of the said Counties be deemed to take away abridge destroy or Affect the Right and Title of Any Bodies Politic or Corporate or of any Patentee or others holding under any Patentee or Patentees in any Manner or by any ways or means whatsoever.

AND BE IT FURTHER ENACTED by the same Authority that so much of the Lines of partition between the County of Albany as restricted by this Act, and the said new Counties of Charlotte & Tryon, as the Judges of the Inferior Court of Common pleas or the Major Part of them for the Time being of the said Counties, shall think fit, shall be actually run out and marked by such Person or Persons and in such Manner, and at such Time and Times as to them the said Justices or the Majority of them shall seem meet, and the Expences of the Service shall be equally divided between the said Counties, and raised in their respective Counties as part of the County Charge thereof, are usually raised and levied, and such Agreements and the Return of the Survey, and other their Transactions in the Business aforesaid, shall be entered in their respective County Records, and the same or an Office Copy thereof shall be conclusive Evidence concerning their respective Partition Lines and County Bounds.

PROVIDED ALWAYS That Nothing in this Act contained shall be construed, deemed or taken to alter or derogate from the Rights and Royal Prerogative of his Majesty his Heirs and Successors in the granting Letters of Incorporation granting Markets and fairs to be kept and held in the said Counties of Charlotte and Tryon, but that the said Rights and Prerogatives and all other the Prerogatives of the Crown shall and may at all Times hereafter be exercised therein by his said Majesty his Heirs and Successors in as full and ample a Manner to all intents and purposes as if this Act had never been made.

[CHAPTER 1535.]

[Chapter 1535 of Van Schaack, where the title only is printed.]

An Act to revive and continue an Act intitled. "An Act for raising and collecting "the Arrears of Taxes due to this Colony "from the City and County of New York." with some Additions thereto.

[Passed, March 12, 1772.]

WHEREAS some of the Collectors chosen and appointed for collecting the Taxes in the above Act mentioned have not been able to collect in the same within the Time limited by the said Act for that purpose.

BE IT THEREFORE ENACTED by his Excellency the Governor the Council and the General Assembly and it is hereby enacted by the Authority of the same. That the abovementioned Act intitled "An Act for raising and collecting the Arrears of "Taxes due to this Colony from the City and County of New York." passed in the eleventh Year of his present Majesty's Reign, and every Article and Clause therein contained, shall be in force from the Publication hereof until the first Day of November now next ensuing, and the several and respective Collectors chosen and appointed to collect in the Taxes in the said recited Act mentioned shall and are hereby authorized and impowered to take all such Modes and Methods for collecting in the Taxes that are now outstanding and uncollected, and which ought to have been collected by virtue of the above recited act, as they could, ought or might, have taken by virtue of the said Act for collecting the same.

AND WHEREAS the Collectors for the Dock Ward, Montgomerie Ward, and Bowry Division of the Outward of the said City, were by the said recited Act impowered and enabled to collect in the Taxes and Assessments that had been laid by virtue of former Acts of this Colony, but no Provision or Allowance was made for them therein for their Fees or Trouble in collecting the same.

BE IT THEREFORE ENACTED by the Authority aforesaid. That the said Colectors for the Dockward Montgomerie Ward and Bowry Division of the Outward shall out of the Money which they have or shall collect for Taxes that were laid by virtue of former Acts of the Legislature of this Colony, retain and keep in their Hands the Sum of six pence for every Pound which has been and shall be collected by them for their Trouble in collecting and paying the said Taxes.

AND WHEREAS it may happen that the Collectors for the three Wards abovementioned may not be able to collect in all the Money that is now outstanding upon former Assessments by reason of the Insolvency or absence of the persons taxed or some other Cause, and may be charged with a Neglect of duty herein.

BE IT THEREFORE FURTHER ENACTED by the Authority aforesaid. That in Case of such Deficiency, it shall and may be lawful for the Mayor Recorder and Alderman of the city of New York or the major Part of them, whereof the Mayor or Recorder to be one, and they are hereby authorized and impowered to examine the said Collectors and their Tax Rolls, and to adjudge and determine which Taxes could have been collected by the said Collectors, and which not, and upon such Determination the said Collectors shall be only liable and chargeable for such Taxes as the said Magistrates shall determine could have been collected, and for no others.

[CHAPTER 1536.]

[Chapter 1536 of Van Schaack, where the act is printed in full. Amended by chapter 1586.]

An Act for the better laying out, regulating and keeping in Repair, Common and Public Highways, and Private Roads in the County of Dutchess.

[Passed, March 12, 1772.]

WHEREAS the laying out regulating and keeping in good Repair, Public Highways and Roads, contributes greatly to the Ease and Advantage of the Inhabitants of a Country.

BE IT THEREFORE ENACTED by his Excellency the Governor, the Council and the General Assembly, and it is hereby enacted by the Authority of the same. That from and after the Publication of this Act, the Freeholders and Inhabitants of each Precinct in the County of Dutchess, shall be and hereby are authorized at their annual Town Meetings for electing Town Officers, to choose and elect at the same Time, three Freeholders in each Precinct for Commissioners to lay out and regulate Highways in the Precinct for which they shall be so chosen, and also as many Overseers of the Highways in each Precinct as there shall be districts in the said Precinct, who are to oversee, repair and keep in Order, the several Highways within the respective Districts for which they shall be elected and chosen as aforesaid, and the Persons so to be chosen Commissioners, as well as those who are to be Overseers are hereby required to take their several Offices respectively upon them.

AND BE IT FURTHER ENACTED by the Authority aforesaid, That the Commissioners or the Major Part of them, in the respective Precincts for which they shall be chosen Commissioners, are hereby impowered and authorized to regulate the Roads already laid out, and if any of them shall appear inconvenient, and an Alteration absolutely necessary, and the same be certified upon Oath by twelve Principal Freeholders of the said County, the Commissioners may, provided they all judge it necessary, alter the same, and lay out such other Public Highways and Roads as they, or the major Part of them shall think most convenient as well for Travellers as for the Inhabitants of each Precinct. PROVIDED that Nothing in this Act contained shall extend or be construed to impower the Commissioners aforesaid, to alter any Roads that are already commodious; neither shall they lay out any Roads through any Persons Land without the Consent of the Owner or Owners thereof, or paying to him or them the true value of the Lands so to be laid out into an Highway or Road with such Damages as he may sustain by said Road, which value of the Land, and the Amount of the Damages the owner may sustain by such Road shall be determined, and the true value set and appraised by two Justices of the Peace and by the Oaths of twelve principal Freeholders not having any Interest in the Land so to be laid into an Highway or Road. And the said Freeholders shall be summoned by the High Sheriff of the said County or his Deputy, or any Constable of the Precinct in which such Road or Highway shall be laid out as aforesaid by virtue of a Warrant to be issued by the said two Justices for that purpose, and if any Road within any Precinct of said County so laid out be a common Public Highway, and the same be laid out at the request of twelve Principal Freeholders of the County, then the whole charge of the value of the said Lands and Damages, together with the Charge of the Commissioners, and calling and charge of the Jury, and the whole proceeding thereon had, shall be paid as the other contingent Charges of the County are paid; and the Highway so laid out shall be a common Public

Highway. PROVIDED ALWAYS. That no Road or Highway shall be laid through any Orchard or Garden without the Consent of the Owner or Owners thereof, any Thing herein contained to the contrary notwithstanding.

AND BE IT FURTHER ENACTED That the Commissioners to be chosen by virtue of this Act shall before they execute any of the Powers herein mentioned, take an Oath upon the Holy Evangelists or if a Quaker an Affirmation in the words following, to wit. "I A. B. do solemnly swear or Affirm, that I will faithfully "and impartially execute the Powers to me given and granted "by an Act entitled, "An Act for the better laying out, regu-"lating and keeping in repair, Common and Public Highways, "and private Roads in the County of Dutchess." according to the best of my Skill and understanding. so help me God."

AND BE IT FURTHER ENACTED by the Authority aforesaid. That if any Person or Persons within the said Precincts, do, or hereafter shall alter, Stop up or encroach on any Highway or Road that has been heretofore laid out by former Commissioners, or shall be hereafter laid out by the Commissioners to be elected and chosen by virtue of this Act, such Person so offending, contrary to the meaning of this Act, shall for every such Offence, forfeit the Sum of forty Shillings to be recovered before any one Justice of the Peace upon the Oath or Affirmation of one or more credible Witness, which Justice shall issue his Warrant directed to the Constable of the Precinct where such Offence shall be committed to levy the said Forfeiture by distress and sale of the Goods and Chattels of the Offender and the said Constable after five Days Public Notice, shall make Sale of the said Goods and Chattels, and out of the Produce thereof pay the forfeiture and Charges, and return the Overplus, if any there be to the Owner or Owners, which said Forfeiture of forty Shillings, shall be applied by the Commissioners for and towards repairing the Public Roads or Highways within the District where such Forfeiture shall arise.

AND BE IT ENACTED by the Authority aforesaid. That the Width of all the Roads in the said Precincts hereafter to be laid out shall be left to the discretion of the Commissioners for the Time being of the Precinct in which such Road may be laid out, so that they do not exceed the Breadth of four Rods, and not less than two Rods.

AND BE IT FURTHER ENACTED by the Authority aforesaid. That the Roads and Highways within the said Precincts, shall be cleared, worked upon, repaired and maintained by the Freeholders and Inhabitants hereafter made liable to work upon the same, as often as they or any of them shall have Notice from the Overseers for the Time being of the District to which they belong, not exceeding six Days in a Year.

AND to prevent all manner of Disputes that may arise respecting the Persons who are obliged by this Act to work upon the Highways. BE IT ENACTED by the Authority aforesaid. That every Freeholder, Housekeeper and other Person exercising any Business for themselves and on their own Accounts within the said Precincts shall either in Person or by an able sufficient Man in his Room, be obliged to work upon the Highways.

AND BE IT FURTHER ENACTED by the Authority aforesaid, That every Freeholder and Inhabitant who by this Act are obliged to work on Highways shall work at least three Days between the first Day of April and the first Day of July, and three Days between the first Day of August and the first Day of November in every Year, and at least eight Hours in every such Day, of which the Overseers are to give Notice to the Freeholders and Inhabitants of their respective Districts accordingly under the Penalty herein aftermentioned: And in order that the good Effects intended by this Act may not under any pretence be eluded,

BE IT FURTHER ENACTED by the Authority aforesaid. That every Overseer in each District, shall keep a List of the Persons within his District, who by this Act are obliged to work upon the Highways, and shall as nearly as he conveniently can keep an Account of the Time that every Such Person shall have worked, and for every Hour which any Person is obliged to work, and doth neglect, he shall forfeit and pay the sum of six pence to the Overseer of the District to which he doth belong, and in Case the same is not paid within eight Days after such Default, it shall be recovered and applied in the Manner hereinafter Mentioned.

AND BE IT FURTHER ENACTED that every Overseer in each Precinct shall deliver an Account to one of the Commissioners of the Precinct to which he doth belong, and shall take an Oath before the said Commissioners or one of them who is hereby impowered to administer the same in the Words following, to wit. "I A. B. do declare upon the holy Evangelists (or if a Quaker "affirm) that this Account now delivered by me, contains the "Names of all the Persons within my District who by Law are "obliged to work on Highways, as far as have come to my knowl-"edge, and that each Person therein named (except such as are "mentioned to have been fined or excused) has worked himself or "by a Man in his stead six Days since the first Day of April last, "and as nearly as I could judge to the Amount of eight Hours "in each Day; three of which Days Work were done between the "first Day of April and the first Day of July, and the other three "Days between the said first Day of July, and the first Day "of November, and I have laid out or disposed of agreeable to "Law, the Monies by me received of such Persons as are therein "mentioned to be excused from Working or fined for not working "as aforesaid, and that within twenty five Days after the Time "in which such Person ought to have worked or was excused as "aforesaid according to the best of my knowledge and belief, so "help me God."

AND BE IT FURTHER ENACTED by the Authority aforesaid. That the Commissioners for the Time being for each Precinct with the Assistance of two Justices of the Peace of said County, may at any Time after the first Day of June next and that once in every year divide their respective Precincts into as many Districts as they or the major Part of them shall think most equitable and convenient, and the Freeholders and Inhabitants at their next annual Town Meetings after such Division shall choose as many Overseers, as there shall then be Districts.

AND BE IT FURTHER ENACTED by the Authority aforesaid. That all Forfeitures which shall arise by any Persons not working on the Roads or High-Ways agreeable to the Directions of this Act, shall be recovered with five Shillings Costs, by Warrant under the Hand and Seal of the Overseer of the District where such Forfeiture shall arise, to be directed to any Constable within the said Precinct who is to seize and sell as is usual in other Cases, the Offenders Goods and Chattels, and after paying the Forfeiture to the said Overseer with two shillings for issuing the Warrant the Constable shall retain three Shillings for his Services; and all Forfeitures which shall be paid to the said Overseer in the Manner aforesaid, and also every Sum of Money which he may receive from any Person for not working on the Public Roads or High-Ways shall be by him well and faithfully laid out in mending and repairing the Roads and Highways within his District within the Time above limited.

AND BE IT FURTHER ENACTED by the Authority aforesaid That all Trees that stand in any Highway which has or shall be laid out through any Persons Land, shall belong to the Owner or Owners thereof, but the said Owner shall not hinder the Public from making use of so much Timber which is standing or lying on the Road as will amend and repair the same.

AND BE IT FURTHER ENACTED by the Authority aforesaid. That if any Overseers shall think fit, and have Occasion of any Teams, Carts or Waggons, and a Man to manage the same, such Team, Cart or Waggon with the Person to manage the same, shall, be esteemed for and in lieu of two Days work of a single Man, and the fine for Neglect to be proportionably, that is double the Fine of a single Person, and every working Man shall be obliged to bring such Utensils as he is directel to bring by the Overseer of his District.

AND BE IT FURTHER ENACTED by the Authority aforesaid, that the Commissioners of the respective Precincts for which they shall be chosen, or the Major part of them shall from Time to Time during the continuance of this Act, enter a Return in Writing of all the Highways or Roads by them laid out altered or stopped up and sign their Names thereto and cause the same to be entered in the County Records by the Clerk of the Peace, who is hereby directed and required to record the same, and whatsoever the said Commissioners shall do according to the Power given them by this Act being so entered in the County Records shall be deemed valid and good to all Intents and purposes whatsoever.

AND BE IT FURTHER ENACTED by the Authority aforesaid, That each Commissioner shall be allowed a Sum not exceeding six Shillings for every Day as a Reward for his Care and Trouble in doing the Business required by this Act; and they shall transmit their Accounts to the Supervisors of the said County of Dutchess at their annual Meetings, and the Supervisors shall add so much as they find the Commissioners of each Precinct have a Right to claim, to the Quota of such Precinct from whence such Accounts shall be brought, and shall raise the same with the County Tax, which shall be paid by the County Treasurer to the Commissioners; upon a Warrant from the Supervisors as in other Cases, except where the Commissioners are paid by private persons, as is herein after directed.

AND BE IT FURTHER ENACTED by the Authority aforesaid. That any one of his Majesty's Justices of the Peace for the Time being in the County of Dutchess, or any one Commissioner for the Time being may at any Time or Times within the Times above particularly specified for working on Highways, order any Overseer to work upon and repair any Road or Highway that he shall think necessary within his District, and such Overseer shall within eight Days thereafter, warn and set to work the Persons of his District who are obliged to work on Highways upon that Part of the Road or Highway, which he shall be so ordered to work upon and repair.

AND BE IT ENACTED by the Authority aforesaid. That every Overseer of Highways to be chosen for any of the said Precincts or Districts who shall neglect or refuse to do and perform any of the Duties and Services required of him by this Act shall forfeit and pay the Sum of forty Shillings for every such Neglect or Refusal, and the Commissioners for the Time being of the Precinct where such Forfeiture shall arise are hereby impowered and required to issue their Warrant to any Constable of the said Precinct commanding him to seize and sell the Goods and Chattels of the said Offender to the amount of the said Forfeiture with reasonable Costs, which said Forfeiture shall be laid out and expended by the said Commissioners in repairing of the Roads within the District where such Forfeiture shall arise; And if any Overseer shall die, neglect or refuse to serve in his Office, in that Case the Commissioners of the said Precincts respectively or the Major part of them shall and are hereby impowered to appoint some other fit person in the Room and stead of such Overseer so dying refusing or neglecting to serve in the said Office, who shall take the Oath above prescribed for an Overseer, and have the same Powers and be subject to the same Fines, Forfeitures and Penalties, as Overseers chosen by virtue of this Act, have are liable and subject to.

AND BE IT FURTHER ENACTED by the Authority aforesaid, That upon an Application to the Commissioners of any Precinct for a Private Road, the Commissioners for the Precinct where such private Road is desired to be laid shall view the same, and if they are of Opinion such Road is absolutely necessary, and twelve principal Freeholders under Oath, shall be of the same opinion, the said Commissioners are hereby impowered to lay out such Road observing the same steps in ascertaining what shall be paid for the Land as before directed to be taken in laying out Public Roads, and the Value of the Land over which such Road shall be laid, and all the Expences and Charges attend ing the laying out and valuing the same shall be paid by the Person or Persons applying for the same; and the said Road when so laid out shall be for the only use of the Person or Persons who shall pay for the same, his and their Heirs and Assigns; but not to be converted to any other use or purpose than that of a Road. PROVIDED ALWAYS, the Owner or Owners of the Land through which such Private Road may be laid shall not be prevented from making use of such Road if he shall signify his Intention of making use of the same, at the Time when the Jury are to ascertain the value of the Land, and the Damages by means of laying out such Road, and it shall and may be lawful for such Person or Persons by and with the Approbation of the said Commissioners for such Precinct or District to hang good Swinging Gates on such Highways, and he she or they keeping the same in repair at their own Cost.

AND BE IT FURTHER ENACTED by the Authority aforesaid. That all Laws heretofore made and enacted relative to Public Highways or Roads so far as they relate to the said County of Dutchess, shall be, and are hereby suspended to all Intents Constructions and purposes whatsoever during the continuance of this Act.

AND BE IT ALSO ENACTED by the Authority aforesaid. That this Act shall continue and be of force until the first Day of February which will be in the Year of our Lord one thousand seven hundred and seventy six.

[CHAPTER 1537.]

[Chapter 1537 of Van Schaack, where the title only is printed.]

An Act to raise one thousand Pounds in the Precincts of Goshen and Cornwall in the County of Orange to build a Court House in the Town of Goshen, and for other Purposes therein mentioned.

[Passed, March 12, 1772.]

WHEREAS the Court House and Goal in the Precinct of Goshen in Orange County are insufficient for holding of Courts, and securing of Prisoners.

BE IT THEREFORE ENACTED by his Excellency the Governor the Council and the General Assembly, and it is hereby enacted by the Authority of the same. That the Justices of the

Peace of the Precincts of Goshen and Cornwall in the County of Orange, with Daniel Everit, Jesse Woodhull, Elihu Marvin and Benjamin Gale shall meet at the Court-House in Goshen, on the second Tuesday in April next, and they or the greater Number of them, then and there present are hereby impowered and required to fix the place where the Court House and Goal shall be erected in the Town of Goshen in the County of Orange aforesaid and to determine the Plan and of what Materials the same shall be built.

AND BE IT FURTHER ENACTED by the Authority aforesaid That for building and erecting the same Court House and Goal the Supervisors of the said County for the Time being shall and they are hereby directed and required to order to be levied on the Freeholders and Inhabitants of the said Precincts of Goshen and Cornwall a Sum not exceeding one thousand Pounds with the Additional Sum of three pence for every Pound for collecting the same, five hundred Pounds of which said one thousand Pounds shall be raised in the first Tax that shall be levied after the publication of this Act, and the remainder thereof, with the second Tax which said Sum of one thousand Pounds shall be raised levied and collected in the same Manner as the other necessary and contingent Charges of the said County are.

AND BE IT FURTHER ENACTED by the Authority aforesaid That the Monies so to be raised by virtue of this Act shall from Time to Time be paid by the several and respective Collectors of the said Precincts of Goshen and Cornwall unto Daniel Evert, Benjamin Tusteen, Jesse Woodhull Elihu Marvin and Benjamin Gale who are hereby appointed Trustees for laying out the said one thousand Pounds for the purposes aforesaid, and the said Trustees or any three of them shall and may from Time to Time inspect examine and audit all the several and respective Accounts for Workmanship and Materials to be employed for and towards making and erecting the Court House and Goal beforementioned, and of the due Disposition of the said Sum of one thousand Pounds or so much thereof as shall come into their Hands, they the said Trustees appointed as aforesaid shall render a true Account thereof upon Oath unto the Justices of the said Precincts at the General Sessions of the Peace at Goshen.

AND BE IT FURTHER ENACTED by the Authority aforesaid That the said Daniel Evert, Benjamin Tusteen, Jesse Wood.

hull, Elihu Marvin and Benjamin Gale, or the Major Part of them shall and they are hereby impowered to sell the present Court House and Goal in the Town of Goshen at public Vendue to the highest Bidder (after giving one Months public Notice thereof) and give and execute good and sufficient Deeds of conveyance in the Law to the purchaser for the same. And the Monies arising by such Sale (after deducting the Charges attending the same, shall be applied towards finishing the new Court House and Goal. PROVIDED ALWAYS that such Sale shall not be made until the new Court House and Goal to be so built shall be fit for confining Prisoners and holding the Courts in

[CHAPTER 1538.]

[Chapter 1538 of Van Schaack, where the act is printed in full. See chapter 1205.]

An Act to divide the Precinct of New Burgh in the County of Ulster into two Precincts.

[Passed, March 12, 1772.]

WHEREAS the Precincts of New Burgh in the County of Ulster is very extensive and the Inhabitants thereof greatly increased, whereby it is not only become extreamly inconvenient for the people to assemble and transact the public Business at their annual Meetings, but the Duties of it's several Officers are become very burthensome, for remedy whereof.

BE IT ENACTED by his Excellency the Governor the Council and the General Assembly, and it is hereby enacted by the Authority of the same, That the said Precinct of New Burgh in the County of Ulster shall be and hereby is divided into two Precincts by the following Lines, to wit, Beginning on the West side of Hudson's River in the North East Corner of a Tract of Land formerly granted by Letters Patent under the broad Seal of the Province of New York, to Francis Harrison and Company commonly called the five thousand Acre Tract, and from thence running Westerly along the North Bounds of the said Tract and another Tract granted to the said Francis Harrison to the Tract of Land commonly called Wallace's Tract, thence along the Lines of the same Northerly and Westerly to the North Easterly Bounds of a Tract of Land formerly granted to Jacobus Kip, John Cruger and others, commonly called Kip and Cruger's Tract, thence Westerly along the North Easterly and Northerly Bounds thereof to the Eastermost Bounds of the Tract formerly belonging to Richard Bradly and William Jamison, thence Northerly and Westerly along the Lines thereof to the North East corner of the Tract of Land formerly granted to Peter Barberie and commonly called Barberie's Tract, and then Westerly along the North bounds thereof to the Westermost Bounds of the said Precinct of New Burgh.

AND BE IT FURTHER ENACTED by the Authority aforesaid. That all the Lands heretofore comprehended within the said Precinct of New Burgh lying to the Northward of the aforesaid Division Lines, shall be called by the Name of New Marlborough Precinct, and that all the Lands heretofore comprehended within the said Precinct of New Burgh lying to the Southward of the aforesaid Division Lines shall continue to be called New Burgh Precinct.

AND BE IT FURTHER ENACTED by the Authority aforesail, That the Freeholders and Inhabitants of each of the aforesaid two Precincts called New Burgh Precinct and New Marlborough Precinct shall have full Power and Authority to assemble together and hold annual Meetings within their respective Precincts, and then and there by plurality of Voices to elect and choose one Supervisor, three Assessors, one Collector, one Constable, two Overseers of the Poor, two Commissioners for Highways with so many Overseers of the Highways as to them shall seem necessary and convenient, who when so chosen and elected shall be respectively vested with, and have the same Authorities and Powers, and be subject to the like Rules, Regulations, Fines and Penalties as are by Law prescribed for the like Officers respectively in other Precincts in the said County.

BE IT FURTHER ENACTED by the Authority aforesaid, That the Freeholders and Inhabitants of each of the aforesaid Precincts at their respective annual Meetings shall have the same power and Authority by Majority of Voices to make such By Laws and Regulations as the Freeholders and Inhabitants of the said New Burgh Precinct might heretofore lawfully have done.

AND BE IT FURTHER ENACTED that the annual Meetings for the said two Precincts respectively shall be held on the first Tuesday in April in every year, and that the Freeholders and Inhabitants of New Burgh Precinct aforesaid shall hold their first Annual Meeting at the now Dwelling House of Jonathan Haasbrook Esquire on the first Tuesday in April next. And that the Freeholders and Inhabitants of New Marlborough Precinct shall hold their first annual Meeting at the now dwelling House of Hendrickus Dijo, on the said first Tuesday in April next; and that the beforementioned two places for holding the first annual Meetings, shall continue and be the places for holding the annual Meetings in the aforesaid two Precincts respectively, until such Time as other places shall be agreed upon by a Majority of the Freeholders and Inhabitants of said Precincts respectively at their respective annual Meetings, which places so agreed upon shall then remain the place for holding the annual Meetings until altered as aforesaid.

AND BE IT ENACTED by the Authority aforesaid, That the Constable Overseers of the Poor, Commissioners of Highways and other Precinct Officers of the said Precinct of New Burgh, shall continue to exercise their respective Offices throughout the said Precinct as fully and amply until the first Tuesday in April next, as they might lawfully have done before the passing of this Act, any Thing herein contained to the contrary thereof in any wise notwithstanding.

AND BE IT FURTHER ENACTED by the Authority aforesaid, That the Freeholders and Inhabitants of the said Precincts of New Burgh and New Marlborough respectively shall continue to pay and contribute as well to the future Relief of such Poor Persons as were chargeable to or maintained by the said Precinct of New Burgh before the Division thereof as towards the Expence and Charge, the same was put to or chargeable with on Account of any such Poor Persons, in the same proportion as they formerly did, unless the Overseers of the Poor to be chosen for the said Precincts respectively shall agree to divide as well such Poor Persons between their respective Precincts, as to pay and discharge their respective proportionable Parts and Shares of such Expence and Charges, any Thing herein contained to the contrary thereof in any wise notwithstanding.

[CHAPTER 1539.]

[Chapter 1539, of Van Schaack, where the act is printed in full.]

An Act to fix and ascertain from whence the Mileage Fees of the respective Constables of the Manor of Cortlandt in the County of West Chester shall be computed.

[Passed, March 12, 1772.]

WHEREAS frequent Disputes have arisen about the places from whence the Mileage Fees of the respective Constables of the

Manor of Cortlandt in the County of Westchester should be computed, for Remedy whereof

BE IT ENACTED by his Excellency the Governor the Council and the General Assembly, and it is hereby enacted by the Authority of the same, That from and after the first Tuesday in April next, the Mileage Fees for all Precepts to be served by any of the respective Constables of the Manor of Cortlandt in the County of Westchester shall be computed from the places herein after respectively mentioned, to wit, the Mileage Fees for all Precepts to be served by either of the Constables aforesaid, in the West Division, North of Croton River shall be computed from the House of Abraham John Lent, situate on the rear of front Lot Number five in the said Manor, and that the Mileage Fees for all precepts to be served by either of the Constables aforesaid in the Middle Division of said Manor on the North side of Croton River, shall be computed from the House of Joseph Walters, situate on North Lot Number five in said Manor, and that all precepts to be served by either of the Constables aforesaid, in the East-Division of said Manor shall be computed from the House of John Purdy, situate on North Lot Number nine in said Manor, and that the Mileage Fees for all Precepts to be served by either of the Constables aforesaid, on the Lots South of Croton River, from Lot Number one to Lot Number ten inclusive shall be computed from the House of Bartow Underhill situate on South Lot Number six south of Croton River in said Manor, any Law usage or Custom to the contrary in any wise notwithstanding.

[CHAPTER 1540.]

[Chapter 1540, of Van Schaack, where the title only is printed.]

An Act for the payment of the Salaries of the several Officers of this Colony, and other purposes therein mentioned.

[Passed, March 24, 1772.]

BE IT ENACTED by his Excellency the Governor the Council and the General Assembly, and it is hereby enacted by the Authority of the same, That the Treasurer of this Colony shall, and hereby is directed and required out of the Monies arisen or which may arise by virtue of the following Acts vizt: An Act entitled, "An Act further to continue an Act entitled "An Act for "granting to his Majesty the several Duties and Impositions "on Goods, Wares and Merchandizes imported into this Colony "therein mentioned:" AN ACT entitled "An Act for collecting "the Duty of Excise on Strong Liquors retailed in this Colony "from the first Day of February one thousand seven hundred "and seventy two, to the first Day of February, one thousand "seven hundred and seventy three inclusive;" AN ACT entitled, "An Act to regulate the sale of Goods at Public Vendue, Auction "or Outcry within this Colony," and, AN ACT entitled "An Act "further to continue an Act entitled An Act to restrain Hawk-"ers and Pedlars within this Colony from selling without "Licence," to pay.

UNTO his Excellency William Tryon Esquire for Firewood and Candles for his Majesty's Fort George in the City of New York from the eighth Day of July one thousand seven hundred and seventy one to the first Day of September one thousand seven hundred and seventy two, after the Rate of four hundred Pounds per Annum.

UNTO the Honorable Daniel Horsemanden Esquire as Chief Justice of the Supreme Court of this Colony, and for going the Circuits from the first Day of September one thousand seven hundred and seventy one, to the first Day of September one thousand seven hundred and seventy two after the Rate of three hundred Pounds per Annum.

UNTO the Honorable David Jones Esquire one of the Puisne Justices of the Supreme Court of this Colony, and for going the Circuits from and to the Time aforesaid after the Rate of two hundred Pounds per Annum.

UNTO the Honorable Robert R Livingston Esquire one other of the Puisne Justices of the Supreme Court of this Colony, and for going the Circuits from and to the Time aforesaid, after the Rate of two hundred Pounds per Annum.

UNTO the Honorable George D Ludlow Esquire the other Puisne Justice of the Supreme Court of this Colony, and for going the Circuits from and to the Time aforesaid, after the Rate of two hundred Pounds per annum.

UNTO the Secretary of this Colony for the Time being for engrossing and enrolling the Acts of the General Assembly, from and to the Time aforesaid, after the Rate of forty Pounds per Annum.

UNTO the Clerk of the Council for the Time being, for his Services in that Station from and to the Time aforesaid the Sum of thirty Pounds.

UNTO the Door keeper of the Council for the Time being for his Services in that Station from and to the Time aforesaid the sum of thirty Pounds.

UNTO Hugh Gaine for services performed as public printer of this Colony, and in discharge of his Account for printing the Bills emitted by virtue of the Loan Office Act, and for furnishing six thousand Mortgages, sundry Blank Books, and other Articles for the use of the Loan Officers the Sum of three hundred Pounds.

UNTO John Kip as Guager of Liquor subject to a Duty within this Colony, or to the Guager thereof, for the Time being, from and to the Time aforesaid after the Rate of thirty Pounds per Annum.

UNTO Thomas Hill and Josias Smith Land and Tide Waiters, or to the Land and Tide Waiters for the Time being for their Services in that Station from and to the Time aforesaid after the Rate of fifty Pounds per Annum to each of them.

ALL which aforesaid several sums of money shall be paid by the Treasurer on Warrants issued by his Excellency the Governor or the Commander in Chief for the Time being, by and with the Advice and Consent of his Majesty's Council of this Colony, and the Receipts of the several persons endorsed on the said Warrants, shall be to the Treasurer good Vouchers and Discharges for so much as shall be thereby acknowledged to be received.

AND BE IT ENACTED by the authority aforesaid, That the Treasurer shall, and hereby is directed and required out of the Funds aforesaid to pay the several Allowances following (to wit.)

UNTO Abraham Lott Esquire Treasurer of this Colony, or to the Treasurer thereof for the Time being for his Services in that Station, from the first Day of September one thousand seven hundred and seventy one, to the first Day of September one thousand seven hundred and seventy two after the Rate of two hundred Pounds per Annum.

UNTO to the said Treasurer or the Treasurer for the Time being, for the extraordinary Services which he is now obliged to perform beyond the usual Duty of his Office after the Rate of the further Sum of one hundred Pounds.

UNTO Edmund Burke Esquire or Order Agent for this Colony in Great Britain, as a Reward for his Care, Trouble, and Diligence in attending upon his Majesty and his Ministers of State in that Station from and to the Time aforesaid after the Rate of five hundred Pounds per Annum.

UNTO John Tabor Kemp Esquire for extraordinary Services performed by him as Attorney General of this Colony from and to the Time aforesaid after the Rate of one hundred and fifty Pounds per Annum.

UNTO Edmund Seaman Esquire as Clerk to the General Assembly for his Services in that Station from and to the Time aforesaid twenty Shillings per Diem, payable upon a Certificate from the General Assembly signed by the Speaker for the Number of Days he has or may serve the General Assembly.

UNTO the said Edmund Seaman for sundry Disbursements by him made for the use of the General Assembly the Sum of fifty five Pounds nine Shillings and five Pence.

UNTO Gerard Bancker as Assistant Clerk to the General Assembly for his Services in that Station from and to the Time aforesaid, twenty shillings per Diem payable upon a Certificate from the General Assembly signed by the Speaker for the Number of Days he has or may serve the General Assembly.

UNTO Alexander Lamb Doorkeeper of the General Assembly for his Services in that Station from and to the Time aforesaid six Shillings per Diem payable upon a Certificate from the General Assembly signed by the Speaker, for the Number of Days he has or may serve the General Assembly.

UNTO the said Alexander Lamb for providing FireWood and Sundry Necessaries for the use of the General Assembly the sum of fifty five Pounds.

UNTO William Scott Sergeant at Arms for his Services in that Station from and to the Time aforesaid six Shillings per Diem payable upon a Certificate from the General Assembly signed by the Speaker for the Number of Days he has or may serve the General Assembly.

UNTO John Martin as Gunner and keeper of the Colony stores from the twenty eighth Day of July one thousand seven hundred and seventy one to the twenty eighth Day of July one thousand seven hundred and seventy two, after the Rate of twenty Pounds per Annum.

AND BE IT ENACTED by the Authority aforesaid That for Answering the Expences of Contingencies and extraordinary Emergencies, that have or may happen for the Services of this Colony, from the first Day of September one thousand seven hundred and seventy one, to the first Day of September one thousand seven hundred and seventy two, Warrants may issue for the same, on the Treasurer from Time to Time, if drawn by his Excellency the Governor or Commander in Chief for the Time being with the Advice and Consent of his Majesty's Council, which the Treasurer is hereby ordered and directed to pay out of the Monies arising by virtue of the Acts herein before mentioned provided the Amount of the said Warrants do not exceed the sum of one hundred Pounds during that Time.

AND BE IT ENACTED by the Authority aforesaid, That the Treasurer shall, and hereby is directed and required out of the Funds aforesaid to pay the several sums following, to wit,

UNTO his Excellency the Governor or Commander in Chief for the Time being to defray one half the Expence of running and ascertaining the Boundary Line between this Colony and the Colony of Quebec, from the Station fixed by his Excellency Sir Henry Moore at the forty fifth Degree of North Latitude to Connecticut River provided the said one half does not exceed the Sum of two hundred and eighty Pounds including the sum of one hundred and fifty Pounds pursuant to a Resolution of the General Assembly the fourteenth Day of February one thousand seven hundred and seventy one.

UNTO his Majesty his Heirs and Successors for defraying the Expence of making the necessary Repairs to the Fortifications in this City provided the same does not exceed the Sum of one thousand Pounds; to be paid by the Treasurer of this Colony unto the Commissioners hereafter mentioned at such Time, and in such proportion as his Excellency the Governor or Commander in Chief by and with the Advice and Consent of his Majesty's Council shall think necessary: And that James Jauncey and Jacob Walton Esquires are hereby appointed Commissioners and fully impowered, Authorized and required to lay out the foregoing Sum or so much thereof as may be necessary for the purposes abovementioned, and to and for no other use or purpose whatsoever.

UNTO Anthony Van Dam for a Flag for Fort George and Repairs, the Sum of thirty five Pounds seven Shillings and three Pence.

UNTO William Scott Sergeant at Arms for extraordinary Services performed by him during the present Sessions the sum of seven Pounds.

UNTO Aarie King and Jacob Blauvelt the Sum of two Pounds two Shillings unto each of them for their Attendance agreeable to summons from the General Assembly

UNTO the following Persons for sundry Repairs done to the House in Fort George and to the Barracks, to wit,

UNTO Jonathan Hampton the Sum of one hundred and ninety seven Pounds sixteen Shillings and seven pence.

UNTO George Stanton and Jonathan Blake the Sum of two Pounds.

UNTO William Winterton the Sum of twenty six pounds seventeen Shillings and four Pence half Penny.

UNTO Anthony Dodane the Sum of twenty Shillings.

UNTO Stephen Callow the Sum of one Pound seven shillings and two pence.

UNTO Stephen Steel the Sum of eleven Pounds six Shillings and nine pence.

UNTO Robert Andrews the Sum of twenty seven Pounds five Shillings and eight pence three Farthings.

UNTO John Bailey and James Youle the sum of forty two Pounds eleven Shillings and four Pence.

UNTO Thomas and John Barrow the sum of fifteen Pounds twelve Shillings and one penny.

UNTO Peter Goelet the Sum of fifteen Pounds six Shillings and four Pence half penny.

UNTO James Gutherie the Sum of one Pound sixteen Shillings and four Pence.

AND BE IT FURTHER ENACTED by the Authority aforesaid That the said Treasurer shall and is hereby directed and required out of the Interest Money arisen or that may arise by virtue of the Act entitled "An Act for emitting the Sum of one "hundred and twenty thousand Pounds in Bills of Credit to be "put out on Loan, and to appropriate the Interest arising thereon "to the payment of the Debts of this Colony, and to such Public "Exigencies as the Circumstances of this Colony may from Time "to Time render necessary," to pay the several Sums following (to wit)

UNTO Leonard Lispenard for Necessaries furnished for the use of this Colony in the year one thousand seven hundred and sixty nine, the sum of one thousand and seventeen Pounds nine shillings and nine pence half Penny.

UNTO John De Peyster Junior and Dirck Ten Broeck for Necessaries furnished for the use of this Colony in the Years one thousand seven hundred and sixty seven and one thousand seven hundred and sixty eight the sum of two hundred and sixty nine Pounds and ten pence half penny.

UNTO his Majesty the sum of one thousand Pounds for making good a Deficiency of that Sum granted by an Act passed the fifth Day of January one thousand seven hundred and seventy, entitled "An Act for making a further Provision of two thousand "Pounds for furnishing his Majesty's Troops quartered in this "Colony with Necessaries for one year," which sum of one thousand Pounds, the Treasurer is hereby directed and required to pay (after the other Grants out of this Fund are paid) on Warrant or Warrants to be drawn for that purpose by his Excellency the Governor or Commander in Chief for the Time being, by and with the Advice and Consent of his Majesty's Council.

UNTO Elisha Gallaudet for cutting the Stamps for the new Loan Office Money, the Sum of twenty two Pounds one shilling.

AND BE IT FURTHER ENACTED that the Treasurer shall and is hereby directed to place the sum of one hundred and fifty five Pounds ten Shillings and six pence part of the Sum of three hundred Pounds allowed to Hugh Gaine in this Act to the Account of the Interest of the Loan Office Money any Thing herein contained to the Contrary notwithstanding.

AND BE IT FURTHER ENACTED by the Authority aforesaid That the Treasurer shall and he is hereby directed to keep exact Books of his several Receipts and payments in virtue of this Act, and shall render true and distinct Accounts thereof upon Oath to his Excellency the Governor or Commander in Chief for the Time, the Council or the General Assembly when by them or any of them thereunto required.

[CHAPTER 1541.]

[Chapter 1541, of Van Schaack, where the act is printed in full.]

AN ACT for regulating the Militia of the Colony of New York.

[Passed, March 24, 1772.]

WHEREAS a due and proper Regulation of the Militia of this Colony tends not only to the security and Defence thereof, but likewise to the Honor and Service of his Majesty.

BE IT THEREFORE ENACTED by his Excellency the Governor the Council and the General Assembly, and it is hereby enacted by the Authority of the same, that every Person from sixteen to fifty Years of Age residing within this Colony shall within one Month after he arrives at the Age of sixteen, and every sojourner above the same Age having resided within this Colony above three Months, shall inlist himself with the Captain, or in his absence with the next Commanding Officer either of the Troop of Horse in the City or County where he dwells or resides, or in such Company of Foot, whose Captain or next Commanding Officer has the Command thereof in the City, Town, Borough, Manor or Precinct where such person shall reside or sojourn under the Penalty of five Shillings, and three Shillings for every Month that such Person shall remain so unlisted after Notice given: and all Captains of Troops of Horse, and Companies of Foot in the several Cities, Boroughs, Townships, Manors and Precincts of this Colony, are hereby commanded to take due Care to inlist all Inhabitants and Sojourners from sixteen to fifty Years of age, which Age in Case of Doubt is to be proved by the Oath of the Person whose Age is in Question, or the Oath of his Parent, or some other credible Witness to be taken by the Officer before whom the Dispute shall happen to be, who shall administer the same in the Words following, "I A. B. do swear upon the Holy Evangelists of Almighty God, "that C. D. summoned before Captain E. F. in order to be in- "listed is Years old, and no more, according to the "best of my knowledge, so help me God." which Oath being duly administered by the Captain or other Officer who hath summoned such Person before him in order to be inlisted, and it appearing that he is under sixteen, he shall be for that Time dismissed; and if any Dispute shall arise about elder Persons, and it appearing that he or they are above the Age of fifty, such Person or Persons shall be exempted at all Times thereafter.

AND BE IT ENACTED by the Authority aforesaid that all Captains of Troops of Horse and Companies of Foot shall within three Months from the Commencement of this Act, provide for their Companies and Troops, Drums and Trumpets, Colours and Banners, and Drummers and Trumpeters at the proper Charge of their respective Captains of Troops and Companies under the Penalty of Three Pounds, and for every Month such Captain shall remain unprovided thereof, the sum of two Pounds.

BE IT ENACTED by the same Authority, That the Colonels or Commanding Officers of all Regiments or Battalions, Troops, or unregimented Companies within this Colony shall at least once in every Year issue out their Warrants to their Inferior Officers commanding him or them to make diligent Search and Enquiry in their several Precincts that all Persons be duly listed, armed and equipped, and to return to them the Names of such Defaulters as he or they shall find, to the End they may be punished according to this Act.

AND BE IT FURTHER ENACTED by the Authority aforesaid. That twice in every Year command be given by the Colonel, and in his absence by the next Commanding Officer of the respective Regiments or Battalions, that the several Companies in each Regiment or Battalion, and the Captains or next Commanding Officers of the several Troops of Horse and Independent Companies of the several Cities and Counties shall meet at the most convenient places therein to be appointed by the respective Officers commanding the Regiment to be then and there mustered and exercised, and that every Soldier belonging to the Horse shall at the Time and place commanded, appear and be provided with a good serviceable Horse not less than fourteen Hands high, covered with a good Saddle, Houlsters, Housing, Breast-plate, and Crupper, a Case of good Pistols, a good sword or Hanger, half a Pound of Gun Powder, and twelve sizeable Bullets, a pair of Boots, with suitable Spurrs, and a Carabine well fixed, with a good Belt, Swivel and Bucket, under the Penalty of ten shillings for want of a sizeable Horse, and the Penalty of five Shillings for want of each or either of the Articles of the Troopers Furniture, and the Troopers in the City and County of New York shall be cloathed with a Blue Coat and Breeches, with yellow Metal Buttons, and a scarlet Waistcoat, and their Hats laced with Gold Lace: And the Troopers for the City and County of Albany, shall be cloathed with blue Coats and the Hats shall be laced with silver Lace under the Penalty of five shillings for the Want of each Article of such Cloathing, the whole Penalty on a Trooper for the Defaults of one Day not to exceed the Sum of forty shillings.

AND BE IT PROVIDED AND ENACTED by the Authority aforesaid that in Case of a general Alarm or Invasion all unregimented or Independant Companies and Troops shall in the Absence of the Captain General or Commander in Chief, be under the immediate Command and direction of the Colonel, and in his Absence the next commanding Officer of the Regiment or Battalion of the City or County where such unregimented or Independant Companies or Troops are or may be, any Thing herein to the contrary hereof notwithstanding.

AND BE IT FURTHER ENACTED by the Authority aforesaid, that the Number of the Troopers in each Company in the City and County of Albany shall be sixty besides Officers; and the Number of all other Troops in this Colony shall be fifty Troopers besides Officers; and for a constant supply of Troopers in each City and County within this Colony where Troops of Horse have been, or are, or shall be whensoever it shall happen by Death or otherwise, that there be fewer Troopers in Number than are limited by this Act, and the same cannot be supplied by Volunteers, that then the Captain of such Troop shall under his Hand certify unto the Colonel of the Regiment of Foot or Battalion, or in his absence to the next Commanding Officer in the City or County where such Want shall happen, how many Troopers are wanting in his List of the Troop under his Command and thereupon the said Colonel or next Commanding Officer of such Regiment or Battalion shall nominate out of the same the Number that shall be so wanting as aforesaid. PROVIDED that such Person or Persons so nominated by the said Colonel or next Commanding Officer, be not under the Age of twenty one Years, nor above ten Miles distant from the place of the Captains abode: upon which nomination the Person or Persons so nominated shall within the space of three Months equip themselves as is hereby directed. And every Trooper that shall be so nominated to serve in any of the Troops, and refusing to equip himself and serve, he shall for such Offence forfeit the sum of five Pounds, and upon payment thereof shall not be liable to any other or further Forfeiture for any Offence respecting the Troop but shall nevertheless be subject to serve in the Foot service as if no such Nomination had ever been made. And all Troopers already inlisted or who shall consent to be inlisted in manner as aforesaid refusing or neglecting to appear shall for every such Offence forfeit the sum of ten shillings for the first Default in not appearing, for the second Default the sum of fifteen shillings, and for the third Default twenty shillings, and for every Default after the third twenty shillings until he doth appear; and every Trooper or Soldier belonging to the Horse, shall always have at his Habitation or Place of abode, one Pound of Gun Powder, and three Pounds of sizeable Bullets, on Penalty of ten Shillings for every Default.

AND BE IT ENACTED by the Authority aforesaid that the Companies of Cadets, and Blue Artillery in the City of New York are to consist each of one hundred Men besides Officers, and if the Colonel of the Regiment of the said City or in his Absence the next Commanding Officer thereof, doth suspect that the Captain or Captains of the said Companies have inlisted a greater Number than is limited above, the Captain of the Company so suspected shall be obliged within fourteen Days after Notice to deliver to the Captain General or Commander in Chief, a true and compleat Roll of the Name and Names of all the Persons he or they have on his or their List: And if it thereby appears that more are inlisted than the Number abovementioned, all such Supernumerary Men are immediately to be discharged out of such List, and the Captain is to give a List of their Names to the Colonel or next Commanding Officer aforesaid, and the person and persons so discharged shall within fourteen Days thereafter inlist him or themselves in one of the Foot Companies of the said Regiment, and such of the persons so discharged as shall omit to inlist themselves accordingly, shall be subject to the Fines inflicted in this Act, on persons omitting or neglecting to inlist in the Militia.

AND BE IT ENACTED by the Authority aforesaid, that every Foot Soldier in any of the Regiments or Battalions, or Independant Companies of Foot in this Colony, shall be provided with a good well fixed Musket or Fuzee, a good Sword, Belt and Cartridge Box, six Cartridges of Gun Powder, and six sizeable Bullets, and so provided shall appear when and where required upon Penalty of five shillings for each Musket or Fuzee not well fixed, and for want of a sufficient sword, Belt, or Cartridge Box shall forfeit one shilling, and the same for want of each Cartridge or Bullet, the whole penalty for the Default of one Person for one Day not to exceed ten shillings, and the sufficiency of the Musket or Fuzee, Sword, Belt, and Cartridge Box to be judged of and determined by the Captain, or in his Absence the next commanding Officer of each Company, and every Foot soldier shall at his Habitation or place of abode have one Pound of good Gun Powder, and three Pound of sizeable Bullets upon Penalty of ten shillings for each soldier of Foot, and if any Soldier of Foot or Horse shall refuse to shew to his Captain or person sent by him, or other Officer for that purpose by this Act appointed, all or any of the Equipage, Furniture or Ammunition herein mentioned, he shall be deemed and esteemed to be unprovided thereof, and shall be fined accordingly.

AND BE IT ENACTED by the Authority aforesaid, that upon Notice given of a general Muster, or of the Review or Appearance in the Field of any particular Troop or Troops Company or Companies, no person whatsoever inlisted in Horse or Foot in manner aforesaid, shall withdraw himself from that Service without having first acquainted his Captain, and in his Absence the next Commanding Officer therewith, and without his leave or authority so to do, under the Penalty of ten shillings, and no Commission Officer shall remove himself out of Town or withdraw from the Service without Leave from his superior Officer, under the Penalty of twenty Shillings, and no sergeant, Corporal or Drummer whether of Horse or Foot, shall absent themselves in Manner aforesaid under Penalty of twenty Shillings.

AND BE IT FURTHER ENACTED by the same Authority, that no Person or Persons being thereunto required by their Superior and proper Officer shall refuse to be Sergeant, Corporal or Drummer in any Troop or Company under the Penalty of forty Shillings and in Case any Sergeant or Corporal so appointed shall refuse to warn the people to appear under Arms when thereunto required by his Captain or next Commanding Officer, he shall for every such Neglect or Refusal forfeit the Sum of twenty Shillings.

AND BE IT FURTHER ENACTED by the same Authority that every Soldier under Arms that shall not give due Obedience to his Superior Officer shall forfeit the sum of ten shillings for each Offence, and if any Person inlisted to serve either in Horse or Foot, and appearing under Arms, and during such Appearance shall refuse or neglect to perform such Military Duty as shall be required from him, or shall depart from his Colours or Guard without Leave from such Officer, he shall forfeit the Sum of twenty Shillings, and for nonpayment thereof shall be committed by Warrant from the Captain or Commanding Officer there present of the Company or Troop to which such Offender doth belong to the next Goal till the said twenty shillings be paid with the Prison Charges, and the Sheriff of each City and County is hereby impowered and required to receive the Body or Bodies of such Offender or Offenders against this Act as shall be brought to him by virtue of a Warrant or Warrants under the Hand and Seal of such Officers as aforesaid, and him or them to keep in safe Custody until such Fees and Fines mentioned in such Warrant are paid, and it is hereby declared that such sheriffs or keepers of Goals shall in such Cases as aforesaid be entitled to the same Fees as are allowed in all other Cases. PROVIDED LIKEWISE that in Case of a Military Watch or Night Guard where a Captain doth not command in person, the Warrant of Distress or Warrant of Imprisonment granted by an inferior Officer, who did command the Guard or Watch, shall be of the same Authority against all Offenders, as if the same Warrants were issued by the Captain, any Thing in this Act to the contrary thereof in any wise notwithstanding.

AND BE IT ENACTED by the Authority aforesaid. That the several Fines Penalties and Forfeitures in this Act mentioned shall be levied recovered and disposed of as followeth that is to say, that all such Forfeitures as do relate to any person under the Degree of a Captain shall be adjudged by and be taken to the respective Captains, to defray the Charges of their Troops and Companies and to be levied before the next exercising Day, by Distress and Sale of the Offenders Goods, by the Captains Warrant directed to the Sergeant or Corporal of the Company wherein said Offence was committed: But if the Offender be a Servant or under his Parents Care, then in such Case the Master's or Parents Goods shall be liable to such Distress and Sale as aforesaid, 'till Satisfaction be made, and if any Sergeant or Corporal shall refuse to execute such Warrant so to him directed, such Sergeant or Corporal shall for every such Offence forfeit for the uses abovementioned the sum of forty Shillings to be levied in Manner before expressed by such Other Officer, Sergeant or Corporal as such Warrant shall be directed to, and for all other Penalties and Forfeitures in this Act mentioned, the same shall be levied by Distress and Sale of the Offenders Goods, by Warrant from the Colonel or the next Field Officer where such Offenders are, which Forfeiture and Penalties shall be for the use and Benefit of the Regiment or Battalion in the City and County where the Offence is committed, and if the Fines that relate to Persons under the Degree of a Captain shall not amount to a Sum sufficient to defray the Charges of Captains of Troops and Company, that then what is wanting shall and may be levied upon the several Soldiers equally by Warrant of the Colonel or Chief Officer of the Regiment or Battalion, Troops or Companies, and if no Goods are to be found whereon to distrain, the Person Offending is to be sent to the next Goal there to remain till Satisfaction be given and the Prison Fees paid, and the Sergeants, Corporals or Clerk of the Regiment or Battalion are to reserve to themselves out of the Distress or Forfeiture the sum of three Shillings for executing each Warrant from their Captain or other superior Officer.

AND BE IT FURTHER ENACTED That all Drummers and Trumpeters lately in service, or that shall be put in service by the several Captains during pleasure, shall serve upon the Salary of forty shillings per Annum for a Trumpeter and twenty shillings for a Drummer, finding their Trumpet or Drum: and twenty Shillings for a Trumpeter, and ten Shillings for a Drummer, if the Captain do provide the Drum or Trumpet, and each Drummer or Trumpeter refusing to serve to forfeit forty shillings to be levied in Manner aforesaid, ALWAYS PROVIDED. That all the Members of his Majesty's Council and Members of the General Assembly, Justices of the Peace, High Sheriffs, Coroners, and other Civil Officers of his Majesty's Government in this Colony, and all other Officers of Courts, Ministers of the Gospel, Schoolmasters, Physicians, Surgeons all Firemen within this Colony and one Miller to a Grist-Mill, shall be free from being listed in any Troop or Company within this Colony.

AND BE IT ENACTED by the Authority aforesaid. That no Commission Officer of the Militia of this Colony legally superceded, shall afterwards be obliged to do the Duty of a Private Soldier, unless he be casheered for Cowardice, nor shall it be in the Power of any Commission Officer to throw up or Quit his Commission, unless he is superseded in his Rank, until he has served in Commission fifteen Years at the least, any Thing in this Act to the contrary thereof notwithstanding.

AND BE IT ENACTED by the Authority aforesaid That no Military Commission Officer, as well of Foot Companies or Troops of Horse, whether Regimented or Independent as likewise the Troopers in the City and County of New York shall be liable or subject to serve as Constable tho' chosen, any Law or usage to the contrary notwithstanding. PROVIDED NEVERTHELESS, That a Commission obtained by any Person after he is elected a Constable, shall not entitle him to the Exemption abovementioned.

AND BE IT ENACTED by the Authority aforesaid that in Case of any Alarm, Invasion, Insurrection or Rebellion, every Officer of the Militia shall have full power and Authority by virtue of this Act, and is hereby required forthwith to raise the Militia or Company under his Command and to send immediate Intelligence to the Commanding Officer of the Regiment to which he belongs, who also are hereby required and commanded to send forwards the Intelligence forthwith to the Commanding Officers of the next adjacent Counties, informing him and them at the same Time, in what Manner he intends to proceed: and every Commanding Officer in every County upon any Alarm or receiving Intelligence of any Insurrection, Invasion or Rebellion shall forthwith dispatch an Express to the Governor or Commander in Chief for the Time being notifying the Danger, and shall therewith signify the Strength and Motions of the Enemy, & the said Commanding Officer hath hereby full Power to impress Boats and Hands, Men and Horses, as the Services may require, and shall draw together the Militia of his County, and march them to such place or places as he shall judge most convenient for opposing the Enemy, and to such Place or Places within this Colony, as shall be directed by the Governor or Commander in Chief for the Time being and every Captain or other Commission Officer under the Degree of Major, that shall neglect or refuse to perform his Duty hereby required shall forfeit the Sum of twenty Pounds: and every non Commission Officer or Private Man for his Neglect or Refusal of such Duty shall forfeit the sum of five Pounds, and every Commission Officer besides paying such Forfeiture shall be degraded, and rendered incapable thereafter of holding or exercising any Office Civil or Military within this Colony.

AND WHEREAS the County of Suffolk is so scituated that a Descent may be made on the Eastern Part thereof by water, and the said County being extensive, the remote Parts which are most exposed, are generally at a great Distance from the Colonel or Commanding Officer of the Regiment, and consequently the waiting for Orders from the said Commanding Officer may greatly expose such remote Places to the Ravages of small Parties of the Enemy.

BE IT THEREFORE ENACTED That the Captains or next Commanding Officer of the several and respective Companies within the said County, nearest to any place where such Descent may happen to be made, shall immediately call together his or their Company or Companies and forthwith proceed to use their utmost endeavours to repel and drive off, the Enemy, and on the first Notice of such Descent, shall dispatch an Express to the Commanding Officer of the Regiment of the said County, with Intelligence thereof and of the Number and Motions of the Enemy, according to the best Information he or they shall have obtained, any Thing herein before contained to the contrary notwithstanding.

BE IT FURTHER ENACTED by the Authority aforesaid. That if any Person or Persons shall be sued, molested or impleaded for any Matter or Thing lawfully done and commanded in the Execution and performance of this Act, he or they shall plead the general Issue, and give this Act in Evidence, and if the Plaintiff discontinue his Action, be nonsuited, or Verdict pass against him, the Defendant shall recover treble Costs, nor shall any such suit or suits be admitted or allowed to be brought unless it be done within three Months next after the Offence is Committed.

AND BE IT ENACTED by the Authority aforesaid. That once every Year and oftner if thereunto required, each particular Captain shall give to his Colonel or in his absence to the next Field Officer, and such Field Officer and the Captains of unregimented Troops and Companies, to the Captain General or Commander in Chief for the Time being fair Written Rolls of their respective Regiments, Troops and Companies on the Penalty of forty Shillings for a Field Officer and twenty shillings for an inferior Commanding Officer, and if any Person be wounded or disabled upon any Invasion, or in any other Military Service, he shall be taken care of, and provided for by the Public during the Time of such Disability.

AND BE IT FURTHER ENACTED by the same Authority. That the Majority of the Officers in the Regiment on the south Side of the Mountains in Orange County shall before any Training or meeting of the said Regiment assemble and agree by a Majority of Voices on a convenient place as near the Center as shall be for the good of the Public Service which place of Training so agreed on and fixed shall be afterwards notified to the respective Companies by an Instrument under the Hand of such Majority, and read by the Captain or his Order at the Head of each respective Company.

PROVIDED ALWAYS and be it enacted by the Authority aforesaid, That all persons above the Age of fifty and not exceeding sixty years of Age shall in Case of Alarm, Invasion or Insurrection be obliged to appear under Arms under the Captain or the Commanding Officer of the District where they dwell or reside, any Thing herein contained to the contrary thereof in any wise notwithstanding.

AND BE IT ENACTED by the Authority aforesaid That this Act and evry Clause Article and Thing therein contained shall commence from the first Day of May next, and remain of full force and virtue until the first Day of May, which will be in the Year of our Lord one thousand seven hundred and seventy four.

[CHAPTER 1542.]

[Chapter 1542, of Van Schaack, where the act is printed in full. See chapters 411 and 856.]

An Act more effectually to prevent private Lotteries.

[Passed, March 24, 1772.]

WHEREAS the Laws now in being for the suppression of Private Lotteries have been found ineffectual to answer the salutary Purposes intended by the Legislature in enacting the same. AND WHEREAS many mischievous Consequences have been experienced from this Practice, which has proved highly prejudicial to Trade, has occasioned Idleness and Inattention to Business, been productive of Fraud and Imposition, and has given Birth to a dangerous spirit of Gaming. For Remedy whereof and to suppress a Practice which may be attended with Distress, Impoverishment and Ruin to many Families.

BE IT ENACTED adjudged and declared, and it is hereby enacted adjudged and declared by his Excellency the Governor, the Council and the General Assembly, and by the Authority of the same. That all Lotteries other than such as are authorized by the Legislature are common and Public Nuisances.

AND BE IT FURTHER ENACTED by the Authority aforesaid That no Person or Persons from and after the first Day of August next, shall open, set on Foot, carry on, or draw Publickly or Privately any Lottery, Game or Device of Chance of whatever nature or kind it may be or by whatever Name Denomination or Title it may be called known or distinguished or shall by any such Ways or Means expose or set to sale any Houses, Lands Tenements and real Estate, or any Merchandize, Goods, Wares or any other Goods or Chattels of any kind whatsoever; and every Person or Persons who shall offend in the Premises against the true Intent and meaning of this Act and shall be thereof convicted on the Oath of one or more credible Witness before three Justices of the Peace (one whereof being of the Quorum) where such Offence shall be committed, or the Offender found the Person so convicted shall forfeit double the amount of the whole Sum or value for which such Lottery was made, and if such Sum or Value cannot be ascertained, then the said Offender shall forfeit five hundred Pounds, one half of the said Forfeiture to be paid to the Treasurer for the use of his Majesty his Heirs and Successors for and towards the support of Government: the other half to the person giving information thereof, to be levied by Distress and sale of the Offenders Goods and Chattels by Warrant of the said Justices or any two of them, and for want of Goods and Chattels the Offender to be committed to the common Goal till the said Penalty be paid. PROVIDED that if any Person or Persons shall think himself aggrieved he may appeal to the next Quarter or General Sessions of the Peace for the County where such Offence shall be committed whose Judgment shall be final.

AND BE IT FURTHER ENACTED by the Authority aforesaid That if any Person shall vend or sell or offer to vend or sell any Ticket or Tickets, or if any Person or Persons shall purchase the same or shall in any wise become Adventurer or Adventurers, or be any ways concerned in any such Lotteries or Games of Chance, or in promoting the same, each person so Offending shall upon being convicted thereof as above forfeit ten Pounds for every Offence to be recovered before any one Justice of the Peace, and applied in Manner above directed.

AND BE IT FURTHER ENACTED by the Authority aforesaid That if any Person or Persons who shall be Adventurers in such Lotteries or Games as aforesaid for transferring Property by Lot or Chance, shall become entitled to any prize or prizes he or they shall be liable to forfeit the same to such Person or Persons who shall give Information thereof so that such Offender may be convicted in Manner above directed; for the recovery whereof the said Person or Persons so informing shall be entitled to maintain an Action in any Court of Record in this Colony against the Person who shall set up the said Lottery or Game, or Person or Persons selling or offering to sale any Ticket or Tickets; and if the person or persons so informing as aforesaid be himself an Adventurer in such Lottery or Game, he shall upon giving such Information as aforesaid be exempted from the Penalty which he would otherwise incurr by this Act: And every Person or Persons adventuring as aforesaid whose Ticket or Tickets shall prove or turn up Blank, shall upon giving Information as aforesaid, so that the Person or Persons setting up and drawing the said Lottery or other Game, or selling or offering for sale such Ticket or Tickets, may be convicted according to this Act be entitled to recover against such Person or Persons, the Money he or they adventured therein with double Costs of Suit by Action of Debt in any Court of Record in this Colony: And if the person or persons setting on Foot and drawing such Lottery or Game as aforesaid, shall either before or after the drawing or finishing the same, give Information thereof so that the Persons adventuring therein may be convicted in Manner before directed, he or they shall not only be exempted from the Penalty he or they would otherwise have incurred by this Act, and be entitled to the Reward allowed to Persons informing in such Case, but shall also have a Right to retain all such Monies, as he or they may have received in the sale of Tickets.

AND for the more easy Detection of the said Lotteries or Games BE IT FURTHER ENACTED by the Authority aforesaid, That it shall be lawful for any one Justice of the Peace having reasonable Cause to suspect that any such Lottery or Game as aforesaid is set on Foot or carrying on to summon any Person or Persons whom he shall suspect to be privy to the same, and to examine him or them touching the same, and in Order that such persons may not be excused from answering any Questions which shall be asked them by the said Justice by Colour of any Plea or Pretence that they may thereby incur any Penalty inflicted by this Act; it is hereby declared that they shall upon being examined as aforesaid, and declaring all they know touching the matters enquired of them by the said Justice, be exempted from any such Penalty, and from all prosecutions in virtue of this Act: And in Case any Person summoned as aforesaid shall refuse to be sworn or answer such Questions as shall be asked thereupon, the Justice shall and hereby is impowered to commit such Person to the common Goal, there to remain till he shall comply or be from thence delivered by due Course of Law.

AND BE IT FURTHER ENACTED by the Authority aforesaid. That every Conveyance Grant, Bargain Sale or Transfer of any Lands Tenements Hereditaments and real Estate, or of any Goods or Chattels whatsoever, which shall hereafter be made in pursuance of any such Lottery Game or other Device to be determined by Chance or Lot are hereby declared void and of none Effect.

AND for the more effectual suppressing and preventing such unlawful Lotteries, be it further Enacted that the Justices of the Peace and all Mayors, Bailiffs, Constables & other his Majesty's Civil Officers within their respective Jurisdictions are hereby impowered directed and required to use their utmost Endeavours to prevent the drawing of any such unlawful Lotteries, by all lawful Ways and Means, according to the true Intent and meaning of this Act.

AND BE IT FURTHER ENACTED by the Authority aforesaid, That where any two or more persons shall be concerned in setting on Foot, carrying on, or drawing any Lottery or Game of Chance or be joint Adventurers in the same, the Penalties abovesaid may be recovered against all or either of them, any Thing in this Act, or any Law to the contrary notwithstanding.

[CHAPTER 1543.]

[Chapter 1543, of Van Schaack, where the act is printed in full.]

An Act to revise digest and print the Laws of this Colony.

[Passed, March 24, 1772.]

WHEREAS the Laws of this Colony are at present irregularly bound up, and not properly digested, which often occasions Difficulties and Inconveniencies, it is therefore conceived necessary that all the Laws from the happy Revolution down to the End of the Present Session, should be revised and digested, and that the same be new printed on good paper and bound in one or more Volumes of a suitable Size. AND WHEREAS Peter Van Schaack Esquire hath declared his willingness for the Consideration herein after mentioned to undertake to revise digest and collect exact Copies of all the Laws in force in this Colony from the said Revolution to the End of the present Session of the General Assembly, and to perform the whole in Manner following, That is to say, to make search where it may be necessary in the Council Books, and in the Journals of the General Assembly in order to distinguish what Acts have had the Royal Assent, what are repealed, and which remain probationary, to insert in their Order, the Titles of all the Acts passed within the said Series of Time distinguishing if Temporary, when revived, when expired, when repealed, to distribute the Acts into Chapters, each Act into a Chapter, and each Chapter subdivided into Sections and numbered, to abstract the Substance of each Section in the Margin; to make of all this a compleat and fair Copy for the press, and to examine in transcribing, to supervise and correct the press with the Utmost exactness and Attention, to make an Index and Table of all the Principal Matters in the Acts alphabetically digested, with reference to each matter in every Act, Section and page, to make References from one Act to another, where the Matter in one Act may have relation to a head Matter in another: AND in as much as several temporary Acts, and some others may be wholly useless, and unnecessary to be printed, the Legislature put Trust and Confidence in him the said Peter Van Schaack Esquire to distinguish and determine the same, and in Case he should be in doubt thereof, he may apply to the Justices of the Supreme Court or any of them, and govern himself accordingly, only taking Notice of the Title of such Acts, when passed, and when expired.

BE IT THEREFORE ENACTED by his Excellency the Governor the Council and the General Assembly, and it is hereby enacted by the authority of the same, that he the said Peter Van Schaack Esquire, shall be and hereby is fully authorised and appointed to do the said Work, and for the better enabling him to perform the same in the Manner beforementioned, he shall and may from Time to Time have recourse to the original Acts, the Council Books, and the Journals of the General Assembly.

AND BE IT ENACTED by the Authority aforesaid That upon the said Peter Van Schaack's producing to the Treasurer of this Colony a Certificate to be signed by the Governor or Commander in Chief for the Time being, and by three or more of the Council and likewise by the Speaker of the General Assembly for the Time being, certifying, that they take the same Work to be conformable to the true Intent and meaning of this Act, the said Treasurer shall thereupon be, and hereby is impowered and required to pay unto him the said Peter Van Schaack or to his Assigns the Sum of two hundred and fifty Pounds out of any Monies which shall then be in the Treasury granted or to be granted for the support of the Government of this Colony any Law to the contrary thereof notwithstanding; and a proper Receipt upon the said Certificate shall be to the Treasurer a good Voucher and Discharge for the same.

AND BE IT ENACTED by the Authority aforesaid, That Hugh Gaine shall and hereby is impowered to print the said Work on the best paper and large Folios, and with the usual Types for such Work, and to deliver one printed Book thereof compleatly Bound in Calves Skin to the Governor or Commander in Chief for the Time being, one other for the use of the Council and four for the use of the General Assembly of this Colony.

BE IT ENACTED by the Authority aforesaid, That upon the said Hugh Gaine's producing to the Treasurer aforesaid a Certificate from the Governor or Commander in Chief from the Council, and from the Speaker of the General Assembly for the Time being, certifying, That they have respectively received the said printed Books compleatly bound as aforesaid, according to the true Intent and meaning hereof the said Treasurer shall thereupon be, and he is hereby impowered and required to pay unto the said Hugh Gaine the Sum of twenty Shillings for every Sheet of paper in the said printed Books, so compleatly bound up as aforesaid, out of any Monies in the Treasury as aforesaid, and a proper Receipt signed by the said Hugh Gaine for the same shall be to the Treasurer a sufficient Voucher and discharge provided the same do no not exceed the Sum of twenty Shillings for each Sheet as aforesaid.

PROVIDED ALWAYS and be it Enacted by the Authority aforesaid, That they the said Peter Van Schaack and Hugh Gaine shall with all convenient speed fulfil accomplish and compleat the Work aforesaid by them undertaken in Manner as aforesaid.

[CHAPTER 1544.]

[Chapter 1544, of Van Schaack, where the act is printed in full. Revived by chapter 1726.]

An Act to oblige the Justices of the Peace at their general or Quarter Sessions to determine Appeals made to them according to the Merits of the Case, notwithstanding Defects of Form in the Original proceedings, and to oblige Persons suing forth Writs of Certiorari to remove Orders made on such Appeals, into the Supreme Court of this Colony, to give Security to prosecute the same to effect.

[Passed, March 24, 1772.]

WHEREAS in many Cases where his Majesty's Justices of the peace by Law are impowered to give or make Judgment or Orders, great Expences have been occasioned by reason that such Judgments or Orders have, on Appeals to the Justices of the Peace at their respective General or Quarter Sessions been quashed or set aside upon exceptions or Objections to the Form or Forms of the proceedings without hearing or examining the Truth and Merits of the Matter in Question between the Parties concerned, therefore to prevent the same for the future.

BE IT ENACTED by his Excellency the Governor the Council and the General Assembly, and it is hereby enacted by the Authority of the same, That after the first Day of May next upon all Appeals to be made to the Justices of the Peace at their respective General or Quarter Sessions to be holden for any County City, Borough or place within this Colony against Judgments or Orders given or made by any Justices of the Peace as aforesaid, such Justices so assembled at any General or Quarter sessions shall, and they are hereby required from Time to Time within their respective Jurisdictions upon all and every such Appeals so made to them, to cause any Defect or Defects of Form that shall be found in any such Original Judgments or Orders to be rectified and amended without any Cost or Charge to the Parties concerned, and after such Amendment made, shall proceed to hear examine and consider the Truth and Merits of all Matters concerning such Original Judgments or Orders and likewise to examine all Witnesses upon Oath and hear all other Proofs relating thereto, and to make such Determinations thereupon as by Law they should or ought to have done in case there had not been such Defect or want of Form in the original Proceeding, any Law, Usage or Custom to the contrary notwithstanding.

AND WHEREAS divers Writs of Certiorari have been procured to remove such Judgments or Orders into the Supreme Court of this Colony in hopes thereby to discourage and weary out the Parties concerned in such Judgments or Orders by great Delays and Expences. BE IT THEREFORE ENACTED by the Authority aforesaid That no Certiorari shall be allowed to remove any such Judgment or Order unless the Party or Parties prosecuting such Certiorari before the Allowance thereof, shall enter into a Recognizance with sufficient sureties before one or more Justices of the Peace of the County or Place, or before the Justices at their General or Quarter Sessions of the Peace where such Judgment or Order shall have been given or made, or before any one of his Majesty's Justices of the said Supreme Court in the Sum of fifty Pounds with Condition to prosecute the same at his or their own Costs and Charges to Effect, without any wilful or Affected Delay, and to pay the Party or Parties in whose favour and for whose Benefit such Judgment or Order was given or Made within one Month after the said Judgment or Order shall be confirmed, their full Costs and Charges to be taxed according to the Course of the Court where such Judgments or Orders shall be confirmed, and in Case the Party or Parties prosecuting such Certiorari shall not enter into such Recognizance, or shall not perform the Conditions aforesaid, it shall and may be lawful for the said Justices to proceed and make such further Order or Orders for the Benefit of the Party or Parties for whom such Judgment shall be given, in such Manner as if no Certiorari had been granted.

AND IT IS HEREBY FURTHER ENACTED by the Authority aforesaid That the Recognizance and Recognizances to be taken as aforesaid shall be certified into the Supreme Court, and there filed with the Certiorari and Order or Judgment removed thereby, and if the said Order or Judgment shall be confirmed by the said Court, the persons entitled to such Costs for the Recovery thereof within ten Days after Demand made of the Person or Persons who ought to pay the said Costs upon Oath made of the making such Demand and Refusal of payment thereof, shall have an Attachment granted against him or them by the said Court for such Contempt, and the said Recognizance so given upon the allowing of such Certiorari shall not be discharged, until the Costs shall be paid, and the Order so confirmed shall be complied with and obeyed.

AND BE IT FURTHER ENACTED by the Authority aforesaid, That this Act shall continue and be in force until the first Day of February which will be in the Year of our Lord one thousand seven hundred and seventy five.

[CHAPTER 1545.]

[Chapter 1545, of Van Schaack, where the act is printed in full.]

An Act to enable any one of the Coroners for the different Counties within this Colony, to make Return to process.

[Passed, March 24, 1772.]

WHEREAS Justice has been frequently delayed on Account of the Difficulty and Expence in procuring all the Coroners of such Counties in this Colony, in which there are two or more, to make and sign Returns to Process to them directed, occasioned by the Remoteness of their situations from each other.

BE IT THEREFORE ENACTED by his Excellency the Governor, the Council and the General Assembly, and it is hereby enacted by the Authority of the same. That from and after the publication of this Act, any Return made and signed by any one of the Coroners in any of the Counties in this Colony respectively for the Time being, to any future process which shall issue from and out of any of his Majesty's Courts of Record within this Colony, directed to the Coroners of the said Counties respectively, shall and is hereby declared to be as good and valid in Law to all Intents Constructions and purposes as if such Return was made and signed by all the Coroners of the said Counties respectively, any Law, usage or Custom to the Contrary notwithstanding. PROVIDED ALWAYS and be it also enacted that the Act or Return of one or more of the Coroners shall in no degree prejudice the rest, and that nothing in this Act contained shall be construed to extend to any Venire Facias or other Jury process in any Cause whatsoever.

[CHAPTER 1546.]

[Chapter 1546, of Van Schaack, where the act is printed in full.]

An Act for carrying into execution Judgments obtained by virtue of an Act entitled, "An Act to impower Justices of the Peace "Mayors, Recorders and Aldermen to try "Causes to the Value of ten Pounds and under "and for suspending an Act therein mentioned."

[Passed, March 24, 1772.]

WHEREAS his Majesty by his Order in Council at the Court of St. James's bearing date the ninth Day of December one thousand seven hundred and seventy hath been pleased with the Advice of his privy Council to declare his disallowance of the abovesaid Act, AND WHEREAS several Judgments have been given by virtue of the above said Act, before the Disallowance thereof as aforesaid; but have not been fully carried into execution by which means many honest Creditors have been kept out of their just Dues, to remedy which.

BE IT THEREFORE ENACTED by his Excellency the Governor, the Council and the General Assembly, and it is hereby enacted by the Authority of the same. That where any such Judgment hath been given by any Justice of the Peace, Mayor, Recorder or Aldermen by virtue of the abovesaid Act entitled. "An Act to impower Justices of the Peace, Mayors, Recorders "and Aldermen to try Causes to the value of ten Pounds and "under and for suspending an Act therein mentioned," before the Disallowance thereof as abovesaid, shall and may be carried into execution, and all other proceedings had thereon, in the same Manner as fully and effectually as if the abovesaid Act had not been disallowed, any Thing in the aforesaid Act to the contrary hereof notwithstanding

PROVIDED ALWAYS And be it further enacted by the Authority aforesaid. That Nothing in this Act shall extend or be construed to extend to affect any Action already brought or had in any Inferior Court of Common pleas or before any Justice of the peace, Mayor, Recorder or Aldermen to recover such Debts or Demands given by such Judgment as aforesaid.

[CHAPTER 1547.]

[Chapter 1547, of Van Schaack, where the act is printed in full. See chapter 1855.]

An Act to amend an Act entitled "An Act "to ascertain the size of Casks in which white "Bread shall be packed within the City of New "York, and to regulate the Manner in which the "same shall be sold."

[Passed, March 24, 1772.]

WHEREAS by the aforesaid Act passed the sixth Day of February one thousand seven hundred and sixty eight, it is among other Things enacted that no white Bread shall be packed in Casks less than eighteen Inches and an half long, and eleven Inches wide in the Head, nor shall contain less than twenty Pounds weight of Bread which being found inconvenient.

BE IT THEREFORE ENACTED by his Excellency the Governor the Council and the General Assembly and it is hereby enacted by the Authority of the same, That from and after the first Day of May next, all white Bread may be packed in Casks not being less than fifteen Inches long, and ten Inches wide in the Head and not containing less than fifteen Pounds weight of Bread, any Thing in the said Act to the contrary notwithstanding.

[CHAPTER 1548.]

[Chapter 1548, of Van Schaack, where the act is printed in full.]

An Act for the Inspection of Flax in the City of New York.

[Passed, March 24, 1772.]

WHEREAS the cleaning of Flax in this Colony to prepare it for spinning and Rope Making has become an Object of some Importance, and as abuses are committed in the sale of Flax altogether unfit for the said purposes, to the great Damage of the purchasers, for the prevention therefore of the said Evil for the future.

BE IT ENACTED by his Excellency the Governor the Council and the General Assembly, and it is hereby enacted by the Authority of the same, that from and after the tenth Day of April next ensuing no Person or Persons whatsoever shall sell or expose to sale any Flax in the City of New York, before the same shall have been submitted to the view and examination of the

Inspecter herein after named, who shall try the same by opening the Bundles, and then carefully examine if it be clean and well dressed, and shall sort the same if necessary, putting that which is Merchantable by itself in Bundles, which he shall Mark and distinguish by affixing thereto a Label, having on it the Words, "inspected," and, "New York." together with the initial Letters of his Christian Name and Sirname; for which Trouble the said Inspecter shall have and receive one Farthing per pound, for every Pound he shall so inspect; one half whereof to be paid by the purchaser, and the other half by the vender.

AND BE IT ENACTED by the Authority aforesaid That if any Dispute shall happen to arise between the Owner and Inspecter in regard to the cleanness and Quality of the Flax, the Owner shall choose one skilful Person and the said Inspecter one other, and if the Persons so chosen do not agree, they shall choose a third Person, and the three Persons so chosen or any two of them, shall finally determine the Dispute.

AND BE IT ENACTED by the Authority aforesaid That if any Person or Persons whatsoever shall sell, dispose of, or offer for sale, any Flax within the City of New York until it shall have been inspected and marked as aforesaid, that every such Person and Persons shall forfeit three pence per pound for every Pound of Flax so sold contrary to this Act, and at and after that Rate for every greater Quantity, to be sued for and recovered by Action of Debt with Costs of Suit, in a Summary way, by any Person who will sue for and prosecute the same before any Justice of the Peace within the City of New York to be levied by process to be directed to either of the Constables or other proper Officer of the City commanding them, or either of them to levy the same by Distress and sale of the Offenders Goods and Chattels, which Forfeiture, when recovered as aforesaid, to be applied by the Person recovering the same, to his or her own use; And if any person or persons shall presume to counterfeit the Label or Mark of the said Inspector, he, she, or they so offending shall forfeit for every such Offence the sum of five Pounds to be sued for, recovered and applied in manner aforesaid.

AND BE IT FURTHER ENACTED that Obadiah Wells, shall be, and hereby is appointed Inspector of Flax within the City of New York, which said Inspector, before he does any Thing in execution of the said Office, shall take an Oath before the Mayor or Recorder of the City of New York, in the Words following, to wit. "I A. B. do swear that I will faithfully, truly and impartially

" according to the best of my Judgment skill and Understanding, " execute, do and perform the Office and Duty of an Inspector and " examiner of Flax according to the true Intent and meaning of " an Act entitled "An Act for the inspection of Flax in the City " of New York, and I will not directly or indirectly buy or sell " any Flax during the Time I continue Inspector of the same, " except for the private use of my Family, so help me God." and if the Officer hereby appointed shall by any accident be rendered incapable or neglect to execute the said Office or misbehave himself therein or shall happen to die, then and so often and from Time to Time in such Cases, it shall and may be lawful to and for the Mayor Recorder and Aldermen of the City of New York or the Major part of them to supply his place by some other fit and capable person, who shall thereupon be the Officer for putting this Act in Execution until another be appointed by Act or Acts hereafter to be passed for that purpose, which Officer so appointed shall take the Oath abovementioned, have the same Powers, and be liable to the same penalties as the Officer particularly appointed by this Act, any Law Usage or Custom to the contrary notwithstanding.

PROVIDED ALWAYS and be it enacted by the Authority aforesaid, That the said Inspecter shall be obliged to procure a House or Store proper for the inspection of the said Flax, to be situated near the Water, between Peck's and Burling's slips in this City.

This Act to continue in force from the tenth Day of April next, until the first Day of February one thousand seven hundred and seventy four.

[CHAPTER 1549.]

[Chapter 1549, of Van Schaack, where the act is printed in full.]

An Act to prevent the Danger arising from the pernicious Practice of lodging Gun Powder in dwelling Houses Stores or other Places within the City of New York or on board of Vessels within the Harbour.

[Passed, March 24, 1772.]

WHEREAS the City of New York has lately been greatly endangered by the Storing of Gun Powder to the Southward of Freshwater contrary to Law, notwithstanding the Corporation have long Since provided a Powder House for that Purpose. BE IT THEREFORE ENACTED by his Excellency the Governor the Council and the General Assembly and it is hereby enacted by the Authority of the same, That from and after the passing of this Act it shall not be lawful for any Person or Persons, other than Shopkeepers and Retailers of Gun Powder, to have or keep in any Place within two Miles of the City Hall of the said City, more than Six Pounds of Gun Powder, nor for Shopkeepers and Retailers more than twenty eight Pounds weight of Gun Powder, and that in four Separate Stone Jugs or leathern Bags, each of which shall not contain more than seven Pounds of Gun Powder upon Pain of forfeiting all such Gun Powder, and the sum of Forty Pounds for every hundred weight, and in that Proportion for a greater or less Quantity, and upon Pain of forfeiting all such Quantities which any Person may lawfully keep as aforesaid, and which shall not be separated as above directed with full Costs of Suit to any Person or Persons who will inform and sue for the same, by any Action Bill or Information in any of his majesty's Courts of Record in this Colony; which Courts are hereby impowered and required to give special Judgment in such Actions Bills or Informations to be brought upon this Act, as well for the recovery of such Gun Powder in Specie, as for the Penalty aforesaid, besides Costs, and to award effectual Execution thereon.

AND BE IT FURTHER ENACTED by the Authority aforesaid, that it shall be lawful for the Mayor or Recorder or any two Justices of the Peace of the City and County of New York, upon Demand made by any one or more Householder or Householders being an Inhabitant or Inhabitants of the said City, within two Miles of the City Hall of the said City, assigning a reasonable Cause of Suspicion on Oath, of the sufficiency of which Cause the said Mayor or Recorder or Justices is and are to judge, to issue his or their Warrant or Warrants under his or their Hands and Seals, for searching in the Day Time for Gun Powder within the Limits aforesaid any such Building or Place whatsoever, or any such Ship or Vessel within twelve Hours after her Arrival and fastening to the Wharf or to any other Ship or Vessel along side of the Wharf or Key of which Building Place Ship or Vessel such reasonable Cause of Suspicion shall be assigned on Oath as aforesaid; and that upon every or any such Search it shall be lawful for the Searchers or Persons finding the same immediately to seize and then or at any Time within twelve Hours after such Seizure to amove or cause to be amoved all such Gun Powder as shall be found within the Limits aforesaid, or on Board of such

Vessel as aforesaid upon any such search, exceeding the Quantity allowed by this Act, to some proper Magazine now or to be built for the Purpose of Storing of Gun Powder, and the same being so amoved, it shall be lawful to detain and keep the same until it shall be determined in one of his Majesty's Courts of Record of this Colony, whether the same shall be forfeited by virtue of this Act, and the Person or Persons so detaining the same, shall not in the mean Time be Subject or liable to any Action or Suit for the keeping or detaining the Same, until it shall be determined whether the same be forfeited as aforesaid.

PROVIDED ALWAYS AND BE IT ENACTED by the Same Authority that nothing in this Act contained shall be construed to countenance or Authorize any Person having such Warrant to take Advantage of the same for serving any Civil Process of any Kind whatsoever, but that all such Service shall be absolutely null and void.

PROVIDED ALSO AND IT IS HEREBY FURTHER ENACTED by the Authority aforesaid That it shall not be lawful for any Person or Persons interested in such Gun Powder or any Person or Persons by Collusion with the Owners or Proprietors thereof to have or maintain any Action Bill or Information upon this Act, any Thing herein contained to the contrary notwithstanding.

AND for preventing the dangerous Carriage of Gun Powder in and through the Streets of the City of New York within two Miles of the City Hall of the said City BE IT ENACTED by the Authority aforesaid That from and after the passing of this Act it shall not be lawful for any Person or Persons to carry or convey in or through any of the Streets or Lanes within the Limits aforesaid more than five hundred Pounds weight of Gun Powder at a Time; and that all Gun Powder which shall be carried or conveyed in any Carts or Carriages, or by Hand or otherwise in or thro' any of the Streets or Lanes aforesaid after the Time aforesaid shall be in tight Casks well headed and hooped and shall be put into Bags or Cases of Leather and intirely covered therewith so as that no Such Gun Powder be spilt or Scattered in the Passage thereof; AND if at any Time after the Passing of this Act any Gun Powder shall be carried or conveyed by any Person or Persons in or through any of the Streets or Lanes aforesaid in any greater Quantity, or in any other Manner than as aforesaid all such Gun Powder shall be forfeited, and shall and may be seized by any Person or Persons to his or their own Use and Benefit the Person or Persons so offending being thereof lawfully convicted before two Justices of the Peace PROVIDED ALWAYS that this Act or any Thing herein contained shall not extend or be construed to extend in any wise to affect any Ship of War, Store house or Magazine belonging to his Majesty his Heirs or Successors wherein Gun Powder or other Stores shall be kept for the use of the Publick or the Powder House abovementioned.

AND BE IT FURTHER ENACTED by the Authority aforesaid That if any Suit or Action shall be commenced or prosecuted against any Person or Persons for any Thing done in pursuance of this Act, in every such Case such Person or Persons shall and may plead the General Issue, and give this Act and the special Matter in Evidence at any Tryal to be had thereupon, and that the same was done in pursuance or by the Authority of this Act; And if a Verdict shall pass for the Defendant or Defendants, or the Plaintiff or Plaintiffs shall become Nonsuit or Discontinue his her or their Suit or Action after Issue joined; or if upon Demurrer or otherwise Judgment shall be given against the Plaintiff or Plaintiffs, the Defendant or Defendants shall and may recover treble Costs and shall have the like Remedy for the same as any Defendant or Defendants hath or have in any other Case by Law.

PROVIDED ALWAYS AND BE IT ENACTED by the Authority aforesaid. That all Suits Actions and Prosecutions to be brought, commenced or Prosecuted against any Person or Persons for any thing done or to be done in pursuance or by Authority of this Act shall be laid and tryed in the County where the Fact was committed, and shall be commenced and prosecuted without wilful Delay within six Calendar Months next after the Fact committed and not otherwise.

AND BE IT FURTHER ENACTED by the Authority aforesaid That if any Powder other than such Quantity as any Person by this Act may lawfully keep in his Custody, shall be found during any Fire or Alarm of Fire in the said City by any of the Firemen of the said City it shall be lawful for him to seize the same without Warrant from a Magistrate and to hold and have the same to his own Use any Thing in this Act to the contrary notwithstanding.

THIS ACT to be and continue of Force from the passing thereof until the twenty fifth Day of March One Thousand seven hundred and Seventy four.

[CHAPTER 1550.]

[Chapter 1550, of Van Schaack, where the act is printed in full.]

An Act for the better support of the Hospital to be erected in the City of New York for Sick and Indigent Persons.

[Passed, March 24, 1772.]

WHEREAS his Majesty has been graciously pleased by Letters Patent or Charter under the Great Seal of this Colony to establish a Corporation under the Name of, "The Society of the Hospital in the City of New York in America." for the benevolent Design of healing such Sick Persons, who from their extreme Indigence are become Objects of Charity AND WHEREAS the said Society have by their Petition to the General Assembly, not only suggested that without the Aid of the Public the Institution is in Danger of failing; but given the fullest and most explicit Assurances that the Benefits thereof shall not be denied to any Poor diseased Persons, and that they mean to proceed uninfluenced by any contracted or partial Attachments and without Civil or Religious Distinctions of any kind. AND WHEREAS a Society established for Ends so laudable and conducted by Principles so Generous, Humane and Benevolent, deserves the Encouragement of the Public.

BE IT THEREFORE ENACTED by his Excellency the Governor the Council and the General Assembly, and it is hereby enacted by the Authority of the same, That the Treasurer of this Colony for the Time being shall out of any Fund in the Treasury pay, and he is hereby required to pay unto the Treasurer for the Time being of the said Society of the Hospital in the City of New York in America, the sum of eight hundred Pounds annually for and during the Term of twenty Years to be computed from the first Day of February next, which Sum of eight Hundred Pounds so to be paid shall become chargeable upon the Duty of Excise laid or to be laid on Strong Liquors retailed in the City of New York.

AND BE IT ALSO ENACTED by the same Authority That the Monies that may hereafter arise by the Duty of Excise to be laid on Strong Liquors retailed in the several Cities Counties Towns Boroughs and Manors within this Colony for and during the Term of twenty Years to be computed from the first Day of February next; and not appropriated by this Act, shall be paid by the Commissioners to be appointed for collecting the Duty of Excise on Strong Liquors retailed within this Colony unto the Treasurer of the Counties severally, where such Duty shall be collected to be annually disposed of and applied to the use of such Counties, in such Manner as the Majority of the Supervisors of the Counties respectively shall think proper, PROVIDED ALWAYS, That if the Duty on Excise in the City of New York should in any Year exceed the said sum of eight hundred Pounds, that such Excess shall be paid, and the Commissioner to be appointed is hereby required to pay the same unto the Chamberlain of the Corporation of the City of New York to be applied by the said Corporation in keeping in repair the Highways in the said City and County of New York.

AND BE IT FURTHER ENACTED by the Authority aforesaid That all such Sick Persons who from their Extreme Indigence are become Objects of Charity and may reside in any of the Counties of this Colony shall and may receive the Benefits of the said Hospital in common with such Sick and Indigent Persons as reside in the said City of New York, and shall be received into the said Hospital without any Expence any Thing in this Act or the said Charter or Letters Patent to the contrary hereof notwithstanding

AND BE IT ALSO ENACTED by the same Authority. That the Admission and Continuance of any Person in the said Hospital shall not be construed to give such Person a Residence or Settlement in the City of New York but that every such Person shall and may be sent when removed from the same Hospital to the place of his or her last Residence next before such Admission any Thing in this or any other Law of this Colony to the contrary notwithstanding.

AND BE IT FURTHER ENACTED by the same Authority. That the Governors of the said Corporation for the Time being and all and every the Physicians, Surgeons and Officers, and Servants employed by the said Governors in the Service of the said Hospital for and during the Time of such Service shall be privileged and discharged from the Office of Constable in the said City of New York and from Serving in the Militia (except on Actual Invasion) any Law or Custom to the contrary notwithstanding.

[CHAPTER 1551.]

[Chapter 1551, of Van Schaack, where the title only is printed. Repealed and provided for by chapter 1584. See chapter 1664.]

An Act for the better Laying out Regulating, Clearing and Keeping in repair the public Roads and Highways in the Counties of Albany and Tryon.

[Passed, March 24, 1772.]

WHEREAS it hath been found by Experience that the several Acts lately in force for regulating, clearing and further laying out public Highways throughout the City and County of Albany, have not fully answered the good purposes thereby intended.

BE IT THEREFORE ENACTED by his Excellency the Governor, the Council and the General Assembly, and it is hereby Enacted by the Authority of the same, that from and after the publication of and during the Continuance of this Act the persons hereinafter named shall be and hereby are appointed Commissioners for regulating the Highways and public Roads already laid out, and for laying out and regulating such other Highways and public Roads as may still be necessary within the said City and County of Albany and within the said County of Tryon, and they or the Majority of them in each District for which they are appointed, are hereby Authorized and impowered to put in Execution the several Services intended and required of them by this Act in such City, Towns, Manors or Districts only for which they shall be respectively named and appointed, that is to say.

FOR the District of the City of Albany, the Mayor, Recorder, Aldermen and Commonalty of the said City.

FOR the District of the Manor of Livingston, Robert Livingston Junr. Robert R. Livingston and Dirck W: Ten Broeck.

FOR the District of Claverack John Van Renselaer, Casparus Conyn Jun'r. Robert Van Renselaer, Peter Van Ness, Joseph Pixly, Jacob Hagedorne. Stephen Hogeboom, Solomon Hutchinson & Evert Knickerbaker Junr.

FOR the District of Kinderhook, Peter S Van Alstyn, Francis Van Buren LUCAS I Goes, Cornelius Van Schaack Junr. Melgert Van Derpool.

FOR Kings District, James Savage, William Whiting, Nathaniel Culver, Samuel Baldwin, Robert Bullis, and Isaac Pebody.

FOR the District of Renselaerwyck, Renselaer Nicoll, Killian Van Renselaer, Abraham Ten Broeck, John H. Beekman, Teunis Slingerlandt, Stephen Schuyler Lucas Van Veghten, and Stephen J. Schuyler.

FOR Schactikoke District Johannis Knickerbacker, Marte Winne, Wouter Groesbeeck, and Peter Williams.

FOR Hosick District, Daniel Bradt, John Munroe, Bliss Willoughby, Cornelius Van Ness, Ebenezer Cole & John Abbott

FOR Cambridge District, Isaiah Younglove, Thomas Morrison & Archibald Campbell.

FOR Saratoga District, Philip Schuyler, Killian De Ridder, Jonathan Jones, Jacobus Swart, George Palmer, Dirck Swart, Cornelius Van Der Bergh, James Mc Crea & Jeremiah Taylor.

FOR Half Moon District, Guert Van Schoonhoven, Anthony Van Schaick, Cornelius Tymese, Nicholas Fisher, Abraham Fort & Hendrick V: D: Werken.

FOR Schenectady District, Jacobus Van Slycke, Joseph R Yates, Isaac Vroman Ryer Schermerhorn John Glen, and John Duncan.

FOR the united Districts of Duansburgh and Schoharie Johannis Lawyer, Hendrick Haynes, Jacob Sternberger, Herman Sidney, and Peter Snyder.

FOR Cocksakie District, John Barclay, Anthony Van Bergen, Jacob Halenbeeck, Sybrant G. VanSchaick and Teunis Van Veghten.

FOR the great Imbocht District, John Ten Broeck, Abraham Pearse, Jury William Dederick, John B. Dumond, and John Van Orden.

AND FOR the Districts in the County of Tryon Vizt.

FOR the Mohawk District, Sir William Johnson, Sir John Johnson, Jellis Fonda, John Butler, and Peter Conyn.

FOR Stone Arabia District, Safrinus Tyger, Adam Louse, Jury Copernol, Arent Brouwer, and Hendrick Merchel.

FOR Canajoharie District, Harmanus Van Slyck, Hendrick Frey, Nicholas Herkemer, William Seeber, and Johannis Feling.

FOR the German Flatts District, Marcus Petri, Nicholas Weaver, & Martin Smith.

FOR Kingsland District John Joost Herkemer Junr. Rudolph Schoonmaker, Coenradt Frank & Peter Ten Broeck.

THE Major part of which said Commissioners in each District shall have full power to do and execute what in this Act is required, and injoined as the Duty of the said Commissioners.

AND BE IT ENACTED by the Authority aforesaid that the Commissioners or the Major part of them in the respective Districts, for which they are named and appointed Commissioners, are hereby impowered and authorized to regulate the Roads already laid out, and to lay out such other public Roads in the several Districts for which they are appointed Commissioners, as to them or the Major part of them, shall seem necessary and convenient, and if need be to take a review of the Roads already laid out, and such of them as appear to be really inconvenient, the said Commissioners shall and may alter and lay out such other public Ways and Roads as they shall think most convenient, as well for Travellers as for the Inhabitants of the next adjacent Districts, Provided that nothing in this Act contained shall extend or be construed to impower the Commissioners aforesaid to lay any new Road through any inclosed or improved Lands without either the Consent of the Owners thereof or paying the true Value of the Lands so laid out into an Highway, AND if any Dispute shall arise by that Means the same shall be determined, and the true Value set and appraised by two Justices of the peace, not being Commissioners in the District where the Dispute shall happen, And by the Oath of Twelve of the principal Freeholders of the Neighborhood not having any Interest in the Lands ABOUT which such Dispute may arise. the said Freeholders to be summoned by any one of the Constables of the said County by Virtue of a Warrant to be issued by the said two Justices for that purpose: And if the said Roads by the Commissioners so laid out shall be found by such Jury to be public Roads, and of public and general Benefit, then the Value of such cleared and improved Lands, through which the said Roads shall be laid out, shall be paid by the said Commissioners, and they are hereby required to pay the same out of the Monies to be raised by this Act, together with the Charge of calling a Jury, their Verdict and the whole proceedings thereon had: BUT if the Roads so laid out shall be found by such Jury to be private Roads and for the particular Convenience of one or more particular person or persons, then such person or persons requiring the same shall defray the whole Charge of the Value of the said cleared or improved Lands to be paid to the person or persons injured, and through whose cleared and improved Lands a private Road shall be laid, together with the charge of calling a Jury and of their Verdict, and of the whole proceedings thereon had.

AND BE IT FURTHER ENACTED by the Authority aforesaid, that the Overseers of the Highways in each District respectively or any one of them are hereby impowered, directed and required to order such a Number of the Inhabitants of said District, with their Sleds Horses, or Oxen, as they the said Overseers, or any one of them shall think sufficient and proper to break up the Roads where deep Snows happen to fall; And if any person or persons being ordered as aforesaid shall refuse to break up said Road, such person or persons shall respectively forfeit the Sum of ten Shillings for every Day they shall so neglect or refuse said Service to be levied by the Constable in each District by Distress and Sale of the Offenders Goods and Chattels, by Warrant from any one of the Overseers for the respective District for which they shall be appointed returning the Overplus of such Sale if any there be, to the Owner or Owners, after deducting thereout the Constables Fees as is Common in other Cases, and one Shilling for the Warrant, and the said Forfieture of ten Shillings, shall be paid to the Clerk of the Commissioners of the Highways FOR the District where such Forfeiture shall arise; to be by them applied in the same Manner as the other Monies to be raised by this Act are hereafter directed to be applied.

AND BE IT ALSO ENACTED by the same Authority that if any person or persons within the said City and County do, or hereafter shall without the consent of the Commissioners or the Major part of them for the District to which they are by this Act appointed Commissioners, alter, stop up, or lessen any Highway or Road that has heretofore been laid out by former Commissioners according to Law, or shall hereafter be laid out by the Commissioners named in this Act; such person so Offending contrary to the Meaning of this Act, shall for every such Offence forfiet the Sum of five Pounds to be recovered before any Justice of the peace upon the Oath of any one credible Witness, and levied by Warrant from any Justice of the peace, directed to the Constable of the District where such Offence shall be committed, commanding him to Destrain the Goods and Chattles of the offender, and the said Constable after six Days public Notice given by him of the Time for Sale of said Distress shall make Sale thereof, and out of the produce deduct the said Forfeiture and all the Charges, and return the Overplus if any there be, to the Owner or Owners AND the said Constable is hereby required to pay the said Forfeiture into the Hands of the Clerk of the Commissioners of the Highways, for the District wherein the Offence was committed to be by the Commissioners thereof applied in the same Manner as the other Monies to be raised by this Act, are herein directed to be applied.

AND BE IT ALSO ENACTED by the same Authority that the Breadth of all the public Roads in and throughout the said City and Counties shall be regulated by the Commissioners of each District respectively. PROVIDED ALWAYS that no Road shall be broader than four Rods, nor none less than two Rods.

AND in Order that the Burthen of keeping the Highways in the said City and Counties in repair, and the making other Highways, for the Ease, Benefit and Safety of the Inhabitants may be as equitably proportioned BETWEEN the Inhabitants thereof as the Nature of the Case will admit.

BE IT THEREFORE ENACTED by the same Authority that the Commissioners herein before named for each District respectively are hereby required to meet at such convenient place as any one of them shall appoint within the said District for which they are named, on the first Tuesday in the Month of May next ensuing the publication of this Act, and Annually on the first Tuesday in the Month of May, and as often thereafter as need shall be, and they or a Majority of them being so met on the said first Tuesday in May, they shall immediately proceed to make a List of all the Inhabitants dwelling and residing in their District, and which are by this Act liable to work on and pay towards the Highways, and the List so made out the Commissioners shall cause to be delivered to the Treasurer or Treasurers of the said City and Counties, who are hereby required with all convenient Speed to write against each Persons Name the pounds Quota which such person was rated for the next preceding Year in the Tax laid and raised by Virtue of the Act Entitled "An Act for the better ex-" plaining, and more effectual putting in Execution, an Act of " General Assembly made in the third Year of the Reign of their " late Majesties King William and Queen Mary, Entitled An Act " for defraying of the public and necessary Charge throughout " this Province, and for maintaining the poor, and preventing " Vagabonds." and then the said Treasurers respectively shall return the same to the Clerk of the Commissioners who shall pay unto the Treasurer two Shillings for his trouble, and the Clerk shall deliver the same to the Commissioners at their next Meeting, and if it shall appear to the said Commissioners that the said

is common in Case where Distress is made by a Collector, and the said Forfeitures of six Shillings shall by the Overseer be paid into the Hands of the Commissioner's Clerk to be by the said Commissioners applied in the same Manner as the other Monies directed to be raised by this Act, are to be applied.

AND BE IT ALSO ENACTED by the same Authority, that all the Monies to be raised by Virtue of this Act, or that may accrue from Fines and Forfietures, shall be honestly and fairly applied by the Commissioners of each District respectively for the Use of the Highways, and to and for Building and Repairing Bridges, and such other necessary Work in and concerning the premises in their respective Districts, as shall from Time to Time occur, and also in paying one or more Overseers of the Highways, and a Clerk, And the said Commissioners are hereby required and commanded to keep true and Just Accounts of all the Money by them received and expended by Virtue of this Act, and of all their Transactions, and the same to deliver in upon Oath to the Court of General Sessions held for the said Counties respectively whenever thereunto required.

AND BE IT ALSO ENACTED by the same Authority, that the Commissioners by this Act appointed shall in their Districts respectively agree with one or more Sober, Discreet, and capable person or persons to be an Overseer or Overseers of the Highways in their District, and the same to discharge at pleasure, and other or others in his or their Stead to appoint, and also to appoint a Clerk to keep their Accounts, to receive the Monies arising by this Act, and to write the Orders and Directions that they shall from Time to Time give (and which they are hereby impowered to do,) to the Overseer or Overseers of the Highways, of which Appointments they shall give public Notice in the District by Advertisement put up at the place where the annual Election for Officers of the District are held.

AND BE IT ALSO ENACTED that as soon as the Commissioners of the several Districts respectively, shall have rated the Inhabitants of their District, they shall cause a Copy of the List to be put up in at least two noted places within their District one of which to be the place of Election to the Intent that all the Inhabitants may know how many Days Labour, and how much Money they are respectively rated, and in Order to prevent all disputes that may arise in rating the Inhabitants to Work and Contribute towards the Expence of the Highways.

BE IT ALSO ENACTED by the same Authority, that the Master or Mistress of every Family in each of the said Districts only shall be rated to Work and pay towards the Highways and no other person whatsoever.

AND BE IT ALSO ENACTED that all Trees standing or laying in any persons Lands through which any common public Highway is or shall be laid out be for the proper Use of the Owner or Owners of the same, but the said Owners shall not hinder the Overseer of the Highways of the District from making Use of so much Timber which is standing or laying on that Road or which is standing or laying in any Lands adjacent not actually in Fence as will amend the said Highways or Bridges.

AND BE IT ALSO ENACTED by the same Authority that if any Trees shall fall out of any inclosed Lands into or across any of the public Highways, that the Owner of such Inclosure shall within forty eight Hours after the same be so fallen remove the same or be liable to a Fine of ten Shillings for every Days Neglect in the nonremoval thereof after Notice given to be recovered and applied in the same Manner as the other Fines and Forfietures are recovered and applied by this Act.

PROVIDED ALWAYS, AND BE IT ENACTED by the same Authority that in Case it should happen that the Highways in any of the said Districts should want so little Repair, as that the Money only raised or to be raised in such District by Virtue of this Act may be sufficient to do the Work THEN and in such Case the Overseers of the Highways shall not call upon the Inhabitants to Work upon the Highways. PROVIDED ALSO that in Case it should not be necessary in any one or more of the said Districts to have all the Days wrought by the Inhabitants that this Act requires that then the Commissioners shall direct the Overseers to let each Inhabitant Work in his Just proportion and no more. And PROVIDED ALSO that any person liable to Work on the Highways by Virtue of this Act may be excused from the same on paying to the Commissioners besides the Money such person was rated the Sum of three Shillings for each Days Labour that such person was rated.

AND BE IT ALSO ENACTED by the same Authority, that no person whatever in any of the said Districts shall after the first Day of June next after the publication of this Act set up any Swinging or other Gate or suffer any that may be then already set up to remain across any of the Highways in the said City or Counties respectively unless by a special Licence from the Commissioners of the District under their Hands and Seals, PROVIDED always that before the said Commissioners shall be permitted to grant such a Licence they shall at the request and at the Cost and Charge of the person or persons requesting such Licence apply to two of the nearest Justices of the peace who shall cause the Constable of the District to summon twelve impartial principal Freeholders of the District, and the said Justices together with the said Freeholders, the Freeholders, being first duly Sworn, shall maturely enquire and then declare under their Hands and Seals whether there are any sufficient Obstacles to prevent the setting of Fences, and maintaining the same, and what those Obstacles are if any there be, and if by the return of the inquest, it shall appear that no Fences can be reasonably maintained, then the Commissioners shall grant their Licence for Gates; If otherwise they shall allow one Year to remove the Gates, and no longer, and any person or persons offending contrary to the true Intent and Meaning of this Clause SHALL for every Offence be liable to the like Forfieture that is inflicted in the fourth Clause of this Act, and the said Forfietures shall be recovered and applied in the same Manner as is directed in said fourth Clause.

AND BE IT FURTHER ENACTED by the Authority aforesaid, that in Case any person or persons shall Stake or Shore open any Licenced Gate or Gates or wilfully ride over or through any Lands, Meadow Ground, or Cornfields to the Damage of the Owners thereof, such person or persons shall for every such Offence forfiet the Sum of Twenty Shillings, to be recovered by the overseers of the Highways in each respective District, where such Offence shall be committed, and be recovered and applied in like Manner as the other Forfietures in this Act are recovered and applied, and such Offender shall pay all such Damages with Cost which the possessor of the Soil shall suffer or sustain thereby as shall be ordered and awarded by a Justice of the peace residing nearest to the place where such Offence shall be committed, and the determination of such Justice shall be final and conclusive therein.

AND BE IT FURTHER ENACTED by the same Authority, that if the Commissioners or Overseers of the Highways shall think fit and have Occasion of any Team, Sled, Cart or Waggon, and a Man to Manage the same, the said Cart, Sled or Waggon, and Man shall be esteemed to be in lieu of three Days Work of one Man, and the Fine for neglect or refusal to furnish the same to be proportionable that is treble to the Fine to be imposed for the Neglect of one person, and every Working Man shall be obliged to bring such Tools as Spades, Axes, Crows, Pick Axes, or other Utensils as shall be directed by the Overseers of the Highways, and no person under the Age of Sixteen Years shall be deemed a sufficient Labourer.

AND BE IT FURTHER ENACTED by the same Authority, that if any of the said Commissioners herein appointed, shall neglect, refuse or delay, to qualify themselves, as this Act hereafter directs, or being qualified SHALL happen to die or remove out of the District for which he or they are appointed Commissioners, it shall and may be lawful for the Justices of the peace in the General Sessions held for the said Counties respectively to appoint in his or their Stead another Commissioner or Commissioners for such District where such Refusal, Neglect, delay, Death or Removal shall so happen, and the Commissioner or Commissioners so appointed, shall be under the same Restrictions, and have the same power and Authority, as those appointed by this Act.

AND BE IT ALSO ENACTED by the same Authority, that it shall and may be lawful for the Justices of the peace in the General Sessions held for the said Counties respectively, to appoint such an additional Number of Commissioners to such Districts as have not above three appointed by this Act, as to them shall seem necessary, and the Commissioner or Commissioners so appointed, shall be under the same Restrictions, and have the same power and Authority as those appointed by this Act.

AND BE IT ALSO ENACTED by the Authority aforesaid that the Commissioners of each respective District for which they are respectively appointed shall from Time to Time during the Continuance of this Act, enter in Writing all the Highways by them laid out, altered, or stopped up, and sign the same by putting their Names thereto, and cause the same to be entered in the Records of the said counties respectively by the Clerk of the peace, who is hereby directed and required to Record the same, and whatsoever the s'd Commissioners shall do in layingout, altering or Stopping, and otherwise regulating Highways, according to the power given them in this Act being so entered in the County Records shall be deemed valid and good to all Intents and purposes whatsoever, for which Entry the Clerk shall be paid two Shillings.

AND BE IT FURTHER ENACTED by the same Authority, that upon the order of any one or more of the Justices of the peace of the said Counties respectively, the Overseers of the Highways shall set to Work the RESPECTIVE Inhabitants to mend and repair any part of the Road that may want the same, and if the Overseer or Overseers shall neglect to have the said Highway repaired for the Space of eight Days such Overseer or Overseers shall for every such neglect forfiet the Sum of forty Shillings to be adjudged by and recovered before any one Justice of the peace of the said Counties respectively upon the Oath of one credible Witness, or on the View of such Justice in the common and usual Method, which Fine shall be applied in like manner as the other Fines are applied in this Act.

PROVIDED ALWAYS AND BE IT ENACTED by the same Authority that where the Inhabitants of a small Neighborhood or plantation shall desire to have public Roads laid out the Commissioners aforesaid shall not be allowed to lay out so many Roads as the said Inhabitants may be desirous to have but only one public Road leading from such Neighbourhood to the nearest other public Highway, from whence they can travel and Transport Goods to other Towns or Landing places; and where it shall be necessary to lay out a Road from one District, as they are in this Act Joined to another District, the Commissioners or the Major part of both Districts are to meet and consult where such Road can be laid out in the best and Straightest Manner, and to lay out the same accordingly, to the end that such Roads may not only correspond with each other but be laid and carried on in the most convenient and shortest Manner the Nature of the Land will allow.

PROVIDED ALWAYS AND BE IT FURTHER ENACTED that if it shall so happen that if the improved Farm of any Inhabitant of the said County, shall be divided or thrown into different Districts, as they are described in this Act, that then in such Case every such Inhabitant shall be Subject to work upon and contribute towards the Highways in that District, only in which his Dwelling House is erected.

PROVIDED ALSO, AND BE IT FURTHER ENACTED that if any INHABITANT of the said respective Districts shall conceive it more convenient to use a public main Road not Maintained by the District wherein he resides leading to the City of Albany or other port or place of Embarkation which may hereafter be established; that in every such Case upon Application to the Commissioners both of his own District, and of that through which the Road he prefers may pass, it shall and may be lawful to and for the said Commissioners or the Major part of them, if such Convenience shall appear to them to be Manifest, to relieve him from the Duties required of him by this Act, in the District which he inhabits, and Subject him to the performance of those Duties in the next adjoining District through which such Road passes, and whereby it is supported.

PROVIDED ALSO, AND BE IT FURTHER ENACTED that where a public and Main Road shall be required from any District in which there is a considerable Settlement to the City of Albany, or any other port or place of Embarkation as aforesaid, that in every such Case such public or Main Road shall be continued from District to District, as streight and direct as the Nature of the Ground and other Circumstances will admit, AND that such Main and public Road may be established with more general Conveniepce and Utility to the Inhabitants of the respective Districts through which the same may extend; it shall and may be lawful to and for the Commissioners of the District, which shall require the said Road by Writing under their Hands to appoint and Summons a general Meeting of all the Commissioners of the respective Districts through which the Road proposed shall extend at any Time not less than three nor more than ten Days after the Service of Notice on the said Commissioners, and at such convenient place in that District which shall be most Central to the usual Residence of the Major part of such Commissioners, AND the said Commissioners are hereby directed and required to meet and attend according to such Appointment, AND when the said Commissioners so convened, shall have consulted together and deliberated upon the Subject of the said Meeting they shall then proceed to lay out the Highway or Road proposed and required from District to District, and in the best and most advantageous Manner for public and general Utility and Convenience (that is to say) the Commissioners of each respective District shall lay out that part of the intended Road which shall extend through the District of which they are respectively Commissioners, and the same being so laid out, shall be certified, returned and recorded, as a public Road or Highway in the Manner herein before directed; and shall be maintained and supported in the several Districts thro' which it shall extend as other Highways or public Roads ought by this Act to be maintained in each respective District, BUT if it shall so happen that the Commissioners of either of the other Districts then Assembled shall be dissatisfied with any part of the Road so laid out they shall be at Liberty a[illegible] are hereby Authorized to propose the manner in which the[illegible] ceive that part of the Road which is objected to ought t[illegible] out and if the Commissioners whose Duty it is to l[illegible] same shall not agree to the Alteration insisted upo[illegible] Discription shall be made in Writing signed by all [illegible] sioners present of both the Roads proposed AND it [illegible] ful for three or more of the said Commissioners to [illegible] two of his Majestys Justices of the peace of the s[illegible] respectively not residing or holding Lands in the [illegible] cerning which such Controversy shall have arisen or [illegible] for which such Road shall be required. And such [illegible] hereby Authorized and directed thereupon to issue t[illegible] to one of the Constables of the said County comman[illegible] summons a Jury of twelve good and sufficient Freehol[illegible] said County not interested in the said Road who being [illegible] for that purpose shall enquire and give their Verdict w[illegible] Roads in Controversy will be the best and most comm[illegible] Main and public Highway, and an Inquest being the [illegible]ade under the Hands and Seals of the said Justices and Juro[illegible] shall be final and conclusive according to WHICH the Road shall be laid out, certifyed and returned as a public Road by the respective Commissioners through whose District it shall extend, and the return thereof together with the said Inquisition being filed in the Office of the Clerk of the said County and entered of Record the said Road shall be deemed and esteemed a public Road or Highway to all Intents and purposes, and be supported and maintained in the respective Districts through which the same shall extend in the same Manner as the other Highways in such Districts are directed and required to be maintained and supported by this Act and the Charge and Expence of such Inquest shall be born and paid out of the Monies to be raised by this Act for the Benefit of the District whose Commissioners shall have created the same by refusing to lay out such Road in the Manner which by the said Inquest shall be found the best and most commodious.

PROVIDED ALWAYS, AND BE IT ENACTED by the Authority aforesaid, that the Inhabitants of the united Districts of Duansburgh and Schoharie shall work upon and keep in Repair so much of the Road leading from Schoharie towards the City of Albany, through Renselaerwyck District as lays between the United Districts of Duansburgh and Schoharie and the Foot of the Hill commonly called the Hellebergh, AND the Inhabitants of Renselaerswyck District are hereby excused from Working on or Contributing towards that part of the above said Schoharie Road, any Thing in this Act to the Contrary notwithstanding.

AND BE IT ENACTED by the same Authority that the said ᵕmmissioners appointed by this Act shall respectively before y Execute any of the powers herein contained take an Oath ᵕn the Holy Evangelists before any Justice of the Peace of the 1 County in the Words following.

, A. B. do Solemnly Swear that I will faithfully, diligently, and partially execute the powers to me given and granted by An :t intitled, "AN ACT for the better laying out, regulating, clear- ng and KEEPING in Repair the public Roads and Highways in the City and County of Albany." or the County of Tryon, as ıe Case may be, So help me God.

AND LASTLY, BE IT ENACTED by the same Authority, that ɑis Act shall be and remain in full Force and Virtue, from its ᵕublication until the first Day of February which will be in the ʕear of our Lord One Thousand seven Hundred and Seventy ıeven.

[CHAPTER 1552.]

[Chapter 1552, of Van Schaack, where the act is printed in full. See chapter 1628.]

An Act to divide the Counties of Albany and Tryon into Districts.

[Passed, March 24, 1772.]

WHEREAS the Inhabitants of the Counties of Albany and Tryon labour under many Inconveniencies for want of having the said Counties divided into proper Districts to remedy which BE IT ENACTED by his Excellency the Governor the Council and the General Assembly and it is hereby enacted by the Authority of the same, That all that Part of the said County of Albany which is comprehended by the City of Albany, shall be one separate and distinct District. That all that Part of the said County of Albany which lays to the Northward of Dutchess County and to the Southward of the South Bounds of Claverack continued to the Eastermost Extent of this Colony, and to the Eastward of Hudson's River shall be one separate and distinct District, and be henceforth called and known by the Name of the District of the Manor of Livingston. That all that Part of the said County of Albany which is bounded on the South by the District of the Manor of Livingston on the East by the East Bounds of this Colony, on the West by Hudson's River, on the North by a Line Beginning at the Mouth of Major Abraham's Creek and running thence up to the first Falls, and from thence East as far as this Colony extends, shall be and is hereby declared to be one separate and distinct District and the same shall be from henceforth called and known by the Name of the District of Claverack. That all that Part of the said County of Albany which lays to the Northward of Claverack District, to the Southward of an East Line from Bearen Island in Hudson's River to the Eastward of Hudson's River and to the West of a straight Line to be drawn from a Point in the said East Line from Bearen Island, ten Miles distant from Hudsons River and to be continued due South until it strikes the North Bounds of the District of Claverack, shall be one separate and distinct District, and be henceforth called and known by the Name of the District of Kinderhook.

That all that Part of the said County of Albany which lays to the Eastward of Kinderhook District to the North of Claverack District to the West of the East Bounds of this Colony, and to the South of an East Line from Bearen Island shall be one separate and distinct District and be henceforth called and known by the Name of King's District.

That all that Part of the said County of Albany which is comprehended within the Limits and Bounds of that Part of the Manor of Rensselaerwyck which lays to the Northward of an East and West Line from Bearen Island aforesaid together with all that part of the said County which lays to the Northward of the said East Line from Bearen Island continued to the East Bounds of this Colony, and to the Southward of the South Bounds of the County of Cumberland continued to the East Bounds of the said Manor excepting thereout the City of Albany, shall be one Separate and distinct District and be henceforth called and known by the Name of the District of the Manor of Rensselaerwyck.

That all that Part of the said County of Albany which is bounded as follows to wit on the South by Rensselaerwyck District, on the North by a Line South eighty four Degrees East drawn from the Mouth of Lewis Creek or Kill, and on the East by a Straight Line drawn from a Point in the North Bounds of Rensselaerwyck District thirteen Miles distant from Hudson's

River to a Point in said Line from the Mouth of Lewis Creek or Kill at ten Miles distant from Hudson's River, and on the West by Hudson's River, shall be one Separate and distinct District and be henceforth called and known by the Name of Schactekoke District.

That all that part of the said County of Albany which lays to the Northward of Rensselaerwyck District to the southward of the said Line from the Mouth of Lewis Creek or Kill continued to the West Bounds of the County of Cumberland to the Eastward of Schactekoke District, and to the Westward of the County of Cumberland, shall be one Separate and distinct District, and be henceforth called and known by the Name of Hosick District.

That all that Part of the said County of Albany which lays to the Northward of Schactekoke and Hosick Districts, and to the South of Battenkill and the County of Charlotte, and to the East of the East Bounds of Saratoga so far North as Batten Kill and to the West of the County of Cumberland shall be one separate and distinct District and be henceforth called and known by the Name of Cambridge District.

That all that Part of the said County of Albany which lays on the East Side of Hudson's River to the Westward of Cambridge District and to the Northward of Schaetekoke District together with all that part of the said County of Albany which lays on the West Side of Hudson's River and to the North of Anthony's Kill, and a West Line drawn from that part of the said Kill where it comes out of the round Lake to the County of Tryon, as also all the Islands laying in Hudson's River between the North and South Bounds of this Tract, shall be one separate and distinct District and be henceforth called and known by the Name of Saratoga District.

That all that Part of the said County of Albany which lays to the Southward of Saratoga District, to the Northward of Rensselaerwyck District to the west of Hudson's River, and to the East of the Township of Schenectady and the County of Tryon, shall be one Separate and Distinct District and be henceforth called and known by the Name of Half Moon District.

That all that Part of the said County of Albany which is comprehended by the Township of Schenectady continued Southerly to Rensselaerwyck District shall be one separate and distinct District, and be henceforth called and known by the Name of Schenectady District.

That all that Part of the said County of Albany which is bounded as follows to wit, beginning at the South West Corner of Schenectady District, thence along the North Bounds of Rensselaerwyck District to the North West Corner thereof, thence along the West Bounds of Rensselaerwyck District to the South East Corner of a Tract of Land granted to Johannes Lawyer and others, thence West to the West Bounds of the said County of Albany, thence along the West Bounds of the said County to the Mohawk River, thence along the Mohawk River to Schenectady District, thence along the West Bounds of the same to the place of beginning, shall be one separate and distinct District and be henceforth called and known by the Name of the United Districts of Duanesburg and Schoharie.

That all that Part of the said County of Albany which lays to the South of Rensselaerwyck District and the united Districts of Duanesburgh and Schoharie and to the North of a West line drawn from the South Bank of the Mouth of Katts Kill to the West Bounds of this Colony, and to the Westward of Hudson's River, shall be one separate and distinct District, and be henceforth called and known by the name of Cocksakie District.

That all that Part of the said County of Albany which lays on the West side of Hudson's River, and on the South of Cocksakie District, shall be one separate and distinct District, and be henceforth called and known by the Name of the great Imbocht District.

That all that Part of the County of Tryon which is bounded as follows, to wit on the East by the West Bounds of the County of Albany, on the West by a North and South Line drawn from the Kill commonly called Anthony's Nose continued to the North and South Bounds of this Colony, on the South by the County of Albany, and south Bounds of this Colony on the North by the North Bounds of this Colony, shall be one separate and distinct District and be henceforth called and known by the Name of the Mohawk District.

That all that Part of the said County of Tryon which is Bounded as follows to wit, on the East, and on the North side of the Mohawk River by the Mohawk District on the West by a North Line from the Little Falls on the North by the North Bounds of this Colony, and on the South by the Mohawk River shall be one separate and distinct District, and be henceforth called and known by the Name of Stone Arabia District.

That all that Part of the said County of Tryon which is comprehended by the following Bounds to wit, on the East by the Mohawk District, on the West by a south Line from the Little Falls, on the South by the South Bounds of this Colony on the North by the Mohawk River shall be one separate and distinct District and be henceforth called and known by the Name of Canajoxharie District.

That all that Part of the said County of Tryon which is comprehended within the following Bounds, to wit, on the East by Stone Arabia District, on the south by the Mohawk River, on the West and North by the Bounds of this Colony shall be one separate and distinct District, and be henceforth called and known by the Name of the German Flatts District.

That all that Part of the said County of Tryon which is comprehended within the following Bounds to wit, on the East by Canajoxharie District on the North by the Mohawk River, southerly and Westerly by the Limits of this Colony shall be one separate and Distinct District, and be henceforth called and known by the Name of Kingsland District.

AND BE IT FURTHER ENACTED by the same Authority, That none of the Lines or Bounds by this Act assigned for the Limits of either of the said Districts shall be deemed to take away abridge destroy or affect the Right and Title of any Body Politic or Corporate or of any Patentee or Patentees or others holding under any Patentee or Patentees in any Manner or by any ways or Means whatsoever, neither shall they be deemed taken or construed as a Confirmation of the Bounds and Rights of any Patent or Patents whatsoever.

AND for the easier assessing and collecting the Taxes in the said Counties of Albany and Tryon, and better payment of the Charges thereof, BE IT ALSO ENACTED by the same Authority, That the Freeholders and Inhabitants of every District in the said Counties as by this Act ascertained are hereby required and authorized yearly and every year upon the first Tuesday in May to elect and appoint one Freeholder to be a Supervisor, two Freeholders to be assessors, one Freeholder to be Collector, two Freeholders to be Overseers of the Poor, two Constables, two Fence Viewers and one Clerk, which Supervisors Assessors and Collectors for the said Districts respectively shall have the same Power and Authority to perform execute and serve, and be liable to the same Pains and Penalties as the Supervisors Assessors and Collectors of the several Counties within this

Colony have or intended to have, or ought to do, or be liable to, by an Act passed in the Year one thousand seven hundred and three entitled "An Act for the better explaining and more effec- "tual putting in Execution an Act of General Assembly made "in the third Year of the Reign of their late Majesties King "William and Queen Mary entitled An Act for defraying the "Public and necessary Charge throughout this Province, and for "maintainin the Poor and preventing Vagabonds."

PROVIDED ALWAYS and be it further enacted by the same Authority, That the Freeholders and Inhabitants of the City of Albany shall and may, and they are hereby required Yearly and every Year on the first Tuesday in May to elect and appoint one Supervisor, two Assessors and one Overseer of the Poor being Freeholders, and two Constables in each of the Wards of the said City and one Collector, and that the Freeholders and Inhabitants of the District of Rensselaerwyck, shall and may and they are hereby required Yearly and every Year on the said first Tuesday in May to elect and appoint two Freeholders to be Supervisors, four Freeholders to be Assessors, and two Freeholders to be Collectors, six Constables and six Fence Viewers, any Thing in this or any other Act or Acts of this Colony to the contrary hereof notwithstanding.

PROVIDED ALSO and be it Enacted by the same Authority That if the Courts of General Sessions of the Peace of the said Counties should hereafter conceive that more Constables and Fence Viewers should be requisite in any of the Districts aforesaid than are by this Act given, that it shall and may be lawful for the said Courts in their respective Counties to order such additional Number of Constables and Fence Viewers to be elected as to them shall seem necessary, any Thing in this or any other Act of this Colony to the contrary hereof notwithstanding.

AND BE IT FURTHER ENACTED by the same Authority that every Supervisor within the said Counties of Albany and Tryon upon entering into his Office shall take the following Oath before any one of his Majesty's Justices of the Peace who is hereby authorized and required to administer the same. "I. "A. B. do swear that I will well truly and impartially, and to the "best of my Understanding, cause the Quotas of the Public "Taxes as well as the contingent Charges of the City and County "of Albany," or County of Tryon as the case may be, "to be "raised levyed collected and paid in such manner that the same, "as near as may be, be equally borne and paid by the Inhabit-

"ants of each respective District in the said County: and that "I will not pass any Account or any Article thereof, wherewith "I do not think the County justly chargeable, nor will I dis-"allow any Account or any Article thereof, wherewith I think "the county justly chargeable, so help me God," of the administration of which Oath the Justice who shall administer the same shall give a Certificate under his Hand and Seal, which Certificate shall be filed with the Clerk of the Supervisors at their first Meeting next after their having been qualified as aforesaid, any Thing in this Act or any other Act to the contrary notwithstanding.

AND BE IT ENACTED by the Authority aforesaid That in Case any of the Supervisors so to be chosen and elected as aforesaid shall after their being chosen and elected refuse to take the said Oath, he or they so refusing shall forfeit and pay the Sum of five Pounds to be recovered before any one of his Majesty's Justices of the Peace of the said City or Counties respectively, by any Person who shall or will prosecute the same to effect, one half of which Fine to be for the proper use and behoof of the person prosecuting as aforesaid and the other half for the use of the Poor of such District for which such supervisor shall have been elected.

AND BE IT FURTHER ENACTED by the same Authority, That it shall and may be lawful for the Freeholders and Inhabitants of such District upon any such refusal made by the Supervisors or any of them as aforesaid, and they are hereby directed and required as soon as may be thereafter to choose and elect another Supervisor or Supervisors in the place and stead of him or them so refusing to be qualified as aforesaid, public Notice being first given of the Day of Election by one or more of his Majesty's Justices of the Peace of such District by Advertisement fixed up at the Usual place of Meeting at least eight Days before such Day of Election, which Supervisor or Supervisors so to be chosen shall and he or they are hereby directed and required to take the Oath and qualify him or themselves in Manner herein before directed: and be liable to the same Fines and Penalties and have the same Powers, as are in this Act directed and required.

BE IT ALSO ENACTED by the authority aforesaid That all and every Person or Persons within the Counties aforesaid who shall be elected and chosen as assessor, Overseer of the Poor, Collector, Constable or Fence Viewer, and shall refuse to execute

that Office, every such Person or Persons shall pay as a Fine for every such Refusal the sum of five Pounds for the use of the Poor in the District where such Refusal shall happen, to be levied by Warrant under the Hand and Seal of any one of his Majesty's Justices of the Peace of the said Counties.

AND BE IT FURTHER ENACTED by the same Authority. That it shall and may be lawful for the Freeholders and Inhabitants of such District upon any such Refusal made by any Assessor, Collector Overseer of the Poor, Constable or Fence Viewer, and they are hereby directed and required as soon as may be thereafter to choose and elect one other Assessor, Collector, Overseer of the Poor, Constable or Fence Viewer in the place and stead of him or them so refusing, Notice being given as aforesaid for electing a Supervisor, which Assessor, Collector, Overseer of the Poor, Constable or Fence Viewer shall have the same Power and Authority to perform execute and serve, and be liable to the same Pains and Penalties as are in this Act directed and required.

PROVIDED ALWAYS and be it enacted by the same Authority that the Freeholders and Inhabitants of the King's District aforesaid may Elect such Supervisors Assessors and Collectors in and for the same District, of Persons being substantial Householders within the same who are not Freeholders.

[CHAPTER 1553.]

[Chapter 1553, of Van Schaack, where the act is printed in full. Revived by chapter 1696.]

An Act to prevent the Waste of Fire Wood in the County of Albany.

[Passed, March 24, 1772.]

BE IT ENACTED by his Excellency the Governor the Council and the General Assembly and it is hereby enacted by the Authority of the same, That no person or persons whatsoever shall either by themselves their Servants or Slaves bring any Wood to be used as firewood into the City of Albany or into that part of the Manor of Rensselaerwyck which lays on the West side of Hudson's River, and between the North Bounds of the said City, and the Creek commonly called the fifth Creek and to the Eastward of a due North Line drawn from a certain point in the North Bounds of the said City, one Mile distant from Hudson's River either for Sale or otherwise, under the Diameter of six Inches if such Wood

· of the Pine kind, and four Inches Diameter if of any other kind Wood at the Stump end on Penalty of forfeiting and paying the ım of six Shillings for every Load of Wood which shall contain ore than six Sticks or Pieces of Wood under the size aforesaid, · be recovered before the Mayor Recorder or any one of the ldermen of the said City, or before any other of the Justices of ıe Peace for the City and County of Albany, on the Oath of one : more credible Witnesses, which said Penalty shall be paid into ıe Hands of the County Treasurer and applied from Time to ime to such Public uses as the Supervisors of the said City and ounty or the major Part of them shall direct by Warrant under ıeir Hands and Seals

BE IT ALSO ENACTED by the same Authority That this Act ıall be in force from the Publication thereof until the first Day f February, one thousand seven hundred and Seventy seven.

[CHAPTER 1554.]

[Chapter 1554, of Van Schaack, where the act is printed in full.]

An Act to Divide the Precinct of the Wallkill in Ulster County into two Precincts and other Purposes therein mentioned.

[Passed, March 24, 1772.]

WHEREAS the Precinct of the Wallkill in the County of Ulster is so extensive and the Inhabitants thereof so much increased that it is not only become very inconvenient for the People to Assemble in Order to Transact the Public Business at their annual Meetings, but the Duties of the several Officers are become Difficult and Burthensome, for Remedy whereof

BE IT THEREFORE ENACTED by his Excellency, the Governor the Council and the General Assembly And it is hereby enacted by the Authority of the same, That the said Precinct of the Wallkill in the County of Ulster shall be and hereby is Divided into two Precincts by the following Lines to wit, BEGINNING at the Southwest Corner of a Tract of Land granted to Phineas McIntosh, which said Corner is also the Southeast Corner of a Tract of Two thousand Acres of Land granted to Patrick MacNight and running thence along the Southward Bounds of the last mentioned Tract of Patrick MacNight and along the Southwest Bounds of a Tract of Two thousand Acres of Land granted to Thomas Noxon. and along the Southwest Bounds of a Tract of Five thousand Acres of Land granted to Francis Harrison and others, and along the Southwest Bounds of a Tract of Eight thousand Acres of Land granted to Philip Schuyler and others, and so continuing a Line on the same Course with the Southwest Bounds of the last mentioned Tract to the River commonly called Peakadasinck River or Chawangonk Kill.

AND BE IT FURTHER ENACTED by the Authority aforesaid that all the Lands heretofore comprehended within the said Precinct of the Wallkill lying to the Northeast of the aforesaid Division Lines shall be called by the Name of HANOVER Precinct, and that all the Lands heretofore comprehended within the said Precinct of the Wallkill lying to the Southwest of the aforesaid Division Lines shall continue to be called Wallkill Precinct

AND BE IT FURTHER ENACTED by the Authority aforesaid that the Freeholders and Inhabitants of each of the aforesaid two Precincts called Hanover and Wallkill shall have full Power and Authority to assemble and hold Annual Meetings within their respective Precincts and then and there by Plurality of Voices to elect and chuse One Supervisor, one Clerk, Two Assessors, Two Collectors, Two Constables, Three Overseers of the Poor, Three Fence Viewers, Two Commissioners for Highways, with so many Overseers of the Highways as to them shall seem necessary and convenient who when so chosen and elected shall be respectively Vested with and have the same Authorities and Powers, and be subject to the like Rules, Regulations, Fines and Penalties as are by Law prescribed for the like Officers respectively in other Precincts in the said County.

AND BE IT FURTHER ENACTED by the Authority aforesaid that the Freeholders and Inhabitants of each of the aforesaid Precincts at their respective Annual Meetings shall have the same Power and Authority by Plurality of Voices to make such By Laws and Regulations as the Freeholders and Inhabitants of the said Wallkill Precinct might heretofore lawfully have done. And that the Annual Meetings for the said two Precincts respectively shall be held on the first Tuesday in April in every Year.

AND BE IT FURTHER ENACTED that the Freeholders and Inhabitants of Hanover Precinct aforesaid shall hold their first Annual Meeting at the now Dwelling House of Stephanus Crist on the first Tuesday in April next And that the Freeholders and Inhabitants of Wallkill Precinct aforesaid shall hold their first Annual Meeting at the now Dwelling House of Samuel Watkins on the first Tuesday in April next, and that the before mentioned two Places for holding the first Annual Meetings shall continue and be the Places for holding the Annual Meetings in the aforesaid two Precincts respectively until such Time as another Place shall be agreed upon by a Majority of the Freeholders and Inhabitants of the said Precincts respectively at their respective Annual Meetings, which Place so agreed upon shall remain the Place for holding the Annual Meetings until altered in Manner as aforesaid.

AND WHEREAS great Tumults, Disorders and Contentions frequently arise at Precinct Meetings for the want of proper Order and Method in taking the Votes of the Inhabitants BE IT ENACTED That the Magistrates living in each of the said Precincts shall and are hereby Required to give their Attendance at the said Annual Meetings of the Inhabitants at the Times and Places hereinbefore mentioned who shall preside at the said Elections for the keeping good Order and Decorum And the Clerk of the said Precincts shall be in the Presence and under the Inspection of the said Magistrates so met at such Hour as they shall Direct proceed to open the Poll if demanded and take down in Writing the Names of the Electors as they respectively present themselves, and also the several Names of the several and respective Persons by the said Electors severally nominated for Executing the several and respective Offices hereinbefore mentioned, and the said Magistrates are hereby Authorized to Examine and Inspect the said Poll List when closed, and Return to the Clerk the Names of the several Persons they find are duly Elected by a Majority of Voices in the several Offices aforesaid of which an Entry shall be made in the Precinct Books and being so entered shall be a sufficient Authority to each of the Person or Persons so Elected to proceed to the Execution of his and their Duties. PROVIDED always that each and every Officer shall previous thereto take the Oaths of Office directed by Law and also that every Collector and Constable shall enter into Bond with good Security in such Penalty as the Magistrates shall think suf. ient well and faithfully to discharge the Duties of their respective Offices and in due Time pay into the Hands of such Person or Persons as they are or shall by Law be directed, all such Sum and Sums of money as shall be by them received in their respective Offices of Collector and Constable

AND WHEREAS divers Disputes and Controversies have heretofore arisen and Yearly arise between the Assessors, Collectors and Constables of the Precinct of the Wallkill and the Assessors, Collectors and Constables of the Precinct of Mamecoting respecting the Limits and Bounds of said Precincts along the Shawangonk Mountains To Render the same for the future indubitable BE IT ENACTED That from and after the first Monday in April next, All the Lands from the Westerly Bank of the said River commonly called the Peakadasinck or Shawangonk Kill Southward of the Platta Kill and North of the Division Line between the Counties of Ulster and Orange shall be and hereby are annexed to the Precinct of Mamecoting, And that the said Westerly Bank of the said River commonly called the Peakadasinck River or Shawangonk Kill shall be the Western Bounds of the said Precinct of the Wall kill and Hanover

PROVIDED always and be it also Enacted by the same Authority that nothing in this Act contained shall be construed deemed or adjudged to extend, benefit or establish the Claims of the Proprietors of the Patent commonly called the Patent of Minisink or of any Persons that have held or still do hold Lands within the same or to defeat or prejudice or in any Manner to alter or affect the Claims of any Patentees their or either of their Heirs or Assigns in any Patent or Grant within the said County of Ulster; It being the Intention of the Legislature that the private Claims of all Parties concerned and the Bounds of all Patents and Lands in the same County shall remain for any Thing in this Act contained to the contrary in the same State and Condition with respect to all Disputes and Controversies that now or may hereafter subsist as if this Act had never been passed.

AND BE IT ENACTED by the Authority aforesaid, that the Freeholders and Inhabitants of the Precinct of Mamecoting at their Annuai Meetings for chusing and electing Precinct Officers shall and may choose one Supervisor, who shall have the same Powers and perform the same Duties as the Supervisors of any other Town or Precinct within the said County have or are subject to any Law, Usage or Custom to the contrary thereof in any wise notwithstanding. Provided always that the whole of the Lands comprehended in the Patent lately granted to Lieutenant James Mc. Donald shall be considered as in the Precinct of the Walkil any Thing in this Act contained to the contrary notwithstanding.

[CHAPTER 1555.]

[Chapter 1555, of Van Schaack, where the act is printed in full. See chapters 652, 756.]

An Act for dividing the South Precinct in the County of Dutchess into three Precincts.

[Passed, March 24, 1772.]

WHEREAS the South Precinct in the County of Dutchess is so extensive that many of the Inhabitants cannot attend the Annual Meetings for Election of Officers without great inconveniency, and is become so populous that the Election can no longer be held with due Order and Regularity.

BE IT THEREFORE ENACTED by his Excellency the Governor the Council, and the General Assembly, and it is hereby enacted by the Authority of the same, That the said South Precinct, shall after the first Day of April next be divided into three Precincts in the Manner following, the West Division or Precinct to be called Philip's Precinct and bounded as follows, to wit, southerly by Westchester County, Easterly by the East Line of Beverly Robinson's long Lot number four, Northerly by the Division Line between Rumbout and Philip's Patent and Westerly by Hudson's River; and the Middle Division or Precinct to comprehend that part of Philip's Patent within the said South Precinct, known by the Name of the three East short Lots, and the two Eastern Long Lots, to be called Fredricksburgh, and bounded as follows, to wit Southerly by Westchester County, Northerly by Pauling's Precinct, Easterly by the Oblong and Westerly by Philip's Precinct: The Eastermost Division or Precinct to comprehend the Lands called the Oblong, lying within the said South Precinct to be called the South East Precinct and Bounded as follows, to wit, Southerly by Westchester County, Westerly by Fredricksburgh Precinct, Northerly by Pauling's Precinct until it comes to the Connecticut Line, and Easterly by the Connecticut Line, in which said three Precincts there shall be annually chosen by the Majority of Voices of the Freeholders and Inhabitants in each respective Precinct, one Clerk, one Supervisor, two Assessors, one Collector two Constables, three Overseers of the Poor, three Fence Viewers, two Pound Masters and six Overseers of the Highways or as many Pound Masters and Overseers of Highways as the Majority of the Inhabitants at their said Annual Meetings respectively shall think fit, which said Officers so elected shall each and every of them have the same Powers and Authorities, that any of the like Officers have in any other of the Precincts in the said County, and shall be liable to the same Pains and Penalties, any Thing in this or any other Act to the contrary thereof notwithstanding.

AND BE IT ENACTED by the Authority aforesaid, That the Justices and Overseers of the Poor shall as soon as possible after the Division of the said precinct as aforesaid call together all and every of the Poor of the said Precincts and make as equal Distribution of them as is possible in the said Precincts to be for the future maintained by, and reside in the Precinct they shall then be allotted to, and that all such Sum or Sums of Money that shall or may be due by the said Precinct at the Division thereof for the Maintenance of the Poor, shall be levied proportionably on each of the respective precincts at the next meeting of the Supervisors and Assessors.

AND BE IT ENACTED That the Inhabitants of Fredricksburgh Precinct shall annually meet on the first Tuesday of April for the Election of Officers for said Precinct at the House of Thomas Smith, in Fredricksburgh, and the Inhabitants of Philipses Precinct shall meet on the same Day for the like purposes at the House of John Crompton in Philipses Precinct, and the Inhabitants of the South East Precinct shall meet on the same Day for the like purposes at the Dwelling House of John Rider in the said Precinct.

AND BE IT ENACTED That it shall and may be lawful for the Inhabitants of each of the aforesaid Precincts, at any of their annual Meetings for electing Officers as aforesaid by a Majority of Voices of the Inhabitants so met, to appoint any other certain Place for the next Election, which shall continue to be the Place of Election till another appointment be made in the same Manner.

AND BE IT ENACTED by the Authority aforesaid. That the Inhabitants of Philipses and Fredricksburgh Precincts having personal Estates to the value of sixty Pounds free from all In cumbrance, shall be and hereby are made liable to serve as Jurors on the Trial of Causes in Justices Courts in the said Precincts of Philips and Fredricksburgh, any Thing in the afore said Act to the contrary notwithstanding.

[CHAPTER 1556.]

[Chapter 1556, of Van Schaack, where the act is printed in full. Continued by chapter 1694.]

An Act to prevent the Destruction of Fish in the County of Suffolk.

[Passed, March 24, 1772.]

WHEREAS the Fish in the Bays, Rivers and Creeks in the County of Suffolk are greatly diminished, and are likely in a very short Time to be entirely destroyed, by reason of the Inhabitants fishing with long Seins or Nets in their Winter Quarters, to the great Damage of the Inhabitants of said County and the Public in general; to prevent the same for the future.

BE IT ENACTED by his Excellency the Governor the Council and the General Assembly, and it is hereby enacted by the Authority of the same, That if any person or persons after the publication of this Act, shall draw any Sein or net of any length whatsoever; or set any sein or Net of more than six Fathoms in length with Mashes not less than three Inches square, from the fifteenth Day of November, to the fifteenth Day of April in any Year during the continuance of this Act, in any of the Bays, Rivers or Creeks in said County, such Person or Persons shall for each Offence forfeit the Sum of one hundred Pounds with Costs of Suit, to be recovered in any Court of Record within this Colony, by any Person or Persons, that will sue for the same, the one half of the Forfeiture when recovered shall belong to the prosecutor or prosecutors, and the other half to be paid to the Treasurer of the said County to be disposed of by the Supervisors towards defraying the Public Expence of the said County.

BE IT FURTHER ENACTED by the Authority aforesaid, That if any Person or Persons shall be discovered to have any Quantity of Fish or to have sold any Quantity of Fish, from the fifteenth Day of November to the fifteenth Day of April, such person or persons shall be deemed guilty, and shall suffer the same Penalty as aforesaid to be recovered and applied as above directed by this Act, unless he can make it appear that he has caught them otherwise, than by such Seins or Nets prohibited by this Act.

AND BE IT FURTHER ENACTED by the Authority aforesaid. That if any Person or Persons shall be seen to carry any Seins or Nets, in any fishing Craft in any of the Bays, Rivers or

Creeks in the said County, within the aforesaid Time from the fifteenth Day of November to the fifteenth Day of April, of more than six Fathoms in length, and shall be convicted thereof, such Person or Persons shall forfeit the Sum of five Pounds to be recovered by any Person or Persons who will sue for the same with Costs of Suit, before any one of his Majesty's Justices of the Peace of said County, and disposed of as the other Forfeitures of this Act are directed. This Act to continue in force from the publication hereof until the fifteenth Day of April which will be in the Year of our Lord one thousand seven hundred and seventy six.

[CHAPTER 1557.]

[Chapter 1557, of Van Schaack, where the act is printed in full. See chapter 1785.]

An Act to prevent infectious Distempers in the Counties therein mentioned.

[Passed, March 24, 1772.]

WHEREAS the Practice of Inoculation for the small pox is carried on in Houses situate near the Public Roads and landing places in the Counties of West Chester, Dutchess and Orange greatly prejudicial to the Inhabitants thereof.

BE IT THEREFORE ENACTED by his Excellency the Governor the Council and the General Assembly, and it is hereby enacted by the Authority of the same, That in Case any Person or Persons whatsoever shall carry on the Practice of Inoculation for the small pox in the Counties of West Chester and Dutchess, and in the precincts of Goshen and Cornwall in the County of Orange within the distance of a quarter of a Mile of any Dwelling House, Public Road, or Landing Place within the Counties aforesaid shall forfeit the sum of five Pounds for every such Offence, which Offence is to be proved by two credible Witnesses before any one of his Majesty's Justices of the Peace within the Counties aforesaid where the Offence is committed who is hereby impowered to hear, try and determine the said Offence or Offences, to give Judgment and grant Execution for the same, with Cost of Suit against the Offender or Offenders Goods and Chattels within the space of three Months, one third of the said Forfeiture to be for the prosecutor, and the other two thirds for the use of the Poor of the Town, Borough, Manor or Precinct within the said Counties where the Offence shall be committed and in Case no Goods or Chattels can be found, then the Offender or Offenders shall be committed to Goal for the space of three Months without Bail or Main-prize, except such Fine as aforesaid shall be sooner paid.

PROVIDED ALWAYS, and be it further Enacted by the Authority aforesaid. That Nothing herein contained shall be construed to prevent any private Family from being inoculated in their own Dwelling Houses within the said Counties and precincts, provided the same shall be a Quarter of a Mile distant at the least from any public Landing, and provided also that no person whatsoever shall be there Inoculated except their own Family, any Thing herein contained to the contrary notwithstanding.

This Act to continue in force until the first Day of February one thousand seven hundred and seventy five.

[CHAPTER 1558.]

[Chapter 1558, of Van Schaack, where the act is printed in full. See chapter 172.]

An Act to amend an Act entitled "An Act "for the more effectual preservation of Deer "and other Game and the Destruction of "Wolves, Wild Cats and other Vermin." so far "as it relates to the Township of Huntingtown "and the precinct of Islip in Suffolk County.

[Passed, March 24, 1772.]

WHEREAS by the third Clause in the aforesaid Act entitled "An Act for the more effectual preservation of Deer and other "Game, and the Destruction of Wolves, Wild Cats and other "Vermin." passed in the seventh year of her late Majesty Queen Ann, it is among other Things provided and enacted that whosoever whether Christian or Indian Freeman or Slave after the publication thereof should kill or destroy any Heath Hens, Partridges or Quails, their Eggs or Young ones, within the Counties of Suffolk Queens or Kings at any Time in the Months of April. May, June, or July should for every such Offence forfeit and pay the Sum of two Shillings and six pence, or in Default thereof suffer two Days and an half Imprisonment. AND WHEREAS it is conceived that the Penalty mentioned in the said Act is too low and the Time therein allowed for the Killing of the said Game too long to answer the good purposes thereby intended.

BE IT THEREFORE ENACTED by his Excellency the Governor the Council and the General Assembly and it is hereby enacted by the Authority of the same That if any Person or Persons whatsoever within the Township of Huntingtown, or the Precinct of Islip in Suffolk County after the publication of this Act shall kill or destroy any Heath Hen, Partridge or Quail their Young ones or Eggs at any Time from the first Day of March to the fifth Day of October in any of the Years during the continuance of this Act every such person or persons shall forfeit the sum of ten shillings with Costs of suit for every Offence contrary to the true Intent and meaning of this Act, the one half of all such Forfeitures shall be to him that will sue for the same, to be recovered before any one of his Majesty's Justices of the Peace in this Colony, who is hereby authorized and required to hear and determine the same, and the other half to the use of the Poor of the aforesaid Town or precinct where the Offence shall be committed; and for want of Effects whereon to levy the aforesaid Forfeitures with Costs of suit, such person or persons shall be committed to the common Goal of the County where the Offence is committed, for the space of one Month if not sooner discharged by paying the aforesaid Forfeitures with Costs.

And for the better conviction of Offenders against this Act BE IT ENACTED by the Authority aforesaid, That every person or persons in whose Custody shall be found, or who shall expose to sale, any Heath Hens, Partridges, Quails, their young ones or Eggs from the first Day of March to the fifth Day of October, and shall be convicted thereof by the Oath of one credible Witness or by the Confession of the person shall be deemed and adjudged Guilty of the Offence and suffer as aforesaid, this Act to be and remain in force until the first Day of February in the Year of our Lord one thousand seven hundred and eighty.

[CHAPTER 1559.]

[Chapter 1559, of Van Schaack, where the act is printed in full.]

An Act for the better ascertaining the Boundaries of the Counties of Cumberland and Gloucester.

[Passed, March 24, 1772.]

WHEREAS his present most gracious Majesty by his Royal Letters Patent under the Great Seal of this Colony bearing Date the nineteenth Day of March in the Year of our Lord one thousand seven hundred and sixty eight was pleased to erect and constitute into one Distinct and separate County. ALL that Tract or District of Land situate in this Colony on the West side of Connecticut River, Beginning at a Point on the West Bank of the same River opposite to where the Line run for the Partition Line betwen the Colonies of the Massachusetts Bay and New Hampshire touches the East side of the same River, and running thence West ten Degrees North on a direct Line about twenty six Miles to the south East Corner of a Tract of Land called Stamford, thence North about thirteen Degrees East on a direct Line fifty six Miles to the south East Corner of the Township of Socialborough in the County of Albany: thence North about fifty three Degrees East on a direct Line thirty miles to the south West Corner of the Township of Tunbridge;—thence along the south Bounds thereof, and of Stratford and Thetford about eighteen miles to Connecticut River aforesaid, and thence along the West Banks of the same River to the place of beginning. And did thereby ordain, establish and declare that all and singular the Lands comprized within the Limits aforesaid should forever thereafter be continue and remain a distinct and separate County to be called known and distinguished by the Name of the County of Cumberland: and did further Grant and declare that his loving Subjects then residing, and who thereafter should Inhabit within the same County might at their own Charge erect a Court House and Goal in the Township of Chester, which as nearest to the center of the said County would be most convenient AND WHEREAS his said most gracious Majesty by other Letters Patent under the Great Seal of the said Colony bearing date the sixteenth Day of March in the Year of our Lord one thousand seven hundred and seventy was further pleased to erect and constitute into another distinct and separate County. ALL that certain Tract or District of Land situate in this Colony on the West Side of the said Connecticut River to the Northward of the said County of Cumberland, Beginning at the North West Corner of the said County of Cumberland, and thence running North fifty Miles; thence East to Connecticut River, thence along the West Bank of the same River as it runs to the North East Corner of the said County of Cumberland on the said River, and thence along the North Bounds of the said County of Cumberland to the place of beginning above mentioned, and did thereby ordain establish and declare that all and singular the said Lands so comprized within the Limits last above-mentioned should forever thereafter be continue and remain a County distinct and separate by itself to be called distinguished and known by the Name of the County of Gloucester, and that the Township of Kingsland contained within the said County of Gloucester should forever thereafter be the County Town of and for the said County, and that it should and might be lawful for the Inhabitants of the said County of Gloucester at their own Expence and charge to erect within the said Township of Kingsland a Court House and Goal for the said County of Gloucester AND WHEREAS the Limits of several of the Townships upon which by the said first recited Letters Patent the said County of Cumberland is bounded have never been fixed, surveyed nor ascertained by Lawful Authority, nor the said Townships hitherto been granted under the great seal of this Colony, and the said County of Gloucester being bounded and depending upon the said County of Cumberland, both the said Counties are thereby at present exposed to the Danger and Inconveniencies of an Obscure precarious and uncertain Jurisdiction, which must be productive of future Controversy and disquiet, and greatly embarrass the Courts, Ministers and Officers of Justice in the exercise of their authority and Duty, for Remedy whereof,

BE IT ENACTED by his Excellency the Governor the Council and the General Assembly, and it is hereby enacted by the Authority of the same, That the said County of Cumberland shall forever hereafter be bounded and limited as follows, to wit. BEGINNING on the West Bank of Connecticut River opposite to the point where the Partition Line between the Colonies of the Massachusetts Bay and New Hampshire touches the East side of the said River, and extending from thence North eighty Degrees West until such Line shall meet with and be intersected by another Line proceeding on a Course south ten Degrees West from the North West Corner of a Tract of Land granted under the Great Seal of this Colony on the fourth Day of September one thousand seven hundred and seventy to James Abeel and nine other persons and extending from the said Point of intersection North ten Degrees East until such Line shall meet with and be intersected by another Line to be drawn on a Course North sixty Degrees West from the South West Corner of a Tract of Land granted under the Great Seal of this Colony on the thirteenth Day of November in the Year of our Lord one thousand seven hundred and sixty nine and erected into a Township by the Name of Royalton, and running from the last mentioned Point of intersection south sixty Degrees East to the

West Bank of Connecticut River, and so down along the West Bank of the said River as the same River winds and turns to the place of beginning; all and singular which Lands included and comprized within the Limits and Description last aforesaid shall be continue and forever remain a distinct and separate County to be called known and distinguished by the Name of the County of Cumberland.

AND BE IT FURTHER ENACTED by the Authority aforesaid That the said County of Gloucester shall forever hereafter be bounded and limited as follows, to wit, on the South by the North Bounds of the County of Cumberland on the East by the East Bounds of this Colony, on the North by the North Bounds thereof, on the West and North West partly by a Line to be drawn from the North west Corner of the said County of Cumberland on a Course North ten Degrees East until such Line shall meet with and be intersected by another Line proceeding on an East Course from the south Bank of the Mouth of Otter Creek, and partly by another Line to be drawn and continued from the said last mentioned point of Intersection on a Course North fifty Degrees East until it meets with and terminates at the said North Bounds of the Colony all and singular which Lands included and comprized within the Limits and description last aforesaid shall be continue and forever remain a distinct and separate County, to be called known and distinguished by the Name of the County of Gloucester.

[CHAPTER 1560.]

[Chapter 1560, of Van Schaack, where the act is printed in full.]

An Act for erecting a more convenient Court House and Goal; for altering the Terms appointed for holding the Courts of Common Pleas and General Sessions of the Peace; and for enabling the Inhabitants to elect Supervisors and other County Officers, in and for the County of Cumberland.

[Passed, March 24, 1772.]

WHEREAS it is necessary to the Administration of Justice that a more convenient Court House and Goal should be built in some convenient place in the County of Cumberland which his Majesty hath been pleased to erect into a separate County with the power of holding an Inferior Court of Common pleas, and a Court of General Sessions of the Peace; And it is also highly expedient, that the Inhabitants of the said County should be enabled to elect and choose Supervisors and other County Officers for the said County.

BE IT THEREFORE ENACTED by his Excellency the Governor the Council and the General Assembly, and it is hereby enacted by the Authority of the same, That the Supervisors to be chosen for the said County in the manner hereafter directed shall assemble and meet together on the last Tuesday in May next, at the Court-House in the Township of Chester in the said County, and shall then and there, by plurality of Voices of such of them as shall then and there be assembled, agree upon determine and ascertain the Township or Place within the said County, where a Court House and Goal shall be erected and built and shall certify and declare the same by an Instrument under their Hands and Seals, which shall be filed with the Clerk of the said County and recorded in his Office; and such Township or Place so to be agreed upon and ascertained shall be and remain the County Town of and for the said County; if not disapproved of by the Governor or Commander in Chief for the Time being with the Advice and Consent of the Council.

AND BE IT FURTHER ENACTED by the authority aforesaid. That it shall and may be lawful to and for the Supervisors of the said County, or the major Part of them, and they are hereby directed and required after ascertaining the Township or Place wherein the said Court House and Goal shall be erected to raise levy and collect upon and from the Freeholders and Inhabitants of the said County a sum not exceeding two hundred and fifty Pounds to be applied towards the erecting and building such Court House and Goal in and for the said County, and that the same shall be raised levied and collected in the same manner as the Necessary and contingent Charges of other Counties of this Colony are by Law directed to be raised and levied.

AND BE IT FURTHER ENACTED by the Authority aforesaid, That the Supervisors of the said County, or the major Part of them shall nominate and appoint three fit Persons to superintend and direct the Building of the said Court-House and Goal, and the laying out and expending the Monies to be raised for that purpose, and who shall, and are hereby enjoined to render a just Account thereof upon Oath to the Court of General Sessions of the Peace when thereunto required, and the respective Collectors who shall levy and collect the said money shall and are hereby directed and required to pay the same into the Hands of the said three Persons so to be appointed as aforesaid to superintend the said Business.

AND BE IT FURTHER ENACTED by the Authority aforesaid That the Judges and Justices of the Peace of the said County shall assemble and meet together at the Court House in the said Township of Chester on the first Tuesday in May next, and that they or the major Part of them so to be assembled, shall and they are hereby authorized and required to form divide and distinguish such Parts of the said County as are not erected into Townships under the Great Seal of this Colony into Convenient Districts of which a Description shall be made in Writing and subscribed by them and filed with the Clerk of the said County and the same shall also be recorded by him in a Book to be kept for that purpose, and the said Districts so to be formed, shall remain and continue Districts until the same shall be erected into Townships by Letters Patent under the Great Seal of this Colony. And it shall and may be lawful to and for the Freeholders and Inhabitants of each respective District on the third Tuesday in May next to elect and choose from among the Freeholders and Inhabitants of the same respectively one Supervisor, two Assessors, two Collectors, two Overseers of the Poor three Commissioners for laying out the Highways, & also so many Persons to be Surveyors & Overseers of the Highways, as the Major Part of the Freeholders and Inhabitants of each Town and District shall judge necessary, two Fence Viewers, and four Constables, which Officers so from Time to Time to be elected and chosen shall have and enjoy, and are hereby invested with all the Rights and powers which such County Officers have and enjoy within the other Counties of this Colony, and shall be and are hereby made subject and liable to all the Regulations and Penalties directed by an Act passed in this present sessions entitled. "An Act to enable the Inhabitants "of the County of Charlotte to raise and defray the Public and "Necessary Charges of the said County and to choose County "Officers," and that it shall and may be lawful to and for the Freeholders and Inhabitants of each respective Township now or hereafter to be erected, and of each respective District yearly and every year forever thereafter to choose other Freeholders and Inhabitants of each respective Township and District to succeed to and supply the said several Offices, the Elections for Townships to be made at the Times and Places prescribed by their respective Charters, and for Districts on the third Tuesday in May in every Year: And that a County Treasurer shall also be annually appointed and chosen for the said County of Cumberland in the Manner and Form, and for the purposes, and to be subject to the Regulations and Penalties prescribed and directed in and by the said last mentioned Act with respect to the County Treasurer of the said County of Charlotte.

AND BE IT FURTHER ENACTED that the Public and necessary Charges of the said County of Cumberland, shall be raised levied and defrayed in the same Manner as the Public and necessary Charges of the other Counties of the said Colony are by Law directed to be raised and defrayed.

AND BE IT FURTHER ENACTED by the Authority aforesaid, That from and after the first Tuesday in June now next ensuing, the Inferior Courts of Common Pleas and General Sessions of the Peace for the said County shall begin sit and be held in and for the said County, in the County Town so to be appointed in pursuance of this Act, and at the four several Times following (to wit) on the second Tuesday in June, the second Tuesday in September, the second Tuesday in December, and the second Tuesday in March in every Year, which said several Terms or sittings shall be held and continue for any Time not exceeding four Days respectively: And the said respective Courts shall have, exercise and enjoy all the Powers and Authorities lawfully exercised and enjoyed by any other the like Courts within this Colony. PROVIDED ALWAYS and be it further enacted that the first and next of the said Courts of Common Pleas and General Sessions of the Peace shall be opened for the said County at the Time and place to which the same now stand adjourned, and shall from thence be adjourned with all presentments, Indictments, Suits, Causes, Plaints, Writts, processes and proceedings, whether Criminal or Civil, and all Parties charged, prosecuting or defending therein, to the next following Term established by this Act, and to the Place which in pursuance hereof shall be appointed for the County Town of the said County, and the same shall then and there be proceeded upon as the Law directs, any Thing in this Act, or any Law Ordinance, Usage or Custom to the contrary thereof in any wise notwithstanding.

PROVIDED ALWAYS and be it also enacted by the Authority aforesaid, That notwithstanding any Thing in this Act, or the Letters Patent erecting the said County of Cumberland contained to the contrary, it shall and may be lawful for the

Governor or Commander in Chief for the Time being with the Advice and Consent of the Council, by Ordinance under the Great Seal of this Colony from Time to Time to fix the Terms and Times for the sittings of the several Courts in this Act mentioned, as hath been anciently used in the other Counties of this Colony.

[CHAPTER 1561.]

[Chapter 1561, of Van Schaack, where the act is printed in full. Amended by chapter 1685.]

An Act for the better laying out regulating and keeping in repair the Common and Public Highways in the County of Charlotte.

[Passed, March 24, 1772.]

WHEREAS Nothing is more highly conducive to the settlement and Improvement of a new Country and the Ease Credit and Advantage of it's Inhabitants, than the well regulating laying out and keeping in repair the Public Roads and Highways; and none having hitherto been established by lawful Authority within the County of Charlotte.

BE IT THEREFORE ENACTED by his Excellency the Governor the Council and the General Assembly, and it is hereby enacted by the Authority of the same, That Philip Skene, William Duer, Patrick Smith, Alexander McNathan, Jonathan Baker, Archibald Campbell, Thomas Clark, Jacob March, Benjamin Spencer, Simon Metcalf Philip Ombury Jeremiah French and James Gray, shall be and are hereby appointed Commissioners of the Highways for the said County, and it shall and may be lawful to and for the said Commissioners to assemble and meet at the House of Colonel Philip Skene on the third Tuesday in May next, and they the said Commissioners or the major Part of them being so met are hereby authorized and required then and there to agree, determine upon, alter regulate, and establish all such Public Roads and Highways as they or the major Part of them shall conceive and judge to be convenient or necessary, provided that all Main Roads shall be of the Breadth of four Rods and all Cross and other Roads of the Breadth of two Rods at least; and the said Commissioners at their said first Meeting shall and may agree upon such place and Times as to the Majority of them shall seem meet for any future Meeting.

AND for the better execution of the Trust hereby reposed in the said Commissioners. BE IT FURTHER ENACTED that regular Minutes and Entries shall be made and preserved of all their Acts and proceedings in a Book to be kept for that purpose by the Clerk of the Peace of the said County, and all Orders or Certificates for the laying out establishing or altering such Public Roads shall be made in writing and signed by the said Commissioners and recorded in the said Book. And it shall and may be lawful to and for the said Commissioners and they are hereby directed and required to nominate any two of them the said Commissioners to whom it shall be found most convenient to superintend and direct the laying running out or altering the respective Roads to be from Time to Time agreed upon and established by them, And the said Commissioners shall also and they are hereby authorized and required to distribute and divide such parts of the said County as are not erected into Townships by Letters Patent under the great Seal of this Province into convenient Districts and to assign and appoint to the respective Inhabitants of each Township and District the part and proportion of the several Roads on which they shall labour and be employed, and also to elect and choose out of each respective District to be formed by them two or more of the Inhabitants of the same respectively to be surveyors of the Highways for the District in which they reside, and such Persons so chosen shall accept and faithfully discharge the said Office and together with the Surveyors of the Highways to be chosen for the several Townships which are invested with that Privilege by Royal Grant, shall and are hereby required to be obedient to the Orders and Instructions of the said Commissioners in all Things touching the Duties of their respective Offices.

AND BE IT FURTHER ENACTED by the Authority aforesaid that the Clerk of the Peace of the said County for the Time being shall and he is hereby directed and required to furnish and transmit to each of the respective Surveyors of the Highways of the said County certified Copies of all such Acts Orders and Instructions of the said Commissioners as may concern each of them respectively. And the said Clerk in Consideration of the several Duties enjoyned upon him by this Act, shall be and is hereby exempted from contributing to the laying out and repairing the Highways of the said County.

AND BE IT FURTHER ENACTED by the Authority aforesaid That every Inhabitant of the said County being a Freeholder or Householder shall by virtue of this Act be compellable to work upon the Highways six Days in every Year, and every other Inhabitant not being the son or Servant of a Freeholder or Householder and of the Age of eighteen Years and upwards, three Days in every year and to furnish themselves respectively with an Ax Crow-bar, Spade or Mattock, according as they shall be required by the respective Surveyors of the Township or District in which they reside and whenever it may be necessary to employ Teams and Carriages in repairing the Highways it shall and may be lawful to and for each respective Surveyor of the Highways to direct and appoint such and so many of the Inhabitants of the Township or District under his superintendance as he shall think proper to provide a Team, Cart or Waggon and an able man to manage the same, to labour on the Highway, and such Inhabitant so appointed, shall and is hereby required to comply therewith accordingly, and one Days Work with such Team, Carriage and able Man to manage the same shall be esteemed and accepted as equal to and in lieu of three Days labour of a single Man, and to prevent the Idleness and Negligence which too frequently prevail in the Discharge of this Necessary Service, eight Hours actual Labour and not less shall be computed and accepted for a Days work and the Surveyors of each respective Township and District, shall and are hereby respectively required to keep an Account according to the best of their Judgment of the Hours such Inhabitant shall refuse or neglect to work of the Time required of him by this Act and to transmit the same annually to the Clerk of the Peace of the said County with a List of the Names of all the Inhabitants under their respective Superintendance, on whom the Duty of repairing the Highways is hereby enjoyned, to be by the said Clerk exhibited to the said Commissioners at their then succeeding Meeting.

AND BE IT FURTHER ENACTED That the several Surveyors, of the Highways shall and they are hereby authorized and required to fix and appoint the Times when the Inhabitants of the Township or District under their respective Superintendance shall work on the Highways, and shall give them at least two Days Notice thereof, unless where a sudden Injury or Obstruction happens to the Roads of the Township or District under his superintendance, in which Case he shall and is hereby required upon Notice of such injury or Obstruction without

Delay to summons as many of the Inhabitants as he shall find necessary to assist in removing and repairing the same, and if the Clerk of the Peace of the said County or any Surveyor of the Highways or Inhabitant of the said County, shall neglect or refuse to perform any or either of the Duties required of them respectively by this Act they shall respectively forfeit and pay the several Sums and Penalties following to wit, the Clerk of the Peace shall forfeit for every Refusal or Neglect of his Duty the Penalty of forty shillings to be sued for and recovered in the Name of the first Judge of the Court of Common Pleas of the said County whose Duty it shall be to see that the same is recovered, and every Surveyor of the Highways who shall transgress or neglect any of the Duties required of him by this Act, shall forfeit for every Offence the sum of twenty shillings, and every Inhabitant being duly warned and summoned to work on the Highways and refusing or neglecting so to do shall forfeit for every Hours Omission of his Duty therein six pence, and in Case he shall be required to work with a Team and Carriage, and shall refuse or Neglect the same, he shall forfeit for every Hour such Neglect one shilling and six pence: All which Penalties inflicted on the Surveyors of the Highways and Inhabitants shall be respectively sued for and recovered in the Name of the Clerk of the Peace of the said County whose Duty it shall be to prosecute for the same, and all the said several Penalties shall be sued for and recovered in a summary way before any Justice of the Peace of the said County, and on the Oath of a credible Witness to be levied by the Distress and Sale of the Offenders Goods and shall be paid into the Hands of the said Commissioners and by them be applied for the Repair of the public Roads and Highways of the said County, And for as much as some of the said Penalties are very small, and all of them are enjoyned for the enforcing a public Duty, no other Costs shall be awarded or recovered against the Offender than six pence to the Constable for serving the Summons to require the Offender's Appearance and one shilling for levying the Penalty by Execution.

AND BE IT FURTHER ENACTED by the Authority aforesaid, That the said Commissioners who shall attend the actual laying and running out the said public Highways, shall be entitled to and receive a Reward of six Shillings for every Day they shall be necessarily employed in that Service which is to be determined and ascertained by the Certificate of the said

Commissioners at any Meeting, and to be raised upon the Inhabitants of the said County together with the other contingent Charges of the said County as shall be hereafter directed by Law.

AND BE IT FURTHER ENACTED by the Authority aforesaid, That the said Commissioners before they enter upon the Execution of the Trust reposed in them by this Act, shall at their said first meeting, before any Justice of the Peace, be respectively qualified on Oath well and truly to discharge the Trust reposed in them respectively by this Act without favour or partiallity and according to the best of their Skill and judgment, of which Qualification an Entry shall be made in the Record of their proceedings, and the several surveyors of the Highways shall in like Manner before they enter upon their Office be sworn in the presence of a Justice of the Peace, that they will respectively faithfully and impartially discharge the Trust reposed in them by this Act according to the best of their skill and Judgment of which Qualification such Justice shall transmit a Certificate to the Clerk of the Peace of the said County to be filed and preserved among the proceedings of the said Commissioners, and which service such Justice shall perform without Fee or Reward.

AND BE IT FURTHER ENACTED by the Authority aforesaid That this Act shall remain and continue in force until the first Day of February which will be in the Year of our Lord one thousand seven hundred and seventy five.

[CHAPTER 1562.]

[Chapter 1562, of Van Schaack, where the act is printed in full. See chapters 133, 1446.]

An Act to enable the Inhabitants of the County of Charlotte to raise and defray the Public and necessary Charges of the said County and to choose County Officers.

[Passed, March 24, 1772.]

WHEREAS the Inhabitants of the County of Charlotte cannot have the Benefit of an Act entitled "An Act for the better ex-"plaining and more effectual putting in Execution an Act of "General Assembly made and passed in the third year of the "Reign of their late Majesties King William & Queen Mary en-

"titled An Act for defraying of the Public and necessary Charge "throughout this Province and for maintaining the Poor and "preventing Vagabonds," without an Appointment of the several Officers who are necessary to carry the same into Execution.

BE IT THEREFORE ENACTED by his Excellency the Governor the Council and the General Assembly and it is hereby enacted by the Authority of the Same. That it shall and may be lawful to and for the Freeholders and Inhabitants as well of each respective Township within the said County erected by Letters Patent under the Great Seal of this Colony as of the several Districts to be formed and laid out in pursuance of an Act made and passed in this present Sessions entitled "An Act for the "better laying out regulating and keeping in Repair the common "and Public Highways in the County of Charlotte," annually to elect and choose for each respective Township and District from among the Freeholders and Inhabitants of the same respectively one Supervisor, two Assessors, two Overseers of the Poor, one Collector and four Constables, that is to say, for each respective Township at the Times and Places prescribed in their respective Charters, and for each respective District on the first Tuesday in May in every Year.

AND BE IT FURTHER ENACTED by the Authority aforesaid That the said Supervisors so to be chosen shall in every year hold their first Meeting at the County Town of the said County on the Day of opening the General Sessions of the Peace which shall succeed the Time of their Election and afterwards for that Year at such Time and place as they or the major part of them shall agree upon and appoint, at which first Meeting in each and every year they shall and are hereby authorized and directed to nominate and appoint one of the Freeholders and Inhabitants of the said County, to be Treasurer of the said County, who shall enter into Bond to the said Supervisors with such Security and in such sum as they or the major Part of them shall think proper, And in Case of the Breach of the Condition thereof the same shall be put in suit, and the Monies recovered thereon be applied according to the Directions of an Act passed in the tenth Year of the Reign of his present Majesty entitled. "An Act "to enable the Supervisors of the several Counties of this Colony "therein mentioned to take Security of their respective County "Treasurer before he enters upon the Execution of his Office." for the faithful Discharge of the Office of Treasurer of the said

County which Bond shall be lodged by them in the Office of the Clerk of the Peace of the said County.

AND BE IT FURTHER ENACTED by the Authority aforesaid. That the said Supervisors, Treasurer, Assessors Overseers of the Poor Collectors and Constables to be elected chosen and appointed in pursuance of this Act shall and are hereby vested with all the Rights and Powers and made subject to all the Laws which such Officers respectively of the other Counties within this Colony are vested with and subject to, and that the necessary and Public Charges of the said County shall be raised and defrayed in the same Manner as the public and Necessary Charges of the other Counties of the said Colony are directed by Law to be raised and defrayed.

AND BE IT FURTHER ENACTED by the Authority aforesaid That every Supervisor and Assessor before he enters upon the Execution of his Office shall take an Oath to be administered to him by any Justice of the Peace of the said County in the Words following to wit, "I A B do swear that I will well and "truly execute the Office of Supervisor (or Assessor) without "favor or partiality and according to the best of my Skill and "judgment, so help me God." a Certificate of which Qualification shall be given under the Hand of the Justice who shall Administer the Same and be filed with the Clerk of the Peace of the said County.

AND BE IT FURTHER ENACTED by the Authority aforesaid That if any of the Freeholders and Inhabitants of the said County being duly chosen to either of the said respective Offices shall neglect or refuse to take on themselves the execution thereof they shall for every such Offence severally forfeit the following Penalties (to wit) for refusing the Office of Supervisor and Treasurer respectively ten pounds, the Office of Overseer of the Poor five Pounds, the Office of Collector and Constable respectively four Pounds, to be sued for and recovered with Costs of Suit, by Plaint Bill or Information in the Inferior Court of Common Pleas of the said County, and in the Name of the Clerk of the Peace of the said County, who is hereby authorized and required to prosecute for the same and to be applied towards the better laying out and repairing the Public Highways of the said County by the Commissioners thereof.

[CHAPTER 1563.]

[Chapter 1563, of Van Schaack, where the act is printed in full. Amended by chapter 1701. See chapter 27.]

An Act to extend an Act intitled. "An "Act for the supervising intestates Estates "and regulating the Probate of Wills, and "granting Letters of Administration." to the Counties therein mentioned.

[Passed, March 24, 1772.]

WHEREAS an Act of the Governor, the Council and the General Assembly, of this Colony made and passed in the fourth year of the Reign of their late Majesties King William and Queen Mary entitled "An Act for the supervising Intestates "Estates and regulating the probate of Wills, and granting "Letters of Administration," it is enacted among other Things. That the Courts of Common Pleas for the several remote Counties in this Colony, should be impowered and authorized to take the examination of Witnesses to any Will within the said respective remote Counties upon Oath, and to grant Letters of Administration as by the said Act at large doth appear. AND WHEREAS the Counties of Tryon, Charlotte Cumberland and Gloucester are far remote from the City of New York, and the Inhabitants thereof do now labour under the like Inconveniencies, which those remote Counties did before the Remedy provided by the said Act.

BE IT THEREFORE ENACTED by his Excellency the Governor, the Council and the General Assembly, and it is hereby enacted by the Authority of the same. That from and after the Publication of this Act, the said Act entitled. "An Act "for the supervising Intestates Estates and regulating the Pro- "bate of Wills, and granting Letters of Administration." shall extend to the Counties of Tryon Charlotte Cumberland and Gloucester, and the Court of Common Pleas for the said Counties respectively, and the Judges and Justices thereof in the Time of the Vacations of the said Courts of Common Pleas and the Clerks of the said Counties shall have and hereby are vested with the like Power and Authority to take the Examination of any Witnesses to Wills upon Oath within the said Counties, and to grant Letters of Administration in like Manner and form, and to Act do and perform every Matter and Thing in the said

Act mentioned, as fully and amply to all Intents purposes, and Constructions as the said Court of Common Pleas, and the said Judges Justices and Clerks of the Courts of the said remote Counties, have power to do, by virtue of the aforesaid Act, any Thing contained in the said Act to the contrary notwithstanding.

[CHAPTER 1564.]

[Chapter 1564, of Van Schaack, where part of the act only is printed.]

An Act for naturalizing the several Persons therein named.

[Passed, March 24, 1772.]

WHEREAS Francis Phifster, George Cramer, Michael Berringer, Peter Hodler, Jurry Bear, Coenradt Crock, Jurry Karel Jacob Conjes, Jacob France, Michael Leinhart, Joost Coons, Johan N. Cremer, Anthony Baron, John Luca Foeshay, Michael Staller, Adam Leonard Remsen, Claude Joseph Sauthier, John Martin and Ernest Aadig have by their Petitions presented to the General Assembly desired they may be naturalized and become. his Majesty's liege Subjects within this Colony.

BE IT THEREFORE ENACTED by his Excellency the Governor the Council and the General Assembly, and it is hereby enacted by the Authority of the same, That the before named Francis Phifster, George Cramer, Michael Berringer, Peter Hodler, Jurry Bear, Coenradt Crock, Jurry Karel, Jacob Conjes, Jacob France, Michael Leinhart, Joost Coons, Johan N. Cremer, Anthony Baron, John Luca Foeshay, Michael Staller, Adam Leonard Remsen, Claude Joseph Sauthier, John Martin, and Ernest Aadig, and each and every of them shall be and are hereby declared to be naturalized to all Intents Constructions and purposes whatsoever, and from henceforth and at all Times hereafter shall be entitled to have and enjoy all the Rights, Liberties, Privileges, and Advantages which his Majesty's natural born subjects in this Colony have and enjoy, or ought to have and enjoy, as fully to all Intents and purposes whatsoever, as if all and every of them had been born within this Colony.

PROVIDED ALWAYS and it is hereby further Enacted by the Authority aforesaid. That each of the above mentioned Persons shall take the Oaths appointed by Law instead of the Oaths of Allegiance and Supremacy, subscribe the Test, and make, repeat swear to and subscribe the abjuration Oath, in any of his Majesty's Courts of Record within this Colony, which Oaths the said Courts are hereby required upon Application to them made to administer, take the Subscriptions, and cause the Names of the Persons so swearing and subscribing to be entered upon Record in the said Courts; and the said beforementioned persons are hereby, each of them required to pay the several Sums hereafter mentioned, that is to say to the Speaker of the General Assembly the Sum of ten shillings; to the Judge of such Court the Sum of six Shillings; and to the Clerk of such Court the Sum of three Shillings.

AND BE IT FURTHER ENACTED by the Authority aforesaid That if the said Persons or any of them, having so sworn and subscribed as aforesaid shall demand a Certificate of his or their being entered upon Record in the Manner before directed, the Court or Courts in which such Oaths and subscriptions shall be made are hereby directed and required to grant such under the Hand of the Judge and Seal of the said Court or Courts in which such Oaths and Subscriptions as aforesaid shall be made, countersigned by the Clerk of the said Courts: for which Certificate each of them shall pay over and above the Sums above mentioned, the sum of six Shillings, one half to the Judges of such Court or Courts, and the other half to the Clerk thereof, which Certificate or Certificates shall be at all Times to the Person or Persons therein named, a sufficient Proof of his or their being naturalized by virtue of this Act in as full and effectual a Manner as if the Record aforesaid was actually produced by the Person or Persons so named in such Certificate

PROVIDED ALSO and be it enacted by the Authority aforesaid, That such of the Persons hereby naturalized, as shall not take the Oath, Test and Abjuration in Manner herein before directed within twelve Months next after the Publication hereof, shall have no Manner of Benefit by this Act, any Thing herein contained to the contrary notwithstanding.

AND BE IT ENACTED by the same Authority, That the Public Printer of this Colony, shall and hereby is directed and required to print this Act, as if the same was a public Law of this Colony.

[CHAPTER 1565.]

[Chapter 1565, of Van Schaack, where the title only is printed.]

An Act for the Relief of Insolvent Debtors within this Colony.

[Passed, March 24, 1772.]

BE IT ENACTED by his Excellency the Governor the Council and the General Assembly and it is hereby enacted by the Authority of the same, That Israel Horsfield Junior, Elias DeGrushe, Frederick Wisenfels, Charles Moore, James Sloan, Joseph Hauser Peter Shackerly, John Godfreid Muller, William Young, David Irish, Joseph Hopkins, Seth Sherwood, Eliathan Ashman, Isaac June, Godfreid Stock, John Dewey Cornelius Malone, John Roff and Richard Hilton, Insolvent Debtors in this Colony, shall and may, and hereby are allowed to take the Benefit of the several Acts continued by an Act entitled. "An Act to continue the "several Acts therein mentioned respecting the relief of in-"solvent Debtors," passed the nineteenth Day of December one thousand seven hundred and sixty six and which are expired by their own Limitation as fully and effectually, as if the said Acts respecting the Relief of insolvent Debtors were now in actual and full force.

AND WHEREAS it appears by the joint Petition of Frederick Wisenfels and a considerable Number of his Creditors, that a Debt was due from the said Fredrick Wisenfels unto Isaac Man an insolvent Debtor at the Time that he the said Isaac became insolvent, AND WHEREAS the Assignees of the said Isaac do not conceive themselves Authorized by any Law of this Colony to join in a Petition for the Relief of the said Fredrick.

BE IT THEREFORE ENACTED by the Authority aforesaid, That it shall and may be lawful to and for the Assignees of the said Isaac Man or the Major part of them to join in a Petition with the said Fredrick and with the Creditors of the said Fredrick in order to his obtaining the Benefit of said Acts, provided it appears to them the said Assignees or the major Part of them by the Books of said Isaac Man or otherwise that the said Debt was actually due from the said Fredrick to the said Isaac at the Time that the said Isaac became insolvent, and the Assignees of the said Isaac shall certify under their Hands to the Judge or Judges to whom such Petition shall be preferred the Sum that to them appears due from the said Fredrick to the said Assignees, which Certificate shall be as full and effectual as if the said Assignees had taken the Oath prescribed by the said Acts, or one of them for Petitioning Creditors to take, any Thing in the said Acts to the contrary notwithstanding.

PROVIDED ALWAYS That Nothing in this Act shall extend or be construed to extend to the discharge of any of the said Debtors if he shall stand chargeable at the Suit of the Crown or to affect any Creditors residing in Great Britain.

[CHAPTER 1566.]

[Chapter 1566, of Van Schaack, where the title only is printed.]

An Act for the Relief of insolvent Debtors within this Colony with respect to the Imprisonment of their persons.

[Passed, March 24, 1772.]

WHEREAS in Imitation of the Wise and Benevolent Example of the British parliament the Legislature of this Colony hath frequently passed occasional Laws for the Relief of such unfortunate persons who are become unable to discharge their whole Debts, and who by Means of their Confinement are rendered not only miserable to themselves and Families but useless to the Community. AND WHEREAS it has been represented to the General Assembly that the several persons hereinafter mentioned imprisoned in different Goals in this Colony are destitute even of the common Necessaries of Life, and it is conceived reasonable if their Creditors will not consent to their Enlargement or Contribute to their Subsistence, that such persons should be relieved by the Legislature, TO THIS END

BE IT ENACTED by his Excellency the Governor, the Council, and the General Assembly, and it is hereby Enacted by the Authority of the same, That such of the Creditors of the following persons Vizt. of Simon Losee confined in Queens County Goal, John P Smith, and Jacob Mace, In Orange County Goal: George Johnson, James Wilson, John Graham, Dennis Woortman, James Way, William Peek, Frederick Groome, and John Smith, In New York Goal: Seth Scofield in Ulster County Goal: John Christy, and George Charters in Albany Goal; and Thomas Robinson in Suffolk County Goal, who shall insist upon such their Debtor's being detained under their respective Confinement shall within one Month after the publication of such Advertisements as are herein after directed agree by Writing under their Hands to pay and allow four Shillings per Week unto the said prisoners respectively to be paid the Monday of every Week so long as he shall continue in prison at his or their Instance, AND if such Agreement as afore said shall not be entered into, or if entered into not punctually complied with, and on Failure of the payment of such Weekly Sum at any Time such of the said prisoners whose Creditor or Creditors shall not enter into such Agreement OR shall fail Complying with it as aforesaid shall be entitled to the benefit of this Act upon Complying with the Terms and Conditions herein after Imposed.

AND BE IT FURTHER ENACTED by the Authority aforesaid that it shall and may be lawful for each and every of them the said Simon Losee, John P Smith, Jacob Mace, George Johnson, James Wilson, John Graham, Dennis Woortman, James Way, William Peek, Frederick Groome, John Smith, Seth Scofield, John Christy, George Charters, and Thomas Robinson to present a Petition to the Court out of which any process against them respectively hath issued, and upon which they are imprisoned, or to any two of the Judges. of such Court, certifying the Cause or Causes of his Imprisonment, and exhibiting an Account and Inventory of his whode real and personal Estate, and of the Securities relating to the same, Which Petition with the said Account and Inventory shall be lodged with the Clerk of the said Court for the Inspection of the Creditors, AND after such Petition presented and Account and Inventory filed such prisoners shall respectively publish Advertisements in one or more of the public News Papers of this Colony Notifying their Creditors that they intend to apply to the said Court or to any two of the Judges thereof at a certain Day not less than four Weeks from the Publication of such Advertisements respectively to be discharged according to the prayer of his or their said Petition. At which Day the said Court or the said two Judges may (and are hereby required by precept under their Hands and Seals directed to the Sheriff, Goaler or Officer in whose Custody such prisoner or prisoners may be, to) order the said prisoner or prisoners respectively to be brought up before such Court or such Judges, and if such provision as is aforesaid hath not been made for the Subsistence of the said prisoner or prisoners by his or their Creditors respectively, the said Court or Judges may then respectively administer the following Oath or Affirmation.

I, A. B. do Solemnly Swear or Affirm that the Account by me now delivered is a just and true Account of all my Creditors, and the Monies owing to them respectively BY me to the best of my Knowledge and Remembrance, And that the Inventory and Account now delivered by me is a just and true Account of all my Estate real and personal both in Law and Equity, either in possession, Reversion or Remainder (the necessary Wearing Apparel of myself, my Wife and Children, and Family immediately under my Care excepted) and I have not directly or indirectly Sold, Leased, Assigned, or otherwise disposed of or made over either in Trust for myself or otherwise, except as set forth in the same Account any part of my Estate real or personal for my future benefit, or in order to defraud my Creditors, and that none of my Creditors reside in Great Britain, So help me God.

WHICH Oath or Affirmation being taken if the Truth thereof shall be denied or controverted by any of the Creditors the said Court or Judges may appoint some farther Day for hearing the parties as well Debtors as Creditors, and upon such farther hearing may in their Discretion either remand the said Debtors or proceed to their Discharge, as if no such farther hearing had been required. BUT if the said Oath or Affirmation shall not be controverted or denied then the said Court or Judges may immediately order the Lands, Goods and Effects contained in such Account and Inventory to be by a Short Indorsement on the back of such petition executed by the prisoner, assigned to the said Creditors or one or more of them in Trust for all his or their Creditors, or to some other person or persons to be appointed by the said Court or Judges respectively in Trust for all the Creditors, and also for all Attornies, Sheriffs, Goalers, and other Officers with respect to their Fees for which they shall come in as the Creditors of the Insolvent, abating pro Rata, By which Assignment such Estate shall actually vest in and be taken in possession of by the said Trustee or Trustees, according to the purport of such Assignment, and shall be divided by the Assignees from Time to Time among all the Creditors in proportion, after six Months previous Notice published in one of the public News papers of such Assignment, and requiring all the Creditors to send in their Demand and if any part thereof is in the possession of any other person or persons the SAME shall be recoverable in the Name or Names of such Trustee or Trustees who are hereby fully authorized to dispose of and execute good and sufficient Deeds for the same or any part thereof, and to divide and distribute as well the Monies thence arising, as such other Monies which shall come into their Hands by Virtue of this Act among the Creditors of the said Debtors respectively, and the Officers aforesaid to whom any Fees may be due in proportion to their respective Debts or Demands, according to the true Intent and Meaning of this Act, to which no Release from the Insolvent shall be any Bar. AND immediately upon such Assignment being made, and the Effects of the Insolvent delivered to the said Trustee or Trustees. The said prisoner or prisoners shall by order of the said Court or Judges be discharged out of Custody, And such Order shall be a sufficient Warrant to the Sheriff, Goaler or keeper of such prisoner to discharge such prisoner or prisoners if detained for no other Cause or Causes than mentioned in such his or their petition, and he is required forthwith to discharge, and set him or them at Liberty without Fee, And upon such discharge the said Debtors shall be finally released from all Debts contracted and all Judgments obtained, before that Time, and shall not be liable to be sued or arrested or to have their Lands or Tenements, Goods or Chattels seized by Virtue or in Consequence thereof. AND every person who shall be convicted of wilful false Swearing in any Matter or Article contained in the said Oath he or she shall be guilty of Felony and suffer the pains of Death without Benefit of Clergy.

AND BE IT FURTHER ENACTED by the Authority aforesaid, that if any of the said Debtors shall be sued for any Debts accrued before the publication of this Act, or if any Judge or other Officer shall be sued for any Thing done in pursuance and under the Authority of this Act such Defendant may plead the General Issue, and give this Act and the special Matter in Evidence. PROVIDED that this Act shall not extend to discharge any PERSON who shall stand committed at the Suit of the Crown, And PROVIDED ALSO that this Act shall not be construed to affect any Creditor or Creditors residing in Great Britain, any Thing herein contained to the Contrary Notwithstanding.

[CHAPTER 1567.]

[Chapter 1567, of Van Schaack, where the title only is printed.]

An Act for the Relief of John Cox and Catharine Heysham Insolvent Debtors confined in Goal in the City of New York.

[Passed, March 24, 1772.]

WHEREAS the distressing Situation of such unfortunate Persons who have been rendered incapable of discharging their Debts, has ever been an Object of the Attention of the Legislature. AND WHEREAS it appears by the Petition of John Cox and Elizabeth Heysham that they have been respectively under a long Confinement, by Reason whereof their Effects which they are desirous of applying as far as they will go to the Satisfaction of their Creditors are daily diminishing. WHEREFORE,

BE IT ENACTED by his Excellency the Governor the Council and the General Assembly, and it is hereby enacted by the Authority of the same That it shall and may be lawful to and for the said John Cox and Catharine Heysham and each of them to present a Petition to the Court out of which any Process against them respectively hath issued or to any two of the Judges of such Court (exhibiting at the same Time an Account and Inventory of all Monies owing by and of all Estate real and personal belonging, and of all Debts due to them respectively.) praying to be discharged from his or her said Imprisonment, upon which Petition being so presented such Court may by Rule or Order of Court if it shall be in Term Time, or if in the Vacation any two of the Judges thereof by Warrant under their Hands and Seals directed to the Goaler in whose Custody he or she is may order such Prisoner to be brought up, and being so brought up administer to him or her the following Oath, (to wit) "I A. B. do "solemnly swear that the Account by me now delivered is a just "and true Account of all my Creditors, and the Monies owing to "them respectively by me to the best of my knowledge and "Remembrance, and that the Inventory and Account now de- "livered by me is a just and true Account of all my Estate real "and personal both in Law and equity either in possession Re- "version or Remainder (the necessary wearing Apparel of myself "and Family immediately under my Care excepted) and I have "not directly or indirectly, sold, leased assigned or otherwise "disposed of or made over either in Trust for myself or otherwise "except as set forth in the same Account, any part of my Estate "Real and Personal for my future Benefit or in order to defraud "my Creditors, so help me God."

Which Oath being so taken as aforesaid if Proof shall be made to the said Court or Judges that Notice has been given in one or more of the Public News Papers of this Colony (which the said Debtors are hereby required to do in Order to entitle them to the Benefit of this Act) by such Debtor of his or her intending to apply to such Court or Judges for his or her Discharge at least three Weeks before such Application made, and if the Truth of such Oath shall be denied or controverted; the Court or Judges may appoint some further Day for hearing what can be alledged on either Side, and either remand the Prisoners or discharge them after such further hearing in Manner herein after directed; but if such Oath shall not be denied or controverted, then such Court or Judges as aforesaid may immediately order the Lands Goods and Effects contained in such Accounts to be by a short Indorsement on the Back of such Petition subscribed by the Prisoner assigned to the said Creditors or to any one or more of them in Trust for his or her Creditors, or to some proper Person to be by the said Court or Judges appointed in Trust for all the Creditors, and also for all Attornies Sheriffs, and other Officers of the Court with the Goaler as to their Fees in any Causes depending against such Debtor, for which Fees such Officers shall come in only as Creditors, and abate in the same proportion, by which Assignment all the Estate of the said Debtors respectively shall instantly vest according to the purport of such Assignment, and such of it as is in possession of any other person shall be recoverable in the Name or Names of such Trustees, who are hereby fully authorized to dispose of and execute good and sufficient Deeds for the same or any Part thereof, and after six Months previous Notice published in one of the Public News Papers of such Assignment, and requiring all the Creditors to send in their Demands, to divide and distribute as well the Monies thence arising, as such other Monies which shall come into their Hands by virtue of this Act, among the Creditors of the said Debtors respectively, and the Officers aforesaid to whom any Fees may be due, in proportion to their respective Debts or Demands according to the true Intent and meaning of this Act: which Assignment being made, and all the Lands Goods and Effects in the Debtors possession according to such Inventory being delivered to such Trustee or Trustees the said Prisoner shall be discharged out of the Custody by order of Court if such Court shall be sitting, or by Order of such Judges if in Vacation Time, and such Order as aforesaid shall be a sufficient Warrant to the Sheriff Goaler or Keeper, and he is hereby required to discharge the said Prisoner if detained for no other Causes than such mentioned in his or her said Petition: (PROVIDED that this Act shall not be construed to affect any Creditor or Creditors residing in Great Britain). and such Debtors or either of them shall never after be liable to be sued for any Matter or Cause accrued, or to have his or her Body or Estate taken in Execution upon any Judgment obtained, before such Discharge unless he or she shall be convicted of perjury in any Matter or Article contained in the said Oath.

AND BE IT FURTHER ENACTED by the Authority aforesaid, That if any Action or Suit shall be brought for any Thing done in pursuance of this Act, the Defendant or Defendants may plead the General Issue, and give this Act in Evidence, PROVIDED that this Act shall not authorize the Discharge of the said Debtors if he or she shall stand chargeable at the Suit of the Crown.

PROVIDED ALSO and be it further Enacted that if the said Debtors or either of them shall be convicted of wilful false swearing in any Matter or Article contained in the said Oath he or she shall be guilty of Felony, and suffer the Pains of Death without Benefit of Clergy.

[CHAPTER 1568.]

[Chapter 1568, of Van Schaack, where the title only is printed. See chapter 1405.]

An Act for defraying a Moiety of the Expenses accrued on settling the contested Boundaries between the patented Lands commonly called Cheesecocks and Kakiate.

[Passed, March 24, 1772.]

WHEREAS in pursuance of a former Act passed the twentieth Day of May one thousand seven hundred and sixty nine, intitled "An Act for settling the contested Boundaries between the Patented Lands commonly called Cheesecocks and Kakiate," the Honourable George Duncan Ludlow Esquire, one of the Justices of the Supreme Court of Judicature for this Colony, William Nicoll of Suffolk County, Thomas Hicks of Queens County and Benjamin Kissam and Samuel Jones of the City of New York Esquires were duly Authorized and appointed Commissioners to settle and determine the contested Boundaries between the said Patented Lands of Cheesecocks and Kakiate, who have accordingly settled and determined the same, and their Determination thereof is by the said Act become final and conclusive, On all parties claiming under the said two Patents respectively. AND WHEREAS before any proceedings in virtue of the said Act, it was stipulated and agreed by the Committees named and appointed therein for the Proprietors of the said Patents of Kakiate and Cheesecocks respectively, that the one Moiety of all Expences which should accrue in the Execution of the Powers given by the said Act should be sustained by the Proprietors of the said Patent of Kakiate, and the other Moiety by the Proprietors of the said Patent of Cheescocks. AND WHEREAS the said Commissioners have by a Certificate under their Hands dated the twenty third Day of January one thousand seven hundred and seventy two, certified That all the Lands claimed by the Proprietors of Kakiate lying to the Northward and Westward of a Line from the Head of Welsh's Island near where Syme's Mill stood, East to Hudson's River, and from the Head of the said Island along Demareest's Kill to Gurney's Spring, and from thence to the Head of Verdreedige Mountain at a place called the Table Rock, and from thence nearly West to a parcel of Laurel on the South Branch of Minners Fall, and from thence along the said Branch to the Head thereof near Symmond's Spring and from thence due West until a North Line from the Tree commonly called John Wood's Tree on Wessegroreap Plain will intersect the said Line, were in controversy with the said Proprietors of Cheescocks in the said Dispute so submitted to them. AND WHEREAS it is represented by the Committee named for the Proprietors of Kakiate in the above recited Act, that by reason of the many Shares and Interests into which the controverted Lands mentioned in the said Certificate are multiplied subdivided and dispersed, and by Reason that part of the Lands therein mentioned remain in common and undivided, and because of the disparity in value of the said Lands so in Controversy, and of the Absence of some of the Claimants thereof, and the Coverture and Infancy of others, it is very difficult if not impracticable to make such an Assessment of the Moiety of the Expence of the Settlement of the said Boundary which falls upon the said Proprietors of Kakiate as will be in any Degree satisfactory or will not be productive of endless Controversy and Litigation. AND WHEREAS it is most just and reasonable that the said Expences should be paid, and that every Person concerned in the said Controversy should sustain and contribute a due proportion thereof according to the Value of his Right and Share in the said controverted Lands.

BE IT THEREFORE ENACTED by his Excellency the Governor the Council and the General Assembly, and it is hereby enacted by the Authority of the same, That it shall and may be lawful to and for the said Commissioners or any three of them to audit settle adjust and pass the Accounts of all Expences and Charges which have accrued in the Settlement of the said Contested Boundaries and to fix and determine the proportion thereof which ought to be contributed and paid by that Part of the said Patented Lands of Kakiate which were so contested, and that their Certificate of the Amount thereof shall be final and conclusive to all the parties interested under the said Patent of Kakiate.

AND BE IT FURTHER ENACTED by the Authority aforesaid, That the said Commissioners or any three of them shall within three Months after the Publication of this Act issue a precept under their Hands and Seals to be directed to the Sheriff of the said County of Orange commanding and requiring him to Summons all the Freeholders of the Precinct of Haverstraw in the said County within which Precinct the said patented Lands of Kakiate are included, to be and appear at the House of Daniel Coe in the said Precinct at a Time therein to be prefixed which shall not be more than twelve nor less than six Days after the Date of the said Precept, then and there by plurality of Voices of the Freeholders so assembled, and having a Right or Claim in the said controverted Land as above described to elect and choose three good and sufficient Freeholders of the said County of Orange in no wise interested in the said Controversy to be Assessors, and to execute the Power and Authority to them hereafter given and granted by this Act, and if any Question shall arise concerning the Right of any Person to vote for such Assessors, that then the Sheriff shall administer to the Person so objected against an Oath to declare the Truth touching his Right of Election which shall be the Test for admitting or rejecting such Voter.

AND BE IT FURTHER ENACTED by the Authority aforesaid, That the Sheriff of the said County shall Return on the back of the Precept so to him to be directed the Names of the Persons to be chosen and elected Assessors for the purposes aforesaid, which precept and Return being filed in the Clerks Office of the said County shall be full Evidence of such Election, and that thereupon the said Assessors shall take an Oath to be Administered to them by one of the Judges of the Inferior Court of common Pleas of the said County of Orange truly and impartially to assess the Sum to be raised by virtue of this Act, on the Lands so in Controversy according to the best of their Skill and Judgment.

AND BE IT FURTHER ENACTED by the Authority aforesaid. That the said Assessors being so duly chosen and Qualified shall proceed in a just and equitable manner to rate and Assess the Quotas and Proportion of each respective Lot and parcel of Land whether divided or undivided within the said Controversy according to it's Quantity and Quality in order to raise upon the whole of the said controverted Lands the Sum which shall be fixed and certified to be the proportion of the said Patent of Kakiate of the Expences which have accrued on the Settlement of the said contested Boundary together with the further Sum of one Shilling in the Pound as a Reward for the Trouble of the said Assessors in assessing collecting and paying the same, and also the further Sum of thirty Shillings as a Fee to the Sheriff for the Duty required of him by this Act, and that the said Assessors shall within six Months after their being so qualified finally compleat the said Assessment and make and subscribe a Roll thereof containing the several Lots and parcels of Land so assessed and distinguishing whether they are divided or undivided, the Proprietors Names of each as far as shall come to their knowledge and the Quota and Proportion of each respective Lot and Tract, and the particular Sums or Proportion which each Proprietor thereof shall pay, and having finished the same shall file and lodge a Duplicate thereof under their Hands in the Clerks Office of the said County to which all Persons shall have free recourse at all seasonable Hours without any Charge or Expence, and that the said Assessors or the Survivors or Survivor of them shall within one Month thereafter publish an Advertisement in the New York Gazzette to be continued for four Weeks, and shall also affix Copies thereof at the Court House at Orange Town in the said County, and at the Door of the Presbyterian Meeting House in Kakiate giving Notice to and requiring from all persons concerned in the late contested Boundary between the said Patents to pay their respective Quotas of the Expence of the settlement thereof at such Time and place and to such Person as they the said Assessors shall agree upon and appoint PROVIDED ALWAYS That the Time to be so prefixed for such payment shall not be more than four Months nor less than six Weeks after the Date of such Notification and Demand.

AND BE IT FURTHER ENACTED by the Authority aforesaid That if the Quota so to be assessed on any or either of the Tracts or Lots of Land whether divided or undivided within the Limits of the said Controversy shall not be duly paid and discharged according to the said Notice and Demand, that then it shall and may be lawful to and for the said Assessors or the Survivors or Survivor of them, to sell and dispose the undivided

Right Interest share and proportion of any Person or Persons having any Estate or Interest in any of the said undivided Tract or Tracts of Land, or any other Lot or parcel of Land so charged as aforesaid with a proportion of said Expence, who shall not on or before that Day have paid and discharged his her or their Proportion of the said Expence so as aforesaid to be assessed at Public Vendue or Outcry first giving one Months Notice of such intended Sale by Advertisement to be affixed in the said County of Orange at the Places aforesaid and after retaining out of the Monies arising by such Sale so much as the Assessment shall amount unto together with the contingent Expence of such Sale shall render the Overplus Money if any be to the Owner or Owners of the said undivided Tracts or other Lot or Lots so to be sold.

AND BE IT FURTHER ENACTED by the Authority aforesaid. That the Deed of Conveyance of the said Assessors or the Survivors or Survivor of them, to every respective purchaser shall be good and effectual in the Law to convey such undivided Right and Rights, share and shares, Lot and Lots to the purchasor his Heirs and Assigns in fee simple and shall be and operate as a full and effectual Bar both in Law and equity against all persons claiming or to claim the same by virtue of or under the said Patent of Kakiate.

AND BE IT FURTHER ENACTED by the Authority aforesaid That the said Assessors or the Survivors or Survivor of them shall account for and pay the Monies which shall from Time to Time come into their Hands in pursuance of this Act to the Committee named and appointed by the Act herein recited for the Proprietors of the said Patent of Kakiate to be by them applied in discharge of the Expences accrued by the Settlement of the said contested Boundary on the Part of Kakiate.

[CHAPTER 1569.]

[Chapter 1569, of Van Schaack, where the act is printed in full.]

An Act to raise the Sum of one hundred and fifty Pounds on the Lands therein mentioned for the use of clearing and opening the Creek, Commonly called Crommeline's Creek, and for other purposes therein mentioned.

[Passed, March 24, 1772.]

WHEREAS there are several large parcels of swamp and Bog-Meadow in a Tract of Land commonly called Grey Court situate in the Patent of Wawayanda in the County of Orange and Province of New York, which are frequently drowned and rendered unfit for use by the overflowing of the Creek called Crommeline's Creek which runs through the said Tract. AND WHEREAS the Proprietors of the said Swamps and Bog-Meadow conceive the same may be made fit for Tillage or Pasturage by clearing out and enlarging the said Creek.

BE IT THEREFORE ENACTED by his Excellency the Governor the Council and the General Assembly, and it is hereby enacted by the Authorities of the same, That Samuel Gale, Jesse Woodhull, and Nathaniel Roe Junior Esquires or any two of them or the survivor or Survivors of them shall be Inspectors to settle and finally ascertain the Number of Acres of swamp and Bog Meadow belonging to each Proprietor in the said Tract which may in their Opinion be benefited by clearing and enlarging the said Creek, which Determination shall be delivered in Writing to the Treasurer hereafter to be chosen by Virtue of this Act.

AND BE IT FURTHER ENACTED by the Authority aforesaid That in order to clear and enlarge the said Creek the sum of one hundred and fifty Pounds shall be paid by the Proprietors of the said Swamps and Bog-Meadow in proportion to the Number of Acres they shall respectively own and that will, as settled by the said Inspectors be benefited thereby: which sum of one hundred and fifty Pounds shall be paid to Elihu Marvin, Hector Saint John, and Joseph Drake to be by them applied in paying all incidental Charges and for clearing and enlarging the said Creek, as they or any two of them shall think proper from thirty Rods below to forty Rods above the Outlet Bridge, and from thence in clearing and enlarging the said Creek at least ten feet wide and three feet deep to the south Bounds of the said Grey Court Tract.

AND BE IT FURTHER ENACTED by the Authority aforesaid That the Proprietors of the said Swamps and Bog-Meadow for the clearing and scouring of the said Creek shall for every Acre as settled by the said Inspectors pay one Penny annually for fifteen Years to be computed from the first Day of January one thousand seven hundred and seventy three, that the said penny per Acre shall be paid annually on the first Day of April into the Hands of a Treasurer to be chosen by the Majority of the said Proprietors on the first Monday in January in every Year at the House of Bezalel Seily, situate in the said Grey Court Tract: and in Case any Proprietor shall neglect to pay annually on the said first Day of April his proportion of the Monies to be raised by the Assessment of one Penny per Acre, the Treasurer for the Time being shall sue for and recover the same before any one of his Majesty's Justices of the Peace with Interest and Costs of suit. And the said Treasurer for the Time being shall lay out the Money or such part thereof as he may think necessary in clearing the said Creek or in enlarging the same, and on the said first Monday in January in every Year the Treasurer for the Time being shall render an Account unto the said Proprietors then met, and the Monies (if any he may have in his Hands) together with all Accounts, papers and Things respecting the said swamps and Bog-Meadow he shall then deliver to the Treasurer who may be chosen to succeed him.

AND BE IT FURTHER ENACTED by the Authority aforesaid That each Proprietor shall within one Month after the said Inspectors have made their Determination pay his respective proportion of the said one hundred and fifty Pounds to the said Elihu Marvin, Hector Saint John, and Joseph Drake or either of them, and in Default of payment it shall be lawful for the said Elihu Marvin, Hector Saint John and Joseph Drake, or the survivor or survivors of them to recover the same by due Course of Law with Interest and Costs of suit.

AND WHEREAS there are many Ditches between the Lots of Swamp and Bog-Meadow (commonly called Line Ditches) and several Main Ditches to lead the Waters into the said Creek already made, and for the more effectual draining of the said swamps and Bog-Meadow it may be necessary to have one or more main Ditches made, and also many Line Ditches in order to lead the Waters either into the Main Ditches or into the Creek. AND WHEREAS it will be also necessary that the said Ditches should be sufficiently Scouered at least once in two Years.

BE IT THEREFORE FURTHER ENACTED by the Authority aforesaid That any Proprietor who shall be desirous of having a Line Ditchmade shall give at least one Months Notice of his Intention to the Person or Persons owning the Meadow or Swamp adjoining, and in Case the Owner of the Meadow or swamp adjoining shall neglect or refuse to make one equal half Part of such Line Ditch, the Person so giving Notice may proceed to dig the Ditch, and may sue the other party for one half of the Expence thereof before any one of his Majesty's Justices of the Peace and shall recover the same with Interest and Costs of suit: all Line Ditches shall be cut five Feet wide and two Feet and an half deep unless the Parties shall otherwise agree.

AND BE IT FURTHER ENACTED by the Authority aforesaid That when one or more of the said Proprietors shall think it necessary that any other Ditch or Ditches should be cut in the said swamps and Bog-Meadows and the Parties interested cannot agree respecting the same, the said Inspectors or any two of them shall determine whether such Ditch is necessary, and if so, then in what place the same shall be made, the Size of the Ditch, and who shall pay the Expence thereof with all incidental Charges; And in Case either of the Parties shall neglect to comply with such Determination, the Person or Persons desirous of having such Ditch made may proceed to make the same, and shall then be fully authorized to sue for and recover in the Manner directed respecting Line Ditches, of each Person interested their respective proportions of the Expence thereof, together with all incidental Charges.

AND BE IT FURTHER ENACTED by the Authority aforesaid That all or so many of the Ditches in the said swamps and Bog-Meadow as the said Inspectors or any two of them may think necessary shall be cleared and scoured at such Time in this present Year and in the Manner they or any two of them shall direct, and every Ditch which shall hereafter be made as well as those already made shall once at least in every two Years be scoured and enlarged to the same Breadth & Depth as they were at first made: the Expence of Scouring and enlarging said Ditches shall be paid by the Person or Persons at whose Charge the respective Ditches were or shall be made: And upon the Neglect or Refusal of any Person or Persons to contribute his or their Proportion of the Expence, it shall be lawful after twenty Days Notice for any one or more of the said Proprietors to cause the said Ditch or Ditches to be scoured and enlarged as aforesaid, and to sue for and recover the respective proportions in the same Manner as is herein directed respecting Line Ditches.

AND BE IT FURTHER ENACTED by the Authority aforesaid That in Case the said one hundred and fifty Pounds shall not be sufficient for clearing and enlarging the said Creek agreeable to the Directions of this Act; such further sum not exceeding fifty Pounds shall be raised as the majority of the Proprietors shall think proper, which further sum shall be paid to the said Commissioners by the respective Proprietors in the same Proportion as the one hundred and fifty Pounds is to be paid.

AND BE IT FURTHER ENACTED by the Authority aforesaid That the Inspectors for the Services required of them by virtue of this Act shall be paid after the Rate of ten Shillings per Day each, and the said Commissioners after the Rate of six Shillings per Day each.

This Act to be in force till the first Day of January, one thousand seven hundred and eighty eight.

[CHAPTER 1570.]

[Chapter 1570, of Van Schaack, where the act is printed in full.]

An Act to settle and establish the Line or Lines of Division between the City of New York, and the Township of Harlem, so far as concerns the right of Soil in Controversy.

[Passed, March 24, 1772.]

WHEREAS Disputes and Controversies have long subsisted between the Mayor Aldermen and Commonalty of the City of New York, and divers persons claiming under the Township of Harlem in the Outward of the said City respecting the Division Line between the Lands granted to the said Mayor Aldermen and Commonalty of the City of New York, and the said Township of Harlem, which are productive of great Trouble expence and vexation to both Parties: For prevention whereof as well the said Mayor Aldermen and Commonalty of the said City of New York as the Proprietors and Claimants under the said Township of Harlem have humbly prayed that the Boundary of property in the said contested Lands may be finally settled and adjusted by Commissioners to be appointed and Authorized by an Act of the Legislature.

BE IT THEREFORE ENACTED by his Excellency the Governor the Council and the General Assembly, and it is hereby enacted by the Authority of the same, that William Nicoll Esquire of Suffolk County, Thomas Hicks Esquire Attorney at Law, of Queens County, and George Clinton Esquire of Ulster County. shall be and hereby are appointed Commissioners to agree, fix upon, settle and finally ascertain the Boundary between the Township of Harlem and the Lands granted to the Mayor Aldermen and Commonalty of the City of New York within the said City of New York aforesaid, and the said Commissioners or the Major Part of them, or the Survivors or Survivor of them, or the Major Part of such Survivors shall be and hereby are fully authorized and impowered to meet for the purpose aforesaid at such place or places within the City of New

York aforesaid as often as they the said Commissioners or the Major Part of them, or the Survivors or Survivor of them or the Major Part of such Survivors shall think proper, and shall be and hereby are Authorized and impowered to summon and order any Person or Persons within this Colony to appear before them when and as often as they the said Commissioners or the major Part of them or the Survivors or Survivor of them or the Major part of such Survivors shall think necessary, to be examined and give Evidence touching the Matters in controversy, and also to bring along with them all such Books, Deeds, Papers, Records or other written Evidence as the said Commissioners or the major Part of them, or the Survivors or Survivor of them or the major Part of such Survivors shall from Time to Time think proper to order and direct, for the Execution of the Trust reposed in them by this Act, and that it shall and may be lawful to and for the said Commissioners or either of them to administer an Oath, or Affirmation in Cases where the Law directs an Affirmation to the Witnesses to be examined before them to declare the Truth touching the Matters in question, and if any Witness so to be examined shall give false Evidence or wilfully and knowingly affirm or depose falsely on such Examination, and shall thereof be duly convicted, such Witness shall for such Offence suffer the Pains and Penalties inflicted by Law for wilful and corrupt perjury. And if any Person or Persons being summoned or ordered by the said Commissioners to attend in order to give Evidence before the said Commissioners or to bring along with him or them any Book Deed paper or Record, or any Books Deeds papers or Records by a writing under the Hands of the said Commissioners or any of them duly served on such Person or Persons or left at his or their last place of abode, if the same shall be within the City of New York five Days, and if in any other Part of the Colony thirty Days before the Day required by such Summons for his or their attendance as aforesaid shall neglect refuse or delay to give such Attendance, or to bring such written Evidence as shall be required by the said Commissioners or any of them such person or Persons shall forfeit for every such Neglect refusal or delay the Sum of ten Pounds current Money of New York to be recovered in the Name and for the use of the Mayor Aldermen and Commonalty of the City of New York if the Summons for the Appearance of such Witness shall have issued at the Instance of the said Mayor Aldermen and Commonalty; but if the same shall have issued at the instance of the said Township of Harlem, then in the Name of the Committee of the said Township of Harlem herein after named, and for the use of the said Township, and that in a summary way before any one of his Majesty's Justices of the Supreme Court of Judicature of this Colony, who is hereby authorized and required to hear and determine the same, and to award Execution for the same against the Goods and Chattels of every such Offender.

AND BE IT FURTHER ENACTED by the Authority aforesaid That the said Commissioners or the major Part of them, or the Survivors or Survivor of them, or the major Part of such Survivors are hereby authorized and impowered to settle and ascertain the said Line or Lines of Division at such place or Places as they or the Major Part of them or the Survivors or Survivor of them or the major Part of such Survivors shall think just right and equitable and most agreeable to the Grants under which the Township of Harlem and the Mayor Aldermen and Commonalty of the City of New York hold their Lands, and shall after they have agreed upon such Line or Lines of Division aforesaid Choose and elect one or more proper person or persons to survey, run out, and mark in the presence of some of them such Line or Lines as they the said Commissioners or the Major Part of them or the Survivors or Survivor of them or the major Part of such Survivors shall determine to be the Boundary or Division Line or Lines between the said Township of Harlem and the Lands of the said Mayor Aldermen and Commonalty of the City of New York.

AND BE IT FURTHER ENACTED by the Authority aforesaid that the said Commissioners or the Major Part of them or the Survivors or Survivor of them, or the major Part of such Survivors shall within some convenient Time after this Act shall have received the Royal Approbation, not exceeding one Year, settle fix upon and ascertain the Line or Lines of Division aforesaid, and cause the same to be run out in Manner and form aforesaid, a Description of which Line or Lines so settled agreed upon, ascertained, and caused to be run out and marked by the said Commissioners or the Major Part of them, or the Survivors or Survivor of them, or the Major Part of such survivors as aforesaid specifying the Places of Beginning and ending, the course or Courses and Distance thereof shall be entered upon Record in the Secretary's Office of this Colony within one Month thereafter, and shall for ever afterwards be and remain within the Boundary or division Line or Lines between the said Township of Harlem and the Lands of the Mayor Aldermen and Commonalty of the City of New York, and shall operate as a total Extinguishment of all the Right Title Interest Claim or pretences of Claim whatsoever of the Township of Harlem and of all and every Person and Persons whatsoever claiming under the said Township of Harlem of in and to all the Lands Tenements and Hereditaments, which shall lie to the Southward and Westward of such Division Line or Lines, and shall also at the same Time operate as a total Extinguishment of all the Right Title Interest Claim or pretences of Claim whatsoever of the said Mayor Aldermen and Commonalty of the City of New York, and of all and every Person and Persons claiming under the said Mayor Aldermen and Commonalty of the City of New York of in and to all the Lands Tenements Hereditaments which shall lie to the Eastward and Northward of the said Division or Boundary Line or Lines, so as aforesaid to be ascertained, fixed upon, run out, and marked by virtue of this Act, the Lands lying and being between high and low Water Mark within the City of New York to the Eastward and Northward of the said Division or Boundary Line or Lines only excepted.

AND BE IT FURTHER ENACTED by the Authority aforesaid, That all such Expences Costs and Charges as shall arise or accrue in fixing ascertaining and running out the Boundary Line or Lines of Division before mentioned or for or by reason of any other Matter or Thing respecting the Execution of the Powers given by this Act and other the Premises, shall be paid in equal Proportions, (that is to say,) the one equal half Part or Moiety thereof by the Mayor Aldermen and Commonalty of the City of New York, and the other equal half Part thereof by the Township of Harlem, except all such Expences as have arisen, been paid, or as shall hereafter arise or be paid by either the Mayor Aldermen and Commonalty of the City of New York or the Town ship of Harlem to their Counsel for advice in about or any ways relating to the Settlement of the Boundary Line or Lines aforesaid, PROVIDED ALWAYS and be it further Enacted that the settlement and Establishment of the said Boundary Line or Lines, or any Matter or Thing to be done or concerted in pursuance of this Act shall not operate or be construed to lessen diminish or affect the Bounds Limits or Extent of the said City of New York in point of Jurisdiction or to alter abrogate or defeat any of the Powers Pre-eminences Privileges or

Immunities over or in respect of the said Township of Harlem which are vested in, or have ever lawfully been, or may be claimed or exercised by the said Mayor Aldermen and Commonalty of the City of New York in virtue of the respective Royal Charters to them given & granted; but the same shall operate and be for ever received and adjudged as an absolute and final Determination and Establishment of the Right and Property of the Soil so in controversy between the said Mayor Aldermen and Commonalty of the City of New York and all claiming or to claim by from or under them, and the said Township of Harlem and all claiming or to claim by from or under the same, any Thing in this Act to the contrary thereof in any wise notwithstanding.

AND BE IT FURTHER ENACTED by the Authority aforesaid That John Livingston, John Sickels, David Waldron, John Nagle, and John Myer, or the Majority of them who are appointed by the Township of Harlem to be a Committee to manage the said Controversy before the Commissioners aforesaid, shall and may have Authority to treat with them concerning the Satisfaction to be made to the said Commissioners for their Trouble in the Execution of the Trust reposed in them by this Act, and shall enter into a Bond to the said Commissioners to secure their Wages in such Manner as the said Commissioners and Committee shall agree, before the Commissioners shall proceed to hear any Witnesses or Proofs relative to the same Dispute, to the Intent that the said Commissioners may be under no Bias of interest in the Execution of the residue of the Trust herein after assigned to them.

AND for the defraying of all such Charges and Expences as have accrued or shall accrue on the Part of the Township of Harlem towards obtaining a final settlement of the Controversy abovementioned.

BE IT FURTHER ENACTED by the same Authority That the said Commissioners or the Majority or survivor of them shall have Authority to adjudge and determine which of the Proprietors of Lands in the said Township, are chargeable with, or liable to contribute to any Part of the same Burthen, and in what particular sum, of which they shall give a Certificate under their Hands and seals and therein fix a Day for the payment thereof, and the same Certificate and adjudication shall be final and conclusive to all parties therein named, and the several Sums so certified, shall be recoverable from the several Persons so certified to be chargeable therewith by Action or Actions grounded on this Act, in the Name of the said Committee or the Majority or

Survivors of them in any Court of Law having Cognizance of such Suit or Suits to the Intent that the said Committee may thereby be reimbursed for all the Money they shall expend or be liable for, in the Service aforesaid, and if the said Committee shall not be able to commence any such suit or Action against any Person or Persons so certified to be chargeable to contribute to the Settlement of the said Controversy on the Part of the said Township by reason of the Absence of the Defendant or Defendants from the Colony Infancy or other Impediment, then it shall be lawful for the said Committee or the Majority or Survivor of them to sell the Lands, Tenements and Hereditaments of the Person or Persons whose Proportions of the Expence shall so remain unpaid and to retain to their own use out of the Produce of the Sale the sum so certified to be due as the Proportion of the Proprietor or Proprietors thereof with lawful Interest thereon from the Time so fixed for payment thereof together with the Costs and Charges attending the same Sale returning the Surplus to the Proprietor or Proprietors thereof when thereunto lawfully required, and every sale of such Lands Hereditaments and Tenements shall convey as good an Estate and Title to the purchaser as the Proprietor or Proprietors thereof held in the same at the Time of making such sale.

AND BE IT ALSO ENACTED by the same Authority, That every such Sale shall be made by the said Committee or the Majority or Survivor of them at public Auction or Vendue to be held on the Premises to be so sold, of which eight Weeks previous Notice shall be given by Advertisement one Copy whereof shall be inserted from Week to Week in one of the Public NewsPapers of this Colony, and the other to be fixed up for the space of Time aforesaid on the Outside of the Church Door of the said Town of Harlem; but no such sale shall be made on the Day appointed for the Auction, if the Person or Persons chargeable with such Proportion, or any other Person for him or them shall before such Sale tender or offer to pay the Sum intended to be raised by the same for the purposes aforesaid to the said Committee, any or either of them.

PROVIDED ALWAYS, and be it further enacted by the Authority aforesaid that this Act, nor any Thing herein contained shall be of force until the same shall have received his Majesty's Royal Approbation.

[CHAPTER 1571.]

[Chapter 1571, of Van Schaack, where the act is printed in full.]

An Act for dividing and setting apart such Lands in the Patent of Wawayanda in the County of Orange as are held by the Owners of Goshen Town Rights in Common with the Proprietors of those Lots in the said Patent which were divided and ballotted for by Commissioners pursuant to an Act of this Colony entitled "An Act for the more effectual collecting of his "Majesty's Quit-Rents in the Colony of New "York and for Partition of Lands in order "thereto," and also to prevent Doubts respecting the Division of the said Patent made by the said Commissioners.

[Passed, March 24, 1772.]

WHEREAS a certain Tract of Land commonly called the Wawayanda Patent situate in the County of Orange in the Province of New York hath been divided by Commissioners appointed in pursuance of an Act of this Colony entitled. "An Act "for the more effectual collecting of his Majesty's Quit-Rents in "the Colony of New York and for partition of Lands in order "thereto," AND WHEREAS some Doubts have arisen whether the said Division was in every respect made agreeable to the Directions of the said Act, AND WHEREAS there are several thousand Inhabitants in the said Patent, many of whom in Case the said Division should be overturned, would be greatly prejudiced and some utterly ruined thereby, for Remedy whereof.

BE IT ENACTED by his Excellency the Governor, the Council and the General Assembly, and it is hereby enacted by the Authority of the Same, That the said Division of the said Patent shall be as valid and effectual to all Intents Constructions and purposes whatsoever as if all the said Division had been made in every respect exactly agreeable to the Directions of the said Act.

AND WHEREAS the Proprietors of those Rights in the said Patent commonly called the Goshen Town Rights are entitled to one undivided sixth part of all those Lots in the said Patent commonly called the Ballotted Lots, which Lots are of too small Value to be divided agreeable to the Directions of the said Act.

BE IT THEREFORE ENACTED by the Authority aforesaid That any Person or Persons interested in any of the said balloted Lots, inclined to have Partition thereof may subscribe a writing, and publish the same in any of the Public News Papers of this Colony twelve Weeks successively, directed to all Persons interested in said Lot or Lots specifying the Number thereof, and to what Patentee Right the same doth belong, giving Notice that three Commissioners (one of whom shall be a Surveyor) not interested in such Lot or Lots naming them and their places of abode, are appointed to make such Partition, and that they will meet at a certain Day and place to be also mentioned to proceed to the partition of the said Lot or Lots and requiring all persons interested therein to attend either by themselves or their Attornies a Copy of which writing shall be affixed to the Court House and Presbyterian Church in the said Town of Goshen, and if no Objection to any of the said Commissioners be offered in writing to any one of the Judges of the Inferior Court of Common Pleas for the said County of Orange, nor any Notice thereof in Writing be served upon the Subscriber or Subscribers to the Notice so directed to be published or any one of them, and within nine Weeks after the first Publication thereof, then the Commissioners so named shall perform the Duty required of them by this Act; but if such Objection and Notice be made and given, the Judge to whom it was offered shall appoint the Parties a Day and place within ten Days after nine Weeks from the first Publication of the Notice are expired, and then and there hear and determine such Objection and appoint other fit and uninterested persons in the Room of those he may think Proper to remove as unfit, and such Persons so appointed shall thenceforth be the Commissioners for executing the Powers given to Commissioners by virtue of this Act, and shall before they proceed to execute their Offices be severally sworn before any one of his Majesty's Justices of the Peace, to perform the Trust and Services required of a Commissioner by this Act, fairly and impartially, according to the Directions thereof and the best of his Skill and Judgment, a Certificate of their being so Sworn from the Person Administring the Oath, shall be filed with the rest of the proceedings as hereafter directed,

AND BE IT FURTHER ENACTED by the Authority aforesaid That the same Commissioners so to be appointed or any two of them shall set apart as the share and proportion of the Person or Persons who shall be entitled to the same, by virtue of the said Goshen Town Rights, or any of them, one sixth Part (having due Regard to the situation and Quality.) of the Lands so to be divided, and shall make two Maps of the same, which with two Copies of their Field Book signed by them or any two of them and proved before any Judge of the Inferior Court of Common Pleas for the said County of Orange shall be filed, one Map and Field Book in the Secretary's Office and the other in the Clerk's Office for the said County, which Partition so made shall be as valid and effectual in the Law to divide and Separate the said Land, as if the same had been made on Writs of Partition according to the Course of the Common Law.

AND BE IT FURTHER ENACTED by the Authority aforesaid That the Person or Persons who shall subscribe such Notice as is before mentioned shall pay the Expence attending such Partition, and may at any Time after six Months from the filing of the said Maps and Field-Books, sue for, and recover of each person interested in the Lands so to be divided his respective share of such Expence with Interest and Costs of suit.

AND BE IT FURTHER ENACTED by the Authority Aforesaid, That when the said sixth part of any of the Balloted Lots shall have been so set apart as aforesaid, any person or persons interested in the same may have his or their share or Proportion thereof set apart by proceeding in the same Manner as is herein before directed for the Division of the said sixth Part from the said Balloted Lots.

PROVIDED ALWAYS AND BE IT ENACTED That Nothing herein contained shall in any wise affect the Right or Interest of his Majesty his Heirs or Successors, or the Right or Interest of any Bodies Politick or Corporate, or any Person or Persons except such as are interested in the said Patent.

AND BE IT FURTHER ENACTED that this Act shall not be in force until the same shall have received his Majesty's Royal approbation.

[CHAPTER 1572.]

[Chapter 1572, of Van Schaack, where the title only is printed.]

An Act for discharging the present Assignees of Joseph Forman an Insolvent Debtor and for appointing a New Assignee and for other Purposes therein mentioned.

[Passed, March 24, 1772.]

WHEREAS Joseph Forman formerly of the City of New York Merchant an Insolvent Debtor, Robert Ray, John Harris Cruger and Lewis Pintard his Assignees and the Major Part of the

Creditors of the said Joseph Forman by their humble Petition presented to the General Assembly of this Colony having represented, That the said Joseph Forman being an Insolvent Debtor did on or about the first Day of December which was in the Year of our Lord one thousand seven hundred and sixty seven, together with divers of his Creditors present a Petition to the Honorable Daniel Horsmander and William Smith Esquires then two of the Judges of the Supreme Court of Judicature of this Colony in Order to obtain a General Discharge of the said Joseph Forman by Virtue of Sundry Acts of the Legislature of this Colony, then in Force for the Relief of Insolvent Debtors That the above named Robert Ray, John Harris Cruger and Lewis Pintard were nominated for Assignees of the Estate of the said Joseph Forman by the Majority of the then Petitioning Creditors as the said Acts directed, and that the said Judges having directed an Assignment thereof to them, and the said Joseph having made and executed the same accordingly afterwards on the Sixteenth day of January in the Year of our Lord one thousand seven hundred and sixty eight obtained a Discharge from the said Judges as the said Acts direct — That the said Robert Ray, John Harris Cruger and Lewis Pintard consented to become Assignees upon an express Stipulation with the Majority of the said Creditors, that they the said Assignees should not be expected in their own Persons to collect in the Debts due to the said Joseph Forman or in any other Manner to act personally in that Business, their own private Affairs not permitting them so to do, but only occasionally to overlook the said Joseph Forman, whom they the said Creditors considered as best capable of transacting the same for their Common Benefit, and whom they were desirous of employing therein and to allow him ten per Cent for his Encouragement — That the said Assignees in Consideration of this Stipulation accepted of the said Assignment upon the express Terms of not being allowed any Thing for their Trouble out of the said Insolvent Estate and by the desire of the Major Part of the said Creditors constituted the said Joseph Forman their Attorney for the Purpose of collecting in the Monies owing to him, and settling his Affairs with an Allowance of Ten Pounds on every hundred Pounds of the Monies so collected That after the Assignment so made by the said Joseph Forman, and his Discharge as above mentioned it was discovered that a Mistake had been made in the Computation of the Accounts annexed to the said Petition presented to the said Judges as aforesaid; on rectifying which Mistake it appeared that the Amount of all the Debts of his then Petitioning Creditors fell short of three fourths of all his Debts, which it is apprehended may give Occasion for drawing into Question the Legality of the aforesaid Assignment and Discharge That the said Joseph Forman from his Age and Infirmities hath been able of the many Debts due to his Estate to collect only a very inconsiderable Part. That the said first above mentioned Petitioners and Creditors of the said Joseph Forman convinced that very little Benefit of the Estate of the said Joseph Forman will be derived to his Creditors unless some more vigorous Methods are used to settle the same, and to collect in what may be due to him, and being desirous that the said Assignees should not be compelled to undertake beyond their said Engagements, and being willing to remove all Inconveniencies that may arise from any Doubts of the Validity of the said Assignment and Discharge have in a Meeting lately held by them on that Subject agreed humbly to Petition the General Assembly of this Colony for Relief by a Law discharging the said Joseph and his Assignees and vesting all the Estate in Law and Equity which belonged to the said Joseph Forman at the Time he became Insolvent in such Person as to the Legislature should seem fit, the said Doubt notwithstanding in order that the most might be made thereof for the Benefit of the Creditors of the said Joseph Forman, and also for a Provision for the Discharge of the said Petitioner Joseph Forman as fully to all Intents and Purposes, as he would have been had no Doubt arisen about the Validity of the said Proceedings — That at their said Meeting Bernardus La Grange Esquire was proposed to and approved by the Petitioners as a very proper Person for that Trust who has declared himself willing to accept thereof — The General Assembly pray that it may be enacted.

AND BE IT ENACTED by his Excellency the Governor, the Council and the General Assembly and it is hereby enacted by the Authority of the same that the said Robert Ray, John Harris Cruger and Lewis Pintard Assignees as aforesaid in Order to their Discharge and Releasement from the said Trust shall and do respectively within one Month after the passing of this Act exhibit in Writing under their Hands on Oath to one of the Judges of the Supreme Court of Judicature of this Colony a full and true Account of all the Monies received and paid by them respectively as Assignees as aforesaid, and of all Mortgages, Bonds,

Notes or other Securities Assigned to them by the said Joseph Forman or by them respectively taken for securing the Payment of any Debt or Debts due and owing to the said Joseph Forman at the Time he became Insolvent as aforesaid, or to his Estate or as due and owing to them the said Robert Ray, John Harris Cruger and Lewis Pintard as Assignees as aforesaid, And that such Accounts being exhibited as aforesaid by them or the Survivors or Survivor of them it shall and may be lawfull for them the said Robert Ray, John Harris Cruger and Lewis Pintard or the Survivors or Survivor of them to execute an Assignment to Bernardus La Grange of New Brunswick in the Colony of New Jersey Esquire in the words following to wit, KNOW ALL MEN by these Presents that We [naming the said Assignees or the Survivors or Survivor of them] by Virtue of an Act of the Governor, the Council and the General Assembly of the Colony of New York, Entitled an Act for Discharging the present Assignees of Joseph Forman an Insolvent Debtor, and for appointing a new Assignee and for other Purposes therein mentioned HAVE granted assigned and set over and by these Presents DO grant assign and set over unto Bernardus La Grange of New Brunswick in the Colony of New Jersey Esquire appointed in and by the said Act to receive the same. All and Singular the Estate Real and Personal both in Law and Equity formerly belonging to the said Joseph Forman, and all the Books, Vouchers and Securities relating to the same, To have and to hold the same to the said Bernardus La Grange his Executors, Administrators, and Assigns and to his and their use and Behoof for ever IN TRUST nevertheless for the Benefit of the Creditors of the said Joseph Forman IN WITNESS whereof We have hereunto set our Hands and Seals this [naming the Day of the Month] in the Year of our Lord One thousand seven hundred and Seventy two.

Sealed and Delivered in the Presence of

Which said Assignment being executed as aforesaid in the Presence of two Credible Persons attesting the same as Witnesses thereto, all and singular the Estates Real and Personal both in Law and Equity, Chattels, Rights, Thing and Things in Action whatsoever which did belong to the said Joseph Forman and were assigned or intended to be assigned as aforesaid to the said Robert Ray, John Harris Cruger and Lewis Pintard by the said Joseph Forman, together with all and Singular the Books, Vouchers and Securities whatsoever relating to the same shall thereby be vested in the said Bernardus La Grange his

Executors Administrators and Assigns as fully and absolutely and for and upon the like Trusts, Intents and Purposes as the same were assigned or intended to be assigned to the said Robert Ray, John Harris Cruger and Lewis Pintard as aforesaid or are or could have become vested in them as Assignees as aforesaid by any Law of this Colony in Force on the said Sixteenth day of January one thousand seven hundred and Sixty eight any Doubt or Doubts that have arisen or may hereafter arise concerning the Regularity or Validity of the said Discharge of the said Joseph Forman or of any the Proceedings relative thereto, or any Matter or Thing whatsoever to the Contrary in any wise notwithstanding.

PROVIDED ALWAYS AND BE IT FURTHER ENACTED by the Authority aforesaid, that nothing in this Act shall extend or be construed to extend to defeat or make void any Sale or other Disposal of any the said Estate or Effects or any Part or Parts thereof by the said Robert Ray, John Harris Cruger and Lewis Pintard in Pursuance of their Trust as Assignees as aforesaid, but that the same and every other Act and Act bona fide done and transacted by them in Pursuance of their said Trust is hereby confirmed and declared to be valid and effectual, and shall be so adjudged any Thing contained in this Act or any Doubt or other Matter or Thing as aforesaid in any wise notwithstanding.

AND BE IT FURTHER ENACTED by the Authority aforesaid that they the said Robert Ray, John Harris Cruger and Lewis Pintard or the Survivors or Survivor of them shall deliver to the said Bernardus La Grange a Duplicate of the said Account hereinbefore directed and required to be made and exhibited before one of the Judges of the Supreme Court of Judicature of this Colony as aforesaid and thereupon and the said Assignment being made to the said Bernardus La Grange as above directed they the said Robert Ray, John Harris Cruger and Lewis Pintard, and every of them, their and every of their Heirs Executors and Administrators shall from thence forward be totally and absolutely discharged from being Assignees as aforesaid and of and from all Manner of Trusts Accounts, Suits Reckonings or Demands whatsoever of to from or by the said Joseph Forman or any of his Creditors for or by Reason of their having been Assignees as aforesaid, and shall only be accountable as having been Assignees as aforesaid to the said Bernardus La Grange his Executors and Administrators for such Sum and Sums of money as they the said Robert Ray, John Harris Cruger and Lewis Pintard or either of them is, are, or shall be indebted to the Estate of the said Joseph Forman by Reason of the Premises.

AND BE IT FURTHER ENACTED by the Authority aforesaid that the said Assignment being made and the Duplicate of the said Account delivered to the said Bernardus La Grange as is herein before directed and appointed, he the said Bernardus La Grange shall thenceforward be by Virtue of the said Assignment and of this Act Assignee of the said Joseph Forman fully and absolutely to all Intents and Purposes whatsoever according to the true Intent and Meaning of this Act, for the Benefit of the Creditors of the said Joseph Forman and be invested with all and every the Powers and Authorities Benefits and Advantages whatsoever and subjected to all the Trusts, Regulations and Directions, which they the said Robert Ray, John Harris Cruger and Lewis Pintard, were or might have been invested with or Subject to as Assignees of the said Joseph Forman by Virtue of any and every Law or Laws of this Colony in Force on the said Sixteenth day of January one thousand seven hundred and Sixty eight as fully and absolutely to all Intents and Purposes whatsoever, as if he the said Bernardus La Grange had been appointed solely Assignee to the said Joseph Forman preparatory to the Discharge of the said Joseph as aforesaid and all the Proceedings relating thereto had been in all Things strictly regular; and as if all and singular the Articles and Things in the said Laws of this Colony contained and expressed in Force on the Day last abovementioned were herein at large particularly repeated and reenacted at length.

PROVIDED nevertheless that the said Bernardus La Grange his Executors and Administrators shall be allowed the same Time to be computed from the Date of the Assignment to be made to him by Virtue of this Act for making the Divisions of the Monies he shall raise from the Estate of the said Insolvent as any other Assignees under the said Laws in Force on the said Sixteenth day of January One thousand seven hundred and sixty eight, were by such Laws allowed for the like Purpose.

AND BE IT FURTHER ENACTED by the Authority aforesaid that if any Creditor of the said Joseph Forman who shall not have already given Notice of and proved his Debt according to the true Intent and Meaning of the said Laws in Force on the said Sixteenth day of January one thousand seven hundred and sixty eight, shall not within Eighteen Months from the Date of the Assignment by this Act directed to be made to the said Bernardus La Grange give Notice of and prove such his Debt such Creditor shall not be thereafter admitted to prove his Debt in order to entitle himself to any Share in the Estate of the said Joseph Forman, but shall by this Act be debarred from any Share thereof.

AND BE IT FURTHER ENACTED by the Authority aforesaid, That the said Bernardus La Grange shall immediately after the said Assignment made to him as aforesaid take an Oath to be Administred by any one of the Judges of the Supreme Court of Judicature of this Colony well and faithfully to manage the Estate of the said Joseph Forman Assigned to him as aforesaid and keep and render a true Account of all that shall come to his Hands of the same, and for that Purpose shall keep regular Books of Accounts to which every Creditor at all reasonable Times may have recourse, and for the Care and Trouble Incumbent on the said Bernardus La Grange in the Premises he shall be allowed out of the said Estate such a Consideration as the Petitioning Creditors, signing the Petition hereinbefore mentioned to the Judges of the Supreme Court for the Discharge of the said Joseph Forman as hereinbefore recited, or a Major Part of them shall agree and fix upon.

AND BE IT FURTHER ENACTED by the Authority aforesaid, That for the more full Discovery of the said Insolvents Estate any one of the Judges of the Supreme Court of Judicature of this Colony at the Request of the said Bernardus La Grange Assignee as aforesaid his Executors or Administrators or any of them shall have full Power and are hereby required to Summon and examine on Oath any Person whomsoever known or suspected to detain any Part of the said Insolvents Estate or to be indebted thereto. And in Case any Person on such Summons shall refuse to attend having no reasonable Excuse or shall refuse to be Sworn or Answer, or if a Quaker to affirm and Answer, then it shall be lawfull for any of the said Judges to commit the Person so refusing to Goal until he or she shall submit to be examined and discover what he or she shall know of the said Insolvents Estate or Effects, And if any such Person shall wilfully and knowingly Swear or Affirm falsely the Person so offending shall on Conviction incur the same Pains and Penalties as those who are convicted of wilfull and corrupt Perjury.

AND WHEREAS the said Joseph Forman hath been employed by the said Robert Ray, John Harris Cruger and Lewis Pintard by the Desire of the Creditors of the said Joseph Forman as above mentioned to collect in the Monies due to him, with an Allowance after the Rate of Ten Pounds for every hundred Pounds so collected by him as aforesaid. BE IT FURTHER ENACTED by the Authority aforesaid That the said Joseph Forman shall and do before he shall receive any Benefit or Advantage of this Act or be in any wise discharged from any of his said Debts, exhibit a just and true Account in Writing to one of the said Judges of all the Monies or Effects so received by him or any other Person or Persons for him as far as the same shall have come to his Knowledge as and for Payment of any Debt or any Part or Parts of any Debt or Debts due to him at the Time he became Insolvent as aforesaid and of all Securities taken by him or any other Person or Persons for him, in the Name of the said Joseph Forman or in the Name or Names of any other Person or Persons whomsoever for securing the Payment of any such Debt or any Part or Parts of any such Debt or Debts as far as the same shall have come to his Knowledge and how such Monies and Effects so received hath been paid over disposed of or applied by the said Joseph Forman or any Person or Persons for him, and in whose Hands any such Securities now are, and shall also pay over to the said Bernardus La Grange his Executors or Administrators all and Singular the Monies so received by him, or by any Person or Persons for him, not already paid over into the Hands of the said Robert Ray, John Harris Cruger and Lewis Pintard, or one of them or to some other Person or Persons by their Order, first deducting thereout for the use of him the said Joseph Forman at and after the Rate of Ten Pounds for every hundred Pounds of the said Monies so actually received and paid over as aforesaid. On exhibiting which said Account the said Judge shall Administer an Oath to the said Joseph Forman to the following Effect.

"I Joseph Forman do solemnly swear in the Presence of Al-"mighty God, that the Account by me delivered is a just and "true Account of all the Monies and Effects received by me since "I was entrusted by Robert Ray, John Harris Cruger and Lewis "Pintard, or any of them with the collecting the Debts due to me "before I become Insolvent, and by every Person for me as far "as the same have come to my Knowledge, as and for Payment "of any Debt or any Part or Parts of any Debt or Debts due to "me, at the Time I became Insolvent; And also of all Securities "taken by me or any other Person or Persons for me in my

"Name or in the Name of any other Person or Persons whomso-"ever for securing the Payment of any such Debt or any Part or "Parts of any such Debt or Debts, as far as the same, have come "to my Knowledge. And that the Monies and Effects so re-"ceived have been respectively paid over disposed of and applied "in such Manner and Form as in and by the said Account is "expressed and stated concerning the same respectively, And "that the said Securities and every of them are to the best of my "Knowledge and Belief now in the Hands of the Person or Per-"sons mentioned in the said Account to be possessed of them "respectively, And that I have not directly or indirectly done or "willingly suffered to be done any Act or Thing whatsoever to "defraud my Creditors or any of them So help me God." Which Oath being taken by the said Joseph Forman, and the said Joseph having as above directed made Payment to the said Bernardus La Grange as hereinbefore is directed and appointed, Notice shall be given by the said Bernardus La Grange his Executors or Administrators to all the Creditors of the said Joseph Forman by Advertising the same in one of the Public News Papers printed in this Colony to shew Cause before one of the Judges of the Supreme Court of Judicature of this Colony if any they have by such a Day as shall be appointed by any of the said Judges why the said Joseph Forman should not be discharged of and from all the Debts owing by him before the said Sixteenth day of January one thousand seven hundred and sixty eight, at which Day it shall and may be lawfull to and for one fourth Part of the Creditors of the said Joseph Forman in respect to the Value of all the Debts due and owing by him on the said sixteenth day of January one thousand seven hundred and sixty eight having first respectively made Oath of the Justness of their said Debts, and that the same was and were due and owing to them respectively on the Day last above mentioned to signify their Dissent in Writing under their Hands to his being so discharged: AND if on the said Day such Dissent shall not be signified as aforesaid according to the true Intent and Meaning hereof, the said Joseph Forman shall from thenceforth be discharged from all Debts owing by him on the said Sixteenth day of January one thousand seven hundred and Sixty eight or contracted for before that Time though payable afterwards, And if he the said Joseph Forman his Executors or Administrators or any of them should be at any Time hereafter Prosecuted for any such Debt or Contract, he, she or they may plead the General Issue and give the Special Matter in Evidence.

AND BE IT FURTHER ENACTED by the Authority aforesaid that if such Dissent shall be shewn in Writing as above mentioned according to the true Intent and Meaning hereof against the said Joseph Forman's being discharged from his said Debts, that then and in this Case the said Joseph shall not be discharged from any of his said Debts, nor shall any his said Creditors be prevented from recovering either in Law or Equity their just Demands against him the said Joseph Forman his Executors or Administrators or of levying the same by Execution on all and every such Estates and Effects as he the said Joseph hath acquired or become entitled to in Law or Equity since the said Sixteenth day of January one thousand seven hundred and sixty eight, Yet Nevertheless the said Judge to whom such Dissent as aforesaid shall be given, shall Discharge the said Joseph Forman if in Prison from his Imprisonment, which Discharge or the Record thereof shall be a sufficient Warrant to the Sheriff or Goaler for setting the said Joseph Forman at large: And if the said Joseph shall at any Time thereafter be imprisoned for or by Reason of any of the said Debts or Contracts, upon every such Arrest it shall and may be lawfull for any Judge of the Court whence the Process issued upon producing to him the Discharge last above mentioned or the Record thereof or a Certified Office Copy thereof to release and discharge the said Joseph Forman out of Custody, and the said Judge is hereby required so to do, so as the said Joseph Forman do give a Warrant of Attorney to appear to every such Action and Plead thereto.

AND BE IT FURTHER ENACTED by the Authority aforesaid, That if the said Joseph Forman shall be guilty of Perjury in any Matter or Particular contained in the said Oath herein before mentioned or shall secret any Books, Vouchers, Writings or other Things appertaining to his Estate with an Intent to Defraud his Creditors he shall in such Case be deemed and adjudged Guilty of Felony without Benefit of Clergy.

AND BE IT FURTHER ENACTED by the Authority aforesaid that if any Action of Escape or any Suit or Action shall be brought against the Judge of any Court or any Justice of the Peace or any Sheriff Goaler or Keeper of any Prison for performing their Office in Pursuance of this Act he or they may Plead the General Issue, and give this Act, and any other Special Matter in Evidence, and if the Plaintiff be nonsuited or discontinue his Action or Verdict, or Judgment on Demurrer pass against him, the Defendant shall have treble Costs awarded to him: AND if the said Robert Ray, John Harris Cruger and Lewis Pintard or any of them their or any of their Heirs, Executors or Administrators or any of them, they the said Robert Ray, John Harris Cruger and Lewis Pintard or the Survivors or Survivor of them, having in all Things complied with and performed the Matters and Things in this Act directed for them to do and perform according to the true Intent and Meaning hereof, shall at any Time hereafter be sued in any Court of Law or Equity for any Matter or Thing in any wise relating to their said Trust as Assignees as aforesaid, or for any Matter or Thing by them done by Virtue of this Act, or if any other Person or Persons shall be sued for any Matter or Thing done by Virtue of this Act, it shall be lawfull for them and every of them so sued to plead the General Issue and give this Act and any other Special Matter in Evidence.

THIRTY-FIRST ASSEMBLY.

Fifth Session.

(Begun Jan. 5, 1773, 13 George III, William Tryon, Governor.)

[CHAPTER 1573.]

[Chapter 1573, of Van Schaack, where the title only is printed. This act re-enacts chapter 948. See chapter 1509.]

An Act further to continue an Act intitled. "An Act for granting to His Majesty the several Duties and Impositions on Goods, Wares "and Merchandizes imported into this Colony, "therein mentioned."

[Passed, February 6, 1773.]

WHEREAS the several Duties and Impositions on Goods, Wares and Merchandizes imported into this Colony, and granted for the support of the Government of his late Majesty King George the second by the above mentioned Act, have by several subsequent Acts, been continued to the first Day of February one thousand seven hundred and seventy three, and the General Assembly being willing to make provisions for the further Support of his Majesty's Government.

BE IT THEREFORE ENACTED by his Excellency the Governor the Council and the General Assembly, and it is hereby enacted by the Authority of the same. That the abovementioned Act entitled. "An Act for granting to His Majesty the several "Duties and Impositions on Goods Wares and Merchandizes imported into this Colony therein mentioned". passed in the twenty seventh year of his late Majesty's Reign shall be, and is hereby continued, and every Clause, Matter and Thing therein contained enacted to be and remain in full Force, to all Intents, Constructions and purposes whatsoever until the first Day of February which will be in the year of our Lord one thousand seven hundred and seventy four inclusive, and that Nicoll Havens of Shelter Island in Suffolk County be the Officer to collect the Colony Duties in the said County, in the Room of Isaac Hubbard deceased appointed in the abovementioned Act. PROVIDED, ALWAYS. That so much of the first Clause or Section of said Act as relates to European or East-India Goods imported from the British Islands into this Colony shall be construed taken and deemed to be from the British Islands in America only, any Thing in the said Act to the contrary hereof notwithstanding.

[CHAPTER 1574.]

[Chapter 1574, of Van Schaack, where the act is printed in full. See chapter 1486.]

An Act to continue an Act entitled. "An "Act to amend an Act entitled An Act to prevent Frauds in Debtors, by extending the "same to Executors and Administrators residing out of this Colony, whose Testators or "Intestates have Effects within the same."

[Passed, February 6, 1773.]

WHEREAS an Act entitled. "An Act to amend an Act entitled An Act to prevent Frauds in Debtors, by extending the "same to Executors and Administrators residing out of this "Colony, whose Testators or Intestates have Effects within the "same." will expire by it's own Limitation on the first Day of February one thousand seven hundred and seventy three.

BE IT THEREFORE ENACTED by his Excellency the Governor the Council and the General Assembly, and it is hereby enacted by the Authority of the same. That the said Act entitled. "An Act to amend an Act entitled An Act to prevent Frauds in

"Debtors by extending the same to Executors and Adminis-"trators residing out of this Colony, whose Testators or Intestates "have Effects within the same," shall be and hereby is continued from the Expiration thereof, until the first Day of February one thousand seven hundred and seventy five, any Thing in the said Act contained to the contrary hereof in any wise notwithstanding.

[CHAPTER 1575.]

[Chapter 1575, of Van Schaack, where the act is printed in full. See chapter 1488.]

An Act to continue an Act entitled. "An "Act for apprehending of Persons in any "County or Place upon Warrants granted by "Justices of the peace of any other County or "place."

[Passed, February 6, 1773.]

BE IT ENACTED by his Excellency the Governor the Council and the General Assembly, and it is hereby enacted by the Authority of the same That the abovementioned Act entitled. "An "Act for apprehending of Persons in any County or place upon "Warrants granted by Justices of the Peace of any other County "or place." passed the sixteenth Day of February one thousand seven hundred and seventy one, shall be and is hereby continued and every Clause Matter and Thing therein contained enacted to be and remain in full force to all Intents Constructions and purposes whatsoever until the first Day of February which will be in the Year of our Lord one thousand seven hundred and eighty.

[CHAPTER 1576.]

[Chapter 1576, of Van Schaack, where the title only is printed.]

An Act to facilitate the Return of his Majesty's Commission under the Great Seal of Great Britain, and the proceedings thereon, for settling the Boundary Line between this Colony and New Jersey.

[Passed, February 6, 1773.]

WHEREAS his Majesty's Commission under the Great Seal of Great Britain for settling the Boundary Line between this Colony and New Jersey hath not hitherto been returned, but remains together with all the proceedings of the Commissioners thereupon, in the Hands of John Jay Esquire the Clerk of the said Commissioners, who is doubtful whether he can legally deliver up the said Commission and proceedings to any Person not authorized under the Great Seal of Great Britain, or by Act of Legislature to receive the same.

BE IT THEREFORE ENACTED by his Excellency the Governor, the Council and the General Assembly, and it is hereby enacted by the Authority of the same, That it shall and may be lawful to and for the said John Jay, and he is hereby authorized and required forthwith to deliver to the Commissioners named and appointed in and by his Majesty's said Commission or to either of them, the said Commission and the Acts and proceedings of the said Commissioners thereupon, together with all the Maps, Evidence, and papers which remain in his Custody relative thereto, in order that a Copy of the same proceedings and proofs may be transmitted to his Majesty in privy Council.

[CHAPTER 1577.]

[Chapter 1577, of Van Schaack, where the title only is printed.]

An Act to impower the Mayor Recorder and Aldermen of the City of New York or the major Part of them to order the raising a Sum not exceeding sixteen hundred pounds for the uses therein mentioned.

[Passed, February 6, 1773.]

WHEREAS the providing a sufficient Number of Watchmen and lighting of Lamps within the City of New York has not only been found convenient but also necessary for the safety of it's Inhabitants and others.

BE IT THEREFORE ENACTED by his Excellency the Governor, the Council and the General Assembly, and it is hereby enacted by the Authority of the same. That the Mayor Recorder and Aldermen of the City of New York for the Time being or the Major Part of them whereof the Mayor or Recorder to be one, shall have full power and Authority, and are hereby fully impowered and authorized on the second Tuesday in the Month of February one thousand seven hundred and seventy three, or within twenty Days thereafter to order the raising a Sum not exceeding sixteen hundred Pounds by a Tax upon the Estates real and personal of all and every the Freeholders, Freemen, Inhabitants Residents and sojourners within the City of New York on the South Side of Fresh-Water for the payment of so many Watchmen as the Mayor Aldermen and Commonalty of the City of New York shall think necessary for guarding the City and for purchasing Oil providing Lamps and for repairing and attending the Lamps which now are or hereafter may be erected, which Sum of sixteen hundred Pounds shall be rated and Assessed by the Vestrymen who shall rate and assess the Tax for the Minister and poor of the said City, the Vestrymen first taking the Oath prescribed to be taken in and by an Act entitled. "An Act to enable "the Inhabitants of the City of New York to choose annually two "Vestrymen for each respective ward within the said City". made and passed in the nineteenth Year of the Reign of his late Majesty King George the second, and the Tax so to be laid shall be collected levied and paid at the same Time as the Tax for the Maintenance of the Minister and poor of the said City hath been accustomed into the Hands of the Church Wardens of the said City for the Time being, who are hereby required and directed to pay the same into the Hands of the Chamberlain of the said City to be by him paid as shall be directed by Warrant or Warrants of the said Mayor Aldermen and Commonalty in Common Council convened for uses aforesaid.

AND BE IT FURTHER ENACTED by the Authority aforesaid, That over and above the sum of sixteen hundred Pounds to be levied and paid by virtue of this Act, the sum of three pence in the Pound as a Reward to the Constables for their Trouble shall be assessed levied and paid to the respective Constables for collecting and paying the same and no more, according to the true Intent and meaning of this Act, any Thing herein or in any other Act or Acts contained to the contrary hereof in any wise notwithstanding.

AND BE IT FURTHER ENACTED by the Authority aforesaid, That if the said Mayor Recorder or Aldermen, Church-Wardens, Vestrymen or Constables of the said City, who are hereby authorized impowered and required to take effectual care that this Act be executed according to the true Intent and meaning thereof, or any of them shall deny refuse or delay to perform execute or comply with all or any of the Powers Authorities and Duties in this Act given and required to be done and performed by them or either of them, and thereof shall be lawfully convicted in any Court of Record in this Colony, he or they so denying refusing or delaying to perform the Duties as aforesaid shall suffer such Pains and Penalties by Fine and Imprisonment as by the Discretion of the said Court shall be adjudged.

AND BE IT FURTHER ENACTED by the Authority aforesaid, That if any Person or Persons shall wilfully break or damage any of the Lamps whether private or Public now erected or hereafter to be erected within the said City, he she or they so offending shall forfeit the sum of twenty Pounds for every Lamp he she or they shall damage or break as aforesaid to be levied by Warrant or Warrants under the Hands and seals of two or more of his Majesty's Justices of the Peace for the City and County of New York by Distress and sale of the Offender's Goods and Chattels on due Conviction made upon the Oath of one or more credible Witness or Witnesses, rendering the overplus if any there be to the Owner or Owners, and for want of such Distress, the Offender or Offenders shall be imprisoned by Warrant under the Hands and Seals of the said Justices who are hereby required to issue the same, for the space of three Months unless the said Forfeiture or Forfeitures be sooner paid, which Forfeitures shall be applied towards providing and repairing of Lamps and paying the Watchmen.

AND BE IT FURTHER ENACTED by the Authority aforesaid. That all such Persons as shall be employed to guard the said City and attend the Lamps shall be under the Direction of and obey such Orders as they shall from Time to Time receive from the Mayor Aldermen and Commonalty of the said City, any Custom Law or Usage to the contrary thereof in any wise notwithstanding.

[CHAPTER 1578.]

[Chapter 1578, of Van Schaack, where the act is printed in full. See chapter 956.]

An Act to extend an Act entitled "An Act "to enable and impower the Mayor Aldermen "and Commonalty of the City of New York, "and their Successors to prevent & remove the "particular Nusances within the same to the "Southward of Fresh Water", to the Outward of the said City.

[Passed, February 6, 1773.]

WHEREAS the Act entitled. "An Act to enable and impower "the Mayor Aldermen and Commonalty of the City of New York, "and their Successors to prevent and remove the particular Nu-"sances within the same to the southward of Fresh Water", has by Experience been found of great use. AND WHEREAS extending the same to the Outward of the said City will answer the good purposes thereby intended.

BE IT THEREFORE ENACTED by his Excellency the Governor the Council and the General Assembly, and it is hereby enacted by the Authority of the same. That the said Act is hereby extended to the Outward of the City of New York and all the Matters and Things therein contained, are hereby enacted to be in force in the said Outward of the said City, to all Intents Constructions and purposes whatever.

[CHAPTER 1579.]

[Chapter 1579, of Van Schaack, where the act is printed in full. See chapters 1198 and 1367 and 670.]

An Act to increase the Number of Firemen in the City of New York.

[Passed, February 6, 1773.]

BE IT ENACTED by his Excellency the Governor, the Council and the General Assembly, and it is hereby enacted by the Authority of the same. That the Mayor Aldermen and Commonalty of the City of New York, or the Major Part of them in Common Council convened shall with all convenient speed after the Publication of this Act elect nominate and appoint twenty more able honest sober discreet Men (willing to accept) being Freemen of, or Freeholders within the said City and County to be added to the Firemen of the said City appointed in virtue of several Acts heretofore passed, who when elected shall be hereby excused from the several Offices and Duties as the Firemen are by an Act entitled. "An Act for the better extinguishing of Fires that "may happen within the City of New York," passed in the eleventh Year of the Reign of his late Majesty King George the second, and be liable to the Rule, Order, Ordinance and Regulation, Fines and Penalties as the Firemen are liable and subject to by the said recited Act.

AND BE IT FURTHER ENACTED by the Authority aforesaid. That the Mayor Aldermen and Commonalty of the City of New York, or the major Part of them in Common Council convened, may displace any of the Firemen to be appointed by this

Act for Default or neglect of Duty, and others to appoint in their Room and stead from Time to Time, and so often as they shall think necessary.

[CHAPTER 1580.]

[Chapter 1580, of Van Schaack, where the act is printed in full.]

An Act to prevent the Defacing the Statues which are erected in the City of New York.

[Passed, February 6, 1773.]

WHEREAS there has been erected in the City of New York an Equestrian Statue of our most gracious Sovereign as a Monument of the deep Sense with which the Inhabitants of this Colony are impressed of the Blessings they enjoy under his illustrious Reign, as well as their great Affection for his Royal Person AND ALSO a Statue of the Right Honorable William Pitt Esquire, now Earl of Chatham, in commemoration of the many eminent Services which he has rendered by his patriotic Conduct in Parliament to his fellow subjects in North America.

BE IT THEREFORE ENACTED by his Excellency the Governor, the Council and the General Assembly and it is hereby enacted by the Authority of the same. That if any Person or Persons shall wilfully break, deface, disfigure or otherwise damage the said statues or either of them, the person or persons so breaking, defacing, disfiguring or otherwise damaging them or either of them, shall forfeit for every such Offence the sum of five hundred Pounds Current Money of this Colony, to be recovered in any Court of Record within the same, by Bill, plaint or Information by any Person or Persons who will sue for the same, the one half to be applied to the use of such Person or Persons so suing, and the other half to be paid to the Treasurer of this Colony for and towards the support of the Government thereof, and if the said Forfeiture be not immediately paid, the person or persons who shall commit said Offence, shall be committed to the Common Goal, there to remain one whole Year without Bail or Mainprize, unless the Forfeiture be sooner paid.

[CHAPTER 1581.]

[Chapter 1581, of Van Schaack, where the act is printed in full. See chapter 1494.]

An Act to continue and amend an Act entitled. "An Act for the more effectual punish-" ment of Persons who shall be guilty of any of "the Trespasses therein mentioned in the Cities "of New York and Albany, and Township of "Schenectady."

[Passed, February 6, 1773.]

WHEREAS an Act entitled. "An Act for the more effectual "punishment of Persons who shall be guilty of any of the Tres-"passes therein mentioned in the Cities of New York and Al-"bany and Township of Schenectady." will expire by it's own Limitation on the first Day of February one thousand seven hundred and seventy three, and the same being found useful and necessary.

BE IT THEREFORE ENACTED by His Excellency the Governor the Council and the General Assembly, and it is hereby enacted by the Authority of the same. That the Act entitled "An Act for the more effectual punishment of persons who shall "be guilty of any of the Trespasses therein mentioned in the "Cities of New York and Albany, and Township of Schenectady," shall be and hereby is continued and every Article Matter and Clause therein contained enacted to be and remain in full force until the first Day of February which will be in the Year of our Lord one thousand seven hundred and eighty.

AND BE IT FURTHER ENACTED by the Authority aforesaid. That all and every Person or Persons, who shall or may be present when any of the Trespasses in the said Act mentioned shall be committed, shall be deemed to be guilty thereof, and be subject to the Penalties inflicted by the said Act, altho he or they shall not be aiding abetting or assisting therein; unless such person or persons shall give Evidence whereby to convict the person or persons really guilty thereof, or unless he or they shall declare upon Oath, that he or they came there accidentally, and that he or they do not know who the Offender or Offenders is or are.

[CHAPTER 1582.]

[Chapter 1582, of Van Schaack, where the act is printed in full. Continued by chapter 1714.]

An Act for regulating the practice of Innoculation for the Small Pox in the City of Albany.

[Passed, February 6, 1773.]

BE IT ENACTED by his Excellency the Governor the Council and the General Assembly and it is hereby enacted by the Authority of the same. That from and after the Publication of this Act, and during the continuance thereof, no person or persons whatever shall make use of any House or Building within the City of Albany as a Hospital or House of reception for receiving people with intent to Inoculate or cause them to be Inoculated for the small pox unless by a Licence previously obtained from the Mayor Recorder Aldermen and Commonalty of the said City, in Common Council convened. PROVIDED ALWAYS. That Nothing in this Act shall extend or be construed to deprive or prevent any Person or Persons from Inoculating any Person or Persons, belonging to his her or their Family in their own House.

AND BE IT FURTHER ENACTED by the same Authority, That if any Person or Persons shall offend contrary to the true Intent and Meaning of this Act, such Offender or Offenders shall be liable to and pay a Fine of fifty Pounds to be recovered in any Court of Record in the City and County of Albany, one half to the Informer, the other to the poor of the said City.

AND BE IT FURTHER ENACTED by the same Authority That this Act shall be and remain in force until the first Day of May which will be in the Year of our Lord, one thousand seven hundred and seventy five.

[CHAPTER 1583.]

[Chapter 1583, of Van Schaack, where the title only is printed.]

An Act to enable the Mayor Recorder Aldermen and Commonalty of the City of Albany for the Time being or the major Part of them to order the raising a Sum not exceeding one hundred and fifty Pounds for the purposes therein mentioned.

[Passed, February 6, 1773.]

WHEREAS the establishing of a regular well constituted Night-Watch and lighting of Lamps within the City of Albany, has not only been found convenient, but also necessary for the safety of it's Inhabitants and others.

BE IT THEREFORE ENACTED by his Excellency the Governor the Council and the General Assembly, and it is hereby enacted by the Authority of the same That the Mayor Recorder Aldermen and Commonalty of the City of Albany for the Time being or the major Part of them whereof the Mayor or Recorder to be one, shall have full power and Authority and are hereby fully impowered and authorized at any Time before the last Day of March one thousand seven hundred and seventy three to order the raising a Sum not exceeding one hundred and fifty Pounds by a Tax upon the Estates real and personal lying and being within the said City, of all and every the Freeholders, Freemen, Inhabitants, Residents and sojourners living within a half Mile of Hudson's River, and to the North of a West Line drawn from the old Fort, for the payment of so many Watchmen and Lamps as the Mayor Recorder Aldermen and Commonalty of the said City in Common Council convened shall think necessary for guarding the said City and lighting the Lamps in the same, which Tax so to be laid shall be rated and assessed at the same Time and by the Assessors who shall rate and assess the Tax which shall be raised by virtue of an Act of the Governor, the Council and the General Assembly of the Colony of New York entitled. "An Act for the better explaining and more effectual "puting in Execution an Act of the General Assembly made in "the third year of the Reign of their late Majesties King "William and Queen Mary entitled An Act for defraying the "Public and necessary Charge throughout this Province, and for "maintaining the Poor and preventing Vagabonds," made and passed the nineteenth Day of June one thousand seven hundred and three, the Assessors first taking the Oath prescribed to be taken by the last mentioned Act, and the Tax so to be laid, shall be collected levied and paid by the same Collector and at the same Time as the Tax raised by virtue of the Act aforesaid hath been accustomed, and shall be paid into the Hands of such persons as the Mayor Recorder, Aldermen and Commonalty in Common Council convened shall appoint for the uses aforesaid.

AND BE IT FURTHER ENACTED by the Authority aforesaid. That the Collector shall retain in his Hands three pence in the pound for every pound so raised by virtue of this Act as a Reward for his Trouble in collecting and paying the same and no more.

AND BE IT FURTHER ENACTED by the Authority aforesaid. That if the said Mayor Recorder Aldermen and Commonalty, Assessors or Collectors of the said City of Albany who are hereby authorized impowered and required to take effectual care that this Act be executed according to the true Intent and meaning thereof, or any of them shall deny or refuse or delay to perform, execute or comply with all or any of the powers Authorities and Duties in this Act given and required to be done and performed by them or either of them, and thereof shall be lawfully convicted in any Court of Record in this Colony, he or they so denying refusing or delaying to perform the Duties as aforesaid shall suffer such Pains and Penalties by Fine and Imprisonment as by the Discretion of the said Court shall be adjudged.

AND BE IT FURTHER ENACTED by the Authority aforesaid, That if any person or persons shall neglect or refuse to pay the several Rates and Assessments wherewith he or they shall be charged by this Act, for or in respect of his and their Goods and Chattels, Lands or Tenements upon Demand of the Collector appointed to receive the same that it shall and may be lawful to and for such Collector, and he is hereby required on non-payment thereof, to distrain upon the Goods and Chattels of the person or persons so refusing or neglecting to pay; and the Distress so taken to carry away, and the same to expose to sale within the said City for the payment of the said Rate or Assessment, and the Overplus if any be after paying the Charges of taking, carrying away and exposing the same Distress to sale, to be immediately returned to the Owner or Owners thereof.

AND BE IT FURTHER ENACTED by the Authority aforesaid. That all such persons as shall be employed to guard the said City shall be under the Directions of, and obey such Orders as they shall from Time to Time receive from the Mayor Recorder Aldermen and Commonalty in Common Council convened, any Custom Law or Usage to the contrary in any wise notwithstanding.

[CHAPTER 1584.]

[Chapter 1584, of Van Schaack, where the act is printed in full.]

An Act for the better laying out, regulating and keeping in repair the Public Roads and Highways in the City and County of Albany, and County of Tryon.

[Passed, February 6, 1773.]

WHEREAS it hath been found by Experience that the Act now in force for the better laying out regulating clearing and keeping in repair the Public Highways in the Counties of Albany and Tryon doth not fully answer the good purposes thereby intended.

BE IT THEREFORE ENACTED by his Excellency the Governor, the Council and the General Assembly, and it is hereby enacted by the authority of the same. That from and after the publication of and during the Continuance of this Act, the persons hereinafter named shall be and hereby are appointed Commissioners in the Districts for which they are named, for regulating the Highways and Public Roads already laid out and for regulating such other Highways and Public Roads as may still be necessary within the said City and Counties, that is to say.

For the City of Albany, the Mayor, Recorder, Aldermen and Commonalty of the said City.

For the District of the Manor of Livingston, Robert Livingston Junior, Robert R Livingston, Dirk W. Ten Broeck and Casparus Conyn.

For the District of Claverack, Robert Van Renselaer, Peter Van Ness, Casparus Conyn, Isaac Vosburgh Junior, John Van Allen, William Henry Ludlow, Richard Esseltyn, Henry Dible Martin Crumb and Abraham Carley.

For the District of Kinderhook Peter S. Van Alstyn, Franse Van Beuren, Lucas J. Goes, Cornelius Van Schaack Junior and Melgert Vanderpool.

For Kings District William Bradford Whiting, James Savage, Nathaniel Culver Samuel Baldwin Robert Bullis and Isaac Peabody.

For the District of Renselaerwyck, Renselaer Nicholl, Killyaen Van Renselaer, Abraham Ten Broeck, John H Beekman, Teunis Slingerlandt, Stephen Schuyler, Lucas Van Veghten, Stephen J Schuyler, and Anthony Van Schajck.

For Schactikoke District, Johannes Knickerbacker, Marte Winne, Wouter Groesbeek and Peter Williams.

For Hosick District Daniel Bradt, John Munro, Bliss Willoughby, Cornelius Van Ness, Ebenezer Cole, John Abbot and John Mc. Comb.

For Cambridge District Isaiah Younglove, Thomas Morrison and Archibald Campbell.

For Saratoga District Philip Schuyler, Killyaen De Ridder, Jonathan Jones, Jacobus Swart, George Palmer, Dirk Swart, Cornelius Van der Bergh, James Mc. Cree, Jeremiah Taylor, Stephen Potter, and James Gorden.

For Half-Moon District, Guert Van Schonhoven, Cornelius Tymesse, Nicholas Fisher, Abraham Fort, and Hendrick Van der Werken.

For Schenectady District, Jacobus Van Slyck, Isaac Vrooman, Ryer Schermerhorn, John Glen Christopher Yates, Abraham Mempel and John Cuyler Junior.

For the united Districts of Duanesburgh and Schoharie, Johannis Lawler, Hendrick Hens, Jacob Sternbergh, Harman Sidney, and Peter Snyder.

For Cocksackie District, Anthony Van Bergen, Jacob Hallenbeck, Sybrant G. Van Schajck, Teunis Van Veghten and Henry Hogeteeling.

For the Great Inboght District John Ten Broeck, Abraham Pearse, Jury William Dedrick, John B Dumont, and John Van Norden.

AND for the Districts in the County of Tryon vizt:

For the Mohawk District, Sir William Johnson, Sir John Johnson, Guy Johnson, Jellis Fonda, John Butler, Peter Conyn and Christian Ernest.

For Stone Arabia District, Harmanus Van Slyck, Jacob Klock, John Frey, Adam Loucks, and Isaac Paris.

For Canajoharie District, Hendrick Frey, Nicholas Herkemer, William Seeber, Robert Wells, and Frederick Young.

For the German Flatts District, Marcus Petri, Nicholas Weaver, and John Cunningham.

For Kingsland District John Jost Herkemer Junior, Rudolph Schumaker, Peter Ten Broeck, and Fredrick Orendorf.

AND BE IT ENACTED by the Authority aforesaid That the Commissioners in the respective Districts for which they are named and appointed Commissioners are hereby impowered and authorized to regulate the Roads already laid out, and to lay out such other Public Roads in the several Districts for which they are appointed Commissioners as to them shall seem necessary and convenient, and if need be to take a Review of the Roads already laid out, and such of them as appear to be really inconvenient, the said Commissioners shall and may alter, and lay out such other public Ways and Roads as they shall think most convenient, as well for travellers as for the Inhabitants of the next adjacent Districts. Provided that Nothing in this Act contained shall extend or be construed to impower the Commissioners aforesaid to lay any new Road through any inclosed or improved Lands, without either the Consent of the Owners thereof or paying the true Value of the Lands so laid out into an Highway, and if any Dispute shall arise by that means, the same shall be determined, and the true Value set and appraised by two Justices of the Peace, not being Commissioners in the District where the Dispute shall happen, and by the Oath of twelve of the Principal Freeholders of the Neighbourhood not having any Interest in the Lands about which such Dispute may arise, the said Freeholders to be summoned by any one of the Constables of the said County by virtue of a Warrant to be issued by the said two Justices for that purpose, and if the said Roads by the Commissioners so laid out shall be found by such Jury to be Public Roads, and of Public and General Benefit, then the value of such cleared and improved Lands through which the said Roads shall be laid out, shall be paid by the said Commissioners, and they are hereby required to pay the same together with the Charge of calling a Jury, their Verdict, and the whole proceedings thereon had; but if the Roads so laid out shall be found by such Jury to be private Roads, and for the particular Convenience of one or more particular person or persons, then such person or persons requiring the same shall defray the whole Charge of the value of the said cleared or improved Lands, to be paid to the person or persons injured, and through whose cleared or improved Lands a private Road shall be laid, together with the Charge of calling the Jury, and of their Verdict, and of the whole proceedings thereon had.

AND BE IT FURTHER ENACTED by the Authority aforesaid, That the Overseers of the Highways in each District respectively, or any one of them, are hereby impowered directed and required to order such a Number of the Inhabitants of said District with their Sleds, Horses or Oxen, as they the said Overseers or any one of them shall think sufficient and proper to break up the Roads where deep Snows happen to fall, and if any Person or Persons being ordered as aforesaid shall refuse to break up said Road, such person or persons shall respectively forfeit the Sum of Ten Shillings for every Day they shall so neglect or refuse said Service, to be levied by the Constable in each District, by Distress and Sale of the Offender's Goods and Chattels, by Warrant from any one of the Overseers for the respective District for which they shall be appointed returning the Overplus of such Sale, if any there be, to the Owner or Owners, after deducting thereout the Constable Fees, as is common in other Causes, and one Shilling for the Warrant, and the said Forfeiture of ten Shillings shall be paid to the Clerk of the Commissioners of the Highways for the District where such Forfeiture shall arise to be by them applied in the same Manner as the other monies to be raised by this Act are hereafter directed to be applied.

AND BE IT ENACTED by the same Authority. That if any Person or Persons within the said City and Counties do, or hereafter shall without the Consent of the Commissioners for the District to which they are by this Act appointed Commissioners alter, stop up, or lessen any Highway or Road that has heretofore been laid out by the former Commissioners according to Law, or shall hereafter be laid out by the Commissioners appointed or to be appointed by this Act, such Person or Persons so offending contrary to the Meaning of this Act, shall for every such Offence forfeit the Sum of five Pounds, to be recovered before any Justice of the Peace, upon the Oath of any one credible Witness, and levied by Warrant from any Justice of the Peace, directed to the Constable of the District where such Offence shall be committed, commanding him to distrain the Goods and Chattels of the Offender, and the said Constable after six Days Public Notice given by him of the Time for sale of said Distress, shall make sale thereof, and out of the produce deduct the said Forfeiture, and all the Charges, and return the Overplus if any there be, to the Owner or Owners and the said Constable is hereby required to pay the said Forfeiture into the Hands of the Clerk of the Commissioners of the Highways for the District wherein the Offence was committed, to be by the Commissioners thereof applied in the same Manner as the other Monies to be raised by this Act are herein directed to be applied.

AND in Order. That the Burthen of keeping the Highways in the said City and Counties in Repair, and the making other Highways for the ease, benefit, and safety of the Inhabitants may be as equitably proportioned between the Inhabitants thereof, as the Nature of the Case will admit. BE IT FURTHER ENACTED by the same Authority, That the Commissioners of each District respectively shall and are hereby required to meet annually on the second Tuesday in May at such Convenient place within the District for which they are Commissioners as they shall agree upon, and as often thereafter as need shall be, at such Times and places as they shall think meet, and being so met on the said second Tuesday in May annually shall proceed to make a List of all the Inhabitants in their District liable by this Act to work on the Highways, and shall then proceed either on that Day or as soon thereafter as the said List shall be compleated to affix to each persons Name the Number of Days that such person shall be liable to work on the Highways for the Year ensuing Copies of which List so compleated and signed by the Commissioner's Clerk shall be put up in two of the most Public places within the District, one, of which to be the place where the preceeding Election for District Officers was last held to the Intent that all the Inhabitants may know how many Days Labour they are respectively rated: PROVIDED ALWAYS. That if any Person's Name should be left out of such Lists, or the District increase by the accession of New Inhabitants such Omission and increase shall from Time to Time be added to the said List, and the persons be rated by the said Commissioners to work on the Highways. Provided also. That it shall not be in the Power of the Commissioners to rate any one Person rateable by this Act at more than twenty five Days annually nor less than five.

AND WHEREAS it may be necessary to build or repair Bridges in some of the said Districts, be it therefore also enacted by the same Authority. That such Persons as by this Act are liable to work on the Highways, and who are Carpenters or Masons, and who may be employed as such by the Commissioners, shall for every Day they work at such their Trade on the said Highways be allowed two Days in lieu of the Days that they were rated by the said Commissioners. BUT WHEREAS it may so happen that neither the Labour of such Carpenters or Masons, nor the Monies arising by Fines, Forfeitures or Compositions will be sufficient effectually to build or repair such Bridges, and to answer the other necessary exigencies that may arise. Be it therefore Enacted by the same Authority. That in such Case the Commissioners shall certify such Deficiency to the Supervisors of the County who are hereby required to add the same to the other Charges of the said District, and cause the same to be levied in the same Manner as said other Charges are usually levied, and order the same to be paid unto the said Commissioners: Provided always that such Deficiency shall in no one Year exceed the sum of twenty Pounds.

AND WHEREAS it may in some Cases be absolutely necessary to expend such a Sum of Money in one Year as that the Deficiency would exceed the said Sum of twenty Pounds BE IT THEREFORE ENACTED by the same Authority. That in Case the Commissioners should think it necessary to carry on a Work which would cause a greater Deficiency than twenty Pounds, they shall and are hereby required to apply to the Supervisor or Supervisors of the District who shall cause three Weeks Notice to be given by at least three Advertisements, appointing a Time and place for the persons ratable by this Act to meet and by majority of Voices to determine whether they will or will not agree to the proposal of the Commissioners, which proposals shall be contained in the said Advertisements together with a Computation of what such Deficiency will amount to, and if it appears that a Majority of such ratable persons approve of the Proposals of the Commissioners, the Supervisors shall then give a Certificate thereof subscribed by himself and countersigned by at least three of the Principal Freeholders then present which Certificate shall be directed to the Supervisors of the County of which such District is a part, and the said Supervisors shall thereupon at their next Meeting cause the same to be levied collected and paid in like Manner as the other Deficiency in this Act mentioned is directed to be levied collected and paid. PROVIDED ALWAYS. That no greater Sum shall be raised by virtue of this Clause in any Year than two hundred Pounds.

AND BE IT FURTHER ENACTED by the same Authority, That upon Complaint made to any Justice of the Peace, by any Person, that the Highways in any District are not kept in sufficient Repair, that in such Case it shall and may be lawful to and for such Justice to whom such Complaint has been preferred, and he is hereby required to issue his summons requiring the Commissioners of the District or some or one of them to appear on a certain Day, not less than ten Days from the Date of such Summons, at such place as he shall appoint, at which Time and place the said Justices shall have a Jury of twelve Men out of the next District, who shall hear Evidence and enquire into the Matter, and if it shall appear by the Verdict of such Jury given under

Oath that the insufficiency of the Highways is owing to the Neglect of the Commissioners, the Commissioners of the District shall pay all the Cost attending such Enquiry and be severally fined in the sum of forty shillings to be recovered together with the proportion of Cost by Distress and sale of their Goods and Chattels respectively, one half of which Fine shall go to the Complainants, and the other half to the Poor of the District. PROVIDED ALWAYS That if the Complaint should appear to the Jury to be frivolous and vexatious, that the Jury shall give such Damages to the Commissioners as they shall appear to have suffered, and the Complainant shall pay all the Cost, which Cost and Damages shall be recovered in the same Manner as the Cost and Fine is to be recovered if the Verdict goes against the Commissioners: and provided also, That every Complainant shall give Security for the Cost and Damages to such Justice of the Peace before any proceedings against the Commissioners shall commence.

AND BE IT FURTHER ENACTED by the same Authority That all the Inhabitants of the respective Districts who shall be rated to work on the Highways, shall as often as they or any of them shall receive Notice from the Overseer or Overseers of the Highways, for the Time being, to work on the Highways, punctually attend the said Service either by themselves, their Slaves or Servants with proper Tools, and faithfully Work all the Number of Days which they are rated if required, and in Case any Person or Persons duly warned, shall refuse or neglect to appear, or being come to work on the Highways, shall remain Idle, or not Work faithfully, or hinder or deter others from doing their Duty, such Offender shall for each Day forfeit the Sum of four Shillings to be recovered by the Overseer or Overseers of the Highway, by distress and sale of the Offender's Goods and Chattels, returning the Overplus to the Owner or Owners, if any there be, after deducting the usual Charges, as is common in Case where Distress is made by a Collector, and the said Forfeiture of four Shillings shall by the Overseer, be paid into the Hands of the Commissioners Clerk, to be by the said Commissioners applied in the same Manner as the other Monies directed to be raised by this Act, are to be applied.

AND BE IT ALSO ENACTED by the same Authority. That all the monies to be raised by virtue of this Act, or that may accrue from Fines, Forfeitures and Compositions, shall be honestly and fairly applied by the Commissioners of each District respectively, for the use of the Highways, and to and for building and repairing Bridges, and such necessary Work in and concerning the premises, in their respective Districts, as shall from Time to Time occur, and also in paying one or more Overseers of the Highways and a Clerk, and the said Commissioners are hereby required and commanded to keep true and just Accounts of all the Monies by them received and expended by virtue of this Act, and the same to deliver in upon Oath to the Court of General Sessions, held for the said Counties respectively, whenever thereunto required.

AND BE IT ALSO ENACTED by the same Authority That the Commissioners by this Act appointed, shall in their Districts respectively agree with one or more sober discreet and capable person or persons to be an Overseer or Overseers of the Highways in their District, and the same to discharge at pleasure, and other or others in their stead to appoint, and also to appoint a Clerk to keep their Accounts, to receive the Monies arising by this Act, and to write the Orders and directions that they shall from Time to Time give, and which they are hereby impowered to do, to the Overseer or Overseers of the Highways, of which Appointments they shall give Public Notice in the District, by Advertisement put up at the place where the annual Election for Officers of the District are held.

AND in Order to prevent all Disputes that may arise in rating the Inhabitants to work on the said Highways. BE IT ENACTED by the same Authority. That the Master or Mistress of every Family in each of the said Districts only, shall be rated to Work and pay towards the Highways, and no other person or persons whatsoever.

AND BE IT ALSO ENACTED. That all Trees standing or laying in any Person's Land, through which any Common Public Highways is or shall be laid out, be for the proper use of the Owner or Owners of the same, but the said Owners shall not hinder the Overseer of the Highways of the District from making use of so much Timber which is standing or laying on that Road, or which is standing or laying in any Lands adjacent, not actually in Fence, as will amend the said Highways or Bridges.

AND BE IT ALSO ENACTED by the same Authority, That if any Tree shall fall out of any inclosed Lands, into or across any of the Public Highways, that the Owner of such Inclosures shall within twenty four Hours after the same be so fallen, remove the same, or be liable to a Fine of ten Shillings for every

Day's Neglect in the non-removal thereof after Notice given to be recovered and applied in the same Manner as the other Fines and Forfeitures are recovered and applied by this Act.

PROVIDED ALWAYS, AND BE IT ENACTED by the same Authority, That in Case it should not be necessary in any one or more of the said Districts, to have all the Days wrought by the Inhabitants, that this Act requires, that then the Commissioners shall direct the Overseers to let each Person work, in his just proportion to the Days such Person is rated and no more: AND PROVIDED ALSO, That any Person liable to work on the Highways by virtue of this Act may be excused from the same on paying to the Overseer or Overseers the Sum of three shillings for each Days Labour that such person was rated.

AND BE IT ALSO ENACTED by the same Authority. That no person whatever in any of the said Districts, shall after the first Day of June, next after the Publication of this Act, set up any swinging or other Gate, or suffer any that may be then already set up to remain across any of the Highways in the City and Counties respectively unless by a special Licence from the Commissioners of the District, under their Hands and Seals: PROVIDED ALWAYS. That before the said Commissioners shall be permitted to grant such a Licence, they shall, at the Request, and at the Cost and Charge of the Person or Persons requesting such Licence apply to two of the nearest Justices of the Peace, who shall cause the Constable of the District to summon twelve impartial principal Freeholders of the District, and the said Justices together with his said Freeholders being first duly sworn, shall maturely inquire and then declare under their Hands and seals whether there are any sufficient Obstacles to prevent the setting of Fences and Maintaining the same, and what those Obstacles are, if any there be, and if by the Return of the Inquest, it shall appear that no Fences can be reasonably maintained, then the Commissioners shall grant their Licence for Gates; if otherwise they shall allow three Months to remove the Gates and no longer, and any Person or Persons offending contrary to the true Intent and meaning of this Clause, shall for every Offence be liable to the like Forfeiture that is inflicted in the fourth Clause of this Act, and the said Forfeitures shall be recovered and applied in the same Manner as is directed in the said fourth Clause.

AND BE IT FURTHER ENACTED by the Authority aforesaid. That in Case any Person or Persons shall stake or shore open any Licenced Gate or Gates, or wilfully Ride over or through any Lands, Meadow Ground, or Cornfields to the Damage of the Owners thereof, such Person or Persons shall for every such Offence forfeit the sum of twenty Shillings, to be recovered by the Overseers of the Highways in each respective District where such Offence shall be committed, and be recovered and applied in like Manner as the other Forfeitures in this Act are recovered and applied, and such Offender shall pay all Damages with Costs which the possessor of the soil shall suffer or sustain thereby, as shall be ordered and awarded by a Justice of the Peace residing nearest to the place where such Offence shall be committed, and the Determination of such Justice shall be final and conclusive therein.

AND BE IT FURTHER ENACTED by the same Authority. That if the Commissioners or Overseers of the Highways shall think fit and have occasion of any Team, Sled, Cart or Waggon and a Man to manage the same, the said Cart Sled or Waggon and Man shall be esteemed to be in lieu of three Days Work of one Man, and the Fine for Neglect or Refusal to furnish the same to be proportionable, that is treble to the Fine to be imposed for the Neglect of one Person, and every working Man shall be obliged to bring such Tools, as Spades, Axes, Crows, Pick-Axes, or other Utensils as shall be directed by the Overseers of the Highways: and no Person under the Age of sixteen Years shall be deemed a sufficient Labourer.

AND BE IT FURTHER ENACTED by the same Authority. That if any of the said Commissioners herein appointed shall neglect, refuse or delay to qualify themselves as this Act hereafter directs, or being qualified shall happen to die or remove out of the District for which he or they are appointed Commissioners, it shall and may be lawful for the Justices of the Peace in the General Sessions held for the said Counties respectively to appoint in his or their stead, another Commissioner or Commissioners for such District where such Refusal Neglect, Delay, Death or Removal shall so happen, and the Commissioner or Commissioners so appointed shall be under the same Restrictions, and have the same Power and Authority as those appointed by this Act.

AND BE IT ALSO ENACTED by the Authority aforesaid, That the Commissioners of each respective District for which they are respectively appointed, shall from Time to Time during the Continuance of this Act, enter in writing all the Highways so by them laid out, altered, or stopped up, and sign the same by puting their Names thereto, and cause the same to be entered in the Records of the said Counties respectively, by the Clerk of the Peace, who is hereby directed and required to record the same, and whatsoever the said Commissioners shall do in laying out, altering or stopping, and otherwise regulating Highways according to the Power given them in this Act, being so entered in the County Records, shall be deemed valid and good to all Intents and purposes whatsoever, for which Entry the Clerk shall be paid two shillings.

PROVIDED ALWAYS, AND BE IT ENACTED by the same Authority, That where the Inhabitants of a small Neighbourhood or Plantation shall desire to have public Roads laid out, the Commissioners aforesaid shall not be allowed to lay out such and so many Roads as the said Inhabitants may be desirous to have, but only one Public Road leading from such Neighbourhood to the nearest other Public Highway which is central in the said District, from whence they can travel and transport Goods to other Towns or Landing-places, and where it shall be necessary to lay out a Road from one District, as they are in this Act, joined to another District, the Commissioners or the major Part of both Districts, are to meet and consult where such Road can be laid out and carried on in the most convenient and shortest Manner the Nature of the Land will allow.

PROVIDED ALSO, AND BE IT FURTHER ENACTED. That if it shall so happen That if the improved Farm of any Inhabitant of the said Counties shall be divided or thrown into different Districts, as they are described in this Act, that then in such Case, every such Inhabitant shall be subject to work upon the Highways in that District only in which his Dwelling House is erected.

PROVIDED ALSO, AND BE IT FURTHER ENACTED. That if any Inhabitant of the said respective Districts, shall conceive it more convenient to use a Public main Road not maintained by the District wherein he resides, leading to the City of Albany or other port or place of embarkation which may hereafter be established, that in every such Case, upon application to the Commissioners, both of his own District, and of that through which the Road he prefers may pass, it shall and may be lawful to and for the said Commissioners or the major Part of them, if such Convenience shall appear to them to be manifest, to relieve him from the Duties required of him by this Act, in the District which he Inhabits, and subject him to the performance of those Duties in the next adjoining District through which such Road passes, and whereby it is supported.

PROVIDED ALSO, AND BE IT FURTHER ENACTED. That where a Public and Main Road shall be required from any District in which there is a considerable settlement to the City of Albany or any other port or place of Embarkation as aforesaid, that in every such Case, such Public or main Road shall be continued from District to District, as straight and direct as the Nature of the Ground and other Circumstances will admit, and that such main and Public Road may be established with more general Convenience and Utility to the Inhabitants of the respective Districts, through which the same may extend, it shall and may be lawful to and for the Commissioners of the District which shall require the said Road by Writing under their Hands to appoint and Summons a general Meeting of all the Commissioners of the respective Districts through which the Road proposed shall extend, at any Time, not less than three, nor more than ten Days after the Service of Notice on the said Commissioners, and at such convenient place in that District which shall be most central to the usual Residence of the major Part of such Commissioners, and the said Commissioners are hereby directed and required to meet and attend according to such Appointment, and when the said Commissioners so convened, shall have consulted together and deliberated upon the Subject of the said Meeting, they shall then proceed to lay out the Highway or Road proposed and required from District to District, and in the best and most advantageous Manner for Public and general Utility and Convenience, that is to say, the Commissioners of each respective District, shall lay out that Part of the Intended Road which shall extend through the District of which they are respectively Commissioners, and the same being so laid out shall be certified, returned and recorded, as a Public Road or Highway in the Manner herein before directed, and shall be maintained and supported in the several Districts through which it shall extend as other Highways or Public Roads ought by this Act to be maintained in each respective District: But if it shall so happen that the Commissioners of either of the other Districts then assembled shall be dissatisfied with any Part of the Road so laid out, they shall be at liberty, and are hereby authorized to propose the Manner in which they conceive that Part of the Road which is objected to, ought to be laid out, and if the Commissioners whose Duty it is to lay out the same shall not agree to the Alteration insisted upon, that then a Description shall be made in Writing, signed by all the Commissioners present of both the Roads proposed and it shall be lawful for three or more of the said Commissioners to apply to any two of His Majesty's Justices of the Peace of the said Counties respectively, not residing or holding Lands in the District concerning which such controversy shall have arisen, or the District for which such Road shall be required, and such Justices are hereby Authorized and directed thereupon to issue their precept to one of the Constables of the said County, commanding him to summon a Jury of twelve good and sufficient Freeholders of the said County, not interested in the said Road, who being duly sworn for that purpose shall inquire and give their Verdict, which of the Roads in controversy will be the best and most commodious as a main and Public Highway, and an Inquest being thereof made under the Hands and seals of the said Justices and Jurors, shall be final and conclusive according to which the Road shall be laid out, certified and returned, as a Public Road by the respective Commissioners through whose District it shall extend, and the Return thereof, together with the said Inquisition, being filed in the Office of the Clerk of the said County, and entered of Record, the said Road shall be deemed and esteemed a Public Road or Highway to all Intents and purposes, and be supported and maintained, in the respective Districts through which the same shall extend, in the same manner as the other Highways in such Districts are directed and required to be maintained and supported by this Act, and the Charge and Expence of such Inquest, shall be borne and paid out of the Monies to be raised by this Act, for the Benefit of the District whose Commissioners shall have created the same, by refusing to lay out such Road, in the Manner which by the said Inquest shall be found best & most commodious.

AND BE IT ALSO ENACTED by the same Authority. That the Commissioners for the Time being for each District shall and may at any Time during the continuance of this Act, divide the District of which they are Commissioners into such and so many Parts as to them shall seem most necessary and assign the Case of one or more such Parts to one or more Overseers, and such partition to alter whenever they shall think it necessary.

AND BE IT FURTHER ENACTED by the same Authority. That every Person compellable to work on the Highways in any of the said Counties, shall actually work for each Day he is obliged to work eight Hours, and shall be liable to pay a Fine of six pence for every Hour such person shall be in Default, to be recovered in like manner as the other Fines and Forfeitures are by this Act directed to be recovered.

AND BE IT FURTHER ENACTED by the same Authority. That the several Overseers of the Highways in the several Districts or parts of Districts for which they shall be appointed by this Act, shall whenever thereunto required by the Commissioners of the District to which they belong, deliver an Account to the Commissioners Clerk attested to before any Justice of the peace, which Attestation shall be in the Words following to wit. "I. A B. do declare upon the Holy Evangelists of Almighty God, "that the Account now delivered by me contains the Names of "all the persons assigned by the Commissioners of the Highways "in .... District to be under my Direction in working "on the Highways, and that I have affixed to each persons Name "the Number of Days such Person has worked or some other in "such Person's stead, as also the Names of all such persons that "have paid three shillings per Day in lieu of the Days they were "required to work, and also of such persons as have been fined "for refusing to work as the Law requires, so help me God."

AND BE IT FURTHER ENACTED by the same Authority. That the Commissioners of the respective Districts, shall be respectively allowed a Sum not exceeding six Shillings for every Day that such Commissioner shall absolutely and necessarily be employed in the Execution of his Office, and they shall transmit their Accounts on Oath to the Supervisors of the County to which they belong, at their annual Meetings; and the Supervisors shall cause the same to be raised as the Monies by the seventh Clause of this Act, are directed to be raised and paid.

AND BE IT ALSO FURTHER ENACTED by the same Authority. That the Commissioners for the Highways by this Act appointed or to be appointed, shall respectively before they execute any of the Powers herein given to them, take an Oath before any Justice of the Peace of the said City or Counties, in the Words following. "I. A B. do solemnly Swear, That I will faith- "fully diligently and impartially execute the powers to me given "and granted by an Act entitled, An Act for the better laying "out regulating and keeping in repair the Public Roads and "Highways in the City and County of Albany and County of Tryon, so help me God."

AND BE IT ALSO ENACTED by the same Authority. That in Case any Overseer or Overseers to be appointed by virtue of this Act shall refuse to serve as such, or shall neglect or delay the putting in Execution any Services which he or they are required to do by this Act or shall refuse to return an Account upon Oath as in this Act is directed, that in either of these Cases, such Overseer or Overseers so offending contrary to the meaning of this Act, such Offender or Offenders shall be subject to the like Penalty as is inflicted by the fourth Clause of this Act on Persons altering, stopping up, or lessening any Highway, and be recovered in like manner as the said Penalty is directed to be recovered.

AND BE IT ALSO ENACTED by the same Authority, That the major Part of the Commissioners, or the major Part of the Survivors of them in any of the Districts within the said City and Counties, shall and hereby are authorized to do and execute all or any of the Powers given unto them by this Act, in their respective Districts, and their proceedings shall be as effectual and legal as if all the Commissioners of such Districts were present and concurring any Thing in this Act to the contrary hereof notwithstanding.

AND BE IT ALSO LASTLY ENACTED by the same Authority, That the Act now in force entitled. "An Act for the "better laying out regulating clearing and keeping in repair the "Public Roads and Highways in the Counties of Albany and "Tryon." passed the twenty fourth Day of March one thousand seven hundred and seventy two, shall be and is hereby repealed, and that this Act shall be and continue in force from the Publication thereof, unto the second Tuesday in May, which will be in the Year of our Lord one thousand seven hundred and seventy five.

[CHAPTER 1584a.]

[Chapter 1584a, there being two chapters of this number in Van Schaack, this is designated as 1584a in order to preserve continuity. See chapters 1413 and 1496.]

An Act to impower the Justices of the Peace residing in that part of the Township of Schenectady therein mentioned to establish and regulate a Night-Watch, and for other purposes therein mentioned.

[Passed, February 6, 1773.]

WHEREAS the establishing a Night-Watch and appointing Firemen to manage the Fire Engine in that part of the Township of Schenectady which lays to the southward of the Mohawks River, and not more than three Quarters of a Mile from the Dutch Church, will tend to the safety and preservation of the Inhabitants thereof in their persons and Effects.

BE IT THEREFORE ENACTED by his Excellency the Governor the Council and the General Assembly, and it is hereby enacted by the Authority of the same, That it shall and may be lawful to and for the Justices of the Peace or the majority of them for the Time being, living or dwelling in that part of the Township of Schenectady which lays to the southward of the Mohawks River, and not more than three Quarters of a Mile distant from the Dutch Church to meet together with all convenient Speed after the publication of this Act, and being so met, they are hereby required and directed to order establish and regulate a Night Watch, which Watch shall consist of six Men and an Officer for each Night out of the Inhabitants of that part of the said Township hereinbefore described, who shall and are hereby required and directed in their Turns to keep Watch and Guard in such Manner, and at such Times and places as the said Justices shall order and direct.

AND BE IT FURTHER ENACTED by the same Authority, That it shall and may be lawful to and for the said Justices or the major Part of them to make establish and ordain such Rules Orders Ordinances and Regulations for the Government Conduct Duty and Behaviour of the said Watch and Watchmen, and to impose and establish such reasonable Fines, Penalties and Forfeitures upon them or any of them for Default or Neglect of the Duties and services enjoined or required by such Orders or Ordinances as to the said Justices shall from Time to Time seem meet and convenient. PROVIDED ALWAYS that no greater Fine Penalty or Forfeiture shall be levied for any one Offence than six Shillings on an Officer, and three Shillings on every other Person or Watchman.

AND BE IT FURTHER ENACTED by the same Authority. That it shall and may be lawful to and for the said Justices of the Peace or the major Part of them, and they are hereby required with all convenient speed to elect nominate and appoint a sufficient Number of Men willing to accept, not exceeding twenty in Number out of the Inhabitants residing in that part of the said Township abovementioned, to have the Care management working and use of the Fire Engine or Engines belonging to the said Township and the other Tools and Instruments for extinguishing of Fires that may happen therein who are hereby required and enjoined in Case of Fires happening to manage work and use the said Engine or Engines and the other Tools and Instruments for the extinguishing of Fires.

BE IT FURTHER ENACTED by the same Authority, That the said Justices of the peace or the major Part of them are hereby authorized and impowered to remove and displace all or any of the Firemen so as aforesaid to be elected nominated and appointed when & as often as they shall think fit, and others in lieu of such as shall be removed to elect nominate and appoint from Time to Time as they the said Justices shall see convenient.

AND BE IT ALSO ENACTED by the Authority aforesaid, That such persons as shall be elected and appointed Firemen, and each and every of them during the Time such Person or Persons shall remain Firemen and no longer, shall and hereby are declared to be freed and exempted from serving in the Office of Constable and Overseer of the Highways, and of and from serving as Jurors, and of and from serving in the Militia, except in Cases of Invasion or other imminent Danger.

AND BE IT FURTHER ENACTED by the same Authority. That it shall and may be lawful to and for the said Justices or the major Part of them to make establish and ordain such Rules, Orders, Ordinances and Regulations for the Government Conduct Duty and Behaviour of the Persons from Time to Time to be by them Elected nominated or appointed Firemen by virtue of this Act.

AND BE IT ALSO ENACTED by the same Authority, That the Assessors for the District of Schenectady shall annually (at their usual Meeting) during the continuance of this Act, levy the Sum of fifteen Pounds, to be raised levied and collected of and from the Inhabitants residing in that part of the Township of Schenectady herein before described, and the Collector of the said Township is hereby required as soon as he shall have collected the same, to pay the same (after deducting therefrom six pence in the Pound for his trouble) unto the said Justices or such other person as they shall appoint to receive the same, to be by the said Justices applied in paying a Person by them to be appointed to take care of the Watch-House, and supplying the same with Fire Wood and Candles.

AND WHEREAS there is still a Debt due amounting to the sum of thirty Pounds for building the Watch House that has been erected in the said Township. BE IT THEREFORE ALSO

ENACTED by the same Authority, That the Assessors before mentioned shall cause the said sum of thirty Pounds to be raised and levyed in like Manner as is directed in the preceding clause with regard to the annual Sum of fifteen Pounds, and the Collector to collect and pay the same to the said Justices after deducting six pence in the pound for his trouble.

AND BE IT FURTHER ENACTED by the Authority aforesaid. That this Act shall be in force from the Publication thereof until the first Day of February which will be in the year of our Lord one thousand seven hundred and seventy eight.

[CHAPTER 1585.]

[Chapter 1585, of Van Schaack, where the title only is printed.]

An Act for repairing the Court House and Common Goal in the County of Ulster.

[Passed, February 6, 1773.]

WHEREAS the Court House and Goal in Kingston in the County of Ulster are not only inconvenient, but greatly out of repair.

BE IT THEREFORE ENACTED by his Excellency the Governor, the Council and the General Assembly and it is hereby enacted by the Authority of the same. That it shall and may be lawful to and for the Justices of the Peace and Supervisors of the said County of Ulster, and they are hereby directed and required to assemble and meet together at the said Court-House on the first Tuesday in May next and they the said Justices and Supervisors, or the major Part of them so to be assembled and met together are hereby authorized and required to agree and determine upon the Manner in which the said Court-House and Goal shall be altered and repaired and to compute the amount of the Charge and Expence that may attend the same, so always as that the Sum to be expended for that purpose shall not exceed four hundred Pounds. which Agreement the said Justices and Supervisors shall reduce to writing, and subscribe with their respective Names, and cause the same to be filed with the Clerk of the Supervisors of said County, and the Sum so by them to be agreed upon shall be raised levied and collected of and from the Freeholders and Inhabitants of the said County in the same Manner, as the other necessary and contingent Charges of the said County are by Law directed to be raised and assessed

AND BE IT FURTHER ENACTED by the Authority aforesaid, That the Monies so to be raised by virtue of this Act shall from Time to Time be paid by the Collectors of the respective Towns Manor and Precincts within the said County, as the same shall come into their Hands, unto the County Treasurer, to be by him paid to Dirck Wynkoop Junior, Johannes Sleght, Abraham Low, John Beekman and John Elmendorph or to any three of them, who are hereby appointed Commissioners for directing, manageing and inspecting the said Repairs, and for laying out the Money to be expended for that purpose, agreeable to the said Determination of the said Justices and Supervisors, which said Commissioners shall, and are hereby required to render a just true and particular Account on Oath of the Trust hereby reposed in, and of the Monies to be expended by them, to the Justices of the said County at the next General Sessions of the Peace to be holden for the said County after the completion of the said Repairs.

AND BE IT ALSO ENACTED by the same Authority. That in Case the Monies so to be estimated by the said Justices and Supervisors, and to be levied on the said County should exceed the Sum that may be expended for the said Repairs, that such excess shall by the said Commissioners be repaid into the Hands of the said Treasurer to be disposed of by the said Supervisors for the use of the said County, in such Manner as to them shall seem most convenient.

[CHAPTER 1586.]

[Chapter 1586, of Van Schaack, where the act is printed in full. See chapter 1536.]

An Act to amend an Act entitled. "An "Act for the better laying out regulating and "keeping in Repair, Common and public High- "ways, and private Roads in the County of "Dutchess."

[Passed, February 6, 1773.]

WHEREAS by the beforementioned Act entitled. "An Act "for the better laying out, regulating and keeping in repair "Common and Public Highways and private Roads in the County "of Dutchess," passed the twelfth Day of March in the twelfth Year of his present Majesty's Reign, sufficient Authority is not given to the Overseers of the said public Highways and Roads, to compel the Inhabitants of their several and respective Districts to work on said Highways and Roads at certain Seasons in the Year when the same may be necessary nor to provide Timber for building, amending and repairing the Bridges on said Highways and Roads.

BE IT THEREFORE ENACTED by his Excellency the Governor the Council and the General Assembly, and it is hereby enacted by the Authority of the same. That the Freeholders and Inhabitants mentioned in the Act aforesaid, shall be obliged to work on the said Highways and Roads six Days in the Year agreeable to the Directions in said Act, and as many more as occasion shall or may require, not exceeding three Days.

AND BE IT FURTHER ENACTED by the Authority aforesaid, That any one of his Majesty's Justices of the Peace for the Time being in the County of Dutchess aforesaid or any one Commissioner for the Time being, may as often as occasion shall or may require order any Overseer to work upon and repair any Road or Highway that he shall think necessary within his District, and such Overseer under the Penalty in said Act mentioned agreeable to the Directions in said Act to be recovered, shall within three Days thereafter warn and set to work the persons of his District who are obliged to work on Highways upon that part of the Road or Highway which he shall so be ordered to work upon and repair, and that the person or persons so ordered to work, in Case of Refusal shall forfeit the like Penalty in said Act mentioned to be recovered according to the Directions of the Act aforesaid.

AND BE IT FURTHER ENACTED by the Authority aforesaid. That if any Timber or other Materials shall be necessary and wanting further than for which Provision is made in the Act aforesaid, for building, amending and repairing the Bridges and Causeways on the Roads and Highways in the County aforesaid, That it shall and may be lawful for the said Overseers of the said Roads and Highways respectively, by and with the Consent of the major Part of the Commissioners of Highways of their respective Precincts signified by a Certificate in writing under their Hands, and they are hereby required to purchase at as reasonable a Rate as they can so much Timber and other Materials as shall be necessary for the purposes aforesaid; and that the respective Overseers of the said Roads and Highways, respectively shall on the third Tuesday in March in every Year, deliver under Oath to the Supervisor of their respective Precincts a true Account of all such Sum and sums of Money as they shall have respectively paid, or for which they are become engaged, for the purposes aforesaid, together with the said Certificate subscribed by the major Part of the said Commissioners, signifying their Consent thereto as aforesaid, which Account and Certificate, the said Supervisor shall deliver in to the Supervisors of the said County at their annual Meeting; And the said Sum and Sums of Money so by the said Overseers respectively paid and engaged for as aforesaid shall be raised and levied of and from the Freeholders and Inhabitants of the respective precincts in which the same shall have been expended, in like manner and after the same Rate and proportion as the other necessary and contingent Charges of the said County are raised and paid.

AND BE IT FURTHER ENACTED by the Authority aforesaid. That this Act shall continue and be in force until the first Day of February which will be in the Year of our Lord one thousand seven hundred and seventy six.

[CHAPTER 1587.]

[Chapter 1587, of Van Schaack, where the act is printed in full. See chapter 1457.]

An Act to revive an Act entitled "An Act "for the more equal Taxation of Estates in "Orange County."

[Passed, February 6, 1773.]

WHEREAS an Act entitled. "An Act for the more equal "Taxation of Estates in Orange County." passed in the tenth Year of his present Majesty's Reign, expired by it's own Limitation the first Day of January one thousand seven hundred and seventy three, and the same having been found useful and necessary.

BE IT THEREFORE ENACTED by his Excellency the Governor the Council and the General Assembly, and it is hereby enacted by the Authority of the same. That the Act entitled, "An Act for the more Equal Taxation of Estates in Orange "County". shall be and hereby is revived, and every Article Matter and Clause therein contained enacted to be and remain in full Force from the publication hereof until the first Day of February which will be in the Year of our Lord one thousand seven hundred and seventy six.

[CHAPTER 1588.]

[Chapter 1588, of Van Schaack, where the act is printed in full.]

An Act to raise fifteen hundred Pounds for draining the drowned Lands in the Precinct of Goshen in Orange County.

[Passed, February 6, 1773.]

WHEREAS there is a large Tract of Land situate in the Patent of Wawayanda in the Precinct of Goshen in the County of Orange commonly called the drowned Lands which for many Months in a Year is overflowed and thereby rendered unfit for any use. AND WHEREAS it is imagined that the said Lands may be drained, so that a great part of them may be fit for Tillage or pasturage, AND WHEREAS it is represented, that some Parts of the drowned Lands are owned by Infants, Feme Coverts or Persons not within this Colony, notwithstanding which it is just and equitable that the Expence of draining the same ought to be borne by the Proprietors of the Lands which will be benefited thereby.

BE IT THEREFORE ENACTED by his Excellency the Governor the Council and the General Assembly, and it is hereby enacted by the Authority of the same. That Samuel Gale, Jesse Woodhull and Nathaniel Roe Junior Esquires or any two of them or the survivors or survivor of them shall be Inspectors or Inspector to settle and finally ascertain the Quantity of Land (Cedar Swamps and Upland excepted) within the said Precinct which in their Opinion may be benefited by draining the said drowned Lands and shall then proceed to rate and Assess the Quotas and Proportion of each respective Lot and Parcel of Land (Cedar Swamps and Upland excepted) which in their Opinion may be so benefited, according to it's Quantity and Quality, in order to raise upon the whole of the said Land the Sum of fifteen hundred Pounds: And that the said Inspectors after they have finally compleated the said Assessment, shall make and subscribe a Roll thereof containing the several Lots or parcels of Land so assessed, and distinguishing whether they are divided or undivided, the Proprietors Names of each as far as shall come to their knowledge, and the Quota or Proportion of each respective Lot or Tract in the said Sum of fifteen hundred Pounds, and the particular sums or Proportion thereof which each Proprietor of such respective Lots or Parcels of Land shall pay, and having finished the same shall file a Copy thereof under their Hands in the Clerk's Office of the said County and in the Secretary's Office in the City of New York, and that the said Inspectors or any two of them, or the Survivors or Survivor of them shall when desired by the Trustees hereafter named or the major Part of them publish an Advertisement in the Public News paper of this Colony commonly called the New York Gazette and Weekly Mercury, to be continued for four Weeks successively, and to contain an exact Transcript of such Assessment as aforesaid, and shall also fix a Copy thereof at the Court House in Goshen in the said County giving Notice to and requiring all persons interested in the said drowned Lands to pay their respective Quotas of the said fifteen hundred Pounds to the Trustees hereafter mentioned within two Months from the Date of the said Advertisement.

AND BE IT FURTHER ENACTED by the Authority aforesaid. That if the Quota so to be assessed on any or either of the Tracts or Lots of Land whether divided or undivided being so notified as aforesaid, shall not be duly paid and discharged according to the said Notice and Demand that then it shall and may be lawful to and for the said Inspectors or any two of them, or the survivors or survivor of them, at one or more Sale or Sales, to sell and dispose of so much or so great a part of the undivided right, Interest, share and Proportion of any Person or Persons having any Estate or Interest in any of the said undivided Tract or Tracts of Land, or any other Lot or parcel of Land so charged as aforesaid with a proportion of the said fifteen hundred Pounds so as aforesaid to be assessed, which Sale or Sales shall be made at Public Vendue or Outcry at the Court-House in Goshen, first giving two Months Notice of such intended Sale by Advertisement to be affixed in the said County of Orange at the said Court-House, and by advertising the same in the Public Newspaper as aforesaid, four Weeks successively: and after retaining out of the Monies arising by such Sale, so much as the Assessment shall amount unto, together with the Contingent Expence of such sale, shall render the Overplus Money, (if any be) to the Owner or Owners of the said undivided Tracts or other Lot or Lots, that shall so have been sold.

AND BE IT FURTHER ENACTED by the Authority aforesaid, That the Deed or Deeds of Conveyance of the said Inspectors or of any two of them, or the Survivors or Survivor of them to every respective purchaser shall be good and effectual in the Law to convey such undivided Right or Rights, share and Shares,

Lot and Lots, to the purchaser his Heirs and Assigns in fee Simple, and shall be and operate as a full and effectual Barr both in Law and Equity against all persons or Bodies corporate and Politic, claiming or to claim the same, by virtue of or under any Right or Title whatsoever.

AND BE IT FURTHER ENACTED by the Authority aforesaid That the said Inspectors, or the Survivors or Survivor of them shall also pay to the Trustees hereafter named, or the Survivors or Survivor of them, the Monies which shall from Time to Time come into their Hands by virtue of any Sale to be made in pursuance of this Act, and that the proprietor or proprietors of any and every such undivided Lands, and of every such Lot or parcel of Land shall according to the said Assessment pay his and their respective Proportion of the said fifteen hundred Pounds to the Trustees hereafter named (to wit) William Wickham, Henry Wisner, Samuel Gale, William Allison and Gilbert Bradner, and the Survivors or Survivor of them, to be by them, and the Survivors or Survivor of them applied towards draining the said drowned Lands, at such Times and by such Ways and Means as they or any three of them, or the survivors or Survivor of them shall think proper.

AND BE IT FURTHER ENACTED by the Authority aforesaid, That the said Inspectors before they proceed upon the Business required of them by this Act, shall take an Oath before one of the Judges of the Inferior Court of Common Pleas for the said County of Orange, truly and impartially, according to the best of their Skill and Judgment, to assess the said fifteen hundred Pounds on the Lands made liable by this Act for the payment of the same.

AND BE IT FURTHER ENACTED by the same Authority, That exact accounts shall kept by the said Trustees of all monies expended by them in pursuance of this Act, one Copy of which, under Oath, shall be filed in the said Secretary's Office, and another in the Clerk's Office in the County of Orange: And that in Case the whole of the said fifteen hundred Pounds shall not be expended the Overplus shall be divided by the said Trustees among the respective Proprietors of the Lands mentioned in the Assessment to be made by the said Inspectors, and that in the same proportion as the said sum was raised.

AND BE IT FURTHER ENACTED by the same Authority. That in Case the said Trustees, or the major Part of them shall think proper to proceed upon the Business required of them by this Act before the said fifteen hundred Pounds shall be raised, they may advance such Sum or sums of Money as they or the major Part of them shall think proper, and Interest shall be allowed for the same.

AND WHEREAS the said William Wickham and Henry Wisner did in the Year of our Lord one thousand seven hundred and seventy two expend several Sums of Money in clearing the Outlet of the said drowned Lands.

BE IT THEREFORE FURTHER ENACTED by the Authority aforesaid, That the said Inspectors or any Two of them shall examine the Accounts of the said William Wickham and Henry Wisner, and view the Outlet of the said drowned Lands, and shall certify under their Hands the Sum of Money which in their Opinion ought to be paid to the said William Wickham and Henry Wisner, for the Services by them done towards the clearing of the said Outlet, which Sum so certified the said William Wickham and Henry Wisner may retain in their Hands out of the said fifteen hundred Pounds to be raised by virtue of this Act. PROVIDED ALWAYS. That Nothing in this Act contained shall affect his Majesty, his Heirs or Successors, or any Estate Right, Title, or Interest belonging to him or them, any Thing in this Act contained to the contrary thereof in any wise notwithstanding.

[CHAPTER 1589.]

[Chapter 1589, of Van Schaack, where the act is printed in full.]

An Act to raise one hundred and fifty Pounds for lowering a Pond commonly called Wickham's Pond, in the Precinct of Goshen in the County of Orange.

[Passed, February 6, 1773.]

WHEREAS there are several large Tracts of Swamp and Bog Meadow adjoining to the said Pond and the Creek that runs out of the same, which are frequently rendered unfit for use by the overflowing of the said Pond.

BE IT THEREFORE ENACTED by his Excellency the Governor the Council and the General Assembly, and it is hereby enacted by the Authority of the same. That Samuel Gale, Richard Edsall, and Nathaniel Roe Junior Esquires, or any two of them or the Survivor or Survivors of them shall be inspectors to settle and finally ascertain the Number of Acres of Swamp and Bog-Meadow which may in their Opinion be benefited by lowering the said Pond, and clearing out the said Creek and to make an assessment of what each Person interested in the said Swamps and Bog-Meadows, ought to pay towards the said Sum of one hundred and fifty Pounds.

AND BE IT FURTHER ENACTED by the Authority aforesaid, That in order to lower the said Pond, and to clear out and enlarge the said Creek, the said Sum of one hundred and fifty Pounds shall according to the assessment which shall be made by the said Inspectors be paid to William Wickham, John Bard, and Henry Wisner the third, to be by them applied in paying all incidental Charges, and for lowering the said Pond, and in clearing and enlarging the said Creek from the said Pond to forty Rods below that part of the Lands of the said John Bard whereon Israel Wood formerly had a Mill, and that by such Ways and Means as they or any two of them shall think proper.

AND BE IT FURTHER ENACTED by the authority aforesaid. That each proprietor shall within one Month after the said Inspectors shall have made their Assessment pay his respective proportion of the said one hundred and fifty Pounds to the said William Wickham, John Bard, and Henry Wisner or either of them, and in default of payment it shall be lawful for the said William Wickham, John Bard and Henry Wisner or either of them to recover the same by due Course of Law with Interest and Costs of Suit, in like Manner as other Actions of Debt are recovered within this Colony.

AND BE IT FURTHER ENACTED by the same Authority, That in Case the said one hundred and fifty Pounds shall not be sufficient for effectually lowering the said Pond and clearing and enlarging the said Creek, such further Sum not exceeding fifty Pounds shall be raised as the majority of the Proprietors shall think proper, which further Sum shall be paid to the said William Wickham, John Bard and Henry Wisner by the respective proprietors in the same proportion as the one hundred and fifty Pounds is to be paid.

[CHAPTER 1590.]

[Chapter 1590, of Van Schaack, where the act is printed in full. See chapter 804.]

An Act for altering the place of Meeting of the Supervisors in the County of West Chester.

[Passed, February 6, 1773.]

WHEREAS an Act was passed on the twenty ninth Day of November one thousand seven hundred and forty five entitled. "An Act to alter the place of the supervisors Meeting in the "County of West Chester." by which it was Enacted, that the annual Meeting of the Supervisors should be at the School-House in the Town of Rye. AND WHEREAS by the increase of the Inhabitants in the Northerly Part of the said County, the said place of meeting is become extremely inconvenient.

BE IT THEREFORE ENACTED by his Excellency the Governor, the Council and the General Assembly, and it is hereby enacted by the Authority of the same, That the Supervisors for the Time being of the said County of West Chester, shall for the future hold their annual Meetings at the Court-House at the White Plains in said County, and being so met, shall have power to adjourn for such Time and to such place as they or the major Part of them shall think expedient any Thing in the said Act, or any other Act or Acts to the contrary thereof notwithstanding.

[CHAPTER 1591.]

[Chapter 1591, of Van Schaack, where the act is printed in full.]

An Act to prevent the killing and destroying of Game in the Manor of Philipsborough in the County of West Chester.

[Passed, February 6, 1773.]

WHEREAS a Number of idle Persons have for sometime past carried on a pernicious practice of killing and destroying Partridges, Pheasants and Quails within the manor of Philipsborough insomuch that unless some Remedy be provided the whole Breed of them within the said Manor is in danger of being extirpated.

BE IT THEREFORE ENACTED by his Excellency the Governor, the Council and the General Assembly, and it is hereby enacted by the authority of the same. That no person or persons whatsoever from and after the passing this Act, for and during the Term of three Years from thenceforth shall take kill or destroy any Partridges, Pheasants or Quails, their Eggs or Young with Nets, Snares, Gins, or any other Engines or Devices, or by any other Ways or means whatsoever within the said Manor upon Pain and Forfeiture for every Partridge, Pheasant or Quail young or old, or their Egg or Eggs so taken killed or destroyed as aforesaid the Sum of twenty Shillings Current Money of this Colony, which Forfeiture shall be recovered before any one Justice of the Peace in the County of West Chester, upon the Oath of one credible Witness, or upon proof made by such Witness, that any such Partridge, Pheasant or Quail or their Egg or Eggs hath been seen in his or their possession, one Half of the said Forfeiture to be paid to the said person giving Information of such Offence, and the other Half to the Overseers of the Poor, to be applied to the use of the Poor on said Manor, and in Case the said Forfeiture shall not be paid upon Conviction, the Offender or Offenders shall be committed to the Common Goal of the said County without Bail or Mainprize, and shall there remain for the Space of twenty Days: and in Case any Slave or Slaves shall commit such Offence or Offences, and the Forfeiture or Forfeitures shall not be paid upon Conviction, such Justice shall order him or them to be whipped thirty Lashes on the bare Back at the Public whipping Post.

AND BE IT FURTHER ENACTED by the Authority afo:esaid, That no person or persons after the Expiration of the said Term of three Years shall presume to kill or take any Partridges, Pheasant or Quail, from the tenth Day of February to the tenth Day of October in every year forever after; and if any Person or Persons shall offend contrary hereto, he or they so offending shall forfeit the like Sum of twenty shillings to be recovered and applied in manner and form aforesaid.

[CHAPTER 1592.]

[Chapter 1592, of Van Schaack, where the act is printed in full. See chapter 575.]

An Act to amend an Act entitled "An Act "for the better clearing regulating and further laying out Public Highways in the "County of Suffolk."

[Passed, February 6, 1773.]

WHEREAS the aforementioned Act which was passed in the fifth Year of the Reign of his late Majesty King George the second, by several subsequent Acts has been continued to the Year one thousand seven hundred and seventy five, and it has been found by Experience, that the Clause in the same, enacting that the penalties for not working on the Highways, as in that Act directed shall be recovered by Warrant from the Commissioners or the major Part of them, is attended with great Inconvenience, for the Commissioners being usually chosen in separate Districts in the Towns for the Ease of the Inhabitants, it generally happens that the Commissioners must travel many Miles before such a Majority can be obtained, for remedy whereof.

BE IT ENACTED by his Excellency the Governor, the Council and the General Assembly and it is hereby enacted by the Authority of the same. That each Commissioner in such his District, shall and is hereby impowered and authorized to issue his Warrant for the Recovery of every Penalty or Forfeiture that may arise within his District by virtue of the said Act, notwithstanding any Thing contained therein to the contrary.

[CHAPTER 1593.]

[Chapter 1593, of Van Schaack, where the act is printed in full.]

An Act declaring Winthorp's Patent to be under the Jurisdiction of the Town of Brookhaven in Suffolk County.

[Passed, February 6, 1773.]

WHEREAS there is a certain Tract of Land in the said County known by the Name of Winthorp's Patent, and Disputes have arisen whether the Lands contained in the said Patent are within the Jurisdiction of the said Township, though the Lands are within it's Boundaries, and it being judged most reasonable that the said Patent should be under the Jurisdiction thereof, therefore, to prevent any further Disputes.

BE IT ENACTED by his Excellency the Governor the Council and the General Assembly, and it is hereby enacted by the Authority of the same. That from and after the publication of this Act, the Lands contained in the said Patent shall be and remain under the Jurisdiction of the said Town of Brookhaven, and the Inhabitants dwelling and residing within the said Patent shall be subject to all the Laws and Regulations that the other Inhabitants of the said Town are liable and subject to, and invested with all the powers and privileges that the Inhabitants of the said Town are invested with: AND that the Freeholders and Inhabitants of the said Town, are hereby impowered to choose one Constable more at their annual Elections, who shall be chosen out of the Freeholders or Inhabitants dwelling and residing within the said Patent. PROVIDED ALWAYS that Nothing contained in this Act shall be construed to affect the Title or property of any Lands, but only the Jurisdiction thereof, any Law, Usage or Custom to the contrary in any wise notwithstanding.

[CHAPTER 1594.]

[Chapter 1594, of Van Schaack, where the title only is printed.]

An Act to raise the Sum of sixteen hundred pounds in the County of Tryon to compleat the Court-House and erect a Goal at Johnstown in said County.

[Passed, February 6, 1773.]

WHEREAS the Court House for the County of Tryon is begun, and the Building hitherto carried on by some of the Inhabitants of the said County. AND WHEREAS the same cannot be compleated neither can the Goal be erected without the Assistance of a Law for raising a Sum to defray the Charge of the same.

BE IT THEREFORE ENACTED by his Excellency the Governor, the Council and the General Assembly, and it is hereby enacted by the Authority of the same. That for building and erecting the same Court-House and Goal, the Supervisors of the said County, or the major Part of them for the Time being, shall and they are hereby required and directed to order to be levied on the Freeholders and Inhabitants of the said County a Sum not exceeding sixteen hundred pounds with the Additional sum of three pence for every pound for collecting the same eight hundred pounds of said sixteen hundred Pounds shall be raised in the first Tax that shall be levied after the publication of this Act, and the Remainder thereof with the second Tax, which said Sum of sixteen hundred pounds shall be raised levied and collected in the same Manner as the other necessary and contingent Charges of the said County are.

AND BE IT FURTHER ENACTED by the Authority aforesaid, That the Monies so to be raised by virtue of this Act, shall from Time to Time be paid by the several and respective Collectors of the said County unto the Honorable Sir William Johnson Baronet, Daniel Claus, Hendrick Fry, John Butler and Robert Adems Esquires, who are hereby appointed Trustees for laying out the said sum of sixteen hundred Pounds for the purposes aforesaid; and the said Trustees or any three of them, shall and may from Time to Time, inspect, examine and audit, all the several and respective Accounts for Workmanship and Materials to be employed for and towards making and erecting the Court-House and the Goal beforementioned, and of the due Disposition of the said Sum of sixteen hundred pounds or so much thereof as shall come into their Hands, they, the said Trustees or any three of them appointed as aforesaid, shall render a true Account upon Oath unto the Justices at the General Sessions of the Peace for the said County.

[CHAPTER 1595.]

[Chapter 1595, of Van Schaack, where the act is printed in full.]

An Act to encourage the destroying of Wolves and Panthers in the County of Tryon.

[Passed, February 6, 1773.]

WHEREAS the giving of an Encouragement for the destroying of Wolves in the adjacent Counties has by Experience, been found very beneficial to the Freeholders and Inhabitants of the same. AND WHEREAS there is no Law for that purpose extending to the County of Tryon.

BE IT THEREFORE ENACTED by his Excellency the Governor, the Council and the General Assembly, and it is hereby enacted by the Authority of the same, That from and after the Publication of this Act, and during the continuance thereof, every Person whether Christian or Slave, and every native Indian who shall kill or destroy a Wolf or Panther, or it's Whelp in the County of Tryon, shall have and receive the following Reward, That is to say, for every grown Wolf or Panther the Sum of twenty Shillings, and for every Wolf or Panther under the Age of one Year the Sum of fifteen Shillings.

AND to the End the Reward before mentioned may be truly paid and discharged. BE IT ENACTED by the Authority aforesaid. That the person or Persons killing or destroying a Wolf or Wolves, Panther or Panthers, and carrying the Head or Heads thereof with the intire Skin thereon within three Days after killing the same to a Justice of the Peace residing in the said County, before whom (if a Christian and thereunto required by the said Justice of the Peace) he shall make Oath that he killed the same within the said County, and within the Time limited by this Act, or if not a Christian, shall afford some other satisfactory proof, of the Truth thereof at the Discretion of the said Justice, and the said Justice shall and hereby is obliged thereupon to give a Certificate thereof gratis, and to mention therein the Name or Names of the person or persons that killed such Wolf or Wolves, Panther or Panthers, the Time when and whether the same were full grown or under the Age of one Year, after which the Ears of the Wolf or Wolves, Panther or Panthers so certified are to be cut off in the presence of the said Justice, and such Certificate being produced to the Supervisors of the said County, the said Supervisors shall, and hereby are obliged, at their annual Meetings, to order the Treasurer of the said County to pay unto the person or persons who so killed or destroyed the same or to his or their Assigns, the Reward allowed and established by this Act: and the said Reward shall be a County Charge and raised together with the other necessary, and contingent Charges of the said County.

This Act to be of force from the publication hereof until the first Day of February one thousand seven hundred and seventy eight.

[CHAPTER 1596.]

[Chapter 1596, of Van Schaack, where the title only is printed.]

An Act for making a further Provision of one thousand Pounds, for furnishing his Majesty's Troops quartered in this Colony with Necessaries to the first Day of January next.

[Passed, March 8, 1773.]

BE IT ENACTED by his Excellency the Governor, the Council and the General Assembly, and it is hereby enacted by the Authority of the same, That the Treasurer of this Colony shall pay and he is hereby directed and required out of the Interest arising from the Money in the Loan Office, to pay such Sum or Sums of Money as shall from Time to Time be necessary for quartering his Majesty's Troops in this Colony to the first Day of January one thousand seven hundred and seventy four, on Warrant or Warrants to be drawn for that purpose by his Excellency the Governor or Commander in Chief for the Time being, by and with the Advice and Consent of his Majesty's Council, provided the whole Sum to be drawn for does not exceed the Sum of one thousand Pounds.

AND BE IT ENACTED by the Authority aforesaid, That the Treasurer shall keep exact Books of his payments by virtue of this Act, and a true and just Account thereof shall render upon Oath, to the Governor or Commander in Chief for the Time being, the Council or the General Assembly, when by them or any of them thereunto required.

[CHAPTER 1597.]

[Chapter 1597, of Van Schaack, where the title only is printed.]

An Act for the Payment of the Salaries of the several Officers of this Colony and other purposes therein mentioned.

[Passed, March 8, 1773.]

BE IT ENACTED by his Excellency the Governor the Council and the General Assembly and it is hereby enacted by the Authority of the same That the Treasurer of this Colony shall and hereby is directed and required out of the Monies arisen, or which may arise by virtue of the following Acts to wit, the Act entitled. "An Act further to continue an Act entitled An Act for granting " to his Majesty the several Duties and Impositions on Goods " Wares and Merchandizes imported into this Colony therein " mentioned." the Act entitled "An Act to regulate the sale of " Goods at Public Vendue Auction or Outcry within this Colony." the Act entitled. "An Act to revive an Act entitled An Act to " restrain Hawkers and Pedlars within this County from selling " without Licence with an Addition thereto." and in Case the said Funds are insufficient to pay the following several Allowances, the Deficiency to be paid out of the Interest Money arisen or that may arise by virtue of the Act entitled "An Act for " emitting the Sum of one hundred and twenty thousand Pounds " in Bills of Credit to be put on Loan and to appropriate the Interest arising thereon to the payment of the Debts of this Colony, and to such public Exigencies, as the Circumstances of " this Colony may from Time to Time render necessary," to pay.

UNTO his Excellency William Tryon Esquire for Fire Wood and Candles for his Majestys Fort George in the city of New York from the first Day of September one thousand seven hundred and seventy two, to the first Day of September one thousand seven hundred and seventy three after the Rate of four hundred Pounds per Annum.

UNTO the Honorable Daniel Horsemander Esquire as Chief Justice of the Supreme Court of this Colony and for going the Circuits from and to the Time aforesaid after the Rate of three hundred Pounds per Annum.

UNTO the Honorable David Jones Esquire, one of the puisne Justices of the Supreme Court of this Colony, and for going the Circuits from and to the Time aforesaid after the Rate of two hundred Pounds per Annum.

UNTO the Honorable Robert R. Livingston Esquire one other of the Puisne Justices of the Supreme court of this Colony, and for going the Circuits from and to the Time aforesaid after the Rate of two hundred Pounds per Annum.

UNTO the Honorable George D. Ludlow Esquire the other puisne Justice of the Supreme Court of this Colony, and for going the Circuits from and to the Time aforesaid after the Rate of two hundred Pounds per Annum.

UNTO such of the Justices of the Supreme Court of this Colony as may attend the Circuit Courts in the Counties of Tryon, Charlotte, Cumberland and Gloucester, or either of them the Sum of fifty Pounds to each Justice that shall so attend; and for the Attendance of such Justice or Justices on any special Commission of Oyer and Terminer and General Goal Delivery in either of the said Counties other than such Special Commission which may be held when the Circuit Courts in the said Counties are held, the further Sum of fifty Pounds to the Justice or Justices so attending, and for the Attendance of such Justice or Justices on such Special Commission in the County of Albany the Sum of thirty Pounds, and for the other Counties in this Colony, not already provided for, the Sum of twenty Pounds.

UNTO the Secretary of this Colony for the Time being for engrossing and enrolling the Acts of the General Assembly from and to the Time aforesaid after the Rate of forty Pounds per Annum.

UNTO the Clerk of the Council for the Time being for his Services in that Station from and to the Time aforesaid the Sum of thirty Pounds.

UNTO the Doorkeeper of the Council for the Time being for his Services in that Station from and to the Time aforesaid the Sum of thirty Pounds.

UNTO Hugh Gaine for Services performed by him as Public Printer of this Colony as per Account the Sum of one hundred and ninety one Pounds.

UNTO Thomas Moore and John Griffiths as Gaugers of Liquor subject to a Duty within this Colony, or to the Gaugers thereof for the Time being, from the Time of their respective Appointments to the first Day of September one thousand seven hundred and seventy three, after the Rate of thirty Pounds per Annum unto each of them.

UNTO Thomas Hill and Josias Smith Land and Tide Waiters, or to the Land and Tide Waiters for the Time being for their Services in that Station from the first Day of September one thousand seven hundred and seventy two, to the first Day of September one thousand seven hundred and seventy three after the Rate of fifty Pounds per annum unto each of them.

ALL which aforesaid several Sums of Money shall be paid by the Treasurer on Warrants issued by his Excellency the Governor or the Commander in Chief for the Time being by and with the Advice and Consent of his Majesty's Council of this Colony, and the Receipts of the several Persons endorsed on the said Warrants shall be to the Treasurer good Vouchers and Discharge for so much as shall be thereby acknowledged to be received.

AND BE IT FURTHER ENACTED by the Authority aforesaid, That the Treasurer shall and hereby is directed and required out of the Funds aforesaid to pay the several Allowances following to wit.

UNTO Abraham Lott Esquire Treasurer of this Colony, or to the Treasurer for the Time being for his Services in that Station from and to the Time aforesaid after the Rate of two hundred Pounds per Annum.

UNTO the said Treasurer or to the Treasurer for the Time being for the extraordinary Services which he is obliged to perform beyond the usual Duty of his Office after the Rate of the further Sum of one hundred Pounds per Annum.

UNTO Edmund Burke Esquire Agent of this Colony in Great Britain or to the Agent for the Time being from and to the Time aforesaid after the Rate of five hundred pounds per Annum: which said Sum shall be paid unto him the said Edmund Burke by an Order of the General Assembly of this Colony signed by the Speaker for the Time being and not otherwise.

UNTO John Tabor Kemp Esquire for extraordinary services performed by him as Attorney General of this Colony from and to the Time aforesaid after the Rate of one hundred and fifty Pounds per Annum.

UNTO Edmund Seaman Esquire as Clerk to the General Assembly for his Services in that Station from and to the Time aforesaid twenty shillings per Diem payable upon a Certificate from the General Assembly signed by the speaker for the Number of Days he has or may serve the General Assembly.

UNTO the said Edmund Seaman for sundry Disbursements by him made for the use of the General Assembly the sum of fifty three Pounds nineteen shillings and two Pence.

UNTO Gerard Bancker as Assistant Clerk to the General Assembly for his Services in that Station from and to the Time aforesaid twenty shillings per Diem, payable upon a Certificate from the General Assembly signed by the Speaker for the Number of Days he has or may serve the General Assembly.

UNTO the said Edmund Seaman and Gerard Bancker for extraordinary Services performed by them this session the further Sum of twenty five Pounds unto each of them.

UNTO Alexander Lamb Doorkeeper of the General Assembly for his Services in that Station from and to the Time aforesaid six Shillings per Diem payable upon a Certificate from the General Assembly signed by the Speaker for the Number of Days he has or may serve the General Assembly.

UNTO the said Alexander Lamb for providing FireWood and sundry Necessaries for the use of his Majesty's Council and the General Assembly the Sum of sixty Pounds.

UNTO William Scott Serjeant at Arms for his Services in that Station from and to the Time aforesaid six Shillings per Diem payable upon a Certificate from the General Assembly signed by the speaker for the Number of Days he has or may serve the General Assembly.

UNTO John Martin as Gunner and keeper of the Colony Stores from the twenty eighth Day of July one thousand seven hundred and seventy two, to the first Day of September one thousand seven hundred and seventy three after the Rate of twenty Pounds per Annum.

AND BE IT ENACTED by the Authority aforesaid. That for answering the Expences of Contingencies and extraordinary Emergencies that have or may happen for the Services of this Colony from the first Day of September one thousand seven hundred and seventy two to the first Day of September one thousand seven hundred and seventy three, Warrants may issue for the same on the Treasurer from Time to Time, if drawn by his Excellency the Governor or Commander in Chief for the Time being, with the Advice and Consent of his Majesty's Council, which the Treasurer is hereby ordered and directed to pay out of the Monies arising by virtue of the Acts herein beforementioned. Provided the Amount of the said Warrants, does not exceed the Sum of one hundred Pounds during that Time.

AND BE IT ENACTED by the Authority aforesaid, That the Treasurer, shall and hereby is directed and required out of the Funds aforesaid to pay the several Sums following, to wit.

UNTO his excellency William Tryon Esquire the Sum of three hundred and twenty three Pounds thirteen Shillings and six pence for Monies advanced by his Excellency for running the Line between this Colony and Quebec from Lake Champlain to Connecticut River in the forty fifth Degree of North Latitude.

UNTO his said Excellency for sundry Repairs in Fort George and the Mansion House therein, and on the Battery the Sum of one thousand seven hundred and twenty one Pounds twelve Shillings.

UNTO his said Excellency to compleat the running of the Boundary Line between this Colony and Quebec a Sum not exceeding two hundred Pounds.

UNTO his said Excellency to purchase Brass Field pieces to carry Ball of six pounds weight, with proper Carriages for the use of this Colony, a Sum not exceeding three hundred Pounds.

UNTO his said Excellency such a Sum as will be sufficient to purchase one thousand Weight of Gun Powder for the use of Fort George and the Battery in the City of New York.

UNTO Richard Morris Esquire Clerk of the Courts of Oyer and Terminer and General Goal Delivery for his past Services in that Station throughout this Colony the Sum of one hundred and fifty Pounds.

UNTO Jacob Walton Esquire for a Ballance due to him for providing Carriages for the Cannon on the Battery the Sum of twenty six pounds nine Shillings and four Pence.

UNTO Jacob Walton and James Jauncey Esquires for a Ballance due to them for repairing the Battery, the Sum of ninety four Pounds six Shillings and six pence.

UNTO Benjamin Kissam Esquire Attorney at Law for his Services in assisting the Attorney General as Counsel for the King at the Request of his late Excellency Sir Henry Moore, at the Special Court of Oyer and Terminer and General Goal Delivery held in the counties of Dutchess and Albany, in the Year one thousand seven hundred and sixty six the Sum of fifty Pounds.

UNTO John Mc. Kesson Esquire attorney at Law for the like Services the Sum of fifty nine Pounds nine Shillings.

UNTO Samuel Jones Esquire Attorney at Law for the like Services in Dutchess County the Sum of forty Pounds ten Shillings.

UNTO Gerard Bancker for sundry Services performed by him respecting the Controversy about the Line of Boundary between this Colony and New Jersey as per his Account the Sum of twenty six Pounds seven Shillings and six pence.

UNTO James and Alexander Stewart for repairs to the Flag in Fort George as per Account the Sum of three pounds one Shilling and nine Pence.

UNTO Daniel Ebbets for sundry Repairs at Fort George, the Store House, and Fences, from the Year one thousand seven hundred and sixty eight to the fourth Day of February one thousand seven hundred and seventy three as per Accounts the Sum of sixty three Pounds five Shillings and ten pence half penny.

UNTO Daniel Buck for extraordinary Services performed and Monies disbursed by him out of the ordinary Duty of his Office as Constable in the County of Albany in apprehending sundry Persons charged and since convicted for Counterfeiting and passing Bills of Credit of this Colony the Sum of fifty seven Pounds; and also the further Sum of forty three Pounds as a Reward for his Activity and Diligence on that Occasion.

UNTO Esra Hickock Junior for his Expences and extraordinary Services, in assisting and apprehending sundry Persons charged and since convicted for counterfeiting and passing Bills of Credit of this Colony the Sum of thirty four Pounds thirteen Shillings and eleven pence.

UNTO Asa Holmes for his Expences and extraordinary Services as above the Sum of twenty two Pounds sixteen Shillings and four Pence.

AND BE IT ENACTED by the Authority aforesaid That the Treasurer shall and he is hereby directed to keep exact Books of the several payments which he is directed to make by this Act, and shall render true and Distinct Accounts thereof upon Oath to his Excellency the Governor, or Commander in Chief for the Time being, the Council or the General Assembly, when by them or any of them, he shall be thereunto required.

[CHAPTER 1598.]

[Chapter 1598, of Van Schaack, where the act is printed in full. See chapters 1550 and 1692.]

An Act to lay a Duty of Excise on Strong Liquors in this Colony, and to appropriate the Money arising therefrom.

[Passed, March 8, 1773.]

BE IT ENACTED by his Excellency the Governor the Council and the General Assembly, and it is hereby enacted by the authority of the same. That the several and respective persons and Officers herein after named shall be and are hereby appointed Commissioners for collecting the Duty of Excise of and from the several Retailers of Strong Liquors within the several Cities, Counties, Towns, Boroughs Manors Precincts and Districts, and the Harbours, Bays and Rivers thereunto adjoining or belonging in this Colony, for which they shall be respectively appointed from the first Day of February in the Year of our Lord one thousand seven hundred and seventy three, to the first Day of February which will be in the Year of our Lord one thousand seven hundred and seventy four inclusive. That is to say.

For the City and County of New York Cornelius Clopper.

For the City and County of Albany, Peter Lansingh, and Gysbert G Marcelis Esquires.

For the County of Ulster Joseph Gashery, and James McClaghrie Esquires.

For the County of Dutchess, the supervisor and Assessors in each Precinct respectively for the Time being.

For the County of Orange as follows. for Haverstraw Precinct David Pye Esquire. for Orange Town John Perry Esquire, for Goshen Precinct William Ellison Esquire, and for Cornwall precinct Daniel Coleman Esquire.

For Richmond County Hezekiah Wright, Jacob Rezeau, and Richard Conner Esquires.

For Kings County Theodorus Polhemus Esquire.

For Queens County Benjamin Townshend and Samuel Clowes Esquires.

For Suffolk County Colonel William Smith, Samuel Landon and Malby Gelston Esquires.

For Tryon County Jellis Fonda and John Frey Esquires.

For Cumberland County. The Judges of the Inferior Court of Common Pleas in said County.

For the Manor of Cortlandt and Rykes Patent in the County of West Chester Hackaliah Brown Esquire, with three or more of the Justices of the Peace residing in the said Manor or on the said Patent.

For the Borough Town of West Chester the Mayor thereof for the Time being.

For the Manor of Philipsburgh in the County of West Chester, William Davids, Isaac Deane, Israel Underhill, and Gabriel Purdy Esquires, and,

For the remaining part of West Chester County Stephen Ward and John Thomas Junior Esquires.

AND BE IT FURTHER ENACTED by the Authority aforesaid. That the said Commissioner for the City and County of New York, or such other or others as shall hereafter be appointed shall annually appoint the several Retailers of Strong Liquors in the said City and County, and agree with and ascertain what each Retailer shall pay for the said Duty from the first Day of February in any one Year unto the first Day of February in the next succeeding Year, during the Continuance of this Act. PROVIDED ALWAYS. That the whole sum so to be laid in any one Year on the several Retailers in the said City and County shall not be less than the full sum of ten hundred Pounds, together with the additional sum of Sixty Pounds for the trouble of such Commissioner: PROVIDED ALSO. That if the said Commissioner or such other or others as may hereafter be appointed should not in his or their first Assessment on the Retailers within the said City and County, assess the said Sum of Ten hundred Pounds annually, so to be paid by the said Retailers, that he or they shall in such Case add to the Excise each Retailer was to have paid his or her proportional part of such Deficiency according to the first Assessment so made by the said Commissioner or such other or others as may hereafter be appointed.

AND BE IT FURTHER ENACTED by the same Authority. That the said Commissioner for the City and County of New York, or such other or others as shall hereafter be appointed shall annually on or before the first Day of February in every Year pay the Sum of eight hundred Pounds into the Treasury of this Colony to be by the Treasurer for the Time being applied paid and disposed of as is directed by an Act of this Colony passed on the twenty fourth Day of March one thousand seven hundred and seventy two, entitled "An Act for the better support "of the Hospital to be erected in the City of New York for Sick "and indigent Persons." and the Overplus of the Duty of Excise collected in the said City and County if any there be shall by the said Commissioner or such other or others as shall hereafter be appointed, be annually paid for the first five Years next after the passing of this Act to the Treasurer of the Corporation of the Chamber of Commerce to be by the said Corporation disposed of in such Manner as they shall think most proper for encouraging a Fishery on the sea Coast for the better supply of the Markets in the City of New York; and for the remaining fifteen Years shall be annually paid into the Hands of the Chamberlain of the said City to be disposed of for and towards keeping in Repair the Public Roads of the said City and County.

AND BE IT ENACTED by the same Authority, That the aforesaid several and respective Commissioners, or such other or others as may hereafter be appointed (other than the Commissioner appointed by this Act for the City and County of New York, or such other or others as may hereafter be appointed for the same) shall annually as soon as they conveniently can after the first Day of February in each Year during the Continuance of this Act, meet at the County Hall of their several and respective Counties, or at such other place or places as they the said Commissioners of the respective Counties and Districts shall respectively appoint for putting in Execution the Powers and Authorities with which they are severally invested by this Act, at which Time or at such other Times as they shall judge necessary, they respectively shall for the Counties or Districts for which they are or may be Commissioner, fix the Number and appoint the several Retailers within their respective Counties and Districts, and direct and ascertain what each Retailer shall pay for the said Duty of Excise annually from the first Day of February in any one Year during the Continuance of this Act, to the first Day of February in the next succeeding Year. PROVIDED ALWAYS, and be it Enacted by the same Authority, That no Retailer of Strong Liquors in any of the Cities or Counties of this Colony shall pay less than the Sum of twenty shillings for one Years Duty of Excise, except such as shall retail strong Liquors not to be drank in their Houses, and such as may retail strong Liquors at or near the County Hall in the County of Suffolk during the sitting of their Courts or other public Meetings there, who shall be rated at the discretion of the Commissioners of said County for the Time being.

AND BE IT FURTHER ENACTED by the same Authority, That the several Commissioners so appointed as aforesaid or such other or others as may hereafter be appointed shall on or before the first Day of February annually during the Continuance of this Act render just true and particular Accounts on Oath to the several persons to whom by this Act they are directed to pay the same, of all the Sums of Money so annually to be raised by virtue of this Act on the several Retailers within the Cities Counties and Districts for which they are or may hereafter be appointed Commissioner or Commissioners as aforesaid specifying the Name of every Retailer, together with the Name of the City County and District in which such Retailer does reside and of the Sums they have been respectively rated at.

AND BE IT FURTHER ENACTED by the same Authority, That the said several Commissioners for the respective Cities Counties and Districts herein before mentioned, or such as may hereafter be appointed (except the Commissioner for the Time being for the City and County of New York) shall annually on or before the first Day of February in every Year during the Continuance of this Act, pay the several Sums of Money which they shall rate to be paid by the several Retailers of strong Liquors, in Manner following, that is to say.

The Commissioners that by this Act are or hereafter may be appointed for the City and County of Albany, and for the County of Tryon, shall pay the Money so annually to be rated by them into the Hands of the Clerk for the Time being of the Commissioners of the Highways of the District in which the same was raised, to be by the said Commissioners of the Highways applied to the use of the Highways.

The Commissioners that by this Act are or hereafter may be appointed for the several Counties of Ulster, Kings, Suffolk, Richmond, Cumberland and West Chester (except the Commissioners of so much of the last mentioned County as are appointed for the Borough and Town of West Chester the Manors of Cortlandt and Philipsburgh and Rykes Patent,) shall pay the Money so annually to be rated by them into the Hands of the Treasurer for the Time being of the said Counties respectively to be applied by the Supervisors of the said Counties respectively, as to them shall appear most conducive to the public Weal of their respective Counties.

The Commissioners that by this Act are, or that may hereafter be appointed for the several Counties of Dutchess and Orange, and for the Manors of Cortlandt and Philipsburgh, and for Rykes Patent, shall pay the Money so annually to be rated by them into the Hands of the respective Overseers of the Poor for the Time being of the several precincts in the said Counties and of the said Manors and Patents to be by the said Overseers applied to the Support of the Poor in their respective Districts.

The Commissioner that by this Act is or such other or others as may hereafter be appointed for the Borough and Town of West Chester shall pay the Money so annually to be rated by him or them into the Hands of the Recorder of the said Borough and Town for the Time being to be by the Mayor Recorder Aldermen and Commonalty of the same applied as to them shall appear most conducive to the Public Weal thereof.

The Commissioners that by this Act are, or may hereafter be appointed for the County of Queens, shall pay the Money so annually to be rated by them into the Hands of the Treasurer of the said County for the Time being to be applied by the Supervisors thereof in discharge of the public Taxes of said County, and the Overplus if any there be, shall by the said Treasurer be paid into the Hands of the Church Wardens or Overseers of the Poor of each respective Town in said County in the same proportion that each Town hath paid of the last Public Tax, to be by the said Church Wardens or Overseers of the Poor applied to the use of the Poor of their respective Towns.

AND in order the better to secure the payment of the said Sums so to be rated and raised by them by virtue of this Act. BE IT FURTHER ENACTED by the same Authority. That the said Commissioners or such other or others as may hereafter be appointed before they take upon themselves the Execution of the Powers and Authorities given by this Act, shall respectively enter into Bonds to the several Persons and Officers herein mentioned, and in the several Sums following. That is to say.

The said Commissioner by this Act appointed for the City and County of New York or such other or others as may hereafter be appointed to the Treasurer of this Colony for the Time being in the penal Sum of one thousand six hundred Pounds.

AND the said several other Commissioners or such other or others as may hereafter be appointed, to the several persons or Officers by this Act impowered to receive the Monies so to be rated and raised by virtue of this Act in the respective Counties and Districts following, that is to say.

The said Commissioners by this Act appointed, or such as may hereafter be appointed for the City and County of Albany in the penal Sum of three hundred Pounds.

The said Commissioners or such as may hereafter be appointed for the County of Tryon in the penal Sum of one hundred Pounds.

The said Commissioners or such as may hereafter be appointed for the respective Counties of Ulster Queens and Suffolk, severally in the Penal Sum of two hundred Pounds.

The said Commissioners or such as may hereafter be appointed for Richmond County and for the several precincts in the Counties of Dutchess, Orange and Kings, severally in the penal Sum of sixty Pounds.

The said Commissioners or such other or others as may hereafter be appointed for the Borough and Town of West Chester, the Manors of Cortlandt and Philipsburgh and Rykes Patent severally in the Penal Sum of fifty Pounds. and,

The said Commissioners or such other or others as may hereafter be appointed for the remaining part of West Chester County, and for the County of Cumberland in the Penal Sum of one hundred Pounds.

CONDITIONED That the said respective Commissioner or Commissioners or such as may hereafter be appointed, his or their Executors or Administrators, shall render a just and true account upon Oath in manner following, that is to say, the Commissioner for the City and County of New York for the Time being to the Treasurer of this Colony, for the Time being; and all other the Commissioners in the several Counties of this Colony for the Time being, to the Treasurer of the respective Counties for the Time being of all the Sums that may by him or them be rated or raised upon the several Retailers of strong Liquors within the City County or District for which he or they is or are, or shall be appointed Commissioner or Commissioners, (and well and truly pay the same except the Sum allowed him or them by this Act in Manner as herein before is directed) on or before the first Day of January next ensuing the Date of such Bond, which Bond shall be delivered to and remain with the said Treasurers respectively for the Time being. PROVIDED ALWAYS. That if any Commissioner or Commissioners that during the Continuance of this Act shall have entered into such Bond, and shall produce an Attested Account of the Monies so by him rated, with a Receipt from the person or persons to whom by this Act such Commissioner or Commissioners was or were to pay the same acknowledging the Receipt of such Money, that in such case the said Treasurer shall cancel the Bond entered into by such Commissioner or Commissioners; but if Default shall be made in the performance of the Condition of any or either of the said Bonds, it shall and may be lawful to and for the said Treasurers for the Time being, and they are respectively hereby directed and required at the Expiration of three Calender Months after the same ought to have been paid as herein directed to cause Suits to be brought in their respective Names upon each and every of the said Bonds so forfeited and prosecute the same to effect and no suit to be brought upon any or either of the said Bonds shall be abated or discontinued by the Death or Removal of any of the said Treasurers. but shall be continued and prosecuted to Effect by the new Treasurer or Treasurers.

AND BE IT FURTHER ENACTED by the Authority aforesaid, That the said Commissioners or such as may hereafter be appointed shall be allowed and may deduct out of the Sum to be by them respectively laid on the several Retailers within the Counties or Districts for which they are or shall be appointed Commissioners, the following Sums annually for their Trouble and Charge in the Execution of the Powers vested in them by this Act, that is to say. The Commissioners for the City and County of Albany each the Sum of fourteen Pounds: Those for the County of Ulster each the Sum of eight Pounds Those for the Counties of Dutchess, Richmond and Cumberland each one Pound; Those for the County of Orange each one Pound ten Shillings; Those for Queens County each five Pounds; Those for Suffolk County each four Pounds; Those for the County of Tryon each five Pounds; Those for the Manor of Cortlandt and Rykes Patent jointly Four Pounds; Those for the Manor of Philipsburgh jointly four Pounds; The Commissioner for the Borough Town of West Chester one Pound four shillings and those for the remaining Part of West Chester County each five Pounds; The Commissioner for Kings County five Pounds.

AND BE IT FURTHER ENACTED by the Authority aforesaid. That the several and respective Retailers of Strong Liquors within this Colony shall pay unto the Commissioner or Commissioners, that by this Act are or hereafter may be appointed, the several and respective Sums of Money to be laid on them respectively by virtue of this Act, before they shall be permitted to retail any Spirituous Liquors.

AND BE IT FURTHER ENACTED by the Authority aforesaid, That in Case any Person or Persons whomsoever, other than such as the said Commissioners so appointed or hereafter to be appointed shall permit, shall presume to sell any strong Liquors by Retail directly or indirectly, the Offender or Offenders shall for each such Offence forfeit the Sum of five Pounds to be recovered by the said Commissioners or Commissioners respectively, or by any other Person or Persons whatsoever, on the Oath of any one credible Witness in a Summary way in the Cities of New York and Albany and Borough of West Chester before the Mayor or Recorder and one or more Aldermen of the said Cities and Borough respectively, and in the several Counties before any Justice of the Peace within the several Counties respectively: and if upon Conviction the said Forfeitures be not paid, the same shall be levied on the Goods and Chattels of the Offender or Offenders, by Warrant or Warrants under the Hands and Seals of the Person or Persons before whom such Conviction shall happen, and if no Goods and Chattels are found on which to distrain, it shall and may be lawful for the Person or Persons who heard and determined the same to commit the Offender or Offenders to Goal without Bail or Main-prize for the space of three Months unless the Penalties are sooner discharged and the said respective Magistrates shall be and are hereby fully impowered directed and required to hear and determine those Matters in the Manner aforesaid and to give Judgment, if need be to award Execution thereon, and to issue a Warrant or Warrants for the Commitment of the Offenders, as the Case may require; one half of which Forfeiture shall be to the prosecutor or prosecutors, and the other half to the Poor of the Town Manor or Precinct where the Offence shall be committed to be paid into the Hands of the Church Wardens or Overseers of the Poor of the said respective place or places, by the Officer or Officers by whom the same shall be levied, any Thing in any of the Acts of this Colony to the contrary notwithstanding.

AND BE IT FURTHER ENACTED by the Authority aforesaid, That the several Retailers who shall be permitted and allowed to retail by the said Commissioner or Commissioners, or such as may hereafter be appointed, shall before they do so retail any strong Liquors enter into Recognizance unto our sovereign Lord the King, that is to say, in the Cities of New York and Albany and Borough of West Chester, before the respective Mayors, thereof, and in the several Counties in this Colony before two Justices of the Peace in the Penal Sum of twenty Pounds with sufficient Sureties in the like Sum, Conditioned to keep an orderly House according to Law during the Time they shall be permitted to retail as aforesaid, and thereupon the respective Mayors, or the said Justices shall grant to such person or persons who have entered into such Recognizance, a Licence under his or their Hands and Seals to retail Strong Liquors in such House and place as shall be mentioned therein from the Date of such Licence unto the first Day of February next succeeding; which Recognizances are to be lodged by the Person or Persons before whom the same shall be taken vizt: In the Cities of New York and Albany and Borough of West Chester with the Town Clerks, and in the several Counties with the respective Clerks thereof, and upon Complaint of the Breach of the said Condition, it shall be lawful for the said Mayor and Aldermen of New York and Albany and Borough of West Chester respectively or the greater Number of them, and in the Counties for the Justices of the General and Special Sessions of the peace, to suppress the Licence or Licences of such Offender or Offenders.

AND BE IT ENACTED by the Authority aforesaid, That in Case any of the Persons who shall be permitted to retail strong Liquors as aforesaid, shall presume to retail before he she or they have obtained a Licence and entered into Recognizance to keep an orderly House as aforesaid, he she or they so offending shall respectively forfeit the Sum of five Pounds for each Offence to be recovered in a summary way in the Manner before directed, one half thereof to the prosecutor and the other half to the Poor of the Town Manor Precinct or District where the Forfeiture shall arise: And that the Expence of being qualified to retail may be within the Bounds of Moderation.

BE IT ENACTED by the Authority aforesaid, That no more shall be taken for a licence and Recognizance in the Cities of New York and Albany and Borough of West Chester than the usual and accustomed Fees, and in the respective Counties than the Sum of three Shillings.

AND BE IT ENACTED by the Authority aforesaid, That such Persons permitted to retail as aforesaid, who retail Strong Liquors not to be drank in their own Houses, but carried elsewhere shall not be obliged to enter into Recognuzance, and take Licence as aforesaid, any Thing contained in this Act to the Contrary notwithstanding.

AND BE IT ENACTED by the Authority aforesaid, That in Case of the Death or refusal of any of the aforesaid Commissioners, or those that may hereafter be appointed the surviving or other Commissioner or Commissioners where such Death or Refusal may happen, shall be and hereby is and are entitled to the whole Reward, and vested with the same Powers and Authorities to execute this Act as if no such Death or Refusal had happened: And in Case of the Death or Refusal of all the Commissioners of any of the respective Cities, Counties, Towns, Manors Precincts or Districts, then the Sheriff or Sheriffs for the Time being for the Cities, Counties, Towns, Manors, precincts or Districts, where such Death or Refusal shall happen, shall be and hereby is and are vested until the first Day of the Month of February next succeeding such Death or Refusal, with all the powers and Authorities given to the Commissioners by this Act, be under the same Regulations, and entitled to the same Rewards to all Intents Constructions and purposes whatsoever, as if they had been particularly named and appointed in this Act, any Thing in this Act to the contrary notwithstanding.

PROVIDED ALWAYS and be it further Enacted by the same Authority, That if it should so happen that no future Law or Laws should be passed within one Month next after the said first Day of February which will be in the year of our Lord one thousand seven hundred and seventy four, or within one Month next after the first Day of every succeeding February during the Continuance of this Act, that then and in such Case it shall and may be lawful to and for the Supervisors of the several and respective Counties of this Colony for the Time being, and for the Mayor Recorder and Aldermen of the City of New York for the Time being, to nominate and appoint the several Commissioners of Excise in their respective Cities and Counties, and such Commissioner or Commissioners so nominated and appointed shall exercise the said Office until the first Day of the next succeeding February in as full and ample a Manner as any of the Commissioners appointed by this Act, and be liable to the same Penalties and receive the like Rewards, any Thing in this Act to the contrary hereof notwithstanding.

AND BE IT ENACTED by the same Authority, That the major Part of the Commissioners appointed or to be hereafter appointed, as also the major Part of the Supervisors for the Time being Shall have all the Powers and Authorities that the whole of the said Commissioners or Supervisors are invested with by this Act, any Thing to the contrary hereof in this Act notwithstanding.

PROVIDED ALWAYS That Nothing in this Act shall be construed to make void, abridge, or any wise lessen the several Rights and Privileges granted unto the Cities of New York and Albany, and Borough of West Chester by their respective Charters any Thing contained in this Act to the contrary thereof notwithstanding.

AND BE IT FURTHER ENACTED. That this Act shall be in force from the passing thereof, until the first Day of February which will be in the Year of our Lord one thousand seven hundred and ninety three.

[CHAPTER 1599.]

[Chapter 1599, of Van Schaack, where the act is printed in full. See chapter 1472.]

An Act to remedy the Evil this Colony is exposed to from the great Quantities of counterfeit Money introduced into it.

[Passed, March 8, 1773.]

WHEREAS the Credit of the paper Currency of this Colony hath been of late greatly injured by the flagitious Practices of artful and wicked Men who have counterfeited and altered the same, and passed such counterfeited and altered Bills knowing the same to be counterfeited and altered: And as it is of the utmost Importance to the trade and Interest of the Colony to prevent the Mischiefs arising from the circulation of counterfeit Currency; and as it may tend greatly to defeat the Designs of the Counterfeitors if the true and genuine Bills be distinguished from such as are false and Counterfeited. And the Bills of Credit of this Colony which have chiefly been of late counterfeited are those which were emitted by virtue of an Act entitled "An Act for emitting the Sum of one hundred and "twenty thousand Pounds in Bills of Credit to be put out on "Loan and to appropriate the Interest arising thereon to the "payment of the Debts of this Colony and to such public Exi- "gences as the Circumstances of this Colony may from Time to "Time render necessary."

BE IT THEREFORE ENACTED by his Excellency the Governor the Council and the General Assembly, and it is hereby enacted by the Authority of the same That the Treasurer of this

Colony for the Time being, Samuel Verplank, Theophilact Bache, and Walter Franklin and the major Part of them are hereby constituted Commissioners, and authorized to cause such plate or plates, and Device or Devices to be formed and engraved as they shall judge to be most difficult to be immitated and counterfeited as they or the major Part of them may think proper; and forty four thousand Copies thereof to be struck off upon thin paper to be pasted, glued or affixed to each of the Bills emitted by the Act aforesaid.

AND BE IT FURTHER ENACTED by the same Authority, That the Person by whom the said plate or plates shall be made, shall deliver the same to the said Commissioners or one of them, and then take an Oath, that the Plate or Plates by him so delivered, hath or have not been out of his Custody from the Time of his commencing to engrave the same to the Time of such Delivery, and that he hath not made, nor will attempt to make any Imitation thereof, and that no paper Copies have been taken or Struck off from or with the same other than such as he shall have struck off or cause to be struck off in the presence of the said Commissioners, some or one of them.

AND BE IT FURTHER ENACTED by the same Authority, That as soon as the above number of Copies are struck off, the said plate or plates shall be melted down in the presence of the Majority of the said Commissioners.

AND BE IT ALSO ENACTED by the same Authority, That the said paper Copies so to be made of the said plate or plates shall be lodged with the said Treasurer who shall give a Receipt for the same to the Speaker of the General Assembly for the Time being, and affix one Copy to the reverse Side of each of as many of the said Bills of credit as may be presented to him or come to his Hands, and which he shall adjudge and agree to be genuine true and good Bills of the Emission authorized by virtue of the Act aforementioned taking an Account of the Number and Value of each Bill, and of the Names of the Signers in a Book to be kept for that purpose; And in Case any of the Bills tendered to have such Device affixed thereto as aforesaid shall appear to him to be suspicious, he shall call to his Assistance the other Signers of such Bills emitted by the said first recited Act or one of them together with the printer thereof, to inspect and determine the same, whose Opinion and Judgment of such inspected Bills shall be a full Justification of the Conduct of the Treasurer thereon.

AND in Order that any Person or Persons tendering such true and genuine Bills emitted by the said first recited Act may not be detained until the Device or Devices be thereunto affixed as by this Act is directed. BE IT ENACTED by the same Authority. That it shall and may be lawful to and for the said Treasurer to give such person or persons so tendering any of the said true and genuine Bills any other Money that may then be in the Treasury in lieu thereof, other than such Bills of credit emitted by former Laws of this Colony, the Limitation of whose Currency is or may be expired.

AND BE IT FURTHER ENACTED by the same Authority, That from and after the first Day of February next, no Bill of Credit shall pass for or be deemed to be a Bill of Credit issued by virtue of the said Act until it shall have on the reverse thereof a Copy of such plate or plates as may be made in pursuance of the Directions of this Act.

AND BE IT ALSO ENACTED by the same Authority, That the Treasurer may pay such Sums out of the Treasury for procuring the plate or plates, paper and Copies aforesaid as the Majority of the said Commissioners shall think requisite, not exceeding two hundred Pounds, of which the said Treasurer shall render an Account as well as of the Services of the said Commissioners respectively that Provision may be made for satisfying the same by a future Law of this Colony.

AND forasmuch as the Neglect of the Commissioners by any Accident to exercise the great and important Trust committed to them by this Act would stagnate and discredit the Bills made Current by the Act aforesaid. BE IT THEREFORE ENACTED by the same Authority, that Nothing in this Act beforementioned shall be of force until the said Commissioners or the major Part of them have taken an Oath or Affirmation well and faithfully to perform the Trust aforesaid. PROVIDED ALWAYS. that Nothing in this Act contained shall be construed or taken to constitute the said paper Copies of the said Device to be a new Emission of Money, but only a Mark for distinguishing the Genuine and true Bills of Credit emitted by the said Act from the false and Counterfeit Bills.

BE IT FURTHER ENACTED by the same Authority. That there shall be given and paid to such Person or Persons as shall apprehend any felonious Offender or Offenders against either of the Laws aforementioned such Sum or Sums as the Governor or Commander in Chief of this Colony with the Advice and Consent of the Council shall promise by Proclamation to be specially issued from Time to Time for that purpose PROVIDED ALWAYS that such Offender or Offenders be convicted in a due Course of Law and that all the Rewards so to be promised by Proclamation do not exceed the Sum of two hundred Pounds.

AND BE IT ALSO ENACTED by the same Authority. That the Treasurer of this Colony for the Time being shall pay the Rewards aforesaid to such Person or Persons as the Majority of the Judges before whom the Offender shall be convicted, shall certify to be due to him or them by virtue of such Proclamation, out of any Money then in the Treasury, and every such Certificate with a Receipt thereon indorsed by the Bearer of the same for the Sum therein mentioned shall be a sufficient Voucher to the said Treasurer in his Account with this Colony.

[CHAPTER 1600.]

[Chapter 1600, of Van Schaack, where the act is printed in full.]

An Act for the settlement and relief of the Poor.

[Passed, March 8, 1773.]

WHEREAS the Laws of this Colony relating to the settlement and support of the Poor, are very deficient and ineffectual for that purpose.

BE IT THEREFORE ENACTED By his Excellency the Governor the Council and the General Assembly and it is hereby enacted by the Authority of the same. That from and after the passing hereof it shall and may be lawful upon Complaint made by the Church-Wardens or Overseers of the Poor of any Parish Town Precinct or District Within this Colony to any Justice of the Peace within forty Days after any Person or Persons shall come to settle in such Parish, Town, Precinct or District in any Tenement under the Yearly Value of five Pounds, for any two Justices of the Peace whereof one to be of the Quorum, in or next unto the Parish Town Precinct or District where any such person or persons that are likely to be chargeable to the Parish Town Precinct or District, shall come to inhabit by their Warrant to remove and convey such person or persons to such Parish, Town, Precinct or District where he she or they were last legally settled either as a Native, Householder sojourner Apprentice or Servant for the space of forty Days at the least unless he she or they give sufficient security for the Discharge of the said Parish Town Precinct or District to be allowed by the said two Justices.

PROVIDED ALWAYS, That all such Persons who think themselves aggrieved by any such Judgment of the said two Justices may appeal to the Justices of the Peace of the County wherein the Parish Town Precinct or District from which such poor person or persons is or are removed doth lie, at their next General or Quarter sessions of the peace who are hereby required to do them Justice according to the Merits of their Cause.

AND forasmuch as poor persons at their first coming to any Place, may conceal themselves. BE IT THEREFORE HEREBY PROVIDED AND ENACTED by the same Authority, That the forty Days continuance of such Person or Persons in any such place intended by this Act to make a Settlement shall be accounted from the Entry or Record of a Notice in writing which he or she shall deliver of the House of his or her abode and the Number of his or her Family if he or she have any, to one of the Church Wardens or Overseers of the Poor of such place to which they shall so remove; and the said Church Wardens or Overseers of the Poor is or are hereby required to register or cause to be registered the said Notice in Writing in the Book kept for the Poors Accounts, and within forty eight Hours after the Receipt thereof.

PROVIDED ALWAYS, AND BE IT ENACTED by the Authority aforesaid. That no Soldier, Seaman, Shipwright or other Artificer or Workman employed in his Majesty's Service shall have any settlement in any Place by delivery and publication of a Notice in writing as aforesaid unless the same be after the Dismission of such person out of his Majesty's service.

AND BE IT FURTHER ENACTED by the Authority Aforesaid, That if any Church Wardens or Overseers of the Poor shall refuse or neglect to register or cause to be registered such Notice in Writing as aforesaid in such Manner and Time as aforesaid he or they for every such Offence (upon proof thereof by two credible Witnesses upon oath before any Justice of the Peace for the same County, City or Town Corporate where complaint thereof shall be made) shall forfeit the Sum of forty shillings to the use of the party grieved, to be levied by Distress and Sale of the Offender's Goods, by Warrant under the Hand and Seal of any Justice of the Peace within the said Jurisdictions respectively, directed to the Constable of the City Parish, Town, Precinct or District where such Offender or Offenders dwell, the

Overplus, if any be, to be returned to the Owner or Owners, and for want of such sufficient Distress, the said Justice shall commit him or them to the common Goal of the said County City or Town Corporate there to remain without Bail or Mainprize for the space of twenty Days.

PROVIDED ALWAYS, AND BE IT FURTHER ENACTED by the same Authority. That if any Person who shall come to Inhabit in any City Parish Town Precinct or District, shall for himself and on his own Account execute any public annual Office or charge in the said City, Parish, Town Precinct or District during one whole year, or shall be charged with and pay his share towards the Public Taxes or Levies of the said City, Parish, Town, Precinct or District for the space of two years, then he shall be adjudged and deemed to have a legal Settlement in the same, though no such Notice in writing be delivered and registred as before required.

AND IT IS HEREBY FURTHER ENACTED. That if any unmarried person not having a Child or Children shall be lawfully hired in any City, Parish, Town, Precinct or District for one Year and shall continue and abide in the same Service during the Space of one whole year, such Service shall be adjudged and deemed a good settlement therein though no such Notice be delivered and registred as is herein before required.

AND BE IT FURTHER ENACTED, That if any Person shall be bound an apprentice by Indenture or by any Deed Writing or Contract not Indented and inhabit in any City Town Parish Precinct or District, such binding and inhabitation shall be adjudged a good settlement, though no such Notice in writing be delivered and published as aforesaid.

PROVIDED ALWAYS AND BE IT HEREBY ENACTED, That if any Person or Persons shall find him her or themselves aggrieved by any Determination which any Justice of the Peace shall make in any of the Cases abovesaid, the said Person or Persons shall have liberty to appeal to the next General or Quarter Sessions of the Peace to be held for the said County City or Town Corporate, who upon full hearing of the said Appeal shall have full power finally to determine the same.

AND BE IT FURTHER ENACTED by the Authority aforesaid, That if any person be removed by virtue of this Act from one County City Town Corporate precinct or District to another by Warrant under the Hands and seals of two Justices of the Peace, the Church Wardens or Overseers of the Poor of the said

City Parish Town, Precinct or District to which the said person shall be so removed are hereby required to receive the said person, and if he or they shall refuse so to do he or they so refusing or neglecting (upon proof thereof by two credible witnesses upon Oath before any Justice of the Peace of the County City or Town Corporate to which the said person shall be removed.) shall forfeit for each Offence the Sum of ten pounds to the use of the Poor of the City, Parish, Town, Precinct or District from which the said person was removed to be levied by Distress and Sale of the Offender or Offenders Goods by Warrant under the Hand and Seal of any Justice of the Peace of the County City or Town Corporate to which such person was removed, directed to the Constable of the City, Parish, Town precinct or District where such Offender or Offenders dwell, which Warrant the said Justice is hereby impowered and required to make the Overplus if any be to be returned to the Owner or Owners, and for want of such sufficient Distress, then the said Justice shall commit the said Offender or Offenders to the Common Goal of the said County City or Town Corporate there to remain without Bail or Mainprize for the Space of forty Days, provided always and be it hereby enacted, That all such persons who think themselves aggrieved with any such Judgment of the said two Justices may appeal to the Justices at their next General or Quarter sessions of the Peace to be held for the County, City or Town-Corporate from which the said Person was so removed, who are hereby required to determine the same.

AND BE IT FURTHER ENACTED by the same Authority, That if any Person or Persons whatsoever, that from and after the passing of this Act shall come into any Parish Town Precinct or District there to inhabit and reside shall at the same Time procure bring and deliver to the Church Wardens or Overseers of the Poor of the Parish or place where any such person shall come and inhabit, or to any or either of them a Certificate under the Hands and seals of the Church Wardens or Overseers of the Poor of any other Parish Township, Precinct District or place, or the major Part of them, to be attested respectively by two or more credible Witnesses thereby owning and acknowledging the Person or Persons mentioned in the said Certificate to be an Inhabitant or Inhabitants legally settled in that City Parish Town, Precinct District or place every such Certificate having been allowed of, subscribed by, & duly proved before two or more of the Justices of the Peace of the County, City or Town-Corporate wherein the Parish or Place from whence any such Certificate shall come doth lie, by the Oath of the said Witnesses who attest the Execution thereof, or one of them to have been executed by the Church Warden or Church Wardens, Overseer or Overseers signing and sealing the same in the presence of the said Witnesses, and (in Case it is proved by the Oath of one of the Witnesses only,) that the Names of such witnesses are of their own proper Hand writing and the said Justices of the Peace certifying that such Oath was made before them shall oblige the said Parish or Place to receive and provide for the person mentioned in the said Certificate together with his or her Family as Inhabitants of that Parish or place whenever he she or they shall happen to become chargeable to, or be forced to ask relief of the Parish Town or Place to which such Certificate was given, and then and not before it shall and may be lawful for any such Person, and his or her children though born in that Parish or Place, not having otherwise acquired a legal Settlement there to be removed conveyed and settled in the Parish or place from whence such Certificate was brought.

AND BE IT FURTHER ENACTED, That every such Certificate so allowed, and Oath of the execution thereof so certified as aforesaid by the said Justices of the Peace shall be taken deemed and allowed in all Courts whatsoever within this Colony as duly and fully proved, and shall be taken and received as Evidence without other proof thereof.

AND BE IT FURTHER ENACTED by the same Authority, That no Person or Persons whatsoever who shall come into any Parish or Place by any such Certificate as aforesaid, shall be adjudged by any Act whatsoever to have procured a legal settlement in such Parish or Place unless he or they shall really and bona fide rent a Tenement of the Yearly Value of five Pounds or shall execute some annual Office in such Parish or Place, being legally placed in such Office.

AND BE IT FURTHER ENACTED by the same Authority. That if any person whatsoever who shall be an Apprentice bound by Indenture to or shall be an hired servant to or with any Person whatsoever who did come into or shall reside in any city Parish Town or Place within this Colony by means or Licence of such Certificate as aforesaid and not afterwards having gained a legal settlement in such City, Town, Parish or Place, such Apprentice by virtue of such Apprenticeship, Indenture or binding and such

Servant by being hired by or serving as a Servant as aforesaid to such Person shall not gain or be adjudged to have any settlement in such City Parish Town or Place by reason of such Apprenticeship or binding or by reason of such hiring or serving therein, but every such apprentice and Servant shall have his and their Settlements in such Parish Town or place as if he or they had not been bound Apprentice or Apprentices or had not been an hired Servant or Servants to such Person as aforesaid.

AND BE IT FURTHER ENACTED by the same Authority. That when any Overseer or Overseers of the Poor of any Parish or Place or other Person shall remove back any Person or Persons or their Families residing in such Parish or Place, or sent thither by Certificate and becoming chargeable as aforesaid to the Parish or Place to which such Person or Persons shall belong, such Overseers or other Person shall be reimbursed such reasonable Charges as they may have been put unto in maintaining and removing such person or persons by the Church Wardens or Overseers of the Poor of the Parish or Place to which such Person or Persons is or are removed the said Charges being first ascertained and allowed of by one or more of his Majesty's Justices of the Peace for the County or Place to which such removal shall be made, which said Charges so ascertained and allowed shall in Case of refusal of payment be levied by Distress and Sale of the Goods and Chattels of the Church Wardens or Overseers of the Poor of the Parish or Place to which such Certificate Person or Persons is or are removed, by Warrant or Warrants under the Hand and Seal or Hands and Seals of such Justice or Justices returning the Overplus if any there be, which Warrant or Warrants he or they are hereby required to grant.

AND BE IT ENACTED by the Authority aforesaid. That from and after the passing of this Act no person or persons shall be deemed adjudged or taken to acquire or gain any settlement in any Parish or Place for or by virtue of any purchase of any Estate or Interest in such Parish or Place, whereof the Consideration for such purchase doth not amount to the Sum of thirty Pounds bona fide paid for any longer or further Time than such Person or Persons shall inhabit in such Estate, and shall then be liable to be removed to such parish or place where such person or persons were last legally settled before the said purchase and Inhabitancy therein.

AND BE IT FURTHER ENACTED by the same Authority, That no appeal or Appeals from any Order or Orders of removal of any Poor person or persons whatsoever from any Parish or Place to another shall be proceeded upon in any Court of General or Quarter Sessions of the Peace unless reasonable Notice be given by the Church Wardens or Overseers of the Poor of such parish or place, who shall make such Appeal unto the Church Wardens or Overseers of the Poor of such Parish or Place from which such poor person or persons shall be removed; The reasonableness of which Notice shall be determined by the Justices of the Peace at the General or Quarter Sessions to which the Appeal is made; and if it shall appear to them that reasonable Time of Notice was not given, then they shall adjourn the said Appeal to the next General or Quarter sessions, and then and there finally hear and determine the same.

AND for the preventing vexatious Removals and frivolous Appeals BE IT FURTHER ENACTED by the Authority aforesaid. That the Justices of the Peace of any County, City or Town Corporate in their General or Quarter Sessions of the Peace upon any Appeal before them there to be had for and concerning the Settlement of any Poor person or upon any Proof before them there to be made of Notice of any such Appeal to have been given by the proper Officer to the Church-Wardens or Overseers of the Poor of any Parish or Place (though they did not after wards prosecute such Appeal) shall at the same General or Quarter Sessions award and order to the Party for whom and in whose Behalf such Appeal shall be determined, or to whom such Notice did appear to have been given as aforesaid such Costs and Charges in the Law as by the said Justices in their Discretion shall be thought most reasonable and just to be paid by the Church-Wardens, Overseers of the Poor, or any other person against whom such Appeal shall be determined, or by the person that did give such Notice as aforesaid, and if the Person ordered to pay such Costs shall happen to live in any County City or Town Corporate or elsewhere out of the Jurisdiction of the said Court, it shall and may be lawful for any Justice of the Peace of the county City or Town Corporate wherein such Person shall inhabit, and every such Justice is hereby required upon request to him for that purpose to be made and a true Copy of the Order for the payment of such Costs produced and proved by some credible Witness upon Oath, by Warrant under his Hand and Seal to cause the Money mentioned in that order to be levied by Distress and Sale of the Goods of the Person that is ordered and ought to pay the same and if no such Distress can or may be had to commit such person to the common Goal of that County or City there to remain by the space of three Months.

AND BE IT FURTHER ENACTED by the Authority aforesaid. That if the Justices of the Peace shall at their General or Quarter Sessions upon any Appeal before them there had concerning the settlement of any Poor Person determine in favor of the Appellant that such Poor Person or Persons was or were unduly removed, that then the said Justices shall at the same General or Quarter Sessions order and Award to such Appellant so much Money, (besides his Costs and Charges,) as shall appear to the said Justices to have been reasonably paid by the Parish or other place on whose behalf such Appeal was made, for or towards the Relief of such Poor Person or Persons between the Time of such undue removal and the Determination of such Appeal, the said Money so awarded to be recovered in the same Manner as Costs and Charges upon an Appeal are above prescribed to be recovered.

AND BE IT FURTHER ENACTED by the Authority aforesaid. That the Father and Grandfather, Mother and Grandmother (being of sufficient Ability) of any Poor lame or decrepit Person or Persons whomsoever not being able to maintain themselves, and becoming chargeable to any City, Town Manor, Precinct or District within this Colony, and the Children and Grand Children (being of sufficient Ability) of every Poor, old, blind, lame or impotent person not being able to maintain themselves, and becoming chargeable as aforesaid, shall severally at his, her or their Charges and Expences relieve and maintain every such Poor Person as aforesaid in such Manner as the Justices of the Peace of the County, City or Town Corporate where such sufficient person shall dwell at their General or Quarter Sessions of the Peace shall order and direct, on Pain of forfeiting and paying ten Shillings for each Person so ordered to be relieved for every Week they shall fail therein to be sued for and recovered by the Church Wardens or Overseers of the Poor of the place to which such Poor Person or Persons shall be chargeable for the use of the Poor of the same place, in the Manner herein before directed, with respect to Costs and Charges upon an Appeal.

AND WHEREAS it sometimes happens that Persons run away, or abscond from their places of abode and legal Settlement, and leave their Wives and Families a Charge to the Public although such Persons may have some Estate real or Personal whereby the place might be eased in whole or in part, which is most just and reasonable. BE IT THEREFORE ENACTED by the Authority aforesaid. That it shall and may be lawful for the Church Wardens or Overseers of the Poor of any City Town Manor Precinct or District within this Colony where any Father or Husband shall run away or absent himself from his Wife and Children, or any Widow shall run away or absent herself from her Children and leave them a public Charge, to apply to any two Justices of the Peace of the County, City or Town Corporate where such Estate Real or personal, or any part thereof may be, and by Warrant under the Hands and Seals of the said two Justices to take and seize so much of the Goods and Chattels, and to let out and receive so much of the annual Rents and Profits of the Lands and Tenements of such Father Husband or Mother so absconding as aforesaid as such two Justices shall order and direct for and towards the maintaining bringing up and providing for such Wife Child or Children so left as aforesaid; and so soon as the said Seizure shall be allowed of, and confirmed by the Justices in their General or Quarter Sessions of the Peace, it shall and may be lawful for the said Overseers or any two of them from Time to Time and as often as the Case may require to sell and dispose of so much and so many of the said Goods and Chattels at Public Vendue to the highest Bidder, and to receive the said Rents and profits or so much of them as shall be ordered by the said Sessions, and to apply the Money arising thereby towards the Maintenance of such Poor Family so left as aforesaid.

AND BE IT ENACTED by the Authority aforesaid, That the Freeholders and Inhabitants of each respective Town Manor or Precinct not already impowered by Law to appoint Church Wardens or Overseers of the Poor shall and may on the first Tuesday in April in every Year, or at their annual Meetings for the electing of Officers, elect and choose so many Persons to be Overseers of the Poor as the Majority of the Freeholders and Inhabitants then present, shall judge necessary, which Overseers of the Poor so elected shall have all the Powers and be subject to all the Duties and Penalties required by this Act, or any general Law of the Colony, relating to the Poor, and this Act shall extend to every City and Manor in this Colony as well as to other places.

PROVIDED NEVERTHELESS, That Nothing herein before enacted shall extend or be construed to extend to set aside or make void any Judgment Order or Decree which hath been made or shall be made by any Court in this Colony respecting the settlement of any Poor Person before the making of this Act, which is to continue and be in force from the passing hereof until the first Day of May which will be in the Year of our Lord one thousand seven hundred and seventy six. Provided also that all Suits or Processes that shall be commenced by virtue of this Act may be proceeded on and determined notwithstanding the Expiration hereof.

[CHAPTER 1601.]

[Chapter 1601, of Van Schaack, where the act is printed in full.]

An Act to appoint Commissaries to settle a Line or Lines of Jurisdiction between this Colony and the Province of the Massachusetts Bay.

[Passed, March 8, 1773.]

BE IT ENACTED by his Excellency the Governor the Council and the General Assembly, and it is hereby enacted by the Authority of the same. That the Honorable John Watts, the Honorable William Smith, the Honorable Robert R. Livingston and William Nicoll Esquires shall be Commissaries on the Part of this Colony, who shall be commissionated by the Governor or Commander in Chief for the Time being, and who shall have full power, and are hereby authorized to meet with the Commissaries who are or may be appointed and in like Manner authorized and impowered by the Governor, Council and General Court or Assembly of the Province of the Massachusetts Bay, at such Time or Times, place or places, as shall be agreed upon and determined by the Governors or Commanders in Chief for the Time being of this Colony and the Province of the Massachusetts Bay; then and there to agree upon a Line or Lines of future Jurisdiction between the said Province of the Massachusetts Bay and this Colony on the Easterly part of this Colony, to begin at the south-West corner of the Province of New Hampshire on the West Bank of Connecticut River, and from thence in such Manner, and by such Line or Lines as shall be found eligible with due Regard to the Rights of this Colony to the Colony of Connecticut: the Governor or Commander in Chief of this Colony for the Time being, and the Governor of the said Province being present, and such Line or Lines so agreed upon and approved of, and consented to by the said Governor or Commander in Chief of this Colony, and the Governor of the province of the Massachusetts Bay for the Time being, shall be presented by the said Governors respectively to his Majesty for his Royal Approbation: and being ratified and confirmed by his Majesty, shall at all Times thereafter be the Line or Lines of Jurisdiction between this Colony and the Province of the Massachusetts Bay; the true and real Extent or Boundary of this Colony by the Royal Grants, or any Law Act Declaration or Ordinance to the contrary thereof in any wise notwithstanding.

AND BE IT FURTHER ENACTED by the same Authority. That after such Line or Lines shall be so agreed upon approved ratified and confirmed the Commissaries appointed by this Act, are hereby authorized and impowered to employ a Surveyor or Surveyors, Chainbearers, and such and so many other persons as may be found necessary to perform the executive part in running, marking and ascertaining the said Line or Lines in conjunction with such as may be appointed on the part of the said Province of the Massachusetts Bay for that purpose.

AND to the Intent that the good Ends of this Act may not be defeated by the Death, Sickness or unavoidable Absence of either of the Commissaries above named.

BE IT ENACTED by the same Authority. That in Case of any such Accident happening to any of the Commissaries, the major Part of the said Commissaries, or the survivors and Survivor of them shall and may execute and perform all such Acts as they may conceive to be expedient and necessary for settling the said Line or Lines of Jurisdiction between this Colony and the Province abovementioned, and that as fully to all the Intents and purposes aforementioned, as all the Commissaries could or might execute and perform the same.

[CHAPTER 1602.]

[Chapter 1602, of Van Schaack, where the act is printed in full.]

An Act to regulate the gauging of Liquors, and for other purposes therein mentioned.

[Passed, March 8, 1773.]

BE IT ENACTED by his Excellency the Governor the Council and the General Assembly, and it is hereby enacted by the Authority of the same, That all Casks containing Rum, Brandy, Oyl, or other Commodities usually sold by the Gallon within this Colony, shall before the Sale thereof, be gauged by the sliding

Gunter, and the full Contents marked on each Cask by the Gauger thereof, with the initial Letter of his Name, which gauging shall be performed by Thomas Moore and John Griffiths, or one of them, or by any Deputy or Deputies appointed by them, unless the Buyer and Seller shall agree to the contrary, which said Gaugers and their Deputies shall first be duly sworn truly to execute the said Office, and sue for the Penalties that may be incurred by this Act, as often as any Breach of the same shall come to his knowledge, for which gauging and marking the Gauger thereof shall receive for each Cask four pence, and no more. PROVIDED NEVERTHELESS that all Spirituous Liquors subject to a Duty by an Act of this Colony shall for said Duties be gauged by the said Gaugers or either of them, or by either of their Deputies only, and that the said Gaugers or one of them, and no other Person, shall deliver the Contents thereof to the Treasurer of this Colony, in order that he receive the Duties imposed therein.

AND BE IT FURTHER ENACTED by the Authority aforesaid. That if any Person or Persons during the Continuance of this Act shall presume to sell any Rum, Brandy or other Commodities usually sold by the Gallon in this Colony, without first causing the same to be gauged and the Casks marked in the Manner directed by this Act, he she or they shall for every such Offence forfeit the Sum of forty Shillings to be recovered in the like Manner as Debts of five Pounds and under are recoverable in this Colony, for the use of any Person or Persons who will sue for the same with full Costs of Suit.

AND BE IT ALSO ENACTED by the Authority aforesaid That all Wine imported into this Colony, shall from and after the first Day of June in this present Year be in pipes containing not less than one hundred and twenty Gallons, or in Hogsheads containing not less than sixty Gallons, or in Quarter Casks containing not less than thirty Gallons: And every Person who shall import into this Colony, or dispose of any Wine containing less than is above directed, shall forfeit and pay the Sum of five Pounds for every Pipe, and in like proportion for every Hogshead or Quarter Cask so imported or sold contrary to the true Intent and meaning of this Act, the Contents of all such pipes, Hogsheads or Quarter Casks to be determined by the Gaugers appointed by this Act, or either of them, to be sued for and recovered as aforesaid: the one half of said Forfeiture to be for any Person or Persons who shall sue for the same to effect, and the other half to be paid to the

Treasurer of this Colony, to be applied for and towards the support of the Government thereof. PROVIDED ALWAYS, that neither of the Gaugers appointed by this Act shall employ more than two Deputies.

This Act to continue from the passing thereof until the first Day of February, which will be in the Year of our Lord one thousand seven hundred and eighty.

[CHAPTER 1603.]

[Chapter 1603, of Van Schaack, where the act is printed in full.]

An Act to ascertain the Size of Casks in which Fish shall be sold within this Colony.

[Passed, March 8, 1773.]

WHEREAS the Casks in which Fish are packed and exposed to sale in this Colony are of various Sizes and Dimensions, which often causes the Buyer to be greatly imposed upon, for remedy whereof.

BE IT ENACTED by his Excellency the Governor, the Council and the General Assembly, and it is hereby enacted by the Authority of the same, That every Cask in which Fish shall be packed and exposed to sale being a Barrel shall contain thirty one Gallons and an half of Wine Measure each, and in the same proportion for a greater or lesser Cask, and shall be well packed and filled, and of good Quality, upon the Penalty of twenty shillings for each Cask exposed to sale contrary to the Directions of this Act, to be paid by the Vender or Venders, one half thereof to the use of the Poor of that place where such Offence shall happen, and the other Half to the use of any person who will sue for the same to be recovered in any Court within this Colony having Cognizance of the same, by the usual practice and process of such Court.

AND BE IT ENACTED by the Authority aforesaid. That this Act shall continue and be in force from the first Day of May next, until the first Day of May in the Year of our Lord one thousand seven hundred and eighty.

[CHAPTER 1604.]

[Chapter 1604, of Van Schaack, where the act is printed in full. See chapter 1433.]

An Act to revive an Act entitled. "An Act "to restrain Hawkers and Pedlars within this "Colony from selling without Licence," with an Addition thereto.

[Passed, March 8, 1773.]

BE IT ENACTED by his Excellency the Governor the Council and the General Assembly, and it is hereby enacted by the Authority of the same, That the Act entitled, "An Act to restrain Hawkers and Pedlars within this Colony from selling "without Licence," passed the twenty seventh Day of January one thousand seven hundred and seventy. shall be and hereby is revived, and every Article Matter and Clause therein contained, enacted to be and remain in full force until the first Day of February, which will be in the Year of our Lord one thousand seven hundred and seventy four.

AND BE IT FURTHER ENACTED by the same Authority. That if any Hawker or Pedlar, shall sell any kind of Goods, Wares or Merchandize whatsoever unto any Slave without the Leave and permision of the person owning such Slave, and shall be thereof accused by any Person and convicted before any one Justice of the Peace of this Colony, shall for every such Offence forfeit and pay the Sum of five Pounds, which Justice is hereby strictly required and directed to hear and finally determine the same, and give Judgment, and award Execution in the usual Manner of proceeding on the Trial of Causes of the Value of five Pounds and under before Justices of the Peace, the one half of which Forfeiture shall go to the Person suing for the same, and the other half to the Overseers of the Poor in the District where such Offence shall be committed, to be by the Overseers of the Poor applied to the use of the Poor of such District, any Law usage or Custom to the contrary notwithstanding.

[CHAPTER 1605.]

[Chapter 1605, of Van Schaack, where the act is printed in full.]

An Act to regulate the Office of Under or Deputy Sheriff within this Colony.

[Passed, March 8, 1773.]

Business incident to the Office of Sheriff throughout v is of late much increased and in many of the Coun- ,articularly in the City and County of New York, the ?art of it is committed to Under Sheriffs or Deputies ıot sworn to the faithful Execution of their Offices; and 'eing too long continued in their Offices, they are more ·orruption, whereby the Rights of the Crown as well as 'ty of the Subject may be greatly injured, for preven- 'of.

NACTED by his Excellency the Governor the Council neral Assembly, and it is hereby enacted by the Au- he same. That from and after the passing of this Act ev... ɔn that shall be admitted to the Office of an Under-Sheriff or Deputy within this Colony before he enters upon the Execution of the said Office shall take an Oath before one of the Justices of the Supreme Court or a Judge of the Inferior Court of Common pleas or the Mayors of the Cities of New York and Albany, respectively for the true and impartial Execution of his Office in the form and Words following to wit. "I. A B. do in the "presence of Almighty God swear that I will well and truly "serve our Sovereign Lord the King in the Office of Under Sheriff "or Deputy during my Continuance therein, and will duly, faith-"fully and truly execute all Writs and precepts that shall be "delivered to me or come to my Hands for that purpose, and will "faithfully and truly return the same according to the best of "my knowledge Skill and Judgment and that I will not know-"ingly corruptly or unjustly use or exercise the Office of under-"Sheriff or Deputy during the Time I shall remain therein, neither "will I directly or indirectly accept receive or take by any Colour "Means or Device whatsoever, or consent to the taking of any "Manner of Fee or Reward of or from any person or persons "whatsoever for the impanneling or returning of any Inquest, "Jury or Tales in any Court for the King or between party and "party, or for the serving any legal process whatsoever more "than such Fees or Rewards as now are or hereafter shall be "appointed allowed and established, but will demean myself "truly and impartially in all Things that shall belong to the "Duty of my Office of under Sheriff or Deputy according to the "best of my Skill and power. so help me God," which Oath shall be taken by such Officers already appointed, within thirty Days after passing this Act. AND BE IT FURTHER ENACTED by the Authority aforesaid, That no Under Sheriff or Deputy, that now is, or that hereafter shall be appointed to Act in the Office of Under-Sheriff or Deputy within the City and County of New York shall continue in the same more than three Years, and every such Officer shall be and is hereby rendered incapable of holding the same Office again until he shall have been at least three Years out of the said Office.

AND BE IT FURTHER ENACTED by the same Authority. That if any Under Sheriff or Deputy at any Time or Times from and after thirty Days next after the passing of this Act, shall presume to Act in the said Office of under Sheriff or Deputy within this Colony without taking the Oath herein before directed, or if any Under Sheriff or Deputy in and for the City and County of New York, shall continue in that Office longer at any one Time than the Term herein before limitted, or if any of the said Under Sheriffs or Deputies shall do or commit any Act or Thing by virtue of his Office contrary to the true Intent and Meaning of this Act that then and in such Case every person so Offending shall forfeit for every such Offence the Sum of ten pounds Current Money of New York the one Moiety for the use of the Poor of the City or County where the Offence shall happen, the other Moiety to any person who shall sue for the same to be recovered by Action of Debt Bill Plaint or Information in any of his Majesty's Courts of Record within this Colony, in which Actions, Suits, Plaints or Informations no Essoign or Wager of Law, and but one Imparlance shall be allowed. PROVIDED ALWAYS That neither this Act, nor any Thing herein contained shall extend or be construed to extend to Cases of Special Deputations made by any High Sheriff and indorsed on any Writ at the Special Instance and request, and at the Risque of any Plaintiff or Plaintiffs; But every Person who shall assist the Sheriff of any County in the Service of more than three Writs or Processes shall be deemed to be an Under Sheriff within the Meaning of this Act.

This Act to be in force from the passing thereof until the first Day of February which will be in the Year of our Lord one thousand seven hundred and seventy six.

[CHAPTER 1606.]

[Chapter 1606, of Van Schaack, where the act is printed in full.]

An Act to oblige Collectors and Constables to give Security for the faithful performance of their respective Offices.

[Passed, March 8, 1773.]

WHEREAS several of the Counties within this Colony have sustained considerable Losses by the Insolvency and Misconduct of the Collectors of the said Counties and many of the Inhabitants of the said Counties have sustained Losses by the Misconduct and Insolvency of the Constables of the said Counties, for Remedy whereof for the Future

BE IT ENACTED by his Excellency the Governor the Council and the General Assembly, and it is hereby enacted by the Authority of the same. That every Collector hereafter to be chosen for any of the Wards in the City and County of New York immediately after he shall be elected, and before he shall enter upon the Business of the said Office of Collector shall enter into Bond with sufficient Security to the Mayor of the said City and County for the Time being in such Sum as the said Mayor for the Time being shall think proper well and faithfully to execute the Office of Collector of such Ward as he shall be so elected for during the Time he shall continue to be collector.

AND BE IT FURTHER ENACTED by the Authority aforesaid. That if the Collector of any of the respective Wards within the City and County of New York, shall not comply with the Condition of the Bond or Obligation above directed to be given, whereby the Penalty of such Bond or Obligation shall be forfeited, in such Case it shall be lawful for the said Mayor of the said City and County of New York for the Time being to sue for and recover the same with Costs of Suit, in any Court of Record within this Colony, and the Monies that shall be recovered in such Suit or Action shall be applied towards making good any such Deficiency as shall happen or accrue by reason or means of the Neglect or Misconduct of such Collector.

AND BE IT FURTHER ENACTED by the Authority aforesaid, That every Collector hereafter to be chosen in such of the other respective Counties, Towns, Boroughs, Manors Precincts or Districts within this Colony immediately after he shall be elected Collector for such County, Town, Borough, Manor, Precinct or District, and before he shall enter upon the Business of the said Office of Collector, shall enter into Bond or Obligation with sufficient Security, (if required by twelve Freeholders,) to the Clerk of each respective Town Borough Manor Precinct or District for the Time being, in double the Sum to be by him collected within the same, well and faithfully to execute the Office of Collector of such respective County, Town, Borough, Manor, Precinct or District during the Time of his continuing to be Collector.

AND BE IT ENACTED by the Authority aforesaid. That if the Collector of each respective County, Town, Borough, Manor, Precinct or District shall not comply with the Condition of the Bond or Obligation above directed to be given, whereby the Penalty of such Bond or Obligation shall be forfeited in such Case it shall and may be lawful for the Clerk of each respective Town, Borough, Manor, Precinct or District, for the Time being by the Name of the Clerk of such Town, Borough, Manor, Precinct or District, to sue for and recover the same with Costs of Suit in any Court of Record within this Colony and the Monies that shall be recovered in any such Suit or Action shall be applied towards making good any Deficiencies that may arise or accrue by reason or means of the Neglect or Misconduct of such Collector.

AND BE IT ENACTED by the Authority aforesaid, That every Constable hereafter to be chosen in each respective City, County, Town Borough Manor, precinct or District within this Colony shall (unless he shall make Oath before a Magistrate at the Time of his being so chosen, that he was chosen against his Inclination,) immediately after he shall be elected Constable for any such City, County, Town, Borough, Manor, Precinct or District, and before he shall enter upon the Business of the said Office of Constable enter into Bond or Obligation with sufficient Security, (if required by twelve Freeholders,) to any one of his Majesty's Justices of the Peace of such respective County for the Time being in the Sum of one hundred Pounds well and faithfully to execute the Office of Constable of such respective City, County, Town, Borough, Manor, Precinct or District, for which he shall be so chosen as aforesaid.

AND BE IT ENACTED by the Authority aforesaid. That if any Constable hereafter to be chosen shall not comply with the Condition of the Bond or Obligation above directed to be given, in such Case it shall and may be lawful for any Person or Persons aggrieved by the Misconduct or Negligence of such Constable or Constables their Executors or Administrators to commence his or their Action or Actions against such Constable or Constables, his or their Security or Securities, or either of them, or their respective Heirs Executors or Administrators if the Sum in Demand amounts to upwards of five Pounds in any of the Courts of Common Pleas within this Colony, and if five Pounds or under before any of his Majesty's Justices of the Peace residing in the County for which the said Constable shall be chosen, who is hereby authorized and commanded in a summary way to hear try and determine the same and to give Judgment, and award Execution thereupon, in the usual Manner of proceeding for Trial of Causes of the Value of five Pounds and under, in which Action or Actions so to be commenced, if it shall appear that the said Constable hath been guilty of Neglect or Misconduct, the Plaintiff or Plaintiffs shall recover his or their Damages with Costs of Suit any Law Usage or Custom to the contrary notwithstanding. PROVIDED ALWAYS, That such Action or Actions be commenced within one Year from the Time that the Cause of such Action or Actions shall accrue.

AND WHEREAS many Inconveniencies might arise from the Difficulty of producing the original Bond or Obligation in Evidence in Actions to be Commenced, by virtue of this Act, for the preventing whereof, BE IT ENACTED by the Authority aforesaid, That in all Actions hereafter to be commenced by virtue of this Act against any Constable his Security or Securities, or either of them, or their respective Heirs Executors or Administrators a Copy of the said Bond certified under the Hand of the said Justice shall be good and effectual Evidence on the Trial of any such Action or Actions to all Intents and purposes as if the said original Bond was produced and proved.

AND BE IT ENACTED by the Authority aforesaid. That this Act shall be of force from the passing thereof, until the first Day of April which will be in the Year of our Lord one thousand seven hundred and seventy seven.

[CHAPTER 1607.]

[Chapter 1607, of Van Schaack, where the act is printed in full. See chapter 1501.]

An Act to prevent the firing of Guns and other Fire Arms within this Colony.

[Passed, March 8, 1773.]

WHEREAS great Damages are frequently done on the Eve of the last Day of December, and on the first and second Days of January by Persons going from House to House with Guns and other Fire Arms, and being often intoxicated with Liquor, have not only put the Inhabitants in great Terror, but committed many Mischiefs; for prevention whereof for the future.

BE IT ENACTED by his Excellency the Governor the Council and the General Assembly, and it is hereby enacted by the Authority of the same, That if any Person or Persons of any Age or Quality whatsoever shall fire or discharge any Gun Pistol Rocket, Cracker Squib or other Fire Work in any House Barn or other Building, or before any Door, or in any Garden, Street, Lane or other Inclosure on the said Eve or Days before mentioned; that then every such person or persons so offending and being thereof convicted before one or more Justice or Justices of the Peace in the County where such Offence shall be committed either by the Confession of the party or parties so offending, or the Oath of one or more Witnesses, which Oath said Justice or Justices of the Peace is or are hereby impowered and required to administer, shall for every such Offence forfeit the sum of twenty shillings with Costs of Suit: the said Forfeiture to be levied by Distress and Sale of the Offenders Goods and Chattels by Warrant under the Hand and seal of the said Justice or Justices of the Peace before whom such Conviction or Convictions shall be as aforesaid made, the which Forfeitures to be to the use of the Poor of the Town or place wherein such Offender shall be discovered: and if the said Offender or Offenders shall not pay the said Forfeiture or Forfeitures upon Conviction as aforesaid and for want of sufficient Distress whereon to levy the same, that then every such Justice or Justices of the Peace is and are hereby impowered and required by Warrant under his or their Hands and Seals to commit every such person or persons so as aforesaid offending, to the common Goal of the County where the said Forfeiture shall arise, there to remain without Bail or Mainprize for the Space of one

Month unless such Forfeiture or Forfeitures be sooner paid, but in Case such Offender or Offenders in the premises last abovementioned shall happen to be a Slave or Slaves, and the Forfeiture or Forfeitures aforesaid on conviction as aforesaid shall not be forthwith paid, that then it shall and may be lawful to and for said Justice or Justices before whom the Conviction shall be to cause such Slave or Slaves to be publickly whipped on the naked Back such Number of Stripes as he or they shall think proper, not exceeding thirty nine, which punishment shall be in lieu and instead of the said Forfeiture.

AND BE IT FURTHER ENACTED by the Authority aforesaid. That This Act be in force from the passing hereof until the first Day of February one thousand seven hundred and eighty.

[CHAPTER 1608.]

[Chapter 1608, of Van Schaack, where the act is printed in full.]

An Act to prevent aged and decrepit Slaves from becoming burthensome within this Colony.

[Passed, March 8, 1773.]

WHEREAS there have been repeated Instances in which the Owners of Slaves have obliged them after they are grown aged and decrepit, to go about begging for the common Necessaries of Life, whereby they have not only been reduced to the utmost Distress themselves, but have become Burthens on the Humanity and Charity of others; and sometimes also such Owners by Collusive Bargains, have pretended to transfer the property of such Slaves to persons not able to maintain them, from which the like evil Consequences have followed: For the Prevention whereof, and effectually to suppress such unjust and inhuman practices.

BE IT ENACTED by his Excellency the Governor the Council and the General Assembly, and it is hereby enacted by the Authority of the same, That from and after the passing of this Act if any Person or Persons within this Colony shall knowingly and willingly suffer and permit his, her, or their Slave or Slaves to go about begging of others, Victuals Cloathing or other Necessaries, such Person or Persons being thereof convicted before two Magistrates (who are hereby fully impowered and strictly enjoined to inquire into, hear, and determine the same) shall forfeit for every such Offence the sum of ten pounds, to be levied by Distress and Sale of the Offender's Goods by Warrant of the said Justices and to be applied, the one half to the Person giving Information thereof, and the other half to the Poor of the place where such Offence shall be committed.

AND BE IT FURTHER ENACTED by the Authority aforesaid, That if any Person or Persons shall by such collusive Conveyance or fraudulent Agreement as aforesaid pretend to sell or dispose of any such aged and decrepit Slave or Slaves to any Person or Persons who is or are unable to keep and maintain such Slave or Slaves, such Sale or Sales shall be absolutely void, and the person or persons making such pretended Sale shall incur the Penalty of twenty Pounds and shall moreover be deemed to be the Owner and Owners of such Slave or Slaves within the Intent and Meaning of the first section of this Act; which last mentioned Forfeiture shall be recovered levied and applied in the Manner herein before directed.

[CHAPTER 1609.]

[Chapter 1609, of Van Schaack, where the act is printed in full. See chapter 1484.]

An Act to amend an Act entitled, "An Act "to confirm certain Ancient Conveyances and "directing the Manner of proving Deeds to be "recorded."

[Passed, March 8, 1773.]

WHEREAS by the aforesaid Act passed in the eleventh Year of the Reign of his present Majesty it is among other Things enacted with respect to Conveyances of Estates in this Colony by Persons living abroad in other parts of the British Dominions that no such Conveyances executed after the publishing of the said Act shall be recorded here unless acknowledged and certified as in the said Act is directed and as the Mode of proof thereby required may in some Instances be inconvenient.

BE IT THEREFORE ENACTED by his Excellency the Governor the Council and the General Assembly, and it is hereby enacted by the Authority of the same, That all Conveyances of, and Letters of Attorney relating to, Real Estates in this Colony executed in Europe or any part of the British Dominions and proved by a subscribing Witness before one of his Majesty's Council or one of the Judges of the Supreme Court of this Colony, or acknowledged by the Grantor or proved by a subscribing Witness before one of the Judges of the Superior or

Supreme Court of any of his Majesty's Colonies in America and transmitted together with a Certificate under the Great Seal of such Colony, purporting that the person therein named to have taken such acknowledgment or Proof is a Judge of the Superior or Supreme Court of such Colony, or duly acknowledged by the Grantor or proved by one of the subscribing Witnesses before the Lord Mayor of the City of London, the Mayors of the Cities of Bristol or Liverpool, the Lord Provoost of the City of Edinburgh, the Lord Mayor of the City of Dublin, or the Mayors of the Cities of Londonderry and Cork in the Kingdom of Ireland, and certified and transmitted under the Seals of Office of such Mayors or Provoost respectively may be recorded here in any of the Public Offices and such Deed, or the Record thereof may be read in Evidence in any of the Courts of Law in this Colony and any such Conveyances and Letters of Attorney which have been proved and certified as above directed before the Publication of this Act or the Records thereof may in like Manner be given in Evidence. AND WHEREAS also there are many Real Estates in this Colony vested in Feme Coverts residing out of the said Colony, and it is very inconvenient and often imposible for them to acknowledge Conveyances of their said Estates in the Manner directed by the above recited Act, and it would be much more practicable and easy for them to grant such Estates were they enabled to do it by Conveyances to be executed in this Colony by their attorneys duly thereto appointed.

BE IT THEREFORE ENACTED by the Authority aforesaid, That all Deeds of Conveyance which have been executed since the passing the aforesaid Act, and which shall be hereafter executed by any Feme Covert living out of this Colony in conjunction with her Husband for the conveying of the real Estate of such Feme Covert lying and being in this Colony and duly acknowledged or hereafter to be acknowledged by such Feme Covert before any of the Persons authorized by the said former Act, or by this Act, to take proofs and acknowledgements of Conveyances of Real Estates in this Colony executed by Persons living out of the same shall be good and sufficient to pass the Estate of such Feme Covert purported to be therein conveyed by her, provided such Acknowledgment of such Feme Covert (to be written on such Conveyance and signed by the Judge or other Officer by whom such acknowledgment shall be taken,) shall specify or purport that such Feme Covert was examined by him separate from her Husband and that she confessed she executed such Conveyance as her Act and Deed freely without any Fear or Compulsion of her Husband, and provided also that the Execution of such Deed by the Husband of such Feme Covert be proved or acknowledged by him and certified in the Manner directed by the before recited Act, or by this Act, with respect to conveyances of Estates in this Colony by Persons living out of the same.

AND BE IT FURTHER ENACTED by the Authority aforesaid, That any Lands or Real Estates in this Colony vested as aforesaid in any Feme Covert living or residing out of the same which have been since the passing of the said Act or shall hereafter be conveyed in the Name of such Feme Covert, by any Attorney or Attornies of such Feme Covert to any Person or Persons whatsoever, in virtue of a Letter of Attorney from such Feme Covert and her Husband for that purpose, shall be good and sufficient in the Law to pass to and vest in the Grantee or Grantees respectively and their Heirs, the Lands and real Estate of such Feme Covert so conveyed or to be conveyed according to the purport and Intention of such Letter of Attorney and Conveyance provided that such Letter or Letters of Attorney is or shall be acknowledged by such Feme Coverts respectively in the Manner herein before directed, to be her free Act and Deed without any Fear or Compulsion from her Husband and such acknowledgment be written on the said Letters of Attorney respectively, and signed by such Judge or other Officer as aforesaid, and provided also that such Letter or Letters of Attorney, and the acknowledgment thereon to be Written, and also the Execution thereof by the Husband of such Feme Covert be acknowledged by him or proved and certified in the Manner directed by the before recited Act, or by this Act.

AND BE IT FURTHER ENACTED by the Authority aforesaid, That all such Deeds and Letters of Attorney executed or to be executed and acknowledged as aforesaid by Feme Coverts living out of this Colony and Proved and certified in the Manner directed by this Act, or in the Manner directed by the last Section of the before recited Act, may be recorded here in any of the Public Offices and such Deeds and Letters of Attorney, or the Records thereof may be read as Evidence in any of the Courts of Law in this Colony.

AND BE IT ENACTED by the Authority aforesaid That the Copies of any Last Will or Testament whatsoever heretofore made, or hereafter to be made, within any Part of the Kingdoms of Great Britain or Ireland by which any Lands, Tenements, Hereditaments or other Estate within this Colony, are devised or bequeathed, certified under the Seal of such Office where such Will or Testament is proved and lodged, may be given and Shall be received in Evidence before any of the Courts of Judicature within this Colony, and be esteemed as valid and sufficient as if the original Will or Testament was then and there produced and proved.

[CHAPTER 1610.]

[Chapter 1610, of Van Schaack, where the act is printed in full.]

An Act for the amendment of the Law, and the better advancement of Justice.

[Passed, March 8, 1773.]

BE IT ENACTED by his Excellency the Governor the Council and the General Assembly, and it is hereby enacted by the Authority of the same That from and after the passing hereof where any Demurrer shall be joined and entered in any Action or Suit in any Court of Record within this Colony, the Judges shall proceed and give Judgment according as the very Right of the Cause and Matter in Law shall appear unto them, without regarding any Imperfection Omission or Defect in any Writ, Return Plaint, Declaration or other Pleading, Process or Course of Proceeding whatsoever, except those only which the party demurring shall specially and particularly set down and express, together with his Demurrer as Causes of the same, notwithstanding that such Imperfection Omission or Defect might have heretofore been taken to be Matter of Substance; so as sufficient Matter appear in the said Pleadings upon which the Court may give Judgment according to the very Right of the Cause, and therefore from and after the passing hereof no Advantage or Exception shall be taken of or for an immaterial Traverse, or of or for the Default of entering Pledges upon any Bill or Declaration; or of or for the Default of alledging the bringing into Court any Bond, Bill, Indenture or other Deed whatsoever mentioned in the Declaration or other pleading; or of or for the Default of alledging of the bringing into Court Letters Testamentary or Letters of Administration; or of or for the Omission of, with force and Arms, and, against the Peace, or either of them, or of or for the want of Averment of, this he is ready to verify, or, this he is ready to verify by the Record, or of or for not alledging as appears by the Record;

but the Court shall give Judgment according to the very Right of the Cause, as aforesaid, without regarding any such Imperfections Omissions and Defects or any other Matter of like Nature, except the same shall be specially and particularly set down and shewn for Cause of Demurrer.

AND BE IT FURTHER ENACTED by the Authority aforesaid. That from and after the passing hereof all the Statutes of Jeofails, shall be extended to Judgments which shall at any Time afterwards be entered upon Confession, Nihil dicit, or non sum informatus in any Court of Record, and no such Judgment shall be reversed, nor any Judgment upon any Writ of Inquiry of Damages executed thereon be staid or reversed for or by reason of any Imperfection, Omission, Defect, Matter or Thing whatsoever which would have been aided and cured by any of the said Statutes of Jeofails in Case a Verdict of twelve Men had been given in the said Action or Suit, so as there be an original Writ or Bill, and Warrants of Attorney duly filed according to the Law as is now used.

PROVIDED ALWAYS AND BE IT ENACTED by the Authority aforesaid That the Attorney for the Plaintiff or Demandant in any Action or Suit, shall file his warrant of Attorney with the proper Officer of the Court where the Cause is depending the same Term he declares; and the Attorney for the Defendant, or Tenant shall file his Warrant of Attorney as aforesaid, the same Term he appears under the Penalties inflicted upon Attornies by any former Law, for Default of filing their Warrants of Attorney.

AND BE IT FURTHER ENACTED by the Authority aforesaid, That from and after the passing hereof, it shall and may be lawful for any Defendant or Tenant in any Action or suit, or for any Plaintiff in Replevin in any Court of Record with the Leave of the same Court to plead as many several Matters thereto, as he shall think necessary for his Defence.

PROVIDED NEVERTHELESS, That if any such Matter shall upon a Demurrer joined, be judged insufficient. Costs shall be given at the Discretion of the Court, or if a Verdict shall be found upon any Issue in the said Cause for the Plaintiff or Demandant, Costs shall be also given in like Manner, unless the Judge who tried the said Issue shall certify, that the said Defendant or Tenant, or Plaintiff in Replevin had a probable Cause to plead such Matter, which upon the said Issue shall be found against him.

PROVIDED ALWAYS AND BE IT ENACTED by the Authority aforesaid, That Nothing in this Act before contained shall extend to any Writ Declaration or Suit of Appeal of Felony or Murder, or to any Indictment or presentment of Treason, Felony or Murder or other Matter, or to any Process upon any of them, or to any Writ, Bill, Action or Information upon any Penal Statute or Act.

AND BE IT FURTHER ENACTED by the Authority aforesaid, That from and after the passing hereof in any Actions brought in any Courts of Record, where it shall appear to the Court in which such Actions are depending, that it will be proper and necessary, that the Jurors who are to try the Issues in any such Actions should have the view of the Messuages, Lands or Place in Question in order to their better understanding the Evidence that will be given upon the Trial of such Issues, in every such Case the respective Courts in which such Actions shall be depending, may order special Writs of Distringas or Habeas Corpora to issue, by which the Sheriff, or such other Officer to whom the said Writs shall be directed, shall be commanded to have six out of the first twelve of the Jurors named in such Writs, or some greater Number of them, at the place in Question, some convenient Time before the Trial, who then and there shall have the Matters in Question shewn to them by two persons in the said Writ named to be appointed by the Court; and the said Sheriff or other Officer, who is to execute the said Writs, shall by a special Return upon the same, certify that the view hath been had according to the Command of the said Writs.

AND BE IT FURTHER ENACTED by the Authority aforesaid, That from and after the passing hereof all Grants or Conveyances thereafter to be made by Fine or otherwise, of any Manors or Rents, or of the Reversion or Remainder of any Messuages or Lands shall be good and effectual to all Intents and purposes without any Attorenment of the Tenants of any such Manors, or of the Lands out of which such Rent shall be issuing, or of the particular Tenants upon whose particular Estates any such Reversions or Remainders shall and may be expectant or depending as if their Attorenment had been had and made.

PROVIDED NEVERTHELESS, That no such Tenant shall be prejudiced or damaged by payment of any Rent to any such Grantor or Conusor, or by breach of any Condition for non payment of Rent, before Notice shall be given to him of such Grant by the Conusee or Grantee.

AND BE IT FURTHER ENACTED by the Authority aforesaid That from and after the passing hereof no dilatory Plea shall be received in any Court of Record unless the party offering such plea do by Affidavit prove the Truth thereof, or shew some probable Matter to the Court to induce them to believe that the Fact of such Dilatory plea is true.

AND BE IT FURTHER ENACTED by the Authority aforesaid, That from and after the passing of this Act, where any Action of Debt shall be brought upon any single Bill, or where any Action of Debt or Scire Facias, shall be brought upon any Judgment if the Defendant has paid the Money due upon such Bill or Judgment such payment shall and may be pleaded in Barr of such Action or Suit, and where an Action of Debt is brought upon any Bond which hath a Condition or Defeazance to make void the same upon payment of a Lesser Sum at a Day or Place certain, if the Obligor his Heirs, Executors or Administrators have before the Action brought paid to the Obligee his Executors or Administrators, the principal and Interest due by the Defeazance or Condition of such Bond, though such payment was not made strictly according to the Condition or Defeazance, yet it shall and may nevertheless be pleaded in Barr of such Action, and shall be as effectual a Barr thereof, as if the Money had been paid at the Day and place according to the Condition or Defeazance, and had been so pleaded.

AND BE IT FURTHER ENACTED by the Authority aforesaid, That if at any Time, pending an Action upon any such Bond with a Penalty, the Defendant shall bring into the Court where the Action shall be depending all the principal Money, and Interest due on such Bond, and also all such Costs as have been expended in any Suit or Suits in Law or Equity upon such Bond, the said Money so brought in shall be deemed and taken to be in full Satisfaction and discharge of the said Bond, and the Court shall and may give Judgment to discharge every such Defendant of and from the same accordingly.

AND BE IT FURTHER ENACTED by the Authority aforesaid, That all Suits and Actions in the Court of Admiralty for Seamen's Wages which shall become due shall be commenced and sued within six Years next after the Cause of such Suit or Suits shall accrue and not after; PROVIDED NEVERTHELESS and be it further Enacted That if any Person or Persons who is or shall be entitled to any such Suit or Action for Seamen's Wages be or shall be at the Time of any such Cause of suit or Action accrued fallen or come, within the Age of twenty one Years, Feme Covert, non Composmentis, imprisoned or beyond the Seas, that then such Person or Persons shall be at liberty to bring the same Actions so as they take the same within six years next after their coming to or being of full age, discovert, of sane Memory, at large, and returned from beyond the Seas.

AND BE IT FURTHER ENACTED by the Authority aforesaid, That if any Person or Persons against whom there is or shall be any such Cause of suit or Action for Seamen's Wages, or against whom there shall be any Cause of Action of Trespass Detinue, Action sur Trover, or Replevin for taking away any Goods or Chattels, or of Action of Account, or upon the Case, or of Debt grounded upon any lending or Contract without specialty or Debt for Arrearages of Rent, or Assault, Menace, Battery, Wounding and imprisonment or any of them, be or shall be, at the Time of any such Cause of suit or Action given or accrued, fallen, or come, beyond the Seas, That then such Person or Persons who is or shall be entitled to any such Suit or Action, shall be at Liberty to bring the said Actions against such Person or Persons after their Return from beyond the seas, so as they take the same after their return from beyond the Seas within such Times as are respectively limited for the bringing of the said Actions before by this Act.

AND BE IT ENACTED by the Authority aforesaid, That if any Person or Persons shall be arrested from and after the passing hereof by any Writ, Bill or Process issuing out of any Court of Record, at the Suit of any common Person, and the Sheriff or other Officer taketh Bail from such Person against whom such Writ Bill or Process is taken out, the Sheriff or other Officer at the Request and Costs of the Plaintiff in such Action or suit, or his lawful Attorney, shall assign to the Plaintiff in such Action the Bail Bond, or other Security taken from such Bail by indorsing the same and attesting it under his Hand and Seal in the presence of two or more credible Witnesses; And if the said Bail Bond or Assignment or other Security taken for Bail be forfeited, the plaintiff in such Action after such Assignment made may bring an Action and Suit thereupon in his own Name, and the Court where the Action is brought may by Rule or Rules of the same Court give such Relief to the Plaintiff and Defendant in the original Action, and to the Bail upon the said Bond or other Security taken from such Bail as is agreeable to

Justice and Reason, and that such Rule or Rules of the said Court shall have the Nature and Effect of a Defeazance of such Bail Bond or other Security for Bail.

AND BE IT FURTHER ENACTED by the Authority aforesaid, That all Warranties which shall be made after the passing hereof by any Tenant for Life of any Lands Tenements or Hereditaments, the same descending or coming to any person in Reversion or Remainder, shall be void and of none Effect, and likewise all Collateral Warranties which shall be made after the passing of this Act, of any Lands, Tenements or Hereditaments by any Ancestor who has no Estate of Inheritance in possession in the same, shall be void against his Heir.

AND BE IT FURTHER ENACTED by the Authority aforesaid, That no Subpoena or any other process for Appearance do issue out of any Court of Equity till after the Bill is filed with the proper Officer in such Court, except in Cases of Bills for Injunctions to stay Wastes, or stay Suits at Law commenced.

AND for the better preventing Vexatious Suits in Courts of Equity, BE IT FURTHER ENACTED, That upon the Plaintiffs dismissing his own Bill, or the Defendants dismissing the same for want of prosecution, the Plaintiff in such Suit shall pay to the Defendant or Defendants his or their full Costs to be taxed by a Master, and that no Copy Abstract or Tenor of any Bill in Equity do go with the Dedimus or commission for taking the Defendants Answer.

AND BE IT FURTHER ENACTED by the Authority aforesaid That this Act and all the Statutes of Jeofails shall extend to all Suits in any Court of Record for recovery of any Debt immediately owing or any Revenue belonging to His Majesty his Heirs and Successors, and shall also extend to all Courts of Record within this Colony.

AND for preventing great Vexation from suing out defective Writs of Error, BE IT ENACTED by the Authority aforesaid, That upon the quashing any Writ of Error to be sued out after the passing hereof for Variance from the Original Record or other Defect, the Defendant in such Writ of Error shall recover against the Plaintiff or Plaintiffs issuing out such Writ, his Costs as he should have had if the Judgment had been affirmed, and to be recovered in the same Manner.

AND BE IT ENACTED by the Authority aforesaid, That from and after the passing hereof, Actions of Account shall and may be brought and maintained against the Executors and Administrators of every Guardian Bailiff and Receiver; and also by one Joint Tenant and Tenant in Common his Executors and Administrators against the other as Bailiff for receiving more than comes to his just Share or Proportion and against the Executor and Administrator of such Joint Tenant, or Tenant in common, and the Auditors appointed by the Court where such Action shall be depending shall be and are hereby impowered to administer an Oath, and examine the Parties touching the Matters in Question, and for their Pains and trouble in Auditing and taking such Account, have such Allowance as the Court shall adjudge to be reasonable, to be paid by the Party on whose side the Ballance of the Account shall appear to be.

[CHAPTER 1611.]

[Chapter 1611, of Van Schaack, where the act is printed in full.]

An Act for punishing Accessories to Felonies and Receivers of Stolen Goods.

[Passed, March 8, 1773.]

WHEREAS Thieves and Robbers are much encouraged to commit Felonies because a great Number of Persons make it their Trade and Business to deal in buying Stolen Goods. AND WHEREAS the Counsellors and contrivers of Theft and other Felonies, and Receivers of Goods that have been stolen, are the principal Cause of the Commission of such Felonies, and as no Accessory can be convicted 'or suffer Punishment, where the Principal is not attainted, or hath the Benefit of his Clergy; for Remedy whereof.

BE IT ENACTED by his Excellency the Governor the Council and the General Assembly, and it is hereby Enacted by the Authority of the same. That from and after the Publication of this Act, if any Person or Persons shall buy or receive any Goods or Chattels that shall be feloniously taken or stolen from any other Person, knowing the same to be stolen, he she or they shall be taken and deemed an Accessory or Accessories to such Felony after the Fact and shall incur the same Punishment as an Accessory or Accessories to the Felony, after the Felony committed.

AND BE IT ENACTED by the Authority aforesaid, That if any Principal Offender shall be convicted of any Felony, or shall stand mute or peremptorily challenge above the Number of twenty Persons returned to serve of the Jury, it shall and may be lawful to proceed against any Accessory either before or after the Fact, in the same manner as if such Principal Felon had been attainted thereof, notwithstanding any such Principal

Felon shall be admitted to the Benefit of his Clergy, Pardoned or otherwise delivered before Attainder, and every such Accessory shall suffer the same Punishment if he or she be convicted, or shall stand mute or peremptorily challenge above the Number of twenty Persons returned to serve of the Jury, as he or she should have suffered if the Principal had been attainted.

AND BE IT FURTHER ENACTED by the Authority aforesaid, That it shall and may be lawful to prosecute and punish every such Person and Persons buying or receiving any stolen Goods knowing the same to be stolen as for a Misdemeanor to be punished by Fine and Imprisonment, although the principal Felon be not before convicted of the said Felony, which shall exempt the Offender from being punished as Accessory, if the Principal shall be afterwards convicted.

[CHAPTER 1612.]

[Chapter 1612, of Van Schaack, where the act is printed in full.]

An Act for giving Relief on Promissory Notes.

[Passed, March 8, 1773.]

BE IT ENACTED by his Excellency the Governor the Council and the General Assembly, and it is hereby enacted by the Authority of the same, That all Notes in writing already made or hereafter to be made and signed by any Person or Persons, or by the Factor or Agent of any Merchant or Trader who is usually intrusted by him her or them to sign such promissory Notes for him her or them, whereby such person or persons, his her or their Factor or Agent as aforesaid doth or shall promise to pay to any other person or persons, Body Politick or Corporate, his her or their Order, or unto Bearer any sum of Money mentioned in such Note shall be taken and construed to be by virtue thereof due and payable to any such person or persons, Body Politick or Corporate to whom the same is made payable, and also every such Note payable to any person or persons, Body Politick or Corporate, his her or their Order shall be assignable or indorsable over to any other person or persons Body Politick or Corporate; and that the person or persons Body Politick or Corporate to whom such sum of Money is or shall be by such Note made payable, shall and may maintain an Action for and recover the Money made payable by such Note against the Person or Persons who, or whose Factor or Agent as aforesaid signed the same, and that any Person or persons, Body Politick or Corporate to whom such Note that is payable to any person or persons, Body Politick or Corporate, his her or their Order is or shall be indorsed or assigned or the Money therein mentioned ordered to be paid by Indorsement thereon shall and may maintain his her or their Action for such sum of Money either against the person or persons, who or whose Factor or Agent as aforesaid signed such Note or against any of the Persons who indorsed the same, and in every such Action the Plaintiff or Plaintiffs shall recover his her or their Damages and Costs of suit, and if such Plaintiff or Plaintiffs shall be nonsuited or a Verdict be given against him her or them, the Defendant or Defendants shall recover his her or their Costs against the Plaintiff or Plaintiffs, and every such plaintiff or plaintiffs, Defendant or Defendants respectively recovering may sue out Execution for such Damages and Costs by Capias or Fieri Facias, as is usual in other Cases.

AND BE IT FURTHER ENACTED by the Authority aforesaid That all and every such Action upon any such Note already made shall be commenced sued and brought within six years next after the End of this present Session and not after, and that all and every such Action upon any such Note hereafter to be made shall be commenced sued and brought within six Years next after the Cause of such Action and not after.

PROVIDED NEVERTHELESS, and it is hereby enacted by the Authority aforesaid. That if any person that is or shall be entitled to any such Action, be or shall be at the Time of such Action accrued within the Age of one and twenty Years, Feme Covert, non Compos mentis, imprisoned or beyond the Seas, that then such person or persons shall be at liberty to bring the same Actions, so as they take the same within such Time as is before limited after their coming to, or being of full Age, discovered of sane Memory, at large and returned from beyond the seas, as other persons having no such Impediment should have done.

[CHAPTER 1613.]

[Chapter 1613, of Van Schaack, where the act is printed in full. Revived by chapter 1705.]

An Act to prevent Frauds in the Sale of Bread.

[Passed, March 8, 1773.]

WHEREAS great Complaints are made of Frauds committed in the City of New York by the Sale of Bread made of unmerchantable Flour, tho' the Assize of Bread be regulated by the Price of Flour of the Quality of such as ought to pass the Inspection as good and Merchantable.

BE IT THEREFORE ENACTED by the Governor the Council and the General Assembly, and it is hereby enacted by the Authority of the same, that from and after the tenth Day of April next, no Baker in the said City shall directly or indirectly sell any Loaf of Bread at the Price and Weight at which white Bread of the best or finest Flour is or may be assized by the Corporation of the said City, unless the same be wholly made of Flour that has duely pass'd the Inspection as good and merchantable Flour agreeable to the Laws for that Purpose made and now in Force, to prevent the Exportation of unmerchantable Flour under the Penalty of Four Shillings for every Offence to be recovered by him who will sue for the same before any Justice of the Peace in a summary Way with Costs of Suit. And whenever the Proof shall upon a View of the Bread or otherwise appear to the Magistrate, before whom any Suit may be brought against any Baker for the Penalty aforesaid to be not direct and full, but only of a probable and presumptive Nature, the same shall nevertheless be deemed and adjudged to be sufficient and conclusive unless the Defendant shall acquit himself by clear and satisfactory Proof that the same Bread was wholly made of Flour that had been inspected and branded in due Form of Law. This Act to be in Force until the first Day of January which will be in the year one Thousand seven hundred & seventy five.

[CHAPTER 1614.]

[Chapter 1614, of Van Schaack, where the act is printed in full. See chapter 138.]

An Act to regulate the Sale of Bricks within the City and County of New-York.

[Passed, March 8, 1773.]

WHEREAS the Regulations respecting the Quality and Sale of Bricks in this Colony, prescribed by a certain Act of the Governor, the Council, and General Assembly, entitled, [An Act to ascertain the Size of Casks, Weights and Measures, and Bricks within this Colony] have not prevented the Mischiefs intended to be remedied thereby,

I. BE IT ENACTED by his Excellency the Governor, the Council, and the General Assembly, and it is hereby Enacted by Authority of the same, That from and after the first Day of November next ensuing, no Bricks shall be deemed merchantable and exposed to Sale, or imported within the City and County of New-York, but such as shall be skilfully made and burnt, consist of proper Materials, and measure nine Inches in length, four Inches and one Quarter of an Inch in breadth, and two Inches and one Half of an Inch in thickness.

II. AND BE IT FURTHER ENACTED by the Authority aforesaid, That all Bricks, which shall be exposed to Sale in the said City and County after the said first Day of November, that shall not answer the aforesaid Description of merchantable Bricks, shall be forfeited to the Use of the Society of the Hospital in the City of New-York in America; and the Mayor, Recorder, and Aldermen of the said City of New-York, and each and every of them, are hereby authorized and required in a summary Way to hear and determine all Complaints, relative to the Size and Quality of Bricks exposed to Sale as aforesaid, within the said City and County; and shall cause all such as shall not be of the Size and Quality as herein before directed, to be seized and taken to the Use of the Hospital as aforesaid. Provided nevertheless, That nothing in this Act contained shall extend to such Bricks as any Person or Persons in the said City and County may make for their own Use, or to Bricks commonly called soft Bricks, provided their Dimensions be agreeable to the aforesaid Directions, nor to Well Bricks, or to any Bricks imported from Europe.

III. AND BE IT ENACTED by the Authority aforesaid, That this Act shall continue in Force unto the End of the first sessions of the General Assembly of this Colony which will be after the first Day of November in the Year of our Lord One thousand Seven hundred and Seventy-Seven, and no longer.

[CHAPTER 1615.]

[Chapter 1615, of Van Schaack, where the act is printed in full.]

An Act to prevent the Sale of Goods at Night by Vendue Auction or Outcry in the City of New York.

[Passed, March 8, 1773.]

WHEREAS a Practice of selling Goods by Auction at Night, when their Qualities cannot be accurately distinguished, has obtained in the City of New York, whereby the unwary have been frequently imposed upon, and great Frauds committed, for prevention whereof.

BE IT ENACTED by his Excellency the Governor the Council and the General Assembly, and it is hereby enacted by the Authority of the same, That from and after the passing of this Act if any Person or Persons shall be convicted of selling or putting up for Sale within the said City, any Goods Wares or Merchandizes or any other Article or Thing whatsoever by way of Vendue Auction or Outcry at any Time after Sunset, such Person or Persons so offending contrary to the true Intent and meaning of this Act shall forfeit and pay for every such Offence the Sum of five Pounds to be recovered by Action of Debt before any one of his Majesty's Justices of the Peace in the said City and County, who is hereby required to hear and determine the same in a summary way: one half of which Forfeiture shall be to the use of the person suing for the same, and the other half to be applied for the Benefit of the Poor of the said City or County.

[CHAPTER 1616.]

[Chapter 1616, of Van Schaack, where the act is printed in full. Amended by chapter 1683. The acts hereby repealed are chapters 805, so far as it relates to Orange county, 1118, 1455 and 1502.]

[Passed, March 8, 1773.]

WHEREAS the keeping in good repair public Roads and Highways contributes greatly to the Ease and Advantage of the Inhabitants of a Country.

BE IT THEREFORE ENACTED by his Excellency the Governor the Council and the General Assembly and it is hereby enacted by the Authority of the same, That from and after the passing of this Act, the Freeholders and Inhabitants of the Precincts within the County of Orange shall be and are hereby authorized at their annual Town Meetings for electing Town Officers to choose and elect at the same Time three Freeholders in each Precinct for Commissioners to lay out and regulate Highways in the Precinct for which they shall be so chosen, and also as many Overseers of the Highways in each precinct as there shall be Districts in the said precinct, who are to oversee repair and keep in order the several Highways within the respective Districts for which they shall be elected and chosen as aforesaid, and the Persons so to be chosen Commissioners as well as those who are to be Overseers, are hereby required to take those several Offices respectively upon them.

AND BE IT FURTHER ENACTED by the Authority aforesaid, That the Commissioners or the major Part of them in the respective Precincts for which they shall be chosen Commissioners, are hereby impowered and authorized to regulate the Roads already laid out, and if any of them shall appear inconvenient and an Alteration absolutely necessary, and the same be certified upon Oath by twelve principal Freeholders of the said County, the Commissioners may provided they all judge it absolutely necessary, alter the same, and also to lay out such other public Highways and Roads as they or the major Part of them shall think most convenient as well for Travellers as for the Inhabitants of each Precinct and the next adjacent Towns, Villages and Neighbourhoods. PROVIDED that Nothing in this Act contained shall extend or be construed to impower the Commissioners aforesaid to alter any Roads that are already commodious, neither shall they lay out any Roads through any Person's Land without the Consent of the Owner or Owners thereof, or agreeing with and paying to him or them the value of the Land so to be laid out into an Highway or Road, with such Damages as he or they may sustain by said Road; Provided the whole Sum to be paid to any one person shall not exceed five Pounds, and in Case they cannot agree or the Sum demanded should exceed five Pounds then the true value shall be set and appraised by two Justices of the Peace and by the Oaths of twelve principal Freeholders not having any Interest in the Land concerning which such Dispute may arise; which Freeholders may be summoned by the High Sheriff, his Deputy or any Constable of the County of Orange, by virtue of a Warrant to be issued by the said two Justices for that purpose, and if any Road within the said County so laid out be a common public Highway and the same be laid out at the Request of twelve Principal Freeholders of the County, then the whole Charge of purchasing the said Road, together with the Charge of the Commissioners and calling and charge of the Jury, and the whole proceedings thereon had shall be paid as the other contingent Charges of the County are paid, and the Highway so laid out shall be a common Public Highway. Provided always that no Road or Highway shall be laid through any Garden without the Consent of the Owner or Owners thereof.

AND BE IT FURTHER ENACTED, That the Commissioners to be chosen by virtue of this Act shall before they execute any of the Powers therein contained take an Oath upon the Holy Evangelists in the Words following, to wit, "I. A B. do Solemnly "swear that I will faithfully and impartially execute the powers "to me given and granted by an Act entitled An Act for the "better laying out regulating and keeping in repair common "public and private Highways in the County of Orange, accord-"ing to the best of my Skill and understanding so help me "God."

AND BE IT FURTHER ENACTED by the Authority aforesaid, That if any person or persons within the said County do or hereafter shall alter, stop up, or encroach on any Highway or Road that has been heretofore laid out by former Commissioners or shall be hereafter laid out by the Commissioners to be elected and chosen by virtue of this Act such person so offending contrary to the meaning of this Act shall for every such Offence forfeit the Sum of forty Shillings to be recovered before any one Justice of the Peace by Warrant directed to the Constable of the precinct where such Offence shall be committed, by distraining the Goods and Chattels of the Offender, and the said Constable after public Notice is given by him of the selling the said Distress, shall make sale thereof, and out of the produce pay the said Forfeiture and Charges, and return the Overplus if any there be to the Owner or Owners thereof which said Forfeiture shall be applied by the Commissioners for and towards repairing the Public Roads or Highways within the Precinct where the same may arise.

AND BE IT ENACTED by the Authority aforesaid, That the width of all the Roads in the said precincts hereafter to be laid out shall be left to the discretion of the Commissioners for the Time being of the Precinct in which such Road may be laid out, so that they do not exceed the Breadth of four Rods, and not less than two Rods.

AND BE IT FURTHER ENACTED by the Authority aforesaid, That the Roads and Highways within the said County shall be cleared repaired and maintained by the Freeholders and Inhabitants hereafter made liable to work on the same, and that as often as they or any of them shall have Notice from the Overseer for the Time being of the District to which they belong, not exceeding the Number of Days hereafter mentioned. And to prevent all Manner of Disputes that may arise respecting the persons who are obliged by this Act to work upon the Highways.

BE IT FURTHER ENACTED by the Authority aforesaid, That every Male Freeholder and Inhabitant, (and no other Person) between the Age of twenty one Years and sixty Years shall either in person, or by an able sufficient Man in his Room be obliged to work upon the Highways.

BE IT FURTHER ENACTED by the Authority aforesaid, That every Person who may be liable by this Act to work on Highways shall Work faithfully eight Hours at the least in every Day, and in order that the good Effects intended by this Act may not under any pretence be eluded.

BE IT FURTHER ENACTED by the Authority aforesaid, That every Overseer in each Precinct shall keep a List of the Persons within his District who by this Act are obliged to work upon the Highways, and shall keep an exact Account of the Time that every such Person shall have worked, and for every Hour which any Person shall neglect to work he shall forfeit and pay the Sum of six pence to the Overseer of the District to which he doth belong, and in Case the same is not paid within eight Days after such Default, it shall be recovered and applied in the manner hereafter mentioned.

AND BE IT FURTHER ENACTED by the Authority aforesaid. That every Freeholder and Inhabitant who by this Act shall be obliged to work on Highways shall work at least four Days within their Districts, between the first Day of April, and the first Day of July, and one Day between the first Day of April and the first Day of December, in every Year, and the Overseers are to give Notice to the Freeholders and Inhabitants of their respective Districts accordingly under the Penalty hereafter mentioned.

AND BE IT FURTHER ENACTED by the Authority aforesaid. That every Overseer in each Precinct shall on or before the first Monday of December in every Year deliver under Oath to one or more of the Commissioners of the Precinct to which he doth belong an Account of the Labour done on the Highways within his District and shall take an Oath before the said Commissioner who is hereby impowered to administer the same in the Words following, to wit. "I. A. B. do declare upon the Holy "Evangelists that this Account now delivered by me contains "the Names of all the persons within my District which by Law "are obliged to work on Highways, that each Person therein "named has worked agreeable to Law, five Days since the first

"Day of April last to the Amount of eight Hours in each Day, "or I have laid out or disposed of agreeable to Law the Fines "of such persons as have not worked, and the Monies by me "received for excusing person from working and that within "twenty five Days after the Time in which such person as I "have fined ought to have worked, according to the best of my "knowledge and belief, so help me God," and if any Overseer shall neglect or refuse to deliver an Account or take the Oath hereby required he shall forfeit the Sum hereafter mentioned.

PROVIDED NEVERTHELESS, That if any Freeholder or Inhabitant who by this Act is obliged to work on Highways shall move into any Overseers District or any person shall remove out after the said Overseer has worked part of his Time, the said Overseer shall make such exception in his Account and Oath according to the Number of Days every such person did work.

AND BE IT FURTHER ENACTED by the Authority aforesaid, That the Bridges and Causeways herein after mentioned in the Precincts of Goshen and Cornwall are to be made and kept in repair by a Public Tax, and are as follow, to wit, one Bridge and Causeway near the House of Zachariah DuBois; one other Bridge and Causeway near Richard Goldsmiths; one other Bridge and Causeway near Stephen Gilbert's; one other Bridge and Causeway near Colonel Benjamin Tusteen's; one other Bridge and Causeway across Pochuck Creek, where the old Bridge now stands; one other Bridge and Causeway near Warwick Meeting House; one other Bridge and Causeway near Grey Court; one other Bridge and Causeway near Curtis Coleman's; one other Bridge and Causeway over Murderer's Creek near Cornwall; one other Bridge and Causeway upon Schunemunck Creek near Smith's Mill; and one other Bridge on said Creek called Coal House Bridge; one other Bridge and Causeway near the Widow Tutle's; one other Bridge and Causeway near John Carpenter's Mill; one other Bridge and Causeway near the House of Daniel Denton; one other Bridge and Causeway near the House of Jeremiah Curtice; one other Bridge and Causeway over Murderer's Creek near the House of John McClean; one other Bridge and Causeway over the Walkill at the Outlet of the drowned Lands; one other Bridge and Causeway across Warwick Creek near where Israel Wood's Mill formerly stood; and one other Bridge and Causeway where the New Road will cross the Trout Brook, South of Alexander Gilchrist's on Sterling Road: And the Commissioners for the Time being, for each of the said Precincts of Goshen and Cornwall are directed and required to have the aforementioned Bridges and Causeways well and sufficiently made and kept in Repair and the Account of the Expences for doing the same shall be transmitted to the Supervisors of the said County of Orange at their annual Meeting, who are hereby directed and required to divide the whole Amount of the said Expence between the two last mentioned precincts, in the same Proportion as the County Charges for the Time being shall be divided between the said two Precincts, and the said Expence shall be raised with the County Tax, and in the same Manner and shall be paid by the County Treasurer to the respective Commissioners upon a Warrant or Warrants from the Supervisors as in other Cases: And inasmuch as it may frequently happen that the Commissioners or some of them will to obliged to advance Money towards making and repairing of Bridges and Causeways, the Supervisors are hereby required in the making up the Amount of the Expence to allow lawful Interest for any Money that may be advanced from the Time of the advancing it to the Time the same is to be repaid by the County Treasurer.

AND WHEREAS a Road was formerly laid out from the House of Captain Nathaniel Roe Junior, in the Precinct of Goshen through the Valley towards Sterling and another from Doctor John Bard's Mill in the said Precinct to the first mentioned Road near the House of Jacob Mace, and it is difficult to ascertain where the said Roads were laid out.

BE IT ENACTED by the Authority aforesaid that the Commissioners of the Precinct of Goshen shall take a view of the said Roads, and shall lay out and alter the same Roads in such Manner as they or any two of them shall think proper which Alterations being entered as usual in the Town Clerks Book of the said Precinct shall be good and effectual, any Law Usage or Custom to the contrary notwithstanding.

AND BE IT FURTHER ENACTED by the Authority aforesaid That the Commissioners of the Precinct of Goshen for the Time being who shall divide the said Sterling Roads into Districts shall by the first Day of June next, and once in every Year during the Continuance of this Act, appoint a Man who lives on said Roads to have the Care and Direction to shew every Overseer where he shall Work on said Roads and to work with him, and for every Days Work he shall be paid the Sum of four Shillings, which Charges as well as the Charges the Commissioners shall be put to by laying out the aforesaid Roads and dividing them into Districts shall be raised on the respective Precincts of Goshen and Cornwall as the other Charges of the said precincts are raised.

BE IT FURTHER ENACTED by the Authority aforesaid, That every Person who by this Act is obliged to work on Highways and does dwell in that part of the Precinct of Cornwall within the following Bounds, to wit, Beginning on the West Side of the Murderer's Creek where the reputed Line of Jurisdiction between the Counties of Ulster and Orange crosses the same, from thence South Westerly along the West Side of the said Creek until it comes opposite to the North End of Schunemunk Hill or Mountain, then along the West Side of the said Hill or Mountain to the Southerly End of it, so as to include all the Inhabitants on the West Side of said Hill, and from thence to and including the House in which John Smith now lives, and from thence to the Division Line of Cornwall and Goshen Precincts and from thence along the last mentioned Line Until it intersects the said reputed Line of Jurisdiction between the said Counties of Ulster and Orange, and from thence along the said last mentioned Line to the place of beginning: and also every Person who by this Act is obliged to work on Highways and doth dwell in the said Precinct of Goshen to the Eastward of the Walkill and to the North of the following Lines, to wit, Beginning at the Black Walnut Island, from thence to and including the House of Captain John Wisner, from thence to and including the House of Francis Armstrong, from thence to and including the House of John Sayre, from thence to and including the House of Timothy Clark Junior, from thence to the House where David Benjamin now lives, then beginning on the last mentioned Bounds on the West Side of those Companies that live on the Warwick Water side Road, and running Northerly along the West Bounds of the said Companies until it intersects the Division Line of Goshen and Cornwall precincts, thence along the last mentioned Line, the reputed Line of Jurisdiction between the said Counties of Ulster and Orange and along the East Side of the said Walkill to the place of beginning, shall during the continuance of this Act work one Day in a Year between the first Day of April and the first Day of July on the Water side Roads in the precinct of Cornwall, from the said Division Line of the said Precincts near Barnabas Horten Junior down to New Windsor, and the Road from the said

Division Line of the said Precincts near John Manney's, and so along by Stephen Gilbert's down to New Windsor and that Captain John Wisner Captain Elihu Mervin, Mr. Zachariah Dubois and John Gale Esquire, are hereby directed and required by the first Day of May next, and that once in every Year to view the said Roads, and that they or any three of them shall give Directions to every Overseer in the said Precincts of Goshen and Cornwall who are obliged to work on the said Roads, what place they shall work upon, and in Case any Overseer shall refuse or neglect to work according to such Directions, he shall forfeit the Sum hereafter particularly mentioned.

AND BE IT FURTHER ENACTED by the Authority aforesaid That every Person who by this Act is obliged to work on Highways and does dwell in that Part of the Precincts of Goshen and Cornwall within the following Bounds to wit, Beginning at the Black Walnut Island, from thence running along the aforementioned Lines, by Captain John Wisner's, Francis Armstrong's, John Sayre's, Timothy Clark Junior's and along the said Line to the Companies that work on the Warwick Water Side Road, then along the West Side of those Companies that work on the said Warwick Water side Road Northerly until it intersects the Division Line of Goshen and Cornwall Precincts, then Southerly along the said Line until it comes to Goose Pond Mountain, then along the East Side of those Companies that work on Sterling Road until it comes to the Jersey Line, then running Westerly along the Jersey Line to the Walkill, then Northerly along the Walkill to the place of beginning (except such of the Inhabitants as live in Warwick Mountains to the Southward of William Blain's) shall during the continuance of this Act work one Day in a Year between the first Day of April and the first Day of July on the Sterling Road from Captain Nathaniel Roe Junior's and along the Valley towards Sterling until it meets with the Jersey Line and the Road from Doctor John Bard's Mill across the Mountains until it meets with the aforementioned Road, and that the Commissioners of the Precinct of Goshen for the Time being are hereby directed and required by the first Day of June next, and shall once in every Year view the said Roads and divide them into Districts, and that they or any two of them shall give Directions to every Overseer within the said Bounds, who are obliged to work n the said Roads, what place they shall Work upon, and in Case any Overseer shall refuse or neglect to Work according to such Directions he shall forfeit the Sum hereafter mentioned.

AND BE IT FURTHER ENACTED, That Captain John Wisner, Captain Elihu Mervin, Zachariah Dubois, and John Gale Esquire, or the major Part of them shall order any three of the Overseers of the Districts that are obliged to work on the said Waterside Roads to work with the Men of their respective Districts on the new Road which turns out of the Goshen Road opposite to Carpenter's Mills and runs by Sharrick Van deursen's to the Landing at new Cornwall, which Days Work shall be in lieu of the one Day which they are obliged to work on the said Water side Roads, any Thing in this Act contained to the contrary notwithstanding.

AND WHEREAS many Persons choose rather to pay Money, than be obliged to Work on the said Roads. BE IT THEREFORE ENACTED by the Authority aforesaid, That each person who by this Act is obliged to work one Day in a Year on the said Waterside Roads and the new Road in the Precinct of Cornwall, and on the said Sterling Roads from Nathaniel Roe Jun'r to the Jersey Line, and from Warwick to the aforesaid Road shall be excused from working on the same provided he will (before, or on the Day appointed for him to work,) pay the Sum of three Shillings to the Overseer of the District to which he doth belong.

AND BE IT FURTHER ENACTED. That every Overseer shall pay all the Money which he shall or may receive for excusing persons from working on the said Waterside Roads, and for Fines for their not working thereon, into the Hands of John Gale Esquire John Brewster and Zachariah Du Bois, who are hereby directed to lay out the same in repairing the said Waterside Roads, in such Manner as they or any two of them shall think proper, and to render an Account thereof on Oath to the Justices at the annual Town Meetings of the Precincts of Goshen and Cornwall, that every Overseer shall pay all the Money which he shall or may receive for excusing persons from working on the said Sterling Roads or for Fines for their not Working thereon into the Hands of the Commissioners of the Precinct of Goshen for the Time being, who are hereby directed to lay out the same in repairing the said Sterling Roads in such Manner as they or any two of them shall think proper, and to render an Account thereof on Oath to the Justices at the annual Town Meeting of the Precinct of Goshen.

AND BE IT FURTHER ENACTED by the Authority aforesaid, That the Freeholders and Inhabitants of the respective precincts in said County of Orange at their next annual Town Meeting shall choose one Overseer of the Highways for each District in the said Precincts respectively; and in Case of the Death Absence or Refusal of any Overseer another shall be appointed in his stead by the next Commissioner to the District where such Death, Absence or Refusal may happen, and the Overseer so appointed shall be under the same Circumstances in every respect, as if he had been chosen by the Freeholders and Inhabitants at an annual Town Meeting.

AND BE IT FURTHER ENACTED by the same Authority, That the Commissioners for the Time being if needful may at any Time after the passing of this Act and that once in every Year, if they shall judge the same Necessary, divide their respective precincts into as many Districts as they or the major Part of them shall think most convenient and necessary by Writing under their Hands to be lodged with the Town or Precinct Clerk and the Freeholders and Inhabitants at their next annual Town Meeting after such Division shall choose as many Overseers as there shall then be Districts.

AND BE IT FURTHER ENACTED by the Authority aforesaid, That all Forfeitures which shall arise by any Persons not working on the Roads or Highways agreeable to the Directions of this Act shall be recovered (with five Shillings Costs,) by a Warrant under the Hand and Seal of the Overseer of the District where such Forfeiture shall arise to be directed to any Constable within the said Precinct, who is to seize and sell (as is usual in other Cases,) the Offender's Goods and Chattels, and after paying the Forfeiture to the said Overseer with two Shillings for issuing the Warrant, the Constable shall retain three Shillings for his Services, and all Forfeitures which shall be paid to the said Overseer in the Manner aforesaid, and also every Sum of Money which he may receive from any Person for not working on the Public Roads or Highways shall be by him well and faithfully laid out within his District or disposed of according to Law.

AND BE IT FURTHER ENACTED by the Authority aforesaid, That every Overseer within the said County, who shall not give notice to the Persons within his District who are obliged to work on Highways and work four Days between the first Day of April and the first Day of July, and one other Day between the first Day of April and the first Day of December in every Year, shall forfeit the Sum of five Pounds; and in Case any Overseer shall refuse or neglect to deliver an Account on or before the first Monday in December in every Year as herein before directed he shall forfeit the Sum of five Pounds and in Case any Overseer who by this Act is obliged to work one Day in a Year on the Water Side Roads in the precinct of Cornwall, that shall refuse or neglect to work agreeable to the Direction he shall receive from the aforesaid Captain John Wisner, Captain Elihu Mervin, Mr. Zachariah Dubois and John Gale Esquire or any three of them, shall forfeit the Sum of five Pounds, and in Case any Overseer who by this Act is obliged to work one Day in a year on the aforesaid Sterling Roads shall refuse or neglect to work agreeable to the Directions he shall receive from the Commissioners of the Precinct of Goshen for the Time being or any two of them shall forfeit the Sum of five Pounds, all which Forfeitures shall be recovered with usual Charges in the recovery thereof, and the Commissioners for the Time being or any two of them of the Precinct where such Forfeiture shall arise, are hereby ordered directed and required to issue their Warrant to any Constable for the recovery of the said Penalties, who is ordered to take and sell the Offender's Goods and Chattels as is usual in other Cases, and the Commissioners shall lay out the said Fines in repairing the Roads within the Districts where such Overseer ought to have worked.

AND BE IT FURTHER ENACTED by the Authority aforesaid. That all Trees that stand in any Highway which has or shall be laid out through any Person's Land shall belong to the Owner or Owners thereof but the said Owner shall not hinder the Public from making use of so much Timber which is standing or lying on the Road as will make and repair the same.

AND BE IT FURTHER ENACTED by the Authority aforesaid, That if any Overseer shall think fit and have occasion of any Teams, Carts, Waggons, Ploughs or Sleds and a Man to manage the same; such Team, Cart, Waggon Plough or Sled with a person to manage the same, if with four Creatures shall be esteemed for and in lieu of three Days work of a single Man, and if with two Creatures for and in lieu of two Days work of a single Man, and the Fine to be proportionable, that is if with four Creatures treble and if with two, twice as much as the Fine of a single person; and every Workman shall be obliged to bring such Utensils as he is directed to bring, by the Overseer of his District.

AND BE IT FURTHER ENACTED by the Authority aforesaid, That the Commissioners of each Precinct for which they shall be chosen and elected shall from Time to Time enter in Writing all the Highways or Roads laid out or altered, and sign the same by putting their Names thereto and cause the same to be entered into their Town Book and whatsoever the Commissioners shall do according to the Powers given them in this Act being so entered into their Town Book shall be valid and good to all Intents and purposes whatsoever.

AND BE IT FURTHER ENACTED by the Authority aforesaid, That no greater Fees or Charges shall be allowed or taken for altering or laying out any Highways and for Services done by virtue of this Act, than the following, to wit, To each Commissioner and Justice six Shillings per Day, to the Justices for issuing their Warrant to summons a Jury three Shillings; to the Sheriff his Deputy or a Constable for summoning a Jury six Shillings, for his Attendance on a Jury each Day four Shillings, to each Jury Man four Shillings per Day; to Captain John Wisner, Captain Elihu Mervin, Mr. Zachariah Dubois, and John Gale Esquire four Shillings per Day as a Reward for their Care and Trouble in doing the Business required of them by this Act: which Fees or Charges shall be raised upon the respective Precincts where they shall so arise, as other contingent Charges of the said Precincts in the said County are raised.

AND BE IT FURTHER ENACTED by the same Authority, That any one of his Majesty's Justices of the Peace for the Time being in the County of Orange, or any one Commissioner for the Time being may order any Overseer to Work upon any Road or Highway within his District that he shall think necessary, the Number of Days he is obliged to work by this Act, and such Overseer shall within eight Days thereafter warn and set to work the persons within his District who are obliged to work on Highways, upon that part of the Road or Highway which he shall be so ordered to amend and if any Overseer shall neglect or refuse to warn and set to work the persons aforesaid of his District to amend such Road or Highway as he shall be so ordered to amend, he shall for every such Neglect or Refusal pay a Fine of forty Shillings with usual Costs of Suit, to be adjudged by and recovered before any one of his Majesty's Justices of the Peace for the County of Orange upon the Oath of any one credible Witness, or on the View of such Justice or Commissioner or Confession of the party in the common or usual Method, which Fines shall be delivered to one of the Commissioners, and applied towards repairing the said Highways in such place where such Fine may arise.

AND WHEREAS it may be absolutely necessary to lay out private Roads within the said County, BE IT THEREFORE ENACTED by the Authority aforesaid That upon Application to the Commissioners of either Precinct for a private Road the Commissioners for the Precinct where such Road is desired to be laid, shall view the same, and if they are of Opinion such Road is absolutely necessary, and twelve principal Freeholders under Oath shall be of the same opinion, the said Commissioners are hereby impowered to lay out such Road, observing the same Steps in ascertaining what shall be paid for the Land as are before directed to be taken in laying out Public Roads, and all the Expences and Charges attending the said Road shall be paid by the Person or Persons applying for the same, and the said Road when laid shall be for the only use of the Person or Persons who shall pay for the same, his and their Heirs and Assigns, but for no other use and purpose than that of a Road: PROVIDED ALWAYS That the Owner or Owners of the Land through which such private Road may be laid shall not be prevented from making use of such Road, if he shall signify his Intention of making use of the same at the Time when the Jury are to ascertain the Value of the Land and the Damages by means of laying out such Road.

AND inasmuch as it is thought practicable at a small Expence to open a Road through the Mountains from the Neighbourhood of Haverstraw on the south side of the Highlands to the Murderer's Creek or Schunemuck Clove which if effected will not only contribute greatly to the Ease and Advantage of the Inhabitants of the said County by affording a more short and easy Communication between those parts thereof which lie on the different Sides of the said Mountains; but to Travellers passing from the Southern to the Northern Parts of the Colony, as the Post Road from the City of New York to Albany on the West Side of Hudson's River would be shortened thereby many Miles.

BE IT THEREFORE ENACTED by the same Authority, That John DeNoyelles, David Pye, Ann Hawkes Hay, John Griffiths and Jesse Woodhull Esquires, or the Majority of them, shall be and hereby are appointed Commissioners for the Special purposes of viewing, laying out opening and improving a Public

Road or Highway through the Highlands from Haverstraw aforesaid to the Schunemuck Clove Road, and so to the North Bounds of the County of Orange near the Murderers Creek, in such Manner, and upon such Course or Courses as they shall think most expedient and beneficial, and to make a Return thereof and have the same entered of Record, and they shall have all the powers and Authorities for the purposes aforesaid which are given to the Commissioners of Highways to be elected by virtue of this Act, any Thing herein contained to the contrary notwithstanding: and the said Road so to be laid out by the said Commissioners shall be a public Road or Highway to all Intents and purposes as if the same had been laid out by the Commissioners to be chosen by virtue of this Act, and as such shall be worked upon and improved.

AND BE IT FURTHER ENACTED by the same Authority, That the said John DeNoyelles, David Pye, Ann Hawkes Hay, John Griffiths and Jesse Woodhull, and the major Part of them shall, and are hereby impowered and authorized to, receive all such sum and Sums of Money as may be collected or given as voluntary Donations by any Person or Persons whomsoever for the opening working and improving the said Road and erecting and building Bridges thereon, and the same to lay out and expend for the purposes aforesaid in such Manner as they shall think best, rendering an Account of the Monies so by them received and expended annually to the Court of General Sessions of the peace for the said County under Oath if required.

AND BE IT ALSO ENACTED by the same Authority, That all the Inhabitants residing on the North of a West Line from the Mouth of Floras Fall, to the East and south of the Bounds of the Precinct of Cornwall aforesaid shall be considered as one distinct District, and be subject to no future Division by virtue of this Act; and the Inhabitants residing in Cornwall precinct within one Mile south of the said Road so to be laid out to the East of the West side of Schunemuck Clove, and to the Southward of a North East Line to be drawn from Smith's Mill to Hudson's River shall likewise be considered as one distinct District, and be subject to no future Division by virtue of this Act; and the Inhabitants of those two Districts shall be compellable to work upon such Road so to be laid out and such other public Roads as are or may be laid out in their said Districts respectively under the directions of the Overseers that shall be appointed for said respective Districts by the Commissioners aforesaid: And the said Commissioners shall have full power and are hereby required to appoint Overseers of Highways for the said Districts respectively, who shall have all the Powers and Authorities, and be subject to the same Fines Rules and Regulations, that are given to Overseers to be elected or appointed by this Act: And the Inhabitants of those two Districts shall not be compellable to Work on any other Public Roads in the said County, any Thing herein before contained to the contrary hereof in any wise notwithstanding.

AND BE IT FURTHER ENACTED by the Authority aforesaid, That all Laws heretofore made respecting Roads or Highways so far as they relate to the County of Orange shall be and hereby are repealed, made Null and void to all Intents Constructions and purposes whatsoever.

AND BE IT FURTHER ENACTED by the Authority aforesaid, That this Act shall be and continue in force from the passing thereof, until the first Day of February which will be in the Year of our Lord one thousand seven hundred and seventy eight.

[CHAPTER 1617.]

[Chapter 1617, of Van Schaack, where the act is printed in full. See chapter 1666. The act amended is chapter 1287, and the act repealed hereby is chapter 1451.]

An Act to amend an Act entitled. "An Act "for the better clearing mending and further "laying out Public High Roads and others in "the County of Ulster."

[Passed, March 8, 1773.]

WHEREAS it is found by Experience that the Laws for regulating and improving the Public Highways in the County of Ulster, do not fully answer the good purposes thereby intended, for remedy whereof.

BE IT ENACTED by his Excellency the Governor, the Council and the General Assembly, and it is hereby enacted by the Authority of the same, That every Person liable to Work on the Public Roads or Highways in the said County of Ulster by virtue of an Act entitled, "An Act for the better clearing mending and "further Laying out Public High Roads and others in the County "of Ulster," passed in the third Year of his present Majesty's Reign, shall actually work thereon for each Day he is by the said Act obliged to work, at least eight Hours and for Default shall be liable to pay a Fine of six Pence for every Hour he shall neglect his Duty therein to be sued for and recovered in the same Manner as other Fines and Penalties are recoverable by the said Act, and applied as is herein after directed.

AND WHEREAS Disputes have arisen, and hereafter may arise concerning what persons are by the said Act compellable to work on the Public Roads and Highways in the said County, for prevention whereof for the future, BE IT ENACTED by the Authority aforesaid, That every Freeholder House keeper and other Person exercising any Trade or Business for themselves and on their own Accounts within the said County shall be liable to work upon the Public Roads and Highways, and that no Person living with and working for their Master or Parents, and not exercising any Trade or Business for themselves or upon their own Account shall be compellable to work upon the same, any Thing herein or in the said Act contained to the Contrary thereof in any wise notwithstanding.

PROVIDED ALWAYS AND BE IT FURTHER ENACTED by the same Authority, That it shall be lawful nevertheless for any Person compellable to work on the Public Roads or Highways aforesaid to commute for and pay Money at the Rate of two Shillings and six pence a Day instead of working, which Money shall be paid to the Overseer of the Highway of the District in which the Person or Persons paying the same do reside, to be by the said Overseer applied and expended in the improvement of the said Roads and Highways in such District, and towards purchasing Materials and other Necessaries for, and in erecting and building the most Public and useful Bridges in the same District according to the Directions of the major Part of the Commissioners of such Town or Precinct.

AND inasmuch as many of the Commissioners of Highways named in the said Act are since the passing thereof dead, some removed out of the Places for which they were appointed, others have declined acting, and a Number of new Precincts have been made. And an increase of the Number of Commissioners in the several Towns and Precincts in the said County will not only be an Ease and Advantage to the Inhabitants but also tend to the better and more effectual putting in Execution the good Design of said Law

BE IT THEREFORE ENACTED by the same Authority. That the following Persons shall be and are hereby appointed Commissioners for Highways for the several Towns and Precincts in the said County in the Room and stead of those appointed in and by the said Act, to wit.

For the Town of Kingston Andreas DeWitt Junior, Adam Swart, Joseph Gashery Esquire, Henry Jansen and Jacobus Persen.

For the Town of Hurley Matthias Lafever, Adrian Wynkoop, John Van deursen Esquires, Petrus Crispell and Matthewis Ten Eyck.

For Marble Town, Jacob Hassbrook, Nathaniel Contine, Esquire, David Bevier, Cornelius E. Wynkoop, and Andries J. De-Witt Esquire.

For Rochester Jacob Hornbeek, Andries DeWitt Esquires, Benjamin Hornbeek, Cornelius Hardenbergh, and Ephraim De-Pue.

For the Township of the New Paltz and the Neighbourhood thereunto belonging Cornelius DuBois, Noah Eltinge Esquires, Abraham Dojo, Abraham Donaldson and Peleg Ransom.

For the Precinct of Shawangunk, Jacobus Bruyn, Benjamin Smeedes, Isaac Haasbrouck, Johannes Jansen Esquires, and Cornelius Decker.

For the Precinct of New Marlborough, Samuel Carpenter Esquire, Lewis DuBois, Caleb Merit, Joseph Moorey, and Richard Woolsey Esquire.

For the Precinct of New Burgh, Jonathan Haasbrouck, Samuel Sands Esquire, Samuel Stratton, Arthur Smith, and Henry Smith.

For the Precinct of New Windsor John Nicoll Esquire, George Denniston, James Falkner, John Nicholson Esquire and Samuel Brewster.

For the Precinct of Hanover Hendricus Vankeuren, Cadwallader Colden Junior Esquire, Matthew Rea Esquire, Patrick Barber and Jacob Crist.

For the Precinct of the Wallkill, Abimal Young, Moses Philips, Daniel Butterfield, George Booth, and Nathaniel Owen, and.

For the Precinct of Mamacotting Benjamin DePue, Jacob Rutsen DeWitt, William Cuddeback, Jacob Gemaar and Philip Swartwout.

Which said Commissioners or any three of them shall have all the Powers and Authorities in the Towns and Precincts for which they are respectively appointed, and perform all the Duties enjoyned upon the Commissioners of Highways and Public Roads in and by the said Act, shall be entitled to the same Rewards, and be subject to the same regulations, Fines Forfeitures and Penalties, any Thing therein contained to the contrary notwithstanding: And the said Commissioners abovenamed shall before they do any Thing in consequence of their Appointment respectively take an oath before one of his Majesty's Justices of the Peace for the said County who is hereby impowered and required to administer the same in the Words following to wit. "I. A. B. do "swear that I will faithfully fairly and impartially execute the "Powers given to me as a Commissioner of Highways by virtue of "two Acts of the Legislature of this Colony, the one entitled, "An Act for the better clearing mending and further laying out "Public High Roads and others in the County of Ulster; and the "other entitled, An Act to amend an Act entitled An Act for the "better clearing mending and further laying out Public High "Roads and others in the County of Ulster, in such Manner as "shall appear to me to be most for the Public good so help me "God." And if any of the said Commissioners shall die, remove out of the place for which they are appointed, or refuse or neglect to act in their Office, others shall be elected in their Room and stead in the same Manner as in the aforesaid Act is directed.

AND BE IT FURTHER ENACTED by the Authority aforesaid, That the Commissioners of the respective Towns and Precincts in the said County or the major Part of them shall if needful at least Ten Days before their next annual Town or Precinct Meeting, and so annually, if they shall Judge the same necessary by writing under their Hands to be lodged with the Town or Precinct Clerk by him to be entered on the Town or Precinct Book, divide their respective Towns and Precincts into as many Districts as they shall Judge most equitable and convenient, and for each of which Districts there shall be annually elected and chosen by the Freeholders and Inhabitants of such Towns and Precincts in the said County respectively an Overseer of the Highways, who shall do the Duties and be subject to the same Fines and Penalties for any Neglect or Refusal to Act or Misconduct in his Office, as Overseers of Roads or Highways are by the said Act, and to whom the Commissioners of the Towns and Precincts respectively shall deliver a List in Writing containing the Names of all the Persons in such his District compellable to work on the Public Roads or Highways: and in order that the good purposes hereby intended may in no wise be evaded, but that the same may be faithfully executed.

BE IT ALSO ENACTED, That the Overseer of each District in said county so to be chosen shall keep a just and true Account in writing, wherein he shall distinctly set down or mention all such Persons as have commuted for and paid Money instead of working as aforesaid, and such as have been fined and the Sums they were so respectively fined, and also those who shall have actually worked on the Public Roads or Highways with the Number of Days they have so worked, which said Account together with the said List, the said Overseer shall on or before the Determination of his Office deliver to one of the Commissioners of the Town or Precinct to which he doth belong, and shall duly take an Oath before such Commissioner, who is hereby impowered to administer the same in the Words following, to wit. " I. A B. do declare (or if " a Quaker affirm) that this Account now delivered by me con" tains the Names of all the Persons within my District who by " Law are compellable to work on Highways as far as have come " to my knowledge and that each Person therein named (except " such as are mentioned to have commuted for and paid Money " instead of working or have been fined,) has worked himself or " by a Man or Team in his stead since the Day I was last elected " into the Office of an Overseer of the Roads or Highways the " Number of Days in this Account particularly mentioned, and as " nearly as I could well compute eight Hours in each Day, and I " have laid out and disposed of agreeable to Law the Monies by " me received from such Persons as are therein mentioned to have " been fined, and from those who have commuted for and paid " Money instead of working; together with all such other Sums as " have come to my Hands for the purpose of improving of the " Roads, or erecting of Bridges within my District, the Ballance " mentioned in this Account (if any there be) only excepted, " fairly honestly and impartially according to the best of my " Skill and knowledge so help me God," which Account so sworn to the said Commissioner shall file with the Town or Precinct Clerk, and the said Overseer shall pay the Ballance mentioned in the said Account (if any,) to his Successor in Office to be expended in the Course of the next Year.

AND WHEREAS the Monies that may arise by Fines and from Persons commuting for and paying Money instead of working may not be sufficient for purchasing Materials and other Necessaries for erecting and building Bridges and in making such Improvements on the Public Roads as are absolutely necessary, and yet cannot be well accomplished in the ordinary way of working thereon.

BE IT THEREFORE ENACTED by the same Authority, That if the major Part of the Commissioners of any Town or Precinct in the said County shall judge it necessary to raise a further Annual Sum, for the Purposes aforesaid, they shall in that Case meet together annually, and agree upon the Sum necessary to be so raised for that year, and shall deliver a Certificate of such Sum so agreed upon in writing subscribed with their Names to the Supervisor of such Town or Precinct, which Supervisor shall lay the same before the Supervisors of the County at their next annual Meeting for raising the contingent Charges of the said County, who shall and are hereby required to order the raising and collecting of that Sum of and from the Freeholders and Inhabitants of such Town or Precinct in the same Manner and after the same Rate that the contingent Charges of the County are raised: which Sum as soon as the Collector shall have collected the same, he shall and is hereby required to pay into the Hands of the Clerk of the Town or Precinct in which it was levied, to be by him paid to the Overseer or Overseers of the Public Roads or Highways for said Town or Precinct on an Order or Orders under the Hands of the major Part of the Commissioners being produced and delivered to him for that purpose. PROVIDED ALWAYS that the annual Sum so agreed upon to be raised shall not exceed a Sum equal to the Amount of two Shillings for each Freeholder and Housekeeper residing in such Town or Precinct which Sum or Sums shall be laid out and expended in the said Town or Precinct in the same Manner and for the like purposes that Fines are directed to be applied by virtue of this Act.

AND BE IT FURTHER ENACTED by the same Authority, That the Act entitled, "An Act for the better laying out, regu-"lating and keeping in Repair the common and public High-"ways in such Precincts in the County of Ulster as is therein "mentioned", passed the twenty seventh Day of January one thousand seven hundred and seventy, shall be and is hereby repealed.

PROVIDED ALWAYS AND BE IT FURTHER ENACTED by the same Authority, That if there shall be any Money remaining in the Hands of any of the Clerks of Precincts or Overseers of the Highways which was raised by virtue of the Act last mentioned it shall be laid out and expended for the purposes therein expressed, any Thing herein contained to the contrary notwithstanding.

This Act to be in force from the passing thereof until the first Day of January one thousand seven hundred and seventy six.

[CHAPTER 1618.]

[Chapter 1618, of Van Schaack, where the act is printed in full.]

An Act for the more equal Taxation of Estates, and providing for Deficiencies in the Taxes of the County of West-Chester.

[Passed, March 8, 1773.]

WHEREAS it often happens by the removal of some persons out of the Manors, Townships and Districts in which they were assessed and taxed before the same Tax has been collected, and by the poverty of some others, that their proportion of the Taxes of the Manor Township or Districts in which they lived cannot be collected, and by the Misconduct of the Collectors who sometimes apply the Monies or Part thereof to their Own use, and are unable to replace the same, that the Taxes or part of the Taxes of some of the Manors, Townships or Districts in the said County of West Chester are in Arrear and unpaid to the great Injury of the Inhabitants of the said County in general, for Remedy whereof.

BE IT ENACTED by his Excellency the Governor the Council and the General Assembly, and it is hereby enacted by the Authority of the same, That in all Cases where there has or may happen any Deficiencies in the Taxes of any of the Manors, Townships or Districts in the said County of West Chester for the Space of six Months after the same ought to have been paid unto the Treasurer of the said County then and in such Case the Supervisors of the said County shall be and hereby are fully authorized impowered and required to add in the next succeeding Tax or Rate of the same nature to the Quota or Assessment of such Manor, Township or District respectively as do and shall appear to be so in arrear of former Taxes or Rates as aforesaid, so much as their respective Deficiencies shall amount to which being so added to the said Quota is to be collected therewith and paid in the same manner and to the same use and uses as in the original Tax or Rate is or shall be directed: And as much as may be to remedy the Inconvenience arising from the misconduct of the several Assessors and Collectors in the said County.

BE IT FURTHER ENACTED by the Authority aforesaid That the several Assessors for the said County shall within ten Days after they are respectively elected and before they enter upon their Business as Assessors, take the following Oath before any one Justice of the Peace for the said County, who are hereby fully authorized and impowered to administer the same. Vizt: "That they shall well and truly execute the Office of an Assessor and well and truly equally impartially and in due proportion assess and rate the Estate real and personal of the Freeholders and Inhabitants within their several and respective Districts according to the best of their Skill and knowledge, and therein shall spare no person for favour or affection, or grieve any Person for Hatred or ill will," of which Oath the said Justice shall give a Certificate to be filed with the Clerk of the County.

AND BE IT FURTHER ENACTED by the Authority aforesaid, That the respective Collectors for the said County shall before they respectively enter upon the Execution of their Office give Bond with one security at least (to the supervisor of the Manor Township or District for which he shall be chosen collector and his successors in Office) in a penalty which shall be double the Sum to be collected by the said Collector, which Bond shall be conditioned for the faithful Execution of the said Collector's Office in every respect, and for the payment of the Monies to be raised within the said District or such part thereof as can be collected to the County Treasurer by a Day certain in the said Bond to be mentioned, which Bond or Bonds so to be given to the supervisor of any particular Manor Town or District and to his Successors in Office shall and is hereby declared to be a good Bond in Law and shall and may be either put in suit in the Name of the supervisor who took the same or in the Name of his successor in Office for the Benefit of the Manor, Township or District for which he shall be chosen as aforesaid any Law Usage or Custom to the contrary in any wise notwithstanding: and that this Act may be duly observed and complied with.

BE IT FURTHER ENACTED by the Authority aforesaid. That the Supervisor and Supervisors Assessor and Assessors as well as the Collector and Collectors for the said County of WestChester shall be and hereby are strictly charged and enjoined to comply with the Directions of this Act, and in Default thereof, they and each of them respectively shall be subject and liable to the same Fines and Penalties as in such Cases are provided by the several Acts by virtue of which any former Taxes or Rates have been laid Assessed and collected.

[CHAPTER 1619.]

[Chapter 1619, of Van Schaack, where the act is printed in full. See chapters 801, 1672 and 1458.]

An Act for the better regulating and keeping in repair the Public Roads in the Borough and Town of West-Chester, and to levy Money to defray the Expence thereof.

[Passed, March 8, 1773.]

WHEREAS the several Laws which relate to the repairing of the Highways have been found insufficient for that purpose in the Borough and Town of West Chester.

BE IT THEREFORE ENACTED by his Excellency the Governor the Council and the General Assembly, and it is hereby enacted by the Authority of the same, That for and during the space of three years from and after the first Day of March which will be in the Year of our Lord one thousand seven hundred and seventy three, and to the End of the next Session of the General Assembly thereafter, the Mayor and other Members of the Corporation of the said Borough and Town for the Time being shall have full power and lawful Authority to raise and levy from the Freeholders and Inhabitants of the same Borough and Town the annual Sum of one hundred and ten pounds in such Manner as the Corporation of the said Borough and Town, or the Majority thereof shall at their Common Council think proper, which Sum shall be received by the Mayor of the said Corporation; and the said Sum when so raised, the said Mayor shall yearly and every Year pay into the Hands of Lewis Graham Esquire, on every last Monday in April, for the use and purpose of mending and repairing, first the Post Road, and then other the Highways and Bridges within the Limits of the said Borough and Town excepting the Bridge called Queens Bridge between West Chester and New York.

AND BE IT FURTHER ENACTED by the Authority aforesaid, That if any of the said Freeholders or Inhabitants shall refuse to pay the proportion to him or them in manner aforesaid Allotted of the said Sum, the said Mayor shall issue his Warrant in Writing to the Serjeant of the Mace of the said Borough to distrain the Goods and Chattels of such Person or Persons as shall so refuse, and to sell the same at public Auction for the payment of said proportion, returning the Overplus if any there be to the Owner or Owners thereof after deducting thereout the legal Charges.

AND BE IT FURTHER ENACTED by the Authority aforesaid, That every Member of the said Corporation who shall refuse or neglect to assist in raising the said Sum shall forfeit the Sum of twenty Pounds to be recovered by the said Lewis Graham by Action of Debt in any Court of Record with Costs of suit, one half of which shall be applied to the Repairs of the Roads in the said Borough: And if the said Mayor for the Time being shall refuse to pay on the said last Monday in April into the Hands of him the said Lewis Graham the said sum of one hundred and ten pounds; the said Lewis Graham shall prosecute an Action of Debt against the said Mayor in any Court of Record within this Colony, and shall recover against him the Sum of one hundred and twenty Pounds together with the Costs of Suit; sixty Pounds whereof to be to the use of him the said Lewis Graham and the remainder to be for the uses and purposes abovementioned.

AND BE IT FURTHER ENACTED by the Authority aforesaid, That the said Lewis Graham upon the Receipt of the said annual Sum of one hundred and ten pounds shall use and employ one hundred Pounds thereof yearly and every Year during the continuance of this Act in the mending and repairing of the Highways and Bridges abovementioned and in removing all Nuisances which shall be in the same, and shall retain the remaining ten Pounds for his Trouble.

AND BE IT FURTHER ENACTED by the Authority aforesaid, That the said Lewis Graham upon the Receipt of the said every Year deliver in upon his Corporal Oath unto the said Corporation at their Common Council aforesaid a just true and particular Account of the Manner in which the said Sum of one hundred Pounds hath been expended, and in Default thereof, or if the said Sum hath not been expended for the purposes aforesaid, then the said Corporation shall prosecute an Action of Debt against him the said Lewis Graham in any Court of Record within this Colony, and recover thereon the Sum of one hundred Pounds to the use of the said Corporation in the mending and repairing the Highways and Bridges aforesaid with the Costs of such Suit.

AND BE IT FURTHER ENACTED by the Authority aforesaid. That if any Person or Persons shall leave the Carcass of any dead Beast, or any broken Carriage on any of the Bridges or Highways within the Limits of the said Borough for any longer Time than is necessary for the Removal of the same, shall for every such Offence forfeit the Sum of twenty shillings to be recovered by the said Lewis Graham by Action of Debt with Costs of Suit, in a Summary way, before any one of the Aldermen of the said Borough, and to be employed and laid out by the said Lewis Graham in the repairing and improving the said Highways and Bridges: And if any Person or Persons shall make or burn any Lime Kilns or Coal Kilns upon the said Highways or shall plow up or pare off and remove the Soil of any Highway for the purposes of Manure or sodding Land or any other, but repairing the Road, shall for every such Offence forfeit the Sum of twenty shillings to be recovered paid and applied as aforesaid.

AND BE IT FURTHER ENACTED by the Authority aforesaid. That the Owner or Owners of any dead Beast or other Nuisance placed or left on any of the said Highways or Roads, shall be deemed to have placed or left the same thereon, unless such Owner or Owners do upon Oath deny his or their knowledge of the Existence of such Nuisances, before one of the Magistrates of the said Corporation, or prove who is the true Author thereof, to the satisfaction of such Magistrates.

AND BE IT ENACTED by the Authority aforesaid. That in case the said Lewis Graham who is hereby appointed Commissioner of the Highways for the said Borough as aforesaid, shall die or refuse to serve, or remove from the said Borough the Mayor, Aldermen and Common Council or the Major Part of them shall nominate and appoint some other sufficient Freeholder to act in his stead, who shall be invested with the same powers herein before given to the said Lewis Graham, and liable to the same Penalties.

AND BE IT ENACTED by the Authority aforesaid, That the said Lewis Graham or any Commissioner hereafter to be appointed by virtue of this Act shall be and hereby is obliged upon Information being given by any two Freeholders in the aforesaid Borough within six Days after such Information to mend and repair every Highway Bridge and Causeway, (except as is above excepted) which shall be either washed away damaged or broken; and in Case the abovementioned Lewis Graham or the Commissioner for the Time being, shall refuse or neglect after the abovementioned Information being given to amend and repair the said Highways Causeways and Bridges, he shall for every Neglect forfeit the sum of forty Shillings to be recovered by the Person or Persons who shall prosecute or sue for the same by Action of Debt before any Alderman of said Borough in Manner as aforesaid, and in Case the above Sum of one hundred Pounds shall not be sufficient to answer the above mentioned purposes.

BE IT ENACTED by the Authority aforesaid, That the Mayor of the said Borough as aforesaid shall have full Power and lawful Authority as aforesaid to raise and levy upon the Freeholders and Inhabitants of the said Coroporation annually, in Manner aforesaid such further sum as shall be thought necessary for the purposes aforesaid, not exceeding the sum of twenty Pounds.

AND BE IT FURTHER ENACTED by the Authority aforesaid, That all former Acts heretofore passed for keeping in repair the Public Highways as far as they relate to the Borough and Town of West Chester shall be and hereby are repealed.

[CHAPTER 1620.]

[Chapter 1620, of Van Schaack, where the act is printed in full. See chapter 1557.]

An Act to repeal an Act entitled "An Act "to prevent Infectious Distempers in the "Counties therein mentioned," so far as it re-"lates to the Borough and Town of West Chester and Manor of Philipsborough.

[Passed, March 8, 1773.]

WHEREAS the Act entitled, "An Act to prevent Infectious "Distempers in the Counties therein mentioned," has been found inconvenient in the Borough and Town of West Chester, and the Manor of Philipsborough, and is judged by the Inhabitants thereof to have a bad Tendancy.

BE IT THEREFORE ENACTED by his Excellency the Governor the Council and the General Assembly, and it is hereby enacted by the Authority of the same. That every Clause and part of the aforesaid Act is repealed so far as the same relates to the Borough and Town of West Chester and the Manor of Philipsborough any Thing in the said Act to the contrary notwithstanding.

[CHAPTER 1621.]

[Chapter 1621, of Van Schaack, where the act is printed in full. The acts hereby repealed are chapter 905 (so far as it relates to Richmond) and chapter 1267.]

An Act for the better laying out regulating and keeping in repair common and public Highways in Richmond County.

[Passed, March 8, 1773.]

WHEREAS Nothing contributes more to the Ease and Advantage of the Inhabitants, than the well regulating, laying out and keeping in Repair Public Highways. BE IT THEREFORE ENACTED by his Excellency the Governor the Council and the General Assembly and it is hereby enacted by the Authority of the same, That from and after the passing hereof the Freeholders and Inhabitants of the County of Richmond shall be and are hereby authorized at their annual Town Meetings for electing Town Officers to choose and elect at the same Time two Freeholders in each Manor precinct or Division to be Commissioners for laying out and regulating Highways, and also as many Freeholders in each Manor and precinct as the majority of the people shall think necessary, to be Surveyor and Overseer thereof for the Mending repairing and keeping in order the several Highways in the respective precinct and Divisions for which they shall be elected and chosen in manner as aforesaid and the person or persons so chosen and elected as well those who are to regulate and lay out Highways as those who are to be Overseers and Surveyors thereof, are hereby required to take the several Offices upon them, and in Case of the Death or Removal of any of the Commissioners or Overseers aforesaid, it shall and may be lawful for two Justices of the Peace living in the Precinct and in Case there should be but one, then the next Justice to the said Precinct in conjunction with the Justice of the Precinct to appoint some fit person to execute the Office of Commissioner or Overseer as the Case may require until a new Election shall be made at the Time or Times beforementioned, and every such Commissioner or Overseer so appointed as aforesaid shall have the same powers, and be liable to the same Penalties as if chosen and Appointed by this Act.

AND BE IT ENACTED by the Authority aforesaid, That the Commissioners chosen in each precinct or Manor as aforesaid joined with one Commissioner out of each of the other respective Precincts of said County are hereby impowered and authorized to lay out all such Public Roads or Highways as they or the major Part of them shall think necessary and also take a view of the Roads already laid out, and if any of them shall appear inconvenient, and in their Opinion an Alteration absolutely necessary, may alter the same, and lay out such other Public Highways as they or the major Part of them shall think convenient, and if they find upon view any of the above Roads are lessened or blocked up, they the said Commissioners or the major Part of them shall have power and are hereby authorized to open the same to such widths as they shall think proper not exceeding four Rods nor less than two, and if any of the Roads lessened or blocked up as aforesaid shall run between two persons Lands and a Dispute arise which of them hath encroached upon the Road the said Commissioners shall hear all the Allegations and Proofs on both Sides of the Question, and after mature Deliberation give their Judgment thereon as they or the major Part of them shall think equitable and just being first Sworn in the words following vizt: "You " will well and truly try this Matter in Dispute between A B. and " C D. respecting the Road running between them, and give a true " Judgment thereon according to Evidence, so help you God," and shall open and lay out the said Highways agreeable thereto, and when any Roads so opened as aforesaid shall take away Land from any Person or Persons which were actually measured to him or them as part of their Land purchased, the possessor of such Lands shall have his Remedy against the Person or Persons they respectively purchased from. PROVIDED ALWAYS, That Nothing in this Act shall extend or be construed to impower the Commissioners aforesaid to lay out any Road through any Person's Lands or Meadows without the Consent of the Owner or Owners thereof, or paying to him or them the true Value of the Lands so to be laid out into a Highway or Road with such Damages as he shall sustain thereby, and in Case of Public Highways or Roads if any Dispute shall arise respecting the Value of the Land or the Necessity of laying said Road in that Case the said Commissioners shall deliver all their proceedings signed by themselves or the Majority of them to the Supervisors at their next Meeting thereafter, who after examining the same and hearing the Objections shall have it in their power to approve or reject the same, as it shall appear to them or the major Part of them to be reasonable or Necessary and shall likewise have power to agree with the Owner or Owners for the value of the Land and Damages, and if it shall happen that the Supervisors shall be equally divided in their Opinion, so that no Majority appears, then and in that Case they shall call to their Assistance the Treasurer of the said County, who agreeing with either Side shall determine, and if the same be approved and confirmed, the said Supervisors shall Cause the same with all their proceedings thereon to be entered in the County Records, and the Clerk is hereby directed and required to enter the same, and the Supervisors shall then endeavor to agree with the Owners of the Lands respecting the Value thereof, and the Amount of Damages, and if they cannot agree, the same shall then be determined, and the true Value set and appraised by the Oath of twelve principal Freeholders not having any Interest in the Land so laid out into an Highway or Road, the said Freeholders to be summoned by the Sheriff of said County by virtue of a Warrant to be issued by any one Justice of the Peace of said County, who shall attend at the Time and place mentioned in the said Warrant and swear the Jury, and sit with them upon hearing the Dispute and swear the Witnesses, but shall not give his Vote with the said Jury in assessing the said Value and Damages; but if no Dispute arises about the Necessity of laying out such Public Highway then the said Commissioners shall report the same to the Supervisors at their next Meeting and the said Supervisors shall then endeavour to agree with the Owner or Owners of the Land over which such Highway shall be laid out, for the value of the Land and Damages; and if they cannot agree, the same shall be determined by a Jury in the Manner aforesaid, and in all Cases of Public Highways so laid out or altered as aforesaid, the Value of the Lands and Damages, whether agreed on as aforesaid or assessed by a Jury, together with the Charges of the Commissioners, and calling and charges of a Jury if there be a Jury, and of the whole proceedings thereon had shall be levied and paid in like Manner as the other contingent Charges of the County: And the Highways, so laid out shall be a common Public Highway, but if the Road laid out be for the private use and benefit of any particular person or persons, then the said Commissioners shall hear and determine all Disputes concerning the necessity of such private Road, and the Value of the Land Damages and Charges aforesaid shall be paid by the person or persons who desire the same to be laid out, and the Road to be for the only proper use of such Person or Persons and their Heirs and Assigns who shall pay for the same; and in Case the Person or Persons applying for such private Road cannot agree with the Owner or Owners of the Land over which such private Road shall go, respecting the Value of the Land and Damages, then the same shall be assessed by a Jury in the Manner above directed: ALWAYS PROVIDED, That the Person through whose Land the said Road shall be so laid out, his Heirs or Assigns, shall not be debarred from crossing or using said Road.

AND BE IT FURTHER ENACTED by the Authority aforesaid, That if any Person or Persons within the said County do or hereafter shall alter stop up or lessen any Highway or Road, that has been heretofore laid out by former Commissioners according to Law or shall be hereafter laid out by Commissioners elected and chosen by virtue of this Act without the Consent of the Commissioners, shall for every such Offence forfeit the Sum of forty shillings to be recovered before any Justice of the Peace, upon the Oath of any one credible Witness and levied by Warrant from any Justice of the Peace directed to the Constable of the Town or Place where such Offence is committed by distraining the Goods and Chattels of the Offender, and the said Constable after six Days Notice is given by him of the selling the said Distress, shall make sale thereof and out of the produce pay the said Forfeiture and Charges and return the Overplus (if any there be) to the Owner or Owners thereof: which said Forfeiture of forty Shillings shall be applied by the Surveyor of the Highways, for and towards repairing the Public Roads or Highways within the Precinct where such Forfeiture shall arise.

AND BE IT FURTHER ENACTED by the Authority aforesaid, That all common public Roads or Highways which shall be hereafter laid out by the aforesaid Commissioners shall not exceed four Rods in Breadth nor be less than two, and where any Private Road for any Person or Persons particular use or benefit as aforesaid shall be laid out through any Person's Land or Meadow, it shall not exceed the Breadth of twenty Feet.

AND BE IT FURTHER ENACTED by the same Authority, That the Inhabitants of the Manor and Precincts where any Common Public Roads or Highways have or shall run, or be hereafter ascertained or laid out, are hereby obliged to clear and maintain the same by draining banking, cutting or stubbing the Brush, carrying off the Stones, and the Limbs of Trees hanging over the said Road to be lopped and carried off, or the Trees cut down as the same may be necessary; and so often as they or any of them shall have Notice from the respective Surveyors or Overseers of the Highways for the Time being shall by themselves or Servants, clear level and amend the Highways in such place and Manner as they shall be directed by the said Overseers or Surveyors respectively, not exceeding six Days in the year nor less than three, under the Penalty of four Shillings for each Day every Person shall neglect or refuse such Service, to be levied by the Constable in each Precinct or Division by Distress and Sale of the Offender's Goods and Chattels, by Warrant from any one of the Surveyors or Overseers of the Highways for the Time being where such Neglect or Refusal shall happen, returning the Overplus of such Sale if any there be, to the Owner or Owners, the Constable to be first paid for his pains and Trouble out of the Distress as is common in other Cases, and the said Forfeiture of four shillings shall be applied for repairing the Public Roads or Highways within the Precincts where such Forfeiture shall arise.

AND BE IT ENACTED by the Authority aforesaid, That all trees that stand in any Person's Land, through which any Common Public Road or Highway is or may hereafter be laid out shall be for the proper use of the Owner or Owners of the same, but the Owner shall not hinder the Public from making use of so much Timber which is standing or lying on that Road as will amend and repair the Highways or Road running through that Land, and if there should not be sufficient Timber on the Public Roads to amend and repair the same, or should any other Materials for that purpose be necessary or wanting the Overseers shall have power to purchase any of the aforesaid Materials in the best and cheapest Manner they can, and shall carry in their respective Accounts to the supervisors who shall add so much to the respective precincts where the same did arise, and be by them raised in the same Manner as the other contingent Charges are raised and levied.

AND BE IT ALSO ENACTED by the same Authority, That where any Highway from any Plantation to any Meadow, Mills or Common Landing places shall run through any Person or Persons Land or Meadow it shall and may be lawful for any such person or persons by the Approbation of the Commissioners as aforesaid to place and hang good and easy swinging Gates on such Highways, and keep them in good Repair at their own proper Costs, and the several Gates already standing and allōwed, may or shall be approved and continued or altered, as the Commissioners shall judge most convenient.

AND BE IT FURTHER ENACTED by the same Authority, That if the Overseers of the Roads and Highways shall think fit and have Occasion for any Team, Cart or Waggon and a Man to manage the same, the said Team, Cart or Waggon shall be esteemed to be for and in lieu and stead of three Days Work of a single Man and the Fine proportionable, and every Person when called to work on the Roads shall bring such Materials as spades Axes and other Utensils as shall be directed and approved by the Surveyors or Overseers of the Highways respectively.

AND BE IT FURTHER ENACTED by the same Authority, That the Commissioners or the majority of them, shall from Time to Time enter in writing all the Highways or Roads by them laid out altered or stopped up, and sign the same and cause them to be entered in the County Record, and the Clerk is hereby directed and required to enter the same, unless in Case of public Roads where a Dispute arises about the Necessity of laying out such Road, in which Case the said Commissioners are to return their said proceedings to the supervisors as is herein before directed, and whatsoever the said Commissioners shall do according to the Powers given them in this Act being so entered in the County record shall be valid and good to all Intents and purposes whatsoever.

AND BE IT FURTHER ENACTED by the Authority aforesaid, That each Commissioner shall have take and receive a sum not exceeding six Shillings for every Day he shall be employed in laying out and regulating or opening Highways as aforesaid for his Care and Trouble in doing the Business required by this Act: and the said Commissioners shall transmit their Accounts to the supervisors of the said County at their annual Meetings, of the Number of Days they have respectively spent in doing the Business required by this Act, and the supervisors shall raise the same with the County Tax which shall be paid by the County Treasurer to the Commissioners and Overseers upon a warrant from the supervisors as in other Cases except where the Commissioners are paid by private persons as before directed.

AND BE IT FURTHER ENACTED by the Authority aforesaid, That upon the Ordering of any one Justice of the Peace the surveyors or Overseers of the several precincts and Divisions shall within eight Days after warn and set to work the respective

Inhabitants and persons made liable to mend and repair the Highways and Roads which by Law they are obliged to repair, and if any of the surveyors or Overseers shall neglect or refuse to warn and set to work the Inhabitants as aforesaid, and see the said Highways and Roads amended and repaired, such Surveyor or Overseer shall for every such Neglect or Refusal forfeit and pay a sum of forty shillings to be adjudged by and recovered before any one Justice of the Peace of said County where such Neglect or Refusal shall happen which Fine shall be applied towards repairing the said Highways in such Precinct or Manor wherein such Fine shall arise.

AND BE IT FURTHER ENACTED by the Authority aforesaid, That one certain Act passed the twenty ninth Day of November one thousand seven hundred and forty-five entitled, "An Act "for the better clearing,. regulating, and further laying out Public Highways in King's County, Queen's County, Richmond "County, and Orange County", as far as it respects the County of Richmond aforesaid, and the Act entitled, "An Act for the "better laying out regulating and keeping in Repair common "and public Highways in Richmond County," passed the twentieth Day of October one thousand seven hundred and sixty four, shall be and hereby are repealed.

AND BE IT FURTHER ENACTED by the Authority aforesaid. That this Act shall be in force from the passing thereof until the first Day of February which will be in the Year of our Lord one thousand seven hundred and seventy seven.

[CHAPTER 1622.]

[Chapter 1622, of Van Schaack, where the act is printed in full. See chapter 1483.]

An Act to revive an Act entitled "An Act "to appoint Inspectors of Flour and Repackers "of Beef and Pork in the several Counties "therein mentioned."

[Passed, March 8, 1773.]

BE IT ENACTED by his Excellency the Governor the Council and the General Assembly, and it is hereby enacted by the Authority of the same, That the Act entitled, "An Act to ap"point Inspectors of Flour and Repackers of Beef and Pork in "the several Counties therein mentioned," passed in the eleventh year of his present Majesty's Reign, shall be and hereby is revived, and every Article Matter and Clause therein contained enacted to be and remain in full force from the passing hereof until the first Day of February which will be in the Year of our Lord one thousand seven hundred and seventy five.

[CHAPTER 1623.]

[Chapter 1623, of Van Schaack, where the act is printed in full.]

An Act to ascertain the place, from whence the Mileage Fees of the respective Sheriffs of the several Counties therein named, shall be computed, and for other purposes therein mentioned.

[Passed, March 8, 1773.]

WHEREAS it has been usual for the sheriffs of the respective Counties herein after mentioned to compute their Mileage Fees on the Service of Writs from their respective places of abode or from their respective County Goals although they are remote from the Center of the said respective Counties, which greatly increases the Charge for Mileage in the Service of Writs on such Persons as live at a Distance from their Goals or the Habitations of the said sheriffs, to remedy which for the future.

BE IT ENACTED by his Excellency the Governor the Council and the General Assembly, and it is hereby enacted by the Authority of the same, That from and after the passing of this Act, the respective Sheriffs of the respective Counties herein after named for the Time being, shall compute their Mileage Fees for the Service of all Writs and process hereafter by them served, and subject to the payment of Mileage Fees from the respective places herein after mentioned, and from no other place whatsoever, that is to say.

The sheriffs of the Counties of Cumberland and Kings respectively from the place where the respective Court Houses and Goals now stand in the said Counties.

The sheriff of the County of Suffolk from a Path commonly known by the Name of the Wading River path, about seven Miles to the Westward of the County Hall in the said County, at the Junction of the said Path with the County Road which passes through Nassau Island about the Middle thereof.

The sheriff of Queens County from a certain Pond commonly called the Wind-Mill Pond near the North side of Hempstead Plains.

AND the sheriff of Dutchess County from the House where Myndert Veale Esquire now lives in Beekman's Precinct: any

Law, Ordinance Usage or Custom to the contrary notwithstanding.

AND forasmuch as the returning of Process issued out of the Supreme Court of this Colony by the Sheriff of the said County of Cumberland is attended with extraordinary Trouble and Expence, the Sheriff in many Cases being obliged to travel a great Distance in order to facilitate the Return thereof.

BE IT FURTHER ENACTED by the Authority aforesaid. That it shall and may be lawful to and for the sheriff of the said County of Cumberland for the Time being to ask demand and receive the usual and Customary Mileage Fees for every Mile he shall necessarily travel in or out of the said County in order to facilitate the Return of each and every Writ and process which shall be issued out of the supreme Court of this Colony, and by him served and returned, and that an Affidavit to be by him made in each Case before one of the Judges of the Inferior Court of Common pleas for the same County of the Number of Miles he necessarily travelled in order to facilitate such Return, shall be a sufficient proof of the same, and an Authority to the Judges of the said Supreme Court, or one of them to tax such Mileage Fees in all Bills of Cost in Causes where the Defendant resides within the said County of Cumberland any Law Usage or Custom to the contrary notwithstanding.

AND BE IT FURTHER ENACTED by the Authority aforesaid, That it shall and may be lawful to and for the sheriff of the said County of Cumberland for the Time being and his Deputies, and they are hereby impowered to serve and execute all Summonses, Warrants, Executions, and other precepts which Justices of the Peace are impowered to issue in pursuance of an Act of the Legislature of this Colony entitled, "An Act to im-"power Justices of the Peace, Mayors, Recorders and Alder-"men to try Causes to the Value of five Pounds and under, and "for suspending the Act therein mentioned," made and passed on the twelfth Day of March one thousand seven hundred and seventy two: and that the said sheriff for the Time being and his Deputies shall and hereby are declared to be entitled to the like Fees for their respective Services as are allowed by the said Act to the Constables who are by the said Act impowered to perform the same.

This Act to continue of force until the ninth Day of April which will be in the Year of our Lord one thousand seven hundred and seventy eight.

[CHAPTER 1624.]

[Chapter 1624, of Van Schaack, where the act is printed in full. See ers 1453, 1500, 1526.]

An Act for the better Regulation of the Public Inns and Taverns in the several Counties therein mentioned.

[Passed, March 8, 1773.]

EREAS the Laws for the better regulation of Public Inns verns within the several Counties herein after mentioned, er expired or found ineffectual, and thereby the original f instituting Inns and Taverns for the accommodation lers is in a great Measure defeated.

THEREFORE ENACTED by his Excellency the Gov- e Council and the General Assembly, and it is hereby by the Authority of the same, That every Person who ter the first Day of May next keep any Public Inn or in either of the Counties of Albany, Tryon, Dutchess, range West Chester, Richmond Kings, or Queens, shall keep three good spare Beds, two of which to be Feather Beds, with good and sufficient sheeting and Covering for such Beds respectively, and good and sufficient Stabling and Provender of Hay in the Winter, and Hay or Pasturage in the Summer, and Grain for six Horses or other Cattle, for the accommodation of Travellers their Horses and Cattle, upon Pain of forfeiting for every Offence the Sum of twenty Shillings to be sued for and recovered by Action of Debt in a summary way with Costs of Suit before any Justice of the Peace of the County where such Offence shall be committed, one half of such Forfeiture to be applied to the use of the person so suing for and recovering the same, and the other half thereof, to be paid into the Hands of the Overseers of the Poor in such Town, Manor, Precinct or District where the Offence shall have been committed, to be applied to the Maintenance of the Poor thereof.

PROVIDED ALWAYS, AND IT IS HEREBY FURTHER ENACTED, That Whereas in some Parts of the aforesaid Counties, so little Resort is had to some Inns and Taverns as would make the last mentioned Regulations burthensome, and yet it being necessary, that in those places some sort of Entertainment should be provided, it shall therefore be in the Discretion of any three Justices of the Peace residing in, or next adjacent to the said Town, Manor, Precinct or District, to exempt by writing under their Hands and Seals, one or more Innholders or Tavern-keepers in every such Town, Manor, Precinct or District from being subject to the Regulations prescribed in and by the foregoing Clause any Thing therein contained to the contrary notwithstanding.

AND WHEREAS by two Acts of the Legislature of this Colony heretofore passed it is enacted, That if any Tavernkeeper or Innholder shall sell any Spirituous Liquor to any Apprentice, Servant, or Negro or other Slave without the Consent of his, her or their Master or Mistress, every such person or persons so offending shall forfeit forty Shillings: which Forfeiture being conceived insufficient; in order therefore more effectually to prevent so pernicious a practice.

BE IT FURTHER ENACTED by the Authority aforesaid, That if any Inn-holder or Tavern-keeper shall after the passing of this Act, be convicted of Selling Spirituous Liquor of any Kind, to any Apprentice, Servant, or Negro or other Slave in either of the aforesaid Counties, contrary to the true Intent and meaning of the abovementioned Acts, the Licence of every Innholder or Tavern-keeper so offending shall be and is hereby declared void from the Time of such Conviction, and such Innholder or Tavern-keeper shall be and is hereby declared in capable of receiving any further or other Licence for holding a Public Inn or Tavern for the Space of three Years from the Time of such Conviction.

AND BE IT FURTHER ENACTED by the Authority aforesaid, That every Inn-holder or Tavern-keeper within the said Counties shall on or before the first Day of May next after the passing hereof put up and fix a proper Sign on or adjacent to the Front of his or their House, with his or their Names at the Foot thereof, under the Penalty of five Shillings for every Months neglect thereof.

AND BE IT FURTHER ENACTED by the Authority aforesaid, That the Clerk of each respective Town, Manor, Precinct and District within the Counties aforesaid shall publickly read this Act, at the next annual Town, Manor, Precinct or District Meeting for which he is Clerk, and so every Year during the Continuance of this Act.

AND BE IT FURTHER ENACTED by the Authority aforesaid, That this Act shall be and continue in force from the passing thereof until the first Day of February which will be in the Year of our Lord one thousand seven hundred and seventy eight.

[CHAPTER 1625.]

625, of Van Schaack, where the act is printed in full. Chap-
ended to the county of Albany.]

An Act for the Relief of the Poor in the County of Albany.

[Passed, March 8, 1773.]

ENACTED by his Excellency the Governor the Council General Assembly and it is hereby enacted by the Au- f the same, That the Act entitled "An Act for the Re- the Poor in the Counties of Ulster and Orange and to the Freeholders and Inhabitants of the several Towns ecincts thereof to elect Overseers of the Poor at their l Meetings," passed the thirty first Day of December usand seven hundred and sixty eight; shall be and is extended to every District in the City and County ...any, any Law, Usage or Custom to the contrary thereof notwithstanding. PROVIDED ALWAYS That Nothing in the said Act shall be construed to abridge or diminish the Rights and Privileges of the Corporations of the Reformed Protestant Dutch Churches in the City of Albany and of the Township of Schenectady.

[CHAPTER 1626.]

[Chapter 1626, of Van Schaack, where the act is printed in full. See chapter 1339.]

An Act to revive an Act entitled. "An Act "to prevent the Destruction of Deer by Blood "Hounds or Beagles in the Counties of Albany "Ulster and Orange."

[Passed, March 8, 1773.]

WHEREAS the Act entitled, "An Act to prevent the De- "struction of Deer by Blood-Hounds or Beagles in the Counties "of Albany Ulster and Orange", passed in the eighth Year of his present Majesty's Reign, expired by it's own Limitation on the first Day of January last, and the same having been a beneficial Law.

BE IT THEREFORE ENACTED by his Excellency the Governor the Council and the General Assembly. and it is hereby enacted by the Authority of the same, That the said Act entitled, "An Act to prevent the Destruction of Deer by Blood-

"Hounds or Beagles in the Counties of Albany, Ulster and "Orange," shall be and hereby is revived, and every Article Matter and Clause therein contained enacted to be and continue in full force from the passing hereof until the first Day of February which will be in the Year of our Lord one thousand seven hundred and eighty five.

[CHAPTER 1627.]

[Chapter 1627, of Van Schaack, where the act is printed in full. See chapter 1534 and chapter 1552.]

An Act to run out the Lines of Division between the Counties of Albany, Tryon and Charlotte, and also the Lines of the several Districts in the said Counties of Albany and Tryon.

[Passed, March 8, 1773.]

WHEREAS it is necessary that the Lines between the Counties of Albany Tryon and Charlotte, as they are ascertained by an Act passed the twelfth Day of March one thousand seven hundred and seventy two, entitled, "An Act to divide the County "of Albany into three Counties," should be run out and marked.

BE IT THEREFORE ENACTED by his Excellency the Governor the Council and the General Assembly, and it is hereby enacted by the Authority of the same, That the Judges of the Inferior Court of Common Pleas for the Time being of the Counties of Albany, Tryon and Charlotte respectively, or the major Part of any five of them shall and are hereby required to meet on the first Tuesday in May next after the passing of this Act at the House of Thomas Clinch, Vintner at Schenectady in the County of Albany, and being so met shall by majority of Voices appoint one or more Surveyors with Chain Bearers and such other Assistants as they shall deem necessary to run out and mark the said Lines, and such Surveyor or Surveyors shall run the said Lines as they are directed to be run in and by the last before recited Act, and the Expence arising by such Survey shall be equally born by the said Counties in their just proportion, of which the said Surveyor or Surveyors shall keep an exact Account and the said Judges shall certify to the Supervisors of their respective Counties the Amount of such Expence, and the supervisors of the said Counties respectively are hereby required to raise levy and cause the same to be collected in like Manner as the usual Charges of their Counties respectively are raised levied and collected, and the Sum so collected shall by the several Collectors thereof be paid, and they are hereby required to pay the same into the Treasury of their respective Counties to be by the Treasurers respectively paid unto such persons as shall by the said Judges or a Majority of any five of them be authorized to receive the same.

AND WHEREAS it is also necessary that the Lines which divide the several Districts in the said Counties of Albany and Tryon should be run out and Marked, BE IT THEREFORE ALSO ENACTED by the same Authority That it shall and may be lawful to and for the Supervisors or the major Part of them, of the said Counties respectively and they are hereby directed and required at their respective Meetings next after the passing of this Act to appoint one or more Surveyors with Chain Bearers, and such other Assistants as may be necessary to run out and Mark the said Lines as they are described by an Act of this Colony passed the twenty fourth Day of March one thousand seven hundred and seventy two, entitled, "An Act to divide "the Counties of Albany and Tryon into Districts," and the Expences accruing thereby to raise levy and cause to be collected of and from the Inhabitants of the said Counties respectively, in like Manner as the other Charges of the said Counties are usually raised, and the Sum so collected shall by the several Collectors thereof be paid, and they are hereby required to pay the same into the Treasury of their respective Counties to be by the Treasurers respectively paid unto such Persons as shall by the Supervisors or a Majority of them, be authorized to receive the same.

[CHAPTER 1628.]

[Chapter 1628, of Van Schaack, where the act is printed in full. See chapter 1552.]

An Act to change the Names of certain Districts in the County of Tryon and to alter the Bounds of others in the County of Albany.

[Passed, March 8, 1773.]

WHEREAS by an Act passed on the twenty fourth Day of March one thousand seven hundred and seventy two, entitled. "An Act to divide the Counties of Albany and Tryon into Dis-"tricts," certain Districts therein described were to be thenceforth called and known by the Names of Stone-Arabia German-Flatts, and Kingsland Districts, and it being thought expedient, that the Names of the said Districts should be altered.

BE IT THEREFORE ENACTED by his Excellency the Governor the Council and the General Assembly, and it is hereby enacted by the Authority of the same, That Stone Arabia District as the same is described in the said Act shall henceforth be called and known by the Name of Palatine District; And that the German Flatts District as the same is described in the said Act shall henceforth be called and known by the Name of Kingsland District, and that Kingsland District as the same is described in the said Act shall henceforth be called and known by the Name of the German Flatts District, any Thing in the said Act to the contrary hereof notwithstanding.

AND WHEREAS the Bounds of the united District of Duanesburgh and Scholiarie as it is described in the said Act are found to be inconvenient, BE IT THEREFORE ENACTED by the Authority aforesaid, That the united Districts of Duanesburgh and Schoharie shall henceforth be bounded as follows to wit, Beginning at the South West Corner of Schenectady District, thence along the North Bounds of Renselaerwyck District to the North West Corner thereof, thence along the West Bounds thereof, so far as to meet an East Line drawn from the North East Corner of the Township of Blenheim, thence West along the last mentioned Line and the North Bounds of the said Township to the West Bounds of the County of Albany, thence along the West Bounds of the said County to Schenectady District, thence along the West Bounds of the same to the place of beginning aforesaid, any Thing in the said Act to the contrary hereof notwithstanding.

[CHAPTER 1629.]

[Chapter 1629, of Van Schaack, where the act is printed in full. See chapters 26 and 1716.]

An Act respecting Fairs in the Counties of Albany, Cumberland and Tryon.

[Passed, March 8, 1773.]

WHEREAS the seventh Clause of an Act entitled, "An Act "for settling Fairs and Markets in each respective City and "County throughout the Province," passed the eleventh Day of November one thousand six hundred and ninety two, enacts "That there be held in the City and County of Albany two Fairs "Yearly; the first Fair to be kept at Albany and to commence "the third Tuesday of July, and to end on the Friday then next "following, being in all four Days inclusive and no longer; the "second Fair to be held at Crawlier in Ranselaerwyck on the

"third Tuesday in October, and to end on the Friday following "being in all four Days inclusive and no longer," AND WHEREAS it would be beneficial to the Inhabitants of the said County, if more Fairs were established within the same: AND WHEREAS it would also be beneficial to the Inhabitants of the Counties of Cumberland and Tryon if Fairs were established therein.

BE IT THEREFORE ENACTED by his Excellency the Governor the Council and the General Assembly, and it is hereby enacted by the Authority of the same, That there be held and kept two Fairs in every Year in the Town of Schenectady, the first to commence on the first Tuesday in June annually and to continue unto the Evening of the Thursday next ensuing and no longer, and the second Fair to commence on the second Tuesday in November annually, and to continue unto the Evening of the Thursday next ensuing and no longer; And that there be also held and kept two other Fairs in every Year at Still Water in the said County, the first to commence on the first Tuesday in May annually, and to continue to the Evening of the Thursday next ensuing and no longer, and the second Fair to commence on the first Tuesday in November annually and to continue to the Evening of the Thursday next succeeding and no longer and that there be also held and kept two Fairs in every Year at the Township of Westminister in the said County of Cumberland, the first of the said Fairs to commence on the first Wednesday in June annually, and to continue until the Evening of the Friday next ensuing and no longer; and the second of the said Fairs to commence on the first Wednesday in September annually, and to continue until the Evening of the Friday next ensuing and no longer. AND that there be also held and kept two ffairs in every Year at the Town of Johnstown in the said County of Tryon; the first of the said Fairs to commence on the second Tuesday in June annually, and to continue until the Evening of the Thursday next ensuing and no longer, and the second of the said Fairs to commence on the second Tuesday in November annually, and to continue until the Evening of the Thursday next Succeeding and no longer: and that the same Fairs be held and kept as in and by the tenth Clause of the said Act is directed, and that Governors and Rulers of the said Fairs be appointed, as in and by the eleventh Clause of the said Act is directed; and such Governors or Rulers so appointed, shall and are hereby required to conduct themselves in the execution of their Office as by the twelfth Clause in the said Act is directed, any Law Usage or Custom to the contrary hereof notwithstanding.

AND BE IT ALSO ENACTED by the same Authority That the Fair at Crawlier in Ranselaerwyck shall henceforth be kept on the Tuesday next after the Tenth day of November annually, and continue to the Evening of the Saturday next ensuing, any Thing in the said Act to the contrary hereof notwithstanding.

[CHAPTER 1630.]

[Chapter 1630, of Van Schaack, where the title only is printed.]

An Act for raising the further Sum of two hundred and fifty Pounds in the County of Cumberland towards finishing the Court-House and Goal already erected in the said County.

[Passed, March 8, 1773.]

WHEREAS the Court House and Goal in the County of Cumberland are insufficient for holding of Courts and secyring of Prisoners.

BE IT THEREFORE ENACTED by his Excellency the Governor the Council and the General Assembly, and it is hereby enacted by the Authority of the same, That it shall and may be lawful to and for the Supervisors of the said County, or the major Part of them, and they are hereby directed and required to raise levy and collect upon and from the Freeholders and Inhabitants of the said County the sum of two hundred and fifty Pounds, with the additional Sum of three pence for every Pound for collecting the same: one hundred and twenty five Pounds of which said two hundred and fifty Pounds shall be raised in the first Tax that shall be levied after the passing of this Act, and the Remainder thereof with the second Tax; to be applied towards the finishing the Building of the Court House and Goal already erected in and for the said County, and that the same shall be raised levied and Collected in the same Manner as the necessary and contingent Charges of other Counties of this Colony are by Law directed to be raised and levied.

AND BE IT FURTHER ENACTED by the Authority aforesaid, That the Monies so to be raised by virtue of this Act, shall from Time to Time be paid by the several and respective Collectors of the said County unto Ephraim Ranny Esquire, John Norton and Benjamin Burt, who are hereby appointed Trustees to superintend the building of the said Court House and Goal and for laying out the said Sum of two hundred and fifty Pounds for the purpose aforesaid, and the said Trustees or the majority of them shall and may from Time to Time inspect examine and Audit all the several and respective accounts for Workmanship and Materials to be employed for and towards making and finishing the Court House and Goal before mentioned, and of the due Disposition of the said Sum of two hundred and fifty Pounds, or so much thereof as shall come into their Hands, they the said Trustees appointed as aforesaid shall render a true Account thereof upon Oath unto the Judges of the said County at the Court of General Sessions of the Peace in and for the same County.

[CHAPTER 1631.]

[Chapter 1631, of Van Schaack, where the act is printed in full.]

An Act for fixing the Allowance to the Representatives of the Counties of Tryon and Cumberland.

[Passed, March 8, 1773.]

WHEREAS the Representatives of the people of the Counties of Tryon and Cumberland cannot officiate and discharge that honorable Trust reposed in them without being at great Charge and Expence.

BE IT THEREFORE ENACTED by his Excellency the Governor the Council and the General Assembly, and it is hereby enacted by the Authority of the same, That the Allowance of each Representative in General Assembly of the said Counties of Tryon and Cumberland shall from the first Day of this Sessions and forever hereafter be twelve Shillings Current Money of this Province for every Day from their attending their Duty in any Session of General Assembly, until their leaving the same together with the further Allowance of ten Days to each for coming to the said General Assembly and as many for returning therefrom to their respective Counties.

AND BE IT FURTHER ENACTED by the Authority aforesaid, That each of the said Counties shall bear and defray the Charge of their own Representatives, which Charge or Allowance as aforesaid shall be paid to the respective Representatives by the Treasurer of each respective County by Warrant from the Supervisors or the Major Part of them to the Treasurer of the respective Counties after the Return of the said Representatives from the General Assembly: which said Charge or Allowance shall be assessed and collected as the other Necessary and Contingent Charges of the respective Counties are assessed and collected, and shall be paid within ten Days after the collecting of the same.

[CHAPTER 1632.]

[Chapter 1632, of Van Schaack, where the act is printed in full.]

An Act to extend an Act entitled "An "Act to prevent Damages by Swine in Dutchess "County", to the Counties of Tryon and Cumberland.

[Passed, March 8, 1773.]

WHEREAS the Act to prevent Damages by Swine in Dutchess County, has by long Experience been found highly beneficial to the Freeholders and Inhabitants thereof, and may be productive of much advantage if extended to the Counties of Tryon and Cumberland.

BE IT THEREFORE ENACTED by his Excellency the Governor the Council and the General Assembly, and it is hereby enacted by the Authority of the same, That a certain Act of the Legislature of this Colony, passed the twenty ninth Day of November one thousand seven hundred and forty five entitled. "An Act to prevent Damages by Swine in Dutchess County," and continued by several subsequent Acts until the first Day of January which will be in the Year of our Lord one thousand seven hundred and seventy five, shall be and hereby is extended to the Counties of Tryon and Cumberland to all Intents Constructions and purposes whatsoever, any Thing in the said Act to the contrary notwithstanding.

[CHAPTER 1633.]

[Chapter 1633, of Van Schaack, where the act is printed in full. See chapter 1532.]

An Act for establishing and regulating Ferries in the County of Tryon.

[Passed, March 8, 1773.]

WHEREAS there are at present no established Ferries within the County of Tryon; and the same being much wanted therein for the Ease and Convenience of it's Inhabitants

BE IT THEREFORE ENACTED by his Excellency the Governor the Council and the General Assembly, and it is hereby enacted by the Authority of the same, That the Judges and Assistant Justices of the Inferior Court of Common Pleas for the said County shall have full power and Authority at the first Court for said County to be held after the first Day of June next to appoint and settle Ferries along the Mohock River, wheresoever the same shall appear necessary for the Ease and Convenience of the said Inhabitants, and to fix and ascertain the Ferriage for Travellers, and their Effects who shall pass the said Ferries or any of them respectively. Provided the Number of Ferries so established do not in the whole exceed eight, and to alter or discontinue any of them, at their Quarter Sessions, as they may be found improper or useless.

AND BE IT FURTHER ENACTED by the same Authority. That if any Person or Persons not impowered as afore directed, to keep a Ferry, shall presume to keep any Ferry, or to transport any Person or Persons, or their Effects for pay, over the said River, such person or persons so presuming to keep Ferry, or transporting any Person or Persons, or their Effects as aforesaid, shall forfeit and pay the Sum of twenty Shillings for every such Offence to the nearest Ferryman, to be recovered upon Proof thereof before any Justice of the Peace in said County.

AND BE IT FURTHER ENACTED by the same Authority That all such person or persons who shall hereafter undertake to keep a Ferry or Ferries by Appointment of the said Judges and Justices under this Act, and do not provide good and sufficient Boats or other proper Craft and keep the same in good repair and well and sufficiently attended for the passage of all Travellers and their Effects, or shall demand or receive more Ferriage from any Person or Persons than shall be directed as aforesaid, shall forfeit and pay the Sum of five Pounds for every such Neglect or Extortion; one half of which Sum to go to the Informer, and the other half towards lessening the County Tax, to be recovered on due proof, in the Manner directed in and by a certain Act of the Legislature of this Colony entitled, "An Act to impower Justices of the Peace, Mayors, Recorders, "and Aldermen to try Causes to the value of five Pounds and "under and for suspending an Act therein mentioned."

AND BE IT FURTHER ENACTED by the Authority aforesaid That this Act shall be and continue in force until the first Day of February which will be in the Year of our Lord one thousand seven hundred and seventy six and no longer.

[CHAPTER 1634.]

[Chapter 1634, of Van Schaack, where the act is printed in full. See chapter 1551.]

An Act to extend an Act entitled, "An Act "for laying out and regulating and keeping in "repair common and public Highways in the "County of Cumberland," to the County of Gloucester.

[Passed, March 8, 1773.]

BE IT ENACTED by his Excellency the Governor the Council and the General Assembly, and it is hereby enacted by the Authority of the same, That the Act entitled, "An Act for laying "out regulating and keeping in repair common and public High-"ways in the County of Cumberland," passed the twenty sixth Day of February one thousand seven hundred and seventy two, shall be and hereby is extended to the County of Gloucester, any Thing in the said Act to the contrary hereof notwithstanding.

[CHAPTER 1635.]

[Chapter 1635, of Van Schaack, where the act is printed in full. See chapter 1530.]

An Act to amend an Act entitled "An Act "for regulating Inns and Taverns in the County "of Cumberland," and to extend the same to the County of Gloucester.

[Passed, March 8, 1773.]

BE IT ENACTED by his Excellency the Governor the Council and the General Assembly, and it is hereby enacted by the Authority of the same, That no Person or Persons within the said County shall sell by retail any Rum Brandy Wine or Spirits of any kind, under the Quantity of five Gallons except thereunto licenced as in the said Act entitled, "An Act for regulating "Inns and Taverns in the County of Cumberland", passed the twenty sixth Day of February one thousand seven hundred and seventy two, is directed, on pain of incurring the Forfeiture in the said Act mentioned to be recovered in the Manner and to be applied to the uses in the said Act directed.

AND BE IT FURTHER ENACTED by the Authority aforesaid, That no person who hath, or shall obtain Licence to retail

Strong Liquors in the said County, shall sell any mixt Liquors directly or indirectly on pain of forfeiting the Sum of twenty Shillings Current Money of this Colony for every Offence to be recovered in the like Manner and to be applied to the like uses as the Forfeiture of twenty Shillings is in the said Act hereby amended expressed and directed.

AND BE IT FURTHER ENACTED by the Authority aforesaid That the Judges of the Inferior Court of Common Pleas for the said County of Cumberland shall be and hereby are authorized and impowered to grant Licences at the Court of General Sessions of the Peace in and for the said County to such persons as they shall think proper to sell and retail Strong Liquors within the said County in the Manner directed by the said Act, any Thing in the said Act, or any other Act of this Colony to the contrary hereof notwithstanding.

AND BE IT FURTHER ENACTED by the Authority aforesaid That the said Act entitled, "An Act for regulating Inns and "Taverns in the County of Cumberland," as the same is amended by this present Act, shall be and hereby is extended to the County of Gloucester, any Thing in the said Act to the contrary hereof notwithstanding.

[CHAPTER 1636.]

[Chapter 1636, of Van Schaack, where the title only is printed.]

An Act for the Relief of Insolvent Debtors within this Colony.

[Passed, March 8, 1773.]

BE IT ENACTED by his Excellency the Governor the Council and the General Assembly and it is hereby enacted by the Authority of the same, That John Clandenning, Nathaniel Peck, James Dunscomb, John Dalley Junior, Matthias Compton, Stephen Seaman, William Miller, John Borrowe, Thomas Carmer, Anthony Fowler, John O Farrel, Peter Harris, Henry Webb, Amos Dickenson, Jacobus C. Swarthout, Jeremiah Bakehorn, Joseph Thorn, Luke Noorstrant, Peter Noorstrant, William Schutt Junior, John Nicholas Hinneke, James Cable, Gale Yelverton, John Foster, Peter Nefies, Samuel Simmons, Joseph Higgins John Way and James Seaman, Insolvent Debtors in this Colony shall and may, and are hereby allowed to take the Benefit of the several Acts continued by an Act entitled, "An Act "to continue the several Acts therein mentioned respecting the

"Relief of Insolvent Debtors", passed the nineteenth Day of December, one thousand seven hundred and sixty six, and which are expired by their own Limitation as fully and effectually as if the said Acts respecting the Relief of Insolvent Debtors were now in actual and full force.

AND WHEREAS the aforenamed Nathaniel Peck stands indebted in a considerable Sum to the Estate of Abraham De-Peyster Esquire deceased late Treasurer of this Colony; and it is thought that it will be most to the Interest of the Colony for the Trustees of said Estate to compound for and accept of a Dividend of the Debts so due with the other Creditors of the said Nathaniel Peck. BE IT THEREFORE ENACTED by the same Authority, that it shall and may be lawful to and for the said Trustees or the major Part of them, or the major Part of the survivors of them to join in a Petition with the said Nathaniel Peck, and with his other Creditors in order to his obtaining the Benefit of the said Acts, and the said Trustees shall not be held to swear or attest to the Debt due to them as Trustees as aforesaid, from the said Nathaniel Peck, but having ascertained the same in the best Manner they are able, their subscription of the said Petition shall be as effectual without any further attestation as if the said Trustees had taken the Oath or Oaths prescribed by the said Act or Acts; any Thing herein or in the said Act or Acts before mentioned contained to the contrary thereof in any wise notwithstanding.

PROVIDED ALWAYS, That Nothing in this Act shall extend, or be construed to extend to the Discharge of any of the said Debtors, if he shall stand chargeable at the suit of the Crown, or to affect any Creditors residing in Great Britain.

[CHAPTER 1637.]

[Chapter 1637, of Van Schaack, where the title only is printed.]

An Act for the Relief of Insolvent Debtors within this Colony with respect to the Imprisonment of their Persons.

[Passed, March 8, 1773.]

WHEREAS it has been represented to the General Assembly that the several Persons herein after mentioned imprisoned in different Goals in this Colony are destitute even of the Common Necessaries of Life, & it is conceived reasonable if their Creditors will not consent to their Enlargement or contribute to their

Subsistance, that such Persons should be relieved by the Legislature. To this End.

BE IT ENACTED by his Excellency the Governor the Council and the General Assembly, and it is hereby enacted by the Authority of the same. That such of the Creditors of the following Persons. Vizt: David Still, William Kennedy, Henry Dawkins, Benjamin Willet, Alexander McDonald, Benjamin Dassigny, James Shaw, Francis Humbert De LaRoche, Henry Kilgrow, Thomas Stilwell, William Valentine, Thomas Barry, Daniel McInley, Isaac Bratt, John Hiscock, and George Ellis all confined in the Goal of the City and County of New York; Cornelius Balsom, Abraham Onderdonck and Samuel Ferguson confined in Orange County Goal, Zebulon Scoffield, confined in Ulster County Goal, Gilbert Willet, confined in the Goal of the Borough Town of West Chester, Jacob Simderer, Adam Smith, Hendrick Klauw, Daniel Pierce, Hugh Mulloy, Cornelius Malone, Owen Daly, Petrus Egbertson, Christopher Haak, Benedict or Benedictus Falkenier, confined in Albany County Goal, Jeremiah Bennet confined in King's County Goal, Isaiah Ismond, William Tompkins, Paul Davison, Gerardus Lewis, Daniel Seaman, Hendrick Ackart, John Calkin, Christian Sachrider, Thomas Freer, John Vandervoort, John Van Vleckere, Isaac Bull and Simon Newcomb confined in Dutchess County Goal, who shall insist upon such their Debtors being detained under their respective Confinements, shall within one Month after the publication of such Advertisements as are herein after directed agree by writing under their Hands to pay and allow three shillings and six pence per Week, unto the said Prisoners respectively, to be paid the Monday of every Week so long as he shall continue in prison at his her or their Instance, and if such Agreement as aforesaid shall not be entered into, or if entered into, not punctually complied with and on Failure of the payment of such Weekly sum at any Time, such of the said Prisoners whose Creditor or Creditors shall not enter into such Agreement or shall fail complying with it as aforesaid, shall be entitled to the Benefit of this Act, upon complying with the Terms and Conditions herein after imposed.

AND BE IT FURTHER ENACTED by the Authority aforesaid, That it shall and may be lawful for each and every of them the said David Still, William Kennedy, Henry Dawkins, Benjamin Willet, Alexander Mc Donald, Benjamin Dassigny, James Shaw, Francis Humbert De LaRoche, Henry Kilgrow,

Thomas Stilwell, William Valentine, Thomas Barry, Daniel McInley, Isaac Bratt, John Hiscock, George Ellis, Cornelius Balsom, Abraham Onderdonck, Samuel Ferguson, Zebulon Scofield, Gilbert Willet, Jacob Simderer, Adam Smith, Hendrick Klauw, Daniel Pierce, Hugh Mulloy, Cornelius Malone, Owen Daly, Petrus Egbertson, Christopher Haak, Benedict or Benedictus Falkenier, Jeremiah Bennet, Isaiah Ismond, William Tompkins, Paul Davison, Gerardus Lewis, Daniel Seaman, Hendrick Ackart, John Calkin, Christian Sachrider, Thomas Freer, John VanderVoort, John Van Vleckere, Isaac Bull and Isaac Newcomb, to present a Petition to the Court, out of which any process against them respectively hath issued, and upon which they are imprisoned, or to any two of the Judges of such Court certifying the Cause or Causes of his Imprisonment, and exhibiting an Account and Inventory of his whole real and personal Estate, and of the securities relating to the same, which Petition with the said Account and Inventory, shall be lodged with the Clerk of the said Court, for the inspection of the Creditors, and after such Petition presented, and Account and Inventory filed, such Prisoners shall respectively publish Advertisements in one or more of the Public Newspapers of this Colony, notifying their Creditors that they Intend to apply to the said Court, or to any two of the Judges thereof, at a certain Day, not less than four Weeks from the Publication of such Advertisements respectively, to be discharged according to the prayer of his or their said Petition, at which Day the said Court, or the said two Judges may and are hereby required by precept under their Hands and Seals directed to the Sheriff, Goaler, or Officer in whose Custody such Prisoner or Prisoners may be, to order the said Prisoner or Prisoners respectively to be brought up before such Court, or such Judges and if such Provision as is aforesaid, hath not been made for the subsistance of the said Prisoner or Prisoners by his or their Creditors respectively, the said Court or Judges may then respectively administer the following Oath or Affirmation to wit. "I A. B. do solemnly Swear or Affirm, That the "Account by me now delivered is a just and true Account of "all my Creditors, and the Monies owing to them respectively "by me, to the best of my knowledge and remembrance: And "that the Inventory and Account now delivered by me, is a "just and true Account of all my Estate real and personal, "both in Law and Equity, either in possession, Reversion or

"Remainder (the Necessary wearing Apparel of myself my wife "and Children, and Family immediately under my Care ex- "cepted), and I have not directly or indirectly, sold, leased, "assigned or otherwise disposed of or made over, either in Trust "for myself or otherwise, except as set forth in the same Ac- "count any part of my Estate real or personal for my future "Benefit, or in order to defraud my Creditors, and that none of "my Creditors reside in Great Britain so help me God," which Oath or Affirmation being taken if the Truth thereof shall be denied or controverted by any of the Creditors, the said Court or Judges may appoint some further Day for hearing the Parties, as well Debtors as Creditors, and upon such further Hearing, may in their Discretion, either remand the said Debtors, or proceed to their Discharge as if no such further Hearing had been required; But if the said Oath or Affirmation, shall not be controverted or denied, then the said Court or Judges may immediately order the Lands Goods and Effects contained in such Account and Inventory to be by a short Indorsement on the Back of such Petition executed by the Prisoner assigned to the said Creditors or to one or more of them, or to some other Person or Persons to be appointed by the said Court or Judges respectively in Trust for all the Creditors, and also for all Attornies, sheriffs, Goalers, and other Officers with respect to their Fees, for which they shall come in as the Creditors of the Insolvent, abating pro rata, by which Assignment such Estate shall actually vest in, and be taken in possession by the said Trustee or Trustees according to the purport of such Assignment, and shall be divided by the Assignees from Time to Time, among all the Creditors in proportion, after six Months previous Notice published in one of the public News-papers of this Colony of such Assignment, and requiring all the Creditors to send in their Demands, and if any Part thereof is in possession of any other person or persons, the same shall be recoverable in the Name or Names of such Trustee or Trustees, who are hereby fully authorized to dispose of and execute good and sufficient Deeds for the same, or any Part thereof, and to divide and distribute as well the Monies thence arising as such other Monies which shall come into their Hands by Virtue of this Act among the Creditors of the said Debtors respectively, and the Officers aforesaid to whom any Fees may be due in proportion to their respective Debts or Demands according to the true Intent and meaning of this Act, to which no Release from the Insolvent shall be any Bar; And immediately upon such Assignment being made, and the Effects of the Insolvent delivered to the said Trustee or Trustees, the said Prisoner or Prisoners, shall by order of the said Court or Judges be discharged out of Custody: and such Order shall be a sufficient Warrant to the Sheriff, Goaler, or Keeper of such Prisoner to discharge such Prisoner or Prisoners, if detained for no other Cause or Causes than those mentioned in such his or their Petition, and he is required forth with to discharge and set him or them at liberty without Fee, and upon such Discharge the said Debtors shall be finally released from all Debts contracted and all Judgments contained before that Time, and shall not be liable to be sued or arrested or to have their Lands or Tenements, Goods or Chattels seized by virtue or in Consequence thereof, and every Person who shall be convicted of wilful false swearing, in any Matter or Article contained in the said Oath, he or she shall be guilty of Felony, and suffer the Pains of Death without Benefit of Clergy.

AND BE IT FURTHER ENACTED by the Authority aforesaid, That if any of the said Debtors shall be sued for any Debts accrued before the passing of this Act, or if any Judge or other Officer shall be sued for any Thing done in pursuance and under the Authority of this Act, such Defendant may plead the general Issue, and give this Act and the special Matter in Evidence: Provided that this Act shall not extend to discharge any Person who shall stand committeed at the Suit of the Crown, and Provided also, That this Act shall not be construed to affect any Creditor or Creditors residing in Great Britain any Thing herein contained to the contrary notwithstanding.

PROVIDED ALSO, AND BE IT ENACTED by the same Authority That Nothing in this Act contained shall operate as a Discharge to the aforenamed Gilbert Willet from any Debts Legacies or Demands due from him to any Person or Persons as Executor or one of the Executors of the last Will and Testament of his Father Thomas Willet deceased, any Thing herein contained to the contrary there of in any wise notwithstanding.

[CHAPTER 1638.]

[Chapter 1638, of Van Schaack, where the act is printed in full.]

An Act for naturalizing the several Persons therein named.

[Passed, March 8, 1773.]

WHEREAS Michael Kleyne, John Fretcher, Michael Stoller, Michael Warner, Henry Haan, Jacob Waggoner, Christian

Schorer, Michael Witherick, Johannes Kelthsh, Christian Hoffsteder, Honnicol Rhyne, Matthias Clemens, Philip Clemens, William Bender, George Shiff, George Brown, Lawrence Ringle, Jost Kough, George Sneck Junior, George Witherick, Theobald Bacher, Philip Bellanger, George Ough, Faltin Miller, Baltus Breitenbeger, George Bower, John George Groundhart, John Rhyma, Nicholas Keller, Peter Multer, John Kellar Junior, Johannes Wolf, Jacob Myer, Hendrick Schafer, John Leuz, Christopher Stuble, Jacob Tynges, Adam Hartman, Jacob Byrkey, Jacob Byrkey Junior, Peter Byrkey, Peter Gardner, Arnold Steinwas, Johannes Kleyne, Johannes Munderbach, Fredrick Ayrer, John Eisenlord, Julius Bush, Simon Bydeman, Philip William Stuart, Andreas Heintz, John Conradt Smith, John Forneyee, Jacob Moore, William Goodbrode, Jacob Walter, Francis Fry, Jacob Myer, Peter Whitmore, George Kough, John Kough, Michael Kermer Junior, Jacob Sheets, Jacob Merkley, Christian Hill, Hendrick Hagner, John Siemon, Philip Cool, Leonard Kratzer, Adam Bengle, Coenradt Hoining, Philip Smith, Henry Smith, John Ronlaff, Samuel Millur, Jacob Flander, Johan Soll, Johan Jost Volz, Johan Daniel Gros, Adam Dumm, Nicholas Dumm, Melicher Dumm, Henry Becker, Jacob Joran, Peter Eigebrode, Johan Smith, John Hortigh, Jacob Duslar, Christian Graf, Henry Herring, George Bartholemew Jean Haumaid and John Fisher, have by their Petitions presented to the General Assembly desired that they may be naturalized and become his Majesty's liege Subjects within this Colony.

BE IT THEREFORE ENACTED by his Excellency the Governor the Council and the General Assembly, and it is hereby enacted by the Authority of the same, That the beforenamed Michael Kleyne, John Fretcher, Michael Stoller, Michael Warner, Henry Haan Jacob Waggoner, Christian Schorer, Michael Witherick, Johannes Kelthsh, Christian Hofsteder, Honnicol Rhyne, Matthias Clemens, Philip Clemens, William Bender, George Shiff, George Brown, Lawrence Ringle, Jost Kough, George Sneck Junior, George Witherick, Theobald Bacher, Philip Bellanger, George Ough, Faltin Miller, Baltus Breitenbeger, George Bower, John George Groundhart, John Rhyma, Nicholas Keller, Peter Multer, John Kellar Junior, Johannes Wolf, Jacob Myer, Hendrick Shafer, John Leuz, Christopher Stuble, Jacob Tynges, Adam Hartman, Jacob Byrkey, Jacob Byrkey Junior, Peter Byrkey, Peter Hardner, Arnold Steinwas, Johannes Kleyne, Johannes Munderbach, Fredrick Ayrer, John Eisenlord, Julius

Bush, Simon Bydeman, Philip William Stuart, Andreas Heintz, John Conradt Smith, John Forneyee, Jacob Moore, William Goodbrode, Jacob Walter Francis Fry, Jacob Myer, Peter Whitmore, George Kough, John Kough, Michael Kermer Junior, Jacob Sheets, Jacob Merkley, Christian Hill, Hendrich Hagner, John Siemon, Philip Cool, Leonard Kratzer, Adam Bengle, Coenradt Hoining, Philip Smith, Henry Smith, John Ronlaff, Samuel Millur, Jacob Flander, Johan Soll, Johan Jost Volz, Johan Daniel Gros, Adam Dum, Nicholas Dum, Melicher Dum, Henry Becker, Jacob Joran, Peter Eigebrode, Johan Smith, John Hortigh, Jacob Duslar, Christian Graf, Henry Herring, George Bartholemew, Jean Haumaid and John Fisher, and each and every of them shall be and are hereby declared to be naturalized to all Intents, Constructions and purposes whatsoever, and from henceforth and at all Times hereafter shall be entitled to, have, and enjoy all the Rights, Liberties, Privileges and Advantages which his Majesty's natural born subjects in this Colony have and enjoy, or to have and enjoy, as fully to all Intents and purposes whatsoever as if all and every of them had been born within this Colony.

PROVIDED ALWAYS and it is hereby further Enacted by the Authority aforesaid, That each of the abovenamed persons, shall take the Oaths appointed by Law instead of the Oaths of Allegiance and Supremacy, subscribe the Test, and make, repeat, swear to, and subscribe the Abjuration Oath, in any of his Majesty's Courts of Record within this Colony, which Oaths, the said Courts are hereby required upon Application to them made, to administer, take the Subscriptions, and cause the Names of the Persons so swearing and subscribing to be entered upon Record in the said Courts, and the said beforementioned persons are hereby each of them required to pay the several Sums hereafter mentioned, that is to say. To the Speaker of the General Assembly the Sum of ten Shillings, to the Judge of such Court the Sum of six Shillings, and to the Clerk of such Court the Sum of three Shillings.

AND BE IT FURTHER ENACTED by the Authority aforesaid, That if the said persons or any of them having so sworn and subscribed as aforesaid shall demand a Certificate of his or their being entered upon Record in the manner before directed, the Court or Courts in which such Oaths and Subscriptions shall be made, are hereby directed and required to grant such under the Hand of the Judge and seal of the said Court or

Courts, in which such Oaths and subscriptions as aforesaid shall be made, countersigned by the Clerk of the said Courts, for which Certificate each of them shall pay over and above the Sums abovementioned the Sum of six Shillings, one half to the Judges of such Court or Courts, and the other half to the Clerk thereof, which Certificate or Certificates shall be at all Times to the person or persons therein named a sufficient proof of his or their being naturalized by virtue of this Act, in as full and effectual a Manner as if the Record aforesaid was actually produced by the Person or Persons so named in such Certificate.

PROVIDED ALSO and be it Enacted by the Authority aforesaid, That such of the Persons hereby naturalized as shall not take the Oath Test and Abjuration and pay the Fees in Manner herein before directed within twelve Months next after the passing hereof shall have no manner of Benefit by this Act, any Thing herein contained to the contrary notwithstanding.

AND BE IT ENACTED by the same Authority, That the Public Printer of this Colony, shall and hereby is directed and required to print this Act as if the same was a public Law of this Colony.

THIRTY-FIRST ASSEMBLY.

Sixth Session.

(Begun Jan. 6, 1774, 14 George III, William Tryon, Governor.)

[CHAPTER 1639.]

[See chapter 948, continued by chapter 1691.]

An Act further to continue an Act entitled, "An Act for granting to his Majesty the Several Duties and Impositions on Goods Wares and Merchandizes imported into this Colony therein Mentioned."

[Passed, February 8, 1774.]

WHEREAS the several Duties and Impositions on Goods Wares and Merchandizes imported into this Colony and granted for the support of the Government of his late Majesty King George the Second by the abovementioned Act, have by several subsequent Acts been continued to the first Day of February one thousand seven hundred and seventy four, and the General Assembly being willing to make Provision for the further support of his Majesty's Government.

Be it therefore Enacted by his Excellency the Governor, the Council and the General Assembly and it is hereby enacted by the Authority of the same That the abovementioned Act, entitled, "An Act for granting to his Majesty the several Duties and Impositions on Goods Wares and Merchandizes imported into this Colony therein mentioned," passed in the twenty seventh Year of his late Majesty's Reign, shall be and is hereby continued and every Clause Matter and Thing therein contained, enacted to be and remain in full force, to all Intents, Constructions and Purposes whatsoever until the first Day of February which will be in the Year of our Lord one thousand seven hundred and seventy five inclusive; and that Nicoll Havens of Shelter Island in Suffolk County, be the Officer appointed to collect the Colony Duties in the said County in the abovementioned Act.

Provided always, That so much of the first Clause or Section of said Act, as relates to European or East India Goods imported from the British Islands into this Colony, shall be construed, taken and deemed to be from the British Islands in America only, any Thing in the said Act to the contrary hereof notwithstanding.

[CHAPTER 1640.]

An Act to enable posthumous Children to take Estates as if born in their Father's Lifetime.

[Passed, February 8, 1774.]

WHEREAS it often happens that by marriage and other Settlements, Estates are limited in remainder to the Use of the Sons and Daughters the Issue of such marriage, with Remainder over without limiting an Estate to Trustees to preserve the contingent Remainders limited to such Sons and Daughters, by which means such Sons and Daughters, if they happen to be born after the Decease of their Father, are in Danger to be defeated of their Remainder, by the next in Remainder after them, and left unprovided for by such Settlements, contrary to the Intent of the Parties that made those Settlements,

Be it Enacted by his Excellency the Governor the Council and the General Assembly, and it is hereby Enacted by the Authority of the same, That where any Estate already is, or shall hereafter by any marriage or other Settlement be limited in remainder to, or to the use of the first or other Son or Sons of the Body of any Person lawfully begotten, with any Remainder or

Remainders over to, or to the use of any other Person or Persons; or in Remainder to, or to the use of a Daughter or Daughters lawfully begotten with any Remainder or Remainders to any other Person or Persons, that any Son or Sons, or Daughter or Daughters of such Person or Persons lawfully begotten or to be begotten, that shall be born after the Decease of his, her, or their Father, shall and may by virtue of such Settlement, take such Estate so limited to the first and other Sons, or to the Daughter or Daughters in the same Manner as if born in the Lifetime of his, her or their Father, although there shall happen no Estate to be limited to trustees after the Decease of the Father, to preserve the contingent Remainder to such afterborn Son or Sons, Daughter or Daughters, until he she or they come *in esse*, or are born, to take the same, any Law or usage to the contrary in any wise notwithstanding.

Provided always, That nothing in this Act shall extend, or be construed to extend to devest any Estate in Remainder, that by virtue of any Marriage or other Settlement is already come to the Possession of any Person or Persons, or to whom any Right is accrued though not in actual Possession by Reason or Means of any afterborn Son or Sons or Daughter or Daughters not happening to be born in the Lifetime of his, her or their Father.

[CHAPTER 1641.]

[See chapter 1598.]

An Act to appoint Commissioners for collecting the Duty of Excise on strong Liquors retailed in this Colony from the first Day of February one thousand seven hundred and seventy-four, to the first Day of February one thousand seven hundred and seventy-five inclusive.

[Passed, February 8, 1774.]

Be it Enacted by his Excellency the Governor the Council and the General Assembly, and it is hereby enacted by the Authority of the same, That the several and respective Persons and Officers herein after named, shall be and are hereby appointed Commissioners for collecting the Duty of Excise laid by an Act entitled, "An Act to lay a Duty of Excise on Strong Liquors in this Colony, and to appropriate the Money arising therefrom," passed the eighth Day of March in the Year of our Lord one thousand seven hundred and seventy-three; of and from the several Retailers of Strong Liquors within the several Cities, Counties Towns, Boroughs, Manors, Precincts and Districts, and the Harbours, Bays and Rivers thereunto adjoining or belonging in this Colony, for which they shall be respectively appointed, from the first Day of February in the Year of our Lord one thousand seven hundred and seventy-four, to the first Day of February which will be in the Year of our Lord one thousand seven hundred and seventy-five inclusive, That is to say,

For the City and County of New York Cornelius Clopper Esquire.

For the City and County of Albany, Peter Lansing, and Gysbert G. Marcelis Esquires.

For the County of Ulster Joseph Gashery and James McClagrie Esquires.

For the County of Dutchess the Supervisor, and Assessors in each Precinct respectively for the Time being.

For the County of Orange as follows, for Haverstraw Precinct, David Pye Esquire; for Orange Town John Perry Esquire; for Goshen Precinct William Ellison Esquire, and for Cornwall Precinct Daniel Coleman Esquire.

For Richmond County John Micheau and Christian Jacobson Esquires.

For Kings County, Theodorus Polhemus Esquire.

For Queens County, Benjamin Townshend and Samuel Clowes Esquires.

For Suffolk County, Colonel William Smith, and Samuel Landon and Malby Gelston Esquires.

For Tryon County, Jellis Fonda and John Frey Esquires.

For Cumberland County the Judges of the Inferior Court of Common Pleas in said county.

For the Manor of Cortlandt and Rykes Patent in the County of West Chester, Hachaliah Brown Esquire, with three or more of the Justices of the Peace residing on the said Manor, or on the said Patent.

For the Borough Town of West Chester, the Mayor thereof for the Time being.

For the Manor of Philipsburgh in the County of West Chester, William Davids, Isaac Deane, Israel Underhill and Gabriel Purdy Esquires.

And for the remaining Part of West Chester County Stephen Ward, and John Thomas Junior Esquires.

[CHAPTER 1642.]

An Act to impower the Mayor Recorder and Aldermen of the City of New York, or the major Part of them, to order the raising a sum not exceeding eighteen hundred Pounds for the uses therein mentioned.

[Passed, February 8, 1774.]

WHEREAS the providing a sufficient number of Watchmen and lighting of Lamps within the City of New York, has not only been found convenient, but also necessary for the safety of its Inhabitants and others,

Be it therefore Enacted by his Excellency the Governor, the Council, and the General Assembly, and it is hereby enacted by the Authority of the same That the Mayor Recorder and Aldermen of the City of New York for the Time being, or the major Part of them whereof the Mayor or Recorder to be one, shall have full Power and Authority, and are hereby fully impowered and authorized, on the Second Tuesday in the Month of February one thousand seven hundred and seventy-four, or within twenty Days thereafter, to order the raising a Sum not exceeding eighteen hundred Pounds, by a Tax on the Estates real and personal of all and every the Freeholders, Freemen, Inhabitants Residents and Sojourners within the City of New York on the South Side of Fresh-Water for the payment of so many Watchmen as the Mayor Aldermen and Commonalty of the City of New York shall think necessary for guarding the City, and for purchasing Oil, providing Lamps, and for repairing and attending the Lamps which now are or hereafter may be erected; which Sum of eighteen hundred pounds, shall be rated and assessed by the Vestrymen who shall rate and assess the Tax for the Minister and Poor of the said City, the Vestrymen first taking the Oath prescribed to be taken in and by an Act entitled "An Act to enable the Inhabitants of the City of New York to choose annually two Vestrymen for each respective Ward within the said City." made and passed in the nineteenth Year of the Reign of his late Majesty King George the second, and the Tax so to be laid shall be collected, levied and paid at the same Time as the Tax for the Minister and Poor of the said City hath been accustomed into the Hands of the Church Wardens of the said City for the Time being, who are hereby required and directed to pay the same into the Hands of the Chamberlain of the said City, to be by him paid as shall be directed by

Warrant or Warrants of the said Mayor Aldermen and Commonalty in Common Council convened for the Uses aforesaid.

And be it further Enacted by the Authority aforesaid, That over and above the Sum of eighteen hundred pounds to be levied and Paid by virtue of this Act, the Sum of three Pence in the Pound as a Reward to the Constables for their Trouble, shall be assessed levied and paid to the respective Constables for collecting and paying the same, and no more, according to the true Intent and Meaning of this Act, any Thing herein or in any other Act or Acts contained to the contrary hereof in any wise notwithstanding.

And be it further Enacted by the Authority aforesaid, That if the said Mayor Recorder or Aldermen, Church-Wardens, Vestrymen or Constables of the said City who are hereby authorized impowered and required to take effectual care that this Act be executed according to the true Intent and Meaning thereof, or any of them shall deny, refuse or delay to perform, execute or comply with all or any of the Powers, Authorities and Duties in this Act given and required to be done and performed by them or either of them, and thereof shall be lawfully convicted in any Court of Record in this Colony, he or they so denying refusing or delaying to perform the Duties as aforesaid shall suffer such Pains and Penalties by Fine and Imprisonment, as by the Discretion of the Court shall be adjudged.

And be it further Enacted by the Authority aforesaid, That if any Person or Persons shall wilfully break or damage any of the Lamps whether private or public, now erected or hereafter to be erected within the said City, he she or they so offending shall forfeit the Sum of twenty Pounds for every Lamp he she or they shall damage or break as aforesaid to be levied by Warrant or Warrants under the Hands and Seals of two or more of his Majesty's Justices of the Peace for the City and County of New York by Distress and Sale of the Offenders Goods and Chattels on due Conviction made upon the Oath of one or more credible Witness or Witnesses, rendering the Overplus, if any there be, to the Owner or Owners, and for want of such Distress, the Offender or Offenders shall be imprisoned by Warrant under the Hands and Seals of the said Justices, who are hereby required to issue the same, for the Space of three Months unless the said Forfeiture or Forfeitures be sooner paid, which Forfeitures shall be applied towards providing and repairing of Lamps and paying the Watchmen.

And be it further Enacted by the Authority aforesaid, That all such Persons as shall be employed to guard the City and attend the Lamps shall be under the Direction of, and obey such Orders as they shall from Time to Time receive from, the Mayor Aldermen and Commonalty of the said City, any Custom Law or Usage to the contrary thereof in any wise notwithstanding.

[CHAPTER 1643.]

[See chapter 1549. Expired, February 1, 1775.]

An Act to continue an Act entitled "An Act to prevent the Danger arising from the pernicious Practice of lodging Gunpowder in Dwelling Houses, Stores, or other Places within the City of New York, or on board of Vessels within the Harbour."

[Passed, February 8, 1774.]

Whereas the Act entitled "An Act to prevent the Danger arising from the pernicious practice of lodging Gunpowder in Dwelling Houses, Stores or other places within the City of New York, or on board of Vessels within the Harbour, passed in the twelfth Year of his present Majesty's Reign, will expire by its own limitation on the twenty fifth Day of March one thousand seven hundred and seventy four; and the same being found useful and necessary,

Be it therefore Enacted by his Excellency the Governor, the Council, and the General Assembly, and it is hereby enacted by the Authority of the same, That the said Act shall be, and is hereby continued, and every Clause, Matter and Thing therein contained, enacted to be and remain in full force to all Intents Constructions and Purposes whatsoever, until the first Day of February which will be in the Year of our Lord one thousand seven hundred and eighty five.

[CHAPTER 1644.]

An Act for the better fixing and ascertaining the Division Line between Montgomerie Ward and the Out Ward of the City of New York, on the Easterly Side of Montgomerie Ward.

[Passed, February 8, 1774.]

Whereas the Line of Division between Montgomerie Ward and the Out Ward of the City of New York on the Easterly Side of Montgomerie Ward, by the Charter granted by his late Majesty King George the second to the said City, was a Rivulet that run from Fresh Water into the East River until the said Rivulet emptied itself into the said East River, and from thence to run a South East Line four hundred Feet beyond low Water Mark into the said East River, *And Whereas* the said Rivulet has been long since filled up, and Disputes have arisen of late, about the Place where it did run; to avoid which for the future, and to fix the said Line of Division with more certainty,

Be it Enacted by his Excellency the Governor, the Council and the General Assembly, and it is hereby enacted by the Authority of the same, That from and after the passing of this Act, the Division between the said Montgomerie Ward, and the Out Ward on the Easterly Side of Montgomerie Ward, shall be a Line, Beginning at the most Northerly Corner of Montgomerie Ward, where it joins the North Ward as fixed by the abovementioned Charter, at the Place where the Rivulet formerly run from Fresh Water, now near the Tanyards, and shall run from thence to the Middle of a Street which runs Southerly along the East Side of Land belonging to George Janeway; thence through the Middle of said Street, Southerly to the Middle of the Bowry Lane, thence Easterly along the Middle of the Bowry Lane until it comes opposite to the Middle of Roosevelt Street, and from thence to run Southerly through the Middle of Roosevelt street until it comes to the Middle of Rutgers Street, and from thence to run Easterly through the Middle of Rutgers Street until it comes to the Middle of Saint James's Street, and from thence to run through the Middle of Saint James's Street, South Six Degrees East as the Magnetic Needle now points, so far into the East River as the Corporation of the City of New York have, or may have Right to the Soil under Water; And the Westerly Side of said Line shall be deemed and taken to be Montgomerie Ward, and the Easterly Side thereof shall be deemed and taken to be the Out Ward, any Law or Usage to the contrary thereof in any wise notwithstanding.

[CHAPTER 1645.]

An Act to enable the Mayor Recorder Aldermen and Commonalty of the City of Albany for the Time being, or the major Part of them, to order the raising a Sum not exceeding one hundred and sixty Pounds for the Purposes therein mentioned.

[Passed, February 8, 1774.]

Whereas the establishing of a regular well constituted Night Watch, and lighting of Lamps within the City of Albany, has not only been found convenient, but also necessary for the safety of its Inhabitants and Others.

Be it therefore Enacted by his Excellency the Governor the Council and the General Assembly, and it is hereby enacted by the Authority of the same That the Mayor Recorder Aldermen and Commonalty of the City of Albany for the Time being, or the major Part of them, whereof the Mayor or Recorder to be one, shall have full Power and Authority, and are hereby fully impowered and authorized at any Time before the last Day of March one thousand seven hundred and seventy-four, to order the raising a Sum not exceeding one hundred and sixty Pounds by a Tax upon the Estates real and personal lying and being within the said City, of all and every the Freeholders, Freemen Inhabitants, Residents and Sojourners living within a half Mile of Hudson's River, and to the North of a West Line drawn from the old Fort, for the Payment of so many Watchmen and Lamps, as the Mayor Recorder Aldermen and Commonalty of the said City in Common Council convened shall think necessary for guarding the said City and lighting the Lamps in the same, which Tax so to be laid, shall be rated and assessed at the same Time, and by the Assessors who shall rate and assess the Tax which shall be raised by virtue of an Act of the Governor, the Council and the General Assembly of the Colony of New York entitled, "An Act for the better explaining, and more effectual putting in Execution an Act of the General Assembly made in the third Year of the Reign of their late Majesties King William and Queen Mary entitled An Act for defraying the Public and necessary Charge throughout this Province, and for maintaining the Poor and preventing Vagabonds," made and passed the nineteenth Day June one thousand seven hundred and three, the Assessors first taking the Oath prescribed to be taken by the last mentioned Act, and the Tax so to be laid shall be collected levied and paid by the same Collector, and at the same Time as the Tax raised by virtue of the Act aforesaid hath been accustomed, and shall be paid into the Hands of such Persons as the said Mayor, Recorder, Aldermen and Commonalty in Common Council convened shall appoint, for the Uses aforesaid.

And be it further Enacted by the Authority aforesaid, That the Collector shall retain in his Hands three Pence in the Pound for every Pound so raised by virtue of this Act, as a Reward for his Trouble in collecting and paying the same, and no more.

And be it further Enacted by the Authority aforesaid, That if the said Mayor Recorder Aldermen and Commonalty, Assessors or Collectors of the said City of Albany, who are hereby authorized, impowered and required to take effectual care that this Act be executed according to the true Intent and Meaning thereof, or any of them shall deny, refuse or delay to perform, execute or comply with all or any of the Powers Authorities and Duties in this Act given and required to be done and performed by them or either of them, and thereof shall be lawfully convicted in any Court of Record in this Colony, he or they so denying refusing or delaying to perform the Duties as aforesaid, shall suffer such Pains and Penalties by Fine and Imprisonment, as by the Discretion of the said Court shall be adjudged.

And be it further Enacted by the Authority aforesaid, That if any Person or Persons shall neglect or refuse to pay the several Rates and Assessments wherewith he or they shall be charged by this Act, for or in respect of his and their Goods and Chattels, Lands or Tenements, upon the Demand of the Collector appointed to receive the same, that then it shall and may be lawful to and for such Collector, and he is hereby required on non-payment thereof, to distrain upon the Goods and Chattels of the Person or Persons so refusing or neglecting to pay; and the Distress so taken to carry away, and the same to expose to Sale within the said City for the Payment of the Rate or Assessment, and the Overplus, if any be after paying the Charges of taking, carrying away, and exposing the same Distress to sale, to be immediately returned to the Owner or Owners thereof.

And be it further Enacted by the Authority aforesaid, That all such Persons as shall be employed to guard the said City, shall be under the Directions of, and obey such Orders as they shall from Time to Time receive from the Mayor, Recorder, Aldermen and Commonalty of the said City in Common Council convened, any Law or usage to the contrary in any wise notwithstanding.

[CHAPTER 1646.]

An Act to increase the Number of Constables in the County of Ulster.

[Passed, February 8, 1774.]

Be it Enacted by his Excellency the Governor the Council and the General Assembly, and it is hereby enacted by the Authority of the same, That in every Town and Precinct in the County of Ulster wherein but one Constable has heretofore been elected, it shall and may be lawful for the Freeholders and Inhabitants of every such Town and Precinct to elect and choose at their annual Meetings, by majority of voices, two constables who shall be the constables of the said Towns and Precincts respectively for which they shall be so chosen, and shall have the same powers and be subject to the same Regulations Fines and Penalties as the other Constables in the said County now are.

[CHAPTER 1647.]

An Act for making a further Provision of two thousand Pounds for furnishing his Majesty's Troops quartered in this Colony with Necessaries for one Year.

[Passed, March 9, 1774.]

Be it Enacted by his Excellency the Governor the Council and the General Assembly and it is hereby enacted by the Authority of the same, That the Treasurer of this Colony shall, and he is hereby directed and required out of the Interest arisen or that may arise from the Money in the Loan Office to pay such Sum or Sums of Money as shall from Time to Time be necessary for quartering his Majesty's Troops in this Colony to the first Day of January next, on Warrant or Warrants to be drawn for that Purpose by his Excellency the Governor or Commander in Chief for the Time being, by and with the Advice and Consent of his Majesty's Council, provided the whole Sum to be drawn for, does not exceed the Sum of two thousand Pounds.

And be it Enacted by the Authority aforesaid, That the Treasurer shall keep exact Books of his Payments by virtue of this Act, and a true and just Account thereof shall render upon Oath to the Governor or Commander in Chief for the Time being the Council or the General Assembly, when by them or any of them thereunto required.

[CHAPTER 1648.]

An Act for making an Allowance of five thousand Pounds to his Excellency the Governor, as a compensation in Part for the Damage he sustained by the late dreadful Fire.

[Passed, March 9, 1774.]

WHEREAS by the late dreadful Fire in his Majesty's Fort in the City of New York the Edifice erected by this Colony for the residence of the Governor, was destroyed, together with the Furniture and other valuable Effects therein, belonging to his Excellency William Tryon Esquire the present Governor in Chief; and the General Assembly of this Colony having thereupon resolved to allow to his Excellency the Sum of five thousand Pounds as well to repair in some Measure his great and heavy Loss on this Occasion; as to manifest their high respect and Esteem for his Person and Family: Therefore pray that it may be Enacted,

And be it Enacted by his Excellency the Governor the Council and the General Assembly, and it is hereby enacted by the Authority of the same, That the Treasurer of this Colony shall pay, and he is hereby directed and required out of any Monies in his Hands, to pay, unto his said Excellency William Tryon Esquire, or to his Order the Sum of five thousand Pounds for the Purposes aforesaid, whose Receipt endorsed on the Warrant to be drawn for the same by the Governor or Commander in Chief of this Colony, by and with the Advice and Consent of his Majesty's Council, shall be a good Voucher and Discharge for the Sum so paid, and of which the said Treasurer is to render Account on Oath to the Governor, the Council or to the General Assembly, when by them or any of them thereunto required.

[CHAPTER 1649.]

An Act for the better Settling of Intestates Estates.

[Passed, March 9, 1774.]

Be it Enacted by his Excellency the Governor the Council and the General Assembly and by the Authority of the same, That all Governors or Commanders in Chief, Judges and Officers and every of them for the Time being having power as a Prerogative Court to commit Administration of the Goods of Persons dying Intestate, shall and may upon their respective granting and committing of Administrations of the Goods of Persons dying Intestate, after the passing of this Act of the respective Person or Persons to whom any Administration is to be committed, take sufficient Bonds and Conditions with two or more able Sureties, Respect being had to the Value of the Estate, in Form and Manner following, *mutatis mutandis*, Vizt. *Know all Men* by these Presents that We are held and firmly bound unto our Sovereign Lord by the Grace of God of Great Britain France and Ireland King Defender of the Faith and so forth, in the Sum of Pounds current Money of the Province of New York, To be paid to his said Majesty his Heirs and Successors, To the which Payment well and truly to be made we do bind us and every one of us our and every of our Heirs Executors and Administrators jointly and severally firmly by these Presents Sealed with our Seals, dated the Day of in the Year of his said Majesty's Reign and in the Year of our Lord The Condition of this Obligation is such, that if the above bounden Administrator of all and singular the Goods Chattels and Credits of Deceased, do make or cause to be made a true and perfect Inventory of all and singular the Goods Chattels and Credits of the said Deceased, which have or shall come to the Hands Possession or Knowledge of him the said or into the Hands and Possession of any other Person or Persons for him, and the same so made do exhibit or cause to be exhibited into the Registry of the Prerogative Court of the Province of New York at or before the Day of next ensuing; and the same Goods Chattels and Credits, and all other the Goods Chattels and Credits of the said Deceased at the Time of his Death which at any Time after shall come to the Hands or Possession of the said or into the Hands and Possession of any other Person or Persons for him, do well and truly Administer according to Law; And further do make, or cause to be made a true and just Account of Administration, at or before the Day of next following. And all the rest and residue of the said Goods Chattels and Credits which shall be found remaining upon the said Administrator's Account, the same being first examined and allowed of by the Judges or Judges for the Time being, of the said Court, shall deliver and pay unto such Person or Persons respectively, as the said Judge or Judges, by his or their Decree or Sentence pursuant to the true Intent and Meaning of this Act, shall limit and appoint; And if it shall hereafter appear, That any last Will and Testament was made by the said Deceased, and the Executor or Executors therein named do exhibit the same into the said Court, making Request to have it allowed and approved accordingly, if the said above bounden being thereunto required, do render and deliver the said Letters of Administration (Approbation of such Testament being first had and made) in the said Court; then this Obligation to be void and of none Effect, or else to remain in full Force and Virtue.

Which Bonds are hereby declared and enacted to be good to all intents and purposes and pleadable in any Courts of Justice; And also that the said Governors and Commanders in Chief, Judges and Officers respectively, shall and may and are enabled to proceed and call such Administrators to Account, for and touching the Goods of any Person dying Intestate; and upon Hearing and due Consideration thereof, to order and make just and equal Distributition of what remaineth clear (after all Debts, funerals and just Expenses of every sort first allowed and deducted) amongst the Wife and Children or Children's Children, if any such be, or otherwise to the next of Kindred to the dead Person in equal Degree, or legally representing their Stocks *pro suo cuique Jure*, according to the Laws in such Cases, and the Rules and Limitations hereafter set down; and the same Distributions to decree and settle, and to compel such Administrators to observe and pay the same by the due Course of the Laws: Saving to every one, supposing him or themselves agrieved, such Right of Appeal as in such Cases used.

Provided always, and be it Enacted by the Authority aforesaid, That every Person who by this Act is enabled to make Distribution of the Surplusage of the Estate of any Person dying intestate shall distribute the whole surplusage of such Estate or Estates in manner and form following: That is to say, One third part of the Surplusage to the Wife of the Intestate, and all the residue by equal portions, to and amongst the Children of such Persons dying Intestate and such Persons as legally represent such Children, in case any of the said Children be then Dead, other than such Child or Children (not being Heir at Law) who shall have any Estate by the Settlement of the Intestate, or shall be advanced by the Intestate in his Life time, by Portion or Portions equal to the Share which shall by such

Distribution be allotted to the other Children to whom such Distribution is to be made: And in case any Child, other than the Heir at Law, who shall have any Estate by Settlement from the said Intestate, or shall be advanced by the said Intestate in his Life time by Portion not equal to the Share which will be due to the other Children by such Distribution as aforesaid; then so much of the Surplusage of the Estate of such Intestate to be distributed to such Child or Children as shall have any Land by Settlement from the Intestate, or were advanced in the Life time of the Intestate, as shall make the Estate of all the said Children to be equal as near as can be estimated: But the Heir at Law notwithstanding any Land that he shall have by Discent or otherwise from the Intestate, is to have an equal Part in the Distribution with the rest of the Children, without any Consideration of the value of the Land which he hath by Discent, or otherwise from the Intestate.

And in Case there be no Children, nor any legal Representatives of them, then one Moiety of the said Estate to be allotted to the Wife of the Intestate, the Residue of the said Estate to be distributed equally to every of the next Kindred of the Intestate, who are in equal Degree, and those who legally represent them.

Provided, That there be no Representations admitted among Collaterals after Brothers and Sisters Children: And in Case there be no Wife, then all the said Estate to be distributed equally to and amongst the Children: And in case there be no Child then to the next of Kindred in equal Degree of, or unto the Intestate, and their legal Representatives as aforesaid, and in no other Manner whatsoever.

Provided also, and be it likewise Enacted by the Authority aforesaid To the End that a due Regard be had to Creditors, that no such Distribution of the Goods of any Person dying Intestate be made, till after one Year be fully expired after the Intestates Death; And that such and every one to whom any Distribution and Share shall be alloted, shall give Bond with sufficient Sureties in the said Courts, that if any Debt or Debts truly owing by the Intestate shall be afterwards sued for and recovered, or otherwise duly made to appear; that then and in every such Case he or she shall respectively refund and pay back to the Administrator his or her rateable Part of that Debt or Debts, and of the Costs of Suit and Charges of the Administrator by reason of such Debt, out of the Part and Share so as aforesaid allotted to him or her, thereby to enable the said Administrator to pay and satisfy the said Debt or Debts so discovered after the Distribution made as aforesaid.

Provided always and be it Enacted by the Authority aforesaid, that in all Cases where the said Court Judge or Officers or either of them hath or have used heretofore to grant Administration *cum Testamento annexo,* he and they shall continue so to do, and the Will of the Deceased in such Testament expressed, shall be performed and observed, in such Manner as it should have been if this Act had never been made.

Provided always, and it is hereby further Enacted, That no Administrator shall after the Passing of this Act, be cited to any the Courts, to render an Account of the personal Estate of his Intestate (otherwise than by an Inventory or Inventories thereof) unless it be at the instance or prosecution of some Person or Persons in behalf of a Minor, or having a demand out of such personal Estate as a Creditor or next of Kin, nor be compellable to account before any the Governors or Commanders in Chief Judges or Officers impowered and appointed to take the same, otherwise than as is aforesaid; any thing in this Act or any Law Usage or Custom to the contrary notwithstanding.

Provided also, and it is further Enacted by the Authority aforesaid, that if after the Death of a Father any of his Children shall Die Intestate without Wife or Children, in the Life time of the Mother, every Brother and Sister, and the Representatives of them, shall have an equal Share with her; any thing in this Act or any Law Usage or Custom to the Contrary notwithstanding. And all former Acts and Proceedings, and all Rights and Claims agreable to the Provisions of this Act are hereby confirmed.

And be it Enacted by the Authority aforesaid, That neither this Act nor any Thing herein contained shall be construed to extend to the Estates of Feme Coverts that shall die Intestate; but that their Husbands may demand and have Administration of their Rights, Credits and other Personal Estates, and recover and enjoy the same as they might have done before the Passing hereof.

[CHAPTER 1650.]

An Act for the Relief of Creditors against fraudulent Devises.

[Passed, March 9, 1774.]

Whereas it is not reasonable or just, that by the Practice or Contrivance of any Debtors, their Creditors should be defrauded of their just Debts, and nevertheless it hath often so happened, that where several Persons having by Bonds or other Specialties bound themselves and their Heirs, and have afterwards died seized in fee Simple of and in Manors, Messuages, Lands, Tenements and Hereditaments, or had Power or Authority to dispose of, or charge the same by their Wills or Testaments have, to the defrauding of such their Creditors, by their last Wills or Testaments, devised the same or disposed thereof, in such manner as such Creditors have lost their said debts, for remedying of which, and for the Maintenance of just and upright Dealing,

Be it Enacted by his Excellency the Governor the Council and the General Assembly, and it is hereby enacted by the Authority of the same, That all Wills and Testaments Limitations, Dispositions or Appointments of, or concerning any Manors, Messuages, Lands, Tenements or Hereditaments, or of any Rent, Profit Term or Charge out of the Same, whereof any Person or Persons at the Time of his her or their Decease, shall be seized in Fee Simple in Possession Reversion or Remainder, or have Power to dispose of the same, by his her or their Last Wills or Testaments that have, or hereafter shall be made, shall be deemed and taken, (only as against such Creditor or Creditors as aforesaid, his her and their Heirs Successors, Executors, Administrators and Assigns, and every of them,) to be fraudulent and clearly absolutely and utterly void, frustrate and of none Effect, any Pretence, Colour feigned, or presumed Consideration, or any other Matter or Thing to the contrary notwithstanding.

And for the Means that such Creditors may be enabled to recover their said Debts, *Be it further Enacted by the Authority aforesaid,* that in the Cases beforementioned, every such Creditor shall and may have and maintain his her and their Action and Actions of Debt, upon his her and their said Bonds and Specialties, against the Heir and Heirs at Law of such Obligor or Obligors, and such Devisee and Devisees jointly by virtue of this Act; and such Devisee or Devisees shall be lyable and chargeable for a false Plea by him or them pleaded, in the same Manner as any Heir should have been, for any false Plea by him pleaded, or for not confessing the Lands or Tenements to him descended.

Provided always and be it Enacted by the Authority aforesaid, That where there hath been, or shall be any Limitation or Appointment, Devise or Disposition of, or concerning any Manors, Messuages, Lands, Tenements or Hereditaments, for the raising or Payment of any real and just Debt or Debts, or any Portion or Portions, Sum or Sums of Money, for any Child or Children of any Person other than the Heir at Law according to, or in pursuance of, any Marriage Contract or Agreement in Writing, *bona fide* made before such Marriage, the same and every of them shall be in full force, and the same Manors, Messuages, Lands, Tenements and Hereditaments, shall and may be holden and enjoyed by every such Person or Persons, his her and their Heirs, Executors, Administrators and Assigns for whom the said Limitation, Appointment, Devise or Disposition was made, and by his her and their Trustee or Trustees, his her and their Heirs, Executors, Administrators and Assigns for such Estate or Interest as shall be so limited or appointed, devised or disposed until such Debt or Debts, Portion or Portions shall be raised, paid and satisfied, any Thing in this Act contained to the contrary notwithstanding.

And Whereas several Persons being Heirs at Law, to avoid the Payment of such just Debts, as in regard to the Lands Tenements and Hereditaments descending to them, they have by Law been lyable to pay, have sold, aliened or made over, such Lands Tenements or Hereditaments, before any Process was or could be issued out against them.

Be it further Enacted by the Authority aforesaid, That in all Cases, where any Heir at Law shall be lyable to pay the Debt of his Ancestor, in regard of any Lands, Tenements or Hereditaments descending to him, and shall sell, alien or make over the same, before any Action brought, or Process sued out against him, that such Heir at Law shall be answerable for such Debt or Debts, in an Action or Actions of Debt to the Value of the said Land so by him sold aliened or made over, in which Cases all Creditors shall be preferred, as in Actions against Executors and Administrators, and such Execution shall be taken out, upon any Judgment or Judgments so obtained, against such Heir to the Value of the said Land, as if the same were his own proper Debt or Debts, saving that the Lands, Tenements and Hereditaments *bona fide* aliened before the Action brought, shall not be lyable to such Execution.

Provided always and be it further enacted by the Authority aforesaid, That where any Action of Debt upon any Specialty is brought against any Heir, he may plead *Riens per Descent,* at the Time of the original Writ brought, or the Bill filed against him, any Thing herein contained to the contrary notwithstanding, and the Plaintiff in such Action may reply, that he had Lands Tenements or Hereditaments from his Ancestor before the original Writ brought, or Bill filed; and if upon Issue joined thereupon, it be found for the Plaintiff, the Jury shall enquire of the value of the Lands Tenements or Hereditaments so descended, and thereupon Judgment shall be given, and Execution shall be awarded as aforesaid; but if Judgment be given against such Heir, by Confession of the Action, without confessing the Assets descended, or upon Demurrer or *Nihil Dicit*, it shall be for the Debt and Damages, without any Writ to enquire of the Lands Tenements or Hereditaments so descended.

Provided also, and be it further enacted, That all and every Devisee and Devisees, made lyable by this Act, shall be lyable and chargeable in the same Manner as the Heir at Law by force of this Act, notwithstanding the Lands, Tenements and Hereditaments to him or them devised, shall be aliened before the Action brought.

[CHAPTER 1651.]

An Act for the better preventing of excessive and deceitful Gaming.

[Passed, March 9, 1774.]

WHEREAS the Laws now in force for preventing the Mischiefs which happen by Gaming, have not been found sufficient for that Purpose; therefore for the further preventing of all excessive and deceitful Gaming,

Be it Enacted by his Excellency the Governor, the Council and the General Assembly, and it is hereby enacted by the Authority of the same, That from and after the first Day of May next all Notes, Bills, Bonds, Judgments, Mortgages or other Securities or Conveyances whatsoever, given granted drawn or entered into, or executed by any Person or Persons whatsoever, where the whole or any Part of the Consideration of such Conveyances or Securities, shall be for any Money or other valuable Things, whatsoever won by Gaming or Playing at Cards Dice, Tables, Tennis, Bowls or other Game or Games whatsoever, or by betting on the Sides or Hands of such as do Game at any of the Games aforesaid, or for the reimbursing or repaying any Money knowingly lent or advanced for such Gaming or Betting as aforesaid, or lent or advanced at the Time and Place of such Play to any Person or Persons so Gaming or Betting as aforesaid, or that shall during such Play, so Play or Bett, shall be utterly void, frustrate and of none Effect to all Intents and Purposes whatsoever, any Law or Usage to the Contrary thereof in any wise notwithstanding; and that where such Mortgages Securities or other Conveyances shall be of Lands Tenements or Hereditaments, or shall be such as incumber or affect the same, such Mortgages Securities or other Conveyances shall enure and be to and for the sole Use and Benefit of, and shall devolve upon such Person or Persons as should or might have, or be entitled to such Lands Tenements or Hereditaments, in Case the said Grantor or Grantors thereof, or the Person or Persons so incumbring the Same had been naturally dead, and as if such Mortgages Securities or other Conveyances had been made to such Person or Persons so to be intitled after the Decease of the Person or Persons so incumbring the same; And that all Grants and Conveyances to be made for the preventing of such Lands Tenements or Hereditaments from coming to, or devolving upon such Person or Persons hereby intended to enjoy the same as aforesaid, shall be deemed fraudulent and void, and of none Effect, to all Intents and Purposes whatsoever.

And be it further Enacted by the Authority aforesaid, That from and after the said first Day of May next, any Person or Persons whatsoever who shall at any Time or Sitting, by playing at Cards Dice Tables or other Game or Games whatsoever, or by betting on the Sides or Hands of such as do play at any of the Games aforesaid lose to any one or more Person or Persons so playing or betting, in the whole Sum or Value of ten Pounds, and shall pay or deliver the Same or any Part thereof, the Person or Persons so losing and paying or delivering the Same, shall be at Liberty within three Months then next, to sue for and recover the Money or Goods so lost, and paid or delivered or any Part thereof from the respective Winner and Winners thereof with Costs of Suit, by Action of Debt founded on this Act, to be prosecuted in any of his Majesty's Courts of Record within this Colony, having Cognizance of the same, in which Action or Suit no Essoin Protection Wager of Law, or more than one Imparlance shall be allowed: In which Actions it shall be sufficient for the Plaintiff to alledge that the Defendant or Defendants are indebted to the Plaintiff or Plaintiffs, or received to the Plaintiff's Use, the Monies so lost and paid, or converted the Goods won of the Plaintiffs to the Defendants Use, whereby the Plaintiff's Action accrued to him, according to the Form of this Act, without setting forth the special Matter: And in Case the Person or Persons who shall lose such Money or other Thing as aforesaid, shall not within the Time aforesaid really and *bona fide*, and without Covin or Collusion, sue and with Effect prosecute for the Money or other Thing so by him or them lost, and paid or delivered as aforesaid, it shall and may be lawful to and for any Person or Persons, by any such Action or Suit as aforesaid to sue for and recover the Same, and treble the Value thereof, with Costs of Suit against such Winner or Winners as aforesaid, the one Moiety thereof to the Use of the Person or Persons that will sue for the Same, and the other Moiety to the Use of the Poor of the Parish or Place where the Offence shall be committed.

And for the better Discovery of the Monies or other Thing so won, and to be sued for and recovered as aforesaid, *It is hereby further Enacted by the Authority aforesaid,* That all and every the Person or Persons, who by virtue of this present Act shall or may be liable to be sued for the Same, shall be obliged and compellable to answer upon Oath such Bill or Bills as shall be preferred against him or them for discovering the Sum and Sums of Money or other Thing so won at Play as aforesaid.

Provided always and be it nevertheless enacted by the Authority aforesaid, That upon the Discovery and Repayment of the Money or other Thing so to be discovered and repaid as aforesaid, the Person or Persons who shall so discover and repay the Same as aforesaid shall be acquitted, indemnified and discharged from any further or other Punishment, Forfeiture or Penalty which he or they may have incurred by the playing for or winning such Money or other Thing so discovered and repaid as aforesaid any former or other Law or Usage, or any Thing in this present Act contained to the contrary thereof in any wise notwithstanding.

And be it further Enacted by the Authority aforesaid, That if any Person or Persons whatsoever at any Time or Times after the said first Day of May next do, or shall by any Fraud or Shift, Cousenage, Circumvention, Deceit or unlawful Devise or ill Practice whatsoever in playing at or with Cards, Dice or any the Games aforesaid, or in or by bearing a Share or Part in the Stakes, Wagers or Adventures, or in or betting on the Sides or Hands of such as do or shall play as aforesaid, Win, obtain or acquire to him or themselves, or to any other or others, any Sum or Sums of Money or other valuable Thing or Things whatsoever, or shall at any one Time or Sitting, win of any one or more Person or Persons whatsoever, above the Sum or Value of ten Pounds, that then every Person or Persons so winning by such ill Practice as aforesaid, or winning at any one Time or Sitting above the said Sum or Value of ten Pounds, and being convicted of any of the said

Offences, upon any Indictment or Information to be exhibited against him or them for that Purpose shall forfeit five Times the value of the Sum or Sums of Money or other Things so won as aforesaid, and in Case of such ill Practice as aforesaid shall be deemed infamous, and suffer such corporal Punishment as in Cases of wilful Perjury, and such Penalty to be recovered by such Person or Persons as shall sue for the Same by such Action as aforesaid.

And Whereas divers leud and dissolute Persons live at great Expences, having no visible Estate, Profession or Calling to maintain themselves, but support those Expences by gaming only, *Be it therefore further Enacted by the Authority aforesaid,* That it shall and may be lawful for any two or more of his Majesty's Justices of the Peace, in any County City or Place whatsoever, to cause to come, or be brought before them, every such Person or Persons within their respective Limits whom they shall have just Cause to suspect, to have no visible Estate, Profession or Calling to maintain themselves by, but do for the most Part support themselves by gaming, and if such Person or Persons shall not make it appear to such Justices, that the principal Part of his or their Expences is not maintained by gaming; that then such Justices shall require of him or them sufficient Securities for his or their good Behaviour for the Space of twelve Months; and in Default of his or their finding such Securities, to commit him or them to the common Goal there to remain until he or they shall find such Securities as aforesaid.

And be it Enacted by the Authority aforesaid, That if such Person or Persons so finding Sureties as aforesaid, shall during the Time for which he or they shall be so bound to the good Behaviour, at any one Time or Sitting, play or bett for any Sum or Sums of Money or other Thing exceeding in the whole the Sum or Value of twenty Shillings that then such playing shall be deemed or taken to be a Breach of his or their Behaviour, and a Forfeiture of the Recognizance given for the Same.

[CHAPTER 1652.]

An Act for the better Security, and more easy recovery of Rents, and renewal of Leases, and to prevent Frauds committed by Tenants.

[Passed, March 9, 1774.]

Be it Enacted by his Excellency the Governor the Council and the General Assembly, and it is hereby enacted by the Authority of the Same, That from and after the passing of this Act, where any Goods or Chattels shall be distrained for any Rent reserved and due upon any Demise, Lease or Contract whatsoever; and the Tenant or Owner of the Goods so distrained shall not within five Days next after such Distress taken, and Notice thereof (with the Cause of such taking,) left at the chief Mansion House, or other most notorious Place on the Premises charged with the Rent distrained for, replevy the same with sufficient Security to be given to the Sheriff according to Law, that then in such Case after such Distress and Notice as aforesaid, and Expiration of the said five Days, the Person distraining shall and may with the Sheriff or under Sheriff of the County, or with the Constable or other Officer of the Town or Place where such Distress shall be taken, (who are hereby required to be aiding and assisting therein,) cause the Goods and Chattels so distrained to be appraised by two sworn Appraisers (whom such Sheriff under Sheriff, Constable or other Officer as aforesaid are hereby impowered to summon for that Service and to swear well and truly to perform it,) to appraise the same truly according to the best of their Understandings, and after such Appraisment, shall and may lawfully sell at Public Vendue the Goods and Chattels so distrained for the best Price that can be gotten for the same (giving three Days Public Notice,) towards satisfaction of the Rent for which the said Goods and Chattels shall be distrained, and of the Charges of such Distress, Appraisment and sale, leaving the Overplus (if any,) in the Hands of the said Sheriff, Under Sheriff, Constable or Officer for the Owners Use.

Be it further Enacted by the Authority aforesaid That from and after the passing of this Act, it shall be lawful for any Person or Persons having Rent, arrear and due upon any such Demise, Lease or Contract as aforesaid to seize and secure any Sheaves or Cocks of Corn, or Corn loose, or in the Straw, or Hay lying or being in any Barn or Granary or upon any Hovel Stack or Rick, or otherwise, upon any Part of the Land charged with such Rent, and to lock up or detain the same in the Place where the same shall be found, for or in the Nature of a Distress until the same shall be replevied upon such Security to be given as aforesaid, and in Default of Replevying the same as aforesaid within the Time aforesaid, to sell the same after the Appraisment thereof in Manner as above directed: *And also* it shall be lawful for such Landlord or Lessor to take and seize as aforesaid any Cattle or Stock of such Tenant or Tenants feeding or depasturing upon any common appendant or appurtenant, or any ways belonging to the Premises demised or holden, *And also* to take and seize all Sorts of Corn and Grass Roots or other Produce growing thereon as Distress for Arrears of Rent, and the same to cut gather, make, cure, carry and lay up in some convenient Place on the Premises and for Want thereof in some other Place to be procured by such Landlord (due Notice of such Place being given to such Tenant or Lessee, or left at his Place of abode) and within the Time, and in manner herein before directed to appraise sell or dispose of the same.

And be it further Enacted, That it shall be lawful for any Person lawfully taking any Distress to impound or otherwise secure the Distress so made, of whatever Nature or Kind it may be in such Place, or on such Part of the Premises as shall be most convenient for the Purpose, and to appraise sell and dispose of the same upon the Premises in like Manner as any Person taking a Distress for Rent may do off the Premises by virtue of this Act: And it shall be lawful for any Person or Persons to come and go to and from such Place or Part of the said Premises in order to view appraise and buy, and also to carry off and remove the same.

And be it further Enacted by the Authority aforesaid, That upon any Pound Breach or Rescous of Goods or Chattels distrained for Rent, the Person or Persons grieved thereby shall in a special Action upon the Case for the Wrong thereby sustained recover his and their treble Damages and Costs of Suit against the Offender or Offenders in any such Rescous or Pound Breach, any or either of them, or against the Owner of the Goods distrained, in Case the same be afterwards found to have come to his use or Possession.

Provided always and be it further Enacted, That in Case any such Distress and Sale as aforesaid, shall be made by virtue or colour of this present Act, for Rent pretended to be arrear and due, where in truth no Rent is arrear or due to the Person or Persons distraining, or to him or them in whose Name or Names or Right such Distress shall be taken as aforesaid, that then the Owner of such Goods or Chattels distrained and sold as aforesaid, his Executors or Administrators, shall and may by Action of Trespass, or upon the Case, to be brought against the Person or Persons so distraining any or either of them, his or their Executors or Administrators recover double of the Value of the Goods or Chattels so distrained and sold together with full Costs of Suit.

And be it further Enacted by the Authority aforesaid, That from and after the passing hereof where any Distress shall be made for any Kind of Rent justly due, and any irregularity or unlawful Act shall be afterwards done by the Party or Parties distraining, or by his her or their Agents, the Distress itself shall not be therefore deemed to be unlawful, nor the Party or Parties making it be deemed a Trespasser or Trespassers *ab initio;* but the Party or Parties aggrieved by such unlawful Act or Irregularity, shall or may recover full Satisfaction for the special Damage, he she or they shall have sustained thereby and no more, in an Action of Trespass, or on the Case at the Election of the Plaintiff or Plaintiffs: *Provided always* That where the Plaintiff or Plaintiffs shall recover such Action, he she or they shall be paid his her or their full costs of Suit, and have all the like Remedies for the same as in other Cases of Costs. *Provided nevertheless,* That no Tenant or Tenants, Lessee or Lessees, shall recover in any Action for any such unlawful Act or Irregularity as aforesaid, if Tender of Amends hath been made by the Party or Parties distraining, his her or their Agent, or Agents, before such Action brought.

And be it further Enacted by the Authority aforesaid, That in all Actions of Trespass or upon the Case to be brought against any Person or Persons intitled to any Rents or Services of any Kind, his her or their Bailiff or Receiver, or other Person or Persons relating to any Entry by virtue of this Act, or otherwise upon the Premises chargeable with such Rents or Services, or to any Distress or Seizure, Sale or Disposal of any Goods or Chattels thereupon, it shall and may be lawful to and for the Defendant or Defendants in such Actions to plead the general Issue and give the special Matter in Evidence, any Law or Usage to the contrary notwithstanding, and in Case the Plaintiff or Plaintiffs shall become nonsuit, discontinue his her, or their Action, or have Judgment against him her or them, the Defendant or Defendants shall recover double Costs of Suit.

And be it further Enacted That no Goods or Chattels whatsoever in or upon the demised Premises shall be liable to be taken by virtue of any Execution on any Pretence whatsoever, unless the Party at whose Suit the said Execution is sued out, shall before the Removal of such Goods from off the said Premises by virtue of such Execution or Extent, pay to the Landlord of the said Premises or his Bailiff all Sum or Sums of Money due for Rent for the said Premises at the Time of the taking such

Goods or Chattels by virtue of such Execution, provided the said Arrears of Rent do not amount to more than one Years Rent, and in Case the said Arrears shall exceed one years Rent, then the said Party, at whose Suit such Execution is sued out, paying the said Landlord or his Bailiff one Years Rent, may proceed to execute his Judgment as he might have done before the making of this Act: and the Sheriff or other Officer is hereby impowered and required to levy and pay to the Plaintiff, as well the Money so paid for Rent as the Execution Money.

And be it further Enacted by the Authority aforesaid, That in Case any such Lessee for Life or Lives, Term of Years, at Will or otherwise shall from and after the passing of this Act, convey or carry off or from such demised Premises his Goods or Chattels, leaving the Rent unpaid, it shall and may be lawful for such Lessor or Landlord or any Person or Persons by him for that Purpose lawfully impowered within the Space of thirty Days next after such conveying away, or carrying off such Goods or Chattels as aforesaid, to take and seize such Goods and Chattels where-ever the same shall be found, as a Distress for the said Arrears of Rent; and the same to sell or otherwise dispose of in such Manner as if the said Goods and Chattels had actually been distrained by such Lessor or Landlord in and upon such Premises for such Arrears of Rent, any Law custom or usage to the contrary in any wise notwithstanding.

Provided nevertheless, That Nothing in this Act contained shall extend or be construed to extend to impower such Lessor or Landlord to take or seize any Goods or Chattels as a Distress for Arrears of Rent, which shall be sold *bona fide*, and for a valuable Consideration before such Seizure made to any Person not privy to such Fraud any Thing herein contained to the contrary notwithstanding.

And to deter Tenants from such conveying away their Goods and Chattels leaving the Rent unpaid, and others from wilfully aiding or assisting therein or concealing the same, *Be it further Enacted by the Authority aforesaid,* That if any such Tenant or Lessee shall remove and convey away his or her Goods or Chattels as aforesaid, or if any Person or Persons shall wilfully and knowingly aid or assist any such Tenant or Lessee in such conveying away or carrying off of any Part of his or her Goods or Chattels, or in concealing the same; all and every Person and Persons so offending shall forfeit and pay to the Landlord or Landlords, Lessor or Lessors, their Heirs or Assigns, from whose

Estate such Goods and Chattels were so carried off as aforesaid, double the value of the Goods by him her or them respectively carried off, or concealed as aforesaid, to be recovered by Action of Debt in any Court of Record wherein no Essoin, Protection or Wager of Law shall be allowed, nor more than one Imparlance.

And be it further Enacted by the Authority aforesaid, That where any Goods or Chattels shall be conveyed or carried away as aforesaid by any Tenant or Tenants, Lessee or Lessees, his her or their Servant or Servants, Agent or Agents, or other Person or Persons, aiding or assisting therein, shall be put, placed, or kept in any House, Barn, Stable, Out House, Yard, Close or Place locked up, fastened or otherwise secured, so as to prevent such Goods or Chattels from being taken and seized as a Distress for arrears of Rent it shall and may be lawful for the Landlord or Landlords Lessor or Lessors, his or their Heirs or Assigns, his or their Steward, Bailiff, Receiver or other Person or Persons empowered to take and seize as a Distress for Rent, such Goods and Chattels (first calling to his her or their Assistance the Constable or other Peace Officer of the Town or Place where the same shall be suspected to be concealed, who are hereby required to aid and assist therein; and in Case of a Dwelling House Oath being also first made before some Justice of the Peace of a reasonable Ground to suspect that such Goods or Chattels are therein,) in the Daytime to break open and enter into such House, Barn, Stable, Out House, Yard, Close and Place, and to take and seize such Goods and Chattels for the said Arrears of Rent, as he she or they might have done by virtue of this or any former Act, if such Goods and Chattels had been put in any open Field or Place.

Be it further Enacted by the Authority aforesaid, That it shall be lawful for any Person or Persons, having any Rent in Arrear or due upon any Lease or Demise for Life or Lives to bring an Action or Actions of Debt for such Arrears of Rent in the same Manner they might have done in Case such Rent were due, and reserved upon a Lease for Years.

And Whereas Tenants *per Auter Vie,* and Lessees for Years or at will frequently hold over the Tenements to them demised, after the Determination of such Lease: *And Whereas* after the Determination of such or any other Leases no Distress can by Law be made for any Arrears of Rent that grew due on such respective Leases before the Determination thereof: *It is hereby further Enacted by the Authority aforesaid,* That it shall be lawful for any Person or Persons having any Rent in arrear and due upon any Lease for Life or Lives, or for Years or at Will ended or determined to distrain for such Arrears, after the Determination of the said respective Leases, in the same Manner as they might have done if such Lease or Leases had not been ended or determined.

Provided, That such Distress be made within the Space of six Kalender Months after the Determination of such Lease and during the Continuance of such Landlord's Title or Interest, and during the Possession of the Tenant from whom such Arrear became due.

Provided always and it is hereby enacted and declared by the Authority aforesaid, That Nothing in this Act contained shall extend or be construed to extend to let hinder or prejudice his Majesty, his Heirs or Successors in the levying recovering or seizing any Debts Fines Penalties or Forfeitures that are or shall be due payable or answerable to his Majesty his Heirs or Successors; but that it shall and may be lawful for his Majesty his Heirs and Successors to levy recover and seize such Debts Fines Penalties and Forfeitures in the same Manner as if this Act had never been made, any Thing in this Act contained to the contrary thereof in any wise notwithstanding.

And be it further Enacted, That in Case any Tenant or Tenants for any Term of Life Lives or Years or other Person or Persons who are or shall come into Possession of any Lands Tenements or Hereditaments by from or under, or by Collusion with such Tenant or Tenants, shall wilfully hold over any Lands Tenements or Hereditaments after the Determination of such Term or Terms, and after Demand made and Notice in writing given for delivering the Possession thereof, by his or their Landlords or Lessors, or the Person or Persons to whom the Remainder or Reversion of such Lands Tenements or Hereditaments shall belong, his or their Agent or Agents thereunto lawfully authorized, then and in such Case, such Person or Persons so holding over, shall for and during the Time he she or they shall so hold over or keep the Person or Persons intitled, out of Possession of the said Lands Tenements and Hereditaments as aforesaid, pay to the Person or Persons so kept out of possession their Executors Administrators or Assigns at the Rate of double the Yearly Value of the Lands Tenements and Hereditaments so detained, for so long Time as the same are detained to be recovered in any of the Courts of Record in this Colony, by Action of Debt, whereunto the Defendant or Defendants shall be obliged to give special

Bail, against the recovering of which said Penalty there shall be no Relief in Equity.

And be it further Enacted by the Authority aforesaid, That in Case any Tenant or Tenants shall give Notice of his, her, or their Intention to quit the Premises by him her or them holden, at a Time mentioned in such Notice, and shall not accordingly deliver up the Possession thereof at the Time in such Notice contained, that then the said Tenant or Tenants his her or their Executors or Administrators shall from thenceforward pay to the Landlord or Landlords, Lessor or Lessors their Heirs or Assigns double the Rent or Sum which he she, or they should otherwise have paid; to be levied, sued for and recovered at the same Times and in the same Manner as the single rent or Sum before the giving such Notice could be levied, sued for, or recovered, and such double Rent or Sum shall be continued to be paid, during all the Time such Tenant or Tenants shall continue in possession as aforesaid.

And Whereas great Inconveniencies may happen to Lessors and Landlords in Cases of Re-entry for non-payment of Rent by reason of the many Nicities that attend Re-entries at Common Law, and for asmuch as when a legal Re-entry is made, the Landlord or Lessor must be at the Expence Charge and Delay of recovering in Ejectment before he can obtain the actual Possession of the demised Premises, for Remedy whereof.

Be it Enacted by the Authority aforesaid That in all Cases between Landlord and Tenant from and after the passing this Act as often as it shall happen that one half Years Rent shall be in arrear, and the Landlord or Lessor to whom the same is due hath Right by Law to re-enter for the nonpayment thereof such Landlord or Lessor, shall and may without any formal Demand or Re-entry, serve a Declaration in Ejectment, for the Recovery of the demised Premises, or in Case the same cannot be legally served, or no Tenant be in actual possession of the Premises, then to affix the same upon the Door of any demised Messuage, or in Case such Ejectment shall not be for the Recovery of any Messuage, then upon some notorious Place of the Lands, Tenements or Hereditaments comprized in such Declaration in Ejectment, and such affixing shall be deemed legal Service thereof, which Service or affixing such Declaration in Ejectment shall stand in the Place and stead of a Demand and Re-entry, and in Case of Judgment against the casual Ejector or nonsuit for not confessing Lease Entry and Ouster, it shall be made appear to the Court where the said Suit is depending, by Affidavit or be proved upon the Trial in Case the Defendant appears, that half a Years Rent was due before the said Declaration was served, and that no sufficient Distress was to be found on the demised Premises, countervailing the Arrears then due, and that the Lessor or Lessors in Ejectment had Power to Re-enter, then and in every such Case the Lessor or Lessors in Ejectment shall recover Judgment and Execution in the same Manner as if the Rent in arrear had been legally demanded and Re-entry made; and in Case the Lessee or Lessees, his her or their Assignee or Assignees or other Person or Persons claiming or deriving under the said Lease shall suffer Judgment on such Ejectment, and Execution to be executed thereon, without paying the Rent and Arrears together with full Costs, and without filing any Bill or Bills for Relief in Equity, within six Kalender Months after such Execution executed, then and in such Case the said Lessee or Lessees his her or their Assignee or Assignees, and all other Persons claiming and deriving under the said Lease shall be barred and foreclosed from all Relief or Remedy in Law or Equity, other than by Writ of Error for reversal of such Judgment in case the same shall be erroneous, and the said Landlord or Lessor shall from thenceforth hold the same demised Premises discharged from such Lease or Contract, and if on such Ejectment, verdict shall pass for the Defendant or Defendants, or the Plaintiff or Plaintiffs shall be nonsuited therein except for the not confessing Lease, Entry and Ouster, then and in every such Case such Defendant or Defendants shall have and recover his her and their full Costs, *Provided always*, That Nothing herein contained shall extend to bar the Right of any Mortgagee or Mortgagees of such Lease, or any Part thereof, who shall not be in Possession, so as such Mortgagee or Mortgagees shall and do within six Kalender Months after such Judgment obtained and Execution executed pay all Rent in Arrear, and all Costs and Damages sustained by such Lessor, Person or Persons intitled to the remainder or Reversion as aforesaid and perform all the Covenants and Agreements which on the Part and behalf of the first Lessee or Lessees are and ought to be performed.

And be it further Enacted by the Authority aforesaid, That in Case the said Lessee or Lessees, his, her, or their Assignee or Assignees or other Person or Persons claiming any Right Title or Interest in Law or Equity of in or to the said Lease shall within the Time aforesaid file one or more Bill or Bills for relief in any Court of Equity, such Person or Persons shall not have or continue any Injunction against the Proceedings at Law on such Ejectment unless he she or they do or shall within forty Days next after a full and perfect Answer shall be filed by the Lessor or Lessors of the Plaintiff, in such Ejectment, bring into Court and lodge with the proper Officer such Sum and Sums of Money as the Lessor or Lessors of the Plaintiff in the said Ejectment shall in his, her, or their Answer swear to be due and in arrear over and above all just Allowances, and also the Costs taxed in the said Suit, there to remain till the hearing of the Cause, or to be paid out to the Lessor or Landlord on good Security, subject to the Decree of the Court, and in Case such Bill or Bills shall be filed within the Time aforesaid and after Execution is executed, the Lessor or Lessors of the Plaintiff shall be accountable only for so much and no more, as he she or they shall really and *bona fide* without Fraud Deceit, or wilful Neglect make of the demised Premises, from the Time of his her or their entering into the actual Possession thereof, and if what shall be so made by the Lessor or Lessors of the Plaintiff happen to be less than the Rent reserved on the said Lease, then the said Lessee or Lessees, his her or their Assignee or Assignees, before he she or they shall be restored to the Possession or Possessions, shall pay such Lessor or Lessors, or Landlord or Landlords with the Money so by them made, fell short of the reserved Rent, for the Time such Lessor or Lessors of the Plaintiff, Landlord or Landlords held the said Lands.

Provided always and be it further Enacted by the Authority aforesaid That if the Tenant or Tenants, his her or their Assignee or Assignees shall at any Time before the Trial in such Ejectment pay or tender to the Lessor or Landlord, his Executors or Administrators, or his her or their Attorney in that Cause, or pay into the Court where the same Cause is depending, all the Rent and Arrears, together with the Costs, then and in such Case, all further Proceedings on the said Ejectment shall Cease, and be discontinued; and if such Lessee or Lessees, his her or their Executors Administrators or Assigns shall upon such Bill filed as aforesaid be relieved in Equity, he she and they shall have hold and enjoy the demised Lands according to the Lease thereof made, without any new Lease to be thereof made to him her or them.

And be it further Enacted by the Authority aforesaid, That from and after the passage of this Act, all and every Person or Persons, Bodies Politic and Corporate, shall and may have the like Remedy by Distress and by impounding and selling the same in Cases of Rents-Seck, Rents of Assize, and Chief Rents, which have been duly answered or paid for the Space of three Years, within twenty Years next before the first Day of this present Session of the General Assembly, or shall be hereafter created, as in Case of Rent reserved upon Lease, any Law or Usage to the contrary notwithstanding.

And for making the renewal of Leases More easy for the future. *Be it Enacted by the Authority aforesaid,* That in Case any Lease shall be duly surrendered in order to be renewed, and a new Lease made and executed by the Chief Landlord or Landlords the same new Lease shall without a Surrender of all or any the under Leases be as good and valid to all Intents and Purposes, as if all the under Leases derived thereout, had been likewise surrendered at, or before the taking of such new Lease, and all and every Person and Persons in whom any Estate for Life or Lives, or for Years shall from Time to Time be vested by virtue of such new Lease, and his her and their Executors and Administrators shall be intitled to the Rents Covenants and Duties, and have like Remedy for recovery thereof and the under Lessees shall hold and enjoy the demised Premises respectively, as if the original Leases, out of which the respective under Leases are derived had been still kept on Foot and continued, and the Chief Landlord or Landlords shall have and be intitled to such and the same Remedy by Distress or Entry in and upon the demised Premises, for the Rents and Duties reserved by such new Lease, so far as the same exceed not the Rents, and Duties reserved in the Lease, out of which such under Lease was derived, as they would have had in case such former Lease had been still continued, or as they would have had in case the respective Under Leases had been renewed under such new principal Lease any Law, Custom or Usage to the contrary hereof notwithstanding.

And be it Enacted by the Authority aforesaid, That where any Tenant for Life shall happen to die before or on the Day on which any Rent was reserved or made payable upon any Demise or Lease of any Lands Tenements or Hereditaments which Determined on the Death of such Tenant for Life, that the Executors or Administrators of such Tenant for Life shall and may in an Action on the Case recover of and from such under Tenant or under Tenants of such Lands, Tenements or Hereditaments if such Tenant for Life die on the Day on which the same was made payable, the whole, or if before such Day, then a Proportion of such Rent according to the Time such Tenant for Life lived of the last Year, or Quarter of a Year, or other time in which the said Rent was growing due as aforesaid, making all just Allowances or a proportionable Part thereof respectively.

And whereas the Possession of Estates in Lands Tenements and Hereditaments is rendered very precarious by the frequent and fraudulent Practice of Tenants, in attorning to Strangers who claim Title to the Estates of their respective Landlord or Landlords, Lessor or Lessors, who by that Means are turned out of Possession of their respective Estates, and put to the Difficulty and Expence of recovering the Possession thereof by actions or Suits at Law, for remedy whereof.

Be it Enacted by the Authority aforesaid, That all and every such Attornment and Attornments of any Tenant or Tenants of any Messuages Lands Tenements or Hereditaments shall be absolutely null and void, to all Intents and Purposes whatsoever, and the Possession of their respective Landlord or Landlords, Lessor or Lessors shall not be deemed or construed to be any wise changed altered or affected by any such Attornment or Attornments: *Provided always,* That Nothing herein contained shall extend to vacate or affect any Attornment made pursuant to and in consequence of some Judgment at Law, or Decree or Order of a Court of Equity, or made with the privity and Consent of the Landlord or Landlords, Lessor or Lessors, or to any Mortgagee after the Mortgage is become forfeited.

And be it further Enacted by the Authority aforesaid, That every Tenant to whom any Declaration in Ejectment shall be delivered for any Lands Tenements or Hereditaments shall forthwith give Notice thereof to his or her Landlord or Landlords, or his her or their Bailiff or Receiver under Penalty of forfeiting the Value of three Years improved or Rack Rent of the Premises so demised or holden in the Possession of such Tenant, to the Person of whom he or she holds; to be recovered by Action of Debt to be brought in any Court of Record within this Colony, wherein no Essoin Protection or Wager of Law shall be allowed, nor any more than one Imparlance.

And be it further Enacted by the Authority aforesaid, That it shall be lawful for the Court where such Ejectment shall be brought to suffer the Landlord or Landlords to make him her or themselves Defendant or Defendants, by joining with the Tenant or Tenants to whom such Declaration in Ejectment shall be delivered, in case he or they shall appear but in Case such Tenant or Tenants shall refuse or neglect to appear, judgment shall be signed against the Casual Ejector, for want of such Appearance; but if the Landlord or Landlords of any Part of the Lands Tenements or Hereditaments for which such Ejectment was brought shall desire to appear by himself or themselves and consent to enter into the like Rule, that by the Course of the Court the Tenant in Possession in Case he or she had appeared, ought to have done; then the Court where such Ejectment shall be brought, shall and may permit such Landlord or Landlords so to do, and order a stay of Execution upon such Judgment against the casual Ejector, until they shall make further Order therein.

And to obviate some Difficulties that many Times occur in the Recovery of Rents where the Demises are not by Deed. *Be it further Enacted by the Authority aforesaid*, That it shall be lawful to and for the Landlord or Landlords their Heirs or Assigns, where the agreement is not by Deed to recover a Reasonable Satisfaction for the Lands Tenements or Hereditaments, held or occupied by the Defendant or Defendants, in an Action on the Case for the Use and Occupation of what was so held or enjoyed; and if in Evidence on the Trial of such Action any Parole Demise or any Agreement (not being by Deed.) whereon a certain Rent was reserved shall appear, the Plaintiff in such Action, shall not therefore be non-suited, but may make use thereof as an Evidence of the *Quantum* of the Damages to be recovered.

[CHAPTER 1653.]

An Act for the better Discovery of Judments in the Courts of Record in this Colony.

[Passed, March 9, 1774.]

WHEREAS great Mischiefs arise as well to Persons whilst living as to their Heirs Executors and Administrators, and also to Purchasers and Mortgagees by the Difficulty there is in discovering Judgments entered upon Record.

Be it therefore Enacted by his Excellency the Governor, the Council and the General Assembly and it is hereby enacted by the Authority of the same That the several and respective Clerks of the several and respective Courts of Record in this Province, shall before the last Day of the Term or Court next after the first Day of July in the present Year of our Lord one thousand seven hundred and seventy four, and so in every Term or at every Court or within six Days thereafter make or cause to be made, and put into an Alphabetical Docket by the Name or Names of the Party or Parties against whom such Judgment shall be entered a Particular of all Judgments by Confession, *non sum informatus* or *nil dicit*, and upon Verdicts, Writs of Inquiry, Demurrer, and every other Judgment for Debt or Damages entered in the said respective Courts of the Term or at the Court preceeding, which shall contain the Name and Names of the Plaintiff and Plaintiffs and the Name and Names of the Defendant and Defendants his her or their Place or Places of Abode and Title Trade or Profession (if any such be in the Record of the said Judgment) and the Debt Damages and Costs recovered thereby And that the said respective Dockets shall be fairly put into and kept in Books in the respective Offices of the said respective Clerks to be searched and viewed by all Persons at reasonable Times, paying to the respective Clerks in whose keeping the said Books respectively shall be for every Terms Search for Judgments against any one Person six Pence and no more upon Pain that every Clerk of the said respective Courts shall respectively for every Term or Court in which he shall omit or neglect to do his Duty in the Premisses forfeit the Sum of One Hundred Pounds, the one Moiety to the Party or Parties aggrieved, and the other Moiety to him or them who shall sue for the same, to be recovered in any Court of Record in this Province with Costs of Suit, wherein no Privilege or Essoin or Protection or Wager of Law shall be admitted nor more than one Imparlance.

And be it further Enacted by the Authority aforesaid That no Judgment not Docketed and entered in the Books as aforesaid shall affect any Lands or Tenements as to Purchasers or Mortgagees, or have any Preference against Heirs Executors or Administrators in their Administration of their Ancestors, Testators or Intestates Estates.

And be it further Enacted by the Authority aforesaid That hereafter there shall be paid by the Party or Parties in whose Favour any such Judgments shall be entered, to the Clerk of the Court in which such Judgments shall be respectively entered over and above the Fees now due for the same, the Sum of one Shilling and no more for Docketing the said Judgments, which Sum shall be allowed and taxed in the Bill of Costs against the Party or Parties chargeable therewith.

And Whereas it is the Practice in some of the said Courts for the Attornies of the same Courts, to enter the Judgments of the same Courts on Record and to get the same signed, and it sometimes happens that the Rolls or Records of such Judgments are not filed in the Office of the Clerk of such Court until long after the same are signed as aforesaid by reason whereof many great Mischiefs do happen. *Be it therefore further Enacted by the Authority aforesaid,* That the Clerks of the said respective Courts shall mark upon the Back of the Rolls or Judgments so filed, in their respective offices, the Time of filing the same And that no such Judgment shall affect any Lands or Tenements as to Purchasers or Mortgagees or have any Preference against Heirs Executors or Administrators in their Administration of their Ancestors, Testators or Intestates Estates but from the Time of the actual filing the same in the said respective Offices, And that the Clerks of the several inferior Courts of Record shall and may make the said Dockets from the Minutes of the said Courts, the Proceedings and taxed Bill of Costs in each Cause respectively Any Thing herein contained to the contrary notwithstanding.

[CHAPTER 1654.]

An Act to prevent the depreciating the. Paper Currency of this Colony.

[Passed, March 9, 1774.]

WHEREAS the Paper Currency or Bills of Credit issued in the Neighbouring Colonies are not made a legal Tender by any Act of this Colony, and yet for Convenience do pass therein as Money, and are often received in this Colony at a higher Value than they were emitted for by the Colony issuing the same, to the great Discredit and Depreciation of the Bills of Credit of this Colony, the Prejudice of Individuals; the draining the Colony of the Gold and Silver imported therein; and to the Obstruction and Detriment of Commerce.

Be it therefore Enacted by his Excellency the Governor, the Council and the General Assembly, and it is hereby enacted by the Authority of the same, that after the first Day of May next, No Person shall either pass, exchange, pay or receive any Bill of Credit of any of the Neighbouring Colonies for any Sum, or at any Rate more than the Sum payable therefor at the Treasury of that Colony in which the same was issued upon pain of Forfeiting a Sum equal to the Value of the Bills so passed, exchanged, paid or received at the Rate payable therefor at the Treasury of the Colony issuing the same, to be recovered with Costs of Suit, by

Bill Plaint or Information in any Court of Record, if the Sums or Bills received, passed, paid or exchanged at one time exceed Five Pounds, and if less before any Justice of the Peace according to the Course prescribed by An Act intitled An Act to empower Justices of the Peace, Mayors, Recorders and Aldermen to try Causes to the Value of five Pounds and under, and for suspending an Act therein mentioned; one Moiety of which said Penalty shall belong to the Person suing for the same, together with the whole Costs and the other Moiety thereof to be applyed for the use of the Poor of the City County Town or Place where the Offence was Committed and be paid to such Officer or Officers as are or may be appointed by Law to receive the same for the purposes aforesaid.

Provided always and it is also hereby enacted and declared by the same Authority, that this Act nor any Clause Article or Thing therein contained shall be construed or adjudged to give a Currency in this Colony to any of the Bills of Credit issued or to be issued in any of the neighbouring Colonies, or to oblige any Person to receive the same.

[CHAPTER 1655.]

An Act for the more effectual Prevention of private Lotteries.

[Passed, March 9, 1774.]

Whereas the Laws now in being for the Suppression of Private Lotteries have been found ineffectual to answer the salutary Purposes intended by the Legislature in enacting the Same. *And Whereas* many mischievous Consequences have been experienced from this Practice which has proved highly prejudicial to Trade, has occasioned Idleness and Inattention to Business, been productive of Fraud and Imposition, and has given Birth to a dangerous Spirit of gaming; for remedy whereof, and to suppress a Practice which may be attended with Distress, Impoverishment and ruin to many Families,

Be it Enacted adjudged and declared, and it is hereby enacted adjudged and declared by his Excellency the Governor the Council and the General Assembly, and by the Authority of the same, That all Lotteries after the first Day of May next other than such as are authorized by the Legislature, are common and public Nuisances, and the Justices of the Supreme Court of Judicature of this Colony, and all other Justices of the Courts of Oyer and Terminer, and the Justices of the Courts of General or Quarter Sessions of the Peace at their several Sessions within the respective Counties in this Colony are hereby empowered and required in all and every of their Charges hereafter to be made by them to the Grand Jurors in their several Courts, strictly to order and charge such Grand Jurors diligently to enquire present or indict all Breaches and Offences against this Act and the Court before whom such Indictment shall be made or found, are hereby empowered and required to prosecute such Indictment in the usual Manner of Prosecution, and upon Conviction to order Costs and Execution, and to apply the Penalties when recovered in the Manner herein directed.

And be it further Enacted by the Authority aforesaid, That no Person or Persons from and after the first Day of May next, shall open set on foot, carry on, or draw, publickly or privately, any Lottery, Game or Device of Chance of whatever Nature or Kind it may be, or by whatever Name, Denomination or Title it may be called known or distinguished, or shall by any such Ways or Means expose or set to Sale any Houses, Lands, Tenements and real Estate, or any Goods, Wares, Merchandize Cash or other Thing whatever; and every Person or Persons who shall offend in the Premises against the true Intent and Meaning of this Act, and shall be thereof convicted on the Oath of one or more credible Witness in the Supreme Court of Judicature, or in any of the inferior Courts of Common Pleas in this Colony, where such Offense shall be committed, or the Offender found, the Person so convicted shall forfeit double the Amount of the whole Sum or Value for which such Lottery was made; And if such Sum or Value can not be ascertained, then the said Offender shall forfeit five hundred Pounds, one half of the said Forfeiture to be paid to the Treasurer of this Colony for the use of his Majesty, his Heirs and Successors, for and towards the Support of Government, the other Half to the Person giving Information thereof; to be levied by Distress and Sale of the Offender's Goods and Chattels Lands and Tenements, by Process from the said Courts, and for want of Goods and Chattels Lands and Tenements, the Offender to be committed to the common Goal till the said Penalty be paid

And be it further Enacted by the Authority aforesaid, That if any Person shall vend or sell, or offer to vend or sell any Ticket or Tickets, or if any Person or Persons shall purchase the same, or shall in any wise become Adventurer or Adventurers, or be any ways concerned in any such Lotteries or Games of Chance by aiding or assisting in the same, either by printing writing or any other ways publishing an Account thereof, or where Tickets may be had for the same, every Person or Persons so offending, shall upon being convicted thereof as above forfeit Ten Pounds for every Offense to be recovered and applied in Manner above directed.

And be it further Enacted by the Authority aforesaid, That if any Person or Persons who shall be Adventurers in such Lotteries or Games as aforesaid for transferring of Property by Lot or Chance, shall become intitled to any Prize or Prizes, he or they shall be liable to forfeit the same to such Person or Persons who shall give Information thereof, so that such Offender may be convicted in Manner above directed; for the Recovery whereof the said Person or Persons so informing, shall be intitled to maintain an Action in any Court of Record in this Colony, against the Person who shall set up the said Lottery or Game, or Person or Persons selling or offering to sale any Ticket or Tickets, and if the Person or Persons so informing as aforesaid be himself an Adventurer in such Lottery or Game, he shall upon giving such Information as aforesaid be exempted from the Penalty which he would otherwise incurr by this act; And every Person or Persons adventuring as aforesaid whose Ticket or Tickets shall prove or turn up Blank, shall upon giving Information as aforesaid so that the Person or Persons setting up and drawing the said Lottery or other Game or selling or offering for Sale such Ticket or Tickets may be convicted, be intitled to recover against such Person or Persons the Money he or they adventured therein, with double Costs of Suit by Action of Debt in any of the Courts abovementioned in this Colony: And if the Person or Persons setting on Foot, and drawing such Lottery or Game as aforesaid, shall either before or after the drawing or finishing the same give Information thereof, so that the Persons adventuring therein may be convicted in Manner before directed he or they shall not only be exempted from the Penalty he or they would otherwise have incurred by this Act, and be intitled to the Reward allowed to Persons informing in such Case, but shall also have a Right to retain all such Monies as he or they may have received in the Sale of Tickets.

And for the more easy Detection of the said Lotteries or Games, *Be it further Enacted by the Authority aforesaid.* That it shall be lawful for any of the Justices of the Supreme Court of Judicature; the Judges of the Inferior Courts of Common Pleas, or any Justice of the Peace in this Colony, having reasonable Cause to suspect that any such Lottery or Game as aforesaid is set on foot or carrying on, to summon any Person or Persons who shall be suspected to be privy to the same, and to examine him or them touching the same, and in order that such Persons may not be excused from answering any Questions which shall be asked them by either of the said Judges or Justices by Colour of any Plea or Pretence that they may thereby incur any Penalty inflicted by this Act, or any other Act of this Colony; it is hereby declared that they shall upon being examined as aforesaid, and declaring all they know touching the Matters enquired of them by the said Judges or Justices, be exempted from any such Penalty and from all Prosecutions in virtue of this Act, or any other Act of this Colony: And in Case any Person summoned as aforesaid, shall refuse to be sworn, or answer such Questions as shall be asked thereupon, the Judges or Justices shall, and hereby are impowered to commit such Person to the Common Goal, there to remain till he shall comply, or be from thence delivered by due Course of Law.

And be it further Enacted by the Authority aforesaid, That every Conveyance Grant Bargain Sale or Transfer of any Lands Tenements, Hereditaments and real Estate, or of any Goods or Chattels whatsoever, which shall hereafter be made in pursuance of any such Lottery Game or other Device to be determined by Chance or Lot are hereby declared void and of none Effect.

And for the more effectual Suppressing and preventing such unlawful Lotteries. *Be it further Enacted*, That the Justices of the Peace, and all Mayors Bailiffs, Constables and other his Majesty's Civil Officers within their respective Jurisdictions, are hereby impowered directed and required to use their utmost Endeavors to prevent the drawing of any such unlawful Lotteries, by all lawful Ways and Means, according to the true Intent and Meaning of this Act.

And be it further Enacted by the Authority aforesaid, That where any two or more Persons shall be concerned in setting on Foot, carrying on, or drawing any Lottery or Game of Chance, or be joint Adventurers in the same, the Penalties abovesaid may be recovered against all or either of them, any Thing in this Act, or any Law to the contrary notwithstanding.

[CHAPTER 1656.]

[See chapter 1433. Expired, January 31, 1775.]

An Act to revive an Act entitled "An Act to restrain Hawkers and Pedlars within this Colony from selling without Licence," with an Addition thereto.

[Passed, March 9, 1774.]

Be it Enacted by his Excellency the Governor, the Council and the General Assembly, and it is hereby enacted by the Authority of the same, That the Act entitled "An Act to restrain Hawkers and Pedlars within this Colony from selling without Licence," passed the twenty seventh Day of January, one thousand seven hundred and seventy, shall be and hereby is revived and every Article Matter and Clause therein contained enacted to be and remain in full force until the first Day of February which will be in the year of our Lord one thousand seven hundred and seventy five,

And be it further Enacted by the same Authority, That if any Hawker or Pedlar shall sell any kind of Goods, wares or Merchandize whatsoever unto any Slave, without the Leave and Permission of the Person owning such Slave, and shall be thereof accused by any Person, and convicted before any one Justice of the Peace of this Colony, shall for every such Offence, forfeit and pay the Sum of five Pounds, which Justice is hereby strictly required and directed to hear and finally determine the same, and give Judgment and award Execution in the usual Manner of Proceeding on the Trial of Causes of the value of five Pounds and under before Justices of the Peace; the one half of which Forfeiture shall go to the Person suing for the same, and the other half to the Overseers of the Poor in the District where such Offence shall be committed, to be by the Overseers of the Poor applied to the use of the Poor of such District, any Law, Usage or Custom to the contrary notwithstanding.

[CHAPTER 1657.]

[See chapter 767.]

An Act to amend an Act entitled "An Act for the speedy punishing and releasing such Persons from Imprisonment, as shall Commit any Criminal Offences, under the Degree of Grand Larceny."

[Passed, March 9, 1774.]

WHEREAS the aforesaid Act has been found very beneficial, and it is disputable whether the Justices of the Peace may try an Offender against the said Act, who is of Ability and refuses to give sufficient Bail in the Manner therein directed,

Be it therefore Enacted by his Excellency the Governor, the Council and the General Assembly and it is hereby enacted by the Authority of the same, That when any such Offender shall be in Custody in the Manner mentioned in the said Act, it shall be at his own Election or Choice to give sufficient Bail; and upon Refusal, three Justices of the Peace shall try him in the Manner directed in the said Act, any Thing contained therein to the contrary in any wise notwithstanding: *And also,* That this Act shall extend to the trial of offenders against one other Act, entitled "An Act to relieve the Cities and Counties of this Colony by the speedy Trial of petty Offenders."

[CHAPTER 1658.]

An Act to prevent the Abatement of Suits by the Death of the Parties.

[Passed, March 9, 1774.]

WHEREAS the Practice of the Courts of Equity in Cases where there are many Parties to Suits depending therein, may be attended with great Delays and Expence by the Death of some of the Parties, and the abatement of such Suits in Consequence thereof; And Whereas every Obstacle to the Easy and expeditious Administration of Justice should be removed, every unnecessary Expence prevented, and the Remedy of Suitors be as much as possible facilitated,

Be it therefore declared and Enacted by his Excellency the Governor the Council and the General Assembly and it is hereby declared and enacted by the Authority of the same, That in all

Actions now depending, or which shall hereafter be brought in any Court of Equity in this Colony, if there be two or more Plaintiffs or Defendants, and one or more of them should die, if the Cause of Action shall survive to the surviving Plaintiff or Plaintiffs, or against the Surviving Defendant or Defendants, such Action shall not be thereby abated, but the same shall proceed at the Suit of the Surviving Plaintiff or Plaintiffs, against the Surviving Defendant or Defendants, such Death being suggested by Affidavit or otherwise to the Satisfaction of the Court.

And be it further Enacted by the Authority aforesaid, That in all and every such Action or Actions in which any Bill or Bills is, are, or shall or may hereafter be filed, and in which there shall be two or more Plaintiffs or Defendants, and any of them shall die, and the Cause of Action shall not Survive, but other Persons shall become Parties in Interest, in right of such deceased Party; any such Suit shall by reason of such Death, be abated only with respect to such deceased Person or Persons, and the surviving Plaintiff or Plaintiffs shall and may proceed against the surviving Defendant or Defendants, without reviving the Suit against the Representatives of the deceased Party, *Provided however*, that in such Case such Representatives shall not be bound by any Order or Decree in such Cause, to which they are not made Parties: And in Case the Plaintiff or Plaintiffs shall choose to make the Representatives of the deceased Person, Parties to such Suit, no Bill of Rivivor, or *Subpoena ad revivendum*, shall be necessary, but the Court in which such Action shall be depending, shall and may by Rule or Order as often as there shall be Occasion for it, direct the Suit to stand revived; which Rule or Order shall be served on the adverse Clerk; and unless the Representatives of such deceased Person or Persons shall within eighty Days after such Service as aforesaid, appear and file their Answer, or signify their Disclaimer of the Suit and the Matters in controversy thereby, the Plaintiff or Plaintiffs may cause their Appearance to be entered, and in such Case the Answer of the deceased Person or Persons shall be deemed and taken as and for the Answer of such Representatives.

And be it further Enacted by the said Authority aforesaid, That in Case any Plaintiff or Plaintiffs, in such Suit or Suits in Equity now depending or hereafter to be brought, wherein the Cause of Action shall not survive as aforesaid shall happen to die, pending such Suit or Suits, the lawful Representative or Representatives of such deceased Plaintiff or Plaintiffs shall and may upon Affidavit in such Suit or Suits, by him or them or any other Person or Persons, and on Motion thereon made in open Court be by Rule or Order of such Court inserted as a Complainant or Complainants in the said Suit or Suits, and be permitted to make such Amendments in the Bill or Bills of Complaint as his her or their Title or Interest therein, under such deceased Plaintiff or Plaintiffs may require, to which Amendment or Amendments, the Defendant or Defendants shall be compellable by Rule and Order of the said Court to answer, proceed to Issue and Examinations of Witnesses and Production of Proofs, and all other Proceedings shall be had thereon as in ordinary Cases: And in Case such Person or Persons shall not within Eighty Days after the Death or Deaths of such Plaintiff or Plaintiffs cause himself, herself or themselves to be entered Plaintiff or Plaintiffs as aforesaid in the Room of such deceased Plaintiff or Plaintiffs, that then and in every such Case the surviving Plaintiff or Plaintiffs may insert the Representative or Representatives of such deceased Plaintiff or Plaintiffs as Defendant or Defendants in such Suit or Suits and proceed in such Manner as by this Act is directed in Cases where the lawful Representative or Representatives of a deceased Defendant or Defendants may be made Party or Parties.

[CHAPTER 1659.]

An Act to prevent the breaking or defacing the Mile Stones now or hereafter to be erected in this Colony.

[Passed, March 9, 1774.]

WHEREAS the erection of Mile Stones, Hands Pointers, or any other Monument erected for the Direction of Travellers, along the Public Roads, contributes greatly to the Convenience of Travellers, *And Whereas* a Number of them have been put up in different Parts of this Colony, and probably many more will hereafter be erected,

Be it therefore Enacted by his Excellency the Governor the Council and the General Assembly, and it is hereby enacted by the Authority of the same, That from and after the passing of this Act, if any Person or Persons shall remove or willfully break, deface or in any wise damage any or either of the Mile Stones, Hands, Pointers or any other Monument already erected and put up, or hereafter to be erected or put up within this

Colony, the Person or Persons so removing or willfully breaking defacing or in any wise damaging any or either of the said Mile Stones, Hands, Pointers, or any other Monument, shall forfeit for every such Misdemeanor the Sum of three Pounds, to be recovered before any one of his Majesty's Justices of the Peace of the County where such offence shall be committed, who is hereby impowered in a summary way to hear and determine such Offence, and to cause such Forfeiture to be levied on the Goods and Chattels of the Offender, and in Default thereof to commit him to the common Goal there to remain for the Space of two Months, unless the Forfeiture be sooner paid, the said Forfeiture to be applied, the one Half to the Prosecutor; and the other Half after repairing the Damage, to go to the Poor.

And be it further Enacted by the Authority aforesaid, That if any Slave shall be guilty of the Offence intended to be prevented by this Act, such Slave shall for every such Offence, upon Conviction thereof before any one of his Majesty's Justices of the Peace be committed to the Common Goal and receive thirty nine Lashes on the bare Back unless the said Forfeiture of three Pounds be paid within six Days after such Conviction.

And be it further Enacted by the Authority aforesaid, That all Grand Jurors, and all Judges, Justices, Sheriffs, Constables and other Civil Officers within their respective Jurisdictions shall as much as in them lies endeavor to find out such Offenders, and prevent, prosecute and punish them according to the true Intent and Meaning of this Act.

[CHAPTER 1660.]

[Expired, December 31, 1775.]

An Act for preventing tumultuous and riotous Assemblies in the Places therein mentioned, and for the more speedy and effectual punishing the Rioters.

[Passed, March 9, 1774.]

Whereas a Spirit of Riot and Licentiousness has of late prevailed in some Parts of the Counties of Charlotte and Albany, and many Acts of Outrage and Cruelty have been perpetrated by a Number of turbulent Men, who assembling from Time to Time in Arms have seized insulted and menaced several Magistrates and other Civil Officers, so that they dare not execute their respective Functions; rescued Prisoners for Debt; assumed to themselves Military Commands and Judicial Powers; burned and demolished the Houses and Property, and beat and abused the Persons of many of his Majesty's Subjects; expelled others from their Possessions, and finally have put a Period to the administration of Justice within, and spread Terror and Destruction throughout that Part of the Country which is exposed to their Oppression: Therefore for the Preventing and suppressing such Riots and Tumults; and for the more speedy and effectual punishing the Offenders therein,

Be it Enacted by his Excellency the Governor, the Council and the General Assembly, and it is hereby enacted by the Authority of the same, That if any Persons to the Number of three or more being unlawfully, riotously and tumultuously assembled within either of the said Counties to the Disturbance of the Public Peace at any Time after the Passing of this Act, and being required or commanded by any one or more Justice or Justices of the Peace, or by the High Sheriff, or his Under Sheriff, or by any one of the Coroners of the County where such Assembly shall be; by Proclamation to be made in the King's Name, in the Form herein after directed to disperse themselves and peaceably to depart to their Habitations, or to their lawful Business, shall to the Number of three or more notwithstanding such Proclamation made, unlawfully riotously and tumultuously remain or continue together after such Command or request made by Proclamation, that then every Person or Persons so continuing together to the Number of three or more, after such Command or request made by Proclamation, shall for every such Offence upon Conviction thereof in due Form of Law, either in the Supreme Court of Judicature of this Colony, or at the Courts of Oyer and Terminer and general Goal Delivery, or at the General Sessions of the Peace to be held respectively in and for the said Counties of Albany or Charlotte or either of them suffer twelve Months Imprisonment without Bail or Mainprize, and such further Corporal Punishment as the respective Courts before which he she or they shall be convicted, shall judge fit, not extending to Life or Limb, and before his her or their Discharge shall enter into Recognizance with two sufficient Securities in such Sums as the said Courts shall respectively direct, to be of the good Behaviour, and to keep the Peace towards his Majesty and all his Subjects for the Term of three Years from such his her or their Discharge out of Prison.

And be it further Enacted by the Authority aforesaid, That the Order and Form of the Proclamation which shall be made by the Authority of this Act, shall be as hereafter follows, *that is to say*, the Justice or other Person authorized by this Act to make the said Proclamation, shall among the said Rioters, or as near to them as he can safely come, with a loud Voice command or cause to be commanded, Silence to be kept while Proclamation is making, and shall then openly with a loud Voice, make or cause to be made Proclamation in these Words or to the like Effect: "Our Sovereign Lord the King chargeth and commandeth all Persons being assembled, immediately to disperse themselves, and peaceably to depart to their Habitations, or to their lawful Business upon the Pain contained in the Act made in the fourteenth Year of the Reign of King George the third for preventing tumultuous and Riotous Assemblies," and every such Justice and Justices of the Peace, Sheriff, under Sheriff or Coroner within the Limits of the respective Counties where they reside are hereby authorized impowered and required on Notice or Knowledge of any such unlawful riotous and tumultuous Assembly, forthwith to repair to the Place where such unlawful riotous and tumultuous Assembly shall be, to the Number of three or more, and there to make or cause to be made Proclamation in Manner aforesaid.

And be it further Enacted by the Authority aforesaid, That if any Person or Persons do or shall with Force and Arms wilfully and knowingly oppose obstruct or in any Manner wilfully and knowingly let, hinder or hurt any Person or Persons who shall begin to proclaim, or go to proclaim according to the Proclamation hereby directed to be made whereby such Proclamation shall not be made; that then every such opposing, letting hindering or hurting such Person or Persons so beginning or going to make such Proclamation as aforesaid shall be adjudged Felony without Benefit of Clergy; and that the Offenders therein shall be adjudged Felons and shall suffer Death as in Cases of Felony without benefit of Clergy, and that also every such Person or Persons so being unlawfully riotously and tumultuously assembled to the Number of three as aforesaid or more to whom Proclamation should or ought to have been made if the same had not been hindered as aforesaid shall in Case they or any of them to the Number of three or more shall continue together, and not forthwith disperse themselves after such Let or Hinderence so made, having knowledge of such Let or Hinderence; shall likewise for every such Offense upon Conviction thereof in Manner aforesaid suffer the same Pains and Penalties as are hereby inflicted on those who shall continue together to the Number of three or more after they shall be commanded to depart to their Habitations or lawful Business by Proclamation as aforesaid.

And be it further Enacted by the Authority aforesaid, That if such Persons so unlawfully riotously and tumultuously assembled or any three or more of them after Proclamation made in Manner aforesaid shall continue together and not forthwith disperse themselves, it shall and may be lawful to and for every Justice of the Peace Sheriff under-Sheriff, Coroner or Constable of any County or Township, where such Assembly shall be, and to and for such Person or Persons as shall be commanded to be assisting unto such Justice of the Peace Sheriff under Sheriff Coroner or Constable who are hereby authorized and impowered to command all his Majesty's Subjects of age and ability to be aiding and assisting to them therein, to seize and apprehend, and they are hereby required to seize and apprehend such Persons so unlawfully riotously and tumultuously assembled together after Proclamation made as aforesaid and forthwith to carry the Persons so apprehended before any one or more of his Majesty's Justices of the Peace of the said Counties of Charlotte or Albany in order to their being proceeded against for such their Offences according to Law. And that if the Persons so unlawfully, riotously and tumultuously assembled, or any of them shall happen to be killed maimed or hurt in the dispersing seizing or apprehending or endeavoring to disperse seize or apprehend them, by reason of their resisting the Persons so dispersing seizing or apprehending or endeavoring to disperse seize or apprehend them, that then every such Justice of the Peace, Sheriff, under Sheriff, Coroner or Constable and all and singular Persons being aided and assisting to them, or any of them, shall be freed, discharged and indemnified as well against the King's Majesty his Heirs and Successors as against all and every other Person and Persons, of for or concerning the killing, maiming or hurting of any such Person or Persons so unlawfully riotously and tumultuously assembled that shall happen to be so killed maimed or hurt as aforesaid.

And be it further Enacted by the Authority aforesaid, That if any Person or Persons within the said Counties or either of them, not being lawfully authorized as a Judge, Justice or Magistrate, shall assume Judicial Power, or shall try, fine, sentence or condemn any Person who shall either be absent or shall unlawfully or forcibly be seized taken or brought before him or them for Trial or Punishment; or if any Person or Persons shall aid or Assist in such illegal Proceedings, or shall inforce execute or carry the same into effect, or if any Person or Persons shall unlawfully seize detain or confine, or assault and beat any Magistrate or Civil Officer, for or in the respect of any Act or Proceeding in the due Exercise of his Function, or in order to compel him to resign, renounce or surcease his Commission or Authority, or to terrify, hinder or prevent him from performing and discharging the Duties thereof, or if any Person or Persons either secretly or openly, shall unlawfully wilfully and maliciously burn or destroy the Grain Corn or Hay of any other Person, being in any enclosure, or if any Persons unlawfully riotously and tumultuously assembled together to the Disturbance of the Public Peace, shall unlawfully and with Force demolish or pull down, or begin to demolish or pull down any dwelling House Barn Stable, Grist Mill, Saw Mill or Out House within either of the said Counties, that then each of the said Offences respectively shall be adjudged Felony without Benefit of Clergy, and the Offenders therein shall be adjudged Felons, and shall suffer Death as in Cases of Felony without Benefit of Clergy.

And Whereas Complaint and Proofs have been made as well before his Excellency the Governor in Council as before the General Assembly, That Ethan Allen sometime of Saulsbury in the Colony of Connecticut, but late of Bennington in the County of Albany Yeoman, Seth Warner late of Bennington in the said County Yeoman, Remember Baker late of Arlington in the said County Yeoman, Robert Cockran late of Rupert in the County of Charlotte Yeoman, Peleg Sunderland & Sylvanus Brown late of Socialborough in the same County Yeoman, James Brackenridge late of Wallumschack in the County of Albany Yeoman, and John Smith late of Socialborough in the County of Charlotte Yeoman, have been principal Ringleaders of, and Actors in the Riots and Disturbances aforesaid; and the General Assembly have thereupon addressed his Excellency the Governor to issue a Proclamation offering certain Rewards for apprehending and securing the said Offenders, and for bringing them and the other Perpetrators and Authors of the said Riots to Justice; and forasmuch as such disorderly Practices are highly Criminal and destructive to the Peace and settlement of the Country, and it is indispensably necessary for want of Process to Outlawry (which is not used in this Colony,) that special provision be made for bringing such Offenders in future to Trial and Punishment without exposing the Colony to the Expence of extraordinary Rewards and Bounties for apprehending such Offenders.

Be it therefore Enacted by the Authority aforesaid, That it shall and may be lawful to and for his Excellency the Governor, or the Governor or Commander in Chief for the Time being by and with the Advice of the Council as often as either of the abovenamed Persons or any other person shall be indicted in either of the Counties aforesaid for any Offence perpetrated after the passing of this Act made capital by this or any other Law, or where any person may stand indicted for any of the Offences abovementioned, not made Felony by this Act to make his Order in Council thereby requiring and commanding such Offender and Offenders to surrender themselves respectively within the Space of seventy Days next after the first Publication thereof in the New York *Gazette* and Weekly *Mercury*, to one of his Majesty's Justices of the Peace for either of the said Counties respectively, who are hereby required thereupon to commit him or them without Bail or Mainprize to the Goal of the City of New York, or of the City and County of Albany, to the End that he or they may be forthcoming to answer the Offence or Offences wherewith he or they shall stand charged according to the ordinary Course of the Law which Order the Clerk of his Majesty's Council or his Deputy shall cause to be forthwith printed and published in eight successive Papers of the New York *Gazette* and Weekly *Mercury*, the two first of which to be forthwith transmitted to the Sheriffs of the Counties of Albany and Charlotte, and the said Sheriffs respectively shall within six Days after the Receipt thereof cause the same printed Orders to be affixed upon the Door of the Court House of the County of Albany, and upon the Door of the Dwelling House of Patrick Smith Esquire, where the Courts are now usually held for the said County of Charlotte, and upon the Doors of two other Public Houses in each of their respective Counties; And in Case the said Offenders shall not respectively surrender themselves pursuant to such Order of his Excellency the Governor, or of the Governor or Commander in Chief for the Time being to be made in Council as aforesaid, he or they so neglecting or refusing to surrender himself or themselves as aforesaid, shall from the Day to be appointed for his or their Surrender as aforesaid be adjudged deemed and taken (if indicted for a Capital Offence hereafter to be perpetrated,) to be convicted and attainted of Felony, and shall suffer Death as in Cases of Persons convicted and attainted of Felony by Verdict and Judgment without Benefit of Clergy; and that it shall and may be lawful to and for the Supreme Court of Judicature of this Colony, or the Courts of Oyer and Terminer or General Goal Delivery for the respective Counties aforesaid to award Execution against such Offender or Offenders so indicted for a Capital Offence perpetrated after the passing of this Act in such Manner as if he or they had been convicted or attainted in the said Supreme Court of Judicature or before such Courts of Oyer and Terminer or General Goal Delivery respectively; and if any Offender being indicted for a lesser Offence under the Degree of Felony shall not surrender himself within the Time fixed by such Order and after such Notice as aforesaid, he shall thenceforth be deemed guilty of the Offence for which he may be charged, by such Indictment, and it shall be lawful for the Court wherein such Indictment is found to proceed to pronounce such Judgment against the Offender as might lawfully be done if he was present in Court, and convicted in the ordinary Course of the Law, of the Crime wherewith he shall so stand charged as aforesaid.

Provided always and be it further enacted by the same Authority, That if any Person so neglecting to surrender himself as aforesaid within the said seventy Days shall at any time afterwards surrender himself to the Sheriff of the City of New York or Albany, or of the Counties of Dutchess or West Chester, (who are to receive and safely keep such Offender,) and being actually in custody exhibit reasonable Proof to the Satisfaction of the Judges of the Supreme Court of this Colony, or either of them, that he was not within either of the said Counties of Albany or Charlotte, or within either the Counties of Cumberland or Gloucester at any Time after the Publication and Notice above directed, and before such Surrender of himself as aforesaid, then such Judge before whom such Proof is made shall forthwith notify the same in Writing to the Sheriff to whom any Warrant of Execution for the Executing such Offender or any other Process for any lesser Punishment, hath been or may be issued, and thenceforth such Prisoner or Offender shall not be liable to suffer Death or any other Punishment for not surrendering himself within the said seventy Days as aforesaid. *Provided also*, That Nothing in this Act contained shall be construed to exempt any Offender so surrendering himself after the seventy Days as aforesaid from any Punishment to which he may be liable for any other Crime than for not surrendering himself within the seventy Days as aforesaid, nor to deprive any Person who shall so surrender himself within the seventy Days from being bailed in Cases where he shall be bailable by Law; any Thing herein contained to the contrary thereof in anywise notwithstanding.

And be it further Enacted by the same Authority, That all and every Person and Persons who shall after the expiration of the Time to be appointed as aforesaid for the surrender of the respective Offenders herein before named, harbour, receive conceal, abet or succour such Offender or Offenders knowing him or them to have been required to surrender him or themselves by such Order or Orders as aforesaid, and not to have surrendered pursuant thereto, shall upon Conviction thereof in due Form of Law suffer the same Pains and Penalties as are by this Act inflicted on those who shall continue together to the Number of three or more after they shall be commanded to depart to their Habitations or lawful Business by Proclamation as aforesaid.

And whereas the said County of Charlotte hath but lately been set off from the said County of Albany, and there is yet no Goal or Court House erected within the same, and a great Part of the said County being involved in a state of Anarchy and Confusion by reason of the Violent Proceedings of the aforesaid riotous and disorderly People, from whence it must at present be extremely difficult if not impracticable to bring Offenders to Justice within the said County.

Be it therefore further Enacted by the Authority aforesaid That all Treasons Felonies, Crimes, Misdemeanors and Offences whatsoever at any Time heretofore committed or perpetrated to be committed or perpetrated within the said County of Charlotte shall and may be proceeded against and presented by any Grand Jury for the County of Albany, from Time to Time to be impanelled and sworn at any Court of criminal Jurisdiction to be held in and for the said County of Albany, who shall and may charge any of the said Offences to have been committed in any Part of the said County of Charlotte, and all Indictments so found by them shall be adjudged to be good and valid, notwithstanding that the Place of perpetrating any of the said Offences be in the said Indictments alledged to be out of the said County of Albany; and all such Offences and Offenders which shall be presented or indicted as aforesaid, shall and may be tried within the County of Albany and by a Jury thereof, and there heard determined and punished in the same Manner and Form, as if such Treason, Felony, Crime, Misdemeanor or Offence had arisen and been perpetrated within the said County of Albany.

Provided always and be it further Enacted, That if at any Time hereafter the Justices to be appointed for holding Courts of Oyer and Terminer and General Goal Delivery for the said County of Charlotte, in Cases cognizable before them; or the Justices of the General Sessions of the Peace for the said County of Charlotte, in Cases cognizable before them; shall concieve that any Prisoner or Offender, may be safely brought to Justice within, and by a Jury of the said County of Charlotte; that then it shall and may be lawful to and for each of the said Courts respectively to proceed against, and try such Prisoner or Offender, having lawful Cognizance of his Cause, within and by a Jury of the said County of Charlotte, and him there to acquit and deliver, or to sentence condemn and punish as the Law directs; any Thing in this Act to the contrary thereof notwithstanding.

And be it further Enacted by the Authority aforesaid, That this Act shall be publickly read in every Court of General Sessions of the Peace to be held in each of the said Counties of Albany and Charlotte respectively.

And be it further Enacted by the Authority aforesaid, That this Act shall remain and continue in full Force and Effect from the passing thereof, until the first Day of January which will be in the Year of our Lord one thousand seven hundred and seventy six.

[CHAPTER 1661.]

[Expired, April 30, 1777.]

An Act for the better regulating the Public Roads in the City and County of New York.

[Passed, March 9, 1774.]

Be it Enacted by his Excellency the Governor the Council and the General Assembly, and it is hereby enacted by the Authority of the same, That the Mayor Aldermen and Commonalty of the City of New York and their Successors shall be and hereby are appointed Commissioners to regulate and keep in repair the present Highways, and to lay out regulate and keep in repair such other Public Roads or Highways in the said City and County as shall hereafter be laid out by Act or Acts hereafter to be passed for that Purpose, and they are hereby fully authorized and impowered to put in execution the several Services in tended by this Act, *that is to say*, That the said Commissioners are hereby authorized and impowered to widen all Public Roads and Highways already laid out in the said City and County to such convenient Breadth not exceeding four Rods nor less than two, (provided that the Main Road leading to King's Bridge shall not be of less Breadth than it is at present, nor any part thereof less than four Rods wide,) as the said Commissioners shall judge fit to make them passable for Horses and Carriages, paying the Owner or Proprietor the Value thereof as shall be assessed by a Jury summoned as usual, (Provided that no Person be paid for any Land which they have incroached on the Road,) and also to make all such other Public Roads or Highways as they shall think necessary or convenient to lay out in the said City and County in Manner as aforesaid, if the Owner or Owners of the Lands through which such new Roads are to run will on reasonable Recompence consent to the same, and to alter any old Roads which they shall think proper, provided such Alteration be made and done with the Consent of the Owner or Owners of the Lands contiguous thereto; And also to make and build Bridges and Causeways where they shall think it necessary, and to dig Ditches from the said Road or Roads through any Person's Land where they shall judge it necessary for carrying off the Water and keeping the Roads dry, and also to appoint one or more Surveyors or Overseers of the said Roads, and to employ Labourers and Workmen on the best Terms they can to make and keep in repair the said Public Roads or Highways.

And be it further Enacted by the Authority aforesaid, That the said Commissioners shall from Time to Time during the Continuance of this Act enter in Writing all the Roads or Highways by them widened laid out or altered to be signed by the Clerk of the said Mayor Aldermen and Commonalty, and cause the same to be entered in the Records of the said City and County; and whatever the said Commissioners shall do according to the Power given them by this Act being so entered on Record shall be deemed valid and good to all Intents, Constructions and Purposes in the Law whatsoever

And be it further Enacted by the Authority aforesaid, That in Case any Person or Persons shall wantonly spoil or damage any such Roads, Bridges or Causeways or fill up or destroy any of the Ditches aforesaid, or Fence across any of the said Roads or Highways, or erect or set up any Gates thereon, or put or leave in them any unnecessary Obstruction without Leave of the said Commissioners, such Person or Persons shall for every such Offence forfeit and pay to the Chamberlain of the City of New York the Sum of forty Shillings to be applied to the repairing and embellishing the said Roads or Highways as the said Commissioners shall think fit, and to be recovered by the said Chamberlain by Action of Debt with Costs of Suit in a Summary way, before any Justice of the Peace within the said City: And in Case any Person or Persons shall leave a dead Horse or the Carcase of any other Beast, or any broken Carriage on any of the said Roads or Highways, for any longer Time than is necessary in order to remove the same, or set up near the said Roads or Highways, any Thing by which Horses are usually affrighted, or shall by any improper Behaviour Affright any Horse or Traveller on any of the said Roads, every such Person or Persons shall for every such Offence forfeit the Sum of forty Shillings, and any Person leaving a dead Dog in any of the said Roads or Highways shall forfeit the Sum of ten Shillings, to be recovered, paid and applied as aforesaid.

And be it further Enacted by the Authority aforesaid, That in Case any Person or Persons shall fell or any way destroy any Tree or Trees standing on any of the said Roads or within the Distance of one Rod of any of them, without the Leave of the said Mayor Aldermen and Commonalty, or of the Owner of such Tree or Trees, such Person or Persons shall for every such Offence forfeit the Sum of three Pounds, to be recovered paid and applied as aforesaid.

And be it Enacted by the Authority aforesaid, That all Persons meeting each other on any of the said Roads or Highways in Carriages or Sleighs, those going out shall give way to such as are coming towards the Town, under the Penalty of forty shillings to be recovered and applied as aforesaid.

And be it further Enacted by the Authority aforesaid That on information being given by any Person whatsoever to the Overseers of the said Roads or Highways of any of the said Nuisances or Obstructions, he shall immediately proceed to the removing thereof, and shall also use his best Endeavors to discover the Person or Persons who committed the same, who upon Discovery shall not only be liable to the Penalties hereinbefore appointed according to the Nature of the Offense, but also to the Costs of removing them, and a reasonable Allowance to the said Overseer for his Time and Trouble therein to be recovered by him in a Summary Way with Costs of Suit before any Justice of the Peace within the said City, and every such Overseer neglecting or refusing to do his Duty according to the true Intent and Meaning of this Act, shall for every such Neglect or Refusal Forfeit the Sum of five Pounds to be recovered paid and applied as aforesaid. And in Order as far as possible to prevent the Evasion of the good Purposes intended by this Act.

Be it further Enacted by the Authority aforesaid, That the Owner of any Dead Horse or other Nuisance left on any of the said Roads or Highways shall be deemed to have put or left the same thereon unless he proves the contrary.

And be it further Enacted by the Authority aforesaid, That the first Process to be issued against any Offender or Offenders against this Act shall be by Warrant and not otherwise, and the Execution on every such Process shall be against the Goods and Chattels of the Offender or Offenders, and for want of such Goods and Chattels against his her or their Bodies, and shall be contained in one and the same Precept and not otherwise, any Law Usage or Custom to the contrary thereof in any wise notwithstanding.

This Act to be in force from the passing thereof, until the first Day of March which will be in the Year of our Lord one thousand seven hundred and Seventy seven.

[CHAPTER 1662.]

[See chapter 1492. Expired, January 31, 1780.]

An Act to revive an Act entitled "An Act for the better regulation of the Election of Officers in the City of New York, chosen by virtue of the Charters granted to the said City, and other Purposes therein mentioned."

[Passed, March 9, 1774.]

Be it Enacted by his Excellency the Governor the Council and the General Assembly, and it is hereby enacted by the Authority of the same, That the Act entitled "An Act for the better Regulation of the Election of Officers in the City of New York chosen by virtue of the Charters granted to the said City, and other Purposes therein mentioned," passed in the eleventh Year of his present Majesty's Reign, shall be and hereby is revived, and every Clause Matter and Thing therein contained enacted to be and to continue in force from the passing hereof, until the first Day of February which will be in the Year of our Lord one thousand seven hundred and eighty.

[CHAPTER 1663.]

[See chapter 1551. Expired, April 30, 1777.]

An Act to lay a Tax on Dogs in the Cities of New York and Albany, and Counties of Queens and Suffolk.

[Passed, March 9, 1774.]

Be it Enacted by his Excellency the Governor the Council and the General Assembly, and it is hereby enacted by the Authority of the same, That it shall and may be lawful for the Persons appointed to collect the Poor Tax in each Ward in the Cities of New York and Albany, and in each respective Town Manor Precinct or District within the Counties of Queens and Suffolk, once in every Year after the first Day of May next, during the continuance of this Act, and not oftner, to demand and receive of and from all Persons within their several Districts having the Property in, or keeping any Dog or Dogs of what kind or size soever of six Months old and upwards the Sum of one Shilling for each Dog, and if there should be more than one Dog kept by any one Person or Family then he she or they shall pay the Sum of two Shillings for the second Dog, and the Sum of four Shillings for every Dog above the Number of two kept as aforesaid.

And be it further Enacted by the Authority aforesaid, That if any Person or Persons having Property in, or keeping any Dog or Dogs of what size or kind soever as aforesaid, shall neglect or refuse to pay unto the Collector or Collectors of their several and respective Districts, the Sum or Sums as above fixed, when thereunto required; it shall and may be lawful for the Collectors of the respective Districts within the Cities and Counties aforesaid, them and each of them in their respective Districts to levy the same by Distress and Sale of the Offenders Goods returning the Overplus if any be, and for Want thereof, to commence and prosecute his or their Action or Actions against any Delinquent or Delinquents within their respective Districts for the recovery of the same with Costs of Suit before any one Justice of the Peace for the Cities or Counties aforesaid and if any Person or Persons shall deny that he she or they have Property in, or keep any Dog, yet if it can be proved that such Person or Persons are in possession of, or suffer the same to remain in or about his or her House, thirty Days before the

Demand made by the Collector, he she or they shall be deemed to be the Owner or Owners of such Dog or Dogs, and liable to the Payment of the aforesaid Tax, to be recovered as above. and if any Dog or Dogs shall keep about any Person's House twenty Days, and no Person appearing within that time to claim the same, it shall and may be lawful for such Person having such Dog or Dogs about his or her House as aforesaid, to kill him or them at any Time after the said twenty days.

And be it Enacted by the Authority aforesaid, That the Collector or Collectors of each respective District within the Cities and Counties aforesaid, shall each keep a Book and therein enter the Names of every Person in their several and respective Districts keeping Dog or Dogs, and the Number, with the Tax or Sums Collected by virtue of this Act and the same shall pay into the Hands of the Church Wardens or Overseers of the Poor of the several and respective Districts within the Counties of Queens and Suffolk, to be by them applied for the Use of their Poor respectively: And the Money arising from the Tax in the City and County of New York shall be paid into the hands of the Chamberlain of the said City, to be applied by the Mayor Aldermen and Commonalty of the said City as a Bounty for Tiles to be made in this Colony, and sold in the City of New York in such Manner, and under such Regulations as they shall think necessary: And the Money arising from the Tax in the City of Albany shall be paid to the Chamberlain of the said City to be applied by the Mayor Aldermen and Commonalty for and towards keeping in repair the Public Roads within the said City: each Collector retaining in his Hands one Shilling in the Pound for collecting and paying the same.

And be it Enacted by the Authority aforesaid, That if any of the Collectors, Church Wardens, Constables or Overseers of the Poor within either of the Cities or Counties aforesaid shall neglect or refuse to do what is enjoined them by this Act, shall respectively forfeit the Sum of five Pounds to be recovered by Action of Debt, before any one of his Majesty's Justices of the Peace of the City or County where the Offence is committed, with Costs of Suit by any Person or Persons who will prosecute the same to Effect, one Half to the Prosecutor and the other Half to the Use of the Poor as aforesaid.

And be it further Enacted by the same Authority, That all Manors and Patentships in the Counties of Queens and Suffolk, that are not legally impowered to choose Town Officers, are hereby impowered and required to meet together annually at the most convenient Place of the Manors or Patentships on the last Tuesday in April, and then and there by a majority of Voices to choose one Collector and two Overseers of the Poor who shall be vested with the same Power and Authority, and be liable to the same Penalties as other Collectors and Overseers of the Poor are subject and liable to in the said Counties respectively.

This Act to be in force from the twelfth Day of April next, until the first Day of May which will be in the Year of our Lord one thousand seven hundred and seventy-seven.

[CHAPTER 1664.]

[See chapter 1551.]

An Act to amend and Act entitled, "An Act for the better laying out, regulating and keeping in repair the Public Roads and Highways in the City and County of Albany, and County of Tryon."

[Passed, March 9, 1774.]

WHEREAS in and by the second Section of the said Act it is enacted That where Public Roads are laid through cleared or improved Land, the Value of such Land shall be paid to the Owner by the Commissioners who are thereby required to pay the same, together with the Charges of the proceedings thereon; but no Mode of levying the said Money being prescribed by the said Act; and no provision made thereby for enabling the Commissioners to defray such Expence.

BE IT THEREFORE ENACTED by his Excellency the Governor the Council and the General Assembly, and it is hereby enacted by the Authority of the same That in such Cases as aforesaid where Public Roads shall be laid through improved or cleared Land, as soon as the Value thereof and the Charges of such Proceedings, as in the said Act are directed shall be ascertained, it shall be lawful for the Commissioners of the District or Districts, in which such Roads shall be so Laid out as aforesaid, to transmit to the Supervisor or Supervisors of the District an Account of such Value and Charges, and the Supervisor or Supervisors shall thereupon allow, and cause the same to be rated assessed and levied as a Public contingent District Charge.

And in order the more clearly to ascertain what Persons shall be compellable to work on the Highways. *Be it further Enacted by the Authority aforesaid,* That every Freeholder Houskeeper and other Person exercising any Trade or Business for themselves and on their own Accounts within the said Counties of Albany and Tryon shall be liable to work on the Public Roads and Highways; and that no Person living with and working for their Master or Parents, and not exercising any Trade or Business for themselves or upon their own Accounts, shall be compellable to work upon the same, any Thing herein or in the said Act contained to the Contrary thereof in any wise notwithstanding.

And Whereas during the Continuance of the Act entitled "An Act for the better laying out regulating clearing and keeping in repair the Public Roads and Highways in the Counties of Albany and Tryon," passed the twenty fourth Day of March one thousand seven hundred and seventy two; sundry Expences and Charges were incurred in the Execution thereof, and the said Act being afterwards repealed before the same were levied or paid.

Be it further Enacted by the same Authority, That the Accounts of all such Expences and Charges shall be transmitted by the Commissioners of the respective Districts, to the Supervisors of the said Counties respectively, who shall allow the same as a Public County Charge, in the same Manner as is above directed with respect to the Payment of the Charges of laying out Public Roads through improved Lands.

[CHAPTER 1665.]

An Act to settle a Line of Jurisdiction between the Counties of Ulster and Albany.

[Passed, March 9, 1774.]

WHEREAS by a Law of this Colony passed on the first Day of October in the year of our Lord one thousand six hundred and ninety one, the County of Ulster is to contain the Towns of Kingston, Hurley, Marble Town, Fox Hall and the New Paltz, and all Villages, Neighbourhoods and Christian Habitations on the West Side of Hudson's River, from the Murderer's Creek near the Highlands to the Sawyer's Creek; and the County of Albany to contain the Manor of Renselaerwyck, Schenectady and all the Villages, Neighbourhoods and Christian Plantations on the East Side of Hudsons River from Roelof Jansen's Creek, and on the West Side from Sawyer's Creek to the utmost End of Saraghtoga.

And Whereas Doubts have arisen concerning the Division Line between the said Counties of Ulster and Albany, more especially as the Christian Plantations on the West Side of Hudson's River at the Time of passing the said Act extended no farther to the Westward than the Westerly Bounds of the Township of Schenectady; and since an uncertainty of Jurisdiction is productive of Discord and Violence, involving the Inhabitants of the contested Districts in all the numberless and complicated Miseries of a Lawless State,

Be it therefore Enacted by his Excellency the Governor, the Council and the General Assembly, and it is hereby enacted by the Authority of the same, That a direct Line running from the most Northerly End or Part of Wanton Island in Hudson's River to the Head of Kaater's Creek or Kill where the same issues out of the Southerly Side or End of a certain Lake or Pond lying in the blue Mountains, from thence a direct Line to the Lake Utsayantho being the South Eastermost Bounds of the County of Tryon, from thence along the Easterly Bounds of the said County of Tryon, to the Western Limits of this Colony, shall and are hereby declared to be from henceforth the Lines of Jurisdiction between the said Counties of Albany Ulster and Tryon.

And Whereas many Disputes have arisen or may hereafter arise between different Persons claiming under Grants of this Colony, in which Controversy the Northern Bounds of said County of Ulster, as formerly declared by Act or Acts of the Legislature heretofore passed, may in a great Measure be Evidence in fixing the Property conveyed by the said Grants.

Be it therefore further Enacted by the Authority aforesaid, That the Lines of Jurisdiction abovementioned nor any Thing in this Act contained shall be construed deemed or adjudged to extend, benefit or establish the Claims or Possessions of any Patentees, their or either of their Heirs Successors or Assigns in any Patent or Grant of Land lying within either of the said Counties of Ulster and Albany, or to defeat or prejudice, or in any Manner to alter or affect the same, it being the Intention of the Legislature that the private Claims of all Parties concerned, and the Bounds of all Patents and lands in the said Counties shall remain (for any Thing in this Act contained to the contrary) in the same State and Condition with respect to all Disputes Suits and Controversies, that now, or may hereafter subsist, as if this act had never been passed.

And be it further Enacted by the Authority aforesaid, That the Inhabitants to the Southward of the Northern Limits prescribed for the said County of Ulster, and to the Eastward of Sawyer's Creek, shall be liable to be taxed and do all Public Duties as within the Town of Kingston, and intitled to give their Votes at the annual Elections of said Town, for such Town Officers as are made elligible in and for the said Town by virtue of any Law of this Colony.

And forasmuch as there have been, now are, and hereafter may be Suits at Law, which may in some degree depend upon, or may be affected by, or connected with the Question, what the Northern Limits of the said County of Ulster were before the passing of this Act, but such suits can only relate to Lands situate West of the Sawyer's Creek aforesaid, and East of the blue Mountains; And to the Intent that all such Suits may be fairly and impartially tried and determined.

Be it further Enacted by the same Authority, That whenever it shall appear probable to the Court in which Suits are or may be pending, that the same may in any Manner relate to the Lands situate as aforesaid, the Jury for the Trial of the same shall not come from the said Counties of Ulster or Albany, or either of them, but from such other County as the Court shall in their Discretion by special Rule order and direct, nor shall this Act or any Thing herein contained be offered as Evidence in favor of the Claim of any or either of the Parties in any such Suit or Suits, directly or indirectly, but only to prove the Line of Jurisdiction between the said Counties now by this present Act established, and the Court where such Trial or Trials may be had shall so charge the Jury with the same any Law Usage or Custom to the contrary notwithstanding.

And be it further Enacted, That the Jurisdiction Line aforesaid from the North Part of Wanton Island, to the Head of Kaaters Kill shall be run out and marked in the Presence of two of the Justices of the Peace for the County of Albany, and two Justices of the Peace for the County of Ulster residing near the said line, by such Person as they or any three of them shall appoint within six Months after the passing hereof, and the Expence thereof shall be defrayed equally by the said Counties, to be raised of and from the Freeholders and Inhabitants of the said Counties respectively, in the same Manner as the other contingent Charges of the said Counties are, and paid to the said Justices for the Purposes aforesaid, and the said Justices are hereby authorized and required to cause the said Line to be run out and marked accordingly.

[CHAPTER 1666.]

[See chapters 1287 and 1617. Expired, April 30, 1776.]

An Additional Act for laying out and improving Public Roads in Ulster County.

[Passed, March 9, 1774.]

WHEREAS a Public Road to be made from the King's Highway leading from Kingston to Rochester near a Place called Hunk, and to proceed thence to and through a Neighbourhood called Sagawack is necessary for the convenience of the Inhabitance, and will open a farther communication with the more interior Parts of the Country,

Be it therefore Enacted by his Excellency the Governor the Council and the General Assembly, and it is hereby enacted by the Authority of the same, That Jacob Hornbeek and Andries De-Witt Esquires, Benjamin Hornbeek, Cornelius Hardenbergh and Ephraim Depue the Commissioners for the Township of Rochester or any three of them shall and may be Commissioners to lay out, and are hereby authorized and required to lay out and regulate a Road from the Rochester Road near the said Place called Hunk, to and through the said Place called Sagawack, and as far into the interior Parts of the Country as they shall think necessary as near to the old Path there used by the Inhabitants as conveniently may be, which Road shall be worked upon and improved by the Inhabitants living near the same in like Manner as the other Roads in the said County of Ulster are worked and improved.

And Whereas by the Laws now in force relating to Roads in the said County of Ulster the Overseers of the Highways have a discretionary Power to warn and call out the Inhabitants thereby compellable to work upon the Highways any Number of Days that they shall think necessary not exceeding six Days in each Year by which Means it is often the Case that a sufficient Portion of Labour is not bestowed on the Highways to keep them in good Repair.

Be it therefore Enacted by the Authority aforesaid That for the future the several Overseers of the Highways in the respective Districts within the said County shall annually call out the Inhabitants put under their superintendance respectively to work upon the Highways within their respective Districts at least six Days in every Year four of which Days shall be between the first Day of April and the first Day of August, any Thing in the said Acts or either of them to the contrary thereof in any wise notwithstanding.

And be it Enacted by the Authority aforesaid, That an Act entitled "An Act for the better clearing mending and further laying out Public High Roads & others in the County of Ulster," passed in the sixth Year of his present Majesty's Reign, and also another Act entitled "An Act to amend an Act entitled An Act for the better clearing mending and further laying out Public High Roads and others in the County of Ulster" passed in the thirteenth Year of his Majesty's Reign, and also this Act, shall be in force until the first Day of March one thousand seven hundred and seventy six and all Proceedings had or to be had thereon shall be good and valid notwithstanding any misrecital of the Date or Time of passing of the first abovementioned act.

[CHAPTER 1667.]

[Expired, January 31, 1780.]

An Act to prevent Damages by Swine in the Township of Marbletown in the County of Ulster.

[Passed, March 9, 1774.]

Be it Enacted by his Excellency the Governor the Council and the General Assembly, and it is hereby enacted by the Authority of the same, That from and after the passing of this Act, it shall and may be lawful for the Freeholders of the said Township of Marbletown, or the major Part of them, at their Annual Meetings for the Election of Town Officers, to make such prudential Rules Orders and Regulations, either for restraining Swine from running at large, or for compelling the Owner or Owners of such Swine as shall hereafter commit any Damage, to make satisfaction for such Damage to the Person or Persons who shall sustain the same, or otherwise, as by them shall be thought most convenient; all which Rules, Orders and Regulations so to be made as aforesaid, the Clerk of the said Township for the Time being, shall from Time to Time enter in the Town Books, and shall make out and deliver a true Copy thereof certified under his Hand, to the Clerk of the Peace of the said County, to be by him filed in his Office.

And be it Enacted by the Authority aforesaid, That this Act shall continue and be in force until the first Day of February, which will be in the Year of our Lord, one thousand seven hundred and eighty.

[CHAPTER 1668.]

An Act to raise the Sum of four hundred Pounds to finish the Court House and Goal in Goshen in the County of Orange.

[Passed, March 9, 1774.]

Whereas by virtue of an Act entitled "An Act to raise one thousand Pounds in the Precincts of Goshen and Cornwall in the County of Orange to build a Court House in the Town of Goshen, and for other Purposes therein mentioned" the Sum of one thousand Pounds has been raised, which being found insufficient for the Purpose intended thereby,

Be it therefore Enacted by his Excellency the Governor the Council and the General Assembly, and it is hereby enacted by the Authority of the same, That for finishing the said Court House and Goal the Supervisors of the said County for the Time being shall, and they are hereby directed & required to, order to be levied on the Freeholders and Inhabitants of the Precincts of Goshen and Cornwall a sum not exceeding four hundred Pounds with the additional Sum of three Pence for every Pound for collecting the same; which said Sum shall be raised with the first Tax that shall be levied after the passing of this Act, and shall be levied and collected in the same Manner as the other necessary and contingent Charges of the said County are.

And be it further Enacted by the Authority aforesaid, That the Monies so to be raised by virtue of this Act, shall from Time to Time be paid by the several and respective Collectors of the said Precincts of Goshen and Cornwall unto Daniel Everitt, Benjamin Tusteen, Jesse Woodhull, Elihu Mervin, and Benjamin Gale; who are appointed Trustees for building the said Court House, for the Purposes aforesaid and the said Trustees or any three of them shall and may from Time to Time inspect examine and audit all the several and respective Accounts, for Workmanship and Materials to be employed for and towards finishing the Court House and Goal before mentioned, and of the due Disposition of the said four hundred Pounds or so much thereof as shall come into their hands, they shall render a true Account upon Oath, unto the Justices of the said Precincts at the General Sessions of the Peace at Goshen, and the said Justices at the same General Sessions, shall allow unto each of the said Trustees such Sum per Day as they shall think reasonable for their Services.

[CHAPTER 1669.]

An Act to confine Rams at certain Seasons of the Year in the Counties of Ulster Orange and Dutchess.

[Passed, March 9, 1774.]

Whereas the Yeaning of Ewes in the severity of a Winter Season, frequently occasions the Loss of the Yeanlings,

Be it therefore Enacted by his Excellency the Governor the Council and the General Assembly, and it is hereby enacted by the Authority of the same, That every Person in either of the Counties of Ulster Orange or Dutchess owning or keeping a Ram shall between the first Day of July, and the tenth Day of November in every Year keep the same within his or her own Inclosure, and if any Ram shall between the said first Day of July and the tenth Day of November after the passing of this Act be found on any Common or uninclosed Lands, or on the inclosed Lands of any Person other than the Owner of such Ram, it shall and may be lawful to and for the Owner or Possessor of such inclosed Lands where such Ram may be so found, or for any other Person or Persons (where such Ram may be found on any common or uninclosed Lands) to take up, impound, or detain such Ram, and if the Owner or Owners of such Ram so taken up do not within twenty Days after Notice given to him or her personally, or to some or one of his Family of suitable Age, or by Advertisement fixed up in two Public Places in the Neighbourhood where such Ram may be so taken up describing his Marks and Colour, and a Coby of such Advertisement being delivered to the Clerk of the Town or Precinct wherein the same shall happen, which he is hereby directed to file and preserve; pay or cause to be paid unto the Person so taking up such Ram, the Sum of eight Shillings, such Ram shall become the Property of the Person or Persons so taking up the same, and he or they may lawfully dispose of the said Ram to and for his her or their own proper use and Benefit; and in Case the Original Owner or Owners of such Ram shall sue for the same, the Person or Persons having taken up such Ram, may plead the General Issue, and give this Act in Evidence on the Trial, and recover treble Costs.

[CHAPTER 1670.]

An Act for the more easy collecting his Majesty's Quit Rents in the Oblong Patent in the Counties of Dutchess and West Chester, and for dividing the same into three Districts.

[Passed, March 9, 1774.]

WHEREAS the Oblong Patent in the Counties of Dutchess and West Chester is near seventy Miles in length and divided into a great Number of Farms, and but one Collector therein at present, whose Duty is not only extreamly difficult and burthensome; but he altogether incapable of discharging the same in the Manner the Law directs; for Remedy whereof,

Be it Enacted by his Excellency the Governor the Council and the General Assembly, and it is hereby enacted by the Authority of the Same, That the said Oblong Patent in the Counties of Dutchess and West Chester, shall be and hereby is divided into three Districts in the following Manner, to wit, The first and South Division to extend so far North till it comes to the hove out Lands, South of Jois Hills, and shall be called the Lower District; The second and middle Division to begin at the hove out lands south of Jois Hills, and go so far North till it comes to the hove out Lands, North of ten Mile River, and shall be called the Middle District; And the third and last Division to begin at the hove-out Lands North of ten Mile River, and extend to the upper End of said Patent, and shall be called the Upper District.

And be it further Enacted by the Authority aforesaid, That the Freeholders of each of the aforesaid three Districts called, the Lower District; the Middle District, and the Upper District shall have full Power and Authority to assemble and hold annual Meetings within their respective Districts, and then and there by plurality of Voices to elect and choose two Assessors and one Collector.

And be it further Enacted, That the Freeholders of the lower District aforesaid, shall hold their first annual Meeting on the first Tuesday of May next, at the Upper MeetingHouse in Salem; That the Freeholders of the Middle District aforesaid, shall hold their first annual Meeting on the said first Tuesday of May next, at the Quaker MeetingHouse on Quaker Hill; and that the Freeholders of the Upper District aforesaid shall hold their first annual Meeting on the said first Tuesday of May next at the now Dwelling House of Samuel Johnson, and that the before mentioned three Places for holding the first annual Meetings shall continue and be the Places for holding the annual Meetings in the aforesaid three Districts respectively.

And be it further Enacted by the same Authority, that the Assessors chosen by Virtue of this Act, shall within six Months thereafter meet at the Quaker Meeting House on Quaker Hill in the Middle District; to rate and assess the several Owners and Freeholders of the said Patent, according to the Part share and Proportion of land each Owner and Freeholder shall have hold possess and enjoy within the same, in Manner as directed by a certain Act of the Lieutenant Governor, the Council, and the General Assembly of this Colony, passed the eighth day of January in the second Year of his present Majesty's Reign entitled, "An Act for the more effectual collecting of his Majesty's Quit Rents in the Colony of New York, and for Partition of Lands in Order thereto:" And the said Assessors when met in Manner aforesaid, shall by plurality of Voices choose and elect a Treasurer to whom the Collectors of the three Districts respectively shall pay the several Sums by them collected, as soon as conveniently may be and in Default thereof the said Treasurer is hereby authorized and impowered to sue and prosecute such Collector for the same in any Court of Record within this Colony; and the said Treasurer when the several Sums assessed by the Assessors shall be paid to him by the several Collectors respectively shall pay the same to the Receiver General or his Deputy and take his Receipt for the same, and shall within three Months after paying the same, produce and shew the Receipt thereof to the Assessors.

And be it further Enacted by the Authority aforesaid, That the several Owners and Freeholders of the said Grant or Patent respectively shall be rated and assessed over and above the Amount of the whole Quit Rent annually due to his Majesty, one Shilling and six Pence in every Pound as a Reward to the Collectors for collecting the same, six Shillings per Day for each of the Assessors, and six Pence in the Pound to the Treasurer for what Monies he shall receive and pay away to the Receiver General. *Provided* that Nothing in this Act contained shall be construed to affect any other Lands than the Great Patent to Hawley and others commonly distinguished by the Name of the Oblong Patent.

[CHAPTER 1671.]

[See chapter 433.]

An Act to amend an Act entitled "An Act for the better clearing regulating and further laying out public Highways in the County of West Chester."

[Passed, March 9, 1774.]

Whereas by the Laws now in force for laying out public Highways in West Chester County, the Commissioners or the major Part of them in the respective Places for which they are appointed Commissioners, are authorized and impowered to lay out such public Roads through inclosed or improved Lands in the several Places for which they are appointed Commissioners; But no Provision is made how the Owner or Owners of such Land shall receive the Value thereof, and Damages thereby sustained,

Be it therefore Enacted by his Excellency the Governor, the Council and the General Assembly, and it is hereby enacted by the Authority of the same, That all Public Highways hereafter to be laid out through inclosed or improved Lands in any Town or Place in West Chester County, without the Consent of the Owner or Owners thereof if any Dispute shall arise by that Means, the true Value of the Lands so laid out into a public Highway shall be determined, and the true Value thereof, and the Damages sustained thereby set and appraised by two Justices of the Peace, and by the Oaths of twelve Freeholders of one of the neighbouring Towns or Places to be summoned by one of the Constables of the said County, by virtue of a Warrant to be issued by the said two Justices of the Peace for that Purpose, and the Freeholders and Inhabitants of the Town or Place where such Public Highway shall be laid out, shall defray and pay the whole charges of the Value of the Land and Damages aforesaid to the Person or Persons through whose Land such Highway shall be laid out together with the Wages of the Commissioners, and the Charges of the whole Proceedings thereon had to be raised and paid in the same Manner as the Wages of the Supervisors of said County are or ought to be by virtue of an Act entitled "An Act to increase the Number of Supervisors' in the County of West Chester and that no Wages of the Supervisors shall be any Part of the said County Rate for the future," passed the first Day of November in the Year of our Lord one thousand seven hundred and twenty two, any Law Usage or Custom to the contrary notwithstanding.

And be it further Enacted by the Authority aforesaid, That instead of the Number of Days which by the aforesaid Act, the Inhabitants were respectively compellable to work on the Highways, it shall and may be lawful for the respective Commissioners or Overseers of the Highways for the Time being to encrease the Number of Days as to them from Time to Time shall be found necessary, so that no Person be obliged to work more than twelve Days in one Year; any Law Usage or Custom to the Contrary notwithstanding.

[CHAPTER 1672.]

[See chapter 1619.]

An Act to repeal an Act entitled "An Act for the better regulating and keeping in Repair the Public Roads in the Borough and Town of West Chester, and to levy Money to defray the Expence thereof."

[Passed, March 9, 1774.]

INASMUCH as the Act entitled "An Act for the better regulating and keeping in Repair the Public Roads in the Borough and Town of West Chester, and to levy Money to defray the Expence thereof," passed the eighth Day of March in the thirteenth Year of his present Majesty's Reign, is by Experience found not to answer the salutary Purposes for which it was intended; and the Laws now in force for regulating and keeping in repair the Public Roads in the County of West Chester which also extend to the said Borough are found to be effectual.

Be it therefore Enacted by his Excellency the Governor the Council and the General Assembly, and it is hereby enacted by the Authority of the same, That the said Act entitled "An act for the better regulating and keeping in repair the Public Roads in the Borough and Town of West Chester, and to levy Money to defray the Expence thereof," and every Clause Article and Thing therein contained shall be, and is hereby repealed and made void to all Intents Constructions and Purposes whatsoever.

[CHAPTER 1673.]

An Act to declare Harrison's Purchase a Precinct independent and distinct from Rye.

[Passed, March 9, 1774.]

Whereas it has been usual heretofore for the Freeholders and Inhabitants of Harrison's Purchase in the County of West Chester to join with the Freeholders and Inhabitants of the Township of Rye in electing Town Officers; and the said Tract of Land being extensive, it is found to be very inconvenient, for Remedy whereof,

Be it Enacted by his Excellency the Governor the Council and the General Assembly, and it is hereby enacted by the Authority of the same, That the said Tract of Land called Harrison's Purchase, shall after the passing hereof be a Precinct independent and distinct from Rye, and shall be called Harrison's Precinct; in which there shall be annually chosen one Clerk, one Supervisor, two Assessors, one Collector, one Constable, two Fence Viewers, one Pound Master, and two Overseers of the Highways, or as many more Overseers of the Highways as the Majority of the Inhabitants at their annual Meetings for the Election of Officers shall think fit; which Officers so elected as aforesaid, shall each and every of them respectively have the same Powers and Authority, as any of the like Officers have in any of the Towns or Manors of the said County, and shall be liable to the same Pains and Penalties, any thing in this, or any other Act to the contrary hereof notwithstanding.

And be it further Enacted by the Authority aforesaid, That the Inhabitants of the said Precinct shall annually meet on the first Tuesday in April for the Election of Officers for the said Precinct, at the present SchoolHouse, near the Dwelling House of Josiah Fowler.

Provided always, and be it also enacted by the same Authority, That Nothing in this Act contained shall be construed deemed or adjudged to abridge the Powers and Authorities of the Several Officers appointed, or to be appointed for raising the Sums of Money leviable for the Maintenance of a Ministry in the said County of West Chester pursuant to any former Law or Laws of this Colony, or for repealing or altering the said Laws or either of them, so far as the same respects the Setling or raising a Maintenance for a Ministry in the County aforesaid.

[CHAPTER 1674.]

[See chapter 1311. Expired, February 28, 1777.]

An Act to amend an Act entitled "An Act for laying out regulating and keeping in repair common and public Highways in the County of Cumberland," and to facilitate the raising the County Charges in the said County.

[Passed, March 9, 1774.]

WHEREAS in and by the said Act abovementioned it is amongst other Things enacted, "That if any Disputes shall arise with respect to the most convenient Place of making a Road, or the joining of Roads from Town to Town, that then it shall be in the Power of the Commissioners or the major Part of them in such Town or Towns to call in three Commissioners one from each neighbouring Town who shall determine where the said Road shall be, as they or the major Part of them shall think to be most convenient, as well for Travellers as for the Inhabitants of every such Town and the next adjacent towns," which Mode so prescribed hath not been found to answer the good Ends thereby proposed, more especially as sufficient Powers are not therein given for carrying the Matters thereby enacted into execution, for remedy whereof.

Be it Enacted by his Excellency the Governor the Council and the General Assembly, and it is hereby Enacted by the Authority of the Same, That if any Disputes have already arisen or shall hereafter arise with respect to the most convenient Place of making a Road or the joining of Roads from Town to Town, or District to District, or upon the Complaint of three or more Freeholders or Inhabitants of the said County of the Inconvenience of any public Road or Roads, now or hereafter to be laid out through the same, to the Court of General Sessions of the Peace for the same County, in all Cases of such Disputes or Complaint as beforementioned, it shall and may be lawful to and for the said Court of General Sessions of the Peace, and they are hereby directed and required if they see just Cause to appoint Commissioners for the Purposes aforesaid, which Commissioners so appointed are hereby authorized required and commanded to go to the Place or Places about which such Controversy arose, or Complaint shall have been made, and to determine and fix where such Roads respectively shall be laid out and made, or where any such Road or Roads from Town to Town or District to District shall join, and to certify the same to the said Court at their next Meeting, which being approved of by the said Court shall be recorded by the Clerk of the Township or District through which such Road or Roads shall be so laid out, and shall be the Public Road or Highway through the Place or Places where the same shall have been so laid out by the Commissioners appointed by the said Court, which said Commissioners shall be paid in equal Proportions by the several Townships or Districts in which they shall perform the Services required by this Act, the like Sums, and to be levied in the same Manner as the Sums allowed to the Commissioners of the several Townships and Districts in the said County; And that when the said Commissioners or the major Part of them shall have determined where the said Road shall be, or where the said Roads from Town to Town, or District to District shall join, That the Surveyor and Overseer or Surveyors and Overseers of the respective Town or Towns District or Districts where such Road or Roads shall be determined or ordered to be laid out or be, shall proceed to warn the Inhabitants respectively, and set them to work, and cause the same to be laid out opened and made, and from Time to Time worked on and kept in repair in the same Manner as the other Roads in the said County are by Law ordered and directed to be done, and that all other Road or Roads to be hereafter laid out in the said County, shall be also recorded by the Clerk of each respective Township or District within the same through which such Road or Roads shall be laid out; and that no Road or Roads hereafter laid out, shall be deemed or taken as a public Road or Roads, except the same be so recorded as aforesaid.

And be it further Enacted by the Authority aforesaid, That the Inhabitants being Freeholders of the Township of Westminster in the said County, and who live on the Town Street of the said Township, or who own Lands bounded thereon shall each of them work three Days in the present year in clearing opening and repairing the said Town Street to the Breadth of ten Rods, which Service the Surveyors of the said Township or any one or more of them shall warn the said Inhabitants to perform and shall see the same performed accordingly, and which said three Days shall be deducted from the Number of Days such Inhabitants are directed to work according to Law, and that any Overseer or Surveyor of Highways who shall refuse or neglect to do his Duty in any of the Matters aforesaid as by this Act is directed, shall forfeit for each such Neglect or Refusal the Sum of ten Pounds lawful Money of New York to be sued for recovered, levied and applied as herein after is directed.

And be it further Enacted by the Authority aforesaid, that every Inhabitant within any Township or District in the said County of Cumberland being a Labourer or Tradesman and no Freeholder or Housekeeper, shall be obliged to work only three days in each Year on the Highways at such Times as they shall be warned or summoned for that Purpose by the Surveyors or Overseers of the Highways or one of them in the Township or District where such Person or Persons shall statedly reside, and that indented Servants who live with and labour for their Masters, and Young Men who live with and labour for their Parents not being Freeholders shall be exempted from the Burthen of working on the Roads on their own Accounts.

And Whereas some few of the Inhabitants of the said County of Cumberland have lately with great Labour and Expence, laid out and opened a Road from Connecticut River towards the City of Albany running Westward through the Townships and Tracts of Land called Brattleborough, New Marlborough, Whiting and Draper in the County of Cumberland, and the Townships or Tracts of Land called Readesborough, New Stamford and Pownal in the County of Albany, which Road if well made and kept in good Repair will be very beneficial to all the Inhabitants in those Townships and Tracts of Land, enable them to carry their Produce to Market and raise the Value of their Lands.

Be it therefore Enacted by the Authority aforesaid, That every Freeholder or Housekeeper dwelling and residing in any of the said Townships or Tracts of Land called Brattleborough, New Marlborough, Whiting, Draper, Readesborough, New Stamford, and Pownal shall by himself or by some able sufficient Person in his Room and stead work so long Time as the Commissioners herein after named or any two of them shall judge necessary not exceeding three Days in every Year on the said Road last mentioned where the same passes through the Township or District in which such Freeholders or Housekeepers respectively dwell, and that the respective Overseers of Highways within the respective Towns and Districts above mentioned do warn and call out the Inhabitants hereby made liable to work on the said Road to perform the Work and Labour hereby enjoined, and that every Person refusing or neglecting his Duty in the Premises shall be liable to the like Forfeitures as other Persons in like Cases are made liable to by this Act, to be sued for, recovered, levied and applied as in such Cases respectively by this Act is declared and enacted.

And be it further Enacted by the Authority aforesaid, That the Work and Labour above directed to be done and performed on the Road leading from Brattleborough towards Albany, shall be done and performed on the same as it is now laid out, unless the same Road shall be altered by the Commissioners herein after named or any two of them. And that Samuel Anderson of the County of Albany and John Houghton and Malachi Church of the Township of Brattleborough in Cumberland County are hereby appointed Commissioners from Time to Time to inspect and view the said Road, and to make such Alterations in the Place or Places where the same is or shall be run or made, as they or any two of them shall think best, and most advantageous for the general Interest and Benefit of all the Inhabitants, each of which said Commissioners shall be, and hereby are entitled to the Sum of eight Shillings for each Day he or they shall be actually employed in the Service aforesaid; the Number of Days to be ascertained by the Oath of the said Commissioners respectively and the Sum which shall be due and owing to them and each of them respectively shall be raised levied and collected in the same Manner as the contingent Charges in the said Counties of Albany and Cumberland are directed to be raised and levied.

And to prevent Idleness and Negligence which too frequently prevail in the Discharge or the necessary Services on the Highways, *Be it Enacted by the Authority aforesaid,* That Eight Hours actual Labour and not less shall be computed and accepted for a Days Work and the Surveyors or Overseers of the Highways in each respective Township or District shall and are hereby respectively required to keep an Account according to the best of their Judgment of the Hours that each Person under their respective superintendence on whom the Duty of working on the Highways is enjoined, shall refuse or neglect to work of the Time required of him by this Act to work in each Day and for every such Hours Neglect or Refusal each such Person having been duly summoned shall forfeit the sum of one Shilling, to be levied by Distress and Sale of the Defaulters Goods and Chattels, which Distress and Sale shall be made by Warrant under the Hand and Seal of such Surveyor or Overseer of the Highways and directed to the nearest Constable, who is hereby required to execute the same and pay such Forfeiture to the Overseer who issued such Warrant.

And to facilitate the raising the County Charges in the said County of Cumberland, and more fully to carry into execution, the good Purposes intended by this Act, *Be it Enacted by the Authority aforesaid,* That in Case the Freeholders and Inhabitants of any Township or District in the said County shall neglect to elect and choose a Supervisor Assessors or Collectors or either of them at the Time or Times when the Same respectively ought to have been chosen in such Township or District; That the Justices of the Peace of the said County at their next Court of General Sessions of the Peace after such Neglect shall have happened, or the major Part of them at such Court are hereby authorized impowered and required from Time to Time under their Hands and Seals to nominate and appoint a Supervisor Assessors and Collectors or either of them that shall have been omitted to be chosen or refuse to act, in the Room and stead of such so omitted to be chosen or refusing to act, who shall be Supervisor or Assessors or Collectors according to his or their Appointment to all Intents and Purposes, with the like Powers and subject to the same Rules Pains Forfeitures and Penalties as any Supervisor Assessor or Collector chosen and elected by virtue of any of the Laws of this Colony; and any Assessor elected by the Freeholders or Inhabitants of any Township or District in the said County or so appointed as aforesaid by the said Justices at any Court of General Sessions of the Peace who shall refuse or neglect to do the Duty of his Office, shall be subject to the Penalty of ten Pounds to be sued for levied and recovered in like Manner as the other Penalties and Forfeitures mentioned in this Act, and directed to be sued for and recovered, and to be applied by order of the Court of General Sessions of the Peace to make mend or repair the Highways in the said County in such Place and Manner as the said Court of General Sessions of the Peace shall order and direct.

And be it Enacted by the Authority aforesaid, That the Supervisors of the said County of Cumberland shall meet annually at the County Town of the said County on the second Tuesday in June, and afterwards for that Year at such Time and Place as they or the major Part of them shall agree upon, and that the Supervisors so met at any one Meeting or a Majority of them shall and may proceed to fix the Proportion of the contingent Charges of the said County to be raised and levied in each Particular Township or District of the said County and to do all Matters and Things to be done by the Supervisors of the said County as fully and perfectly as if a Majority of all the Supervisors of the said County were present any Law, Usage or Custom to the contrary notwithstanding.

And be it Enacted by the Authority aforesaid, That when and as often as any of the Penalties or Forfeitures of the Sum of ten Pounds each in this Act mentioned shall have accrued by reason of the Neglect or refusal of any Person or Persons to perform the Duty or Service on him or them thereby enjoined. And also, That when and as often as any Collector shall by the Space of ten Days retain any Monies raised and levied or to be raised and levied by Tax on the Inhabitants of any Township or District in the said County of Cumberland having been first requested to pay the same to the Treasurer of the said County by the Sherif of the said County or any one of his Deputies at the request of any Justice of the Peace in the said County, that each of the Sums so forfeited as aforesaid or any Sum or Sums of Money so detained by such Collector or Collectors as aforesaid shall be sued for and recovered with Costs of Suit by Action of Debt Bill Plaint Information or otherwise in the Inferior Court of Common Pleas of the said County, and in the Name of the County Treasurer of the said County for the Time being, who is hereby required and authorized to prosecute for the same, such Forfeiture or Forfeitures to be applied in such Place, and in such Manner as the Court of General Sessions of the Peace of the said County shall direct for the better laying out clearing and repairing the Public Highways of the said County, and such Sum or Sums of Money retained by any Collector or Collectors as aforesaid when recovered, to be applied for the use or uses for which the same were laid as a Tax or levied in the said County, and in any such Suit or Suits to be commenced by the Treasurer of the said County no Essoin Protection or Wager of Law, and no more than one Imperlance shall be allowed. This Act to continue of force from the passing thereof until the first Day of March one thousand seven hundred and seventy seven.

[CHAPTER 1675.]

[See chapter 924.]

An Act to amend an Act entitled "An Act to prevent Damages by Swine in the Manor of Livingston."

[Passed, March 9, 1774.]

WHEREAS the Act aforesaid, which was passed in the twenty sixth Year of the Reign of his late Majesty King George the second, and which is since continued to the twentieth Day of October in the Year of our Lord one thousand seven hundred and eighty, is found insufficient to answer the Purposes thereby intended,

Be it therefore Enacted by his Excellency the Governor, the Council and the General Assembly and it is hereby Enacted by the Authority of the same, That all such Swine as by the said Act might have been impounded, which shall hereafter be found running at large unyoked and unringed may lawfully be killed: and if any Dispute shall arise concerning the same; it shall be finally settled and determined in the Manner prescribed by the said Act for settling the Damages sustained by the Trespasses therein mentioned.

[CHAPTER 1676.]

An Act for the Payment of the Salaries of the several Officers of this Colony and other Purposes therein mentioned.

[Passed, March 19, 1774.]

Be it Enacted by his Excellency the Governor the Council and the General Assembly and it is hereby Enacted by the Authority of the same, That the Treasurer of this Colony shall and hereby is directed and required to pay:

Unto his Excellency William Tryon Esquire or the Commander in Chief for the Time being for Fire Wood and Candles for his Majesty's Fort George in the City of New York from the first Day of September one thousand seven hundred and seventy three to the first Day of September one thousand seven hundred and seventy four, after the Rate of four hundred Pounds per Annum.

Unto his said Excellency for purchasing Gun Powder for the use of Fort George and the Battery in the City of New York the sum of one hundred Pounds.

Unto his said Excellency for Monies paid by him to the Surveyors which have been employed on the Part of this Colony to run out and mark the Partition Line between this Colony and the Colony of Quebec as per account the sum of three hundred and thirty one Pounds three Shillings and Nine Pence.

Unto his said Excellency for his Expences and incidental Charges on a Journey to Hartford last Spring to meet his Excellency Governor Hutchinson in order to assent to and confirm the agreement entered into by the Commissaries appointed by this Colony and the Province of the Massachusett's Bay for settling the Line of Jurisdiction between the two Governments, the sum of two hundred and fifteen Pounds sixteen Shillings and nine Pence three Farthings.

Unto his said Excellency for Repairs in Fort George and for four additional Rooms Built at the Battery as per Account the Sum of seven hundred and five Pounds.

Unto the Honorable Daniel Horsemanden Esquire as Chief Justice of the Supreme Court of this Colony, and for going the Circuits from the first day of September one thousand seven hundred and seventy three, to the first Day of September one thousand seven hundred and seventy four after the Rate of three hundred Pounds per Annum.

Unto the Honorable Robert R. Livingston Esquire one of the Puisne Justices of the Supreme Court of this Colony, and for going the Circuits from and to the Time aforesaid, after the Rate of two hundred Pounds per Annum.

Unto the Honorable George D. Ludlow Esquire, one other Puisne Justice of the Supreme Court of this Colony, and for going the Circuits from and to the Time aforesaid after the Rate of two hundred Pounds per Annum.

Unto the said George D. Ludlow Esquire, as a Compensation in some Measure for the Loss of his Library lately consumed by Fire, the Sum of five hundred Pounds.

Unto the Honorable Thomas Jones Esquire the other Puisne Justice of the Supreme Court of this Colony, and for going the Circuits from the twenty ninth day of September one thousand seven hundred and seventy three, to the first Day of September, one thousand seven hundred and seventy four, after the Rate of two hundred Pounds per Annum.

Unto such of the said Justices of the Supreme Court of this Colony as may attend the Circuit Courts in the Counties of Tryon, Charlotte, Cumberland and Gloucester, or either of them, the Sum of fifty Pounds to each Justice that shall so attend; And for the Attendance of such Justice or Justices on any special Commission of Oyer and Terminer and General Goal delivery in either of the said Counties other than such special Commission which may be held when the Circuit Courts in the said Counties are held, the further Sum of fifty Pounds to the Justice or Justices so attending; and for the Attendance of such Justice or Justices on such special Commission in the County of Albany the Sum of thirty Pounds; and for the other Counties in this Colony not already provided for, the Sum of twenty Pounds.

Unto Richard Morris Esquire for his services for the Year past in going the Circuits and for attending thereon for the Trial of Criminals the Sum of one hundred and fifty Pounds.

Unto the Secretary of this Colony for the Time being, for engrossing and enrolling the Acts of the General Assembly from the first Day of September one thousand seven hundred and seventy three to the first day of September one thousand seven hundred and seventy four, after the Rate of forty Pounds per Annum.

Unto the Clerk of the Council for the Time being for his Services in that Station from and to the Time aforesaid after the Rate of thirty Pounds per Annum.

Unto the Doorkeeper of the Council for the Time being for his Services in that Station from and to the Time aforesaid after the Rate of thirty Pounds per Annum.

Unto Hugh Gaine for Services performed by him as public Printer of this Colony (including the Sum of two hundred Pounds which he received from the said Treasurer pursuant to a Resolution of the General Assembly of the twentieth Day of March one thousand seven hundred and seventy two) as per Account amounting to three hundred and ninety four Pounds.

Unto Thomas Moore and John Griffiths as Gaugers of Liquor subject to a Duty within this Colony, or to the Gaugers thereof for the Time being from and to the Time aforesaid after the Rate of thirty Pounds per Annum unto each of them.

Unto Thomas Hill and Josias Smith Land and Tide Waiters, or to the Land and Tide Waiters for the Time being from and to the Time aforesaid, after the Rate of fifty Pounds per Annum unto each of them.

All which aforesaid several Sums of Money shall be paid by the Treasurer on Warrants issued by his Excellency the Governor or the Commander in Chief for the Time being, by and with the Advice and Consent of His Majesty's Council of this Colony, and the Receipts of the several Persons endorsed on the said Warrants shall be to the Treasurer good Vouchers and Discharges for so much as shall be thereby acknowledged to be received.

And be it further Enacted by the Authority aforesaid, That the Treasurer shall and hereby is directed and required to pay the several Allowances following, to wit:

Unto Abraham Lott Esquire Treasurer of this Colony, or to the Treasurer for the Time being for his Services in that Station from the first Day of September one thousand seven hundred and seventy three, to the first Day of September one thousand seven hundred and seventy four after the rate of two hundred Pounds per Annum.

Unto the said Treasurer, or to the Treasurer for the Time being for the extraordinary Services which he is obliged to perform beyond the usual Duty of his Office, after the Rate of the further Sum of one hundred Pounds per Annum.

Unto Edmund Burke Esquire Agent of this Colony in Great Britain or to the Agent for the Time being from and to the Time aforesaid after the Rate of five hundred Pounds per Annum.

Unto the said Edmund Burke Esquire for the Contingent Charges he has been at the further Sum of one hundred and forty Pounds: which said Sums shall be paid unto him the said Edmund Burke by an Order of the General Assembly of this Colony signed by the Speaker for the Time being and not otherwise.

Unto John Tabor Kempe Esquire for extraordinary Services performed by him as Attorney General of this Colony from and to the Time aforesaid after the Rate of one hundred and fifty Pounds per Annum.

Unto Edmund Seaman Esquire as Clerk to the General Assembly for his Services in that Station from and to the Time aforesaid twenty Shillings per diem payable upon a Certificate from the General Assembly signed by the Speaker for the Number of Days he has or may serve the General Assembly.

Unto the said Edmund Seaman for sundry Disbursements by him made for the use of the General Assembly the Sum of Forty six Pounds one Shilling and eight Pence.

Unto Gerard Bancker as Assistant Clerk to the General Assembly for his Services in that Station, from and to the Time aforesaid twenty Shillings per Diem, payable upon a Certificate from the General Assembly signed by the Speaker for the Number of Days he has or may serve the General Assembly.

Unto the said Gerard Bancker for his Services as Clerk to the Commissaries appointed on the Part of this Colony to meet with the Commissaries of the Province of the Massachusett's Bay in order to settle a Line of Partition between the two Governments and Expences, the Sum of forty five Pounds eighteen Shillings and five Pence.

Unto the said Gerard Bancker for his Services as Surveyor in running in Part the Line of Partition between this Colony and the Province of the Massachusett's Bay and Expences, the Sum of sixty nine Pounds three Shillings and five Pence.

Unto Alexander Lamb Door keeper of the General Assembly for his Services in that Station from the first Day of September one thousand seven hundred and seventy three to the first Day of September one thousand seven hundred and seventy four six Shillings per Diem, payable upon a Certificate from the General Assembly signed by the Speaker for the Number of Days he has or may serve the General Assembly.

Unto the said Alexander Lamb for providing FireWood and sundry Necessaries for the use of his Majesty's Council and the General Assembly the Sum of sixty five Pounds.

Unto William Scott Serjeant at Arms for his Services in that Station from and to the Time aforesaid eight Shillings per Diem, payable upon a Certificate from the General Assembly signed by the Speaker for the Number of Days he has or may serve the General Assembly.

Unto John Martin as Gunner and keeper of the Colony Stores, for his Services in that Station, from and to the Time aforesaid, after the Rate of twenty Pounds per Annum.

Unto the Honourable John Watts Esquire one of the Commissaries appointed on the Part of this Colony to meet with the Commissaries of the Massachusett's Bay in order to settle a Line of Partition between the two Governments, the Sum of fifty six Pounds thirteen Shillings and three Pence.

Unto the Honourable William Smith Esquire one other of the Commissaries appointed on the Part of this Colony for the Purpose aforesaid and other Services the Sum of sixty seven Pounds fifteen Shillings and three Pence.

Unto the Honourable Robert R. Livingston Esquire one other of the Commissaries appointed on the Part of this Colony for the purpose aforesaid the Sum of fifty six Pounds thirteen Shillings and three Pence.

Unto William Nicoll Esquire the other Commissary appointed on the Part of this Colony for the Purpose aforesaid the Sum of fifty six Pounds thirteen Shillings and three Pence.

Unto the said William Nicoll Esquire appointed to superintend the running out and marking the said Line of Partition, for his attending that Service and Expences, the Sum of one hundred and twenty five Pounds nine Shillings and ten Pence.

Unto Robert Yates Surveyor, employed by the Commissaries above named for traversing Hudson's River, and running two Lines; the one from the North West Corner of the Province of the Massachusetts's Bay to Hudson's River, the other from the North West Corner of the Oblong to the said River, including the Sum of fifty Pounds voted for that Service at the last Session of the General Assembly, the Sum of ninety three Pounds four Shillings and six Pence.

Unto Mary Valentine, Relict and Executrix of Thomas Valentine Surveyor deceased, in full for his Services and Expences in running in Part the Partition Line between this Colony and the Colony of Quebec, the Sum of three hundred Pounds.

Unto Claude J. Sauthier Surveyor, for the Ballance of his Account of Days Wages and Expences in running and marking Part of the Line of Partition between this Colony and the Colony of Quebec the Sum of seventy seven Pounds four Shillings.

Unto John Collins of Quebec Surveyor, a Ballance due to him, as per his Account of Expences accrued in running the Quebec Line the Sum of seven Pounds thirteen Shillings and six Pence.

Unto Jacob Walton Esquire for Monies advanced by him for carting of Stone for flaging the Battery, the Sum of eight Pounds one Shilling.

Unto James Hallet for Wheel Barrows for the use of the Battery the Sum of Six Pounds.

Unto Anthony Van Dam for a Flag for his Majesty's Fort George, and Repairs, the Sum of thirty one Pounds sixteen Shillings and six Pence.

Unto John Zunicher and George Lindsay for Stone for flaging the Battery the Sum of eleven Pounds seventeen Shillings and nine Pence.

Unto William Winterton for his Account of Mason's Work done on the Battery the Sum of fourteen Pounds nineteen Shillings and nine Pence.

And be it further Enacted by the Authority aforesaid, That for answering the Expences of Contingencies and extraordinary Emergencies that have or may happen for the Services of this Colony, from the first Day of September one thousand seven hundred and seventy three to the first Day of September one thousand seven hundred and seventy four, Warrants may issue for the same on the Treasurer from Time to Time if drawn by his Excellency the Governor or Commander in Chief for the Time being, with the Advice and Consent of his Majesty's Council, which the Treasurer is hereby ordered and directed to pay, provided the Amount of the said Warrants does not exceed the Sum of one hundred Pounds during that Time.

All which aforesaid several Sums shall be paid by the Treasurer out of the Monies arisen or which may arise by virtue of the Act entitled, "An Act further to continue an Act entitled An Act for granting to his Majesty the several Duties and Impositions on Goods Wares and Merchandizes imported into this Colony therein mentioned." The Act entitled "An Act to regulate the Sale of Goods at Public Vendue Auction or Outcry within this Colony," and the Act entitled "An Act to revive an Act entitled An Act to restrain Hawkers and Pedlars within this Colony from selling without Licence with an Addition thereto." And the Treasurer is hereby directed to repay himself the Sum of thirty Pounds which he has paid to Robert McGinnis; out of the aforesaid several Acts.

And be it further Enacted by the Authority aforesaid, That the said Treasurer shall, and hereby is directed and required out of the Ballance due to the Colony on the Act entitled "An Act for emitting Bills of Credit to the Amount of one hundred and fifty thousand Pounds to enable his Majesty's General to pay the Debts contracted, and to carry on his Majesty's Service in North America, and for sinking the same in twelve Months," to pay to John Duncan Esquire as a Compensation for a Loss he sustained on Lake Ontario, of so much of the Bills of Credit of this Colony, emitted by virtue of the last recited Act, the Sum of sixty Pounds.

And be it further Enacted by the Authority aforesaid, That the said Treasurer shall, and hereby is directed and required out of the Interest arising or that may arise by virtue of an Act of this Colony entitled "An Act for emitting the Sum of one hundred and twenty thousand Pounds in Bills of Credit to be put out on Loan, and to appropriate the Interest arising thereon to the Payment of the Debts of this Colony, and to such Public Exigencies as the Circumstances of this Colony may from Time to Time render necessary," to pay unto Hugh Gaine for printing the Devices intended to be pasted on the Backs of the Bills emitted in virtue of the aforesaid Act as per Account the Sum of two hundred and twelve Pounds.

And the Treasurer is hereby directed to repay himself out of the last recited Act, the Sum of forty two Pounds, which he has paid to Henry Dawkins for engraving and cleaning seven Plates to print the Devices intended to be pasted on the Backs of the Bills emitted by virtue of said Act.

And be it Enacted by the Authority aforesaid That the Treasurer shall and hereby is directed and required to keep exact Books of the several Payments which he is directed to make by this Act, and shall render true and distinct Accounts thereof upon Oath, to his Excellency the Governor or Commander in Chief for the Time being, the Council or the General Assembly when by them or any of them he shall be thereunto required.

[CHAPTER 1677.]

[See chapter 945.]

An Act for the more effectual Registry of Mortgages and for securing the Purchasers of Mortgaged Estates.

[Passed, March 19, 1774.]

WHEREAS an Act passed in this Colony on the twelfth day of December one thousand seven hundred and fifty three for registring Mortgages tends to Prevent Fraud; But with Intention to elude the same, absolute Conveyances of real Estates are now made and conditional Defeazances given instead of Mortgages in common Form.

Be it therefore Enacted by his Excellency the Governor the Council and the General Assembly, and it is hereby Enacted by the Authority of the same that every Deed conveying a real Estate made after the first day of June next which shall appear by any other Instrument or Writing to have been intended only as a Security in the Nature of a Mortgage tho' it be an absolute Conveyance in Terms shall be considered as a Mortgage and be deemed and adjudged to be liable to be registered as other Mortgages are by Virtue of the said Act. And that the Person or Persons for whose Benefit such Deed shall be made shall not have the Advantages given by the said Act to Mortgagees unless every Instrument and Writing operating as a Defeazance of the same or explanatory of its being designed to have the Effect only of a Mortgage or Conditional Deed be also therewith registred in Substance as in Case of Mortgage.

And Whereas many real Estates are held under Sales made by Mortgagees who were authorized by the Mortgagor to make Conveyance of the same in Fee for the Payment of the Debt or Demand secured by the Mortgage and to return the Surplus of the Purchase Money to the Mortgagor, and as many Inconveniences may arise, if such Estates should be redeemable in Equity, vexatious Suits be promoted and *bona Fide* Purchasers ruined.

Be it therefore further Enacted by the same Authority that no good and *bona Fide* Sale of Lands Tenements or Hereditaments made or to be made by Mortgagees or others authorized thereunto by special Power for that Purpose in due form of Law from him or them who had the Equity of Redemption shall be defeated to the Prejudice of the *bona Fide* Purchaser thereof in Favor or for the Advantage of any Person or Persons claiming a Right of Redemption in Equity.

Provided always that Nothing in this Act contained shall be construed to prejudice any other Mortgagee of the same Lands Tenements and Hereditaments or any Part thereof whose Title accrued prior to such *bona Fide* Sale or any Creditor to whom the Mortgaged Premises or any part thereof was before bound by any Judgment at Law or Decree in Equity.

And to prevent fraudulent Advantages from being taken to the Prejudice of young and extravagant Persons.

Be it also Enacted by the same Authority that nothing in this Act contained shall operate for the Security of any Purchaser in Fee under a Power hereafter to be executed for that Purpose to the Mortgagee unless the Person giving such Power be of the Age of at least twenty-five years: And all Powers to Mortgagees now or hereafter to be made for making Sales in Fee shall be acknowledged or proved and recorded as other Deeds usually are before the Conveyances for the Sale be executed, and every such Sale shall be at public Auction or Vendue, of which said Auction or Vendue public Notice shall be given by Advertisements, one Copy thereof to be inserted for six Months previous thereto in one of the public News Papers in this Colony and the other to be fixed up on the outward Door of the Court House of that County where the Mortgaged Premisses or the greater Part of them lay.

And be it further Enacted by the same Authority that every Mortgage hereafter to be executed shall have Priority and the Benefits thereof given by the Act abovementioned according to the Time of the actual Registry thereof And such Priority and the Benefits thereof shall extend to all future Mortgages of the same real Estates or Parts thereof whether made by the same or different Persons Except as to such Lands and Tenements which lay in the remote Counties of Albany, Tryon, Charlotte, Cumberland or Gloucester with Respect to which all Mortgages upon Lands and Tenements therein respectively contained whether of the same real Estates or Parts thereof or by the same or different Persons shall not have such Priority and the Benefits thereof from the Registry of such Mortgage but only from the Time of the actual Execution thereof if the same be registred within four Weeks after such Execution, and no Instrument or Writing in the Nature of a Mortgage of any kind whatsoever hereafter to be made or executed shall in any manner defeat prejudice or Affect the Title or Interest of any *bona Fide* Purchaser of Lands Tenements or Hereditaments unless the same shall have been duly registred according to this and the other Act of this Colony herein before mentioned any Thing in this and the above mentioned Act to the Contrary notwithstanding.

[CHAPTER 1678.]

An Act for the Amendment of the Law for prevention of Frauds and Perjuries.

[Passed, March 19, 1774.]

Whereas the Statute for the Prevention of Frauds and Perjuries hath been received by Usage as Law in this Colony, and amended by a subsequent Statute passed after the Establishment of a Legislature within this Colony.

Be it therefore Enacted by the Governor, the Council, and the General Assembly, and it is hereby enacted by the Authority of the same, That all Declarations or Creations of Uses, Fines or Confidences of any Fines or common Recoveries of any Lands, Tenements or Hereditaments, manifested and proved or which hereafter shall be manifested and proved by any Deed already made or hereafter to be made by the Party who is by Law enabled to declare such Uses or Trusts after the levying or suffering of any such Fines or Recoveries are and shall be good and effectual in the Law.

And be it also enacted by the same Authority that all such Witnesses as are and ought to be allowed to be good Witnesses upon Trials at Law by the Laws and Customs of England and of this Colony shall be deemed good Witnesses to prove any Nuncupative Will or any Thing relating thereto.

[CHAPTER 1679.]

An Act for the Relief of Parishes and other Places from such Charges as may arise from Bastard Children born within the same.

[Passed, March 19, 1774.]

Whereas the Laws now in being are not sufficient to provide for the securing and indemnifying Parishes and other Places, from the Great Charges frequently arising from Children begotten and born out of lawful Matrimony, for Remedy thereof

Be it Enacted by his Excellency the Governor, the Council and the General Assembly, and it is hereby Enacted by the Authority of the same, That from and after the passing hereof, if any Single Woman shall be delivered of a Bastard Child, which shall be chargeable, or likely to become chargeable to any Parish or Place, or shall declare herself to be with child, and that such Child is likely to be born a Bastard, and to be chargeable to any Parish or Place and shall in either of such Cases, in an Examination to be taken in Writing upon Oath before any one or more Justice or Justices of the Peace of any County, City, Borough or Place, wherein such Parish or Place shall lie, charge any Person with having gotten her with Child, it shall and may be lawful to and for such Justice or Justices upon Application made to him or them by the Overseers of the Poor, of such Parish, or by any one of them, or by any Substantial Householder of such Place to issue out his or their Warrant or Warrants for the immediate apprehending such Person so charged as aforesaid, and for bringing him before such Justice or Justices or before any other of his Majesty's Justices of the Peace of such County, City, Borough, Parish or Place, and the Justice or Justices before whom such Person shall be brought is, and are hereby Authorized and required to commit the Person so charged as aforesaid, to the common Goal or House of Correction of such County, City, Borough, Parish or Place, unless he shall give Security to indemnify such County, City, Borough, Parish or Place or shall enter into a Recognizance with sufficient Surety, upon Condition to appear at the next General or Quarter Sessions of the Peace to be holden for such County, City, Manor or Place, and to Abide and Perform such Order or Orders as shall be made in Pursuance of an Act passed in the Eighteenth Year of the Reign of her Majesty Queen Elizabeth concerning Bastards begotten and born out of lawful Matrimony.

Provided nevertheless, And be it Enacted by the Authority aforesaid, That if the Woman so charging any Person as aforesaid, shall happen to die or be married before she shall be delivered, or if she shall miscarry of such Child, or shall appear not to have been with Child at the Time of her Examination, Then and in any of the said Cases, such Person shall be discharged from his Recognizance at the next General or Quarter Sessions of the Peace, to be holden for such County, City, Borough or

Place, or immediately released out of Custody by Warrant under the Hand and Seal, or Hands and Seals of any one or more Justice or Justices of the Peace residing in or near the Limits where such Parish or Place shall lie.

Provided also, And be it Enacted by the Authority aforesaid, That upon Application made by any Person who shall be committed to any Goal or House of Correction by Virtue of this Act, or by any Person on his Behalf to any Justice or Justices residing in or near the Limits where such Parish or Place shall lie, such Justice or Justices is and are hereby authorized and required to Summon the Overseer or Overseers of the Poor of such Parish or one or more of the Substantial Householders of such Place to appear before him or them at a Time and Place to be mentioned in such Summons to shew Cause why such Person should not be discharged and if no Order shall appear to have been made in Pursuance of the said Act of the Eighteenth Year of the Reign of her Majesty Queen Elizabeth within six Weeks after such Woman shall have been delivered, such Justice or Justices shall and may discharge him from his Imprisonment, in such Goal or House of Correction, to which he shall have been committed.

Provided always, And be it further Enacted by the Authority aforesaid, That it shall not be lawful for any Justice or Justices of the Peace to send for any Woman whatsoever, before she shall be delivered and one Month after, in order to her being examined concerning her Pregnancy or supposed Pregnancy or to compel any woman before she shall be delivered to Answer to any Questions relating to her Pregnancy any Law, Usage or Custom to the contrary notwithstanding.

And Whereas the putative Fathers and lewd Mothers of Bastard Children run away out of the Parish or Place and sometimes out of the County, and leave the said Bastard Children upon the Charge of the Parish or Place where they are born, although such putative Father and Mother have Estates sufficient to discharge such Parish or Place *Be it therefore Enacted by the Authority aforesaid,* that it shall and may be lawful for the Church Wardens or Overseers of the Poor of such County, City, Manor, Parish or Place where any Bastard child shall be born, to take and seize so much of the Goods and Chattels and to receive so much of the Annual Rents or Profits of the Lands of such putative Father or lewd Mother, as shall be ordered by any two Justices of the Peace, for or towards the Discharge of the Parish or Place to be confirmed at the Sessions for the bringing up and providing for such Bastard Child, and thereupon it shall be lawful for the Sessions to make an Order for the Church Wardens or Overseers for the Poor of such Parish or Place to dispose of the Goods by Sale or otherwise or so much of them for the Purposes aforesaid as the Court shall think fit, and to receive the Rents and Profits, or so much of them as shall be Ordered by the Sessions as aforesaid of his or her Lands.

[CHAPTER 1680.]

[See chapters 488, 535. Expired, January 31, 1778.]

An Act to Amend an Act entitled an Act to impower the Justices of the Peace of the County of Albany living or Dwelling in the Township of Schenectady in the said County to Regulate the Streets and Highways and to prevent Accidents by Fire in the said Town.

[Passed, March 19, 1774.]

WHEREAS by an Act of the Legislature passed the Eleventh Day of November One thousand Seven Hundred and Twenty six entitled "An Act to Impower the Justices of the Peace of the County of Albany living or dwelling in the Township of Schenectady in the said County to Regulate the Streets and Highways and to prevent Accidents by Fire in the said Town." The Inhabitants and Freeholders are impowered and directed Annually on the first Tuesday in April to Elect and Choose by Majority of Voices, Two able and discreet Persons to be Overseers of the Chimnies and Ovens. But there being no Penalty inflicted by the said Law in Case the said Overseers should Neglect or Refuse to serve; Difficulties for want thereof have arisen

Be it therefore Enacted by his Excellency the Governor, the Council and the General Assembly, and it is hereby enacted by the Authority of the same that every Overseer of Chimnies and Ovens to be chosen for the future by Virtue of the said Act shall in Case of any Refusal or Neglect to serve as such Forfeit the Sum of Ten Pounds to be recovered by Action of Debt in any Court of Record within the said County, wherein but one Imparlance shall be allowed, one half of which Forfeiture shall be for the use of the Person suing for the same, and the other half to the use of the Poor of the District of Schenectady.

And be it further Enacted by the same Authority that the Overseers of the Chimnies and Ovens so to be chosen by Virtue of the said Act shall and they are hereby directed and impowered once in every Fortnight to enter the Houses of the Inhabitants of the said Town in order to examine and View the Chimnies and Fire places instead of once in every Month as is by the said Act directed any Thing therein contained to the contrary notwithstanding

And be it further Enacted by the Authority aforesaid that this Act and the Act entitled an Act to continue an Act entitled an Act to revive an Act entitled an Act to impower the Justices of the Peace of the County of Albany living or Dwelling in the Township of Schenectady in the said County to Regulate the Streets and Highways and to prevent Accidents by Fire in the said Town shall continue and be in Force from the Passing hereof until the First Day of February One Thousand seven Hundred and Seventy eight.

[CHAPTER 1681.]

An Act for running out and marking the Division Line between the Counties of Ulster and Orange, from the East Side of the Shawangunk Mountains to the Delaware River.

[Passed, March 19, 1774.]

WHEREAS the Line dividing the Counties of Ulster and Orange, has never been run and marked farther Westward than to the East Side of the Shawangunk Mountains, and for want of a Continuance of that Line to the Delaware River, the Jurisdiction of those Parts of the said Counties lying West of the said Mountains is uncertain and the Inhabitants thereof are frequently taxed and compelled to perform Public Duties in both of the said Counties; To remedy which Evils,

Be it Enacted by his Excellency the Governor the Council and the General Assembly, and it is hereby enacted by the Authority of the same, That the said Line shall be continued run out and marked as soon as conveniently may be, from the East Side of the Shawangunk Mountains aforesaid to the Delaware River on a Course of South eighty nine Degrees and fifty Minutes West, as the Magnetic Needle now points, by such Person as shall be appointed for that Purpose by William Allison, John Gale, Jonathan Smith, Jesse Woodhull and Joseph Watkins Esquires or any three of them, which Person shall be sworn to perform the same truly, agreeable to the Directions of this Act, and the Expences attending the same shall be paid by the said Counties respectively in equal Proportion, and raised as the Contingent Charges of the said Counties respectively are; and the said Line so to be run shall be the Line of Jurisdiction between the said two Counties in such Parts thereof as adjoin the same.

Provided always, and be it further enacted That Nothing in this Act contained shall be construed to affect any Person's Title Estate or Possession but the same shall remain in the same Condition as if this Act had never passed.

[CHAPTER 1682.]

[Expired, January 31, 1775.]

An Act for the more equal Taxation of Estates in the County of Orange.

[Passed, March 19, 1774.]

FORASMUCH as the Method heretofore practiced for the Taxation of Estates in the County of Orange hath not been done in that due equal and just Proportion as it is conceived it might be, and as Justice and Equity demand that all the Freeholders and Inhabitants thereof should be rated and Taxed in due Proportion to the Estates they enjoy,

Be it therefore Enacted by his Excellency the Governor the Council and the General Assembly, and it is hereby enacted by the Authority of the same, That from and after the first Day of April next, it shall and may be lawful for the Freeholders and Inhabitants of each of the respective Towns and Precincts within the said County to choose and elect at their annual Meetings a Person being a Freeholder inhabiting within the said Town or Precinct for one of the Assessors of the County, which Assessor so chosen in each of the Towns or Precincts as aforesaid shall meet on the second Tuesday of April next at the House of Daniel Coe in Kakiate in said County, and before they enter on the Duties of their Office shall take an Oath before any one of his Majesty's Justices of the Peace for said County to the following Effect, *to wit,* That they shall and will well truly equally and impartially according to the best of their Skill knowledge and Judgment assess the Real Estates (Wood Land only excepted) and Personal Estates of all the Freeholders and Inhabitants of the said County as nearly as they can discover the same to be, within the same County.

And be it further Enacted by the Authority aforesaid, That the said Assessors so chosen and qualified shall as soon as they conveniently can after such Qualification make an Assessment in the Manner following, *to wit,* they shall proceed all together from House to House throughout the said County, till they have gone through the whole and shall make out a true and exact List of all the Names of the Freeholders and Inhabitants of the said County, and against the Names of every such Person, shall set down the Value of all his or her Estate real and personal as nigh as they can discover the same to be within the same County setting down for every hundred Pounds real Value stated as aforesaid four Pounds, and in that Proportion for a greater or lesser Sum, which List or Lists the said Assessors shall deliver to the Supervisors of the said County on or before the first Tuesday of June then next ensuing.

And be it further Enacted by the same Authority, That the said Supervisors shall make the Quota of each respective Person or Persons according to the Total Sum of the List or Lists returned as aforesaid and not otherwise, and that the Clerk of the Supervisors shall transcribe the List or Lists and add to each Persons Rate the Sum or Proportion such Person is to pay of what the Supervisors find the said County chargeable with, and when the said List or Lists are compleated the said Supervisors or the greater Number of them are hereby required to issue their Warrants commanding the Collector or Collectors of each Town or Precinct to collect and pay the same as by the Warrant shall be directed.

And be it further Enacted by the Authority aforesaid, That if any Assessor or Assessors, Collector or Collectors chosen and elected at the annual Town Meetings for choosing of officers shall either refuse to take the Charge upon him or them, or if having accepted the same shall neglect his or their duty therein required, each so refusing or neglecting shall respectively forfeit the Sum of five Pounds, to be recovered by the Supervisors of the said County, or any one of them with full Costs of Suit. before any one of his Majesty's Justices of the Peace for said County, to be by them applied towards defraying the contingent Charges of said County.

And be it Enacted by the Authority aforesaid, That the said Assessors as a Reward for their Trouble shall receive five Shillings per Day, and the same shall be raised levied and paid in the same Manner as the other Contingent Charges of the said County are.

And be it further Enacted by the Authority aforesaid, That the Act entitled. "An Act for the more equal taxation of Estates in Orange County" passed the twenty seventh Day of January one thousand seven hundred and seventy shall be and hereby is suspended during the continuance of this Act.

And be it Enacted by the same Authority, That this Act shall be in force from the passing hereof till the first Day of February which will be in the Year of our Lord one thousand seven hundred and seventy five and no longer.

[CHAPTER 1683.]

[See chapter 1616.]

An Act to amend an Act entitled. "An Act for the better laying out and keeping in repair common public and private Highways in the County of Orange."

[Passed, March 19, 1774.]

WHEREAS by the eleventh Section of an Act of this Colony passed the eighth Day of March one thousand seven hundred and seventy three entitled. "An Act for the better laying out and keeping in repair common public and private Highways in the County of Orange," it is enacted, That every Overseer in each Precinct shall on or before the first Monday in December in every Year deliver under Oath to one or more of the Commissioners of the Precinct to which he doth belong, an Account of the Labour done on the Highways within his District. *And Whereas* it may hereafter happen that a Quaker may be chosen an Overseer of a District,

Be it therefore Enacted by his Excellency the Governor the Council and the General Assembly, and it is hereby enacted by the Authority of the same, That whenever a Quaker shall be chosen an Overseer of a District it shall and may be lawful for him, and he is hereby required to deliver an Account of the Labour done on the Highways within his District under a solemn Affirmation instead of the Oath aforesaid any Thing in the said in part recited Act to the contrary thereof notwithstanding.

And Whereas Disputes have frequently happened respecting the Time that Persons ought to reside within the said County of Orange before they can be compelled to work on the Highways, for remedy of which, *Be it further Enacted by the Authority aforesaid,* That every Person who shall reside in the said

County of Orange for the Space of forty Days shall be deemed and adjudged an Inhabitant, for the purpose of working on the Highways and shall be compelled to work on the same.

And be it further Enacted by the same Authority, That Peter Townshend, Nathaniel Roe and Thomas Welling or any two of them are hereby authorized impowered and required to take a Review of the Road that runs from the House of Jacob Mace to Sterling Iron Works, from thence to Stephen Slot's, and from thence to the Line of Partition between this Colony and the Colony of New Jersey, near the House of Coenrad Frederick and the same to lay out alter and regulate as they shall think proper; which being entered as usual in the Town Clerk's Book of the Precinct of Goshen Cornwall and Haverstraw, shall be good and effectual, any Law Usage or Custom to the contrary in any wise notwithstanding.

And be it further Enacted by the Authority aforesaid, That the Roads within the said County of Orange on the West Side of the Wallkill that were within the Jurisdiction of New Jersey until the late final Settlement of the said Line of Partition between the said Colonies, shall be worked upon by the Freeholders and Inhabitants of that Part of the County as any other District in the said Precinct of Goshen is worked upon, until the Commissioners for the Time being for the said Precinct of Goshen shall think proper to new lay or alter the same.

And be it further Enacted by the Authority aforesaid, That in Case the Court of General Sessions of the Peace for the said County of Orange shall be of Opinion, that the Freeholders and Inhabitants of the said County ought to work on the Highways a greater Number of Days, than five in a year, it shall and may be lawful, and the said Court when it shall be held at Goshen, is hereby authorized and impowered by Rule or Order of the same annually to direct the Number of Days, not exceeding five in one Year, and the Times when the Freeholders and Inhabitants shall work, over and above the five Days already established by Law, on the Highways within their respective Districts in the Precincts of Goshen and Cornwall, and the said Court when it shall be held on the South Side of the Highlands, shall have the like Power to direct the Number of Days, and the Times when the Freeholders and Inhabitants of the Precincts of Haverstraw and Orange Town shall work on the Highways, and the Overseers of the respective Districts within the said County shall order the Freeholders and Inhabitants of their respective

Districts under the like Penalties in the said Act mentioned to work on the Highways agreeable to the Directions of the said Court: and if any Overseer shall refuse or neglect to work agreeable to the Directions of the said Court, he shall for every Offense forfeit the Sum of five Pounds, to be recovered with Costs of Suit before any Justice of the Peace in the said County, one half of which Forfeiture shall be for the use of the Prosecutor, and the other half shall be laid out on the Highways in the District where such Overseer shall reside.

[CHAPTER 1684.]

An Act for raising a Sum not exceeding One Thousand Pounds for building a Court House and Goal in the County of Orange and for other Purposes therein mentioned.

[Passed, March 19, 1774.]

WHEREAS the Court House and Goal in the Township of Orange on the South side of the Mountains in Orange County were lately destroyed by Fire. *And Whereas* by the late Settlement of the Line between this Colony and the Colony of New Jersey, the situation where said Court House stood is within a few Rods from said Line, and therefore altogether inconvenient to the Inhabitants thereof,

Be it therefore Enacted by his Excellency the Governor, the Council and the General Assembly, and it is hereby Enacted by the Authority of the same, That the Justices of the Precincts of Orange Town and Haverstraw in the County of Orange. together with the Supervisors for the Time being and Cornelius Cornelius Smith and Roeloff Van Houten shall meet at the House of Daniel Jeroe on the first Tuesday in May next, and they, or the greater Number of them then and there present, are hereby impowered and required to fix on the most Convenient Spot where the Court House and Goal shall be erected at a place commonly called the City near the House of the said Daniel Jeroe in the Precinct of Haverstraw in the said County of Orange, and to determine the Plan and of what Materials the same shall be built.

And be it further Enacted by the Authority aforesaid that for building and erecting the same Court House and Goal, the Supervisors of the said County for the Time being shall and they are hereby directed and required to order to be levied on the Freeholders and Inhabitants of the said Precints of Orange Town and Haverstraw a Sum not exceeding One thousand Pounds with the Additional Sum of Three Pence for every Pound for collecting the same, Two hundred and fifty Pounds, of which said One thousand Pounds shall be raised in the first Tax that shall be levied after the Publication of this Act and so Annually for three Years next after the said first Tax, the Sum of Two hundred and fifty Pounds; which said Sum of One thousand Pounds shall be raised levied and collected in the same manner as the other necessary and contingent Charges of the said County are.

And be it further Enacted by the Authority aforesaid, That the Monies so to be raised by Virtue of this Act shall from Time to Time be paid by the several and respective Collectors of the said Precincts of Orange Town and Haverstraw unto John Coe, David Pye, Edward William Keirs, Cornelius Cornelius Smith and Roeloff Van Houten who are hereby appointed Trustees for laying out the said One thousand Pounds for the Purposes aforesaid, and the said Trustees or any three of them shall and may from Time to Time inspect, examine Audit and Settle all the several and respective Accounts for Workmanship and the Materials to be employed or used or other Expences for and towards building and erecting the said Court House and Goal before mentioned, and of the due Disposition of the said Sum of One thousand Pounds, or so much thereof as shall from Time to Time come to their Hands, they the said Trustees appointed as aforesaid shall render a true and just Account upon Oath unto the Justices of the Peace at the General Sessions of the Peace for said County when by them thereunto required.

And be it further Enacted by the Authority aforesaid, That the said John Coe, David Pye, Edward William Keirs, Cornelius Cornelius Smith and Roeloff Van Houten or the Major Part of them shall and they are hereby impowered to sell or otherwise dispose of all the Materials remaining of the old Court House lately destroyed by Fire, and in the Name of the Trustees, or the Major Part of them appointed by this Act to call Persons to Account who may have taken away or embezzled any Part of the said Materials, and if need be to sue for and recover the same in any of his Majesty's Courts within this Colony, and the Monies arising by such Sales or Recoveries shall be applied towards the Building and Finishing the said Court House and Goal.

And Whereas the said Trustees may want some Part or the whole Sum of One thousand Pounds for the Purpose of building said Court House and Goal before any Part of the said Sum hereby directed to be raised can come into their hands. Be it further Enacted by the same Authority, that the said John Coe, David Pye, Edward William Keirs, Cornelius Cornelius Smith and Roeloff Van Houten or any three of them may from Time to Time take up at Interest, the whole or so much of the said One thousand Pounds as shall appear to them to be necessary towards carrying on building and finishing the said Court House and Goal with convenient Expedition. And of the Interest of such Sum or Sums so to be taken up by the said Trustees for the Purposes aforesaid, they shall keep a particular Account and deliver the same Certified under their Hands or the Hands of the Major Part of them to the Supervisors of the said County, who shall and are hereby directed and impowered thereupon to order the raising of the Sum or Sums due or to become due for Interest as aforesaid, of and from the Freeholders and Inhabitants of the said Precincts of Orange Town and Haverstraw, in the same Manner as the Contingent Charges of the said County are raised, which Money when collected shall be paid by the respective Collectors of said Precincts, into the hands of the Trustees aforesaid to be by them applied for the Purposes aforesaid.

[CHAPTER 1685.]

[See chapter 1561. Expired, January 31, 1778.]

An Act to amend an Act entitled. "An Act for the better laying out, regulating and keeping in repair the Common and Public Highways in the County of Charlotte."

[Passed, March 19, 1774.]

WHEREAS the Commissioners appointed by an Act entitled. "An Act for the better laying out regulating and keeping in repair the Common and Public Highways in the County of Charlotte," did not assemble and meet at the Time and Place in and by the said Act directed, to execute the Powers in them thereby vested; by means whereof the said Act hath not hitherto been carried into Effect; and the said Act will expire on the first Day of February next,

Be it therefore Enacted by his Excellency the Governor, the Council and the General Assembly and it is hereby enacted by the Authority of the same. That it shall and may be lawful to and for the Commissioners in the said Act named or the Major Part of them who shall continue Residents in the said County of Charlotte, and they are hereby required to assemble and meet together at the Dwelling House of Patrick Smith Esquire where the Courts of Justice, in and for the said County are now usually held, and at such Day between the passing of this Act, and the first Day of August next, as shall be notified by William Duer Esquire, the said Patrick Smith and Thomas Clarke three of the said Commissioners or by any two of them, And the said Commissioners so appointed by the said recited Act, or the Major Part of them who shall continue Residents in the said County, shall then and there proceed to execute the Trust reposed in them by the said Act, and at such their first Meeting, shall and may agree upon such Place and Time for any Future Meeting as to the major Part of them, shall appear most convenient.

And be it further Enacted by the Authority aforesaid, That the said recited Act shall continue and remain in full force until the first Day of February which will be in the Year of our Lord one thousand seven hundred and seventy eight, any Thing therein contained to the Contrary notwithstanding.

[CHAPTER 1686.]

An Act for the Relief of Insolvent Debtors within this Colony, with respect to the Imprisonment of their Persons.

[Passed, March 19, 1774.]

WHEREAS it has been represented to the General Assembly That the several Persons herein after mentioned imprisoned in different Goals in this Colony, are destitute even of the common Necessaries of Life, and it is conceived reasonable if their Creditors will not consent to their Enlargement, or contribute to their Subsistance, that such Persons should be relieved by the Legislature; to this End,

Be it Enacted by his Excellency the Governor the Council and the General Assembly and it is hereby Enacted by the Authority of the same, That such of the Creditors of the following Persons Vizt: Frederick Donaldson, Michael Jacobs, James Light Junior, John Cannon, Louis Andrew Gautier, John Godfrey Muller, Justus Rodgers, William Sloo, George Fach, Jeremiah Moor, John Campbell Taylor, James Dunscomb, James McMillan, Jedediah Beckwith, and Anthony Fowler insolvent Debtors in the City of New York; Daniel Angevine and James Green insolvent Debtors in the County of West Chester; Simon Laraway, John

O'Farrel and Casparus VanSalsbury insolvent Debtors in the City of Albany, John Wallace and John Concklin insolvent Debtors in the County of Orange; John Johnson an insolvent Debtor in the County of Ulster; and Peter Harris, Amos Dickinson, John Nicholas Hannike, John Way, Jacobus C. Swartwout, Gale Yelverton, Joseph Higgins, John Coopman, Louis Winter, Joseph Cock, Peter Phillips, and John Laroy insolvent Debtors in the County of Dutchess who shall insist upon such their Debtors being detained under their respective Confinements shall within four Weeks after the first Publication of such Advertisements as are herein after directed, agree by writing under their Hands to pay and allow three Shillings and six Pence per Week unto the said Prisoners respectively to be paid the Monday of every Week, so long as he shall continue in Prison at his her or their Instance; and if such Agreement as aforesaid shall not be entered into, or if entered into, not punctually complied with, and on failure of the Payment of such Weekly Sum at any Time, such of the said Prisoners whose Creditor or Creditors shall not enter into such Agreement, or shall fail complying with it as aforesaid, shall be intitled to the Benefit of this Act, upon complying with the Terms and Conditions herein after imposed.

And be it further Enacted by the Authority aforesaid That it shall and may be lawful for each and every of the above named Persons to present a Petition to the Court out of which any Process against them respectively hath issued and upon which they are imprisoned, or to any two of the Judges of such Court, certifying the Cause or Causes of his Imprisonment, and exhibiting an Account and Inventory of his whole real and personal Estate, and of the securities relating to the same, which Petition with the said Account and Inventory shall be lodged with the Clerk of the said Court for the Inspection of the Creditors; and after such Petition presented and Account and Inventory filed, such Prisoners shall respectively publish Advertisements in one or more of the Public News Papers of this Colony notifying their Creditors that they intend to apply to the said Court or to any two of the Judges thereof who shall attend, at a certain Day not less than four Weeks from the Publication of such Advertisements, respectively, to be discharged according to the Prayer of his or their said Petition, at which Day the said Court or the said two Judges may and are hereby required by Precept under their Hands and Seals directed to the Sheriff, Goaler, or Officer in whose Custody such Prisoner or Prisoners may be to order the said Prisoner or Prisoners respectively to be brought up before such Court or such Judges; and unless it be made appear that such Provision as aforesaid hath been made for the Subsistance of the said Prisoner or Prisoners by his or their Creditors respectively the said Court or Judges may then respectively administer the following Oath or Affirmation to wit:

"I, A B. do solemnly swear or affirm That the Account by me filed in the Office of the Clerk of the Supreme Court, (or in the Office of the Clerk of the County of naming the County, as the Case may be,) is a just and true Account of all my Creditors and the Monies owing to them respectively by me to the best of my knowledge and Remembrance; and that the Inventory and Account by me filed in the said Clerk's Office, is a just and true Account of all my Estate real and personal both in Law and Equity, either in Possession Reversion or Remainder (the necessary wearing Apparel of myself and wife and Children; and Family immediately under my Care excepted,) and I have not directly or indirectly sold, Leased, assigned or otherwise disposed of, or made over either in Trust for myself or otherwise except as set forth in the same Account and Inventory any Part of my Estate real or Personal for my future Benefit, or in order to defraud my Creditors, and that none of my Creditors reside in Great Britain, so help me God."

Which Oath or affirmation being taken, if the Truth thereof shall be denied or controverted by any of the Creditors, the said Court or Judges may appoint some further Day for hearing the Parties as well Debtors as Creditors, and upon such further hearing, may in their Discretion either remand the said Debtors or proceed to their Discharge, as if no such further hearing had been required; but if the said Oath or Affirmation shall not be controverted or denied, then the said Court or Judges may immediately order the Lands Goods and Effects contained in such Account and Inventory to be by a short Indorsement on the Back of such Petition executed by the Prisoner assigned to the said Creditors, or to one or more of them, or to some other Person or Persons, to be appointed by the said Court or Judges respectively in Trust for all the Creditors; and also for all Attornies, Sheriffs, Goalers and other Officers with respect to their Fees, for which they shall come in as the Creditors of the Insolvent abating *pro rata*, by which Assignment such Estate shall actually vest in, and be taken in possession by the said Trustee or Trustees, according to the Purport of such Assignment, and shall be divided by the Assignees from Time to Time among all the Creditors in proportion after six Months previous Notice published in one of the Public News Papers of this Colony of such Assignment, and requiring all the Creditors to send in their Demands, and if any Part Thereof is in possession of any other Person or Persons, the same shall be recoverable in the Name or Names of such Trustee or Trustees, who are hereby fully authorized to dispose of and execute good and sufficient Deeds for the same or any Part thereof, and to divide and distribute as well the Monies thence arising, as such other Monies which shall come into their Hands by virtue of this Act, among the Creditors of the said Debtors respectively, and the Officers aforesaid to whom any Fees may be due in proportion to their respective Debts or Demands, according to the true Intent and meaning of this Act, to which no Release from the Insolvent shall be any Bar; And immediately upon such Assignment being made, the said Prisoner or Prisoners shall by order of the said Court or Judges be discharged out of Custody: and such Order shall be a sufficient Warrant to the Sheriff Goaler or Keeper of such Prisoner, to discharge such Prisoner or Prisoners, if detained for no other Cause or Causes than those mentioned in such his or their Petition; and he is required forthwith to discharge and set him or them at liberty without Fee, and upon such Discharge the said Debtors shall be finally released from all Debts contracted, and all Judgments obtained before that Time, and shall not be liable to be sued or arrested, or to have their Lands or Tenements Goods or Chattels seized by virtue or in consequence thereof: And every Person who shall be convicted of willful false-swearing, in any Matter or Article contained in the said Oath, he shall be guilty of Felony and suffer the Pains of Death without Benefit of Clergy.

Provided nevertheless and be it also enacted by the same Authority, That if any or either of the said insolvent Persons other than such as are confined in the Goal of the City and County of New York, shall be imprisoned by virtue of Process of the Supreme Court, it shall be lawful for such Persons respectively to take such Oath or Affirmation as aforesaid before any one of the Judges of the Inferior Court of Common Pleas of the County in which they are respectively imprisoned, and such Oath or Affirmation being subscribed by such Debtor and certified by such Judge to transmit to the said Judges of the Supreme Court at the Day mentioned in such Advertisement for the Purpose aforesaid;

and on such Day, such Judges of the Supreme Court may proceed to issue their Order or Warrant commanding the Sheriff in whose Custody such insolvent Debtor may be, to discharge such Debtor immediately after he shall have executed such Assignment as by this Act is directed in the Presence of two Witnesses, of whom the said Sheriff or one of his Deputies shall be one.

And be it further Enacted by the Authority aforesaid, That if any of the said Debtors shall be sued for any debts accrued before the passing of this Act, or if any Judge or other Officer shall be sued for any Thing done in pursuance, and under the Authority of this Act, such Defendant may plead the General Issue, and give this Act and the special Matter in Evidence. *Provided*, That this Act shall not extend to discharge any Person who shall stand committed at the suit of the Crown, *And Provided also*, That this Act shall not be construed to affect any Creditor or Creditors residing in Great Britain any Thing herein contained to the contrary notwithstanding.

Whereas by an Act of this Colony passed in the year of our Lord one thousand seven hundred and seventy two, entitled, "An Act for the Relief of insolvent Debtors within this Colony with respect to the imprisonment of their Persons," it was enacted, that John P. Smith a Prisoner confined in Orange County Goal, should have the Benefit of the said Act. *And Whereas* the said Prisoner did pursuant to the said Act, petition the Judges of the Supreme Court, and did duly advertise his Intentions of applying for a Discharge, and was afterwards by order of the said Court brought before the same on Saturday the first Day of August one thousand seven hundred and seventy two, being the last Day of the Term to be discharged pursuant to the said Act. *And Whereas* the said Prisoner did accordingly attend the Court, but imagining he was to be called neglected to apply to the Court till the same was adjourned. *And Whereas* the said Prisoner did afterwards again advertise his intention of being discharged, and no objection being made was discharged by the Judges of the said Court pursuant to the said Act; But as the said Prisoner was not discharged on the said first Day of August, nor any order made on that Day respecting him by the said Court, doubts have since arisen whether the Sheriff or other Officer who had the custody of the said Prisoner was not guilty of an Escape for remedy whereof.

Be it Enacted by the Authority aforesaid, That the said Sheriff or other Officer in whose Custody the said Prisoner was, shall be and is hereby discharged from all Actions which have or may be brought against him by reason of the supposed escape, and it is hereby declared that the said Prisoner shall be deemed in all Courts of Law and Equity to have been legally discharged on the said first Day of August pursuant to the said Act, and the said Sheriff or other Officer in any Suit may give this Act in Evidence without specially pleading the same.

[CHAPTER 1687.]

An Act for the Relief of Insolvent Debtors within this Colony.

[Passed, March 19, 1774.]

Be it Enacted by his Excellency the Governor the Council and the General Assembly, and it is hereby Enacted by the Authority of the same That Henry Bickers, John Burrow, John Hutt, William Stone, Johannes Duryee, James O'Brien, John Shaw, John Haumaid, Matthias Compton, Isaac De Lyon, Moses Hart, William Upton, John Osborn, Robert Welsh, Thomas Dunn, George Traile, Thomas Lupton, John Campbell Shopkeeper, James McKendless, David McKendless, William Norman, and John Griffiths insolvent Debtors in the City of New York; Volkert Dawson, Arent Wempel, Sebastian Keyserick, John Johnson, Francis Martin, John W. Wendell and Philip Cuyler insolvent Debtors in the City of Albany; and Charles Giles an insolvent Debtor in Ulster County in this Colony shall and may, and are hereby allowed to take the Benefit of the several Acts continued by an Act entitled, "An Act to continue the several Acts therein mentioned respecting the Relief of Insolvent Debtors." passed the nineteenth Day of December one thousand seven hundred and sixty six, and which are expired by their own Limitation as fully and effectually as if the said Acts, respecting the Relief of Insolvent Debtors were now in actual and full force.

Provided nevertheless and be it enacted by the same Authority that with respect to such of the said several abovenamed Insolvent Debtors who may have been arrested by process out of the Supreme Court of this Colony (other than such as are confined in the Goal of the City and County of New York,) it shall be lawful for the said Insolvent Debtors, and for any or either of their Creditors respectively to take such Oaths or Affirmations as are directed to be taken by the said Acts hereby revived, before one or more of the Judges of the Inferior Courts of Common Pleas within this Colony instead of taking such Oaths or Affirmations before one or more of the Judges of the Supreme Court as is required by the said revived Acts, which Oaths or Affirmations such Judges of the Inferior Courts are hereby authorized to administer, And such Oaths or Affirmations respectively being reduced to Writing shall be transmitted to the Justices of the Supreme Court or any two of them, who may and shall proceed to the Discharge of such Insolvent Debtors respectively, as if such Oaths or Affirmations had been taken before them or either of them, any Thing in the said hereby revived Acts to the contrary notwithstanding.

[CHAPTER 1688.]

An Act for laying a Road through the Land of Adolph Myer to Mutie David's Fly in the Township of Harlem.

[Passed, March 19, 1774.]

Whereas the laying out of a Road from the King's Highway to Mutie David's Fly on Hudson's River will be very convenient and useful to many Inhabitants of the Township of Harlem; *and Whereas* the Heirs of Peter Waldron through whose Land the greatest Part of the said Road will run have consented to the same being laid out, *and Whereas* Adolph Myer through whose Land a small Part of the said Road will run has refused to consent to the same,

Be it therefore Enacted by his Excellency the Governor, the Council and the General Assembly, and it is hereby enacted by the Authority of the same That the Commissioners for regulating laying out and keeping in repair the Public Highways in the City and County of New York shall, and are hereby impowered to lay out a Road not exceeding two Rods wide, from the King's Highway or road leading from New York to King's Bridge, through the Land of the said Adolph Myer not exceeding two hundred Yards, until it meets with the land belonging to the Heirs or Assigns of Peter Waldron and from thence along the Division Fence between the Lands of the said Adolph Myer and the Heirs or Assigns of Peter Waldron until it comes to Mutie David's Fly, and from thence to Hudson's River, provided the Persons for whose Benefit the said Road through the Lands of the said Adolph Myer shall be laid out, and shall use the same shall keep the said Road in repair, and a good and sufficient

Fence on both sides of it, and the Part adjoining the King's Highway with a good and sufficient swinging Gate thereon, to be regulated by the above Commissioners, and shall pay to the said Adolph Myer the true Value of the Same, and the Damages he shall sustain thereby, to be set appraised and assessed by two Justices and twelve Freeholders of the County of West Chester to be summoned by the High Sheriff of the said County by virtue of a Warrant to be issued by the said two Justices for that purpose.

Provided nevertheless, That if the Persons for whose Benefit the said Road shall be laid out, shall hereafter neglect or refuse to keep the Part of the said Road through the Land of the said Adolph Myer in the Manner above directed, it shall and may be lawful for the said Adolph Myer to stop up and inclose the same.

[CHAPTER 1689.]

An Act to enable Lewis Morris and John Sickles to erect and build a Bridge across Harlem River.

[Passed, March 19, 1774.]

WHEREAS the laying out of Highways in such Manner as to shorten the Distance from the City of New York to any Part of this or the neighbouring Colonies, or to render them more easy safe or convenient is an Object highly deserving the Attention of the Legislature. *And Whereas* a Bridge over Harlem River, and a Road through Harlem Morrissania, and the Borough of West Chester will greatly conduce to both of the aforesaid Purposes,

Be it therefore Enacted by his Excellency the Governor the Council and the General Assembly, and it is hereby Enacted by the Authority of the same, That Lewis Morris of the Manor of Morrissania Esquire and John Sickles of the Township of Harlem be, and they hereby are impowered at any Time within three Years from the passing of this Act to erect and build a Bridge over Harlem River, from the Land of the said John Sickles to the Land of the said Lewis Morris, as they the said Lewis Morris and John Sickles shall judge most fit, and that the said John Sickles shall be and hereby is obliged to open and make a good and sufficient High Road from the Public Highway in the Township of Harlem to the said Bridge; and that the said Lewis Morris shall open and make a good and sufficient High Road from that End of the said Bridge on the Side of Morrissania to the Road now laid out leading to the Borough Town of West Chester. *Provided*, That in such Bridge there shall be three or more Apertures of at least twenty five Feet each, for the Convenience of navigating the said River by Small Boats: And the said Bridge when so built shall be and is hereby declared to be a free and public Highway for the Use Benefit and Behoof of all his Majesty's Subjects whatsoever.

[CHAPTER 1690.]

An Act to impower certain Persons therein named to compleat a Ditch that is partly dug from Gawanes Bay to the East River in Kings County under certain Restrictions.

[Passed, March 19, 1774.]

Whereas the Inhabitants of Gawanes in Kings County have by their Petition to the General Assembly set forth the great Inconveniences under which they have laboured, by Reason of the difficult and dangerous Navigation to which they are exposed in going round Red Hook in their Passage to the City of New York, *And Whereas* it has also been represented, That in Order to remove the said Inconveniences the Petitioners or those whose Estates they hold did for the Consideration of One hundred and Seventeen Pounds Purchase of Isaac Sebring a certain piece or streak of Meadow Ground through which to dig a Canal, whereby to open a Communication for small Craft between Gawanes Bay and the Bay of New York as appears in and by certain Indentures bearing Date the Twenty fourth Day of August in the Year of our Lord One thousand seven hundred and fifty one and made between the said Isaac Sebring of the one Part and Nicholas Veghte and eight other Persons of the other Part, And Whereas sundry Obstructions have hitherto prevented the entire Accomplishment of the said Canal and the aid of the Legislature is necessary effectually to finish and compleat the same,

Be it therefore Enacted by his Excellency the Governor the Council and the General Assembly and it is hereby Enacted by the Authority of the same, That from and after the passing of this Act it shall and may be lawful for Nichlaes Veghte, Peter Staats, Deborah Bergen, Anthony Holst, John Rapalje Esquire,

Wineant Bennet Jacob Bennet, Tuenis Bergen, Tuenis Tiebout and Simon Bergen their Heirs and Assigns or the Major Part of them to build and erect a good and sufficient Bridge well railed on the sides over the said Canal or Ditch [in that Part of it where a Road, sometime since laid out by the Commissioners of Highways in Kings County aforesaid for John Van Dyke, crosses the same: Which said Bridge shall be laid directly across the said Canal] and shall in other Respects be finished and compleated in such Manner as the said John Van Dyke his Heirs and Assigns shall think proper And the Expence of building and erecting the said Bridge as well as of upholding, maintaining and keeping the same in good Repair shall be sustained by and between them in such equitable Manner and Proportion as such Majority shall agree upon. And the said Nicklaes Veghte and the other Persons above named their Heirs and Assigns shall in like manner be obliged to keep in good Repair the said Road on each side of the said Ditch for the Space of two Rods.

And be it further Enacted by the Authority aforesaid, That it shall and may be lawful for the said Isaac Sebring his Heirs and Assigns after the Passing of this Act to make, dig, finish and compleat the said Ditch or Canal in such Direction as the same is already begun and laid out through the said Meadow Ground from Gawanes Bay to the Bay or Harbor of New York Which said Ditch or Canal shall be Twelve and an Half Feet wide and Six Feet deep throughout But in Case the said Isaac Sebring his Heirs and Assigns shall not dig and finish the said Ditch or Canal within Three Months after he or they shall be thereunto requested by Notice in Writing to be Subscribed by the said Nicklaes Veghte, Peter Staats, Deborah Bergen, Anthony Holst, John Rapalje, Wineant Bennet, Jacob Bennet, Tuenis Bergen, Tuenis Tiebout and Simon Bergen or any three of them, That then and in such Case it shall be lawful for them the said several Persons last above named their Heirs and Assigns to make, dig, finish and compleat the said Ditch or Canal in the Manner aforesaid; And of the Expence and Charge which shall attend the carrying on and finishing the said Work they the said Nicklaes Veghte and the several other Persons last above named their Heirs and Assigns shall keep fair and exact Accounts which they shall render to the said Isaac Sebring his Heirs and Assigns who shall be obliged to discount and set off the Amount thereof against a certain Bond or Bonds to the said Isaac Sebring from the said Nicklaes Veghte and others for the Purchase money of the said Meadow Ground mentioned in the said recited Deed.

And be it further Enacted by the same Authority That the said Nicklaes Veghte, Peter Staats, Deborah Bergen, Anthony Holst, John Rapalje, Wineant Bennet, Jacob Bennet, Tuenis Bergen, Tuenis Tiebout and Simon Bergen their Heirs and Assigns shall and may continue the said Ditch to the East River or Harbour of New York and for that Purpose it shall be lawful for them to dig a Trench or Channel through the Beach on the East River aforesaid, and from Time to Time to clear and keep open the said Trench or Channel without any Hindrance or Impediment of or from any Person whatever, And it shall also be lawful to and for the said Nicklaes Veghte and the other Persons aforesaid their Heirs and Assigns to use occupy and enjoy the Ground adjoining the said Ditch or Canal so to be finished as aforesaid, for the Space of Two Feet and an Half on each side thereof for the Purpose of a Foot Path whereon to drag or hawl along their Canoes and other Craft agreeable to the Tenor and Purport of the said recited Deed.

And Whereas it is apprehended that the said Canal or Ditch may be attended with Damage to the Mill now in the Occupation of Jacob Sebring Junior by Reason of the back Water which may possibly be occasioned thereby or otherwise. *Be it therefore Enacted by the same Authority,* That upon Complaints made by the said Jacob Sebring Junior his Heirs and Assigns that any Loss or Damage has happened to the said Mill by Means of the said Canal or Ditch it shall be lawful for any one of the Judges of the Inferior Court of Common Pleas for Kings County aforesaid and he is hereby required from Time to Time and as often as such Complaint shall be made to issue his Warrant to the High Sheriff commanding him to Summon a Jury of Freeholders of the Neighbourhood not interested in the Matters in Controversy to appear before such Judge at a certain Day and Place in the Warrant to be expressed to hear the said Complaint And the said Judge shall at such Day and Place Administer an Oath to the said Jurors well and truly to enquire and determine whether the Owner or Owners of the said Mill have really sustained any Loss Damage or Injury occasioned by the said Ditch or Canal, and if so what the Amount of such Loss, Damage or Injury to the said Mill is And also whether any such Loss Damage or Injury is in future likely to be occasioned by the said Ditch or Canal And if such

Jury shall find that the Owner of the said Mill has really sustained and is likely further to sustain any Loss Damage or Injury thereto by Reason of the said Ditch or Canal then the Damages so to be assessed and also the Costs and Charges of calling such Jury and of the Proceedings thereon shall be borne and paid by the said Nicklaes Veghte and the several other Persons aforesaid in such Proportion as aforesaid which said Costs and Charges shall be Taxed by the said Judge and together with the said Damages if not paid within Twenty Days shall and may be levied by Distress and Sale of the Goods and Chattels of any or either of them the Persons last aforesaid their Heirs and Assigns. And upon such finding of such Jury the said Nichlaes Veghte and the several other Persons above named their Heirs and Assigns shall at their proper Charge and Expence make a flood or draw Gate so constructed as occasionally to prevent the Passage of the Water through the said Canal or Ditch. But in Case such Jury shall determine that the said Jacob Sebring Junior his Heirs and Assigns have not Sustained any Loss, Damage or Injury to the said Mill by Means of such Canal or Ditch then the Costs and Charges of calling such Jury and of the Proceedings thereon shall be paid by the Complainant or Complainants to be levied as aforesaid. Of which finding the said Judge shall make an Entry in Writing to be Subscribed by himself and the said Jurors. *Provided nevertheless* that it shall not be lawful for the said Jacob Sebring Junior his Heirs or Assigns at any Time to prosecute such Complaint or to carry on such Proceedings as aforesaid until the said Nichlaes Veghte, Peter Staats, Deborah Bergen, Anthony Holst, John Rapalje, Wineant Bennet, Jacob Bennet, Tuenis Bergen, Tuenis Tiebout and Simon Bergen their Heirs and Assigns or the Major Part of them shall first have refused to make Amends for such Damages and to put up such Gate as aforesaid. *Provided also* that it shall be lawful for the said Nicklaes Veghte and the said several other Persons before named to make and erect such Gate as aforesaid before such finding of the Jury as aforesaid, and at any time they shall think proper after the Passing of this Act.

And be it also Enacted by the Authority aforesaid, that the said Nicklaes Veghte, Peter Staats, Deborah Bergen, Anthony Holst, John Rapalje, Wineant Bennet, Jacob Bennet, Tuenis Bergen, Tuenis Tiebout and Simon Bergen their Heirs and Assigns shall be, and are hereby made liable, at their joint Expence to be defrayed in such equitable Proportions as they or the Major Part of them shall agree among themselves to make, erect, uphold and maintain such and so many Dams upon the several canals which intersect and run across the said Ditch or Canal so to be made as aforesaid, as will be sufficient to preserve the Water in the several Mill Ponds now belonging to Jacob Sebring Senior and the said John Van Dyke; And to enable them so to do it shall be lawful for them to enter upon the Meadow adjoining to and on each side of the said Canals and Ditches and from Time to Time to come and go to and from the same And if the said Nicklaes Veghte and the several other Persons abovementioned shall neglect to maintain such Dams as aforesaid whereby Damages shall arise to the Owners of the Mills of the said Jacob Sebring Senior and John Van Dyke then and in such Case they shall be liable to repair such Damages, And it shall be lawful for the Owners of such Mills to proceed against them in the Manner above directed with Respect to the Damages which may arise to the Mill of the said Jacob Sebring Junior.

And be it also Enacted by the same Authority, That in Case any of the Inhabitants of Gawanes aforesaid not named herein or in the Neighbourhood thereof shall make use of the said Ditch or Canal such Persons shall respectively be liable to contribute a proportionable share of the Expence and Charges of erecting and keeping in Repair the said Bridge and Gate.

Provided nevertheless that if the said Nicklaes Veghte and the said several other Persons above named their Heirs and Assigns or the Major Part of them shall find the Damages occasioned by the said Ditch or Canal which they are made liable to pay by this Act to be more than the Benefits they shall derive from the same, that then it shall be in their Power to stop up the said Ditch or Canal whenever they shall think proper.

Provided always and be it also Enacted by the same Authority that nothing herein contained shall be construed to make void the said Deed or Conveyance from Isaac Sebring or any Agreement Matter or Thing therein contained, but that the same shall remain in all respects not altered or affected hereby as if this Act had not been passed.

THIRTY-FIRST ASSEMBLY.

Seventh Session.

(Begun Jan. 10, 1775, 15 George III. Cadwallader Colden, Lieut. Governor.)

[CHAPTER 1691.]

[See chapters 948 and 1639. Expired, January 31, 1776.]

An Act further to continue an Act entitled, "An Act for granting to his Majesty the several Duties and Impositions on Goods Wares and Merchandizes imported into this Colony therein mentioned."

[Passed, January 31, 1775.]

WHEREAS the several Duties and Impositions on Goods Wares and Merchandizes imported into this Colony, and granted for the Support of the Government of his late Majesty King George the second by the abovementioned Act, have by several subsequent Acts been continued to the first Day of February one thousand seven hundred and seventy five; and the General Assembly being willing to make Provision for the further Support of his Majesty's Government,

Be it therefore Enacted by his Honor the Lieutenant Governor the Council and the General Assembly, and it is hereby enacted by the Authority of the same, That the abovementioned Act entitled, "An Act for granting to his Majesty the several Duties and Impositions on Goods Wares and Merchandizes imported into this Colony therein mentioned." passed in the twenty seventh Year of his late Majesty's Reign, shall be, and is hereby continued, and every Clause Matter and Thing therein contained, (excepting the Duty on the Article of Cocoa therein mentioned.) enacted to be and remain in full force to all Intents Constructions and Purposes whatsoever until the first Day of February which will be in the year of our Lord one thousand seven hundred and seventy six inclusive; and that Nicoll Havens of Shelter Island in Suffolk County, be the Officer appointed to collect the Colony Duties in the said County, in the abovementioned Act. *Provided always,* That so much of the first Clause or Section of said Act as relates to European or East India Goods imported from the British Islands into this Colony, shall be construed taken and deemed to be from the British Islands in America only, any Thing in the said Act to the contrary hereof notwithstanding.

[CHAPTER 1692.]

[See chapter 1598.]

An Act to appoint Commissioners for collecting the Duty of Excise on Strong Liquors retailed in this Colony from the first Day of February one thousand seven hundred and seventy five, to the first Day of February one thousand seven hundred and seventy six inclusive.

[Passed, January 31, 1775.]

Be it therefore Enacted by his Honor the Lieutenant Governor the Council and the General Assembly, and it is hereby enacted by the Authority of the same That the several and respective Persons and Officers herein after named, shall be and are hereby appointed Commissioners for collecting the Duty of Excise on Strong Liquors, laid by an Act entitled "An Act to lay a Duty of Excise on Strong Liquors in this Colony, and to appropriate the Money arising therefrom," passed the eighth Day of March one thousand seven hundred and seventy three, of and from the several Retailers of Strong Liquors within the several Cities, Counties, Towns, Boroughs, Manors, Precincts and Districts, and the Harbours Bays and Rivers thereunto adjoining or belonging in this Colony, for which they shall be respectively appointed, from the first Day of February in the Year of our Lord one thousand seven hundred and seventy five to the first Day of February which will be in the Year of our Lord one thousand seven hundred and seventy six inclusive; that is to say,

For the City and County of New York Cornelius Clopper Esquire.

For the City and County of Albany, except the District of the Manor of Rensselaerwyck, the District of the Manor Livingston, and the District of the German Camp in said County, Gysbert G. Marcelis, and Gysbert Marcelis Esquires.

For the District of the Manor of Rensselaerwyck in the County of Albany, Lucas Van Veghten Esquire.

For the District of the Manor of Livingston in the County of Albany Robert Livingston Junior Esquire.

For the District of the German Camp in the said County, John Curts Esquire.

For the County of Ulster, Joseph Gashery and James Mc-Clagry Esquires.

For the County of Dutchess, the Supervisors and Assessors in each Precinct respectively for the Time being.

For the County of Orange as follows; for Haverstraw Precinct David Pye Esquire; for Orange Town John Perry Esquire, for Goshen Precinct William Ellison Esquire, and for Cornwall Precinct Daniel Coleman Esquire.

For Richmond County John Micheau and Christian Jacobson Esquires.

For Kings County, Theodorus Polhemus Esquire.

For Queens County, Benjamin Townshend and Samuel Clowes Esquires.

For Suffolk County, Colonel William Smith, Samuel Landon and Malby Gelston Esquires.

For Tryon County Jellis Fonda and John Frey Esquires.

For Cumberland County the Judges of the Inferior Court of Common Pleas in said County.

For the Manor of Cortlandt and Rykes Patent in the County of West Chester Abraham Purdy and Jeremiah Drake Esquires.

For the Borough Town of West Chester the Mayor thereof for the Time being.

For the Manor of Philipsburgh in the County of West Chester, William Davids, Isaac Deane, Israel Underhill, and Gabriel Purdy Esquires.

And for the remaining Part of West Chester County Stephen Ward, and John Thomas Junior Esquires.

And be it further Enacted by the Authority aforesaid That the Commissioners hereby appointed for the different Districts in the County of Albany, shall be allowed the following Sums for their Trouble and Charge in the execution of the Powers vested in them, that is to say.

To the Commissioner of the District of the Manor of Rensselaer-wyck the Sum of five Pounds.

To the Commissioner of the District of the Manor of Livingston the Sum of one Pound.

To the Commissioner of the District of the German Camp the Sum of one Pound.

Provided always, and be it further enacted by the Authority aforesaid, that Nothing in this Act or any Clause or Part thereof shall be construed to abridge or lessen the Rights and Privileges of the Corporations of the Cities of New York and Albany.

[CHAPTER 1693.]

[See chapter 1516. Expired, January 31, 1780.]

An Act to continue an Act entitled "An Act to regulate the Sale of Goods at Public Vendue Auction or Outcry within this Colony."

[Passed, January 31, 1775.]

Be it Enacted by his Honor the Lieutenant Governor, the Council and the General Assembly, and it is hereby enacted by the Authority of the same, That the Act entitled. "An Act to regulate the Sale of Goods at Public Vendue Auction or Outcry within this Colony," passed the twenty sixth Day of February one thousand seven hundred and seventy two, shall be, and hereby is continued, and every Clause Matter and Thing therein contained, enacted to be in full force, until the first Day of February which will be in the Year of our Lord one thousand seven hundred and eighty, and from thence to the End of the then next Session of the General Assembly.

[CHAPTER 1694.]

[See chapter 1556. Expired, April 14, 1780.]

An Act to continue and amend an Act entitled an Act to prevent the Destruction of Fish in the County of Suffolk.

[Passed, January 31, 1775.]

Whereas the abovesaid Act passed the Twenty fourth Day of March in the Year of our Lord One thousand seven Hundred and Seventy two has been found in a great Measure to answer the good Purposes thereby Intended and if further continued with some Amendments must prove of great Advantage to the Community,

Be it Enacted by his Honor the Lieutenant Governor, the Council and the General Assembly And it is hereby enacted by the Authority of the same, That the first enacting Clause in the said Act is hereby repealed and declared null and void, and the following Clause substituted and enacted by the Authority aforesaid instead thereof, That if any Person or Persons shall draw any Sein or Net of any Length whatsoever or set any Sein or Net above six Fathoms in Length from the Fifteenth Day of November to the Fifteenth Day of April in any Year during the Continuance of this Act in any of the Bays, Rivers or Creeks within the County of Suffolk shall for each Offence forfeit the Sum of one Hundred Pounds, And if any Person or Persons shall set any Net whatsoever in Ketchabanuck Channel or within Thirty Rods of the Mouth of said Channel leading into Quantuck Bay or out of said Bay shall forfeit the Sum of Ten Pounds; Or if any Person or Persons shall set any Net or Nets in any other Place in any of the Bays, Rivers or Creeks in the County abovesaid within four Rods of another Net or Nets, and that with Mashes less than three Inches Square shall for each Offence Forfeit the Sum of Five Pounds; Which Forfeitures shall be recovered with Costs of Suit in any Court in this Colony having Cognizance of the same by any Person or Persons who shall sue for the same, the one half of all the Forfeitures shall be paid to the Prosecutor or Prosecutors and the other half to be paid to the Treasurer of the said County to be disposed of by the Supervisors of said County towards defraying the Public Expence of the County, and for want of Estate to levy the same, the Offender or Offenders shall be committed to the common Goal of the County wherein he shall be Convicted there to remain until the Forfeiture or Forfeitures be paid with Cost of Suit.

Be it further Enacted by the same Authority, That it shall be no legal Objection or Disqualification against any Freeholder or Inhabitant in the said County otherwise lawfully qualified as a Juror or Evidence to serve on any Jury or give Evidence in any Suit or Suits, that shall be brought by Virtue of this or the abovesaid Act, notwithstanding the one half of the forfeitures are made payable into the County Treasury and to be disposed of by the Supervisors as aforesaid.

Be it further Enacted by his Honor the Lieutenant Governor, the Council and the General Assembly, And it is hereby enacted by the Authority of the same, That the abovesaid Act to prevent the Destruction of Fish in the County of Suffolk passed the Twenty fourth Day of March in the Year of our Lord One Thousand seven Hundred and Seventy two, Except the first enacting Clause shall be and is hereby continued and every Clause, Matter and Thing therein contained with this Amendment, enacted to be and remain in full Force to all Intents and Purposes whatsoever until the Fifteenth Day of April which will be in the Year of our Lord one Thousand seven hundred and eighty.

[CHAPTER 1695.]

An Act for altering the Time of assessing and collecting the Taxes for the Support of a Minister, and the Poor in the City of New York.

[Passed, January 31, 1775.]

WHEREAS the Taxes for the support of a Minister in the City of New York and the Poor of the said City, have heretofore been assessed and collected in the Winter Season, which has been found to be inconvenient to the Assessors from the coldness of the Weather; and also inconvenient to the inhabitants in general to pay their taxes at that Time when there is but little circulation of Money and their Family expenses higher than at any other Season of the Year,

Be it therefore Enacted by his Honor the Lieutenant Governor, the Council and the General Assembly, and it is hereby enacted by the Authority of the same, That the Taxes that shall be laid and assessed in the Year of our Lord one thousand seven hundred and seventy six, and in every Year forever thereafter for the Support of a Minister in the City of New York and the Poor of the said City, shall be assessed and made on the first Tuesday in May or within ten Days thereafter in every Year, and shall be collected and paid to the Church Wardens of the said City by the Constables to whom the Tax Rolls shall be delivered on or before the first Day of August next following in every Year; any Act or Acts, Usage or Custom to the contrary in any wise notwithstanding.

And be it further Enacted by the Authority aforesaid, That if any Justice of the Peace, Vestryman or Constable shall neglect refuse or delay to do and perform his Duty herein, he and they so offending shall be liable to, and suffer all such Penalties and Forfeitures, and be liable to be proceeded against in the same Manner as they are now liable to, and may be proceeded against by any Act or Acts of the Legislature of this Colony passed for settling a Minister in the said City, and for raising Money for his Maintenance, and for supporting of the Poor of the said City, or any other Act or Acts respecting the same, for Neglect or Refusal of Duty in their respective Offices.

[CHAPTER 1696.]

[See chapter 1553. Expired, January 31, 1785.]

An Act to revive an Act entitled "An Act to prevent Frauds in the Sale of Damaged Goods imported into this Colony."

[Passed, January 31, 1775.]

Be it Enacted by his Honor the Lieutenant Governor, the Council and the General Assembly and it is hereby enacted by the Authority of the same; That the Act entitled "An Act to prevent Frauds in the Sale of damaged Goods imported into this Colony," passed the first Year of the Reign of his present Majesty, shall be, and hereby is revived, and every Clause, Matter and Thing therein contained, enacted to be and remain in full Force from the passing hereof until the first Day of February which will be in the Year of our Lord one thousand seven hundred and eighty five, and from thence to the End of the then next Session of the General Assembly.

[CHAPTER 1697.]

An Act to impower the Mayor, Recorder and Aldermen of the City of New York or the Major Part of them to order the raising a Sum not exceeding Two Thousand Pounds for the Uses therein mentioned.

[Passed, January 31, 1775.]

WHEREAS the providing a sufficient Number of Watchmen, and lighting of Lamps within the City of New York and keeping the public Roads in the said City and County in good repair is convenient and necessary for the Inhabitants and others

Be it therefore Enacted by his Honor the Lieutenant Governor, the Council and the General Assembly, and it is hereby enacted by the Authority of the same, That the Mayor, Recorder and Aldermen of the City of New York for the Time being, or the Major part of them whereof the Mayor or Recorder to be one, shall have full Power and Authority, and are hereby fully impowered and authorized on the second Tuesday in the Month of February One Thousand seven Hundred and Seventy five or within Twenty Days thereafter to order the raising a Sum not exceeding Two Hundred Pounds by a Tax on the Estates real and personal of all and every the Freeholders, Freemen, Inhabitants, Residents and Sojourners within the City and County of New York for keeping the public Roads in the said City and County in good repair And also a further Sum not exceeding One Thousand eight Hundred Pounds by a Tax on the Estates real and personal of all and every the Freeholders, Freemen, Inhabitants, Residents and Sojourners within the City of New York on the South side of Fresh Water for the payment of so many Watchmen as the Mayor, Aldermen and Commonalty of the City of New York shall think necessary for guarding the City and for purchasing Oil, providing Lamps and for repairing and attending the Lamps which now are or hereafter may be erected: which Sums above mentioned shall be rated and assessed by the Vestrymen who shall rate and assess the Tax for the Minister and Poor of the said City, the Vestrymen first taking the Oath prescribed to be taken in and by an Act Entitled "An Act to enable the Inhabitants of the City of New York to choose annually two Vestrymen for each respective Ward within the said City," made and passed in the Nineteenth Year of the Reign of his late Majesty King George the second; And the Tax so to be laid shall be collected levied and paid at the same Time as the Tax for the Minister and Poor of the said City hath been accustomed into the Hands of the Church Wardens of the said City for the Time being, who are hereby required and directed to pay the same into the Hands of the Chamberlain of the said City, to be by him paid as shall be directed by Warrant or Warrants of the said Mayor, Aldermen and Commonalty in Common Council convened for the Uses aforesaid.

And be it further Enacted by the Authority aforesaid, That over and above the Sums of two hundred Pounds and one Thousand eight Hundred Pounds to be levied and paid by Virtue of this Act the Sum of Three Pence in the Pound as a Reward to the Constables for their Trouble, shall be assessed, levied and paid to the respective Constables for collecting and paying the same and no more, according to the true Intent and Meaning of this Act any Thing herein or in any other Act or Acts contained to the contrary hereof in any wise notwithstanding.

And be it further Enacted by the Authority aforesaid, That if the said Mayor, Recorder or Aldermen, Church Wardens, Vestrymen or Constables of the said City, who are hereby authorized, impowered and required to take effectual Care that this Act be executed according to the true Intent and Meaning

thereof, or any of them shall deny, refuse or delay to perform, execute or comply with all or any of the Powers, Authorities and Duties in this Act given and required to be done and performed by them, or either of them, and thereof shall be lawfully Convicted in any Court of Record in this Colony, he or they so denying, refusing or delaying to perform the Duties as aforesaid shall suffer such pains and Penalties by Fine and Imprisonment as by the Discretion of the Court shall be adjudged.

And be it further Enacted by the Authority aforesaid That if any Person or Persons shall wilfully break or damage any of the Lamps whether private or public now erected or hereafter to be erected within the said City, he, she or they so offending shall forfeit the Sum of Twenty Pounds for every Lamp he, she or they shall damage or break as aforesaid to be levied by Warrant or Warrants under the Hands and Seals of two or more of his Majesty's Justices of the Peace for the City and County of New York by Distress and Sale of the Offenders Goods and Chattels, on due conviction made upon the Oath of one or more credible Witness or Witnesses rendering the overplus if any there be to the Owner or Owners: And for want of such Distress the Offender or Offenders shall be imprisoned by Warrant under the Hands and Seals of the said Justices (who are hereby required to issue the same) for the space of Three Months unless the Forfeiture or Forfeitures be sooner paid, which Forfeitures shall be applied towards providing and repairing of Lamps and paying the Watchmen.

And be it further Enacted by the Authority aforesaid, That all such Persons as shall be employed to guard the City and attend the Lamps shall be under the Direction of, and obey such Orders as they shall from Time to Time receive from the Mayor, Aldermen and Commonalty of the said City, any Custom, Law or Usage to the contrary thereof in any wise notwithstanding.

[CHAPTER 1698.]

An Act to impower the Mayor, Recorder Aldermen and Commonalty of the City of Albany for the Time being or the Major Part of them to order the raising a Sum not exceeding one hundred and Sixty Pounds for the Purposes therein mentioned.

[Passed, January 31, 1775.]

WHEREAS the establishing of a regular well constituted Night-Watch, and lighting of Lamps within the City of Albany, has not only been found convenient, but also necessary for the safety of its Inhabitants and others.

Be it therefore Enacted by his Honor the Lieutenant Governor, the Council and the General Assembly, and it is hereby enacted by the Authority of the same, That the Mayor Recorder Aldermen and Commonalty of the City of Albany for the Time being or the major Part of them whereof the Mayor or Recorder to be one, shall have full Power and Authority, and are hereby fully impowered and authorized, at such Time as they shall think convenient on or before the first Day of June one thousand seven hundred and seventy five, to order the raising a Sum not exceeding one hundred and sixty Pounds by a Tax upon the Estates real and personal lying and being within that Part of the said City herein after mentioned of all and every the Freeholders, Freemen Inhabitants Residents and Sojourners living within a half Mile of Hudson's River, and to the North of a West Line drawn from the old Fort, for the Payment of so many Watchmen and lamps, as the Mayor Recorder Aldermen and Commonalty of the said City in Common Council convened shall think necessary for guarding the said City, and lighting the Lamps in the same; which tax so to be laid shall be rated and assessed by the Assessors who shall rate and Assess the Tax which shall be raised by virtue of an Act of the Governor the Council and the General Assembly of the Colony of New York entitled "An Act for the better explaining and more effectual putting in Execution an Act of the General Assembly, made in the third Year of the Reign of their late Majesties King William and Queen Mary entitled An Act for defraying the Public and necessary Charge throughout this Province and for maintaining the Poor and preventing Vagabonds," made and passed the nineteenth Day of June one thousand seven hundred and three, the Assessors first taking the Oath prescribed to be taken by the last mentioned Act, and the Tax so to be laid shall be collected levied and paid by the Collector appointed under the Act aforesaid within twenty Days next after he shall have received a Warrant for that Purpose and shall pay the same into the Hands of such Persons as the said Mayor Recorder Aldermen and Commonalty in Common Council convened shall appoint, for the Uses aforesaid.

And be it further Enacted by the Authority aforesaid, That the Collector shall retain in his Hands three Pence in the Pound for every Pound so raised by Virtue of this Act as a Reward for his Trouble in collecting and paying the same, and no more.

And be it further Enacted by the Authority aforesaid, That if the said Mayor Recorder Aldermen and Commonalty Assessors or Collector of the said City of Albany who are hereby authorized impowered and required to take effectual Care that this Act be executed according to the true Intent and Meaning thereof, or any of them shall deny refuse or delay to perform execute or comply with all or any of the Powers Authorities and Duties in this Act given and required to be done and performed by them or either of them. and thereof shall be lawfully convicted in any Court of Record in this Colony. he or they so denying refusing or delaying to perform the Duties as aforesaid, shall suffer such Pains and Penalties by Fine and Imprisonment as by the Discretion of the said Court shall be adjudged.

And be it further Enacted by the Authority aforesaid, That if any Person or Persons shall neglect or refuse to pay the several Rates and Assessments wherewith he or they shall be charged by this Act, for or in respect of his and their Goods and Chattels, Lands or Tenements, upon the Demand of the Collector appointed to receive the same, that then it shall and may be lawful to and for such Collector, and he is hereby required on non-payment thereof to distrain upon the Goods and Chattels of the Person or Persons so refusing or neglecting to pay; and the Distress so taken to carry away, and the same to expose to sale within the said City, for the Payment of the Rate or Assessment, and the Overplus, if any be, after paying the charges of taking, carrying away, and exposing the same Distress to sale, to be immediately returned to the Owner or Owners thereof.

And be it further Enacted by the Authority aforesaid, That all such Persons as shall be employed to guard the said City, shall be under the Directions of, and obey such Orders as they shall from Time to Time receive, respecting the Premises, from the Mayor Recorder Aldermen and Commonalty of the said City in Common Council convened, any Law, Usage or Custom to the contrary in any wise notwithstanding.

[CHAPTER 1699.]

An Act for the Payment of the Salaries of the several Officers of this Colony and other Purposes therein mentioned.

[Passed, April 1, 1775.]

Be it Enacted by his Honor the Lieutenant Governor, the Council and the General Assembly, and it is hereby Enacted by the Authority of the same, That the Treasurer of this Colony shall and hereby is directed and required to pay,

Unto his Honor the Lieutenant Governor or the Commander in Chief for the Time being for Administring the Government of this Colony from the seventh Day of April last, to the first Day of September one thousand seven hundred and seventy five after the Rate of Two thousand Pounds per Annum.

Unto his said Honor or to the Commander in Chief for the Time being for Fire Wood and Candles for his Majesty's Fort George in the City of New York from the first Day of September One thousand seven hundred and seventy four to the first Day of September One thousand seven hundred and seventy five after the Rate of four Hundred pounds per Annum.

Unto the Honorable Daniel Horsmanden Esquire as Chief Justice of the Supreme Court of this Colony and for going the Circuits from and to the Time last aforesaid after the Rate of three Hundred pounds per Annum.

Unto the Honorable Robert R. Livingston Esquire one of the Puisne Justices of the Supreme Court of this Colony, and for going the Circuits from and to the Time aforesaid after the Rate of two Hundred Pounds per Annum.

Unto the Honorable George Duncan Ludlow Esquire one other Puisne Justice of the Supreme Court of this Colony and for going the Circuits from and to the Time aforesaid after the Rate of two hundred Pounds per Annum.

Unto the Honorable Thomas Jones Esquire the other Puisne Justice of the Supreme Court of this Colony and for going the Circuits from and to the Time aforesaid after the Rate of two Hundred Pounds per Annum.

Unto such of the said Justices of the Supreme Court of this Colony as may attend the Circuit Courts in the Counties of Tryon, Charlotte, Cumberland and Gloucester the Sum of Fifty Pounds to the Justice or Justices that shall so attend in each or either of the said Counties, and for the Attendance of such Justice or Justices on any special Commission of Oyer and Terminer and General Goal Delivery in either of the said Counties, other than such special Commission, which may be held when the Circuit Courts in the said Counties are held, the further Sum of Fifty Pounds to the Justice or Justices so attending; And for the attendance of such Justice or Justices on such special Commission in the County of Albany the Sum of Thirty Pounds, and for the other Counties in this Colony not already provided for the Sum of Twenty Pounds.

Unto the Secretary of this Colony for the Time being, for engrossing and enrolling the Acts of the General Assembly from the first Day of September one thousand seven hundred and Seventy four to the first Day of September one thousand seven hundred and Seventy five after the Rate of Forty Pounds per Annum.

Unto the Clerk of the Council for the Time being for his Services in that Station from and to the Time aforesaid after the Rate of Thirty Pounds per Annum.

Unto the Door Keeper of the Council for the Time being for his Services in that Station from and to the Time aforesaid after the Rate of Thirty Pounds per Annum.

Unto Hugh Gaine for Services performed by him as public Printer of this Colony as per Account the sum of One hundred and Twenty one Pounds four Shillings and three Pence.

Unto Thomas Moore and John Griffiths as Gaugers of Liquor Subject to a Duty within this Colony, or to the Gaugers thereof for the Time being from and to the Time aforesaid after the Rate of Thirty Pounds per Annum unto each of them.

Unto Thomas Hill, Jacob Roome and Henry Law, Land and Tide Waiters or to the Land and Tide Waiters for the Time being from and to the Time aforesaid after the Rate of Fifty Pounds per Annum unto each of them, for the Time they serve.

All which aforesaid several Sums of money shall be paid by the Treasurer on Warrants issued by his Honor the Lieutenant Governor or the Commander in Chief for the Time being, by and with the Advice and Consent of his Majesty's Council of this Colony; And the Receipts of the several Persons endorsed on the said Warrants shall be to the Treasurer good Vouchers and Discharges for so much as shall be thereby acknowledged to be received.

And be it further Enacted by the Authority aforesaid, That the Treasurer shall and hereby is directed and required to pay the several Allowances following to wit

Unto Abraham Lott Esquire Treasurer of this Colony, or to the Treasurer for the Time being for his Services in that Station from the first Day of September One Thousand seven Hundred and Seventy four to the first Day of September one Thousand seven Hundred and seventy five after the Rate of two Hundred Pounds per Annum.

Unto the said Treasurer, or to the Treasurer for the Time being, for the extraordinary Service which he is obliged to perform beyond the usual Duty of his Office after the Rate of the further Sum of One Hundred Pounds per Annum.

Unto Edmund Burke Esquire Agent for this Colony in Great Britain, or to the Agent for the Time being, from and to the Time aforesaid after the Rate of Five Hundred Pounds per Annum.

Unto the said Edmund Burke Esquire for the contingent Charges he has been at the further Sum of One Hundred and Forty Pounds. Which said Sums shall be paid unto him the said Edmund Burke by an Order of the General Assembly of this Colony, signed by the Speaker for the Time being and not otherwise.

Unto John Tabor Kempe Esquire for extraordinary Services performed by him as Attorney General of this Colony from and to the Time aforesaid, after the Rate of one Hundred and Fifty Pounds per Annum.

Unto Richard Morris Esquire for his Services in going the Circuits, and attending thereon for the Trial of Criminals from the Nineteenth Day of March one thousand seven Hundred and seventy four to the first Day of September one thousand seven Hundred and Seventy five after the Rate of One Hundred and Fifty Pounds per Annum.

Unto Edmund Seaman Esquire as Clerk to the General Assembly for his Services in that Station from the first Day of September one Thousand seven hundred and Seventy four to the first Day of September One thousand seven Hundred and Seventy five Twenty Shillings per Diem payable upon a Certificate from the General Assembly signed by the Speaker for the Number of Days he has or may serve the General Assembly.

Unto the said Edmund Seaman for sundry Disbursements by him made for the Use of the General Assembly the Sum of Forty Pounds.

Unto Gerard Bancker as Assistant Clerk to the General Assembly for his Services in that Station from and to the Time aforesaid Twenty Shillings per Diem payable upon a Certificate from the General Assembly signed by the Speaker for the Number of Days he has or may serve the General Assembly.

Unto the said Gerard Bancker for Services performed by him for the Use of the General Assembly and Disbursements the Sum of Fifty one Pounds and Eight Shillings.

Unto William Scott Serjeant at Arms to the General Assembly for his Services in that Station from and to the Time last aforesaid Eight Shillings per Diem payable upon a Certificate from the General Assembly signed by the Speaker for the Number of Days he has or may serve the General Assembly.

Unto the Widow of Alexander Lamb deceased late Door Keeper of the General Assembly, for his Services in that Station from the beginning of the present Session until the Ninth Day of March one Thousand seven Hundred and Seventy five, Six Shillings per Diem payable upon a Certificate from the General Assembly signed by the Speaker for the Number of Days he has served the General Assembly.

Unto the said widow of Alexander Lamb for Fire Wood and sundry Necessaries provided by the said Alexander Lamb for the use of his Majesty's Council and the General Assembly the Sum of Sixty five Pounds.

Unto John Johnson the present Door Keeper to the General Assembly for his services in that Station from the Ninth Day of March one thousand seven Hundred and Seventy five to the first Day of September following Eight Shillings per Diem payable upon a Certificate from the General Assembly signed by the Speaker for the Number of Days he has or may serve the General Assembly.

Unto John Martin as Gunner and Keeper of the Colony Stores for his Services in that Station from the first day of September one Thousand seven Hundred and seventy four to the first Day of September one thousand seven hundred and seventy five Twenty Pounds per Annum.

Unto the Honorable James Jauncey Junior Esquire Master of the Rolls for this Colony for his Services in that Station from the Twenty fourth Day of March One Thousand seven Hundred and Seventy four to the first Day of September one thousand seven hundred and Seventy five after the Rate of Two Hundred and Fifty Pounds per Annum.

Unto his Excellency William Tryon Esquire or his Order for money paid by him to Theophilus Hardenbrook for Repairs in Fort George the Sum of Sixty four Pounds, Sixteen Shillings and four Pence.

Unto Gerard Bancker a Sum not exceeding Forty Pounds to be by him laid out in repairing the Secretarys Office.

Unto Joseph Cox for lodging one of the Commissioners appointed to settle the Boundary Line between this Colony and the Province of New Jersey in the Year One Thousand seven Hundred and sixty nine the Sum of Eleven Pounds three Shillings and three Pence.

Unto John Van Dalsam for Repairs done to the Battery as per his Account the Sum of Thirty three Pounds Eight Shillings and two Pence.

Unto Theophilus Hardenbrook for Repairs done on the Battery and the Garden at Fort George as per his Account the Sum of nine Pounds eleven Shillings and one Penny.

Unto Joshua Root and Abijah Rood of the County of Albany for their Expences and Loss of Time in assisting an Officer in the Service of this Government in executing a Warrant issued by the Judges of the Supreme Court the Sum of Ninety Pounds.

Unto Robert Yates Esquire in full of his Account of Expences and Services in assisting as a Surveyor to the late Commissioners appointed for settling the Boundary Line between this Colony and the Province of the Massachusetts Bay the Sum of Thirty six Pounds, sixteen Shillings and eleven Pence.

Unto Samuel Holland Esquire for his Services on the Part of this Colony in Conjunction with Mr. Rittenhouse on the Part of Pennsylvania in fixing the beginning of the Forty third Degree of Latitude upon the River Delaware as per Account the Sum of Two Hundred and two Pounds, Thirteen Shillings and six Pence.

Unto John Collins for compleating the extension of the Boundary Line between this Colony and the Province of Quebec to Lake St. Francois agreeable to a Resolution of this House the Sixteenth of March last the Sum of Eighty five Pounds.

Unto Samuel Gale and William Wickham Esquires for running the Partition Line between the Province of New York and New Jersey the Sum of one Hundred and sixty nine Pounds, Fifteen Shillings and seven Pence.

Unto the Governors of the Society of the Hospital of the City of New York in America the Sum of Four Thousand Pounds for rebuilding the said Hospital lately consumed by Fire; Instituted for the Reception and Relief of Poor, Sick and Indigent Persons in this Colony.

And be it further Enacted by the Authority aforesaid, That for Answering the Expences of Contingencies and extraordinary Emergencies that have or may happen for the Services of this Colony from the First Day of September one Thousand seven Hundred and Seventy four to the first Day of September one thousand seven Hundred and Seventy five, Warrants may issue for the same on the Treasurer from Time to Time, if drawn by his Honor the Lieutenant Governor or Commander in Chief for the Time being with the Advice and Consent of his Majesty's Council, which the Treasurer is hereby ordered and directed to pay, *Provided* the Amount of the said Warrants, does not exceed the Sum of one Hundred Pounds during that Time.

All which aforesaid several Sums shall be paid by the Treasurer out of the Monies arisen or which may arise by Virtue of the Act entitled "An Act further to continue an Act entitled an Act for granting to his Majesty the several Duties and Impositions on Goods Wares and Merchandizes imported into this Colony therein mentioned." The Act entitled "an Act to continue an Act entitled An Act to regulate the Sale of Goods at Public Vendue, Auction or Outcry within this Colony." And the Act entitled "An Act to revive an Act entitled An Act to restrain Hawkers and Pedlars within this Colony from selling without Licence with an Addition thereto."

And be it Enacted by the Authority aforesaid, That the Treasurer of this Colony is hereby directed and required to place the following Ballances in his Hands due to this Colony as per his Accounts delivered in, to the General Assembly this present Session to the account of the Fund for Support of Government *to wit* the Ballance of one thousand and Eighty one Pounds, fifteen Shillings and nine Pence half Penny on the Act of the Twentieth day of October one thousand seven Hundred and Sixty four for cancelling Fifty nine Thousand two Hundred and fifty Pounds. The Ballance of Twenty five Pounds, ten Shillings and eleven pence Farthing on the Act of the fourth Day of July one thousand seven Hundred and Fifty three for paying the Debts of the Colony; The Ballance of one Hundred and Ninety five Pounds, thirteen Shillings and one penny half penny on the Act of the third Day of June one Thousand seven Hundred and Fifty eight for paying the Debts of the Colony; the Ballance of two Hundred and Thirty six Pounds, one Shilling and six Pence on the Act of the Tenth Day of June one thousand seven Hundred and Sixty for paying the Debts of the Colony; the Ballance of Twelve Pounds on the Act of the Twentieth Day of October one Thousand seven Hundred and Sixty four for paying the Debts of the Colony, and the Ballance of Fifty four Pounds on the Act of the third Day of June one Thousand seven hundred and Fifty nine for granting one Hundred and fifty Thousand Pounds to General Amherst and also the Sum of Three Hundred and two Pounds, Eighteen Shillings and nine Pence put into his Hands by the Honorable John Cruger Esquire Commissary and Paymaster to the Troops in the last War, And also the Sum of Eighty one Pounds received from Paul Micheau Esquire of Richmond County being money taken out of the Treasury in the late Treasurer's Time to encourage a Linen Manufactory in the said County, and the said Treasurer is hereby also directed and required to place the following Ballances due to himself as per the said Accounts to the said Fund for support of Government *to wit*, the Ballance of Three thousand five Hundred and Thirty eight Pounds nine Shillings and three Pence three farthings on the Act of the Eleventh Day of December one thousand seven Hundred and sixty two for settling the Boundary Line between this Colony and New Jersey the Ballance of two Pounds, eleven Shillings and nine Pence on the Act of the Twentieth Day of December one Thousand seven Hundred and Sixty three for granting a Bounty on Hemp and the Ballance of Five Thousand Pounds on the Act of the Ninth day of March one Thousand seven Hundred and seventy four for granting that Sum to his Excellency Governor Tryon as a Compensation in some Measure for the Losses he sustained by the Fire in Fort George; and the said Treasurer is also hereby directed to place the Sum of Fifteen Hundred Pounds due to himself on an Act of the Twenty first Day of December one Thousand seven Hundred and sixty seven for granting that Sum for supplying the Kings Troops with Necessaries to the Interest of the Loan Office money of the Year one Thousand seven Hundred and seventy one.

Provided always, That Nothing in this Clause contained shall be construed to deprive any Person or Persons from receiving their Debts due from the Colony and provided for by the four different Acts passed for the Purpose of paying sundry Debts due from the Colony, the Ballances whereof are directed by this Clause to be placed to the Account of the Fund for Support of Government; but that the Treasurer shall nevertheless pay the said Debts in the same Manner as if this Clause had never been passed, and when paid to charge them to the Account of the Fund for Support of Government, any Law, Usage, or Custom to the contrary notwithstanding.

And be it Enacted by the Authority aforesaid, That the Treasurer shall and hereby is directed and required to keep exact Books of the several Payments which he is directed to make by this act; and shall render true and distinct Accounts thereof upon Oath to his Honor the Lieutenant Governor, or the Commander in Chief for the Time being, the Council or the General Assembly when by them or any of them, he shall be thereunto required.

[CHAPTER 1700.]

[Expired, April 30, 1778.]

An Act for the better regulating the Militia of the Colony of New York.

[Passed, April 1, 1775.]

WHEREAS a due and proper regulation of the Militia of this Colony tends not only to the Security and Defence thereof, but likewise to the Honor and Service of his Majesty,

Be it therefore Enacted by his Honor the Lieutenant Governor, the Council and the General Assembly, And it is hereby enacted by the Authority of the same, That from and after the First Day of May next every Person from Sixteen to Fifty Years of Age, residing within this Colony not already inlisted shall within one Month after he Arrives at the Age of Sixteen, and every Sojourner above the same Age having resided within this Colony above three Months shall inlist himself with the Captain, or in his Absence with the next Commanding Officer either in the Troop of Horse or Independent Companies in the City or County, or in such Company of Foot where he dwells or resides under the Penalty of Five Shillings, and Three Shillings for every Month that such Person shall remain unlisted, and all Captains of Troops of Horse and Companies of Foot in the several Cities, Manors, Boroughs, Townships, Precincts or District within this Colony are hereby commanded to take due Care to inlist all Inhabitants and Sojourners from Sixteen to Fifty Years of Age not already inlisted, which Age in Case of doubt is to be proved by the Oath of the Person whose Age is in question or the Oath of his Parent, or some other credible Witness to be taken by the Officer before whom the dispute shall happen to be, who shall administer the same in the words following I A. B. do Swear upon the Holy Evangelists of Almighty God, that C. D. Summoned before Captain E. F. in order to be inlisted is Years old and no more, according to the best of my Knowledge so help me God, which Oath being duly Administred by the Captain or other Officer who hath Summoned such Person before him in order to be inlisted, and it appearing that he is under Sixteen he shall be for that Time dismissed, and if any dispute shall arise about Elder Persons and it appearing that he or they are above the Age of Fifty such Persons shall be exempted at all Times thereafter.

And be it Enacted by the Authority aforesaid, That all Captains of Troops of Horse and Companies of Foot shall within Three Months from the Commencement of this Act, provide for their Troops and Companies Trumpets and Drums, Colours and Banners and Drummers and Trumpeters at the proper Charge of the respective Captains of Troops and Companies under the Penalty of Three Pounds, and for every Month such Captain shall remain unprovided thereof, the Sum of Two Pounds.

Be it Enacted by the same Authority, That the Colonels or Commanding Officers of all Regiments or Battalions, Troops or unregimented Companies within this Colony shall at least once in every Year issue out their Warrants to their inferior Officers commanding him or them to make diligent Search and Inquiry in their several Precincts or Districts, that all Persons be duly Listed, Armed and Equipped, and to return to them the Names of such Defaulters, as he or they shall find, to the End they may be punished acording to this Act.

And be it further Enacted by the Authority aforesaid, That once in every Year and no more command be given by the Colonel, and in his Absence, by the next Commanding Officer of the respective Regiments or Battalions that the several Companies in each Regiment or Battalion shall meet at the most convenient Place therein to be appointed by the respective Officer commanding the Regiment or Battalion and the Captains or next Commanding Officers of the several Troops of Horse and Independent Companies of the several Cities and Counties shall meet twice in every Year at the most convenient Places therein to be appointed by the respective Officers commanding the Troop of Horse or Independent Company to be then and there mustered and Exercised, And that every Soldier belonging to the Horse shall at the Time and Place commanded appear and be provided with a good serviceable Horse not less than Fourteen Hands high covered with a good Saddle, Houlsters, Housing, Breast Plate and Crupper, a Case of good Pistols a good Sword or Hanger Belt and Cartridge Box, Twelve Cartridges of Gun Powder and Twelve sizeable Bullets, a pair of Boots with suitable Spurs and a Carabine well fixed with a good Belt, Swivel and Bucket under the Penalty of Ten Shillings for the want of a sizeable Horse, and the Penalty of Five Shillings for want of each or either of the Articles of the Troopers Furniture; And the Troopers of the City and County of New York shall be cloathed with a blue Coat and Breeches with yellow metal Buttons and a scarlet Waistcoat, and their Hats laced with Gold Lace, And the Troopers for the City and County of Albany shall be cloathed with blue Coats with white metal Buttons and their Hats laced with Silver Lace and the Troopers of Kings County shall be cloathed with blue Coats and red Jackets and their Hats laced with Silver Lace under the Penalty of Five Shillings for the want of each Article of such Cloathing, the whole Penalty on a Trooper for the Defaults of one Day not to exceed the Sum of Forty Shillings, And every Captain of a regimented Company who shall fail to appear as directed by this Act or appearing fail or neglect to exercise the Company under his Command as directed by the Commanding Officer there present every such Captain for every such Default or Neglect shall forfeit the Sum of Five Pounds, and every Lieutenant, Cornet or Ensign who shall not appear at such Times, or appearing shall not perform his Duty shall forfeit and pay the Sum of Three Pounds.

And be it Enacted by the Authority aforesaid, that once in every Year and not oftner command be given by the Captain and in his Absence by the next commanding Officer of the respective Companies in each Regiment or Battalion of the several Cities, Counties and Manors of this Colony, that the Company under his Command shall meet at some place within his District to be appointed by the said Officer to be then and there mustered and Exercised.

And be it Provided and Enacted by the same Authority, That in Case of a General alarm or Invasion all Unregimented or Independant Companies and Troops shall in the Absence of the Captain General or Commander in Chief be under the immediate Command and Direction of the Colonel, and in his Absence the next Commanding Officer of the Regiment or Battalion of the City, County or District where such Unregimented or Independant Companies or Troops are or may be, any Thing herein to the contrary notwithstanding.

And be it further Enacted by the Authority aforesaid, That the Number of the Troopers in each Company in the City and County of Albany shall be Sixty besides Officers, and the Number of all other Troops in this Colony shall be Fifty Troopers besides Officers, and for a constant supply of Troopers in each City and County within this Colony, where Troops of Horse are or shall be, whensoever it shall happen by Death or otherwise, that there is fewer Troopers in Number than are limited by this Act, and the same cannot be supplied by Volunteers, That then the Captain of such Troop, shall under his Hand certify unto the Colonel of the Regiment of Foot or Battalion or in his Absence to the next Commanding Officer in the City or County where such want shall happen how many Troopers are wanting in his List of the Troop under his Command, and thereupon the said Colonel or next Commanding Officer of such Regiment or Battalion shall nominate out of the same, the Number that shall be so wanting as aforesaid; *Provided* that such Person or Persons so nominated by the said Colonel or next Commanding Officer be not under the Age of Twenty one Years, nor above Ten Miles distant from the Place of the Captains abode, Upon which Nomination the Person or Persons so nominated shall within the Space of Three Months equip themselves as is hereby directed, And every Trooper that shall be so nominated to serve in any of the Troops and refusing to equip himself and serve, he shall for such Offence forfeit the Sum of Five Pounds, and upon Payment thereof shall not be liable to any other or further Forfeiture for any Offence respecting the Troop, but shall nevertheless be Subject to serve in the Foot Service, as if no such nomination had ever been made And all Troopers inlisted in manner as aforesaid refusing or neglecting to appear shall for every such Offence, forfeit the Sum of Ten Shillings for the first Default in not appearing, for the second Default the Sum of Fifteen Shillings and for every Default after the second the Sum of Twenty Shillings until he doth appear; and every Trooper or Soldier belonging to the Horse, shall always have at his Habitation or place of abode, one Pound of Gun Powder and Three Pounds of sizeable Bullets on Penalty of Ten Shillings for every Default.

And be it Enacted by the Authority aforesaid that the Companies of Cadets, and blue Artillery in the City of New York and Company of Cadets in Queens County are to consist each of One hundred Men besides Officers And if the Colonel of the Regiment of the said City or County or in his Absence the next Commanding Officer thereof doth suspect that the Captain or Captains of the said Companies have inlisted a greater Number than is limited above, the Captain of the Company so suspected, shall be obliged within Fourteen Days after Notice, to deliver to the Captain General or Commander in Chief a true and compleat Roll of the Name and Names of all the Persons, he or they have on his or their List; And if it thereby appears, that more are inlisted than the Number above mentioned all such Supernumerary Men are immediately to be discharged out of such List, and the Captain is to give a List of their Names to the Colonel, or next Commanding Officer aforesaid, and the Person and Persons so discharged shall within Fourteen Days thereafter inlist him or themselves in one of the Foot Companies of the said Regiment, and such of the Persons so discharged as shall omit to inlist themselves accordingly shall be subject to the Fines inflicted in this Act, on Persons omitting or neglecting to inlist in the Militia.

And be it further Enacted by the Authority aforesaid, That every Foot Soldier in any of the Regiments or Battalions or Independant Companies of Foot in this Colony shall be provided with a good well fixed Musket or Fuzee, a good Sword, Belt and Cartridge Box, Six Cartridges of Gun Powder and Six sizeable Bullets and so provided shall appear when and where required as aforesaid upon Penalty of Five Shillings for each Musket or Fuzee not well fixed, and for want of a sufficient Sword, Belt or Cartridge Box shall forfeit One Shilling, and the same for want of each Cartridge or Bullet, the whole Penalty for the Default of one Person for one Day not to exceed Ten Shillings, and the sufficiency of the Musket or Fuzee, Sword, Belt and Cartridge Box to be judged of and determined by the Commanding Officer then present, and every Foot Soldier shall at his Habitation or Place of Abode, have one Pound of good Gun Powder, and three Pounds of sizeable Bullets, upon Penalty of Ten Shillings, for each Soldier of Foot; And if any Soldier of Foot or Horse shall refuse to shew to his Captain, or Person sent by him, or other Officer for that Purpose by this Act appointed all or any of the equipage, Furniture or Ammunition herein mentioned, he shall be deemed and esteemed to be unprovided thereof and shall be fined accordingly.

And be it Enacted by the Authority aforesaid, That upon Notice given of a general Muster, or of the Review or Appearance in the Field of any particular Troop or Troops, Company or Companies no Person whatsoever inlisted in Horse or Foot in Manner aforesaid shall absent or withdraw himself from that Service without having first acquainted his Captain and in his absence, the next Commanding Officer therewith and without his leave or Authority so to do, under the Penalty of Ten Shillings, and no Commission Officer shall remove himself out of Town, or withdraw from the Service without Leave from his

Superior Officer, under the Penalty of Twenty Shillings, And no Serjeant, Corporal or Drummer whether of Horse or Foot shall absent themselves in manner aforesaid, under the Penalty of Twenty Shillings.

And be it further Enacted by the same Authority That if any Person or Persons being duly inlisted if thereunto required by their Superior and proper Officer, shall refuse to warn the People to appear under Arms when thereunto required by his Captain or next Commanding Officer, he shall for every such Neglect or refusal forfeit the Sum of Twenty Shillings.

And be it further Enacted by the same Authority That every Soldier inlisted to serve either in Horse or Foot, and appearing under Arms, and during such Appearance shall refuse or neglect to perform such Military Duty as shall be required from him, or shall depart from his Colours or Guard without Leave from the Commanding Officer, he shall forfeit the Sum of Twenty Shillings; and for non payment thereof shall be committed by Warrant from the Commanding Officer there present to the next Goal till the said Twenty Shillings be paid with the Prison Charges; and the Sheriff of each City and County is hereby impowered and required to receive the Body or Bodies of such Offender or Offenders against this Act, as shall be brought to him by Virtue of a Warrant or Warrants under the Hand and Seal of such Officer as aforesaid and him or them to keep in safe Custody until such Fees and Fine mentioned in such Warrant are paid, And it is hereby declared that such Sheriffs or Keepers of Goals shall in such Cases as aforesaid, be intitled to the same Fees, as are allowed in all other Cases, and the Fines so recovered shall be disposed of by the Commanding Officer for the Benefit of the Company to which the Offender doth belong.

And be it Enacted by the Authority aforesaid That the several other Fines, Penalties and Forfeitures in this Act mentioned, shall be levied, recovered and disposed of as followeth *that is to say* That all such Forfeitures as do relate to any Person under the Degree of a Captain shall be adjudged by and be taken to the respective Captains to defray the Charges of their Troops and Companies, and to be levied before the next exercising Day by Distress and Sale of the Offenders Goods by the Captains Warrant directed to the Serjeant or Corporal of the Company wherein such Offence was committed. But if the Offender be a Servant or under his Parents Care, then in such Case the Masters or Parents Goods shall be liable to such Distress and Sale as aforesaid till Satisfaction be made, and if any Serjeant or Corporal shall refuse to execute such Warrant to him directed he shall for every such Offence forfeit for the uses above mentioned, the Sum of Forty Shillings to be levied in Manner before expressed by such other Officer, Serjeant or Corporal as such Warrant shall be directed to, and for all other Penalties and Forfeitures in this Act mentioned, the same shall be levied by Distress and Sale of the Offenders Goods by Warrant from the Colonel or the next Field Officer where such Offenders are, which Forfeiture and Penalty shall be for the use and Benefit of the Regiment or Battalion in the City and County where the Offence is committed, and the Serjeants or Corporals of the Regiment or Battalion are to reserve to themselves out of the Distress or Forfeiture the sum of Three Shillings for executing each Warrant from their Captain or other Superior Officer.

And be it further Enacted, That all Drummers and Trumpeters lately in Service, or that shall be put in Service by the several Captains during pleasure shall serve upon the Salary of Forty Shillings per annum for a Trumpeter, and Twenty Shillings for a Drummer, finding their Trumpet or Drum; and Twenty Shillings for a Trumpeter and Ten Shillings for a Drummer, if the Captain do provide the Drum or Trumpet, and each Drummer or Trumpeter refusing to serve, to Forfeit Forty Shillings to be levied in Manner aforesaid.

Always provided, That all the Members of his Majestys Council, Members of the General Assembly and the Officers of the same, Justices of the Peace, High Sheriffs, Coroners and other Officers of his Majestys Government and all Persons that have held any Civil or Military Commission in this Colony and all other Officers of Courts, Ministers of the Gospel, Physicians, Surgeons, School-masters, all Firemen within this Colony, One Miller to a Grist Mill, and one Ferryman to every Public Ferry, All Supervisors, One Founder and six Men to every Furnace and six Men to every Forge, all Colliers and their necessary Servants employed in burning of Coal and all bought Servants during their Servitude shall be free from being listed in any Troop or Company within this Colony.

And be it Enacted by the Authority aforesaid, That no Commission Officer of the Militia of this Colony legally superseded, shall afterwards be obliged to do the Duty of a private Soldier unless he be Casheered for Cowardice or other Misdemeanor,

nor shall it be in the Power of any Commission Officer to throw up or quit his Commission unless he is Superseded in his Rank until he has served in Commission Fifteen Years at the least, any Thing in this Act to the contrary thereof notwithstanding.

Provided always, That if any Officer shall die or be removed by the Commander in Chief or shall be Casheered for Cowardice or other Misdemeanor in either of which Cases, if the Officer next in Rank shall refuse to be promoted to the Rank such Officer held he shall nevertheless be obliged to serve in the Rank he holds altho' a Junior Officer or any other person should be promoted over him. *Provided always*, that no Senior Officer shall be obliged to continue to serve in any Regiment of Militia or Independant Company or Troop over whom a Junior Officer or any other person is promoted (unless in the Case before mentioned) and unless by his own Consent.

Provided also And be it further Enacted by the same Authority, That in Case any Officer or Officers shall die, or be removed, That then the Governor or Commander in Chief for the Time being shall appoint another or others within the same County to serve in his or their Stead.

And be it Enacted by the Authority aforesaid, That no Military Commission Officer as well of Foot Companies or Troops of Horse, whether Regimented or Independent, as likewise the Troopers in the City and County of New York and Albany shall be liable or subject to serve as Constable though chosen, any Law or Usage to the contrary notwithstanding. *Provided nevertheless* That a Commission obtained by any Person after he is elected a Constable, shall not entitle him to the exemption above mentioned.

And be it Enacted by the Authority aforesaid, That in Case of any Alarm, Invasion Insurrection or Rebellion, every Officer of the Militia shall have full Power and Authority by Virtue of this Act and is hereby required forthwith to raise the Militia or Company under his Command, and to send immediate Intelligence to the Commanding Officer of the Regiment to which he belongs, who also are hereby required and commanded to send forwards the Intelligence forthwith to the Commanding Officer of the next Adjacent Counties informing him and them at the same Time in what Manner he intends to proceed, and every Commanding Officer in every County, upon any Alarm or receiving Intelligence of any Insurrection, Invasion or Rebellion shall forthwith Dispatch an Express to the Governor or Commander in Chief for the Time being, notifying the Danger, and shall therewith signify the Strength and Motions of the Enemy; and the said Commanding Officer hath hereby full Power to impress Boats and Hands, Men and Horses as the Service may require, and shall draw together the Militia of his County or such part thereof as he shall think necessary and March them to such Place or Places as he shall judge most convenient for opposing the Enemy, and to such Place or Places within this Colony, as shall be directed by the Governor or Commander in Chief for the Time being and every Captain or Commission Officer under the degree of Major, that shall neglect or refuse to perform his Duty hereby required shall forfeit the Sum of Twenty Pounds, and every non Commission Officer or private Man for his Neglect or Refusal of such Duty shall forfeit the Sum of Five Pounds, and every Commission Officer, besides paying such Forfeiture, shall be degraded, and rendered incapable thereafter of holding or exercising any Office, Civil or Military within this Colony.

And Whereas the County of Suffolk is so Situated, that a Descent may be made on the Eastern part thereof by Water and the said County being extensive, the remote Parts which are most exposed are generally at a great Distance from the Colonel or Commanding Officer of the Regiment, and consequently the waiting for Orders from the said Commanding Officer may greatly expose such remote Places to the Ravages of small Parties of the Enemy.

Be it therefore Enacted, That the Captains or next Commanding Officer of the several and respective Companies within the said County, nearest to any Place where such Descent may happen to be made shall immediately call together his or their Company or Companies, and forthwith proceed to use their utmost Endeavours to repel and drive off the Enemy: And on the first Notice of such Descent shall dispatch an Express to the Commanding Officer of the Regiment of the said County with Intelligence thereof, and of the Number and Motions of the Enemy according to the best Information he or they shall have obtained, any Thing herein contained to the contrary notwithstanding.

Be it further Enacted by the Authority aforesaid, That if any Person or Persons shall be sued molested or impleaded for any Matter or Thing lawfully done and commanded in the Execution and Performance of this Act, he or they shall plead the general Issue, and give this Act in Evidence; and if the

Plaintiff discontinue his Action, be Nonsuited or Verdict pass against him, the Defendant shall recover treble Costs; nor shall any such Suit or Suits be admitted, or allowed to be brought unless it be done within three Months next after the Offence is committed.

And be it Enacted by the Authority aforesaid, That once every Year, and oftner if thereunto required each particular Captain shall give to his Colonel or in his Absence to the next Field Officer, and such Field Officer and the Captains of unregimented Troops and Companies to the Captain General or Commander in Chief for the Time being fair written Rolls of their respective Regiments, Troops and Companies, on the Penalty of Forty Shillings for a Field Officer, and Twenty Shillings for an inferior Commanding Officer, and if any Person be wounded or disabled upon any Invasion, Insurrection or Rebellion he shall be taken Care of, and provided for by the Public during the Time of such Disability.

And be it further Enacted by the same Authority, That the Majority of the Officers in the Regiment on the South side of the Mountains in Orange County, shall before any Training or Meeting of said Regiment assemble and agree by a Majority of Voices on a convenient Place as near the Center as shall be, for the good of the Public Service; which Place of Training so agreed on and fixed, shall be afterwards notified to the respective Companies by an Instrument under the Hand of such Majority, and read by the Captain or his Order, at the Head of each respective Company.

Provided always and be it Enacted by the Authority aforesaid, That all Persons above the Age of Fifty, and not exceeding Sixty Years of Age, shall in Case of Alarm, Invasion or Insurrection be obliged to appear under Arms under the Captain, or the Commanding Officer of the District where they dwell or reside, any Thing herein contained to the Contrary thereof in any wise notwithstanding.

And be it further Enacted by the Authority aforesaid, That the Independant Companies of Foot in the City and County of New York shall and are hereby formed into a seperate and distinct Battalion, and that the Captain of the said Companies shall have Power and Authority to call out and exercise their respective Company with the Approbation of the Governor or Commander in Chief for the Time being as often as they shall think necessary not exceeding once in each Month, and that every Person who shall have inlisted or shall hereafter inlist in the said Companies shall not absent or withdraw himself without a Discharge under the Hand of his respective Captain with the Approbation of the Colonel or other Field Officer commanding the said Battalion under the Penalty of Ten Shillings for each Offence any Law, Usage or Custom to the contrary notwithstanding

And be it Enacted by the Authority aforesaid, That the Captains of the Independant Companies in the City and County of Albany shall have Power and Authority to call out and exercise with the Approbation of his Excellency the Governor or the Commander in Chief for the Time being their Companies as often as they shall think necessary not exceeding once in each Month, and that no Person that has inlisted or hereafter shall voluntarily inlist in any of the said Independant Companies shall absent or withdraw himself without a Discharge from his Captain or the Commanding Officer of the Company any Thing in the said Act contained to the contrary in any wise notwithstanding.

Be it further Enacted by the same Authority, That the Colonel or Commanding Officer of the Regiment in Queens County shall and is hereby directed and required to Order the said Regiment to meet at two different Places *Viz:* That Part of the Regiment that is in the Parish of Jamaica at or near the Beaver Pond within the Parish of Jamaica aforesaid, and the other Part of the said Regiment which is in the Parish of Hempstead at or near the House of Samuel Nicols or at or near the House of Jordan Lawrence on the Great Plains in said Parish and at no other Places whatsoever any Thing in this Act or any Law, usage or Custom to the contrary hereof in any wise notwithstanding.

Provided always And be it Enacted by the Authority aforesaid, That every Person professing himself to be of the People commonly called Quakers and producing to the Captain or Commanding Officer of the Company in whose Beat he resides a Certificate from one of their Monthly Meetings signed by six or more of the Principal People of such Meeting, that such Person had been deemed and allowed one of the People called Quakers for the Space of One whole Year or upwards before the producing such Certificate, such Person so producing such Certificate shall be and is hereby exempted from the ordinary Duties of Training or Mustering unless upon an Alarm, Invasion, Insurrection or

Rebellion any Thing herein contained to the contrary thereof in any wise notwithstanding.

Be it further Enacted by the Authority aforesaid, That this Act shall be in Force from the first Day of May next until the first Day of May which will be in the year of our Lord one Thousand seven Hundred and Seventy eight.

[CHAPTER 1701.]

[See chapter 1103.]

An Act to amend an Act entitled "An Act for the more effectual Prevention of Fires, and for regulating of Buildings in the City of New York."

[Passed, April 1, 1775.]

WHEREAS the said Act has not had its Effect, and it is necessary to that good End, that it be amended and inforced,

Be it therefore Enacted by his Honor the Lieutenant Governor the Council and the General Assembly, and it is hereby enacted by the Authority of the same, That from and after the passing hereof till the first Day of January next, the abovementioned Act entitled, "An Act for the more effectual Prevention of Fires and for regulating of Buildings in the City of New York," and every Clause Matter and Thing therein contained shall be and is hereby declared to be suspended any Thing in the said Act to the contrary notwithstanding.

And be it Enacted by the Authority aforesaid, That it shall be lawful any Thing in the said Act to the contrary notwithstanding, to erect any Building in the said City with Wood or other Materials and cover the same with Shingles or Boards, that shall be situated to the Northward or North Eastward of a Line. Beginning on the Easterly Edge of Hudson's River in the Middle of Partition Street and running South Easterly through the Middle of the said Street, and through the Middle of Fair Street to the Middle of Nassau Street; thence North Easterly through the Middle of Nassau Street until it comes opposite to the Middle of Frankford Street, thence South Easterly through the Middle of Frankford Street till it comes opposite to the Middle of VandeWater Street, thence Easterly through the Middle of Vande Water Street till it comes to the Middle of Queen Street, thence Southerly through the Middle of the same till it comes to the Middle of Saint Georges Square, thence Easterly through the Middle of Cherry Street till it comes opposite to the Middle of Saint James's Slip, thence Southerly through the Middle of the said Slip to the East River, *Provided* such Buildings shall not exceed fourteen Feet in Height from the Level of the Street on which the same is erected, to the Eaves of the Roof, and that the Elevation of such Roof do not exceed one third Part of the Span or Breadth thereof, and that the upper Part thereof be nearly a Flat of at least two equal fifth Parts of the whole Span of such Roof.

And be it further Enacted by the same Authority, That any Thing in the said Act to the contrary notwithstanding, it shall be lawful on the Southward and South Westward of the Line above mentioned to cover the Flat of any roof with Boards or Shingles, provided such Flat do not exceed two equal fifth Parts of the Span of such Roof and there be erected around the same Flat a substantial Balcony or Balustrade and a Platform and Steps to the top of every Chimney, and that all Roofs, Coverings of Steeples, Cupolas and Spires of Churches and other Public Buildings may be also made of Boards and Shingles any Thing in the said Act to the contrary hereof in any wise notwithstanding. And if any Dwelling House or other Building whatsoever shall be erected or roofed contrary to the true Intent and Meaning of this Act, the Proprietor or Proprietors thereof shall forfeit and pay for every such Offence the Sum of fifty Pounds, to be sued for and recovered in any Court of Record in this Colony by Bill Plaint or Information, wherein no Essoin Protection or Wager of Law, or any more than one Imparlance shall be allowed; And the Workmen who shall build or roof such House or Building contrary to the true Intent and Meaning of this Act, shall each of them forfeit and pay for every such Offence the Sum of five Pounds to be levied by Warrant under the Hands and Seals of two or more of his Majesty's Justices of the Peace of the said City and County of New York by Distress and Sale of the Offenders Goods, upon due Conviction upon Oath or upon the View of one or more of such Justices, rendering the Overplus, if any there be to the Owner or Owners, and for want of such Distress the Offender shall be imprisoned by Warrant from the said two Justices, who are hereby impowered and required to issue such Warrant until Payment as aforesaid, which said Forfeitures shall be paid to the Chamberlain of the said City to be applied by the Mayor Aldermen and Commonalty as a Bounty on Tile made in this Colony, and sold in the City of New York; and every such Dwelling House or other Building whatsoever so built or roofed contrary to the true Intent and

Meaning of this Act, shall be and hereby is adjudged deemed and declared to be a Public Nuisance.

And Whereas it may be expedient to erect Houses and other Buildings on new made Ground in divers Parts of the said City where no sufficient Foundation can be laid for heavy Edifices of Stone or Brick.

Be it therefore Enacted by the same Authority, That no Person shall incur any Penalty for erecting any Wooden Buildings on such new made Grounds if Previous to the Erection of the same an Inquisition be filed in the Town Clerk's Office, and the Sheriff of the said City and County, and a Jury of at least twelve Freeholders who have had a View of the Place, therein Certify that no sufficient Foundation could be laid in such Place for a Building of Stone or Brick without exposing the Proprietor to the Expence at least of the Sum of one hundred Pounds.

And to the Intent that every Inquisition to be taken either by virtue of this Act or the Act aforementioned in an Affair of so much Consequence to the Public may be fairly taken.

Be it further Enacted by the same Authority, That the Jurors for every such Inquisition shall be struck from a compleat Book or List of the Freeholders of the said City to be made by the said Sheriff and by order of the Mayor thereof for the Time being, on request to him made for that Purpose, and that the Party applying for Leave to build, may in the Presence of the said Mayor, out of the forty eight Names first struck by the said Mayor from the said Book, strike out twelve Names, and such other indifferent Person as the Mayor shall appoint twelve other Names, until by alternate strikings, there remain twenty four who shall be all summoned by the Sheriff to attend such Inquisition, and as many as attend shall sit thereon provided that no more than twenty three Persons be sworn, and that no such Inquisition shall be valid, unless it be found by at least twelve of the Jurors chosen and summoned as aforesaid.

And be it further Enacted by the Authority aforesaid, That every Proprietor or Proprietors of such Ground so inspected as aforesaid, shall pay and satisfy unto the Sheriff for summoning such Jury and taking such Inquest the Sum of forty Shillings.

And be it further Enacted by the same Authority, That every Building erected or made contrary to this or the Act aforesaid, shall be indictable as a Public Nusance and be so adjudged, and that the Judges of the Supreme Court shall in every subsequent Term charge the Grand Jury to cause diligent Enquiry to be made of all such Offences, and all the Offenders presented, that they may be prosecuted and punished by Fine and Imprisonment according to the Nature of the Offence, and after the Conviction of any Proprietor or Proprietors of the Soil in a due Course of the Law for erecting any Building contrary to this or the aforementioned Act, the Owner or Owners thereof as long as the same Conviction shall remain unreversed, and the same Nusance continue; shall in every Assessment for Taxes in the said City and County be liable to pay double the Sum for which such House or Building would have been taxable if this Law had not been made, and such double Tax shall by the Assessors be imposed thereon accordingly, and be recoverable as the single Tax may be over and above all other Forfeitures and Penalties incurred for erecting the Same contrary to this and the Act aforesaid or either of them.

And be it also Enacted by the same Authority, That the Aldermen of all the several Wards of the said City except the Out-Ward shall respectively present to one of the Judges of the Supreme Court five Days before the first Day of every Term a List of every Building erected in their respective Wards since the last Term, to the Intent that the same may be delivered to the Grand Jury, and in Default thereof without sufficient Excuse to be assigned to the said Court (concerning which the Judges shall inquire in a summary way,) they shall impose a Fine adequate to the Offence and cause the same to be levied as in Cases of Contempt of any Rule or Order of the said Court together with reasonable Costs to the Officers of the said Court, which said Fine shall by the Clerk of the said Court be paid to the Overseers of the Poor, for the use of the Poor of the said City.

Provided always that nothing herein contained shall be construed to affect any Thing done before the passing hereof.

[CHAPTER 1702.]

An Act to regulate the Pilots and establish their Pilotage between Sandy Hook and the Port of New York and other Purposes therein mentioned.

[Passed, April 1, 1775.]

Whereas the subjecting the Pilots of the Port of New York to proper Regulations, tends greatly to the Safety and Convenience of the Navigation to and from the said Port,

Be it therefore Enacted by his Honor the Lieutenant Governor the Council and the General Assembly, and it is hereby enacted by the Authority of the same, That it shall and may be lawful for the Governor or Commander in Chief of this Colony for the Time being, by and with the Advice and Consent of his Majesty's Council to appoint one fit and proper Person to be Master, and three or more fit and proper Persons to be Wardens of the said Port of New York who shall be called by the Name of *the Master and Wardens of the Port of New York;* and in like Manner to appoint and commissionate a sufficient Number of Persons to be Branch-Pilots for the said Port, who shall be and are hereby impowered to appoint each one Deputy under him, *Provided* that no Person shall hereafter be commissionated as a Branch-Pilot, or appointed a Deputy-Pilot, until he shall have been examined before, and obtained a Certificate from the Master and Wardens of the said Port, or any three or more of them under their Hands and Seals, of his being duly qualified for such Office; and if any Person not so commissionated or appointed shall Pilot any Ship or other Vessel going into or out of the said Port from or to Sandy Hook when a Branch or Deputy Pilot offers, such Person shall forfeit and pay the Sum of five Pounds.

And be it Enacted by the Authority aforesaid, That if any Branch Pilot or his Deputy shall neglect or refuse to give all the Aid and Assistance in his Power to any Ship or other Vessel appearing in Distress on the Coast or in want of a Pilot, such Branch-Pilot or Deputy, if the Governor or Commander in Chief with the Advice and Consent of his Majesty's Council shall think fit, shall forfeit his Branch or Deputation, or be fined at the Discretion of the Master and Wardens aforesaid or any three or more of them, not less than the Sum of ten Pounds, nor more than the Sum of twenty Pounds; which said Master and Wardens or any three or more of them are hereby impowered to impose such Fine, and also to make such prudential Rules and Orders (to be approved of by the Governor or Commander in Chief for the Time being with the Advice and Consent of the Council,) for the better regulating the said Pilots, as they shall judge necessary and expedient, and to impose and lay any Fine for the Breach of such Rules and Orders not less than the Sum of ten Pounds, nor more than the sum of twenty Pounds; And as a Reward for such Branch Pilots, or their Deputies who shall be the most active and ready to give all the Aid and Assistance in their Power to any Ship or other Vessel appearing in Distress or in want of a

Pilot on the Coast, the Master or Owner of such Ship or other Vessel shall pay unto every Branch-Pilot or Deputy who shall give his Aid and Assistance in Manner aforesaid, such reasonable Sum for all extra Services and Assistance as the Master or Owner of such Vessel and the Pilot or Deputy shall agree upon, and in Case no Sum can be agreed upon by them, then the Master and Wardens shall fix and ascertain what to them appears a reasonable Compensation and Reward for such Services.

And to the End such Pilots may have due Encouragement to attend and perform such Services. *Be it Enacted by the Authority aforesaid,* That it shall and may be lawful to and for every such Pilot to ask demand and receive of and from every Person or Persons that shall employ him or them to pilot any Ship or other Vessel from the Eastward of the false Hook unto the Port of New York, and from the Port of New York down to the Eastward of the false Hook so far as that such Vessel may proceed from thence safely to Sea, from the fifteenth Day of March until the first Day of December yearly, the Rates and Pilotage of four Shillings for every Foot of Water such Ship or other Vessel shall draw, *Provided always* That no more than half Pilotage shall be demanded and received by every such Pilot who shall take Charge of any Ship or other Vessel coming to the Port of New York to the Westward of the false Hook: And from the first Day of December to the fifteenth Day of March yearly, the Sum of twenty Shillings more for every such Ship or other Vessel drawing ten feet Water and upwards, and for every Ship or other Vessel drawing less than ten feet Water the Sum of ten Shillings more; And for every Ship or other Vessel which such Pilot shall be required to Pilot clear of the Middle Ground out to Sea the Sum of ten Shillings more, for every such Ship or Vessel drawing ten Feet Water or under; and the Sum of twenty Shillings more for such as draw more than ten feet Water: And for every Day such Pilot shall be required to remain and is detained on Board by the Master while waiting for a fair Wind, such Pilot shall be paid, and he is hereby authorized to ask demand and receive the Sum of ten Shillings per Day.

And to the End the said Master and Wardens may be disinterested and impartial Directors, as by this Act is intended; *Be it Enacted,* That neither of them so long as they are employed in this Trust, shall be direcly or indirectly concerned in any Pilot-Boat, or with any Person whatever commissionated as a Branch-Pilot.

And be it Enacted by the Authority aforesaid, That the Branch-Pilots and Deputy Pilots of the Port of New York already appointed and deputized, shall within one Month after the passing hereof; and the Branch-Pilots and Deputy Pilots hereafter to be appointed and deputed, shall before they take upon them the Execution of such Office respectively enter into Recognizances with two Sufficient Securities to be approved of by the Master and Wardens aforesaid or any three or more of them in the Penal Sum of one hundred Pounds Current Money of this Colony, conditioned that such Pilot or Deputy shall and will in all Things diligently and faithfully perform and execute the Trust reposed in him according to the Directions true Intent and Meaning of this Act, and according to such Orders and Directions as he or they shall from Time to Time receive from the said Master and Wardens of the Port of New York, or any three or more of them, and on breach of such Recognizance, the same may and shall be put in Suit at the Request of any Party complaining, who shall be intitled to and receive such Part of the Penalty if recovered as shall be awarded and determined by the said Master and Wardens or any three or more of them, who are hereby authorized to take Cognizance of such Matter and award the Damages accordingly: *Provided always* that if the Branch Pilot or Deputy Pilot so offending shall pay to the Party so aggrieved such Damages as shall be assessed by the said Master and Wardens or any three or more of them with the Costs accrued, the Proceedings upon such Recognizance shall be stayed or discontinued.

And be it further Enacted, That every Branch Pilot that shall hereafter be appointed, shall be such and remain in his office as Branch-Pilot no longer than while he is a bona fide Owner or Part Owner of a Pilot-Boat, and while such Boat shall be really and only employed and used in that Service as a Pilot Boat, and in Case any such Branch-Pilot as aforesaid sells or disposes of his Property in such Boat, or employs her, or suffers her to be employed in any other Service such Branch-Pilot shall forfeit his Branch and be immediately dismissed from his Office of Branch-Pilot by the Master and Wardens or any three or more of them with the Consent of the Governor or Commander in Chief for the Time being, by and with the Advice of the Council.

And be it further Enacted, That the Master and Wardens of the Port of New York for the Time being shall be, and they, or any two or more of them are hereby appointed Surveyors for the surveying of all damaged Goods brought into the Port of New York in any Ship or other Vessel, and in like Manner with the Assistance of one or more able Carpenter or Carpenters to survey all vessels that shall or may be deemed or thought unfit to proceed to Sea, and thereupon shall give proper Certificates under their Hands and Seals as the Matter shall appear to them; An Entry whereof they shall Cause to be made in a Book to be kept for that Purpose, for which Certificate and Entry their Clerk shall be intitled to a Fee of eight Shillings and no more; And the Master and Wardens shall be allowed at the Rate of twenty Shillings each per Day, and in that Proportion for half or quarter of a Day; and no Survey on such Goods or Vessels performed or made in any other Manner than is herein directed and prescribed shall be valid or authentic.

And be it further Enacted, That before the said Master or Wardens enter upon the Execution or Discharge of the said Office, they shall severally take an Oath before one of the Judges of the Supreme Court of this Colony in the Words following, that is to say, "I, A. B. will well truly and impartially according to the best of my Skill and Understanding execute the Powers vested in me by virtue of an Act of the Colony of New York entitled An Act to regulate the Pilots and establish their Pilotage between Sandy Hook and the Port of New York and other Purposes therein mentioned; so help me God."

And be it further Enacted That the said Master and Wardens shall keep an Office in the City of New York, and provide and keep a Clerk, and a proper Book or Books, and therein shall cause regular and fair Entries to be made of all their Transactions and Proceedings in virtue of this Act, to which all Persons may have recourse; which Clerk so to be appointed is hereby impowered to receive all the Pilotage Money which shall from Time to Time become due to all or any of the Pilots by virtue of this Act, and on Refusal of Payment, in his own Name to sue for the same before the Mayor or any other Magistrate of the City of New York who are hereby respectively impowered to hear try and determine the same in a summary way, and to award Execution thereon with Costs; and to keep a distinct and separate Account with each and every of the said Pilots, of all such Monies as he shall or may receive to their Use, and every three Months to pay the same to them severally, retaining in his Hands four Per Cent for his Trouble; And all Fines and Forfeitures arising by this Act, shall and may be sued for and recovered by and in the Name of the said Clerk in like Manner as aforesaid, and all the said Fines and Forfeitures, and such Part of the Penalty of any Recognizance recovered and unapplied as aforesaid shall be paid into the Hands of the said Master and Wardens, and by them applied towards defraying such necessary Expences as they shall be put to in the Discharge of the Trust reposed in them; And the said Clerk is hereby required and ordered to enter into Bond with good Security to the said Master and Wardens in the Sum of five hundred Pounds for the faithful discharge of the Duty and Trust reposed in him by this Act.

And be it further Enacted, That the Pilotage which shall or may become due to any of the Pilots who shall take charge of any Vessel outward Bound, shall be paid or secured to be paid to the said Clerk before the breaking Ground of such Vessel in the Port of New York; and in Case the said Pilot for whose Use such Money is paid, shall fail in doing his Duty, the Money shall be returned or the Security be void, as may happen to be the Case.

Be it further Enacted, That the Master or Owners of every Vessel going out of this Port of New York, shall pay to the Clerk of the Master and Wardens of said Port, in Case he or they shall carry off any Pilot or Deputy Pilot, through his or their own Default when a Boat Attends for taking off such Pilot from on board such Vessel, for the Use of such Pilot or Deputy Pilot, the same Wages per Month that the Mate of such Vessel in which such Pilot or Deputy Pilot is carried off, over and above the Pilotage of such Vessel, until he can return to the Port of New York; *Provided* such Pilot or Deputy Pilot performs on his part the Duties of him required by this Act; and *Provided also* that he performs on board such Vessel, the usual Services and Work of a Seaman as far as in his Power; And if any Money shall be advanced to such Pilot or Pilots by the Master Owner or Factor of such Vessel, such Money to be deducted accordingly.

And be it also Enacted by the Authority aforesaid, That during the Continuance of this Act it shall and may be lawful for the Governor or Commander in Chief of this Colony for the Time being by and with the Advice and Consent of his Majesty's Council to appoint so many Branch-Pilots as shall be judged necessary for the safe Pilotage of Vessels (when required) through the Channel in the East River or Sound commonly called Hell-Gate, to and from the Port of New York, the Master and Wardens aforesaid to establish the Pilotage and also to make such Rules and Regulations for the ordering and directing the said Pilots as shall be by them judged necessary and expedient.

And be it further Enacted by the same Authority, That in Consideration that the said Master and Wardens to be appointed by virtue of this Act must necessarily give their Attendance to the Duty of their Offices, they shall not be liable therefore to serve as Grand or Petit Jurors, during their Continuance in the said Office.

And be it further Enacted, That the Branch and Deputy Pilots of the Port of New York shall be obliged and they are hereby required to keep a good and sufficient Whale-Boat at all Times on Sandy Hook at their Joint Expence, which Boat shall be purchased and ready at the Place aforesaid on or before the first Day of October next, and the Clerk of the Master and Wardens of the Port aforesaid is hereby required and authorized to keep and retain in his Hands out of the Pilotage of the said Pilots a sufficient Sum by that Time for the Purpose of paying for such Boat to the Contractor or Builder thereof, which Boat so to be purchased and kept at Sandy Hook aforesaid shall be furnished with a sufficient Number of Oars, and at all Times to be kept by the said Pilots in good and sufficient Repair, the Expence of which also shall be retained by the said Clerk and paid out by him as aforesaid from the Earnings of the said Pilots.

And Whereas several Buoys are already, and more may hereafter be placed over and at the Shallows and most dangerous Places for Vessels coming in from, and going out to Sea, so that many Masters of Vessels may perhaps refuse taking a Pilot on board.

Be it therefore further Enacted by the Authority aforesaid, That such Masters who shall so refuse such Pilot as aforesaid, shall pay to such Pilot half Pilotage according to the place such Pilot shall offer himself at.

And be it further Enacted, That the Wardens of the said Port shall furnish every Pilot with printed or written Instructions, to be delivered by every such Pilot to the Master of every Vessel, as soon as he goes on board to take Charge of such Vessel to bring her into the Port of New York, which Instructions shall be strictly observed by every Branch-Pilot or Deputy Pilot, Master or Masters of Vessels, at their Peril.

This Act to continue in force from the passing thereof until the first Day of February which will be in the Year of our Lord one thousand seven hundred and eighty five, and from thence to the End of the then next Session of the General Assembly.

[CHAPTER 1703.]

An Act to confirm a Submission to Referees of a Controversy concerning the Bounds of the Patent of Jan Hendrickse Van Baal and for binding the Title of the respective Claimants agreeable to the Award of the said Referees.

[Passed, April 1, 1775.]

Whereas by Letters Patent under the Great Seal of the Province of New York bearing Date the Twenty first Day of August in the Year of our Lord One Thousand six hundred and Seventy two a certain Parcel of Land was granted to Jans Hendrickse Van Baal in Fee *to wit* a Certain Parcel of Land near Schenectady lying and being by the Kill or Creek called by the Indian name Tawalsontha otherwise the Normans Kill, the said lands stretching from the Sandy Hills North West on to an Out Hook of Land the which it also includes Containing in Breadth and Length on both sides of the Kill all the Land as it lies in a Square together with the Wood Land Valley or Meadow Ground Kills and Creeks therein included. *And Whereas* by Letters Patent under the Great Seal of the Province of New York bearing Date the Fourth Day of November in the Year of our Lord One Thousand six Hundred and Eighty five the Manor of Rensselaerwyck was granted in Fee to Killian Van Rensselaer the Son of Johannes Van Rensselaer and to Killian Van Rensselaer the Son of Jeremiah Van Rensselaer Comprehending two different Tracts of Land the one of which is described in the same Letters Patent as follows Beginning at the South end or part of Berrent Island on Hudsons River and extending Northwards up along both sides of the said Hudsons River unto a Place heretofore called the Kahoos or the great Falls of the said River and extending itself East and West all along from each side of the said River backwards into the Woods Twenty four English Miles To have and to hold the same (except as therein is excepted) unto the said Killian the Son of Johannes Van Rensselaer and Killian the Son of Jeremiah Van Rensselaer their Heirs and Assigns for ever In Trust to and for the only use and Behoof of the Right Heirs and Assigns of Killian Van Rensselaer their Grand Father, which said Manor of Rensselaerwyck is claimed by Catherine Van Rensselaer Widow and Relict of Stephen Van Rensselaer

nesses and that such Witnesses shall be examined and cross examined by Peter Silvester Esquire on the Part of the said Manor of Rensselaerwyck and by Robert Yates Esquire in behalf of the other party hereto. *Fourthly*, That the said Examiners and such Clerk and Clerks as they shall appoint to assist them shall take an oath well and truly to discharge the several Trusts reposed in them concerning the Premisses and also not to divulge or make known or suffer to be divulged or made known directly or indirectly by any Ways or Manner whatsoever any of the Contents of the said Depositions or any of them untill they are to be published as herein is after mentioned, That each of the said Depositions when taken as aforesaid together with the rough Draft thereof be sealed up by the said Examiners as soon as compleated and indorsed with the Deponants Name and when the said Examinations are fully compleated then the Depositions of the Witnesses produced on each part respectively together with the rough Draft thereof be sealed up by the said Examiners those of the Parties of the first Part to be kept by the said Peter Silvester and those of the Parties of the second Part to be kept by the said Robert Yates, which affidavits and every of them so taken as aforesaid are hereby mutually agreed shall and may without Objection to be made by either of the said Parties respectively or those claiming under them be given and received in Evidence before the said Arbitrators or on any future Trial or Hearing in Law or Equity between any of the said Parties or those claiming under them concerning the Premisses or any Part thereof in Case the Witness so making the same shall be dead or in Case it shall be Proved to the satisfaction of the said Referees or the said Court of Law and Equity that the Witness making such Deposition or Depositions cannot be got to attend to give Evidence *viva voce* saving all just Exceptions to each Party as to the legality and Character of the Witness as if he was present and personally offered as a Witness. *Fifthly*, That whenever the said Arbitrators shall meet for the Purposes aforesaid and the Majority of them at the Request of either Party shall require any of the said Depositions to be read in Evidence to them agreeable to the true Intent and Meaning of these Presents that then it shall and may be lawfull for the said Peter Silvester and Robert Yates or either of them to deliver such Deposition and Depositions to the Party so applying for it and an original Duplicate thereof to the opposite Party to be read in evidence as aforesaid. *Sixthly* And it is further agreed, that after the said Arbitrators shall have compleated and delivered in their Award or in Case the said Arbitration by any Accident shall be entirely frustrated that then it shall and may be lawfull for the said Peter Silvester and Robert Yates to deliver and give up to any of the first and second Parties respectively the Depositions of their Witnesses respectively and the Duplicate thereof and rough Draft thereof so taken as aforesaid, the same Depositions to be given in Evidence on all future Ocasions in manner and form as aforesaid. *Seventhly* In order to expedite the Determination by the Arbitrators aforesaid and in order to strengthen the Security to the Parties aforesaid it is further agreed that Rules of Referrence be severally entered by the Consent of Parties at the next Supreme Court of Judicature for the Province of New York in two several Actions of Ejectment brought for Part of the Premises in Question and now pending undetermined the one at the Suit of James Jackson on the Demise of the said Catharine Van Rensselaer against Simon Johannise Veeder, Volkert Veeder, Simon M. Veeder and Abraham Veeder the other at the Suit of James Jackson on the Demise of Barnardus Legrange against Robert Freeman and the said Catharine Van Rensselaer, by which Rules the said Causes shall be severally referred to the Determination of the Arbitrators mentioned in and according to the true Intent and Meaning of the Bonds of Arbitration herein before mentioned. *Eighthly* It is also agreed that the Award of the said Arbitrators shall bind the Possession of the Lands in Controversy only but not the Title of either of the Parties to any Part or Parcel thereof unless an Act of the Legislature of the Province of New York be passed within Two Years from the Date hereof either confirming the aforesaid Submission and authorizing the said Referrees finally to determine the Title of the Lands in Question and the Bounds of the said Patent granted to the said Jan H. Van Baal as aforesaid or confirming such Award as the said Arbitrators shall before that Time have made concerning the Premisses nor unless such Act shall within four Years from the Date hereof be confirmed by his Majesty. *Ninthly* It is also further agreed, that the Parties of the first and second Part to these Presents shall at their joint Expence respectively use their utmost Endeavours to procure the passing of such an Act of the Legislature of the said Province as is above mentioned and the Confirmation thereof by his Majesty as aforesaid in order to which they shall jointly Petition the House of Assembly for the said Province for the same that the said Parties or some or more of them on or before the first Day of July then and now next ensuing and with Condition on the Part of the said Claimants of the aforesaid Manor to deliver up to the said other Parties within Six Months after the delivery of the said Award full peaceable and quiet Possession of all and singular such Lands, Tenements, Hereditaments and Appurtenances as should be included within the Lines Awarded or ascertained by the said Award to be the Bounds of the Lands granted in and by the said first above mentioned Letters Patent to the said Jans Hendrickse Van Baal which then was or should be held as of the said Manor of Rensselaerwyck or be in Possession of the said Claimants of the said Manor any or either of them their or either of their Tenants or Assigns Except such Persons as held under the said Manor by Grant or Lease in Writing with respect to whose Possession Provision is made by the Articles of Agreement aforesaid, By which said Bonds the said Parties are reciprocally bound to each other to keep observe, execute, do, perform abide by and fulfill all and singular the Covenants Articles, Matters and Things whatsoever mentioned and contained in the Articles of Agreement aforesaid, which on their Parts respectively ought to be kept, observed, executed, done, performed abided by and fulfilled according to the true Intent and Meaning of the said Articles of Agreement as by the said respective Bonds or Obligations and the Conditions thereof reference being thereunto had may appear, which said Articles of Agreement are in the words following *to wit*

Articles of Agreement Indented had made and concluded upon this Fifth Day of July in the Year of our Lord one Thousand seven Hundred and Seventy four Between Catharine Van Rensselaer Widow and Relict of Stephen Van Rensselaer late of the Manor of Rensselaerwyck Esquire Deceased, Philip Livingston of the City of New York Esquire and Abraham Ten Broeck of the City of Albany Esquire of the first Part and Simon Johannis Veeder of the City of Albany Merchant, Arie Legrange of the same place Mariner, John M. Veeder of Schenectady in the County of Albany Yeoman, Volkert Veeder of the Normans Kill in the same County Yeoman, Abraham Veeder, Christian Legrange, Omie Legrange, Isaac Legrange, Coenradt Legrange, Omie Legrange the Younger, John Legrange the Younger, Myndert Legrange all of the last mentioned place Yeoman, Bernardus Legrange of New Brunswick in the Province of New Jersey Esquire and John Legrange of the County of Bergen in the said Province of New Jersey Yeoman of the second part.

Whereas divers disputes have arisen by and between the Parties to these Presents and those under whom they respectively claim concerning certain Lands in the County of Albany claimed by the Parties of the first Part as belonging to the Manor of Rensselaerwyck and by the Parties of the second Part as included within the Bounds of a certain Tract of Land also in the said County of Albany granted to Jan H. Van Baal by Letters Patent under the Great Seal of the Province of New York bearing Date the Twenty first Day of August in the Year of our Lord One Thousand six Hundred and Seventy two, which Disputes having occasioned great Expences to the said Parties; For the Prevention whereof for the future and for settling the said Disputes between the said Parties they have mutually referred the same to Arbitration by Bonds bearing even Date with these Presents in the Penalty of Fifty Thousand Pounds with Condition as is thereunder written Now for the preventing all unnecessary Delays in determining the same and to increase their mutual Security concerning the Premisses the Parties to these Presents of the first and second Parts respectively for themselves their Heirs Executors, Administrators and Assigns jointly and severally do hereby mutually covenant promise and agree with the parties of the other Part their Heirs Executors Administrators and Assigns in manner and form following *that is to say Imprimis* the said Parties do hereby mutually fix and appoint the Twenty second Day of August next for the Meeting of the said Arbitrators at the City of Albany in order to proceed on the said Arbitration And that the said Parties shall use their best Endeavours to procure the said Meeting at the Time and Place aforesaid *Secondly* if it should so happen that the said Arbitrators should not meet at the Time and Place aforesaid, that it shall and may be lawfull for them to meet on the Business aforesaid at the place aforesaid at any other Time or Times to be appointed by them (so as they compleat their Award within the Time limited by the Bonds above referred to) provided previous Notice in Writing by them or any three of them of such Meeting be given to one of the Parties of the first Part and one of the Parties of the second Part at least Twenty Days. *Thirdly*, That the Parties of the first and second Part to these Presents shall be at liberty to examine such Witnesses as they respectively shall think proper one of the said Examiners herein after mentioned giving to the other two Days Notice in Writing of the Time and Place for examining such Witnesses and that such Witnesses shall be examined and cross examined by Peter Silvester Esquire on the Part of the said Manor of Rensselaerwyck and by Robert Yates Esquire in behalf of the other party hereto. *Fourthly*, That the said Examiners and such Clerk and Clerks as they shall appoint to assist them shall take an oath well and truly to discharge the several Trusts reposed in them concerning the Premisses and also not to divulge or make known or suffer to be divulged or made known directly or indirectly by any Ways or Manner whatsoever any of the Contents of the said Depositions or any of them untill they are to be published as herein is after mentioned, That each of the said Depositions when taken as aforesaid together with the rough Draft thereof be sealed up by the said Examiners as soon as compleated and indorsed with the Deponants Name and when the said Examinations are fully compleated then the Depositions of the Witnesses produced on each part respectively together with the rough Draft thereof be sealed up by the said Examiners those of the Parties of the first Part to be kept by the said Peter Silvester and those of the Parties of the second Part to be kept by the said Robert Yates, which affidavits and every of them so taken as aforesaid are hereby mutually agreed shall and may without Objection to be made by either of the said Parties respectively or those claiming under them be given and received in Evidence before the said Arbitrators or on any future Trial or Hearing in Law or Equity between any of the said Parties or those claiming under them concerning the Premisses or any Part thereof in Case the Witness so making the same shall be dead or in Case it shall be Proved to the satisfaction of the said Referees or the said Court of Law and Equity that the Witness making such Deposition or Depositions cannot be got to attend to give Evidence *viva voce* saving all just Exceptions to each Party as to the legality and Character of the Witness as if he was present and personally offered as a Witness. *Fifthly*, That whenever the said Arbitrators shall meet for the Purposes aforesaid and the Majority of them at the Request of either Party shall require any of the said Depositions to be read in Evidence to them agreeable to the true Intent and Meaning of these Presents that then it shall and may be lawfull for the said Peter Silvester and Robert Yates or either of them to deliver such Deposition and Depositions to the Party so applying for it and an original Duplicate thereof to the opposite Party to be read in evidence as aforesaid. *Sixthly* And it is further agreed, that after the said Arbitrators shall have compleated and delivered in their Award or in Case the said Arbitration by any Accident shall be entirely frustrated that then it shall and may be lawfull for the said Peter Silvester and Robert Yates to deliver and give up to any of the first and second Parties respectively the Depositions of their Witnesses respectively and the Duplicate thereof and rough Draft thereof so taken as aforesaid, the same Depositions to be given in Evidence on all future Ocasions in manner and form as aforesaid. *Seventhly* In order to expedite the Determination by the Arbitrators aforesaid and in order to strengthen the Security to the Parties aforesaid it is further agreed that Rules of Referrence be severally entered by the Consent of Parties at the next Supreme Court of Judicature for the Province of New York in two several Actions of Ejectment brought for Part of the Premises in Question and now pending undetermined the one at the Suit of James Jackson on the Demise of the said Catharine Van Rensselaer against Simon Johannise Veeder, Volkert Veeder, Simon M. Veeder and Abraham Veeder the other at the Suit of James Jackson on the Demise of Barnardus Legrange against Robert Freeman and the said Catharine Van Rensselaer, by which Rules the said Causes shall be severally referred to the Determination of the Arbitrators mentioned in and according to the true Intent and Meaning of the Bonds of Arbitration herein before mentioned. *Eighthly* It is also agreed that the Award of the said Arbitrators shall bind the Possession of the Lands in Controversy only but not the Title of either of the Parties to any Part or Parcel thereof unless an Act of the Legislature of the Province of New York be passed within Two Years from the Date hereof either confirming the aforesaid Submission and authorizing the said Referrees finally to determine the Title of the Lands in Question and the Bounds of the said Patent granted to the said Jan H. Van Baal as aforesaid or confirming such Award as the said Arbitrators shall before that Time have made concerning the Premisses nor unless such Act shall within four Years from the Date hereof be confirmed by his Majesty. *Ninthly* It is also further agreed, that the Parties of the first and second Part to these Presents shall at their joint Expence respectively use their utmost Endeavours to procure the passing of such an Act of the Legislature of the said Province as is above mentioned and the Confirmation thereof by his Majesty as aforesaid in order to which they shall jointly Petition the House of Assembly for the said Province for the same that the said Parties or some or one of both the said Parties shall with all convenient speed jointly give such Notifications of their Intention to apply for the same as are required by the Royal Instructions relative to the passing of private Acts in this Province. *Tenthly* In Order to prevent either Party from any undue Bias that may lead them directly or indirectly to obstruct the passing of such Act of the Legislature or the Confirmation thereof as aforesaid in Case the said Arbitrators shall have met and examined into the Matters in Controversy before the passing of said Act the Parties do hereby mutually request the said Arbitrators to compleat their Award ready to be delivered to the Parties but to keep the same and every Part thereof and their Sentiments and Opinions concerning the Premisses secret from all Persons whatever untill the rising or other Termination of the next Sessions of the said General Assembly for said Province, and if such Act shall be passed untill also Nine Months from the passing thereof shall be expired that an Opportunity may be given of Soliciting the Royal Confirmation of the said Act And in Case by a sudden Desolution or Prorogation of the said General Assembly such Act should be prevented from passing at the next Sessions of the said General Assembly, that then the Parties shall in manner aforesaid endeavour to procure the passing such Act at the then next subsequent Sessions of the said General Assembly and in such Case the said Arbitrators are hereby requested to keep their Sentiments concerning the Premises secret as aforesaid until the rising or other Termination of the said Subsequent Session of Assembly and untill Nine Months from the passing such Act shall be expired that an opportunity may be given of Solliciting the Royal Confirmation thereof. *Eleventhly* That in Case the said Act shall pass the said Legislature it is further agreed that neither of the said Parties directly or indirectly shall use any Means whatever which may in any wise tend to prevent his Majestys Confirming such Act of the Legislature or to bring about the Royal annulling or disallowing thereof. *Twelfthly*, That the said Arbitrators before the making of their said Award do have a View of the Premises in Question. *Thirteenthly* It is further agreed that the Costs in the Actions of Ejectment aforesaid shall follow the Determination of the Arbitrators according as the Lands controverted therein respectively shall appear to be within the said Tract of Land granted to Van Baal or not as the Boundaries thereof shall be adjudged by the said Arbitrators, and the said Parties shall accordingly pay the said Costs to the other in such Case to be taxed. *Fourteenthly,* That the Expence attending the said Arbitration shall be jointly paid by the Parties to these Presents to be ascertained by the Certificate of the said Referrees who shall determine the said Controversy or any three of them excepting that each Party shall provide for and pay their respective Council and Witnesses. *Fifteenthly* And it is further agreed that in a certain Action of Debt now depending in the Supreme Court of the Province of New York between Philip Livingston Esquire Administrator *de bonis non* of Jeremiah Van Rensselaer deceased Plaintiff and Simon Johannise Veeder surviving Executor of the last Will and Testament of Johannise Simonse Veeder deceased Defendant there shall be a Rule of Referrence entered at the next Supreme Court for the Province of New York submitting the said Cause to the Determination of the Arbitrators who shall take upon them the Detemination of the Matters in Controversy hereinbefore mentioned or any three or more of them; It is agreed between the said Parties that in the Determination of the said Controversy the Title of either Party shall not be controverted before the said Referrees. And that it shall be admitted, that the said Manor of Rensselaerwyck doth surround the Lands in Question and the only Point to be settled by the said Referrees shall be to fix the Boundaries of the said Patent to Van Baal, it being agreed to be admitted before the said Referrees that the said Parties claiming under the said Patent to Van Baal have Title to all the Lands comprehended within the Boundaries of the aforesaid Grant to Van Baal, that the said Parties respectively shall not take or cause to be taken any new Possession or Possessions of any Part of the said Controverted Lands or Settle any Tenant or Tenants thereon during the Time the said Disputes are depending undetermined before the said Arbitrators. *And Whereas* the said Proprietors of the said Manor have leased or granted by Writing on Rents reserved Parts of the Premisses in Controversy to the Persons following *to wit* To Jacob Truax, John Banker, Nicholas Van Patten, John Long, John Redliff, William Venton, Isaac Ostrander, Gerrit Slingerlandt, Cornelius Van Den Bergh, Jacob Cooper, John Van Deusen, Adrian Bradt and to Coenradt Luke a small Parcell and also a small Parcell thereof to Major General John Bradstreet as by the said Leases and Grants may appear, and have received from some of the said Grantees the following Considerations (to wit) from the said Jacob Truax the sum of Fifty Pounds, Jacob Cooper the Sum of One Hundred and Thirty one Pounds, John Van Deusen the Sum of Ninety Pounds, Adrian Bradt the Sum of Ten Shillings, Cornelius Van Den Bergh the Sum of Five Shillings, Gerrit Slingerlandt the Sum of Five Shillings, Isaac Ostrander the Sum of Five Shillings and the said William Venton the Sum of Five Shillings. And the Owners of the Tract Granted to the said Van Baal have on their Part also Granted and Leased in Writing on Rents reserved Parts of the said Premisses in Controversy to the Persons following to wit Andrew Makans, Christopher Yates, Johannis Van Der Wilgen, John Oliver, Ephraim Hudson, Daniel Hungerford and Frederick Wormer as by the last mentioned Leases and Grants may appear *Now therefore* the said Parties of the first Part do further covenant and agree with the said Parties of the second Part their Heirs Executors Administrators and Assigns, That in Case the Lines which shall be adjudged by the said Referrees to be the Boundaries of the Lands granted to the said Jan Hendrickse Van Baal shall include the Lands so as aforesaid Leased and Granted under the said Manor or any Part thereof within the Bounds of the aforesaid Patent to the said Van Baal, then the said Parties of the first Part shall pay to the said Parties of the second Part their Heirs Executors Administrators or Assigns such Consideration money as hath been received as aforesaid by the Proprietor of the said Manor of Rensselaerwyck for the Lands so Awarded to be within the Bounds of the said Jan Hendrickse Van Baals Patent with Interest thereon and all such Rents as have been received thereon And also shall deliver and assign to the said Parties of the second Part the respective Leases and Grants aforesaid made of such Lands so included within the said Bounds of Van Baals Patent, and the Rents then in Arrear and thereafter to become due thereon respectively And the said Parties of the second Part do further covenant and agree with the said Parties of the first Part their Heirs Executors Administrators and Assigns that they will make the like Payments and Assignments to the Parties of the first Part of all such Monies, Leases, Grants and Rents of such of the said Lands in Controversy as shall in manner as aforesaid appear to be without the Boundary of the Lands so as aforesaid Granted to the said Van Baal. And it is hereby declared to be the true Intent and Meaning of the Parties to these Presents, that the Possession of the said Jacob Truax to be retained by him or his Assigns in case his Farm aforesaid shall be included within the Lines so to be settled as aforesaid for the Boundaries of the said Patent granted to the said Jan Hendrickse

Van Baal shall contain only the Lands granted to him by Omie Legrange deceased And that in such Case the Party claiming under the said Manor shall not be obliged to assign to the other Party the Lease from the said Jacob Truax nor to pay to the other Party the Consideration paid for the said Lease or the Rents already paid and in Arrear and to grow due thereon. *In Witness whereof* the Parties to these Presents have hereunto interchangeably set their Hands and Seals the Day and Year first above written Provided the said Award be made by the Time and in the Manner herein before mentioned.

And Whereas pursuant to the Terms of the said Submission and Agreement the Honorable George Duncan Ludlow Esquire, Thomas Hicks Esquire Samuel W. Johnson Doctor of Laws, Samuel Jones and Goldsbrow Banyar Esquires Referees above mentioned have taken upon themselves the Burden of the said Award and have met at the City of Albany, viewed the said Lands in Controversy and fully heard the Proofs and Allegations of all the said Parties thereto and of their witnesses respectively All which Proceedings of the said Referees have been had and done according to the true Intent and Meaning of the said Articles of Agreement and to the full satisfaction of the several and respective Parties thereto. *And Whereas* the said Parties have given public Notice pursuant to his Majestys Instruction to the Governor and Commander in Chief of this Colony in that Behalf, That they intended to apply to the Legislature of this Colony at this present Sessions of the General Assembly for a Law either to confirm the aforesaid Submission and to authorize the said Referees finally to determine the Title and Bounds of the Land in Question as aforesaid or to confirm such Award as the said Referees should before the passing such Act have made concerning the Premises. *And Whereas* the said Parties by their joint Petition to the General Assembly have prayed that a Bill may be passed for confirming such Award as the said Referees last mentioned or any three of them shall make in the Premises and for binding the Title of the Parties agreeable thereto,

Be it therefore Enacted by his Honor the Lieutenant Governor the Council and the General Assembly, And it is hereby enacted by the Authority of the same, That the said Bonds, Articles of Agreement and Submission be, and the same are hereby confirmed and made valid and effectual between the said Parties and Claimants and the said Meeting of the said Referees, their view of the Premises and all and singular other their Proceedings heretofore had as aforesaid shall at all Times hereafter be adjudged, deemed and taken to have been held, had and done according to the true Intent and Meaning of the Conditions of the said Bonds of Arbitration and of the said Articles of Agreement hereinbefore mentioned And the said last mentioned Referees or any three of them are hereby authorized finally to determine the Right and Title of the said Lands in Controversy between the said Parties and Claimants and the Bounds of the said Tract of Land granted by the aforesaid Letters Patent to the said Jan Hendrickse Van Baal.

And it is also hereby further Enacted by the same Authority, That in Case the said last mentioned Referees or any three of them shall already have made or shall hereafter make their Award in the Premises by the Time hereinbefore mentioned for that Purpose such their said Award is and shall be hereby confirmed and made valid and effectual in the Law And that from thenceforth the said Parties above named claiming as aforesaid under the said Letters Patent to the said Jan Hendrickse Van Baal their Heirs and Assigns for ever (except such of their Tenants who are excepted in the said Articles of Agreement) are hereby and shall for ever hereafter be barred and excluded of and from all Claim, Right, Title and Interest whatsoever derived from and under the said Letters Patent to the said Jan Hendrickse Van Baal of in or to any Lands lying not included within the Lines adjudged or to be adjudged by the last mentioned Referees or any three of them in and by their said Award to be the Boundaries of the Land granted by the first said Letters Patent to Jan Hendrickse Van Baal and within the Out Lines of the said Manor. And in like manner the said other Parties above named claiming as aforesaid under the said Letters Patent granting the said Manor or under any other Grant or Confirmation thereof and all others claiming or to claim or having or to have any Right or Title under and by Virtue of the said last mentioned Will and Testament of the said Stephen Van Rensselaer deceased their Heirs and Assigns for ever (except such of their Tenants as are excepted in the said Articles of Agreement) are hereby and shall be for ever from and after the making the said Award barred and excluded of and from all Claim, Right, Title and Interest whatsoever derived from and under the said recited Letters Patent granting the said Manor of Rensselaerwyck or any other Subsequent Grant or Confirmation thereof of in or to any Land lying within the said Lines so adjudged or to be adjudged by the said last mentioned Referees or any three of them in and by their said Award to be the Boundaries of the Land granted by the said Letters Patent to the said Jan Hendrickse Van Baal and comprehended within the Out Lines of the said Manor of Rensselaerwyck.

And be it further Enacted by the Authority aforesaid, That from and after the Time of making the said Award the Parties aforesaid claiming under the said Letters Patent to the said Jan Hendrickse Van Baal and all others claiming or to claim or having or to have any Right, Title or Interest under them or any of them to any of the Lands comprehended within the Lines or Limits which are or shall be Awarded or adjudged by the said last mentioned Referees or any three or more of them to be the Boundaries of the Lands granted by the said Letters Patent to the said Jans Hendrickse Van Baal shall in all Courts of Law and Equity be deemed, adjudged and taken to have a good legal and valid Title thereto against all Rights, Titles, Claims or Demands thereto made or to be made by the said Parties hereinbefore named claiming under the said or any other Letters Patent, Deed or Instrument granting or confirming the said Manor of Rensselaerwyck and against all others claiming or to claim or having or to have any Right, Title or Interest thereto either as Heirs at Law to or under or by Virtue of the said last Will and Testament of the said Stephen Van Rensselaer. And in like manner after the Time of making the said Award the said Parties hereinbefore mentioned claiming the Lands so in Controversy as Part of the said Manor of Rensselaerwyck and all others claiming or to claim or having any Right either as Heirs at Law to or under or by Virtue of the said last Will and Testament of the said Stephen Van Rensselaer to any of the Lands in Controversy as aforesaid within the Bounds of the said Manor and which are or shall not be Comprehended within the Lines or Limits awarded or adjudged or which shall be awarded or adjudged by the said last mentioned Referees or any three of them to be the Boundaries of the said Letters Patent to the said Jan Hendrickse Van Baal shall in all Courts of Law or Equity be deemed, adjudged and taken to have a good legal and valid Title thereto against all Rights, Titles, Claims or Demands thereto made or to be made under the said Letters Patent to the said Jan Hendrickse Van Baal by the said Parties hereinbefore named claiming under the said Letters Patent to the said Jan Hendrickse Van Baal and against all others claiming or to claim or having any Right thereto in Virtue of the said last mentioned Letters Patent and under the said Parties claiming as last aforesaid. And further that such Lines or Boundaries as the said Referees or any three or more of them shall Award as aforesaid to be the Bounds of the Land granted as aforesaid to the said Jan Hendrickse Van Baal shall for ever thereafter be deemed, esteemed and taken in all Courts of Law and Equity against the said Parties and Claimants respectively their Heirs and Assigns and against all others claiming or to claim by from or under them or any of them respectively by any Ways or Means whatsoever and against all others claiming or to claim by from or under the last Will and Testament of the said Stephen Van Rensselaer, as and for the true Limits and Bounds of the Land granted to the said Jan Hendrickse Van Baal by the said Letters Patent to him.

Provided Always, That nothing herein contained shall be construed in any wise to affect the Claim Right or Title of his Majesty his Heirs or Successors or of any Person or Persons to the said Controverted Lands or any Part thereof who are not Parties to the said Submission or who do not or shall not claim by from or under them or any of them or as Heir or under the last Will and Testament of the said Stephen Van Rensselaer deceased Nor shall any Thing herein contained be construed to alter, change, make void or defeat the Right or Title to any of the Lands in Controversy of any Tenant or Tenants of the said Parties respectively who are mentioned and excepted as aforesaid in the said Articles of Agreement. And this Act shall be deemed and adjudged to be a Public Act and nothing herein contained shall be of Force until this Act shall be approved or confirmed by his Majesty his Heirs or Successors.

[CHAPTER 1704.]

[See chapter 1393. Expired, January 31, 1785.]

An Act to revive an Act entitled "An Act for the better and more effectual collecting of Taxes in the City of New York."

[Passed, April 1, 1775.]

Be it Enacted by his Honor the Lieutenant Governor the Council and the General Assembly, and it is hereby Enacted by the Authority of the same, That the Act entitled. "An Act for the better and more effectual collecting of Taxes in the City of New York." passed the Twentieth Day of May one thousand seven hundred and sixty nine, shall be and hereby is revived and every Clause Article Matter and Thing therein contained enacted to be and remain in full force from the passing hereof until the first Day of February one thousand seven hundred and eighty five, and from thence to the End of the then next Session of the General Assembly.

[CHAPTER 1705.]

[See chapter 1613. Expired, 1785.]

An Act to revive an Act entitled "An Act to prevent Frauds in the Sale of Bread."

[Passed, April 1, 1775.]

WHEREAS the above mentioned Act expired by its own Limitation on the first Day of January last,

Be it therefore Enacted by his Honor the Lieutenant Governor the Council and the General Assembly, and it is hereby Enacted by the Authority of the same, That the said Act entitled. "An Act to prevent Frauds in the Sale of Bread" passed the eighth Day of March one thousand seven hundred and seventy three, and every Clause Article Matter and Thing therein contained, shall be and hereby is revived from the passing hereof until the first Day of January which will be in the Year of our Lord one thousand seven hundred and eighty five, and from thence to the End of the then next Session of the General Assembly.

[CHAPTER 1706.]

[See chapter 1382. Expired, January 31, 1785.]

An Act to revive an Act entitled "An Act to raise a Fund for defraying Damages done by Dogs in the County of Richmond."

[Passed, April 1, 1775.]

WHEREAS the Act entitled. "An Act to raise a Fund for defraying Damages done by Dogs in the County of Richmond." passed the thirty-first Day of December one thousand seven hundred and sixty eight, expired by its own Limitation on the first Day of January last, and the same having been found useful and necessary,

Be it therefore Enacted by his Honor the Lieutenant Governor the Council and the General Assembly, and it is hereby Enacted by the Authority of the same, That the abovementioned Act and every Clause Matter and Thing therein contained, shall be and hereby is revived, from the passing hereof until the first Day of February which will be in the Year of our Lord one thousand seven hundred and eighty five.

[CHAPTER 1707.]

[See chapter 1343. Expired, January 31, 1785.]

An Act to revive an Act entitled "An Act to impower the Freeholders of the Towns of Hempstead and Oyster Bay in Queens County to make prudential Orders for the better regulating the parting their Sheep feeding on the Great Plains, and to sell such stray Sheep as shall be left at such Time of parting."

[Passed, April 1, 1775.]

Be it Enacted by his Honor the Lieutenant Governor the Council and the General Assembly, and it is hereby enacted by the Authority of the same, That the Act entitled. "An Act to impower the Freeholders of the Towns of Hempstead and Oyster Bay in Queen's County to make prudential Orders for the better regulating the Parting their Sheep feeding on the Great Plains, and to sell such Stray Sheep as shall be left at such Time of parting," passed the thirteenth Day of January one thousand seven hundred and sixty eight, shall be and hereby is revived, and every Article Matter and Clause therein contained, enacted to be and continue in full force from the passing hereof until the first Day of February which will be in the Year of our Lord one thousand seven hundred and eighty five, and from thence to the End of the then next Session of the General Assembly.

[CHAPTER 1708.]

An Act to appropriate certain Monies in the Treasury of Queens County for the Uses therein mentioned.

[Passed, April 1, 1775.]

Whereas by virtue of two certain Acts of the Legislature of the Colony of New York, one of them entitled. "An Act for the regulating the Militia of the Colony of New York." and the other entitled, "An Act to continue an Act entitled An Act for regulating the Militia of the Colony of New York with some Additions thereto," passed in the twenty eighth and twenty ninth Years of the Reign of his late Majesty King George the second, the several County Treasurers in this Colony for the Time being were empowered to levy certain Fines and Forfeitures from the People called Quakers, and from the People called Unitus Fratrum, or the

United Brethern, AND WHEREAS the present Treasurer of Queens County during the continuance of the above recited Acts, and in Virtue thereof hath received divers Sums of Money from the People as abovementioned: Part of which Monies still remain in the Hands of the said Treasurer unaccounted for and unappropriated to the Uses specified in the above mentioned Acts.

Be it therefore Enacted by his Honor the Lieutenant Governor the Council and the General Assembly, and it is hereby enacted by the Authority of the same, That the present Treasurer of Queens County aforesaid shall, and is hereby required and directed on the first Tuesday in October next to render unto the Supervisors of Queens County, a just and true Account on Oath of all the Monies heretofore received by him from the People called Quakers, and also from the People called *Unitus Fratrum* or the United Brethren in virtue of the two Acts abovementioned, and likewise what Sum or Sums of Money hath been appropriated to the Uses in the said Acts herein before mentioned; and that he pay the Ballance remaining in his Hands within three Months thereafter into the Hands of the Church Wardens or Overseers of the Poor of each respective Town in said County, in the same Proportion that each Town hath paid of the last Public Tax of said County to be by the Church Wardens or Overseers of the Poor applied to the Use of the Poor of their respective Towns; and the Receipt of the Church Wardens or Overseers of the Poor to the said Treasurer shall be a full Discharge to him for the same, any Thing contained in the two Acts herein beforementioned or either of them to the Contrary in any wise notwithstanding.

[CHAPTER 1709.]

[See chapters 575, 686, 795, 1592, 1005, 1503, 1081, 1208, 1460. Expired, December 31, 1784.]

An Act to revive the several Acts therein mentioned, as they relate to the Counties of Queens and Suffolk.

[Passed, April 1, 1775.]

WHEREAS the several Acts, the Titles whereof are herein after particularly mentioned and described have been found by Experience to be very beneficial and useful in the Counties of Queens and Suffolk for which they were made, but are now expired by their own Limitation.

Namely, the Act entitled "An Act for the better clearing regu-

as the Overseers of the Poor, Assessors and Collectors elected by the Manor in general now have, or are subject to.

And be it further Enacted by the Authority aforesaid, That the Overseers of the Poor so as aforesaid to be chosen for the said Districts or Divisions respectively shall not receive any Poor Person under their Care charging the Manor aforesaid with the Support or Maintenance of such Person unless by Consent of two of his Majesty's Justices of the Peace residing in said Manor in Writing under their Hands first had and obtained for that Purpose any Thing in the first abovementioned Act to the contrary notwithstanding.

Provided always and be it further Enacted by the Authority aforesaid That nothing herein contained shall be construed to exempt the Overseers of the Poor aforesaid from receiving and providing for such Poor Persons and performing other the Duties enjoined on the Overseers of the Poor by virtue of an Act entitled. "An Act for the settlement and Relief of the Poor." passed the eighth Day of March one thousand seven hundred and seventy three.

[CHAPTER 1711.]

An Act to erect the East Camp in the District of the Manor of Livingston in the County of Albany into a separate District, and to alter the District of Saraghtoga and erect a new District by the name of Balls Town.

[Passed, April 1, 1775.]

Whereas by an Act passed the twenty fourth Day of March one thousand seven hundred and seventy two, entitled. "An Act to divide the Counties of Albany and Tryon into Districts." all that Part of the County of Albany which lays to the Northward of Dutchess County, and to the Southward of the South Bounds of Claverack continued to the Easternost Extent of this Colony, and to the Eastward of Hudson's River was made one separate and distinct District called and known by the Name of the District of the Manor of Livingston, And Whereas the Freeholders and Inhabitants of the Camp commonly called and known by the Name of the German Camp on the East Side of Hudson's River find many Inconveniencies by their being included in said District, and being desirous to be made a separate and distinct District,

Be it therefore Enacted by his Honor the Lieutenant Governor the Council and the General Assembly, and it is hereby Enacted by the Authority of the same, That all that Tract of Land commonly called and known by the Name of the German or East Camp on the East Side of Hudson's River, shall be, and hereby is separated from the District of the Manor of Livingston, and made a distinct District to be hereafter called the German Camp District.

And be it also Enacted by the same Authority, That the District of Saraghtoga shall be henceforth limited on the West by the East Side of Balls Town and a North Line to the Northern Bounds of the County of Albany, and a South Line to Half Moon District, and that the Residue of the Lands formerly assigned to the District of Saraghtoga by the said Act, shall be henceforth one separate District, distinguished by the Name of the District of Balls Town.

And be it further Enacted by the same Authority, That the Freeholders and Inhabitants of each of the said Districts are hereby severally required and authorized annually on every first Tuesday in May to elect and choose the like District Officers as are annually elected and chosen by the aforesaid Act in the different Districts therein mentioned.

And be it further Enacted by the same Authority, That none of the Lines or Bounds by this Act assigned for the Limits of either of the said Districts, shall be deemed to take away abridge destroy or affect the Right and Title of any Body Politic or Corporate or of any Patentee or Patentees, or others holding under any Patentee or Patentees in any Manner or by any ways or Means whatsoever, neither shall they be deemed taken or construed as a Confirmation of the Bounds and Rights of any Patent or Patents whatsoever.

[CHAPTER 1712.]

[See chapters 1286 and 1414. Expired, January 31, 1785.]

An Act to revive the two Acts therein mentioned for preventing Damages by Swine in the Manor of Rensselaerwyck.

[Passed, April 1, 1775.]

Be it Enacted by his Honor the Lieutenant Governor the Council and the General Assembly, and it is hereby enacted by the Authority of the same, That the Act entitled. "An act to prevent

such Slave, or to any such Native or free Indian or free Negro in the same Manner and form as is herein before directed to be given, and such Master or Mistress native or free Indian or free Negro shall be intitled to & receive the same reward as is given by this Act as aforesaid, This Act to be in force from the passing thereof, until the first Day of January which will be in the Year of our Lord one thousand seven hundred and eighty five.

[CHAPTER 1714.]

[See chapter 1582. Expired, December 31, 1784.]

An Act to continue an Act entitled "An Act for regulating the Practice of Inoculation for the small Pox in the City of Albany."

[Passed, April 1, 1775.]

WHEREAS the above mentioned Act will expire on the first Day of May next by its own Limitation, and the same being found very necessary,

Be it therefore Enacted by his Honor the Lieutenant Governor the Council and the General Assembly, and it is hereby enacted by the Authority of the same, That the said Act entitled "An Act for regulating the Practice of Inoculation for the Small Pox in the City of Albany," and every Clause Article Matter and Thing therein contained shall be and hereby is continued to be in full force from and after the first Day of May next, until the first Day of January which will be in the Year of our Lord one thousand seven hundred and eighty five, and from thence to the End of the then next Session of the General Assembly.

[CHAPTER 1715.]

[See chapter 1257. Expired, January 31, 1785.]

An Act to revive an Act entitled "An Act for the more equal Taxation of Estates in the City of Albany."

[Passed, April 1, 1775.]

Be it Enacted by his Honor the Lieutenant Governor the Council and the General Assembly, and it is hereby enacted by the Authority of the same, That the Act entitled "An Act for the more equal Taxation of Estates in the City of Albany," passed in the fourth Year of his Majesty's Reign, shall be and hereby is revived from the passing hereof until the first Day of February which will be in the Year of our Lord one thousand seven hundred and eighty five.

[CHAPTER 1716.]

[See chapter 1629.]

An Act for altering the Time of keeping Fairs in the Town of Schenectady.

[Passed, April 1, 1775.]

Be it Enacted by his Honor the Lieutenant Governor the Council and the General Assembly, and it is hereby enacted by the Authority of the same, That the two Fairs to be held and kept in every Year in the Town of Schenectady by virtue of an Act entitled "An Act respecting Fairs in the Counties of Albany Cumberland and Tryon" passed the eighth Day of March one thousand seven hundred and seventy three, shall for the future be held and kept as follow; The first to commence on the third Tuesday in June annually, and to continue until the Evening of the Thursday next ensuing and no longer, and the second Fair to commence on the first Tuesday in November annually, and to continue until the Evening of the Thursday next ensuing and no longer, any Law Usage or Custom to the Contrary hereof notwithstanding.

[CHAPTER 1717.]

An Act to raise a Sum not exceeding nine hundred Pounds in the County of Tryon, to compleat the Court House and Goal erected at John's Town in the said County.

[Passed, April 1, 1775.]

Whereas the Money raised to compleat the Court House and erect a Goal at John's Town in the County of Tryon has been found insufficient,

Be it therefore Enacted by his Honor the Lieutenant Governor the Council and the General Assembly, and it is hereby enacted by the Authority of the same, That for compleating the said Court House and Goal the Supervisors of the said County, or the Major Part of them for the Time being shall, and they are hereby directed and required to order to be levied on the Freeholders and Inhabitants of the said County a Sum not exceeding nine hundred Pounds with an additional Sum of three Pence in every Pound for col-

erly Corner thereof, and thence on a direct Course to the Southerly Corner Bounds of the Township of Hulton, where it meets with and is intersected by the West Boundary Line of the County of Cumberland as established in and by the Act herein before mentioned; shall be the Westerly Boundary Line and Lines of the said County of Cumberland in all Places so far as the same is altered by this present Act, any Thing in the said Act to the contrary hereof notwithstanding.

[CHAPTER 1720.]

An Act to prevent Causes being tried in Taverns by Justices of the Peace in the County of Cumberland.

[Passed, April 1, 1775.]

WHEREAS by a law of this Colony every Justice of the Peace is impowered to hold a Court for the Tryal of Causes to the Value of five Pounds and under. And Whereas such Courts have been frequently held at Taverns in the said County, to the great Prejudice of the Suitors and Damage of the Inhabitants, for Remedy whereof.

Be it Enacted by his Honor the Lieutenant Governor the Council and the General Assembly, and it is hereby enacted by the Authority of the same, That from and after the second Tuesday in June next, it shall not be lawful for any Justice within the said County to hold his Court at a Tavern, and every Justice of the Peace who shall hold his Court at a Tavern shall for every Offence forfeit ten Pounds, and all the Proceedings of the said Court are hereby enacted and declared to be Null and Void, which Forfeiture shall be sued for and recovered with Costs of Suit by any Person or Persons in any Court of Record within this Colony one half for the Use of the Person or Persons who may sue for the same, and the other half for the Poor of the Township or District where such Offence shall be committed.

[CHAPTER 1721.]

An Act for annexing the two Tracts of Land therein mentioned to the Township of the New Paltz in Ulster County.

[Passed, April 1, 1775.]

WHEREAS the Tract of Land granted by Letters Patent to Noah Eltinge and Nathaniel Lafever, and the Tract granted to Anne

Mullinder commonly called Mullinder's Tract lay contiguous to the Town of the New Paltz in Ulster County, and it will be much more convenient for the Inhabitants residing on those Tracts to attend the annual Elections of Precinct Officers, and perform other the Public Duties required of them by Law in the Township or Precinct of the New Paltz, than in that to which they now belong.

Be it therefore Enacted by his Honor the Lieutenant Governor the Council and the General Assembly, and it is hereby enacted by the Authority of the same, That the said two Tracts of Land shall be and hereby are annexed to and made Part of the Township or Precinct of the New Paltz, and the Inhabitants residing or to reside thereon shall enjoy the same Privileges and be subject to the same Duties as other the Inhabitants of the said Township or Precinct enjoy or are subject to by any former Law of this Colony, any Law Usage or Custom to the contrary in any wise notwithstanding.

[CHAPTER 1722.]

An Act for enabling the Persons therein named to finish the Court House and Goal in Ulster County and other Purposes therein mentioned.

[Passed, April 1, 1775.]

WHEREAS a Sum of Money was raised by virtue of an Act of the Legislature, for repairing the Court House and Goal in Ulster County, which has proved insufficient to compleat the same,

Be it therefore Enacted by his Honor the Lieutenant Governor the Council and the General Assembly, and it is hereby enacted by the Authority of the same That the Supervisors of the said County shall at their next annual Meeting for raising the contingent Charges of the said County; order the raising a further Sum not exceeding four hundred Pounds; to be raised levied and collected in the same Manner as the other necessary and contingent Charges of the said County are by Law directed.

And be it further Enacted by the Authority aforesaid, That the Monies so to be raised by virtue of this Act shall from Time to Time be paid by the Collectors of the respective Towns Manor and Precincts within the said County into the Hands of the County Treasurer as the same shall come into their Hands; to be by him paid to Dirck Wynkoop Junior, Johannes Sleght, Abraham Low, John Beekman, and John Elmendorph or any three of them, who are hereby appointed Commissioners for compleating the said Court House and Goal, and for reimbursing the Sum of Money already advanced by them in repairing the same, over and above the Sum heretofore raised for that Purpose, and also for digging and making a Well near the said Court House, and making such other useful and necessary Repairs as by the said Commissioners or the major Part of them shall be thought most convenient and proper, which said Commissioners shall and are hereby required to render a just and true Account on Oath of the Trust hereby reposed in them to the Supervisors of the said County after the Completion of the said Court House and Goal and other Repairs.

And be it also Enacted by the same Authority, That in Case the Monies so to be raised by virtue of this Act, should exceed the Sum to be expended for the Purposes herein mentioned, such Excess shall be repaid by the Commissioners into the Hands of the County Treasurer, to be disposed of by the said Supervisors for the use of the said County in such Manner as to them shall seem most convenient.

[CHAPTER 1723.]

An Act for removing the Prisoners from the old Goal in the Precinct of Goshen in the County of Orange, to the new Goal built in the said Precinct.

[Passed, April 1, 1775.]

Whereas a new Court House and Goal in the Town of Goshen in the County of Orange has been lately erected, with proper and commodious Appartments therein for the safe Custody of Prisoners; and it is expedient that the Prisoners now confined in the Goal in the Town of Goshen aforesaid should be removed from thence to, and confined in the said new Goal.

Be it therefore Enacted by his Honor the Lieutenant Governor the Council and the General Assembly, and it is hereby enacted by the Authority of the same That the new Court House and Goal aforesaid and the Appartments therein shall be a Goal or Goals of and for the said County of Orange, and that the Sheriff of the said County for the Time being shall have the keeping of the same, and shall remove all his Prisoners from the old Court House and Goal aforesaid to the new Court-House and Goal, when and as soon as one of the Judges of the Court of Common Pleas, and two of his Majesty's Justices of the Peace for the said County by order in Writing under their respective

Hands and Seals to be served on the said Sheriff shall direct, and shall there keep them the said Prisoners and every of them in safe Custody until they be respectively discharged by due Course of Law.

And be it further Enacted by the Authority aforesaid That the said Sheriff shall not be liable to any Action or Actions of escape or other Actions at Law for the removing of the said Prisoners or either of them, and that if any Action Plaint Suit or Information, shall be commenced or prosecuted against the said Sheriff for removing the said Prisoners or either of them in Pursuance of this Act that it shall and may be lawful for him to plead the General Issue; and upon any Issue joined may give this Act and the Special Matter in Evidence, and if the Plaintiff or Prosecutor shall become nonsuit, or forbear further to prosecute, or suffer a Discontinuance, or if a Verdict pass against the Plaintiff, the Defendant shall recover double Costs, for which he shall have like Remedy as in Cases where Costs by Law are given to Defendants.

Provided always and it is hereby enacted, That in Case any Prisoner or Prisoners shall escape from the Custody of the said Sheriff in the Time of his her or their Removal, and the said Sheriff shall not retake him her or them, and actually confine such Prisoner or Prisoners in the new Goal or Goals provided as aforesaid, within sixty Days after such Escape made, the said Sheriff shall be liable to all Actions for such Escape or Escapes in the same Manner as he would have been if this Act had not been made.

[CHAPTER 1724.]

An Act for an indulgence to Persons of Scrupulous Consciences in the manner of Administring Oaths.

[Passed, April 1, 1775.]

Whereas a considerable Number of his Majesty's Subjects have preferred sundry humble Petitions to the General Assembly, setting forth the great Hardships they suffer on Account of their scrupling to use the common Ceremony of laying the Hand upon and kissing the Book, when they are called to make Oath, and soliciting to be indulged in using no Other Ceremony than that of holding up the Right Hand, according to the Custom of that Part of Great Britain called Scotland, And Whereas it is most conducive to the Discovery of Truth to exact Oaths with such Solemnities as the Persons taking them conceive to be most binding, And Whereas it is most agreeable to the mild Genius of the British Constitution, and highly expedient for promoting the Welfare of this Colony, as well as just in itself to give all due Indulgence to his Majesty's Subjects in Matters relating to Conscience.

Be it therefore Enacted by his Honor the Lieutenant Governor the Council and the General Assembly, and it is hereby enacted by the Authority of the same, That all Oaths administred or to be administred only with the Ceremony of holding up the right Hand shall be deemed and adjudged in all Cases to be corporal Oaths, as valid as if they were administred with the Ceremonies used in England, and that Persons swearing falsely with the aforesaid Ceremony of holding up the right Hand, shall be deemed guilty of wilful and corrupt Perjury, and suffer accordingly.

Provided always, That such Persons only shall have the Indulgence allowed by this Act, as shall produce a Certificate of their being of that religious Persuasion commonly distinguished by the Name of the Associate Presbyteries and Synods (who publicly and notoriously object to corporal Oaths administred in the English Form,) and that they are of good Fame and Reputation, which Certificate shall not only be signed by the Minister but by the Majority of the Elders and Deacons of that Congregation, to which the Person having such Certificate shall at the Date thereof belong, or of that Congregation nearest to his then Place of Residence being of the Persuasion or Denomination aforesaid.

And be it further Enacted by the Authority aforesaid, That the signing of the aforesaid Certificate being proved before one of Judges of the Inferior Court of Common Pleas of the County in which the said Congregation is, and attested under the hand of such Judge shall be sufficient in all Courts without further Proof, to intitle the Persons in whose Favor such Certificate was given, to the Indulgence granted by this Act.

[CHAPTER 1725.]

[See chapters 1061 and 1213. Expired, January 31, 1785.]

An Act to revive the two Acts therein mentioned relative to the bringing in and spreading infectious Distempers in this Colony.

[Passed, April 1, 1775.]

Be it Enacted by his Honor the Lieutenant Governor the Council and the General Assembly, and it is hereby enacted by the Authority of the same, That the Act entitled "An Act to prevent the bringing in and spreading of infectious Distempers in this Colony," passed the twenty fourth Day of March one thousand seven hundred and fifty eight, and the Act entitled "An Act to revive an Act entitled An Act to prevent the bringing in, and spreading infectious Distempers in this Colony with an Addition thereto," passed the thirteenth Day of December in the Year of our Lord one thousand seven hundred and sixty three, shall be and hereby are revived and every Article Matter and Clause therein contained enacted to be and remain in full Force from the passing hereof until the First Day of February which will be in the Year of our Lord one thousand seven hundred and eighty five, and from thence to the End of the then next Session of the General Assembly.

[CHAPTER 1726.]

[See chapter 1544. Expired, January 31, 1785.]

An Act to revive an Act entitled "An Act to oblige the Justices of the Peace at their General or Quarter Sessions to determine Appeals made to them according to the Merits of the Case notwithstanding Defects of Form in the original Proceedings; and to oblige Persons suing forth Writs of Certiorari, to remove Orders made on such Appeals into the Supreme Court of this Colony to give Security to prosecute the same to Effect."

[Passed, April 1, 1775.]

Be it Enacted by his Honor the Lieutenant Governor the Council and the General Assembly, and it is hereby enacted by the Authority of the same, That the Act entitled "An Act to oblige the Justices of the Peace at their General or Quarter Sessions to determine Appeals made to them according to the Merits of the Case notwithstanding Defects of Form in the original Proceedings; and to oblige Persons suing forth Writs of Certiorari to remove Orders made on such Appeals into the Supreme Court of this Colony; to give Security to prosecute the same to Effect," passed in the twelfth Year of his present Majesty's Reign shall be, and hereby is revived, and every Clause Matter and Thing therein contained, enacted to be in full force until the first Day of February which will be in the Year of our Lord one thousand seven hundred and eighty five.

[CHAPTER 1727.]

An Act to discourage Tortious Entries and Possessions.

[Passed, April 1, 1775.]

Whereas Persons trespassing upon Lands often defend against Suits brought for the same under feigned Pretences, until Judgment passes for the Plaintiff and then abscond or taking Advantage of the contracted Limits of the Colony, escape to other Provinces to the great Injury of the Plaintiff or true Proprietors for want of Bail given by the Defendant at the Commencement of the Suit.

Be it therefore Enacted by his Honor the Lieutenant Governor the Council and the General Assembly, and it is hereby enacted by the Authority of the same, That the Plaintiff or Plaintiffs shall in all such Actions of Trespass be intitled to special Bail and that an Ac-aetiam or proper Clause for that Purpose may be accordingly inserted in the first Process, and that the Plaintiff or Plaintiffs shall have all the Advantages as well thereupon, as upon the Bail Bonds, that may be taken on the Arrest as in Assumption and other Actions where the Defendant is held to Bail, and that both Parties shall be subject to such discretionary Rules and Orders of Court respecting such Suits in Trespass and on the Bail Bonds as are used in other Cases.

[CHAPTER 1728.]

[Expired, January 31, 1778.]

An Act for giving Remedy where Defendants in Courts of Equity neglect to enter their Appearances after being served with a Subpoena and cannot be served with Process of Contempt.

[Passed, April 1, 1775.]

Whereas Mortgagors residing in this Colony who have been served with Subpoenas to appear upon Bills filed against them in the Court of Equity for the said Colony, have been guilty of many Frauds in refusing or neglecting to enter their Appearances upon such Bills, and secrete themselves within the said Colony, in such a Manner that no Process of Contempt can be served upon them, whereby Mortgagees are prevented from recovering their just Debts, and the Course of public Justice is impeded, And Whereas it is highly expedient that a Remedy should be provided in this Behalf.

Be it therefore Enacted by his Honor the Lieutenant Governor the Council and the General Assembly, and it is hereby enacted by the Authority of the same, That where any Bill has been or hereafter shall be filed by any Mortgagee or Mortgagees in the Court of Equity for this Colony, and the Mortgagor or Mortgagors, his or their Grantees, Heirs or Devisees, after being regularly served with a Subpoena or other Process to appear, shall neglect or refuse to enter his her or their Appearance and cannot be taken upon an Attachment, Attachment with Proclamations, and Commission of Rebellion regularly issued against him her or them to the Sheriff of, and Commissioners in, the County where such Mortgagor or Mortgagors his or their Grantees Heirs or Devisees resided, or were found when such Subpoena or Process was served as aforesaid, that then and in such Case the said Court wherein such Bill was filed, shall and may upon the Return of the said Commission of Rebellion, make an Order directing such Mortgagor or Mortgagors, his or their Grantees Heirs or Devisees to appear in the said Court within a certain Time therein to be limited, a Copy of which shall within twenty Days be inserted in one of the public News Papers in this Colony, and a Copy of the same Order shall also be posted up within the Time aforesaid at the Parish Church or Place of Public Worship, or where there shall be no Parish Church or Place of Public Worship, at some other Public Place in the Parish, District or Precinct in which such Mortgagor or Mortgagors his or their Grantees Heirs or Devisees resided or were found when such subpoena was served as aforesaid, and if such Mortgagor or Mortgagors his or their Grantees Heirs or Devisees shall not appear in the said Court within the Time limited by the said Order, then the said Court shall and may upon being satisfied that the said Order was duly published, order that the Complainant's Bill be taken pro confesso, and thereupon such further Decree shall be made, and such Sale and other Proceedings be had as in and by an Act entitled "An Act for making Process in Courts of Equity effectual against Mortgagors who abscond and cannot be served therewith, or who refuse to appear," are directed and limited in Cases of Bills being taken pro confesso, in Suits commenced and prosecuted in pursuance of the said Act. This Act to continue in force from the passing thereof to the first Day of February in the Year of our Lord one thousand seven hundred and seventy eight, and from thence to the End of the then next Session of the General Assembly.

[CHAPTER 1729.]

[See chapter 1433. Expired, January 31, 1776.]

An Act to revive an Act entitled " An Act to restrain Hawkers and Pedlars within this Colony from selling without Licence, with an addition thereto.

[Passed, April 1, 1775.]

Be it therefore Enacted by his Honor the Lieutenant Governor the Council and the General Assembly, and it is hereby enacted by the Authority of the same, That the Act entitled " An Act to restrain Hawkers and Pedlars within this Colony from selling without Licence," passed the twenty seventh Day of January one thousand seven hundred and seventy, shall be and hereby is revived, and every Clause Matter and Thing therein contained, enacted to be and remain in full force until the first Day of February which will be in the Year of our Lord one thousand seven hundred and seventy six, and from thence to the End of the then next Session of the General Assembly.

Provided always, and be it further Enacted by the same Authority, That the Penalty for travelling without Licence, or for refusing to shew the same, as mentioned in the third Clause of said Act, shall henceforth be twenty Pounds, to be recovered as directed by the said Act, the one Moiety thereof to the Informer, and the other Moiety to the Commissioners of the Highways for the Town Manor Precinct or District in which the Offence was committed to be by them expended in repairing the Highways thereof, any Thing in the said Act to the contrary thereof in any wise notwithstanding.

And be it further Enacted by the same Authority, That if any Hawker or Pedlar shall sell any kind of Goods Wares or Merchandize whatsoever unto any Slave without the Leave and Permission of the Person owning such Slave, and shall be thereof accused by any Person, and convicted before any one Justice of the Peace of this Colony, he shall for every such Offence forfeit and pay the Sum of five Pounds; which Justice is hereby strictly required and directed to hear and finally determine the same, and give Judgment and award Execution in the usual Manner of proceeding on the Trial of Causes of the value of five Pounds and under before Justices of the Peace, the one half of which Forfeiture shall go to the Person suing for the same, and the other half to the Overseers of the Poor in the District where such Offence shall be committed, to be by the Overseers of the Poor applied to the use of the Poor of such District, any Law Usage or Custom to the contrary notwithstanding.

[CHAPTER 1730.]

An Act for the better laying out regulating, and keeping in repair the Public Roads and Highways in the City and County of Albany and County of Tryon.

[Passed, April 3, 1775.]

Be it Enacted by his Honor the Lieutenant Governor the Council and the General Assembly, and it is hereby enacted by the Authority of the same, That from and after the passing and during the continuance of this Act the Persons herein after named, together with all such Persons as have been appointed Commissioners by the Court of General Sessions in either of the said Counties since the sixth Day of February one thousand seven hundred and seventy three; shall be and hereby are appointed Commissioners, in the Districts for which they are named or appointed, for regulating the Highways and Public Roads already laid out, and for regulating such other Highways and Public Roads as may be necessary within the said City and Counties, that is to say:

For the City of Albany, the Mayor Recorder Aldermen and Commonalty of the said City.

For the District of the Manor of Livingston, Robert Livingston Junior, Robert R. Livingston, Peter R. Livingston, Walter Livingston and Dirck W. Ten Broeck Esquires.

For the District of the German Camp, John Curts, Peter Sharp and Peter Cosper Esquires.

For the District of Claverack, Robert Van Rensselaer, Peter Van Ness, Casparus Conyn, Isaac Vosburgh Junior, John Van Alen, William Henry Ludlow, Richard Esselstyn, Henry Dible, Martin Crumb, and Abraham Carly.

For the District of Kinderhook, Peter S. Van Alstyn, Frans Van Beuren, Lucas J. Goes, Cornelius Van Schaack Junior, and Melgert Vander Pool.

For King's District, William Bradford Whiting, James Savage, Nathaniel Culver, Samuel Baldwin, Robert Bullis, and Isaac Peabody.

For the District of the Manor of Rensselaerwyck, Rensselaer

Nicoll, Killyaen Van Rensselaer, Abraham Ten Broeck, John H. Beekman, Teunis Slingerlandt, Stephen Schuyler, Lucas Van Veghten, Stephen J. Schuyler and Anthony Van Schajck.

For Schactikoke District, Johannes Knickerbacker Junior, Marte Winne, John Groesbeek and Dirck Van Veghten.

For Hosick District, Daniel Bradt, John Munro, Bliss Willoughby, Cornelius Van Ness, Ebenezer Cole, John Abbot, and John McComb.

For Cambridge District, Josaiah Younglove, Thomas Morrison and Archibald Campbell.

For Saraghtoge District, Philip Schuyler, Killian DeRidder, Jonathan Jones, Jacobus Swart, George Palmer, Dirk Swart, Cornelius Vanderbergh, Jeremiah Taylor and Nathan Tift.

For Balls Town District, James McCrea, James Gordon.

For Half Moon District, Guert VanSchoonhoven, Cornelius Tymese, Nicholas Fisher, Abraham Fort, and Hendrick Van der Werken.

For Schenectady District Isaac Vrooman, Ryer Schermerhorn, John Glen, Christopher Yates, Abraham Wempel, & John Cuyler Junior.

For the united District of Duanesburgh and Schoharie, Johannes Lawyer, Hendrick Hanes, Jacob Sternbergh, Herman Sidney, Peter Snyder, George Man and Peter Ziele.

For Cocksackie District Anthony Van Bergen, Jacob Hallenbeek, Teunis Van Veghtèn, Casper M. Halenbeek, and Henry Hoogteling.

For the Great Imboght District, John Ten Broeck, Abraham Pearse, Goose Van Schajck, John Van Norden and John B. Dumont.

And for the Districts in the County of Tryon vizt:

For Mohawk District, Sir John Johnson, Baronet, Guy Johnson, Jellis Fonda, John Butler, and Christian Ernest.

For Palatine District, Harmanus Van Slyck, Jacob Klock, John Frey, Adam Louks and Isaac Paris.

For Canajoharie District Hendrick Frey, Nicholas Herkemer, William Seeber, Robert Wells and Frederick Young.

For Kingsland District Marcus Petri, Nicholas Weaver and John Cunningham.

For the German Flats District, John Jost Herkemer Junior, Rudolph Schumaker, Peter Ten Broeck, and Frederick Orendorf.

And be it Enacted by the Authority aforesaid, that the Commissioners in the respective Districts, for which they are named and appointed Commissioners are hereby impowered and authorized to regulate the Roads already laid out, and to lay out such other Public Roads in the several Districts for which they are appointed Commissioners as to them shall seem necessary and convenient; and if need be to take a Review of the Roads already laid out, and such of them as appear to be really inconvenient, the said Commissioners shall and may alter and lay out such other Public Ways and Roads as they shall think most convenient as well for Travellers as for the Inhabitants of the next adjacent District. Provided that Nothing in this Act contained shall extend or be construed to impower the Commissioners aforesaid to lay any new Road through any inclosed or improved Lands without either the Consent of the Owners thereof, or paying the true Value of the Lands so laid out into an Highway, and if any Dispute shall arise by that Means, the same shall be determined, and the true Value set and appraised by two Justices of the Peace not being Commissioners in the District where the Dispute shall happen and by the Oath of twelve of the Principal Freeholders of the Neighbourhood not having any Interest in the Lands about which such Dispute may arise, the said Freeholders to be summoned by one of the Constables of the said County by virtue of a Warrant to be issued by the said two Justices for that Purpose, and if the said Roads by the Commissioners so laid out shall be found by such Jury to be Public Roads and of Public and general Benefit, then the Value of such cleared and improved Lands through which the said Roads shall be laid out shall be paid by the said Commissioners, and they are hereby required to pay the same together with the Charge of calling a Jury, their Verdict and the whole Proceedings thereon had, of which Valuation and Charges the Commissioners shall transmit an Account to the Supervisors of the said City and County at their next meeting who are hereby required to cause the same together with the Collectors Reward for collecting the same, to be rated Assessed and levied, as a Public contingent District Charge and to be paid by the Collector into the Hands of any one of the Commissioners for such District in which it shall be directed to be levied deducting therefrom his Reward for collecting the same; But if the Roads so laid out shall be found by such Jury to be private Roads, and for the particular convenience of one or more particular Person or Persons, then such Person or Persons requiring the same shall defray the whole Charge of the Value of the said cleared or improved Lands, to be paid to the Person or Persons injured and through whose cleared or improved Lands a private Road shall be laid, together with the Charge of calling the Jury and of their Verdict and of the whole Proceedings thereon had, which shall be certified by such Justices.

And be it further Enacted by the Authority aforesaid, That the Overseers of the Highways in each District respectively or any one of them are hereby impowered directed and required to order such a Number of the Inhabitants of said District with their Sleds, Horses or Oxen as they the said Overseers, or any one of them shall think sufficient and proper to break up the Roads where deep Snows happen to fall, and if any Person or Persons being ordered as aforesaid, shall refuse to break up said Road, such Person or Persons shall respectively forfeit the Sum of ten Shillings for every Day they shall so neglect or refuse said Service, to be levied by the Overseer requiring the same, in like Manner as the Forfeiture mentioned in the tenth Clause of this Act is directed to be recovered; and the said Forfeiture of ten Shillings shall be paid to the Clerk of the Commissioners of the Highways for the District where such Forfeiture shall arise, to be by them applied in the Manner directed by the eleventh Clause of this Act.

And be it Enacted by the same Authority, That if any Person or Persons within the said City and Counties do, or hereafter shall without the Consent of the Commissioners for the District to which they are by this Act appointed Commissioners, alter, stop up, or lessen any Highway or Road that has heretofore been laid out by former Commissioners according to Law, or shall hereafter be laid out by the Commissioners appointed or to be appointed by this Act, such Person or Persons so offending contrary to the Meaning of this Act, shall for every such Offence forfeit the Sum of five Pounds to be recovered before any Justice of the Peace upon the Oath of any one credible Witness, and levied by Warrant from any Justice of the Peace directed to any Constable of the District where such Offence shall be committed commanding him to distrain the Goods and Chattels of the Offender, and the said Constable after six Days Public Notice given by him of the Time of Sale of said Distress, shall make Sale thereof, and out of the Produce deduct the said Forfeiture and all the Charges, and return the Overplus if any there be to the Owner or Owners, and the said Constable is hereby required to pay the said Forfeiture into the Hands of the Clerk of the Commissioners of the Highways for the District wherein the Offence was committed, to be by the Commissioners thereof applied in the same Manner as the other Monies to be raised by this Act are in the eleventh Clause thereof directed to be applied.

And in order that the Burthen of keeping the Highways in the said City and Counties in repair, and the making other Highways for the Ease Benefit and Safety of the Inhabitants may be as equitably proportioned between the Inhabitants thereof as the Nature of the Case will admit, be it further Enacted by the same Authority, That the Commissioners of each District respectively shall and are hereby required to meet annually between the second Tuesday in May at the Place of Election for District Officers, and on such a certain Day as they shall agree upon, and as often thereafter as need shall be, at such Times and Places as they shall think meet; and at their first Meeting, they shall proceed to make a List of all the Inhabitants in their District liable by this Act to work on the Highways, and shall then proceed either on that Day, or as soon thereafter as the said List shall be compleated to affix to each Persons Name the Number of Days that such Person shall be liable to work on the Highways for the Year ensuing, Copies of which List so compleated and signed by the Commissioner's Clerk, shall be put up in two of the most Public Places within the District, one of which to be the Place where the Preceding Election for District Officers was held, to the Intent that all the Inhabitants may know how many Days Labour they are respectively rated. Provided always That if any person's Name should be left out of such Lists, or the District increase by the Accession of New Inhabitants, such Omission and Increase shall from Time to Time be added to the said List, and the Persons be rated by the said Commissioners to work on the Highways, Provided also, That it shall not be in the Power of the Commissioners to rate any one Person rateable by this Act, at more than twenty five Days annually.

And Whereas several of the Districts in this Act mentioned contain Tracts of unimproved Land the Value of which Increases in Proportion as the Highways and Public Roads running through the same to settlements beyond them, are made better and more convenient for transporting the Produce of the Country, and whereas it is extremely Unreasonable that the Proprietors of such Lands should be benefited at the Expence of actual Settlers, who are in general in low circumstances.

Be it therefore Enacted by the Authority aforesaid, that where any Road runs through any Lands the Proprietor whereof does not actually reside in the District, and which are not let to Persons actually residing thereon, that it shall and may be lawful to and for

Nicoll, Killyaen Van Rensselaer, Abraham Ten Broeck, John H. Beekman, Teunis Slingerlandt, Stephen Schuyler, Lucas Van Veghten, Stephen J. Schuyler and Anthony Van Schajck.

For Schactikoke District, Johannes Knickerbacker Junior, Marte Winne, John Groesbeek and Dirck Van Veghten.

For Hosick District, Daniel Bradt, John Munro, Bliss Willoughby, Cornelius Van Ness, Ebenezer Cole, John Abbot, and John McComb.

For Cambridge District, Josaiah Younglove, Thomas Morrison and Archibald Campbell.

For Saraghtoge District, Philip Schuyler, Killian DeRidder, Jonathan Jones, Jacobus Swart, George Palmer, Dirk Swart, Cornelius Vanderbergh, Jeremiah Taylor and Nathan Tift.

For Balls Town District, James McCrea, James Gordon.

For Half Moon District, Guert VanSchoonhoven, Cornelius Tymese, Nicholas Fisher, Abraham Fort, and Hendrick Van der Werken.

For Schenectady District Isaac Vrooman, Ryer Schermerhorn, John Glen, Christopher Yates, Abraham Wempel, & John Cuyler Junior.

For the united District of Duanesburgh and Schoharie, Johannes Lawyer, Hendrick Hanes, Jacob Sternbergh, Herman Sidney, Peter Snyder, George Man and Peter Ziele.

For Cocksackie District Anthony Van Bergen, Jacob Hallenbeek, Teunis Van Veghten, Casper M. Halenbeek, and Henry Hoogteling.

For the Great Imboght District, John Ten Broeck, Abraham Pearse, Goose Van Schajck, John Van Norden and John B. Dumont.

And for the Districts in the County of Tryon vizt:

For Mohawk District, Sir John Johnson, Baronet, Guy Johnson, Jellis Fonda, John Butler, and Christian Ernest.

For Palatine District, Harmanus Van Slyck, Jacob Klock, John Frey, Adam Louks and Isaac Paris.

For Canajoharie District Hendrick Frey, Nicholas Herkemer, William Seeber, Robert Wells and Frederick Young.

For Kingsland District Marcus Petri, Nicholas Weaver and John Cunningham.

For the German Flats District, John Jost Herkemer Junior, Rudolph Schumaker, Peter Ten Broeck, and Frederick Orendorf.

And be it Enacted by the Authority aforesaid, that the Commissioners in the respective Districts, for which they are named and

happen that neither the Labour of such Carpenters or Masons, nor the Monies arising by Fines Forfeitures or Compositions, will be sufficient effectually to build or repair such Bridges, and to answer the other necessary Exigencies that may arise, Be it therefore Enacted by the same Authority, That in such Case the Commissioners shall procure a certified Copy of the List of the preceding Assessment for the District, and shall then proceed to affix to each Persons Name the just Proportion of such Deficiency together with a reasonable Reward for the Collector according to the Rates in the said Assessment, and the same being so affixed they shall cause the same to be delivered to one of the Collectors of the District who shall within thirty Days thereafter levy and collect the same in like Manner as the other District Charges are usually levied and collected, and the said Deficiency being so collected, the Collector shall within ten Days thereafter pay the same to the Clerk of the Commissioners to be by them applied as directed in the eleventh Clause of this Act; Provided always that such Deficiency shall in no one Year exceed the Sum of twenty Pounds.

And Whereas it may in some Cases be absolutely necessary to expend such a Sum of Money in one Year as that the Deficiency would exceed the said Sum of twenty Pounds, Be it therefore Enacted by the same Authority, That in Case the Commissioners shall think it necessary to carry on a Work which would cause a greater Deficiency than twenty Pounds, they shall and are hereby required to apply to any two Justices of the Peace not being Commissioners of the Highways in the District, who shall cause three Weeks Notice to be given by at least three Advertisements, appointing a Time and Place for the Persons rateable by this Act to meet, and by a Majority of Voices to determine whether they will or will not agree to the Proposal of the Commissioners, which Proposals shall be contained in the said Advertisements, together with a Computation of what such Expence will amount to, and if it appears that a Majority of such rateable Persons approve of the Proposals of the Commissioners, and determine on the Sum to be allowed, the Justices shall then give a certificate thereof subscribed by themselves, and countersigned by at least three of the Principal Freeholders then present, which Certificate shall be directed to the Commissioner of the District, and the said Commissioner shall thereupon at their next Meeting cause the same to be levied collected and paid in like Manner as the Deficiency mentioned in the preceding Clause of this act, is directed to be levied collected and Paid. Provided always, That no greater Sum shall be raised by virtue of this Clause in any one Year than one hundred Pounds.

And be it further Enacted by the Authority aforesaid, That upon Complaint made to any Justice of the Peace by any Person that the Highways in any District are not kept in sufficient repair, it shall and may be lawful to and for such Justice to whom such Complaint has been preferred, and he is hereby required to issue his Summons requesting the Commissioners of the District or some or one of them to appear on a certain Day, not less than ten Days from the Date of such Summons, at such Place as he shall appoint within the said District at which Time and Place the said Justices shall have a Jury of twelve Men out of the next District, who shall hear Evidence and enquire into the Matter; and if it shall appear by the Verdict of such Jury given under Oath, that the Insufficiency of the Highways is owing to the Neglect of the Commissioners, the Commissioners of the District shall pay all the Cost attending such Enquiry, and be severally fined in the Sum of forty Shillings, to be recovered together with the Proportion of Cost, by Distress and Sale of their Goods and Chattels respectively, one half of which Fine shall go to the Complainants, and the other half to the Poor of the District. Provided always, That if the Complaint should appear to the Jury to be frivolous and vexatious, that the Jury shall give such Damages to the Commissioners as they shall appear to have suffered, and the Complainant shall pay all the Cost, which Cost and Damages shall be recovered in the same Manner as the Cost and Fine is to be recovered if the Verdict goes against the Commissioners. And Provided also, That every Complainant shall give Security for the Cost and Damages to such Justice of the Peace before any Proceedings against the Commissioners shall commence.

And be it further Enacted by the Authority aforesaid, That all the Inhabitants of the Respective Districts who shall be rated to work on the Highways, shall as often as they or any of them shall receive Notice from the Overseer or Overseers of the Highways for the Time being to work on the Highways punctually attend the said Service either by themselves, their Slaves or Servants with proper Tools and faithfully Work all the Number of Days which they are rated if required, and in Case any Person or Persons duly warned shall refuse or neglect to appear, or being come to work on the Highways, shall remain idle or not work faithfully, or hinder or deter others from doing their Duty, such Offender shall for each Day forfeit the Sum of four Shillings to be recovered by the Overseer or Overseers of the Highways without any further Warrant for that Purpose by Distress and Sale of the Offender's Goods and Chattels returning the Overplus if any there be to the Owner or Owners after deducting the usual Charges as is common in Case where Distress is made by a Collector, and the said Forfeiture of four Shillings shall by the Overseer be paid into the Hands of the Commissioners Clerk to be by the said Commissioners applied as directed in the eleventh Clause of this Act.

And be it also Enacted by the same Authority, That all the Monies to be raised by virtue of this Act or that may accrue from Fines Forfeitures and Compositions shall be honestly and fairly applied by the Commissioners of each District respectively, for the Use of the Highways, and to and for building and repairing Bridges and such necessary Work in and concerning the Premises in their respective Districts as shall from Time to Time occur; and in paying a Clerk to be by them appointed and removed at pleasure, and the said Commissioners are hereby required and commanded to keep true and just Accounts of all the Monies by them received and expended by virtue of this Act, and the same to deliver in upon Oath to the Court of General Sessions, held for the said Counties respectively whenever thereunto required.

And in order the more clearly to ascertain what Persons shall be compellable to work on the Highways, Be it therefore Enacted by the authority aforesaid, That every Freeholder Housekeeper and other Person exercising any Trade or Business for themselves and on their own Account within the said Counties of Albany and Tryon, shall be liable to work on the Public Roads and Highways, and that no Person living with and working for their Master Mistress or Parents and not exercising any Trade or Business for themselves or upon their own Accounts shall be compellable to work upon the same.

And be it also Enacted by the same authority, That if any Tree shall fall out of any inclosed Lands into or across any of the Public Highways, that the Owner of such Inclosure shall within twelve Hours after the same be so fallen, remove the same or be liable to a Fine of twenty Shillings for every Days neglect in the non-removal thereof after Notice given by any Person or Persons whatsoever to be recovered and applied in the same Manner as the other Fines and Forfeitures are recovered and applied by the fourth and eleventh Clauses of this Act.

And Whereas several Persons in clearing of their Lands through which the Public Highways run have and yearly do kill the Trees and leave them standing, which Trees so killed upon every high Wind are subject to fall across the Roads and are thereby dangerous to Persons who are travelling along the said Roads, and Cattle feeding near the same.

Be it therefore Enacted by the Authority aforesaid, That whenever any Tree or Trees shall be girdled and killed on or within one Chain of any Public Road or Highway and shall remain standing for two Years after such girdling the Owner or Owners so girdling the same shall cut down or cause to be cut down such Tree or Trees or on Failure thereof shall forfeit and pay the Sum of five Shillings for every such Tree so girdled and left standing as aforesaid, to be recovered and applied in like Manner as the other Forfeitures mentioned in this Act are by the fourth and eleventh Clauses.

Provided Always and be it Enacted by the same Authority, That in Case it should not be necessary in any one or more of the said Districts to have all the Days wrought by the Inhabitants that this Act requires, that then the Commissioners shall direct the Overseers to let each Person work in his just Proportion to the Days such Person is rated and no more, or to pay an Equivalent at the rate of three Shillings a Day.

And be it also Enacted by the same Authority, That no Person whatever in any of the said Districts shall after the first Day of June next after the passing hereof, set up any swinging or other Gate, or suffer any that may be then already set up to remain across any of the Highways in the said City and Counties respectively, unless such Gate or Gates have already been licenced by any former Act or Acts, and unless by a special Licence from the Commissioners of the District under their Hands and Seals, Provided always, That before the said Commissioners shall be permitted to grant such a Licence, they shall at the request and at the Cost and Charge of the Person or Persons requesting such Licence, apply to two of the nearest Justices of the Peace, who shall cause the Constable of the District to summon twelve impartial principal Freeholders of the District, and the said Justices together with the said Freeholders being first duly sworn shall maturely inquire and then declare under their Hands and Seals whether there are any sufficient Obstacles to prevent the setting of Fences and maintaining the same, and what those Obstacles are, if any there be, and if by the Return of the Inquest it shall appear that no Fences can be reasonably maintained, then the Commissioners shall grant their Licence for Gates, if otherwise, they shall allow three Months to remove the Gates and no longer, and any Person or Persons offending contrary to the true Intent and meaning of this Clause, shall for every Offence be liable to the like Forfeiture that is inflicted in the fourth Clause of this Act, and the said Forfeiture shall be recovered in the same Manner as is directed in the said fourth Clause, and applied as is directed in the eleventh Clause of this Act.

And be it further Enacted by the same Authority, That in Case any Person or Persons shall stake or shore open any Licenced Gate or Gates or wilfully ride over or through any Lands, Meadow-Ground or Cornfield to the damage of the Owners thereof such Person or Persons shall for every Offence forfeit the Sum of twenty Shillings to be recovered by any of the Overseers of the Highways, in each respective District where such Offence shall be committed, and be recovered and applied in like Manner as the other forfeitures in this Act are recovered and applied by the fourth and eleventh Clauses of this Act, and such Offender shall pay all Damages with Costs which the Possessor of the Soil shall suffer or sustain thereby as shall be ordered and awarded by a Justice of the Peace residing nearest to the Place where such Offence shall be committed, and the Determination of such Justice shall be final and conclusive therein.

And be it further Enacted by the same Authority, That if the Commissioners or Overseers of the Highways shall think fit and have occasion of any Team Sled Cart or Waggon and a Man to manage the same, the said Cart Sled or Waggon and Man shall be esteemed to be in lieu of three Days work of one Man, and the Fine for Neglect or refusal to furnish the same to be proportionable, that is treble to the Fine to be imposed for the Neglect of one Person, and every Working Man shall be obliged to bring such Tools, as Spades, Axes, Crows, Pick Axes, or other Utensils as shall be directed by the Overseers of the Highways, and no Person under the Age of Sixteen Years shall be deemed a sufficient Labourer.

And be it further Enacted by the same Authority, That if any of the said Commissioners herein appointed, shall neglect refuse or delay to qualify themselves as this Act hereafter directs, or being qualified shall happen to die or remove out of the District for which he or they are appointed Commissioners, it shall and may be lawful for the Justices of the Peace in the General Sessions held for the said Counties respectively to appoint in his or their stead another Commissioner or Commissioners for such District, where such Refusal Neglect Delay Death or Removal shall happen, and the Commissioner or Commissioners so appointed shall be under the same Restrictions, and have the same Power and Authority as those appointed by this Act.

And be it also Enacted by the same Authority, That the Commissioners of each respective District for which they are respectively appointed, shall from Time to Time during the Continuance of this Act enter in writing all the Highways so by them laid out altered or stopped up, and sign the same by putting their Names thereto, and cause the same to be entered in the Records of the said Counties respectively by the Clerk of the Peace, who is hereby directed and required to record the same, and whatsoever the said Commissioners shall do in laying out altering or stopping up, and otherwise regulating Highways, according to the Power given them in this Act, being so entered in the County Records, shall be deemed valid and good to all Intents and Purposes whatsoever, for which Entry the Clerk shall be paid two Shillings.

Provided always and be it Enacted by the same Authority, That where the Inhabitants of a small Neighbourhood or Plantation shall desire to have Public Roads laid out, the Commissioners aforesaid shall not be allowed to lay out such and so many Roads as the said Inhabitants may be desirous to have, but only one Public Road leading from such Neighbourhood to the nearest other Public Highway which is central in the said District, from whence they can travel and transport Goods to other Towns or Landing Places, and where it shall be necessary to lay out a Road from one District, as they are in this Act joined to another District, the Commissioners or the major Part of both Districts are to meet and Consult where such Road can be laid out, and carried on in the most convenient, and shortest Manner the Nature of the Land will allow.

Provided also, And be it further Enacted, That if it shall so happen, That if the improved Farm of any Inhabitant of the said Counties shall be divided and lay in different Districts, that then in such Case, every such Inhabitant shall be subject to work upon the Highways in that District only, in which his Dwelling House is erected.

Provided also and be it further Enacted, That if any Inhabitant of the said respective Districts shall conceive it more convenient to use a Public Main Road not maintained by the District wherein he resides, leading to the City of Albany, or other Port or Place of Embarkation which may hereafter be established, that in every such Case upon Application to the Commissioners both of his own District, and of that through which the Road he prefers may pass, it shall and may be lawful to and for the said Commissioners or the major Part of them, if such Convenience shall appear to them to be manifest, to relieve him from the Duties required of him by this Act in the District which he Inhabits, and subject him to the Performance of those duties in the next adjoining District through which such Road passes, and where it is supported.

And Whereas the Proprietors of Land in many of the said Districts have formerly carried the Highways in such a Manner round their Lands as to save the Expence of fencing without any regard to the Inconvenience to which Travellers were put, And Whereas Such Highways have been since established by former Commissioners to save the Expence that a District would be put to, if the Highway had been laid in a more convenient Place, and through improved Lands, to remedy which Evil and to make the Highways as convenient as possible, Be it further Enacted, That every Public and Main Road leading from any District in which there is a considerable Settlement to the City of Albany or any other Port or Place of Embarkation as aforesaid, or where a new Road shall be so required to be laid out, that then and in every such Case, such Public or Main Road shall be continued from District to District and through the same as straight and direct as the Nature of the Ground will admit, and that such Main and Public Road may be established, or being established may be altered so as to be more generally convenient and useful to the Inhabitants of the respective Districts through which the same may extend, it shall and may be lawful to and for the Commissioners of the District which shall require the said Road to be laid out or altered, by writing under their Hands to appoint and summons a general Meeting of all the Commissioners of the respective Districts through which the Road proposed shall extend at any Time not less than three, or more than ten Days after the Service of Notice on the said Commissioners, and at such convenient Place in that District which shall be most central to the usual Residence of the major Part of such Commissioners, and the said Commissioners are hereby directed and required to meet and attend according to such Appointment, and when the said Commissioners so convened shall have consulted together and deliberated upon the Subject of the said Meeting, they shall then proceed to lay out the Highway or Road proposed and required from District to District, and in the best and most advantageous Manner for Public and General Utility and Convenience, That is to say The Commissioners of each respective District shall lay out that Part of the intended Road which shall extend through the District of which they are respectively Commissioners, and the same being so laid out, shall be certified, returned and recorded as a Public Road or Highway in the Manner herein before directed, and shall be maintained and supported in the several Districts through which it shall extend as other Highways or Public Roads ought by this Act to be maintained in such respective District, but if it shall so happen that the Commissioners of either of the other Districts then Assembled shall be dissatisfied with any Part of the Road so laid out, they shall be at Liberty, and are hereby authorized to propose the Manner in which they concieve that Part of the Road which is objected to ought to be laid out; and if the Commissioners whose Duty it is to lay out the same shall not agree to the Alteration insisted upon, that then a Description shall be made in writing signed by all the Commissioners present of both the Roads proposed, and it shall be lawful for three or more of the said Commissioners to apply to any two of his Majesty's Justices of the Peace of the said Counties respectively not residing or holding Lands in the District concerning which such Controversy shall have arisen, or the District for which such Road shall be required, and such Justices are hereby authorized and directed thereupon to issue their Precept to one of the Constables of the said County, commanding him to summon a Jury of twelve good men sufficient Freeholders of the said County not interested in the said Road, who being duly sworn for that Purpose, shall inquire and give their Verdict, which of the Roads in controversy will be the best and most commodious as a main and public Highway, and an Inquest being thereof made under the Hands and Seals of the said Justices and Jurors, shall be final and conclusive, according to which the Road shall be laid out, certified and returned as a public Road by the respective Commissioners through whose District it shall extend, and the Return thereof together with the said Inquisition being filed in the Office of the Clerk of the said County, and entered of Record, the said Road shall be deemed and esteemed a Public Road or Highway to all Intents and Purposes and be supported and maintained in the respective Districts through which the same shall extend in the same Manner as the other Highways in such Districts are directed and required to be maintained and supported by this Act, and the Charge and Expence of such Inquest shall be borne and paid out of the Monies to be raised by this Act for the Benefit of the District whose Commissioners shall have created the same by refusing to lay out such Road in the Manner which by the said Inquest shall be found best and most commodious. Provided always that if such Road so altered or laid out shall run through any improved Lands, the Proprietor thereof shall be satisfied and paid therefor as directed by the second Clause of this Act.

And be it also Enacted by the same Authority, That the Commissioners for the Time being for each District, shall and may at any Time during the Continuance of this Act divide the District of which they are Commissioners into such and so many Parts as to them shall seem most necessary, and such Partition to alter from Time to Time as they shall think expedient, of which Partition they shall give Notice by Advertisements to be put up at the Place of Election for District Officers at least six Days before the Day of Election, at which Election an Overseer of the Highways shall be chosen for each of the Parts into which the District is so divided, the Names of which Overseers shall be immediately transmitted by the Clerk of the District to the Commissioners of the Highways thereof.

And be it further Enacted by the same Authority, That every Person compellable to work on the Highways in any of the said Counties, shall actually work for each Day he is obliged to work eight Hours and shall be liable to pay a Fine of six Pence for every Hour such Person shall be in default, to be recovered and applied in like Manner as directed by the tenth and eleventh Clauses of this Act.

And be it further Enacted by the same Authority, That the several Overseers of the Highways in the several Districts or Parts of District for which they shall be appointed by this Act, shall whenever thereunto required by the Commissioners of the District to which they belong deliver an Account to the Commissioners Clerk, attested to before any Justice of the Peace which Attestation shall be in the Words following to wit, "I. A. B. do declare upon the Holy Evangelists of Almighty God, that the Account now delivered by me, to the best of my Knowledge and Belief contains the Names of all the Persons assigned by the Commissioners of the Highways in District to be under my Direction in working on the Highways, and that I have affixed to each Person's Name the Number of Days such Person has worked, or some other in such Person's stead as also the Names of all such Persons that have paid three Shillings per Day in lieu of the Days they were required to work; and also of such Persons as have been fined for refusing to work as the Law requires, so help me God."

And be it further Enacted by the same Authority, That the Commissioners of the respective Districts, shall be respectively allowed a Sum not exceeding six Shillings for every Day that such Commissioner shall absolutely and necessarily be employed in the Execution of his Office, and they shall transmit their Accounts on Oath to the Supervisors of the County to which they belong, at their Annual Meetings; and the Supervisors shall cause the same to be raised as the Monies by the seventh Clause of this Act are directed to be raised and paid.

And be it further Enacted by the same Authority, That the Commissioners for the Highways by this Act appointed or to be appointed shall respectively before they execute any of the Powers herein given to them take an Oath before any Justice of the Peace of the said City or Counties in the Words following, to wit, "I. A B, do solemnly swear that I will to the best of my Knowledge impartially execute the Powers to me given and granted by an Act entitled An Act for the better laying out regulating and keeping in repair the Public Roads and Highways in the City and County of Albany and County of Tryon, so help me God."

And be it further Enacted by the same Authority, That all Persons in the said Counties that may meet each other on any of the said Roads or Highways in Carriages or Sleighs those going from the City of Albany shall give way to those going toward the said City, and all Persons travelling Eastward on any of the said Roads or Highways on the East Side of Hudson's River shall give way to those travelling westward, and vice versa on the West Side of the said River under the Penalty of twenty Shillings to be recovered and applied as directed in the fourth and eleventh Clauses of this Act.

And be it further Enacted by the Authority aforesaid, That in Case any Person or Persons shall wantonly spoil or damage any Roads Bridges or Causeways, or fill up or destroy any of the Ditches or Fence across any of the said Roads or Highways, or erect or set up any Gates thereon, or put or leave in them any unnecessary Obstruction without Leave of the said Commissioners, such Person or Persons shall for every such Offence forfeit the Sum of forty Shillings to be recovered and applied as directed in the fourth and eleventh Clauses of this Act, And if any Person or Persons shall leave a Dead Horse or the Carcase of any other Beast or any broken Carriage on any of the said Roads or Highways for any longer Time than twelve Hours after Notice given or set up near the said Roads or Highways, any Thing by which Horses are usually affrighted, or shall by any improper Behaviour affright any Horse or Traveller on any of the said Roads, every such Person shall for every such Offence forfeit the Sum of forty Shillings to be recovered and applied as directed in said fourth and eleventh Clauses of this Act; and any Person leaving a dead Dog or Hog in any of the said Roads or Highways shall forfeit the Sum of twenty Shillings to be recovered and applied in like Manner.

And be it further Enacted by the same Authority, That on Information being given by any Person whatsoever to any of the Overseers of the said Roads or Highways of any of the said Nusances or Obstructions, he shall immediately proceed to the removing thereof, and shall also use his best Endeavours to discover the Person or Persons who committed the same, who upon Discovery, shall not only be liable to the Penalties herein before appointed, according to the Nature of the Offence, but also to the Costs of removing them, and a resonable Allowance to the said Overseer for his Time and Trouble therein, to be recovered by him in a summary way with Costs of Suit before any Justice of the Peace within the said City and Counties, and every such Overseer neglecting or refusing to do his Duty according to the true Intent and Meaning of this Act, shall for every such Neglect or Refusal forfeit the Sum of five Pounds, to be recovered paid and applied as directed in the fourth and eleventh Clauses of this Act.

And in order as far as possible to prevent the Evasion of the good Purposes intended by this Act, Be it Enacted by the same Authority, That the Owner of any dead Horse or other Nusance left on any of the said Roads or Highways, shall be deemed to have put or left the same thereon, unless he proves the contrary.

And be it further Enacted by the same Authority, That the Overseer of the Highways elected for that Part of the Manor of Rensselaerwyck from the North Bounds of the City of Albany to Water Vliet. and continued Northerly nearly along Hudson's River to the Gate at the North End of the Patroon's Farm, shall and he is hereby impowered and directed from and after the said first Tuesday in May and as often as need shall be to order and direct all and every the Inhabitants within the Bounds above described to clear and clean the said Street or Highway every one of them before his and their respective Lots of Ground and dwelling Places of all Fire-Wood, Timber, Lime, Stones, Shavings, Straw and Dung (except Timber, Boards, or Stone for present Building,) and if any Person or Persons shall refuse neglect or delay to yield Obedience to the Orders and Directions of the said Overseer, every such Person or Persons shall forfeit the Sum of Two Shillings for every Days Disobedience, Refusal, Neglect or Delay, to be recovered and applied as directed by the tenth and eleventh Clauses of this Act.

And be it further Enacted by the Authority aforesaid, That each and every Person living and dwelling on both sides of the Street or Highway leading from the City of Albany to Water Vliet shall upon two Months Notice given to them by the said Overseer pave or cause to be paved with Stone in such Manner as the said Overseer shall order and direct, not exceeding ten feet, before his and their respective Dwelling Houses and Lots of Ground, and that each and every Person not living and dwelling, but having a Lot or Lots of Ground on the West Side of the said Street leading to Water Vliet shall upon Notice given to them by the Overseer as aforesaid, lay with Gravel in such Manner as the said Overseer shall order and direct not exceeding ten feet before his and their respective Lots of Ground, and if any Person or Persons shall refuse neglect or delay to yield Obedience to the Orders and Directions of the said Overseer in the Premises, every such Person and Persons shall forfeit the Sum of twenty Shillings for every Months neglect or delay, to be recovered and applied as directed by the tenth and eleventh Clauses of this Act.

And be it also Enacted by the same Authority, That the major Part of the Commissioners or the major Part of the Survivors of them in any of the Districts within the said City and Counties shall and hereby are authorized to do and execute all or any of the Powers given unto them by this Act, and their Proceedings shall be as effectual and legal as if all the Commissioners of such Districts were present and concurring, any Thing in this Act to the contrary hereof notwithstanding. Provided always that in any District where a greater Number than three is a Majority of the Commissioners, and the Clerk of the Commissioners having in writing given Notice as herein after directed of an intended Meeting, that in every such Case the Majority of the Commissioners that shall attend being not less than three, shall and may do and perform every Act and Thing that a Majority of all the Commissioners of the District might or could have performed had they been present, any Thing in this Act to the contrary hereof notwithstanding, Provided also that the Clerk of the Commissioners shall whenever thereunto required by any one of the Commissioners give Notice in writing to all the Commissioners of the District of which he is Clerk at least three Days before such intended Meeting, of which Notice a Minute shall be made in the Book of the Proceedings of such Commissioners.

And be it Enacted by the same Authority, That in Case any Overseer or Overseers to be appointed by virtue of this Act shall refuse to serve as such, or shall neglect or delay the putting in execution any Services which he or they are required to do by this Act, or shall refuse to return an Account upon Oath as in this Act is directed; that in either of these Cases such Overseer or Overseers so offending contrary to the Meaning of this Act, shall be subject to the like Penalty as is inflicted by the fourth Clause of this Act on Persons altering, stopping up, or lessening any Highways, and be recovered in like Manner as the Penalty is thereby directed to be recovered; and applied as directed by the eleventh Clause of this Act.

And be it also Enacted by the same Authority, That the Act entitled "An Act for the better laying out, regulating and keeping in repair the public Roads and Highways in the City and County of Albany and County of Tryon," passed the sixth Day of February one thousand seven hundred and seventy-three, shall be and is hereby repealed, and that this Act shall be and continue in force from the passing thereof until the second Tuesday in May which will be in the year of our Lord one thousand seven hundred and eighty five, and from thence to the End of the then next Session of the General Assembly.

[CHAPTER 1731.]

[Expired in part, January 31, 1785.]

An Act for Relief against absconding and absent Debtors.

[Passed, April 3, 1775.]

Whereas divers Persons being indebted within this Colony and having Estates or Effects in the same, with design to defraud their Creditors of their just Dues do secretly depart the Colony, and procure their Estates and Effects or the Value thereof to be remitted to them, or conceal themselves within the Colony in Order to bring their Creditors to an unreasonable Composition; for Remedy of which evil practices the Laws hitherto provided have been found inadequate,

Be it therefore Enacted by his Honor the Lieutenant Governor the Council and the General Assembly, and it is hereby enacted by the Authority of the same, That from and after the passing of this Act whensoever it shall happen that any Person or Persons whatsoever, being indebted within this Colony, shall either secretly depart the Colony or keep concealed within the same, any one Creditor, or joint Company whose Debt or Demand is due to them jointly, to whom such absconding or concealed Person or Persons is or are indebted in the Sum of Forty Pounds or upwards; or any two, to whom he she or they is or are indebted in the Sum of sixty Pounds or upwards or any three, to whom he she or they is or are indebted in the Sum of Eighty Pounds or upwards, over and above all Discounts, may make application to the Judges of the Supreme Court of this Colony for the Time being, or any of them, and there make Affidavit or Affirmation in Writing, in Cases where by Law an Affirmation is allowed, that the said absconding or concealed Person or Persons is or are indebted to him her or them in the Sum of over and above all Discounts, and that he she or they do verily believe that the said absconding or concealed Person or Persons, is or are either departed the Colony or concealed within it, with Intent and Design to defraud him her or them and other Creditors (if any such there be) of their just Dues or to avoid being arrested by the ordinary Process of Law; which Departure or Concealment shall also be proved to the satisfaction of such Judge or Judges by two Witnesses: And on such Affidavit or Affirmation, and such other Proof made the said Judge or Judges, or any one of them, hereby is and are fully impowered, authorized and required forthwith to issue his or their Warrant or Warrants to the Sheriff of the City or County which contains the last usual Place of Residence of such absconding or concealed Person or Persons or to the Sheriff or Sheriffs of any or every other City or County within this Colony commanding such Sheriff or Sheriffs respectively to attach seize take and safely keep all the Estate as well real as personal of the said absconding or concealed Person or Persons of what kind or nature soever, and every or any Part or Parcel thereof in whatever Part of his Bailiwick they can be found with all Evidences, Books of Accounts, Vouchers and Papers relating thereto: Which Warrant or Warrants the Sheriff or Sheriffs respectively to whom the same shall be directed and delivered are hereby enjoined, required, authorized and commanded well and truly to execute and with the Assistance of two Substantial Freeholders forthwith to make a just and true Inventory of all such Estate and Effects as he shall seize and take by Virtue thereof, and to return the same signed by himself and the said two Freeholders to such Judge or Judges who issued the Warrant or Warrants for taking and seizing thereof.

And be it further Enacted by the Authority aforesaid, That such Judge or Judges who shall issue such Warrant or Warrants, shall immediately thereafter order Notice to be given in all the public News Papers printed in the City of New York, that on Application to him or them made by a Creditor or Creditors, as the Case may be, of such absconding or concealed Person or Persons, he has directed all his her or their Estates Real and Personal within this Colony to be seized, and that unless he she or they by Name, so absconding or concealed return and discharge his her or their Debt or Debts within Three Months after such public Notice given all his her or their Estates Real and personal will be sold for the Payment and Satisfaction of his her or their Creditors.

And be it further Enacted by the Authority aforesaid, That in case any Sheriff or Sheriffs shall by Virtue of any Warrant or Warrants to be issued in Pursuance of this Act, seize and take any perishable Goods or Chattels it shall and may be lawful for the Judge or Judges who issued such Warrant or Warrants, at his or their Discretion, to order the Sale of such Things perishable; and the Monies arising thereby to be delivered and paid to the Trustees, that shall be appointed to manage the Estate and Effects of such absconding or concealed Person or Persons mentioned in such Warrant or Warrants, to be by such Trustees applied according to the directions and Intention of this Act.

And be it further Enacted by the Authority aforesaid, That if any Sheriff or Sheriffs, shall by Virtue of any Warrant or Warrants to be issued in Pursuance of this Act, through Ignorance or want of proper Information seize and take any Goods, Chattels or Effects which shall or may be claimed or challenged by any Person or Persons as his her or their Property, it shall and may be lawful for such Sheriff thereupon to summon and swear a Jury to enquire into and try the Right and Property thereof: And if such Jury shall upon such Inquest find the Right and Property of such Goods, Chattels or Effects to be in the Person or Persons so claiming the same, or in any other than the Person or Persons against whose Effects or Estate such Warrant or Warrants did issue, such Sheriff shall forthwith after such Inquisition had and taken deliver such Goods, Chattels and Effects to the Person or Persons in whom the Property thereof shall be so found, or to his, her or their Agent, Attorney or Assigns; and such Sheriff shall not be liable to any Suit or Prosecution for his having seized and taken such Goods Chattels or Effects, so seized and taken through Ignorance or for want of proper Information; and all reasonable Charges arising by the Sale of such perishable Goods, or by such Inquest as aforesaid shall be allowed and certified by the Judge or Judges who issued such Warrant and paid out of the Effects or Estate of the absconding or concealed Person or Persons against whose Estate and Effects such Warrant issued if the Property of such Goods, Chattels or Effects so claimed shall by such Inquisition be found to be in any other than the Person or Persons against whose Estate or Effects such Warrant issued; But if the Property of the Goods, Chattels or Effects so claimed shall by such Inquisition be found to be in the Person or Persons against whose Estate or Effects the Warrant of Attachment which caused them to be seized did issue then all Costs, Charges and Expenses accrued or arising by such Claim and Inquisition or either of them shall be paid and born by the Person or Persons who claimed the same from the Sheriff or applied for Inquisition to be had, or occasioned the same to be had and taken.

And be it further Enacted by the Authority aforesaid, That if any Person or Persons indebted to any such absconding or concealed Person or Persons, or having the Custody or Possession of any Effects or other Thing or Things whatsoever of any such absconding or concealed Person or Persons shall after such first public Notice as aforesaid given pay any Debt or Demand or deliver any such Effects or other Thing or Things whatsoever to any such absconding or concealed Person or Persons, or his her or their Attorney, Agents, Factors or Assigns, the Person or Persons so paying any such Debt or Demand or delivering such Effects or other Thing or Things whatsoever shall be deemed to have paid the same fraudulently and is and are hereby made liable to answer the same or the Amount or Value thereof to such Trustees or the Survivor of them as shall by Virtue of this Act be appointed to receive and distribute the Estate and Effects of such absconding or concealed Person or Persons towards the Payment and Satisfaction of his her or their Creditors. And if any Person or Persons indebted to or having the Custody or Possession of any Effects or other Thing or Things whatsoever of any absconding or concealed Debtor or Debtors shall after such public Notice as aforesaid given be sued by him or them, or by his her or their order, Attorney or Procurement for any such Debt or Debts, Duty, Demand, Effects or Thing he she or they so sued may plead the general Issue, and give this Act and the special Matter in Evidence.

And be it further Enacted by the authority aforesaid, That all Sales and Conveyances of his her or their Estates, Lands, Goods, Chattels or Effects and all Assignments of any promisory Note, Bill of Exchange, Security or chose in Action, to him her or them due or belonging made by any such absconding or concealed Person or Persons after such public Notice as aforesaid given; and all Powers of Attorney by him her or them, for selling any Estate or Effects or collecting any Debts or Demands, whether made after or before such first public Notice as aforesaid given shall be null and void to all Intents, Constructions and Purposes whatsoever as to all Acts done or to be done after such first public Notice given any Law Usage or Custom to the contrary notwithstanding.

And be it further Enacted by the Authority aforesaid, That if any Person or Persons against whose Estate or Effects such Warrant or Warrants of Attachment as aforesaid shall have issued, shall at any Time before the Appointment of Trustees for all the Creditors of such Debtor be made either by himself or by his Attorney or Agent by Petition to the Judge or Judges who issued such Warrant offer to prove to the Court of which he or they is or are Judge or Judges in open Court that he she or they against whose Estate or Effects such Warrant or Warrants issued, is or are resident within this Colony and were not at the Time such Warrant issued, within Thirty Days preceding, nor at any Time after and is or are not then absconding or concealed and thereby pray that the same may be heard and determined at the then next sitting of such Court; and shall and do at the same Time execute and deliver to the Creditor or Creditors who applied for and obtained such Warrant or Warrants of Attachment a Bond with good and sufficient Security, to be approved of by the said Judge or Judges, if in the Supreme Court in the Sum of Forty Pounds, and if in any of the inferior Courts in the Sum of Twenty Pounds binding the Obligors jointly and severally with a Condition, that if such Person or Persons by Name against whose Estate or Effects such Warrant or Warrants issued, do not prove to the said Court at the then next

Court that he she or they is or are residents in this Colony, and were not at the Time such Warrant or Warrants issued, nor within Thirty Days preceding the issuing thereof, nor at any Time after, and is or are not then absconding or concealed, then such Bond or Obligation to be void otherwise to remain in full Force and Virtue, Then and in every such Case the Judge or Judges who issued such Warrant or Warrants, shall report his or their Proceedings in the Premises to the next Court whereof he or they is or are Judge or Judges; which Court is hereby fully authorized and impowered to compel the Parties and their Witnesses to come into Court and hear the Proofs and Allegations of the Parties and their Witnesses in a Summary way, and thereupon to determine whether the Matters and Things in such Petition have been fully proved and supported. And if such Court shall adjudge and determine that the Matters and Things contained in such Petition have been fully and satisfactorily proved and supported, Then such Court shall Grant a Supersedeas to such Warrant or Warrants, and the Person or Persons whose Estate or Effects such Warrant or Warrants did issue shall recover his her or their Costs, to be taxed by the said Court, in open Court, of the Creditor or Creditors who procured such Warrant or Warrants of Attachment to be issued; But if the said Court shall judge and determine that the Matters and Things in such Petition mentioned have not been fully and satisfactorily supported and proved to the said Court, Then the Person or Persons to whom such Bond as aforesaid shall have been given his her or their Executors or Administrators shall recover the Penalty or Sum of such Bond, together with Costs of Suit, by Action of Debt, Bill, Plaint or otherwise in any Court of Record within this Colony, the one Moiety of such Penalty or Sum to the use of the Obligee or Obligees, his her or their Executors, Administrators or Assigns, And the other Moiety thereof when recovered and received to be paid to such Trustees, or the Survivor of them as shall be appointed to manage and Distribute the Estate and Effects, for seizing whereof such Warrant or Warrants issued; to be by such Trustees or the Survivor of them disposed of and distributed in like manner as all other Monies that may come to their Hands by Virtue of their Appointment as Trustees, is directed to be disposed of by Virtue of this Act.

And be it further Enacted by the Authority aforesaid, That if such absconding or concealed Person or Persons do not return within three Months next after such public Notice as aforesaid given and discharge his, her or their Debt or Debts or otherwise

Compound with or Satisfy his her or their Creditors, not having presented such Petition and given such Bond as aforesaid; or if such absconding or concealed Person or Persons shall have presented such Petition, and the Court shall have adjudged and determined that the Matters and Things in such Petition mentioned have not been fully and satisfactorily supported and proved, or shall have refused to Grant a Supersedeas to such Warrant or Warrants, That then and in either such Case it shall and may be lawful for the Judge or Judges who issued the Warrant of Attachment or the Judges of the same Court for the Time being or any one of them, and either of them is hereby fully authorized and impowered to nominate and Appoint three or more fit Persons to be Trustees for all the Creditors of such absconding or concealed Person or Persons, which Trustees shall take an Oath or Affirmation (in Cases where by Law an Affirmation is allowed) well and truly to execute the Trust by that Appointment reposed in them, according to the best of their Skill and Understanding, which Oath or Affirmation the Judge or Judges appointing the said Trustees is and are hereby required to administer.

And be it further Enacted by the Authority aforesaid, That the said Trustees or any two of them, when so as aforesaid appointed, shall as soon as may be thereafter, cause public Notice to be given in all the News Papers Printed in the City of New York of such their Appointment and thereby require all Persons indebted to such absconding or secreted Person or Persons by a day certain to be appointed by them in their said Notice, to pay all such Sum or Sums of money or other Debt, Duty or Thing, which they owe to the said absconding or concealed Person or Persons, and deliver all other Effects of such absconding or concealed Person or Persons which he she or they may have in their Hands, Power or Custody, to them the said Trustees. And that the said Trustees shall also by public Advertisement in all the said News Papers desire all the Creditors of such absconding or concealed Person or Persons by a certain Time in such Advertisement to be mentioned to deliver to the said Trustees or any one or more of them their respective Account and Demands against such absconding or concealed Debtor or Debtors.

And be it further Enacted by the Authority aforesaid, That such Trustees, and each and every of them when so nominated and appointed under the Hand and Seal or Hands and Seals of the said Judges, or any one of them, hereby is and are fully authorized and impowered to take into their Hands, All the Estate or Estates of such absconding or concealed Person or Persons for the Management of whose Estate or Effects they were appointed, and every Part and Parcel thereof, that shall have been seized as aforesaid and all other his, her or their Estate and Effects which they the said Trustees may afterwards discover in any part of this Colony, And all Evidences, Books of Accounts, Vouchers and Papers relating thereto; and such Trustees immediately from their appointment shall be and are hereby declared to be vested with all the Estate Real and Personal of such absconding or concealed Person or Persons, for the Management of whose Estate they were appointed; And they and the survivors and Survivor of them is and are hereby enabled and made capable to sue for recover and receive all such Estate and Estates as well Real as Personal, Debts, Dues, Effects or other Thing or Things whatsoever as they shall find due, payable or belonging to such absconding or concealed Person or Persons. And such Sheriff or Sheriffs as shall have seized, attached or taken any Estate or Estates, Real or personal or any other Matter or Thing whatsoever by Virtue of any such Warrant or Warrants as aforesaid, shall deliver the same to such Trustees or one of them: And such Trustees and the Survivors and Survivor of them is and are hereby authorized and directed to make Sale by Public Vendue of all such Estates and Effects of such absconding or concealed Person or Persons as shall come to their Hands (after Fourteen Days Notice of each Time and Place of Sale respectively) And of all Estate and Interest which such absconding or concealed Person or Persons had in the same, And Deeds, Releases, Bills of Sale or other Conveyances for the same, or any Part or Parts thereof from Time to Time to make and execute, which being so made and executed by them or any two of them, or the Survivor of them, for such Estates or Effects or any Part or Parts thereof shall be and are hereby declared to be as good, valid and effectual to transfer the Property thereof to all Intents, Constructions and Purposes whatsoever, as if executed by the said absconding or secreted Person or Persons before such first public Notice as aforesaid given, and shall be good, valid and effectual in Law to all Intents and Purposes whatsoever against the said absconding or concealed Person or Persons his, her or their Heirs, Executors, Administrators and Assigns, and all Persons claiming under them or any of them, by virtue of any Act Deed, Matter or Thing after such first public Notice as aforesaid given.

And be it further Enacted by the Authority aforesaid, That if any Person or Persons indebted to such absconding or concealed

Debtor or Debtors, or having the Custody of any Goods, Chattels or Effects, or other Thing or Things whatever of such absconding or concealed Debtor or Debtors, shall conceal the same and not deliver a just Account thereof to such Trustees as aforesaid or one of them, by the Day for that Purpose by them appointed, he, she or they so concealing shall forfeit double the Sum of the Debt or Debts, or double the Value of the Goods, Chattels, Effects or other Thing or Things so concealed to be recovered by the said Trustees in any Court within this Colony having Jurisdiction to the Amount of such Forfeiture, and applied as hereinafter directed; which said Courts are hereby respectively fully impowered to compel to come before them all such concealors or others concerned, and them to examine upon Oath, touching the Premises, and to commit them or either of them if they refuse to be so examined, or being so examined refusing to Answer fully and satisfactorily to such Court.

And be it further Enacted by the Authority aforesaid, That it shall and may be lawful for the Trustees of any Debtor or Debtors Estate, heretofore appointed by Virtue of any of the Laws of this Colony relating to fraudulent or absconding Debtors, or hereafter to be appointed by Virtue of this Act, or the Survivors or Survivor of them, or the Major Part of such Survivors to apply to any Justice of the Peace in this Colony, who is hereby in such Case authorized, required and commanded to grant a Warrant under his Hand and Seal commanding such Debtor or Debtors, the Wife or Wives of such Debtor or Debtors respectively, and every other Person whomsoever, known or suspected to detain any part of such Debtors Estate or to be indebted to it, or knowing or suspected to know any Thing concerning the Concealment or Embezzlement thereof, by their respective Names, forthwith to be brought before such Justice or Trustees at such Place as the said Justice and Trustees or the Major Part of them or Survivors or Survivor of them, or the Major Part of such Survivors, shall at the Time of the Application for or issuing of such Warrant appoint; where the said Justice of the Peace is also hereby required and commanded to be present; Or in Case of his Death, absence or indisposition such other Justice of the Peace as the said Trustees, or the Major Part of them or the Survivors or Survivor shall request to be present: At which Meeting as well the said Justice of the Peace, as the said Trustees or the Survivors or Survivor of them, or the Major Part of such Survivors, shall and may examine on Oath, or if a Person privileged by Law to affirm on his or her Affirmation (which Oath or Affirmation the said Justice of the Peace is hereby required to Administer, as well by word of Mouth, as on Interrogatories in Writing all and every Person or Persons brought before the said Justice and Trustees, by Virtue of such Warrant or Warrants; and any other Person or Persons present at any such Meeting, touching all Matters relative to the Person, Trade, Dealings, Debts, Credits, Estate or Effects of all and every such Debtor or Debtors and also to take down and reduce into Writing, the Answers of every such Person had given or taken before them as aforesaid: which Examination so taken down and reduced into Writing, the Person whose Examination the same is, shall and is hereby required to sign and subscribe. And in Case any Person so brought before them the said Justice and Trustees or the Survivors or Survivor of them, or the Major Part of such Survivors, shall refuse to be sworn, or if a Person so Privileged by Law to affirm, as aforesaid, or being sworn or affirmed, shall refuse to answer or shall not fully answer to the Satisfaction of the said Justice all lawful Questions put to him or them by the said Justice and Trustees or the Major Part of them then present, as well by word of Mouth, as by Interrogatories in Writing; or shall refuse to sign and subscribe his her or their examination so taken down in Writing as aforesaid, not having a reasonable Objection either to the wording thereof or otherwise to be allowed by the said Justice, it shall and may be lawful to the said Justice of the Peace and he is hereby required, by Warrant under his Hand and Seal to commit him or them to Prison, there to remain without Bail or Mainprize, until such time as such Person or Persons respectively shall submit to the said Justice to be sworn or affirmed as aforesaid, and full Answer to make, to the Satisfaction of the said Justice, to such Questions as shall be put to him her or them [illegible] to sign and subscribe such examination as aforesaid, according to the true Intent and Meaning of this Act.

Provided always, That in Case any Person or Persons shall be committed as aforesaid for refusing to be sworn or affirmed, or [illegible] not fully Answering any Question or Questions put to him or them by the said Justice and Trustees, or the Major Part of them then present by word of Mouth, or on Interrogatories, the said Justice of the Peace shall in his Warrant of Commitment specify such default respectively; And if the Commitment be for refusing to Answer any Question or Interrogatory, the said Justice shall in his Warrant specify such Interrogatories Question or Questions.

Provided always also, That in Case any Person or Persons committed by such Warrant or Warrants by virtue of this Act, shall bring any Habeas Corpus in order to be discharged from any such Commitment, and on the return of any such Habeas Corpus there shall appear any insufficiency whatever in the form of the Warrant whereby such Person was committed, by reason whereof the Party might be discharged of such Commitment; That then it shall and may be lawful for the Court or Judge before whom such Party shall be brought by Habeas Corpus as aforesaid, and such Court or Judge shall, and is hereby required by Rule, Order or Warrant, to commit such Person or Persons to the same Prison to which he was first committed there to remain as aforesaid, unless it shall be made appear to such Court or Judge, by the Party committed, that he, she or they have fully answered all lawful Questions put to him, her or them by the said Justice and Trustees, that were then present, or the Major Part of them; Or in Case such Person was committed for not signing his, her or their examination unless it shall be made appear to such Court or Judge, that the party so committed, had a good and sufficient Reason for refusing to sign the same And in Case any Goaler or Keeper of any Prison or Goal to whom any such Person or Persons shall be committed as aforesaid shall willfully suffer any such Person or Persons to escape from such Prison until he she or they shall be duly discharged as aforesaid such Goaler or Keeper shall for every such Offence, being first duly Convicted thereof by indictment or Information forfeit to the Trustees appointed to manage and distribute the Estate and Effects of such absconding or concealed Person or Persons respectively a Sum equal to all such Sum or Sums of money as shall be due or owing to the Creditor or Creditors of such absconding or concealed Person or Persons; provided the same does not exceed the Sum of One Thousand pounds to be sued for recovered and levied by the said Trustees or the Survivors or Survivor of them in any Court of Record within this Colony, and distributed as hereinafter directed.

And be it Enacted by the same Authority, That in Case any Person so to be examined as aforesaid either in Court or before such Justice and Trustees as aforesaid shall wilfully and knowingly swear or affirm falsely the Person so offending, shall be liable to all the same Pains and Penalties as those who are Convicted of wilfull and corrupt Perjury.

And be it Enacted by the Authority aforesaid, That any Person or Persons (other than those who have the Effects in their Custody) who shall discover any Effects of any absconding or concealed Debtor or Debtors secreted contrary to the true Intent and Meaning of this Act, so that they be recovered by the Trustees of such absconding or concealed Person or Persons Estate; shall be and hereby is or are entitled to Ten per Cent on the Value of all Effects so discovered, recovered and received by the said Trustees, to be paid to the discoverer or discoverers, by the said Trustees out of the Estate or Effects of such absconding or concealed Debtor or Debtors.

And be it further Enacted by the Authority aforesaid, That the Trustees of any absconding or concealed Debtors Estate already appointed in Pursuance of any of the said Laws of this Colony relating to absconding and fraudulent Debtors, or hereafter to be appointed in Pursuance of this Act, or any two of them are hereby fully empowered to settle and adjust all Matters, Contracts and Accounts that may be subsisting between such absconding or concealed Person or Persons, and his her or their Debtor or Debtors; And also between such absconding or concealed Person or Persons, and his her or their Creditor or Creditors; and to examine any Person or Persons upon Oath concerning any Matters, Accounts or Settlements between them or either of them; which Oath the said Trustees or any one of them, two of them being present, is and are hereby empowered to Administer.

And for the greater ease and relief of such Trustees as aforesaid, Be it Enacted by the same Authority, That in case any Controversy shall arise concerning any Debt, Matter or Thing claimed by any Creditor or Creditors, of such absconding or concealed Person or Persons; or concerning any Debt due, Duty Matter or Thing claimed by the said Trustees from or against any Person or Persons, as belonging to, or in right of the Effects or Estate of such absconding or concealed Debtor or Debtors; or concerning or relating to any Contract or Agreement entered into or made by such absconding or concealed Debtor or Debtors previous to such public Notice as aforesaid first given, it shall and may be lawful for such Trustees already appointed as aforesaid or hereafter to be appointed in Pursuance of this Act or any two of them or the Survivors or Survivor of them, to have every such Controversy determined in the following manner, that is to say, the said Trustees or any two of them or the Survivors or Survivor of them may nominate two Referees not being Creditors of such absconding or concealed Debtor or Debtors or to them known to be otherwise interested in such Controversy or related to any Person interested in such Controversy, and the other Party or Parties in such Controversy shall also nominate two indifferent Persons to be Referees and their Names shall be separately written on four pieces of paper as nearly as may be of the same size and figure, which shall be rolled up separately in the same manner and put into a Box, and from thence one of the Trustees shall draw out three of the said pieces of paper and the Persons whose names are so drawn, shall finally settle such Controversy; And if any Referees so appointed shall refuse or be incapable of acting in a reasonable Time, a new choice shall be made in like manner as before of another or others in the Room of him or them so refusing or being incapable of acting as aforesaid; And in Case any Person or Persons who shall have any Controversy with any such Trustees as aforesaid shall refuse to nominate fit Persons to be Referees on his or their Part, Then such Trustees or any two of them, or the Survivors or Survivor of them are hereby empowered to nominate Referees for him or them so refusing and to proceed to the final Settlement of such Controversy in manner aforesaid.

And be it further Enacted by the Authority aforesaid, That all Trustees hereafter to be appointed by Virtue of this Act, shall proceed to convert the Estate or Estates Real and Personal of such absconding or concealed Debtor or Debtors for the Management of which Estates respectively they shall be appointed into money, and collect the Debts due to the same, And that the said Trustees or any two of them, or the Survivor or Survivors of them, shall cause public Notice to be given in one or more of the public News Papers printed in the City of New York requesting a general Meeting of all such Creditors as shall choose to attend to examine and see the Debts due to each Person ascertained, at a certain Time and Place by such Trustees in their said Notice to be appointed, which shall not be less than two, nor more than three months after such said Notice given, nor more than one year and an half from the Time of their first Appointment: At which Meeting or other Subsequent Meetings necessary for that purpose, to be continued by Adjournments if necessary, when all Accounts are fairly stated and adjusted, they shall proceed to make a Distribution or Division amongst the Creditors in Proportion to their respective just Demands, of all monies as shall have come to their Hands as Trustees of such Estate or Effects (of which all Forfeitures by them recovered and received by virtue of this Act shall be considered as a part) first deducting thereout all legal Charges and Commissions; in which Payments no preference shall be allowed to Debts due on Specialties: And if the whole of such absconding or concealed

Debtor or Debtors Estate, shall not be then settled and distributed, such Trustees or any two of them or the Survivors or Survivor of them shall within the space of one year thereafter make a second Dividend of all such Monies as shall have come to his or their Hands after the first division, and so from Year to Year until a final Settlement thereof and a just and equal distribution of such Estate or Effects shall have been made amongst the Creditor or Creditors of such absconding or concealed Debtor or Debtors in Proportion to their respective just Demands. And if any surplus shall remain after all just Debts and legal Charges and Commissions are fully paid and satisfied such Surplus shall be paid or delivered to the said Absconding or concealed Person or Persons, his her or their Executors Administrators or Assigns.

And be it further Enacted by the Authority aforesaid, That any Person or Persons who may have given Credit to any such absconding or concealed Debtor or Debtors on a valuable Consideration for any Sum of money which shall not be due or payable at the Time of any such division or distribution as aforesaid, but will become due or payable at some after Time, shall and may nevertheless, be admitted and considered as a Creditor or Creditors, whose Debts were then due, and shall receive a Dividend of the Estate of such absconding or concealed Debtor or Debtors in the same Proportion as other Creditors, deducting thereout only a rebate of legal interest for what shall be received on such Debt or Debts, to be computed from the actual Payment thereof, to the Time of such Debt or Demand respectively would have become due.

And be it further Enacted by the same Authority, That if any Creditor or Creditors shall neglect or refuse to give Notice of, or deliver in to the said Trustees an Account of his, her or their Debt or Demand, or having any Controversy relating to or concerning the Estate of such absconding or concealed Debtor or Debtors, shall refuse to adjust or settle the same with the said Trustees in the manner in and by this Act directed until after a Division shall have been made of the Monies and Effects in the Hands of the said Trustees any such Creditor or Creditors shall not be entitled to any Dividend, and the whole monies then in Hand to be divided shall be divided by the said Trustees among the other Creditors: But in Case the whole of such Debtor or Debtors Estate shall not be divided and settled at the first Division, then if such Creditor or Creditors respectively shall prove and deliver in to such Trustees, his her or their Debt or Demand, before the Time appointed for the second Division; or shall have settled such Controversy as aforesaid with the said Trustees, then such Creditor or Creditors shall have his, her or their first Dividend, or so much money as he would otherwise have been entitled to on the first Division before any second Dividend shall be made.

And be it further Enacted by the Authority aforesaid, That any Creditor or Creditors residing out of this Colony shall be entitled to all the Privileges and Benefits of this Act; And that the Attorney or Attornies of every such Creditor or Creditors residing out of this Colony on producing a Letter of Attorney from such Creditor or Creditors duly Authenticated and legal Proof of the Debt due shall and may in all Respects act do and proceed, for and in behalf of such Creditor or Creditors, in the same manner as such Creditor or Creditors might or could do, for securing or recovering their respective Debts from such absconding or concealed Debtor or Debtors, if such Creditor or Creditors was or were personally present.

And Whereas Persons who dwelt out of this Colony may be indebted within the same and have Estates or Effects sufficient within the same to pay and satisfy such Debts or Parts thereof, Be it also Enacted by the same Authority, That the Estates, Goods, Chattels and Effects real and personal of all and every such Person and Persons (so indebted) as do or may dwell or reside out of this Colony, shall also be Subject and liable to be taken, seized, proceeded against sold, conveyed and disposed of, for the Payment and satisfaction of such of the said Debts as aforesaid, as near as may be in like manner as the Estates and Effects of other Debtors in and by this Act are made subject and liable to.

Provided always, That instead of the Proof of Absconding or Concealment of such Debtor or Debtors the Creditor or Creditors applying for any Attachment, against the Estate or Effects of any Person or Persons residing out of this Colony, shall make Proof by two Witnesses to the satisfaction of the Judge or Judges to whom Application for such Attachment shall be made, that such Debtor or Debtors reside out of this Colony. And also Provided, That in any such Case no Trustees shall be appointed until the Expiration of one Year after such public Notice as aforesaid given.

And be it further Enacted by the Authority aforesaid, That the Judges of the Inferior Court of Common Pleas in each County within this Colony, and the Mayor and Recorder of the City of New York and each and every of them is hereby authorized and impowered to put this Act in Execution in their respective Counties, where the Debt or Sum due to any one Creditor or joint Company applying for relief does not exceed one Hundred Pounds.

Provided always, That where Warrants shall be issued by any Judge or Judges of the Supreme Court and also by any Judge or Judges of any of the said Inferior Courts against the Estate or Effects of the same Person or Persons, in such Case, the Judges of the Supreme Court or any one of them shall award a Writ or Writs of Certiorari to the Judge or Judges of such Inferior Court, as the Case may require, to remove the Proceedings there, before the Judge or Judges of the Supreme Court, that he or they may proceed upon both Warrants or either of them.

And be it further Enacted by the Authority aforesaid, That the Judge or Judges who shall issue any Warrant or Warrants of Attachment in Pursuance of this Act, shall make Report to the Court whereof he or they is or are Judge or Judges, of the Court whereof he or they is or are Judge or Judges, of the Proof of the Debt or Demand made by the Creditor or Creditors, on whose Application such Warrant or Warrants issued, of the issuing of such Warrant or Warrants, of the Notice thereon ordered, of the Publication of such Notice, of the Appointment of Trustees, and of all other Matters required of him or them by this Act, to be done out of Court; and cause that Report to be entered in the Minutes of the said Court, to be Evidence of the Facts so reported. And such Report or the Record or Entry thereof in the Minutes of the said Court, shall be full and conclusive Evidence of the Facts so reported in all Courts of Record within this Colony.

And be it further Enacted by the Authority aforesaid, That the Judge or Judges who shall make any such Appointment of Trustees, shall and is and are hereby required at the request of the Trustees thereby appointed or any one of them, to endorse on such Appointment an allowance that the same may be recorded; which allowance signed by the said judges or any one of them, if a Judge of the Supreme Court shall be a sufficient Warrant and Authority to the Secretary of this Colony, and all or any of the Clerks of the respective Cities or Counties within this Colony to record the same. And if such Judge be a Judge of an Inferior Court of Common Pleas, shall be a sufficient Warrant and Authority to the Clerk of the Court or County whereof he is a Judge to record the same. And any Appointment of Trustees under the Hand and Seal, or Hands and Seals of any Judge or Judges authorized to put this Act in Execution or the Record thereof duly made in the said Secretary's Office, or in the Office of the Clerk of any City or County of this Colony, shall be full and conclusive Proof in all Courts and Places within this Colony, That the Person or Persons against whose Estate or Effects such Warrant or Warrants issued was or were at the Time of issuing thereof, either absent, absconding or concealed Debtor or Debtors, within the meaning of this Act; And that the said Appointment and the Proceedings previous thereto were regular and according to the directions of this Act.

And Whereas the Affidavits or Affirmations of the Creditors, whereon Warrants of Attachment have issued against secreted or absconding Debtors by virtue of sundry Laws of this Colony relating to fraudulent and absconding Debtors, and the Warrants of Attachment issued as aforesaid, and the Sheriffs returns thereof and Inventories therewith returned, have usually remained with the Judge or Judges who issued the same, or one of them; And the Appointment of Trustees made in Pursuance thereof remained in the Hands of the Trustees appointed or one of them; And by reason of the decease of such Judges, and death or removal of such Trustees, are many Times lost or mislaid; By means whereof such Persons as have or may Purchase any Messuages, Lands, Tenements or Hereditaments which were of such absconding concealed or secreted Debtors from or under any Trustees for all the Creditors of any secreted concealed or absconding Person or Persons appointed as aforesaid may be disabled to make out their Rights and Titles to the same; And such Affidavits or Affirmations, Warrants of Attachment or Appointments of Trustees, in Case they can be found are not at present of record, or filed in any public Office of Records; which may be of evil Consequence to such Purchasers as aforesaid, or Persons claiming under them; for remedy whereof.

Be it Enacted by the Authority aforesaid, That any Judge or Judges who shall issue such Warrant or Warrants of Attachment as aforesaid pursuant to this Act, shall, and he or they is and are hereby required and directed, to cause the Affidavits or Affirmations, of the Creditor or Creditors made before him or them previous to the issuing of such Warrant or Warrants respectively, within Thirty Days after the taking of such Affidavit or Affirmation; And such Warrant or Warrants of Attachment as aforesaid, within Thirty Days after the return thereof by such Sheriff as shall return the same, together with the Sheriffs return thereof to be delivered into the Office of the Clerk of that Court, whereof he or they is or are Judge or Judges, which Clerk is hereby required and commanded to mark or cause them to be marked respectively, with the Day and Year on which each of them respectively shall be filed in his office, and to preserve the same amongst the Papers filed in such Office. And all Trustees hereafter to be appointed by Virtue of this Act, or the Survivors or Survivor of them who by virtue of such Appointment, shall sell and convey any Messuages, Lands, Tenements or Hereditaments shall cause such Appointment of Trustees to be duly proved or acknowledged and allowed so that the same may be recorded, and shall cause the same to be entered of Record either in the Secretary's Office of this Colony or in the Office of the Clerk of the City or County wherein such Messuages, Lands, Tenements or Hereditaments do lie; And every Appointment of Trustees for the Estate of any fraudulent or absconding or concealed Debtor heretofore made by any Judge or Judges of the Supreme Court, or any of the Inferior Courts of Common Pleas in this Colony or by the Mayor or Recorder of the City of New York; And every Appointment of Trustees hereafter to be made in Pursuance of this Act or the Record thereof made by such proper Officer as aforesaid, or an Office Copy thereof attested by any such proper Officer as aforesaid, in Case such Record should have perished by Fire or other Accident, together with a legal Title or Conveyance from such Trustees or any two of them, or the Survivors or Survivor of them, proved or to be proved in such due form as by Law required shall be a full, compleat and perfect Title for such Messuages, Lands, Tenements or Hereditaments to such Purchaser or Purchasers, his her or their Heirs and Assigns, against such absconding or concealed Debtor or Debtors, his her or their Heirs and Assigns and all other Persons claiming or to claim by from or under him her or them, by virtue of any Act, Deed, Matter or Thing after such first public Notice as aforesaid given. And all Sales and Conveyances of any Messuages, Lands, Tenements, or Herditaments heretofore bona fide sold and conveyed by any Trustees heretofore appointed by such Judge or Judges as aforesaid for the Management and Distribution of the Estate of any absconding or concealed Debtor or Debtors are hereby confirmed and declared to be valid and effectual to all Intents and Purposes to such Purchaser or Purchasers his her and their Heirs and Assigns against such absconding or concealed or absent Debtor or Debtors his her or their Heirs or Assigns or any Person claiming or to claim by from or under him her or them, by virtue of any Act, Deed, Matter or Thing after such first public Notice as aforesaid given.

Provided always, That such Purchaser or Purchasers his her or their Heirs or Assigns now are and have been for the space of three Years last past in the actual Possession of such Messuages, Lands, Tenements or Hereditaments.

And be it further Enacted by the Authority aforesaid, That such Trustees as shall hereafter be appointed by virtue of this Act, shall keep a regular Book, or regular Books of Account, of all such monies as shall come to their Hands, by reason or on Account of such their Appointment, to which Book or Books every Creditor interested in such monies or Estate, at all reasonable Times, may have recourse. And that such Trustees and each of them shall be Subject to such Orders and Directions for the more effectual puting this Act in Execution and finishing a Distribution of such Estate or Effects as may come to their Hands by virtue of such Appointment, as shall from Time to Time be made and given in the Court by the Judge or Judges whereof such Appointment of Trustees was made. And also that such Trustees shall render unto the Court by the Judge or Judges whereof they were appointed a just and true Account or Accounts in Writing upon Oath made in open Court, of their Proceedings and Accounts in the Premises by virtue of their Appointment, which shall be filed with the Clerk of the said Court for the satisfaction of all Persons concerned: And such Trustees of the Estate of any such absconding or concealed Person or Persons already appointed, or hereafter to be appointed, shall and may retain and keep in their Hands for the Trouble and Services to be by them performed the Sum of Five per Cent on the whole Sum which shall come into their Hands by Virtue of such Appointment before each Dividend made, over and above all necessary Disbursements in the Premises.

And be it further Enacted by the Authority aforesaid, That any Judge or Judges who have issued any Warrant or Warrants in Pursuance and by Virtue of any Act or Acts against fraudulent absconding or concealed Debtors may proceed thereon by Virtue of this Act; And that Trustees appointed by any of the said Acts may exercise all the Powers given by this Act to such Trustees and shall be Subject to such Rules, Orders and Regulations as in and by this Act are appointed.

And be it further Enacted by the Authority aforesaid, That if any Person or Persons shall be sued, for any Matter or Thing done in Pursuance or by virtue of this Act, it shall and may be lawful for him or them to plead the General Issue, and give the special Matter in Evidence. And also that this Act shall be beneficially construed for the Creditors in all Courts of Record within this Colony. And that the same shall continue and be in Force as to the Powers of Judges to grant such Warrants of Attachment, and exercise the Powers hereby given until the First Day of February which will be in the Year of our Lord one Thousand, seven Hundred and Eighty five and from thence to the End of the then next Session of the General Assembly of this Colony: But shall continue and be in full Force, as to the Power of every Court, Person and Trustees, that shall be appointed as aforesaid by virtue of this Act before its above Limitation, and have any Duty or thing thereby enjoined or required to be done until a full and final Settlement and Distribution shall be by them made and finished according to the true Intent and Meaning of this Act.

[CHAPTER 1732.]

An Act for the relief of insolvent Debtors within this Colony, with respect to the Imprisonment of their Persons.

[Passed, April 3, 1775.]

Whereas it has been represented to the General Assembly that the several Persons herein after named imprisoned in different Goals in this Colony are destitute of even the common Necessaries of Life, and it is conceived reasonable if their Creditors will not consent to their Enlargement or contribute to their Subsistence, that such Persons should be relieved by the Legislature, to this End,

Be it Enacted by his Honor the Lieutenant Governor, the Council and the General Assembly, and it is hereby enacted by the Authority of the same, That such of the Creditors of the following Persons, confined in the different Goals in this Colony, to wit, William Hedges and Jeremiah Hedges in the County of Suffolk; Jacobus Van Kleek, Thomas Palmer, Edward Simmonds, Jeremiah Jones, Isaac Finch, Frayer Ter Boss, Alexander Griggs, John Krankhyt, Justus Knap, Frederick Klein and Lewis Bogardus in Dutchess County; Isaac Wood in Richmond County; Isaac Van Valkenburg, John W. Wendell, Volkert Dawson, Dennis Sullivan, Jacob Barney, John R. Wendell, James Pearce, Sibastian Keezer, Samuel Loadman, Stephen Mason, Jonathan Washburn, John Wolf Reighly, and John Smith, in Albany County; Isaac Post in Orange County; Nathan Furman in Kings County; Hendrick Wemple in Tryon County; Thomas Vernon, Isaac Romyn, Thomas Lupton, Hendrick Bogert, John Osburn, Henry Burtsell, John Roberts, Oliver Loshier, Robert Welsh, Mauritz Gobel, John Delanoy, Abraham Wheeler, Samuel Hunt, Samuel Tanner Alexander Forbes, Abraham Klankhyt, Susannah Spencer, Mary Thompson, Sarah Church, & John Burrowe in the City of New York; Henry Coutant, John Anderson, Philip Richie, Henry Bancker, Isaac Jones, Abraham Yeomans, and Oliver Killock in West Chester County; William Brace in Cumberland County; and Henry Rosekrans Junior in Dutchess County who shall insist upon such their Debtors being detained under their respective Confinements shall within four Weeks after the first Publication of such Advertisements as are herein after directed agree by Writing under their Hands to pay and allow three Shillings and six Pence per Week unto the said Prisoners respectively, to be paid the Monday of every Week so long as he or she shall continue in Prison at his her or their Instance, and if such Agreement as aforesaid shall not be entered into, or if entered into not punctually complied with, and on failure of the Payment of such weekly Sum at any Time, such of the said Prisoners whose Creditor or Creditors shall not enter into such Agreement, or shall fail complying with it as aforesaid, shall be entitled to the Benefit of this Act, upon complying with the Terms and Conditions herein after imposed.

And be it further Enacted by the Authority aforesaid, That it shall and may be lawful for each and every of the abovenamed Persons to present a Petition to the Court out of which any Process against them respectively hath issued, and upon which they are imprisoned, or to any two of the Judges of such Court, certifying the Cause or Causes of his Imprisonment, and exhibiting an Account and Inventory of his whole real and personal Estate, and of the Securities relating to the same, which Petition with the said Account and Inventory shall be lodged with the Clerk of the said Court for the Inspection of the Creditors; and after such Petition presented and Account and Inventory filed, such Prisoners shall respectively publish Advertisements in one or more of the public News Papers of this Colony notifying their Creditors that they intend to apply to the said Court or to any two of the Judges thereof who shall attend, at a certain Day not less than four weeks from the Publication of such Advertisements respectively to be discharged according to the Prayer of his her or their said Petition, at which Day the said Court or the said two Judges may and are hereby required by Precept under their Hands and Seals directed to the Sheriff Goaler or Officer in whose Custody such Prisoner or Prisoners may be, to order the said Prisoner or Prisoners respectively to be brought up before such Court or such Judges, and unless it be made appear that such Provision as aforesaid hath been made for the Subsistence of the said Prisoner or Prisoners by his her or their Creditors respectively, the said Court or Judges may then respectively administer the following Oath or Affirmation to wit, "I, A B do solemnly swear or affirm that the Account by me filed in the Office of the Clerk of the Supreme Court (or in the Office of the Clerk of the County of .... naming the County, as the Case may be) is a just and true Account of all my Creditors, and the Monies owing to them respectively by me, to the best of my Knowledge and Remembrance; and that the Inventory and Account by me filed in the said Clerk's Office is a just and true Account of all my Estate real and personal both in Law and Equity, either in Possession Reversion or Remainder (the necessary wearing Apparel of myself and Wife and Children, and Family immediately under my Care excepted,) and I have not directly or indirectly sold leased assigned or otherwise disposed of, or made over, either in Trust for myself or otherwise except as set forth in the same Account and Inventory any Part of my Estate real or personal for my future Benefit, or in order to defraud my Creditors, and that none of my Creditors reside in Great Britain so help me God." Which Oath or Affirmation being taken, if the Truth thereof shall be denied or controverted by any of the Creditors, the said Court or Judges may appoint some further Day for hearing the Parties as well Debtors as Creditors, and upon such further hearing, may in their Discretion, either remand the said Debtor or proceed to their Discharge, as if no such further Hearing had been required; but if the said Oath or Affirmation shall not be controverted or denied, then the said Court or Judges may immediately order the Lands Goods and Effects contained in such Account and Inventory to be, by a short Indorsement on the back of such Petition executed by the Prisoner, assigned to the said Creditors, or to one or more of them, or to some other Person or Persons to be appointed by the said Court or Judges respectively, in trust for all the Creditors; and also for all Attornies, Sheriffs Goalers and other Officers with respect to their Fees, for which they shall come in as the Creditors of the Insolvent, abating pro rata, by which Assignment such Estate shall actually vest in and be taken in Possession by the said Trustee or Trustees according to the Purport of such Assignment, and shall be divided by the Assignees from Time to Time among all the Creditors in Proportion, after six Months previous Notice published in one of the Public News Papers of this Colony of such Assignment, and requiring all the Creditors to send in their Demands, and if any Part thereof is in Possession of any other

Person or Persons, the same shall be recoverable in the Name or Names of such Trustee or Trustees who are hereby fully authorized to dispose of, and execute good and sufficient Deeds for the same, or any Part thereof; and to divide and distribute as well the Monies thence arising, as such other Monies which shall come into their Hands by virtue of this Act, among the Creditors of the said Debtors respectively, and the Officers aforesaid to whom any Fees may be due, in proportion to their respective Debts or Demands, according to the true Intent and Meaning of this Act, to which no Release from the Insolvent shall be any Bar; and immediately upon such Assignment being made, the said Prisoner or Prisoners shall by Order of the said Court or Judges be discharged out of Custody: And such Order shall be a sufficient Warrant to the Sheriff Goaler or Keeper of such Prisoner to discharge such Prisoner or Prisoners, if detained for no other Cause or Causes than those mentioned in such his or their Petition, and he is required forthwith to discharge and set him or them at Liberty without Fee; and upon such Discharge the said Debtors shall be finally released from all Debts contracted and all Judgments obtained, before that Time, and shall not be liable to be sued or arrested, or to have their Lands or Tenements, Goods or Chattels, seized by virtue, or in Consequence thereof, and every Person who shall be convicted of wilful false-swearing in any Matter or Article contained in the said Oath, he or she shall be guilty of Felony and suffer the Pains of Death without Benefit of Clergy.

Provided nevertheless and be it also enacted by the same Authority, That if any or either of the said Insolvent Persons other than such as are confined in the Goal of the City and County of New York, shall be imprisoned by virtue of Process of the Supreme Court it shall be lawful for such Persons respectively to take such Oath or Affirmation as aforesaid before any one of the Judges of the Inferior Court of Common Pleas of the County in which they are respectively imprisoned, and such Oath or Affirmation being subscribed by such Debtor and certified by such Judge to transmit to the said Judges of the Supreme Court at the Day mentioned in such Advertisement for the Purpose aforesaid, and on such Day such Judges of the Supreme Court may proceed to issue their Order or Warrant commanding the Sheriff in whose Custody such Insolvent Debtor may be to discharge such Debtor immediately after he shall have executed such Assignment as by this Act is directed in the Presence of two Witnesses of whom the said Sheriff or one of his Deputies shall be one.

And be it further Enacted by the Authority aforesaid, That if any of the said Debtors shall be sued for any Debts accrued before the passing of this Act, or if any Judge or other Officer shall be sued for any Thing done in pursuance, and under the Authority of this Act, such Defendant may plead the general Issue, and give this Act and the special Matter in Evidence, Provided, That this Act shall not extend to discharge any Person who shall stand committed at the Suit of the Crown, And provided also That this Act shall not be construed to affect any Creditor or Creditors residing in Great Britain, any Thing herein contained to the contrary notwithstanding.

And Whereas the said Henry Rosekrans Junior did heretofore hold and exercise the Office of High Sheriff in and for the County of Dutchess, during which Time sundry Escapes as hath been aledged happened by Means or through the Default of Persons acting under him as Deputies Goalers or Bailiffs in the said Office, And Whereas such Persons may also be liable in other Respects for Matters arising in the Execution of such their Office. Be it therefore provided and enacted, and it is hereby enacted by the Authority aforesaid, That Nothing herein contained shall in any Wise or Manner or by any Construction whatsoever be deemed or held to discharge or release the said Persons so having acted as Deputies, Under Sheriffs, Goalers and Bailiffs to the said Sheriff as aforesaid or any of them, from any Cause Action or Remedy to which they may be liable for or by reason of any Matter or Thing whatsoever, by them or any of them done suffered or permitted in such their Office of Deputy or Under Sheriff, Goalers and Bailiffs as aforesaid, but that all such Person or Persons who before the passing of this Act may have been intitled by Law to any Suit Action Claim or Demand against such Deputies, Under Sheriffs, Goalers or Bailiffs or any of them shall or may, in all respects whatsoever, sue, prosecute and maintain the same in such Manner and Form to all Intents and Purposes as if this Act had never been passed, or as if the said Henry Rosekrans had not been named or mentioned therein, any Thing therein contained to the contrary thereof in any wise notwithstanding.

And be it further also enacted and it is hereby enacted by the Authority aforesaid, That in all Cases whatsoever, wherein the said Henry Rosekrans Junior before the passing of this Act was by Law liable to any Person or Persons for or on Account or by Reason or Means of any Matter or Thing whatsoever done committed suffered or neglected by the said Persons so having acted as the

Deputy or Under Sheriffs or Goalers of the said Henry Rosekrans Junior as aforesaid or any of them, and wherein also upon any Suit Judgment and Recovery against him the said Henry Rosekrans Junior (for or by reason of any such Matters or Things so done committed suffered or neglected by his said Deputies Under Sheriffs, Goalers or Bailiffs as aforesaid, he the said Henry Rosekrans Junior) would have been intitled by Law to any Action Suit or Remedy against such Deputies Under Sheriffs Goalers and Bailiffs or any of them or against their or any of their Securities; that in all such Cases it shall and may be lawful to and for all such Person or Persons having any Claim Demand or Cause of Action for or by Reason of the Premises to sue and prosecute such Action or Actions in the Names of the Trustees of the Estate of the said Henry Rosekrans Junior to be appointed in Virtue of this Act against such Deputies Under Sheriffs, Goalers and Bailiffs or any of them, or their or any of their Securities, as he the said Henry Rosekrans Junior might have sued maintained and prosecuted against them or any of them respectively if any Judgment and Recovery had been obtained against him for or by Reason of any such Matters and Things aforesaid before the passing of this Act; In which said Suits so to be commenced as aforesaid, it shall not be necessary for the Plaintiffs to alledge or prove that any Judgment or Recovery was had or obtained against the said Henry Rosekrans Junior or that the Monies thereby demanded had been paid by him.

Provided nevertheless That in such Suits as aforesaid the said Trustees shall not be liable to pay any Costs, but all such Costs which by Law would have been chargeable on the Plaintiffs, shall be paid by the Person or Persons for whose Benefit such Suits respectively shall be prosecuted as aforesaid, and Provided also that no such Suit or Action shall be discontinued or stayed by the said Trustees.

And be it further Enacted by the Authority aforesaid, That this Act and also one other Act made and passed this present Session of the General Assembly entitled "An Act for the Relief of Insolvent Debtors within this Colony," shall be deemed and construed as Public Laws, and as such shall be pleaded and taken Notice of in all and every the Courts within this Colony. And that all such of the abovenamed persons as may not be actually in a a common Goal in this Colony, but nevertheless in Custody of the Sheriff, or under an Arrest, shall be and hereby are declared intitled to the Benefit of this Act, as fully as if they were in actual Confinement.

[CHAPTER 1733.]

An Act for the Relief of Insolvent Debtors within this Colony.

[Passed, April 3, 1775.]

Be it Enacted by his Honor the Lieutenant Governor, the Council and the General Assembly, and it is hereby Enacted by the Authority of the same, That the following Persons Insolvent Debtors within this Colony, to wit Daniel Jones in the County of Suffolk, Arent Wemple, William Shadacker, Michael Losk, John Cole, Philip I. Bovee, Jacob Hilton, Jan Johannes Van Hoesen and Samuel Rose in the County of Albany, Gilbert Tice in the County of Tryon, Herman Courter, John Lewis, John Calder, John Gallaudet, Philip Simon, John Smallhood, Charles Gilmore, William Welsh, John Bergen, John Campbell, Joseph Maerschalk, Abraham Ferdon, Azor Betts, William Spotten, James Wilmot and Alexander McLean in the City of New York, Joseph Teed Junior and William Brown in the County of Westchester, John Pike in the County of Cumberland, and Thomas Hallett in the County of Queens shall and may and are hereby allowed to take the Benefit of the several Acts continued by an Act entitled, "An Act to continue the several Acts therein mentioned respecting the Relief of Insolvent Debtors." passed the Nineteenth Day of December one thousand seven hundred and sixty six, and which are expired by their own Limitation as fully and effectually as if the said Acts respecting the Relief of Insolvent Debtors were now in actual and full Force.

Provided nevertheless, And be it Enacted, by the same Authority, That all such Oaths as by the said revived Acts, or any of them are required to be taken by the Insolvent Debtors or their Creditors being two or more Judges may be taken before one Judge only, and that with Respect to such of the said several above named Insolvent Debtors, who may have been Arrested by Process out of the Supreme Court of this Colony (other than such as are confined in the Goal of the City and County of New York,) it shall be lawful for the said Insolvent Debtors, and for any or either of the Creditors respectively, to take such Oaths or Affirmations as are directed to be taken by the said Acts hereby revived, before one or more of the Judges of the inferior Courts of Common Pleas within this Colony instead of taking such Oaths or Affirmations before one or more of the Judges of the Supreme Court, as is required by the said revived Acts: Which Oaths or Affirmations such

Judges of the inferior Courts are hereby Authorized to Administer; And such Oaths or Affirmations respectively being reduced to Writing shall be Transmitted to the Justices of the Supreme Court, or any two of them, who may and shall proceed to the Discharge of such insolvent Debtors respectively, as if such Oaths or Affirmations had been taken before them or either of them; any Thing in the said hereby revived Acts to the contrary notwithstanding.

[CHAPTER 1734.]

[Expired, January 31, 1785.]

An Act to prevent the Exportation of unmerchantable Flour, and the false taring of Bread and Flour Casks.

[Passed, April 3, 1775.]

Whereas it is necessary that great Care be taken to preserve the Reputation of Flour, one of the Staple Commodities of this Colony,

Be it therefore Enacted by his Honor the Lieutenant Governor, the Council and the General Assembly, and it is hereby enacted by the Authority of the same, That every Bolter of Flour and Baker of Bread for exportation from the Colony of New York shall each one for himself provide and have a distinguishable Brand-Mark with the initial Letter of his Christian Name, and his Sirname at length, and shall therewith brand each and every Cask of Flour and Biscuit of his own bolting or baking for exportation from this Colony before the same be removed from the Place where the same shall be so bolted or baked under the Penalty of one Shilling for every Cask so removed and not branded as aforesaid.

And be it further Enacted by the Authority aforesaid, That all Wheat Flour bolted for exportation as aforesaid, shall by the Bolter thereof be made Merchantable and of due fineness, and honestly and well packed in good strong Casks well made, and of Staves well seasoned with the Tare of the Cask marked thereon, and each and every Cask thereof shall be well hooped with ten Hoops at least, three of which to be on each Head; and shall be well and sufficiently nailed before the same shall be removed or carried from the Place where the same shall be packed as aforesaid, and every Bolter offending in all or any of the Premises shall forfeit and pay for every such Offence the Sum of one Shilling for every Cask.

And be it further Enacted by the Authority aforesaid, That if any Person or Persons shall put a false or wrong Tare on any Cask of Flour or Bread to the Disadvantage of the Purchaser, he she or they, shall forfeit and pay for every Cask falsely tared as aforesaid the Sum of five Shillings to the Inspector or other Person discovering the same.

And be it further Enacted by the Authority aforesaid, That no Flour shall be shipped for Exportation out of this Colony before the same Flour shall have been submitted to the View and Examination, and been inspected and approved by one, of the Inspectors herein after named or by virtue of this Act to be appointed, who shall bore the Head of each Barrel or Cask, and pierce the same through with an Instrument contrived for that Purpose, and examine try and determine whether the same Flour is of due fineness, and whether it has not been injured by being ground too close, or by some other means, so as to prevent its rising properly and making light Bread, and also whether it be honestly and truly packed, and shall then plug up the Hole, and if the said Inspector shall judge the same Flour to be merchantable and of due fineness, and that the same has not been injured in the Manufacturing or wet or otherwise damaged and that the same is honestly and well packed in such Casks, so made marked and branded as aforesaid then and not otherwise he shall brand every such Cask of Flour on the Quarter in a fair and distinguishable Manner with the Colony Arms and the initial Letters of his Name and Sirname if such Flour is manufactured in this Colony, and if the same is manufactured in any other Colony, he shall likewise brand on each Cask under the Colony Arms, the Name of the Colony where the same Flour is manufactured, for which Trouble the said Inspector who performs the Service shall receive of the Purchaser one Penny per Cask and no more, and the said Inspectors are hereby strictly charged not to brand any Cask of Flour for Exportation although the Flour should be of due fineness, unless it shall appear to them that the same Flour has not been injured in the manufacturing and that it is really Merchantable, nor unless the same be honestly and well packed in good strong Casks well made, and of Staves well seasoned, and hooped and branded in the Manner herein before directed, and the Tare marked on each Cask.

Provided always and be it further enacted by the Authority

aforesaid, That if any Dispute shall arise between the said Inspectors or any or either of them and the Possessor of any Flour concerning the fineness or goodness thereof, on application to the Mayor Recorder or any one of the Aldermen of the Cities of New York or Albany, or to any Justice of the Peace in the County where such Dispute shall happen, he shall and is hereby required to issue his Warrant to three indifferent judicious Persons of Skill and Integrity to view and examine the said Flour one of them to be named by the Possessor of such Flour, one other of them to be named by the said Inspector, and the third by the said Magistrate, which three Persons shall be duly sworn by the said Magistrate carefully to examine the said Flour and make report to the said Magistrate forthwith, how they find the same, and the said Magistrate is hereby impowered and required to give Judgment agreeable to the Report of the Persons so named or to the Report of any two of them, and in Case the said Flour is judged not fit to be exported, the said Inspector shall not brand the same, nor shall any Person or Persons ship the same for Exportation on Pain of forfeiting the same: And the said Magistrate shall also award and order the Owner or Possessor of the said Flour to pay the said Inspector one Penny for each Cask of all such Flour as shall be judged not fit for Exportation as aforesaid with reasonable Costs and Charges, and the said Inspector shall and may recover the said Allowance, Costs and Charges from the Owner or Possessor of the said Flour in the same Manner as Debts of five Pounds and under are or may be recovered in this Colony; but in Case the said Flour upon such Trial shall be found good and merchantable then the Charges of such Trial shall be paid by the Inspector or Purchaser at whose request such Trial is had, and to be recovered in the Manner aforesaid.

And be it further Enacted by the same Authority, That if any Flour upon Inspection is adjudged by the Officer inspecting the same to be unfit for Exportation, and the Owner or Possessor thereof acquiesces in such Judgment, he shall pay the Inspector one Penny per Cask for every Cask so rejected.

And be it further Enacted by the Authority aforesaid, That no Flour whatsoever not branded as aforesaid by one of the said Inspectors as and for good and merchantable Flour shall be shipped for Exportation out of this Colony under the Penalty of the Forfeiture and Loss of all such Flour so shipped, one half Part thereof to be paid to the Treasurer of this Colony for the Time being, to be applied for and towards the Support of the Government thereof, and the other half Part thereof to such Person as shall inform or sue for the same in any Court of Record in this Colony by Bill Information, Plaint or other Action, wherein no Essoin Protection or Wager of Law shall be allowed.

And be it further Enacted by the same Authority, That if any Person shall export out of this Colony any Flour not inspected and branded as aforesaid by one of the said Inspectors, such Exporter and the Master of such Vessel carrying such uninspected and unbranded Flour out of this Colony shall upon Conviction of such Offence in any Court of Record in this Colony severally forfeit the Sum of forty Shillings for every such Cask so exported or carried out of this Colony to be recovered in the Manner directed in the preceding Clause of this Act, the whole of which Fine and Forfeiture shall go to the Person prosecuting for the same, any Thing in this Act to the contrary notwithstanding.

And be it further Enacted by the Authority aforesaid, That the said Inspectors and each and every of them shall have full Power and Authority by virtue of this Act, and without any further or other Warrant to enter on board any Vessel whatsoever in the Harbours of the City of New York, Albany, or in any of the Counties herein after mentioned, to search for and make Discovery of any Flour shipped or shipping on Board any such Vessel for Exportation immediately from thence out of this Colony, and if the said Inspectors or any or either of them shall on such Search discover any Cask or Casks of Flour not branded as before directed the Person or Persons so shipping the same shall forfeit all and every such Cask or Casks of Flour so shipped or shipping and not branded in the Manner before directed, and the Master or Commander of such Vessel who shall knowingly receive any such Cask or Casks of Flour not branded as aforesaid shall forfeit and pay for each cask so received on Board his Vessel the Sum of ten Shillings, and if any person shall obstruct or hinder the said Inspectors or any or either of them in making such search as aforesaid, every Person so offending shall forfeit and pay the Sum of fifty Pounds.

And be it further Enacted by the Authority aforesaid, That all Flour purchased for Exportation shall be inspected in the Manner aforesaid at or after the Time the same shall be so purchased for Exportation, and if any Purchaser of Flour for Exportation shall not have the same inspected as aforesaid, at or after the Time of such Purchase, such Purchaser shall forfeit and pay for every such Cask of Flour the Sum of ten Shillings although the said Flour may have been inspected and branded at any Time before the said Purchase.

And be it further Enacted by the Authority aforesaid, That if any dispute shall arise between the Owner or Possessor of any Flour offered to be inspected and the Inspector or Inspectors, concerning the Place where such Flour offered for Inspection was manufactured, the Owner or Possessor thereof shall prove by himself or one credible Witness upon Oath or Affirmation before any Justice of the Peace to the best of his knowledge & belief where such Flour was manufactured or made.

And be it further Enacted by the Authority aforesaid, That no Inspector of Flour shall brand or mark as inspected any Cask of Flour wherever manufactured unless the initial Letter of the Christian Name and the Sirname at length of the Manufacturer be first branded thereon.

And be it further Enacted by the Authority aforesaid, That Francis Marschalk and Coenrad W. Ham, shall be and hereby are appointed Inspectors of all Flour intended to be shipped for Exportation directly from the Port of New York, and they shall once in every three Months account to each other, and divide the Allowance provided by this Act for their Trouble for inspecting the said Flour equally between them and shall each of them do as near as may be an equal Share of the Duty required of them by this Act, and if either of the said Inspectors hereby appointed for the City of New York shall become incapable or neglect to execute his Office or die, then and in either of those Cases it shall and may be lawful to and for the Mayor, Aldermen and Commonalty of the City of New York, or the Majort Part of them to enquire into the same, and if it shall appear to them that either of the said Inspectors is rendered incapable or doth neglect to execute his Office or is dead, that then and in either of these cases, they are to appoint another fit Person in his stead and such other so by them to be appointed shall have the same Powers, be under the same Restrictions, and take the like Oath as the Inspectors for the City of New York, are by this Act directed to take, but before the said Inspectors hereby or hereafter to be appointed for the City of New York shall do any Thing in the Execution of their said Office, they shall respectively take an Oath or if one of the People called Quakers an Affirmation before the Mayor or Recorder or one of the Aldermen of the City of New York in the Words following to wit: "I, A B. do swear or Affirm, that I will faithfully truly and impartially according to the best of my

Judgment Skill and Understanding execute do and perform the Office and Duty of an Inspector and Examiner of Flour according to the true Intent and Meaning of an Act entitled, An Act to prevent the Exportation of unmerchantable Flour, and the false taring of Bread and Flour Casks and that I will account with the Person appointed with me, or to be appointed as Inspector in the City of New York once in every three Months for the Allowance provided by the said Act for the Trouble of inspecting Flour and pay to him his Proportion thereof, so help me God."

And be it further Enacted by the same Authority, That the Proprietor or Proprietors of any Flour inspected in the City and County of Albany, or in any of the Counties of this Colony, as by this Act is directed, shall and may ship the same directly out of this Colony from the Place where the same was inspected without being obliged to have the same reinspected.

Provided always, That Nothing in this Act contained shall be construed to prevent the Exportation of Cornel, Midling or Ship Stuff, provided the same be marked as such.

And be it further Enacted by the Authority aforesaid, That John Roseboom, Peter Vosburgh, and John A. Van Alen shall be and are hereby appointed Inspectors of Flour in the City and County of Albany; And that Zacharias Van Vorhees, Peter P. Van Kleek and William Radliff shall be and hereby are appointed Inspectors of Flour in the County of Dutchess, and that Peter Mercereau shall be and hereby is appointed Inspector of Flour in the County of Richmond, and that Israel Seaman, Gilbert Bloomer and Joseph Travis shall be and hereby are appointed Inspectors of Flour for the County of West Chester, and that Lawrence Van Gaasbeek, Edward Hallock and John Nicholson shall be and hereby are appointed Inspectors of Flour for the County of Ulster; And that James Peters and Roeloff Van houton shall be and hereby are appointed Inspectors of Flour for the County of Orange; and that such Person or Persons in the Counties of Suffolk and Queens as shall be appointed by a Majority of the Justices of the Peace in the respective Towns of the said Counties of Suffolk and Queens shall be the Inspectors of Flour in the said Counties.

And be it further Enacted by the Authority aforesaid, That in Case either of the Inspectors by this Act appointed or to be appointed shall become incapable or neglect to execute his Office or die, that then and in either of these Cases, it shall and may be lawful to and for the Justices of the Peace or the majority of them met in general or special Sessions for the said City and

County of Albany, and the aforementioned Counties severally, other or others in the Stead of such Person or Persons so becoming incapable, neglecting Duty or dying to appoint, and the Inspectors so by them appointed shall have the same Powers, be under the same Restrictions, and take the like Oath as the Inspectors by this Act appointed or to be appointed are required to take.

And be it further Enacted by the same Authority, That the Inspectors by this Act appointed or to be appointed, shall each of them provide himself with a Brand-Mark in addition to those they are already by this Act required to have to brand the Word Superfine, and they and each of them are hereby required and directed to brand the Word Superfine on all such Casks as they shall have inspected, and which they shall judge to be superfine Flour and no other: And each of the said Inspectors shall if they find any Cask of Flour marked by the Proprietor or Manufacturer with the Word Superfine and which upon Inspection they shall find not to be superfine erase or cut out said Mark.

And be it further Enacted by the same Authority, That the Inspector or Inspectors hereby appointed or to be appointed for the said City and County of Albany, and the said other Counties shall before they do any Thing in the Execution of their said Office respectively take an Oath, or if one of the People called Quakers an Affirmation before one of the Judges of the Inferior Court of Common Pleas for the County for which they are respectively appointed Inspectors in the Words following, to wit: "I, A B. do swear, or Affirm, that I will faithfully truly and impartially according to the best of my Judgment Skill and Understanding, execute do and perform the Office and Duty of an Inspector and Examiner of Flour, according to the true Intent and Meaning of an Act entitled, An Act to prevent the Exportation of unmerchantable Flour, and the false taring of Bread and Flour Casks, and that I will brand every Cask of Flour by me inspected, with the Name of the County where manufactured, and with such other Marks as by the said Act are directed to be put on the same, so help me God."

And be it further Enacted by the Authority aforesaid, That no Inspector of Flour hereby appointed or hereafter to be appointed shall purchase any Flour by them respectively condemned, nor any Flour whatsoever other than for their own particular and private use under the Penalty of fifty Pounds to be recovered by Action of Debt Bill Plaint or Information by any Person or Persons who will sue for the same in any Court of Record in this Colony; the one half thereof to the Use of the Person or Persons so suing; the other half Part thereof to be paid to the Treasurer of this Colony, for and towards the Support of the Government thereof.

And be it further Enacted by the Authority aforesaid, That if any Inspector of Flour not then actually employed in the Examination of Flour according to the Powers and Authorities given by this Act, shall on Application to him made to examine and inspect any Flour as aforesaid refuse neglect or delay to proceed to such Examination for the Space of three Hours after such Application so made, every Inspector so refusing neglecting or delaying to make such Examination and Inspection, shall for each Offence forfeit and pay the Sum of twenty Shillings to the Use of the Person or Persons so delayed.

And be it further Enacted by the Authority aforesaid, That if any Person or Persons shall counterfeit any of the aforesaid Brand Marks, whether Provincial or Private, he she or they shall forfeit and pay for every Offence the Sum of one hundred Pounds.

And be it further Enacted by the Authority aforesaid, That if any Person or Persons shall empty any Cask of Flour inspected and branded as aforesaid, in order to put in other Flour for Sale or Exportation, or shall put any Flour for Sale or Exportation into any Cask so branded as aforesaid without cutting out the said Brand-Marks, every Person so offending shall forfeit and pay the Sum of one hundred Pounds.

And be it further Enacted by the Authority aforesaid, That the said Inspectors hereby appointed or to be appointed, and every or either of them shall be and hereby are authorized impowered and directed to sue for all Fines and Forfeitures mentioned in this Act except such as are herein otherwise applied, and except their own Forfeitures; which Fines and Forfeitures not exceeding five Pounds shall be recovered in the same Manner as other Debts of five Pounds and under by the Laws of this Colony are recoverable; and such as exceed five Pounds, shall and may be sued for and recovered in any Court of Record in this Colony by Bill Plaint or Information, wherein no Essoin Protection or Wager of Law, or any more than one Imparlance shall be allowed: the one half of all which said Fines and Forfeitures when recovered shall be paid to the Treasurer of this Colony towards the support of the Government thereof, and the other half thereof shall be to the Use of the Inspector or Inspectors that shall sue for and recover the same.

And be it further Enacted by the Authority aforesaid, That this

Act shall be and continue in force from the passing thereof until the first Day of February one thousand seven hundred and eighty five, and from thence to the End of the then next Session of the General Assembly.

[CHAPTER 1735.]

[See chapter 1557.]

An Act to confirm the Proceedings of the Commissioners heretofore appointed by a Law of this Colony to settle the Line or Lines of Division between the City of New York and the Township of Haerlem, and for establishing the Boundary between the said City and Township.

[Passed, April 3, 1775.]

Whereas in and by a certain Act of the Legislature of this Colony made and passed on the twenty-fourth Day of March in the Year of our Lord one thousand seven hundred and seventy two, and confirmed by his present Majesty in Privy Council on the twenty eighth Day of July following entitled, "An Act to settle and establish the Line or Lines of Division between the City of New York and Township of Haerlem so far as concern the Right of Soil in Controversy," certain Powers and Authorities are given and delegated to William Nicoll Esquire of Suffolk County, Thomas Hicks Esquire Attorney at Law of Queens County, and George Clinton Esquire of Ulster County, to agree, fix upon, settle and finally ascertain the boundary between the Township of Haerlem and the Lands granted to the Mayor Aldermen and Commonalty of the City of New York within the said City of New York, and when they should have agreed upon such Line or Lines of Division to cause the same to be surveyed run out and marked in the Presence of some of them and a Description thereof within one Month thereafter to be entered on Record in the Secretary's Office for the Province of New York, and that the same should for ever afterwards be and remain the Boundary and Division Line or Lines between the said Township of Haerlem and the Lands of the Mayor Aldermen and Commonalty of the City of New York (except as to such Lands as do lie between high and low Water-Mark in the City of New York to the Eastward and Northward of the said Division or Boundary Line or Lines,) And Whereas the said William Nicoll, Thomas Hicks and George

Clinton in Compliance with the said Act and according to the Mode in the said Act directed, having for this Purpose met and fully heard the Parties and considered the Allegations and Proofs relative to the said Controversy so to them submitted between the said City of New York and Township of Haerlem, did unanimously declare settle, ascertain, fix upon, adjudge, award, and determine that the Lines of Division between the Lands of the Mayor Aldermen and Commonalty of the said City of New York and the Township of Haerlem are and should be forever thereafter as follow to wit, Beginning at a Bass Wood Stump from whence grow several Cyons, being on a certain Point on the East Side of Hudson's River on the South Side of the Bay lying before a certain Piece of Meadow commonly known by the Name of the round Meadow or Mutje David's Fly, from which Stump the South End of Jacob Vreelandt's House on the West Side of the said River bears North eighty five Degrees West, the South Side of Stephen Bourdett's House North four Degrees and fifteen Minutes West; the South Side of Samuel Prince's House North fifty three Degrees and fifteen Minutes West, and the large Bluff Point on the West Side of the said River North nineteen Degrees East; and from thence running South one Degree and thirty Minutes East one hundred and ten Chains and eighty Links, to a Heap of Stones on the South West Side of a large flat Rock, from whence a large White Wood Tree bears North sixty seven Degrees West distant sixty seven Links, and from thence running North fifty six Degrees West four Chains and seventy Links to a red Cedar Stake with a Heap of Stones about it, thence South thirty five Degrees West fifty one Chains and twenty nine Links to a small Pepperage Tree marked with a Blaze and three Notches on three Sides standing four Chains from the Bloomingdale new cross Road measured on a Course from the Tree South thirty five Degrees West, and from the West Bank of Hudson's River fifty seven Chains and seventy five Links measured on a Course from the said Tree North fifty six Degrees West; and from thence running with a direct Line on a Course South eighteen Degrees East one hundred and twenty Chains to an ancient Heap of Stones on the East Side of a Brook, which Stones are said to have been the Foundation of a Saw Mill mentioned in a Patent from Richard Nicoll Esquire formerly Governor of the Colony of New York to the Township of Haerlem, and from thence along the said Brook as it now runs to the East River, the Distance from the said Heap of Stones to where the said Brook empties into the East

River between a Ledge of Rocks being thirteen Chains on a Course of South fifty five Degrees and thirty Minutes East, all which said Courses and Bearings were run and taken as the magnetic Needle then Pointed, and the said Lines of Division being unanimously agreed on by the said Commissioners, were surveyed run out and marked by Francis Marschalk, by the Desire and in the Presence of the said Commissioners, And whereas for the Prevention of all Doubts that may arise concerning the Operation and Effect of the said Lines of Division so fixed upon run out and marked as aforesaid and for a full Confirmation of the Proceedings of the said Commissioners as well the said Mayor Aldermen and Commonalty of the City of New York, as the Committee appointed in behalf of the Township of Haerlem have prayed that an Act of the Legislature of this Colony be passed for this Purpose,

Be it therefore Enacted by his Honor the Lieutenant Governor the Council and the General Assembly, and it is hereby enacted by the Authority of the same That the said Lines of Division so settled ascertained fixed upon and adjudged, and above particularly mentioned and described are and shall forever hereafter be and remain the Boundary and Division Lines between the Lands of the Mayor Aldermen and Commonalty of the City of New York and Township of Haerlem, and that the said Lines of Division so fixed upon run out and marked as the Boundary between the said Lands of the Mayor Aldermen and Commonalty of the City of New York and Township of Haerlem shall be and operate as a total Extinguishment of all the Right Title Interest Claim or Pretences of Claim whatsoever of the Township of Haerlem, and of all and every other Person and Persons whatsoever claiming or to claim under the said Township of Haerlem of in and to all and singular and every the Lands Common of Pasture, Tenements, Hereditaments Appurtenances and Advantages whatsoever which shall lie to the Southward and Westward of such Division Lines: and shall also at the same Time operate as a total Extinguishment of all the Right Title Interest Claim or Pretences of Claim whatsoever of the Mayor Aldermen and Commonalty of the City of New York and of all and every Person or Persons claiming under the said Mayor Aldermen and Commonalty of the City of New York of in and to all the Lands Tenements Hereditaments and Appurtenances whatsoever which shall lie to the Eastward and Northward of the said Division or Boundary Lines (the Lands lying and being between Low and high Water-Mark within the City of New York to the Eastward and Northward of the said Division or Boundary Line or Lines only excepted.)

Provided always and be it further Enacted, That the Settlement and Establishment of the said Boundary Line or Lines or any Matter or Thing touching the same shall not operate or be construed to lessen diminish or affect the Bounds Limits and Extent of the said City of New York in point of Jurisdiction, or to alter abrogate or defeat any of the Powers, Pre-eminences Privileges or Immunities over or in respect of the said Township of Haerlem which are vested in or have ever lawfully been or may be claimed and exercised by the said Mayor Aldermen and Commonalty of the City of New York in virtue of the respective Royal Charters to them given and granted.

Provided also, That Nothing in this Act shall be construed to extend to or affect the Right Title Interest Claim or Demand of any Person or Persons holding Lands under any other Grant from the Crown, or who have been in quiet and peaceable Possession for sixty Years or upwards, but that the same shall be and remain in the same State and situation as they were before the passing of this Act, any thing in the said Act contained to the contrary in any wise notwithstanding.

And be it also Enacted by the Authority aforesaid, That the Committee on the Part of the Township of Haerlem or the major Part of them shall have full Power and Authority to sell and convey in fee Simple so much of the said Common Lands given to the said Township by the said Award as shall be necessary to defray their Part of the Expence attending the final Settlement of the said Controversy, any Law Usage or Custom to the contrary notwithstanding.

[CHAPTER 1736.]

An Act for admitting in Evidence an ancient Record of the Office of the Town Clerk for the City and County of New York of an Indenture of Release from Jacobus Kip and Henrica his Wife to Samuel Ver Planck and others and the several Indorsements thereon for certain Lands therein mentioned.

[Passed, April 3, 1775.]

Whereas in the infant Settlement of the Country it was usual to record in the Town Clerks Office of the City and County of New York Title Deeds for Lands and Tenements lying in other Counties, and altho' the Original Deeds were duly proved or acknowledged yet according to the Rules of Law, such Records thereof or the Exemplification or sworn Office Copy of the Record cannot be admitted in Evidence in Judicial Proceedings.

And Whereas in and by a certain Indenture made the Twenty sixth Day of March in the seventh Year of the Reign of our Sovereign Lord and Lady William and Mary of England, Scotland, France and Ireland King and Queen Defender of the Faith &c and in the Year of our Lord One Thousand six Hundred and Ninety five between Jacobus Kip of the City of New York Merchant and Henrica his wife of the one part and Samuel Ver Planck, Jacobus Ver Planck, Abraham Ver Planck and Guiliana Ver Planck Children of Gulian Ver Planck late of the said City Merchant deceased and former Husband of the said Henrica of the other part, reciting, That Whereas Thomas Dongan late Governor of the Province of New York by his certain Deed or Patent signed with his Hand and Sealed with the public Seal of the said Province bearing Date the Seventeenth Day of October in the Year of our Lord One Thousand six Hundred and Eighty five for the Considerations therein mentioned did grant ratify and confirm unto Francis Rombolts, Stevanis Van Cortland and the aforesaid Jacobus Kip All that Tract or Parcel of Land Scituate lying and being on the East side of Hudsons River at the North side of the high Lands Beginning from the South side of a Creek called the Fish Kill and by the Indians Mattoavoan and from thence Northward along the said Hudsons River five Hundred Rods beyond the great Wappings Kill called by the Indians Mawenawasigh being the Northerly Bounds and from thence into the Woods four Hours going or sixteen English Miles always keeping five Hundred Rodd distant from the North side of the said great Wappings Creek however it runs, as also from the said Fish Kill or Creek called Maneawan along the said Fish Creek into the Woods at the Foot of the said High Hills including all the Reed or low Lands and the South side of the said Creek with an Easterly Line four Hours going or sixteen English Miles into the Woods and from thence Northerly to the End of the four Hours going or the sixteen English Miles or a Line drawn at the North side of the five Hundred Rodd beyond the great Wappings Creek or Kill called Wawenawasigh And also all manner of Rivers Rivulets Runs, Streams with Liberty to make any Mill or Mills thereon, and all Feedings, Pastures, Woods, Underwoods, Trees, Waters, Water Courses, Ponds, Pools, Pits, Swamps, Moors, Marshes, Meadows, Easements, Profits and Commodities, Fishing, Fowling, Hunting,

Judgment Skill and Understanding execute do and perform the Office and Duty of an Inspector and Examiner of Flour according to the true Intent and Meaning of an Act entitled, An Act to prevent the Exportation of unmerchantable Flour, and the false taring of Bread and Flour Casks and that I will account with the Person appointed with me, or to be appointed as Inspector in the City of New York once in every three Months for the Allowance provided by the said Act for the Trouble of inspecting Flour and pay to him his Proportion thereof, so help me God."

And be it further Enacted by the same Authority, That the Proprietor or Proprietors of any Flour inspected in the City and County of Albany, or in any of the Counties of this Colony, as by this Act is directed, shall and may ship the same directly out of this Colony from the Place where the same was inspected without being obliged to have the same reinspected.

Provided always, That Nothing in this Act contained shall be construed to prevent the Exportation of Cornel, Midling or Ship Stuff, provided the same be marked as such.

And be it further Enacted by the Authority aforesaid, That John Roseboom, Peter Vosburgh, and John A. Van Alen shall be and are hereby appointed Inspectors of Flour in the City and County of Albany; And that Zacharias Van Vorhees, Peter P. Van Kleek and William Radliff shall be and hereby are appointed Inspectors of Flour in the County of Dutchess, and that Peter Mercereau shall be and hereby is appointed Inspector of Flour in the County of Richmond, and that Israel Seaman, Gilbert Bloomer and Joseph Travis shall be and hereby are appointed Inspectors of Flour for the County of West Chester, and that Lawrence Van Gaasbeek, Edward Hallock and John Nicholson shall be and hereby are appointed Inspectors of Flour for the County of Ulster; And that James Peters and Roeloff Van houton shall be and hereby are appointed Inspectors of Flour for the County of Orange; and that such Person or Persons in the Counties of Suffolk and Queens as shall be appointed by a Majority of the Justices of the Peace in the respective Towns of the said Counties of Suffolk and Queens shall be the Inspectors of Flour in the said Counties.

And be it further Enacted by the Authority aforesaid, That in Case either of the Inspectors by this Act appointed or to be appointed shall become incapable or neglect to execute his Office or die, that then and in either of these Cases, it shall and may be lawful to and for the Justices of the Peace or the majority of them met in general or special Sessions for the said City and

County of Albany, and the aforementioned Counties severally, other or others in the Stead of such Person or Persons so becoming incapable, neglecting Duty or dying to appoint, and the Inspectors so by them appointed shall have the same Powers, be under the same Restrictions, and take the like Oath as the Inspectors by this Act appointed or to be appointed are required to take.

And be it further Enacted by the same Authority, That the Inspectors by this Act appointed or to be appointed, shall each of them provide himself with a Brand-Mark in addition to those they are already by this Act required to have to brand the Word Superfine, and they and each of them are hereby required and directed to brand the Word Superfine on all such Casks as they shall have inspected, and which they shall judge to be superfine Flour and no other: And each of the said Inspectors shall if they find any Cask of Flour marked by the Proprietor or Manufacturer with the Word Superfine and which upon Inspection they shall find not to be superfine erase or cut out said Mark.

And be it further Enacted by the same Authority, That the Inspector or Inspectors hereby appointed or to be appointed for the said City and County of Albany, and the said other Counties shall before they do any Thing in the Execution of their said Office respectively take an Oath, or if one of the People called Quakers an Affirmation before one of the Judges of the Inferior Court of Common Pleas for the County for which they are respectively appointed Inspectors in the Words following, to wit: "I, A B. do swear, or Affirm, that I will faithfully truly and impartially according to the best of my Judgment Skill and Understanding, execute do and perform the Office and Duty of an Inspector and Examiner of Flour, according to the true Intent and Meaning of an Act entitled, An Act to prevent the Exportation of unmerchantable Flour, and the false taring of Bread and Flour Casks, and that I will brand every Cask of Flour by me inspected, with the Name of the County where manufactured, and with such other Marks as by the said Act are directed to be put on the same, so help me God."

And be it further Enacted by the Authority aforesaid, That no Inspector of Flour hereby appointed or hereafter to be appointed shall purchase any Flour by them respectively condemned, nor any Flour whatsoever other than for their own particular and private use under the Penalty of fifty Pounds to be recovered by Action of Debt Bill Plaint or Information by any Person or Persons who will sue for the same in any Court of Record in this Colony; the one half thereof to the Use of the Person or Persons so suing; the other half Part thereof to be paid to the Treasurer of this Colony, for and towards the Support of the Government thereof.

And be it further Enacted by the Authority aforesaid, That if any Inspector of Flour not then actually employed in the Examination of Flour according to the Powers and Authorities given by this Act, shall on Application to him made to examine and inspect any Flour as aforesaid refuse neglect or delay to proceed to such Examination for the Space of three Hours after such Application so made, every Inspector so refusing neglecting or delaying to make such Examination and Inspection, shall for each Offence forfeit and pay the Sum of twenty Shillings to the Use of the Person or Persons so delayed.

And be it further Enacted by the Authority aforesaid, That if any Person or Persons shall counterfeit any of the aforesaid Brand Marks, whether Provincial or Private, he she or they shall forfeit and pay for every Offence the Sum of one hundred Pounds.

And be it further Enacted by the Authority aforesaid, That if any Person or Persons shall empty any Cask of Flour inspected and branded as aforesaid, in order to put in other Flour for Sale or Exportation, or shall put any Flour for Sale or Exportation into any Cask so branded as aforesaid without cutting out the said Brand-Marks, every Person so offending shall forfeit and pay the Sum of one hundred Pounds.

And be it further Enacted by the Authority aforesaid, That the said Inspectors hereby appointed or to be appointed, and every or either of them shall be and hereby are authorized impowered and directed to sue for all Fines and Forfeitures mentioned in this Act except such as are herein otherwise applied, and except their own Forfeitures; which Fines and Forfeitures not exceeding five Pounds shall be recovered in the same Manner as other Debts of five Pounds and under by the Laws of this Colony are recoverable; and such as exceed five Pounds, shall and may be sued for and recovered in any Court of Record in this Colony by Bill Plaint or Information, wherein no Essoin Protection or Wager of Law, or any more than one Imparlance shall be allowed; the one half of all which said Fines and Forfeitures when recovered shall be paid to the Treasurer of this Colony towards the support of the Government thereof, and the other half thereof shall be to the Use of the Inspector or Inspectors that shall sue for and recover the same.

And be it further Enacted by the Authority aforesaid, That this

Act shall be and continue in force from the passing thereof until the first Day of February one thousand seven hundred and eighty five, and from thence to the End of the then next Session of the General Assembly.

[CHAPTER 1735.]

[See chapter 1557.]

An Act to confirm the Proceedings of the Commissioners heretofore appointed by a Law of this Colony to settle the Line or Lines of Division between the City of New York and the Township of Haerlem, and for establishing the Boundary between the said City and Township.

[Passed, April 3, 1775.]

Whereas in and by a certain Act of the Legislature of this Colony made and passed on the twenty-fourth Day of March in the Year of our Lord one thousand seven hundred and seventy two, and confirmed by his present Majesty in Privy Council on the twenty eighth Day of July following entitled, "An Act to settle and establish the Line or Lines of Division between the City of New York and Township of Haerlem so far as concern the Right of Soil in Controversy," certain Powers and Authorities are given and delegated to William Nicoll Esquire of Suffolk County, Thomas Hicks Esquire Attorney at Law of Queens County, and George Clinton Esquire of Ulster County, to agree, fix upon, settle and finally ascertain the boundary between the Township of Haerlem and the Lands granted to the Mayor Aldermen and Commonalty of the City of New York within the said City of New York, and when they should have agreed upon such Line or Lines of Division to cause the same to be surveyed run out and marked in the Presence of some of them and a Description thereof within one Month thereafter to be entered on Record in the Secretary's Office for the Province of New York, and that the same should for ever afterwards be and remain the Boundary and Division Line or Lines between the said Township of Haerlem and the Lands of the Mayor Aldermen and Commonalty of the City of New York (except as to such Lands as do lie between high and low Water-Mark in the City of New York to the Eastward and Northward of the said Division or Boundary Line or Lines,) And Whereas the said William Nicoll, Thomas Hicks and George

mencing of any such Action, Bill, Plaint, Information, Commission or other Suit or Proceeding as shall at any Time or Times hereafter be filed issued or commenced for recovering the same or in respect thereof as aforesaid.

Provided also, And be it further Enacted by the Authority aforesaid, That all and singular the said Manors, Lands, Tenements and Hereditaments shall at all Times hereafter be holden of his Majesty his Heirs and Successors and of other Person and Persons, Bodies Politic and Corporate, their Heirs and Successors respectively by the same Tenures, Services, Fee Farms, Chief Rents, Heriots, and other Duties to all Intents and Purposes as the same should or ought of Right to have been holden if the Estates, Rights and Interests established and made sure by this present Act had been, before the making of this Act, firm good and effectual in Law.

Saving to every Person and Persons, Bodies Politic and Corporate their Heirs and Successors (other than his most Excellent Majesty his Heirs and Successors, and other than all Patentees or Grantees of Concealments or defective Titles and all and every Person or Persons claiming from by or under them or any of them for or in respect or by Reason of any such Patents or Grants of Concealments or defective Titles) all such Rights, Title, Interest, Estate, Rents, Commons, Customs, Duties, Profits and other Claims and Demands whatsoever in, to, or out of the said Manors, Lands, Tenements or Hereditaments as they or any of them had or ought to have had before the making of this Act any Thing in this Act to the contrary notwithstanding.

Provided also, and be it Enacted by the Authority aforesaid, That where any Fee Farm Rent, or other Rent or Rents have been or shall be answered and actually paid to the Kings Majesty or to any his Predecessors, Heirs or Successors within the Space of Sixty Years next before any Action, Bill, Plaint, Information, Commission or other Suit or Proceeding shall at any Time or Times hereafter be filed issued or commenced for recovering the same or in respect thereof, out of any Manors, Lands, Tenements or Hereditaments of which Manors, Lands, Tenements or Hereditaments the Estates Rights or Interest being defective, are established and made sure by this present Act, that the Kings Majesty his Heirs and Successors shall from henceforth for ever have hold and enjoy the said Rents and Arrearage thereof in such Manner and Form, And as fully and amply as the same are or were enjoyed at any Time within the said Space of Sixty Years.

Provided always, And be it Enacted by the Authority aforesaid, That nothing in this Act contained shall extend or be prejudicial to the Right, Title or Claim of any Person or Persons in or to any Manors, Lands, Tenements or Hereditaments by virtue of or under any Grant or Grants, Letters Patent or Letters Patents, from any of his Majesty's Progenitors, Ancestors or Predecessors or by virtue of or under any Grant or Grants, Letters Patent, or Letters Patents, from his Majesty made or passed before the first Day of January one Thousand seven Hundred and Sixty-nine so as such Right, Title or Claim be prosecuted with Effect, by Bill, Plaint, Information or other Suit or Proceeding in some of his Majesty's Courts of Record within this Colony, within the Space of one Year from the Confirmation of this Act.

Provided always, And be it further Enacted by the Authority aforesaid, That nothing in this Act contained shall extend to any lands appropriated by Letters Patent or laid out for Highways, but the same shall be and remain for that Purpose any Thing in this Act contained to the contrary notwithstanding.

Provided always, And be it further Enacted, by the Authority aforesaid, That all his Majesty's Subjects in this Colony, holding or possessing Lands by virtue of this Act for the Term of Sixty Years or upwards shall be subject and liable to the usual Quit Rent.

Provided always And be it Enacted by the Authority aforesaid, That no putting in Charge nor standing in super, nor taking or Answering the Farm Rents, Revenues of Profits of any of the said Manors, Lands, Tenements or Hereditaments by Force, Colour or Pretext of any Letters Patent or Grants of Concealments or defective Titles, or of Manors, Lands, Tenements or Hereditaments out of Charge, or by Force, Colour or Pretext of any inquisitions, Presentments by or by Reason of any Commission or other Authority to find out Concealments, defective Titles, or Lands, Tenements or Hereditaments out of Charge shall be deemed construed or taken to be putting in Charge, standing in super, or taken or answering the Farm Rents, Revenues or Profits by or to his Majesty, or any of his Progenitors or Predecessors, Heirs or Successors, unless thereupon such Manors, Lands Tenements or Hereditaments have been or shall be, upon some Information or Suit on the Behalf of his Majesty or some of his Progenitors or Predecessors, Heirs or Successors upon a lawful Verdict given or to be given or demurrer in law adjudged, or upon a hearing Ordered or Decreed for his Majesty or some of his Progenitors or Predecessors, sustain or incur by Reason of such Articles Contracts and Agreements made and entered into by virtue of this Act as aforesaid.

[CHAPTER 1738.]

An Act for the General Quiet of his Majesty's Subjects in this Colony against all Pretences of Concealment whatsoever.

[Passed, April 3, 1775.]

Be it Enacted by his Honor the Lieutenant Governor the Council and the General Assembly, And it is hereby Enacted by the Authority of the same, That the Kings Majesty his Heirs or Successors shall not at any time hereafter sue, impeach, question or implead any Person or Persons, Bodies Politic or Corporate for or in any wise concerning any Manors, Lands, Tenements, Rents or Hereditaments whatsoever (other than Liberties or Franchises) or for or in any wise concerning the Revenues, Issues or Profits thereof, or make any Title, Claim, Challenge or Demand of in or to the same, or any of them by Reason of any Right or Title which hath not first accrued and grown or which shall not hereafter first accrue and grow within the Space of Sixty Years next before the filing issuing or commencing of every such Action, Bill, Plaint, Information, Commission or other Suit or Proceedings as shall at any Time or Times hereafter be filed, issued or commenced for recovering the same, or in respect thereof, unless his Majesty or some of his Progenitors, Predecessor or Ancestors, Heirs or Successors or some other Person or Persons, Bodies Politic or Corporate under whom his Majesty his Heirs and Successors any Thing hath or lawfully claimeth, or shall have or lawfully Claim, have or shall have been answered by Force and Virtue of any such Right or Title to the same, the Rents, Revenues, Issues or Profits thereof, or the Rents, Issues or Profits of any Honor, Manor, or other Hereditaments whereof the Premises in Question shall be Part or Parcel within the said space of Sixty Years, or that the same have or shall have been duly in charge to his Majesty, or some of his Progenitors, Predecessors or Ancestors, Heirs or Successors or have or shall have stood in super of Record within the said space of sixty Years: And that all and every Person or Persons, Bodies Politic and Corporate, their Heirs and Successors, and all claiming by from or under them, or any of them, for and according to their and every of their several Estates and Interests which they have or claim to have, or shall or may have or claim to have in the same respectively shall at all Times hereafter quietly and freely have hold and enjoy against his Majesty his Heirs and Successors claiming by any Title which hath not first accrued or grown, or which shall not hereafter first accrue or grow within the Space of Sixty Years all and singular Manors, Lands, Tenements, Rents, and Hereditaments whatsoever (except Liberties and Franchises) which he or they or his or their, or any of their Ancestors or Predecessors or those from by or under whom they do or shall claim have or shall have held or enjoyed or taken the Rents, Revenues, Issues or Profits thereof by the Space of Sixty Years next before the filing issuing or commencing of every such Action, Bill, Plaint, Information, Commission or other Suit or Proceeding as shall at any time or Times hereafter be filed issued or commenced for recovering the same, or in respect thereof, unless his Majesty or some of his Progenitors, Predecessors or Ancestors, Heirs or Successors, or some other Person or Persons, Bodies Politic or Corporate by from or under whom his Majesty his Heirs or Successors any Thing hath or lawfully claimeth, or shall have or lawfully claim in the said Manor, Lands, Tenements, Rents or Hereditaments by force of any Right or Title, have been or shall have been answered by Virtue of any such Right or Title, the Rents, Revenues Issues or other Profits thereof within the said Space of Sixty Years; or that the same have or shall have been duly in charge, or stood in super of Record as aforesaid within the said Space of Sixty Years: And furthermore that all and every Person or Persons, Bodies Politic and Corporate their Heirs and Successors and all claiming or to claim by from or under them or any of them, for and according to their and every of their several Estates and Interests which they have or claim, or shall or may have or claim respectively, shall for ever hereafter quietly and freely have hold and enjoy all such Manors, Lands, Tenements, Rents and Hereditaments (except Liberties and Franchises) as they now have claim or enjoy or hereafter shall or may have claim or enjoy, whereof his Majesty his Progenitors, Predecessors, or Ancestors; or whereof his Majesty his Heirs or Successors, or he or they by from or under whom his Majesty his Heirs or Successors, any Thing hath or lawfully claimeth or shall have or lawfully claim or some of them by Force of some Right or Title to the same have not or shall not have been answered by Virtue of such Right or Title, the Rents, Revenues, Issues or Profits thereof within the space of Sixty Years next before the filing issuing or commencing of every such Action, Bill, Plaint, Information, Commission or Other Suit or Proceeding as shall at any Time or Times hereafter be filed issued or commenced for recovering the same; or in respect thereof, nor the same have been nor shall have been duly in charge or stood in super of Record as aforesaid within the said Space of Sixty Years against all and every Person and Persons their Heirs and Assigns having claiming or pretending to have or who shall or may have claim or pretend to have any Estate, Right, Title, Interest, Claim or Demand whatsoever, of in or to the same by force or colour of any Letters Patents or Grants upon Suggestion of Concealment of wrongful detaining, or not being in charge, or defective Titles or by from or under any Patentees or Grantees or any Letters Patents or Grants upon Suggestion of concealment or wrongful detaining or not being in Charge or defective Titles of or for which said Manors, Lands, Tenements, Rents and Hereditaments or any of them no Verdict, Judgment, Decree, Judicial Order upon Hearing or Sentence of any Court now standing in force, hath been had or given or any such Verdict, Judgment, Decree, Judicial Order upon Hearing or Sentence of Court shall hereafter be had or given in any Action, Bill, Plaint or Information in any of his Majestys Courts of Record within this Colony, for or in the Name of the Kings Majesty or in any of his Ancestors, Progenitors, Predecessors, Heirs or Successors or for any of the said Patentees or Grantees or for their or any of their Heirs or Assigns within the Space of Sixty Years next before the filing issuing or commencing of every such Action, Bill, Plaint, Information, Commission, or other Suit or Proceeding as shall at any Time or Times hereafter be filed issued or commenced for recovering the same, or in respect thereof as aforesaid.

Provided always And be it Enacted, That where the Rents, Revenues, Issues or Profits of any Manors, Lands, Tenements or Hereditaments are or shall be in charge by, to, or with any Auditor or Auditors or other proper Officer or Officers of the Revenue such Rents, Revenues, Issues and Profits shall be held deemed and taken to be duly in charge within the Meaning and Intent of this Act, any Usage or Custom to the contrary notwithstanding.

Provided always, That this Act or any Thing therein contained, shall not extend to bar, impeach or hinder his Majesty his Heirs or Successors, of, for, or from any Manors, Tenements, Rents or Hereditaments whereof any Reversion or Remainder now is in his Majesty for or concerning the Reversion or Remainder, nor of, for or from any Reversion or Remainder or possibility of Reversion or Remainder in any of his Majestys Progenitors or Predecessors or Ancestors which by the Expiration, End or other

which Assessors so chosen in each of the Districts aforesaid, and before they enter on the Duties of their Office shall take an Oath before any one of his Majesty's Justices of the Peace for the said County in the Words following to wit, " I A B, do solemnly swear that I will well and truly, equally and impartially according to the best of my Skill Knowledge and Judgment assess every Part of the real Estate, (Woodland only excepted,) and also every Part of the personal Estate of every Person within the District for which I am chosen assessor and all such as have Estates therein according to the Directions of an Act entitled An Act for the more equal Taxation of Estates in the County of Orange, so help me God." And that the said Assessors so chosen and qualified shall respectively make an Assessment of their Districts; and that the said Assessors of the several Districts of each Precinct shall thereupon meet together, and make out a true and Exact List in one Book of all the Names of the Freeholders and Inhabitants of the several Districts within their Precincts respectively, and against the Names of every such Person shall set down the Value of all his or her Estate real and Personal as near as they can discover the same to be within the same Precinct, setting down for every hundred Pounds real Value in such Assessment as aforesaid five Pounds and in that Proportion for a greater or lesser Sum, which List or Lists the said Assessors shall deliver to the Supervisors of the said County on or before the last Tuesday in September in every Year.

And for the more equal and just Assessment and Collection of the Taxes, or Rates to be imposed upon the said several Precincts in the said County of Orange, Be it further Enacted by the Authority aforesaid, That every Assessor shall assess the real and personal Estate of every Person within his District according to the following Plan, and in no other Manner or way whatsoever, to wit, Improved Lands at the Rate of one Pound ten Shillings per Acre; Horses above the Age of three Years, and under the Age of sixteen Years at six Pounds, above the Age of two and under the Age of three Years at three Pounds, above the Age of one and under the Age of two Years at one Pound ten Shillings; Oxen and Steers of four Years old and upwards at three Pounds ten Shillings; Cows and other neat Cattle of three Years old and upwards (except Oxen and Steers of four Years old and upward) two Pounds; Young Cattle, above the Age of two and under the Age of three Years at one Pound five Shillings; Young Cattle above the age of one, and under the Age of two Years at twelve

mencing of any such Action, Bill, Plaint, Information, Commission or other Suit or Proceeding as shall at any Time or Times hereafter be filed issued or commenced for recovering the same or in respect thereof as aforesaid.

Provided also, And be it further Enacted by the Authority aforesaid, That all and singular the said Manors, Lands, Tenements and Hereditaments shall at all Times hereafter be holden of his Majesty his Heirs and Successors and of other Person and Persons, Bodies Politic and Corporate, their Heirs and Successors respectively by the same Tenures, Services, Fee Farms, Chief Rents, Heriots, and other Duties to all Intents and Purposes as the same should or ought of Right to have been holden if the Estates, Rights and Interests established and made sure by this present Act had been, before the making of this Act, firm good and effectual in Law.

Saving to every Person and Persons, Bodies Politic and Corporate their Heirs and Successors (other than his most Excellent Majesty his Heirs and Successors, and other than all Patentees or Grantees of Concealments or defective Titles and all and every Person or Persons claiming from by or under them or any of them for or in respect or by Reason of any such Patents or Grants of Concealments or defective Titles) all such Rights, Title, Interest, Estate, Rents, Commons, Customs, Duties, Profits and other Claims and Demands whatsoever in, to, or out of the said Manors, Lands, Tenements or Hereditaments as they or any of them had or ought to have had before the making of this Act any Thing in this Act to the contrary notwithstanding.

Provided also, and be it Enacted by the Authority aforesaid, That where any Fee Farm Rent, or other Rent or Rents have been or shall be answered and actually paid to the Kings Majesty or to any his Predecessors, Heirs or Successors within the Space of Sixty Years next before any Action, Bill, Plaint, Information, Commission or other Suit or Proceeding shall at any Time or Times hereafter be filed issued or commenced for recovering the same or in respect thereof, out of any Manors, Lands, Tenements or Hereditaments of which Manors, Lands, Tenements or Hereditaments the Estates Rights or Interest being defective, are established and made sure by this present Act, that the Kings Majesty his Heirs and Successors shall from henceforth for ever have hold and enjoy the said Rents and Arrearage thereof in such Manner and Form, And as fully and amply as the same are or were enjoyed at any Time within the said Space of Sixty Years.

in October make the Quota of each respective Person or Persons according to the Total Sum of the List or Lists returned as aforesaid is directed by this Act and not otherwise, and that the Clerk of the Supervisors shall transcribe the List or Lists, and add to each Person's Rate the Sum or Proportion such Person is to pay of what the Supervisors find the said County chargeable with, and when the said List or Lists are compleated the Supervisors or the major Part of them are hereby required to issue their Warrant commanding the Collector or Collectors of each Town or Precinct to collect and pay the same as by the Warrant shall be directed.

And be it further Enacted by the Authority aforesaid, That if any Assessor or Assessors, Collector or Collectors, chosen and elected at the annual Town Meetings for choosing of Officers shall refuse to take the Office upon him or them, or if having accepted the same shall neglect his or their Duty therein, every Person so refusing or neglecting shall respectively forfeit the Sum of five Pounds to be recovered by the Supervisors of the said County or any one of them with full Costs of Suit before any one of his Majesty's Justices of the Peace for said County to be by them applied towards defraying the contingent Charges of said County: And if any Assessor shall refuse or neglect to serve as aforesaid then and in that Case the Justices of the Peace of the Precinct, (or the major Part of them) wherein the said Assessors lives, are hereby authorized impowered and required under their Hands and Seals to nominate and appoint Assessor or Assessors in the Room Stead and Place of such Assessor or Assessors so refusing or neglecting to serve, who shall be the Assessor or Assessors to all Intents and Purposes, have the like Powers and be subject to the same Rules, Pains and Penalties as any Assessor chosen and elected as is before directed by this Act, any Law Usage or Custom to the contrary in any wise notwithstanding.

And be it further Enacted by the Authority aforesaid, That every Assessor, as a Reward for his Trouble shall be freed and excused from working on the Highways within his District, and the Overseer of the Highways of his District is hereby directed to excuse him accordingly, and in delivering up his Account to the Commissioners of his Work done on the Highways shall make such exception in his Oath.

And be it further Enacted by the Authority aforesaid, That the Act entitled "An Act for the more equal Taxation of Estates in Orange County," passed the twenty seventh Day of January, one

Heirs or Successors or of some of them within the Space of Sixty years next before the filing, issuing or commencing of every such Action, Bill, Plaint, Information, Commission or other Suit or Proceeding as shall at any Time or Times hereafter be filed issued or commenced for recovering the same or in respect thereof as aforesaid.

Provided also, That this Act shall not be in force, until the same shall have received the Royal Approbation.

[CHAPTER 1739.]

[See chapters 1308, 1429, 1533. Expired, January 31, 1783.]

An Act to revive and amend the two Acts therein mentioned respecting Pot and Pearl Ashes.

[Passed, April 3, 1775.]

Be it Enacted by his Honor the Lieutenant Governor the Council and the General Assembly, and it is hereby enacted by the Authority of the same, That the Act entitled, "An Act to prevent Frauds by the adulteration of Pot-Ash and Pearl-Ash," passed in the seventh year of his present Majesty's Reign; and the Act entitled, " An Act the better to ascertain the Quality of Pot and Pearl Ashes," passed in the twelfth Year of his present Majesty's Reign shall be and are hereby revived and every Clause Matter and Thing therein contained enacted to be and remain in full Force from the passing hereof until the first Day of February which will be in the Year of our Lord one thousand seven hundred and eighty three, and from thence to the End of the then next Session of the General Assembly.

And be it further Enacted by the Authority aforesaid, That Joseph Allicocke shall be and hereby is appointed the Officer for viewing and examining all Pot Ashes and Pearl Ashes, that are intended to be shipped for Exportation directly from the Port of New York, in the Room of Abraham De La Montagnie deceased, and shall take the same Oath, have the same Powers, and be liable to the same Penalties as the Officer appointed in and by the last abovementioned Act, any Thing herein or in the beforementioned Acts contained to the contrary thereof in any wise notwithstanding.

Provided always, And be it Enacted by the Authority aforesaid that if a vacancy shall happen in the Office of Inspector for the City and County of New York the same shall and may be supplied in the manner directed by the Act last abovementioned on a Va-

of Orange Town and Haverstraw in the County of Orange, Provided always that the Inhabitants of the said Precincts shall not be obliged to alter any Wheel Carriage now in Use; but that all Carriages hereafter to be made in the said Precincts, or that shall be repaired with new Axle-Trees, shall be made agreeable to the first Clause of this Act any Thing herein to the Contrary notwithstanding. But nothing in this Act shall be construed to relate to any Coach Chariot Chair or other Carriage used for Pleasure and not for Burdens.

[CHAPTER 1742.]

An Act to raise the further Sum of five hundred Pounds for draining the drowned Lands in the Precinct of Goshen in Orange County.

[Passed, April 3, 1775.]

WHEREAS The Sum directed to be raised by an Act entitled " An Act to raise fifteen hundred Pounds for draining the drowned Lands in the Precinct of Goshen in Orange County," passed the sixth Day of February one thousand seven hundred and seventy three, has been almost expended and found insufficient for the good Purposes intended by the said Act.

Be it therefore Enacted by his Honor the Lieutenant Governor the Council and the General Assembly, and it is hereby enacted by the Authority of the same, That the further Sum of five hundred Pounds shall be assessed and raised in the same Manner as the said fifteen hundred Pounds was in and by the said Act directed to be assessed and raised. And the Trustees in the said Act named, and the Survivor or Survivors of them are hereby authorized to apply the said five hundred Pounds towards draining the said drowned Lands at such Times, and by such Ways and Means as they or any three of them shall think proper.

And Whereas sundry large Tracts of Swamps and Bog Meadows are situated at a great Distance from the main Creek or Kill running through the said drowned Lands; and it is conceived that for the more effectual draining of the said Swamps and Bog Meadows it will be necessary to have some Brooks cleared out, and several large Ditches cut to lead the Waters into the said Main Creek or Kill.

Be it therefore Enacted by the Authority aforesaid, That when any Proprietor of the drowned Lands shall think necessary that any

shall on such search Discover any Cask or Casks of Pot Ashes or Pearl Ashes not Branded as before directed the Person or Persons so Shipping the same shall forfeit all and every such Cask and Casks of Pot Ashes and Pearl Ashes so Shipped or Shipping and not Branded in the manner before directed And the Master or Commander of such Vessel who shall knowingly receive any such Cask or Casks of Pot Ashes or Pearl Ashes not branded as aforesaid shall forfeit and pay for each Cask so received on board his Vessel the sum of forty Shillings and if any person shall obstruct or hinder the said Inspectors or any or either of them in making such search as aforesaid every Person so offending shall forfeit and pay the sum of Fifty Pounds.

[CHAPTER 1740.]

[Expired, January 31, 1776.]

An Act for the more equal Taxation of Estates in the County of Orange.

[Passed, April 3, 1775.]

FORASMUCH as the Method heretofore practised for the taxation of Estates in the County of Orange, hath not been as equal and just as it is conceived it might be,

Be it therefore Enacted by his Honor the Lieutenant Governor the Council and the General Assembly, and it is hereby enacted by the Authority of the same, That before the first Tuesday in April next, it shall and may be lawful for Daniel Everitt, Richard Edsall, Nathaniel Roe Junior and Gilbert Bradner Esquires or the major Part of them, and they are hereby directed and required to divide the Precinct of Goshen into ten Districts; and that Captain Elihu Mervin, Nathaniel Strong, Jeremiah Clark and Austin Smith or the major Part of them shall divide the Precinct of Cornwall into six Districts, and that Teunis Cooper, David Pye, and Ann Hawkes Hay Esquires or the major Part of them shall divide the Precinct of Haverstraw into three Districts and the Precinct of Orange Town shall be considered as one District.

And be it further Enacted by the Authority aforesaid, That it shall and may be lawful for the Freeholders and Inhabitants of each of the respective Towns and Precincts within the said County, to choose and elect, at their next annual Meeting, a Person being a Freeholder inhabitant within every such District within the said County and Precincts, for an Assessor of such District,

[CHAPTER 1744]

An Act for making two Bridges in the Precincts of Goshen and Cornwall in the County of Orange.

[Passed, April 3, 1775.]

WHEREAS the making of good Bridges not only tends to the Ease and Benefit of the Inhabitants but also is of great Utility to Strangers travelling through the Country,

Be it therefore Enacted by his Honor the Lieutenant Governor the Council and the General Assembly and it is hereby enacted by the Authority of the same, That the Commissioners of the Precinct of Cornwall for the Time being shall and they are hereby directed and required to make and erect a sufficient Bridge across Murderer's Creek, where the Highway or Post Road crosses the same, to the Eastward of where Smith's Creek empties into Murderer's Creek aforesaid and that the Commissioners of the Precinct of Goshen for the Time being shall and they are hereby directed and required well and sufficiently to make and erect a Bridge across the WallKill where the Highway that runs from Gilbert Bradnor's to John Allison's crosses the said Kill.

And be it Enacted by the Authority aforesaid That the Commissioners for the Time being for each of the said Precincts of Cornwall and Goshen are hereby directed to have the Accounts of the Expences for erecting and building the same transmitted to the Supervisors of the said County of Orange, who are hereby directed and required to order the levying collecting and paying the same, in the same Manner as the Expences of all other public Bridges in the said two Precincts are raised collected and paid.

[CHAPTER 1745.]

An Act to alter the Place of Election for Representatives, and the Place of Meeting of the Supervisors, Judges and Loan Officers on the South Side of the Mountains in the County of Orange.

[Passed, April 3, 1775.]

WHEREAS the Place appointed by two several Acts of the Legislature of this Colony for holding the Election for Representatives, and for the Meeting of the Supervisors Judges and Loan Officers on the South Side of the Mountains in the County of Orange, is

Shillings; Sheep and Hogs upwards of six Months old at five Shillings; Male Slaves above the Age of fifteen and under the Age of forty Years at thirty Pounds; of the Age of forty and upwards, and under the Age of fifty Years at fifteen Pounds; of the Age of ten and upwards, and under the Age of fifteen Years at eighteen Pounds; and above the Age of seven and under the Age of ten Years at ten Pounds; Female Slaves of the Age of fifteen and upwards and under the Age of forty Years at Twenty Pounds, of the Age of forty and upwards and under the Age of fifty Years at ten Pounds, of the Age of ten and upwards and under the Age of fifteen Years at twelve Pounds, and above the Age of seven and under the Age of ten Years at eight Pounds, Furnaces and Forges at the Discretion of the Assessors not exceeding three hundred Pounds, Grist-Mills, Fulling-Mills and Saw-Mills not exceeding three hundred Pounds, nor less than thirty Pounds, every Storekeeper not exceeding two hundred Pounds nor less than twenty Pounds, every Blacksmith that follow his Trade at the Discretion of the Assessors.

And be it further Enacted that every Person subject to such Tax or charges shall at all Times when required by the Assessor of the District wherein he resides, give him a View of all the improved Lands in his Occupation, and a just Account of all the Horses Cattle and Chattels which are his property, and ought to be subject to such Tax or Charge, and if any Person shall secrete or conceal from the Assessor any Part of his improved Land, Horses Cattle or Chattels which ought to have been subject to such Tax or Charge, he shall forfeit and pay for every such Concealment, the Sum of three Pounds to be recovered by the Assessor of the District where the said Delinquent lives, with full Costs of Suit, before any Justice of the Peace by the Oath of one or more credible Witnesses, two thirds of which Forfeiture shall go to the Use of the Poor of the Precinct, and the other third to the Use of the Informer and in Case the said Assessor shall not prosecute for the said Fine of three Pounds when so as aforesaid forfeited, and the same shall come to his knowledge, then and in that Case the said Assessor shall forfeit the Sum of three Pounds to be recovered by the Supervisor of the said Precinct where such Assessor shall live, with full Costs of Suit, before any Justice of the Peace, and be applied to the Use of the Poor of the said Precinct, which said Supervisor is hereby directed to sue for the same.

And be it further Enacted by the same Authority, That the said Supervisors shall at their annual Meeting on the first Tuesday

in October make the Quota of each respective Person or Persons according to the Total Sum of the List or Lists returned as aforesaid is directed by this Act and not otherwise, and that the Clerk of the Supervisors shall transcribe the List or Lists, and add to each Person's Rate the Sum or Proportion such Person is to pay of what the Supervisors find the said County chargeable with, and when the said List or Lists are compleated the Supervisors or the major Part of them are hereby required to issue their Warrant commanding the Collector or Collectors of each Town or Precinct to collect and pay the same as by the Warrant shall be directed.

And be it further Enacted by the Authority aforesaid, That if any Assessor or Assessors, Collector or Collectors, chosen and elected at the annual Town Meetings for choosing of Officers shall refuse to take the Office upon him or them, or if having accepted the same shall neglect his or their Duty therein, every Person so refusing or neglecting shall respectively forfeit the Sum of five Pounds to be recovered by the Supervisors of the said County or any one of them with full Costs of Suit before any one of his Majesty's Justices of the Peace for said County to be by them applied towards defraying the contingent Charges of said County: And if any Assessor shall refuse or neglect to serve as aforesaid then and in that Case the Justices of the Peace of the Precinct, (or the major Part of them) wherein the said Assessors lives, are hereby authorized impowered and required under their Hands and Seals to nominate and appoint Assessor or Assessors in the Room Stead and Place of such Assessor or Assessors so refusing or neglecting to serve, who shall be the Assessor or Assessors to all Intents and Purposes, have the like Powers and be subject to the same Rules, Pains and Penalties as any Assessor chosen and elected as is before directed by this Act, any Law Usage or Custom to the contrary in any wise notwithstanding.

And be it further Enacted by the Authority aforesaid, That every Assessor, as a Reward for his Trouble shall be freed and excused from working on the Highways within his District, and the Overseer of the Highways of his District is hereby directed to excuse him accordingly, and in delivering up his Account to the Commissioners of his Work done on the Highways shall make such exception in his Oath.

And be it further Enacted by the Authority aforesaid, That the Act entitled "An Act for the more equal Taxation of Estates in Orange County," passed the twenty seventh Day of January, one

recovering the same; or in respect thereof, nor the same have been nor shall have been duly in charge or stood in super of Record as aforesaid within the said Space of Sixty Years against all and every Person and Persons their Heirs and Assigns having claiming or pretending to have or who shall or may have claim or pretend to have any Estate, Right, Title, Interest, Claim or Demand whatsoever, of in or to the same by force or colour of any Letters Patents or Grants upon Suggestion of Concealment of wrongful detaining, or not being in charge, or defective Titles or by from or under any Patentees or Grantees or any Letters Patents or Grants upon Suggestion of concealment or wrongful detaining or not being in Charge or defective Titles of or for which said Manors, Lands, Tenements, Rents and Hereditaments or any of them no Verdict, Judgment, Decree, Judicial Order upon Hearing or Sentence of any Court now standing in force, hath been had or given or any such Verdict, Judgment, Decree, Judicial Order upon Hearing or Sentence of Court shall hereafter be had or given in any Action, Bill, Plaint or Information in any of his Majestys Courts of Record within this Colony, for or in the Name of the Kings Majesty or in any of his Ancestors, Progenitors, Predecessors, Heirs or Successors or for any of the said Patentees or Grantees or for their or any of their Heirs or Assigns within the Space of Sixty Years next before the filing issuing or commencing of every such Action, Bill, Plaint, Information, Commission, or other Suit or Proceeding as shall at any Time or Times hereafter be filed issued or commenced for recovering the same, or in respect thereof as aforesaid.

Provided always And be it Enacted, That where the Rents, Revenues, Issues or Profits of any Manors, Lands, Tenements or Hereditaments are or shall be in charge by, to, or with any Auditor or Auditors or other proper Officer or Officers of the Revenue such Rents, Revenues, Issues and Profits shall be held deemed and taken to be duly in charge within the Meaning and Intent of this Act, any Usage or Custom to the contrary notwithstanding.

Provided always, That this Act or any Thing therein contained, shall not extend to bar, impeach or hinder his Majesty his Heirs or Successors, of, for, or from any Manors, Tenements, Rents or Hereditaments whereof any Reversion or Remainder now is in his Majesty for or concerning the Reversion or Remainder, nor of, for or from any Reversion or Remainder or possibility of Reversion or Remainder in any of his Majestys Progenitors or Predecessors or Ancestors which by the Expiration, End or other

Determination of any limited Estate of Fee Simple or of any Fee Tail or other particular Estate hath or ought to have first fallen or become in Possession, or which shall or may or ought hereafter first to fall or come in Possession within the Space of Sixty Years next before the filing, issuing or commencing of any such Action, Bill, Plaint, Information, Commission or other Suit or Proceeding as shall at any Time or Times hereafter be filed issued or commenced for recovering the same, or in respect thereof, nor of, for or from any Right or Title first accrued or grown to his Majesty or any of his Progenitors, Predecessors or Ancestors, or which shall first accrue or grow to his Majesty or any of his Heirs or Successors, of in or to any Manors, Lands, Tenements, Rents or Hereditaments at any Time or Times within the Space of Sixty Years next before the filing issuing or commencing of any such Action Bill, Plaint, Information, Commission or other Suit or Proceeding as shall at any Time or Times hereafter be filed issued or commenced for recovering the same, or in respect thereof, and not before.

Provided also, And be it Enacted by the Authority aforesaid, That this Act or Thing therein contained shall not extend to any Manors, Lands, Tenements, Rents, or Hereditaments mentioned to be granted or conveyed by any of his Majesty's Progenitors, Predecessors or Ancestors, or by any other under whom his Majesty claimeth to any Person or Persons of any limited Estate in Fee Simple or of any Estate in Tail or other particular Estate, which several Estates (if the same had been good and effectual in Law) have or ought to have first to fall or come in Possession within the Space of Sixty years next before the filing, issuing or commencing of any such Action, Bill, Plaint, Information, Commission or other Suit or Proceeding as shall at any time or Times hereafter be filed issued or commenced for recovering the same, or in respect thereof as aforesaid nor to any Manors, Lands, Tenements, Rents or Hereditaments mentioned to be granted or conveyed by any of his Majesty's Progenitors, Predecessors or Ancestors, or by any other under whom his Majesty claimeth to any Person or Persons in Fee Tail or other particular Estate whereof the Reversion or Inheritance (if such Estate Tail or other Particular Estate had been good and effectual in Law) should have been and continued in his Majesty, or any of his Progenitors, Predecessors or Ancestors, or should or ought hereafter to be and continue in his Majesty his Heirs or Successors at any Time within the Space of Sixty Years next before the filing issuing or com-

mencing of any such Action, Bill, Plaint, Information, Commission or other Suit or Proceeding as shall at any Time or Times hereafter be filed issued or commenced for recovering the same or in respect thereof as aforesaid.

Provided also, And be it further Enacted by the Authority aforesaid, That all and singular the said Manors, Lands, Tenements and Hereditaments shall at all Times hereafter be holden of his Majesty his Heirs and Successors and of other Person and Persons, Bodies Politic and Corporate, their Heirs and Successors respectively by the same Tenures, Services, Fee Farms, Chief Rents, Heriots, and other Duties to all Intents and Purposes as the same should or ought of Right to have been holden if the Estates, Rights and Interests established and made sure by this present Act had been, before the making of this Act, firm good and effectual in Law.

Saving to every Person and Persons, Bodies Politic and Corporate their Heirs and Successors (other than his most Excellent Majesty his Heirs and Successors, and other than all Patentees or Grantees of Concealments or defective Titles and all and every Person or Persons claiming from by or under them or any of them for or in respect or by Reason of any such Patents or Grants of Concealments or defective Titles) all such Rights, Title, Interest, Estate, Rents, Commons, Customs, Duties, Profits and other Claims and Demands whatsoever in, to, or out of the said Manors, Lands, Tenements or Hereditaments as they or any of them had or ought to have had before the making of this Act any Thing in this Act to the contrary notwithstanding.

Provided also, and be it Enacted by the Authority aforesaid, That where any Fee Farm Rent, or other Rent or Rents have been or shall be answered and actually paid to the Kings Majesty or to any his Predecessors, Heirs or Successors within the Space of Sixty Years next before any Action, Bill, Plaint, Information, Commission or other Suit or Proceeding shall at any Time or Times hereafter be filed issued or commenced for recovering the same or in respect thereof, out of any Manors, Lands, Tenements or Hereditaments of which Manors, Lands, Tenements or Hereditaments the Estates Rights or Interest being defective, are established and made sure by this present Act, that the Kings Majesty his Heirs and Successors shall from henceforth for ever have hold and enjoy the said Rents and Arrearage thereof in such Manner and Form, And as fully and amply as the same are or were enjoyed at any Time within the said Space of Sixty Years.

covered by the said County Treasurer before any one of his Majesty's Justices of the Peace for the said County with Costs of Suit, three Pounds thereof to the Use of the County, to be appropriated and applied by the Supervisors thereof in such manner as they shall think best, and the other forty Shillings to the Treasurer as a Reward for his Trouble in prosecuting for the same.

And to the End that the Rate of the said Counties may effectually come in annually, Be it further Enacted by the Authority aforesaid, That if the Treasurer of either of the said Counties for the Time being shall at any Time or Times fail in prosecuting to Effect any such Collector or Collectors for the Offences as aforesaid by the Space of three Months after the Time herein before limited, such Treasurer shall forfeit and pay the Sum of five Pounds Current Money of this Colony for every Twenty Days he shall delay or neglect, to be recovered by the Person or Persons who shall be delayed wronged or injured by such Means before any one of his Majesty's Justices of the Peace for such County with Costs of Suit, besides being liable to an Action of Trespass grounded on the Case to such Person or Persons who shall be delayed wronged or injured, one-half of which Forfeiture to be for the Use and Benefit of such County, and the other half to the Person who shall sue for and recover the same; this Act to continue in force from the passing thereof during the Term of two Years, and thence to the End of the th[illegible] Session of the General Assembly.

HAPTER 1749.]

Expired, January 31, 1785.]

o revive an Act entitled "An Act dents by Fire in that Part of usselaerwyck therein men-

[Passed, April 3, 1775.]

he Lieutenant Governor, the Cou[illegible] bly, and it is hereby enacted by the Au[illegible] the Act entitled "An Act to prevent Accid[illegible] at Part of the Manor of Rensselaerwyck therein [illegible] assed in the tenth Year of the Reign of his present M[illegible] all be and hereby is revived from the passing hereof, unt[illegible] first Day of February which will be in the Year of our Lord one thousand seven hundred and eighty five.

Heirs or Successors or of some of them within the Space of Sixty years next before the filing, issuing or commencing of every such Action, Bill, Plaint, Information, Commission or other Suit or Proceeding as shall at any Time or Times hereafter be filed issued or commenced for recovering the same or in respect thereof as aforesaid.

Provided also, That this Act shall not be in force, until the same shall have received the Royal Approbation.

[CHAPTER 1739.]

[See chapters 1308, 1429, 1533. Expired, January 31, 1783.]

An Act to revive and amend the two Acts therein mentioned respecting Pot and Pearl Ashes.

[Passed, April 3, 1775.]

Be it Enacted by his Honor the Lieutenant Governor the Council and the General Assembly, and it is hereby enacted by the Authority of the same, That the Act entitled, "An Act to prevent Frauds by the adulteration of Pot-Ash and Pearl-Ash," passed in the seventh year of his present Majesty's Reign; and the Act entitled, " An Act the better to ascertain the Quality of Pot and Pearl Ashes," passed in the twelfth Year of his present Majesty's Reign shall be and are hereby revived and every Clause Matter and Thing therein contained enacted to be and remain in full Force from the passing hereof until the first Day of February which will be in the Year of our Lord one thousand seven hundred and eighty three, and from thence to the End of the then next Session of the General Assembly.

And be it further Enacted by the Authority aforesaid, That Joseph Allicocke shall be and hereby is appointed the Officer for viewing and examining all Pot Ashes and Pearl Ashes, that are intended to be shipped for Exportation directly from the Port of New York, in the Room of Abraham De La Montagnie deceased, and shall take the same Oath, have the same Powers, and be liable to the same Penalties as the Officer appointed in and by the last abovementioned Act, any Thing herein or in the beforementioned Acts contained to the contrary thereof in any wise notwithstanding.

Provided always, And be it Enacted by the Authority aforesaid that if a vacancy shall happen in the Office of Inspector for the City and County of New York the same shall and may be supplied in the manner directed by the Act last abovementioned on a Va-

covered by the said County Treasurer before any one of his Majesty's Justices of the Peace for the said County with Costs of Suit, three Pounds thereof to the Use of the County, to be appropriated and applied by the Supervisors thereof in such manner as they shall think best, and the other forty Shillings to the Treasurer as a Reward for his Trouble in prosecuting for the same.

And to the End that the Rate of the said Counties may effectually come in annually, Be it further Enacted by the Authority aforesaid, That if the Treasurer of either of the said Counties for the Time being shall at any Time or Times fail in prosecuting to Effect any such Collector or Collectors for the Offences as aforesaid by the Space of three Months after the Time herein before limited, such Treasurer shall forfeit and pay the Sum of five Pounds Current Money of this Colony for every Twenty Days he shall delay or neglect, to be recovered by the Person or Persons who shall be delayed wronged or injured by such Means before any one of his Majesty's Justices of the Peace for such County with Costs of Suit, besides being liable to an Action of Trespass grounded on the Case to such Person or Persons who shall be delayed wronged or injured, one-half of which Forfeiture to be for the Use and Benefit of such County, and the other half to the Person who shall sue for and recover the same; this Act to continue in force from the passing thereof during the Term of two Years, and thence to the End of the then next Session of the General Assembly.

[CHAPTER 1749.]

[See chapter 1440. Expired, January 31, 1785.]

An Act to revive an Act entitled "An Act to prevent Accidents by Fire in that Part of the Manor of Rensselaerwyck therein mentioned."

[Passed, April 3, 1775.]

Be it Enacted by his Honor the Lieutenant Governor, the Council and the General Assembly, and it is hereby enacted by the Authority of the same; that the Act entitled "An Act to prevent Accidents by Fire in that Part of the Manor of Rensselaerwyck therein mentioned," passed in the tenth Year of the Reign of his present Majesty, shall be and hereby is revived from the passing hereof, until the first Day of February which will be in the Year of our Lord one thousand seven hundred and eighty five.

shall on such search Discover any Cask or Casks of Pot Ashes or Pearl Ashes not Branded as before directed the Person or Persons so Shipping the same shall forfeit all and every such Cask and Casks of Pot Ashes and Pearl Ashes so Shipped or Shipping and not Branded in the manner before directed And the Master or Commander of such Vessel who shall knowingly receive any such Cask or Casks of Pot Ashes or Pearl Ashes not branded as aforesaid shall forfeit and pay for each Cask so received on board his Vessel the sum of forty Shillings and if any person shall obstruct or hinder the said Inspectors or any or either of them in making such search as aforesaid every Person so offending shall forfeit and pay the sum of Fifty Pounds.

[CHAPTER 1740.]

[Expired, January 31, 1776.]

An Act for the more equal Taxation of Estates in the County of Orange.

[Passed, April 3, 1775.]

Forasmuch as the Method heretofore practised for the taxation of Estates in the County of Orange, hath not been as equal and just as it is conceived it might be,

Be it therefore Enacted by his Honor the Lieutenant Governor the Council and the General Assembly, and it is hereby enacted by the Authority of the same, That before the first Tuesday in April next, it shall and may be lawful for Daniel Everitt, Richard Edsall, Nathaniel Roe Junior and Gilbert Bradner Esquires or the major Part of them, and they are hereby directed and required to divide the Precinct of Goshen into ten Districts; and that Captain Elihu Mervin, Nathaniel Strong, Jeremiah Clark and Austin Smith or the major Part of them shall divide the Precinct of Cornwall into six Districts, and that Teunis Cooper, David Pye, and Ann Hawkes Hay Esquires or the major Part of them shall divide the Precinct of Haverstraw into three Districts and the Precinct of Orange Town shall be considered as one District.

And be it further Enacted by the Authority aforesaid, That it shall and may be lawful for the Freeholders and Inhabitants of each of the respective Towns and Precincts within the said County, to choose and elect, at their next annual Meeting, a Person being a Freeholder inhabitant within every such District within the said County and Precincts, for an Assessor of such District, which Assessors so chosen in each of the Districts aforesaid, and before they enter on the Duties of their Office shall take an Oath before any one of his Majesty's Justices of the Peace for the said County in the Words following to wit, "I A B, do solemnly swear that I will well and truly, equally and impartially according to the best of my Skill Knowledge and Judgment assess every Part of the real Estate, (Woodland only excepted,) and also every Part of the personal Estate of every Person within the District for which I am chosen assessor and all such as have Estates therein according to the Directions of an Act entitled An Act for the more equal Taxation of Estates in the County of Orange, so help me God." And that the said Assessors so chosen and qualified shall respectively make an Assessment of their Districts; and that the said Assessors of the several Districts of each Precinct shall thereupon meet together, and make out a true and Exact List in one Book of all the Names of the Freeholders and Inhabitants of the several Districts within their Precincts respectively, and against the Names of every such Person shall set down the Value of all his or her Estate real and Personal as near as they can discover the same to be within the same Precinct, setting down for every hundred Pounds real Value in such Assessment as aforesaid five Pounds and in that Proportion for a greater or lesser Sum, which List or Lists the said Assessors shall deliver to the Supervisors of the said County on or before the last Tuesday in September in every Year.

And for the more equal and just Assessment and Collection of the Taxes, or Rates to be imposed upon the said several Precincts in the said County of Orange, Be it further Enacted by' the Authority aforesaid, That every Assessor shall assess the real and personal Estate of every Person within his District according to the following Plan, and in no other Manner or way whatsoever, to wit, Improved Lands at the Rate of one Pound ten Shillings per Acre; Horses above the Age of three Years, and under the Age of sixteen Years at six Pounds, above the Age of two and under the Age of three Years at three Pounds, above the Age of one and under the Age of two Years at one Pound ten Shillings; Oxen and Steers of four Years old and upwards at three Pounds ten Shillings; Cows and other neat Cattle of three Years old and upwards (except Oxen and Steers of four Years old and upward) two Pounds; Young Cattle, above the Age of two and under the Age of three Years at one Pound five Shillings; Young Cattle above the age of one, and under the Age of two Years at twelve

Shillings; Sheep and Hogs upwards of six Months old at five Shillings; Male Slaves above the Age of fifteen and under the Age of forty Years at thirty Pounds; of the Age of forty and upwards, and under the Age of fifty Years at fifteen Pounds; of the Age of ten and upwards, and under the Age of fifteen Years at eighteen Pounds; and above the Age of seven and under the Age of ten Years at ten Pounds; Female Slaves of the Age of fifteen and upwards and under the Age of forty Years at Twenty Pounds, of the Age of forty and upwards and under the Age of fifty Years at ten Pounds, of the Age of ten and upwards and under the Age of fifteen Years at twelve Pounds, and above the Age of seven and under the Age of ten Years at eight Pounds, Furnaces and Forges at the Discretion of the Assessors not exceeding three hundred Pounds, Grist-Mills, Fulling-Mills and Saw-Mills not exceeding three hundred Pounds, nor less than thirty Pounds, every Storekeeper not exceeding two hundred Pounds nor less than twenty Pounds, every Blacksmith that follow his Trade at the Discretion of the Assessors.

And be it further Enacted that every Person subject to such Tax or charges shall at all Times when required by the Assessor of the District wherein he resides, give him a View of all the improved Lands in his Occupation, and a just Account of all the Horses Cattle and Chattels which are his property, and ought to be subject to such Tax or Charge, and if any Person shall secrete or conceal from the Assessor any Part of his improved Land, Horses Cattle or Chattels which ought to have been subject to such Tax or Charge, he shall forfeit and pay for every such Concealment, the Sum of three Pounds to be recovered by the Assessor of the District where the said Delinquent lives, with full Costs of Suit, before any Justice of the Peace by the Oath of one or more credible Witnesses, two thirds of which Forfeiture shall go to the Use of the Poor of the Precinct, and the other third to the Use of the Informer and in Case the said Assessor shall not prosecute for the said Fine of three Pounds when so as aforesaid forfeited, and the same shall come to his knowledge, then and in that Case the said Assessor shall forfeit the Sum of three Pounds to be recovered by the Supervisor of the said Precinct where such Assessor shall live, with full Costs of Suit, before any Justice of the Peace, and be applied to the Use of the Poor of the said Precinct, which said Supervisor is hereby directed to sue for the same.

And be it further Enacted by the same Authority, That the said Supervisors shall at their annual Meeting on the first Tuesday

in October make the Quota of each respective Person or Persons according to the Total Sum of the List or Lists returned as aforesaid is directed by this Act and not otherwise, and that the Clerk of the Supervisors shall transcribe the List or Lists, and add to each Person's Rate the Sum or Proportion such Person is to pay of what the Supervisors find the said County chargeable with, and when the said List or Lists are compleated the Supervisors or the major Part of them are hereby required to issue their Warrant commanding the Collector or Collectors of each Town or Precinct to collect and pay the same as by the Warrant shall be directed.

And be it further Enacted by the Authority aforesaid, That if any Assessor or Assessors, Collector or Collectors, chosen and elected at the annual Town Meetings for choosing of Officers shall refuse to take the Office upon him or them, or if having accepted the same shall neglect his or their Duty therein, every Person so refusing or neglecting shall respectively forfeit the Sum of five Pounds to be recovered by the Supervisors of the said County or any one of them with full Costs of Suit before any one of his Majesty's Justices of the Peace for said County to be by them applied towards defraying the contingent Charges of said County: And if any Assessor shall refuse or neglect to serve as aforesaid then and in that Case the Justices of the Peace of the Precinct, (or the major Part of them) wherein the said Assessors lives, are hereby authorized impowered and required under their Hands and Seals to nominate and appoint Assessor or Assessors in the Room Stead and Place of such Assessor or Assessors so refusing or neglecting to serve, who shall be the Assessor or Assessors to all Intents and Purposes, have the like Powers and be subject to the same Rules, Pains and Penalties as any Assessor chosen and elected as is before directed by this Act, any Law Usage or Custom to the contrary in any wise notwithstanding.

And be it further Enacted by the Authority aforesaid, That every Assessor, as a Reward for his Trouble shall be freed and excused from working on the Highways within his District, and the Overseer of the Highways of his District is hereby directed to excuse him accordingly, and in delivering up his Account to the Commissioners of his Work done on the Highways shall make such exception in his Oath.

And be it further Enacted by the Authority aforesaid, That the Act entitled "An Act for the more equal Taxation of Estates in Orange County," passed the twenty seventh Day of January, one

thousand seven hundred and seventy shall be and hereby is suspended during the Continuance of this Act.

And be it Enacted by the same Authority, That this Act shall be in force from the passing thereof, till the first Day of February, which will be in the Year of our Lord one thousand seven hundred and seventy six, and from thence to the End of the then next Session of the General Assembly.

[CHAPTER 1741.]

An Act to regulate Waggons within the Township of Schenectady, and the Precincts of Orange Town and Haverstraw in the County of Orange.

[Passed, April 3, 1775.]

Be it Enacted by his Honor the Lieutenant Governor the Council and the General Assembly, and it is hereby enacted by the Authority of the same that from and after the fifteenth Day of August next, no Person whatever dwelling and residing in the Township of Schenectady shall make Use of any Wheel Carriage upon any Highway or Public Road in the said Township the Wheels whereof shall make a Track of less than four Feet eight Inches to be computed from the inside of the Fellows of one Wheel to the inside of the Fellows of the Opposite Wheel, on Penalty of five Pounds for every Offence, to be recovered from the Owner or Proprietor of such Carriage in a Summary Way with Costs of Suit before any Justice of the Peace in the said Township, one-half of which Penalty to go to the Informer, and the other half to the Poor of the said Township.

And be it further enacted by the same Authority, That the Proprietor of every Carriage in the said Township to be used on the Highways or Public Roads thereof shall mark or cause the same to be marked with the initial Letter of his Christian Name and his Sirname at length; and every Carriage used on the Highways and public Roads in said Township, and belonging to Persons residing therein that shall not be marked as aforesaid shall forfeit and pay the Sum of twenty Shillings for every Months Neglect from and after the fifteenth Day of August aforesaid to be recovered and applied in like Manner as the Penalty inflicted in the preceding Clause of this Act is directed to be recovered and applied.

And be it further Enacted by the Authority aforesaid, That every Clause and Article of this Act shall extend to the Precincts of Orange Town and Haverstraw in the County of Orange, Provided always that the Inhabitants of the said Precincts shall not be obliged to alter any Wheel Carriage now in Use; but that all Carriages hereafter to be made in the said Precincts, or that shall be repaired with new Axle-Trees, shall be made agreeable to the first Clause of this Act any Thing herein to the Contrary notwithstanding. But nothing in this Act shall be construed to relate to any Coach Chariot Chair or other Carriage used for Pleasure and not for Burdens.

[CHAPTER 1742.]

An Act to raise the further Sum of five hundred Pounds for draining the drowned Lands in the Precinct of Goshen in Orange County.

[Passed, April 3, 1775.]

WHEREAS The Sum directed to be raised by an Act entitled "An Act to raise fifteen hundred Pounds for draining the drowned Lands in the Precinct of Goshen in Orange County," passed the sixth Day of February one thousand seven hundred and seventy three, has been almost expended and found insufficient for the good Purposes intended by the said Act.

Be it therefore Enacted by his Honor the Lieutenant Governor the Council and the General Assembly, and it is hereby enacted by the Authority of the same, That the further Sum of five hundred Pounds shall be assessed and raised in the same Manner as the said fifteen hundred Pounds was in and by the said Act directed to be assessed and raised. And the Trustees in the said Act named, and the Survivor or Survivors of them are hereby authorized to apply the said five hundred Pounds towards draining the said drowned Lands at such Times, and by such Ways and Means as they or any three of them shall think proper.

And Whereas sundry large Tracts of Swamps and Bog Meadows are situated at a great Distance from the main Creek or Kill running through the said drowned Lands; and it is conceived that for the more effectual draining of the said Swamps and Bog Meadows it will be necessary to have some Brooks cleared out, and several large Ditches cut to lead the Waters into the said Main Creek or Kill.

Be it therefore Enacted by the Authority aforesaid, That when any Proprietor of the drowned Lands shall think necessary that any

Ditch or Ditches should be cut in the said Swamps or Bog Meadows, or any Brook cleared out, and the Persons interested cannot agree respecting the same, it shall be lawful for Samuel Gale, Jesse Woodhull and Nathaniel Roe Junior Esquires, or any two of them to determine whether it is necessary to have such Ditch made, or such Brook cleared out; and if it shall be determined to be necessary, they shall direct in what Manner the same shall be done and who shall pay the Expence thereof and in Case either of the Parties shall neglect to comply with such Determination the Person or Persons desirous of having such Ditch or Ditches made, or Brook cleared, may proceed to do the same, and may prosecute each Party interested for his Proportion of the Expence thereof in any of his Majesty's Courts within this Colony and shall recover the same with Interest and Costs of Suit.

[CHAPTER 1743.]

An Act for raising the further Sum of two hundred Pounds for effectually lowering a Pond commonly called Wickham's Pond in the Precinct of Goshen in the County of Orange.

[Passed, April 3, 1775.]

Whereas the Monies raised by Virtue of an Act passed the sixth Day of February one thousand seven hundred and seventy three entitled, "An Act for raising one hundred and fifty Pounds for lowering a Pond commonly called Wickham's Pond in the Precinct of Goshen in the County of Orange," have been expended and found insufficient for the good Purposes intended by the said Act.

Be it therefore Enacted by his Honor the Lieutenant Governor the Council and the General Assembly and it is hereby enacted by the Authority of the same That such further Sum and Sums of Money not exceeding two hundred Pounds shall be raised as William Wickham John Bard, and Henry Wisner the Third, or any two of them may think proper, which Money shall be raised in like Manner as the one hundred and fifty Pounds mentioned in the said Act was directed to be raised, and shall be laid out in lowering the said Pond and clearing the creek that runs out of the same by such Ways and Means as they or any two of them shall think proper.

[CHAPTER 1744]

An Act for making two Bridges in the Precincts of Goshen and Cornwall in the County of Orange.

[Passed, April 3, 1775.]

WHEREAS the making of good Bridges not only tends to the Ease ınd Benefit of the Inhabitants but also is of great Utility to Strangers travelling through the Country,

Be it therefore Enacted by his Honor the Lieutenant Governor the Council and the General Assembly and it is hereby enacted *y the Authority of the same,* That the Commissioners of the Precinct of Cornwall for the Time being shall and they are hereby lirected and required to make and erect a sufficient Bridge across Murderer's Creek, where the Highway or Post Road crosses the ame, to the Eastward of where Smith's Creek empties into Murlerer's Creek aforesaid and that the Commissioners of the Preinct of Goshen for the Time being shall and they are hereby lirected and required well and sufficiently to make and erect a Bridge across the WallKill where the Highway that runs from Gilbert Bradnor's to John Allison's crosses the said Kill.

And be it Enacted by the Authority aforesaid That the Comnissioners for the Time being for each of the said Precincts of 'ornwall and Goshen are hereby directed to have the Accounts f the Expences for erecting and building the same transmitted o the Supervisors of the said County of Orange, who are hereby irected and required to order the levying collecting and paying he same, in the same Manner as the Expences of all other public Bridges in the said two Precincts are raised collected and paid.

[CHAPTER 1745.]

An Act to alter the Place of Election for Representatives, and the Place of Meeting of the Supervisors, Judges and Loan Officers on the South Side of the Mountains in the County of Orange.

[Passed, April 3, 1775.]

WHEREAS the Place appointed by two several Acts of the Legisature of this Colony for holding the Election for Representatives, nd for the Meeting of the Supervisors Judges and Loan Officers n the South Side of the Mountains in the County of Orange, is at the Court House which stood at Orange Town in the said County, which Court House having since been consumed by Fire, a new Court House and Goal is directed by Law to be erected at a place commonly called the City near the House of Daniel Jeroe in the Precinct of Haverstraw in the said County, and the said Court House so to be erected, being set on foot and begun is thought to be the most convenient and proper Place for holding the Election for Representatives, and also for the Meeting of the Supervisors, Judges and Loan Officers in the Southern Part of the said County.

Be it therefore Enacted by his Honor the Lieutenant Governor the Council and the General Assembly, and it is hereby Enacted by the Authority of the same, That the next and all future Elections for Representatives, to be held on the South Side of the Mountains, for the County of Orange, shall and are hereby directed to be holden at the Court House or some other convenient Place in the City so called, in Haverstraw Precinct.

And be it further Enacted by the Authority aforesaid, That the Meeting of the Supervisors, Judges and Loan Officers on the South Side of the Mountains in the said County shall be holden at the Court House or some other convenient Place in the said City, in the said Precinct of Haverstraw, any Law or Laws of this Colony to the Contrary in any wise notwithstanding.

[CHAPTER 1746.]

[Expired, January 31, 1780.]

An Act to prevent Damages by Swine in the County of Ulster, and other Purposes therein mentioned.

[Passed, April 3, 1775.]

Be it Enacted by his Honor the Lieutenant Governor, the Council and the General Assembly and it is hereby Enacted by the Authority of the same That from and after the passing of this Act, it shall and may be lawful for the Corporations of the several incorporated Towns in the County of Ulster and the Freeholders of the several other Towns and Precincts in the said County at their respective annual Meetings for electing Supervisors and other Town and Precinct Officers by major Voice to make all such prudential bye Laws, Rules, and Orders as well for restricting Swine from running at large and for Yoking them and ringing their Noses, as recovering of Damages which may be done by them, and such other necessary Regulations respecting Swine as by the said Corporations and a Majority of the Freeholders of the other Towns and Precincts respectively at their annual Meetings aforesaid from Time to Time shall be thought meet and expedient.

And Whereas it often happens that great Damage is occasioned by Dogs and the increase of Sheep obstructed for Want of proper Regulations, Be it therefore Enacted by the same Authority, that the Corporations of the several Incorporated Towns and the Freeholders of the several other Towns and Precincts of the same County at their said respective annual Meetings, may also in like Manner make such prudential bye Laws Rules and Orders from Time to Time as they may think proper for penning folding regulating and separating of their Sheep, and for preventing any Annoyance of them by Dogs or other noxious Animals; all which said bye Laws, Rules, Orders and Regulations so to be made by virtue of this Act, shall be entered by the Town or Precinct Clerk in his Book, and certified Copies transmitted by him to the Clerk of the County to be filed in his Office; & shall from thenceforth be binding; and the Fines and Penalties thereby imposed recoverable with Cost of Suit before any one of his Majesty's Justices of the Peace in the said County by the Party agrieved Provided always that no penalty for any offence against such prudential bye Laws Rules and Regulations shall exceed the sum of five Pounds.

And be it Enacted by the same Authority, That the Act entitled " An Act to prevent Damages by Swine in the Township of Marble Town in the County of Ulster " is hereby repealed.

And be it Enacted by the same Authority, that this Act shall be in force from the passing thereof until the first Day of February which will be in the Year of our Lord one thousand seven hundred and eighty, and from thence to the End of the then next Session of the General Assembly.

[CHAPTER 1747.]

[Expired, January 31, 1780.]

An Act to guard against destructive Fires and to provide for a Night Watch in the Town of Kingston in Ulster County.

[Passed, April 3, 1775.]

WHEREAS the said Town is at a considerable Expence, provided with Engines for the extinguishment of Fires and it is expedient for preserving them in good order and for the due use of them that certain Persons be specially appointed for that Purpose,

Be it therefore Enacted by his Honor the Lieutenant Governor, the Council and the General Assembly, and it is hereby enacted by the Authority of the same, That it shall and may be lawful to and for the Trustees of the Freeholders and Commonalty of the Town of Kingston to elect nominate and appoint a sufficient Number of Men not exceeding Twenty residing within one half Mile distant from the Dutch Church of the said Town willing to undertake the Care and Management, working and Use of the Fire Engine or Engines belonging to the said Town and the other Tools and Instruments for extinguishing Fires therein who are hereby required and strictly enjoined in Case of Fire happening and need be to work, use and manage the same And the said Trustees are hereby impowered from Time to Time to remove and displace all or any of such Firemen and others in their Lieu and Stead to appoint who shall be subject to the like Duties, And the said Trustees shall have full Power and Authority to make and establish such Bye-Laws, Rules, Orders, Ordinances and Regulations for the Government, Conduct, Duty and Behaviour of the said Firemen in the Performance of their Duty as to the said Trustees shall seem meet and expedient.

And be it further Enacted by the same Authority, That such Persons as shall be appointed Fire Men as aforesaid during the time they shall continue so to be shall and are hereby declared to be freed and exempted from serving in the Office of Constable or Overseers of the Highways and from serving in the Militia except in Cases of Invasion.

And be it also Enacted by the same Authority, That the said Trustees of the Freeholders and Commonalty of the town of Kingston shall have Authority as often as they shall see Cause to make, Rules, Orders and Ordinances for the Appointment and Support of a Night Watch in such part of the said Town and to enforce the same by such Fines and Penalties not exceeding Five Pounds for any one Offence as they shall judge necessary; Which Fines and Penalties shall be recovered in the manner to be expressed in such Rules, Orders and Ordinances and be applied by the said Trustees for the Support of the Night Watchmen to be appointed and established in manner aforesaid.

And be it further Enacted by the same Authority, That the said Trustees shall have full power and Authority Annually during the Continuance of this Act to raise and levy any Sum not exceeding Fifteen Pounds of and from the Inhabitants residing in the said Town and within the Limits aforesaid as nearly as may be in the same Proportion that their Parts of the Contingent Charges of the County are by them respectively paid. And for that Purpose the said Trustees are hereby Authorized and impowered to issue their Warrant under their Common Seal to the Collector or Collectors of the said Town, who is and are hereby directed and required to Collect such Sum and pay the same to the said Trustees or their Treasurer, (deducting therefrom six pence in every Pound for the trouble of collecting the same) to be by the said Trustees applied in defraying the Expence attending the Appointment of a Night Watch in and for the said Town.

And be it further Enacted by the same Authority, That this Act shall be in Force from the passing thereof until the first Day of February which will be in the Year of our Lord One Thousand seven Hundred and Eighty, and from thence to the End of the then next Session of the General Assembly.

[CHAPTER 1748.]

[Expired, April 3, 1777.]

An Act to oblige the Collectors of the Counties of Dutchess and Ulster more effectually to collect and pay the annual Rates of the said Counties and for other Purposes therein mentioned.

[Passed, April 3, 1775.]

WHEREAS the Monies annually raised in the Counties of Dutchess and Ulster for the support of the Poor have hitherto been paid by the Collectors of the several Towns Manors and Precincts to the County Treasurers of the said Counties respectively, by reason whereof the Overseers of the Poor living in Parts of the Counties remote from the Residence of the Treasurers are exposed to great Inconveniences, Trouble and Expence in getting their Proportions of such Monies out of the Treasuries, for remedy whereof for the future,

Be it enacted by his Honor the Lieutenant Governor the Council and the General Assembly, And it is hereby enacted by the Authority of the same, That it shall and may be lawful to and for the Collectors for the Time being of the several Towns Manors and Precincts for the said Counties of Dutchess and Ulster respectively and they are hereby directed and required to pay all such Sums of Money as shall be by them annually collected for the Support or Maintenance of the Poor in their respective Towns

Manors or Precincts to the Overseers of the Poor thereof respectively, whose Receipt for the same, or the Receipt of a major Part of them shall be a good and sufficient discharge to the Collector therefor, any Law Usage or Custom to the contrary notwithstanding.

And be it further Enacted by the same Authority, That if the said Collectors of any of the said Towns Manors or Precincts of the said Counties shall delay neglect or refuse to pay the Money so as aforesaid by them hereafter to be collected for the Use Maintenance or Support of the Poor, to the Overseers of the Poor of their respective Towns, Manors or Precincts as aforesaid for the Space of ten Days after the same has or ought to have been by them collected, then in such Case it shall and may be lawful to and for the Overseers of the Poor of such Town Manor or Precinct where such Delay Neglect or Refusal may be made, to commence and prosecute their Action of Debt by and in the Name of the Overseers of the Poor of such Town Manor or Precinct in any of his Majesty's Courts of Record within this Colony for the Recovery of the same, wherein no Essoin, Protection, Wager of Law, or more than one Imparlance shall be allowed, and on a Recovery shall be intitled to treble Costs, which Suits so to be prosecuted by virtue of this Act shall not abate or be discontinued by the Death or Removal of any or either of the said Overseers, but shall and may be prosecuted to Effect by their Successor in Office, any Law Usage or Custom to the contrary in any wise notwithstanding.

And Whereas, it frequently happens that the Collectors of the said Counties make Delay in collecting the Monies for defraying the contingent Charges thereof, by which Means the Persons to whom such Monies are payable are disappointed, and exposed to Expence and Trouble in getting the same, for remedy whereof,

Be it Enacted by the Authority aforesaid, That if either of the said Collectors for the Time being for the said Counties shall neglect delay or refuse to pay unto the Treasurer of such County. the several Sum or Sums of Money payable into the said Treasury which he shall be impowered and required to collect within his Town District or Precinct pursuant to the Warrants which from Time to Time shall be issued by the Supervisors of the said Counties respectively for that purpose, for the Space of three Months after the said Warrant shall have been issued, such Collector so neglecting delaying or refusing shall forfeit and pay for every ten Days of such Delay, the Sum of five Pounds to be re-

covered by the said County Treasurer before any one of his Majesty's Justices of the Peace for the said County with Costs of Suit, three Pounds thereof to the Use of the County, to be appropriated and applied by the Supervisors thereof in such manner as they shall think best, and the other forty Shillings to the Treasurer as a Reward for his Trouble in prosecuting for the same.

And to the End that the Rate of the said Counties may effectually come in annually, Be it further Enacted by the Authority aforesaid, That if the Treasurer of either of the said Counties for the Time being shall at any Time or Times fail in prosecuting to Effect any such Collector or Collectors for the Offences as aforesaid by the Space of three Months after the Time herein before limited, such Treasurer shall forfeit and pay the Sum of five Pounds Current Money of this Colony for every Twenty Days he shall delay or neglect, to be recovered by the Person or Persons who shall be delayed wronged or injured by such Means before any one of his Majesty's Justices of the Peace for such County with Costs of Suit, besides being liable to an Action of Trespass grounded on the Case to such Person or Persons who shall be delayed wronged or injured, one-half of which Forfeiture to be for the Use and Benefit of such County, and the other half to the Person who shall sue for and recover the same; this Act to continue in force from the passing thereof during the Term of two Years, and thence to the End of the then next Session of the General Assembly.

[CHAPTER 1749.]

[See chapter 1440. Expired, January 31, 1785.]

An Act to revive an Act entitled "An Act to prevent Accidents by Fire in that Part of the Manor of Rensselaerwyck therein mentioned."

[Passed, April 3, 1775.]

Be it Enacted by his Honor the Lieutenant Governor, the Council and the General Assembly, and it is hereby enacted by the Authority of the same; that the Act entitled "An Act to prevent Accidents by Fire in that Part of the Manor of Rensselaerwyck therein mentioned," passed in the tenth Year of the Reign of his present Majesty, shall be and hereby is revived from the passing hereof, until the first Day of February which will be in the Year of our Lord one thousand seven hundred and eighty five.

[CHAPTER 1750.]

An Act to enable the Freeholders and Inhabitants of the District of the Manor of Rensselaerwyck to elect additional District Officers.

[Passed, April 3, 1775.]

WHEREAS in and by an Act entitled "An Act to divide the Counties of Albany and Tryon into Districts," passed the twenty fourth Day of March one thousand seven hundred and seventy two, by the fourth Clause or Section thereof it is enacted, That the Freeholders and Inhabitants of the District of the Manor of Rensselaerwyck shall and may and they are thereby required yearly and every year on the first Tuesday in May to elect and appoint two Freeholders to be Supervisors, four Freeholders to be Assessors, and two Freeholders to be Collectors, six Constables and six Fence Viewers; and it being found necessary for the convenience of the Inhabitants of said District to have two additional Assessors, Collectors, Overseers of the Poor, Constables and Fence Viewers,

Be it therefore Enacted by his Honor the Lieutenant Governor, the Council and the General Assembly, and it is hereby enacted by the Authority of the same, That it shall and may be lawful to and for the Freeholders and Inhabitants of the said District of the Manor of Rensselaerwyck, and they are hereby impowered to elect and choose two additional Assessors, Collectors, Overseers of the Poor, Constables and Fence Viewers, yearly at the Times already fixed for electing the District Officers by virtue of the said in part recited Act, who shall have the same Power, Authority, Office, and Function, and do, perform, execute and serve, and be liable to the same Pains and Penalties as the like Officers by the above in part recited Act have, ought or are entitled to have, do, perform, and be liable to, any Law Usage or Custom to the contrary in any wise notwithstanding.

[CHAPTER 1751.]

An Act to raise the Sum of one hundred and twenty Pounds on the Freeholders and Inhabitants of the City and County of Albany for the Purposes therein mentioned.

[Passed, April 3, 1775.]

Be it Enacted by his Honor the Lieutenant Governor the Council and the General Assembly, and it is hereby enacted by the Authority of the same, That the Supervisors of the City and

County of Albany shall and are hereby required at their first Meeting next after the passing of this Act, to raise and cause to be levied and collected of and from the Freeholders and Inhabitants of the City and County of Albany the Sum of one hundred and twenty Pounds together with the usual Allowance to the Collector for collecting the same, to be raised levied and collected in like Manner as the other County Charges, and when collected to be paid by the Collectors into the Hands of the County Treasurer to be by him paid to the Order of the Mayor Recorder Aldermen and Commonalty of the said City of Albany to be by them applied in purchasing a Bell and repairing the Court House erected in the said City.

[CHAPTER 1752.]

An Act to oblige the Collectors of the different Districts in the County of Albany to deliver in their Accounts upon Oath to the County Treasurer.

[Passed, April 3, 1775.]

Be it Enacted by his Honor the Lieutenant Governor the Council and the General Assembly and it is hereby enacted by the Authority of the same, That every Collector hereafter to be elected in the City and County of Albany, and who shall receive a Warrant from the Supervisors hereafter to be appointed to levy and collect any County Rates whatever, shall together with the Money so by him collected deliver to the Treasurer of the said City and County an Account upon Oath of all the Monies by him collected by virtue of such Warrant, together with another Account on Oath of every Deficiency (if any there be,) specifying the Persons Names who have not paid their Quota, and assigning the reasons therefore, to the Intent that such Accounts may from Time to Time be laid before the Supervisors of the said City and County for their Approbation or Disallowance as to them shall appear proper; And every Collector refusing or neglecting to give such Accounts on Oath shall for every ten Days neglect after the Day on which he was to pay the Money so by him collected forfeit the Sum of forty Shillings to be recovered with Costs of Suit, by the said Treasurer in a Summary way before any Justice of the Peace, and such Forfeiture to go to the Overseers of the Poor of the District where such Collector resides: and the Treasurer of the said City and County for the time being shall and may administer an Oath to every such Collector that the Accounts by him delivered are to the best of his Knowledge just and true.

[CHAPTER 1753.]

[See chapters 1494 and 1581. Expired, January 31, 1780.]

An Act to revive an Act entitled "An Act for the more effectual Punishment of Persons who shall be guilty of any of the Trespasses therein mentioned in the Cities of New York and Albany, and Township of Schenectady."

[Passed, April 3, 1775.]

Be it Enacted by his Honor the Lieutenant Governor the Council and the General Assembly, and it is hereby Enacted by the Authority of the same, That the Act entitled, "An Act for the more effectual Punishment of Persons who shall be guilty of any of the Trespasses therein mentioned in the Cities of New York and Albany and Township of Schenectady," passed the sixteenth Day of February one thousand seven hundred and seventy one, shall be and hereby is revived and every Clause Article Matter and Thing therein contained enacted to be and remain in full force from the passing hereof until the first Day of February one thousand seven hundred and eighty, and from thence to the End of the then next Session of the General Assembly.

[CHAPTER 1754.]

An Act to regulate Elections for Representatives in General Assembly for the City and County of Albany.

[Passed, April 3, 1775.]

Whereas the Inhabitants of the Town of Schenectady and Manors of Rensselaerwyck and Livingston in the County of Albany having Freehold Estates within the same do respectively enjoy by Virtue of royal Grants, the Privilege of electing a Representative in General Assembly, And Whereas Claims have been set up by the said Inhabitants of the Town of Schenectady and Manors of Rensselaerwyck and Livingston in Right of their Freeholds within the Town and Manors aforesaid not only of electing a Representative for such Town and Manors exclusively, but also of voting for the Representatives of the City and County of Albany in common with the Freeholders thereof, And Whereas such Claims have a Tendency to procure to such Freeholders a double Representation in General Assembly for the same Estate, and thereby to diminish the Rights of the Freeholders of the said County of Albany contrary to the royal Intention in granting such Privilege as aforesaid, And Whereas a due Regulation of the Election of Representatives in General Assembly, is of the utmost Importance to the constitutional Rights of the People of this Colony; Wherefore to prevent those Doubts and Disputes which might be occasioned by the said Claims of the Freeholders of the Town and Manors aforesaid, and forever hereafter to extinguish those Claims, as well as to secure a just equal and constitutional Representation of the said County of Albany; the General Assembly pray that it may be declared and enacted, *And be it declared and enacted by his Honor the Lieutenant Governor the Council and the General Assembly, and by the Authority of the same,* That from and after the passing of this Act, it shall not be lawful for any Person or Persons having a Freehold or Freeholds either within the said Town of Schenectady or Manors of Rensselaerwyck and Livingston respectively, in Right of such Freeholds only, to vote at the Election of Representatives in General Assembly for the City and County of Albany; but from voting at such Elections for the said City and County, in Right of such Estates in the said Town and Manors respectively, such Person or Persons shall be utterly disabled, and all and every Vote and Votes given contrary to the true Intent and Meaning of this Act shall be utterly void and of none Effect, any Usage Custom Claim or Pretence to the contrary notwithstanding.

[CHAPTER 1755.

[See chapter 1351. Expired, January 31, 1785.]

An Act to revive an Act entitled "An Act to prevent the Defaults of Grand and Petit Jurors Constables and other Persons."

[Passed, April 3, 1775.]

Be it Enacted by his Honor the Lieutenant Governor the Council and the General Assembly, and it is hereby enacted by the Authority of the same, That the Act entitled. "An Act to prevent the Defaults of Grand and Petit Jurors Constables and other Persons." passed in the eighth Year of his present Majesty's Reign, shall be and hereby is revived, and every Clause Matter and Thing therein contained enacted to be in full force until the first Day of February which will be in the Year of our Lord one thousand seven hundred and eighty five, and from thence to the End of the then next Session of the General Assembly.

[CHAPTER 1756.]

An Act for the more convenient proving of Deeds and Mortgages.

[Passed, April 3, 1775.]

Be it Enacted by his Honor the Lieutenant Governor the Council and the General Assembly, and it is hereby enacted by the Authority of the same, That all Records and Regestries of Deeds, Mortgages and other Writings whatsoever, whether executed within this Colony, or in other Parts of the British Dominions that have been, or hereafter shall be made upon Acknowledgments taken, or Proofs made before the Master of the Rolls, either of the Masters in Chancery, or the Mayors of the Cities of New York or Albany respectively, shall be as good and effectual to all Intents and Purposes, as if the same had been made, recorded or registred upon Acknowledgments taken or Proofs made before any of his Majesty's Council for the Province of New York, or before any of the Judges of the Supreme Court, any Law, Usage or Custom to the contrary thereof in any wise notwithstanding.

[CHAPTER 1757.]

[Expired, January 31, 1785.]

An Act to prevent Frauds by Bills of Sale which shall be made and executed in the Counties therein mentioned.

[Passed, April 3, 1775.]

Whereas divers Frauds have been committed by Persons conveying their Goods Chattels and Effects by Bill of Sale by way of Mortgage or Collateral Security and afterwards selling the same to other Persons who were Ignorant of such former Sales whereby many Persons have been defrauded of very considerable Sums of money for the preventing whereof for the Future,

Be it Enacted by his Honor the Lieutenant Governor, the Council and the General Assembly, and it is hereby Enacted by the Authority of the same, That immediately from and after the passing of this Act, each and every of the Clerks of the several and respective Towns and Precincts within the counties of Queens,

Orange and Dutches and the Clerk of the City and County of Albany, and the County Clerks of Richmond and Kings shall provide a fit and proper Book for Registering of all Bills of Sale of Goods, Chattels and Effects, which are given by way of Mortgage or Collateral Security, not exceeding the Sum of one Hundred Pounds, which shall be made and executed for any Goods, or Chattels within their respective Towns and Precincts after the passing of this Act, in which Register shall be entered the particular Goods, Chattels and Effects conveyed, the Names of the Persons, by and to whom sold the Dates of the respective Bills of Sale the Consideration money and the Time when Registered and recorded, and for the Registering whereof the said Clerk shall have and receive the Sum of one Shilling and six Pence for each Bill of Sale so registered and no more to which Register all Persons whatsoever at proper Seasons shall have recourse and search, he paying to the said Clerk the Sum of six Pence and no more.

Provided always, That before any such Bill of Sale shall be so entered in any such Register, the same shall be proved on Oath by the Grantor or Grantors that executed the same before one of the Judges or Justices of the said County, that it was for a bona fide Debt of the Value specified in the said Bill or Bills of Sale and not given with an Intent to defraud, for which the Judge or Justice shall have and receive the Sum of one Shilling and six Pence for each Bill of Sale so proved and no more, and that the Clerk of every Town or Precinct shall be sworn before any one of the Judges of the Inferior Court of Common Pleas, for the County well and faithfully to execute the Duty required of him by this Act, and to enter no Bill or Bills of Sale, unless the same has been proved as aforesaid and the Proof endorsed on the back of such Bill or Bills of Sale.

And be it further Enacted by the Authority aforesaid, That if any Person or Persons whatsoever shall after the passing of this Act give any Bill of Sale in Writing by way of Mortgage or Collateral Security for any Goods, Chattels or effects whatsoever, for any Consideration not exceeding the Sum of One Hundred Pounds within the said Counties, to two or more Persons, at different Times, and any doubt or dispute shall arise about the priority of such Bill of Sale, That then and in such Case, the Bill of Sale first entered on the Register in manner before directed shall be deemed and taken, and is hereby declared, and shall be adjudged to be the first and prior Bill of Sale any Law, Usage or Custom to the contrary thereof notwithstanding.

And be it further Enacted by the Authority aforesaid, That if any Person or Persons whatsoever shall after the passing of this Act, give any Bill of Sale, or if any Person or Persons have heretofore given any Bill of Sale in Writing by way of Mortgage or Collateral Security, for any Goods, Chattels or Effects whatsoever for any Consideration not exceeding the Sum of One Hundred Pounds within the said Counties, and the same being entered on the Register in manner before directed by this Act, and the Consideration money mentioned in the said Bill of Sale is become due, the Person or Persons to whom the said Bill of Sale was given, and if there be more than one Bill of Sale, the prior Bill of Sale to take Place first, shall and may with the Sheriff or Undersheriff of the County, or with the Constable or other Officer of the Town, Precinct or District where the mortgagor lives or the Effects can be found (who are hereby required to be aiding and assisting therein) to seize and take into his or their Custody, the said Goods, and when so taken the said Sheriff or Undersheriff, Constable, or other Officer shall advertise the said Goods or Chattels for Four Days at least and sell the same at public Vendue, and pay unto the said Mortgagee the Debt and Interest thereon due, and retain in his Hands the Sum of nine Pence for every Pound for his Trouble of taking, advertising and selling the said Goods or Chattels and return the Overplus if any there be to the Owner of the next prior Bill of Sale if any there be, but if there be none, to the Owner of the said Goods or Chattels.

And be it further Enacted by the Authority aforesaid, That whenever any Bill of Sale, so registered as aforesaid (that has or shall be given by way of Mortgage or Collateral Security) shall be redeemed paid off and discharged, the Clerks of the respective Towns and Precincts in the Counties aforesaid on Application to them made, by the Person or Persons giving, or the Persons redeeming, paying off and discharging the same and producing a Certificate to the respective Clerks of the respective Towns and Precincts in the Counties of Queens, Orange and Dutchess or the County Clerk of the City and County of Albany, and the Clerk of the Counties of Richmond and Kings signed by the Person or Persons to whom the same was given, his, her or their Executors Administrators or Assigns and acknowledged by the Party or Parties signing the same or proved by the Oath of one or more of the Witnesses thereto, before one of the said Judges or Justices shall and they are hereby required to enter in the aforesaid Book or Register of Bills of Sale a Minute of the said Discharge or Discharges, for which entry the respective Clerks shall have and receive the Sum of nine pence and no more, which Minute so entered, shall be deemed and taken and hereby is declared to be a full, perfect and absolute Discharge of every such Bill of Sale.

Provided always And be it further Enacted by the Authority aforesaid, That no Bill of Sale hereafter given or executed for the uses aforesaid shall be of any Effect whatsoever until the same be recorded agreeable to the Directions of this Act

And be it also further Enacted by the Authority aforesaid, That the Clerks of the several Counties aforesaid shall publickly read this Act, in the first Court of Sessions of the Peace for their said respective Counties, next after the passing hereof

And be it further Enacted by the Authority aforesaid, That this Act shall continue and be in Force from the passing hereof until the first Day of February which will be in the Year of our Lord One Thousand seven Hundred and Eighty five, and from thence to the End of the then next Sessions of the General Assembly.

[CHAPTER 1758.]

An Act to enable the Persons therein named to build a free draw Bridge over the Narrows from Mineford's Island to Rodman's Neck.

[Passed, April 3, 1775.]

Whereas a free draw Bridge over the Narrows from Rodman's Neck to Mineford's Island in the Manor of Pelham in the County of West Chester, will considerably shorten the Distance of the present Ferry from Rodman's Neck to Great Neck on Long Island, as the said Ferry may then with great Convenience be kept on Mineford's Island aforesaid; and will moreover afford a convenient and proper Station for taking great Quantities of Fish with Nets and Fikes, which will give considerable Employment and Relief to the Poor in the Neighbourhood of the said Bridge, and lessen the Price of that useful Article in the Markets of the City of New York

Be it therefore Enacted by his Honor the Lieutenant Governor the Council and the General Assembly, and it is hereby enacted by the Authority of the same, That Samuel Rodman Senior, and Benjamin Palmer both of the said Manor of Pelham and County of West Chester shall be, and they are hereby impowered to erect and build a draw Bridge over the said Narrows from Rodman's Neck to Minifords Island as aforesaid in such Place as they the said Samuel Rodman Senior and Benjamin Palmer shall judge most fit, Provided that in such Bridge there shall be two or more Apertures of at least twenty five Feet each, for the Convenience of navigating the said River by small Boats: And the said Bridge when so built shall be and is hereby declared to be a free and public Highway for the Use Benefit and Behoof of all his Majesty's Subjects whatsoever.

And be it further Enacted by the Authority aforesaid, That the said Bridge shall be erected and built in the Space of Seven Years after the passing hereof, or in Default thereof, that this Act and every Thing therein contained shall be Null and Void, any Thing herein before contained to the contrary thereof notwithstanding.

[CHAPTER 1759.]

An Act to enable Jesse Hunt to erect and build a Bridge from Applegate Island to the Public Highway on the Main Land opposite the said Island.

[Passed, April 3, 1775.]

WHEREAS the building of a Bridge from Applegate Island to the Public Highway on the Main Land opposite the said Island in West Chester County will greatly tend to the Ease and Convenience of Persons having intercourse between the said Island and the Main Land.

Be it therefore Enacted by his Honor the Lieutenant Governor the Council and the General Assembly, and it is hereby enacted by the Authority of the same, That Jesse Hunt of the City of New York Mariner shall be, and is hereby, impowered at any time within five Years from the passing of this Act, to erect and build a Bridge from Applegate Island to the Public Highway on the Main Land opposite the said Island, where the Highway from said Island to the Main Land is now used and laid out, in such Manner as he the said Jesse Hunt shall judge most fit.

And be it further Enacted by the Authority aforesaid, That the said Bridge when so built shall be a free and common Bridge for the Use and Benefit of all Persons having any intercourse between the said Island and the Main Land.

[CHAPTER 1760.]

[See chapters 1472 and 1599.]

An Act to amend an Act entitled "An Act for emitting the Sum of one hundred and twenty thousand Pounds in Bills of Credit to be put out on Loan and to appropriate the Interest arising thereon to the Payment of the Debts of this Colony and to such Public Exigencies as the Circumstances of this Colony may from Time to Time render necessary," so far only as it relates to the County of Suffolk.

[Passed, April 3, 1775.]

WHEREAS it is enacted in the said Act that the mortgaged Premises the Equity of Redemption of which may be foreclosed shall be exposed to sale by the Loan Officers on the last Tuesday in June Yearly at the Court House of the respective Counties where the Lands lie, by way of Public Vendue to the highest Bidder, which has been found very inconvenient in that extensive County, both for the Attendance of the Loan Officers and Bidders for such Lands and detrimental to the sale thereof, and thereby many Deficiencies may fall upon the County,

Be it therefore Enacted by his Honor the Lieutenant Governor the Council and the General Assembly, and it is hereby enacted by the Authority of the same, That whenever the Equity of Redemption of any such Lands shall be foreclosed in the Manner directed in the aforesaid Act, that then it shall and may be lawful for the Loan Officers or one of them by the Consent and Approbation of the other to sell all such Lands either at the Court House in the said County, or in such Town Manor Precinct or District in which the Lands do lie having first duly observed the Directions in the said Act previous to the Sale thereof, and if it shall appear to the said Loan Officers upon good and sufficient Reasons, that the mortgaged Premises are not a sufficient Security for the Monies advanced thereon, that then the Loan Officers may sell the same and also prosecute an Action or Actions of Debt as shall appear to them most expedient for the Recovery of the Monies so advanced upon Loan, any Thing in the said Act contained to the contrary thereof in any wise notwithstanding.

[CHAPTER 1761.]

An Act for erecting the Tract of Land therein mentioned in the County of Tryon, into one Separate District by the Name of Old England District.

[Passed, April 3, 1775.]

WHEREAS it has been represented to the General Assembly That the erecting the following Tract of Land into one separate District would tend greatly to the Ease and Convenience of the People settled thereon, who by reason of their remote Distance from any Place of Election, and from the Residence of District Officers, cannot without great Trouble and Expence perform the Duties to which the Inhabitants of Districts are made subject by sundry Acts of the Legislature, and by that Means also are deprived of the beneficial Regulations established thereby; for Remedy whereof,

Be it Enacted by his Honor the Lieutenant Governor the Council and the General Assembly, and it is hereby enacted by the Authority of the same, That from and after the passing of this Act, all and singular that certain Tract of Land within the County of Tryon, Beginning at the Head Water of the Lake Otsego in the Patent commonly called the Otsego Patent granted to George Croghan and others, thence along the Northerly Bounds of the said Patent to the North West Corner thereof, thence extending Westerly to the River Tianaderha, so as to include the Patents granted to William and Robert Edminston Esquires, thence down the said River to its Junction with the Susquehanna River, thence across the said River to the South West Corner of the Patent granted to Alexander Wallace and others, thence continuing along the South Bounds to the South East Corner thereof, and thence continuing along the Bounds of the said Patent to the said River Susquehanna, and then up the said River to the Place of Beginning, shall be and hereby is formed and erected into one Separate and distinct District which shall henceforth be called and known by the Name of Old England District.

And be it also enacted by the same Authority, That the Freeholders and Inhabitants of the said District, are hereby required and authorized yearly and every year upon the first Tuesday in May to elect and appoint one Freeholder to be a Supervisor, two Freeholders to be Assessors, one Freeholder to be Collector, two Freeholders to be Overseers of the Poor, two Constables, two Fence Viewers and one Clerk, which said Supervisor Assessors, Collector,

Overseers of the Poor, Constables, Fence Viewers and Clerk, shall have the same Powers and Authority, and be subject to the same Regulations, and liable to the same Pains and Penalties as the Supervisors Assessors Collectors, Overseers of the Poor, Constables, Fence Viewers and Clerk, have or are liable to in and by a certain Act made and passed the twenty fourth Day of March one thousand seven hundred and seventy two entitled, "An Act to divide the Counties of Albany and Tryon into Districts," and also in and by one certain other Act passed in the Year one thousand seven hundred and three entitled, "An Act for the better explaining and more effectual. putting in Execution an Act of General Assembly made in the third Year of the Reign of their late Majesties King William and Queen Mary entitled An Act for defraying the Public and necessary Charge throughout this Colony and for maintaining the Poor and preventing Vagabonds."

And Be it further Enacted by the Authority aforesaid, That the first Election for the said several Officers shall be held at Smiths Hall within the said District, after which such Elections may be carried on at such Place as the Freeholders and Inhabitants shall from Time to Time by major Voice appoint.

And be it further Enacted by the same Authority, That John Johnson, John Hicks, Increase Thurston, Samuel Gardner, and Ralf Falkner Senior shall be and hereby are appointed Commissioners of the Highways in and for the said District and shall have like Powers and Authority, be subject to the same Regulations, and be liable to the same Pains and Penalties as Commissioners of Highways have and are subject and liable to in and by one certain Act made and passed this present Session of the General Assembly entitled "An Act for the better laying out regulating and keeping in Repair the Public Roads and Highways in the City and County of Albany and County of Tryon," which said Act as well as the other Acts herein mentioned, are hereby extended to the said District hereby enacted in as full and ample a Manner as the same affects any District therein mentioned, or as if the said hereby erected District had been particularly mentioned in the said Acts or any of them.

INDEX—VOL. V.

A.

(See Debtors.)

B.

C.

K.

L.

M.

Names of persons — (Continued): Page.

Names of persons — (Continued): Page.

Names of persons — (Continued): Page.

Names of persons — (Continued): Page.

Names of persons — (Continued): Page.

Names of persons — (Continued): Page.

Names of persons — (Continued): Page.

Names of persons — (Continued):

Names of persons — (Continued): Page.

'ames of persons — (Continued): Page.

Names of persons — (Continued:

O.

P.

T.

U.

Lightning Source UK Ltd.
Milton Keynes UK
UKHW010629110219
337000UK00006B/142/P